*Encyclopedia of the Life Course and Human Development*

# *Encyclopedia of the Life Course and Human Development*

VOLUME 3

**LATER LIFE**

**APPENDICES, INDEX**

*Deborah Carr*

EDITOR IN CHIEF

**MACMILLAN REFERENCE USA**

*A part of Gale, Cengage Learning*

Detroit • New York • San Francisco • New Haven, Conn • Waterville, Maine • London

**Encyclopedia of the Life Course and Human Development**
**Deborah Carr, Editor in Chief**



**Library of Congress Cataloging-in-Publication Data**

Encyclopedia of the life course and human development / Deborah Carr, editor in chief.
v. ; cm.
Includes bibliographical references and index.
ISBN 978-0-02-866162-9 (set : alk. paper) – ISBN 978-0-02-866163-6 (vol. 1 : alk. paper) – ISBN 978-0-02-866164-3 (vol. 2 : alk. paper) – ISBN 978-0-02-866165-0 (vol. 3 : alk. paper)
1. Social evolution—Encyclopedias. 2. Human evolution—Encyclopedias. I. Carr, Deborah S.

HM626.E538 2008
305.203—dc22 2008027490

*Gale*
27500 Drake Rd.
Farmington Hills, MI 48331-3535

ISBN-13: 978-0-02-866162-9 (set) ISBN-10: 0-02-866162-1 (set)
ISBN-13: 978-0-02-866163-6 (vol. 1) ISBN-10: 0-02-866163-X (vol. 1)
ISBN-13: 978-0-02-866164-3 (vol. 2) ISBN-10: 0-02-866164-8 (vol. 2)
ISBN-13: 978-0-02-866165-0 (vol. 3) ISBN-10: 0-02-866165-6 (vol. 3)

This title is also available as an e-book.
ISBN-13: 978-0-02-866166-7 ISBN-10: 0-02-866166-4
Contact your Gale sales representative for ordering information.

Printed in the United States of America
1 2 3 4 5 6 7 12 11 10 09 08

# *Editorial Board*

# *Editorial and Production Staff*

**PROJECT EDITORS**

Deirdre S. Blanchfield
Andrew G. Specht

**EDITORIAL TECHNICAL SUPPORT**

Mark Drouillard

**MANUSCRIPT EDITORS**

Judith Clinebell
Laurie J. Edwards
Jessica Hornik Evans
Christine Kelley
Eric Linderman
Eric Lowenkron
Kari Lucke
Raymond Lukens
David E. Salamie

**PROOFREADER**

John Krol

**INDEXER**

Laurie Andriot

**PRODUCT DESIGN**

Pamela A.E. Galbreath

**IMAGING**

Lezlie Light

**GRAPHIC ART**

Pre-PressPMG

**PERMISSIONS**

Leitha Etheridge-Sims

**COMPOSITION**

Evi Seoud

**MANUFACTURING**

Wendy Blurton

**DIRECTOR, NEW PRODUCT DEVELOPMENT**

Leigh Ann Cusack

**PUBLISHER**

Jay Flynn

# *Contents*

# *Introduction to Volume 3, Later Life*

Many students become interested in the social sciences because they want to know how people live their lives—their work lives, their family lives—and they also want to know why people make the choices they do. People who have meaningful experiences and relationships with grandparents and older relatives often become interested in the study of aging. College students often bring stories to the classroom about how their grandparents (and great grandparents) grew up in dramatically different times and as a result had different life experiences that seem unfamiliar to young people today. Grandmothers had far fewer opportunities to earn college degrees and have careers compared to today's young adults. Grandfathers often were the sole breadwinners in their households providing stable wages and a modest standard of living that benefited their families. These kinds of stories are familiar and expected. However, what is also true is that stories that students share about their older relatives are wide ranging. For example, some tell stories of grandmothers who worked and raised children by themselves, or great uncles who never married. Life course scholars agree that all of these diverse life experiences contribute to variations in later life experiences and statuses. It has been the work of life course scholars to disentangle complex relationships between history and biography in order to learn how each generation is different from all others and why there are differences within each generation.

One of the most significant demographic trends in the United States has been the aging of the population. The number of older adults in the United States—defined as persons ages 65 and older—will more than double in size from 2005 through 2050. The number of working-age Americans and children will increase more slowly than the older population, and will shrink as a proportion of the total population. In the United States, and nearly all developed nations, declining fertility rates and mortality rates have led to a large increase in the older adult population, both in relative and total size. This trend is well described in several entries in this volume (see both Age Structure and Population Aging in this volume). The "graying" of the world's population has inspired a large body of research and theorizing about the latter part of the life course. The life course paradigm has provided a guiding framework for much of this research. The entries in Volume 3 summarize much of the best life course scholarship that has led to a greater understanding of later life. I will next provide an overview about how we might think about defining later life. Then, I'll discuss several of the major trends in aging research that are described in this volume.

## WHAT IS "LATER LIFE"?

The definition of later life is itself a subject of debate. Typically later life, or "old age," is considered to begin at age 65. However, beliefs about what constitutes "old age" vary across time and place. In nineteenth century America, when it was much less common to encounter 60 and 70 years olds, defining old age to begin at age 55 may have been more appropriate. Even today, among the younger populations of the world such as those in South Asia and Africa, researchers define old age as 50 or 55+ or even younger. My own research in Nepal has shown that significant physical impairments are common among people as young as age 45 and 50, especially among Nepalese women. I have met women who appear be in their 80s because their skin and teeth are weathered and they are stooped over, their backs appearing "broken" due to years spent doing arduous farm and household labor. When interviewed, these women report they are decades younger than they appear to be. If the goal of defining old age is to direct attention, policy, and resources to those in need—the definition of old age might account for declining physical health. However, if one were to take physical health alone as a mark of old age—age 65 might be too young of a definition—especially in the United States and other wealthy nations, where a great many adults live impairment-free throughout their 60s and 70s (see "Disability and Functional Limitation, Later Life" by Martin).

Definitions of age may also encompass individuals' own perceptions and self-evaluations. It is not uncommon to "feel" decades younger than the chronological age on a driver's license (see "Age Identity" by Westerhof). This may be especially true of baby boomers who might still identify with a youthful 1960s identity that encompassed the then-revolutionary ideals of peace, self-expression, and free love. By and large, however, a definition of 65+ remains useful to researchers because policies, such as Social Security, use age 65 to define cut points for age-related benefits and services.

## THE RISE OF THE "THIRD AGE"

One of the most significant trends in aging research is the recognition that later life, whatever definition is used, is not a time of inevitable decline. In their entry "Theories of Aging," Norella Putney and Vern Bengtson write that disengagement theory, which emphasizes the necessary withdrawal of older persons from social life, has largely been refuted by empirical research. Instead, this theory has been supplanted by activity theory and continuity theory, which stress the importance of active engagement in the social world for optimizing well-being in later life. As a result of this theoretical shift, there has been an explosion of research on topics such as creativity and wisdom (both in this volume). We learn from these entries that later life can be a time of psychological *growth*, rather than decline or stability. Also in this volume, we describe the time that older adults spend doing volunteer work (see "Volunteering, Later Life" by Burr) and traveling (see "Leisure and Travel, Later Life" by Gibson). All of these topics can be summarized using the label of Third Age. Third age represents the point of view, among scholars and laypersons, that later life can be a time to set new life goals and create new meaning. One only has to spend some time using Google and key words like "seniors and art" and "seniors and travel" to know that older adults are an active, vital community.

## SOCIOBIOLOGICAL INFLUENCES ON AGING

Another important trend in aging research is increasing multidisciplinarity of ideas and research, especially the use of both social and biological perspectives to better understand aging. Sociologists, economists, epidemiologists, psychologists, physicians and many others have engaged with one another to investigate the interrelationships among social status and biology in later life. This volume documents the improved physical health of the older population compared to years past. At the same time, there are new health problems in later life that are growing in importance such as diabetes and dementias, both of which are topics covered in this encyclopedia. In addition to social explanations for the trends in health and well-being, there has been increased scholarly attention to biological influences over the life course on later life health (see "Genetic Influences, Later Life" by Gavrilova & Gavrilov).

Greater longevity or lengthening of the life span and better health have also reorganized the social world of older adults. For example, as people live longer and healthier lives it is possible to occupy roles for prolonged periods of time. Thus, we have seen an increase in the amount of time one spends in some roles such as retirement (see "Retirement" by Williamson & Higo ). Also, time spent on various family roles such as the grandparent role and the great grandparent role has increased (see "Grandparenthood" by Szinovacz). Another consequence of greater longevity is a rise in the variability of roles as not only the time spent in roles increases but also the incidence of new roles increases. For example, one of the notable features of the lengthening life course is that more and more older persons are continuing their education during their post-retirement years (see "Lifelong Learning" by Hamil-Luker). Finally, men and women are more likely to have more complicated combinations of roles than in the past. As a result there are many men and women who experience psychological stress from role overload and role strain (see "Stress in Later Life" by Kahana, Kahana, & Hammel). This trend may be particularly true among older caregivers who take on care of a spouse or partner (see "Caregiving" by Silverstein).

## NEW DATA, NEW FINDINGS

Glen Elder (1985), a sociologist who is considered the architect of the life course paradigm, has observed that that theoretical developments combined with new methodological tools and data have spurred considerable growth in later life scholarship over the past four decades. Many of the authors in this volume credit advances in research in their respective areas to availability of new data; especially longitudinal data (see the composite entry "Data Sources, Later Life"). It is difficult to determine what kinds of behaviors or statuses may be apt to change as one ages when data are from one point in time (referred to as cross-sectional data). With cross-sectional data, older people are compared to younger people at one point in time and it is tempting to attribute any observed differences from these data as being related to aging. It is not possible to disentangle age, period and cohort effects with one wave of data. For example, in her entry "Religion and Spirituality, Later Life," Linda George writes that although older people appear more religious than younger people in cross-sectional studies, only longitudinal data (where individuals are interviewed at various points in their lives) can truly reveal whether and how individuals change as they age. Many entries in this volume describe a similar "data dilemma" (see "Sexual Activity, Later Life" by Waite, Das, & Laumann) that has only recently progressed due to the availability of new data.

Two important types of longitudinal data are described in this volume. First, there are long-term longitudinal studies that follow people over many stages of life. For example, The Wisconsin Longitudinal Study (WLS) follows a sample of Wisconsin high school graduates from the class of 1957 from ages 18 through late life. With longitudinal data such as these, it is possible to understand how early family formation and career choices affect later life outcomes such as retirement and health. Other longitudinal studies begin at later points in the life course such as the Health and Retirement Study (HRS). The HRS interviews people at regular, frequent intervals (every 2 years) so that the dynamics of change associated with aging can be better understood. The importance of data such as the HRS should not be underestimated. HRS data have been widely used since the study began in 1992. The HRS has led to similar studies in Europe (see "Data Sources, Later Life: English Longitudinal Study of Ageing [ELSA]" by Marmot & McMunn). Also, many entries in this volume report on findings from the HRS. It has been a monumental data collection effort, offering rich data over time on a wide range of topics. While the HRS initially focused on the aging experiences of the generations that preceded the baby boom generation, younger birth cohorts have been added to the HRS study. So, new information about the baby boom cohort have become available to researchers recently. This design—where multiple cohorts are followed over time—is an important advance in aging research.

## A FINAL NOTE TO THE READER

I began this introduction by discussng about the predictability of life transitions and the importance of one's history in shaping his or her later life chances. Yet I also noted the incredible diversity of experiences from one generation to the next and also within a given generation. When asking authors to prepare their entries for this volume, we asked them to include comments about this diversity. As a result, the entries in this volume discuss generational differences, cross-cultural differences, and differences by age, gender, social class and race within the United States. It is our hope that readers will find the entries in this volume to be informative about both major trends and patterns over the life course yet also provide many unexpected findings.

### BIBLIOGRAPHY

Elder, Glen H., Jr., (ed.) (1985). Life Course Dynamics: Trajectories and Transitions, 1968–1980. (Project of SSRC Committee on the Life Course.) Ithaca, NY: Cornell University Press.

***Amy M. Pienta***
***Associate Editor***

# A-B

## ACTIVE LIFE EXPECTANCY

One of the defining features of the 20th century was a steady increase in life expectancy, accompanied by rapid population aging—a trend that is expected to continue into the foreseeable future as more individuals survive to older ages, and fertility rates remain low. Accompanying the growth of the older population is an increasing need for support services for individuals with physical limitations and disability. Active life expectancy is a measure researchers have developed that can succinctly describe the average amount of time one is expected to live with disabling conditions in a population. It provides a basis for understanding the time individuals in a population are likely to need support from others or be in need of health care.

### DEFINING ACTIVE LIFE EXPECTANCY

Active life expectancy is a summary measure of population health, which integrates age-specific disability and mortality into a single measure, indicating the average number of years of life expected to be spent active after a specified age. The remaining life expectancy is inactive. When life expectancy is divided into these states, *active* years are usually defined as years lived without a specifically defined disability, whereas *inactive* years are usually defined as years lived with a disability. The inactive years are not necessarily lived at the end of life, and can be distributed throughout the remaining lifetime. The term *inactive* is not meant to imply complete physical incapacitation. Definitions of *inactive* vary from having any difficulty performing normal tasks to having severe limitations that would make it difficult to live independently in a community setting and provide self-care. The accompanying figure shows an example of active and inactive life expectancy in the United States at age 65 in 1980 and 1990. As seen in Figure 1, the sum of the active and inactive (sometimes labeled *disabled*) years is life expectancy at a specific age.

Active life expectancy tends to be used synonymously with the term "disability-free" life expectancy—both of which are subsets of the broader term *healthy* life expectancy. Whereas active life expectancy is usually defined as life without some form of physical limitation or disability, healthy life expectancy can be defined as life without a disease or impairment such as diabetes, cognitive loss, obesity, or hypertension.

As with other life table-based measures, active life expectancy measures are not affected by the composition of the population; therefore, the results can be compared over time or across populations, assuming similar measurement of disability or health state. Like life expectancy, active life expectancy does not represent the actual experience of a real population, but rather the number of years a hypothetical life table population would live in active and inactive states if it experienced the observed mortality and morbidity rates.

Active life expectancy data are used by official government publications in the United States, Europe, Asia, and the World Health Organization (WHO), as well as by journalists and public health researchers around the world. It can be used for several purposes including: to provide a summary description of mortality and morbidity for a population; to indicate health inequalities for subgroups in a single population; to make comparisons

## LIFE TABLE

A life table shows the life expectancy of individuals at different ages. It is a series of calculations based on age-specific mortality rates that summarize the effect of mortality on the number of survivors at a given age, and the expected length of life after that age. Life table measures are valuable because they are succinct indicators that reflect mortality conditions across the life course and are unaffected by the number of people in each age group in the actual population, making them comparable across populations and subgroups of the population. Life tables are usually based on mortality data for a short period of time rather than for a real cohort of people throughout life. Because of falling mortality rates over time, actual life expectancy lived by generations has usually been higher than the life expectancy at birth from the life table in the year of their birth.

across populations; to monitor changes in the health of a population; and to asses the contribution of specific risk factors to population health outcomes and thus inform policy debates. *Years of inactive life* can provide an indicator of the average time individuals will need health care or social or institutional support, and is a measure that can also be used to provide a sense of the magnitude of the potential or realized impact of public health programs or other health interventions.

It should be noted that there is no single number alone that is considered the active life expectancy of a population at a given moment because the value depends on the definition of *active* and the method used to calculate the estimate. The definition of *active* can vary from study to study. When the estimate covers all ages, general definitions of disability are used; with older individuals, the definition of disability (also referred to as inactive) is often related to the ability to care for one's own needs independently based on scales that gauge one's capacity to perform various activities of daily living. In addition, inactive years can be further subdivided by levels of severity from the debilitating (e.g., being unable to bathe oneself or eat without assistance) to the more mild (being unable to go shopping or manage money, for instance), depending on the extent to which the disability limits participation in normal roles and daily activities.

### METHODS OF CALCULATION

The first and most commonly used approach to calculating active life expectancy is the prevalence-based life table method, also known as the Sullivan method (1971), named after its designer. This method, developed in the late 1960s, combines age-specific disability, or another indicator of health status prevalence, with the life table functions derived from a set of age-specific mortality rates, to divide the life table years lived into active and inactive. This method remains the most widely used since cross-sectional data on the prevalence of disability and mortality have been readily available. There are multiple advantages to Sullivan's method: (a) it has a straightforward protocol that does not require special software; (b) it can be applied to cross-sectional disability data (a one-point-in-time observation) that are more available than panel surveys (multiple observations); (c) only moderate sample size in the disability survey is required to produce reliable age-specific prevalence estimates; (d) an abridged life table is sufficient for mortality information because the method is not sensitive to the size of the groups; and (e) prevalence-based methods are less influenced by survey design and model assumptions than longitudinal approaches. For a detailed description of this method see *Health Expectancy Calculation by the Sullivan Method: A Practical Guide* (Jagger, Hauet, & Brouard, 2001).

There are some limitations and disadvantages to this widely used approach. The biggest disadvantage is that this method provides little information about the process of health change, which figures into the estimated length of healthy life. Increases in healthy life could come from reductions in the onset of disability, improvements in recovery from disability, or changes in mortality. Second, it may not be a sensitive indicator of change over time because the prevalence of disability may not change as quickly as disability incidence rates. Finally, mortality rates are usually assumed to be the same for both active and inactive individuals, and this assumption is not likely to be accurate. The Sullivan method has been widely used around the world in order to compare change in health or disability over time, differences across countries, and differences within countries.

Building on the Sullivan approach, the WHO uses a measure called *disability-adjusted life expectancy* (DALE). This measure weights different levels of disability as less than full years based on severity, as well as the duration of the disability, so the years lived do not really add up to the total length of life expectancy. This approach is based on cross-sectional data and thus has all of the same limitations as the Sullivan approach; however, it has been used in international comparison studies because the WHO collected relevant data for this measure. The WHO used the DALE measure to compare the health of 191 member state populations in their Global Burden of Disease publications (Lopez et al., 2006).

Incidence based methods estimate active life using longitudinal data that indicate changes in health or disability state over time. Analysis of active life expectancy based on longitudinal data from a panel study of the population is of increasing importance as researchers investigate the causal mechanisms driving changes in population health. Disability is based on incidence, the new occurrence of a condition at a follow-up interview, and thus is focused on recent health events rather than lifetime events. Mortality among the active is also estimated separately from mortality among the inactive based on the panel study, allowing variation in mortality to be reflected in the estimates of active life expectancy. The data input into the life table are the age-specific transition rates that reflect bidirectional transitions between the active and inactive states as well as to death from either an active or inactive state. This is the theoretically preferred method of estimating active life expectancy and has more potential to provide useful information about the processes of disability onset, recovery, and death.

However, this analytic approach is significantly more complicated to model. The major difficulty in adopting this approach is that it requires extensive longitudinal data, with a substantial sample size in order to model the onset of and recovery from disability and transitions to death. The model is also somewhat sensitive to the assumptions underlying the estimation process such as the functional forms of the transition schedules. Several methods have been developed to analyze longitudinal data including: a hazard model approach (Crimmins, Hayward, & Saito, 1994); an algorithm based on Markov chains called IMaCh (Liévre, Brouard, & Heathcote, 2003); a Markov transition model; and a Bayesian Monte Carlo estimation technique.

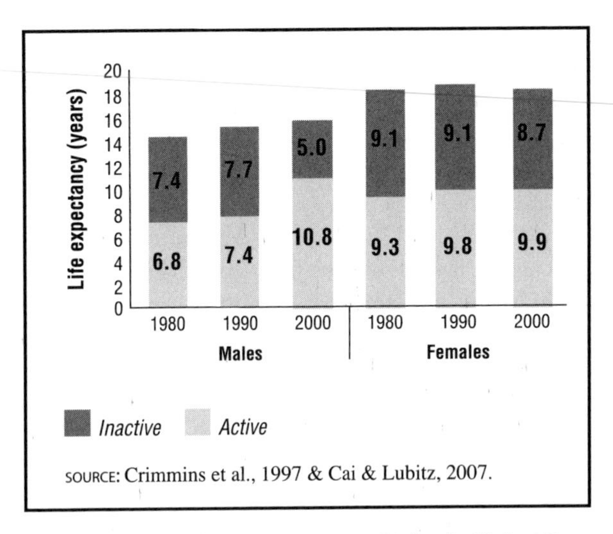


***Figure 1.*** *Active life expectancy at age 65 for the United States. (Crimmins, Saito, & Ingegneri, 1997; Cai & Lubitz, 2007.)* CENGAGE LEARNING, GALE.

## RELATED CONCEPTS

Additional summary measures of active life expectancy have been developed using similar conceptual approaches. In the 1940s the concept of *years of life lost* was developed to assess the health burden associated with deaths prior to the age of average life expectancy based on a simple calculation of the number of deaths multiplied by the life expectancy at the age at which death occurred. More recent measures of life lost have incorporated information on years lived in a disabled state and the time lost to death. For example, in 1993 the WHO introduced *disability-adjusted life years* (DALY) to summarize the effect of both premature death and disability, with each DALY representing one year lost of nondisabled life. The DALY is a health gap measure that identifies years lost to lower quality of life, as well as death. One criticism of the DALY is that it is based on an arbitrary definition of ideal health, with subjectively defined disability weights. DALYs have been used to compare health care cost-effectiveness, with recommendations based on a cost per DALY gained. Both the DALY and the DALE (described earlier) can be used to link potential disease-specific and risk factor interventions with population health outcomes.

*Quality-adjusted life years* (QALY) is usually used as a quantifiable measure of the impact of a medical intervention. In this measure, each year in perfect health is assigned the value of 1.0, each year of non-perfect health (e.g., disabled or otherwise physically limited) is assigned a fractional value relative to its impact on quality of life, and death is assigned a value of 0. The values assigned for non-perfect health are the subject of some debate, and can be calculated by several methods including what follows: the time-trade-off method, where respondents choose between remaining ill for a period of time or being restored to good health with shorter life expectancy; the standard gamble method, in which respondents choose between remaining ill or choosing a risky treatment that has a chance of restoring health or killing them; the visual analog scale in which individuals rate ill health on a scale from 0 (*death*) to 100 (*perfect health*); or the EuroQol EQ-5D questionnaire, a classification system based on dimensions such as mobility, pain, and anxiety (Murray et al., 2002). Multiple question responses can be collapsed into a single health state utility score. Additional information about each of these methods can be found in the *Global Burden of Disease and Risk Factors* report (Lopez et al., 2006) and the WHO's *Summary Measures of Population Health* (Murray et al., 2002).

## TRENDS IN ACTIVE LIFE EXPECTANCY

Active life expectancy became a popular measure with rising interest in whether there has been a compression of morbidity. (Compression of morbidity refers to the concept of pushing all the illness and disability of one's life into as small a time period as possible.) This interest has grown with increasing focus on the quality, as well as the quantity, of life. Many analyses have addressed the issue of how changes in total life expectancy are divided into changes in active and inactive life. A compression of disability or morbidity would be an increase in life expectancy resulting in a greater proportion of life lived active or without disability; an expansion of disability or morbidity would be an increase in the proportion of life lived in the inactive state or with disability or morbidity. It is also possible that both changes occur together, proportional increases in both active and inactive life expectancy, resulting in no change in the relative proportion of life years lived disabled or nondisabled. Understanding which of these scenarios is occurring can potentially have an important impact on planning for the health and support needs of a society, and is of increasing importance as the proportion of the population at older ages increases.

Cross-sectional estimates of expected life that is free of bedridden disability and institutionalization were first attempted in the 1960s. These first estimates of the expectation of healthy life showed increasing healthy life expectancy between the years 1958–1966, whereas life expectancy as a whole did not change. Between 1970 and 1980 life expectancy in the United States increased by about three years and most of the increase was in years of disability. Studies for the mid-1980s through the mid-1990s suggest that disability, particularly severe disability, has declined over this time period, leading to overall increases in active life expectancy. Trends in England and Wales, Canada, and France have been similar to those in the United States: Before 1980 increases in life expectancy were concentrated in disabled years; after 1980 life expectancy in the active state accounted for the majority of the increase in life expectancy.

A small number of studies of trends in active life expectancy based on longitudinal data have been published to date and these are limited to analysis of the older population. Results appear to be similar to studies for the whole population based on cross-sectional data that indicate increases in active life expectancy and decreases in life expectancy with severe disability from the mid-1980s through the late 1990s (Cai & Lubitz, 2007). In addition to calculating estimates of active life expectancy, longitudinal (or over-time) analyses of active life expectancy also investigate trends in disability onset, recovery, and mortality, helping to explain the ways in which the processes leading to disability prevalence may be changing over time. Studies suggest that there have been declines in disability onset through the mid-1980s and the mid-1990s as well as decreases in mortality for both those who are disabled and those who are not.

## DIFFERENCES IN ACTIVE LIFE EXPECTANCY BY SEX, RACE, AND SOCIOECONOMIC STATUS

Researchers have used active life expectancy to summarize differentials in disability and mortality for different subgroups of the population. For example, many studies have addressed differences in active life expectancy by gender, socioeconomic status, and race. Women generally have longer life expectancy than men, and when disability is defined in a yes-or-no fashion, studies show that women tend to have both longer active and longer inactive life than men. Most studies show that women live a greater proportion of their longer lives with disability. In studies where disability severity is taken into account, such as those based on the DALE measure, the proportion of remaining life in disability is more similar for both sexes. This could result from men spending less time with disability, but having more severe disability, which is more heavily weighted in the DALE calculation.

Health expectancy indicators are comparable across groups with different age structures, and are useful for comparing socioeconomic differences across groups, or over time. Socioeconomic differences in active life provide a summary indicator of the effects of inequality on health or disability. Most studies find that people who have lower socioeconomic resources have shorter life expectancy and live a greater proportion of their lives in a disabled state. Differences by social class in expected active life are usually larger than differences in total life expectancy. Reducing socioeconomic differences in active life has become a public health goal in many countries. Trends over recent decades suggest that differences between low and high socioeconomic status groups have been growing, led by increased morbidity differentials (Crimmins & Saito, 2001). Although many different measures of socioeconomic status are used in the literature, education level is the most common measure because it does not generally change after adulthood, and it is not affected by poor health in later life, as income or occupation might be.

In the United States race and ethnic differences in active life expectancy have become an important area of inquiry as these are, of course, highly related to socioeconomic differences. African Americans in the United States have a shorter active life expectancy and a longer disabled life expectancy (Hayward & Heron, 1999). Race and gender also appear to interact; a number of studies conclude that African American women live a notably greater percentage of their lives with disability than

African American men, who have the shortest life expectancy and largest numbers of life years lost.

## INTERNATIONAL COMPARISONS

Measures of active life expectancy have been developed for many countries around the world, led in part by the *Réseau Espérance de Vie en Santé* (REVES) International Network on Healthy Life Expectancy and the Disability Process, and the WHO. The WHO's major contributions are part of a larger initiative called The Global Burden of Disease, which was an attempt to summarize and compare the health needs of countries all over the world. Efforts have been made by researchers to harmonize data collection on disability and health measures in surveys across countries, and many new studies are designed with international comparisons in mind.

International comparison studies by academics generally use the Sullivan method or DALE to calculate expected years active and inactive, as well as the proportion of remaining life expected to be lived in an active state. Precise rankings of countries on active life expectancy are difficult to make, as residents of different countries may evaluate health problems differently and different definitions of disability are employed in different surveys.

Rankings of countries on active life made by the WHO generally parallel rankings of life expectancy. More developed nations report both longer lives and more years active; less developed countries report shorter lives, with a smaller percentage of remaining life expected active. For example, the WHO estimated years of healthy life lost in different regions of the world and found developed countries average about 8% of healthy life lost (of a 77 year life expectancy), while a comparable measure for sub-Saharan Africa is 15% (of a 50 year life expectancy) (Mathers, Sadana, Salomon, Murray, & Lopez, 2001).

Large variations in active life expectancy exist between regions within national borders as well. In Australia, for example, active life expectancy can vary by as much as eight years across states; a comparison of small regions in Canada found differences of active life expectancy as large as 11.5 years; in both Spain and France studies examining active life expectancy in the 1980s and 1990s found increases of up to 4 years in some regions, and declines of 4 years in other regions (Robine, Jagger, Mathers, Crimmins, & Suzman, 2003).

Active life expectancy can be affected by lifestyle and behavioral choices, physical activity, social interactions, random events such as accidents or catastrophic health problems, and preventable strategies to avoid injurious situations. Recovery can be affected by these issues as well, in addition to medical interventions and the availability of compensatory services.

## SUMMARY

Active life expectancy can provide a succinct indicator of the health and mortality of a population as well as a summary of differences within populations, changes over time, or differences between countries. Trends in active life expectancy appear to show increasing length of active life expectancy, especially when severe disability is used to define inactive, and little change over time when mild disability is used to define inactive. Early 21st-century trends suggest widening differences across socioeconomic classes. A valuable summary of information on the concept of active life expectancy, methodological approaches, and empirical findings can be found in *Determining Health Expectancies* (Robine et. al, 2003), which is written and edited by the members of the REVES International Network on Health Expectancy and the Disability Process.

**SEE ALSO** Volume 3: *Disability and Functional Limitation, Later Life; Health Differentials/Disparities, Later Life; Life Expectancy; Mortality; Population Aging.*

### BIBLIOGRAPHY

Cai, L., & Lubitz, J. (2007). Was there compression of disability for older Americans from 1992 to 2003? *Demography, 44*(3), 479–495.

Crimmins, E. M., Hayward, M.D., & Saito, Y. (1994). Changing mortality and morbidity rates and the health status and life expectancy of the older population. *Demography, 31,* 159–175.

Crimmins, E. M., Saito, Y., & Ingegneri, D. (1997). Trends in disability-free life expectancy in the U.S.: 1970–1990. *Population and Development Review, 23*(3), 555–572.

Crimmins, E. M., & Saito, Y. (2001). Trends in disability-free life expectancy in the United States, 1970–1990: Gender, racial, and educational differences. *Social Science and Medicine, 52,* 1629–1641.

Hayward, M., & Heron, M. (1999). Racial inequality in active life among adult Americans. *Demography, 36*(1), 77–91.

Jagger, C., Hauet, E., & Brouard, N. (2001, June 13). Health expectancy calculation by the Sullivan method: A practical guide. Réseau Espérance de Vie en Santé (REVES) International Network on Health Expectancy. Retrieved January 28, 2008, from http://www.reves.net

Laditka, S. B., & Wolf, D. (1998). New methods for analyzing active life expectancy. *Journal of Aging and Health, 10,* 214–241.

Liévre, A., Brouard, N., & Heathcote, C. (2003). The estimation of health expectancies from cross-longitudinal surveys. *Mathematical Population Studies, 10,* 211–248.

Lopez, A. D., Mathers, C. D., Ezzati, M., Jamison, D. T., & Murray, C. J. L. (2006). *Global burden of disease and risk factors.* New York: Oxford University Press.

Mathers, C. D., Sadana, R., Salomon, J.A., Murray, C. J., & Lopez, A. D. (2001). Healthy life expectancy in 191 countries, 1999. *Lancet, 357*(9269), 1685–1691.

Murray, C. J. L., Salomon, J. A., Mathers, C. D., & Lopez, A. D. (Eds.). (2002). *Summary measures of population health: Concepts, ethics, measurement, and applications*. Geneva, Switzerland: World Health Organization.

Robine, J. M., Jagger, C., Mathers, C. D., Crimmins, E. M., & Suzman, R. M. (Eds.). (2003). *Determining health expectancies*. Chichester, UK: John Wiley & Sons.

Sullivan, D.F. (1971). A single index of mortality and morbidity. *HSMHA Health Reports, 86*, 347–354.

***Aaron T. Hagedorn***
***Eileen M. Crimmins***

# ACTIVITIES OF DAILY LIVING (ADLS) AND INSTRUMENTAL ACTIVITIES OF DAILY LIVING (IADL)

SEE Volume 3: *Disability and Functional Limitation, Later Life.*

# ACTIVITY PARTICIPATION, LATER LIFE

SEE Volume 3: *Leisure and Travel, Later Life; Time Use, Later Life; Volunteering, Later Life.*

# AGE, PERIOD, COHORT EFFECTS

Life course and human development research has long concerned itself with time-specific phenomena that can be represented in age, period, or cohort (APC) effects. The search for these effects—APC analysis—permeates sociological, demographic, and epidemiologic studies of aging and the life course. Because APC analysis has the unique capacity to depict the entire complex of social, historical, and environmental factors that shape individual life courses, its importance for constructing and refining theory, measurement, and analysis can hardly be overstated. This entry briefly introduces the intellectual history of various conceptual and analytic issues in contemporary APC analysis, discusses the consequences and implications of misspecifications of APC effects in previous studies, reviews the state-of-the-art development of APC models in recent research, and concludes with the challenges that remain for studies of APC phenomena in human societies.

## DEFINITIONS OF AGE, PERIOD, AND COHORT EFFECTS

Age, period, and cohort effects all refer to some type of time-related variation in the phenomena of interest, yet they carry distinct substantive meanings.

*Age effects* are defined as variations associated with different chronological age groups brought about by physiological changes, accumulation of social experience, and/or role or status changes. Age effects, therefore, reflect biological and social processes of aging internal to individuals and represent developmental changes across the life course. This can clearly be seen in the considerable regularities of age variations across historical time and place in many outcomes such as mortality, fertility, disease prevalence and incidence, schooling, employment, marriage, and family structure. The identification of age changes is especially important in studies of health and aging because age has been shown to be the most important source of variation in vital rates and has frequently been used to understand the etiology of diseases (Hobcraft, Menken, & Preston 1982).

*Period effects* are defined as variation over time periods or calendar years that influence all age groups simultaneously. Period effects subsume a complex set of historical events and environmental factors such as world wars, economic crises, famine, epidemics and pandemics of infectious diseases, public health interventions, and technologic breakthroughs. Shifts in social, cultural, economic, or physical environments may in turn induce similar changes in the lives of all people at a given point in time. Thus, period effects are evident from a correspondence of changes in demographic events and social and epidemiologic conditions that are expected to influence these events.

*Cohort effects* are defined as changes across groups of people who experience an initial event such as birth or marriage in the same year or years. Birth cohorts are the most commonly examined unit of analysis in demographic and aging research. A birth cohort moves through life together and encounters the same historical and social events at the same ages. Birth cohorts that experience different historical and social conditions at various stages of their life course, therefore, have diverse experiences. Conceived as the essence of social change (Ryder, 1965), cohort effects arise when each succeeding cohort carries with it the imprint of physical and social exposures from gestation to old age that bear on its members' fortunes in a way specific to that cohort. Cohort effects thus represent the effects of formative experiences that subsume both the effects of early life conditions and the continuous exposures to historical and social factors throughout the life course.

Conceptually distinguishing APC effects is theoretically important in three ways. First, it is crucial for attributions of etiology or social causation. Age effects represent aging-related developmental changes in the life course, whereas temporal trends across time periods or birth cohorts reflect exogenous contextual changes in broader social conditions. Second, this distinction also relates to the generalizability of research findings. In the absence of period and cohort effects, age changes are broadly applicable across individuals in different time periods and cohorts. However, differences among periods and/or cohorts indicate the existence of social forces and exposures affecting changes that are period and/or cohort specific. Third, to the extent that these effects serve as aggregates and proxies for different sets of structural correlates, the distinction is especially valuable for better understanding and identifying the underlying social and environmental factors that are amenable to modifications.

## THE HISTORY OF AGE, PERIOD, AND COHORT EFFECTS

Although studies of age and time variations have long existed in the history of science, those that jointly consider age, period, and cohort variations as distinct entities appeared in the scholarly literature only relatively recently. Examinations using APC analysis are most common in demographic studies of human population and have been most rigorously developed in analyses of mortality (Hobcraft et al., 1982). The earliest attempts can be found in descriptive studies of 19th-century English death rates that clearly indicated the importance of cohort variations, relative to period variations, in projecting mortality (Derrick, 1927; Kermack, McKendrick, & McKinlay, 1934). The relevance of this approach was then recognized in subsequent epidemiologic investigations of public health issues, the earliest of which is the well-known study on tuberculosis mortality conducted by Frost (1939). Frost's study emphasized the influence of early life conditions, rather than current conditions, on cohort experiences for a disease that has long latency. The usefulness of APC analysis demonstrated by these early studies and the convenience of using simple indicators that are widely available in many kinds of data facilitated the quick spread of APC analysis not only in the demography of mortality and fertility but also in the epidemiology of diseases. Although APC analysis has taken root in these two fields relatively independently of one another, the common interest and similarities in the development of analytic techniques unite them as one cottage industry.

Early studies mostly relied on descriptive analyses such as graphical displays of age-standardized or age-specific data by time period or birth cohort. They are useful for providing *qualitative* impressions about temporal patterns, but they provide no *quantitative* assessment of the sources of change. The question of how these factors simultaneously operate to shape the observed patterns require the use of statistical regression modeling (Kupper, Janis, Karmous, & Greenberg, 1985). The first successful implementation of a statistical model for APC analysis was by Greenberg, Wright, and Sheps (1950), who found statistically significant variations that can be attributed to all three effects.

The APC accounting or multiple classification model was more fully developed by Mason, Mason, Winsborough, and Poole (1973) and has served for over three decades as a general methodology for estimating separate APC effects using conventional linear regression models. Mason and associates also formally defined the model identification problem that is induced by the unique relationship between the three variables: period = age + cohort. A vast literature in demography, biostatistics, and sociology subsequently used this methodology, with only the solutions to the identification problem varying (Hobcraft et al., 1982). Differences among these solutions often produce ambiguous and inconsistent results. Researchers do not agree on methodological solutions to these problems and have concluded that APC analysis is still in its infancy (Kupper et al., 1985; Mason & Wolfinger, 2002).

## DISENTANGLING AGE, PERIOD, AND COHORT EFFECTS: ILLUSTRATIVE EXAMPLES

Disentangling APC effects in empirical analysis is without a doubt an arduous task. Failure to attend to this confounding problem, however, can constitute model misspecification and seriously bias one's understanding of the true social and biological processes that generated the observed data. The following examples illustrate this point by showing how omitting one or more factors leads to differences in inference.

First, some widely embraced images of the baby boom cohorts do not mean the presence of cohort effects. For example, the *boomers* have been frequently conceived of as the innovators rewriting the rules and remaking society. They have also been thought of as the *Me Generation,* which consists of self-indulgent consumers obsessed with health and youth and rely on products such as Botox or Viagra to fight against the effects of biological aging (Hughes & O'Rand, 2004). Although it is intuitively appealing to attribute these as cohort effects, they could have been driven by other forces that are independent of cohort effects, such as period changes. One key assumption on which the expectation of cohort effects rests is that individuals do not change their attitudes and behaviors in response to changes in political, economic, or social context over time. It is possible that

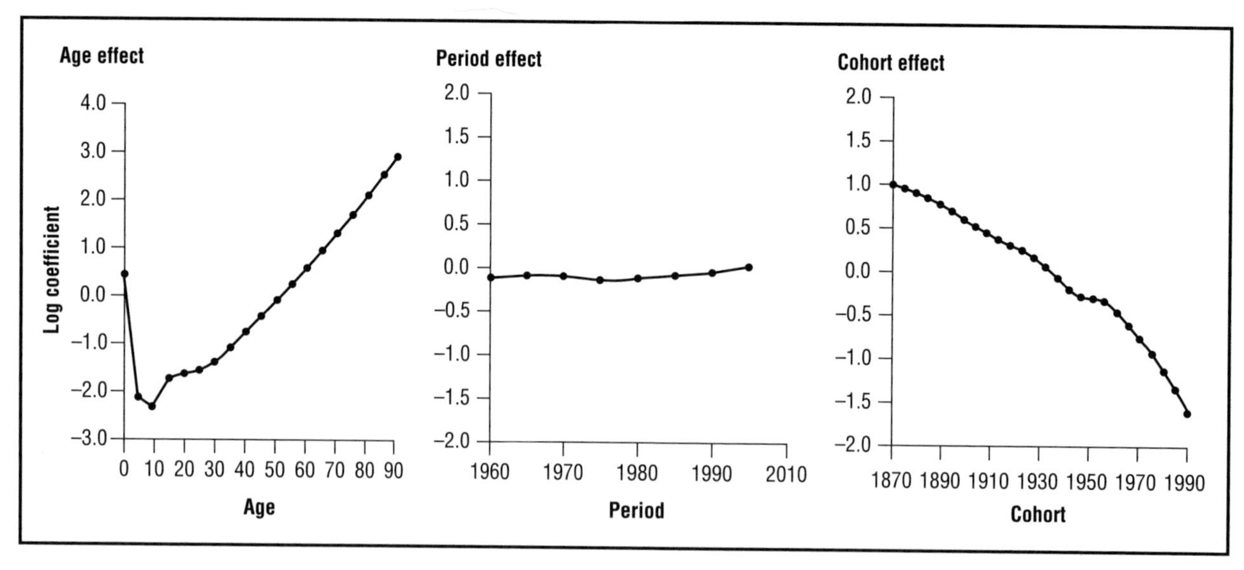


***Figure 1.*** *Hierarchical APC model estimates of age, period, and cohort effects on U.S. verbal ability: GSS 1972–2000.* CENGAGE LEARNING, GALE.

the characteristics observed in the baby boomers have resulted from their adaptations to period conditions. Such period conditions could have also changed other cohorts in a similar way.

Consider another case in which one omits cohort effects in studies of temporal trends in adult mortality in the United States. Substantial mortality declines in the United States for a large part of the past 100 years have been widely documented. However, the sources of mortality reductions in the most recent 50 years are not well understood. Empirical investigations are usually confined to changes in age and/or period trends. The cohort effect is less frequently tested. If it is present, then it implies that certain assumptions currently employed by demographers and other social scientists can be misleading. For instance, it is frequently assumed that rates of mortality declines over time are equal across birth cohorts. It is also assumed that these declines depend on rates of change in period-specific conditions such as economic advance and health care technology that are independent of birth year. These assumptions ignore cohort effects and greatly simplify estimations, but they are increasingly inconsistent with the accumulating evidence of cohort differences in a variety of health outcomes that predict mortality. Recent APC analyses, conversely, relate these temporal patterns of mortality to specific demographic components by delineating APC effects (Yang, Fu, & Land, 2004). They provide new evidence of persistent cohort differences in mortality rates—namely, the substantial survival improvements across most birth cohorts. As shown in Figure 1, the most striking finding is the dominance of cohort effects in explaining recent trends of mortality reductions. Period effects are generally small or modest when birth cohort and age effects are simultaneously controlled in the analysis. Thus, the role of cohort effects in recent mortality declines suggests that the assumptions employed in previous studies are untenable. This undeniably has serious implications for measurement and analysis in future research.

A third example is confounding cohort and aging effects in the life-course study of mental health. Is old age depressing? Most cross-sectional studies found that depression changes with age. However, findings are inconsistent with regard to the direction of this relationship. This inconsistency has been referred to as a *scientific myth.* Cross-section data, however, do not substantiate real-time aging as a risk factor for depression, nor do they suggest true life course changes of individuals. More important, age and birth cohort differences are confounded and cannot be disentangled with observations obtained at a point in time. Using longitudinal data with multiple follow-ups and statistical models that distinguish the age and cohort effects, Yang (2007) found evidence of substantial cohort variations in age trajectories of depression. Earlier cohorts have higher levels of depression on average (Figure 2), which are largely due to their lower levels of education and income relative to more recent cohorts. Taking this cohort effect into account explains away the aging effect.

## AGE-PERIOD-COHORT MODELS: NEW DEVELOPMENTS AND CHALLENGES

The conventional linear model of additive APC effects (Mason et al., 1973) has been the most widely used model

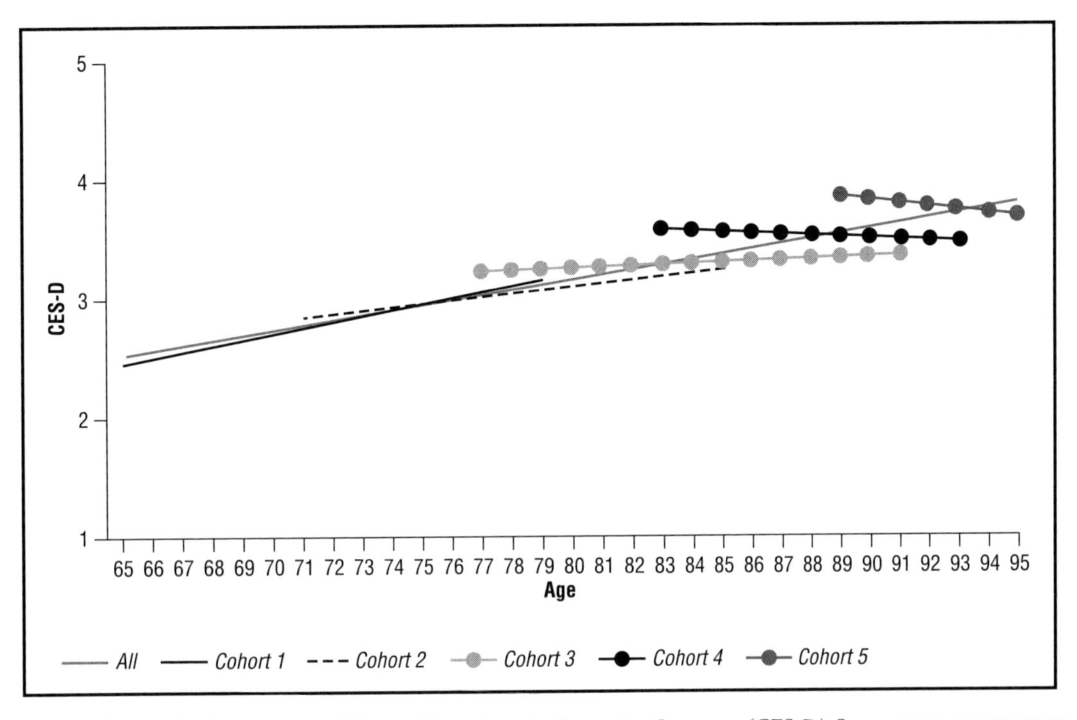


***Figure 2.*** *Expected Growth Trajectories and Cohort Variations in Depressive Symptom (CES-D) Scores.* CENGAGE LEARNING, GALE.

for analysis of tabular population level data. As mentioned already, one has to resolve the identification problem by imposing certain identifying constraints to estimate such a model. The most common approach to solving this problem is to place at least one equality constraint on two or more of the age, period, or cohort coefficients. For example, one can constrain the effect coefficients of two adjacent age groups, periods, or cohorts to be equal to identify the model (see, e.g., Mason & Smith, 1985; Yang et al., 2004). The main criticisms of this approach and its variants are that (a) different equality constraints yield different effect coefficient estimates but identical model fit and (b) estimates of the effect coefficients and thus of the patterns of change across the age, period, and cohort dimensions are sensitive to the choice of the identifying constraints that depends on strong a priori or external information that rarely exists or can be well verified (Mason & Wolfinger, 2002).

The problem with much of the extant literature is that there is a deficiency of useful guidelines on how to conduct an APC analysis. Rather, the literature often leads to the conclusion that it is either impossible to obtain meaningful estimates of the distinct contributions of age, time period, and cohort to the study of social change or that conducting an APC analysis is an esoteric art that is best left to a few skilled methodologists. New models and methods have been developed to redress this situation for three common research designs in social science research. These developments not only have better addressed the limitations in conventional APC models but also have extended the reach of APC analysis to a new family of models. They consist of (a) a new statistical estimator, called the Intrinsic Estimator, for estimating the conventional APC multiple classification models for the aggregate population level data on occurrence/exposure rates (Yang et al., 2004); (b) a hierarchical or mixed (fixed and random) effects model for repeated cross-section sample surveys with multilevel data (Yang & Land, 2006; Yang, 2006); and (c) a hierarchical or individual change model for accelerated longitudinal cohort data (Miyazaki & Raudenbush, 2000; Yang, 2007).

The APC identification problem is inevitable only under the specification of conventional linear models of fixed APC effects that are assumed to be additive. However, additivity is only one approximation to the process of how social change occurs. The models described above in items (b) and (c) bypass this problem by specifying nonlinear models for multilevel data, thereby allowing researchers to capture the contextual effects of cohort membership and historical time on a wide range of social demographic processes. In addition, the possibility of testing explanatory hypotheses using these kinds of models greatly enhances researchers' ability to construct theories about the specific social forces that produce general cohort and period trends.

The developments summarized above mark the beginning of a new era of APC analysis. New models and methods are needed for testing other theories of social change. Two prominent examples (Hobcraft et al., 1982) that need additional methodological development are (a) *cohort-inversion models* that suggest that cohorts experiencing exceptionally adverse or beneficial events early in life will respond inversely later in life and (b) *continuously accumulating or evolving cohort effects models* that suggest that, contrary to what conventional linear models assume, cohorts are continuously exposed to influences that alter their developmental trajectories over the life course. There currently are few, if any, statistical models with which to apply these conceptually appealing models. The development of such analytic devices and tools thus should be a priority for future research.

**SEE ALSO** Volume 3: *Aging; Cohort.*

**BIBLIOGRAPHY**

Derrick, V. P. A. (1927). Observations on (1) errors of age in the population statistics of England and Wales, and (2) the changes in mortality indicated by the national records. *Journal of the Institute of Actuaries, 58,* 17–146.

Frost, W. H. (1939). The age selection of mortality from tuberculosis in successive decades. *American Journal of Hygiene, 30,* 91–96.

Greenberg, B. G., Wright, J. J., & Sheps, C. G. (1950). A technique for analyzing some factors affecting the incidence of syphilis. *Journal of the American Statistical Association, 45,* 373–399.

Hobcraft, J., Menken, J., & Preston, S. H. (1982). Age, period, and cohort effects in demography: A review. *Population Index, 48,* 4–43.

Hughes, M. E., & O'Rand, A. M. (2004). *The American people census 2000: The lives and times of the baby boomers.* New York: Russell Sage Foundation.

Kermack, W. O., McKendrick, A. G., & McKinlay, P. L. (1934). Death rates in Great Britain and Sweden: Some general regularities and their significance. *Lancet, 1,* 698–703.

Kupper, L. L., Janis, J. M., Karmous, A., & Greenberg, B. G. (1985). Statistical age-period-cohort analysis: A review and critique. *Journal of Chronic Disease, 38,* 811–30.

Mason, K. O., Mason, W. M., Winsborough, H. H., & Poole, W. K. (1973). Some methodological issues in cohort analysis of archival data. *American Sociological Review, 38,* 242–258.

Mason, W. M., & Wolfinger, N. H. (2002). Cohort analysis. In *International encyclopedia of the social and behavioral sciences* (pp. 151–228). New York: Elsevier.

Mason, W. M., & Smith, H. L. (1985). Age-period-cohort analysis and the study of deaths from pulmonary tuberculosis. In W. M. Mason & S. E. Fienberg (Eds.), *Cohort analysis in social research* (pp. 151–228). New York: Springer-Verlag.

Miyazaki, Y., & Raudenbush, S. W. (2000). Tests for linkage of multiple cohorts in an accelerated longitudinal design. *Psychological Methods, 5,* 44–63.

Ryder, N. B. (1965). The cohort as a concept in the study of social change. *American Sociological Review, 30,* 843–861.

Yang, Y. (2006). Bayesian inference for hierarchical age-period-cohort models of repeated cross-section survey data. *Sociological Methodology, 36,* 39–74.

Yang, Y. (2007). Is old age depressing? Growth trajectories and cohort variations in late life depression. *Journal of Health and Social Behavior, 48,* 16–32.

Yang, Y., & Land, K. C. (2006). A mixed models approach to age-period-cohort analysis of repeated cross-section surveys: Trends in verbal test scores. *Sociological Methodology, 36,* 75–97.

Yang, Y., Wenjiang J. Fu, & Land, K. C. (2004). A methodological comparison of age-period-cohort models: Intrinsic estimator and conventional generalized linear models. *Sociological Methodology, 34,* 75–110.

*Yang Yang*

# AGE IDENTITY

The concept of age identity refers to the inner experience of a person's age and aging process. Age identity is the outcome of the processes through which one identifies with or distances oneself from different aspects of the aging process. In scientific research a person's age identity is measured with questions such as "How old do you feel?"; "To which age group do you belong?"; and "How do you perceive and understand your own aging process?"

Age identity belongs to the domain of the subjective experience of aging. Key measures of age identity thus are subject to personal biases and misinterpretation, yet researchers in the field of gerontology have long taken the personal experience of one's own age and aging process to be a subject worthy of investigation. Different aspects of age identity have been studied empirically since the 1950s (Barak & Stern, 1986). There are two reasons why it is important to study this topic. First, age identities, however biased they may be, have important consequences for individual development over the life course. Second, age identities represent visions of aging that come from older persons. It is important to highlight these perspectives in research, as they are not paid much attention in contemporary society.

## FEELING YOUNG

Consistent with the saying that "you're only as old as you feel," one of the most widely replicated findings in age identity research is that older individuals tend not to feel old. In 1986 S. R. Kaufman conducted a series of in-depth interviews about the personal experiences of aging. Despite changes in their physical and social functioning, many older persons had a strong inner experience of continuity that was not affected by their rising chronological age. Kaufman concluded that older people have an "ageless self." Many older persons also do not feel that they belong to the elderly age group and tend to see

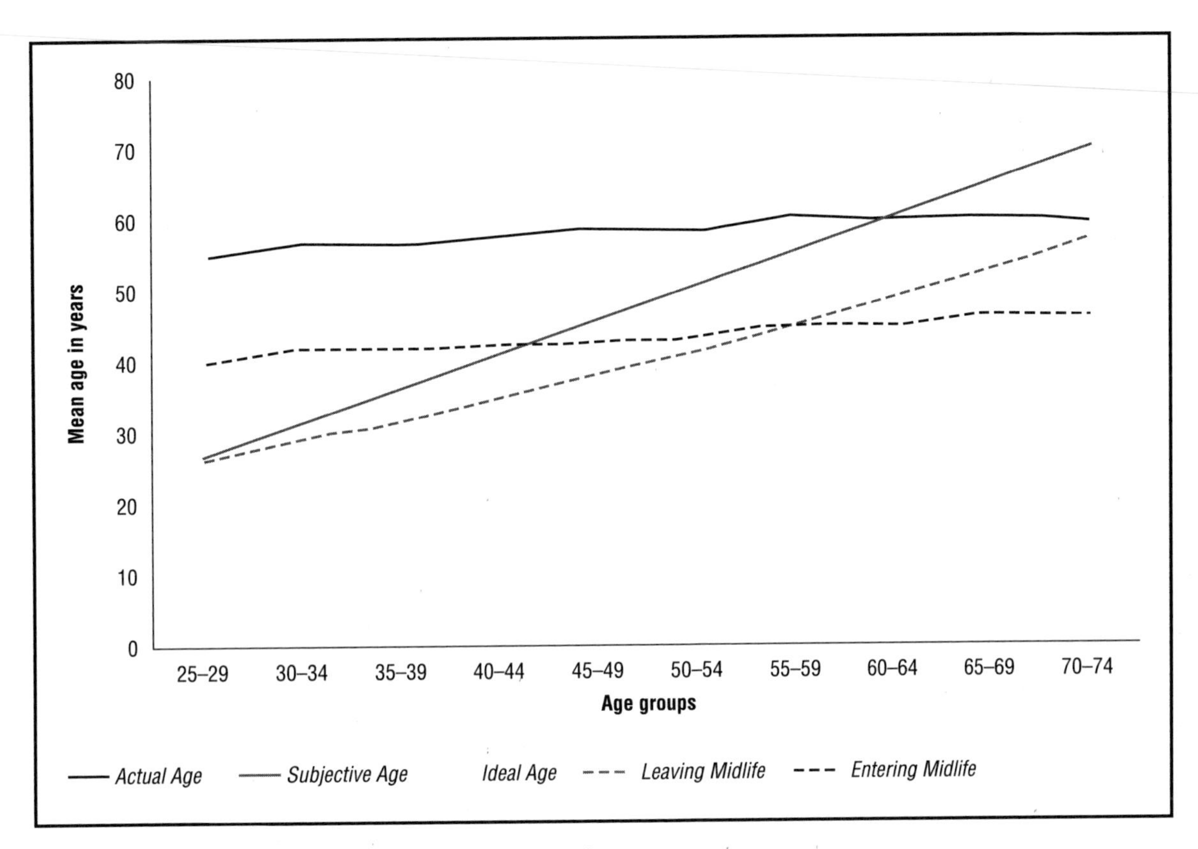


***Figure 1.*** *Different aspects of age identity as compared to actual age.* CENGAGE LEARNING, GALE.

themselves as doing better than their peers. In general they see themselves as an exception to the general belief that aging is related to decline.

Many studies have shown that older individuals feel younger than their chronological age. Figure 1 illustrates this phenomenon by using data from the study on Midlife Development in the United States (MIDUS), one of the few nationally representative American surveys that have measured age identity. The figure shows the mean actual age and the mean subjective age for 5-year age groups. It can be seen that in the youngest age group (25 to 29 years old) there is almost no discrepancy between one's actual age and one's felt age. Each consecutive age group has a younger age identity, up to the oldest individuals, who feel about 13 years younger than their actual age. This pattern has been found consistently in studies comparing different age groups (Barak & Stern, 1986, Westerhof, Barrett, & Steverink, 2003). However, when the same individuals are followed over time, it is found that not all individuals experience an increase in perceived youthfulness; unhealthy people tend to feel less young (Uotinen, Rantanen, Suutuma, & Ruoppila, 2006).

To understand why older people tend to feel younger than their actual age, it is useful to look at the standards individuals use in judging their subjective age. An important standard is people's ideal age: how old individuals want to be. This is an important standard because it provides information about how satisfied older persons are with their chronological age (Uotinen et al., 2006). It can be seen in Figure 1 that the average ideal age is much lower than the chronological age. On average, persons in the oldest age group (70 to 74 years old) want to be almost half their actual age and therefore appear to be very unsatisfied with their age. It also can be seen that individuals on average want to be younger than they actually feel.

Another standard that individuals use in judging their own subjective age are their ideas about when a person enters or leaves a certain stage in the life course. Individuals who participated in the MIDUS study were asked to report the age at which they believe men and women enter and leave middle age. On average, midlife was believed to start at age 44 and end at age 59. In each age group, the mean ideal age is below the age of entering middle age and the mean subjective age is below the age of leaving middle age. Individuals want to be younger than midlife and do not feel older than midlife. It can be concluded that individuals have much younger age identities than their objective age, and their norms about midlife provide support for these perceptions.

## PSYCHOLOGICAL PROCESSES

How can this bias toward younger age identities be understood? Life-span psychologists have described the phenomenon of feeling younger than one's actual age as resulting from a process of adaptation to age-related changes (Sneed & Whitbourne, 2003). When individuals are confronted with age-related changes such as the loss of paid employment and the onset of physical decline, they may strive to maintain their existing identity. For example, when an individual who sees himself as an athlete is confronted with limitations in his physical mobility, he may strive to overcome those limitations by exercising and thus maintain his identity as an athlete. This process is called assimilation. Conversely, an individual may react to new experiences by changing her identity, a process called accommodation. In this case the athlete may give up her identity and search for a new one, for example, being an artist or a writer. From this developmental perspective, feeling younger than one's actual age is the result of an assimilation process that maintains an existing identity.

From a psychological perspective, researchers have argued that motives such as self-continuity and self-enhancement may shape age identity. Self-continuity refers to the desire and motivation to remain the same person over time. Identifying with the younger ages one has been thus results in a feeling of consistency with one's past. Self-enhancement refers to the motive to maintain or increase a positive image of oneself. Youthful identities are a way to satisfy this desire in a culture that associates aging with decline and associates youth with vigor and physical attractiveness, reflecting prevailing negative cultural images of old age in American society.

## CULTURAL CONTEXTS

According to modernization theory, cultural changes create a social context in which youth is a more valued status than old age. For example, historically, the status of older persons declined as a result of increases in literacy and the dissemination of information through formal educational systems and the mass media, which deprived the elderly of their traditional advantage in knowledge. Because there were no systematic observations on age identities in earlier historical periods, it is impossible to assess whether modernization resulted in an increase in the youthfulness of the identities of older persons. However, cross-cultural studies have shown that there are differences in age identities that are based on the way modernization processes unfolded. Although individuals in many cultures tend to feel younger than their actual age, the discrepancy and the age differences are less pronounced in European and Asian cultures than in the United States. For example, a nationally comparative study showed that 74-year-olds feel about 8 years younger in Germany, compared with 14 years in the United States (Westerhof, Barrett, & Steverink, 2003). These differences were attributed to differences in welfare systems and individualistic values resulting from differences in the modernization process in the two countries.

## INTERINDIVIDUAL VARIATION

The focus on average age identities across large groups of persons conceals the fact that there is also clear variability between individuals. Although about three-quarters of Americans feel younger than their actual age, the MIDUS study shows that 15% feel about the same age as they actually are and that 10% feel older than their chronological age. How can this individual variation be understood?

From a life-course perspective, cultural norms provide guidelines for what is considered the optimal chronological age at which life transitions should occur. For example, people judge whether marriage, parenthood, or retirement happens on time or whether an individual is too young or too old for it. In general, when there is a cultural age norm for a particular transition, one can expect that those who experienced that transition will feel older than those who did not. The most consistent evidence for this line of reasoning is found for physical health. Individuals who have poorer health have a less youthful age identity than do their age peers who are in better health (Barrett, 2003). In a culture that largely equates aging with physical decline, individuals tend to use their physical health status as an indicator of their personal aging process. A few studies have examined other life-course transitions, such as the empty-nest phase, retirement, widowhood, and grandparenthood. Although the findings are inconclusive, they tend to confirm that these transitions and their timing in the life course are related to older age identities.

However, life-course transitions tend not to occur at a single uniform age. Life-course theorists have documented that the timing and nature of transitions vary with one's social position, such as socioeconomic status, gender, and race. For example, persons of lower socioeconomic status (less education, less income, and lower-status jobs) experience a pattern of cumulative disadvantage over the life course as well as a temporally more compressed life course; that is, they experience life transitions during a shorter, more densely packed period. Thus, one might expect that persons from backgrounds with lower socioeconomic status have older age identities in that they experience health problems and major transitions such as marriage, parenthood, and grandparenthood earlier than do their wealthier peers. This has been found in many studies. The relative health disadvantage of those with lower status is the most important explanation for this finding (Barrett, 2003).

From a feminist perspective, it has been argued that women in Western cultures suffer from a double standard of aging. Whereas aging comes with grace for men, it comes with disrespect and disregard for older women.

One therefore might expect that women will try to escape this double standard by overstating their own youthfulness more than men do. Few if any empirical studies provide support for this hypothesis, however. Similarly, one might expect that ethnic minorities feel older than Whites, as they have disadvantages similar to those of persons in lower socioeconomic positions. Growing older might pose double jeopardy to aging ethnic minorities that might make them feel even older. However, few studies have assessed this proposition rigorously.

## INTRAINDIVIDUAL VARIATION

Life span psychologists emphasize that the aging process is multidirectional and multidimensional; in other words, there is a balance between gains and losses in different life domains, such as family, health, and personal development. Therefore, it might be expected that one's age identity is more complex than a simple snapshot measure of whether one feels older or younger than one's chronological age.

Qualitative studies of age identities have revealed that individuals perceive both losses and gains in their personal aging process (Keller, Leventhal, & Larson, 1989). In a nationally representative study of middle-age and older persons in the Netherlands, respondents completed two sentence stems: "what I like about getting older ..." and "what I don't like about getting older ..." (Westerhof, 2003). Negative perceptions of aging mainly concern physical and social decline. Physical decline is experienced in terms of increasing vulnerability, a loss of vitality, and complaints about specific functional losses such as losses in mobility, vision, and hearing, which are attributed to normal aging. Social losses pertain to the death of loved ones, the loss of independence, and the loss of respect in society. Positive perceptions of one's own aging process were found mainly in social and psychological functioning. The increasing freedom and autonomy, the continuity of relationships, and the birth of grandchildren are the most important social gains, whereas increases in life experience, wisdom, and tranquillity are the most frequently mentioned psychological gains.

In an effort to incorporate these more complex aspects of age identities into gerontological research, researchers have developed and used multidimensional instruments. For example, the frequently used cognitive age measure (Barak, 1987) characterizes subjective age as feel-age ("I feel as though I am ..."), look-age ("I look as though I am ..."), do-age ("I do things as though I am ..."), and interest-age ("My interest are mostly those of a person of ... years"). Although the answers to these questions are related, individuals may have a feel-age that is different from their look-age, do-age, or interest-age.

New multidimensional measurement instruments have been designed to capture perceptions of different aspects of the aging process. For example, Steverink, Westerhof, Bode, and Dittmann-Kohli (2001) developed an instrument for measuring the experience of one's own aging in terms of physical decline, social loss, and continued personal growth. Older persons experienced more physical and social decline in their aging process than did middle-aged persons and also felt that they had fewer opportunities to continue their personal growth.

In addition to exploring the different domains that shape age identities, researchers have investigated the ways in which social context affects those identities. Symbolic interactionism is a sociological framework that focuses on the ways individuals present themselves in different social interactions in their daily lives. Nikolas Coupland and Justine Coupland (1995) reported a case study of May, a 79-year-old woman. In a conversation with a woman her own age, May presented herself as active and independent, resisting stereotypical images of older persons. In a conversation with a 38-year old woman, however, May suddenly offered a negative portrait of herself, confirming stereotypical images of being old and dependent. These different ways of presenting oneself are related to who has the initiative in the interaction and to the infantilizing mode of communication of the younger partner.

## THE IMPORTANCE OF AGE IDENTITY FOR LIFE-SPAN DEVELOPMENT

As a potentially biased interpretation and characterization of one's own aging process, age identity has important consequences for one's further life-span development. Psychological theories of self-continuity and self-enhancement suggest that one's age identity is typically younger than one's chronological age and that younger age identities are related to mental health and well-being. Many studies have supported this expectation (Barak & Stern, 1986; Steverink et al., 2001). Well-being often is taken as the outcome of successful aging; thus, these studies suggest that age identities are related to a successful outcome of the aging process. However, existing studies have not shown definitively whether age identity influences mental health or mental health affects age identity in later life.

Research shows persuasively that good physical health is one of the strongest correlates of youthful age identities. Although physical health may affect age identities, the causality also may be reversed: One's age identity may affect one's physical health later in life. Studies have shown that more positive self-perceptions of aging and more youthful age identities are related to better health over time and even to longevity (Levy, 2003).

Perceptions of one's aging process have important consequences for one's further psychological development, physical health, and even mortality. However, individuals' denial of aging may contribute unwittingly to the perpetuation of cultural beliefs about old age as a period of decline at the societal level. It is therefore important to construct identities of old age that are positive in and of themselves.

**SEE ALSO** Volume 3: *Ageism/Age Discrimination; Self.*

**BIBLIOGRAPHY**

Barak, B. (1987). Cognitive age: A new multidimensional approach to measuring age identity. *International Journal of Aging and Human Development, 25*(2), 109–128.

Barak, B., & Stern, B. (1986). Subjective age correlates: A research note. *Gerontologist, 26*(5), 571–578.

Barrett, A. E. (2003). Socioeconomic status and age identity: The role of dimensions of health in the subjective construction of age. *Journals of Gerontology Series B: Psychological Sciences and Social Sciences, 58B,* S101–S109.

Coupland, N., & Coupland, J. (1995). Discourse, identity and aging. In J. F. Nussbaum & J. Coupland (Eds.), *Handbook of communication and aging* (pp. 79–103). Mahwah, NJ: Lawrence Erlbaum.

Kaufman S. R. (1986). *The ageless self: Sources of meaning in late life.* Madison: University of Wisconsin Press.

Keller, M. L., Leventhal, E. A., & Larson, B. (1989). Aging: The lived experience. *International Journal of Aging and Human Development, 29*(1), 67–82.

Levy, B. R. (2003). Mind matters: Cognitive and physical effects of aging self-stereotypes. *Journals of Gerontology Series B: Psychological Sciences and Social Sciences, 58B,* P203–P211.

Sneed, J. R., & Whitbourne, S. K. (2003). Identity processing and self-consciousness in middle and later adulthood. *Journals of Gerontology: Psychological Sciences and Social Sciences, 58,* P313–P319.

Steverink, N., Westerhof, G. J., Bode, C., & Dittmann-Kohli, F. (2001). The personal experience of growing old, resources and subjective well-being. *Journals of Gerontology: Psychological and Social Sciences, 56B,* P364–P373.

Uotinen, V., Rantanen, T., Suutama, T., & Ruoppila, I. (2006). Change in subjective age among older people over an eight-year follow-up: "Getting older and feeling younger?" *Experimental Aging Research, 32*(4), 381–393.

Westerhof, G. J. (2003). De beleving van het eigen ouder worden: Multidimensionaliteit en multidirectionaliteit in relatie tot succesvol ouder worden en welbevinden [The experience of aging: Multidimensionality and multidirectionality in relation to successful aging and well-being]. *Tijdschrift voor Gerontologie en Geriatrie, 34,* 96–103.

Westerhof, G. J., Barrett, A. E., & Steverink, N. (2003). Forever young: A comparison of age identities in the United States and Germany. *Research on Aging, 25*(4), 366–383.

*Gerben J. Westerhof*

# AGE SEGREGATION

*Age segregation* refers to the separation of age groups in society. This separation may be physical, in terms of spatial location, or social, in terms of social networks and supports. The separation of age groups can reduce contact between younger and older persons. Because segregation separates members of groups, age segregation may perpetuate stereotypes between generations by limiting opportunities for them to interact. Age-segregated social networks limit the exposure of individuals to others who are not their age. At the same time, age-homogeneous social networks may be perceived as biased or discriminatory because social networks serve to integrate individuals into the greater social context and provide opportunities.

## AGE SEGREGATION AND THE LIFE COURSE

The impact of age segregation varies across the life course. Segregation from other age groups is quite high for younger persons due to the time they spend pursuing education. On entering the workforce, age segregation decreases. As individuals age and retire they may once again become more separated from other age groups. Hence, exposure to age segregation is most common at the younger ages and then later in life. With the aging of the baby-boom cohort and the growth in sheer numbers of older persons, scholars and practitioners are increasingly interested in "age integration," the bringing together of persons of all groups as well as the breaking down of age-based structures in society (Riley & Riley, 2000). By understanding how social structures shape lives, life course researchers are able to distinguish a transition to an increasing degree of age integration in social contexts such as education and work (Riley & Riley, 1994).

Age segregation occurs at multiple levels in society. Individuals are embedded in social contexts. Those social contexts tend to shape their access to other individuals and resources in society. It is well established that individuals are attracted to and associate with others who are like themselves. The principle of homophily suggests that individual's social networks are sorted by characteristics including age, race, and gender. This tendency toward homogeneous networks implies that individuals who are dissimilar will be less likely to maintain relationships (McPherson, Smith-Lovin, & Cook, 2001). Although social networks are likely to be age homogeneous, family-based social supports will vary over the life course (Burt, 1991). Younger adults may turn to their parents for social support. As they age, the focus may shift from parents to their own children.

In the life course context, transitions may be either gradual or discrete. Age is an example of a gradual component of change across the life course and marital status is an example of a discrete transitional stage. Because age is closely related to marital status, the spatial clustering of groups (such as younger married couples in suburbs) can contribute to age segregation in social networks (Kalmijn

& Vermunt, 2007). Age boundaries tend to be stronger among younger adults and women. Possible explanations for this include increased age integration associated with the transition from school to the workforce and the persistence of gender roles associated with child rearing. Although age segregation may be distinguished in terms of individual and group-level network characteristics, age segregation can also be identified in spatial contexts such as residential communities or occupational distributions.

## MEASURING AGE SEGREGATION

Age segregation can be measured using traditional spatial segregation measures as well as through social network analysis. Typically, the preferred method depends on the dimensions of age segregation being measured and the focus of the particular study. The analysis of residential segregation is based on characteristics that may be either ascribed, such as age or race, or achieved, such as economic status. Researchers have refined a number of measures of residential segregation based on the spatial distribution of characteristics.

Scholars of residential segregation distinguish between five distinct dimensions of segregation: evenness, exposure, concentration, centralization, and clustering (Massey & Denton, 1988). One of the best-known measures of residential segregation, the index of dissimilarity, is a measure of evenness. In the age segregation context, it would measure the extent to which different age groups are distributed among dimensions such as neighborhoods or occupations. The index of dissimilarity ranges between zero and one (zero representing no segregation and one representing complete segregation) and is often interpreted as the proportion of one group that would have to move between areas (or occupations) to create an even age distribution.

Other commonly used measures of segregation include the isolation index and correlation ratio, which measure exposure. The isolation index could be used to measure the extent to which one age group has contact with another age group in an area. The correlation ratio measures the degree to which an area is composed of age-homogeneous units. In segregation studies, measures of concentration, centralization, and clustering are related concepts representing the physical space occupied by a group and the adjacency of the group's space to other groups. Researchers have increasingly recognized that no single summary measure fully characterizes all dimensions of spatial segregation (Reardon & O'Sullivan, 2004).

Examining the composition of individuals' social networks, the people they have contact with and to whom they turn to for social support, is another approach to the measurement of age segregation. Data on social networks can be presented descriptively, either in summary tables or through diagrams. Networks diagrams facilitate the visualization of the connections between individuals. There are a growing number of statistical methods used in network analysis (see Wasserman & Faust, 1994).

## CAUSES AND CORRELATES OF AGE SEGREGATION

Age segregation has cultural, social, and spatial contexts. Many Western cultures tend to focus on "youth culture." This focus highlights the language, tastes, and consumption of younger cohorts (Hagestad & Uhlenberg, 2006). A cultural focus on youth may overshadow cohort differences in socialization experiences and exaggerate differences between age groups.

There are both voluntary and involuntary causes of social and spatial age segregation. Voluntary segregation often occurs at the individual or group levels in relation to social networks (or spatial location) and may offer group members supports they might not have access to in the larger society. Involuntary segregation occurs when individuals and groups are denied access to resources or opportunities because of their age. Generally, voluntary and involuntary age segregation can be cast in terms of individual preferences versus age discrimination. In both cases, differential status is assigned to groups based on their age.

Age segregation can occur at any stage of the life course but is most likely at the youngest and oldest ages. Educational and socialization activities are primarily age-segregated for the young. An aging population has contributed to the development of age-segregated retirement communities as well as leisure activities. Involuntary age segregation can be based on either legal justification or socially condoned discriminatory behavior. Examples of involuntary age segregation include mandatory retirement ages as well as the increasing use of long-term care facilities to house the oldest old.

Because social networks are relatively homogeneous, individuals embedded in age-segregated environments will have limited exposure to individuals unlike themselves. They may be unaware of disparities that exist or lack the means to overcome them. For aging adults, an additional consequence of age segregation may be a shrinking social support network. By maintaining ties to family members across generations, older adults are able to increase their age integration and levels of social support (Hagestad & Uhlenberg, 2005).

## PHYSICAL AND PSYCHOLOGICAL CONSEQUENCES OF AGE SEGREGATION

The consequences of age segregation will depend on whether the segregation is at the micro level (individual's connections and membership in social group) or the macro level (society and social institutions; de Jong Gierveld & Hagestad, 2006). Some key institutions associated with age segregation include education, work (retirement), and leisure (Riley & Riley, 2000). At the individual (micro) level, age segregation is contrasted to age integration and associated with social isolation. At the macro level, age segregation may not necessarily be bad for a group. The type of institution associated with the age segregation and whether the segregation is voluntary or involuntary will influence the consequences of segregation.

Successful aging has been associated with both age segregation and integration. Age-segregated communities are often marketed as life style communities, highlighting amenities and active lifestyles (McHugh, 2003). At the same time, older persons may interact with younger age groups through volunteer activities at schools or in the community. Many large universities increasingly offer programs that encourage lifelong learning. In fact, university towns often seek to attract retirees. Voluntary age segregation is generally associated with successful aging, leisure, and active retirement. The rise of age-segregated retirement communities suggests that voluntary segregation can serve a supportive function for elders. These aging "enclaves" may offer support, social capital, and economic opportunities. Yet voluntary age segregation may also represent a disconnect with previously active social networks and general social disengagement. In this situation it can have negative effects on the individual, including psychological stress or depression.

In an involuntarily segregated context, groups may have little or no contact with each other. This lack of contact between groups contributes to the negative consequences associated with segregation through both lack of exposure and unequal access to resources. Many of the negative consequences of segregation result from the extent to which involuntary segregation is embedded in the social fabric. As an individual ages, there may also be cumulative effects of advantage or disadvantage that have accrued over an individual's life course. For example, the cumulative effects of an individual's gender, race, ethnicity, or economic status may mean that some individuals are advantaged as they age whereas others may need more supports. For the less advantaged, age segregation may exacerbate their lower levels of social integration, poorer health, and greater potential for loneliness and depression.

## AGE SEGREGATION AND INDIVIDUAL EXPERIENCES

The segmentation of the life course into three broad periods (education, family and work, and retirement) that are associated with established social institutions has contributed to age segregation over the life course (Hagestad & Uhlenberg, 2005). As the workforce ages, ageism, or age discrimination, at work becomes a greater concern. Traditionally older workers would socialize younger workers, teaching them how to function in the workplace. With the increasing prevalence of technology, younger persons may have stronger skills (Uhlenberg & de Jong Gierveld, 2004). Older workers are more likely to have stronger credentials, whereas the changing nature of the labor force may make younger workers more attractive to employers (MacLean, 2006). Both older and younger workers experience more stereotyping and less power than middle-aged adults (Nelson, 2002).

The aging of the baby-boom cohort has raised concerns about age segregation and discrimination. To the extent that residential patterns are associated with the family life course, unmarried younger adults are more likely to cluster in urban areas whereas married couples may move to suburban areas to raise their families. Older adults may age in place, either in a neighborhood or community. In rural areas, the out-migration of younger age groups may leave the older generations behind. The absence of stable, ongoing interactions between age groups can contribute to a lack of age integration that, in turn, may contribute to increased ageism (Hagestad & Uhlenberg, 2006).

Increases in age segregation may have important consequences for the well-being of community members. To the extent that segregation contributes to discrimination, the consequences of age segregation can have significant physical, psychological, and financial costs for both individuals and communities.

## THE FUTURE OF AGE SEGREGATION

Age segregation is most likely to occur in the early and later stages of the life course. Children are segregated in school by age. Cohorts of children progress through the educational system together. Age integration increases as young adults enter the workforce. On retirement, older adults may have fewer nonfamily connections, and, outside their family interactions, the age integration of their social networks may decrease. With the population aging and the increasing proportion of older persons in many developed societies, researchers and policy makers will need to understand the factors that contribute to both age segregation and age integration over the life course.

Some important research issues to be addressed include the costs of age segregation for communities and societies, whether age-restricted residential communities create or decrease support for elders, and whether increased life expectancy and aging populations will contribute to greater segregation. Such studies should also assess the heterogeneity of social networks across the life course. It has been suggested that greater age integration in a society will promote a more civil society (Riley & Riley, 2000; Uhlenberg & de Jong Gierveld, 2004). A better understanding of the costs and benefits of age segregation across the life course will enable researchers and policy makers to better address the future consequences of age segregation for both individuals and society.

**SEE ALSO** Volume 3: *Ageism/Age Discrimination; Aging in Place; Lifelong Learning; Long-term Care; Riley, Matilda White.*

**BIBLIOGRAPHY**

Burt, R. S. (1991). Measuring age as a structural concept. *Social Networks, 13,* 1–34.

Chevan, A. (1982). Age, housing choice, and neighborhood age structure. *American Journal of Sociology, 87,* 1133–1149.

de Jong Gierveld, J., & G. O. Hagestad. (2006). Perspectives on the integration of older men and women. *Research on Aging, 28*(6), 627–637.

Gorard, S., & Taylor, C. (2002). What is segregation? A comparison of measures in terms of "strong" and "weak" compositional invariance. *Sociology, 36,* 875–895.

Hagestad, G. O., & Uhlenberg, P. (2005). The social separation of old and young: A root of ageism. *Journal of Social Issues, 61*(2), 343–360.

Hagestad, G. O., & Uhlenberg, P. (2006). Should we be concerned about age segregation? Some theoretical and empirical explorations. *Research on Aging, 28*(6), 638–653.

Kalmijn, M., & Vermunt, J. K. (2007). Homogeneity of social networks by age and marital status: A multilevel analysis of ego-centered networks. *Social Networks, 29*(1), 25–43.

MacLean, A. (2006). Age stratification at work: Trends in occupational age segregation in the United States, 1950–2000. *Research in Social Stratification and Mobility, 24,* 299–310.

Masotti, P. J., Fick, R., Johnson-Masotti, A., & MacLeod, S. (2006). Healthy naturally occurring retirement communities: A low-cost approach to facilitating healthy aging. *American Journal of Public Health, 96*(7), 1164–1170.

Massey, D. A., & Denton, N. A. (1988). The dimensions of residential segregation. *Social Forces, 67*(2), 281–315.

McHugh, K. E. (2003). Three faces of ageism: Society, image and place. *Ageing and Society, 23,* 165–185.

McPherson, M., Smith-Lovin, L., & Cook, J. M. (2001). Birds of a feather: Homophily in social networks. *Annual Review of Sociology, 27,* 415–444.

Nelson, T. D. (2002). *The psychology of prejudice.* New York: Allyn & Bacon.

Reardon, S. F., & O'Sullivan, D. (2004). Measures of spatial segregation. *Sociological Methodology, 34,* 121–162.

Riley, M. W., & Riley, J. W. (1994). Age integration and the lives of older people. *The Gerontologist, 34,* 110–115.

Riley, M. W., & Riley, J. W. (2000). Age integration: Conceptual and historical background. *The Gerontologist, 40,* 266–270.

Uhlenberg, P., & de Jong Gierveld, J. (2004). Age segregation in later life: An examination of personal networks. *Ageing and Society, 24,* 5–28.

Ward, R. A., LaGory, M., & Sherman, S. R. (1985). Neighborhood and network age concentration: Does age homogeneity matter for old people? *Social Psychology Quarterly, 48,* 138–149.

Wasserman S., & Faust, K. (1994). *Social network analysis: Methods and applications.* New York: Cambridge University Press.

***Regina M. Bures***

# AGE STRUCTURE

Age is one of the most significant dimensions of the composition of a population. There are important links between the age structure and the social structure of a society. Understanding the age structure provides insight into the history and future potential of a population. There are several measures and methods for summarizing the age structure of a population and for making comparisons across populations and time.

Demographers use the term *age structure* to describe the distribution of people in a population by age. The current distribution of the population by age is the result of past patterns of mortality, fertility, and migration in a population and evolves over time as those processes change. Populations often are referred to as being young or old. Although those terms do not have precise definitions, a young population is generally one in which a large proportion of the people are below working or reproductive age and there is a large potential for future population growth. In contrast, an old population is one in which a relatively large proportion of the people are past working age and the growth rate is small or potentially negative.

## POPULATION PYRAMIDS

A common way to depict the age structure of a population is through the use of a population pyramid. These figures consist of bar graphs showing the proportion of the total population in each age group (usually presented in 5-year age groups) by sex. The bars are arranged horizontally with males on the left side of the *y* axis and females on the right side. In this manner population pyramids summarize both the age structure and the sex structure of the population in a single visual image.

A population that is growing rapidly will have a younger age structure than will one that has a slower growth rate. This can be seen in the shape of the population pyramid, which has a classic pyramid shape with a wide bottom and a narrow top. The youngest age groups constitute the largest proportion of the population, and each age group is larger than the one above it. This shape comes about primarily as a result of high levels of fertility that add new members to the youngest

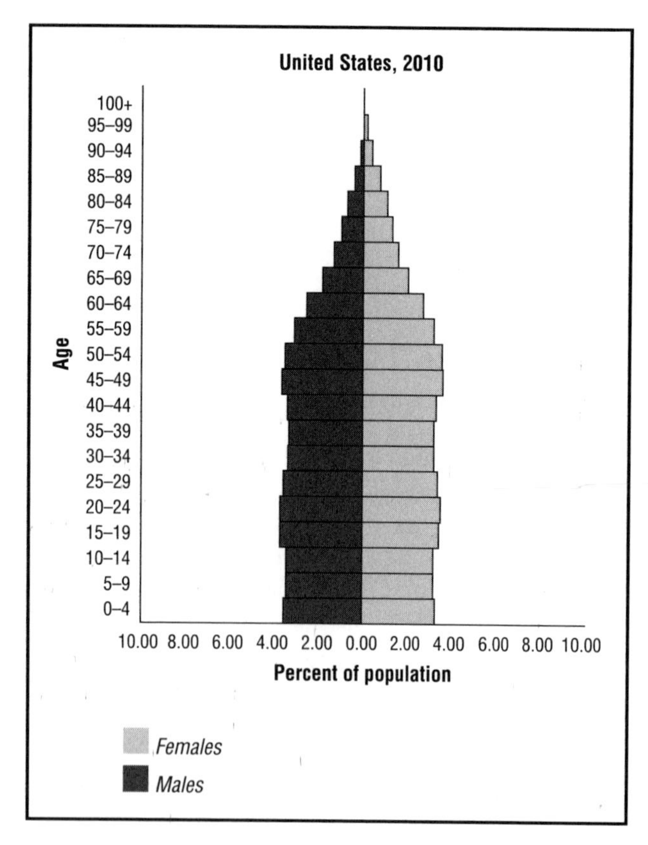


***Figure 1.*** *An estimated population pyramid for the United States.* CENGAGE LEARNING, GALE.

age group. As the younger members age, they enter the reproductive years and, even if fertility rates are falling, create a large number of future births.

A population that is growing more slowly will have a more rectangular shape that represents a relatively even distribution of the population across age groups. In these countries, the base of the pyramid is narrowing and there is little difference in cohort size from one age group to the next. As fertility and mortality levels fall, this rectangular shape emerges. Some populations experience zero or even negative growth. In these cases the base of the pyramid is smaller than the upper age groups because fertility is below the replacement level. (That means that the total fertility rate of an area is not high enough to replace the population.) This creates a pyramid shape that is more barrel- or football-shaped: narrow at the bottom and the top with a bulge in the middle.

## DEPENDENCY RATIO

Another way to summarize the age structure of a population is through the calculation of a dependency ratio. The dependency ratio compares the size of the non-working-age population, both young and old, with that of the working-age population. The age range used to define working is most commonly ages 15 to 64, and the dependent population consists of those under age 15 and those age 65 or older. The ratio of the dependent-age population to the working-age population generally is multiplied by 100 to create the dependency ratio. The higher this ratio is, the more people each individual of working age supports. Countries with high dependency ratios historically are those with high fertility and a large proportion of the population under working age. The higher the dependency ratio, the greater the need for the working-age population to provide economic resources. Dependency ratios of approximately 50 are typical for the United States and Western European countries (Population Reference Bureau, 2007). In this case each dependent is supported by two people of working age. In less developed countries the dependency ratio may be 70 or 80. In those countries each dependent is supported by fewer than 1.5 people of working age.

In young populations the dependency ratio is determined primarily by the relative number of children and youths in the population. As a population ages, the dependency ratio is driven more by the relative size of the elderly population. In the more developed countries the proportion of the population age 65 and older is roughly equal to the proportion under age 15. A more refined measure, the old age dependency ratio, often is used for populations that are aging. Because this index places only those past working age in the numerator, it better captures the dependency needs of aging populations. In the United States this ratio is now close to 20, meaning that there are five people of working age supporting each person over age 65 (Population Reference Bureau, 2007).

## DETERMINANTS OF AGE STRUCTURE

The age structure of a population is determined by the three basic demographic processes: birth, death, and migration. Together those processes shape the age and sex distribution of the population and provide momentum for population growth or decline. Current age structure reflects the past levels and patterns of those processes and the potential for future growth.

Changes in fertility tend to have the most dramatic effect on the age structure of a population. Birthrates determine the number of entrants into a population. Births add new people only to the bottom of the pyramid, but those people stay in the population as they age. For most of history populations had a high proportion of people in the youngest age groups because fertility was very high.

The number of babies born into a population is a function of the number of women of reproductive age (generally 15 to 45 years) and the age-specific fertility rates of those women. If fertility remains constant, large birth cohorts moving into the reproductive ages will create a large number of births. As birthrates fall, the size of the new cohorts decreases. This creates an echo effect in future years as the women in those smaller cohorts reach childbearing age. This smaller group of women, in combination with lower fertility rates, leads to even smaller birth cohorts.

If birthrates temporarily increase, as they did around the 1950s in the United States, an opposite effect—a baby boom—is seen in the age structure. This creates a bulge at the bottom of the age pyramid that travels upward as the cohorts age. The cohorts born before and after the boom are smaller, magnifying the bulge. As the baby boom cohorts reach reproductive age, they create an echo effect as well, this time in the form of a usually smaller baby boom. This boomlet is the artifact of the large number of women in the reproductive ages and occurs even if fertility levels have fallen.

Death rates determine how many people leave the population and at what ages. Because mortality rates are highest among the young and the old, declines in mortality affect those at the youngest and oldest ages to the greatest extent. Mortality declines create population increases at the youngest and oldest ages. In that sense a mortality decline at young ages has an effect on age structure similar to that of an increase in fertility. However, because declines in mortality tend to affect all age groups to some extent, a general decline in mortality without a change in fertility will have only a modest effect on the age structure of the population. In general, declines in mortality create a more rectangular age pyramid.

Unusual patterns of mortality can be detected in the age pyramids of a population. For instance, the effects of war often can be seen in a smaller than expected proportion of older males in a population. Similarly, mortality from HIV creates an unusually high rate of mortality among young men and women in some African populations. This mortality pattern is evident in the population pyramid as a deficit in the expected proportion of the population in the adult ages. Similarly, this type of mortality pattern affects the dependency ratio by decreasing the size of the working-age population.

Migration can both add to and subtract from a population. Migration tends to occur at very specific ages. Most migrants are young adults, and so in-migration adds people to the age structure of the receiving population in a narrow range. In the sending country, conversely, a deficit of young adults is found. These changes have an immediate impact on the age structure, but there is a long-term effect as well because these age groups affect the number of births in the population.

### FEMINIZATION OF OLD AGE

In nearly all countries the relatively longer life expectancy of women compared with men is evident in the larger proportion of females in the older population. This can be seen in the population pyramids of the United States and Italy, where the bars representing females are longer than those representing males, beginning at about age 40. The difference is remarkably evident above age 65. In the United States there were 70 men for every 100 women age 65 and older and 41 men for every 100 women ages 78 or older in 2000 (Hetzel & Smith, 2001). This pattern emerged slowly during the 20th century as mortality improvement was realized faster for women than for men. Men slowly are closing the mortality gap at older ages, and as time goes by, this imbalance in the sex ratio is expected to diminish.

## EFFECTS OF AGE STRUCTURE

These differences in age structure have wide-ranging impacts on a population. As cohorts move through time, their size and characteristics influence the social structure. Younger people in a society have different needs, are treated differently, and have different status compared with those who are older. Those at the upper end of the age spectrum hold a different place in society. As cohorts age, they take with them their characteristics, experiences, and expectations. These differences continue to influence the society throughout the life of the cohort.

Young populations have a large proportion of the population under age 15. A young population can be a resource because its members represent future workers and an anticipated increase in the workforce. At the same time they can stress the economic system. Young members of the population are consumers but not producers. Young populations need services, such as health care and education, that require an economic investment. Those investments can limit investment in industrial development. The social concerns of younger populations are different from those of the adult population as well. In rapidly changing cultures the young may find themselves alienated from traditional cultural ideals and values. This alienation and cultural shift may affect the entire society as those groups age. Some ascribe the major social changes of the 1960s and 1970s in the United States to the dramatic changes in age structure resulting from the baby boom generation.

Older populations face different sets of problems. As a population ages, the workforce also ages. An aging workforce may be associated with a decline in productivity, although little support has been found for that premise. More significant to a society is the rapid growth of the population over age 65 or, more important, over age 85. The members of this segment of the population have greater needs for health care than do those of other ages, and the stress they place on the health care system can be extreme. In addition, families are often responsible for providing large amounts of informal care to the oldest generation, stressing family resources and having a negative impact on productivity. In the United States and other more developed countries the social services provided for the oldest segment of the population sometimes are seen as competing for investment in younger generations.

Age is only one of the population characteristics that influence society. Sex, race, ethnicity, occupation, and marital status are among the many other factors that can affect the growth of a society, economic productivity, allocation of resources, and culture. Understanding the role of each of these factors and their interaction is important in understanding social change.

SEE ALSO Volume 3: *Demographic Transition Theories; Global Aging; Population Aging.*

**BIBLIOGRAPHY**

Hetzel, L., & Smith, A. (2001). *The 65 years and over population: 2000.* Census 2000 Brief. Washington, DC: U.S. Bureau of the Census.

Population Reference Bureau. (2007). *2007 World population data sheet.* Washington, DC: Author.

*Christine L. Himes*

# AGEISM/AGE DISCRIMINATION

In 1969, Robert Butler coined the term *ageism.* At that point it joined *racism* and *sexism* as descriptors for irrational biases toward a social group. However, unlike its counterparts, ageism is the only prejudice for which everyone ultimately can become a target. It is a common experience in the later life course that can have a range of negative consequences for its targets.

Ageism is defined as stereotyping, prejudice, and discrimination against people on the basis of age. Stereotyping is the formation of beliefs and expectations about an age group. The age stereotypes underlying ageism generally focus on health, appearance, and cognitive and physical functioning. Although these stereotypes can be both positive and negative, the negative ones tend to be more prevalent in the United States (Palmore, 1999). Prejudice and discrimination, respectively, describe the attitudinal response to and behaviors toward members of that age group that result from the stereotypes. Ageism can be experienced throughout the life span but is most common later in the life course.

## ORIGINS OF AGEISM

Both societal-level and individual-level factors have been said to contribute to the contemporary forms of ageism. On the societal level, modernization, exposure to television, and cultural norms have been found to be associated with ageism. The early contribution of modernization to ageism followed from the invention of the printing press and the Industrial Revolution (Nelson, 2005). The printing press and the related rise in literacy across social classes contributed to the view of elders as less valued in their long-held respected roles as village historians and resources for useful information (Branco & Williamson, 1982). The Industrial Revolution increased the demand for greater mobility of families, frequently eliminating the extended family structure and often leaving elders behind in less developed areas with fewer opportunities to contribute to the growth of society (Stearns, 1986). The growing appreciation of technological skills over experience further displaced elders from their economic roles.

Research suggests that the advent of television also has contributed to ageism. Older characters on television are underrepresented relative to their proportion in the population (Vasil & Wass, 1993). This relative invisibility communicates the idea that older persons are not valuable members of society. Older characters on television are often one-dimensional and serve as comic relief by displaying physical or mental deficits (Kubey, 1980; Montepare & Zebrowitz, 2002). A study found that greater lifetime television exposure is associated with more negative stereotypes (Donlon, Ashman, & Levy, 2005).

It has been suggested that cultural norms underlie ageism. A cross-cultural look at ageism provides support for this societal-level contributor. For instance, modernized countries such as Canada and many Western European countries have experienced historical events and technological developments similar to those that have been suggested to underlie ageism in the United States. Those countries exhibit some of the same cultural norms held in the United States, such as reverence for youth and devaluation of the old (Westerhof & Barrett, 2005).

Consequently, these countries tend to exhibit ageist attitudes and behaviors similar to those found in the United States (McConatha, Schnell, Volkwein, Riley, & Leach, 2003; Palmore, 2004; Westerhof & Barrett, 2005).

Asian countries, in contrast, traditionally have been presented as the antithesis of the United States in terms of their cultural perspectives on aging and expressions of ageism (Levy & Langer, 1994; Palmore, 1999). Asian cultures generally have revered and respected elders because of their age and the experience and wisdom that it represents. This respect has been cultivated over generations through traditions of filial piety (respect and caring for one's parents) and perpetuation of a vertical social structure (Palmore & Maeda, 1985). However, increasing evidence suggests that Asian cultures are becoming less positive toward older adults as they are exposed to European and North American norms and behaviors, in part through television and the Internet, that favor youth and demonstrate prejudice toward older generations (Boduroglu, Yoon, Luo, & Park, 2006).

On an individual level researchers have explored several major antecedents to ageism. First, humans have an innate tendency to categorize the objects, events, and people they encounter (Cuddy & Fiske, 2002). This categorization reduces the amount of information individuals need to process and allows them to make sense of the world more easily. The categories used for groups of people are stereotypes that serve as the basis for initial judgment and interaction with members of specific categories and ultimately lead to the perception of those belonging to categories different from one's own as more similar to one another and thus further removed from oneself. This process can be adaptive by satisfying inherent needs for affiliation and understanding. It also can lead to an us-versus-them mentality, which is suggested to contribute to the development of ageism among the young.

A second individual-level antecedent to ageism consists of implicit processes or automatic cognition without conscious awareness or control (Levy & Banaji, 2002). Theorists suggest that implicit ageism begins early in life in an explicit form, with children observing ageist attitudes and behaviors among adults or in their entertainment sources. Research has shown that children as young as age 6 know the age stereotypes of their culture (Isaacs & Bearison, 1986). Children's continued exposure to and conscious activation of these stereotypes eventually leads to automatic, uncontrolled activation (Levy & Banaji, 2002). The pervasiveness of age stereotypes and the information-processing efficiency achieved through stereotyping trigger and reinforce this implicit ageism throughout adulthood. The strength of the age stereotypes achieved allows the stereotypes to survive both encounters with individuals who contradict them and the transition of individuals to an age at which they become targets of the stereotypes and the stereotypes become self-relevant (Levy, 2003). Put another way, age stereotypes of others can become self-stereotypes.

A third individual-level antecedent to ageism is death anxiety (Greenberg, Schimel, & Mertens, 2002). This fear and the assumed physical and mental decline leading up to death may be one of the fundamental causes of negative ageism. Americans tend to view death as an unnatural part of the life course (Greenberg et al., 2002). Many associate old age with death and consequently fear aging. This may lead to individuals avoiding and belittling older people as a way to circumvent this fear.

## CONSEQUENCES OF AGEISM

The consequences of ageism are numerous and span several domains. Health care is one area in which ageism is particularly prominent. Five key consequences of this ageism are: (a) insufficient geriatrics training for health care professionals, (b) less aggressive preventive care for older patients, (c) less aggressive disease testing and screening of older patients, (d) inappropriate or incomplete treatment of older patients because of failure by clinicians to provide proven medical interventions, and (e) consistent underrepresentation or exclusion of older patients from clinical trials of drugs for which they will be the primary consumers (Alliance for Aging Research, 2003). In addition, older adults frequently are excluded from trials aimed at improving health behaviors (Levy, Kosteas, Slade, & Myers, 2006). They also may experience lower-quality interactions with their clinicians, as there is research suggesting that clinicians are less supportive, patient, and respectful and provide less medical information when interacting with older compared to younger patients (Greene, Adelman, Charon, & Hoffman, 1986).

Ageism is also well documented in the workplace: Its consequences are felt in the form of age discrimination, with older workers less likely to be hired, less likely to be promoted, and more likely to be the earliest victims of company downsizing (McCann & Giles, 2002). Stereotypes of inferior job performance and productivity are thought to lie behind those practices. In fact, research has found that in many settings older individuals are more reliable and productive than their younger coworkers (McCann & Giles, 2002).

The Age Discrimination in Employment Act (ADEA) of 1967, which was amended in 1978 and 1986, has limited overt discrimination in the workplace but has not eliminated age discrimination entirely. In fact, in fiscal year 2006, 16,548 charges of workplace age discrimination were filed with the Equal Employment Opportunity Commission (EEOC), the government agency overseeing the ADEA

(Equal Employment Opportunity Commission, 2007). Of the 14,146 of those charges that reached resolution, the EEOC dismissed more than 60% because of lack of evidence and nearly 20% for administrative reasons. These figures highlight the difficulty of proving discrimination and the lack of effective enforcement of the ADEA.

Ageism also can affect the behaviors of older adults. Stereotypes can become self-stereotypes and ultimately self-fulfilling prophecies, with belief in the stereotypes leading individuals to confirm them (Levy, 2003). For instance, experimental studies have linked negative age stereotypes to cognitive outcomes such as worsened memory performance (Levy, 1996) and physiological measures such as increased cardiac stress (Levy, Hausdorff, Hencke, & Wei, 2000). Stereotypes also have been shown to affect older individuals' reported will to live, with negative stereotypes leading to greater refusal of life-prolonging treatment in hypothetical medical scenarios (Levy, Ashman, & Dror, 1999–2000). Longitudinal studies have corroborated these findings by demonstrating that older persons with more positive self-perceptions of aging reported better functional health status over an 18-year period (Levy, Slade, & Kasl, 2002) as well as extended survival (Levy, Slade, Kunkel, & Kasl, 2002; Uotinen, Rantanen, & Suutama, 2005).

## INTERSECTION OF AGEISM WITH GENDER AND RACE

The experience of ageism can be affected by other social characteristics that affect the life course. Some research suggests a situation of multiple jeopardy in which older adults who belong to another stereotyped group experience a combined effect of the prejudices that is greater than the individual effects (Palmore, 1999). Evidence supports an intersection of ageism with both sexism and racism. The phenomenon among women has been paid particular attention. A clear age-related double standard exists for women so that women are believed to enter middle and old age earlier than men do (Kite & Wagner, 2002). Women thus are stereotyped at a younger age and tend to be the devalued sex when a gender bias is observed. This bias tends to be greatest in reference to physical attractiveness, sexuality, and competence, with older women often thought to be lower on these traits than older men.

The ageism experience of older persons who are part of a racial or ethnic minority group may be particularly challenging (Williams & Wilson, 2001). Older minorities tend to experience greater rates of poverty or near poverty and consequently poorer health and decreased survival. Moreover, the health care consequences of ageism probably are exacerbated among older members of minority groups in light of long-persisting racial differences in access to and quality of medical care. However, older minorities have been found to be higher in certain resources, such as spirituality, that may help them cope with ageism (Taylor, Chatters, & Jackson, 2007).

## FUTURE DIRECTIONS

Research on ageism has evolved over time. The literature, however, is far from complete and has highlighted several issues for future research. More information is needed about how older adults perceive, experience, and report ageism. Questions regarding multiple stigmatized groups also require further exploration. Any future research questions, however, should remain secondary to the ultimate goal of ageism research: reducing ageism or at least ameliorating its effects. The literature suggests several strategies for reaching this goal, including increasing awareness of old age stereotyping, increasing opportunities for high-quality intergenerational interactions, increasing exposure to stereotype-inconsistent information, emphasizing the heterogeneity of older adults, and increasing the involvement of older adults in meaningful social roles such as policy planning (Braithwaite, 2002). The increased awareness of ageism illustrated by the proliferation of research studies and exploration of legislative responses to ageism through the implementation of the ADEA and several hearings of the U.S. Senate regarding ways to address ageism in media, marketing, and health care provides hope of reaching this goal.

**SEE ALSO** Volume 3: *Age Identity; Cultural Images, Later Life.Policy, Later Life Well-Being.*

### BIBLIOGRAPHY

Alliance for Aging Research. (2003). *Ageism: How healthcare fails the elderly.* Washington, DC: Author.

Boduroglu, A., Yoon, C., Luo, T., & Park, D. C. (2006). Age-related stereotypes: A comparison of American and Chinese cultures. *Gerontology, 52*(5), 324–333.

Braithwaite, V. (2002). Reducing ageism. In T. D. Nelson (Ed.), *Ageism: Stereotyping and prejudice against older persons* (pp. 311–337). Cambridge, MA: MIT Press.

Branco, K. J., & Williamson, J. B. (1982). Stereotyping and the life cycle: Views of aging and the aged. In A. G. Miller (Ed.), *In the eye of the beholder: Contemporary issues in stereotyping* (pp. 364–410). New York: Praeger.

Butler, R. N. (1969). Ageism: Another form of bigotry. *Gerontologist, 9*(4), 243–246.

Cuddy, A. J. C., & Fiske, S. T. (2002). Doddering but dear: Process, content, and function in stereotyping of older persons. In T. D. Nelson (Ed.), *Ageism: Stereotyping and prejudice against older persons* (pp. 4–26). Cambridge, MA: MIT Press.

Donlon, M. M., Ashman, O., & Levy, B. (2005). Re-vision of older television characters: A stereotype-awareness intervention. *Journal of Social Issues, 61*(2), 307–319.

Equal Employment Opportunity Commission. (2007). *Age Discrimination in Employment Act (ADEA) charges FY 1997–FY 2006.* Retrieved December 8, 2007, from http://www.eeoc.gov/stats

Greenberg, J., Schimel, J., & Mertens, A. (2002). Ageism: Denying the face of the future. In T. D. Nelson (Ed.), *Ageism: Stereotyping and prejudice against older persons* (pp. 27–48). Cambridge, MA: MIT Press.

Greene, M. G., Adelman, R., Charon, R., & Hoffman, S. (1986). Ageism in the medical encounter: An exploratory study of the doctor-elderly patient relationship. *Language & Communication, 6*(1–2), 113–124.

Isaacs, L. W., & Bearison, D. J. (1986). The development of children's prejudice against the aged. *International Journal of Aging and Human Development, 23*(3), 175–194.

Kite, M. E., & Wagner, L. S. (2002). Attitudes toward older adults. In T. D. Nelson (Ed.), *Ageism: Stereotyping and prejudice against older persons* (pp. 129–161). Cambridge, MA: MIT Press.

Kubey, R. W. (1980). Television and aging: Past, present, and future. *The Gerontologist, 20*(1), 16–35.

Levy, B. R. (1996). Improving memory in old age through implicit self-stereotyping. *Journal of Personality and Social Psychology, 71,* 1092–1107.

Levy, B. R. (2003). Mind matters: Cognitive and physical effects of aging self-stereotypes. *Journals of Gerontology Series B: Psychological Sciences and Social Sciences, 58*(4), P203–P211.

Levy, B. R., Ashman, O., & Dror, I. (1999–2000). To be or not to be: The effects of aging stereotypes on the will to live. *Omega: Journal of Death and Dying, 40,* 409–420.

Levy, B. R., & Banaji, M. R. (2002). Implicit ageism. In T. D. Nelson (Ed.), *Ageism: Stereotyping and prejudice against older persons* (pp. 49–75). Cambridge, MA: MIT Press.

Levy, B. R., Hausdorff, J. M., Hencke, R., & Wei, J. Y. (2000). Reducing cardiovascular stress with positive self-stereotypes of aging. *Journals of Gerontology Series B: Psychological Sciences and Social Sciences, 55,* P205–P213.

Levy, B. R., Kosteas, J., Slade, M., & Myers, L. (2006). Exclusion of elderly persons from health-risk behavior clinical trials. *Preventive Medicine, 43*(2), 80–85.

Levy, B. R., & Langer, E. (1994). Aging free from negative stereotypes: Successful memory in China and among the American deaf. *Journal of Personality and Social Psychology, 66*(6), 989–997.

Levy, B. R., Slade, M. D., & Kasl, S. V. (2002). Longitudinal benefit of positive self-perceptions of aging on functional health. *Journals of Gerontology Series B: Psychological Sciences and Social Sciences, 57,* P409–P417.

Levy, B. R., Slade, M. D., Kunkel, S. R., & Kasl, S. V. (2002). Increased longevity by positive self-perceptions of aging. *Journal of Personality and Social Psychology, 83*(2), 261–270.

McCann, R., & Giles, H. (2002). Ageism in the workplace. In T. D. Nelson (Ed.), *Ageism: Stereotyping and prejudice against older persons* (pp. 163–199). Cambridge, MA: MIT Press.

McConatha, J. T., Schnell, F., Volkwein, K., Riley, L., & Leach, E. (2003). Attitudes toward aging: A comparative analysis of young adults from the United States and Germany. *International Journal of Aging and Human Development, 57*(3), 203–215.

Montepare, J. M., & Zebrowitz, L. A. (2002). A societal-developmental view of aging. In T. D. Nelson (Ed.), *Ageism: Stereotyping and prejudice against older persons* (pp. 77–125). Cambridge, MA: MIT Press.

Nelson, T. D. (2005). Ageism: Prejudice against our feared future self. *Journal of Social Issues, 61*(2), 207–221.

Palmore, E. B. (1999). *Ageism: Negative and positive* (2nd ed.). New York: Springer.

Palmore, E. B. (2004). Ageism in Canada and the United States. *Journal of Cross-Cultural Gerontology, 19*(1), 41–46.

Palmore, E. B., & Maeda, D. (1985). *The honorable elders revisited.* Durham, NC: Duke University Press.

Stearns, P. J. (1986). Old age family conflict: The perspective of the past. In K. A. Pillemer & R. S. Wolf (Eds.), *Elder abuse: Conflict in the family* (pp. 3–24). Dover, MA: Auburn House.

Taylor, R. J., Chatters, L. M., & Jackson, J. S. (2007). Religious and spiritual involvement among older African Americans, Caribbean Blacks, and non-Hispanic Whites: Findings from the National Survey of American Life. *Journals of Gerontology Series B: Psychological Sciences and Social Sciences, 62*(4), S238–S250.

Uotinen, V., Rantanen, T., & Suutama, T. (2005). Perceived age as a predictor of mortality: A 13-year prospective study. *Age and Ageing, 34*(4), 368–372.

Vasil, L., & Wass, H. (1993). Portrayal of the elderly in the media: A literature review and implications for educational gerontologists. *Educational Gerontology, 19*(1), 71–85.

Westerhof, G. J., & Barrett, A. E. (2005). Age identity and subjective well-being: A comparison of the United States and Germany. *Journals of Gerontology Series B: Psychological Sciences and Social Sciences, 60*(3), S129–S136.

Williams, D. R., & Wilson, C. M. (2001). Race, ethnicity, and aging. In R. H. Binstock & L. K. George (Eds.), *Handbook of aging and the social sciences* (5th ed., pp. 160–178). San Diego, CA: Academic Press. Cultural Images, Later Life.Policy, Later Life Well-Being.

***Erica Leifheit-Limson***
***Becca Levy***

# AGING

In 2000, persons age 65 and older comprised about 12.4% of the American population. By 2100 the population of older adults will be about 23% of the total population, nearly one out of every four persons. One reason for the tremendous growth of the older population in the 20th century is the increase in life expectancy among older persons, which is the average number of years an individual can expect to live in old age. As the population continues to age, continued efforts toward a better understanding of aging are essential. Why humans age, how they age, and what happens as age are all important but complex processes related to childhood and early adulthood life. This entry they will outline the fundamental aspects of individual aging, from biological, psychological, and sociological perspectives.

## BIOLOGICAL AGING

Generally, biologists view aging as changes that represent both growth and decline with time. For example, physical development (a sign of growth) occurs from birth to adulthood, while declines in physical functioning are characterized as part of the aging process. *Senescence* refers to the latter of the two processes that marks decline over time and underlies the progressive loss of function with age, which results from an inability to grow and/or repair damages (Williams, 1957). Multiple biological theories attempt to explain aging: why it occurs, how it happens, and who it affects. Programmed theories of aging are synonymous with "why" theories, which denote the driving forces that cause aging to take place. The "how" theories focus on the mechanisms through which we age. Lastly, the "who" theories examine why some individuals or populations age earlier than others.

**Programmed aging** While the importance of biological processes on aging is largely agreed upon, the reason why aging occurs is often debated. Some scientists argue that aging is based on a programmed, molecular clock, whereas others assert that aging is due to random events resulting from an accumulation of physiological insults or damage to the body over time (wear and tear theory). The programmed aging view is supported in the finding of common pathways of aging among various animal models that exhibit similar life trajectories. For instance, the glucose or insulin-like growth factor-1 (IGF-1) pathways are similar among yeast, worms, flies, mice, and humans. These pathways regulate energy and fat accumulation and ultimately affect growth, aging, and mortality. In contrary some researchers argue that aging is due to physiological insults imposed by the environment (e.g., UV-induced damage to DNA) or internal deviations in homeostasis, the maintenance of equilibrium in response to changes in the internal and external environment (e.g., changes in hormone levels or declines in the immune system). Despite this debate, most investigators agree that aging is a result of more than a single cause. Theories of programmed aging suggest that a biological clock drives the process of human development and aging. Proposed explanations of these conserved molecular pathways (e.g., the previously mentioned glucose or IGF-1 pathways found in multiple animal models) include cellular aging and related genetics.

***Cellular aging.*** Cellular aging, an example of programmed aging, is rooted in the discovery that most cellular tissues can divide only a finite number of times. On average, human cells from embryonic tissues stop dividing after fifty cumulative population doublings (CPDs). This phenomenon, introduced by Leonard Hayflick and Paul Moorhead in 1961, is known as Hayflick's limit or replicative senescence (RS) (for further information, see Kirkwood, 1999). Across species, there is an association between the number of CPDs and longevity. For instance, cells from a Galapagos tortoise, which can live more than 100 years, divide approximately 110 times, while cells from mice, which live less than 5 years, divide about 15 times. Moreover, cells from individuals with Werner syndrome (WS), a progeroid syndrome in which individuals undergo accelerated aging, have far fewer CPDs than cells from normal, non-WS individuals. However, exceptions to Hayflick's limit do exist, with some cell lines never reaching RS. These "immortal" cells include embryonic germ cells and cells from tumors.

Biological indicators, or biomarkers, serve as measurements of biological processes that are difficult to observe directly. A potentially universal biomarker of cellular aging (i.e., a marker of cell division cessation), is the enzyme β-galactosidase (SA β-gal) (Campisi, 2003). SA β-gal is a lysosomal hydroblast, an enzyme that aids in the digestion of excess or worn out organelles, that exhibits abnormal behavior in senescent cells and becomes active at a higher pH in senescent cells compared to normal cells (pH 6 compared to pH 4, respectively). Additionally, the percentage of cells undergoing SA β-gal activity (or positive for SA β-gal) increases with CPDs and age; however, immortal cell lines (e.g., HeLa tumor cells) show no association between percentage of cells positive for SA β-gal and CPDs. Using biomarkers, such as SA β-gal, to determine cellular activity could enable the physiologic measurement of cellular aging across species.

***Genetics.*** In addition to cellular aging, genetic influences are another example of programmed aging. The gene that encodes for Apolipoprotein E (ApoE), for example, has been associated with longevity and age-related diseases, such as Alzheimer's Disease (AD) (Vijg and Suh, 2005; Raber, Hugan, and Ashford, 2004). ApoE is a protein involved in cholesterol and lipid transport to neurons. A growing body of research suggests greater associations between AD and specific ApoE isoforms (i.e., a protein with the same function as another protein but encoded by either a different gene or a mutated form of the same gene). For instance, the ApoE ε4 isoform has a stronger association with AD compared with the ε2 and ε3 isoforms. While the precise mechanism behind this remains unknown, it is clear that the ApoE ε4 is less effective in binding sterols necessary for neuronal repair, compared to the ε2 and ε3 isoforms. Further, studies suggest that the ApoE ε2 isoform confers a decreased risk of AD. ApoE is only one example of an identified genetic influence on aging and longevity.

A more in-depth review of the genetic influences on aging can be found in a separate entry within this volume.

**How Humans Age** Several mechanisms as to "how" organisms age have been proposed. Most of the theories behind this have come from experimental research that attempts to determine the causes and consequences of aging on physiological systems. In the last two decades, oxidative stress and caloric restriction have garnered substantial attention in the scientific literature.

***Oxidative stress.*** In 1956 Denham Harman first proposed the free radical theory of aging. This theory is based on the idea that oxidative damage, caused by free radicals, accumulates in tissues and cells over time. Free radicals include molecules or atoms with at least one unpaired electron. This unpaired state causes the molecule or atom to be unstable and seek stability by either giving its unpaired electron to another atom/molecule or by taking an electron from another atom/molecule with an unpaired electron. In this sense, free radicals are highly reactive and can cause damage to the important biomolecules, including lipids, proteins, and carbohydrates. Ultimately, this accumulation of oxidative damage (through free radical formation) contributes to declines in physiologic function with age.

In turn, the oxidative stress hypothesis posits that an age-related decline in function is due to the progressive and irreversible accumulation of oxidative damage. Oxidative stress results in molecular damage to living tissues and is found to increase with aging. This vulnerability to damage of DNA, proteins, and lipids, resulted in the evolution of repair systems that protect against these damaging reactive oxygen species (ROS) (i.e., oxygen free radicals). However, these repair systems do not prevent all oxidative damage, giving way to one of the mechanisms of aging.

Mitochondria are membrane-enclosed regions responsible for producing chemicals that cells use for energy. This process occurs through a mechanism called the "electron transport chain," in which electrons are passed between different molecules to produce vital chemical energy. In the final step, oxygen is required, and on occasion, the electron incorrectly interacts with oxygen, thereby producing oxygen free radicals. Hence, mitochondria are likely the link between age-related accumulation of oxidative damage due to ROS and changes in physiologic function related to aging.

***Caloric restriction.*** Calorie restriction (CR) is the practice of limiting dietary energy intake while maintaining nutrition levels. In 1935, Clive M. McCay and colleagues found that CR extended the maximum lifespan (MLS) of laboratory rats and mice by 33%, from three to four years. However, this phenomenon remained relatively under-investigated until the mid-1970s. Since then much research has focused on the biochemical and physiological effects of dietary restriction.

In animal models, when nutrients are readily available, early reproduction, high fecundity, and a shorter life span are exhibited. Conversely, when nutrients are limited and starvation conditions occur, late reproduction, low fecundity, and a longer life span ensue. It is likely that natural selection may play some role in explaining this finding. As a premise, the body requires energy for maintenance and survival. During life, there exists a tradeoff between priorities given to self-investment (e.g., during periods of extended starvation or growth and development) and reproduction. Currently, CR is used as a model for understanding the basic mechanisms of aging, due to its robust and reproducible extension of MLS and delay of several age-associated physiological, biochemical, and behavioral changes in a number of non-human species.

It is now known that CR increases the life span across organisms including yeast, rats, worms, mice, and possibly humans. Yeast cells that were grown in nutrient-rich environments lived an average of 6 days; those grown in water or with fewer nutrients lived greater than 17 days; those grown in only 1% potassium acetate, the most restricted environment, lived for years. In comparison to non-CR rodents, CR rodents have also been found to have lower levels of blood glucose, insulin, insulin-like growth factor-1, and inflammation; higher insulin efficiency and resistance to oxidative damage; and lower incidence rates of tumors, kidney disease, vascular calcification, and chronic pneumonia.

While the beneficial effects of CR on non-mammalian taxa are apparent, its effects on humans are still debated. Given the complexity of the mechanisms that affect health and longevity in humans, it is difficult to determine if, and to what extent, the benefits of CR outweigh the energetic and reproductive costs of living in near hibernation. However, some recent studies have attempted to investigate the effects of CR on humans.

Perhaps the most well-known human example of CR is the Biosphere 2 (Poynter, 2006). The Biosphere 2 team lived in a human-made, closed ecosystem in Oracle, Arizona, for 2 years (1991–1992). This eight-member team consisted of individuals who were relatively healthy, with most being young adults. Inhabitants decreased their usual 2,500-calorie intake to 1,800 calories per day. After 6 months, all members had improved levels of physiological state: 15% weight loss, 35% lower blood cholesterol, 18% lower blood glucose, and 18–to 21% (systolic/diastolic) lower blood pressure.

Additionally, favorable changes in biomarkers predictive of human mortality, including dehydroepiandrosterone-sulfate (DHEA-S), body temperature, and insulin levels,

## THIRD AGE

The *third age* refers to the period of life after completing employment and family duties and before the onset of poor health and old age. Given increases in the adult lifespan, reduction in fertility, and, until recently, reductions in age at retirement, this period comprises an increasingly large proportion of the lifespan. The primary proponent of the concept of the third age was Peter Laslett. His seminal work proposed a post-retirement life full of meaning, purpose, and choice (i.e., the third age) that is distinct from the *fourth age,* a stage characterized by decline and decrepitude.

Critics find fault with the subtle implication that attainment of health and happiness depends on engagement in healthy behaviors and those who do not age successfully have not tried hard enough. Furthermore, the popular media have co-opted the concept, conveying the message that buying consumer goods can ensure the attainment of health and happiness in old age. Advocates see the concept as empowering. The concept of the third age may help to promote institutional and normative changes so that newer generations of older persons will have the power to choose a fulfilling lifestyle not tied to meaning found in paid employment.

were found. DHEA-S is a steroid hormone that normally decreases with age. However, in CR-humans, DHEA-S is higher than non-CR humans at the same age. Insulin and body temperature decreased in calorie-restricted individuals as well. Consistent with the beneficial CR effects seen in other animal models, human men with lower temperature, lower insulin, and higher DHEA-S levels had increased survival rates compared to their normal diet counterparts. All in all, CR seems to extend the life span of organisms ranging from yeast to mammals. It may extend longevity in mammals by decreasing both diseases (such as cancers) and inflammation (a response of the body's immune system that protects against infection and foreign bodies, including bacteria and viruses) during aging. However, substantial reductions in caloric intake are difficult to maintain. While the physiologic benefits of CR on yeast and mice are remarkable, it was also found that they lived in states of near hibernation throughout life. Such findings question whether altering metabolic rates in humans via CR is viable and desirable.

**Who Ages** Although aging is inevitable for all, in humans, some populations age more quickly than others. Bio-psycho-social theories attempt to explain who is most vulnerable to adverse changes connected to aging based on person-environment interactions. For example, ethnic minority populations and individuals with low socioeconomic status exhibit both a higher level and earlier onset of age-related disease, including cardiovascular disease and diabetes. To explain this, several theories have been proposed, including the stress theory of aging (Finch and Seeman, 1998). Stress theories of aging suggest that excess stress, due to greater exposure to chronic and acute strains, leads to increased risk for disease and disability. Stress has been involved in disrupting the regulation of several body systems, including the sympathetic nervous system, the immune system, the hypothalamic-pituitary-adrenal axis, and inflammatory responses. Such theories allow researchers to investigate the underlying reasons why health disparities exist across populations and contribute to the overall understanding of aging processes.

### PSYCHOLOGICAL AGING

Some aspects of human psychology undergo changes with age. Psychological aging is not necessarily a series of losses and physiological decrements; rather, aging can also bring improvements in psychological functioning, such as enhanced optimization of positive emotions, or relative stability, as exemplified by personality. Here the authors will describe the relative stability of personality, the positive changes in emotion regulation, and the onset of common psychological disorders with age.

**Personality and Aging** Two different views of personality and aging are presented in trait and growth models of personality development (Staudinger, 2005). Growth models, akin to Erik Erikson's developmental model, suggest that individuals continually adapt to internal and external (i.e., biological and sociocultural) changes in the environment. Such changes allow for personal growth, with the ultimate goal of achieving purpose in life, competence, and wisdom. Conversely, trait models, which are often used in studying personality, focus on individual traits (i.e., dispositional behaviors and attributes) as indicators of personality. These models suggest that personality remains relatively stable after age 30. Studies have shown, however, that a combination of these two models most accurately portrays changes in personality across the lifespan. Simply, both stability and change, or development in personality, occur from adulthood to later life.

Trait models focus on both the structure and content of personality. For instance, personality is measured along the "Big Five" dimensions: extraversion, openness to experience, neuroticism, conscientiousness, and agreeableness (McCrae and Costa, 1990). While personality generally remains stable with age, some specific changes in each of the "Big Five" dimensions are related to age. Neuroticism, for example, decreases across adulthood but may then increase in late life. With age, there is some decrease in extraversion and openness to experience, while conscientiousness and agreeableness increase slightly. These findings appear to be similar in cross-sectional (studies examining different age groups at one point in time) and longitudinal studies (studies using data at more than one time point, respectively), as well as across countries.

Self-regulation is the set of abilities and skills that an individual uses to monitor experiences and behavior. It is a source of the underlying stability and relatively minor change in personality with age (Staudinger, Kessler, & Dörner, 2006). This view suggests that individuals aim for a relatively constant state across life and utilize self-regulating mechanisms to achieve a state of dynamic homeostasis. Self-evaluation, emotion-regulation, and goal setting are a few examples of methods of self-regulation.

With age, individual may employ compensatory mechanisms of self-evaluation more often, such as reinterpreting reality. Such reinterpretations allow for consistent perceptions of oneself, despite behavioral and experiential changes. Emotion regulation, discussed below, generally does not decline with age, and some increases with age in the balance of positive to negative emotions have been found. Older adults also report greater control of their emotions with age. This may reflect changes in life goals or a shift in priorities from information seeking in younger years to emotion regulation in older adulthood (Carstensen, Isaacowitz, and Charles, 1999). This perspective, known as socioemotional selectivity theory, will be discussed later. Despite experiencing more adverse health events and losses of close friends and family, older adults, on average, maintain their sense of control and agency (Smith & Baltes, 1999). However, this stability cannot be viewed as a moment of standstill, with little growth and learning, but should be seen as an indicator of successful self-regulation.

**Emotions** Compared to younger adults, older adults generally have better emotion regulation and tend to remember negative information less well than positive information (Mather & Carstensen, 2003). Although poorer health conditions are more common among older adults, the shift toward selectively remembering positive instead of negative memories enables them to regulate their emotions and obtain better levels of well-being.

Among older adults, the maintenance of positive levels of affect (the experience of a feeling or emotion) while facing challenging life experiences is a paradox to researchers. This paradox may be explained by three theories of optimization: affective optimization, socioemotional selectivity theory, and differential emotions theory. In 1989 Lawton introduced affective optimization, which states that older adults control their social and environmental surroundings in order to minimize negative contacts and maximize positive situations. As indicated above, socioemotional selectivity theory posits that when the time remaining in one's future is perceived as limited (e.g., in late life and among individuals with terminal medical conditions), there is a reorganization of goals, with a greater emphasis on emotion-regulation as opposed to information-seeking. During this period, close, interpersonal relationships take precedence over educational and career-oriented goals that might have been priorities in earlier life. There is a reduction in peripheral or more distant relationships (e.g., an acquaintance) and a greater focus on core relationships, thereby enhancing and maximizing time spent in positive emotions. This suggests a remarkable adaptive "resiliency" among older adults.

Differential emotions theory suggests that a limited number of primary emotion systems evolved to provide safe, reliable, and automatic ways to deal with states of emergency (Darwin, 1955). These primary emotion systems include negative emotions, such as fear, sadness, anger, and disgust, and positive emotions, such as happiness, interest, and love. The greater positive emotional balance that commonly occurs among older adults reflects the systematic decline in negative emotions over the life course, while positive emotions remain relatively stable or increase slightly. Further, older adults exhibit greater levels of self-control in regulating their emotions, by showing less reactivity when inducted to negative emotions and utilize different defense and adaptation mechanisms. Older adults are more likely to use a defense that gives an abstract meaning to an event or reverses its meaning, while younger adults employ less mature defenses. For example, during times of hardship, older adults are more likely to cognitively reassess the situation toward a more positive light (e.g., view the situation as a valuable learning experience) as opposed to younger adults who more commonly employ escape and avoidance strategies (Diehl, Coyle, & Labouvie-Vief, 1996). Additionally, older adults both recognize and recall fewer negative images compared to positive or neutral images.

**Psychological Disorders** In general, mental health problems, including schizophrenia, anxiety disorders, and major depression, decrease with age. Among adults age 65 and older, only 0.6% have schizophrenia compared to 1.3% of younger adults aged 20. For anxiety disorders, most begin in childhood, adolescence, and early adulthood, so their onset is much lower among older adults. The average age of onset for major depressive disorder is 25, and it is most common among adults age 25 to 44 and least common among adults age 65 and older. Despite this, older adults are more likely to suffer from mild depression and dementias than younger persons (Woods, 2005). The high prevalence of depressive disorders and dementias in later life have attracted great attention in relation to theory, assessment, and treatment for older adults. The next two sections discuss two major psychological disorders encountered in older adults: dementia and depression.

***Alzheimer's disease.*** Alzheimer's disease (AD), the most common form of dementia, is perhaps the most feared disease of aging, as older adults fear losing their memory and their sense of self while their physical bodies remain intact. AD is the eighth leading cause of death among individuals over age 65 (Alzheimer's Association, 2007). It is a progressive disease involving loss of memory, then of functional ability, and ultimately, loss of life.

Advancing age is the number one risk factor for AD. In 2007, 5.1 million people in the United States were living with AD, and 4.9 million of these individuals were age 65 and older. At age 65, one out of eight people (15%) are estimated to have AD. While the prevalence of AD continues to increase with age, this number dramatically increases for individuals ages 85 and older; such that by age 85, nearly one out of every two people is thought to have AD (Plassman, Langa, Fisher, Heeringa, Weir et al, 2007). Due to declines in death rates after age 65, current and future generations will survive to older ages, where risk of AD is greatest.

The two hallmark abnormalities of AD include beta (B)-amyloid plaques and neurofibrillary tangles (NFTs); however, it is unclear whether these changes cause neuron death or are indicators of a separate, more complex process (DiGiovanna, 2000). Plaques and tangles are present in the brain when the individual is still asymptomatic. As neuron death persists, the individual begins to exhibit declines in short-term memory. Later, declines in verbal and spatial abilities occur, and ultimately, people with AD lose the ability to complete activities of daily living. During the disease progression, brain size decreases, namely in the frontal, temporal, and parietal lobes, in addition to the amygdala, hippocampus, and nucleus basalis.

Common patterns of symptom progression among individuals with AD have been documented and modeled into a progression of "stages." Although staging systems provide a useful frame of reference for understanding how the disease unfolds in the population, it is important to note that not all individuals with AD will experience the same symptoms nor progress at the same rate. Key symptoms characterizing seven stages of AD are indicated below (Reisberg, 2008).

In Stage 1, no impairments in memory are evident during medical interview. The individual appears to have normal cognitive function but plaques and tangles may be detected via other means, such as functional magnetic resonance imaging (fMRI). Individuals in Stage 2, with very mild cognitive decline, may notice some memory lapses, especially in forgetting familiar words, names, or location of keys or eyeglasses. However, these problems are not noticeable to friends, family, co-workers, or upon medical interview. Mild cognitive decline (Stage 3) can be diagnosed in some individuals. Family, friends, and co-workers begin to notice problems in the AD individual, and problems with concentration and memory are now measurable in medical testing. Some common difficulties include: problems recalling words or names of people, retaining little material from recently read passages, losing or misplacing valuable objects, and performance issues in social or work settings.

Medical interviews of people with moderate cognitive decline, also known as mild or early-stage AD (Stage 4) indicate clear deficiencies in: recollection of recent events, ability to perform challenging arithmetic (e.g., serial sevens) and complex tasks, recollection of personal history, and interaction with others in socially or mentally challenging situations. Moderate or mid-stage AD (Stage 5) is indicative of major gaps in memory and deficits in cognitive functioning. During this stage, the individual requires some help with activities of daily living (ADLs). Moderately severe AD (Stage 6) shows a worsening of memory difficulties, significant changes in personality, and extensive help with ADLs. Here, individuals imperfectly recall their personal history, lose most awareness of recent events, exhibit disruptions in their normal sleeping cycle, increasingly exhibit urinary or fecal incontinence, and begin to wander and become lost. Lastly, severe or late-stage AD (Stage 7) marks the time when individuals are unable to respond to the environment, unable to speak, and unable to control their own movement.

***Depression.*** Categories of depression, including major depressive disorder and dysthymia, are characterized in the Diagnostic and Statistical Manual for Mental Disorders (DSM-IV) (American Psychiatric Association, 2000) and the International Classification of Diseases (ICD-10) (World Health Organization, 2004). Major depressive disorder is defined as having both: (a) a depressed mood or loss of interest or pleasure for at least two weeks, (b) at least 5 of 9 other symptoms, including: physical agitation or psychomotor retardation, significant weight loss or appetite changes, feelings of worthlessness or guilt, and difficulty concentrating or making decisions. Dysthymia, by contrast, is defined as having depressive symptoms less severe than major depression, but lasting for a minimum of 2 years. Major depression disorder and dysthymia may co-occur, known as *double depression.*

Depression is often characterized by different symptoms in younger and older adults (Fiske and Jones, 2005). As such, it is not appropriate to apply the same diagnostic instruments for depression across all age groups and compare rates across age. For example, emotional and cognitive circumstances, including sadness and negative self-attitude, are better indicators of depression in younger adults; however, somatic symptoms (such as fatigue, insomnia, and changes in appetite), feelings of apathy, hopelessness, and thoughts about death are more appropriate indicators of depression among older adults.

Also, older adults more commonly present symptoms that are not characterized by any one diagnostic criterion. This has been referred to in several terms: subsyndromal depression, minor depression (provisionally characterized in DSM-IV), or mild depression (in ICD-10). These differential criteria for older adults reveal the complexity of evaluating depression in this population. This is further illustrated when determining the low and wide-ranging prevalence of depression among older adults. Dysthymia affects about 2% of adults age 65 and older. Major depressive disorder occurs in 12% of older adults, while minor depression is present in 3 13%. To further complicate diagnoses, depression and dementia may coexist, with nearly a quarter of older adults with dementia also having depression.

Late-life depression can be conceptualized as the interplay among biological, psychological, and social influences. For instance, the developmental diathesis-stress model (Gatz, 1996) states that genetic influences on depression onset are more important early in life, while the effects of some biological risk factors (e.g., neuroanatomical changes) and some medical conditions increase with age. Further, susceptibility to depression may decrease with age as adults learn to better adjust expectations and deal with stressors.

On the other hand, having a previous history of depression increases the likelihood of having late-life depression; half of all older adults with depression were depressed earlier in life. Depression onset occurs in conjunction with, and after, certain medical conditions, such as Parkinson's disease, stroke, and general pain. Depression in middle-aged to older adults has also been associated with occurrence of first heart attack, poorer outcomes after a heart attack, mortality post-stroke, and other cardiovascular conditions. Hence, the reciprocal relationship between depression and poor health places other adults at greater risk of comorbidities, or co-existing conditions.

Negative life events and social influences, including bereavement, caregiving, and illness, are associated with depression in older adults. Within the first year of bereavement, depressive symptoms are common among widowed spouses but triggers for depressive symptoms vary for widows and widowers. Concerns about income trigger symptoms in widows, while loss of emotional support triggers depressive symptoms among widowers. Ultimately, depressive disorder is a complex process that often involves consideration of a combination of biological, psychological, and social influences.

## SOCIAL AGING

Social roles and relationships change with age and time. In fact, social scientists view aging as a series of transitions resulting from changing roles connected to sets of rights and responsibilities. Traditionally, transitioning from one social role to the next coincided closely with one's age. In other words, roles in life were traditionally age-segregated. Children and adolescents were students; adult males worked and provided for the family; adult females cared for children; and old age was spent in retirement and caring for oneself.

Over time, however, the links between age and social roles have blurred. For example, as the length of schooling has increased and the idea of retraining has become accepted, "nontraditional age" students now represent nearly 50% of college enrollment. Women, especially women who are mothers, in the work force have increased markedly since the 1960s as women's roles have expanded. More grandparents are providing care and parenting to grandchildren than in earlier decades. It is also true that until recently the age at retirement had been decreasing so that the modal age was 62. This loosening of age structures in work, family, and education is termed the *deinstitutionalization* or *destandardization* of the life course (Sackmann & Wingens, 2003) and represents changes in social aging processes.

The link between social roles and chronological age is not the same in all societies or at all times. As indicated above, the links have been changing in the United States, and such changes have been occurring in much of the world. It is also true that the expected roles and opportunities for older persons are not always those that they desire. For instance, while the age at retirement has been decreasing, there have been many people who were forced to retire when they would prefer to keep working. It is also not always true that the social structure encourages—and in the case of retirement in the past, even legislates—roles that have resulted in the most appropriate fit for the social and economic circumstances of the society. This lack of fit between expected social roles and societal needs has been termed *structural lag*. One can view the elimination of mandatory retirement in the United States several decades ago as an attempt to achieve a better fit between the desires of individuals, the needs of the society, and the legislated options for working.

**A Quiet Revolution** Biological and psychological aging focus on individuals but social aging examines societal or population-level as well as individual-level change. Population aging has been ongoing in much of the world for more than a century: The proportion of older individuals has been growing and the absolute number of older adults has been increasing. It results not only from improvements in life expectancy at older age, but from increased survival throughout life and the decrease in fertility that results from declining infant mortality. As a result of these forces, there are significant changes in the age structure of societies. In many countries there has been an interest in the implications of aging because of the increase in the number of older dependents to workers. In countries where aging has been taking place for a long time, there has already been a significant increase in the number of older persons supported by each worker. This ratio is closely tracked by national governments because most countries provide living and medical expenses for older persons. What has sometimes not been noted, but is of relevance to the interest in changing age structures, is that at the same time there has been an increase in the number of older dependents, there has been a decrease in the number of younger persons supported by each worker. The expectation is that aging is going to continue in most countries of the world for the foreseeable future and an older age structure will require further adaptation of the link between social roles and age.

**Family Structure** Aging in families has occurred in parallel with population aging. Demographic changes have resulted in a "quiet revolution" that has lead to the transformation of multiple facets of the family (Lowenstein, 2005). Declines in fertility and increases in life expectancy have changed the structure of families and the interactions between generations. In the beginning of the 20th century most family structures, like most populations, resembled a pyramid. They had a large, bottom-heavy base of children, a smaller number of parental age persons, and a small number of grandparents. In many countries both populations and families are changing from a pyramid structure to resemble a beanpole. In this case, over time there may be relatively equal numbers of people at most ages up to the very old and close to equal numbers of family members within each generation. This change in family structure leads to fewer members in each generation but more generations alive at any one time. This will mean fewer younger members available to care for the growing older population.

## MARRIAGE, PARENTHOOD, AND GRANDPARENTHOOD

With the decrease in the number of children and increases in requirements of skilled jobs, more recent generations have been more likely to delay marriage and parenthood in order to devote more time to education and advancing their careers. In 2005 the median age of marriage for men had risen to 27 years and 26 years for women, with a majority (72%) of both men and women having been married at least once by the time they were 30 and 34 years old. There has also been a decline in the traditional family and greater diversity among families, including truncated families, reconstituted families, single-parent families, and alternate families.

Families have traditionally been the source of caregiving for both older and younger members. With reductions in the number of children and increasing variety of family forms, relationships with siblings, extended kin, and non-kin peers (i.e., alternative families) may play increasingly important roles. Caregiving, often provided by children to parents in later life, may be more difficult to obtain in the future as the availability of children is reduced. As the rates of divorce have increased, the number of reconstituted families has also increased. These families, as well as single-parent families and grandparents raising grandchildren, are at greater risk of intergenerational strain and familial disorder.

Despite these changes, intergenerational relationships may not be negatively affected. Parents and children appear to retain relatively close relationships even in societies that have undergone significant familial change. Relatively strong social norms for the provision of intergenerational support appear to have survived even though the family has undergone dramatic change. It is even possible that such changes could have positive benefits. Due to longer years lived, there is more time to share with other generations and this could result in stronger relationships across generations. Despite geographic distance, adult children and parents are able to maintain frequent contact and interaction with improved means of communication. Extended families appear to maintain their intergenerational cohesion.

Research has found that across generations, there are shared values, normative obligations to provide care, and lasting ties between parents and children. Generally, research suggests that parents and children provide needed support to each other and that such support improves emotional states throughout life and contributes to better adjustments to crises, such as widowhood, encountered during later life.

While there have been major changes in expected social roles and their link to age, most people still marry, have children, and become grandparents. Based on current cohorts of older adults, three-quarters of adults will become grandparents, with a fifth of all women who die after 80 having spent some time in a five-generation family as great-great-grandmothers. Nearly one-third of grandparents will experience great-grandparenthood and will be part of a four-generation family. Not only are families more likely to consist of more generations, but they are also more likely to be grandparents for longer, with some people as grandparents for more than half of their lifetimes. As more people become grandparents for longer periods of their lives, grandparents could occupy an expanding, and increasingly important, role within the family as the opportunity for more and longer interaction across generations increases. Custodial grandparents, or grandparents raising grandkids, have recently garnered increasing attention. The number of grandparent-headed households increased since the late 1990s by more than 50% with 1.3 million children raised solely by a grandparent as of 2005. The increase in grandparents raising grandkids can be attributed to increasing difficulties experienced by the "middle" or parent generation, including substance abuse, mental illness, imprisonment, and HIV/AIDS.

## LIFE COURSE PERSPECTIVE

The life course perspective is a theoretical orientation that guides research and contributes to our current understanding of humans' lives (e.g., changing roles and relationships with age and time) within historical and biographical contexts (Elder, 2003). The life course perspective is a framework for studying issues central to social change and developmental trajectories. Development is understood to be a lifelong process of fundamental biological, psychological, and social changes. It is also true that people create their own life course via decisions and actions taken in response to personal, social, and historical circumstances. These choices may affect future trajectories. For instance, a woman's choice to delay marriage and parenthood may then delay her age of grandparenthood. Individuals are shaped by the historical atmosphere and places experienced throughout life. For instance, people who experience devastating events like a war early in life may have their lives forever changed by their experience.

Depending on the time of occurrence during the life course, the same experiences or events affect individuals in varying ways. For instance, early parenthood can have detrimental effects on educational and occupational attainment. It is also true that lives are interdependent and relationships are impacted by social and historical influences. Due to this interdependence, transitions in one individual's life often result in transitions for others as well. For instance, a daughter's early role transition to motherhood results in her mother's early transition to grandparenthood, altering both of their roles and social identities. Interestingly, women who enter parenthood in early life often also enter grandparenthood at an earlier age.

Ultimately, the life course perspective considers individual choice and the process of decision-making. It acknowledges social and historical context, timing of events, role changes, and the interdependency of life. Future generations of researchers will continue to use the life course perspective to expand knowledge of how aging is affected by social influences and how aging, itself, affects social structures and societal roles.

Aging reflects a complex interplay among biological, psychological, and social influences combined. Hence, an interdisciplinary perspective of all three aspects of aging is essential to understanding life from childhood to late adulthood. All make clear that aging is a process that begins early in life and is affected by all one's exposure and experiences, and because the social world changes, aging is not a static experience.

**SEE ALSO** Volume 2: *Personality; Roles;* Volume 3: *Active Life Expectancy; Cognitive Functioning and Decline; Dementias; Frailty and Robustness; Genetic Influences, Later Life; Life Expectancy; Mental Health, Later Life; Population Aging; Self; Social Support, Later Life.*

## BIBLIOGRAPHY

Alzheimer's Association. (2007). Alzheimer's disease facts and figures. Retrieved June 26, 2008, from http://www.alz.org

American Psychiatric Association. (2000). *Diagnostic and statistical manual of mental disorders DSM-IV-TR.* Washington, DC: American Psychiatric Association.

Bass, S. A. (2000). Emergence of the third age: Toward a productive aging society. *Journal of Aging & Social Policy, 11,* 7–17.

Campisi, J. (2003). Cellular senescence. In F. M. Hisama, S. M. Weissman, & G. M. Martin (Eds.), *Chromosomal instability and aging: Basic science and clinical implications* (pp. 29–50). New York: Marcel Dekker.

Carstensen, L. L., Isaacowitz, D. M., & Charles, S. T. (1999). Taking time seriously: A theory of socioemotional selectivity theory. *American Psychologist, 54,* 165–181.

Darwin, Charles. (1955). *The expression of the emotions in man and animals.* New York: Philosophical Library.

Diehl, M., Coyle, N., & Labouvie-Vief, G. (1996). Age and sex differences in strategies of coping and defense across the life span. *Psychology and Aging 11,* 127–139.

DiGiovanna, A. G. (2000). *Human aging.* (2nd ed.). Boston, MA: McGraw-Hill.

Elder, G. H., Jr. (2003). The emergence and development of life course theory. In J. T. Mortimer & M. J. Shanahan (Eds.), *Handbook of the life course* (pp. 3–19). New York: Kluwer Academic/Plenum Publishers.

Finch, C. E., & Seeman, T. E. (1998). Stress theories of aging. In V. B. Bengtson & K.W. Schaie (Eds.), *Handbook of Theories of Aging* (pp. 81–97). New York: Springer.

Fiske, A., & Jones, R. S. (2005). Depression. In M. L. Johnson (with V.L. Bengtson, P. G. Coleman, and T. B. L. Kirkwood) (Eds.), *The Cambridge handbook of age & ageing* (pp. 245–251). Cambridge, U.K.: Cambridge University Press.

Gatz, M. (1996). Toward a developmentally informed theory of mental disorder in older adults. In J. Lomranz (Ed.), *Handbook of aging and mental health: An integrative approach* (pp. 101–120). New York: Plenum Press.

Gilleard, C., & Higgs, P. (2005). The third age: Class, cohort, or generation? *Ageing and Society, 22*: 369–382.

Harman, D. (1956). Aging: A theory based on free radical and radiation chemistry. *Journal of Gerontology, 11*, 298–300.

Kirkwood, T. (1999). *Time of our lives: The science of human aging* (pp. 81–99). Oxford, U.K.: Oxford University Press.

Labouvie-Vief, G. (2005). The psychology of emotions and ageing. In M. L. Johnson (with V.L. Bengtson, P. G. Coleman, and T. B. L. Kirkwood) (Eds.), *The Cambridge handbook of age & ageing* (pp. 229–236). Cambridge, U.K.: Cambridge University Press.

Laslett, P. (1989). *A fresh map of life: The emergence of the third age*. London: Weidenfeld and Nicolson.

Lawton, M. P. (1989). Environmental proactivity and affect in older people. In S. Spacapan & S. Oskamp (Eds.), *Social psychology of aging* (pp. 135–164). Newbury Park, CA: Sage.

Lowenstein, A. (2005). Global ageing and challenges to families. In M. L. Johnson (with V. L. Bengtson, P. G. Coleman, and T. B. L. Kirkwood) (Eds.), *The Cambridge handbook of age & ageing* (pp. 403–412). Cambridge, U.K.: Cambridge University Press.

Mather, M., & Carstensen, L. L. (2003). Aging and attentional biases for emotional faces. *Psychological Science, 14*, 409–415.

McCay, C. M., Cromwell, M., F., & Maynard, L. A. (1935). The effect of retarded growth upon the length of life and upon ultimate size. *Journal of Nutrition 10*, 63–79.

McCrae, R. R., & Costa, P. T. (1990). A five-factor theory of personality. In L. A. Pervin (Ed.), *Handbook of personality: Theory and research* (2nd ed., pp. 139–153). New York: Guilford Press.

Parrott, T. M., Mills, T. L., & Bengtson, V. L. (2000). The United States: Population demographics, changes in the family, and social policy challenges. In V. L. Bengston, K. D. Kim, & G. C. Myers (Eds.), *Aging in East and West: Families, states, and the elderly* (pp. 191–224). New York: Springer Publishing Company.

Plassman, B. L., Langa, K. M., Fisher, G. G., Heeringa, S. G., Weir, D. R., Ofstedal, M. B. et al. (2007). Prevalence of dementia in the United States: the aging, demographics, and memory study. *Neuroepidemiology, 29*, 125–132.

Poynter, J. (2006). *The human experiment: Two years and twenty minutes inside Biosphere 2*. New York: Thunder's Mouth Press.

Raber, J., Hugan, Y., & Ashford, J. W. (2004). ApoE genotype accounts for the vast majority of AD risk and AD pathology. *Neurobiology of Aging 25*, 641–650.

Reisberg, B. (2008). Stages of Alzheimer's. Retrieved June 26, 2008, from http://alz.org

Riley, M. W., Foner, A., & Waring, J. (1988). Sociology of age. In N. J. Smelser (Ed.), *Handbook of sociology* (pp. 243–290). Newbury Park, CA: Sage.

Rusting, R. L. (1992). Why do we age? *Scientific American*, Dec., 130–141.

Sackmann, R., & Wingens, M. (2003). From transitions to trajectories: Sequence types. In W. R. Heinz & V. W. Marshall (Eds.), *Social dynamics of the life course: Transitions, institutions, and interrelations*. Piscataway, NJ: Aldine de Gruyter.

Silverstein, M., & Bengtson, V. L. (1997). Intergenerational solidarity and the structure of adult child-parent relationships in American families. *American Journal of Sociology 103*, 429–460.

Smith, J., & Baltes, P. B. (1999). Trends and profiles of psychological functioning in very old age. In P. B. Baltes and K. U. Mayer (Eds.), *The Berlin Aging Study: Aging from 70 to 100* (pp. 197–226). New York: Cambridge University Press.

Staudinger, U. M. (2005). Personality and ageing. In M. L. Johnson (with V. L. Bengtson, P. G. Coleman, and T. B. L. Kirkwood) (Eds.), *The Cambridge handbook of age & ageing* (pp. 237–244). Cambridge, U.K.: Cambridge University Press.

Staudinger, U. M., Kessler, E.-M., & Dörner, J. (2006). Wisdom in social context. In K. W. Schaie & L.L. Cartensen (Eds.), *Social structures, aging, and self-regulation in the elderly*. New York: Springer.

Vijg, J., & Suh, Y. (2005). Genetics of longevity and aging. *Annual Review of Medicine, 56*, 193–212.

Williams, G. C. (1957). Pleiotropy, natural selection, and the evolution of senescence. *Evolution, 11*, 398–411.

Woods, R. T. (1999). *Psychological problems of ageing: Assessment, treatment, and care*. Chinchester, NY: Wiley.

Woods, B. (2005). Dementia. In M. L. Johnson (with V.L. Bengtson, P. G. Coleman, and T. B. L. Kirkwood) (Eds.), *The Cambridge handbook of age & ageing* (pp. 252–260). Cambridge, U.K.: Cambridge University Press.

World Health Organization. (2004). *International statistical classification of diseases and health related problems (ICD-10)*. (2nd ed.). Geneva, Switzerland: World Health Organization.Social Integration/Isolation, Adulthood

***Sarinnapha Vasunilashorn***
***Eileen M. Crimmins***

# AGING IN PLACE

As people reach the final stages of their life course, most want to remain as active and independent as possible for as long as possible. They want to age at home surrounded by friends and family, not in institutions such as nursing homes (Marek and Rantz, 2000). According to an American Association of Retired Persons' (AARP) 2005 *State of 50+ American Survey*, 89% of people over age 50 want to remain in their home for as long as possible, and 85% want to stay in their community for as long as possible. Among the reasons for remaining in the community is continuing to be close to friends and family (AARP, 2006). As people age they may be forced to move when characteristics of their home environment, such as stairs, width of doors and hallways, and bathroom and kitchen design, may no longer accommodate changes in health and functional status or when supportive services to accommodate their needs are unavailable. The goal of aging in place is to allow seniors to remain in the environment of their choice with supportive services as needed (Marek and Rantz, 2000).

Traditionally, older adults have been forced to move as health status deteriorates, needs change, and living environments no longer support successful aging. For older adults who choose to reside in long-term care residential facilities rather than in private homes in the community, state and federal regulations define building safety features, care that can be provided, staffing standards, as well as potential public payment for living in senior housing, residential (assisted living) facilities, or nursing homes. These regulations differ from state to state, but often require an older adult to maintain a certain level of ability to remain in senior housing or residential care. Although relocation has been associated with stress-related illness in older adults, regulations and discharge criteria force older adults to move from senior housing to residential care/assisted living, and finally to a nursing home as health deteriorates (Rantz, Marek, Aud, Johnson, Otto, et al., 2005a). For example, Mr. Jones may be satisfied living in senior housing, having some meals provided. He then experiences pneumonia and a minor stroke. After hospitalization and some rehabilitation in a Medicare skilled nursing facility, he returns to his apartment but has problems with frequent falls and is unable to get up on his own. The housing manager considers him a safety risk and insists he move to the residential care facility nearby so that staff can look after him and help him when he falls. After a few months in residential care, Mr. Jones has another stroke, is hospitalized, and enters a nursing home for rehabilitation in the Medicare unit. Following three weeks of rehabilitation, the physical therapist determines that he will need continuing nursing home care because he cannot walk sufficient distances as required in fire safety drills in his former residential care facility.

*Aging in place* is defined as older adults remaining at home with the services they need for continued residence as they grow older. The key to facilitating aging in place is to separate the type of care provided from the place of the care. In this model, people will not have to move from one level of care delivery to another as their needs change; instead, all the services they need will be delivered in their home. The concept of home includes all residential settings where medical services are not delivered. Home could mean residential care/assisted living, senior housing, an apartment, or private homes (Marek and Rantz, 2000).

The term *aging in place* first emerged in the research literature in the 1980s as researchers were focusing on quality of care and housing needs of older adults. Quality of care was a major issue during the 1980s because of numerous problems in nursing homes that led to U.S. government legislation in 1987 establishing resident rights and standards of care. As one could anticipate with publicity about nursing home problems, people wanted to remain at home as long as possible.

The idea of helping people age at home is not new. Many older individuals age naturally in the environment of their choice with the help of family and friends. Others receive services from a variety of community organizations and businesses. Indeed, many services exist to help older adults age in place. Services are available to help with meals; transportation; housekeeping; shopping for groceries, clothing, or health care items; and help with daily activities like bathing, dressing, or eating. Technologies are also making it easier for people to access health care and communicate with health care professionals. Technologies like such as, the Internet, videophones, and telehealth are helping to make many services more accessible (Demiris, Rantz, Aud, Marek, Tyler, et al., 2004).

Unfortunately, many of these services may not available in rural areas. Rural populations lag behind more populated areas in the variety and amount of services offered, particularly transportation, making aging in place harder. However, many rural people still manage to age in place with the support of family and friends. This option is not always available to older adults; as their children reach young adulthood, many move away from the rural areas to metropolitan areas for employment.

The home itself can affect an individual's ability to age in place. Most homes are not designed with the aging population in mind. The majority of residential housing is tailored to healthy young adults and does not take into account age-related changes such as limited mobility or reduced sensory function (Senior Resources, 2008). Age-related changes may affect one's ability to remain at home, but simple changes can dramatically enhance the home environment. For example, adding grab bars in the bathroom; replacing bathtubs with step-in showers; or moving laundry equipment to the same floor as primary living space will facilitate aging in place.

The term aging in place has been taken over by the senior housing industry to promote a variety of housing options with a range of health care services. The term has been used to market several types of facilities, including assisted living facilities and continuing care retirement communities. However, these settings offer a model of aging in place that differs from the model described here.

Assisted living facilities offer an alternative to nursing home care. Assisted living facilities provide 24-hour care in a residential setting to individuals who need help with some activities of daily living such as bathing, eating, dressing, going to the bathroom, or taking

***Nursing Home.*** *Ebony Martin, 17, and Lilly Maud Walton, 113, in the common area of Ansley Pavilion Nursing Home playing Balloon Volleyball. Many services exist to help older adults age in place.* © MARTIN H. SIMON/CORBIS.

medication, but who do not need the intensive skilled nursing and medical care provided in nursing homes. Assisted living facilities offer the promise of aging in place. However, people move out of assisted living to a higher level of care if health care needs exceed the capacity of the facility to provide care (Chapin and Dobbs-Kepper, 2001; Frank, 2001; Aud, 2004; Ball, Perkins, Whittington, Connell, et al., 2004).

The continuing care retirement community model encompasses different levels of care in one building or on a campus. For example, a community may include independent housing, assisted living, and a nursing home in different buildings within a campus. The continuing care retirement community does allow people to age in place; however the model still requires people to move from place to place within the building or on the campus as their health deteriorates.

In Missouri a demonstration project has been undertaken to evaluate whether aging in place really works. Legislation in 1999 and 2001 enabled the creation of this project within the highly regulated long-term care environment. The purpose of this program was to create innovative approaches to senior housing that incorporate health care services that adjust to the residents' changing needs. One of the four sites chosen for the demonstration, TigerPlace, is a prime example of this new kind of facility.

TigerPlace, a unique senior retirement community, was developed by faculty from the University of Missouri Sinclair School of Nursing and is based on the concept of aging in place. Rather than forcing residents to move as their needs change, TigerPlace offers varied services as needed. TigerPlace not only promotes the independence of its residents (Rantz, 2003) but also helps residents remain healthier and active longer by providing nursing care coordination, direct personal care as needed, ongoing nursing assessment (complete assessment every six months), early illness recognition, health promotion activities, and social activities—all within well-designed housing. TigerPlace is built to nursing home standards, licensed as the state's only aging in place building, and is designed to help residents avoid expensive and debilitating hospitalizations, and for most residents, avoid relocation to a long-term care facility.

The preliminary findings from the demonstration project indicate that this approach positively affects the residents and their families. Satisfaction, overall well-being, social engagement, and maintaining physical function are high while discharges to traditional nursing home care are very infrequent. Several residents died after moving to TigerPlace; most of these deaths were expected, and each resident died with his or her wishes respected, receiving personal care and hospice services as needed, with family and staff close by. These are the truly successful outcomes of aging in place: enjoying life until the end in one's own home with family and friends, getting the required care and services when they are needed.

An important feature of TigerPlace is the interdisciplinary research that takes place there. It is focused on using technology to enhance people's ability age in place and prevent or delay the decline associated with aging (Rantz, Marek, Aud, Tyrer, Skubic, et al., 2005b). Researchers are using sensors to collect physiological data including heart rate, blood pressure, bed restlessness, as well as activity levels (motion sensors). These data are being used to detect changes in health status so health care professionals may intervene to prevent or delay declines in health status (Rantz, Skubic, Burks, Yu, Demiris, et al., 2008).

Others are working on technology that automatically controls room temperature, windows, doors, locks, and other environmental factors (Haigh, Kiff, and Ho, 2006; Plocher, Kiff, and Krichbaum, 2004). Additionally, technology can also provide a safer environment. For example, lights can be automatically switched on when someone enters a room or the stove can automatically turn off if left on too long. All of these technological advances are making it easier for people more safely to age in place.

Aging in place is an idea that is here to stay. People want the independence, privacy, and social support that come with remaining at home. Politicians, researchers, health care providers, and businesses are listening to the wishes of the aging population and are changing to meet their demands.

**SEE ALSO** Volume 3: *Assisted Living Facilities; Assistive Technologies; Neighborhood Context, Later Life; Residential Mobility, Later Life; Retirement Communities.*

**BIBLIOGRAPHY**

AARP. (2006). *The state of 50+ America.* Retrieved April 27, 2008, from http://www.aarp.org

Aud, M. A. (2004). Residents with dementia in assisted living facilities: The role of behavior in discharge decisions. *Journal of Gerontological Nursing, 30,* 16–26.

Ball, M. M., Perkins, M. M., Whittington, F. J., Connell, B. R., Hollingsworth, C., King, S. V., et al. (2004). Managing decline in assisted living: The key to aging in place. *Journal of Gerontology, 59B,* S202–S212.

Chapin, R., & Dobbs-Kepper, D. (2001). Aging in place in assisted living: Philosophy versus policy. *The Gerontologist 41,* 43–50.

Demiris, G., Rantz, M., Aud, M., Marek, K., Tyrer, H., Skubic, M., et al. (2004). Older adults' attitudes towards and perceptions of "smart home" technologies: A pilot study. *Medical Informatics & The Internet in Medicine, 29,* 87–94.

Frank, J. (2001). How long can I stay? The dilemma of aging in place in assisted living. In B. Schwarz (Ed.), *Assisted living: Sobering realities* (pp. 5–30). New York: Haworth Press.

Haigh, K. Z., Kiff, L. M., & Ho, G. (2006). The independent lifestyle assistant: Lessons learned. *Assistive Technology, 18,* 87–106.

Marek, K. D., & Rantz, M. J. (2000). Aging in place: A new model for long-term care. *Nursing Administration Quarterly, 24,* 1–11.

Plocher T., Kiff, L., & Krichbaum, K. (2004). Promoting and maximizing independence through new technologies, *AAHSA Future of Aging Services Conference,* 15 March 2004, Washington, DC.

Rantz, M. J. (2003). Aging in place. *Nurseweek,* Midwest/ Heartland Edition, 4, 7.

Rantz, M. J., Marek, K. D., Aud, M. A., Johnson, R. A., Otto, D., & Porter, R. (2005a). TigerPlace: A new future for older adults. *Journal of Nursing Care Quality, 20,* 1–4.

Rantz, M. J., Marek, K. D., Aud, M. A., Tyrer, H. W., Skubic, M., Demiris, G. & Hussam, A.A. (2005b). Technology and nursing collaboration to help older adults age in place. *Nursing Outlook, 53,* 40–45.

Rantz, M. J., Skubic, M., Burks, K., Yu, J., Demiris, G., Hensel, B. K., et al. (2008). Functional Assessment Technologies. In R.A. Felder & M. Alwan (Eds.), *Eldercare Technology for Clinical Practitioners* (pp. 5–32). Totowa, NJ: Humana.

Senior Resource. (2008). Aging in place. Retrieved April 25, 2008 from http://www.seniorresource.com

Tilson, D. (Ed). (1999). *Aging in place: Supporting the frail elderly in residential environments.* Glenview, IL: Scott, Foresman.

***Marilyn J. Rantz***
***Myra A. Aud***
***Steven J. Miller***

# ALLOSTATIC LOAD

In recent years, many scholars have used allostatic load to explain how various hardships associated with poor social environments "get under the skin" to affect disease and mortality risks, particularly in later life (Seeman, Singer, Ryff, Love, & Levy-Storms, 2002, p. 395). Allostatic load is based on the concept of *allostasis*, or "the ability of the body to increase or decrease vital functions to a new steady state on challenge" (McEwen & Stellar, 1993, p. 2093). Broadly speaking, these vital functions include cardiovascular health, body composition, stress hormones, and the immune system (Seeman, Singer, Rowe, Horwitz, & McEwen, 1997; Seplaki, Goldman, Weinstein, & Lin, 2006). The definition of allostasis is reflected in its etymology, which involves the ancient Greek terms *allo* and *stasis*, meaning change and stability, respectively (Szanton, Gill, & Allen, 2005). Indeed, one conception of allostasis is simply physiological "stability through change" (Sterling, 2004, p. 18). Some scholars view allostasis as a complement to the traditional medical concept of homeostasis, which describes the body's ability to maintain internal conditions such as heart rate and body temperature within a normal, well-tolerated set of parameters (McEwen & Wingfield, 2003). Other scholars have argued that because allostasis more accurately describes physiologic processes, it should overthrow homeostasis as the primary model for internal biological maintenance (Sterling, 2004).

Allostasis is vital for short-term adaptation to physical stressors such as caloric imbalance and psychological stressors such as marital distress, but it is not without long-term physiological cost. *Allostatic load* is a concept that attempts to understand the cumulative effect, or "wear and tear" of repeated physiological adjustments to stress (McEwen & Seeman, 1999). It is important to distinguish allostatic load from an *allostatic state*, which "can be defined as a state of chronic deviation of the regulatory systems from their normal state of operation" (Koob & Le Moal, 2001, p. 102). Over time, an allostatic state can result in allostatic load by overwhelming an organism's ability to cope with repeated adaptations to challenging conditions. For example, excessive production of stress hormones such as cortisol (i.e., one form of an allostatic state) over long periods of time may eventually result in elevated blood pressure (Fraser et al, 1999), which has traditionally been viewed as one key marker of allostatic load (Seeman et al., 1997).

## MEASUREMENT

Allostatic load (AL) was initially measured as an index of 10 biomarkers that were believed to measure the level of physiologic dysregulation, which is simply the overall level of bodily duress (Seeman et al., 1997). These biomarkers are defined as follows (MedicineNet.com, 2008; Seeman et al., 1997):

1. Systolic blood pressure: top number in a blood pressure reading that measures the maximum arterial pressure as the heart contracts; included in AL as an indicator of cardiovascular health.
2. Diastolic blood pressure: bottom number in a blood pressure reading that measures the minimum arterial pressure as the heart relaxes; included in AL as an indicator of cardiovascular health.
3. Ratio of (waist circumference / hip circumference): measures adiposity; included in AL to assess calorie imbalance and metabolism.
4. High-density lipoprotein (HDL) cholesterol: good form of cholesterol that protects arteries from plaque accumulation; included in AL to assess risk of developing atherosclerosis (higher values reflect lower risk).
5. Ratio of (total cholesterol / HDL cholesterol): proxy indicator for plaque inducing low-density lipoprotein (LDL) cholesterol; included in AL to assess risk of developing atherosclerosis (higher values reflect higher risk).
6. Glycosylated hemoglobin: blood sugar that has become attached to the hemoglobin molecule in red blood cells; included in AL to measure glucose metabolism and diabetes mellitus (higher values reflect higher risk).
7. Cortisol: a corticosteroid hormone released by the adrenal gland in response to stress; included in AL to measure stress hormones that may weaken the immune system and cause other health issues (e.g., weight gain) at elevated levels.
8. Epinephrine: often referred to as adrenaline, this adrenal hormone causes arterial dilation and increases heart rate; included in AL to assess stress hormone levels.
9. Norepinephrine: an adrenal hormone that causes vasoconstriction and increases blood pressure; included in AL to assess stress hormone levels.
10. Dehydroepiandrosterone sulfate (DHEA-S): an adrenal hormone that is similar to testosterone in its physical effects; included in AL to assess stress hormone levels.

When operationalized in the traditional way, each biomarker is dichotomized into a high-risk quartile (the worst 25% of research participants) with a score of one and a "normal range" category (the remaining 75% of research participants) with a score of 0 and then summed—yielding an index ranging from 0 to 10, with 10 being the maximal score for allostatic load. Since this initial attempt to measure the concept of allostatic load, researchers have developed more complicated and nuanced techniques. This research suggests that some biomarkers may be more important measures of allostatic load than others. For instance, one study (Karlamangla Singer, McEwen, Rowe, & Seeman, 2002) found that epinephrine and diastolic blood pressure were particularly important measures of allostatic load, whereas other measures such as HDL cholesterol were unnecessary. Similarly, Burton Singer, Carol Ryff, and Teresa Seeman (2004) found that diastolic blood pressure was a particularly important measure of allostatic load. However, unlike Karlamangla et al.'s analysis, Singer and colleagues found that HDL cholesterol was an important contributor to the allostatic load construct.

Despite these improvements, Christopher Seplaki and colleagues (2006) have identified a number of limitations of previous efforts to measure allostatic load. For instance, existing measures tend to capture health risks associated with elevated biomarkers (e.g., high blood pressure) but not risks associated with unusually low levels of those same biomarkers (e.g., hypotension). Another limitation is that allostatic load may not operate in the same matter for men and women, suggesting that gender insensitive measures of allostatic load may be inappropriate. Also, most research on allostatic load is based on a single study (the MacArthur Study of Successful Aging), raising serious questions about the generalizability of existing knowledge. Importantly, most research to date has failed to account for immune function, which is a potentially important component of the allostatic load construct.

To account for these shortcomings, Seplaki and colleagues (2006) devised a measure of allostatic load that incorporated a total of 16 biomarkers. In addition to the 10 biomarkers used previously, these scholars included dopamine, body mass index, triglycerides, fasting glucose, insulin-like growth factor-1, and interleukin-6. The latter two biomarkers provided an assessment of immune function, whereas the others offered a more comprehensive picture of stress response, body composition, metabolic function, and cardiovascular health. Using a sample of 972 Taiwanese adults age 70 or older from the 2000 Social Environment and Biomarkers of Aging Study, Seplaki et al. used an advanced statistical technique to create five distinct allostatic load profiles for various sorts of health risk (e.g., low stress hormones but elevated biomarkers for metabolic and cardiovascular function). Analyses showed that this new measure of allostatic load performed better than the traditional 10-count measure in terms of the strength of its associations with health outcomes. In addition to this important finding, the study found only relatively minor gender differences in allostatic load in this sample of older Taiwanese adults, suggesting that previous concerns about gender differences may have been overstated.

## CAUSES OF ALLOSTATIC LOAD

Extant literature suggests that allostatic load is caused by repeated exposures to various stressors across the life course. These stressors have been defined as "external and internal challenges to the body and brain" (Koob & Le Moal, 2001, p. 99) and also as "events that are threatening to an individual and elicit physiological and behavioral responses" (McEwen, 2004, p. 67). These stressors may include (a) physical challenges such as hunger, exhaustion, temperature variations, and infections and (b) emotional and psychological difficulties such as anxiety and depression. (McEwen & Stellar, 1993; Schulkin, 2004). As various body systems—including the autonomic nervous system, the hypothalamo-pituitary-adrenal axis, and the immune system—respond to these challenges, allostasis results; as noted, this is functional for short-term adaptation (McEwen, 2002).

However, overexposure to stressors can provoke allostatic load, which is influenced by "repeated cycles of allostasis as well as the inefficient turning-on or shutting-off of these responses" (p. 32). For instance, depressed individuals are often beset with anxiety about future circumstances, provoking the release and chronic elevation of stress hormones such as cortisol (Schulkin, 2004). This has deleterious consequences, including high metabolic rates in the amygdala (a portion of the brain involved in processing emotions such as fear and anger), which may cause a "biasing of the brain" that further predisposes depressed persons toward negative and fearful affect (p. 9).

Although intuitively appealing, studies on the influence of stressors on allostatic load have produced mixed results. Analyses of data from the Wisconsin Longitudinal Study and the MacArthur Studies of Successful Aging demonstrated that individuals with positive social relationships were significantly less likely than individuals without such bonds to have elevated allostatic load scores (Seeman et al., 2002). To illustrate, women in the Wisconsin Longitudinal Study cohort with positive relationship histories were 78% less likely than women with negative histories to score high on the allostatic load index. Despite these compelling findings, some research has yielded less consistent results. For instance, analyses of 13 different scales of work conditions in a manufacturing plant in southern Germany found that only one of these scales—job demands—was significantly (but only weakly) associated with allostatic load (Schnorpfeil et al., 2003). Contrary to Seeman et al., Schnorpfeil et al. did not find significant associations between allostatic load and social support.

Another study (Glei, Goldman, Chuang, & Weinstein, 2007) found only weak support for the association between chronic stressors and allostatic load in the same sample of older Taiwanese adults examined by Seplaki et al. Similarly, an analysis of 290 Dutch managers failed to find any significant differences in allostatic load between "burned out" and exhausted managers and those with better mental health (Langelaan, Bakker, Schaufeli, van

Rhenen, & van Doornen, 2007). Clearly, further research is needed to sort through these findings and elucidate the causes of allostatic load.

## CONSEQUENCES OF ALLOSTATIC LOAD FOR HEALTH AND WELL-BEING

Research has shown that allostatic load is associated with a number of different health outcomes. In a seminal study documenting the health effects of allostatic load, Seeman et al. (1997) found that higher levels of allostatic load predicted decline in both the cognitive and functional capabilities of research participants in the MacArthur Studies of Successful Aging. These results were supported and extended by Karlamangla et al. (2002), who used canonical correlation analyses to show substantially stronger associations between allostatic load and health outcomes than initially found by Seeman et al. Additional research using the MacArthur Studies of Successful Aging cohort has shown that allostatic load is a strong predictor of mortality risk, independent of baseline health conditions and several other covariates such as sex, age, income, and education (Seeman, McEwen, Rowe, & Singer, 2001). Other research has used sophisticated statistical modeling to demonstrate that allostatic load is significantly associated with self-rated health, physical functioning, and depression in a cohort of older Taiwanese individuals (Seplaki et al., 2006).

In addition to health differences among individuals, Szanton et al. (2005) have suggested that allostatic load may explain health disparities across socioeconomic status groups. As resources such as income and education decline, the risk for exposure to chronic stressors increases (House et al., 1994; Marmot et al., 1991). Consequently, it is not surprising that studies have found higher levels of allostatic load in lower socioeconomic status groups (Seeman et al., 2004; Weinstein, Goldman, Hedley, Lin, & Seeman, 2003). Such findings are potentially important, as the elimination of health disparities is currently a top public health priority in the United States (U.S. Department of Health and Human Services, 2000).

## LIMITATIONS

Allostatic load has provided an innovative and useful way to conceptualize the physiological mechanisms that may mediate physical and psychological stressors and deleterious health outcomes. Prior research has shown that allostatic load predicts a range of health outcomes and, to a lesser extent, is associated with an assortment of stressors. Nevertheless, as Jay Schulkin (2004) pointed out, "There are no knock-down arguments for the concept of allostasis" (p. 12) and important questions remain about the validity of allostatic load.

For instance, studies have shown that some biomarkers used to measure allostatic load are more consequential for health than others and even that some biomarkers have no effect (Karlamangla et al., 2002; Singer et al., 2004). This raises the possibility that allostatic load is simply a new term used to describe previously established threats to health such as high blood pressure and elevated levels of cortisol. Furthermore, although research has shown that stress hormones and biomarkers associated with syndrome X (i.e., high cardiovascular risk) independently predict certain health outcomes, it has yet to show that the subcomponents of allostatic load combine to form a single underlying construct. In fact, preliminary analyses of MacArthur data failed to detect significant associations between latent constructs for stress hormones and syndrome X (Reither & Seeman, 2004). Should further research confirm this finding, would it be fair to say that allostatic load is an overarching construct that describes multiple, co-occurring physiological processes?

Despite these questions, ongoing research is continually refining allostatic load and addressing its limitations. For instance, several studies have adopted sophisticated methodologies to help improve the measurement of allostatic load (Karlamangla et al., 2002; Seplaki et al., 2006; Singer et al., 2004). Also, Seplaki et al. have expanded the number of biomarkers used to measure allostatic load, including two measures of immune function. With additional refinement, allostatic load promises to fulfill its potential as a valid and reliable measure of cumulative, physiological dysregulation. With better measurement comes the promise of superior detection of the preclinical signs of a wide range of diseases that afflict older individuals, which is particularly important given the rapid aging of the world's population.

**SEE ALSO** Volume 3: *Aging; Chronic Illness, Adulthood and Later Life; Diabetes, Adulthood and Later Life; Health Differentials/Disparities, Later Life; Stress in Later Life.*

**BIBLIOGRAPHY**

Fraser, R., Ingram, M. C., Anderson, N. H., Morrison, C., Davies, E., & Connell, J. M. C. (1999). Cortisol effects on body mass, blood pressure, and cholesterol in the general population. *Hypertension, 33*(6), 1364–1368.

Glei, D. A., Goldman, N., Chuang, Y.-L., & Weinstein, M. (2007). Do chronic stressors lead to physiological dysregulation? Testing the theory of allostatic load. *Psychosomatic Medicine, 69*(8), 769–776.

House, J. S., Lepkowski, J. M., Kinney, A. M., Mero, R. P., Kessler, R. C., & Herzog, A. R. (1994). The social stratification of aging and health. *Journal of Health and Social Behavior, 35*(3), 213–234.

Karlamangla, A. S., Singer, B. H., McEwen, B. S., Rowe, J. W., & Seeman, T. E. (2002). Allostatic load as a predictor of functional decline: MacArthur Studies of Successful Aging. *Journal of Clinical Epidemiology, 55*, 696–710.

Koob, G. F., & Le Moal, M. (2001). Drug addiction, dysregulation of reward, and allostasis. *Neuropsychopharmacology, 24*(2), 97–129.

Langelaan, S., Bakker, A. B., Schaufeli, W. B., van Rhenen, W., & van Doornen, L. J. P. 2007. Is burnout related to allostatic load? *International Journal of Behavioral Medicine, 14*(4), 213–221.

Marmot, M. G., Smith, G. D., Stansfeld, S., Patel, C., North, F., Head, J., White, I., et al. (1991). Health inequalities among British civil servants: The Whitehall II Study. *The Lancet 337*(8754), 1387–1393.

McEwen, B. S. (2002). Sex, stress, and the hippocampus: Allostasis, allostatic load and the aging process. *Neurobiology of Aging, 23*(5), 921–939.

McEwen, B. S. (2004). Protective and damaging effects of the mediators of stress and adaptation: Allostasis and allostatic load. In J. Schulkin (Ed.), *Allostasis, homeostasis, and the costs of physiological adaptation* (pp. 65–98). New York: Cambridge University Press.

McEwen, B. S., & Seeman, T. (1999). Protective and damaging effects of mediators of stress: Elaborating and testing the concepts of allostasis and allostatic load. *Annals of the New York Academy of Sciences, 896*(1), 30–47.

McEwen, B. S., & Stellar, E. (1993). Stress and the individual: Mechanisms leading to disease. *Archives of Internal Medicine, 153*(18), 2093–2101.

McEwen, B. S., & Wingfield, J. C. (2003). The concept of allostasis in biology and biomedicine. *Hormones and Behavior, 43*(1), 2–15.

MedicineNet.com. (2008). *MedTerms™ dictionary*. Retrieved June 30, 2008, from http://www.medicinenet.com

Reither, E. N., & Seeman, T. E. (2004). *The sufficiency and validity of allostatic load: An examination of gender differences in stress adaptation.* Paper presented at the annual conference for the American Sociological Association. San Francisco, CA.

Schnorpfeil, P., Noll, A., Schulze, R., Ehlert, U., Frey, K., & Fischer, J. E. (2003). Allostatic load and work conditions. *Social Science & Medicine, 57*(4), 647–656.

Schulkin, J. (2004). Introduction. In J. Schulkin (Ed.), *Allostasis, homeostasis, and the costs of physiological adaptation* (pp. 1–16). New York: Cambridge University Press.

Seeman, T. E., Crimmins, E., Huang, M.-H., Singer, B., Bucur, A., Gruenewald, T., et al. (2004). Cumulative biological risk and socio-economic differences in mortality: MacArthur Studies of Successful Aging. *Social Science & Medicine, 58*(10), 1985–1997.

Seeman, T. E., McEwen, B. S., Rowe, J. W., & Singer, B. H. (2001). Allostatic load as a marker of cumulative biological risk: MacArthur Studies of Successful Aging. *Proceedings of the National Academy of Sciences, 98*(8), 4770–4775.

Seeman, T. E., Singer, B. H., Rowe, J. W., Horwitz, R. I., & McEwen, B. S. (1997). Price of adaptation—Allostatic load and its health consequences: MacArthur Studies of Successful Aging. *Archives of Internal Medicine, 157*(19), 2259–2268.

Seeman, T. E., Singer, B. H., Ryff, C. D., Love, G. D., & Levy-Storms, L. (2002). Social relationships, gender, and allostatic load across two age cohorts. *Psychosomatic Medicine, 64*(3), 395–406.

Seplaki, C. L., Goldman, N., Weinstein, M., & Lin, Y.-H. (2006). Measurement of cumulative physiological dysregulation in an older population. *Demography, 43*(1), 165–183.

Singer, B., Ryff, C. D., & Seeman, T. (2004). Operationalizing allostatic load. In J. Schulkin (Ed.), *Allostasis, homeostasis, and the costs of physiological adaptation* (pp. 113–149). New York: Cambridge University Press.

Sterling, P. (2004). Principles of allostasis: Optimal design, predictive regulation, pathophysiology and rational therapeutics. In J. Schulkin (Ed.), *Allostasis, homeostasis, and the costs of physiological adaptation* (pp. 17–64). New York: Cambridge University Press.

Szanton, S. L., Gill, J. M., & Allen, J. K. (2005). Allostatic load: A mechanism of socioeconomic health disparities? *Biological Research for Nursing, 7*(1), 7–15.

U.S. Department of Health and Human Services. (2000). *Healthy People 2010: Understanding and improving health*, 2nd ed. Washington, DC: U.S. Government Printing Office.

Weinstein, M., Goldman, N., Hedley, A., Lin, Y.-H., & Seeman, T. (2003). Social linkages to biological markers of health among the elderly. *Journal of Biosocial Science, 35*, 433–453.Cardiovascular Disease

**Eric N. Reither**

## ALZHEIMER'S DISEASE

SEE Volume 3: *Cognitive Functioning and Decline; Dementias.*

## ARTHRITIS

Within the past century, scientific and medical advancements have been successful in preserving health and preventing and treating acute, infectious diseases (e.g., polio, tuberculosis) that negatively affect population health. These accomplishments, coupled with the growth of the U.S. population and increased life expectancy, have shifted the attention of medical and public health professionals to the prevalence and incidence of more chronic medical conditions such as hypertension, diabetes, cancer, and arthritis.

Arthritis, a condition characterized by pain, aching, stiffness, and swelling in and around the joint, poses a significant burden on the total U.S. population. It is one of the most common nonfatal chronic diseases (depending on the diagnosis) in the United States and is the leading cause of pain, substantive physical disability, and reduced quality of life, particularly among adults 65 years of age and older. An estimated 21.6% (46.4 million) of the adult U.S. population has been diagnosed by their doctor with an arthritis condition. Specifically, 29.3% (20.5 million) of those ages 45 to 64 years of age report being doctor-diagnosed with an arthritis condition, with another 50% (17.2 million) among those age 65 and older reporting such a condition. With the increase in life expectancy, the number of diagnosed cases is expected to increase to 67 million adults by 2030.

Derived from the Greek words *arthron* ("joints") and *itis* ("inflammation"), arthritis is a general term used to describe more than 100 different conditions that affect the joint(s) and/or connective tissues. The most common types of arthritis are osteoarthritis (OA), which causes deterioration of the cartilage, and rheumatoid arthritis (RA), an autoimmune disease that causes inflammation of the joint lining and severe and irreversible damage to the heart muscle, lungs, kidneys, liver, and other organs and systems of the body. Other common forms of arthritis include fibromyalgia, gout, and systemic lupus erythematosus, which also have a significant impact on performance of routine tasks, leisure activities, and daily physical activities.

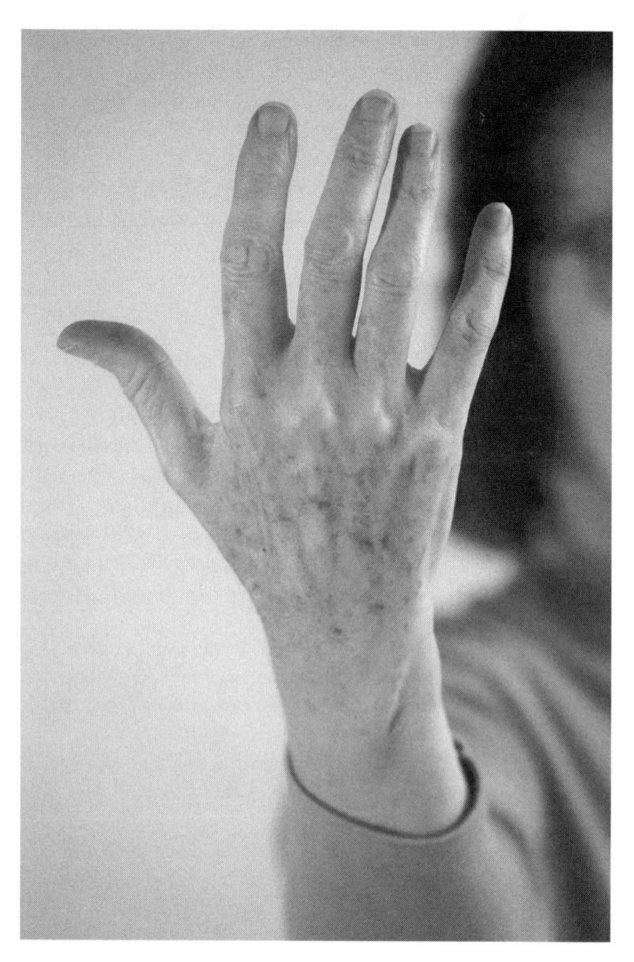

***Rehumatoid Arthritis.*** *Characterized by pain, aching, stiffness, swelling in and around the joint, arthritis poses a significant burden on the US population.* CUSTOM MEDICAL STOCK PHOTO.

## PHYSICAL AND PSYCHOLOGICAL IMPACT OF ARTHRITIS

Defined as the difficulty, inability, or limitation in performing basic functional activities, an estimated 49 million noninstitutionalized persons report some degree of physical impairment or disability due to chronic illness. Whereas the changes in functional status contribute to lost work productivity, they also increase nursing home admissions, health care use, and expenditures. Approximately 16.9.4 million (7.9%) of the adult U.S. population report arthritis-attributable activity limitation (e.g., walking, bathing, dressing). This is projected to increase to 25 million (9.3%) by 2030. This is of growing concern as 54% of all arthritis-attributable activity limitation cases will be among adults 65 years of age and older by 2030. The physical limitations associated with arthritis involve a process in which muscle weakness leads to unstable joints; the resulting stress that is exerted on unstable joints cause physical disability and pain.

Paradoxically, attempts to avoid the pain associated with normal activities may lead to increased muscle weakness or muscle atrophy, in which the individual may lose muscle tone or experience a wasting or loss of muscle tissue. This may initiate a cycle of activity avoidance, physical disability, and pain.

Pain is the predominant manifestation of arthritis and is a significant predictor of disability, particularly for activities involving transfer, mobility, and other instrumental activities of daily living. Defined as an unpleasant sensory and emotional experience that impacts an individual's physical and psychological health and social well-being, the pain experience is not only a major health concern for individuals with arthritis but is also a significant predictor of current and future medication use, future pain experiences, and subsequent physical disability.

The pain experience varies from patient to patient and is contingent on a myriad of factors, including the history of the illness, duration of the medical condition, type (acute versus chronic) and location of the pain, variability of daily pain, number of painful days, number of joints affected, physiological changes (e.g., changes to the body's tissue structure), and side effects of pharmacologic interventions.

Aside from the physical expression of arthritis, many psychosocial factors are associated with the onset and experience of the disease. Psychosocial factors are defined as psychological, behavioral, and social processes that include beliefs, values, perceptions, culture, coping behaviors, personality indicators, and social resources and networks (e.g., social support), all of which influence how the individual detects, interprets, and responds to arthritis.

## CULTURAL DIFFERENCES

Although the biological sensations of pain are universal, the meaning, attitudes, and response to the pain experience differ across race, gender, and age subgroups. For example, some racial and ethnic groups are known to have specific "pain rituals" that shape the expectations and beliefs about pain, as well as strategies to tolerate the pain experience. Factors such as differences in language, ways of understanding and expressing health and disease, preferred modalities of health care management and treatment, the expression and meaning of pain, and the use of identified strategies to cope with pain are among the many factors that define the experience and cultural context of pain. For example, unlike the Western dichotomy of mind and body in explaining the pain experience, pain from a Chinese perspective, is regarded as a complex experience that can be understood only through the understanding of identified Eastern philosophies (e.g., Taoism/Energy Theory, Buddhism, and Confucianism). Social learning is another factor that may explain the contextual patterning and influence lifetime exposure has on how, why, and when this (pain) and other arthritis-related symptoms are experienced.

Race, which comprises ethnicity and culture, is a complex and multidimensional construct that establishes a conceptual framework for how people perceive health, illness, social demands, and environmental changes across the lifespan. To understand the role of race in daily behavior is to understand the extent to which the individual identifies with that particular race (or cultural) group and how experiences throughout the life course influence those experiences.

Social and demographic factors such as age and gender are associated with variability in the arthritis experience. For example, women 65 years of age and older are more likely to experience OA compared to women 35 years of age and younger. Specifically, there is growing evidence of the steady increase in the average age of persons with certain arthritis conditions such as RA, suggesting that RA and related morbidity, mortality, and disability rates are becoming more of an arthritis condition among older adults. Gender also dictates the disease process and its influence on physical health outcomes. Women are more likely to report pain-related chronic conditions such as OA, RA, fibromyalgia, and systemic lupus erythe than their male counterparts. Specifically, arthritis is reported as the most frequent cause of disability among women in general and among those diagnosed with arthritis in particular. National studies corroborate these findings, showing that OA prevalence tends to increase with age and affect woman more frequently than men. Despite the prevalence of these conditions, women are often treated less aggressively for their arthritis-related symptoms. Black women, for example, are at an increased risk for being diagnosed with an arthritis condition that is more severe, physically debilitating, and undertreated when compared to Black men and White men and women. This clearly shows that gender coupled with race has a substantial influence on the arthritis experience.

One's socioeconomic status (SES—e.g., income, education, occupational status), past and current, also influences the experience of arthritis. It is often difficult to determine the effects of SES and race exclusively in reports of arthritis and arthritis-related symptoms. Concatenated data from several national studies show pervasive race differences, with persons from minority populations reporting more severe and debilitating cases of arthritis. Others, however, have found no differences between majority and minority raced populations. Despite these findings, there has been more consistency in documenting the influence of SES on disease onset. Contemporary literature contends that persons with low SES are more likely to report arthritis and experience a decline in functional capacities than those with high SES.

It is important to consider the influence of SES (i.e., social positioning) when examining the etiology, prevalence, and incidence of arthritis, as it may capture lifetime exposure to deprived conditions (social, environmental), which may impact identified health outcomes in general, particularly among persons from more marginalized populations (e.g., minorities, elderly, women, the disabled). This is critical in the attempt to better understand the influence of SES and race on the etiology, progression, and outcome of arthritis among the elderly. For example, it has been shown that, despite equivalent levels of education (i.e., high SES), Whites reported better overall health, whereas Blacks did not enjoy the same health benefits due to higher attained levels of education. Despite these findings, there remains some debate as to whether race and SES function exclusively of one another or as binary constructs. This attests to the difficulty in disentangling the effects of race and SES, as both are cited as being significantly related to one another.

Health reflects a biological, behavioral, and social patterning of differential treatment, rights, and privileges that are defined by the life course, which is embedded in larger historical, geographic, social, cultural, and economic milieus. These constructs become more salient in light the steady increase in the number of older adults. With the increased life expectancy in U.S. society, the focus should extend more to the basic psychological and physical needs of older adults, as many will experience multiple chronic conditions, such as arthritis, within their lifetime. More important, decreasing the impact of arthritis among the aging population will require proven health policies and applied public health interventions that improve functional abilities, decrease pain, and delay the experience of arthritis-related disabilities. Addressing these issues may ultimately help to identify the social, psychological, physical, and cultural factors that have important implications for policy, advocacy, and long-term needs of our growing population.

**SEE ALSO** Volume 3: *Chronic Illness, Adulthood and Later Life; Disability and Functional Limitations, Later Life; Pain, Acute and Chronic.*

**BIBLIOGRAPHY**

Airhihenbuwa, C. O. (1995). *Health and culture: Beyond the Western paradigm.* Thousand Oaks, CA: Sage.

Centers for Disease Control. (2003). Projected prevalence of self-reported arthritis or chronic joint symptoms among persons aged ≥65 years—United States, 2005–2030. *Morbidity and Mortality Weekly Report, 25*(21), 489–512.

Centers for Disease Control. (2006). Prevalence of doctor-diagnosed arthritis and arthritis-attributable activity limitation—United States, 2003–2005. *Morbidity & Mortality Weekly Report, 55*(40), 1089–1092.

Chen, L., Miaskowski, C., Dodd, M., & Pantilar, S. (2008). Concepts within the Chinese culture that influence the cancer pain experience. *Cancer Nursing, 31*(2), 103–108.

Cutler, D. M. (2001). Declining disability among the elderly. *Health Affairs, 20*(6), 11–27.

Dunlop, D. D., Hughes, S. L., & Manheim, L. M. (1997). Disability in activities of daily living: Patterns of change and a hierarchy of disability. *American Journal of Public Health, 87,* 378–383.

Edwards, C. L., Fillingim, R. B., & Keefe, F. (2001). Race, ethnicity and pain. *Pain, 94,* 133–137.

Federal Interagency Forum on Aging-Related Statistics. (2004). *Older Americans 2000: Key indicators of well-being.* Retrieved May 13, 2008, from http://www.agingstats.gov

Helmick, C. G., Felson, D. T., Lawrence, R. C., Gabriel, S., Hirsch, R., et al. (2008). Estimates of the prevalence of arthritis and other rheumatic conditions in the United States. *Arthritis & Rheumatism, 58*(1), 15–25.

Hootman, J. M., & Helmick, C. G. (2006). Projections of U.S. prevalence of arthritis and associated activity limitations. *Arthritis & Rheumatism, 54*(1), 226–229.

King, G., & Williams, D. R. (1995). Race and health: A multidimensional approach to African-American health. In B. C. Amick III, S. Levine, A. R. Taylor, & D. C. Walsh (Eds.), *Society and health* (pp. 93–130). New York: Oxford University Press.

Kraus, L. E., Stoddard, S., & Gilmartin, D. (1996). *Chartbook on disability in the United States.* Washington, DC: U.S. National Institute on Disability and Rehabilitation Research.

Machado, G. P. M., Gignac, M. A. M., & Bradley, E. M. (2008). Participation restrictions among older adults with osteoarthritis: A mediated model of physical symptoms, activity limitations, and depression. *Arthritis & Rheumatism, 59*(1), 129–135.

McIlvane, J. M. (2007). Disentangling the effects of race and SES on arthritis-related symptoms, coping, and well-being in African-American and White women. *Aging & Mental Health, 11*(5), 556–569.

Phinney, J. S. (1996). When we talk about American ethnic groups, what do we mean? *American Psychologist, 51*(9), 918–927.

Sigelman, C. K., & Rider, A. E. (2003). *Life-span human development.* (4th ed.). Belmont, CA: Wadsworth/Thompson Learning.

Theis, K. A., Helmick, C. G., & Hootman, J. M. (2007). Arthritis burden and impact are greater among U.S. women than men: Intervention opportunities. *Journal of Women's Health, 19*(4), 441–453.

Zola, I. K. (1958). Culture and symptoms: An analysis of patients' presenting complaints. *American Sociological Review, 31,* 615–630.

***Tamara A. Baker***

# ASSISTED LIVING FACILITIES

With the dramatic increase in the size of the aged population in the United States, Europe, and Asia, people are seeking new ways to approach how to care for and support the elderly. Traditionally, people remained at home (aging in place), and they transitioned into total care institutions (nursing homes) only when infirmity or health conditions became unmanageable. Until quite recently, individuals and families had few, if any, alternatives to these two extremes in their choice for living arrangements. The formal emergence of intermediate forms of housing, often known as assisted living facilities, has made rapid inroads in filling this need. This approach affords older adults the opportunity to maintain autonomy and independence when they find it difficult to manage some aspects of their day-to-day activities but are not in need of skilled nursing care and the restrictions that are associated with a nursing home facility. Often assisted living facilities work with traditional nursing homes systems so the elderly person can transition from limited levels of care, such as with meals and housekeeping, up to and including 24-hour intensive care. If properly managed and administered, this structured series of transitions offer individuals the opportunity to maintain autonomy for as long as reasonable and can offer a greater sense of dignity and control over their lives.

## HISTORICAL PATTERNS OF CARE

Assisted living is a new development in the ongoing evolution of long-term care for the aged. Historically, most individuals did not retire in a formal sense; instead they worked until they died or until they became too impaired to contribute to the household. Prior to the 20th century,

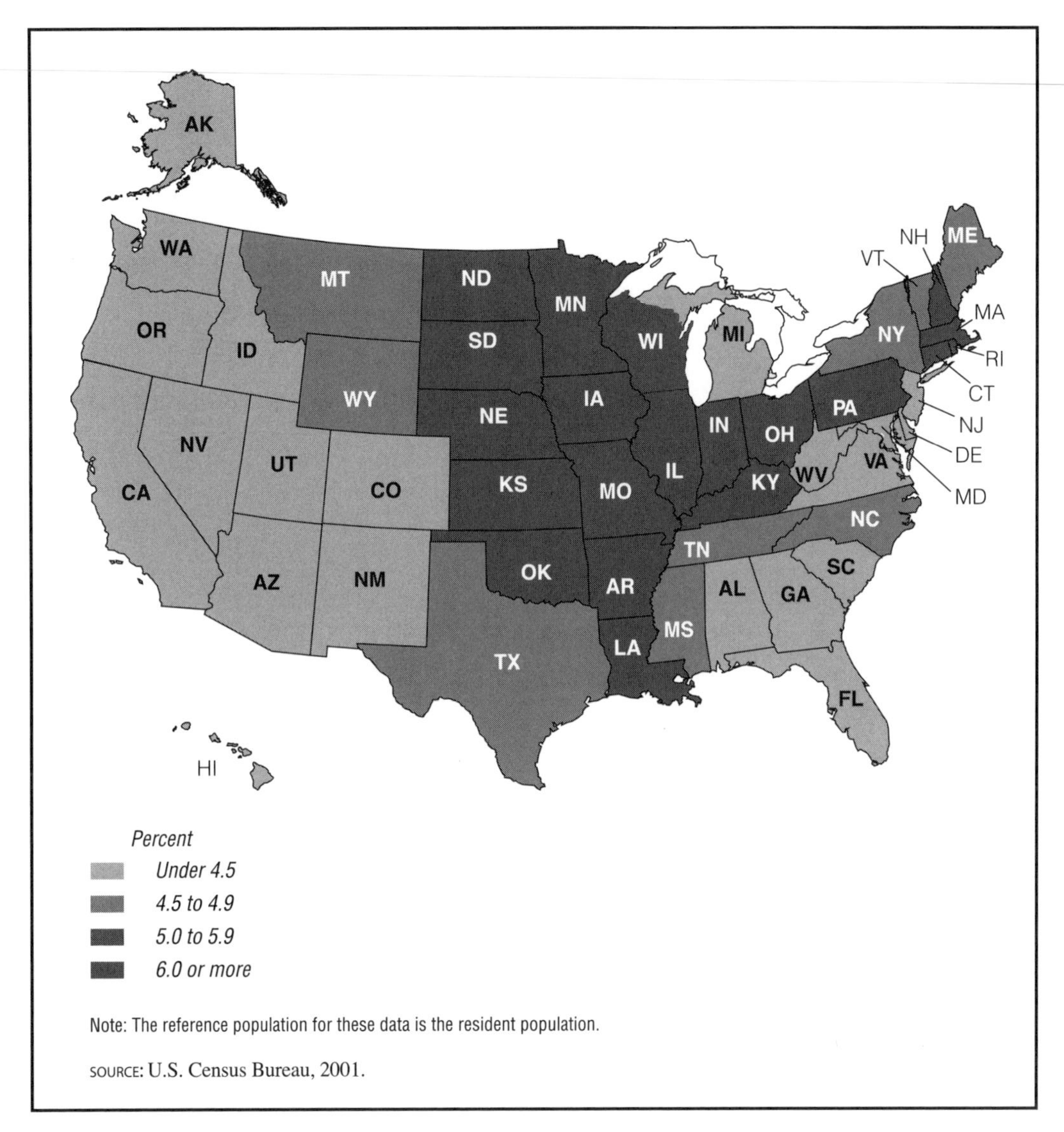


Note: The reference population for these data is the resident population.

SOURCE: U.S. Census Bureau, 2001.

***Figure 1.*** *Percent of the state population aged 65 and over residing in a nursing home, 2000.* CENGAGE LEARNING, GALE.

those people who stopped working in old age normally did so because of physical disability or poor health, although quite often they continued to contribute to the household by performing tasks such as childcare, cooking, and cleaning. With no formal systems of portable economic support (such as pension benefits), the end of work also meant the end of one's income and the capacity to support oneself. Pension systems were rare at that time, and elders who could no longer work and lacked independent resources depended on family, friends, and churches to help them survive. The provision of care was encouraged by social convention and altruism so that most older adults were cared for to some degree—largely by family members. Those who could not depend on family or the community had few alternatives. In the 19th and early 20th centuries, elderly persons who lacked a source of care or support, along with other indigent persons, were frequently required to relocate to state- or locally run homes for the poor. Known under various names, including poorhouses, almshouses, poor farms, infirmaries, and asylums, these residences were often poorly run, overcrowded, and provided only minimal food, shelter, and clothing.

Both home care and state confinement were inadequate sources of care. Home care without an adequate income stream would limit the amount and quality of care a family could provide, and a disabled or infirm elder in the household often represented a strain on family economies. At the other extreme, state confinement in poorhouses was a legislated response to concerns over the destitute population lacking any age-appropriated services or care consideration. Consequently, the elders in these situations had to accept whatever limited services the poorhouse offered and were unable to receive care that focused on their specific needs. When entering these institutions they became part of a general population undifferentiated by age, health concerns, or mental capacity. This represented a place of last resort for the elderly poor—a situation driven by the lack of systematic programs to provide portable income to the elderly when they ceased working.

Although a number of states in the early 20th century recognized older adults as a vulnerable population and offered old-age assistance, the plans varied widely across states and were difficult to maintain because of their noncontributory structure. As the state allocated and controlled all money being distributed, it was seen as simple charity as opposed to a pension system in which the elderly recovered something they had invested in over a period of years.

The introduction of universal social security in 1935 as part of the New Deal was the mechanism by which this system of poverty and dependence among the aged was addressed at the federal level in the United States. Initially it provided an Old-Age Assistance program that matched 50% of the contribution made at the state level. This was a short-term bridge that allowed the more familiar Old-Age Insurance program to accumulate enough funds for disbursements that would not begin until after 1942. Because Old-Age Assistance funds could not be obtained by older adults living in public institutions, this discouraged and eventually eliminated the presence of poorhouses for the elderly and offered incentives that led to the creation of privately run retirement homes that were the precursors to both the nursing home and the assisted living residential models for the elderly. When Social Security allowed residents of public institutions to receive benefits and required state licensing of nursing homes in the 1950s, the nursing homes industry grew tremendously. It was the addition of Medicare and Medicaid as part of the Social Security Act amendments signed into law by President Lyndon Johnson (1908–1973) on July 30, 1965, that allowed nursing homes to provide a wide array of short- and long-term services to the elderly and marked the true beginning of the total care institutionalized nursing care industry.

## NEW MODELS OF CARE AND THE EMERGENCE OF ASSISTED LIVING RESIDENCES

Although the growth of the licensed nursing home industry immeasurably improved the lives of frail and disabled elders who could no longer live in their homes, it was far from the perfect solution for addressing the needs of a growing elderly population. Licensing helped promote the adequate care and protection of the elderly, but he payment of care remained a contentious issue through the 1970s with Congress debating over the amount of care that Medicare and Medicaid would cover. The 1970s was also a period during which the first severe abuses of the new system of nursing homes came to light. Research by Claire Townsend in 1971 on the quality of life for the aged caused consumer advocate Ralph Nader (b. 1934) to coin the term *eldercide* in describing nursing homes (Kelly, 2007).

New legislation, including the Moss and Miller amendments, attempted to address the issues of competent care and adequate compensation for facilities, but these problems remain a concern today. An equally important issue, however, was that home care and institutional care (nursing homes as opposed to poorhouses) continued to represent the primary choices available to the older population, regardless of their overall health and their various levels of need. Nursing homes, although an important component of overall care strategy, remain *total institutions* in that the lives, movements, and activities of residents are regulated to facilitate the efficiency of an organization providing care to a population whose needs ranged from minimum assistance to 24-hour intensive care. As a consequence, individuals with only mild limitations could find their movements severely restricted, and, in essence, they were required to surrender autonomy in exchange for care despite an ongoing ability to manage many of their daily activities. Similarly, many older adults, although desiring to remain in their homes, reached a point where their physical limitations made this dangerous if not impossible. Yet at the same time, the undesirable loss of independence associated with nursing home residence caused them to remain at home unattended despite an inability to successfully manage the complex tasks associated with unassisted living.

## THE FORMALIZATION OF THE ASSISTED LIVING MODEL

As a response to the limited choices available for care in later life, assisted living facilities have rapidly become a diverse middle ground in formal care systems that target older adults. Unlike the absolutes that tend to define home care and institutionalized care as the polar extremes of care provision, assisted living environments are often presented as a broad system of graduated care whereby providers offer services that are tailored to the specific needs of the older population at different stages in their aging life course. Assisted care facilities have expanded in number rapidly since the late 1980s because they fill a necessary niche in the health care marketplace. As a business model, Michael Keslosky and Glenn Stevens

***Holding Hands.*** *Senior citizens hold hands while sitting on a couch at the assisted living facility where they live. Both also suffer from Alzheimer's disease.* AP IMAGES.

(1999) identified four factors that have encouraged the growth of assisted living facilities: (a) Many seniors need assistance with some aspects of daily life but do not need the intensive care of a nursing home, (b) most seniors prefer to live independently as long as they possibly can, (c) the elderly value the ability to age in place, and (d) the largest market for senior housing is in the lower- to middle-income ranges. A fifth factor, not mentioned by Keslosky and Stevens but important nonetheless, was the increase in discretionary income within the retirement-aged population (Hungerford, Rassette, Iams, & Koenig, 2001–2002).

Because of the long-standing lack of intermediate forms of care, the assisted living industry has grown rapidly. This has had positive impacts as it has increased the number and types of support services available to older adults; however, as both definitions and regulatory control varies widely, this array of alternatives can also make it difficult for the general public to make informed decisions about which provider would be best for their needs. The National Center for Assisted Living (NCAL), an advocacy group for long-term care providers, reflects the positive aspects of assisted living as a resource for the aged by stating that about 1 million Americans live in assisted living facilities, including about 115,000 Medicaid recipients. The NCAL stated that many individuals and their families prefer assisted living housing because of its emphasis on residents' privacy, dignity, and choice (Polzer, 2008). In contrast, the formal definition provided by the National Center for Health Statistics (NCHS) introduced some of the complexities associated with defining assisted living facilities and reported the following:

> [Assisted living facilities] provide some assistance with activities of daily living and instrumental activities of daily living but do not provide round-the-clock skilled nursing services. Assisted living facilities and in-home assisted living care stress independence and generally provide less intensive care than that delivered in nursing homes and other long-term care institutions, but there is no standard definition of these places as they are licensed by individual States, if at all. (Bernstein et al. 2003, p. 213)

The definitions given by the NCHS and the NCAL are accurate representations of assisted living, but they represent very different interpretations of what assisted living is. The U.S. Department of Health and Human Services (2003) offers possibly the most reasonable definition, stating that assisted living facilities are "housing alternatives for older adults who may need help with dressing, bathing, eating, and toileting but do not require the intensive medical and nursing care provided in nursing homes." The variations in these definitions are driven by the contrasting missions of the organizations that create them. Advocacy groups such as NCAL tend to focus on licensed facilities that offer excellent care and represent the quality of care they seek to promote as the standard for their constituency. These groups also can provide invaluable services to the public who seek information to help them navigate though the complexities of planning for long-term care.

The NCAL, for example, has offered an annual report since 2001 that summarizes state regulation and oversight of licensed facilities and represents a valuable tool for the public that is informative and user-friendly. In contrast, the NCHS definition is driven by their role as a government agency with a primary focus on health and information dissemination. In this role the organization represents a valuable resource for the issues related to the risks of poor-quality care. The NCAL's definition, although emphasizing the significant benefits of dignity and needs-based care that makes assisted living such a valuable option, glosses over the payment issues and the very limited role that Medicare and Medicaid play in financing this form of care. Similarly, the NCHS definition fails to recognize the growth in both state licensing and professionalism in the assisted living industry entering the 21st century that have helped reduce some of the major abuses seen in the 1980s and 1990s, particularly in the care of older adults suffering from dementia (Tilly & Reed, 2006).

This wide gulf between advocacy and oversight will remain for the foreseeable future, as the term *assisted living* covers an increasingly wide array of circumstances. Again, referring to the U.S. Department of Health and Human Services (2003) summary, such facilities "may be part of a retirement community, nursing home, senior housing complex, or may stand alone. Licensing requirements for assisted living facilities vary by state and can be known by as many as 26 different names including: residential care, board and care, congregate care, and personal care." With this level of variation, it is difficult, if not impossible, to establish a common standard by which assisted living facilities can be evaluated and compared by either the consumer or the state and federal government.

Similarly, complexities and confusions over the financing of assisted living can make educated choices that much more difficult. As of 2008, Medicare and Medicaid insurance covers very little of the cost of assisted living, generally being applicable to the health care and treatment costs that these programs cover regardless of residence. Even the procedures and costs that are covered within assisted living facilities vary depending on the way individual states administer Medicare and Medicaid. In general, assisted living facilities represent a direct out-of-pocket expense to the individual, and costs can run from as low as $10,000 per year to $50,000 or more, comparable to the costs of many nursing homes. Entering the early 21st century, the growing availability of long-term care insurance that is intended to pay these costs has promise for the future, but at present it is still too new a concept to realistically evaluate.

Because this system is often organized around a mixed model of independent living in private apartments or suites, residents within assisted living facilities face many of the challenges that any normal tenant faces in terms of services, rights, and obligations, and in many cases they also need to meet minimum standards for self-care to remain within the facilities; otherwise, they are required to either transition into nursing care or leave the assisted care environment. The selection and negotiating process required to maximize the value of the assisted living experience can be extremely complex, and, like all late-life decisions, it works best when planned for well in advance.

## CONCLUSIONS

In the scheme of long-term care for older adults, assisted living facilities represent a relatively new and potentially invaluable alternative to home care, which is often stressful and inadequate, and to the total institution that is the nursing home model. Although still unregulated in any systematic manner and with wide variations in the quality of care across states, the assisted living model has grown both in popularity and professionalism in the past decade. Increasingly, older adults with minimal support needs can choose from a wide array of alternatives in terms of housing, services, and opportunities to make smooth transitions into more intensive levels of care as needs change. Still, there is much room for improvement. The industry needs to establish internal standards to better serve the needs of the consumer and to better explain the available choices. Funding models also need to change as the long-term care insurance matures and the costs of this investment begin to be felt by the providers. The level of involvement by the federal government, both in terms of financial assistance and regulatory oversight, desperately needs to be addressed as the risks for abuse and mistreatment of older adults are a constant concern for the maturing assisted living system.

Overall, however, the current availability of assisted living facility services is an important and necessary improvement over past systems that left older adults, with only mild to moderate support needs, totally dependent on themselves or their families. It also provides an alternative to an early and often inappropriate move into formal nursing care, offering older adults additional years of the autonomy, productivity, and sense of independence that is essential to successful aging.

**SEE ALSO** Volume 3: *Aging in Place; Long-term Care; Policy, Later Life Well-Being; Retirement Communities.*


**BIBLIOGRAPHY**

Allen, J. E. (2004). *Assisted living administration: The knowledge base.* (2nd ed.). New York: Springer.

Bernstein, A. B., Hing, E., Moss, A. J., Allen, K. F., Siller, A. B., & Tiggle, R. B. (2003). *Health care in America: Trends in utilization.* Hyattsville, MD: National Center for Health Statistics. Retrieved May 25, 2008, from http://www.cdc.gov/nchs

Francese, P. K., & Rogers, J. (1997, August). Big spenders—Household and discretionary income. *American Demographics.*

Hungerford, T., Rassette, M., Iams, H., & Koenig, M. (2001–2002). Trends in the economic status of the elderly, 1976–2000. *Social Security Bulletin, 64*(3), 12–22.

Kelly, N. (2007). *Nursing home abuse: The perils of an institutionalized life.* Dorotha C. White Foundation. Retrieved May 25, 2008, from http://dcwhitefoundation.org/pdf

Keslosky, M. A., & Stevens, G. L. (1999, May). *The assisted living industry: An industry overview and performance analysis of public firms.* Retrieved May 25, 2008, from http://www.aoa.gov/prof

Polzer, K. (2008). *Assisted living state regulatory review.* Washington, DC: National Center for Assisted Living. Retrieved May 25, 2008, from http://www.ncal.org/about/

Schulz, J. H. (1988). *The economics of aging.* (4th ed.). Dover, MA: Auburn House.

Tilly, J., & Reed, P. (Eds.). (2006). *Dementia care practice recommendations for assisted living residences and nursing homes.* Washington, DC: Alzheimer's Association.

Townsend, C. (1971). *Old age: The last segregation.* New York: Grossman.

U.S. Department of Health and Human Services. (2003, August). *Administration on aging fact sheet on assisted living.* Retrieved May 25, 2008, from www.aoa.gov/press

Weir, M., Orloff, A. S., & Skocpol, T. (Eds.). (1988). *The politics of social policy in the United States.* Princeton, NJ: Princeton University Press.


*James W. McNally*

# ASSISTIVE TECHNOLOGIES

Technology is playing an increasingly important role in the lives of older Americans. By facilitating participation in daily activities and promoting independence, the use of assistive technology can influence life-course transitions related to retirement, living arrangements, and long-term care. About 14–18% of adults ages 65 or older use assistive devices (Cornman, Freedman, & Agree, 2005) and two-thirds of older people who report difficulty with personal care activities use a device to meet daily needs (Agree & Freedman, 2000).

## DEFINING ASSISTIVE TECHNOLOGY

Although there is no single agreed-on definition of assistive technology (also often referred to as assistive devices or special equipment), the Assistive Technology Act of 1998 defines assistive technology broadly as "any item, piece of equipment, or product system, whether acquired commercially, modified, or customized, that is used to increase, maintain, or improve the functional capabilities of individuals with disabilities." This definition includes everyday items (so-called mainstream technologies) such as scissors and microwave ovens as well as specialized devices such as wheelchairs or chair lifts. For research purposes the following narrower definition is often used: items intended for and used by individuals to eliminate, reduce, or assist with impairments in functioning (Committee on Disability in America, 2007). Although medications and medical devices implanted in the body (such as pacemakers or artificial joints) can improve functioning, these items generally fall outside both policy and research definitions.

The Committee on Disability in America (2007) broadly categorized forms of assistive technology into (a) personal (or portable) devices, (b) environmental modifications, and (c) adaptive technologies. Within each category, devices may be used to assist with different impairments (such as lower body limitations, difficulty grasping, sensory impairments, or cognitive decline) or with specific tasks (such as walking, dressing, bathing, or managing medications). Personal assistive devices operate as an extension of a person's own capability, may be used in a variety of settings, and include items such as canes, wheelchairs, hearing and vision aids, medication reminders, and reachers or grabbers. Environmental modifications are items that are put into place to adapt a home or building to accommodate a person's disability and include items such as grab bars, raised toilet seats, ramps, wandering prevention systems, and stair glides.

"Smart homes" also incorporate the use of additional technologies including items such as sensors for detecting falls or devices for monitoring blood pressure (see William Mann's *Smart Technology for Aging,*

*Disability, and Independence* [2005] for further details). More comprehensive structural changes, such as widening doorways to accommodate a wheelchair, may also be considered an environmental modification, although this type of change is often excluded from examinations of assistive technology use. Finally, adaptive technologies can be used to make mainstream objects or devices accessible for individuals with differential functional capacities. For example, computers can be fit with screen readers and voice activation software for individuals with sensory impairments, and fixtures can be placed over appliance dials to make them easier for a person with limited hand strength to use.

Two additional concepts that are distinct from but related to assistive technology are durable medical equipment (DME) and universal design. DME is a coverage-related term used by Medicare, the public insurance program for adults age 65 and over, and Medicaid, the public insurance program for poor, blind, and disabled individuals. DME is a class of technologies that are deemed to be medically necessary, reusable, and prescribed by a physician for use in the home. Assistive technologies that fall outside the scope of this definition are generally not covered through Medicare. For low-income individuals, Medicaid can cover the portions of costs that are not covered by Medicare. In addition, Medicaid's state-administered community-based services waiver programs can provide additional funding for the purchase of some assistive technologies and home modifications, although these programs can vary widely across states (Freiman, Mann, Johnson, Lin, & Locklear, 2006).

Universal design refers to the development of "products and environments to be usable by all people, to the greatest extent possible, without the need for adaptation or specialized design" and embraces seven basic principles (Center for Universal Design, 2008). Designs must be equitable for use by people with diverse abilities; be flexible to accommodate different preferences and abilities; be simple and intuitive to use; communicate information efficiently and clearly; minimize hazards and adverse effects of unintended use; be comfortable to use with minimum fatigue; and incorporate the appropriate size and space for use regardless of body size, posture, or mobility. Although it is not likely that an environment or product can accommodate every possible physical or emotional limitation, the spirit behind universal design is to develop products and environments that are accessible to the greatest number of people. Devices that incorporate universal design can be as simple as lever doorknobs or as complex as kitchen sinks that have clear knee space under the sink and adjustable heights so that both users who stand and those who are seated can use them comfortably.

## PEOPLE WHO USE ASSISTIVE TECHNOLOGY

Some individuals are more likely than others to use assistive technology. An individual's underlying capacity (need), various psychosocial factors, the fit between an individual and a device, and selected economic and sociodemographic characteristics all predict whether an individual will use assistive technology. Health and functioning tend to be the most important predictors of whether devices are used, with devices being used more by those with moderate and severe disability and least by those with mild disability (Verbrugge & Sevak, 2002).

Preferences for and attitudes about the use of assistive technology are also related to whether assistive devices are initially adopted and their use sustained. The benefits of device use may include improvements in performing tasks and an increased sense of security and safety. Iezzoni (2003), however, noted that the use of some assistive technologies, particularly those that are highly visible, may be associated with negative psychological consequences such as loss of abilities and independence. Negative feelings toward devices are associated with discontinued use of devices whereas more positive notions (e.g., thinking that devices provide independence and enable individuals to participate in a wider range of activities) are associated with their adoption and continued use (Gitlin, Schemm, Landsberg, & Burgh, 1996).

How well a device fits the needs and lifestyle of an individual also matters. For example, individuals are less likely to use devices that do not do what they were meant to do, do not fully meet the needs of the individual, or do not meet expectations about comfort, safety, and ease of use (Phillips & Zhao, 1993). Discontinuing the use of devices can also result from a lack of adherence to user preferences, inadequate training on the device, or the prescription of devices that are inappropriate or inadequate for the environment in which they are to be used (Iezzoni, 2003; Phillips & Zhao, 1993).

Less clear is the role of economic resources such as income and health insurance and sociodemographic characteristics. Even though more than half the costs of assistive technology are paid for out-of-pocket (Freiman et al., 2006), level of income does not consistently predict the use of assistive technology. For instance, among individuals with a need for assistance, some studies find no relationship between the use of assistive technology and level of income (Agree, Freedman, & Sengupta, 2004; Verbrugge & Sevak, 2002) and another finds that individuals with lower incomes tend to use assistive technology for mobility more often than individuals with the highest levels of income but individuals with incomes that fall in the middle are the most likely to use assistive technology for bathing (Freedman, Martin, Cornman, Agree, & Schoeni, in press).

Because coverage of assistive technologies is quite limited in many cases, health insurance is also not strongly related to assistive technology use. Although Medicare provides limited coverage of DME to all adults age 65 and over, additional resources for the purchase of assistive technology could come from private insurance that supplements Medicare coverage, Medicaid, Medicaid waivers, benefits for veterans of the armed forces, or cash and counseling demonstration programs that provide a cash benefit to Medicaid recipients (available in about 15 states as of 2007). However, having these supplemental benefits does not translate into greater use of assistive devices (Agree et al., 2004).

Finally, variation in use by sociodemographic factors such as age, sex, race, and education also have been noted. Among individuals who require assistance (e.g., have difficulty with daily tasks), women and those with higher levels of education are more likely to use assistive technology, and rates of its use tend to increase with age (Agree et al., 2004; Freedman et al., in press). Evidence also suggests that ethnic and racial minorities who have a disability are more likely to use assistive technology for mobility difficulty and that non-White Hispanics are more likely to use assistive technology for bathing (Freedman et al., in press). Some of these differences across socioeconomic and demographic groups may be due in part to differences in the types of devices used, the adaptability of the home environment (such as being allowed to or having the resources to instill grab bars in the bathroom), receptivity to and attitudes about the efficacy of using devices, the desire for independence, or difference in expectations, preferences, and opportunities for using specific types of care (e.g., the use and availability of personal care versus devices).

## ASSISTIVE TECHNOLOGY AND LIFE-COURSE TRANSITIONS

Whether used alone or in combination with other accommodations, such as personal help or behavior change (e.g., changes in the way a task is done to compensate for functional difficulties), the use of assistive technology may have a number of positive outcomes, including improved functioning to facilitate independence, prolonged labor force participation, and reduced demand on and need for assistance from personal caregivers.

To live independently, older adults must be able to take care of their daily needs. The use of assistive technology can reduce or even eliminate difficulty with such tasks as dressing, reaching, walking, getting in and out of bed, and going to the toilet (Verbrugge, Rennert, & Maddans, 1997). Use of assistive technology and environmental modifications can also slow the rate of functional decline, potentially prolonging the ability to continue living in the community (Mann, Ottenbacher, Fraas, Tomita, & Granger, 1999).

One report on technology for adaptive aging (Pew & Van Hemel, 2004) noted that the use of assistive technology may also make it possible for adults to continue to work when they otherwise may have left the workforce. A number of changes in physical and cognitive abilities are common as individuals age, which can lead to difficulty in certain work situations. For example, vision loss can make it difficult to read a computer screen, and difficulty with fine motor skills can interfere with the ability to do assembly work or to use common computer input devices such as a mouse or keyboard. However, with assistive technologies such as screen magnifiers, large keyboards, or trackball pointing devices, difficulty with work tasks may be reduced. Although there is little research on the efficacy of assistive technology for enabling people to remain in the labor force, the workforce is getting older (e.g., the proportion of the labor force between 25 and 54 is declining) and employers may need to increasingly adapt the work environment to accommodate functional changes common to the aging process.

Finally, with the high costs associated with formal care and potentially high burden levels for informal caregivers, there is also interest in the potential for assistive technology to substitute for or take the place of personal assistance as well as the potential for assistive technology to reduce the costs of long-term care. In general, the use of assistive devices seems to reduce the amount of care received from another individual, but it rarely replaces human assistance altogether (Agree & Freedman, 2000; Allen, Foster, & Berg, 2001). However, the relationship between personal care and device use may depend on the specific devices used and an individual's underlying functional abilities. For instance, devices such as canes and crutches may reduce the number of hours of informal care needed, but items such as wheelchairs and walkers seem to supplement rather than substitute for the receipt of personal care (Agree & Freedman, 2000; Allen et al., 2001). Similarly, individuals reporting less severe difficulty with tasks are most likely to use equipment alone (potentially substituting devices for human assistance), but those with more severe difficulty are more likely to use equipment in combination with personal care (Agree et al., 2004; Verbrugge & Sevak, 2002). Finally, evidence also suggests that individuals using assistive devices, particularly canes, tend to have lower costs for in-home services and institutional care (Allen et al., 2001; Mann et al., 1999).

***Assistive Elderly Care.*** *A sensor on the left side of the refrigerator records and relays the opening and closing of the door. The refrigerator is monitored from a secure Internet site to make certain that senior citizens are getting food on a regular basis.* AP IMAGES.

**SEE ALSO** Volume 3: *Disability and Functional Limitation, Later Life; Health Care Use, Later Life; Media and Technology Use, Later Life; Sensory Impairments.*

**BIBLIOGRAPHY**

Agree, E.M., & Freedman, V. A. (2000). Incorporating assistive devices into community-based long-term care: An analysis of the potential for substitution and supplementation. *Journal of Health and Aging, 12*(3), 426–450.

Agree, E. M., Freedman, V. A., & Sengupta, M. (2004). Factors influencing community-based long-term care. *Journal of Aging and Health, 16,* 267–307.

Allen, S. M., Foster, A., & Berg, K. (2001). Receiving help at home: The interplay of human and technological assistance. *Journals of Gerontology: Social Sciences, 56*B(6), S374–S382.

Center for Universal Design. (2008). Retrieved April 4, 2008, from http://www.design.ncsu.edu/cud

Committee on Disability in America. (2007). *The future of disability in America.* Washington, DC: National Academies Press.

Cornman, J. C., Freedman, V. A., & Agree, E. M. (2005). Measurement of assistive device use: Implications for estimates of device use and disability in late life. *Gerontologist, 45*(3), 347–358.

Freedman, V. A., Martin, L. G., Cornman, J. C., Agree, E. M., & Schoeni, R. F. (in press). Trends in assistance with daily activities: Racial/ethnic and socioeconomic disparities in the U.S. older population persist. In D. Cutler & D. Wise (Eds.), *Health in older ages: The causes and consequences of declining disability among the elderly.* Chicago: University of Chicago Press.

Freiman, M., Mann, W. C., Johnson, J., Lin, S., & Locklear, C. (2006). *Public funding and support of assistive technologies for persons with disabilities.* Retrieved April 18, 2008, from http://assets.aarp.org/rgcenter

Gitlin, L. N., Schemm, R. L., Landsberg, L., & Burgh, D. (1996). Factors predicting assistive device use in the home by older people following rehabilitation. *Journal of Aging and Health, 8,* 554–575.

Iezzoni, L. I. (2003). *When walking fails: Mobility problems of adults with chronic conditions.* Berkeley: University of California Press.

Mann, W. C. (Ed.). (2005). *Smart technology for aging, disability, and independence: The state of the science.* Hoboken, NJ: Wiley.

Mann, W. C., Ottenbacher, K. J., Fraas, L., Tomita, M., & Granger, C. V. (1999). Effectiveness of assistive technology and environmental interventions in maintaining independence and reducing home care costs for the frail elderly. *Archives of Family Medicine, 8,* 210–217.

Pew, R. W., & Van Hemel, S. B. (Eds.). (2004) *Technology for adaptive aging: Steering Committee for the Workshop on Technology for Adaptive Aging: National Research Council.*

Phillips, B., & Zhao, H. (1993). Predictors of assistive technology abandonment. *Assistive Technology, 5,* 36–45.

Verbrugge, L. M., Rennert, C., & Maddans, J. H. (1997). The great efficacy of personal and equipment in reducing disability. *American Journal of Public Health, 87,* 384–392.

Verbrugge, L. M., & Sevak, P. (2002). Use, type, and efficacy of assistance for disability. *Journals of Gerontology: Social Sciences, 57B*(6), S366–S379.

***Jennifer C. Cornman***

# BALTES, MARGRET
### *1939–1999*

# BALTES, PAUL
### *1939–2006*

Margret Maria Baltes, born in Dillingen, Germany, and Paul B. Baltes, born in Saarlouis, Germany, are two of the world's most prominent lifespan psychologists whose lifework substantially advanced the field of gerontology. They were married in 1963 and had two children—Boris (b. 1965) and Anushka (b. 1971).

Both received their bachelor's and master's degrees from Saarland University in Germany. After also receiving his doctorate in psychology from Saarland University in 1967, Paul Baltes took on his first academic position at West Virginia University, where Margret Baltes completed her doctorate in experimental psychology in 1973. They then both held academic positions in human development at Pennsylvania State University. In 1980 they moved to Berlin, Germany, where he became codirector of the Max Planck Institute (MPI) for Human Development and she became a professor of psychological gerontology at the Free University of Berlin.

Margret and Paul Baltes shared a particular interest in successful aging and the related dynamics between gains and losses. Together they coedited *Successful Aging: Perspectives From the Behavioral Sciences* (1990), an influential book that changed the scope of aging research from focusing on age-related loss of capacity to highlighting older adults' potentials and adaptive competencies. They also introduced one of the most internationally renowned theories of lifespan development: the model of selection, optimization, and compensation (SOC), which proposes three mechanisms thought to promote successful development and aging. In this model *selection* is understood as the principle giving direction to development by focusing a person on particular developmental goal options, *optimization* aims at achieving higher levels of functioning, and *compensation* focuses on using alternative means to maintain functioning in the face of developmental loss. They referred to the pianist Arthur Rubinstein (1887–1982) as a good example for use of SOC processes. Rubinstein once described in a television interview how he dealt with the consequences of aging: He reduced his repertoire to a smaller number of pieces (selection), practiced this smaller repertoire more often (optimization), and slowed down the speed of playing prior to fast passages to produce a contrast that enhanced the impression of speed in fast segments (compensation).

Margret Baltes was a behavioral scientist and gerontologist who enriched the field with valuable and innovative insights into how older persons manage their lives by social means and how it is possible to lead a productive life even with the functional limitations that often accompany old age. Her main contributions include research on dependence in old age, summarized in the book *The Many Faces of Dependency in Old Age* (1996). She conducted groundbreaking observational studies in nursing homes, in which she drew on behavioral concepts such as reinforcement contingencies to explain the direct relationship between professionals' ignoring of patients' independence and enforcement of patients' dependent behavior, resulting in enhanced levels of dependence among patients.

Besides bringing the role of the social environment in caregiving settings to the fore, she also refined the concept of proxy control (exerting control indirectly by enlisting another's help or relying on external means), initiated innovative research on cognitive plasticity in aging by using the testing-the-limits approach as a detection means for early dementia, and developed a model of everyday competence by distinguishing basic (e.g., self-care) and expanded (e.g., leisure and social activities) levels of competence in the Berlin Aging Study (BASE). Marked by her interest in social dynamics, she also proposed a collective perspective for the SOC model to look at how adaptive processes evolve in couples, families or groups, and even societies. Finally, she successfully engaged in translating her research into concrete applications (e.g., training programs for the nursing staff), and she was an important advocate for older adults in policy making throughout her career.

Paul Baltes played a key role in establishing lifespan developmental psychology as an internationally acknowledged discipline, criticizing the predominant focus of developmental psychology on childhood and growth. One key contribution he made to the field was introducing the

*Paul and Margret Baltes.* PHOTO COURTESY OF BORIS BALTES.

notion that development includes the whole lifespan characterized by gains and losses as well as biological and cultural influences (e.g., he created a metamodel of the incomplete architecture of human ontogeny, stating that because human development was not optimized by evolution, loss becomes predominant in old age, which can be compensated by culture, but that the effectiveness of culture also becomes increasingly limited with advancing age). Another contribution of importance was his advancement of the measurement of developmental change and plasticity (e.g., he provided groundbreaking methodological reflections on the distinction between age, cohort, and period effects and advanced the testing-the-limits paradigm).

His work was characterized by an interdisciplinary orientation, connecting psychological, sociological, and biological perspectives of aging, as manifested in his initiating and chairing of the BASE, a large-scale multidisciplinary study of the old (*third age*) and oldest old (*fourth age*). Furthermore, he developed several paradigms, such as the dual-process model of cognitive development, which distinguishes mechanics and pragmatics of intelligence with differential age-related trajectories (i.e., the decline in mechanics and increase in pragmatics), and the Berlin wisdom paradigm—defining wisdom as expert knowledge about fundamental problems of life meaning and conduct and providing criteria to guide the study of wisdom.

Both Margret and Paul Baltes and were devoted to promoting the careers of young scientists; she founded the graduate program Psychiatry and Psychology of Aging, a joint effort connecting MPI and Berlin universities. Paul Baltes initiated the International Max Planck Research School called The Life Course: Evolutionary and Ontogenetic Dynamics (LIFE) (hosted by the MPI), which involves collaborative graduate study at the University of Michigan, the University of Virginia, the MPI, the Free University of Berlin, and Humboldt University in Berlin.

Their years in Berlin were marked by a stronger realization of the problems evolving in the fourth age. Though findings from the BASE had shown enormous plasticity in the third age, they also indicated a bleaker ontogenetic picture among the oldest old. However, their focus was still more on the rich potential of the third age and the need to find ways of using it more creatively. Their Berlin years were also characterized by very close connections to American academic institutions through their participating in many international collaborations and accepting appointments as visiting professors and scholars at Stanford and the University of Virginia. This time period was tragically altered by Margret Baltes' sudden death in 1999 at age 59. In the following years, Paul Baltes' work was characterized by even more awareness of the last phase of life and its problems and his initiatives to integrate a wider variety of disciplines into the study of aging (e.g., law, art history, and mathematics)—as manifested by his last coedited book *Lifespan Development and the Brain: The Perspective of Biocultural Co-Constructivism* (2006) and in founding and directing the MPI International Research Network on Aging. Paul Baltes passed away in the fall of 2006, at the age of 67.

Margret and Paul Baltes's enormous productivity and contributions are evident in many acclaimed books, hundreds of scholarly papers, accomplishments honored with several international awards, honorary doctorates at many European and American universities, editorial positions for numerous respected publications, as well as by the many young scientists whose lives and careers they influenced and supported, and that they continue to support through the Margret and Paul B. Baltes Foundation, which is dedicated to the advancement of research in lifespan psychology and gerontology.

SEE ALSO Volume 3: *Aging; Cognitive Functioning and Decline; Quality of Life; Stress in Later Life; Theories of Aging.*

## BIBLIOGRAPHY

Baltes, M. M. (1996). *The many faces of dependency in old age.* Cambridge, U.K.: Cambridge University Press.

Baltes, P. B., & Baltes, M. M. (Eds.). (1990). *Successful aging: Perspectives from the behavioral sciences.* Cambridge, U.K.: Cambridge University Press.

Baltes, P.B., Reuter-Lorenz, P.A., & Rösler, F. (Eds.). (2006). *Lifespan development and the brain: The perspective of biocultural co-constructivism.* Cambridge, U.K.: Cambridge University Press.

*Kathrin Boerner*
*Daniela Jopp*

## BENGTSON, VERN
### *1941–*

Vern Bengtson, an American sociologist, social psychologist, and human developmentalist, is known primarily for his contributions to family theory and research on the topic of adult intergenerational relationships. Bengtson developed the *intergenerational solidarity paradigm*—a conceptual model that has become the gold standard in measuring social cohesion between generations. Bengtson also originated and, for 35 years, directed the Longitudinal Study of Generations (LSOG), the project with which he is most closely identified.

An only child of Swedish descent, Bengtson was born in Lindsborg, Kansas, on May 2, and had a peripatetic early childhood. At the age of 2, he and his mother moved to North Carolina where his father was stationed in the Army. Half a year later they moved to Stromsberg, Nebraska, to live on his grandfather's farm while his father was overseas. At the age of 5, after his father came back from World War II (1939–1945), he and his family moved to Denver, Colorado, and 1 year later to Wausa, Nebraska. When Bengtson was 9 his family settled in Hilmar, a small agricultural town in central California, where he graduated from high school in June 1959. He attended North Park College in Chicago and received his B.A. in 1963. As a junior in college, Bengtson met his future wife, Denise, whom he married in 1965. After becoming a widower in 1977, Bengtson married his second wife, Hannah, in 1983.

Bengtson attended graduate school at the University of Chicago where, in 1967, he earned a Ph.D. in human development and social psychology. Under the guidance of Bernice Neugarten (1916–2001), an engaged and intellectually demanding mentor, and Robert Havighurst (1900–1991), Bengtson was inspired by the scholarly fervor he experienced at the University of Chicago's Committee for Human Development at a time when it was building the intellectual architecture for the emergent and interdisciplinary field of adult development and aging.

Bengtson's only academic post was at the University of Southern California (USC). He began in the department of sociology in 1967, eventually splitting his appointment with the fledgling Davis School of Gerontology. In 1989 he was appointed American Association for Retired Persons university professor of gerontology. While at USC Bengtson established a significant research program on families and aging and, for several decades, directed a multidisciplinary training program in aging research.

In 1970 Bengtson's scholarly interest in the *generation gap* spawned one of the most enduring studies in the social sciences: the LSOG, a study of families spanning three generations. The conceptual core of the study was intergenerational solidarity, a construct that described the emotional, normative, structural, and behavioral factors that bind the generations. In 1985 Bengtson received funding from the National Institute on Aging to make the study longitudinal and to focus on issues pertinent to aging. Drawing from the emerging life course perspective, he added the notion of family time—the metabolism of family life—to that of biographical and historical time in coming to grips with the ways intergenerational relationships develop and change.

***Vern Bengtson.*** **PHOTO COURTESY OF VERN L. BENGTSON.**

As the study progressed through the 1980s and 1990s, families changed in ways that were difficult to predict when the study started: The protest generation moved into careers and family life; women entered the labor force in large numbers; divorce and remarriage became more prevalent; nuclear families became smaller but more complex; and multigenerational families became increasingly common. In 1991 members of the fourth generation—great-grandchildren in the original family lineages—were added to the study. This provided additional leverage in employing a unique research design that could compare family members in the same lineages across historical periods over which substantial social change had occurred. Most important, each of the linked generations could be assessed at the same chronological age, a feature used in Bengtson's *How Families Still Matter* in 2002.

In developing the LSOG, Bengtson blended a social psychologist's appreciation for the importance of studying multiple perspectives, a sociologist's understanding of social movements, and a developmentalist's appreciation of life course dynamics. His observation that solidarity was persistent over long periods of time (combined with increases in the co-survival of generations) led Bengtson to conclude that adult intergenerational relationships had become increasingly important between the 1970s and the present (the topic of his 1998 Burgess Award lecture). He coined the term *beanpole family* (a name reflecting his rural roots) to describe the vertical extension and horizontal attenuation of family lineages due to increased longevity and reduced fertility.

Bengtson has more than 250 scholarly publications to his credit. He wrote often about the importance of theory to the fields of gerontology and family science, serving as editor of several editions of the *Handbook of the Theories of Aging* and as editor-in-chief of the *Sourcebook of Family Theory and Research*. Bengtson received many honors and awards for his work, including the Ernest W. Burgess Award for outstanding career achievement, the Reuben Hill Award for outstanding contribution to research and theory (both from the National Council on Family Relations), the Distinguished Scholar Award from the American Sociological Association Section on Aging, and two Merit Awards from the National Institute on Aging. He also served as president of the Gerontological Society of America in 1990.

Bengtson retired from his academic position at USC in 2006 and moved with his wife, Hannah, to join their children and grandchildren in Santa Barbara, California. As of 2008, he continues his research with a project funded by the Templeton Foundation that studies the transmission of religion across generations. In attempting to reconcile the dialectic between change and continuity within families, Bengtson's most recent work continues to delve into what remains an enduring paradox in the study of intergenerational relationships.

**SEE ALSO** Volume 2: *Parent-Child Relationships, Adulthood;* Volume 3: *Grandparenthood; Parent-Child Relationships, Later Life; Theories of Aging.*

**BIBLIOGRAPHY**

Bengtson, V. L. (2001). The Burgess Award lecture: Beyond the nuclear family: The increasing importance of multigenerational bonds. *Journal of Marriage and the Family, 63*(1), 1–16.

Bengtson, V. L., Acock, A. C., Allen, K. R., Dilworth-Anderson, P., & Klein, D. M. (2005). *Sourcebook of family theory and research.* Thousand Oaks, CA: Sage.

Bengtson, V. L., Biblarz, T. J., & Roberts, R. E. L. (2002). *How families still matter: A longitudinal study of youth in two generations.* New York: Cambridge University Press.

Bengtson, V. L., & Schaie, K. W. (1999). *Handbook of theories of aging.* New York: Springer.

***Merril Silverstein***

## BLINDNESS

**SEE** Volume 3: *Sensory Impairments.*

# C

## CANCER, ADULTHOOD AND LATER LIFE

*Cancer* refers to a group of diseases in which abnormal cells grow and progress through the body. It is the second-leading cause of death in the United States, behind heart disease, and the major cause of death among persons younger than age 85. Cancer's etiology includes both internal (e.g., hormones and inherited genes) and external (e.g., exposures to environmental toxins and infectious organisms) factors, often acting in concert.

### CANCER INCIDENCE ACROSS THE LIFE CYCLE

As a general rule, one's risk of developing cancer increases with each decade of life, with the majority of cancers disproportionately affecting persons aged 55 years and older. This rate is especially pronounced for the four most prominent cancer sites, namely prostate, breast, colon, and lung.

Prostate cancer affects 1 in 39 men between the ages of 40 and 59 years. These odds increase to 1 in 14 men between the ages of 60 and 69 years and 1 in 7 men ages 70 and older. Between 1975, when the National Cancer Institute (NCI) first began to collect data systematically, and 2004, rates of prostate cancer decreased significantly for Black men over the age of 65 years, but remained unchanged for Black men under the age of 65 years, and all White men. Data on incidence rates (the number of new cancer cases in the United States in a given year, usually presented as rate per 100,000) among Asian/Pacific Islanders, Hispanic, and Native American/Alaska Native men were first reported in the mid-1990s. The three ethnic groups have experienced no change in overall incidence rates since that time (Ries, Melbert, Krapcho, Mariotto, Miller, Feuer, et al., 2007)

Cancer of the breast is the most frequently diagnosed cancer among women. Breast cancer affects 1 in 210 females under age 39 years, 1 in 25 females between the ages of 40 and 59 years, 1 in 27 females ages 60 to 69, and 1 in 15 females ages 70 and older. Incidence rates for breast cancer in women increase slightly during menopause, most likely a result of changes in hormone levels. Incidence rates for breast cancer in Black women under 50 years of age, as well as for all White women, have decreased significantly from 1975 to 2004, while incidence rates among Black women over 50 years of age have remained unchanged. Since the mid-1990s, when data were first collected, incidence rates among Hispanic, Asian/Pacific Islander, and Native American/Alaska Native women remained unchanged.

For men, the odds of developing colorectal cancer increase from 1 in 107 for ages 40 to 59 years, to 1 in 60 for ages 60 to 69 years, to 1 in 20 for ages 70 years and older. A similar pattern is observed among women, in which risk increases from 1 in 138 for ages 40 to 59 years, to 1 in 86 for ages 60 to 69 years, to 1 in 22 for ages 70 and older. Between 1975 and 2004, incidence rates for White men and women and Black women decreased significantly, whereas those of Black men remained unchanged. Incidence rates have also remained stable for Native American/Alaskan Native men and women, Hispanic men and women, and Asian/Pacific Islander women since the mid 1990s, when data were first collected. A significant decrease in incidence rates for colorectal cancer is seen only among Asian/Pacific

| | | Birth to 39 (%) | 40 to 59 (%) | 60 to 69 (%) | 70 and Older (%) | Birth to Death (%) |
|---|---|---|---|---|---|---|
| All sites† | Male | 1.42 (1 in 70) | 8.69 (1 in 12) | 16.58 (1 in 6) | 39.44 (1 in 3) | 45.31 (1 in 2) |
| | Female | 2.03 (1 in 49) | 9.09 (1 in 11) | 10.57 (1 in 9) | 26.60 (1 in 4) | 37.86 (1 in 3) |
| Urinary bladder‡ | Male | .02 (1 in 4381) | .41 (1 in 241) | .96 (1 in 105) | 3.41 (1 in 29) | 3.61 (1 in 28) |
| | Female | .01 (1 in 9527) | .13 (1 in 782) | .26 (1 in 379) | .96 (1 in 105) | 1.14 (1 in 87) |
| Breast | Female | .48 (1 in 210) | 3.98 (1 in 25) | 3.65 (1 in 27) | 6.84 (1 in 15) | 12.67 (1 in 8) |
| Colon & rectum | Male | .07 (1 in 1342) | .93 (1 in 107) | 1.67 (1 in 60) | 4.92 (1 in 20) | 5.79 (1 in 17) |
| | Female | .07 (1 in 1469) | .73 (1 in 138) | 1.16 (1 in 86) | 4.45 (1 in 22) | 5.37 (1 in 19) |
| Leukemia | Male | .16 (1 in 640) | .22 (1 in 452) | .35 (1 in 286) | 1.17 (1 in 86) | 1.49 (1 in 67) |
| | Female | .12 (1 in 820) | .14 (1 in 694) | .20 (1 in 491) | .75 (i in 132) | 1.05 (1 in 95) |
| Lung & bronchus | Male | .03 (1 in 3146) | 1.09 (1 in 92) | 2.61 (1 in 38) | 6.76 (1 in 15) | 8.02 (1 in 12) |
| | Female | .04 (1 in 2779) | .85 (1 in 117) | 1.84 (1 in 54) | 4.52 (1 in 22) | 6.15 (1 in 16) |
| Melanoma of the skin | Male | .13 (1 in 775) | .53 (1 in 187) | .56 (1 in 178) | 1.32 (1 in 76) | 2.04 (1 in 49) |
| | Female | .21 (1 in 467) | .42 (1 in 237) | .29 (1 in 347) | .62 (1 in 163) | 1.38 (1 in 73) |
| Non-Hodgkin lymphoma | Male | .14 (1 in 735) | .45 (1 in 222) | .57 (1 in 176) | 1.56 (1 in 64) | 2.14 (1 in 47) |
| | Female | .08 (1 in 1200) | .32 (1 in 313) | .44 (1 in 229) | 1.30 (1 in 77) | 1.83 (1 in 55) |
| Prostate | Male | .01 (1 in 10373) | 2.59 (1 in 39) | 7.03 (1 in 14) | 13.83 (1 in 7) | 17.12 (1 in 6) |
| Uterine cervix | Female | .16 (1 in 631) | .29 (1 in 346) | .14 (1 in 695) | .20 (1 in 512) | .73 (1 in 138) |
| Uterine corpus | Female | .06 (1 in 1652) | .70 (1 in 142) | .81 (1 in 124) | 1.28 (1 in 78) | 2.49 (1 in 40) |

*For people free of cancer at beginning of age interval. † All sites exclude basal and squamous cell skin cancers and in situ cancers except urinary bladder. ‡ Includes invasive and in situ cancer cases.

SOURCE: DevCan Probability of Developing or Dying of Cancer Software, Version 61.0 Statistical Research and Applications Branch, National Cancer Institute, 2006. www.srab.cancer.gov/devcan.

***Table 1.*** *Probability of developing invasive cancers over selected age intervals by sex, 2001 to 2003.* CENGAGE LEARNING, GALE.

Islander men. The decrease in this group likely has to do with who immigrated between the mid-1990s and 2004.

The probability of men developing lung cancer increases with age. Between ages 40 to 59 years, 1 in 92 men develop lung cancer. This increases to 1 in 38 among men ages 60 to 69 years, and 1 in 15 in men for those ages 70 and older. The risk of developing lung cancer likewise increases with age among women, from 1 in 117 between the ages of 40 and 59 years, to 1 in 54 for ages 60 to 69 years, and 1 in 22 for ages 70 and older. Over time, however, a decrease in incidence has been observed for Black and White men and women under the ages of 65 years, as well as for both Black and White men over the age of 65 years. Between 1975 and 2004, incidence rates of lung cancer increased only for Black women, ages 65 and older. National Cancer Institute data collected between the years 1995 and 2004 show a significant annual percentage decrease in rates of lung cancer among Hispanic men and women as well as among Asian and Pacific Islander men. For Asian/Pacific Islander women and Native American/ Alaskan Native men and women, incidence rates remained unchanged during that period of time.

## CAUSES AND CORRELATES OF CANCER

While both internal and external factors contribute to cancer incidence and mortality, a small percentage of all cancer cases (i.e., 5–10% for female breast, 10–15% for lung and prostate, and 20% for colorectal) are thought to be caused by hereditary mutations (Gronberg, 2003; Lynch and de la Chapelle, 2003; Olopade, Fackenthal, Dunston, Tainsky, Collins, and Whitfield-Broome, 2003; Schwartz, 2004). The overwhelming majority of cancers, however, result from sporadic or acquired mutations. These mutations occur spontaneously over the life course in response to environmental phenomena and may help to explain the relationship between cancer and age. In addition, changes in physiology occur over time that may sensitize the body to environmental insults, such as exposure to environmental toxins and occupational hazards that disproportionately affect vulnerable populations, and attenuate the effects of health behaviors, such as high-fat diets, sedentary life styles, and smoking.

Living in poverty is also associated with cancer incidence and mortality, in a number of ways. The so-called "food deserts" noted in inner-city neighborhoods, which limit the availability of healthful foods such as fresh produce, are associated with the development of cancer (Wrigley, 2002). Likewise, high-technology cancer treatments that increase odds of survival are less likely to be part of health services in those inner-city neighborhoods.

## CONSEQUENCES OF THE ONSET OF CANCER

The point in the life cycle at which a cancer is diagnosed affects both the course of cancer and response to its treatment. Although aggressive cancer treatments such as adjuvant chemotherapy (treatment following surgery) improve survival among all persons, older adults are less likely than younger persons to be offered these treatments. They also are more likely to be undertreated (that is, less likely to be offered treatment and less likely to accept proffered treatment) (Bouchardy, Rapiti, Blagojevic, Vlastos, and Vlastos, 2007). It has been proposed that older adults with co-morbidities, physical disabilities, and cognitive and functional impairments respond less well to cancer treatments and are more subject to adverse outcomes, but this view is still under debate (Bouchardy, et al., 2007; Rodin and Mohile, 2007).

Older adults are significantly more likely to be diagnosed with new cancers than other age groups and also more likely to be socially isolated. Thus cancer may come at a time when social networks have been diminished, increasing the burden of some older adults with cancer. This lack of support almost certainly influences medical decision making and ability to cope with the disease and its treatment.

## DIFFERENCES ACROSS RACE AND CLASS

Group differences in the incidence of cancer occur by race, gender, and social class, as do differences in mortality. On the whole, African Americans are more likely to develop prostate, colorectal, and pancreatic cancer; and Whites to develop breast cancer, leukemia, and skin cancer (Ries et al., 2007). Hispanic women have the highest rates of cervical cancer. It is dangerous to generalize, however, because variation occurs even within racial/ethnic groups. Although Asian Americans/Pacific Islanders have the lowest incidence of breast cancer, for example, Native Hawaiians have particularly high incidence.

When cancers develop also varies by race. In West Africa, the geographic area from which African Americans, and their genes, originated, breast cancer appears prior to menopause in 74% of cases, whereas among White women, the odds of developing the disease increase with each year after menopause (Olopade et al., 2003). There is evidence that African-American women disproportionately experience the earlier, more aggressive form of breast cancer seen among women in West Africa. Little is known, however, about breast cancers among other groups.

The reasons that have been given for these racial and ethnic differences combine biological and environmental factors (Gehlert, Sohmer, Sacks, Mininger, McClintock, and Olopade, 2008). Although breast cancers can be classified into the same five identified subtypes (basal-like, erbb2+, "normal," luminal B, luminal A) experienced by women in the general population and White women, the proportion of subtypes varies by race. Basal-like tumors are more common among African-American than White women and are harder to treat. Yet because 70% to 80% of breast cancers are due to sporadic rather than hereditary gene mutations, environmental factors are thought to "get under the skin" to influence the body's natural ability to repair the day-to-day mutations that occur routinely.

Social class, the effects of which are difficult to disentangle from those of race in the United States, is also associated with cancer incidence and mortality. For all races as well as for Black and White adults considered separately, breast cancer survival rates varied by percent of census tracts living below the poverty line (Ries et al., 2007). Cancer incidence is also associated with social class: Individuals from lower social classes have higher rates of all cancers (Ward, Jemal, Cokkinides, Singh, Cardinez et al., 2004). This is, in part, because social class predicts access to education and health insurance coverage and occupational status. Class also predicts exposure to environmental toxins such as industrial waste, social stressors, and access to foods that may protect against cancer.

Health scholars from the biological, behavioral, and social sciences are beginning to understand the myriad factors that influence cancer development, treatment, and outcomes as they relate to adulthood and later life. Medical researchers' approach, however, must become more sophisticated and incorporate the multiple levels of influence on the disease, including biological and societal factors and how the two may interact. Considering both when conducting research will better allow researchers to target interventions.

**SEE ALSO** Volume 3: *Chronic Illness, Adulthood and Later Life; End of Life Decision-Making; Health Behaviors, Later Life; Health Care Use, Later Life; Health Differentials/Disparities, Later Life.*

## BIBLIOGRAPHY

American Cancer Society. (2007). *Cancer facts & figures 2007.* Atlanta, GA: American Cancer Society.

Bouchardy, C., Rapiti, E., Blagojevic, S., Vlastos, A.-T., & Vlastos, G. (2007). Older female cancer patients: Importance, causes, and consequences of undertreatment. *Journal of Clinical Oncology, 26*(14), 1858–1869.

Gehlert, S., Sohmer, D., Sacks, T., Mininger, C., McClintock, M., & Olopade, O. (2008). Targeting health disparities: A model linking upstream determinants to downstream interventions. *Health Affairs, 27*(2), 339–349.

Gronberg, H. (2003). Prostate cancer epidemiology. *The Lancet 361*, 859–864.

Lynch, H. T., & de la Chapelle, A. (2003). Hereditary colorectal cancer. *New England Journal of Medicine, 348*(10), 919–932.

Olopade, O., Fackenthal, J. D., Dunston, G., Tainsky, M. A., Collins, F., & Whitfield-Broome, C. (2003). Breast cancer genetics in African Americans. *Cancer, 97* (I Supplement), 236–245.

Rodin, M. B., & Mohile, S. G. (2007). A practical approach to geriatric assessment in oncology. *Journal of Clinical Oncology, 25*(14), 1936–1944.

Ries, L. A. G., Melbert, D., Krapcho, M., Mariotto, A., Miller, B. A., Feuer, E. J., Clegg, L., et al. (Eds). (2007). SEER Cancer Statistics Review, 1975–2004. Bethesda, MD: National Cancer Institute. Retrieved May 18, 2008, from http://seer.cancer.gov/csr/1975_2004

Schwartz, A. G. (2004). Genetic predisposition to lung cancer. *Chest, 125*(5), 86–89.

Ward, E., Jemal, A., Cokkinides, V., Singh, G. K., Cardinez, C., Ghafoor, A., & Thun, M. (2004). Cancer disparities by race/ethnicity and socioeconomic status. *CA: A Cancer Journal for Clinicians, 54*, 78–93.

Wrigley, N. (2002). "Food deserts" in British cities: Policy context and research priorities. *Urban Studies, 39*(11), 2029–2040.

***Sarah Gehlert***

# CARDIOVASCULAR DISEASE

Cardiovascular disease (CVD) is common among older adults and is the leading cause of morbidity and mortality in that age group. Some conditions include atherosclerosis, coronary heart disease, heart failure, valvular disease and arrhythmias. A growing number of individuals can expect to live with CVD for a significant portion of the life span. The determinants of CVD include biological, social, psychological, and behavioral factors. Treatment can improve symptoms and promote survival; nonetheless, the impact of CVD can be severe, as can treatment demands and side effects. Effective CVD management, which requires medication adherence and changes in diet and exercise patterns, is influenced by social-cultural and psychological factors.

## PREVALENCE

Approximately 80% of persons in the United States over age 60 have CVD (Rosamund et al., 2008). It is the most common diagnosis in that age group and, as the leading cause of death in the elderly (Centers for Disease Control, 2003), is also costly, with estimated indirect and direct annual costs of $448.5 billion (Rosamund et al., 2008). From 2000 to 2030 the number of older adults in the United States is expected to double (Centers for Disease Control, 2003). Concomitant increases in CVD morbidity, mortality, and costs are likely to occur as well.

## CVD AND AGING

Atherosclerosis, coronary heart disease, heart failure, hypertension, arrhythmias, and valvular diseases are common in older individuals. The increasing risk of such conditions in later life may reflect the increasing lifespan and thus account for the age-related changes in the cardiovascular system, including increases in systolic blood pressure and left ventricular mass, alterations in blood vessels, and reductions in maximal heart rate, cardiac output, and aerobic capacity (Schwartz & Zipes, 2008). These changes may be related to alterations in the autonomic nervous system, oxidative damage, inflammatory responses to stress and cell death (Schwartz & Zipes, 2008). In addition, increases in a high fat and cholesterol diet and a sedentary life style is credited with much of the current cohort-associated diseases that we are discussing.

## ATHEROSCLEROSIS AND CORONARY HEART DISEASE

Coronary heart disease (CHD) is caused by atherosclerotic changes in the inner walls of arteries that supply the heart muscle with blood. Fat deposits within the blood vessels activate macrophage white blood cells, causing inflammation and plaque formation. These narrow the blood vessels and obstruct blood flow. This process may begin early in life and progress asymptomatically for decades. CHD occurs when gradual vessel narrowing becomes severe or when plaque ruptures and initiates a platelet-clotting cascade that culminates in thrombosis that suddenly obstructs blood flow further. This process of blood vessel narrowing is stopped only with medications, diet change, and exercise.

Myocardial ischemia is the result of an inadequate supply of oxygenated blood to the heart and can produce angina pectoris, a syndrome of chest pain and other symptoms. However, myocardial ischemia can be asymptomatic and cause sudden death without warning. Although 50% of men and 64% of women who die suddenly of CHD have no previous symptoms of this disease, some data suggest that 95% of symptomatic respondents accurately recognized chest pain as a myocardial ischemia symptom (Rosamund et al., 2008). Prolonged ischemia can cause a portion of heart muscle to die, leading to myocardial infarction (MI, or"heart attack"). The average age of having a first MI is younger for men (65.8) than for women (70.4; Rosamund et al., 2008), possibly reflecting premenopausal protective effects of estrogen among women.

## HEART FAILURE

In heart failure, a damaged heart is unable to pump adequately. The left side of the heart pumps blood that has been oxygenated in the lungs to the organs (systemic

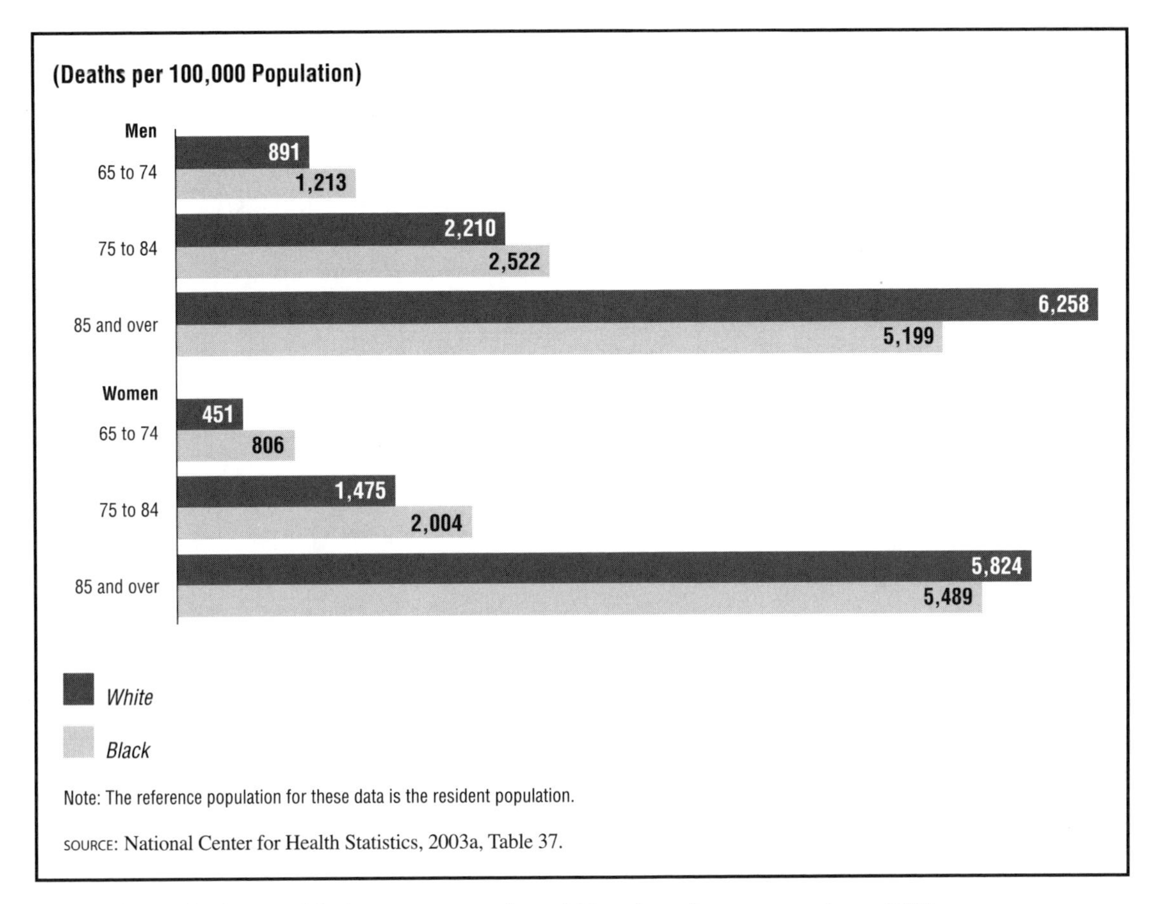


*Figure 1. Death rates for diseases of the heart among people aged 65 and over by age, sex, and race, 2000.* CENGAGE LEARNING, GALE.

circulation), and the right side pumps blood returned from the tissues to the lungs for gas exchange (pulmonary circulation). Impaired systemic circulation can reduce blood supply to organs and cause pulmonary congestion and shortness of breath. Failure of pulmonary circulation can lead to congestion of peripheral tissues and swelling in the lower extremities. The incidence of heart failure is approximately 10 per 1,000 persons among those age 65 and older (Rosamund et al., 2008).

## HYPERTENSION

Hypertension is chronically elevated blood pressure, often as a result of reduced vascular elasticity. Hypertension is a major risk factor for CHD, stroke, heart failure, and kidney disease because it puts an enormous strain on the heart and on blood flow. Approximately 68% of individuals age 65 and older are hypertensive (Rosamund et al., 2008).

## ARRHYTHMIAS

An arrhythmia is any disturbance in electrical activity of the heart that causes an abnormal rhythm. Arrhythmias commonly diagnosed in older persons include atrial tachycardia (rapid heartbeat) and fibrillation (irregular heartbeat). Among the outcomes of arrhythmias are stroke, cardiac arrest, and sudden cardiac death.

## VALVULAR DISEASE

The valves of the heart are made up of leaflets that control the flow of blood with each heart beat. The leaflets become thickened with age and stiffen; they can also be damaged by infections and by bacteria such as streptococcus. When damaged, they become leaky and interfere with flow not only throughout the body but also to the coronary vessels on the heart surface. To prevent strokes and blood clots, medication adherence is critical.

## RISK FACTORS

The traditional risk factors for atherosclerotic CVD are older age, male gender, high total cholesterol levels, hypertension, family history, cigarette smoking, and diabetes. Also implicated are obesity, a sedentary lifestyle, a high fat and carbohydrate diet, low levels of high-density lipoprotein cholesterol, high levels of triglycerides, and high levels of C-reactive protein and other inflammatory markers. Most risk factors have psychosocial and behavioral influences, and those influences also may promote CVD independently of better-established predictors. Potential psychosocial risk factors for CVD include social isolation, loss of spouse or never-married status, transition to retirement, low socioeconomic status (SES), racial/ethnic minority status, religious involvement, type A behaviors (especially hostility), psychological stressors, depression, and anxiety. It is not necessarily the biology of race and gender that elevates CVD risk. Rather, both traits are associated with a variety of social resources and disadvantages, which may shape one's risk of CVD These characteristics are also thought to promote CVD through direct physiological effects and/or by altering health-related behaviors. Some factors, such as gender, race, and SES, cannot be modified, whereas others may be altered through policy changes in health care and educational systems.

In the United States, CVD disproportionately affects African Americans, Hispanic Americans, and Mexican Americans, persons with low SES, and residents of the Southeast and Appalachia (Mensah, Mokdad, Ford, Greenlund, & Croft, 2005). The independent effects of poverty, minority status, and SES are difficult to disentangle. Individuals from disadvantaged backgrounds may be less educated about warning signs or may have cultural beliefs that clash with Western medicine. Additional challenges include the cost of seeking care, proximity to treatment centers, and racial/ethnic discrimination in treatment seeking. However, health care availability and accessibility do not account fully for the inverse relationship between SES and CVD. Whatever the mechanism, a greater portion of life spent in adverse SES conditions appears to increase the risk for MI (Ljung & Hallqvist, 2006).

CVD incidence among menopausal women approximates that among men of the same age. Biological factors specific to women, including postmenopausal estrogen deficiency and altered arterial structure, may delay the diagnosis and promote complications or poorer recovery. The belief among patients and practitioners that CVD is a "male" disease and sex differences in clinical manifestations may lead to underestimation of treatment urgency (Martin & Lemos, 2002), improper utilization of medical services, and unclear indications for medications or procedures. For example, whereas men with acute MI tend to complain mostly about chest pain, women tend to present with atypical symptoms, including abdominal pain, dyspnea, cold sweat, nausea, back and neck pain, indigestion, palpitations, and unexpected fatigue. It is hypothesized that the vagueness of these symptoms may result in delayed help-seeking behavior and increased disease progression. Other factors that contribute to CVD risk in women include a greater prevalence of emotional distress and mood disorders and lower average SES.

Risk factor potency may change from middle adulthood to late life. The effects of hypertension, cholesterol, smoking, and high body mass index may decline with advancing age, whereas diabetes elevates CHD risk across all age groups (Abbott et al., 2002). Nonetheless, older adults without previous cardiovascular events may have significant subclinical or nonsymptomatic vascular disease. Physicians therefore may need to be more vigilant in identifying (lower the threshold for defining) CVD disease in older individuals, attending to even modest elevations in certain risk factors.

## TREATMENT AND MANAGEMENT

Treatment of CVD has improved significantly over the past few decades with the development of thrombi-dissolving drugs, percutaneous transluminal coronary angioplasty (PTCA), and coronary artery bypass grafting (CABG) surgery. In PTCA a balloon is inserted into the occluded vessel and inflated to compress plaque and restore blood flow. A stent (metal scaffold) usually is inserted to keep the vessel open. In CABG, occluded coronary artery segments are bypassed with grafts taken from healthy vessels elsewhere in the body. Evidence suggests that the more beneficial procedure for patients with advanced CVD is CABG (Hannan et al., 2008), which improves survival, reduces recurrence, relieves angina, and enhances the quality of life.

Postintervention patients typically are prescribed medications to decrease the risk of recurrent CVD and mortality. These medications may include cholesterol-controlling, antihypertensive, antiarrhythmic, and/or antithrombotic agents. Drug effectiveness requires long-term continuous treatment. The benefits for those 65 and older are similar to those for younger individuals. Recommended lifestyle changes for CVD patients include smoking cessation, a low-fat and low-salt diet, and increased physical activity. These are also the secondary prevention tools to control and reverse disease in the coronary vessels to avert obstruction and decrease plaque. Secondary prevention are the treatment regimens that are recommended to control a chronic illness after it has been diagnosed.

Medication nonadherence is prevalent and is linked to increased morbidity and mortality. Adherence (taking medications as prescribed by the physician) is suboptimal both after acute CHD and in the larger population of individuals with poor lipid profiles. Nonadherence increases early and rapidly after the initial prescribing of medication, and approximately 65% of patients are non-adherent after 5 years (Benner et al., 2002). Thus, there is significant room for improved secondary prevention for CHD in the older segment of the population.

## SOCIAL AND PSYCHOLOGICAL INFLUENCES ON DISEASE MANAGEMENT

Predictors of medication underuse among individuals over 65 include age, social isolation, depression, and dementia. Although older patients can be highly adherent, the oldest-old (over 77 years) have greater difficulty than do young-old adults (60 to 77 years) in comprehending medication information, which may promote nonadherence (Park, Morrell, Frieske, & Kincaid, 1992). Across age groups females tend to engage in less risk reduction behavior than males.

Because most well-established predictors of nonadherence are nonmodifiable, variables that account for their relationships with secondary prevention behaviors and that are modifiable are being sought. Salient among those predictors are patients' beliefs about CVD and its treatment. Secondary prevention may be undermined when patients overemphasize advancing age or stress as a major cause of CHD while failing to recognize the importance of medication, diet, and exercise; this may be especially likely to occur in women (Cameron, Petrie, Ellis, Buick, & Weinman, 2005). The belief that CVD cannot be controlled, failure to acknowledge illness severity, and the notion that PTCA or CABG is a permanent cure also may discourage secondary prevention. Expectations about the positive consequences of cardiac risk-reduction behaviors may explain why some patients are adherent, but false expectations of negative side effects can discourage adherence. Psychosocial factors, beliefs, and behaviors clearly play a significant role in CVD management and provide opportunities for research and intervention.

**SEE ALSO** Volume 3: *Chronic Illness, Adulthood and Later Life; Epidemiologic Transition; Health Behaviors, Later Life; Health Care Use, Later Life; Health Differentials/Disparities, Later Life.*

**BIBLIOGRAPHY**

Abbott, R. D, Curb, J. D., Rodriguez, B.L., Masaki, K.H., Yano, K., Schatz, I. J., et al. (2002). Age-related changes in risk factor effects on the incidence of coronary heart disease. *Annals of Epidemiology, 12*(3), 173–181.

Benner, J. S., Glynn, R. J., Mogun, H., Neumann, P. J., Weinstein, M. C., & Avorn, J. (2002). Long-term persistence in use of statin therapy in elderly patients. *Journal of the American Medical Association, 288*(4), 455–461.

Cameron, L. D., Petrie, K. J., Ellis, C., Buick, D., & Weinman, J. A. (2005). Symptom experiences, symptom attributions, and causal attributions in patients following first-time myocardial infarction. *International Journal of Behavioral Medicine, 12*(1), 132–141.

Centers for Disease Control. (2003). Public health and aging: Trends in aging—United States and worldwide. *Morbidity and Mortality Weekly Report, 52*(06), 101–106.

Hannan, E. L., Wu, C., Walford, G., Culliford, A. T., Gold, J. P., Smith, C. R., et al. (2008). Drug-eluting stents vs. coronary-artery bypass grafting in multivessel coronary disease. *New England Journal of Medicine, 358*(4), 331–341.

Ljung, R., & Hallqvist, J. (2006). Accumulation of adverse socioeconomic position over the entire life course and the risk of myocardial infarction among men and women: Results from the Stockholm Heart Epidemiology Program (SHEEP). *Journal of Epidemiology and Community Health, 60*(12), 1080–1084.

Martin, R., & Lemos, K. (2002). From heart attacks to melanoma: Do common sense models of somatization influence symptom interpretation for female victims? *Health Psychology, 21*(1), 25–32.

Mensah, G. A., Mokdad, A. H., Ford, E. S., Greenlund, K. J., & Croft, J. B. (2005). State of disparities in cardiovascular health in the United States. *Circulation, 111,* 1233–1241.

Park, D. C., Morrell, R. W., Frieske, D., & Kincaid, D. (1992). Medication adherence behaviors in older adults: Effects of external cognitive supports. *Psychology and Aging, 7*(2), 252–256.

Rosamund, W., Flegal, K., Furie, K., Go, A., Greenlund, K., Haase, N., et al. (American Heart Association Statistics Committee and Stroke Statistics Subcommittee). (2008). Heart disease and stroke statistics—2008 update: A report from the American Heart Association Statistics Committee and Stroke Statistics Subcommittee. *Circulation, 117*(4), e25–e146.

Schwartz, J. B., & Zipes, D. (2008). Cardiovascular disease in the elderly. In P. Libby, R. O. Bonow, D. P. Zipes, & D. L. Mann (Eds.), *Braunwald's heart disease: A textbook of cardiovascular medicine* (8th ed., pp. 1923–1953). Philadelphia: Saunders/Elsevier.

***Julia D. Betensky***
***Richard J. Contrada***
***Elaine Leventhal***

# CAREGIVING

Caregiving is the provision of regular unpaid help to an individual who, because of limited physical or cognitive abilities, is dependent on others for managing activities of daily life. Caregiving represents a broad range of activities that includes providing personal care, doing household chores, preparing meals, shopping, taking care of finances, providing companionship, regular checkups, arranging and supervising activities and outside services, and coordinating medical care. Because of the voluminous empirical literature on the topic, this entry limits its scope to caregiving that involves older adults, primarily focusing on care provided in the immediate family and particularly within intergenerational relationships. Intergenerational caregiving can be divided into two general types: older adults as recipients of care from adult children (upstream caregiving), and older adults as providers of care to grandchildren and disabled adult children (downstream caregiving). Although both upstream and downstream caregiving have unique antecedents and target populations—with the former being more normative and based on disability, and the latter being more extraordinary and based on social conditions—both involve older adults and many of the same care activities.

There is no standardized method for identifying caregivers. Some studies define caregivers based on the number of hours they contribute to care. For example, one study identified primary caregivers as those who either lived with a relative with dementia or who provided at least 8 hours of care per week for an older relative living outside their households (Knight, Longmire, Dave, Kim & David, 2007). Other studies rely on a more liberal time threshold, such as the Health and Retirement Study that originally used a 2 hour per week threshold to distinguish higher from lower intensity caregivers to older adults (Soldo & Hill, 1995). More typical are general screening questions, such as that which follows used in the American Association of Retired Person's (AARP) national study in 2004, which prompted respondents to self-identify as a caregiver:

> Do you currently provide or have you provided in the last year unpaid help to a relative or friend who has a disability or chronic disease? This kind of help includes assistance with health or personal needs or household chores. It might be taking care of finances, arranging for outside services, or visiting regularly to see how they are doing.

Identification of an upstream caregiver is typically made irrespective of living arrangements because most caregivers to older adults do not coreside with their care recipients (AARP, 2004). By contrast, grandparent caregivers are most often defined by their household arrangements. A grandparent caregiver is typically so designated when he or she coresides with a dependent grandchild in the absence of a parent. In some instances, grandparent caregivers include those with part-time responsibility for their grandchildren, either as a dominant or subordinate coguardian, or those who provide regular day care assistance to working parents.

Rarely are upstream and downstream caregiving considered together, yet there are parallels between these two types of caregiving that remain unexplored. In this review, caregiving to and by older adults is considered within the context of the life course perspective, specifically in terms of the importance of timing, context, and linked lives. Timing refers to the onset and duration of care and the demographic and historical conditions that give rise to caregiving and guide caregiving careers. Context refers to the cultural and socioeconomic environments that determine the meanings and resources attached to caregiving roles. Linked lives refer to familial structures and interdependencies that shape caregiving decisions and outcomes.

## CAREGIVING TO OLDER PERSONS

With the increase in life expectancy over the last century, informal caregiving to impaired older people has become increasingly common. Family members form the backbone of the support system of frail older adults who live in the community, with adult children serving most often as main care providers. Before focusing on intergenerational caregiving, it is important to mention other forms of informal caregiving that should not be overlooked. Spouses are among the most prolific caregivers to older adults. However, as age peers to their care recipients, spousal caregivers are vulnerable providers in terms of the relatively few psychological and physical resources they bring to the caregiving situation, the heavy burden they confront in performing the caregiving role, and their greater susceptibility to disease and disability (Pinquart & Sörensen, 2003). These very characteristics of spousal caregivers elevate the importance of adult children in the care portfolio of frail married elders. In addition, while about 10% of frail elders receive care from neighbors and friends, research indicates that nonkin have weaker commitment to caregiving when compared to adult children of the recipient (Barker, 2002).

The role of adult children in providing long-term support and care to their aging parents aroused much interest in social gerontology and family studies in the last quarter of the 20th century. Declines in mortality rates and longer periods of chronic illness in later life have increased older adults' need for prolonged periods of care, thus making caregiving to older parents a normative activity in the lives of adult children. Research shows that older parents expect to rely on their adult children for care, support, and attention when confronting old-age dependencies (Blieszner & Mancini, 1987). Christine Himes (1992) estimates that a majority of middle-aged women with a surviving parent can expect to provide parental caregiving at some point in their lives. In the future, caregiving will occur increasingly later in the lives of caregiving children and their parents. The notion of parent care as an unexpected responsibility now has more to do with the unanticipated duration of the care role than with its entry.

According to a 2004 study by the AARP and the National Alliance for Caregiving, 21% of the U.S.

population provided unpaid care to an adult. This percentage translates into 44.4 million caregivers in the United States, a figure that is certain to rise with the aging of the population. According to this study, the typical caregiver to an adult is a 46-year-old female with some college experience, providing 20 hours of care each week to her older mother. Three out of five caregivers are female, and almost half are employed full time. Slightly more than half of caregivers (55%) are providing care for a recipient living in another household. Although informal caregiving labor is unpaid, it represents a significant economic value to society. Estimates of the value of informal caregiving ranges between $196 and $257 billion annually—an amount greater than the costs of formal home care and nursing home care combined (Staton, Shuy, & Byock, 2001).

**The Stress and Coping Paradigm** The most widely used paradigm in caregiving research today is the general stress and coping model of caregiving (Lazarus & Folkman, 1984). In these models, the psychological and physiological well-being of caregivers are linked to their personal characteristics (e.g., health, gender, martial status, economic status, and race or ethnicity), appraisals of the caregiving situation (perceived burden), stress levels (perceived and physiological), external resources (social support, formal services), and coping styles (active, emotion-focused), as well as the demands placed on them by their care recipients' level of impairment. The deleterious consequences of stress and burden are well-documented. Caregivers are at elevated risk for depression, poor self-reported health, low functional capacity, stress-related diseases, cardiovascular reactivity, impaired immunological function, high blood pressure, and elevated cortisol levels. Several meta-analyses of caregiving studies found that caregivers to dementia patients had greater stress and worse physical and mental health than both noncaregivers and caregivers to nondemented recipients (Pinquart & Sörensen, 2003).

There is also strong evidence that coping skills and support resources produce beneficial effects and serve to ameliorate the impact of burden on negative outcomes. Some coping skills, such as reappraising the situation and creative problem-solving, appear to have a positive impact on the well-being of caregivers, whereas coping styles that deny the problem—also known as avoidant coping—may exacerbate the negative consequences of caregiving (Knight, Silverstein, McCallum, & Fox, 2000). Social support that provides emotional and practical assistance to the care provider also serves to reduce burden and its harmful effect on the well-being of caregivers.

One of the more perplexing paradoxes in caregiving research is the relatively low levels of subjectively perceived burden reported by African-American and Hispanic caregivers, despite providing more hours of care and confronting more objective stressors (Knight et al., 2000). Most explanations of this contradiction have centered on the strong cultural values of familism expressed in African-American families that elevate expectations for caregiving and lead to a more positive appraisal of the experience. Other explanations focus on the greater use of religious coping styles and more active informal support networks in African-American families (Aranda & Knight, 1997).

Less investigated are the positive aspects of caregiving. Although often demanding and challenging in time and effort, caregiving can enhance subjective well-being and produce uplifts in mood as an intrinsic reward for helping a loved one. Taking a life span approach to the topic of family elder care, Karen Roberto and Shannon Jarrott (2008) note the emerging literature on caregiver growth that demonstrates the positive aspects of caregiving, including improvement in problem-solving abilities, increased self-understanding, and a growing sense of competence. However, the assumption that caregiving distress is relieved following the death of the care recipient appears to be overstated. One study found that although former caregivers experienced decreases in stress and negative affect, their depressive symptoms and feelings of loneliness did not rebound 3 years after their caregiving activities ceased.

**Allocating Caregiving Roles in the Family** The literature on intergenerational caregiving and support is replete with evidence for structured differentiation of siblings in their parent care activities. Adult children in larger families tend to provide less support per child than those in smaller families (Wolf, Freedman, & Soldo, 1997), suggesting that siblings resolve their division of labor by offsetting each other's efforts in a coordinated response to their parent's needs. The division of labor in caregiving tends to favor children with less discretionary time. For instance, unmarried sons and daughters are more likely to help their frail older parents, and for longer periods of time, compared to their married counterparts.

Caregiving is increasingly viewed as a team effort, with multiple family (and nonfamily) members trading off their care efforts. Although the structure of caregiving is typically hierarchical with a main care provider who coordinates the efforts of subordinate caregivers, research indicates that there is a good degree of turnover in the composition of caregiver networks, as well as in the primary providers over time. In one national study, more than half the personnel of care networks—including more than one-fourth of primary caregivers—changed over a 2-year interval (Szinovacz & Davey, 2007). As dissatisfaction with caregiving appears to accelerate over time (Walker, Acock, Bowman, & Fuzhong, 1996), the rotation of caregiving networks may help avoid caregiver burnout.

As of 2008, middle-aged children of aging parents—members of the baby boom cohort—have relatively many siblings with whom they can share care duties. However, the next generation of potential caregivers will have fewer siblings than baby boomers, further increasing doubt about the viability of family support to elders. Smaller family size may mean that fewer potential caregivers will be available to support older adults in need. In addition, there have been substantial changes in family structure since the late 1950s, most notably increasing divorce and remarriage rates, and the emergence of stepfamilies as a normative family form. The disruptive effects of divorce and the tenuous nature of stepfamily relations may weaken the responsibility that children feel for their older parents (Silverstein, Bengtson, & Lawton, 1997). Another point of view is that the effects of divorce, remarriage, and family blending may potentially expand the supply of kin available for supporting older family members, and partially compensate for the negative consequences of low fertility and family disruption. However, evidence suggests that caregiving is increasingly focusing on fewer providers. Through the decade of the 1990s, there was a 50% increase in the proportion of primary caregivers who had no secondary partner available to help shoulder the care load, a worrisome trend that may portend greater stress for caregivers and a weaker safety net for care recipients.

One of the most consistent findings in the elder care literature is that women provide more care than men. At the family level of analysis, the presence of daughters appears to suppress the contributions of sons, suggesting that siblings, when they are able, divide caregiving responsibilities along traditional gender lines. Even when sons provide care, they do so with less frequency and intensity. In a review of 223 caregiving studies, Martin Pinquart and Sylvia Sörensen (2006) found that female caregivers provided more hours of care and were more likely to provide personal assistance than male caregivers, and experienced greater burden and depression as a result. Perceived unfairness in the allocation of care duties among siblings may result in feelings of resentment and conflict, particularly if the inequality of effort falls along gender lines.

Scholars using a bargaining framework to better understand family decision-making with respect to parent care explicitly invoke the possibility of intersibling conflict. Adult children negotiate with each other when making decisions about caring for an aged parent based on their own preferences and the anticipation that their siblings will (or will not) provide care or take an aging parent into the household. In such a scenario, adult children may induce their siblings to provide care by bluffing their intention not to provide care.

Finding evidence of systemic familial consequences of caregiving requires examination beyond the caregivers themselves to other family members. Anna Amirkhanyan and Douglas Wolf (2006), for instance, found that noncaregiving sons and daughters of impaired older parents experienced higher rates of depression when compared to their counterparts whose parents were not impaired. Their findings suggest that filial distress in caregiving families may derive from noncaregiving sources, such as concern over unmet need of a frail parent, guilt over not fulfilling an expected role, or intersibling conflict over the allocation of caregiving duties.

**Work-caregiving Stress** One of the most difficult dilemmas facing caregivers who are also working outside the home is the need to balance their labor force participation with their caregiving duties. The number of caregivers who are working at least 30 hours per week has increased between the mid-1980s and mid-1990s, even as the total number of caregivers per recipient has declined (Spillman & Pezzin, 2000). Thus, working caregivers are increasingly common but have fewer colleagues with whom to divide the care load. Not surprisingly, caregivers who are working full time provide lower amounts of care than other caregivers; and while they are also more likely to use supplemental paid providers, their care recipients are at greater risk of having unmet needs (Scharlach, Gustavson, & Dal-Santo, 2007).

Research shows that employed caregivers are at higher risk of health-related problems than nonemployed caregivers. Competing work-family demands adversely affect the physical, mental, social, and economic well-being of workers, elevate their risk of alcohol abuse, and produce stressful home conditions (Bianchi, Casper, & King, 2005). Yet employment also provides income and other work-related benefits that may link the caregiver to ancillary support services, and affords access to coworkers who may serve as an informal support network that lessens the burden and strain associated with caregiving.

Evidence for increasing jeopardy among working caregivers is not gender-neutral. Suzanne Bianchi, Lynne Casper, and Rosalind King (2005) note that women continue to shoulder a disproportionate amount of caregiving even as their responsibilities in the labor market have increased. The continued tilt of caregiving toward adult daughters has raised concerns about the impact of caregiving on their careers. The large time commitment of caregiving appears to reduce working hours more among daughters than among sons, particularly in suppressing full-time employment. Gender imbalances in care work may be viewed as the product of societal norms and social policies that favor men's participation in the labor force. Nations with welfare state regimes, such as Sweden, provide liberal home care benefits to its older citizens (as well as day care for young children), so that women have more equal access to employment.

**Caregiving and Multiple Family Roles** Discussion of the *sandwich generation* in past decades has centered on the challenges faced by working-age adults who simultaneously care for their parents and their dependent children. Brenda Spillman and Liliana Pezzin (2000) found that the number of sandwich generation caregivers has increased, estimating that approximately 3.5 million individuals were dually responsible for an aging parent and a dependent child. A Canadian study found that almost 3 in 10 of those aged 45 to 64 with unmarried children were also caring for an older relative (Raphael & Schlesinger, 1994), with a higher percentage obtained if care for grandchildren is also considered. While delayed fertility has increased the likelihood that middle-aged individuals will be sandwiched between elderly parents and dependent children, some researchers argue that child care and elder care still occur sequentially more often than they do simultaneously (Ward, Logan, & Spitze, 1992).

Because of increases in life expectancy, the sandwich generation increasingly consists of middle-aged individuals embedded within four-generation families. This generation may be responsible for frail older parents, young adult children experiencing economic and social challenges in the transition to adulthood, and grandchildren in need of care. Some research suggests that there are significant intrafamilial strains in families where adult children are dependent on middle-aged parents who are caring for the oldest generation (Hamill, 1994). However, other research finds few negative outcomes in this type of sandwiched family, with one study finding that living with an adult child relieves caregiving burden in midlife caregivers (Raphael & Schlesinger, 1994).

**Caregiving Norms over Time** Life span developmental theories concerning filial responsibility typically focus on psychosocial adjustments made by individuals to meet family demands at successive life course stages. With regard to parent care responsibility, Margaret Blenkner (1965) invoked the concept of *filial maturity* to describe the transition of adult children from being relatively autonomous from their parents to being dependable sources of support for them. This transition involves a change in perspective that allows middle-aged children to view their parents as vulnerable individuals, thereby strengthening their commitment to provide care in the context of an adult relationship. An alternative developmental framework for conceptualizing filial responsibility is based on caregiving anxiety (Cicirelli, 1988). In this framework, filial responsibility is induced when children worry about how they might successfully manage care duties in advance of the time that care is actually needed by their parents.

Cross-sectional studies have found little empirical evidence of midlife exceptionalism with regard to filial duty to older parents, and, to the contrary, describe a linear decline in elder care responsibility across successive age groups (Peek, Coward, Peek, & Lee, 1998). However, a longitudinal study by Daphna Gans and Merril Silverstein (2006) found that normative commitment to caregiving for older parents peaked in middle age and declined thereafter. Filial anxiety and filial maturity may be mutually reinforcing characteristics, as suggested by Mark Bromley's and Rosemary Blieszner's (1997) finding that adult children who worried about the future dependency needs of their parents also collaboratively discussed possible care options with them.

## CAREGIVING FOR GRANDCHILDREN

As of 2000, more than 2.4 million grandparents claimed primary responsibility for at least one coresident grandchild without a parent in the household, a figure that represents a nearly fourfold increase since 1970 (Simmons & Dye, 2003). Over the same period, the percentage of children living in grandparent-headed households not quite doubled, rising from 3% in 1970 to 5.5% in 1997 (Bryson & Casper, 1999). The number of grandchildren being raised by grandparents has increased in all socioeconomic and ethnic groups but rose most dramatically in African-American families of the inner city starting in the 1980s. When their families were hit particularly hard by the crack cocaine epidemic, HIV and AIDS, lack of employment, and incarceration, African-American grandmothers stepped in to raise their grandchildren in greater numbers, continuing a history of grandparent primacy going back several centuries. Custodial grandparents of all races and backgrounds, but particularly those from poor and minority background, subsequently emerged as an important social policy issue in the late 20th century.

**Well-being of Grandparent Caregivers** Grandparents raising grandchildren represent a high-risk group for illness and disease. They are predisposed to poor physical and mental health outcomes even before their care for a grandchild begins as a result of their generally low socioeconomic status and the difficult family circumstances that precipitated their involvement in care. Evidence also suggests that the high demand of grandchild care itself takes a toll on the physical and mental well-being of custodial grandparents, particularly the challenge of meeting the needs of children who are facing physical, behavioral, and mental challenges of their own.

Research has shown that grandparents caring for grandchildren, both in skipped and three-generation households, are at elevated risk for many health problems (Minkler & Fuller-Thomson, 1999). Grandparent caregivers tend to have lower levels of functional health, more chronic conditions, greater risk of coronary heart disease, and less satisfaction with their health compared to noncaregiving grandparents. Physical health and mental health are interrelated such that poor physical health and psychological distress mutually influence each other. Thus it is not surprising that this stressed and distressed group of caregivers is at high risk for developing chronic impairments, acute conditions, and mental health problems.

Grandparents raising grandchildren are more likely to suffer from depressive symptoms than grandparents who are not raising their grandchildren. The degree to which elevated levels of distress are related to the caregiving role itself or to the existential social and family conditions that surround and give rise to this nontraditional family arrangement has not been addressed conclusively. The precipitating adverse conditions that triggered entry into the role are at least as stressful as the daily hassles and sacrifices that come with managing the role itself; indeed, they serve to reinforce each other, producing double (and higher order) jeopardies for grandparent caregivers. Pathways into caregiving that involved drug or alcohol abuse in the parental generation produce the most negative psychological outcomes in custodial grandparents, providing evidence of accumulated disadvantages in this group of grandparents over time (Goodman & Silverstein, 2002). The cluster of risk factors involving preexisting social and economic conditions is exacerbated by entry into the caregiving role.

Caring for grandchildren is associated with poor mental and physical outcomes partially because those engaged in this activity tend to have low income, be of minority status, and be unmarried. Grandparents who care full time for their grandchildren are more likely than noncaregivers to live below the poverty line, receive public assistance, and have less than a high school education (Minkler & Fuller-Thomson, 2005). Low socioeconomic status is consistently related to worse health in this population as a result of the disadvantages associated with poverty, such as lack of access to medical care and insufficient support resources. Unmarried grandparent caregivers have worse health than married caregivers for many of the same reasons.

Beyond economic factors, grandparent caregivers are particularly sensitive to their family and household environments. In coparenting situations, grandparents will have contact with their grandchild's parent(s), often to coordinate care or visits. In such instances, it is not unusual for conflict to emerge over child care decisions and childrearing strategies—particularly if the grandparent and parent are living in the same household. Research shows that custodial grandparents have better mental health when they are the sole caregiver and have autonomy in their caretaking role (Goodman, 2003). In such instances, conflict with the child's parent is minimized because parental authority sits squarely with the grandparent. Conversely, grandparent-parent conflict may be particularly acute when parents exert authority over their children, particularly parents who are involved in substance abuse or suffer from serious mental illness.

Grandparent caregiving often arises in response to parental exigencies, deficits, and crises that may have left grandchildren abused or neglected, further raising the challenges faced by custodial grandparents. Children in grandparent-headed households are at heightened risk of hyperactivity, school difficulties, emotional distress, and forming behavioral problems. Given that parenting can be extremely stressful even under optimal conditions, the mental health of grandparents raising grandchildren is of particular concern given their older age, their exposure to poverty, their greater chance of having special-needs grandchildren to supervise, and their (often) problematic adult children. Not surprisingly, grandparent caregivers exhibit even higher levels of stress than parental caregivers (Musil, Youngblut, Ahn, & Curry, 2002), and their parenting stress is associated with higher levels of depressive symptoms.

In a rare comparison of upstream and downstream caregivers, William Strawbridge, Margaret Wallhagen, Sarah Shema, and George Kaplan (1997) found in a longitudinal study (a study of a sample of individuals at multiple points in time) that while all types of caregivers had greater exposure to stress and confronted more social and economic problems than noncaregivers, grandparent caregivers expressed the most distress 20 years prior to caregiving. These results affirm a life course model of caregiver stress and disadvantage. Caregiving grandparents tend to derive from stressful family, economic, and community contexts that carry over into their caregiving lives.

Despite the challenges they face, caregiving grandparents are generally effective caretakers. Compared to day care, after-school programs, babysitters, nannies, and other formal sources of help, grandparents tend to have a less casual interest with the well-being of their grandchildren. Jennifer Solomon and Jonathan Marx (1999), for instance, found that the health and school adjustment of children raised solely by grandparents was nearly equivalent to children raised by one biological parent.

Research indicates that grandmothers who have been raising a grandchild for at least 2 years were more likely than noncaregiving grandmothers to seek preventive medical treatments; ostensibly, these caregivers were motivated to stay healthy for the sake of their grandchildren (Baker & Silverstein, in press).

While most grandparent caregivers are unquestionably committed to the well-being of the grandchildren in their charge, they often have ambivalent feelings about the disruptive effect their unexpected reengagement in the parent role has on their lives. Some caregiving grandparents report disappointment in having to inhibit their leisure activities or postpone their retirement plans. One grandparent summed it up as follows: "I thought this was the time in my life where I could just go off fishing for three days . . . I can't do it now" (Burton 1992, p. 749). Another grandparent said, "I just don't go places . . . it's just easier to stay home . . . that's just the way it has to be . . . this isn't good" (Jendrek 1993, p. 617).

Similar to the literature on caregiving to older adults, caring for grandchildren can enhance feelings of self-efficacy and a sense of satisfaction that comes from filling a valued family role. Engagement in caregiving has been found to provide numerous psychological benefits to grandparents that include the emotional reward of maintaining a strong affective attachment with the grandchild in their care, a renewed sense of purpose in life, and a second chance at parenting. When asked about the stresses and rewards of raising a grandchildren, four out of five caregiving grandparents found the experience extremely rewarding, and more than one-quarter reported that it was more rewarding than it was stressful (Giarrusso, Silverstein, Feng, & Marenco, 2000).

The cultural meaning attached to skipped-generation caregiving has a bearing on whether grandparent caregivers perceive their role as normative or extraordinary. Such meanings are informative regarding grandparents' legitimate claims to intervene on behalf of their grandchildren, and their eventual success in assuming the authority of a parent. Grandparents from cultures with strong expectations to care for at-risk grandchildren adapt more successfully to their custodial role. For example, a study comparing African-American, Latina, and White grandmothers raising their grandchildren found that African-American grandmothers had the best psychological outcomes once the reason for adopting the role was controlled. Better adaptation of African-American grandmothers was explained by a tradition of extended familism and reliance on surrogate caregivers going back to slavery (Goodman & Silverstein, 2002). African-American custodial grandmothers are also more apt to know others raising grandchildren and to have themselves been raised by grandparents, further legitimating this familiar family form.

The increased prevalence of four-generation families in which middle-aged persons have responsibilities to both their older parents and their grandchildren produces opportunities for the middle-aged or penultimate older generation to engage in multiple caregiving. Some research suggests that there are significant intrafamilial strains in families with both older and younger generations in need of care (Hamill, 1994), whereas other research finds few negative outcomes associated with multiple generation caregiving (Loomis & Booth, 1995). Whether additional roles occupied by caregiving grandparents induce or relieve stress has not been conclusively determined. However, one national study found that additional work and family responsibilities did not detract from the psychological well-being of custodial grandparents. In some instances these added roles reduced levels of depression, providing evidence that engaging in outside social spheres may link grandparents to social support, tangible resources, or social capital that could prove to be beneficial (Baker & Silverstein, in press). Research shows that supportive networks have palliative effects on the emotional well-being of caregiving grandparents by buffering the deleterious effects of caregiving stress.

**Part-time Grandparent Caregiving** A more liberal definition of grandparent caregiving includes those grandparents who provide child care in a secondary, supportive capacity. Women's labor force participation has provided grandparents expanded opportunities to care for grandchildren in dual earner and single-mother households. Mary Elizabeth Hughes, Linda Waite, Tracey LaPierre, and Ye Luo (2007) found that part-time caring for grandchildren is quite common in the United States, with 40% of grandparents providing at least 50 hours of care per year for the children of working parents. In the United Kingdom one in five children under 16 years old is looked after by their grandparents during the daytime (Clarke & Cairns, 2001), and a multinational European study found that 40-60% of grandparents reported taking care of grandchildren over a 1-year period (Attias-Donfut, Ogg, & Wolff, 2005).

While part-time caretakers of grandchildren face challenges, they are qualitatively distinct from grandparents who function as surrogate parents. Custodial grandparents are at risk for negative outcomes far in excess to those who provide part-time child care during the day. The evidence is mixed concerning whether providing part-time care to grandchildren is stressful to grandparents. In a national sample, Hughes and colleagues (2007) found that part-time caregiving produced few negative effects on grandparents. The authors are careful to point out that caregiving is just one of many roles that grandparents may occupy, suggesting that it is important to examine the combination of family and these other roles when assessing the impact of caregiving on the well-being of grandparents.

**Caregiving for a Disabled Grandchild or Child** Providing care for a developmentally or physically disabled grandchild is among the most challenging roles taken on by grandparent caregivers. A review of literature suggests that while these heavily invested grandparents are greatly valued by their families, they are often limited in their capacity to meet the demands of emotionally or physcially challenged grandchildren (Mitchell, 2007). Research by Jennifer Park, Dennis Hogan, and Maryhelen D'Ottavi (2005) reveals that although grandparents are prolific providers of care for special-needs grandchildren, they sometimes face difficulties in bonding with these grandchildren, particularly those exhibiting communication and behavioral problems.

Chronic stressors associated with long-term caregiving interact with aging to produce elevated risk of physical and mental decline among continuing late-life caregivers. Older parents caring for adult children with mental or developmental disabilities report greater health problems due to arthritis, diabetes, heart disease, and depressive symptoms than older parents who were not caregivers (Magana & Smith, 2006). Evidence also shows that older parents who care for adult children with severe mental impairment experience greater economic distress and report lower marital satisfaction compared to their noncaregiving counterparts (Essex & Hong, 2005). Controlled studies of support groups for grandparents caring for grandchildren with developmental delays or disabilities have been shown to reduce depression in these caretakers (McCallion, Janicki, & Kolomer, 2004).

## POLICIES AND PROGRAMS FOR CAREGIVERS

The Family and Medical Leave Act (FMLA), the first U.S. national policy designed to assist working caregivers, mandates the broadest public benefits for family caregivers. The FMLA allows workers in businesses consisting of 50 or more employees to take up to 12 weeks of unpaid leave to care for an ill family member or newborn child; 35 million Americans have taken leave under this law since 1993 (AARP, 2004). Some states have strengthened this coverage by mandating salary replacement rates. Publicly-funded services are also available for family caregivers. In October 2000 Congress established the National Family Caregiver Support Program (NFCSP) to provide support services for family members caring for persons with disabilities and grandparents caring for grandchildren.

According to the Adoption Assistance and Child Welfare Act of 1980, privileged grandparents are now custodians of first choice in the event that parents are not capable guardians of their children; in addition, the Personal Responsibility and Work Opportunity Reconciliation Act of 1996 has allowed public assistance (i.e., grants from the Temporary Assistance for Needy Families [TANF] program) for relative caregivers, even if the caregiver has not adopted the child. Public programs supporting grandparents raising grandchildren are mostly found at the local level. The Departments of Children and Family Services (DCFS) provides formal services such as respite care, public assistance, and legal advice to caregiving grandparents.

However, outside the DCFS foster care system, very few services are specifically targeted at the grandparent caregiver population, as many public benefits depend on whether the grandparent has legal custody of the grandchild. Grandparents who are otherwise eligible to collect public assistance based on their own income do not qualify for full payments for grandchildren if their own children are already covered as eligible dependents. In addition, grandparents raising grandchildren have reported much difficulty obtaining health insurance for their grandchildren; without legal custody, grandparents are usually not able to cover custodial grandchildren under their work-based health insurance. Given that grandparent-headed households are often overcrowded, it is encouraging that special housing specifically designed for grandparents and grandchildren are sprouting up in cities across America, even if there is far more demand than supply as of 2008 (Baker, Silverstein, & Putney, in press).

Programs supporting all types of caregivers include formal therapy sessions, peer-to-peer counseling, and formally organized support groups. Many programs are supported by state and municipal initiatives. Caregivers are taught practical coping skills and relaxation techniques to relieve their stress and are provided with practical information to direct them to appropriate services that could be useful for them. In a meta-analysis of 127 intervention studies with dementia caregivers, Pinquart and Sörensen (2006) found that the best treatments were those therapies and supports that required the most active participation of the caregiver. Informal support groups can be found in all areas of the country, including virtual communities. (Virtual communities are groups of people who interact via letters, telephone, and e-mail for various purposes, rather than face to face.)

Compared to other developed nations, public policy in the United States is not particularly generous with regard to providing relief for long-term chronic caregivers. Because most caregivers are employed, workplace policies and characteristics are arguably more directly important for enhancing the care and support of dependent family members. Several studies have found that positive workplace characteristics—including increased flexibility in the time and place work occurs, supportive supervisors, and a family-friendly work culture—are associated with fewer work-family conflicts and better health of caregivers and their families.

**SEE ALSO** Volume 1: *Grandchildren;* Volume 3: *Grandparenthood; Intergenerational Transfers; Parent-Child Relationships, Later Life; Policy, Later Life Well-Being; Sibling Relationships, Later Life; Singlehood; Stress; Widowhood.*

## BIBLIOGRAPHY


American Association of Retired Persons (AARP) Public Policy Institute. (2004). *Caregiving in the United States.* Retrieved June 13, 2008, from http://assets.aarp.org/rgcenter/il/fs111_caregiving.pdf

Amirkhanyan, A.A., & Wolf, D.A. (2006). Parent care and the stress process: Findings from panel data. *Journals of Gerontology, Series B: Psychological Sciences and Social Sciences, 61*(5), 248–255.

Aranda, M.P., & Knight, B.G. (1997). The influence of ethnicity and culture on the caregiver stress and coping process: A sociocultural review and analysis. *The Gerontologist, 37*(3), 342–354.

Attias-Donfut, C., Ogg, J., & Wolff, F.C. (2005). European patterns of intergenerational financial and time transfers. *European Journal of Aging, 2*(3), 161–173.

Baker, L., & Silverstein, M. (in press). Utilization of preventive health care services among grandmothers raising grandchildren. *Journals of Gerontology, Series B: Psychological Sciences and Social Sciences.*

Baker, L., Silverstein, M., & Putney, N.M. (in press). Grandparents raising grandchildren in the United States: Changing family forms, stagnant social policies. *International Journal of Sociology and Social Policy.*

Barker, J.C. (2002). Neighbors, friends, and other nonkin caregivers of community-living dependent elders. *Journals of Gerontology, Series B: Psychological Sciences and Social Sciences, 57*(3), 158–167.

Bianchi, S.M., Casper, L.M., & King, R.B. (Eds.). (2005). Work, family, health, and well-being. Mahwah, NJ: Erlbaum.

Blenkner, M. (1965). Social work and family relationship in later life with some thoughts on filial maturity. In E. Shanas & G. Streib (Eds.), *Social structure and the family: Generational relations* (pp. 46–61). Englewood Cliffs, NJ: Prentice-Hall.

Blieszner, R., & Mancini, J.A. (1987). *Enduring ties: Older adults' parental role and responsibilities. Family Relations, 36*(2), 176–180.

Bromley, M.C., & Blieszner, R. (1997). Planning for long-term care: Filial behavior and relationship quality of adult children with independent parents. *Family Relations, 46*(2), 155–162.

Burton, L.M. (1992). Black grandparents rearing children of drug-addicted parents: Stressors, outcomes, and social service needs. *The Gerontologist, 32*(6), 744–751.

Bryson, K., & Casper, L.M. (1999). Coresident grandparents and grandchildren. Washington, DC: U.S. Census Bureau. Retrieved June 12, 2008, from www.census.gov/prod/99pubs/p23-198.pdf

Cicirelli, V.G. (1988). A measure of filial anxiety regarding anticipated care of elderly parents. *The Gerontologist, 28,* 478–482.

Clarke, L., & Cairns, H. (2001). Grandparents and the care of children: The research evidence. In B. Broad (Ed.), *Kinship care: The placement choice for children and young people* (pp. 11–20). Dorset, UK: Russell House Publishing.

Essex, E.L., & Hong, J. (2005). Older caregiving parents: Division of household labor, marital satisfaction, and caregiver burden. *Family Relations, 54*(3), 448–460.

Gans, D., & Silverstein, M. (2006). Norms of filial responsibility for aging parents across time and generations. *Journal of Marriage and the Family, 68*(4), 961–976.

Giarrusso, R., Silverstein, M., Feng, D., & Marenco, A. (2000). Primary and secondary stressors of grandparents raising grandchildren: Evidence from a national survey. *Journal of Mental Health and Aging, 6*(4), 291–310.

Goodman, C.C. (2003). Intergenerational triads in grandparent-headed families. *Journals of Gerontology, Series B: Psychological Sciences and Social Sciences, 58*(5), 281–289.

Goodman, C., & Silverstein, M. (2002). Grandmothers raising grandchildren: Family structure and well-being in culturally diverse families. *The Gerontologist, 42*(5), 676–689.

Hamill, S.B. (1994). Parent-adolescent communication in sandwich generation families. *Journal of Adolescent Research, 9*(4), 458–482.

Himes, C.L. (1992). Future caregivers: Projected family structures of older persons. *Journals of Gerontology, Series B: Psychological Sciences and Social Sciences, 47*(1), 17–26.

Hughes M.E., Waite L.J., LaPierre T.A., & Luo Y. (2007). All in the family: The impact of caring for grandchildren on grandparents' health. *Journals of Gerontology, Series B: Psychological Sciences and Social Sciences, 62,* 108–119.

Jendrek, M.P. (1993). Grandparents who parent their grandchildren: Effects on lifestyle. *Journal of Marriage and the Family, 55*(3), 609–621.

Knight, B.G., Longmire, C.V.F., Dave, J., Kim, J.H., & David, S. (2007). Mental health and physical health of family caregivers for persons with dementia: A comparison of African-American and White caregivers. *Aging & Mental Health, 11*(5), 538–546.

Knight, B.G., Silverstein, M., McCallum, T.J., & Fox, L.S. (2000). A sociocultural stress and coping model for mental health outcomes among African-American caregivers in southern California. *Journals of Gerontology, Series B: Psychological Sciences and Social Sciences, 55*(3), 142–150.

Lazarus, R.S., & Folkman, S. (1984). *Stress, appraisal, and coping.* New York: Springer.

Loomis, L.S., & Booth, A. (1995). Multigenerational caregiving and well-being: The myth of the beleaguered sandwich generation. *Journal of Family Issues, 16*(2), 131–148.

Magana, S., & Smith, M.J. (2006). Health outcomes of midlife and older Latina and Black American mothers of children with developmental disabilities. *Mental Retardation, 44*(3), 224–234.

McCallion, P., Janicki, M.P., & Kolomer, S.R. (2004). Controlled evaluation of support groups for grandparent caregivers of children with developmental disabilities and delays. *American Journal on Mental Retardation, 109*(5), 352–361.

Minkler, M., & Fuller-Thomson, E. (1999). The health of grandparents raising grandchildren: Results of a national study. *American Journal of Public Health, 89*(9), 1384–1389.

Minkler, M., & Fuller-Thomson, E. (2005). African-American grandparents raising grandchildren: A national study using the Census 2000 American Community Survey. *Journals of Gerontology, Series B: Psychological Sciences and Social Sciences, 60*, 82–92.

Mitchell, W. (2007). Research Review: The role of grandparents in intergenerational support for families with disabled children: A review of the literature. *Child & Family Social Work, 12*(1), 94–101.

Musil, C.M, Youngblut, J.M., Ahn, S., & Curry, V.L. (2002). Parenting stress: A comparison of grandmother caretakers and mothers. *Journal of Mental Health and Aging, 8*, 197–210.

Park, J.M., Hogan, D.P., & D'Ottavi, M. (2005). Grandparenting children with special needs. In M. Silverstein (Ed.), *Annual review of gerontology and geriatrics* (Vol. 24) (pp. 120–149). New York: Springer.

Pearlin, L.I., Pioli, M.F., & McLaughlin, A.E. (2001). Caregiving by adult children: Involvement, role disruption, and health. In R.H. Binstock & L.K. George (Eds.), *Handbook of aging and the social sciences* (5th ed., pp. 238–255). San Diego, CA: Academic Press.

Peek, M.K., Coward, R.T., Peek, C.W., & Lee, G.R. (1998). Are expectations for care related to the receipt of care? An analysis of parent care among disabled elders. *Journals of Gerontology, Series B: Psychological Sciences and Social Sciences, 53*, 127–136.

Pinquart, M., & Sörensen, S. (2003). Differences between caregivers and noncaregivers in psychological health and physical health: A meta-analysis. *Psychology and Aging, 18*(2), 250–267.

Pinquart, M., & Sörensen, S. (2006). Gender differences in caregiver stressors, social resources, and health: An updated meta-analysis. *Journals of Gerontology, Series B: Psychological Sciences and Social Sciences, 61*(1), 33–45.

Raphael, D., & Schlesinger, B. (1994). Women in the sandwich generation: Do adult children living at home help? *Journal of Women & Aging, 6*, 21–45.

Roberto, K.A., & Jarrott, S.E. (2008). Family caregivers of older adults: A life span perspective. *Family Relations, 57*(1), 100–111.

Scharlach, A.E., Gustavson, K., & Dal-Santo, T.S. (2007). Assistance received by employed caregivers and their care recipients: Who helps care recipients when caregivers work full time? *The Gerontologist, 47*(6), 752–762.

Silverstein, M., Bengtson, V.L., & Lawton, L. (1997). Intergenerational solidarity and the structure of adult child-parent relationships in American families. *American Journal of Sociology, 103*(2), 429–460.

Simmons, T., & Dye, J.L. (2003). *Grandparents living with grandchildren: 2000.* Washington, DC: U.S. Census Bureau. Retrieved June 12, 2008, from http://www.census.gov/prod/2003pubs/c2kbr-31.pdf

Soldo, B.J., & Hill, M.S. (1995). Family structure and transfer measures in the Health and Retirement Study: Background and overview. *Journal of Human Resources, 30*(Suppl.), 108–137.

Solomon, J.C., & Marx, J. (1999). Who cares? Grandparent/grandchild households. *Journal of Women & Aging, 11*(1), 3–25.

Spillman, B.C., & Pezzin, L.E. (2000). Potential and active family caregivers: Changing networks and the "sandwich generation." *Milbank Quarterly, 78*(3), 347–374.

Staton, J., Shuy, R, & Byock, I. (2001). A few months to live: Different paths to life's end. Washington, DC: Georgetown University Press.

Strawbridge, W.J., Wallhagen, M.I., Shema, S.J., & Kaplan G.A. (1997). New burdens or more of the same? Comparing grandparent, spouse, and adult-child caregivers. *The Gerontologist, 37*(4), 505–510.

Szinovacz, M.E, & Davey, A. (2007). Changes in adult child caregiver networks. *The Gerontologist, 47*(3), 280–295.

Walker, A.J., Acock, A.C., Bowman, S.R., & Fuzhong, L. (1996) Amount of care given and caregiving satisfaction: A latent growth curve analysis. *Journals of Gerontology, Series B: Psychological Sciences and Social Sciences, 51*, 130–142.

Ward, R., Logan, J., & Spitze, G. (1992). Influence of parent and child needs on coresidence in middle and later life. *Journal of Marriage and the Family, 54*, 209–221.

Wolf, D.A., Freedman, V., & Soldo, B.J. (1997). The division of family labor: Care for elderly parents. *Journals of Gerontology, Series B: Psychological Sciences and Social Sciences, 52*, 102–109.

**Merril Silverstein**

# CENTENARIANS

Centenarians, persons who have reached the age of 100 years or more, are publicly recognized and honored across cultures. Media accounts of a 120-year-old woman bicycling for exercise, a 100-year-old woman and a 101-year-old man in the United Kingdom becoming the oldest married couple in their country, and centenarian veterans of major wars are inspirational, because centenarians symbolize triumph over frailties of the human body and spirit. What are the secrets to their longevity? What can scientists learn from them about the maintenance of physical and psychosocial health? Do centenarians have helpful tips from their life experience that the rest of us could easily adopt? And, perhaps the question most wondered about, does their quality of life make their longevity fulfilling?

## PATTERNS AND TRENDS IN THE CENTENARIAN POPULATION

Approximately one person in 10,000 living in developed countries of the world attains the age of 100. Women are more likely than men to be centenarians. Among centenarians worldwide, the ratio of women to men is about 5:1. James Vaupel (2000) has estimated that half of all girls born in the developed world in the early 21st century will live to age 100.

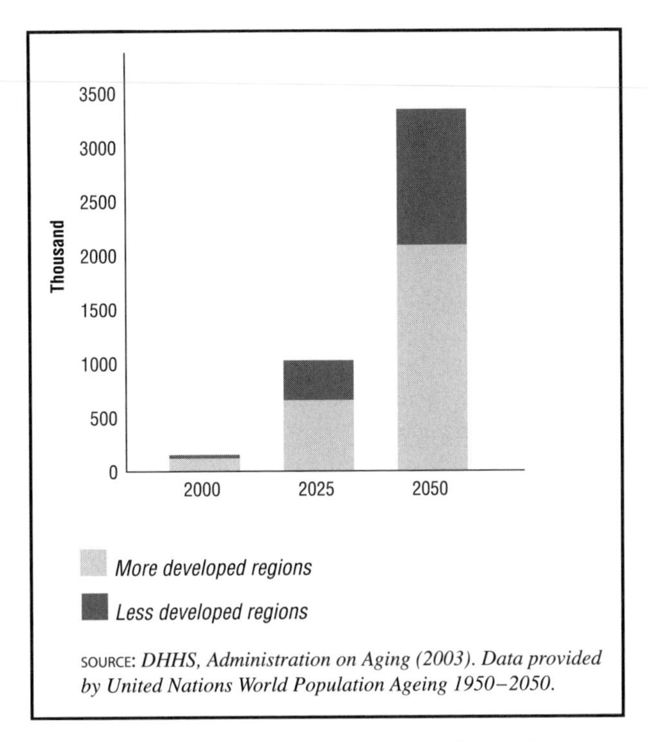


SOURCE: *DHHS, Administration on Aging (2003). Data provided by United Nations World Population Ageing 1950–2050.*

***Figure 1.*** *Distribution of world centenarians by development region, 2000–2050.* CENGAGE LEARNING, GALE.

Persons who attain the age of 110 or older are termed *supercentenarians*. Approximately 90% of supercentenarians are women, according to L. Stephen Coles (2004). The oldest known surviving person was Jeanne Calment of France, who died in 1997 at age 122. The oldest proven age for a male, 115, is attributed to Christien Mortensen, a Danish-born American who died in 1998. The Japanese island of Tokunoshima claims to have produced the oldest man, Shigechiyo Izumi, who reportedly died in 1986 at the age of 120, but he more likely had inherited the name of an older deceased sibling and was actually 105 when he died.

In 1900 only one in 100,000 Americans was a centenarian, compared to one in 8,000 to 10,000 Americans as of 2000 (Perls & Silver, 1999). In the United States, growth in the centenarian population since 1990 and continuing to 2010 is estimated at about 4% per year. The United Nations has projected that the number of centenarians worldwide will increase about 18-fold between the years 2000 to 2050. Although about two-thirds of this increase will occur in developed countries, an increasing portion will occur in regions that are currently less developed (see Figure 1).

Although marked growth in the number of centenarians is a new phenomenon, human survival approaching 100 years is not. In the 16th century the Italian painter Titian lived to be at least age 90 and may have reached age 99. Several accounts of the life of the ancient philosopher Democritus maintain that he lived more than 100 years, perhaps reaching age 109, and other Greek philosophers are also thought to have lived beyond the age of 90. Thus, it is not the maximum life span obtainable that has changed; what has changed dramatically since 1900 is the number of people who are able to achieve their life expectancy potential.

## PROBLEMS OF AGE MISREPORTING

Several geographic areas (e.g., the Russian Caucasus area and Vilacamba, Ecuador) have claimed to have persons with extreme longevity, but the claims were subsequently found to be exaggerated. Validating the age reported by or on behalf of centenarians and supercentenarians is important in studies of the oldest old (Coles, 2004; Perls, Bochen, Freeman, Alpert, & Silver, 1999). Age exaggeration, rather than minimization, is the primary concern.

Some of the factors contributing to error in centenarian reporting include a tendency among young people to cite an older age at the time of immigration in order to qualify for work, poor record-keeping and updating of vital statistics in some locales, and loss or destruction of birth records. The only recording of birth for some persons born at home in rural areas may consist of a baptismal certificate or a birthdate entered in a family Bible, a pattern especially likely to characterize African American persons born in the southern United States.

## CROSS-NATIONAL COMPARISONS OF CENTENARIANS

As of 2008 the United States had the largest total number of centenarians—more than 55,000 (Hall, 2008)—followed by Japan, China, and England-Wales. The higher number of American centenarians in part reflects the large U.S. population in 1890–1905 compared to other countries with a large number of centenarians. Although the United States reports a larger number of centenarians than does Japan, Japan has a higher ratio of centenarians to the overall population than does the United States. Similarly, China reports a larger number of centenarians than does England-Wales, but England-Wales has a higher ratio of centenarians to the overall population than does China.

Areas characterized by geographic clustering of persons who have reached advanced ages are of particular interest, suggesting that people in those areas share environmental influences and/or genes that enable them to reach extreme ages. A concentration of octogenarian and nonagenarian men living in the Tibetan mountains herd livestock and lead physically strenuous lives. Five times as many people living on the island of Okinawa as compared to people living in the rest of Japan live to be 100. A *centenarian belt* in North America extending from Minnesota to Nova Scotia may reflect ethnic backgrounds (e.g., Celtic, French/Acadian, and Scotch) that genetically predispose people to extreme longevity. In areas with geographic clustering of centenarians, the sex ratio becomes more equal, suggesting a shared gene pool. For example, in Sardinia, which has an increased prevalence of centenarians, the ratio of women to men centenarians is only 2:1 (MacKnight, 2007).

## UNIQUE CHARACTERISTICS OF EXCEPTIONALLY LONG-LIVED INDIVIDUALS

Centenarians may share genetic factors that facilitate achieving exceptional old age. Jeremiah A. Barondess (2008) noted that more than half of centenarians have first-degree relatives or grandparents who also reached very old ages. Supercentenarians typically have long-lived siblings (Coles, 2004). After age 80 it is likely that genetics play an increasingly important role in determining survival to an advanced age.

Morbidity profiles, which may be genetically based, suggest that centenarians can be broadly classified as *survivors*, *delayers*, and *escapers*, based on their experience with major age-associated disease states such as hypertension, cancer, and dementia. Persons categorized as survivors have an age of onset of less than 80 years for at least one of the major disease states; delayers' age of onset is between ages 80 and 100; and escapers' age of onset is 100 years or not at all (Evert, Lawler, Bogan, & Perls, 2003). Centenarians are more likely to lack variations of *disease genes* that increase the likelihood of developing particular diseases. Compared with other older persons, centenarians seem to markedly delay or escape life-threatening diseases such as cancer and Alzheimer's disease (Hitt, Young-Xu, Silver, & Perls, 1999). A variation of a gene known for its association with Alzheimer's disease becomes markedly less frequent with advancing age (Frisoni, Louhija, Geroldi, & Trabucchi, 2001) as do some genes that are prominent in cardiovascular disease. Centenarians may also have genes that lower their risk for health problems, such as genes that result in a favorable cholesterol profile. *Longevity enabling genes*, which affect rate of aging, are also hypothesized, although not yet identified. Finally, centenarians may be better able to resist the effects of bad genes, avoiding the inflammatory response that characterizes many chronic conditions.

An estimated 30% of centenarians have physical and mental impairments. The remainder function remarkably well, with about 40% having some vision, hearing, or mobility impairment only and 30% showing very few signs of physical or mental impairment. Thus, generally good health characterizes the majority of centenarians, and they have lived most of their lives in good health, experiencing a fairly rapid decline only near the end of their lives (Hitt et al., 1999). Damage to the immune system may lead to an infection that leads to death, or coronary artery disease may worsen and trigger a heart attack.

Do commonalities exist in the lifestyle of centenarians that are evidenced in health behaviors, social connectedness, and reactions to stress? It has been observed that centenarians are rarely obese and that they exercise and eat healthful foods. Substantial smoking rarely characterizes centenarians, although as many as half of centenarians report enjoying alcoholic beverages on a regular basis. Centenarians vary widely in educational and socioeconomic background, religion, and ethnicity, but most describe having close ties with friends and family. Belle Boone Beard (1991), who interviewed 600 centenarians over a 40-year research career, noted that romance should be considered among the possible so-called secrets of longevity.

Mental health characteristics that have been frequently noted among centenarians include a serene or affirmative outlook on life and the capacity to accept what cannot be changed, such as loss of a spouse. Centenarians demonstrate adaptability to age-related losses and may be individuals who are inherently capable throughout life of progressively adjusting their life styles and accepting their conditions (Dello Buono, Urciuoli, & DeLeo, 1998). Centenarians have been described as *stress-shedders*. They also demonstrate a willingness to assert themselves and their individuality (Beard, 1991). Some have been known to laughingly attribute their longevity to having told themselves that they would live to be 100.

Despite diverse social backgrounds and interests and a vast mosaic of life experiences, centenarians for the most part are individuals who have maximized the portion of their lives spent in good health and independent functioning, and they are content. Compressing the onset and duration of illnesses toward the end of life is a widely shared goal. Centenarians in many ways represent the gold standard for aging well (Perls & Silver, 1999), and there is understandably great interest in identifying the genetic and environmental factors that facilitate the model of aging that centenarians provide.

The discovery of genetic variations associated with survival to extreme old age is a promising route toward understanding cellular and biochemical mechanisms of the aging process and susceptibility to age-related diseases. Studies of centenarian populations in North America, Asia, and Europe increasingly point to clusters of clinical characteristics associated with exceptional longevity that in turn generate genetic investigation. Researchers are also focusing on the significance of non-genetic determinants of long life that are modifiable, including smoking, obesity, and sedentary life style. Registries such as the New England Centenarian Study and the George Centenarian Study facilitate investigation of adaptive mechanisms and functional reserves evident among centenarian survivors. Collectively, centenarian studies not only stimulate the search for new knowledge of the human genome but also have broad potential to improve understanding of how to minimize disability and maximize quality of life in the context of aging.

**SEE ALSO** Volume 1: *Age Norms;* Volume 3: *Active Life Expectancy; Disability and Functional Limitation, Later Life; Frailty and Robustness; Genetic Influences, Later Life; Life Expectancy; Mortality; Oldest Old; Population Aging.*

**BIBLIOGRAPHY**

Barondess, J. A. (2008). Toward healthy aging: The preservation of health. *Journal of the American Geriatrics Society, 56,* 145–148.

Beard, B. B. (1991). *Centenarians: The new generation.* N. K. Wilson & A. J. E. Wilson III (Eds.) New York: Greenwood Press.

Coles, L. S. (2004). Demography of human supercentenarians. *Journal of Gerontology: Biological Sciences, 59A,* 579–586.

Dello Buono, M., Urciuoli, O., & DeLeo, D. (1998). Quality of life and longevity: A study of centenarians. *Age and Ageing, 27,* 207–216.

Department of Health and Human Services, Administration on Aging. (2003). *The number of centenarians is growing worldwide.* Retrieved June 12, 2008, from http://www.aoa.gov/press

Evert, J., Lawler, E., Bogan, H., & Perls, T. (2003). Morbidity profiles of centenarians: Survivors, delayers, and escapers. *Journal of Gerontology: Medical Sciences, 58A,* 232–237.

Frisoni, G. B., Louhija, J., Geroldi, C., & Trabucchi, M. (2001). Longevity and the ϵ2 allele of apolipoprotein E: The Finnish centenarians study. *Journal of Gerontology: Medical Sciences, 56A,* M75–M78.

Hall, W. J. (2008). Centenarians: Metaphor becomes reality. *Archives of Internal Medicine, 168,* 262–263.

Hitt, R., Young-Xu, Y., Silver, M., & Perls, T. (1999). Centenarians: The older you get, the healthier you have been. *The Lancet, 354,* 652.

MacKnight, C. (2007). Centenarians. In E. A. Capezuti, E. L. Siegler, & M. D. Mezey (Eds.), *The encyclopedia of elder care* (2nd ed., pp.127–129) New York: Springer.

Perls, T. T., Bochen, K., Freeman, M., Alpert, L., & Silver, M. H. (1999). Validity of reported age and centenarian prevalence in New England. *Age and Ageing, 28,* 193–197.

Perls, T. T., & Silver, M. H. (1999). *Living to 100: Lessons in living to your maximum potential at any age.* New York: Basic Books.

Vaupel, J. (2000). Setting the stage: A generation of centenarians? *Washington Quarterly, 23*(3), 197–200.

*Nancy Kutner*

# CHILDLESSNESS

**SEE** Volume 2: *Childlessness.*

# CHRONIC ILLNESS, ADULTHOOD AND LATER LIFE

A chronic illness is any health condition that results in sickness or activity limitations that last longer than 3 months. In contrast to acute illnesses, chronic conditions often do not have a distinct onset or a single underlying cause. These conditions can have a global impact on a person's life, with social, psychological, and economic consequences. According to the National Center for Health Statistics (2008), the most common chronic illnesses among older adults in the early 21st century are arthritis, diabetes, cancer, heart disease, and respiratory diseases. Chronic illness claims nearly 7 of 10 lives and account, for more than 75% of annual health care costs in the United States.

## DEFINITION

Chronic illness is a broad category that covers a class of diseases with many different causes and patterns of progression. However, these chronic conditions have two commonalities: They are typically not curable, and they are often degenerative, leading to greater limitations in mental and physical function over time. Thus, the goals of medical care typically are to maintain current levels of function; manage the symptoms of the chronic condition, such as pain; and prevent secondary complications (e.g., pneumonia in persons with chronic obstructive pulmonary disease).

## INCIDENCE AND PREVALENCE

The extension of the human life span in developed nations during the 20th century led to a dramatic shift, and chronic illnesses have become the leading causes of death. Medical advances as well as improvements in living conditions (e.g., sanitation) and nutrition have nearly eradicated infectious diseases as primary causes of death at all ages. More persons survive to adulthood and even into the

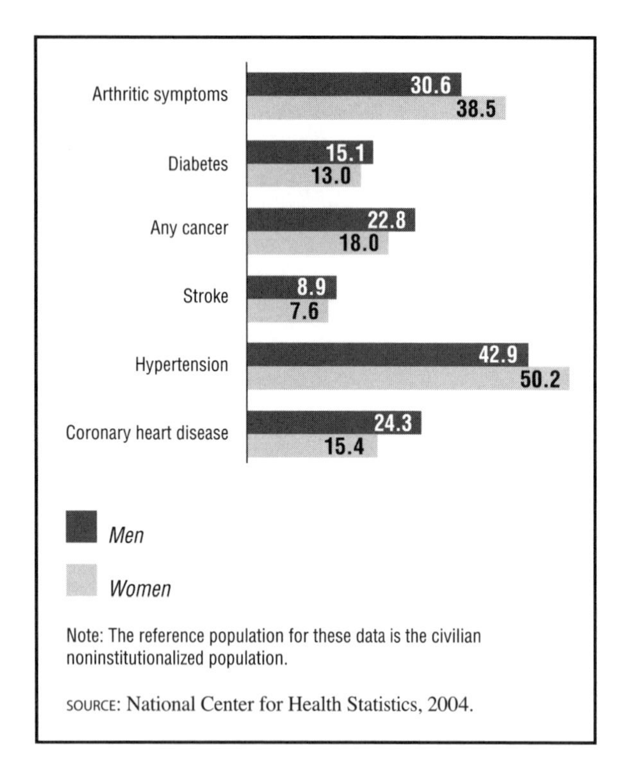


***Figure 1.*** *Prevalence of selected chronic conditions in people aged 65 and over by sex (by percent), 1999–2000.* CENGAGE LEARNING, GALE.

oldest ages than at any other point in history. Five of the six most common causes of death in the United States are chronic illnesses. In 2005 diseases of the heart (27%), cancer (23%), cerebrovascular conditions (6%), respiratory diseases (5%), and diabetes (3%) accounted for 64% of deaths among adults of all ages in the United States.

Considering the population as a whole, nearly 45% of Americans have at least one chronic illness, but there are distinctive patterns of prevalence across age groups. Because the risk of developing most of these conditions accumulates over time, there is a higher concentration of chronic conditions among older adults. 84% of adults age 65 or older report having one or more chronic illnesses. Among people ages 20 to 44, 38% report having at least one chronic condition. Mortality risk from chronic illness peaks from ages 65 to 74, accounting for more than 77% of all deaths in this age group. Although the incidence of chronic illness declines with age, the higher prevalence of these conditions among people of the oldest ages leads to a greater probability of comorbidity and functional limitations. Older Americans are also likely to have chronic conditions that are more disabling, such as arthritis and heart disease. At younger ages, the most prevalent chronic conditions are hypertension and respiratory diseases (asthma and chronic bronchitis).

## CHRONIC ILLNESS OVER THE LIFE COURSE

Even though chronic illness tends to be concentrated among older adults and has a greater influence on functional health in people of advanced age, it is critical to examine chronic illness from a life course perspective. Risk of developing chronic conditions accumulates over a lifetime, influenced by life style factors such as excess body weight, lack of physical activity, poor diet, and tobacco use. These modifiable factors can yield greater gains in long-term health when improved at younger ages. If behavioral interventions and screening are targeted only at older adults, it is likely that there will be only modest gains in the prevention and delay of onset of chronic illnesses.

Over the past decades medical screening procedures have become more specific and sensitive, making it possible to detect chronic diseases at the earliest stages. Early detection can allow early intervention and, for some conditions, treatment. This can have substantial health benefits for individuals, including less disability, a decreased likelihood of secondary complications, and perhaps a slower onset of a condition. Early detection also has increased survivorship, particularly for conditions such as cancer.

Even though a higher proportion of older adults have a chronic illness, the absolute number of persons with chronic conditions is greater among working-age adults. In 2000, 29 million Americans age 65 years and older had one or more chronic conditions, compared to more than 75 million who were age 20 to 64 years. These younger adults are aging with chronic illnesses, which may have significant impact on their social, economic, and mental well-being. Managing a chronic illness can be difficult for working-age adults because many are still employed, raising families, and even perhaps caring for elderly relatives. This directly influences worker productivity, decisions to exit the labor force, ability to fulfill social and familial roles, and long-term functional health. Examining the chronic illness experience from a life course perspective will help researchers and policy makers understand the social, economic, and medical consequences of these conditions not just at advanced ages but over the entire lifetime.

## RISK FACTORS

Although each chronic disease has its own etiology and constellation of risk factors, certain key health behaviors have been linked to nearly every chronic disease: tobacco use, diet, and exercise. According to the Centers for Disease Control, nearly 20% of all premature deaths are due to tobacco use. About 14% of those deaths are caused by a poor diet and lack of exercise. Many of these

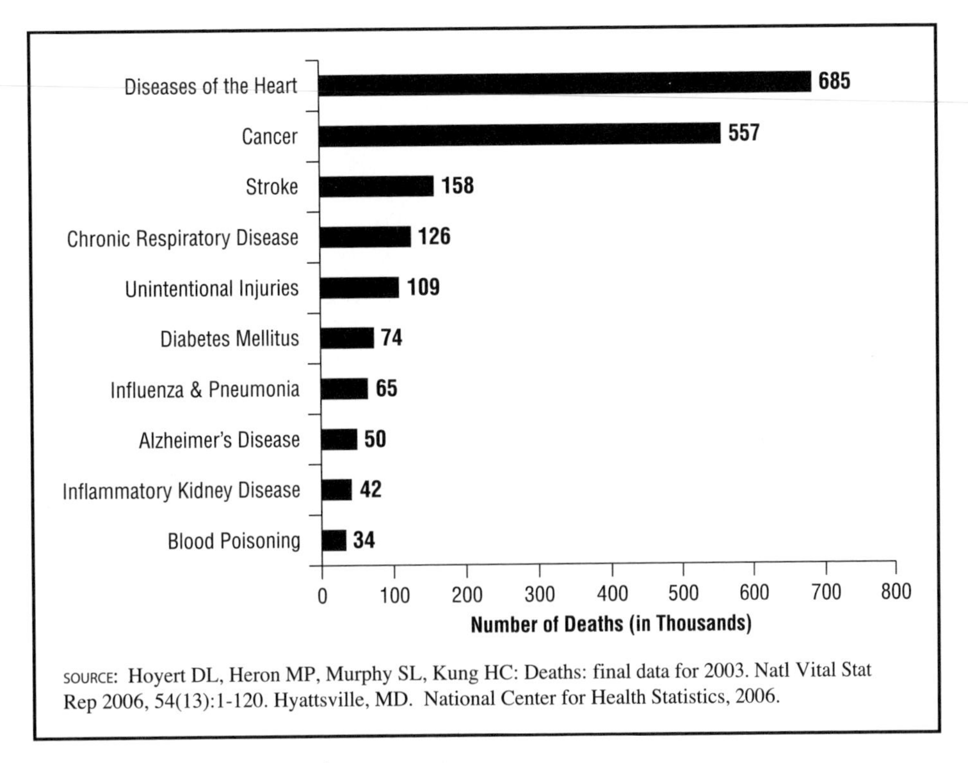


***Figure 2.*** *Leading causes of death in the United States, 2003.* CENGAGE LEARNING, GALE.

risk factors tend to cluster together, so that those who smoke also are more likely to be overweight and have a sedentary life style. Further, these behavioral risk factors can interact with environmental exposures and genetic predispositions to affect the likelihood of developing a chronic condition, the rate of onset, and disease progression over time. The additive and perhaps multiplicative effects of these combined risk factors on the development of chronic illnesses have not been explored sufficiently.

In the last decade of the 20th century and the first decade of the 21st, there were dramatic shifts in mortality risk for specific chronic illnesses among adults age 65 and older. Mortality from diabetes and its complications increased 43% among adults in those two decades. Deaths from chronic lower respiratory diseases increased 62% in the same period (from 185.8 to 300.7 per 100,000 deaths). Largely as a result of advances in life-saving medical treatments, mortality from diseases of the heart and stroke decreased about 35% in those two decades. Deaths from cancer did not change significantly over that period. Heart diseases remain the primary cause of death for older adults.

Disease etiology and long-term consequences for health and functioning vary substantially with the type of chronic condition. For example, more than 60% of adults age 65 and older have one or more types of arthritis. It is the most prevalent chronic illness and the leading cause of disability in older adults. Although arthritis can be disabling, mortality risk is low. Congestive heart failure, in contrast, affects only 6 to 10% of adults age 65 or older, but the mortality risk is very high. About 40% of those with congestive heart failure die within the first year. This occurs because congestive heart failure is a secondary condition caused by complications from other chronic illnesses, most commonly coronary artery disease, hypertension, and/or diabetes. Type 2 (adult-onset) diabetes accounts for about 90% of diabetes prevalence and generally develops in adults over age 40 as a result of accumulated risk associated with chronic obesity and lack of physical activity. The prevalence rate of diabetes increased rapidly in the last decade of the 20th century and the first decade of the 21st, largely because of growing rates of obesity and sedentary life styles among Americans.

## IMPACT AND CONSEQUENCES

The long-term impact of chronic illness is influenced directly by the nature of the disease, the timing of onset, the rate of progression, and effective management of symptoms. Some conditions can lead to a rapid functional decline, whereas others may take years before impairing one's ability to perform activities. Similarly, some chronic illnesses may affect only a few domains, but others may have a more global impact. Nearly 81.8

million Americans have at least one chronic condition but do not report limitation in any life domains. About 43.2 million Americans have a disability as a result of a chronic condition.

The use of health services is substantially higher among adults with chronic illnesses. Chronic medical care accounts for 72% of physician visits, 76% of hospital admissions, 80% of total hospital days, 88% of prescriptions, and 96% of home care visits. Adults with one or more chronic conditions see a physician on average 7.4 times per year, whereas those without chronic conditions have an average of 1.7 physician visits annually. The use of health services increases substantially with each additional chronic condition.

The social consequences of chronic illness can be as life limiting as mental and physical impairment. Symptoms of the chronic illness, particularly pain, fatigue, and mobility limitations, can hinder participation in social activities. Driving cessation is associated with a rapid decrease in social activities, although this decrease is mediated by marital status and the proximity of grown children. The loss of social roles can accumulate over time as a chronic condition progresses, leading to social isolation, depression, and loneliness.

## MANAGEMENT

Because chronic illnesses are long term and can be degenerative or functionally limiting, individuals must engage in active management of their conditions. Effective disease management can include medications or medical treatments, the use of assistive devices, and healthy behaviors such as exercise. The concept of disease management is associated solely with chronic illness. Unlike the goal of acute medical care, which is to heal or cure the patient, chronic medical care focuses on helping the patient manage the symptoms, maintain independence, and prevent secondary complications. It is a long-term investment to prevent further functional decline and requires a partnership between the patient and the physician (often multiple physicians) as well as permanent life style changes.

Adults with a chronic illness play a crucial role in managing their conditions. They must monitor their symptoms, disease progression, the effectiveness of medication, and the onset of secondary complications. Patient reports of changes or stability in their conditions help the medical team determine the course of treatment. Adults with a chronic illness therefore must be critical consumers of medical care and advocate for treatment or screening that will help maintain their long-term health. Barriers to getting necessary care include the prohibitive cost of care and a lack of assistance in coordinating needed services.

## DEMOGRAPHIC FACTORS

Chronic illness prevalence and the associated risk factors tend to be concentrated among certain demographic groups. Effective interventions to prevent and/or delay chronic illness must address the distinctive risk profiles across gender, race, and ethnic groups and levels of socioeconomic status. Overall, chronic conditions disproportionately affect the poor and racial and ethnic minorities primarily because of a lack of access to preventive health care services and a higher likelihood of having risk factors associated with chronic illness.

For example, non-Hispanic Blacks and Hispanic Americans have the highest proportion of sedentary life styles; 30.3 and 33.3%, respectively, were found not to have participated in any physical activity in the previous month. Among all racial and ethnic groups, Black Americans have the lowest percentage of adults with a body mass index in the normal range (27.7%). There are socioeconomic differences in risk factors as well. Thirty-two percent of persons earning less than $15,000 per year currently smoke, more than double the percentage (14.7%) among those earning more than $50,000 per year. Nearly 40% of adults age 18 to 64 who earn less than $15,000 per year are uninsured, limiting their access to preventive medical care and early disease screening at a time in the life course when intervention can be the most effective.

The number and type of chronic illnesses in the population also have distinctive patterns. Among males, heart disease is one of the five most common chronic conditions in those age 45 years and older; among females it is in the top five only at the oldest ages (75 and older). However, women are substantially more likely than men to have arthritis and report more days in pain. Those with higher incomes are less likely to have multiple chronic conditions than are those with lower incomes. Specific conditions are likely to be concentrated in lower socioeconomic groups as well. Asthma rates are nearly double (13.7) for those earning less than $15,000 per year relative to those earning more than $50,000 per year (7.1). The rate of diabetes is nearly triple among those who have less than a high school education (14.2) compared with those who have a college degree or higher (5.4).

The prevention and treatment of chronic illness require a life course perspective of health and healthy behaviors. Early intervention and screening, particularly among high-risk groups, would reduce both the incidence and the prevalence of chronic illness substantially as well as improve functional outcomes. Although many people live with chronic illness for decades, delaying onset, slowing progression, and preventing secondary conditions would extend life and improve the quality of life at all ages.

**SEE ALSO** Volume 3: *Active Life Expectancy; Arthritis; Cancer, Adulthood and Later Life; Cardiovascular*

*Disease; Death and Dying; Diabetes, Adulthood and Later Life; Disability and Functional Limitation, Later Life; Epidemiologic Transition; Health Behaviors, Later Life; Health Care Use, Later Life; Health Differentials/Disparities, Later Life; Older Drivers; Pain, Acute and Chronic.*

**BIBLIOGRAPHY**

Centers for Disease Control and Prevention. (2006). *Behavioral risk factor surveillance system survey data.* Atlanta, GA: U.S. Department of Health and Human Services.

Iezzoni, L. I. (2003). *When walking fails: Mobility problems of adults with chronic conditions.* Berkeley: University of California Press.

Kane, R. L., Priester, R., & Totten, A. M. (2005). *Meeting the challenge of chronic illness.* Baltimore, MD: Johns Hopkins University Press.

McCracken, M., Jiles, R., & Blanck, H. M. (2007). Health behaviors of the young adult U.S. population: Behavioral risk factor surveillance system, 2003. *Preventing Chronic Disease, 4.* Retrieved June 15, 2008, from http://www.cdc.gov/PCD

National Center for Health Statistics. (2008). *Trends in health and aging.* Retrieved June 14, 2008, from www.cdc.gov/nchs

Robert Wood Johnson Foundation. (1996). *Chronic care in America: A 21st century challenge.* Princeton, NJ: Author.

*Jessica Kelley-Moore*

# CIVIC ENGAGEMENT, LATER LIFE

SEE Volume 3: *Political Behavior and Orientations, Later Life; Time Use, Later Life; Volunteering, Later Life.*

# COGNITIVE FUNCTIONING AND DECLINE

Cognitive skills and abilities, such as reasoning, memory, and problem solving, form the foundation for everyday functioning throughout the life span. Cognitive skills are needed to perform activities of daily living, including tasks such as taking medication, procuring meals, and managing finances. Cognitive ability takes on added importance during later life as selective, typical age-related changes occur. In older adulthood, cognitive abilities are essential to additional important health outcomes, including service utilization, mental health, and mortality. Contrary to aging stereotypes, when considering cognitive functioning in adulthood and later life it is important to keep in mind that (a) as a group, older adults' range of functioning and performance tends to be more heterogeneous than that of younger adults; (b) cognitive changes such as dementia are considered "nonnormative" or atypical and do not constitute the majority of cases; and (c) cognitive prevention, enhancement, and intervention efforts are beneficial. Consistent with sociological and psychological perspectives, individual differences as well as ethnicity, socioeconomic status, gender, cohort, and culture are key to understanding cognitive functioning during adulthood and aging.

## PATTERNS OF COGNITIVE FUNCTIONING ACROSS ADULTHOOD AND LATER LIFE

Investigation and assessment of cognitive functioning in adulthood and later life has typically followed three approaches: (a) a psychometric approach aimed at understanding fundamental cognitive abilities and normative aging; (b) examination of higher order skills needed to function within an individual's day-to-day context; and (c) a clinical or neuropsychological approach, which focuses on mechanisms and outcomes of nonnormative cognitive aging such as occurrence of dementia. From the psychometric perspective, normative age-related changes in cognition are well documented, demonstrating that selected abilities decline with age. Consistent trajectories over time of individual cognitive abilities have been described across samples and cohorts. This body of work also indicates that differential change is evident across various types of cognitive abilities and that abilities need to be considered separately (Christensen, 2001).

Cognitive research typically differentiates two broad classes of cognitive abilities, each composed of several individual skills, and this distinction remains important through very late life. Cognitive abilities that rely on accumulated knowledge and experience, and are highly dependent on an individual's culture, have been described as *crystallized intelligence* (Schaie, 2005). A prime example of such ability is verbal comprehension. In contrast, intellectual skills that are considered more "innate" and biologically driven have been labeled *fluid abilities* (Schaie, 2005). Often fluid abilities focus on the ability to deal with novel situations. One such ability is working memory, in which mental information is manipulated before a response is formulated or information is committed to long-term memory (e.g., backward recital of a presented digit span). Inductive reasoning is another example of a fluid ability, in which individual stimuli are used to decipher a larger pattern (e.g., deciding which letter comes next in a presented series of letters). Crystallized abilities tend to remain stable well into later life, whereas fluid abilities peak in young adulthood (Schaie,

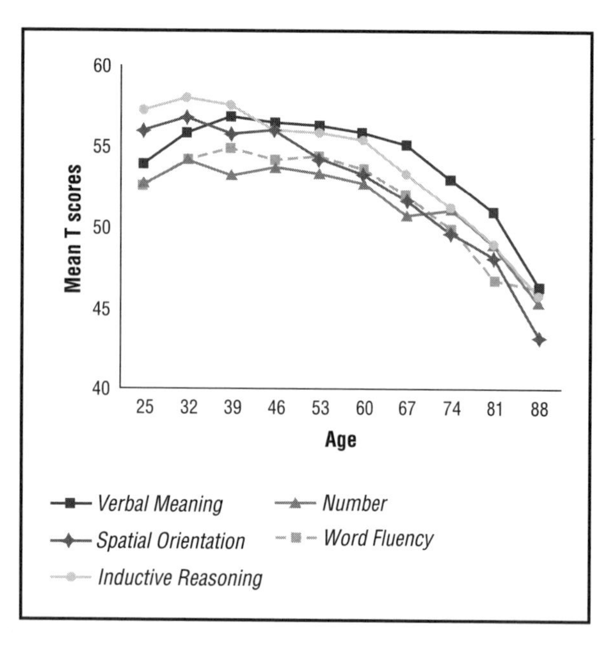


***Figure 1.*** *Estimated age changes from 35-year data for the primary mental abilities.* CENGAGE LEARNING, GALE.

2005). Decreased processing speed (Salthouse, 2000), memory (Christensen, 2001), and attentiveness and inhibition of distracting stimuli/information (e.g., Zacks & Hasher, 1994) in later adulthood have also been observed.

In addition to documenting normative age-related declines, empirical studies have identified two additional developmental phenomena related to cognitive aging. First is the tendency for older adults to demonstrate accelerated cognitive decline close to death. Prior to natural death, some older adults exhibit terminal change (within 3 to 5 years of death) and a drop (within 1 year of death) in their cognitive performance (Bosworth & Siegler, 2002). Second, the very nature and structure of cognitive abilities appears to change throughout older adulthood. Findings suggest that individual cognitive abilities such as memory and verbal knowledge become less differentiated and more similar with increasing age (e.g., deFrias, Lövdén, Lindenberger, & Nilsson, 2007).

Another line of research within the cognitive aging field examines the everyday cognitive and problem-solving skills needed to traverse daily life. In contrast to more narrowly defined individual cognitive skills, problem-solving ability is considered a higher order cognitive skill that depends on the constituent intellectual abilities (Marsiske & Willis, 1995). Within the psychometric approach, there is a reliance on paper-and-pencil measures that are akin to academic tests. However, assessments of problem-solving ability are more contextual and tend to incorporate actual real-life stimuli (e.g., prescription label, transportation schedule). In addition, these assessments are more likely to be experiential and extend beyond paper-and-pencil assessment. For example, participants might be asked to look up a phone number in a telephone book or count out exact change from a lunch bill (e.g., Diehl, Willis, & Schaie, 1995).

Within the cognitive aging literature, everyday problem-solving research has gained momentum as proponents point to the "value added" by using such an approach (see Marsiske & Margrett, 2006). A central issue remains regarding everyday problem solving, namely its relation to everyday functioning and, in part, the difficulty identifying an appropriate standard consistent with actual daily demands by which success can be determined (Marsiske & Margrett, 2006). However, by focusing on what older adults actually do in their day-to-day lives, the primary benefit of examining everyday problem solving is increased ecological validity or relevance, meaning outside of an artificial testing situation. Using this approach, researchers can better approximate how older adults perform in their own real-life settings. These efforts may lead to increased efficiency of assessment using a more concise battery as well as increased participation by older adults and greater self-efficacy when performing the tasks (Marsiske & Margrett, 2006). Additional empirical and theoretical work is needed to explore the nature of everyday problem-solving skills in very late life.

A third approach to understanding cognitive aging stems from a more clinical and neuropsychological perspective aimed at understanding the mechanisms underlying nonnormative cognitive changes such as the occurrence of dementia. From this perspective, global indicators of cognitive functioning and neuropsychological measures are typically employed. For example, a widely used assessment to gauge general cognitive status and distinguish individuals with dementia from those without is the Mini-Mental Status Exam (Folstein, Folstein, & McHugh, 1975). This assessment comprises 11 items that assess orientation to time and place, comprehension and recall of familiar objects, attention and calculation, and language. The maximum score on the Mini-Mental Status Exam is 30, and typically a score of 23 or lower is considered an indication of impairment.

## MEMORY OVERVIEW

Although working memory is often considered an element of fluid abilities, investigation of memory has garnered added attention as this cognitive ability provides a coordinating foundation for higher order cognitive operations with numerous implications for daily functioning. Notably, memory deficiency is linked to mild cognitive impairment and dementia.

Various models have been proposed to describe memory processes. One of the most pervasive models has been the information processing or modal model, which likens memory processes to computer-system processing with input and output. This model focuses on three types of memory: sensory, short-term, and long-term memory (Baddeley, 2007). These three memory constituents vary in capacity and duration. Sensory memory involves very brief retention of sensory input that is either selectively encoded or forgotten. Short-term or working memory involves discrete (limited) tasks such as remembering a telephone number while finding the telephone and waiting to dial. Long-term memory involves more detailed information stored for indefinite periods.

In the process of remembering, people are assumed to engage in three steps. The first step is encoding, in which meaning is ascribed to incoming information. Second, information may then be moved into storage. Third, information may be retrieved via two methods, recognition or recall. Recognition is the easier of the two methods and is conceptually similar to a multiple-choice test. The respondent is presented with several options and asked to identify (remember) which element is the correct answer.

In contrast, recall of information is comparable to an open-ended essay item in which possible responses are not presented. The task is more difficult because respondents must generate (remember) the correct answer. Information may be lost at any stage. For example, the vast majority of received sensory information is not encoded and therefore is not moved into short-term memory. The multicomponent model extends the modal model, particularly in regard to short-term memory and inclusion of an episodic buffer (Baddeley, 2007). In this model, short-term memory is considered very much to be "working," active memory and is distinguished by an attentional (executive) control system with two secondary storage systems that rely on acoustic (auditory) and visuospatial (visual, graphic) representations and processes (Baddeley, 2007). As is discussed later, a link between sensory functioning and processing and cognition is prevalent across differing theories and studies.

As outlined by Bäckman, Small, and Wahlin (2001), long-term memory can be generally classified as episodic (i.e., specific and personal to an individual; memory for events) or nonepisodic (i.e., information related to more general learning and skill building). Age-related differences are evident in storage and retrieval processes across memory type. Generally for nonepisodic memory, younger and older adults' performance is similar; however, differences favoring younger adults may become more pronounced depending on the nature and complexity of the task (Bäckman et al., 2001). In contrast, older adults consistently fare more poorly compared to younger adults on episodic memory tasks, likely reflecting decreased encoding and retrieval abilities by older adults (Bäckman et al., 2001).

## CAUSES AND CORRELATES OF COGNITIVE FUNCTIONING AND DECLINE

The mechanisms underlying both normative or typical cognitive changes, as well as nonnormative (atypical) changes, are debated, and in many ways this work remains in its infancy. Ongoing theoretical and empirical work focuses on factors influencing cognitive functioning and decline, including both individual or micro-level influences (e.g., individual biological factors and sensory functioning) and larger, more macro-level influences occurring within the community or society (e.g., educational system differences between generations). Chronological age alone holds limited predictive value; thus age is usually considered a proxy for other events occurring within and external to the individual. Several theories offer hypotheses related to cognitive change and decline. Neurobiological hypotheses center on cerebral aging, including shrinking of the cortex, impaired neurotransmitter functioning, and development of protein plaques and tangles. Process-oriented explanations focus on individual basic abilities as the foundation for higher order cognitive functioning. From this perspective, older adults' decreased processing speed, attention, and ability to switch tasks and multitask are cited as roots of cognitive decline.

Proponents of a central mechanism theory note that cognitive decline coincides with other declines, including sensory functioning, suggesting a more systemic problem. Related to the latter point is a serious challenge to the investigation of causes and correlates of cognitive functioning. This challenge is the theoretical and practical relationship between cognitive and sensory functioning. Prior work suggests that sensory functioning (particularly hearing and vision) may explain substantial age-related variation in cognitive performance (Li & Lindenberger, 2002). In part these relations could be due to the effect of sensory limitations on cognitive engagement in older adults' daily life, understanding of stimuli in the testing situation, and/or representation of a common mechanism underlying systemic age-related decline.

In a review of studies examining factors related to cognitive change, Christensen (2001) distinguished individual *marker variables* (i.e., fixed characteristics, including early education and genetics) from *risk factors*, which are more dynamic and malleable (e.g., health). Lower education, presence of the APOE $\epsilon 4$ allele (a genetic marker linked to Alzheimer's disease), and poorer objective health indicators have been related to negative cognitive change, although Christensen noted that the relationship may be specific to one or more cognitive abilities. Other individual-level factors have been linked to cognitive performance and change, and these factors vary in duration and malleability. Such factors include nutrition, physical activity, lack of sleep and fatigue, mental health, including depressive symptoms, and prescription and substance use (e.g., Budson & Price, 2005; Poon & Harrington 2006; Starr et al., 2004). Additionally, contextual influences such as the role of significant others, individual and societal attitudes toward aging, changes in emotional regulation, and degree of social and cognitive engagement are important to the development and maintenance of cognitive abilities throughout the life span (e.g., Carstensen, Mikels, & Mather, 2006; Gruber-Baldini, Schaie, & Willis, 1995; Hess, 2006).

In addition to individual, micro-level occurrences, more macro-level factors are also influential in shaping cognition. For instance, differences attributed to cohort or group membership such as generation (e.g., Baby Boomers vs. Generation X), ethnicity, gender, and socioeconomic status impact experiences and access throughout life, which in turn can affect cognitive performance (e.g., Black & Rush, 2002; Orsini et al., 1986; Sloan & Wang, 2005; Willis & Schaie, 1988). In addition to group or cohort affiliation, cognitive ability may also be impacted by historical period. A prime example of cohort and time influence is the generational and period effects related to educational practices and attainment (Schaie, 2005). For instance, Flynn (1987) demonstrated that successive cohorts born in the first half of the 20th century generally evinced superior performance on intelligence (IQ) tests—a phenomenon accounting for several IQ points per generation and one not isolated to the United States. The mechanisms (e.g., nature of intelligence assessment, educational attainment) underlying the observed increase in IQ test performance have been debated as well as how mean-level IQ may or may not correspond with an increase in IQ score variance (Rowe & Rodgers, 2002).

## CONSEQUENCES OF COGNITIVE FUNCTIONING AND DECLINE

Retention of cognitive abilities is linked to critical outcomes in later life, including quality of life and survivorship. Although it is sometimes difficult to distinguish antecedent from consequence, studies and clinical evidence indicate that impaired cognition affects not only cognitive performance but also emotional state, behavior, and day-to-day functioning, including the ability to perform basic and more complex, instrumental activities of daily living (Black & Rush, 2002; Dodge, Du, Saxton, & Ganguli, 2006). The increased heterogeneity observed in older adults' functioning and the increasing prevalence of dementia in very late life provide both challenges as well as the means by which to study successful aging and resiliency in later life.

In contrast to the normative age-related changes described above, dementia and mild cognitive impairment (MCI) are nonnormative and represent significant clinical problems. MCI is usually memory related and a suspected early indicator of dementia (Jorm et al., 2004; Peterson et al., 2001). An individual with MCI experiences subjective memory complaints accompanied by observed impairment; however, activities of daily living are not impaired and the individual is not demented (Peterson et al., 2001). MCI to dementia conversion rates range from 6 to 25% depending on assessment method and study duration (Peterson et al., 2001).

Alzheimer's disease accounts for 50 to 70% of dementia cases, and the characteristic symptom is memory loss for recent events (Alzheimer's Association, 2007). Dementia is linked with an increasing inability to perform activities of daily living. Dementia prevalence rates vary with age. Estimates of the prevalence of early-onset Alzheimer's disease and dementia are 200,000 among persons younger than 65 (Alzheimer's Association, 2007). In contrast, the Alzheimer's Association estimates that 1 in 8 individuals in the United States over the age of 65 have dementia or Alzheimer's disease; this rate dramatically increases among adults 85 and older to 1 in 2 persons. Increased risk associated with greater age raises the question as to the "eventuality" of dementia and the need to delineate risk factors associated with early and late disease contraction or expression. Further research is needed to make clear the transition from normal age-related cognitive changes to cognitive impairment and/or dementia.

A growing area of inquiry within cognitive aging research focuses on cognitive prevention and intervention. To date, intervention approaches have employed a variety of techniques, focusing on specific cognitive abilities (e.g., memory, reasoning), general cognitive processes (e.g., automatic processes), the role of emotions and motivation, as well as incorporation of social partners and everyday life stimuli and activities (Ball et al., 2002; Margrett & Willis, 2006; Park, Gutchess, Meade, & Stine-Morrow, 2007; Rebok, Carlson, & Langbaum, 2007). These interventions hold much promise in the effort to enhance and maintain cognitive acuity throughout adulthood and later life. Providers working both with middle-aged and older adults should be better educated regarding the impact of cognition on adults' day-to-day functioning as well as factors that lead to diminished cognitive abilities. Frequent screening beginning in midlife is essential to ensure early detection of cognitive impairment and to maximize treatment. From a policy perspective, funds and regulations are needed to support screening, prevention, and intervention efforts.

**SEE ALSO** Volume 3: *Aging; Dementias; Older Drivers.*


**BIBLIOGRAPHY**

Alzheimer's Association. (2007). *Alzheimer's disease facts and figures.* Retrieved January 28, 2008, from http://www.alz.org

Bäckman, L., Small, B. J., & Wahlin, Å. (2001). Aging and memory: Cognitive and biological perspectives. In J. E. Birren & K. W. Schaie (Eds.), *Handbook of the psychology of aging* (pp. 349–377). San Diego, CA: Academic Press.

Baddeley, A. (2007). *Working memory, thought, and action.* New York: Oxford University Press.

Ball, K., Berch, D. B, Helmers, K. F., Jobe, J. B., Leveck, M. D., Marsiske, M., et al. (2002). Effects of cognitive training interventions with older adults. *Journal of the American Medical Association, 288*(18), 2271–2281.

Bosworth, H. B., & Siegler, I. C. (2002). Terminal change in cognitive functioning: An updated review of longitudinal studies. *Experimental Aging Research, 28*(3), 299–315.

Black, S. A., & Rush, R. D. (2002). Cognitive and functional decline in adults aged 75 and older. *Journal of the American Geriatrics Society, 50*(12), 1978–1986.

Budson, A. E., & Price, B. H. (2005). Memory dysfunction. *New England Journal of Medicine, 352*(7), 692–699.

Carstensen, L. L., Mikels, J. A., & Mather, M. (2006). Aging and the intersection of cognition, motivation and emotion. In J. E. Birren & K. W. Schaie (Eds.), *Handbook of the psychology of aging* (6th ed., pp. 343–362). Amsterdam: Elsevier.

Christensen, H. (2001). What cognitive changes can be expected with normal ageing? *Australian and New Zealand Journal of Psychiatry, 35*(6), 768–775.

de Frias, C., M., Lövdén, M., Lindenberger, U., & Nilsson, L. G. (2007). Revisiting the dedifferentiation hypothesis with longitudinal multi-cohort data. *Intelligence, 35,* 381–392.

Diehl, M., Willis, S. L., & Schaie, K. W. (1995). Everyday problem solving in older adults: Observational assessment and cognitive correlates. *Psychology and Aging, 10,* 478–491.

Dodge, H. H., Du, Y., Saxton, J. A., & Ganguli, M. (2006). Cognitive domains and trajectories of functional independence in non-demented elderly. *The Journal of Gerontology: Medical Sciences, 61,* 1330–1337.

Flynn, J. R. (1987). Massive IQ gains in 14 nations: What IQ tests really measure. *Psychological Bulletin, 101,* 171–191.

Folstein, M. F., Folstein, S. E., & McHugh, P. R. (1975). Mini-Mental State: A practical method for grading the cognitive state of patients for the clinician. *Journal of Psychiatric Research, 12,* 189–198.

Gruber-Baldini, A. L, Schaie, K. W., & Willis, S. L. (1995). Similarity in married couples: A longitudinal study of mental abilities and rigidity-flexibility. *Journal of Personality and Social Psychology. 69*(1), 191–203.

Hess, T. M. (2006). Attitudes toward aging and their effects on behavior. In J. E. Birren & K. W. Schaie (Eds.), *Handbook of the psychology of aging* (6th ed., pp. 379–406). Burlington, MA: Elsevier Academic Press.

Jorm, A. F., Masaki, K. H., Davis, D. G., Hardman, J., Nelson, J., Markesbery, W. R., et al. (2004). Memory complaints in nondemented men predict pathologic diagnosis of Alzheimer disease. *Neurology, 63*(2), 1960–1961.

Li, K. Z. H., & Lindenberger, U. (2002). Connections among sensory, sensorimotor, and cognitive aging: Review of data and theories. *Neuroscience and Biobehavioral Reviews, 26*(7), 777–783.

Margrett, J. A., & Willis, S. L. (2006). In-home cognitive training with older married couples: Individual versus collaborative learning. *Aging, Neuropsychology, and Cognition, 13*(2), 176–195.

Marsiske, M., & Margrett, J. A. (2006). Everyday problem solving and decision making. In J. E. Birren & K. W. Schaie (Eds.), *Handbook of the psychology of aging* (6th ed., pp. 315–342). Burlington, MA: Elsevier Academic Press.

Marsiske, M., & Willis, S. L. (1995). Dimensionality of everyday problem solving in older adults. *Psychology and Aging, 10,* 269–283.

Orsini, A., Chiacchio, L., Cinque, M., Cocchiaro, C., Schiappa, O., & Grossi, D. (1986). Effects of age, education, and sex on two tests of immediate memory: A study of normal subjects from 20 to 99 years of age. *Perceptual and Motor Skills, 63,* 727–732.

Park, D. C., Gutchess, A. H., Meade, M. L., & Stine-Morrow, E. (2007). Improving cognitive function in older adults: Nontraditional approaches. *Journals of Gerontology, 62B,* 45–52.

Petersen, R. C., Stevens, J. C., Ganguli, M., Tangalos, E. G., Cummings, J. L., & DeKosky S. T. (2001). Early detection of dementia: Mild cognitive impairment (an evidence-based review): Report of the Quality Standards Subcommittee of the American Academy of Neurology. *Neurology, 56,* 1133–1142.

Poon, L. W., & Harrington, C. A. (2006). Commonalities in aging- and fitness-related impact on cognition. In L. W. Poon, W. Chodzko-Zajko, & P. D. Tomporowski (Eds.), *Active living, cognitive functioning, and aging* (pp. 33–50). Champaign, IL: Human Kinetics.

Rebok, G. W., Carlson, M. C., & Langbaum, J. B. S. (2007). Training and maintaining memory abilities in healthy older adults: Traditional and novel approaches. *The Journals of Gerontology, Series B, 62,* 53–61.

Rowe, D. C., & Rodgers, J. L. (2002). Expanding variance and the case of historical changes in IQ means: A critique of Dickens and Flynn (2001). *Psychological Review, 109,* 759–763.

Salthouse, T. A. (2000). Aging and measures of processing speed. *Biological Psychology, 54,* 35–54.

Schaie, K. W. (2005). *Developmental influences on adult intellectual development: The Seattle Longitudinal Study.* New York: Oxford University Press.

Sloan, F. A., & Wang, J. (2005). Disparities among older adults in measures of cognitive function by race and ethnicity. *Journal of Gerontology: Psychological Sciences, 60B,* P242–P250.

Starr, J. M., McGurn, B., Whiteman, M., Pattie, A., Whalley, L. J., & Deary, I. J. (2004). Life-long changes in cognitive ability are associated with prescribed medications in old age. *International Journal of Geriatric Psychiatry, 19,* 327–332.

Willis, S. L., & Schaie, K. W. (1988). Gender differences in spatial ability in old age: Longitudinal and intervention findings. *Sex Roles, 8,* 189–203.

Zacks, R. T., & Hasher, L. (1994). Directed ignoring: Inhibitory regulation of working memory. In D. Dagenbach & T. H.

Carr (Eds.), *Inhibitory processes in attention, memory, and language* (pp. 241–264). New York: Academic Press.

***Jennifer A. Margrett***
***Neha Deshpande-Kamat***

# COHORT

Perhaps the most fundamental premise of the life course perspective is that individuals are both producers and products of a complex historical and socioeconomic context through which their life experiences are shaped and understood. The concept of *cohort* is essential to this perspective in that it provides a mechanism for identifying and interpreting the potentially distinct collective characteristics of individuals who share a common year of birth. These distinct characteristics are commonly referred to as "cohort effects," and their empirical identification is a subject of considerable interest.

## DEFINITION AND USAGE

In the most general sense, *cohort* refers to a group of individuals that experiences an event during a common interval of time. For instance, students matriculating at a college in the same year are often referred to as the "entering cohort." In medicine and epidemiology, the term "cohort study" is used to refer to a study design in which subjects exposed to a treatment or having a particular condition are followed over time and compared to another group not exposed to the condition or treatment. In this example, the cohort is the group of people enrolled in the study at its inception and is defined by the exposure status.

In life course and human development research, the common time interval defining the cohort is often one calendar year, and the shared event is birth. Thus, a birth cohort (often shortened to just "cohort") is the group of people sharing a common year of birth. This is a rather specialized use of the term, and if the subject matter was automobiles or wine rather than people, the analogous term used would be "vintage." In the former cases, the defining event is production, while in the latter, it is birth. Similar to the way in which knowledge of a wine's year of production conveys some information about its characteristics, cohort membership is thought to index the unique historical period in which a group's common experiences are embedded.

Members of a birth cohort have the distinction of potentially experiencing a shared history inasmuch as they are the same age at any given point in time and thus share a common set of political, social, and cultural events at approximately the same point in the life cycle. This confounding of age and birth cohort at any given point in time sometimes leads those unfamiliar with the concepts to refer to an "age cohort." No expression could be more grating to the life course scholar's ear, and the term *age cohort* should always be avoided, for it confuses the source of the group's distinctiveness (i.e., does a particular group characteristic reflect the members' age or birth cohort?) and denies the significance of historical time in shaping life experiences. For example, in many

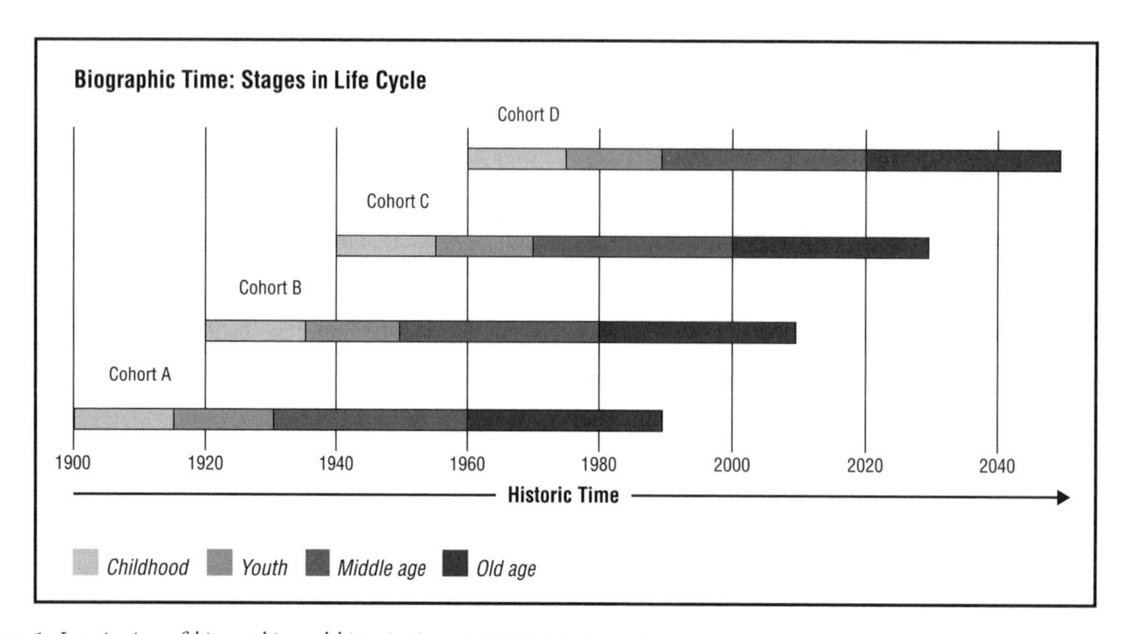


***Figure 1.*** *Interjection of biographic and historic time.* CENGAGE LEARNING, GALE.

areas of interest in the social sciences, 18-year-olds born in 1950 and observed in 1968 are likely much different than 18-year-olds born in 1990 and observed in 2008.

## HISTORICAL DEVELOPMENT: COHORTS AND COHORT EFFECTS

The work of Karl Mannheim (1952) can be credited with bringing the concept of cohort into modern social science and for developing the related idea of *generation* as well as Alwin and McCammon, 2003 for a discussion of the relationship between these concepts). In his work, Mannheim emphasized the role of events experienced early in life in shaping an individual's worldview, stating that "Even if the rest of one's life consisted of one long process of negation and destruction of the natural world view acquired in youth, the determining influence of these early impressions would still be predominant" (1952, p. 298). This idea is central to understanding cohort effects, which are the formative influences of life experiences shared by individuals having the same year of birth.

In his classic 1965 work, Norman Ryder elaborated the role of cohort in shaping social change, emphasizing the demographic procession of cohorts through the life course as a distinct mechanism for social change. Changes in the composition of the population brought on by the succession of early born cohorts by later ones, known as "cohort replacement," is a source of change in society when there are inter-cohort differences in the phenomenon of interest that endure over time. For example, much of the change in racial attitudes in the United States in the late 20th century is attributable to the dying out of earlier-born, more prejudiced cohorts, and their replacement by later-born, less prejudiced ones (Firebaugh & Davis, 1988). Ultimately, the stability of these cohort differences relies on the persistence of individuals' formative characteristics throughout their life spans—a phenomenon known as the *stability of individual differences.* Following from Mannheim, Ryder argues that cohort's place in the study of social change is based on the ideas that "transformations of the social world modify people of different ages in different ways," and that "the effects of these transformations are persistent" (p. 861).

As the works of Mannheim and Ryder reveal, the established view on the origin of cohort effects is that individuals go through a period of impressionable years during youth and young adulthood, and that experiences during these periods shape a variety of socio-individual characteristics: attitudes, beliefs, behaviors, and political orientations, among others. These youthful experiences then become the lens through which the remainder of their lives is experienced and interpreted. While the consequences of the formative experience(s) may differ throughout the life course, the basic idea of cohort effects remains the same, namely that the composition of the population is shaped by persistent birth cohort differences in the experience or interpretation of historical events.

## COHORT VS. GENERATION

Because of its multiple meanings, the term *generation* is frequently a source of confusion. While *generation* may legitimately be used as a kinship term referring to the lineage of individuals in a family, this usage is unrelated to *generations* as a cohort-based phenomenon. A generation is a group of birth cohorts, sometimes overlapping and indistinct with respect to temporal boundaries, that shares a distinctive culture and/or a self-conscious identity by virtue of having experienced the same historical events in the same way at roughly the same time in their lives. Obviously then, there is a common historical referent for cohorts and generations, but unlike *cohort,* a generation "involves more than mere co-presence" in historical and social events (Mannheim, 1952, p. 303). From a more contemporary sociological perspective, a generation is a "joint interpretive construction which insists upon and builds among tangible cohorts in defining a style recognized from outside and from within" (White, 1992, p. 31). As these theorists suggest, a sense of shared identity by its members and recognition of this identity by those outside the group are the essential components of a generation.

## CONTEMPORARY EXAMPLES

The social science literature is replete with examples of cohort effects. As discussed above, these effects commonly arise when a distinctive formative experience which members of a birth cohort (or set of birth cohorts) share shapes their perspectives throughout their lives. Major historical events such as war, economic turmoil, political protest, social upheaval, and technological transformation are frequently identified as sources of cohort effects. For example, people who grew up during the Great Depression of the 1930s have different ideas about money and economic institutions than those who grew up in more prosperous times (Elder, 1974). Other times, cohort differences are of a subtler nature and more diffuse in their origins. For example, it has been

***Greatest Generation.*** *Lines of unemployed people line up in sub-zero weather at a city relief kitchen set up in New York City on January 30, 1934 during the Great Depression. The generation that lived through the Great Depression is often referred to as the Greatest Generation.* AP IMAGES.

suggested that there was a decline in civic involvement in the late 20th century, and that this decline was, in part, attributable to the replacement of earlier-born cohorts of patriotic joiners with later-born and more cynically minded post–World War II cohorts (Putnam, 2000).

Variation in educational experiences and in the quantity and content of formal schooling contributes to cohort differences in a wide range of domains. Knowledge obtained during youth becomes a resource for future intellectual development, and shapes future social and economic opportunities. Given this, it is not surprising that cohort differences in cognitive performance are well documented. Perhaps the best-known example of a systematic cohort effect on cognitive test scores is the so-called "Flynn effect," which is the rise of average IQ test scores over time (Flynn, 1984). While Flynn concludes that a variety of environmental factors contribute to this rise, increases in educational attainment is seen as a substantial contributor. In the area of cognitive aging, significant cohort effects have also been identified. These effects are quite pronounced, and cohort differences may explain a substantial portion of what otherwise might be identified as age-related decline in vocabulary knowledge (Alwin & McCammon, 2001). Similarly, Schaie, Willis, and Pennak, examining longitudinal data (data collected from the same individuals at more than one point in time) from a broad array of cognitive domains, find cohort differences in both absolute levels and rates of change in cognitive performance and that these "cohort differences in intellectual abilities are shaped largely by changes in educational attainment..." (p. 64).

While educational, economic, and other social experiences are obviously important in understanding the nature of cohort effects, duration of exposure may also be an important factor in their strength. Examining the voting behavior of women after the 19th Amendment guaranteed women's suffrage in 1920, Firebaugh and Chen (1995) found an inverse relationship between the duration of women's exposure to political disenfranchisement and their subsequent likelihood of voting relative to their male counterparts. The gender difference in voting behavior was largest in cohorts reaching adulthood prior to the passage of the amendment, and declined to nonexistence in cohorts born after 1925. Many women growing up during the period when women were not permitted to vote retained this norm and remained nonvoters even after the enactment of women's suffrage, whereas later-born women, having never been exposed to gender discrimination in voting rights, were just as likely to vote as men from their same birth cohorts.

Birth cohorts can also be distinctive and exert a unique influence based on their demographic characteristics, such as relative size (i.e., their size relative to other birth cohorts). Easterlin (1987) argues that members of the numerically large birth cohorts making up the post–World War II Baby Boom are at a significant socioeconomic disadvantage relative to members of earlier-born cohorts, because of the effect of their cohort's' size on the opportunity structure. Individuals in large cohorts may experience greater psychological stress in their youth, be less likely to marry, and be more likely to postpone having children (Easterlin, 1987).

### CONCLUSION

Individuals are both cause and consequence of the social context in which their lives are embedded. An individual's year of birth—or *birth cohort*—is the metric used to identify the particular historical context in which they live. In the words of Norman Ryder, "(t)he members of any cohort are entitled to participate in only one slice of life—their unique location in the stream of history" (Ryder, 1965, p. 844). Cohort effects and the phenomenon of cohort replacement demonstrate the reciprocal relationship between individual and society by documenting the role of historically bounded formative experiences in individuals' subsequent interpretation of, and action in, the world around them. Cohort effects are well documented in a variety of domains, and may arise from a number of sources, including economic, political, and educational experiences. Life course scholars are well served to consider birth cohort, and thus, historical context, in their explorations of the interplay between the individual and his environment.

**SEE ALSO** Volume 2: *Baby Boom Cohort; Mannheim, Karl;* Volume 3: *Age, Period, Cohort Effects; Ryder, Norman.*

**BIBLIOGRAPHY**

Alwin, D. F., & McCammon, R. J. (2001). Aging, cohorts, and verbal ability. *Journal of Gerontology: Social Sciences, 56B,* S151–S161.

Alwin, D. F., & McCammon, R. J. (2003). Generations, cohorts and social change. In J. T. Mortimer & M. J. Shanahan (Eds.), *Handbook of the life course* (pp. 23–49). New York: Kluwer Academic/Plenum.

Easterlin, R. A. (1987). *Birth and fortune: The impact of numbers on personal welfare.* (2nd ed.). Chicago: University of Chicago Press.

Elder, G. H., Jr. (1974). *Children of the great depression.* Chicago: University of Chicago Press.

Firebaugh, G., & Chen, K. (1995). Vote turnout of nineteenth amendment women: The enduring effect of disenfranchisement. *American Journal of Sociology, 100,* 972–996.

Firebaugh, G., & Davis, K. (1988). Trends in antiblack prejudice, 1972–1984: Region and cohort effects. *American Journal of Sociology, 94,* 251–272.

Flynn, J. R. (1984). The mean IQ of Americans: Massive gains. *Psychological Bulletin, 95,* 29–51.

Mannheim, K. (1952). The problem of generations. In P. Kecskemeti (Ed.), *Essays in the sociology of knowledge* (pp. 276–322). Boston: Routledge & Kegan Paul.

Putnam, R. D. (2000). *Bowling alone: The collapse and revival of American community.* New York: Simon & Schuster.

Ryder, N. B. (1965). The cohort as a concept in the study of social change. *American Sociological Review, 30,* 843–861.

Schaie, K. W., Willis, S. L., & Pennak, S. (2005). An historical framework for cohort differences in intelligence. *Research in Human Development, 2,* 43–67.

White, H. (1992). Succession and generations: Looking back on chains of opportunity. In H. A. Becker (Ed.), *Dynamics of cohort and generations research* (pp. 31–51). Amsterdam: Thesis.

***Ryan J. McCammon***

## CONSUMPTION, LATER LIFE

**SEE** Volume 2: *Consumption, Adulthood and Later Life.*

## CREATIVITY, LATER LIFE

Creativity is built into the human species, and it is designed to last throughout the entire life cycle (Andreasen, 2005; Cohen, 2000). Howard Gardiner (1993b) who provided information on *multiple intelligences* also amplified the understanding of creativity presenting in some individuals as *Big C* creativity, and in others as *little c* creativity, but in each case its creative essence is real and significant. Big C applies to the extraordinary accomplishments of great artists, scientists, and inventors. These forms of creativity typically change fields of thought and the course of progress, as with Albert Einstein's (1879–1955) theory of relativity, Edison's electrical inventions, and Pablo Picasso's (1881–1973) and Georges Braque's (1882–1963) cubism.

Creativity with a little *c* is grounded in the diversity of everyday activities and accomplishments. "Every person has certain areas in which he or she has a special interest," Gardner explains. "It could be something they do at work the way they write memos or their craftsmanship at a factory—or the way they teach a lesson or sell something. After working at it for a while they can get to be pretty good—as good as anybody whom they know in their immediate world."

Sometimes something little *c* can evolve to big *C* creativity, as with Maria Ann Smith (1799–1870) who during her 60s in the 1860s was experimenting in Australia with different fruit seeds. She took great satisfaction in this work, especially when something different grew—something new that she brought into existence that was valued. One of these successes was a hardy French crabapple seedling from which developed the late-ripening Granny Smith apple, bearing her name, which because of its outstanding taste and keeping qualities formed the bulk of Australia's apple exports for many years.

## DEFINITION OF CREATIVITY

Creativity is difficult to define because it is hard to conceptualize. Is it a product or a process? If it is a product, is it tangible, like a painting, or intangible, like an idea? To encompass each of these possibilities and more, the following definition is offered, borrowing on views of Rollo May (1975), Howard Gardiner (1993a), and Mihaly Csikszentmihalyi (1996): *Creativity is bringing something new into existence that is valued* (Cohen, 2000).

## THE CREATIVITY EQUATION

The *creativity equation* ($C = me^2$) represents an attempt to make an elusive concept—creativity—more graspable (Cohen, 2000). The equation states that creativity ($C$) is the result of one's mass ($m$) of knowledge, multiplied by the effects of one's two dimensions of experience ($e^2$). The first dimension is an individual inner world experience reflecting psychological and emotional growth over the years. The second dimension is the outer world experience reflecting accumulating life experience and wisdom in growing older. All these elements interact in a synergy that sets the stage for creativity. The equation also reflects the positive influence of aging where through the passage of time one is enabled to acquire more knowledge along with increased outer world experience and inner world growth. From a lighter perspective, the $me^2$ is what one realizes when looking at the creative side of oneself in the mirror—"Hey, that's *me* to a higher level!"

## CATEGORIES OF CREATIVITY

Keep in mind that creativity applies not just to artists but is also apparent in all aspects of life, including the social realm where over the history of civilization older adults have assumed the creative role of *keepers of the culture,* transmitting accumulated knowledge, traditions, and perspective.

In general discussions of creativity and aging, to the extent its existence was acknowledged, creative expression in later life was often trivialized as being narrow and simple in form. In reality, not only is creativity relevant and prevalent with aging, it shows itself in a depth and breadth of forms. Consider the following four basic patterns of creativity in the second half of life:

- *Continuing Creativity:* This was certainly the case for Herbert Block (1909–2001), better known as Herblock, the *Washington Post* cartoonist, whose nationally syndicated cartoons informed and enriched American culture for more than 70 years. His first cartoon appeared when he was in his 20s; his last was published less than two months before he died at age 91.
- *Changing Creativity* (while changing creativity can be considered a variant of continuing creativity, it is distinguished by the fundamental change in creative direction that the individual takes as he or she ages): The great mathematician and philosopher Bertrand Russell (1872–1970), for instance, focused tightly on mathematics in his youth and middle age. When he was 42 he and Alfred North Whitehead (1861–1947) published the *Principia Mathematica*, which remains a masterpiece of mathematical logic and synthesis. As he grew older his focus shifted to deeper issues, particularly philosophy, and the many social ills of his time. At the age of 73 he published his renowned work, *A History of Western Philosophy* after which he received the Nobel Prize in Literature, and he remained passionately involved in issues of peace and justice until he died at 98.
- *Commencing Creativity:* Some people first significantly tap into their creative potential around age 65; they are often referred to as *late bloomers*. This author's own ideas about creativity with aging and especially about late bloomers blossomed after a visit to a retrospective exhibit of a half-century of folk art at Washington's Corcoran Gallery of Art in Washington, D.C. The works of 20 of the most highly regarded African American folk artists produced from 1930 to 1980

***Grandma Moses.*** *Artist Anna Mary Robertson Moses, known as Grandma Moses, works on one of her paintings at her home in Eagle Bridge, NY, September 1960, the year before she died at age 101. Grandma Moses is one of the most famous examples of someone who found a new creative outlet late in life.* AP IMAGES.

were exhibited. Reading the artists' brief biographies revealed that of the 20 exhibitors, 16—80%—had begun painting or reached a recognizable mature phase as artists after the age of 65; 30% were 80 years of age or older (Livingston & Beardsley, 1982). The folk art story is particularly important because whenever examples are given of important art by older artists such as Pablo Picasso (1881–1973), Titian (born Tiziano Vecelli, lived ca. 1485–1576), or Georgia O'Keeffe (1887–1986), many fire a reflex response that they are "outliers, exceptions from the rule, not typical of aging." But with folk art, older artists are the rule—across the racial and ethnic diversity of our culture (Hartigan, 1990). With their prominence, their work cannot be diminished as uncommon events. Whenever one can find a field, any field, dominated by older people—such as folk art—then one can no longer deny or trivialize creative potential with aging. And what a statement they make with their numbers about it truly being never too late in life to be creative; they make the ultimate case for late blooming. Grandma Moses (1860–1961) who only at 78 turned her serious attention to painting, with her work selected for 15 international exhibits over the next 23 years until she was 101, was but one of a huge crowd of older folk artists with a major impact. William Edmondson (ca. 1882–1951), who had been a janitor until 65 when he lost his job, turned then full-time to sculpture. Louise Dahl-Wolfe, a photographer, captivated by Edmondson's work, sent a portfolio of images of his sculptures to the Museum of Modern Art (MOMA) in New York. The result was that at 67, Edmondson became the first African American artist in the history of the MOMA to have a solo exhibit, opening the doors to generations that followed (Livingston & Beardsley, 1982).

- *Creativity connected with loss:* There is nothing romantic about loss, but the human condition and the human spirit are such that when loss occurs, it is in our nature to try to transcend it by tapping into unknown or underdeveloped other capacities that we possess. Such is captured in the life and work of William Carlos Williams (1883–1963) of Paterson, New Jersey. Carlos Williams was a pediatrician who also wrote poetry. But a stroke in his 60s left him unable to continue practicing medicine and sent him into a depression that required a year of hospitalization. He gradually emerged from that trauma and loss, turning full-time to poetry; the collection was published in his book *Pictures from Brueghel and Other Poems* when he was 79 years old. It was awarded a Pulitzer Prize. In his later-life poetry, William Carlos Williams wrote about "old age that adds as it takes away."

### PSYCHOLOGICAL GROWTH AND DEVELOPMENT WITH AGING

Psychological growth and development sets the stage for creative expression with aging. Psychoanalytic research has found that older adults are more in touch with their inner psychological life than at any point in the life cycle (Maduro, 1974). What an asset in a creative and artistic sense to be more in touch with one's inner world that negotiates access to potential in new ways as we continue to develop with aging.

Four recently described, overlapping developmental phases in the second half of life set the stage for positive change and creative expression (Cohen, 2004, 2005):

## PRAGMATIC CREATIVITY AND AGING

Pragmatic creativity is a form of creativity that researchers describe as increasing with aging (Cohen, 2005). In his mid-70s Howard Miller, the author's father-in-law, illustrated very well the concept of pragmatic creativity with aging. Stuck in a snowstorm with his wife and unable to find a cab to bring them back home, Howard spotted the steamy windows of a pizza parlor and experienced the flash of a creative solution. He took his wife's arm, carefully crossed the slushy road, entered the pizza place, walked up to the counter, and ordered a large cheese pizza for home delivery. He then asserted, "There's one more thing." "What's that?" asked the clerk, to which Howard convincingly replied, "I'd like you to deliver us with it." And they did.

Two key factors explain the greater frequency of pragmatic creativity with aging: (a) the influence of accumulated life experience over time—reflected in the creativity equation, and (b) the influence of the *liberation phase* ("What can they do to me?"), as illustrated by Howard. This is the other part of the $e^2$ in the creativity equation. The flash of a creative solution that Howard experienced reflects "the New Senior Moment" (Cohen, in press).

**Midlife Reevaluation Phase** The first of four recently described, overlapping developmental phases in the second half of life generally occurs during one's early 40s to late 50s: Plans and actions are shaped by a sense of crisis or quest, although considerably more by quest. Midlife is a powerful time for the expression of human potential because it combines the capacity for insightful reflection with a powerful desire to create meaning in life. This quest is catalyzed in midlife by seriously confronting for the first time one's sense of mortality; on passing the midpoint in the life cycle, one contemplates time left instead of time gone by. This dynamic new inner climate becomes a catalyst for uncovering unrealized creative sides of ourselves, as reflected in Alex Haley's midlife quest that culminated in his publication of *Roots* (1976).

**Liberation Phase** This phase usually emerges from one's mid-50s to mid-70s. Plans and actions are shaped by a new sense of personal freedom to speak one's mind and to do what needs to be done. There are often mounting feelings of "if not now, when," "why not," and "what can they do to me?" that foster a sense of inner liberation. With retirement or partial retirement, common during these years, comes a new experience of external liberation and a feeling of finally having time to experiment with something different.

**Summing-Up Phase** This phase comes most frequently in one's late 60s into one's 80s—or beyond. Plans and actions are shaped by the desire to find larger meaning in the story of one's life as a person looks back, reexamines, and sums up what has happened. This process motivates people to give of the wisdom they have accrued throughout their lives. In the role of keepers-of-the-culture, people who reach this phase begin to share their lessons and fortunes through autobiography and personal story telling, philanthropy, community activism, volunteerism, and other forms of giving back. With Martha Graham (1894–1991), giving back was through choreography from her mid-70s to mid-90s. It is also a time to deal with unresolved conflicts and unfinished business in manners that motivate us to develop creative new strategies.

**Encore Phase** This phase can develop from one's late 70s to the end of one's years. Plans and actions are shaped by the desire to restate and reaffirm major themes in one's life but also to explore novel variations on those themes and to further attend to unfinished business or unresolved conflicts. The desire to live well to the very end has a positive impact on family and community and often influences decisions to have family reunions and other events. The Delany sisters (Sarah [1889–1999] and Bessie [1891–1995]) after a filled century of life, engaged in an encore—a story about themselves with a title that set the stage for an encore: *The Delaney Sisters: The First 100 Years*, which became a best-selling book.

### CONCLUSION

"In the past few years, I have made a thrilling discovery... that until one is over 60, one can never really learn the secret of living. One can then begin to live, not simply with the intense part of oneself, but with one's entire being."

—Pulitzer Prize-winning novelist Ellen Glasgow

**SEE ALSO** Volume 3: *Lifelong Learning; Wisdom.*

**BIBLIOGRAPHY**


Andreasen, N. C. (2005). *The creating brain.* Washington, DC: Dana Press.

Cohen, G. D. (2000). *The creative age: Awakening human potential in the second half of life.* New York: Avon Books/ Harper Collins Publishers.

Cohen, G. D. (2004). United the heart and mind: Human Development in the second half of life. *Mind Alert.* San Francisco, CA: American Society on Aging.

Cohen, G. D. (2005). *The mature mind: The positive power of the aging brain.* New York: Basic Books.

Cohen, G. D (in press). Creativity and aging. In T. Cole, R. Kastenbaum, & R. Ray (Eds.), *A guide to humanistic studies in aging* (3rd ed.).

Csikszentmihalyi, M. (1996). *Creativity.* New York: Harper Collins.

Gardner, H. (1993a). *Creating minds.* New York: Basic Books,

Gardner H. (1993b). *Frames of mind: The theory of multiple intelligences.* New York: Basic Books.

Haley, A. (1976). *Roots.* New York: Doubleday.

Harrison, C. L. (1980). Creative arts for older people in the community. *American Journal of Art Therapy, 19*, 99–101.

Livingston, J., & Beardsley, J. (Eds.). (1982). *Black folk art in America.* Jackson: University of Mississippi Press.

Maduro, R. (1974). Artistic creativity and aging in India. *International Journal of Aging and Human Development, 5*, 303–329.

May, R. (1975). *The courage to create.* New York: Bantam Books.


*Gene D. Cohen*

# CRIME AND VICTIMIZATION, LATER LIFE

The victimization experiences of older adults, defined as persons age 65 and older who have suffered injury or loss due to a crime, is important to the study of the life course and a pressing social concern. Developmental changes associated with advancing age and changing social circumstances occurring in later life affect key indicators of well-being, including health and financial status as well as personal safety. Research has found that the likelihood of victimization consistently differs by age. It also shows that the form victimization takes varies over the life course, and reflects the interrelationship between victims, offenders, the contexts in which crimes occur, and the degree of physical, psychological, and financial harm. The likelihood of being victimized generally follows an age curve—peaking in late adolescence and declining with older age. A life-course understanding considers an individuals' changing social roles over the life span as well as cohort, historical, and cultural differences that impact the relationships between age and victimization.

Most of what is known about victimization in later life comes from victim surveys including the National Crime Victimization Survey, an annual survey of U.S. households of persons 12 years and older, and the British Crime Survey, a nationally representative household survey of adults 16 and older living in England and Wales. These surveys provide information about victimization experiences among older persons and the households in which they reside. A chief finding is older adults are less likely to become victims of violent crimes than persons under the age of 65—a pattern that holds from 1993 to 2006 in the United States and the United Kingdom (Klaus, 2005; Nichols, Kershaw and Walker 2007; Rand and Catalano, 2007).

Similarly, households headed by an older adult reported lower levels of property victimizations compared to households headed by persons under 65 in both the United States and the United Kingdom. In one offense category older adults in the United States had similar victimization rates as persons under the age of 65—personal larceny which includes purse snatching and pocket picking (Klaus, 2005). In 2006 older adults made up 14% of the U.S. resident population 12 years and older and comprised less than 1% of violent and property victimizations (Rand & Catalano, 2007). Among older adults in the United States, violent and property victimization varied across social categories with higher rates found among males and Blacks ages 65 to 74, and households headed by an older adult with lower family income, city residence, and renting residence (Klaus, 2005).

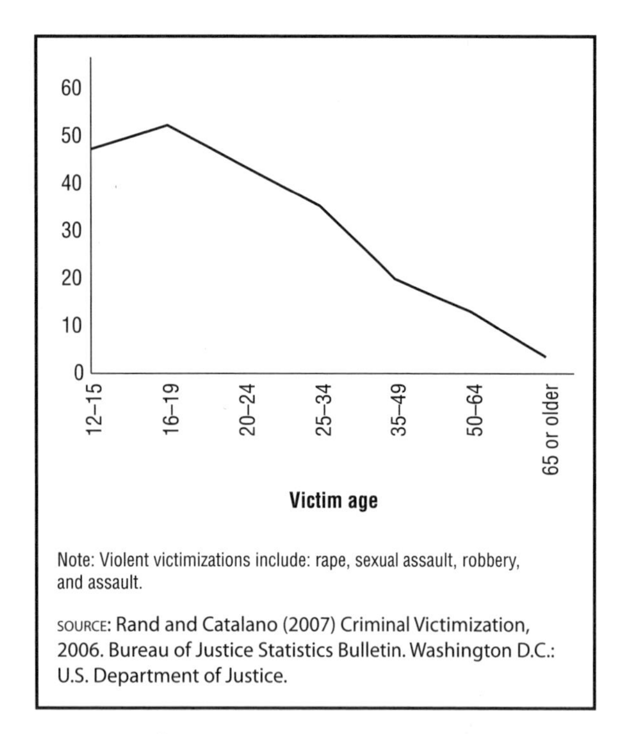


Note: Violent victimizations include: rape, sexual assault, robbery, and assault.

SOURCE: Rand and Catalano (2007) Criminal Victimization, 2006. Bureau of Justice Statistics Bulletin. Washington D.C.: U.S. Department of Justice.

***Figure 1.*** *Violent victimization rate, 2006, per person age 12 years or older.* CENGAGE LEARNING, GALE.

Persons age 65 or older were disproportionately affected by property crimes compared to younger persons. About 9 in 10 victimizations of older adults in the United States were property crimes, including household burglary, motor vehicle theft, and other theft, compared to about 4 in 10 victimizations among younger persons (Rand & Catalano, 2007). Older persons were about as likely as those under age 65 to be victims of personal larceny with contact, including purse snatching (Klaus, 2005). The violent victimization rate of older adults in 2006—including rape, sexual assault, robbery, and aggravated and simple assaults—was about 4 victimizations per 1,000 U.S. residents age 65 and over, compared with 42 victimizations per 1,000 for persons between the ages of 12 and 34 and 17 victimizations per 1,000 for persons between the ages of 35 and 64 (Rand & Catalano, 2007).

Older persons are more likely to be victimized in or near their home and in the daylight hours (Klaus, 2005). In responding to nonfatal violent attacks, older persons in the United States are less likely to resist, about as likely to receive serious injury, and about as likely to be confronted with an armed offender as younger persons (Klaus, 2005). In the United Kingdom, and the United States, older persons are also more likely to report violent incidents of crime than their younger counterparts (Klaus, 2005; Chivite-Matthews & Maggs, 2002). Despite older persons being less likely to experience criminal victimization, fear of crime in the United Kingdom is reported at similar levels among older and younger victims; levels among older women are greater than those reported by older men (Nichols, Kershaw, & Walker, 2007).

Researchers have sought to explain differences in victimization risk by age and other social groupings, including gender, ethnicity, and social class. Lifestyle theory attributes the lower risk of victimization of older persons to differences in lifestyles that decreases exposure to settings associated with greater risk. Examples of settings and lifestyle routines associated with increased risk of victimization include working outside the home, using public transportation, residing in the city, frequenting bars, and going out in public in the evenings. Situational explanations identify contexts that specifically put older persons at higher risk due to the absence of a guardian such as a police officer, or cohabiting family member or roommate. For example, older adults residing alone in crime-prone urban areas less patrolled by police would face greater risks than adults living in more protected contexts.

Importantly, certain contexts are unique to older adults and less understood with respect to victimization occurrence and impact. This includes situations where the older adult is dependent on others—often due to diminishing mental or physical capacities brought on by aging. Unscrupulous caretakers may financially exploit older adults by cashing checks without permission, stealing money and property, and forging and coercing signatures. Older victims may be reticent to report incidents to the police out of concern that it would get a family member in trouble, embarrassment, or out of fear of retaliation from those they depend on for care. Loneliness and isolation of the older adult may also increase susceptibility to being a victim in cases where perpetrators seek out older persons by telephone, mail, and door-to-door solicitation for various types of consumer frauds and identity theft. Further, as health care needs increase, the older person will be more likely to seek care and be subject to charges for unnecessary or unperformed tests, nursing home abuses, misrepresentation of services or quality, and fraudulent medical equipment sales with implications for physical, psychological, and financial harm.

The relatively low property and violent victimization rate of older adults detracts from the potential for serious impact on the aged as well as the alternative contexts unique to older adults where victimizations may go undetected or unreported. A future research agenda on the topic of older adults and crime and victimization includes: improving measurement of victimization by focusing attention on offenses that impact older adults including financial exploitation, neglect, and abuse; extending existing victimization surveys to include nonhousehold, institutional populations such as nursing homes; design more rigorous panel data collections to more effectively disentangle age, cohort, and period effects on criminal victimization over the life span; and developing age-specific strategies for law enforcement and victim service providers that address the needs of the older population from both health and criminal justice policy perspectives (Lachs, Bachman, & Williams, 2004)

**SEE ALSO** Volume 2: *Domestic Violence;* Volume 3: *Elder Abuse and Neglect.*


**BIBLIOGRAPHY**

Chivite-Matthews, N., & Maggs, P. (2002). *Crime, policing, and justice: The experience of older people.* London: Home Office. Retrieved June 18, 2008, from http://www.homeoffice.gov.uk/rds/pdfs2/hosb802.pdf

Klaus, P. (2005). *Crimes against persons age 65 and older, 1993–2002.* Washington, DC: Bureau of Justice Statistics. Retrieved June 18, 2008, from http://www.ojp.usdoj.gov/bjs/pub/pdf/cpa6502.pdf

Lachs, M., Bachman, R., & Williams, C. (2004). Older adults as crime victims, perpetrators, witnesses, and complainants. *Journal of Elder Abuse & Neglect,* 16, 25-40.

Nichols, S., Kershaw, C., & Walker, A. (Eds.). (2007). *Crime in England and Wales, 2006/2007.* London: Home Office. Retrieved June 18, 2008, from http://www.homeoffice.gov.uk/rds/pdfs07/hosb1107.pdf

Rand, M., & Catalano, S. (2007). *Criminal victimization, 2006.* Washington, DC: Bureau of Justice Statistics. Retrieved June 18, 2008, from http://www.ojp.usdoj.gov/bjs/pub/pdf/cv06.pdf


***Mark Motivans***

# CULTURAL CAPITAL, LATER LIFE

**SEE** Volume 1: *Cultural Capital.*

# CULTURAL IMAGES, LATER LIFE

In contemporary technological society cultural views of aging are influenced by and reflected in media portrayals, which provide a snapshot of the aging process and provide a cultural perspective on that process. Cultural images are representations of individuals, groups, and society that are captured by a communication event. That event can be a simple picture, a television program, a speech, or a song; essentially any form of communication can serve as a cultural representation.

## NATURE AND EFFECTS OF CULTURAL REPRESENTATIONS

Cultural representations are important because they influence the way people view other social groups, other cultures, and even themselves; media representations serve as socialization mechanisms related to social groups. For example, exposure to television's portrayals of women in traditional roles is associated with children's development of stereotypical sex-role attitudes (Kimball, 1986). The ways in which viewers perceive other social groups is influenced by television portrayals of those groups (Harwood, 1999, Mastro, 2003). Furthermore, portrayals of social groups in the media have consequences for individuals who belong to social groups, who may come to endorse or reject particular ideas about their groups through exposure to the media (Harwood & Roy, 2005).

Additionally, media images influence the specific cognitive schemas people develop to process information about the world around them. Cognitive schemas are mental structures such as stereotypes that help individuals organize how they think about people and situations. When people are exposed to new messages, their schemas are modified (Schneider, 2004). If media images of older adults are negative, a negative stereotype or schema is likely to develop (Robinson, Gustafson, & Popovich, 2008). The activation of negative stereotypes in perceptions of older adults in turn influences communication with older adults and can lead to age-adapted communication strategies such as patronizing or demeaning communication directed at older people (Hummert, 1994, Hummert, Garstka, Ryan, & Bonnesen, 2004). The activation of age-adapted communication that is based on negative stereotypes can occur even in close family relationships such as grandparent-grandchild relationships (Anderson, Harwood, & Hummert, 2005). Thus, the potential impact of cultural images on people's interactions with one another provides a strong reason for examining the representations of older adults in multiple forms of media.

## PORTRAYALS OF AGING IN MEDIA

Research on media portrayals of aging has focused mainly on prime-time television, daytime television, television advertising, and print advertising, primarily in the United States. That research has examined the presence of older adults in media, the role prominence of older adults in media, and images of aging. The most common form of research works by counting older adult characters and comparing their numbers to those in the population.

Older adult characters are defined in a variety of ways in this research (which has been something of a detriment to effective comparisons across studies). Common methods include defining a range of physical features that define old age (e.g., gray hair, noticeably wrinkled skin, use of a walking cane, etc.), defining based on relational roles (e.g., being a grandparent), or simply defining based on chronological age (e.g., cut-offs from 50 to 65 have been used). Coders demonstrate substantial levels of reliability on all these tasks. One goal for this research area should be to standardize a definition of what counts as an older character. We suspect that definitions based on chronological age are least susceptible to bias; we would advocate for work to consider multiple age groups of older adults (e.g., distinguishing 60 to 70 from 70 and above) and to avoid including characters in their 50s from consideration as "older."

In the context of age distribution estimates from census data, older adults consistently are underrepresented in prime-time television programming (Robinson & Skill, 1995, Harwood & Anderson, 2002), television advertising (Hiemstra, Goodman, Middlemiss, Vosco, & Ziegler, 1983, Miller, Leyell, & Mazachek, 2004, Roy & Harwood, 1997), and advertising in national magazines (Gantz, Gartenberg, & Rainbow, 1990). Older adult women are particularly underrepresented relative to older men (Signorielli & Bacue, 1999). Several authors have concluded that this skewed representation of older women reflects a disproportionate value placed on youth for women (Gerbner, Gross, Signorielli, & Morgan, 1980). In contrast, J. Harwood and K. Anderson (2002) found that older adult men and older adult women were equally underrepresented compared with census estimates, although young adult women were found to be overrepresented relative to middle-aged women, again suggesting a bias toward youth for women.

Studies of role prominence examine whether older adults are portrayed as central characters in television shows and advertisements. Researchers have explored major roles, minor roles, and background roles in various forms of television programming. Most older adult characters in television advertisements play minor or background roles (Roy & Harwood, 1997, Swayne & Greco, 1987, Robinson, 1998). For example, A. Roy and Harwood (1997) determined that more than 50% of older adult characters in television advertisements appear in background roles. However, the percentage of older adult characters in major roles increases when the advertised product targets older adults (Robinson, 1998).

Harwood and Anderson (2002) found that the role prominence of older adult characters in prime-time comedies and dramas does not differ significantly across age groups. However, as female characters age, they become less significant to the plot compared with male characters (Gerbner et al., 1980, Vernon, Williams, Phillips, & Wilson, 1990). J. Robinson and T. Skill (1995) noted that peripheral and minor characters may be more revealing of cultural stereotypes in light of the limited ability for development of depth and complexity in those characters and the need for such characters to serve a "quick and dirty" story function. The current television landscape does not offer many older people in lead roles, but examples from the past include *Matlock*'s Andy Griffith and *Murder, She Wrote*'s Angela Lansbury. A character like the grandfather on *The Simpson's* would qualify as a supporting character, while truly peripheral characters typically have one-off background roles (e.g., a store clerk who is only seen once and says a single line).

Studies of the quality of specific images or portrayals focus on personality traits, cognitive abilities, activities and occupations, physical features, and age stereotypes related to older characters. Much of this research has found negative portrayals of older adults (Gerbner et al., 1980, Harris & Feinberg, 1977). For example, S. R. Stern and D. E. Mastro (2004) found that older adults are substantially less likely to be portrayed in occupational roles than are younger characters; their research also showed that female characters suffer particularly on this front, with virtually no older women being shown in productive occupational roles. Of course, these representations might accurately reflect levels of labor force participation among older women; nonetheless, they do also serve as powerful messages about expectations for this group and for future generations as they age.

Other researchers have uncovered more positive portrayals in prime-time television programming (Bell, 1992, Dail, 1988), cartoons (Robinson & Anderson, 2006), and television advertising (Miller et al., 2004, Roy & Harwood, 1997). For example, J. Bell (1992) focused on the prime-time television shows most watched by older adults and found a combination of positive (e.g., powerful, affluent, healthy, active, admired) and negative (e.g., eccentric, foolish, comical) stereotypical portrayals. P. W. Dail (1988) found a similar pattern of positive and negative portrayals in the perceived cognitive ability of older adult characters. Generally, the older adult characters were seen to have positive mental orientation and verbal interaction but had moments of disorientation, confusion, or forgetfulness. This research focused on a very narrow slice of programming rather than the broad areas of programming examined in studies demonstrating negative portrayals.

Research on television advertising has found that older adults generally are portrayed positively but not as positively as other age groups (Miller et al., 2004, Robinson, 1998, Swayne & Greco, 1987). For example, Roy and Harwood (1997) found that older adults were portrayed as strong, happy, active, and lucid. However, T. E. Robinson (1998) found that the target of the advertisement played a role in the way older adults were portrayed. He examined facial expressions, personal characteristics, and behaviors of older adult characters and found that older adults generally are portrayed as mean, irritable, or grumpy, but are presented as happy when the target of the advertisement is other older adults. Advertisements targeting older adults include products such as medicine, mobility aids, and emergency alerts. Some of these studies reach conclusions about broadly positive portrayals of older adults without doing a relevant comparative examination of younger characters (Harwood, 2007). For instance, T. Robinson and C. Anderson (2006) found predominantly positive portrayals of older characters in cartoons but did not examine younger characters to determine whether those characters are portrayed even more positively. While research has not examined longitudinal trends, reviews of this literature indicate very little in the way of trends towards increasing or more positive portrayals (J. Robinson, Skill, & Turner, 2004).

Most researchers who explore images of aging in media use a quantitative content analysis method. Researchers record a representative sample of programming and analyze the quantity and quality of portrayals through the use of objective coding of characters by independent coders. However, Harwood (2000) took a different methodological approach and provided a textual analysis of one intergenerational interaction in the show *Frasier*. *Frasier* portrays the interactions between the divorced psychiatrist Dr. Frasier Crane; his psychiatrist brother, Niles; and their father, Martin, a retired police officer. Harwood's analysis demonstrated that this intergenerational interaction included a high level of age salience. The intergenerational bonding that occurred demonstrated a duality of tension between portraying the older adult as counterstereotypical and simultaneously using the stereotype of older adults as forgetful to create humor in the interaction. Thus, although the older adult character generally is portrayed positively, Harwood argues that the lurking incoherence of the portrayal is problematic because it relies on and reinforces the negative stereotypes of aging. Harwood and Giles (1992) reached similar conclusions concerning (counter)-stereotypical portrayals in *The Golden Girls*, which focuses on three retired women who live together in Florida, along with the mother of one of the retirees.

## EFFECTS OF MEDIA IMAGES ON VIEWERS

The effects of media portrayals of aging can be divided into effects on older and younger viewers. A concern in regard to older viewers has been with the effects on their own orientation and attitudes toward aging. M. M. Donlon, O. Ashman, and B. R. Levy (2005), for instance, examined the long-term effects of media consumption by measuring an estimate of life-time television consumption—they multiplied number of years of television viewing by the average number of hours viewed in the current year. They found that older individuals (age 60 to 92) with larger life-span exposure to television have significantly more negative stereotypes of aging than do those with less television exposure (e.g., they were more likely to rate other elders as grumpy or senile). Television exposure accounted for more than 10% of the variance in negative stereotyping, more than did health, depression, education, or age. This research illustrates the potential for television to reinforce self-stereotyping among older adults and ultimately lead to more negative experiences of aging.

Experimental studies have examined whether specific types of portrayals affect different types of older people in different ways. M-L. Mares and J. Cantor (1992) examined whether positive versus negative portrayals of older adults affected depression scores among lonely and non-lonely older viewers. Their findings indicated that older people who are not lonely are made more depressed by seeing negative media images of older people (e.g., images portraying an older person as depressed and socially isolated). In contrast, the same images made lonely older people less depressed. The second finding is explained by the authors in terms of social comparison processes: For individuals who are experiencing problems in their lives, seeing that they are not alone and that others are similarly isolated may serve a comforting function, conveying the message that their distress is not unique to them. This work demonstrates that not all older people respond to portrayals of older adults in the same manner and thus draws attention to the fact that an ideal portrayal of older adults on television will be characterized not by simple positivity but by diversity.

Similar concerns exist in regard to younger people. Gerbner et al. (1980) examined whether overall television consumption is associated with perceptions of the prevalence of older people in the population. As might be expected in light of the data on underrepresentation presented above, teens who viewed a lot of television tended to see older adults as constituting a smaller proportion of the total population compared with those who watched less television. These heavy television viewers also had more negative attitudes about aging. The effect sizes here are small, and there has been discussion about whether they persist when other factors are statistically controlled (Passuth & Cook, 1985).

## THEORETICAL FRAMEWORKS

There are relatively limited theoretical frameworks to utilize in examining the content of media portrayals of older adults. One common option is to base such work on media effects theories. For instance, the content analysis of Gerbner et al. (1980) is grounded in cultivation theory, which says that heavy viewers of television will come to view the television world as the "real world," and so their mental representations of the world will come to resemble television. If that is the case, then there is need to understand the television world in more detail. Similar rationales can be developed that are based on, for instance, social cognitive theory (Bandura, 2002). This theory would suggest that individuals are more likely to model (learn and imitate) behavior that is performed by attractive media characters. That approach would recommend examining interactions between younger and older characters on television in terms of the attractiveness of the younger persons. Younger viewers would be more likely to adopt intergenerational behaviors modeled by attractive peers; therefore, seeing discriminatory or patronizing behavior by a younger person on television would be more potentially damaging if the young person was attractive. No such work has been done, but it presents a productive theoretically driven direction for future research. This perspective also draws attention to the need for more extensive examinations of intergenerational interaction on television. Very little work has considered how older people and younger people talk to one another on television or the effects of those images on the well-being of and interactions among young and old adults.

An alternative to the effects-oriented approach has been described by Harwood and Anderson (2002). They suggest examining media content from an ethnolinguistic vitality perspective (Giles, Bourhis, & Taylor, 1977, Harwood, Giles, & Bourhis, 1994). Vitality theory describes the various facets that contribute to a group's strength in society through a systematic examination of sociostructural features such as demography, social status, and institutional support. For instance, groups in the majority with support from government and with a history of societal prestige will exercise more power in most societies than minority groups with a history of exclusion and oppression. Within the category of institutional support, Giles et al. (1977) define media institutions as important, and other work has corroborated the importance of media in determining group vitality (Abrams, Eveland, & Giles, 2003, Harwood & Roy, 2005). Vitality theory specifies media representation as an important topic independent of effects in light of its role as a component of a theoretically grounded understanding of where groups stand in society. Thus, cultural representations provide a socialization function within groups as well as reflecting a broader perception of how the dominant culture views various social groups.

### CULTURAL VALUES AND CHINESE MEDIA

Media representations of aging have been explored in various cultural contexts outside North America, including India, Germany, Britain, South Korea (Lee, Kim, & Han, 2006), and China (Zhang, Harwood, Williams Ylanne-McEwen, Wadleigh, & Thimm, 2006). Y. B. Zhang and J. Harwood (2004) support the conclusion that a norm of respect for older adults is salient in Chinese television advertisements. Filial piety (*Xiao*) is a cultural norm that is based on the traditional Confucian values of hierarchy and respect for elders; it is clear from their research that advertisers use this value to make their products appeal to consumers. Ads for health-related products, for instance, include tag lines suggesting that the parents' health is the responsibility of the child. Zhang and Harwood's (2004) research explores the extent to which modernization and globalization of Chinese culture is reflected in representations on Chinese television. These authors note the continued presence of traditional themes, but often blended with themes relating to progress, technology, and individual gratification. Themes emphasizing a value of "youth" are also strong in Chinese advertising; Lin (2001) suggested that this is in part a function of the one-child policy, which has resulted in a "little emperor/empress" phenomenon for couples with a single child.

## FUTURE RESEARCH DIRECTIONS

As was noted above, research exploring the intergenerational interactions portrayed on prime-time television could provide additional insight into the role of socialization of media portrayals. Researchers could expand their methodological approach by incorporating mixed methods to explore both the presence and the portrayal of older adults through content analysis and the interactions portrayed through discourse analysis. Furthermore, research that explores the effects of these types of interactions on young adults' perceptions of older adults could provide theoretical support for the media effects approach. That approach often is used as a rationale for doing content analytic work on cultural images of aging in the media, but the effects of and impact on real-world intergenerational encounters has not been explored.

Particular areas of content are also deserving of more attention than they have received. In particular, considerable research shows that older adults prefer informational and educational programming (news, etc.) to entertainment programming (sitcoms, etc.) (Riggs, 1996, Robinson, Skill, & Turner, 2004). However, relatively little is known about how older people are portrayed in news programming and other news sources (e.g., newspapers, educational programs, C-Span, quiz shows). Examination of such programs would help researchers understand whether the types of media preferred by older people are the types that portray older people in greater numbers or in a more positive or diverse fashion. Additionally, as generational shifts occur the type of program that older people consume are likely to change. Future research should explore whether the influence of the baby boomers on the media preferences of older adults.

**SEE ALSO** Volume 3: *Age Identity; Ageism/Age Discrimination.*

### BIBLIOGRAPHY


Abrams, J. R., Eveland, W. P., & Giles, H. (2003). The effects of television on group vitality: Can television empower nondominant groups? *Communication Yearbook, 27,* 193–220.

Anderson, K., Harwood, J., & Hummert, M. L. (2005). The grandparent-grandchild relationship: Implications for models of intergenerational communication. *Human Communication Research, 31*(2), 268–294.

Bandura, A. (2002). Social cognitive theory of mass communication. In J. Bryant & D. Zillmann (Eds.), *Media effects: Advances in theory and research* (2nd ed., pp. 121–153). Mahwah, NJ: L. Erlbaum Associates.

Bell, J. (1992). In search of a discourse on aging: The elderly on television. *The Gerontologist, 32*(3), 305–311.

Cheng, H., & Schweitzer, J. C. (1996). Cultural values reflected in Chinese and U.S. television commercials. *Journal of Advertising Research, 36*(3), 27–45.

Dail, P. W. (1988). Prime-time television portrayals of older adults in the context of family life. *The Gerontologist, 28,* 700–706.

Donlon, M. M., Ashman, O., & Levy, B. R. (2005). Re-vision of older television characters: A stereotype-awareness intervention. *Journal of Social Issues, 61*(2), 307–319.

Gantz, W., Gartenberg, H. M., & Rainbow, C. K. (1980). Approaching invisibility: The portrayal of the elderly in magazine advertisements. *Journal of Communication, 30*(1), 56–60.

Gerbner, G., Gross, L., Signorielli, N., & Morgan, M. (1980). Aging with television: Images on television drama and conceptions of social reality. *Journal of Communication, 30*(1), 37–47.

Giles, H., Bourhis, R. Y., & Taylor, D. (1977). Towards a theory of language in ethnic group relations. In H. Giles (Compiler), *Language, ethnicity, and intergroup relations* (pp. 307–348). London and New York: Academic Press.

Harris, A. J., & Feinberg, J. F. (1977). Television and aging: Is what you see what you get? *The Gerontologist, 17*(5), 464–468.

Harwood, J. (1999). Age identity and television viewing preferences. *Communication Reports, 12,* 85–90.

Harwood, J. (2000). "Sharp!" Lurking incoherence in a television portrayal of an older adult. *Journal of Language and Social Psychology, 19,* 110–140.

Harwood, J. (2007). *Understanding communication and aging: Developing knowledge and awareness.* Los Angeles, CA: Sage.

Harwood, J., & Anderson, K. (2002). The presence and portrayal of social groups on prime-time television. *Communication Reports, 15,* 81–97.

Harwood, J., & Giles, H. (1992). "Don't make me laugh": Age representations in a humorous context. *Discourse and Society, 3*(4), 403–436.

Harwood, J., Giles, H., & Bourhis, R. Y. (1994). The genesis of vitality theory: Historical patterns and discoursal dimensions. *International Journal of the Sociology of Language, 108,* 167–206.

Harwood, J., & Roy, A. (1999). Portrayals of older adults in Indian and U.S. magazine advertisements. *Howard Journal of Communications, 10*(4), 269–281.

Harwood, J., & Roy, A. (2005). Social identity theory and mass communication research. In J. Harwood & H. Giles (Eds.), *Intergroup communication: Multiple perspectives* (pp. 189–212). New York: Peter Lang.

Hiemstra, R., Goodman, M., Middlemiss, M. A., Vosco, R., & Ziegler, N. (1983). How older persons are portrayed in television advertising: Implications for educators. *Educational Gerontology, 9*(2–3), 111–122.

Hummert, M. L. (1994). Stereotypes of the elderly and patronizing speech. In M. L. Hummert, J. M. Wiemann, & J. F. Nussbaum (Eds.), *Interpersonal communication in older adulthood: Interdisciplinary research* (pp. 162–184). Thousand Oaks, CA: Sage.

Hummert, M. L., Garstka, T. A., Ryan, E. B., & Bonnesen, J. L. (2004). The role of age stereotypes in interpersonal communication. In J. F. Nussbaum & J. Coupland (Eds.), *Handbook of communication and aging research* (2nd ed., pp. 91–115). Mahwah, NJ: Lawrence Erlbaum Associates.

Kimball, M. M. (1986). Television and sex-role attitudes. In T. M. Williams (Ed.), *The impact of television* (pp. 265–301). Orlando, FL: Academic.

Lee, B., Kim, B-C., Han, S. (2006). The portrayal of older people in television advertisements: A cross-cultural content analysis of the United States and South Korea. *International Journal of Aging & Human Development, 63*(4), 279–297.

Lin, C. A. (2001). Cultural values reflected in Chinese and American television advertising. *Journal of Advertising, 30*(4), 83–94.

Mares, M-L., & Cantor, J. (1992). Elderly viewers' responses to televised portrayals of old age: Empathy and mood management versus social comparison. *Communication Research, 19*(4), 459–478.

Mastro, D. (2003). A social identity approach to understanding the impact of television messages. *Communication Monographs, 70*(2), 98–113.

Miller, D. W., Leyell, T. S., & Mazachek, J. (2004). Stereotypes of the elderly in U.S. television commercials from the 1950s to the 1990s. *International Journal of Aging and Human Development, 58*(4), 315–340.

Passuth, P. M., & Cook, F. L. (1985). Effects of television viewing on knowledge and attitudes about older adults: A critical reexamination. *The Gerontologist, 25*(1), 69–77.

Raman, P., Harwood, J., Weis, D., Anderson, J., & Miller, G. (In press). Portrayals of age groups in U.S. and Indian magazine advertisements: A cross-cultural comparison. *Howard Journal of Communications.*

Riggs, K. (1996). Television use in a retirement community. *Journal of Communication, 46,* 144–156.

Robinson, J., & Skill, T. (1995). The invisible generation: Portrayals of the elderly on prime-time television. *Communication Reports, 8*(2), 111–119.

Robinson, J. D., Skill, T., & Turner, J. W. (2004). Media usage patterns and portrayals of seniors. In J. F. Nussbaum & J. Coupland (Eds.), *Handbook of communication and aging research* (2nd ed., pp. 423–450). Mahwah, NJ: Lawrence Erlbaum Associates.

Robinson, T. E. II (1998). *Portraying older people in advertising: Magazines, television, and newspapers.* New York: Garland.

Robinson, T., & Anderson, C. (2006). Older characters in children's animated television programs: A content analysis of their portrayal. *Journal of Broadcasting and Electronic Media, 50,* 287–304.

Robinson, T., Gustafson, B., & Popovich, M. (2008). Perceptions of negative stereotypes of older people in magazine advertisements: Comparing the perceptions of older adult and college students. *Ageing & Society, 28,* 233–251.

Roy, A., & Harwood, J. (1997). Underrepresented, positively portrayed: Older adults in television commercials. *Journal of Applied Communication Research, 25,* 39–56.

Schneider, D. J. (2004). *The psychology of stereotyping.* New York: Guilford Press.

Signorielli, N., & Bacue, A. (1999). Recognition and respect: A content analysis of prime-time television characters across three decades. *Sex Roles, 70,* 527–544.

Stern, S. R., & Mastro, D. E. (2004). Gender portrayals across the life span: A content analytic look at broadcast commercials. *Mass Communication and Society, 7*(2), 215–236.

Swayne, L. E., & Greco, A. J. (1987). The portrayal of older Americans in television commercials. *Journal of Advertising, 16,* 47–54.

Thimm, C. (1998). *Die sprachliche symbolisierung des alters in der werbung* [The language of old age symbolization in advertising]. In M. Jaeckel (Ed.), *Die umworbene Gesellschaft: Analysen zur Entwicklung der Werbekommunikation [Advertisement and Society - New Approaches in the Analysis of Communication and Advertising]* (pp. 114–140). Wiesbaden, Germany: Westdeutscher Verlag.

Vernon, J. A., Williams, J. A., Phillips, T., & Wilson, J. (1990). Media stereotyping: A comparison of the way elderly women and men are portrayed on prime-time television. *Journal of Women and Aging, 2*(4), 55–68.

Williams, A., Ylänne, V., & Wadleigh, P. M. (2007). Selling the "elixir of life": Images of the elderly in an *Olivio* advertising campaign. *Journal of Aging Studies, 21*(1), 1–21.

Zhang, Y. B., & Harwood, J. (2004). Modernization of tradition in an age of globalization: Cultural values in Chinese television commercials. *Journal of Communication, 54*(1), 156–172.

Zhang, Y. B., Harwood, J., Williams, A., Ylanne-McEwen, V., Wadleigh, P. M., & Thimm, C. (2006). The portrayal of older adults in advertising: A cross-national review. *Journal of Language and Social Psychology, 25*(3), 264–282.

***Karen Anderson***
***Jake Harwood***

# D

## DATA SOURCES, LATER LIFE

*This entry contains the following:*



### I. GENERAL ISSUES

The term *data* is used to define two distinct products: published literature representing the distillation of research findings and research data, the information underlying those publications. Research data include a growing universe of federal and public tabulations, surveys, and other forms of secondary information. These data allow researchers to examine issues that go beyond the findings presented in published research, and the availability of such data has enhanced understanding of aging and the life course. Sources of data on older adults have increased dramatically as a result of the worldwide growth of the aged population and scholars' and policy makers' need to understand the implications of that growth. The value of these data is enhanced by the development of more detailed survey designs, access to more powerful computers, and more sophisticated models for measuring attitudes, behaviors, and change.

#### EARLY STUDIES OF AGING

Although there has always been interest in aging, many historians consider the 1881 publication of *Clinical Lectures on the Diseases of Old Age* by Jean-Martin Charcot as the formal beginning of gerontology. In the eight decades after that publication, studies of aging episodically appeared in the published literature, but, with the exception of articles such as P. K. Whelpton's 1930 article on the aging transition, there was not a significant social science literature on aging until the 1960s.

At that time researchers such as Agnes Brewster (1961) began examining the potential health care costs of a growing aging population, and George Maddox presented the results from one of the earliest longitudinal studies on the aged in 1963; by the late 1960s researchers began exploring family support relationships between aging parents and their adult children (Rosenmayr, 1968). The 1970s saw a growing body of research as studies addressed topics such as living arrangements (Montgomery, 1972), late-life friendships across sexes (Booth & Hess, 1974), and policy research on alternatives to institutionalization (Abdellah, 1978). That work was informative, but it was also static, as researchers could not replicate or build on those published studies because they lacked access to the underlying data resources that measured the outcomes. The growing availability of mainframe computers in the late 1970s changed the state of research. The unprecedented growth and declining costs of computing power introduced a tremendous degree of equity into data analysis, and the subsequent flood of secondary data available for research has made good use of this capacity.

## THE EMERGENCE OF DATA RESOURCES FOR THE STUDY OF LATER LIFE

Like the literature on aging, data sources grew slowly, beginning in the late 1960s. An early example of data focusing on the lives of the elderly was the 1968 National Senior Citizens Survey (Schooler, 1979), a national study of persons 65 years of age and older. It was representative of studies that explored the quality of life by measuring life satisfaction, types of social relationships, and access to community services among the elderly. Most early studies of aging had the common weakness of being cross-sectional, providing a snapshot of complex behaviors at a single point in time rather than allowing researchers to study change across time.

The Retirement History Longitudinal Survey conducted by the U.S. Department of Commerce in 1969 (Social Security Administration, 2002) was an early example of the use of longitudinal (or multiwave) data collected by the federal government and then repeated six times over 10 years to document the transition to retirement as a process that occurred over time. Although the six Retirement History Longitudinal Surveys provided insights into the determinants of retirement, more importantly, they showed the value of longitudinal designs, encouraging the application of this framework to a wide array of studies.

Beginning in 1984, the Longitudinal Study of Aging (LSOA) was another landmark study that examined changes in the aging life course (U.S. Department of Health and Human Services, 2007b). The LSOA followed a sample of persons age 70 years and over across four waves, ending in 1990. Not only did this study provide detailed information about health status, living arrangements, social and economic support, and health insurance, along with detailed Medicare records, it also followed the mortality of the respondents and included interviews with persons named by decedents for additional information. The LSOA reflected the standard for aging research data at that time, and its use in more than 1,000 scholarly publications since its release reveals its value.

From those early studies, a clear set of issues emerged that defined studies of aging and the life course. Health and disability issues predominated, but equally important were issues of economic stability and the structure of support networks. Because all these factors changed as a person aged, it was also clear that longitudinal data offered the best opportunities for addressing questions related to successful aging.

## CONTEMPORARY DATA RESOURCES FOR THE STUDY OF LATER LIFE

Since the early 1990s research data have been used to address many issues related to the life course of aging persons. The National Long-Term Care Survey conducted from 1982 to 2004 (Manton, 2007) addressed a major weakness in most studies of the elderly. This survey collected information on the institutionalized elderly, enabling the study of the health and disability status of all the elderly, not just those living in households. Most studies of aging look only at noninstitutionalized populations, and other studies of the institutionalized elderly, such as the National Nursing Home Study (U.S. Department of Health and Human Services, 2007c), tend to be cross-sectional and thus cannot be used to study changes in health.

Specialized studies of the aged also emerged in more recent years. The Changing Lives of Older Couples Study (Nesse, Wortman, House, Kessler, & Lepkowski, 2003) collected data on marriage and the spousal bereavement process for older adults, and the Resources for Enhancing Alzheimer's Caregiver Health study (Schulz, 2006) examined the burden on those caring for someone with dementia or Alzheimer's disease. The breadth of aging studies has ranged from the Religion, Aging, and Health Survey by Neal Krause (2006), which looked at the impact of religion on health and emotional satisfaction, to the National Social Life, Health, and Aging Project (Waite et. al., 2007), which provided a rare examination of late-life sexuality.

Among the resources that emerged after the 1990s, perhaps the most influential has been the Health and Retirement Study (HRS; U.S. Department of Health and Human Services, 2007a). Begun in 1992, this complex study of aging has been repeated every 2 years, and interviews have been conducted with more than 27,000 individuals age 50 and older. Touching on a broad array of topics from economic stability to health, disability, and family support, the HRS represents a highly successful study measuring the major issues of aging and following the lives of the elderly over time. In later years, the HRS model was expanded internationally with studies such as the Survey of Health, Ageing, and Retirement in Europe (Börsch Supan, 2005), the English Longitudinal Study of Ageing (Taylor, 2003), and the Mexican Health and Aging Study (Soldo, Wong, & Palloni, 2002), which incorporated features comparable to the HRS and allowed a broader understanding of aging trends worldwide.

Many of these data sources are made available to the general public through the National Archive of Computerized Data on Aging (NACDA), which is funded by the National Institute on Aging. The NACDA acquires, preserves, and processes data relevant to gerontological research, disseminates the data to researchers, and facilitates the use of the data. By preserving and making available the largest library of electronic data on aging in the United States, the NACDA offers opportunities for data analysis on major issues of scientific and policy relevance.

**BIBLIOGRAPHY**

Abdellah, F. G. (1978). Long-term care policy issues: Alternatives to institutional care. *Annals of the American Academy of Political and Social Science, 438*(1), 28–39.

Booth, A., & Hess, E. (1974). Cross-sex friendship. *Journal of Marriage and the Family, 36*(1), 38–47.

Börsch Supan, A. (2005). Introduction. In Axel Börsch-Supan, Agar Brugiavini, Hendrik Jürges, Johan Mackenbach, Johannes Siegrist, & Guglielmo Weber (Ed.), *Health, ageing and retirement in Europe—First results from the Survey of Health, Ageing, and Retirement in Europe.* Mannheim, Germany: MEA.

Brewster, A. W. (1961). Meeting the health needs of the aged. *Annals of the American Academy of Political and Social Science, 337*(1), 114–125.

Charcot, J.-M. (1881). *Clinical lectures on the diseases of old age.* Trans. L. H. Hunt. New York: W. Wood.

Krause, N. (2006). *Religion, Aging, and Health Survey, 2001–2004.* Ann Arbor: University of Michigan, School of Public Health, Department of Health Behavior and Health Education and Inter-university Consortium for Political and Social Research.

Maddox, G. L. (1963). Activity and morale: A longitudinal study of selected elderly subjects. *Social Forces, 42*(2), 195–204.

Manton, K. G. (2007). *National Long-Term Care Survey: 1982, 1984, 1989, 1994, 1999, and 2004.* Durham, NC: Duke University; Ann Arbor, MI: Inter-university Consortium for Political and Social Research.

Montgomery, J. E. (1972). The housing patterns of older families. *The Family Coordinator, 21*(1), 37–46.

Nesse, R. M., Wortman, C., House, J., Kessler, R., & Lepkowski, J. (2003). *Changing Lives of Older Couples (CLOC): A study of spousal bereavement in the Detroit area, 1987–1993.* Ann Arbor: University of Michigan, Institute for Social Research and Inter-university Consortium for Political and Social Research.

Rosenmayr, L. (1968). Family relations of the elderly. *Journal of Marriage and the Family, 30*(4), 672–680.

Schooler, K. K. (1979). *National Senior Citizens Survey, 1968.* Ann Arbor, MI: Inter-university Consortium for Political and Social Research.

Schulz, R. (2006). *Resources for enhancing Alzheimer's caregiver health, 1996–2001: Baseline and follow-up data.* Pittsburgh, PA: University of Pittsburgh, University Center for Social and Urban Research; Ann Arbor, MI: Inter-university Consortium for Political and Social Research.

Social Security Administration. (2002). *Retirement History Longitudinal Survey, 1969.* Washington, DC: U.S. Department of Commerce, Bureau of the Census/Social Security Administration, Office of Research and Statistics; Ann Arbor, MI: Inter-university Consortium for Political and Social Research.

Soldo, B., Wong, R., & Palloni, A. (2002, November). *Why should we care about aging in Mexico? The Mexican Health and Aging Study.* Paper presented at the Gerontological Society of America Conference, Boston.

Taylor, R., Conway, L., Calderwood, L., & Lessof, C. (2003). Methodology. In M. Marmot, J. Banks, R. Blundell, C. Lessof, & J. Nazroo, J. (Eds.), *Health, wealth and lifestyles of the older population in England: The 2002 English Longitudinal Study of Ageing.* London: Institute for Fiscal Studies, University College.

U.S. Department of Health and Human Services. (2007a). *Growing older in America: The health and retirement study.* Washington, DC: National Institutes of Health, National Institute on Aging. Retrieved May 30, 2008, from http://www.nia.nih.gov

U.S. Department of Health and Human Services. (2007b). *National Health Interview Survey: Longitudinal study of aging, 70 years and over, 1984–1990.* Hyattsville, MD: Author; Ann Arbor, MI: Inter-university Consortium for Political and Social Research.

U.S. Department of Health and Human Services. (2007c). *National Nursing Home Survey, 2004.* Hyattsville, MD: Author; Ann Arbor, MI: Inter-university Consortium for Political and Social Research.

Waite, L. J., Laumann, E. O., Levinson, W., Lindau, S. T., McClintock, M., O'Muircheartaigh, C. A., et al. (2007). *National Social Life, Health, and Aging Project (NSHAP).* Chicago: National Opinion Research Center; Ann Arbor, MI: Inter-university Consortium for Political and Social Research.

Whelpton, P. K. (1930). Population: Trends in differentials of true increase and age composition. *American Journal of Sociology, 35*(6), 870–880.

***James W. McNally***

## II. BERLIN AGING STUDY (BASE)

The Berlin Aging Study (BASE) was established in 1989 to investigate questions about aging and dying in Germany from the collaborative perspectives of four disciplines: psychiatry, psychology, sociology, and internal medicine (Baltes & Mayer, 1999). Two unique features of the study are (a) an extensive face-to-face protocol of standardized interviews, tests, and clinical examinations and (b) a heterogeneous age-by-sex stratified sample of men and women ages 70 to over 100 years (born between 1883 and 1922).

At baseline (1990–1993), demographic information was obtained from the obligatory Berlin city registry for a verified parent sample of 1908. The initial participation rate was 78%. A total of 516 men and women (27% of the parent sample) agreed to complete the BASE extensive protocol of 14 individual 90-min sessions, which were scheduled over 3 to 5 months. An additional 412 persons (21%) participated at the level of a single 90-min multidisciplinary assessment and 336 (18%) provided a 30-min interview. Information obtained from these subgroups is used to examine the selectivity of the core 516 sample. That means that researchers were able to assess the extent to which the core sample was a positive selection of the original sample. The mean age of the core BASE sample was 85 years at baseline and 14% were living in institutions, such as a nursing home. As of 2007, the study involves seven longitudinal measurement occasions. Subsamples have also been recruited for intensive supplementary studies. Mortality information for the entire sample is obtained regularly from the city registry.

More than 1,000 publications reporting cross-sectional and longitudinal findings from BASE are listed on the project web site (the Internet address is given in the bibliography). These publications deal with a wide range of discipline-specific and multidisciplinary topics regarding the young old (persons ages 70 to 85) and the oldest old (persons 85 and older). Central topics include social inequality, family life, life history and cohort experiences, current life contexts, intergenerational transfer of resources, use of health services, physical health, disability, dental health, dementia, depression, everyday competence, cognitive aging, self and personality, social relationships, social support, and well-being.

**BIBLIOGRAPHY**

Baltes, P. B., & Mayer, K. U. (Eds.). (1999). *The Berlin Aging Study: Aging from 70 to 100.* New York: Cambridge University Press.

*Berlin Aging Study (BASE).* (2008). Retrieved June 11, 2008, from http://www.base-berlin.mpg.de

***Jacqui Smith***

## III. ENGLISH LONGITUDINAL STUDY OF AGING (ELSA)

The English Longitudinal Study of Ageing (ELSA) is a large, national panel study of English people aged 50 and older. The ELSA was established to study processes of aging from an interdisciplinary perspective. ELSA sample members were selected from households that had participated in the Health Survey for England (HSE), an annual, nationally representative cross-sectional survey. Participants aged 50 and over at the time of the first wave of data collection in 2002 were eligible to become ELSA sample members. ELSA participants are interviewed every 2 years, with an additional nurse visit to collect biomedical data every 4 years.

Three waves of ELSA data have been collected (in 2002, 2004, and 2006) with 12,100 participants in the first wave, and 9,432 participants in the second wave. Third wave data will become available in early 2008 and the fourth wave fieldwork will begin in Spring 2008. The ELSA is funded by the National Institute on Aging in the United States and by a consortium of government departments in the United Kingdom. The ELSA was designed to be comparable with its U.S. counterpart, the Health and Retirement Study (HRS), as well as the Survey of Health Ageing and Retirement in Europe (SHARE). The content of the ELSA includes demographics; health; physical and cognitive function, including performance tests; psychosocial factors and well-being; social participation; housing; employment; pensions and retirement; income, assets, and consumption; biomedical measures, including blood pressure, lung function, anthropometric measures, and blood analyses; and links to administrative data, including mortality statistics. Key findings from the first two waves of the ELSA highlighted diversity and inequality, with extreme differences in the distribution of wealth in the older population and strong links between wealth, health, and social participation (Marmot et al., 2003).

**BIBLIOGRAPHY**

*About ESDS longitudinal.* (Updated 2005, July 21). Retrieved June 11, 2008, from http://www.esds.ac.uk/longitudinal

Banks, J., Breeze, E., Lessof, C., & Nazroo, J. (Eds.). (2006). *Retirement, health, and relationships of the older population in England: The 2004 English Longitudinal Study of Ageing.* London: The Institute for Fiscal Studies.

*Institute for Fiscal Studies: English Longitudinal Study of Ageing.* Retrieved June 11, 2008, from http://www.ifs.org.uk/elsa

Marmot, M., Banks, J., Blundell, R., Lessof, C., & Nazroo, J. (Eds.). (2003). *Health, wealth, and lifestyles of the older population in England: The 2002 English Longitudinal Study of Ageing.* London: The Institute for Fiscal Studies.

***Anne McMunn***
***Michael Marmot***

## IV. HEALTH AND RETIREMENT STUDY (HRS)

The Health and Retirement Study (HRS) is a national longitudinal study of more than 20,000 individuals representing the population over age 50 in the United States. The study began in 1992 with a cohort of then preretirement-age individuals born between 1931 and 1941. New cohorts were added in 1993 and 1998 to round out the sample over age 50, and additional cohorts are enrolled every 6 years (e.g., in 2004, 2010) to refresh the sample at the younger ages. The study contains oversamples of African Americans and Hispanics. Participants are followed throughout the life course with biennial interviews and supplemental data collections.

The primary focus of the study is on the intersection between health, retirement, and economic status in later life. The survey provides detailed information on these topics, as well as on employment history and pension portfolio, work disability and related benefits, family composition and resource transfers, health insurance coverage, and utilization of health services. Supplemental data collections have focused on special topics such as consumption, prescription drug coverage, diabetes care and management, and dementia. Since 2003 the study has collected periodic measurements of physical performance (e.g., grip strength, walking speed, and so forth), height, weight, waist size, blood pressure, and several biomarkers.

The HRS is the nation's leading resource for data on the health and economic well-being of America's rapidly growing older population. As of early 2008, more than 900 journal articles, books, book chapters, and dissertations have been completed using HRS data. A few selected publications are listed in the bibliography. Key findings from the study are summarized in a recent publication by the National Institute on Aging (2007).

The HRS has been emulated in numerous international studies, including the English Longitudinal Study of Ageing, the Survey of Health, Ageing, and Retirement in Europe, the Mexican Health and Aging Study, the Korean Longitudinal Study on Aging, as well as studies that are underway or will soon be launched in Japan, China, Ireland, and India. This collection of studies provides rich potential for cross-national analysis.

The HRS is conducted by the University of Michigan with primary support from the National Institute on Aging. HRS data products are available without cost to researchers and analysts and may be downloaded from the HRS Web site (see bibliography). The Web site also includes general information about the study, documentation reports, and a searchable bibliography of publications based on HRS data.

**BIBLIOGRAPHY**

Baker, D. W., Sudano, J. J., Albert, J. M., Borawski, E. A., & Dor, A. (2001). Lack of health insurance and decline in overall health in late middle age. *New England Journal of Medicine, 345*(15), 1106–1112.

Banks, J., Marmot, M., Oldfield, Z., & Smith, J.P. (2006). Disease and disadvantage in the United States and in England. *Journal of the American Medical Association, 295*(17), 2037–2045.

Barsky, R. B., Juster, F. T., Kimball, M. S., & Shapiro, M. D. (1997). Preference parameters and behavioral heterogeneity: An experimental approach in the Health and Retirement Study. *The Quarterly Journal of Economics, 112*(2), 537–579.

Heisler, M., Langa, K. M., Eby, E. L., Fendrik, A. M., Kabeto, M. U., & Piette, J. D. (2004). The health effects of restricting prescription medication use because of cost. *Medical Care, 42*(7), 626–634.

Kington, R., & Smith, J. (1997). Socioeconomic status and racial and ethnic differences in functional status associated with chronic diseases. *American Journal of Public Health, 87*(5), 805–810.

National Institute on Aging. (2007). *The Health and Retirement Study: Growing older in America.* Retrieved May 25, 2008, from www.nia.nih.gov/ResearchInformation

University of Michigan Institute for Social Research. *The Health and Retirement Study.* Retrieved May, 26, 2008, from http://hrsonline.isr.umich.edu

Venti, S. F., & Wise, D. A. (1998). The cause of wealth dispersion at retirement: Choice or chance? *American Economic Review, 88*(2), 185–191.

*Mary Beth Ofstedal*

## V. LONGITUDINAL STUDY OF AGING (LSOA)

There are two Longitudinal Studies of Aging, known as LSOA-I and LSOA-II. Both are cohort studies conducted collaboratively by the National Center of Health Statistics (NCHS) and the National Institutes of Health (NIH). The baseline for the LSOA-I was the 1984 Supplement on Aging (SOA) of the National Health and Interview Survey (NHIS). The NHIS is a continuous cross-sectional household survey conducted annually by the NCHS to monitor trends in illness and disability in the United States. The baseline for the LSOA-II was the 1994 Supplement on Aging. LSOA-I has three follow-up waves (1986, 1988, and 1990); LSOA-II has only two (1997 and 2000). Study populations are all non-institutionalized individuals age 70 years old or older at baseline, living in the United States. The surveys used stratified multistage probability sampling designs. Face-to-face interviews were conducted only at baseline and relied on self-reported information, except when proxy respondents were needed. Respondents of follow-up waves were interviewed by phone or mail in LSOA-I, and with a Computer-Assisted Telephone Interview (CATI) system in LSOA-II. Baseline sample sizes were 7,527 subjects in 1984 and 9,447 in 1994 (Kovar, Fitti, and Chyba, 1992; NCHS, 2003). Respondents who became institutionalized were interviewed during the follow-up waves, except in 1986, when these respondents were purposefully excluded. Hence, this wave was based on a subsample of 5,151. This wave was the only one with a special tracking of non-interviewed persons.

Some important differences between the two studies are that baseline interviews were held at the same time as the NHIS interviews in LSOA-I, but not in LSOA-II; LSOA-II oversampled African Americans; and attrition at last wave was larger for LSOA-II (27%) than for LSOA-I (14%).

LSOA datasets have been valuable in studying the oldest-old Americans and include topics such as: functional limitations and disability over time (Crimmins, Saito and Reynolds, 1997; Freedman, Crimmins, Schoeni, Spillman, et al, 2004; Speare, Avery, and Lawton, 1991; Worobey and Angel, 1990), institutionalization and living arrangements (Speare, Avery, and Lawton, 1991; Worobey and Angel, 1990), mortality determinants (Allison, Gallagher, Heo, Pi-Sunyer, et al, 1997; Grabowski and Ellis, 2001; Rakowski and Mor, 1992; Steinbach, 1992), and health services utilization (Wolinsky and Johnson, 1991).

**BIBLIOGRAPHY**

Allison, D. B., Gallagher, D., Heo, M., Pi-Sunyer, F.X., & Heymsfield, S.B. (1997). Body mass index and all-cause mortality among people age 70 and over: the Longitudinal Study of Aging. *International Journal of Obesity, 21*: 424–431.

Crimmins, E., Saito, Y., & Reynolds, S. L. (1997). Further evidence on recent trends in the prevalence and incidence of disability among older Americans from two sources: the LSOA and the NHIS. *Journals of Gerontology Series B-Psychological Sciences and Social Sciences, 52*: S59–S71.

Freedman, V. A., Crimmins, E., Schoeni, R. F., Spillman, B. C., Aykan, H., Kramarow, E., et al. (2004). Resolving inconsistencies in trends in old-age disability: report from a technical working group. *Demography, 41*: 417–441.

Grabowski, D., & Ellis J. E. (2001). High body mass index does not predict mortality in older people: analysis of the Longitudinal Study of Aging. *Journal of the American Geriatrics Society, 49*: 968–979.

Kovar, M. G., Fitti, J. E., & Chyba, M. M. (1992). *The Longitudinal Study of Aging: 1984–1990.* Vital and Health Statistics, Series 1: Programs and Collection Procedures, 28, Hyattsville, MD: National Center for Health Statistics.

National Center for Health Statistics (NCHS). (2003). *National Health Interview Survey, 1994: Second Longitudinal Study on Aging, Wave 3, 2000. Codebook for Part 1: Survivor Data File.* Ann Arbor, Michigan: United States Department of Health and Human Services, Inter-university Consortium for Political and Social Research. First ICPSR Version. Retrieved June 26, 2008, from http://www.icpsr.umich.edu

Rakowski, W., & Mor, V. (1992). The association of physical activity with mortality among older adults in the Longitudinal Study of Aging (1984–1988). *Journals of Gerontology, 47*: M122–M129.

Speare, A. J., Avery, R., & Lawton, L. (1991). Disability, residential mobility, and changes in living arrangements. *Journal of Gerontology: Social Sciences, 46B*: S133–S142.

Steinbach, U. (1992). Social networks, institutionalization, and mortality among elderly people in the United States. *Journals of Gerontology, 47*: S183–S190.

Wolinsky, F. D., & Johnson, R. J. (1991). The use of health services by older adults. *Journals of Gerontology, 46*: S345–S357.

Worobey, J. L., & Angel, R. J. (1990). Functional capacity and living arrangements of unmarried elderly persons. *Journal of Gerontology: Social Sciences, 45B*: S95–101.

***Gilbert Brenes-Camacho***

## VI. SURVEY OF HEALTH AGEING AND RETIREMENT IN EUROPE (SHARE)

The Survey of Health Ageing and Retirement in Europe (SHARE) is a longitudinal, multidisciplinary, and cross-national database of representative micro data on health, socioeconomic status, and social or family networks of individuals aged 50 and over. Eleven countries contributed to the approximately 30,000 computer-assisted personal interviews conducted during the 2004 SHARE baseline wave. These countries constitute a balanced representation of Continental Europe's regions, ranging from Scandinavia (Denmark and Sweden) through Central Europe (Austria, France, Germany, Switzerland, Belgium, and the Netherlands) to the Mediterranean (Spain, Italy, and Greece). In 2005 and 2006, SHARE data also were collected in Israel. For the second wave of data collection, which was conducted in 2006 and 2007, three additional European Union (EU) member states—the Czech Republic, Ireland, and Poland—joined the SHARE. The survey's third wave, which is scheduled for 2008 and 2009, will focus on the collection of detailed life histories of respondents who participated in previous waves.

The SHARE was modeled after the Health and Retirement Study (HRS) in the United States, and the English Longitudinal Study of Ageing (ELSA). A unique strength of the SHARE is that the data can be used to explore cross-national variations in public policies, cultures, and histories in a variety of European countries. Its measures include health (e.g., self-reported health, physical and cognitive functioning, health behavior, and health care utilization), psychological (e.g., mental health and quality of life), economic (current work situation and job characteristics, sources and composition of current income, wealth, and consumption), and social support (e.g., instrumental help, financial transfers, and volunteer activities) indicators.

The SHARE project is coordinated centrally at the Mannheim Research Institute for the Economics of Aging in Germany. Detailed documentation as well as information on SHARE-based publications is available on the project's Web site. All researchers may download the SHARE data free of charge.

**BIBLIOGRAPHY**

Börsch-Supan, A., Brugiavini, A., Jürges, H., Mackenbach, J., Siegrist, J., & Weber, G. (Eds.). (2005). *Health, ageing, and retirement in Europe. First results from the Survey of Health Ageing and Retirement in Europe*. Mannheim, Germany: Mannheim Research Institute for the Economics of Aging (MEA).

Börsch-Supan, A., Hank, K., & Jürges, H. (2005). A new comprehensive and international view on ageing: Introducing the Survey of Health Ageing and Retirement in Europe. *European Journal of Ageing, 2,* 245–253.

Börsch-Supan, A., & Jürges, H. (Eds.). (2005). *The Survey of Health Ageing and Retirement in Europe—Methodology.* Mannheim, Germany: Mannheim Research Institute for the Economics of Aging (MEA).

*SHARE.* Retrieved June 3, 2008, from http://www.share-project.org

***Axel Börsch-Supan***

## VII. WISCONSIN LONGITUDINAL STUDY (WLS)

The Wisconsin Longitudinal Study (WLS) is a long-term study of a random sample of 10,317 men and women who graduated from Wisconsin high schools in 1957 and of their randomly selected brothers and sisters. Survey data were collected from the graduates or their parents in 1957, 1964, 1975, 1992, and 2004; from a selected sibling in 1977, 1994, and 2005; from the spouse of the original respondent in 2004; from the spouse of the selected sibling in 2006; and from widow(er)s of the graduates and siblings in 2006. The data provide information about: family background; youthful aspirations; schooling; military service; occupational histories and job characteristics; income, assets, and interhousehold transfers; health insurance, access to health care; pension coverage; family formation and relationships among family members; mental and physical health; stressful life events; coping behavior; cognitive functioning; social and civic participation; experiences with the early death, severe mental illness, or disability of a child; and medical, legal, religious, and psychological preparation for the end of life. Many of these measures are repeated across time.

Along with survey data, the WLS has a variety of supplemental data such as mental ability tests and measures of school performance; characteristics of communities of residence, schools and colleges, employers, and industries; information from high school yearbooks; and samples of DNA from both the graduate and the sibling. In-home interviews with the original respondents are planned for 2010. All nonidentifying WLS data are publicly available and most restricted data can be made available to researchers on completion of an application. Data, documentation, and publications are available online at www.ssc.wisc.edu/wlsresearch. The WLS has been supported principally by the National Institute on Aging with additional support from the Vilas Estate Trust, the National Science Foundation, the Spencer Foundation, and the Graduate School of the University of Wisconsin-Madison. The WLS data have been used to study important life course issues, such as inter- and intragenerational social mobility, and were the basis for influential "status attainment model" (Sewell & Hauser, 1975).

**BIBLIOGRAPHY**

Hauser, R. M., & Sewell, W. H. (1986). Family effects in simple models of education, occupational status, and earnings: Findings from the Wisconsin and Kalamazoo studies. *Journal of Labor Economics, 4,* S83–S115.

Hauser, R. M., Tsai, S. L., & Sewell, W. H. (1983). A model of stratification with response error in social and psychological variables. *Sociology of Education, 56,* 20–46.

Sewell, W. H., Haller, A. O., & Ohlendorf, G. W. (1970). The educational and early occupational status attainment process: replication and revision. *American Sociological Review, 35,* 1014–1027.

Sewell, W. H., Haller, A. O., & Portes, A. (1969). The educational and early occupational attainment process. *American Sociological Review, 34,* 82–92.

Sewell, W. H., & Hauser, R. M. (1972). Causes and consequences of higher education: Models of the status attainment process. *American Journal of Agricultural Economics, 54,* 851–861.

Sewell, W. H., & Hauser, R. M. (1975). *Education, occupation, and earnings: Achievement in the early career.* New York: Academic Press.

Sewell, W. H., Hauser, R. M., Springer, K. W., & Hauser, T. S. (2004). As we age: A review of the Wisconsin Longitudinal Study, 1957–2001. In K. T. Leicht (Ed.), *Research in social stratification and mobility* (pp. 3–111). London: Elsevier.

Sewell, W. H., Hauser, R. M., & Wolf, W. C. (1980). Sex, schooling and occupational status. *American Journal of Sociology, 86,* 551–583.

Sewell, W. H., & Shah, V. P. (1967). Socioeconomic status, intelligence, and the attainment of higher education. *Sociology of Education, 40,* 1–23.

***Carol L. Roan***

# DEAFNESS

**SEE** Volume 3: *Sensory Impairments.*

# DEATH AND DYING

Dying is considered the final stage in the life course, and death is the final life course transition. As such, life course sociologists study the ways that values, beliefs, behaviors, and institutional arrangements concerning death are structured by social environments and contexts. Death is a universal human experience, yet societal responses to death vary according to cultural attitudes toward death, contextual factors including the primary causes of death, and normative age at which death occurs. Although death can occur at any point in the life course, the vast majority of all deaths in the early 21st century occur to older adults. In 2006 nearly three-quarters of the 2.4 million deaths in the United States were deaths to persons ages 65 and older (Centers for Disease Control, 2006).

## HISTORICAL CHANGES IN DEATH PRACTICES

Beliefs and practices surrounding death in the United States have come full circle over the past three centuries. In the 18th century, death was public and visible. Death tended to occur at a relatively young age, at home, and was caused by infectious diseases that could not be cured. The loss of a loved one was expressed by dramatic displays of grief among survivors, and elaborate efforts to memorialize the deceased (Aries, 1981). Throughout the late 19th and most of the 20th century, death became "invisible" (Aries, 1981) and "bureaucratized" (Blauner, 1966). Physicians and hospitals assumed control over dying, death and mourning became private, the handling of dead bodies and funeral rites were transferred from private homes to funeral parlors, and people were encouraged to deny death and believe in medical technologies (Blauner, 1966). Treating dying persons in isolation was believed to help smooth the transition beyond death; reducing the social status of those who were about to die would minimize disruption of ongoing social and economic relationships.

The epidemiology of death also changed dramatically (Omran, 1971). In the 19th and early 20th centuries deaths occurred primarily due to infectious diseases, which were not stratified by social class or gender. Men and women, rich and poor were equally likely to become ill and die, and death often occurred relatively quickly after the initial onset of symptoms. Death during the latter half of the 20th and early 21st centuries, in contrast, occurs overwhelmingly due to chronic diseases, including cancer and heart disease. These diseases tend to strike older rather than younger adults, men more so than women, and persons with fewer rather than richer economic resources. Death typically occurs in late life at the end of a long, often debilitating, and painful illness where the dying patients' final days are spent in a hospital or nursing home, and life-sustaining technologies are used.

In the late 20th and early 21st centuries, death is again becoming visible and managed by the dying and their families. Patients' and care providers' recognition that dying is often a socially isolated, physician-controlled experience has triggered a number of political and social movements with the explicit goal of placing control of the dying process in the hands of patients and their families. The Patient Self-Determination Act, passed by Congress in 1990, requires all government-funded health providers to give patients the opportunity to complete an advance directive (or living will) when they are admitted to a hospital. The hospice movement, which began in the United States in the early 1970s to promote palliative care at the end of life, also has grown in popularity. Hospice care, whether in-hospital or at-home, provides an alternative to the medical, scientific model of dying. Pain management, open communication among family, patient, and care providers, and a peacefully accepted death are core goals (National Hospice and Palliative Care Organization, 2001).

## IMPORTANT SOCIOLOGICAL STUDIES OF DEATH

As the social context of death and dying has changed, the foci of research also have shifted. In the 1950s and early 1960s, research was guided by the assumption that the United States was a death-denying society (Gorer, 1965). Influential works included an examination of the problems associated with transferring death and funeral rites from private homes to professional funeral homes (Mitford, 1963), and explorations of the ways that health care providers, dying patients, and their family members mutually ignore and shield one another from their knowledge that the patient is dying (Glaser & Straus, 1965).

In the late 1960s and 1970s, the *death awareness* movement guided research and theory. Key scholarly works of this era offered important advancements in conceptualizing the dying process. Barney Glaser and Anselm Strauss (1968) proposed that dying tends to follow one of three trajectories: lingering, expected quick, and unexpected quick. The latter was considered most distressing for both health care providers and surviving family members. Elizabeth Kübler-Ross (1969) delineated the emotional and cognitive stages that dying persons pass through, before reaching the final stage of *acceptance*.

In the late 20th and early 21st centuries, research on death and dying has flourished. (For a comprehensive compendium, please see Clifton Bryant's *Handbook of Death and Dying* [2003].) Scholarly and public concern about death reflects two broad social patterns. First,

| All races | White | Black | Asian or Pacific Islander | American Indian | Hispanic |
|---|---|---|---|---|---|
| 1 Diseases of heart | Diseases of heart | Diseases of heart | Diseases of heart | Diseases of heart | Diseases of heart |
| 2 Malignant neoplasms | Malignant neoplasms | Malignant neoplasms | Malignant neoplasms | Malignant neoplasms | Malignant neoplasms |
| 3 Cerebrovascular diseases | Cerebrovascular diseases | Cerebrovascular diseases | Cerebrovascular diseases | Cerebrovascular diseases | Cerebrovascular diseases |
| 4 Chronic lower respiratory diseases | Chronic lower respiratory diseases | Diabetes mellitus | Diabetes mellitus | Diabetes mellitus | Diabetes mellitus |
| 5 Alzheimer's disease | Alzheimer's disease | Nephritis | Influenza and pneumonia | Chronic lower respiratory diseases | Alzheimer's disease |

***Figure 1.*** *Leading causes of death among women age 65 and over, by sex, race, and origin, 2004.* CENGAGE LEARNING, GALE.

increasingly large numbers of older adults are living longer than ever before, with most suffering from at least one chronic and terminal disease at the end of life. At the same time, the expanding population of older adults is experiencing the deaths of spouses, siblings, and friends in large numbers. Second, technological innovations to extend life, including life-support systems, organ transplants, and advances in cancer treatment extend the life span, but also raise important questions about the meaning of life and death.

## CONTROL OVER THE DYING PROCESS

One broad theme of the life course paradigm underlies much current research on death: the importance of personal control and agency, both among dying persons and their survivors. Two specific lines of inquiry, which have developed since the late 1990s, are personal control over practical aspects of the dying process and active *meaning making* among the dying and bereaved.

Mounting research explores how older dying persons and their families make decisions about the type, site, and duration of care they want to receive at the end of life. Sociologists' key contributions have included identifying the cognitive, emotional, and structural factors that may enable or prevent individuals from receiving the type of care they hope to receive. Recent research reveals that patients and their family members seldom have sufficient information about their illness trajectory and future lifespan so that they can make informed decisions. Nicholas Christakis (1999) argues that physicians are extremely poor at prognosis, or projecting how much longer a dying patient has to live, and they often convey an unrealistically optimistic picture of their patient's future.

## MEANING MAKING

A second area of inquiry that has attracted renewed scholarly attention is *meaning making*, both among the dying and their loved ones following loss. This concept was first set forth in *Death and Identity*, where Robert Fulton (1965) argued that preserving, rather than losing, personal identity was a critical aspect of the dying process. Sociologist Victor Marshall (1980) proposed that heightened awareness of one's impending death triggers increased self-reflection, reminiscence, and the conscious construction of a coherent personal history. Similarly, developmental theorist Erik Erikson (1902–1994) proposed that preparation for death is the key developmental challenge for older adults. Older adults must simultaneously balance their fear of death and loss, with a heightened capacity for finding meaning in life. More recently, Edwin Shneidman (1995) proposed that dying persons actively construct a post self, or a lasting image of the self that will persist after one's death.

The ways that bereaved survivors actively find meaning in death was articulated early on by Herman Feifel, who observed that the mourning period following loss provides a time for the bereaved to "redefine and integrate oneself into life" (1990, p. 9). Current research explores the ways that active meaning making among the newly bereaved helps to reestablish predictability and one's sense of security. Other goals for the bereaved include personal growth, an adaptive broadening of philosophical perspectives, and an increased appreciation of other interpersonal relations.

## RESEARCH CHALLENGES

Scholars of death and dying face several important methodological challenges. First, bereavement research focuses nearly exclusively on the loss of a spouse, children, and

| | All races | White | Black | Asian or Pacific Islander | American Indian | Hispanic |
|---|---|---|---|---|---|---|
| 1 | Diseases of heart | Diseases of heart | Diseases of heart | Diseases of heart | Diseases of heart | Diseases of heart |
| 2 | Malignant neoplasms | Malignant neoplasms | Malignant neoplasms | Malignant neoplasms | Malignant neoplasms | Malignant neoplasms |
| 3 | Chronic lower respiratory diseases | Chronic lower respiratory diseases | Cerebrovascular diseases | Cerebrovascular diseases | Cerebrovascular diseases | Cerebrovascular diseases |
| 4 | Cerebrovascular diseases | Cerebrovascular diseases | Diabetes mellitus | Chronic lower respiratory diseases | Diabetes mellitus | Diabetes mellitus |
| 5 | Diabetes mellitus | Influenza and pneumonia | Chronic lower respiratory diseases | Influenza and pneumonia | Chronic lower respiratory diseases | Chronic lower respiratory diseases |

***Figure 2.*** *Leading causes of death among men age 65 and over, by sex, race, and origin, 2004.* CENGAGE LEARNING, GALE.

parents; few studies investigate personal responses to the deaths of friends, siblings, or unmarried romantic partners (including gay and lesbian partners) in later life. Life course scholars recognize the importance of *linked lives,* underscoring the value of exploring bereavement across multiple relationships. A further limitation is that studies vary widely in their definition of *dying.* Common measures to define it include one's current illness diagnosis, combinations of diagnoses, symptom expression, and functional capacity (George, 2002). Finally, although most conceptual models of the dying process and bereavement are dynamic, such as the stage theory of dying (Kübler-Ross, 1969), most empirical studies still rely on single point-in-time evaluations that retrospectively recall the dying and bereavement process.

## FUTURE DIRECTIONS

In the future, research may focus increasingly on positive aspects of dying, including psychological resilience in the face of loss, and the characteristics of and pathways to a good death. Important research goals include pinpointing modifiable factors of social contexts and relationships that may help ensure a smooth transition to death and bereavement. Early theories of loss proposed that persons who were not depressed following the loss of a loved one were pathological. Researchers now are documenting that the non-depressed bereaved may experience "resilience" rather than pathological "absent grief" (Bonanno, 2004).

Research on the good death also is accumulating. A *good death* is characterized as one where medical treatments minimize avoidable pain and matches patients' and family members' preferences. A good death also encompasses important social, psychological, and philosophical elements, such as accepting one's impending death and not feeling like a burden to loved ones. As norms for a good death are solidified, a fruitful line of inquiry may be the consequences for bereaved family members and health care providers when a death occurs under conditions that fail to meet the widely accepted ideal. Failure to achieve the good death may reflect enduring social and structural obstacles. Family member (or caregiver) involvement is essential to a patient's participation in hospice; few studies have explored the extent to which unmarried or childless older adults rely on hospice. Such inquiries may further reveal the ways that the experience of death reflects persistent social inequalities and diverse sociohistorical contexts.

SEE ALSO Volume 3: *Hospice and Palliative Care; Life Expectancy; Mortality; Suicide, Later Life.*

### BIBLIOGRAPHY


Aries, P. (1981). *The hour of our death* (H. Weaver, Trans.). New York: Knopf.

Blauner, R. (1966). Death and social structure. *Psychiatry, 29,* 378–394.

Bonanno, G. A. (2004). Loss, trauma, and human resilience: Have we underestimated the human capacity to thrive after extremely aversive events? *American Psychologist, 59,* 20–28.

Bryant, C. D. (Ed.). (2003). *Handbook of death & dying.* Thousand Oaks, CA: Sage.

Centers for Disease Control. (2006, June 28). *National Vital Statistics Reports,* 54 (19). Washington, DC: Author.

Christakis, N. A. (1999). *Death foretold: Prophecy and prognosis in medical care.* Chicago: University of Chicago Press.

Faunce, W. A., & Fulton, R. L. (1958). The sociology of death: A neglected area in sociological research. *Social Forces, 36,* 205–209.

Feifel, H. (1990). Psychology and death: Meaningful rediscovery. *American Psychologist, 45,* 537–543.

Fulton, R. L. (1965). *Death and identity.* New York: John Wiley and Sons.

George, L. K. (2002). Research design in end of life research: State of the science [Special issue]. *The Gerontologist, 42,* 86–98.
Glaser, B. G., & Strauss, A. L. (1965). *Awareness of dying.* Chicago: Aldine.
Glaser, B. G., & Strauss, A. L. (1968). *Time for dying.* Chicago: Aldine.
Gorer, G. (1965). *Death, grief, and mourning.* Garden City, NY: Doubleday.
Kübler-Ross, E. (1969). *On death and dying.* New York: Macmillan.
Marshall, V. (1980). *Last chapters: A sociology of aging and dying.* Monterey, CA: Brooks and Cole.
Mitford, J. (1963). *The American way of death.* New York: Simon and Schuster.
National Hospice and Palliative Care Organization (NHPCO). (2001). *Facts and figures about hospice care in America.* Washington, DC: Author.
Omran, A. R. (1971). The epidemiologic transition: A theory of the epidemiology of population change. *Milbank Memorial Fund Quarterly, 29,* 509–538.
Shneidman, E. S. (1995). The post self. In J. B. Williamson & E. S. Shneidman (Eds.), *Death: Current perspectives* (4th ed., pp. 454–460). Mountain View, CA: Mayfield.

***Deborah Carr***

# DEMENTIAS

*Dementia* is a broad term referring to a syndrome that involves cognitive decline that is sufficiently severe to interfere with an individual's daily functioning. Dementia may encompass a variety of symptoms, including impairment in memory, communication, or personality change, that have a variety of causes (e.g., Alzheimer's disease [AD], cerebrovascular disease, and so forth). Dementia is the behavioral and cognitive expression of an underlying disease process that is causing damage to the brain. For example, AD involves one set of specific brain alterations that lead to a dementia syndrome characterized by severe declines in memory. As AD pathology spreads throughout the brain, additional cognitive, behavioral, and emotional capacities are disrupted. This entry describes several types of dementia including their underlying brain damage, clinical presentation, prevalence, progression, and the extent to which rates of these dementias differ by ethnicity, sex, and geographic region.

Although AD is the most well-known cause of dementia, there are several other pathologies that result in similar symptoms. In general, the dementias are most distinct from one another in the early stages. However, as dementia progresses, the underlying brain damage is more severe and widespread. As a result, more severe dementia involves damage to multiple brain regions and greater impairment in multiple cognitive and behavioral functions. Thus, it is increasingly difficult to find distinctiveness among specific types of dementia as the syndrome progresses over time. An additional source of commonality across types of dementia comes from their overlap in terms of underlying pathology. For example, it is relatively common for individuals to have multiple dementia pathologies, such as both AD and cerebrovascular changes. As a result, some medical experts have advocated a shift in the conceptualization of the various forms of dementia toward the underlying neuropathology rather than the clinical expression of symptoms (Ritchie & Lovestone, 2002). With this distinction in mind, this entry will focus on both the underlying pathology and the expression of symptoms of four types of dementia in their early forms (see Table 1), when their behavioral and cognitive expression is most distinct.

| Symptom | Type of Dementia |
|---|---|
| Memory loss for recent information | AD, VD, LBD, FTD |
| Difficulty performing familiar tasks | AD |
| Difficulties with language and communication | AD, LBD, VD, FTD |
| Disorientation to time and place | AD, LBD, VD |
| Poor or decreased judgment | AD, LBD |
| Misplacing things, especially in unusual places | AD |
| Changes in mood or behavior | AD, LBD, VD, FTD |
| Changes in personality | AD, FTD |
| Difficulty following directions | AD, LBD, VD |
| Recurrent visual hallucinations | LBD |
| Loss of initiative, apathy or unwillingness to talk | AD, VD, FTD |

Note: AD, Alzheimer's disease; VD, vascular dementia; LBD, Lewy body dementia; FTD frontotemporal dementia.

***Table 1.*** *Expression of symptoms of four types of dementia in their early forms.* CENGAGE LEARNING, GALE.

## ALZHEIMER'S DISEASE

AD is the most common and most extensively researched form of dementia, and, as a result, it is treated as the prototypical dementia used to define the broader syndrome itself. Recent estimates suggest that approximately 4.5 million individuals in the United States have AD, and that by the year 2050 this number will grow to more than 13 million with the greatest growth occurring among those over the age of 85 years (Hebert, Beckett, Scherr, & Evans, 2001). The prevalence of AD increases substantially with age. AD is present in roughly 1–1.5% of those in their early 60s (Ritchie & Lovestone, 2002) and in up to 30% among those 80 to 85 years (Blennow, de Leon, & Zetterberg, 2006).

The hallmark neuropathological changes of AD include (a) plaques, which build up between nerve cells and contain deposits of protein fragments; (b) neurofibrillary tangles, which form inside the dying cells and are composed of a protein called tau; and (c) shrinkage of the brain. These changes are initially present in the medial temporal lobes, particularly the hippocampus and related structures, but eventually spread to other regions of the brain, most notably the frontal and parietal lobes. In early AD, these changes are associated with impairment in memory for recent events, names, and locations, but additional changes are observed as the syndrome progresses, including the inability to name common objects, poor judgment, problems with planning and problem-solving, and difficulty with visual-spatial functioning. AD is characterized by a gradual onset and progressive decline. AD can currently only be confirmed by neuropathological evidence (i.e., autopsy); therefore the clinical diagnosis of AD must be considered either possible or probable while the person is still living.

## VASCULAR DEMENTIA

Vascular dementia (VaD) has traditionally been regarded as the second most common form of dementia in late life. Diagnosis requires (a) presence of dementia, or severe cognitive impairment; (b) evidence of cerebrovascular disease such as a stroke; and (c) a temporal connection between the presence of cerebrovascular disease and the onset of dementia. VaD is less homogeneous in its behavioral and cognitive expression than AD because the underlying brain pathology can occur in a variety of locations due to either chronic cerebral ischemia, acute stroke (large or small vessel), or insufficient blood flow to the brain due to hypotensive episodes (O'Brien, 2006; O'Brien et al., 2003). Traditionally, VaD was thought to have a stepwise decline (as opposed to the gradual decline of AD) in which periods of relatively stable functioning were followed by abrupt decrements in function associated with a new vascular event, such as a heart attack or stroke. More recent evidence has suggested that VaD may follow a more progressive course, similar to that of AD (Pedelty & Nyenhuis, 2006). One possible explanation is the considerable overlap between AD and VaD pathology. Many individuals who were clinically diagnosed with VaD demonstrate evidence of both cerebrovascular disease and AD on autopsy, and vascular risk factors appear to place individuals at risk for both VaD and AD. Although the expression of VaD is heterogeneous, it has generally been associated with greater problems with attention, executive functioning that is necessary for tasks such as planning and problem-solving, and slower processing speed in the early stages. VaD is likely to be accompanied by depression and apathy in many cases.

## DEMENTIA WITH LEWY BODIES

Dementia with Lewy bodies (DLB) is becoming increasingly recognized clinically, and some research indicates that DLB may in fact be the second most common type of dementia, representing up to 10–15% of dementia cases (McKeith et al., 1996). DLB is a progressive form of dementia accompanied by the extrapyramidal signs of Parkinson's disease, which are associated with movement (e.g., rigidity, changes in gait, falls, and so forth). Lewy bodies, the underlying pathology, are accumulations of abnormal protein deposits within neurons located in the brain stem, limbic system, and cerebral cortex. Lewy bodies appear to disrupt dopaminergic and cholinergic systems, which play key roles in motor and cognitive functioning (Hou, Carlin, & Miller, 2004). The most prominent clinical symptoms are parkinsonism, fluctuating cognition, and visual hallucinations. Problems with executive functioning and visual-spatial functioning have also been observed in DLB, but memory is relatively spared when compared with AD. DLB has a progression rate similar to that of AD, but may be associated with greater impairment in activities of daily living and greater mortality risk when compared to AD.

## FRONTOTEMPORAL DEMENTIA

Frontotemporal dementia (FTD) is a broad class of dementias characterized by atrophy of the frontal and anterior temporal lobes. These dementias present clinically in several different forms including prominent personality changes or progressive changes in language depending on the region of the brain that is most affected. The frontal variant FTD is characterized by noticeable personality changes, particularly impulsive, disinhibited behavior or apathy and problems with executive functioning. In comparison to AD, memory is relatively preserved. FTD has a gradual and relatively early onset (often younger than 65 years) and is considered to be progressive. Primary progressive aphasia and semantic dementia are related syndromes that fall under the same general category of dementias associated with frontotemporal lobar degeneration, but which differ in that they primarily affect language and communication skills (Neary et al., 2005; Hou et al., 2004).

## RATES OF DEMENTIA BY ETHNICITY, SEX, AND GEOGRAPHIC REGION

The results from research concerning dementia prevalence rates by ethnicity, sex, and global region has been somewhat mixed and additional research is needed to clarify (a) the extent to which the prevalence of dementia varies as a function of these characteristics, and (b) what factors explain any differences that might exist. Highlighted below are several trends observed in the literature, but the reader is advised to consider these to be provisional findings pending additional research. The vast majority of this research has focused on either dementia in general (not specific to type), AD, and, to a lesser extent, VaD. Very little research has addressed prevalence differences in DLB and FTD along these dimensions.

**Ethnicity and Dementia Prevalence** Research suggests that in the United States, African Americans have higher rates of dementia than European Americans (Froehlich, Bogardus, Jr., & Inouye, 2001) although some studies have not found significant differences (Fillenbaum et al., 1998). In relation to specific dementia types, results have been mixed, but some studies suggest that African Americans have AD incidence rates twice those found for European Americans (Evans et al., 2003; Tang et al., 2001). VaD may be more common than AD among African Americans (Froehlich et al., 2001) and this finding has been attributed to high rates of stroke, diabetes, and hypertension among African Americans. However, although there may be differences between ethnic groups in terms of the prevalence of dementia, it is not yet clear whether these reflect true differences in the prevalence of dementia or whether these differences reflect problems with the methods used to detect and diagnose dementia in minority samples. For example, considerable research has documented a relatively high rate of false positives among minority elders, particularly in Hispanic and African-American populations (Fillenbaum, Heyman, Williams, Prosnitz, & Burchett, 1990). In other words, some of the cognitive tests used to identify cognitive impairment (the core feature of dementia) may misclassify some minority elders, potentially leading to overdiagnosis of dementia in these populations.

**Gender Differences in Dementia** Current research suggests that women have a greater prevalence of dementia in general and AD in particular (Baum, 2005). However, because age is the strongest risk factor for dementia and AD, the greater prevalence of dementia may be partially attributable to well-established differences in survival and longevity between men and women. In fact, one comprehensive review of incident dementia research reported minimal differences between men and women. Women had slightly greater risk for AD in the oldest age groups, but men had greater risk for VaD in younger age groups (Jorm & Jolley, 1998). Still other research has shown that gender is not associated with age of onset in AD, incidence of AD or dementia, or risk for developing dementia (Edland, Rocca, Peterson, Cha, & Kokmen, 2002). These conflicting findings point to the need for more research addressing gender differences in dementia, particularly in relation to incidence, and the genetic and environmental factors that contribute to the development of dementia in men and women.

**Cross-national Comparisons of Dementia Prevalence** In addition to differences by race and gender within countries, additional research has examined differences in the rates of dementia across countries and regions of the world. Over the years dementia research on a global scale has found differences in prevalence by country, region, and ethnicity, but research has not progressed sufficiently to provide stable estimates for all regions of the world. An expert panel convened in 2005 to review all available epidemiological evidence concerning prevalence of dementia on a global scale (Ferri et al., 2005). Using World Health Organization (WHO) regions, they determined that outside of North America, Western Europe, and certain western Pacific countries (especially Japan and Australia), there were not sufficient data to estimate the prevalence of dementia with confidence. Using available data, they estimated that developed nations have higher age-adjusted prevalence rates of dementia than developing nations. The lowest rates of dementia were in African and Southeast Asia. Western Pacific, Latin American, and eastern European countries had higher rates than Africa and Southeast Asia, but lower than Western Europe and North American countries.

Results concerning disparities in prevalence of specific types of dementia throughout the world have been even less clear. Throughout the 1980s and 1990s, most studies showed a preponderance of VaD cases over AD cases in Asian countries (Shibayama, Kasahara, & Kobayashi, 1986; Jorm, Korten, & Henderson, 1987; Larson & Imai, 1996). However, more recent research demonstrates that AD has become the most common dementia-related diagnosis in most countries around the world. In a study conducted in Japan, AD accounted for 55% of all dementia cases, whereas VaD only accounted for 26% (Yamada, Hattori, Miura, Tanabe, & Yamori, 2001). A similar study from China found rates of 55% and 37.5% for AD and VaD, respectively (Li et al., 2007). The prevalence of AD is even higher in the United States and most of Europe, where it has been reported to account for 76.9–90% of incident dementia cases in people over the age of 65 (Ganguli, Dodge, Chen, Belle, & DeKosky, 2000). Despite the overwhelming prevalence of AD, one study examining Cree Native Americans over the age of 65 found a prevalence rate of 4.2% for all dementias, but only 0.5% for AD (Hendrie et al., 1993). In Africa the demarcations between different types of dementia have been less obvious, though one study examining an elderly Egyptian sample found that AD accounted for 53% of dementia cases (Ineichen, 2000).

Although there is some uncertainty regarding differences in the prevalence of dementia worldwide, there is even less certainty regarding why these apparent differences might occur. These differences may be due to measurement issues (definitions of dementia and the measurement tools designed to detect them) or to sociocultural differences that affect the reporting of dementia. Many of the tests used to screen for dementia may not be equally effective among different cultures, as demonstrated by high false positives found in minority samples (Gurland, Wilder, Cross, Teresi, & Barrett, 1992). Variation could also be due to properties of the screening tests used, the definition of dementia used, lack of standardization of test administration procedures, biases, and differences in literacy of studied populations (Kukull & Ganguli, 2000). Cultural style of education may also affect scores on dementia screening measures. It is nearly impossible to construct a test that is entirely culture-free. Every test that is created will reflect to some extent the culture in which it was constructed, and its questions may have slightly different meanings for people from other cultures.

Prevalence estimates for developing countries may be lower because of underreporting and lower life expectancy. Dementia could be unreported in some countries because of its stigmatization in certain cultures, and the fact that families in some developing countries may tolerate a wider range of behavior considered to be abnormal by Western standards. Moreover, some of these families may seek help from local healers rather than consult Western doctors.

Despite these challenges with cross-cultural dementia research, there is some evidence to suggest that environmental factors may contribute to legitimate differences in the prevalence of dementia. For example, a study examining elderly Japanese Americans living in Hawaii found prevalence estimates of 9.3% for dementia and 5.4% for AD, which more closely resemble those found for European-American samples as opposed to older adults living in Japan (White et al., 1996). A similar study looking at elderly Japanese adults living in Washington state found an AD prevalence of 14% in people between the ages of 85 and 89, a figure that more closely resembles those found for European-American samples than those found in Asia (Graves et al., 1996). A study comparing an elderly sample from Ibadan, Nigeria, with a matched African-American sample from Indianapolis, Indiana, found dementia rates of 2.29% and 8.24% respectively, indicating that people of African decent living in the United States have dementia rates more similar to those found for European Americans than for elders living in Africa (Ogunniyi et al., 2000). Taken together, these findings seem to suggest that environmental characteristics specific to different geographical regions may play a role in the prevalence of AD and other dementias. Collectively these results highlight the need for further research directed toward identifying these factors.

There is also some evidence suggesting that ApoE4 allele may contribute to potential genetic influences on regional dementia differences. ApoE4 is a gene carried by 20–25% of the population and is known to increase risk for developing AD. In the Nigerian study described above, no association was found between possession of the ApoE4 allele and AD, though a significant association was found for the African-American sample (Ogunniyi et al., 2000). A different study comparing American citizens of different ethnicities presents somewhat conflicting results, as authors found that the presence of the ApoE4 allele was a strong risk factor for AD in European Americans, an intermediate risk factor for Hispanic Americans, and not a risk factor for African Americans (Larson & Imai, 1996). Moreover, some have suggested that the lower incidence of AD in Japanese populations may be related to a lower prevalence of the ApoE4 allele (Jorm & Jolley, 1998). The presence of one or more ApoE4 alleles may increase vulnerability to develop AD, but research examining different populations suggests that the extent to which this occurs may function differently between different ethnic and cultural groups. These conflicting, yet intriguing, findings clearly indicate that more research is warranted on the subject of genetic factors that affect the development of AD and dementia. Future research for policy, practice, screening, and interventions should acknowledge differences in the influence of ApoE4 on different populations.

**SEE ALSO** Volume 3: *Aging; Cognitive Functioning and Decline; Genetic Influences, Later Life; Mental Health, Later Life.*

**BIBLIOGRAPHY**

Baum, L. W. (2005). Sex, hormones, and Alzheimer's disease. *Journals of Gerontology Series A: Biological Sciences and Medical Sciences, 60*(6), 736–743.

Blennow, K., de Leon, M. J., & Zetterberg, H. (2006). Alzheimer's disease. *Lancet, 368*(9533), 387–403.

Edland, S., Rocca, W., Peterson, R., Cha, R., & Kokmen, E. (2002). Dementia and Alzheimer disease incidence rates do not vary by sex in Rochester, Minn. *Archives of Neurology, 59*(10), 1589–1593.

Evans, D., Bennet, D., Wilson, R., Bienias, J., Morris, M., Scherr, P. et al. (2003). Incidence of Alzheimer's disease in a biracial urban community: Relation to the apolipoprotein E allele status. *Archives of Neurology, 60*(2), 185–189.

Ferri, C. P., Prince, M., Brayne, C., Brodaty, H., Fratiglioni, L., Ganguli, M. et al. (2005). Global prevalence of dementia: A Delphi consensus study. *Lancet, 366*(9503), 2112–2117.

Fillenbaum, G. G., Heyman, A., Huber, M. S., Woodbury, M. A., Leiss, J., Schmader, K. E. et al. (1998). The prevalence and 3-year incidence of dementia in older Black and White community residents. *Journal of Clinical Epidemiology, 51*, 587–595.

Fillenbaum, G. G., Heyman, A., Williams, K., Prosnitz, B., & Burchett, B. (1990). Sensitivity and specificity of standardized screens of cognitive impairment and dementia among elderly Black and White community residents. *Journal of Clinical Epidemiology, 43*, 651–660.

Froehlich, T. E., Bogardus, S. T., Jr., & Inouye, S. K. (2001). Dementia and race: Are there differences between African Americans and Caucasians? *Journal of the American Geriatrics Society, 49*(4), 477–484.

*Frontotemporal dementia: Signs and symptoms.* Updated May 8, 2007. Retrieved April 30, 2008, from http://www.ucsfhealth.org/adult/medical_services/memory/fronto/conditions/ftd/signs.html

Ganguli, M., Dodge, H., Chen, P., Belle, S., & DeKosky, S. (2000). Ten-year incidence of dementia in a rural elderly U.S. community population: The movies project. *Neurology, 54*(5), 1109–1116.

Gatz, M., Fiske, A., Reynolds, C.A., Wetherell, J.L., Johansson, B., & Pedersen, N.L. (2003). Sex differences in genetic risk for dementia. *Behavior Genetics, 33*, 95–105.

Graves, A., Larson, E., Edland, S., Bowen, J., McCormick, W., McCurry, S., et al. (1996). Prevalence of dementia and its subtypes in the Japanese-American population of King County, Washington state. *American Journal of Epidemiology, 144*(8), 760–771.

Gurland, B., Wilder, D., Cross, P., Teresi, J., & Barrett, V. (1992). Screening scales for dementia: Toward reconciliation of conflicting cross-cultural findings. *International Journal of Geriatric Psychiatry, 7*, 105–113.

Hebert, L. E., Beckett, L. A., Scherr, P. A., & Evans, D. A. (2001). Annual incidence of Alzheimer's disease in the United States projected to the years 2000 through 2050. *Alzheimer's Disease Association Disorder, 15*, 169–173.

Hendrie, H., Hall, K., Pillay, N., Rodgers, D., Prince, C., Norton, J. et al. (1993). Alzheimer's disease is rare in Cree. *International Psychogeriatrics, 5*(1), 5–14.

Hou, C. E., Carlin, D., & Miller, B. L. (2004). Non-Alzheimer's disease dementias: Anatomic, clinical, and molecular correlates. *Canadian Journal of Psychiatry, 49*, 164–171.

Ineichen, B. (2000). The epidemiology of dementia in Africa: A review. *Social Science & Medicine, 50*(11), 1673–1677.

Jorm, A. F., Korten, A., & Henderson, A. (1987). The prevalence of dementia: A quantitative integration of the literature. *Acta Psychiatrica Scandinavica, 76*(5), 465–479.

Jorm, A. F., & Jolley, D. (1998). The incidence of dementia—A meta-analysis. *Neurology, 51*(3), 728–733.

Kukull, W., & Ganguli, M. (2000). Epidemiology of dementia: concepts and overview. *Neurologic Clinics, 18*(4).

Larson, E., & Imai, Y. (1996). An overview of dementia and ethnicity with special emphasis on the epidemiology of dementia. *Ethnicity and the Dementias, 2*, 9–20.

*Lewy body disease: Signs, symptoms, and treatment.* Updated December 19, 2007. Retrieved April 30, 2008, from http://www.helpguide.org/elder/lewy_body_disease.htm

Li, S., Yan, F., Li, G., Chen, C., Zhang, W., Liu, J. et al. (2007). Is the dementia rate increasing in Beijing? Prevalence and incidence of dementia 10 years later in an urban elderly population. *Acta Psychiatrica Scandinavica, 115*, 73–79.

McKeith, I. G., Galasko, D., Kosaka, K., Perry, E. K., Dickson, D. W., Hansen, L. A., et al. (1996). Consensus guidelines for the clinical and pathologic diagnosis of dementia with Lewy bodies (DLB): Report of the consortium on DLB international workshop. *Neurology, 47*(5), 1113–1124.

Neary, D., Snowden, J., & Mann, D. (2005). Frontotemporal dementia. *Lancet Neurology, 4*, 771–780.

O'Brien, J. T. (2006). Vascular cognitive impairment. *American Journal of Geriatric Psychiatry, 14*, 724–733.

O'Brien, J. T., Erkinjuntti, T., Reisberg, B., Roman, G., Sawada, T., Pantoni, L. et al. (2003). Vascular cognitive impairment. *Lancet Neurology, 2*, 89–98.

Ogunniyi, A., Baiyewu, O., Gureje, O., Hall, K., Unverzagt, F., Siu, S. et al. (2000). Epidemiology of dementia in Nigeria: Results from the Indianapolis-Ibadan study. *European Journal of Neurology, 7*(5), 485–490.

Pedelty, L., & Nyenhuis, D.L. (2006). Vascular cognitive impairment. *Current Treatment Options in Cardiovascular Medicine, 8*, 243–250.

Ritchie, K., & Lovestone, S. (2002). The dementias. *Lancet, 360*(9347), 1759–1766.

Shibayama, H., Kasahara, Y., Kobayashi, H. et al. (1986). Prevalence of dementia in a Japanese elderly population. *Acta Psychiatrica Scandinavica, 74*(2), 144–151.

Tang, M., Cross, P., Andrews, H., Jacobs, D., Small, S., Bell, K. et al. (2001). Incidence of AD in African Americans, Caribbean Hispanics, and Caucasians in northern Manhattan. *Neurology, 56*(1), 49–56.

*Vascular dementia: Signs, symptoms, prognosis, and support.* Updated December 10, 2007. Retrieved April 30, 2008, from http://www.helpguide.org/elder/vascular_dementia.htm

White, L., Petrovitch, H., Ross, G., Masaki, K., Abbott, R., Teng, E. et al. (1996). Prevalence of dementia in older Japanese-American men in Hawaii: The Honolulu-Asia aging study. *Journal of the American Medical Association, 276*(12), 955–960.

Yamada, T., Hattori, H., Miura, A., Tanabe, M., & Yamori, Y. (2001). Prevalence of Alzheimer's disease, vascular dementia, and dementia with Lewy bodies in a Japanese population. *Psychiatry and Clinical Neurosciences, 55*(1), 21–25.

***Benjamin T. Mast***
***Pamela J. Healy***

# DEMOGRAPHIC TRANSITION THEORIES

Social scientists have identified two main demographic transitions. The first or "classic" demographic transition refers to the historical declines in mortality and fertility, as witnessed from the 18th century onward in several European populations, and continuing at present in most developing countries. The end point of the first demographic transition (FDT) was supposed to be an older stationary population (i.e., a population that has an even distribution of age groups), with replacement fertility (i.e., just over two children on average), growth rates oscillating around zero (i.e., the total population size is stable), and life expectancies higher than 70 years. At this stage of the demographic transition, there is a balance between deaths and births, and thus populations would not require sustained immigration for their continuation and growth. Moreover, households in all parts of the world would converge toward the nuclear and conjugal types, composed of married couples and their offspring.

The second demographic transition (SDT), by contrast, sees no such equilibrium as the end point. Rather, a shift in values and tastes brings new developments in the form of sustained below-replacement fertility, a multitude of living arrangements other than marriage, the disconnection between marriage and procreation, and no stationary population. Under these conditions, populations would decline in size if not complemented by new migrants (i.e., "replacement migration"), and they will also be much older than envisaged in the FDT model as a result of lower fertility and additional gains in longevity. Migration streams will not be capable of stemming the aging of national populations but will merely stabilize population sizes. On the whole, the SDT brings new social challenges, including those associated with populations that have disproportionately large numbers of older persons, less stability of households, and higher levels of poverty or exclusion among certain household types (e.g., single persons of all ages, single mothers) and that are dealing with the integration of immigrants and other cultures.

## THE FIRST DEMOGRAPHIC TRANSITION

A typical description of the FDT is that it is an irreversible process of change from a demographic regime with high death rates and high birth rates to a stable regime with low birth and death rates. Moreover, such a change is considered typical for societies that move from a preindustrial to an industrialized economy.

**The Origins of the Concept** The concept of the demographic transition has a long history. In 1890 the French demographer Arsène Dumont (1849–1902) explained the onset of the European fertility decline as an indication of "social capillarity"—that is, the process whereby individuals aspire to upward social mobility. As a result, parents project this aspiration onto their children, invest in their education, and thus place a greater emphasis on the "quality" rather than the "quantity" of their offspring. A century later, economists would call this the "quantity–quality shift." The notion of a systemic demographic transition with distinct phases can be traced to two scientists: the American sociologist Warren S. Thompson (1887–1973) and the French demographer and economist Adolphe Landry (1874–1956).

Thompson developed a three-category typology of nations, based on growth rates. The first group includes populations with low growth rates that had made it through the mortality and fertility declines, and these populations would be on the way to a stationary path or even a declining one. This category comprised the northern and western European countries and the nations settled by European immigrants (e.g., the United States, Canada). The second group consisted of populations where the death rates had fallen but where fertility rates were still high—resulting in high population growth rates. This group comprised southern and eastern European populations. The third group was made up of pretransitional or "Malthusian" populations (referring to Thomas Robert Malthus [1766–1834], the influential English demographer who believed population growth would be limited by resource availability). Countries in this third group had not experienced any of these changes in birth and death rates. Thompson was often pessimistic about the final outcome of the demographic transition given the political and economic problems that such an unequal timing of the transition would produce, but he has the merit of presenting the transition as a global ongoing process.

In 1934 Landry published *La Révolution Démographique*, in which he proposed essentially the same ideas as Thompson, although he did so independently. He also predicted a stationary or declining population for those countries that are in the vanguard of the FDT but also theorized that countries that experience the transition at a later point in history would go through the transition much faster than their predecessors. Landry also provided a much more elaborate account of the reasons for the declines in mortality and fertility.

Neither Thompson nor Landry used the term *demographic transition*, however. The American demographers Frank W. Notestein (1902–1983) and Kingsley Davis (1908–1997) coined the term immediately after World War II.

**The FDT and Economic Development** A core assumption of FDT theory is that the transition follows a period of economic development, marked by specific factors such as urbanization, industrialization, rising real incomes, and increased literacy rates. Another core assumption is that the fertility decline is triggered by a reduction in infant and childhood mortality. Empirical research generated after World War II investigated both of these assumptions by focusing on both industrialized and developing countries. The link between economic development and fertility decline became not only the subject of academic investigation but also the focus of heated political debate. Against the backdrop of a worldwide population explosion in the 1960s and 1970s, "economic developers" and "family planners" debated the primary impetus for fertility declines. The former advocated economic development as the most effective path to fertility reductions, whereas the latter argued that the availability and diffusion of modern contraceptive methods was the answer. To this day, political leaders in developing countries have adopted policies and practices consistent with the family planner model.

During the 1960s and 1970s, tremendous scientific strides were made as well. Among the most notable studies of the FDT were (a) a historical examination of population change in Europe, led by researchers at the Office of Population Research at Princeton University, and (b) the World Fertility Survey, an innovative multination survey of fertility and family formation in developing nations. Both studies amassed large amounts of data and information; analyses of these data played a critical role in reshaping theories about the FDT.

**Institutional and Cultural Factors** In the historical European investigation, or the "Princeton project," researchers reconstructed marriage patterns and marital fertility transitions in all European provinces, from Gibraltar to the Urals. A key finding of the study was that modernization across a broad range of geographic regions only very loosely followed the lines of classic transition theory. Rather, the researchers found a vast number of exceptions, including, for instance, rural areas that experienced the FDT before urban or industrial ones, or areas where fertility declines preceded (rather than resulted from) decreases in childhood mortality. Many areas in France started the control of marital fertility as early as the 18th century, a time when real incomes were declining, mortality rates were not improving, and industrialization had not yet occurred. By contrast, England, the industrial pioneer in Europe, started its marital fertility decline only around 1880—nearly a full century after its initial spell of urban and industrial growth.

Perhaps the most surprising and important finding of the study was that economic factors played a modest and inconsistent role in fertility decline and that a previously overlooked serious series of factors—cultural conditions—were a powerful influence on fertility. For example, language differences emerged as powerful barriers in the widespread acceptance of contraceptive behavior and parity-specific (or rank-specific) fertility control. Put simply, the fertility norms of one region spread or "diffused" most easily to regions that shared a native tongue.

The pace at which demographic modernization occurred also varied widely based on the level of religiosity in a given region, regardless of whether that region was largely Protestant or Catholic. Secular areas that would vote for nonreligious political parties were very often the ones that took the lead in fertility control, and this link proved to be quite robust even when the region's socioeconomic and other demographic characteristics were controlled (e.g., Lesthaeghe & Wilson, 1986). Researchers on the Princeton project also documented the importance of the nuptiality (or marriage) transition for understanding the fertility transition. Specifically, they documented how a pattern of late and nonuniversal marriage in western and northern Europe, also known as the Malthusian marriage pattern, gradually gave way to much younger ages at first marriage and to smaller proportions remaining unmarried (and thus celibate). As a result of this transition in marriage patterns, the overall fertility decline could be broken down into two components referring, respectively, to the modernization of the marriage and marital fertility regimes (see Coale, 1969).

The general conclusion of the Princeton project was that fertility changes were not wholly determined by economic conditions. Rather, a broad array of cultural, religious, and social forces shaped societal-level fertility transitions. The project's findings led the demographer Ansley J. Coale (1973) to reformulate FDT theory. Coale proposed that three preconditions must *all* be satisfied before a fertility transition can occur:

1. *The readiness condition.* The new form of behavior (i.e., adoption of contraception) must have economic advantages for the couple and their already born children.
2. *The willingness condition.* The new form of behavior must be ethically or morally acceptable and not in conflict with one's religious convictions.
3. *The ability condition.* Couples must have access to sufficiently efficient and safe means to accomplish the goal of controlling their number of offspring.

Coale's conditions are commonly referred to as the "ready, willing, and able" model. If any fewer than the three conditions are satisfied simultaneously, then the fertility transition will be delayed. Coale's model adopts a much more holistic approach than the standard FDT, as his model integrates economic and noneconomic factors associated with readiness and willingness, respectively. He also emphasized the importance of the ability factor, which later became known as the family planning effort dimension in less developed countries (see Robinson & Ross, 2007).

A second major collection of studies sprung up around the World Fertility Surveys (WFS), conducted in the 1970s and 1980s in many developing countries. The surveys measured levels of fertility, infant and childhood mortality, and knowledge and use of contraception across many countries. The WFS went beyond these classic demographic topics and also obtained information about "intermediate fertility variables" (Bongaarts, 1978), or those factors that indirectly affect fertility, such as age at first marriage, length of time one breastfeeds, and incidence of contraceptive failures or nonuse (see the concept of "unmet need," Westoff & Ochoa, 1991). Each of these intermediate variables is related to socioeconomic and cultural indicators such as urbanization, literacy levels, gender relations and female empowerment, media penetration and exposure, religious beliefs, existence of consensual unions or polygyny, local networks, and family planning program organization characteristics.

Studies based on the WFS data revealed that many diverse paths may lead to a fertility transition and that all factors related to the "ready, willing, and able" trio were of significance. Moreover, not only individual characteristics but also those at the village or neighborhood level, along with broader patterns of social organization, mattered as significant factors in shaping the fertility and nuptiality transitions. The WFS led to the creation and implementation of the Demographic and Health Surveys, which also obtained information on health and health practices and access to contraception

Data from the Demographic and Health Surveys reveal that the vast majority of developing countries have either completed or are in the middle of their first demographic transition. As Landry predicted several decades ago, many such countries exhibited this demographic transformation faster and in a more compressed time period than did European nations. As a result, demographers have adjusted downward their projections of the size of the total world population by around the middle of the 21st century. Not all countries, however, have experienced rapid transitions. In many nations—such as Bangladesh, the Dominican Republic, Ghana, Kenya, and Peru—fertility declines stalled in mid-transition, well before reaching replacement-level fertility. Finally, in a handful of countries—mostly in West Africa and the Sahel, a border region along the Sahara Desert—the fertility transition has barely started and life expectancy remains low.

## THE SECOND DEMOGRAPHIC TRANSITION

The idea of a distinct phase in the demographic evolution in Western countries stems directly from Philippe Ariès's (1962) analysis of the history of childhood and his much later article, "Two Successive Motivations for the Declining Birth Rate in the West" (1980). In Ariès's view, the decline in fertility during the FDT was "unleashed by an enormous sentimental and financial investment in the child." Ariès referred to this as the "child-king era," and the fertility transition was carried by an altruistic investment in child quality. Yet this motivation has diminished in modern times. Within the SDT, the motivation for parenthood is adult self-realization; as such, fertility rates have declined to well below replacement rates. Ariès postulated that the altruistic element focusing on offspring has weakened, and the adult dyadic relationship has gained prominence instead. In other words, adults are more focused on themselves and their marital relationships and less focused on producing offspring.

Another major influence on SDT theory is the humanist psychologist Abraham H. Maslow's (1954) theory of changing needs. Maslow argued that as populations become wealthier and more educated, individuals shift their attention away from needs associated with survival, subsistence, security, and solidarity. Instead, they focus on individual self-realization, recognition, grassroots democracy, and expressive work and education values.

Maslow's model carries important implications for the SDT. The SDT is an overarching theory that relies on both economic and sociological reasoning to explain the fertility shifts that occurred in all Western nations beginning in the 1960s. This theory treats ideational changes as exogenous influences that contribute to human behavior—even in periods of economic stability. The SDT links cultural shifts to dynamic processes of cohort succession. That is, sweeping social and ideational change occurs when older, traditional cohorts die off and are replaced by younger cohorts who adhere to a new set of norms and behavioral expectations. Values and behaviors are mutually influential, and these mutual influences unfold over the life course.

Consistent with these broad notions, the SDT predicts that the typical demographic outcomes (such as sustained subreplacement fertility and the growth of alternative living arrangements such as cohabitation) are likely to emerge in non-Western societies when they follow in the direction of capitalist economies, with multilevel democratic institutions and greater emphasis on Maslow's "higher order needs" such as self-actualization.

The original statement of the SDT emphasized the connection between fertility trends and the shift in values orientations in the political and ethical domains (secularism, "post-materialist" values, anti-authoritarianism, and so on). Initially certain scholars still had some doubts about whether the new values were capable of sustaining a systemic shift in the demographic regime after 1970, but van de Kaa's 1987 article clearly postulated that Europe's SDT is much more than a short-lived accident of history.

## MAJOR CONTRASTS BETWEEN THE FIRST AND THE SECOND DEMOGRAPHIC TRANSITION

Some scholars argue that the SDT is not necessarily a new regime but is instead a mere continuation of the FDT. Such a "single-transition" view obscures major differences of both a demographic and social nature. The contrasts between the FDT and SDT are listed in Table 1. One of the main differences is found in *nuptiality trends*. In the FDT, ages at first marriage declined and the proportions marrying increased. In the SDT, by contrast, marriage occurred later, and nonmarital cohabitation rates increased—especially after 1990 in central and eastern Europe. Out-of-wedlock fertility also follows the Western trend in such nations. Moreover, such patterns are now also emerging in southern Europe (Italy, Malta, Spain, and especially Portugal).

| FDT | SDT |
|---|---|
| **A. Marriage** | |
| • Rise in proportions marrying, declining age at first marriage | • Fall in proportions married, rise in age at first marriage |
| • Low or reduced cohabitation | • Rise in cohabitation (pre- & postmarital) |
| • Low divorce | • Rise in divorce, earlier divorce |
| • High remarriage | • Decline of remarriage following both divorce and widowhood |
| **B. Fertility** | |
| • Decline in marital fertility via reductions at older ages, lowering mean ages at first parenthood | • Further decline in fertility via postponement, increasing mean age at first parenthood, structural subreplacement fertility |
| • Deficient contraception, parity failures | • Efficient contraception (exceptions in specific social groups) |
| • Declining illegitimate fertility | • Rising extra-marital fertility, parenthood within cohabitation |
| • Low definitive childlessness among married couples. | • Rising definitive childlessness in unions |
| **C. Societal background** | |
| • Preoccupations with basic material needs: income, work conditions, housing, health, schooling, social security. Solidarity prime value | • Rise of "higher order" needs: individual autonomy, self-actualisation, expressive work and socialisation values, grass-roots democracy, recognition. Tolerance prime value. |
| • Rising memberships of political, civic and community oriented networks. Strengthening of social cohesion | • Disengagement from civic and community oriented networks, social capital shifts to expressive and affective types. Weakening of social cohesion. |
| • Strong normative regulation by State and Churches. First secularisation wave, political and social "pillarisation" | • Retreat of the State, second secularisation wave, sexual revolution, refusal of authority, political "depillarisation". |
| • Segregated gender roles, familistic policies, embourgeoisement. | • Rising symmetry in gender roles, female economic autonomy. |
| • Ordered life course transitions, prudent marriage and dominance of one single family model. | • Flexible life course organisation, multiple lifestyles, open future. |

***Table 1.*** *Overview of demographic and societal characteristics respectively related to the FDT and SDT (Western Europe).* CENGAGE LEARNING, GALE.

Another important contrast between the FDT and the SDT involves the background of particular societies. With the exception of the very early fertility decline in France and a few other small European regions, much of the FDT was an integral part of a development phase during which economic growth fostered material aspirations and improvements in material living conditions. The SDT, by contrast, is founded on the rise of the higher order needs. Once the basic material preoccupations are satisfied, further income growth and educational expansion jointly lead to the articulation of more existential and expressive needs. These are centered on a triad: *self-actualization* in formulating goals, *individual autonomy* in choosing means, and claiming *recognition* for their realization. These issues emerge in a variety of domains, and this is why the SDT is related to such a broad array of indicators of ideational or cultural shift.

## RECENT SDT DEVELOPMENTS

Questions about the future development of the SDT mainly pertain to its potential spread to non-Western cultures and to the sequencing of the SDT characteristics in such contexts. In the West, either all SDT traits emerged fairly simultaneously or followed a typical sequence:

1. Postponement of marriage and parenthood, leading to subreplacement fertility.
2. Rise of premarital and postmarital cohabitation.
3. The addition as well of procreation among cohabitors.

Most cross-national differences observed to date reflect differences in the sequencing of the three above patterns. Several non-Western populations have by now experienced the first pattern: Japan, South Korea, Taiwan, Hong Kong, and Singapore all have experienced postponement of marriage and parenthood and have fertility levels well below replacement as a consequence. Demographers speculate that urban China should be added to that list. In addition, premarital cohabitation has emerged in Japan. Furthermore, fertility has dipped below replacement in a number of other settings, several of them Islamic (e.g., Iran, Tunisia, Kazakhstan), others Caribbean (e.g., Puerto Rico, Cuba, Jamaica, Trinidad and Tobago, Surinam) or part of the Indian subcontinent (e.g., the state of Kerala and several large urban areas in India). Studies have not yet documented, however, whether fertility dips in these parts of the world are associated with postponement of marriage and parenthood.

Finally, Scandinavian and western European countries that were in the vanguard of the SDT now have fertility levels that are *higher* than those in countries that transitioned later (Sobotka, in press). In the former countries, parenthood continues to be delayed until later in life, yet many couples quickly proceed to having a second child—a process scholars refer to as the "catching-up" effect. In contrast, other countries with total fertility rates that dipped below 1.5 children generally do not exhibit this same trend. Hence, researchers have observed a major bifurcation within the SDT context between populations that do and do not exhibit a catching-up effect. It is possible that cultural differences regarding gender roles, public policies aimed at establishing gender equity, and greater compatibility between domestic duties and work have helped to facilitate couples' ability to "catch up" in terms of their childbearing. Such policies are much more pronounced in the countries that were the initial SDT trendsetters, such as those in Scandinavia and western Europe. Conversely, the persistence of traditional gender roles and/or the lack of policies facilitating the work and family combination would curtail the catching-up effect and lead to much lower fertility (e.g., McDonald, 2000; Micheli, 2000; Reher, 1998; Tsuya, Bumpass, & Choe, 2000). Such questions will be at the forefront of demographers' and life course scholars' research agendas in the coming decades.

**SEE ALSO** Volume 2: *Age Structure; Epidemiologic Transition; Global Aging; Life Expectancy; Mortality; Population Aging.*

**BIBLIOGRAPHY**


Alwin, D. F. (1989). Changes in qualities valued in children in the United States, 1964 to 1984. *Social Science Research, 18*, 195–236.

Ariès, P. (1962). *Centuries of childhood: A social history of family life.* (R. Baldick, Trans.). New York: Knopf.

Ariès, P. (1980). Two successive motivations for the declining birth rate in the West. *Population and Development Review, 6*, 645–650.

Becker, G. S. (1996). *Accounting for tastes.* Cambridge, MA: Harvard University Press.

Bongaarts, J. (1978). A framework for analyzing the proximate determinants of fertility. *Population and Development Review, 4*, 105–132.

Coale, A. J. (1969). The decline of fertility in Europe from the French Revolution to World War II. In S. J. Behrman, L. Corsa Jr., & R. Freedman (Eds.), *Fertility and family planning: A world view* (pp. 3–24). Ann Arbor: University of Michigan Press.

Coale, A. J. (1973). The demographic transition. In *International Population Conference* (Vol. 1, pp. 53–72). Liège, Belgium: International Union for the Scientific Study of Population.

Davis, K. (1945). The world demographic transition. *Annals of the American Academy of Political and Social Science, 237*, 1–11.

Inglehart, R. (1990). *Culture shift in advanced industrial society.* Princeton, NJ: Princeton University Press.

Kirk, D. (1996). Demographic transition theory. *Population Studies, 50*, 361–387.

Lesthaeghe, R., & Neidert, L. (2006). The second demographic transition in the United States: Exception or textbook example? *Population and Development Review, 32*, 669–698.

Lesthaeghe, R., & Surkyn, J. (2008). When history moves on: The foundations and diffusion of the second demographic transition. In R. Jayakody, A. Thornton, & W. Axinn (Eds.), *International family change: Ideational perspectives* (pp. 81–117). Mahwah, NJ: Lawrence Erlbaum.

Lesthaeghe, R., & Wilson, C. (1986). Modes of production, secularization, and the pace of the fertility decline in western Europe, 1870–1930. In A. J. Coale & S. C. Watkins (Eds.), *The decline of fertility in Europe* (pp. 261–292). Princeton, NJ: Princeton University Press.

Maslow, A. (1954): *Motivation and personality.* New York: Harper & Row.

McDonald, P. (2000). Gender equity in theories of fertility transition. *Population and Development Review, 26*, 427–439.

Micheli, G. A. (2000). Kinship, family, and social network: The anthropological embedment of fertility change in southern Europe. *Demographic Research, 3*, Article 13. Retrieved June 14, 2008, from http://www.demographic-research.org/volumes

Notestein, F. W. (1945). Population: The long view. In T. W. Schultz (Ed.), *Food for the world* (pp. 36–57). Chicago: University of Chicago Press.

Palloni, A. (2001). Diffusion in sociological analysis. In J. B. Casterline (Ed.), *Diffusion processes and fertility transition: Selected perspectives* (pp. 66–114). Washington, DC: National Academy Press.

Reher, D. S. (1998). Family ties in western Europe: Persistent contrasts. *Population and Development Review, 24*, 203–234.

Robinson, W. C., & Ross, J. A. (Eds.). (2007). *The global family planning revolution: Three decades of population policies and programs.* Washington, DC: World Bank.

Sobotka, T. (in press). The diverse faces of the second demographic transition in Europe. *Demographic Research.*

Thompson, W. S. (1929). Population. *American Journal of Sociology, 34*, 959–975.

Tsuya, N. O., Bumpass, L. L., & Choe, M. K. (2000). Gender, employment, and housework in Japan, South Korea, and the United States. *Review of Population and Social Policy, 9*, 195–220.

van de Kaa, D. J. (1987). Europe's second demographic transition. *Population Bulletin, 42*(1), 1–59.

van de Kaa, D. J. (1996). Anchored narratives: The story and findings of half a century of research into the determinants of fertility. *Population Studies, 50*, 389–432.

van de Kaa, D. J. (2003). Second demographic transition. In P. Demeny & G. McNicoll (Eds.), *Encyclopedia of population* (Vol. 2, pp. 872–875). New York: Macmillan Reference USA.

Westoff, C. F., & Ochoa, L. H. (1991). *Unmet need and the demand for family planning.* DHS Comparative Studies No. 5. Columbia, MD: Institute for Resource Development.

***Ron J. Lesthaeghe***

# DIABETES, ADULTHOOD AND LATER LIFE

Diabetes is a significant and growing chronic health problem in the United States (Mokdad et al., 2000, 2003) and around the world (Wild, Roglic, Green, Sicree, & King, 2004). For persons with diabetes, the body cannot make or properly use insulin, the hormone that converts foods (particularly sugars and starches) into the fuel that is needed for daily energy. There are three classifications diabetes diagnoses: Type 1, in which the body cannot make insulin, affects 5 to 10% of Americans diagnosed with diabetes (usually at younger ages); type 2, in which the body does not properly use insulin, affects 90 to 95% of Americans diagnosed with diabetes (usually in midlife and older ages); and gestational diabetes, which occurs during pregnancy, affects about 4% of allpregnant women in the United States (National Institute of Diabetes and Digestive and Kidney Diseases [NIDDK], 2007). More recently, doctors have begun to diagnose a condition known as prediabetes in which the body is at high risk for not properly using insulin. This condition affects more than double the number of people already diagnosed with type 2 diabetes.

The cause of diabetes is unknown, although most experts agree that many factors are involved. That is, although the reason why some people develop diabetes and others do not is unclear, scientists have made great strides in recent years in identifying both biological and environmental factors that are associated with diabetes. For example, middle-age and older adults, women who had gestational diabetes, and members of certain race and ethnic groups are disproportionately represented among those diagnosed with diabetes, particularly type 2 diabetes. Similarly, diabetes rates are higher in people who are overweight, who do not exercise regularly, or who have high blood pressure or high cholesterol (Centers for Disease Control and Prevention [CDC], 2007; NIDDK, 2007). The following sections discuss trends in the prevalence and incidence of diabetes; identify causes and correlates of diabetes; describe the consequences of diabetes; and explain the differences in the onset and management of diabetes by gender, race/ethnicity, and social status.

## TRENDS IN PREVALENCE AND INCIDENCE OF DIABETES

According to researchers at the CDC (Mokdad et al., 2000, 2003), the prevalence (or total number at any point in time) of all types of diabetes in the United States has increased sharply in recent decades—from 4.9% in 1990 to 7.9% in 2001 (or more than 60% since 1990). The increases in the prevalence of diabetes have been observed in both men and women, across all age groups, in all race/ethnicity groups, and in all but five states. Reports of diabetes in men grew from 4.1% in 1990 to 6.8% in 2001 (a 66% increase), and in women from 5.6% in 1990 to 8.9% in 2001 (a 59% increase). The age groups with the greatest changes in reports of diabetes between 1990 and 2001 were adults ages 30 to 39 (from 2.1% to 4.1%, a 95% increase), 40 to 49 (from 3.6% to 6.6%, a 83% increase), and 50 to 59 (from 7.5% to 11.2%, a 49% increase). Although type 2 diabetes has been diagnosed in younger age groups, and more so in recent years, it is still most commonly diagnosed in middle-age and older adults. In fact, about 1 in 10 adults ages 40 to 59 and 1 in 5 adults ages 60 and older have diabetes, comprising the majority of all people with diabetes (NIDDK, 2007). Unfortunately, what is known about diabetes in age groups younger than 20 is currently hampered by a lack of nationally representative data needed to track changes in the risk and onset of diabetes.

The incidence (or number of new cases) of diabetes has increased in recent years as well. Using nationally representative survey data, about 603,000 cases of diabetes were newly diagnosed in 1990, more than doubling (to 1.2 million) by 2001 (NIDDK, 2007). Some 1.5 million cases of diabetes were newly diagnosed in 2005, nearly 9 in 10 (1.3 million) of those in middle-age and older adults. Despite the fact that some of the dramatic increases in the prevalence and incidence of diabetes may be due to greater awareness of the risks for diabetes from public health campaigns and, in turn, more doctor visits resulting in diagnoses, the increases in prevalence and incidence are troubling due to the serious individual and societal consequences of the disease. Government mandates, such as those described in the federal *Healthy People* reports, aim to reverse those trends and related consequences by focusing on the known causes and correlates of diabetes.

## CAUSES AND CORRELATES

As noted earlier, if a person cannot make or properly use insulin to provide needed daily energy, it is likely that the person has higher than normal levels of blood glucose, which may lead to a diagnosis of diabetes. Symptoms common to people with diabetes include increased thirst and urination, extreme tiredness, unexplained weight loss

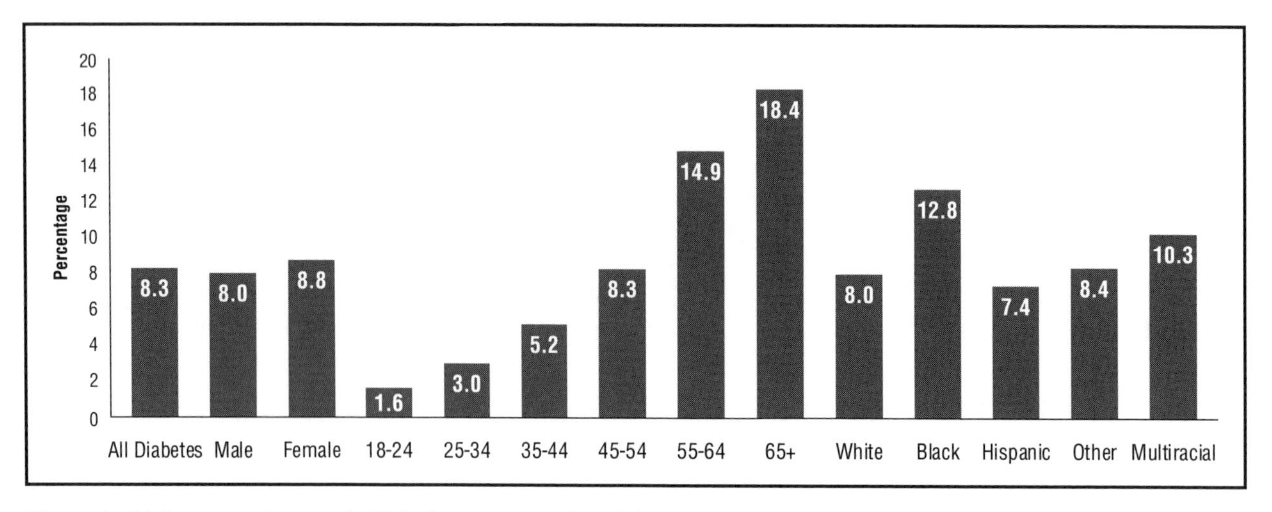


***Figure 1.*** *Diabetes prevalence in the U.S., by sex, age, and race/ethnicity, BRFSS 2006.* CENGAGE LEARNING, GALE.

or weight gain, blurred vision, frequent infections, and slow-healing wounds (NIDDK, 2007). Although the specific causes of diabetes remain a mystery, several biological and environmental factors are associated with the risk for or onset of diabetes, some nonmodifiable and some modifiable. For example, in addition to insulin problems, people with diabetes often have other clinical indicators such as higher than normal levels of blood pressure, LDL (or "bad") cholesterol, and triglycerides, as well as higher than normal waist-to-hip ratios, all indicators with both nonmodifiable and modifiable causes. The risk for diabetes also escalates with increasing age and membership in minority or non-White race/ethnic groups, both nonmodifiable factors.

Excess weight—and particularly obesity—is the modifiable risk factor most often identified with the onset and complications of diabetes. Just as the prevalence of diabetes has risen markedly in recent decades, the prevalence of obesity has also increased by more than 77% since 1990, from 11.8% in 1990 to 20.9% in 2001 (Mokdad et al., 2000, 2003). Many health care providers consider diabetes and obesity to be rising in tandem to epidemic proportions, leading to public health campaigns aimed at reversing the trends in both health problems (American Diabetes Association, 2007; CDC, 2007). Obesity, like diabetes, is disproportionately prevalent in midlife and in ethnic minority groups (Mokdad et al., 2001, 2003).

Because most of the management and consequences of diabetes are in the hands of the person living with diabetes, protective health behaviors such as weight loss and increased physical activity may be critical to good management as well as to fewer and less serious consequences. Despite the recommendations for weight loss, however, obesity is much more prevalent in people with diabetes than in those without (Mokdad et al., 2001; Wray, Blaum, Ofstedal, & Herzog, 2004). Nonetheless, a recent study documented that overweight middle-aged adults were at least 50% more likely to report they had lost 10 pounds of excess body weight if they had been diagnosed with diabetes than if they had not, suggesting that adults with diabetes understand their need to lose weight (Wray et al., 2004). In contrast, adults with diabetes continue to report lower levels of physical activity than do adults without diabetes, perhaps in part due to their higher numbers of health conditions. However, participation in other protective health behaviors may be increasing in recent years. For example, studies have shown that diabetes-related health behaviors such as daily monitoring of blood glucose, as well as getting annual appropriate physical exams, have increased between 1995 and 2001 (Okoro et al., 2004). Similarly, other general practices such as quitting smoking and getting flu and pneumonia vaccines have also increased.

## CONSEQUENCES OF DIABETES

According to NIDDK (2007), adults with diabetes are more likely than those without diabetes to have high blood pressure and other diseases and conditions associated with vascular disease, such as stroke, heart diseases, foot amputations, and vision impairments. High blood pressure is twice as common in persons with diabetes compared to persons without the disease; and up to 75% of cardiovascular disease is attributable to high blood pressure. It is not surprising then that in 2000 one in three people with diabetes reported they had also been diagnosed with cardiovascular disease. Diabetes confers a two-fold to four-fold increased risk of heart attacks and strokes in men and up to a ten-fold increased risk in premenopausal women (Engelgau et al., 2004).

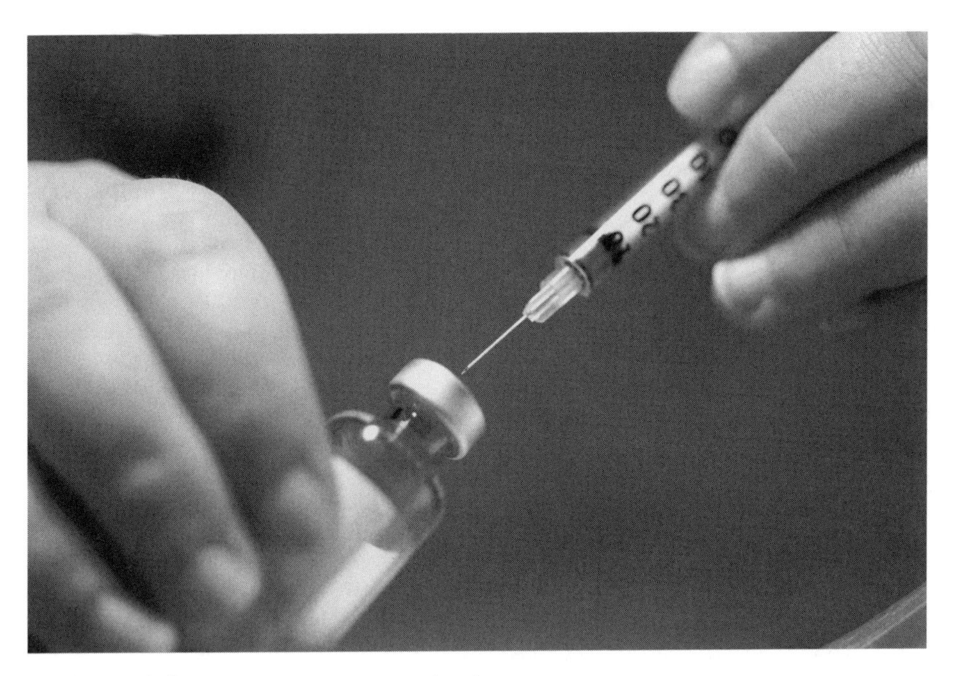

***Insulin.*** *A diabetic person prepares an insulin shot.* NATIONAL GEOGRAPHIC/GETTY IMAGES.

Diabetes is also associated with limitations in physical functioning and disabilities in older adults, lower active life expectancy, and premature mortality (Wray, Alwin, McCammon, Manning, & Best, 2006). For example, age-adjusted mortality in adults with diabetes is about twice that of adults without the disease. Older adults with diabetes are also more likely to have arthritis and geriatric conditions such as incontinence, falls, and poor cognitive performance.

Diabetes killed 73,249 people in the United States in 2002, making it the sixth leading cause of death in the United States. However, that ranking may be an underestimate because diabetes is often left off death certificates as an underlying cause of death, particularly in cases in which there may be multiple causes of death (NIDDK, 2007). For instance, roughly two out of three deaths to people with diabetes are attributed to heart disease and stroke, currently the first and third leading causes of death in the United States (Miniño, Heron, Murphy, & Kochanek, 2007). An estimate of the total costs of diabetes to the United States in 2002 is $132 billion (American Diabetes Association, 2003), including both direct medical costs ($92 billion) and indirect costs from disability, work loss, and premature mortality ($40 billion), accounting for one-tenth of all health care costs in the United States.

Despite these troubling statistics, adults with diabetes can reduce their risk for serious complications by controlling their blood glucose, blood pressure, and cholesterol, as well as participating in the protective diabetes-related health behaviors such as monitoring their blood glucose and having regular foot and eye exams (American Diabetes Association, 2007). According to NIDDK (2007), good glucose control reduces the risk of eye, kidney, and nerve complications; good blood pressure control reduces risks for both heart disease and stroke, as well as eye, kidney, and nerve complications; and good cholesterol control reduces the risk of heart disease and stroke.

## DIFFERENCES BY GENDER, RACE, AND SOCIAL STATUS

The onset of diabetes differs markedly by gender, race, and social status for reasons that are not yet clear. For example, studies using nationally representative data show diabetes and its complications are found disproportionately in women as well as in African American and Hispanic American adults (Mokdad et al., 2000, 2003; Wray et al., 2006). One in every three people born in the United States in 2000—and one in every two African American, American Indian, Hispanic American, and Asian American individuals born in 2000—are projected to develop diabetes in their lifetime (CDC, 2007). Analyses of census and other population-based survey data indicate that the prevalence of diabetes will increase 225% across all ages between 2000 and 2050, a rise from 12 to 39 million, and disproportionately in members of ethnic minority groups (CDC, 2007). Reasons for that projected increase include the overall aging and ethnic diversity of the U.S. population, as well as rising rates of obesity across all ages.

Because there is currently little or no evidence that sex- or race-linked biological differences underlie differences in the prevalence of most diseases, disability, and mortality (Wray & Blaum, 2001), other factors on which males and females differ may be responsible—for example, participation in risky health behaviors (e.g., smoking, drinking, and substance abuse), personality characteristics (e.g., hostility, anger), levels of and responses to stressful situation, and social support. Many of the risky behaviors associated with diabetes and its comorbid conditions (e.g., obesity, physical inactivity, smoking) are disproportionately prevalent in older adults with diabetes, compared to their older and younger counterparts without diabetes, as well as in African American and Hispanic American adults (Wray et al., 2006).

Similarly, middle-aged and older adults with diagnosed diabetes report lower education, income, net worth, and labor force participation than do those without diabetes (Wray, Ofstedal, Langa, & Blaum, 2005; Wray et al., 2006). Many of the risk factors described above also vary widely by social status such that lower levels of schooling, income, or wealth are associated with increasing numbers of risky health behaviors (Wray, Alwin, & McCammon, 2005). Although many existing studies have indicated that these more traditional health risks explain few health and mortality inequalities in general, research on their link to disparities in diabetes in particular is sparse. Wray and colleagues (2006) documented the persistent disproportionate prevalence and incidence of diabetes in African American and Hispanic American adults in midlife and older age, even after accounting for differences in education, income, and net worth. These troubling disparities need further exploration and understanding.

The dramatically increasing rates of diabetes and its serious complications across the United States are raising major concerns with health care providers, health educators, and policy makers, as well as those who have or at risk of getting the disease. Fortunately, studies and public health campaigns stress that people can play a major role in preventing the disease or reducing its complications by adopting a lifestyle that includes eating a healthy diet, maintaining a normal weight, being physically active, not smoking, and seeing a doctor regularly.

**SEE ALSO** Volume 2: *Obesity, Adulthood;* Volume 3: *Chronic Illness, Adulthood and Later Life; Health Behaviors, Later Life; Health Differentials/Disparities, Later Life.*

**BIBLIOGRAPHY**

American Diabetes Association. (2003). Economic costs of diabetes in the U.S. in 2002. *Diabetes Care, 26*, 917–932.

American Diabetes Association. (2007). Clinical practice recommendations. *Diabetes Care, 30*, S3.

Centers for Disease Control and Prevention. (2007). *National diabetes fact sheet 2003*. Retrieved June 11, 2008, from http://www.cdc.gov/diabetes

Engelgau, M. M., Geiss, L. S., Saaddine, J. B., Boyle, J. P., Benjamin, S. M., Gregg, E. W., et al. (2004). The evolving diabetes burden in the United States. *Annals of Internal Medicine, 140*, 945–950.

Miniño, A. M., Heron, M. P., Murphy, S. L., & Kochanek, K. D. (2007). Deaths: Final data for 2004. *National Vital Statistics Reports, 55*(19).

Mokdad, A. H., Ford, E. S., Bowman, B. A., Dietz, W. H., Vinicor, F., Bales, V. S., et al. (2001). The continuing increase of diabetes in the U.S. *Diabetes Care, 24*, 412.

Mokdad, A. H., Ford, E. S., Bowman, B. A., Dietz, W. H., Vinicor, F., Bales, V. S., et al. (2003). Prevalence of obesity, diabetes, and obesity-related health risk factors, 2001. *Journal of the American Medical Association, 289*, 76–79.

Mokdad, A. H., Ford, E. S., Bowman, B. A., Nelson, D. E., Engelgau, M. M., Vinicor, F., et al. (2000). Diabetes trends in the U.S.: 1990–1998. *Diabetes Care, 23*, 1278–1283.

National Institute of Diabetes and Digestive and Kidney Diseases. (2007). *National diabetes information clearinghouse: National diabetes statistics*. Retrieved June 11, 2008, from http://diabetes.niddk.nih.gov/dm

Okoro, C. A., Mokdad, A. H., Ford, E. S., Bowman, B. A., Vinicor, F., & Giles, W. H. (2004). Are persons with diabetes practicing healthier behaviors in the year 2001? Results from the Behavioral Risk Factor Surveillance System. *Preventive Medicine, 38*, 203–208.

Wild, S., Roglic, G., Green, A., Sicree, R., & King, H. (2004). Global prevalence of diabetes: Estimates for the year 2000 and projections for 2030. *Diabetes Care, 27*, 1047–1053.

Wray, L. A., Alwin, D. F., McCammon, R. J., Manning, T., & Best, L. E. (2006). Social status, risky health behaviors, and diabetes in middle-aged and older adults. *Journal of Gerontology: Social Sciences, 61B*, S290–S298.

Wray, L. A., & Blaum, C. S. (2001). Explaining the role of sex on disability: A population-based study. *The Gerontologist, 41*, 499–510.

Wray, L. A., Blaum, C. S., Ofstedal, M. B., & Herzog, A. R. (2004). Diabetes diagnosis and weight loss in middle-aged adults. *Research on Aging, 26*, 62–81.

Wray, L. A., Ofstedal, M. B., Langa, K. M., & Blaum, C. S. (2005). The effect of diabetes on disability in middle-aged and older adults. *Journal of Gerontology: Medical Sciences, 60A*, 1206–1211.

***Linda A. Wray***

# DISABILITY AND FUNCTIONAL LIMITATION, LATER LIFE

At some point in their lifetimes, many people living in the United States experience brief periods of difficulty carrying out everyday activities. For a small minority, having a functional limitation or disability is a lifelong challenge. In old age, when the likelihood of disability is greatest, people follow a variety of trajectories over time, including full functioning until death, onset of limitation followed rapidly by recovery, and steadily increasing limitation.

Many measures and sources of information on disability and functional limitation exist, but analysis of data from the U.S. Census indicates that in 2000, 19.3% of the population aged 5 years and older or almost 50 million people had a limitation or disability. The figures for population aged 65 and older were 41.9% and 14 million (Freedman, Martin, & Schoeni, 2004, Table 1). The definition used was broad and included physical, sensory, and cognitive limitations; self-care and going-outside-the-home disability; and for those aged 21 to 64, disability that affected employment.

Disability and functional limitation may negatively affect individual quality of life and productivity; they are also associated with increased medical expenditures. As the members of the U.S. Baby Boom generation (those born 1946 to 1964) approach old age, policymakers are especially interested in tracking trends in disability over time at the population level and in understanding better who is at greatest risk of having disabilities and how onset can be delayed and recovery facilitated.

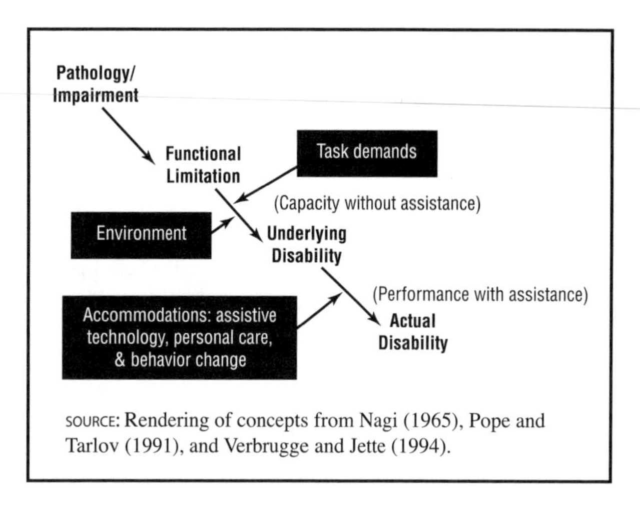


SOURCE: Rendering of concepts from Nagi (1965), Pope and Tarlov (1991), and Verbrugge and Jette (1994).

*Figure 1. The disablement process.* CENGAGE LEARNING, GALE.

## INCONSISTENTLY USED CONCEPTS AND TERMS

The terms *disability* and *functional limitations* are not used consistently by researchers or policymakers in the United States or in other countries around the world. Many employ no conceptual framework at all when considering these constructs, but indeed two widely recognized models exist. The most commonly used in the United States is the so-called *Disablement Process* that draws from the work of Nagi (1965), the Institute of Medicine (Pope & Tarlov, 1991), and Verbrugge and Jette (1994). As indicated in Figure 1, the basic stages of the process are: pathology/impairment, functional limitation, and disability carrying out socially defined roles or activities in a particular environment. Although it is sometimes difficult to distinguish between pathology and impairment, theoretically the former occurs at the cellular level, and the latter at the level of an organ or systems of organs. Functional limitations, which may be physical, sensory, or cognitive, refer to the level of the organism, and disability to how the person interacts with the greater world. For example, arthritis (pathology) may make it difficult to bend the knee (impairment), thus limiting the ability of the person to stoop (functional limitation). Whether such a limitation will in turn lead to a disability regarding, say, bathing may depend on whether a person uses a shower or a bathtub. Similarly, whether arthritis of the fingers leads to a work disability may depend on the demands of the tasks involved in the job. A computer operator or piano player might have a disability, but a night watchman might not have such disability.

Note that it is not the person who is disabled or not. That is, disability is not an inherent attribute of an individual. Rather a disability arises when a person's capacity is not sufficient to meet the demands of a particular task in a specific environment. This conceptualization of disability moves beyond a simple medical perspective that conceives of disability as solely reflecting the health of an individual to a view in which the individual, the task, and the environment are all factors. Moreover, besides built environment, the term *environment* includes the social environment. For example, social role expectations may influence self-assessments of ability to carry out some routine household tasks, such as cooking and cleaning. In the past, at least, women had greater experience with such activities and perceived them as part of their roles. Expected social roles also vary by age, as indicated by the 2000 Census's limiting questioning about work disability to those aged 21 to 64.

As shown in Figure 1, besides task demands and the environment, the use of various accommodations may influence whether a person of a given health status experiences a disability. Accommodations include changes in how the task is carried out, use of assistive technology, and receipt of help or supervision from another person. For example, if one's arthritis is worsening, a person may limit trips up and down stairs each day, use a cane, or take the arm of another person. Verbrugge and Jette (1994) and a few surveys distinguish between an intrinsic or underlying disability—an inability on one's own—and actual or residual disability—an inability even with behavior change, aids, and help.

Internationally, the World Health Organization has been at the forefront of efforts to conceptualize and measure disability since 1980. In the late 1990s, it undertook a consultative process that led to the 2002 publication of its International Classification of Functioning, Disabilities, and Health (known as ICF; World Health Organization, 2002). The ICF emphasizes positive language, focuses on participation in life situations as its ultimate outcome, and, like the Disablement Process, emphasizes the role of the environment, including physical, social, and attitudinal factors. A report by a committee of the U.S. Institute of Medicine (Field & Jette, 2007) encouraged the ICF's further refinement and operationalization with particular attention to developing a clearer distinction between specific activities of life and broader domains of participation. Nevertheless, the report called on various U.S. government statistical agencies to go ahead and adopt the ICF. In the meantime, the language of the Disablement Process framework is more commonly, although not universally or precisely, used in research and data collection in the United States.

## MEASURES

Multiple national-level surveys and the Census in the United States collect information from older people on functional limitations and disability. Typically these data take the form of self-reports, and response categories include difficulty, severity of difficulty, or inability. Some questions are phrased in terms of intrinsic disability, but others in terms of residual disability. Some surveys follow up questions about intrinsic disability with questions about use of assistive technology or personal help. One notable survey, the National Long Term Care Survey (NLTCS), imposes a requirement of chronicity, that is, it asks about disability lasting at least three months. For those who are unable to answer for themselves, proxy responses are sought by most surveys, although such responses in some cases may differ from self-reports if they were possible. Finally, whether the survey includes the institutionalized population as well as those living in the community may influence estimates. Thus, no universal method is used for seeking information about functional limitations and disability (Freedman, Martin, & Schoeni, 2004), although the core concepts are similar, as indicated in the following discussion.

**Functional Limitations** The most commonly used survey indicators of physical functional limitations in old age are the so-called Nagi (1965) measures, which were designed to assess Social Security disability applicants. Although originally used by medical personnel, today population surveys elicit self-reports of difficulty with such functions as standing for two hours, sitting for two hours, walking several blocks, lifting and carrying 10 pounds, stooping, climbing a flight of stairs, reaching over one's head, and grasping a small object. For example, since 1997 the annual National Health Interview Survey (NHIS) has asked one adult per household about nine such functions. Sometimes these measures are analyzed individually, but at other times researchers combine all the measures into a single indicator of ability or difficulty, or into indices of lower-body and upper-body functioning.

Tests in laboratory and clinical settings have indicated that some simple measures of physical performance also are predictive of the onset of disability and mortality (e.g., Guralnik, Simonsick, Ferrucci, Glynn, Berkman, Blazer et al., 1994; Onder, Penninx, Ferrucci, Fried, Guralnik, & Pahor, 2005; Rantanen, Volpato, Ferrucci, Heikkinen, Fried, & Guralnik, 2003). Accordingly, interest is growing in conducting such tests of physical functioning, rather than relying solely on self-reports, during in-person survey data collection efforts. For example, the 2002 wave of the Health and Retirement Study (HRS) included tests of lung function, grip strength, and walking speed. In the 2006 wave, tests of standing balance were added.

Regarding sensory functioning, questions about vision are often phrased in terms of difficulty reading a newspaper even when using glasses or contacts, but sometimes concentrate on blindness. Questions about hearing also range from difficulty hearing a conversation or the television to deafness. For example, the 2000 U.S. Census asked about blindness, deafness, and severe vision or hearing impairment.

A battery of questions are typically used to assess cognitive limitations, which may include difficulty with short- and long-term memory, deterioration of language function, apraxia (impaired ability to execute motor activities), agnosia (inability to recognize objects), and disturbances in executive functioning (inability to think abstractly and process information). The Mini-Mental State Examination (Folstein, Folstein, & McHugh, 1975), which was designed for clinical settings, forms the basis for the Telephone Interview Cognitive Screen (Brandt, Spencer, & Folstein, 1988), which in turn has been modified and adapted by various surveys. For example, the Asset and Health Dynamics of the Oldest Old study (AHEAD) and the HRS focus on memory and executive functioning. In particular, they use an immediate recall test involving 10 words (10 points); a delayed recall test of the same words (10 points); naming the day of the week and date (4 points); naming the object that people usually use to cut paper, the kind of prickly plant that grows in the desert, and the U.S. president and vice president (4 points); a serial 7s test that requires subtracting 7 from 100 five times (5 points); and counting backwards from 20 for 10 consecutive numbers (2 points). Different researchers use different summary measures, but Herzog and Wallace (1997) have suggested that those scoring eight or less (out of 35) are likely severely cognitively impaired.

**Disability** Disability is the most commonly used measure of the "health" of the older population. For members of this group, being able to care for themselves and live independently in the community are typically viewed as extremely desirable. Thus, assessment of disability in U.S. surveys of the older population is most often based on questions about activities of daily living (ADLs) and instrumental activities of daily living (IADL). The ADL battery of questions was originally proposed by Katz and colleagues (Katz, Ford, Moskowitz, Jackson, & Jaffee, 1963; Katz, Downs, Cash, & Grotz, 1970) to gauge the potential for rehabilitation of older hospital patients and involves asking about and observing such personal self-care activities as bathing, dressing, using the toilet, eating, transferring from bed to chair, continence, and grooming. The IADL questions were developed by Lawton and Brody (1969) to assist health care providers and others in assessing competence in taking care of such more routine needs as using the telephone, shopping, preparing meals, housekeeping, doing laundry, taking public transportation, taking medication, and handling finances. In the case of both ADLs and IADLs, some surveys ask about any difficulty or degree of difficulty doing these activities, with some including a response of inability as the most severe category. Some questions are formulated in terms of underlying disability, but others about residual disability, that is, even with help from another person or use of assistive technology. Yet another model is provided by the NHIS, which asks about need for help with these activities.

U.S. government programs to assist those with disability use a variety of definitions of disability (Freedman, Martin, & Schoeni, 2004). The largest program, that of the Social Security Administration, focuses on those under age 65 and on work disability by which it means the "inability to engage in any substantial gainful activity by reason of a medically determinable physical or mental impairment which can be expected to result in death or can be expected to last for a continuous period of not less than 12 months." This definition focuses on the health of the individual and does not take into consideration the environmental considerations of the conceptual frameworks presented earlier. Moreover, it does not focus on a specific job and the task demands of it, but on gainful activity in general. Nor, given the purpose

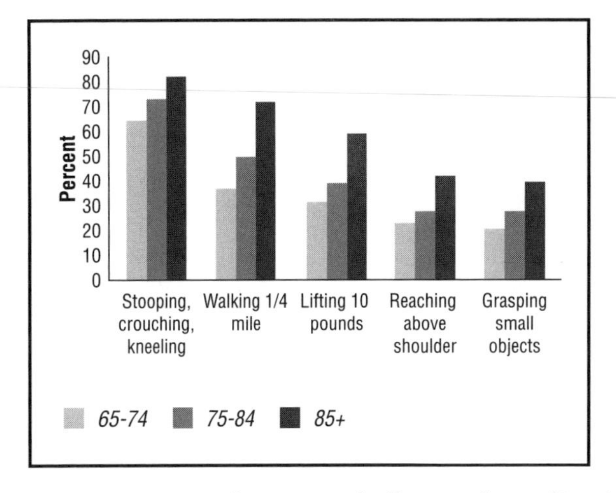


*Figure 2. Percentage of community-dwelling population 65 and over with difficulty with physical functions by age group, 2004.* CENGAGE LEARNING, GALE.

of determining benefit eligibility, does it address the possibility that people who are working might still have limitations associated with work (Jette & Badley, 2000).

Unlike the census, some surveys, such as the Current Population Survey (CPS), do ask older people about work disability. The CPS uses a definition similar to, although not exactly the same as, that of the Social Security Administration. However, as acknowledged by the survey designers, concern exists that answers to questions about work disability may represent rationalization of retirement decisions after the fact (Kreider, 1999) and, in the preretirement years, may be influenced by the availability of disability benefits (Duggan & Ingerman, 2008). Thus, for purposes of understanding the relation between health and work, such questions should be used with care.

## LEVELS OF FUNCTIONAL LIMITATIONS AND DISABILITIES

Figure 2 presents data from the 2004 Medicare Current Beneficiary Survey (MCBS) for five physical functional limitations for the 65 and older population by broad age groups. Clearly limitations increase with age, and such lower-body functions as walking one quarter mile present more difficulty than such upper-body functions as grasping small objects. Overall, almost 70% of the 65 and older population (all age groups combined) reported difficulty with stooping, crouching, and kneeling. However, as noted earlier, the way questions are worded may make a big difference in how people assess their functioning. The National Center for Health Statistics (NCHS) points out that a similar question on the NHIS that substitutes *bending* for *crouching* results in fewer than 50% reporting difficulty (NCHS, 2007a).

| | 65+ | 65–74 | 75–84 | 85+ |
|---|---|---|---|---|
| **IADLs** | | | | |
| Doing heavy housework | 30.59 | 23.12 | 33.46 | 52.95 |
| Shopping | 13.39 | 7.96 | 14.41 | 32.96 |
| Doing light housework | 11.39 | 7.43 | 12.10 | 25.78 |
| Preparing meals | 8.84 | 5.09 | 9.01 | 24.01 |
| Managing money | 6.93 | 3.52 | 7.43 | 21.16 |
| Using the telephone | 6.83 | 3.15 | 7.42 | 18.83 |
| **ADLs** | | | | |
| Walking | 23.37 | 16.53 | 26.18 | 43.20 |
| Getting in/out of bed/chairs | 11.69 | 8.12 | 13.11 | 24.66 |
| Bathing/Showering | 9.59 | 5.31 | 10.52 | 22.17 |
| Dressing | 6.25 | 3.97 | 6.76 | 14.19 |
| Using toilet | 4.67 | 2.62 | 5.06 | 12.05 |
| Eating | 2.17 | 1.33 | 2.30 | 5.33 |

SOURCE: National Center for Health Statistics. Trends in Health and Aging Website, www.cdc.gov/nchs/agingact.htm.

***Table 1.*** *Percentage with difficulty with instrumental activities of daily living and activities of daily living by age, community-dwelling population ages 65 and over, Medicare Current Beneficiary Survey, 2004.* CENGAGE LEARNING, GALE.

Sensory and cognitive limitations also increase with age. In 2004, according to NHIS data for the community-dwelling population, 14% of those aged 65 to 74 reported trouble seeing, even with glasses or contacts, compared with 20% of those ages 75 and older (NCHS, 2007b). The proportions reporting deafness or trouble hearing without a hearing aid were 7% and 15%, respectively. Data from the HRS from the mid-1990s indicate that about 6% of the 70 and older community-dwelling population is cognitively impaired, with percentages ranging from 3% for those aged 70 to 74, to 24% for those 90 and older (Suthers, Kim, & Crimmins, 2003). The proportions for the population in institutions are much higher, roughly 50%, but do not vary much by age. Overall, about 10% of the U.S. population 70 and older is cognitively impaired.

All of these functional limitations—physical, sensory, and cognitive—may contribute to difficulties with IADLs and ADLs. Table 1, which is based on data from the 2004 MCBS, shows the proportions of the older population with specific IADL and ADL disabilities. Reports of IADL difficulty among the 65 and older group range from 7% for using the telephone to almost a third for doing heavy housework.

Less common is difficulty with ADLs, which typically identifies the older population with the greatest needs. Only about 2% of the 65 and older population report difficulty eating, but 10% report difficulty bathing or showering, and mobility within the house is a problem for almost a quarter.

The figures presented in Table 1 are for the non-institutionalized population. Not surprisingly, a much greater proportion of the older population living in long-term care facilities report difficulties. (In the MCBS, facilities are defined as institutions having three or more beds and providing long-term care, such as nursing homes, assisted care homes, and mental health institutions.) For example, more than 90% of the 65 and older population in facilities report difficulty with bathing or showering, which some consider a sentinel ADL.

The variation by age in functional limitation and disability has been highlighted, but significant disparities by other demographic and socioeconomic characteristics also exist. Generally, women are more likely than men to experience limitations and disabilities, as are the unmarried, members of racial and ethnic minorities, the least educated, and the poorest (Freedman, Martin, & Schoeni, 2004). An exception to these patterns is hearing limitation, which is more common among men than women, perhaps reflecting occupational exposure to loud noise.

## POPULATION TRENDS OVER TIME

A central question in the study of aging is whether the extra years of life that result from improvements in survival are spent in good or bad health. Some have argued that there will be an epidemic of disease as older people are kept alive in increasingly frail states (Gruenberg, 1977), whereas others have suggested that there will be a compression of morbidity to a short period before death (Fries, 1980). A third, intermediate, perspective hypothesizes an increase in chronic disease but whose progression is slowed (Manton, 1982).

Although disability is not a pure measure of health, it has been the measure related to late-life health that has been most commonly assessed over time at the population level in the United States. So when studies based on data from the 1970s suggested increasing disability (Waidmann, Bound, & Schoenbaum, 1995), prospects for health in old age were thought to be gloomy.

Subsequently, the research and policy communities were surprised and somewhat cautious in response to the initial report of decline in late-life disability in the 1980s, which was based on NLTCS data (Freedman & Soldo, 1994; Manton, Corder, & Stallard, 1993). But an additional decade of data from the NLTCS and data from other surveys have shown a similar trend (Freedman, Martin, & Schoeni, 2002). In addition, a collaborative effort by the top researchers in the field to understand differences in survey designs and other technical issues has led to the consensus that late-life disability has indeed declined since the late 1980s (Freedman, Crimmins, Schoeni, Spillman, Aykan, Kramarow et al., 2004).

Data from the 1984 to 2006 NHIS, which of all the national surveys provides the longest time series of consistently measured annual observations, indicate that for much of the period decline in needing help with IADLs appears to drive the decline in overall disability. Detecting changes in ADL-type disability has been more challenging, in part because of the smaller numbers involved. One group of experts, however, using all the available data sets and taking into consideration the differences in question wording, concluded that although evidence was mixed for the 1980s, there indeed was a decline in ADL-type disability for the 70 and older population beginning in the mid- to late-1990s (Freedman, Crimmins, Schoeni, Spillman, Aykan, Kramarow et al., 2004).

Among the IADLs, Spillman (2004) has found using NLTCS data that the biggest declines in disability were for managing money, shopping for groceries, and doing laundry. She suggests that the improvement in the first may be less about physical and cognitive functioning and more about the shift of the Social Security Administration to direct deposit of checks in 1987.

Time trends in functional limitations, whether physical, cognitive, or sensory, have been studied less than trends in disability (see Freedman, Martin, & Schoeni, 2002, for a review of work until that date). Data from the Survey on Income and Program Participation show declines in physical and vision limitations from 1984 to 1999 (Cutler, 2001; Freedman & Martin, 1998). Other datasets show little change in hearing limitations over the period. Analysis of more recent data suggest increases in physical functional limitations for the older population (Kramarow, Lubitz, Lentzner, & Gorina, 2007), but clearly more research is needed on these health measures.

There is some controversy about trends in late-life cognitive functioning. Freedman, Aykan, & Martin (2001) analyzed 1993 and 1998 data from the HRS (and its companion AHEAD study) and found a decline in severe cognitive impairment in the 70 and older population, but Rodgers, Ofstedal, & Herzog (2003) found no improvement after they added data from the 2000 wave to the analysis and controlled for the possibility of panel respondents retaining knowledge of the test from one wave to the next. However, analysis of NLTCS data suggests a decline in severe cognitive impairment from 1982 to 1999 (Manton, Gu, & Ukraintseva, 2005).

This discussion of trends in functional limitation and disability has focused on recent decades. However, some research on change in disability from early in the 20th century until recent years compares data on Union Army veterans of the Civil War era with contemporary data. Such comparisons are challenging given differences in sampling, measurements, and so on, but indicate declines in prevalence of physical and sensory limitations over the course of the century (Costa, 2002).

This discussion also has focused on *average* trends in functioning and disability. Only limited research has been done on demographic and socioeconomic disparities in trends. Schoeni, Freedman, & Martin (2008) have found using NHIS data that all major demographic and socioeconomic groups experienced declining disability (ADL and IADL combined) in old-age from 1982 to 2002, but the magnitude of the decrease was larger for those who had higher income, had more years of education, were married, and were younger. For ADL-type disability, there were actual increases in the prevalence of disability for those with the lowest income and those with 8 or fewer years of education (Schoeni, Martin, Andreski, & Freedman, 2005).

## EXPLANATIONS FOR THE DECLINE IN LATE-LIFE DISABILITY

Understanding why late-life disability has declined in recent decades may be helpful in extending the decline into the future and expanding it to subgroups of the population that have not yet benefited. Identifying the reasons, as well as any health costs associated with them, also may inform projections of future Medicare spending (Chernew, Goldman, Pan, & Shang, 2005). Given the plethora of possible explanations (e.g., demographic, socioeconomic, medical, and environmental), however, no single data set allows simultaneous examination of all these influences.

One socioeconomic change that has undoubtedly played a role is the dramatic increase in the educational attainment of older people in the United States over the last few decades of the 20th century (Freedman & Martin, 1999). Data from the Current Population Survey indicate that the proportion of the 65 and older population with eight or fewer years of education declined from 35% in 1985 to 13% in 2005. Over the same period the proportion with more than a high school education doubled from 19% to 38%. Freedman and Martin concluded that, depending on the specific function, from 25% to 75% of the decline in functional limitations among the 65 and older population from 1984 to 1993 could be attributed to increased education attainment. They could not specify the particular mechanisms by which more education reduces limitations but mentioned multiple possibilities, including greater access to health care throughout life, healthier behaviors, less risky occupations, and greater use of assistive devices.

Through a thorough literature review and several new analyses, Schoeni, Freedman, and Martin (2008) eliminated several possible explanations for the disability decline and highlighted several others as promising. Data from the NHIS indicate that from 1997 to 2005, respondents ages 70 and older have become less likely to report some conditions as causing their disability, namely, heart and circulatory conditions, musculoskeletal conditions, and vision problems. This pattern is confirmed by Schoeni and colleagues' analysis of data from 1982 to 2005, as well as by Freedman and colleagues' analysis (Freedman, Schoeni, Martin, & Cornman, 2007) for the period from 1997 to 2004 for the 65 and older population. At the same time, these studies suggest that cancer, diabetes, ear conditions, lung disease, mental conditions, and conditions of the nervous system have not played a significant role in the decline in rates of disability. Although detailed time series data on medical interventions over the same period are not available, the authors note the concurrent increases in the pharmacological treatment of and surgical procedures for heart disease (e.g., beta blockers, balloon angioplasty), musculoskeletal conditions (e.g., nonsteroidal anti-inflammatories, joint replacement surgery), and vision problems (e.g., cataract surgery), which may in part explain the decline in disability.

Schoeni, Freedman, and Martin (2008) also find that increases in the use of assistive technologies, declines in poverty, declines in widowhood, as well as increases in the educational attainment of the older population have likely played a role in the disability decline. They rule out roles for changes in smoking behavior (which thus far have been small, as reported by the surviving population in old age) and changes in some aspects of population composition, namely, race/ethnicity and foreign birth. Overall, Freedman and colleagues (Freedman, Schoeni, Martin, & Cornman, 2007) find that changes in sociodemographic risk factors account for about one third and changes in chronic conditions about two thirds of the decline from 1997 to 2004.

## INDIVIDUAL DISABILITY DYNAMICS AND LIFE-COURSE PERSPECTIVES

The preceding discussion of late-life disability trends was focused on time series of the prevalence of disability, namely, the proportion of the population at any one time reporting having a disability. However, underlying these cross-sectional snapshots are many individual experiences of disability onset, progression, and recovery. Studying dynamic aspects of individual disability requires longitudinal survey data that track respondents' experiences over time. The frequency of observations is critical. Even with one-and two-year intervals between survey waves (which is typical of the best of nationally representative surveys for this purpose, such as the Longitudinal Study on Aging [LSOA] and the HRS), many transitions in disability may be missed. Based on monthly data from a small study in the New Haven, Connecticut, area (sample size: 754 people), Gill and colleagues (Gill, Hardy, & Williams, 2002) found that such intervals often underestimate recovery, as well as disability onset among those who die or who are lost to follow-up during the survey interval. That substantial recovery from disability occurs has been known for some time (e.g., Crimmins & Saito, 1993), but analysis of such monthly data indicates that it is even more common than previously thought. Hardy & Gill (2004) found using the New Haven data that more than 80% of people experiencing onset of disability in at least one of four ADLs recovered within 12 months, most of the recovery took place in the first six months, and more than half of those who recovered maintained independence for at least six months.

In addition to data demands, investigating disability dynamics involves methodological challenges, especially as one moves beyond models of just two periods. As the number of observations, starting states (disabled or not), and outcomes (disabled, not disabled, dead, lost to follow-up) grows, the possible number of trajectories multiplies. Simply summarizing these trajectories, let alone identifying common characteristics of people with similar trajectories, is daunting (Wolinsky, Armbrecht, & Wyrwich, 2000).

In their two-period models of LSOA data on physical functional limitations, ADLs, and IADLs, Crimmins and Saito (1993) found that among the community-dwelling population ages 70 and over, between 1984 and 1986, higher age and being non-White were associated with onset of limitation or disability, but generally not with recovery. Being female was associated with greater risk of onset of functional limitation, but smaller risk of developing a disability among those starting the observation period without one. It could be that those women who experienced disability were more likely to move into institutions and thus not be included in the survey. Generally, having arthritis, vision or hearing problems, or a stroke had the strongest relations with onset.

Evidence is growing that the factors associated with onset indeed are different from those associated with recovery. For example, focusing on functional limitations and using data for the 25 and over population from the Americans' Changing Lives Survey for 1986 and 1994, Zimmer and House (2003) found that income is associated with both onset and recovery, but education is related only to onset, suggesting a relatively greater role for it in the prevention of the development of functional limitation. Similarly, Melzer, Izmirlian, Leveille, and Guralnik (2001) have found, using data for a subnational sample of people aged 65 to 84 who were observed for seven years in the 1980s, that education is associated with the onset of, but not recovery from, inability to climb a flight of stairs or walk half a mile.

These results and the broader literature on the enduring influences of early-life experiences on late-life health (see, for example, Kuh & Ben-Shlomo, 2004) argue for a life-course perspective in research on late-life functioning and disability. Unfortunately, the necessary data for such analyses are rare. The HRS has asked respondents to assess retrospectively their childhood health and socioeconomic status (SES). Using these data, Freedman and colleagues (Freedman, Martin, Schoeni, & Cornman, 2008) found that among the 75 and older population from 1995 to 2004, even after controlling for late-life factors (such as SES and health), being born in the southern United States, reporting less than excellent health as a child, and having eight or fewer years of education are associated with having a disability in late life. The influences of other early-life factors, such as disadvantaged childhood SES and mother's education level being low, are reduced after late-life factors are controlled for, suggesting that they affect late-life disability only indirectly.

Of course, as mentioned at the outset, for some small group, disability is a life-long experience. Using data from a special disability supplement to the 1994 NHIS, Verbrugge and Yang (2002) found that 9% of adults who had a disability reported onset before age 20. Moreover, a recent Institute of Medicine report (Field & Jette, 2007) noted that the survival of children and young adults from previously fatal conditions is increasing the number of people at risk for midlife disability, the development of secondary conditions (i.e., conditions that result from the disability), negative consequences of earlier treatment (e.g., for childhood cancer), and premature aging.

## FUTURE TRENDS AND RESEARCH

Will the declines in late-life disability continue? Most projections have involved either linear extrapolations of past disability trends or have focused on trends in a particular factor associated with disability in the cross-section. For example, much media attention has been given to the growth of obesity in the United States, and some researchers have modeled how a continuation of that trend might affect disability prevalence, assuming that the relation between obesity and disability is stable (Sturm, Ringel, & Andreyeva, 2004). Although this connection warrants close monitoring and obesity is indeed associated with disability, relatively few older people report that obesity causes their disabilities, in comparison with those attributing disabilities to other health conditions such as arthritis and cardiovascular disease (Freedman et al., 2007).

Educational attainment of older people, a very important covariate of late-life disability in the cross-section, can be predicted with much greater certainty, because most people complete their education relatively early in life. Although more education played an important role in the 1984 to 1993 decline in functional limitations mentioned earlier and although the increase in the educational attainment will continue into the future, Freedman and Martin (1999) have cautioned that the rate of increase will be slower. In analyses of disability decline from 1997 to 2004 (Freedman et al., 2007), education did not on balance play a role. The overall increase in educational attainment was offset by the growing disability disadvantage of those with relatively low education, perhaps a more negatively selected group over time.

Given the many influences on the disablement process and without a better overall understanding of the reasons for the recent declines in late-life disability, it is difficult to predict the future. New data collection efforts ideally will track all the elements of the Disablement Process and will obtain frequent observations of disability status for improved analysis of individual onset and recovery. Such information also may facilitate the development and evaluation of interventions to prevent the onset of disability and to enhance the chances of recovery.

Also essential is refinement of the measures used to assess disability in population-based surveys. More than 40 years have passed since the design of the ADL and IADL questions still commonly used in the early 21st century. Daily activities of older people have certainly changed, especially with the revolution in information and communication technologies. Moreover, as labor force participation in late life has grown, greater attention to barriers to and facilitators of work is warranted. More generally, given their relatively low prevalence in the community-dwelling population, alternative measures to ADLs and IADLs that incorporate all levels of functioning are needed to understand and possibly prevent downward transitions. Wider use of self-reports of physical functional limitations and performance-based measures, which provide complementary information, could be helpful.

The subjective nature of self-reports of disability and functional limitations has been the focus of recent innovative research attempting to benchmark responses across different subgroups and periods. The use of so-called *anchoring vignettes* appears promising (Salomon, Tandon, & Murray, 2004). Besides being asked about their own health, respondents are presented with vignettes describing hypothetical persons and asked to rate their health or disability. Responses to the vignettes allows recalibration of own responses and thus more accurate interpersonal comparisons.

Another new approach to understanding late-life disability is the collection of time-use data. Although not measuring disability per se, such data may help identify how behavior changes to accommodate mismatches between underlying capacity, task demands, and the environment. This technique also may provide information on how the onset of or recovery from disability affects time devoted to other tasks, as well as insight into how to enhance fuller participation of older people and those who help them in activities that they enjoy and value.

**SEE ALSO** Volume 3: *Active Life Expectancy; Arthritis; Assistive Technologies; Chronic Illness, Adulthood and Later Life.*

**BIBLIOGRAPHY**

Brandt, J., Spencer, M., & Folstein, M. (1988). The telephone interview for cognitive status. *Neuropsychiatry, Neuropsychology, and Behavioral Neurology, 1,* 111–117.

Chernew, M. E., Goldman, D. P., Pan, F., & Shang, B. (2005). Disability and health care spending among Medicare beneficiaries. *Health Affairs,* Web Exclusive, September 26, W5, R42-R52. Retrieved January 25, 2008, from http://content.healthaffairs.org/cgi/content/abstract/hlthaff.w5.r42

Costa, D. L. (2002). Changing chronic disease rates and long-term declines in functional limitation among older men. *Demography, 39,* 119–137.

Crimmins, E. M., & Saito, Y. (1993). Getting better and getting worse: Transitions in functional status among older Americans. *Journal of Aging and Health, 5,* 3–36.

Cutler, D. M. (2001). Declining disability among the elderly. *Health Affairs, 20,* 11–27.

Duggan, M., & Imberman, S. (2008). Why are the disability rolls skyrocketing? The contribution of population characteristics, economic conditions, and program generosity. In D. Cutler & D. A.Wise (Eds.), *Health at older ages: The causes and consequences of declining disability among the elderly.* Chicago: University of Chicago Press.

Field, M. J., & Jette, A. M. (Eds.). (2007). *The future of disability in America.* Washington: National Academies Press.

Folstein, M. F., Folstein, S. E., & McHugh, P. R. (1975). Mini-mental state: A practical method for grading the cognitive state of patients for the clinician. *Journal of Psychiatric Research, 12,* 189–198.

Freedman, V. A., Aykan, H., & Martin, L. G. (2001). Aggregate changes in severe cognitive impairment among older Americans: 1993 and 1998. *Journals of Gerontology, Series B: Psychological Sciences and Social Sciences, 56B,* S100–S111.

Freedman, V. A., Crimmins, E., Schoeni, R. F., Spillman, B. C., Aykan, H., Kramarow, E. et al. (2004). Resolving inconsistencies in trends in old-age disability: Report from a technical working group. *Demography, 41,* 417–441.

Freedman, V. A., & Martin, L. G. (1998). Understanding trends in functional limitations among older Americans. *American Journal of Public Health, 88*(10), 1457–1462.

Freedman, V. A. & Martin, L. G. (1999). The role of education in explaining and forecasting trends in functional limitations among older Americans. *Demography, 36,* 461–473.

Freedman, V. A., Martin, L. G., & Schoeni, R. F. (2002). Recent trends in disability and functioning among older adults in the United States: A systematic review. *Journal of the American Medical Association, 288,* 3137–3146.

Freedman, V. A., Martin, L. G., & Schoeni, R. F. (2004). Disability in America. *Population Bulletin, 59,* 1–32.

Freedman, V. A., Martin, L. G., Schoeni, R. F., & Cornman, J. C. (2008). Declines in late-life disability: The role of early-and mid-life factors. *Social Science and Medicine, 66,* 1588–1602

Freedman, V. A., & Soldo, B. J. (Eds.). (1994). *Trends in disability at older ages: Summary of a workshop, Committee on National Statistics.* Washington, DC: National Academy Press.

Freedman, V. A., Schoeni, R. F., Martin, L. G., & Cornman, J. C. (2007). Chronic conditions and the decline in late-life disability. *Demography, 44,* 459–477.

Fries, J. F. (1980). Aging, natural death and the compression of morbidity. *New England Journal of Medicine, 303,* 130–135.

Gill, T. M., Hardy, S. E., & Williams, C. S. (2002). Underestimation of disability in community-living older persons. *Journal of the American Geriatrics Society, 50,* 1492–1497.

Gruenberg, E. M. (1977). The failures of success. *Milbank Memorial Fund Quarterly, 55,* 3–24.

Guralnik, J. M., Simonsick, E. M., Ferrucci, L., Glynn, R. J., Berkman, L. F., Blazer, D. G., Scherr, P. A., & Wallace, R. B. (1994). A short physical performance battery assessing lower extremity function: Association with self-reported disability and prediction of mortality and nursing home admission. *Journals of Gerontology, Series A: Medical Sciences, 49,* M85–M94.

Hardy, S. E., & Gill, T. M. (2004). Recovery from disability among community-dwelling older persons. *Journal of the American Medical Association, 291,* 1596–1602.

Herzog, A. R., & Wallace, R. B. (1997). Measures of cognitive functioning in the AHEAD study [Special issue]. *Journals of Gerontology: Psychological Sciences and Social Sciences, 52B,* 37–48.

Jette, A. M., & Badley, E. (2000). Conceptual issues in the measurement of work disability. In N. Mathiowetz & G. S. Wunderlich (Eds.), *Survey Measurement of Work Disability: Summary of a Workshop* (pp. 4-27). Washington, DC: National Academy Press.

Katz, S., Downs, T. D., Cash, H. R., & Grotz, R. (1970). Progress in development of the index of ADL. *Gerontologist, 10,* 20–30.

Katz, S., Ford, A. G., Moskowitz, R. W., Jackson, B. A., & Jaffee, M. W. (1963). Studies of illness in the aged. The Index of ADL, a standardized measure of biological and psychosocial function. *Journal of the American Medical Association, 185,* 914–919.

Kramarow, E., Lubitz, J., Lentzner, H., & Gorina, Y. (2007). Trends in the health of older Americans, 1970–2005. *Health Affairs, 26*(5), 1417–1425.

Kreider, B. (1999). Latent work disability and reporting bias, *Journal of Human Resources, 34,* 734–769.

Kuh, D., & Ben-Shlomo, Y. (Eds). (2004). *A life course approach to chronic disease epidemiology.* Oxford, U.K.: Oxford University Press.

Lawton, M. P., & Brody, E. (1969). Assessment of older people: Self-maintaining and instrumental activities of daily living. *Gerontologist, 9,* 179–186.

Manton, K. G. (1982). Changing concepts of morbidity and mortality in the elderly population. *Milbank Memorial Fund Quarterly, 60,* 183–244.

Manton, K. G., Corder, L. S., & Stallard, E. (1993). Estimates of change in chronic disability and institutional incidence and prevalence rates in the U.S. elderly population from the 1982, 1984, and 1989 National Long Term Care Survey. *Journal of Gerontology, Social Sciences, 48,* S153–S166.

Manton, K. G., Gu, X. L., & Ukraintseva, S. V. (2005). Declining prevalence of dementia in the U.S. elderly population. *Advances in Gerontology, 16,* 30–37.

Melzer, D., Izmirlian, G., Leveille, S. G., & Guralnik, J. M. (2001). Educational differences in the prevalence of mobility disability in old age: The dynamics of incidence, mortality, and recovery. *Journals of Gerontology, Series B: Social Sciences, 56,* S294–301.

Nagi, S. Z. (1965). Some conceptual issues in disability and rehabilitation. In M. B. Sussman (Ed.), *Sociology and Rehabilitation* (pp. 100–113). Washington, DC: American Sociological Association.

National Center for Health Statistics. (2007a). *Guide to functional status/disability tables, trends in health and aging.* Retrieved June 11, 2008, from http://www.cdc.gov/nchs/agingact.htm

National Center for Health Statistics (2007b). *Health, United States, 2007*. Hyattsville, MD: Author. Retrieved May 26, 2008, from http://www.cdc.gov/nchs/data/hus/hus07.pdf

Onder, G., Penninx, B. W., Ferrucci, L., Fried, L. P., Guralnik, J. M., & Pahor, M. (2005). Measures of physical performance and risk for progressive and catastrophic disability: Results from the Women's Health and Aging Study. *Journal of Gerontology: Medical Sciences, 60*, 74–79.

Pope, A. M., & Tarlov, A. R. (Eds.). (1991). *Disability in America: Toward a national agenda for prevention.* Washington, DC: National Academy Press.

Rantanen, T., Volpato, S., Ferrucci, L. Heikkinen, E., Fried, L. P., & Guralnik, J. M. (2003). Handgrip strength and cause-specific and total mortality in older disabled women: Exploring the mechanism. *Journal of the American Geriatrics Society, 51*, 636–641.

Rodgers, W. L., Ofstedal, M.B., & Herzog, A. R. (2003). Trends in scores on tests of cognitive ability in the elderly U.S. population, 1993–2000. *Journals of Gerontology, Series B: Psychological Sciences and Social Sciences, 58B*, S338–S346.

Salomon, J. A., Tandon, A., & Murray, C. J. L. (2004). Comparability of self rated health: Cross sectional multi-country survey using anchoring vignettes. *British Medical Journal, 328*, 258–261.

Schoeni, R. F., Freedman, V. A., & Martin, L. G. (2008). Why is late-life disability declining? *Milbank Quarterly, 86*, 47–87.

Schoeni, R. F., Martin, L. G., Andreski, P. M., & Freedman, V. A. (2005). Persistent and growing socioeconomic disparities in disability among the elderly: 1982–2002. *American Journal of Public Health, 95*, 2065–2070.

Spillman, B. C. (2004.) Changes in elderly disability rates and the implications for health care utilization and cost. *Milbank Quarterly, 82*, 157–194.

Sturm, R., Ringel, J. S., & Andreyeva, T. (2004). Increasing obesity rates and disability trends. *Health Affairs, 23*, 199–205.

Suthers, K., Kim, J. K., & Crimmins, E. (2003). Life expectancy with cognitive impairment in the older population of the United States. *Journals of Gerontology, Series B: Psychological Sciences and Social Sciences*, 58B, S179–S186.

Verbrugge, L. M., & Jette, A. M. (1994). The disablement process. *Social Science and Medicine, 38*, 1–14.

Verbrugge, L. M., & Yang, L. S. (2002). Aging with disability and disability with aging. *Journal of Disability Policy Studies, 12*, 253–267.

Waidmann, T., Bound, J., & Schoenbaum, M. (1995). The illusion of failure: Trends in the self-reported health of the U.S. elderly. *Milbank Quarterly, 73*, 253–287.

Wolinsky, F. D., Armbrecht, E. S., & Wyrwich, K. W. (2000). Rethinking functional limitation pathways. *The Gerontologist, 40*, 137–146.

World Health Organization. (2002). International Classification of Functioning, Disabilities, and Health. Retrieved June 11, 2008, from http://www.who.int/classifications/icf/site/intros/ICF-Eng-Intro.pdf

Zimmer, Z., & House, J. S. (2003). Education, income, and functional limitation transitions among American adults: Contrasting onset and progression. *International Journal of Epidemiology, 32*(6), 1089–1097.

***Linda G. Martin***

# DRINKING, LATER LIFE

SEE Volume 3: *Health Behaviors, Later Life.*

# DRUG USE, LATER LIFE

SEE Volume 3: *Health Behaviors, Later Life.*

# E

## ELDER ABUSE AND NEGLECT

Elder abuse and neglect is controversial. Everyone seems to agree that it is a national, even global, problem with serious consequences for victims. There is little consensus, however, on anything else. Controversy exists on how to define elder abuse and neglect, what forms it takes, how frequently it occurs, and what characterizes victims and perpetrators.

The crux of the controversies rests in scholars' and practitioners' inability to come up with a universally accepted definition of elder abuse and neglect. Since the late 1970s this has challenged researchers and policy makers alike. The areas of contention include whether or not actions against older adults must be intentional (as opposed to passive behaviors), reflect repeated patterns of conduct (versus single incidents), involve only older adults who are vulnerable because of mental or physical impairments (as opposed to including those who are cognitively intact and able-bodied), and be perpetrated by persons who have a close or special relationship with the victim (versus strangers or casual acquaintances).

Lack of consensus has resulted in a proliferation of different elder abuse and neglect definitions in empirical studies and state laws, thus limiting the comparability of research findings and reporting statistics. The National Research Council (2003) convened a panel of experts to evaluate research on elder abuse and neglect and develop recommendations for future directions. In doing so, it proposed a standardized definition that considers the problem in relatively narrow terms. "Elder mistreatment" represents:

> (a) intentional actions that cause harm or create a serious risk of harm, whether or not harm is intended, to a vulnerable elder by caregiver or other person who stands in a trust relationship to the elder, or (b) failure by a caregiver to satisfy the elder's basic needs or to protect the elder from harm. (p. 39).

Definitions lend themselves to classifying elder abuse and neglect into forms. Again, there is no universally accepted set, although those suggested by the National Center on Elder Abuse are commonly used: physical abuse, sexual abuse, emotional abuse, financial/material exploitation, neglect, abandonment, and self-neglect. Missing from the list but frequently found in international descriptions of the problem are violation of rights, abduction, and systemic abuse (in which the failure to adequately or appropriately implement policy or services contributes to abuse occurrences).

### PROBLEM SCOPE AND REPORTING

Although it is uncertain how frequently elder abuse and neglect occurs, there is evidence that the problem is far from rare, with certain forms experienced by older adults more than other forms. Unlike the areas of child mistreatment and partner violence, no national prevalence study of elder abuse and neglect has been conducted in the United States. As a result, knowledge in this area is based on a number of geographically and often methodologically limited investigations. Together these investigations suggest a prevalence rate between 1% and 10% among surveyed older adults (Anetzberger, 2005).

A random sample study of elderly households in the metropolitan Boston area revealed physical abuse to be twice as common as verbal aggression and four times as frequent as neglect. Other forms were not considered (Pillemer & Finkelhor, 1988). These findings contrast with those from the National Elder Abuse Incidence Study (National Center on Elder Abuse, 1998) and compilations of state reports on elder abuse and neglect.

The National Incidence Study's aim was to uncover new domestic cases seen by adult protective services (APS) or community agencies serving older adults during 1996. Using a representative sample drawn from 20 counties in 15 states, researchers suggested an annual elder abuse and neglect incidence rate of 551,011. They also found that only 21% of the cases had been reported to APS, despite the existence of mandatory reporting laws in nearly every state. The largest number of cases (over one-third) represented self-neglect, that is, situations in which an older adult is unable to perform self-care tasks, such as obtaining food and shelter or managing finances, because of impairment or incapacity. Among the remainder of the cases, the most common forms (in order of frequency) were neglect, psychological abuse, exploitation, and physical abuse.

The National Center on Elder Abuse commissioned a nationwide collection of state-level APS data on elder abuse and neglect for 2004 (Teaster et al., 2006). The results revealed that APS received a total of 565,747 reports that year affecting both older and vulnerable younger adults, a nearly 20% increase from 2000. Among reports in which elder abuse was confirmed, the most common form was self-neglect (39.3%), followed by caregiver neglect (21.6%), financial exploitation (13.8%), emotional/psychological/verbal abuse (12.8%), and physical abuse (10.1%). Sexual abuse represented just 1.1% of substantiated reports.

Outside of the United States, elder abuse and neglect prevalence rates seem to fall into the 1% to 10% range as well. This is true for such countries as Canada, Great Britain, Germany, Finland, Australia, and Korea. Rates appear to be higher in only a very few locales, such as Hong Kong at 23.5% (Yan & Tang, 2001); this may result, however, from using a broader definition of elder abuse for research purposes. Moreover, for several of these countries, and in contrast to the situation in the United States, financial exploitation and verbal abuse appear to be more common than other forms.

## HISTORY OF ELDER ABUSE AND NEGLECT RECOGNITION

Elder abuse and neglect has likely existed throughout human history. Examples of it date back centuries in both historical records and literature. Much seems to reflect a perception by younger family members that older relatives are burdens. This is evident in ethnographic accounts of the Fulani of West Africa and the Inuit of North America along with documents on the treatment of elderly widows in 16th- and 17th-century Europe and colonial America, for instance. In literature, elder abuse and neglect is found in such early writings as Greek mythology, old English fairy tales, and even Shakespearean plays such as *King Lear.* Prior to the 20th century, however, nowhere is the phenomenon viewed as a social problem, public health issue, or notable criminal activity.

Recognition of elder abuse and neglect as a societal concern had antecedents in the United States during the 1950s and early 1960s. At that time attention in urban communities, such as Cleveland and Chicago, began focusing on the growing number of adults living to old age and believed to be at risk of neglect and exploitation because they were mentally impaired, lived alone, and lacked nearby or adequate family support. APS evolved from this and then expanded across the country with an infusion of funding from Title XX of the Social Security Act into social welfare agencies during the mid-1970s.

Concurrently, physicians in the United States and Great Britain began recognizing physical abuse and self-neglect among some of their elderly patients, describing the syndromes in medical journals and other publications. By the late 1970s, exploratory studies of elder abuse and neglect were underway, Congressional hearings on the problem were beginning, and states started enacting laws to provide appropriate responses.

Most experts agree that the 1980s represented the watershed decade for elder abuse and neglect recognition. By its end, media portrayals of the problem were fairly common, most states had passed elder abuse reporting laws, research had begun unraveling the dimensions and dynamics of elder abuse and neglect, the first quarterly academic journal devoted to the subject was launched—Haworth Press's *Journal of Elder Abuse & Neglect*—and many relevant national and local advocacy organizations and clearinghouses had been formed, including the National Committee for the Prevention of Elder Abuse and the Clearinghouse on Abuse and Neglect of the Elderly.

Since 1990 research on elder abuse and neglect has advanced, largely as a result of scholarly forums establishing agendas for empirical study and expanded funding opportunities, especially from the National Institute on Aging and the National Institute of Justice. These advancements have generated interest in the topic among investigators new to the field and supported research into aspects of elder abuse and neglect insufficiently studied in the past. Similarly, evaluation of programs and approaches to detect, prevent, and treat the problem have become more common. The effort to learn what works and what does not mirrors broader movements in medicine and criminal justice for evidence-based interventions, as the field of elder abuse and neglect itself has become more medicalized and criminalized.

## THEORETICAL EXPLANATIONS AND RISK FACTORS

Various theories have been proposed to explain elder abuse and neglect. Some have been used to understand other mistreated populations. Conflict theory and feminist theory are good illustrations. Applied to an elderly population, conflict theory suggests that given imbalances in scarce resources, such as available time or money, the potential exists for someone to take advantage of an older adult. Feminist theory sees violence against women, including elderly ones, originating in structural inequities in society that foster gender disadvantage.

Only a few theories have been supported through empirical investigation, most notably psychopathology theory and symbolic interactionism. Psychopathology theory suggests that problems in psychosocial functioning of the perpetrator can promote or provoke elder abuse and neglect. With symbolic interactionism, elder abuse and neglect occurs in social relations with discrepancies between behaviors and role expectations. Caregiving can be such a relationship. Research indicates that mistreatment may result when the caregiver finds the behaviors of the elderly care recipient disturbing or disruptive, particularly when the behaviors also are regarded as deliberate or controllable. If the care recipient is noncompliant, complaining, criticizing, or aggressive, this can represent disturbing behavior for abusive caregivers.

Finally, some theories have been combined into overarching perspectives on the problem. Edward Ansello's (1996) environmental press model also provides operational protocols for interventions to address elder abuse and neglect. The model incorporates various theories to diagnose the origins of inadequate care or neglect of an impaired older adult and to recommend courses of treatment. Accordingly, inadequate care or neglect can result when the demands of the environment are either too strong or too weak for the individual to exercise his or her competence.

A complex problem such as elder abuse and neglect is unlikely to be explained by any single theory, and no theory, alone or in combination with other theories, has been rigorously tested. Instead, empirical study has focused on identifying risk factors for the problem. Risk factors may encompass characteristics of the perpetrator, victim, or environment that tend to predict the occurrence of elder abuse and neglect. Although many risk factors are suggested in the literature, only a handful have been substantiated through research (Lachs & Pillemer, 1995; National Research Council, 2003).

The most important risk factors relate to the perpetrator, and chief among them are pathology and dependency. Perpetrators, more than nonperpetrators, have been found to be alcoholic, to have a diagnosed mental illness, to have spent time in a psychiatric hospital, or to suffer emotional distress (Anetzberger, Korbin, & Austin, 1994; Reis & Nahmiash, 1998; Wolf & Pillemer, 1989). Moreover, they are more likely to be dependent on the victim with respect to finances or housing. Other suggested perpetrator risk factors have less support through research, including caregiver stress and transgenerational violence.

Important victim risk factors are functional incapacity and problem behaviors. Incapacity can be due to physical, cognitive, or mental impairment. It can render the victim dependent on the perpetrator for care, which may be inadequate or inappropriate. Functional declines also can reduce the victim's awareness of elder abuse and neglect or inhibit his or her ability to stop or escape from it. Although problem behavior was discussed previously, one source deserves special mention. Studies suggest that those who care for persons with dementia are two to three times more likely to mistreat care recipients than those caring for persons without dementia (Paveza et al., 1992). Other proposed victim risk factors, such as gender and age, have not been validated.

Shared living arrangements and social isolation are the most salient environmental risk factors. Usually the perpetrator and victim reside together, a situation that can produce tension, conflict, and even mistreatment. The typical perpetrator is either the spouse (Pillemer & Finkelhor, 1988) or adult child (National Center on Elder Abuse, 1998; Teaster et al., 2006). Furthermore, there is evidence that perpetrators and victims tend to be either socially isolated or perceive themselves that way. This can mean there are few, if any, persons around to provide support, monitor the situation, or alert authorities when things go wrong. Other proposed environmental risk factors, such as family disharmony or crowded conditions, lack substantiation.

## PROBLEM RESPONSE AND FUTURE CHALLENGES

The potential effect of elder abuse and neglect on victims can have five dimensions: physical (such as injury and pain), behavioral (including helplessness and reduced coping), psychological (such as fear and anxiety), social (including dependence and withdrawal), and financial (such as loss of property and income). Research suggests that victims are more likely than nonvictims to experience depression, distress, and suicidal thoughts. There is evidence, too, that they tend to die younger (Lachs, Williams, O'Brien, Pillemer, & Charlson, 1998).

The serious and complex nature of the problem means that elder abuse and neglect requires intervention across disciplines, systems, and approaches (Nerenberg, 2008). It is not surprising, therefore, that many organizations and communities establish multidisciplinary teams (Anetzberger, Dayton, Miller, McGreevey, & Schimer, 2005). Although their purposes vary, most seek to resolve difficult cases, identify service gaps or system problems, and advocate for legislation and new programs. Some teams have special foci, such as financial exploitation or fatality review. Most include representation from law enforcement, APS, mental health services, aging service providers, public guardians, and domestic violence advocates.

The need for case coordination and community collaboration also stems from the large number of organizations responsible for responding to elder abuse and neglect (Brandl et al., 2007). Those with federal or state authority include APS, civil and criminal justice, long-term care ombudsman, and public health. Others with useful services for victims or perpetrators include domestic violence and sexual assault programs, health care providers, the Aging Network, humane societies, mental health and substance abuse service providers, and caregiver advocates.

There is a race underway to better understand the dynamics of elder abuse and neglect and to identify effective strategies for preventing and resolving it. The aging of the baby boomers compels action on both fronts, because there is reason to believe that the problem will explode as this generation swells the ranks of older adults. Reasons for concern reflect characteristics of the baby boomers and changes in the larger society. For example, boomer tendencies to have fewer children, higher rates of divorce, and greater geographic mobility relative to earlier cohorts of older adults may translate into fewer available family caregivers and more neglect and self-neglect. Related societal changes may exasperate the situation. These changes include declining numbers of health care providers, particularly in long-term care, and dwindling public revenues to offer economic, medical, and social service support for an extended old age.

**SEE ALSO** Volume 2: *Domestic Violence;* Volume 3: *Caregiving; Crime and Victimization, Later Life; Loneliness, Later Life; Social Integration/Isolation, Later Life.*

**BIBLIOGRAPHY**

Anetzberger, G. J. (2005). The reality of elder abuse. In G. J. Anetzberger (Ed.), *The clinical management of elder abuse* (pp. 1–25). Binghamton, NY: Haworth Press.

Anetzberger, G. J., Dayton, C., Miller, C. A., McGreevey, J. F., Jr., & Schimer, M. (2005). Multidisciplinary teams in the clinical management of elder abuse. In G. J. Anetzberger (Ed.), *The clinical management of elder abuse* (pp. 157–171). Binghamton, NY: Haworth Press.

Anetzberger, G. J., Korbin, J. E., & Austin, C. (1994). Alcoholism and elder abuse. *Journal of Interpersonal Violence, 9,* 184–193.

Ansello, E. F. (1996). Causes and theories. In L. A. Baumhover & S. C. Beall (Eds.), *Abuse, neglect, and exploitation of older persons: Strategies for assessment and intervention* (pp. 9–29). Baltimore, MD: Health Professions Press.

Brandl, B., Dyer, C. B., Heisler, C. J., Otto, J. M., Stiegel, L. A., & Thomas, R. W. (2007). *Elder abuse detection and intervention: A collaborative approach.* New York: Springer.

Lachs, M. S., & Pillemer, K. (1995). Abuse and neglect of elderly persons. *The New England Journal of Medicine, 332,* 437–443.

Lachs, M. S., Williams, C. S., O'Brien, S., Pillemer, K. A., & Charlson, M. E. (1998). The mortality of elder mistreatment. *Journal of the American Medical Association, 280,* 428–432.

National Center on Elder Abuse. (1998, September). *The National Elder Abuse Incidence Study.* Washington, DC: Author.

National Research Council. (2003). *Elder mistreatment: Abuse, neglect, and exploitation in an aging America.* Washington, DC: National Academies Press.

Nerenberg, L. (2008). *Elder abuse prevention: Emerging trends and promising strategies.* New York: Springer.

Paveza, G. J., Cohen, D., Eisdorfer, C., Freels, S., Semla, T., Ashford, J. W., et al. (1992). Severe family violence and Alzheimer's disease: Prevalence and risk factors. *The Gerontologist, 32,* 493–497.

Pillemer, K., & Finkelhor, D. (1988). The prevalence of elder abuse: A random sample survey. *The Gerontologist, 28,* 51–57.

Reis, M., & Nahmiash, D. (1998). Validation of the indicators of abuse (IOA) screen. *The Gerontologist, 38,* 471–480.

Teaster, P. B., Dugar, T. A., Mendiondo, M. S., Abner, E. L., Cecil, K. A., & Otto, J. M. (2006, February). *The 2004 Survey of State Adult Protective Services: Abuse of adults 60 years of age and older.* Washington, DC: National Committee for the Prevention of Elder Abuse; Boulder, CO: National Adult Protective Services Association.

Wolf, R. S., & Pillemer, K. A. (1989). *Helping elderly victims: The reality of elder abuse.* New York: Columbia University Press.

Yan, E., & Tang, C. S.-K. (2001). Prevalence and psychological impact of Chinese elder abuse. *Journal of Interpersonal Violence, 16,* 1158–1174.

***Georgia J. Anetzberger***

## END OF LIFE DECISION-MAKING

Increased longevity and the aging of the baby boom generation are posing substantial challenges to society. The percent of the population aged 65 to 84 years is projected to increase from 10.9% to 15.7% by 2050, an absolute increase of over 35 million people. Those 85 and older will increase from 1.5% (approximately 4 million) to 5% of the population, or nearly 20 million people (President's Council on Bioethics, 2005). However, while average life expectancy at age 65 has increased to over 20 years, only 11.9 of those years are expected to be healthy. After age 85, only one person in 20 is still fully mobile (Sharma, Chan, Liu, & Ginsberg, 2001).

Chronic illnesses, that is, conditions that tend to be long-lasting, persistent in their symptoms, and generally incurable, and including some cancers, organ system failure (primarily heart, lung, liver, or kidney failure), dementia, and stroke, are now the leading causes of death for Americans. Nearly all of the burden of illness and utilization of health care is now concentrated in the last few years of life when people generally live with established, serious chronic diseases and increasing disability that will eventually result in death.

The extension of the life course into very late old age, along with the increasing use of an array of high technology interventions, such as ventilators, cardiopulmonary resuscitation (CPR), and percutaneous endoscopic gastrostomy (PEG) tube for artificial nutrition, that can sustain life in many compromised states, presents individuals, families, and health care professionals with very difficult decisions about the timing and course of the dying process. For example, most people, when asked, would prefer to die at home. However, more than 80% of deaths in the United States occur in hospitals or nursing homes and often with aggressive high technology treatment (Lunney, Lynn, & Hogan, 2002). It is not always clear that these interventions are useful, wanted, or that their application always contributes to quality care or quality of life. An extensive number of end of life care studies indicate that the end of life is associated with a substantial burden of suffering among dying individuals and that there are important negative health and financial consequences that extend to family members and society (Steinhauser et al., 2000).

Traditionally, all medical treatment decisions were made by the physician, who was considered to have the necessary technical knowledge to make decisions regarding patient care. Decisions were based on the physician's assessment of the likely prognosis, risks and benefits of each option, and the physician's belief about the needs of the patient. However, underlying this paternalistic model of decision-making is the assumption that the patient may need to be protected from the facts or may not be capable of understanding the complexities involved in making medical care decisions. With the rise of consumer movements in the 1970s, this traditional model became outdated and the medical community moved toward a more patient-centered model of care focusing on shared decision-making.

## PATIENT AUTONOMY AND PATIENT-CENTERED CARE

Patient autonomy and individual choice are core values in European bioethics and important components of patient and family-centered end of life decision-making (President's Council on Bioethics, 2005). Patient-centered care focuses on the patient's right to participate in making decisions about his or her medical care, and views the physician-patient relationship as a partnership (Gillespie, Florin, & Gillam, 2004). In this shared decision-making model, each participant brings a unique experience and expertise. The patient brings important values, beliefs, personal experience, culture, concerns, and desires, which are central to the decision-making process. The physician brings clinical knowledge, information about disease, treatment, outcomes, effects, risks, and benefits. Where there is an ongoing therapeutic relationship between a patient and a physician, a space for gradually exploring and sharing information, clarifying values, and developing consensus is possible. This process has benefits for both parties, with the patient becoming more empowered and the physician being able to provide the kind of care the patient wants. Where the patient can no longer speak for themselves, the family becomes the surrogate or substitute decision-maker.

## ADVANCE DIRECTIVES AND ADVANCE CARE PLANNING

Advance directives, and more recently, a more comprehensive approach to advance directives called advance care planning (ACP), have been promoted as the most practical means of ensuring patient autonomy and shared decision-making to assist the medical care system in providing quality end of life care (Lorenz et al., 2008). Advance directives are defined as a written instructional health care directive or appointment of an agent, or a written refusal to appoint an agent or execute a directive. In some, but not all, definitions, an advance directive also includes verbal instructions. A health care agent or surrogate is defined as an individual designated in a legal document, known as a durable power of attorney for health care (DPOAHC), who is designated to make a health care decision for the individual granting them power in the event of incapacity (e.g., coma, dementia, and so forth).

Advance directives began as simple requests to avoid medical treatments that would prolong life in undesirable conditions. They have evolved into increasingly complicated, detailed, and specific legal documents containing statements of patient preferences for an assortment of

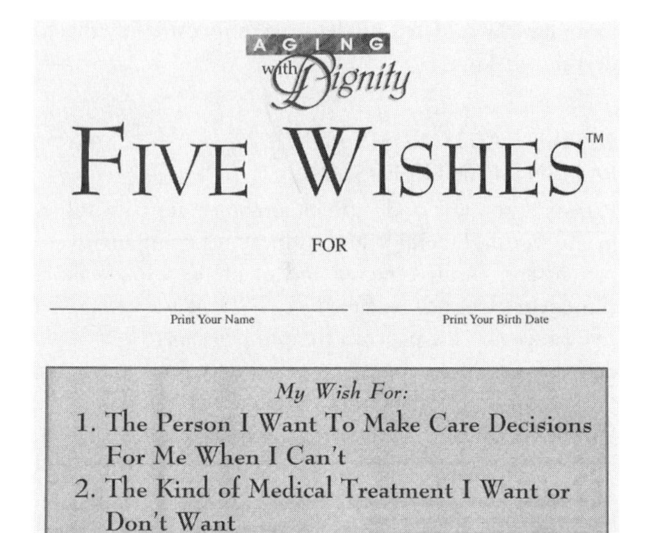
AGING with Dignity

FIVE WISHES™

FOR

Print Your Name

Print Your Birth Date

*My Wish For:*

1. The Person I Want To Make Care Decisions For Me When I Can't
2. The Kind of Medical Treatment I Want or Don't Want
3. How Comfortable I Want To Be
4. How I Want People To Treat Me
5. What I Want My Loved Ones To Know

*Five Wishes* makes it easier for you to let your doctor, family, and friends know how you want to be treated if you become seriously ill and cannot tell them.

*Five Wishes* is a gift to your family members and friends so that they won't have to guess what you want. *Five Wishes* is easy to understand and simple to use.

***Cover of Aging With Dignity's* Five Wishes.** *The* Five Wishes *document helps individuals express how they would want to be treated if they became seriously ill and unable to speak for themselves.* PHOTO BY TIM BOYLE/GETTY IMAGES.

medical treatments under hypothetical medical scenarios. In the early 21st century, all 50 states and the District of Columbia have addressed end of life issues, either by legalizing some form of advance directives, do not resuscitate (DNR) orders, checklists with yes-or-no treatment decisions by the individual regarding the use of life-sustaining medical technology (e.g., ventilators), do not hospitalize (DNH) orders, or by enacting alternative provisions for end of life decisions in the form of family consent, surrogacy, or succession laws that do not require a document to be signed prior to a loss of competency. In addition, the U.S. Congress passed the Patient Self-Determination Act (PSDA) in 1990, which gives legal force to living wills, establishes the legality of the appointment of substitute (e.g., surrogate) health care decision-makers, and allows the possibility of the withdrawal of life support (Brown, 2003).

Since their inception, advance directives have been the focus of intense academic research and broad societal discussion as providers, medical ethicists, policy makers, legislators, and the public have debated important questions concerning patient autonomy, quality of life at the end of life, and the withholding or withdrawal of life-sustaining treatments. In the best case scenario, the patient, family, and physician have held ongoing, comprehensive discussions about treatment options and preferences throughout the course of advanced illness and the individual's wishes have been documented in their medical record. In the absence of such discussions, health care providers or families are left having to choose what they think their loved one would have wanted concerning treatment without guidance from the individual.

However, contrary to widely accepted assumptions about the utility of advance directives, the research conducted to date on the impact of advance directives has generally shown that, despite two decades of legislation and advocacy, advance directive completion rates (that is, the number of people who fill out an advance directive form) remain low (ranging from 15% to 25%) and that advance directives have not been very effective in reducing unwanted aggressive medical treatments or costs at the end of life (Lorenz et al., 2008). End of life care often does not involve explicit, rational decision-making but rather is influenced by a variety of external factors, including the existing medical professional standards and guidelines for care, state and federal laws and regulations, and the financing systems of the health care systems the patient is being treated in; interpersonal factors, such as the patients' age, the nature of the patient's illness, the social, religious, and cultural value systems of participants, including health care providers; and medical care factors, such as the uncertainty of prognosis and the potential benefits and risks associated with various aggressive medical interventions.

Research has shown that few patients have end of life treatment discussions, either with their physician or with their family, and that if these discussions take place, they are often not documented in the medical record. Even when advance directives are executed, physicians are frequently unaware of them, they are not easily available to providers when needed, or they are invoked late in the dying process when the patient is hopelessly ill and actively dying. Advance directives are often too general or are inapplicable to the current clinical circumstances of the patient, or they are overridden by providers and family members. Complicating this situation is the instability of patient preferences; they change over time as the patient's circumstances change and participants, including health care professionals, are often uncomfortable using the rational, analytical decision approach inherent in the legal basis of advance directive documents, particularly amidst the complex and emotion-laden end of life situations. Finally, many patients, families, and providers do not want to face these hard decisions or are not prepared to give up on therapies aimed at cure and life-prolongation in order to focus totally on comfort and the relief of suffering (Lorenz et al., 2008; Street & Ottmann, 2006).

Clinicians, researchers, and advocates have developed new comprehensive, system and community-wide models of end of life planning that build on the original goals of autonomy and self-determination, while addressing the identified shortcomings of advance directives, to better meet the needs of patients and families. Advance care planning (ACP) is defined as a comprehensive and longitudinal process of communication and shared decision-making as circumstances change between the patient, family, and health care providers to determine the patient's goals of care (e.g., from prevention to attempts at cure, or from life prolonging interventions to the use of comfort measures and a focus on the relief of suffering). Many of these ACP models have demonstrated reductions in unnecessary hospitalizations and aggressive care at the end of life, an increase in care that is more consistent with patient goals, and the reduction of caregivers' anxiety, depression, and burden in both hospital and nursing home settings (Lorenz et al., 2008).

### DIRECTIONS FOR THE FUTURE

Though encouraging, these programs have yet to be rigorously evaluated and, while highly successful in terms of completion rates for ACP documents and compliance of end of life care to documented wishes, it is not clear from the methodologically weak and limited research conducted to date which program or contextual variables are the salient features of these program's success. There are a number of ethical, programmatic, conceptual, policy, research, and methodological issues concerning advance care planning and shared decision-making that have yet to be resolved and require continued research—including why advance care planning works when it does, what components of successful programs contribute most to its success, and why it often fails.

In addition, further research is needed on the applicability and utility of advance care planning in various patient populations (such as the elderly, younger and disabled people, ethnically and culturally diverse populations, and so forth); settings (e.g., intensive care units, nursing homes, residential care facilities, or hospitals); and circumstances (of healthy individuals, those with advanced illness, and those facing the end of life). Efforts to date suggest that advance care planning holds great promise, but future efforts should be based on the most successful models. These approaches should integrate change at the community level (e.g., provider practice patterns, institutional protocols, and consumer involvement) with structures and mechanisms at the state and federal level (e.g., legal and health care facility regulations and the financing of care promoting ACP) to facilitate shared decision-making and continuity of care. More flexible legal instruments, the naming of a proxy/surrogate, an emphasis on patient/family/provider communication, and advance care planning educational and skills training tools that support the end of life decision-making process can best inform care in a clinically relevant way.

**SEE ALSO** Volume 3: *Death and Dying; Health Care Use, Later Life; Hospice and Palliative Care.*

**BIBLIOGRAPHY**

Brown, B. (2003). The history of advance directives: A literature review. *Journal of Gerontological Nursing, 29*(9), 4–14.

Gillespie, R., Florin, D., & Gillam, S. (2004). How is patient-centered care understood by the clinical, managerial, and lay stakeholders responsible for promoting this agenda? *Health Expectations, 7*, 142–148.

Lorenz, K. A., Lynn J., Dy, S. M., Shugarman, S. M., Wilkinson A. M., et al. (2008). Evidence for improving palliative care at the end of life: A systematic review. *Annals of Internal Medicine, 148*(2), 147–159.

Lunney, J. R., Lynn, J., & Hogan, C. (2002). Profiles of older Medicare decedents. *Journal of the American Geriatric Society, 50*(6), 1108–1112.

President's Council on Bioethics. (2005). *Taking care: Ethical caregiving in our aging society.* Washington, DC: Author.

Sharma, R. R., Chan, S., Liu, H., & Ginsberg, C. (2001). *Health and health care of the Medicare population. Data from the 1997 Medicare current beneficiary survey.* Rockville, MD: Westat.

Steinhauser, K. E., Christakis, N. A., Clipp, E. C., McNeilly, M., McIntyre, L., & Tulsky, J. A. (2000). Factors considered important at the end of life by patients, family, physicians, and other care providers. *Journal of the American Medical Association, 284*(19), 2476–2482.

Street, A. F., & Ottmann, G. (2006). *State of the science review of advance care planning models.* Victoria, Australia: La Trobe University.

***Anne M. Wilkinson***
***Moira Sim***

## EPIDEMIOLOGIC TRANSITION

Relatively recent historical changes in patterns of death and disability have made fundamental changes in the trajectory of the life course. During the 19th and 20th centuries, most countries experienced a substantial decline in mortality from infectious disease, with a resulting increase in deaths from chronic conditions. One theory of the historical processes of change that describes these shifts in patterns of morbidity and mortality is known as the epidemiologic transition. This theory is relevant to life-course research because of its implications for the aging process and the timing of important life-course transitions related to schooling, marriage, reproduction, and retirement.

## CLASSICAL THEORY OF THE EPIDEMIOLOGIC TRANSITION

The epidemiologic transition as it originally was conceptualized by A. R. Omran (1971) describes recent rapid declines in mortality as a process by which pandemics of infectious diseases (such as influenza) gradually were replaced by degenerative diseases (such as arthritis) and human-made diseases (such as some cancers and heart disease) as the primary causes of morbidity and mortality. According to Omran, the theory of the epidemiologic transition is focused on "the complex change in patterns of health and disease *and* on the interactions between these patterns and their demographic, economic and sociologic determinants and consequences" (Omran, 1971, p. 510).

Omran divided the epidemiologic transition into three historical stages, which he labeled the age of pestilence and famine, the age of receding pandemics, and the age of degenerative and human-made diseases. During the age of pestilence and famine, mortality rates were high and average life expectancy at birth was 20 to 40 years. That stage lasted until the late 17th century for most Western nations and was characterized by death rates that fluctuated greatly in response to periodic occurrences of epidemics of infectious diseases. The leading causes of death included pneumonia, influenza, smallpox, tuberculosis, and other infectious diseases.

The age of receding pandemics was characterized by a sudden rapid and then steady decline in mortality caused by a decrease in epidemics of infectious disease. As those epidemics receded, death rates began to show less fluctuation and average life expectancy increased to around 50 years. The risk of death from infectious diseases was highest among infants, children, and women of reproductive age, because these groups tended to have weaker immune response and because women and infants often died during childbirth. Thus the epidemiologic transition favors the young over the old and women over men in terms of survivorship. In Western nations the mortality decline began during the late 1700s and continued until the early 19th century. Mortality declines in other countries began at various points in the 18th and 19th centuries.

During the age of degenerative and human-made diseases, mortality continued to decline, though less rapidly than it had in the prior stages, and eventually stabilized at relatively low levels toward the end of the transition. With a decrease in mortality at younger ages, more of the population survived to contract diseases associated with middle age and old age. Thus during that period the leading causes of death shifted to the chronic degenerative diseases that characterize the middle and older ages, such as heart disease, stroke, and cancer. As a result of these improvements in survivorship, life expectancy reached 70 years, with little expectation of further improvement.

## VARIATION IN TRANSITION EXPERIENCE

Although dramatic declines in mortality have occurred globally, the specific experience of the epidemiologic transition varies across nations. Omran (1982) proposed four models of epidemiologic transition to account for variations in the pattern, determinants, and consequences of the transition: the Classical (Western), Accelerated, Delayed, and Transitional Variant of Delayed models.

The Classical (Western) model describes the experience of industrialized countries such as the United States, Great Britain, and most other Western European countries. This model is characterized by a gradual transition from high to low mortality rates that accompanied the process of modernization and began as early as the 1750s. In this model, declines in mortality are attributed primarily to economic development, improvements in food supply and nutrition, and advances in sanitation and hygiene. Medical advances are thought to have played a minor role in the initial transition to low mortality, though, as noted by J. B. McKinlay and S. M. McKinlay (1977), the stabilization of mortality at low levels during the third phase is probably attributable to the development of medical technology.

In the Accelerated model, the transition to low mortality occurs in a shorter period and does not begin until the 1850s. Accordingly, the shift to degenerative and human-made diseases also occurs much more swiftly. In addition, the increases in the survival rates of children and young women that are typical of the Classical model occur over shorter periods. As in the Classical model, the primary determinants of the transition are socioeconomic improvements, along with technological and medical advances. This model describes the transition experience in Japan, Eastern Europe, and the former Soviet Union, where the process of modernization occurred in a relatively short period.

The Delayed model describes the relatively recent and incomplete transition experienced by most developing countries. In these countries substantial declines in mortality did not begin until after World War II. Mortality rates among infants, young children, and women of reproductive age did not decline as dramatically as in the Classical and Accelerated models. In fact, mortality declines have begun to recede in most countries, with life expectancy reaching only about 55 years. The

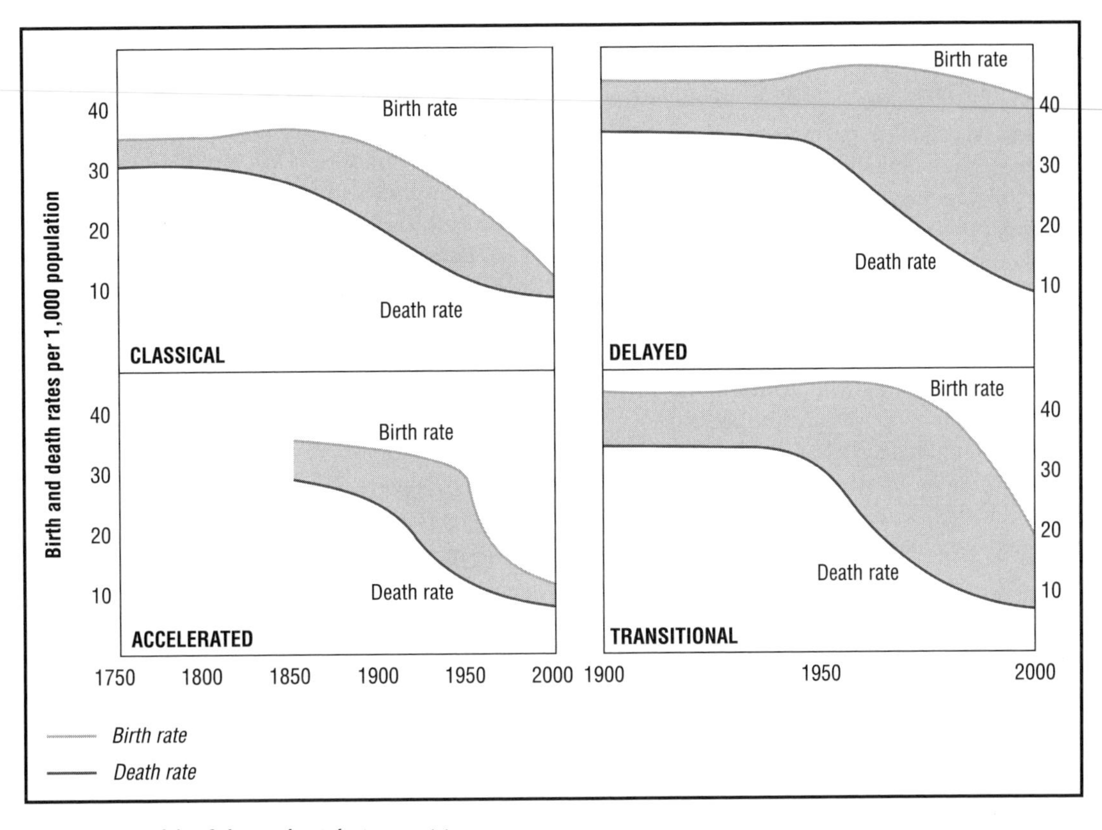


*Figure 1. Models of the epidemiologic transition.* CENGAGE LEARNING, GALE.

decreases in mortality that have occurred are due primarily to medical interventions such as vaccines and public health measures aimed at disease control. Further declines in mortality are not expected to occur until economic and social infrastructures are improved. This model typifies the experience of India and most countries in Africa and Latin America.

The Transitional Variant of the Delayed model has been proposed to describe the experience of countries that have had a delayed transition but where the mortality decline did not lessen to the same extent as in the delayed model with consistent declines in mortality. These countries have the necessary infrastructure, in terms of health-care delivery, to experience sustained declines in mortality. Countries with this transition experience include South Korea, China, and Jamaica.

## CONSEQUENCES FOR POPULATION DYNAMICS

A central proposition of epidemiologic transition theory is that mortality is the main driver of population dynamics. The dramatic decline in mortality from infectious diseases has had a significant impact on population dynamics. A fundamental characteristic of the epidemiologic transition is the shift in the age pattern of mortality. The decrease in infectious disease mortality primarily benefited children and young women, increasing their chances of surviving to middle and older ages. This shift in the age pattern of mortality has had implications for population growth, population aging, and sex differences in survival.

Before the epidemiologic transition both mortality and fertility rates were high, resulting in minimal increases in population sizes. For some time after mortality began to decline, fertility rates remained high, producing an explosion in population growth. During that period, as A. J. Coale (1974) notes, populations grew much faster than they had in earlier human history. In countries that have completed the epidemiologic transition, the declines in mortality eventually were followed by similar declines in fertility. For some countries, such as Italy and other Western European countries, fertility rates eventually fell to below replacement levels. (Women must have, on average, 2.1 children over the course of their childbearing years to maintain population levels.) This phenomenon, which is referred to as the second demographic transition, has resulted in negative population growth in those countries except when immigration has offset the effect of low fertility, as has been the case in the United States. In contrast, in countries experiencing a delayed transition, the decline in fertility has not matched declines in mortality. These countries have experienced sustained population growth, with countries such as India and China experiencing overpopulation.

In addition to overall population growth there have been increases in the population of specific age groups. As a result of the epidemiologic transition, for the first time the human population as a whole has been growing older, as S. J. Olshansky, B. A. Carnes, and A. Désesquelles observe (2001). As mortality from epidemics of infection declined, the leading causes of death shifted to chronic diseases that emerge in middle and later adulthood. Initially, declines in infant, child, and maternal mortality make the population younger, but this improved survival ultimately leads to a drop in births rates and the beginning of population aging. For some countries, such as the United States and Japan, the population has aged dramatically in a relatively short period.

Shifts in the pattern of mortality also have resulted in changes in the sex composition of the population. Changes in cause-specific death rates that accompanied the epidemiologic transition favored women over men. Decreases in maternal mortality resulted in improved survival among women. Men, in contrast, are slightly more susceptible to cardiovascular disease and cancer, two of the leading causes of death that have emerged in the age of human-made degenerative diseases. The male mortality disadvantage is primarily a product of the less healthy life styles of males in terms of diet, risk-taking behavior, health-care utilization, and so on. Thus improvements in life expectancy that result from the epidemiologic transition benefit women more than men.

## SIGNIFICANCE FOR LIFE COURSE TRANSITIONS

The increased life span resulting from the epidemiologic transition has had significant implications for life-course transitions related to schooling, marriage, reproduction, and retirement. The timing of life events depends partly on the average number of years people can expect to live. Increased life expectancy allows individuals to delay life events and increases the chances that individuals will experience certain life events. For instance, the increase in longevity among women and children enabled women to delay childbearing and marriage and spend more of their lives obtaining an education and participating in the labor force. The increased survival of infants and children meant that women could have fewer children than in the past and be assured that most, if not all, of their children would survive to adulthood. When this was combined with increases in their own survival rates, women were able to postpone childbearing and have fewer children.

A longer life span has allowed both men and women to devote more years of their lives to schooling, which in turn may increase life expectancy, and has resulted in more time spent in the workforce. Whereas most of the population did not survive to middle and old age before the epidemiologic transition, the increased longevity that followed the transition has resulted in more of the population experiencing a relatively recent but important life-course transition: retirement. Before the epidemiologic transition, life course transitions related to older age were not experienced by most of the population. Because life expectancy has increased throughout the population, transitions related to older age, such as retirement, have come to be recognized as important stages in the life course.

## RECONCEPTUALIZING CLASSICAL EPIDEMIOLOGIC TRANSITION THEORY

In its original conceptualization, the theory of epidemiologic transition assumes that populations that have completed the transition have achieved a lower limit to mortality (i.e., the risk of death is as low as it can be) and an upper limit to longevity (i.e., the average life expectancy is as long as it can be). This is the case because traditional epidemiologic theory focuses on mortality declines that benefit the young. Because mortality rates among infants and children probably cannot be lowered further, additional increases in life expectancy necessarily will come from mortality declines at older ages. Indeed, after completing the classical epidemiologic transition, many countries experienced further declines in mortality at middle and old ages. To explain continued declines in mortality and increases in longevity, classical epidemiologic transition theory has been reconceptualized to include a fourth stage, the age of delayed degenerative disease, as described by Olshansky and A. B. Ault (1986), and a fifth stage, the age of slowing of senescence, as described by S. Horiuchi (1999).

The age of delayed degenerative diseases describes more recent developments in the epidemiologic experience of populations considered to have completed the classical epidemiologic transition. From the 1950s to the 1970s many countries experienced a decline in cardiovascular and cancer mortality. Classical epidemiologic transition theory emphasizes gains in life expectancy that result from reductions in mortality at younger ages. However, reductions in cardiovascular and cancer mortality occurred primarily among those of middle and older ages, and those declines pushed the upper limit of life expectancy.

A recent development in mortality transition, the age of slowing of senescence, describes reductions in mortality at older ages. Declines in mortality from cardiovascular disease and cancer result in more of the population

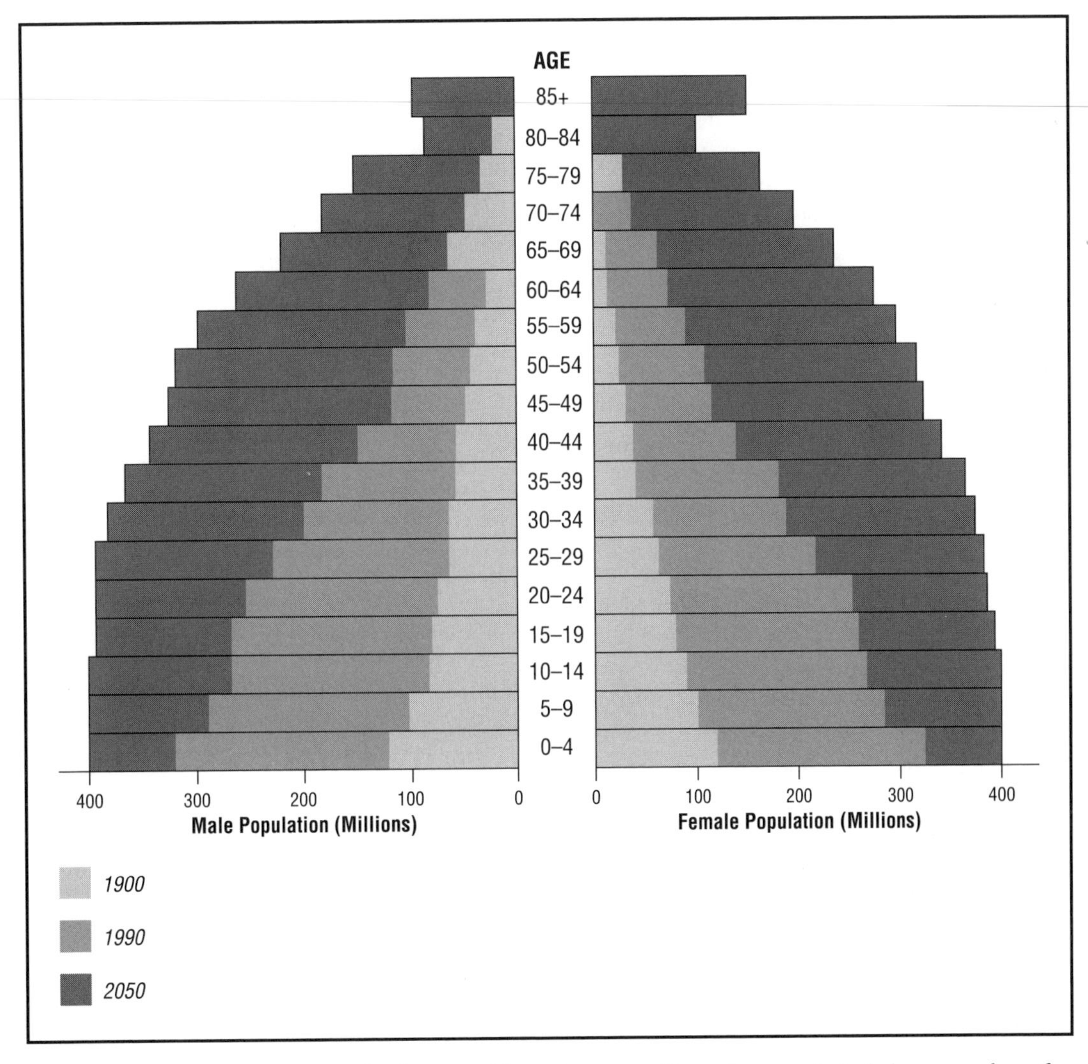


*Figure 2. Since 1990 age structure has become wider and more rectilinear because relatively larger numbers of people in the growing population are surviving to older ages. By the middle of the 21st century it will be very nearly rectangular.* CENGAGE LEARNING, GALE.

surviving to an advanced age. Thus further increases in life expectancy can occur if mortality declines among the elderly. For mortality to decline among the elderly, deaths from old-age physiological frailties would have to be delayed until even later years of the life course. Although there is debate about the biological limits to human longevity, it is clear that a slowing of senescence would push the limits of longevity further, as the work of J. F. Fries (1980); V. Kannisto, J. Lauitsen, A. R. Thatcher, and J. W. Vaupel (1994); J. Oeppen and J. W. Vaupel (2002); and Olshansky et al. (2001) demonstrates.

## THE FUTURE OF THE EPIDEMIOLOGIC TRANSITION

Trends in morbidity and mortality have prompted researchers to address two major limitations of the classical epidemiologic transition theory. First, the theory assumes a unidirectional experience of declining mortality with no attention to the possibility of reversals in the transition to low mortality, as occurred in the former Soviet Union following an economic transition and the resulting health-care finance crisis. Second, the theory was formulated to describe population-level trends in morbidity and mortality. Thus substantial between-group variation in the transition experience within countries has not been explained fully.

Several trends in disease and mortality are not accounted for in classical epidemiologic transition theory. For instance, as noted by R. Barret, C. W. Kuzawa, T. McDade, and G. J. Armelagos (1998), there has been a reemergence of pandemics of infectious disease. HIV/AIDS has increased age-specific mortality in parts of Asia and Africa as well as in some industrialized countries, such as the United States. Furthermore, there is evidence of a global reemergence of infectious diseases, such as tuberculosis, that were thought to be under control. In addition to increases in epidemics of infectious disease, epidemics of noncommunicable disease have emerged. For instance, a significant number of premature deaths in both developed and developing countries can be attributed to smoking-related mortality, as M. Ezatti and A. D. Lopez (2003) note. In addition, there is growing evidence, as B. M. Popkin and C. M. Doak (1998) observe, of the emergence of a global epidemic of obesity that has implications for population health.

These reverse transitions or countertransitions do not fit within the traditional theory because of an implicit assumption of unidirectional transition experience. Furthermore, many developing countries are experiencing a double burden of disease. In these countries mortality rates are high for both communicable and noncommunicable diseases. This burden makes it difficult for those countries to continue to develop in ways that ultimately would improve the health of their populations.

Because the epidemiologic transition focuses on population-level trends in morbidity and mortality, variation within populations tends to be overlooked. The rate of change and the underlying causes of the transition differ among subgroups of the population. For instance, although there has been a rapid and general decline in adult mortality, socioeconomic and racial inequalities have been maintained if not widened, according to R. G. Rogers (1992) and J. Vallin (1980). In addition, the long-term downward trend in U.S. infant mortality has not benefited Blacks and Whites equally. Not only has the disparity persisted, it has increased and is not expected to diminish, as noted by G. K. Singh and S. M. Yu (1995) and I. W. Eberstein and J. R. Parker (1984). Differences in transition experiences among subgroups within populations have produced significant inequalities in health and mortality. Further research is needed to understand the origins of these inequalities.

The epidemiologic transition describes the global historical transition from very high and fluctuating mortality to low and stable mortality. However, populations continue to experience changes related to morbidity and mortality. Thus, the classical epidemiologic transition theory needs to be updated continually in response to changing trends in diseases and death.

**SEE ALSO** Volume 3: *Chronic Illness, Adulthood and Later Life; Demographic Transition Theories; Global Aging; Population Aging; Mortality.*

**BIBLIOGRAPHY**

Barrett, R., Kuzawa, C. W., McDade, T., & Armelagos, G. J. (1998). Emerging and re-emerging infectious diseases: The third epidemiologic transition. *Annual Review of Anthropology, 27,* 247–271.

Coale, A. J. (1974). The history of the human population. *Scientific American, 231*(3), 41–51.

Eberstein, I. W., & Parker, J. R. (1984). Racial differences in infant mortality by cause of death: The impact of birth weight and maternal age. *Demography, 21*(3), 309–321.

Ezatti, M., & Lopez, A. D. (2003). Estimates of global mortality attributable to smoking in 2000. *Lancet, 362*(9387), 847–852.

Fries, J. F. (1980). Aging, natural death, and the compression of morbidity. *New England Journal of Medicine, 303*(3): 130–135.

Horiuchi, S. (1999). Epidemiological transitions in human history. In *Health and mortality: Issues of global concern: Proceedings of the symposium on health and mortality, Brussels, 19–22 November 1997* (pp. 54–71). New York: United Nations.

Kannisto, V., Lauritsen, J., Thatcher, A. R., & Vaupel, J. W. (1994). Reductions in mortality at advanced ages: Several decades of evidence from 27 countries. *Population and Development Review 20*(4): 793–810.

McKinlay, J. B., & McKinlay, S. M. (1977). The questionable contribution of medical measures to the decline of mortality in the United States in the twentieth century. *Milbank Memorial Fund Quarterly. Health and Society, 55*(3), 405–428.

Oeppen, J., & Vaupel, J. W. (2002). Demography: Broken limits to life expectancy. *Science 296*(5570): 1029–1031.

Olshansky, J. S., & Ault, A. B. (1986). The fourth stage of the epidemiologic transition: The age of delayed degenerative diseases. *Milbank Memorial Fund Quarterly, 64*(3), 355–391.

Olshansky, S. J., Carnes, B. A., & Désesquelles, A. (2001). Demography: Prospects for human longevity. *Science, 291*(5508): 1491–1492.

Omran, A. R. (1971). The epidemiologic transition: A theory of the epidemiology of population change. *Milbank Memorial Fund Quarterly, 49*(4), 509–538.

Omran, A. R. (1982). Epidemiologic transition. In J. A. Ross (Ed.), *International encyclopedia of population* (vol. 1., pp. 172–175). New York: Free Press.

Popkin, B. M., and Doak, C. M. (1998). The obesity epidemic is a worldwide phenomenon. *Nutrition Reviews, 56*(4), 106–114.

Rogers, R. G. (1992). Living and dying in the USA: Sociodemographic determinants of death among blacks and whites. *Demography, 29*(2), 287–303.

Singh, G. K., & Yu, S. M. (1995). Infant mortality in the United States: Trends, differentials, and projections, 1950 through 2010. *American Journal of Public Health, 85*(7), 957–964.

Vallin, J. (1980). Socio-economic determinants of mortality in industrialized countries. *Population Bulletin of the United Nations, 13,* 26–41.

***Jennifer A. Ailshire***

# F

## FAMILY AND HOUSEHOLD STRUCTURE, LATER LIFE

Throughout the life course, individuals commonly turn to family members for help when faced with instrumental, emotional, financial, or other types of needs. Although many exchanges of support occur between family members who do not live together, intensive support is facilitated by family members choosing to live in the same household. The ways in which families and households are structured can provide insights into the multidimensional layering of exchanges and attachments that bind family members to one another.

At every stage of the life course, family and household structure evolves in response to changes in family membership and roles, economic resources, and needs for support and assistance. Life course events experienced by an individual, such as changes in marital status or having children, frequently result in changes in the composition of one's household. Events and experiences occurring to others, however, can also impact an individual's household composition. Because individual life trajectories are interconnected with the trajectories of others in one's network, the life course events experienced by close family members may trigger a reconfiguration of living arrangements. For example, an older woman living with her adult daughter may be thrust into a three-generation household if the daughter has a child. Similarly, a frail married woman living with her husband may become widowed and move in with her single "young-old" daughter, transforming her daughter's living situation into a two-person household. The cascading sequences of demographic, social, and economic events experienced by individuals, as well as by others who are close to them, shape family and household structure.

### THE SIGNIFICANCE OF FAMILY AND HOUSEHOLD STRUCTURE

A *household* is defined as the group of individuals who collectively occupy a housing unit (that is, the people who live together in the same home or apartment). The concepts of family and household are closely linked because the vast majority of households are composed of family groups. Only a relatively few people share living quarters with nonrelatives, especially in later life. For example, in 2000 only 3% of individuals aged 65 and over lived exclusively with nonrelatives, a category that includes boarders, roommates, and cohabiting partners. A far larger share of older people—28% in 2000—live alone in a single-person home. Aside from the 6% of older people who live in group quarters such as nursing homes, the rest of the older population, totaling 63% or roughly 22 million people aged 65 and over, share a household with family members (figures calculated based on the Public Use Microdata Sample of the 2000 U.S. Census). This entry focuses on family relationships as they overlap with household relationships among older people. Other entries in this volume report on key family relationships in later life that transcend household boundaries, including relationships with adult children, grandchildren, and siblings.

Household composition has been described as "one of the most basic and essential determinants of the well-being of older adults" (Zimmer, 2003, p. 248), with implications for their economic, physical, and psychosocial well-being. At a minimum, households are economic units, sharing shelter as well as many other resources. Household members, especially those who are related to one another, often pool finances for food and other expenses. The economies of scale realized through sharing living quarters can result in an improved quality of life for older adults, as well as for those with whom they live.

Members of the same household support one another in a variety of noneconomic ways as well. Those who are disabled may receive assistance with activities of daily living (e.g., bathing, dressing) or instrumental activities of daily living (e.g., managing finances, taking medications), effectively forestalling the need for nursing home care. Older individuals in a multigenerational household may support younger family members by providing child care or other services. Indeed, living arrangements may be considered the most visible, though not the only, social indicator of familial embeddedness, support, and solidarity across generations.

## CONCEPTUAL ISSUES UNDERLYING HOUSEHOLD AND FAMILY STRUCTURE

One conceptual theme informing the understanding of household and family structure in later life involves the tension between independence and familial interdependence or mutual support. Just as leaving the parental home and establishing a home of one's own signals adult independence among young adults, relinquishing one's own home by moving in with family members, moving to assisted living, or entering a nursing home may be experienced by many older individuals as a signal of dependency. One of the tasks of the intergenerational family is to facilitate the efforts of different generations to achieve a balance between independence and mutual support, as played out in residential choices. Strong family solidarity may result in the obligation to support dependent family members through coresidence, even when the pull toward independence is strong.

A related theme relevant to any discussion of family and household structure is that of reciprocation, or the give and take of family relationships. Family members are in need of different types of help and support at various stages of the life course, and may experience high levels of dependency at some points but not at others. With the provision of assistance to a family member comes the expectation that help will be reciprocated—if not immediately, then in the future, and if not from the family member who was helped, then from another participant in the family "support bank" (Antonucci, 1990). These interdependencies, and the associated norm of reciprocation, imply that aging family members will make residential choices taking into account both the network members on whom they can rely for help and those members who are counting on them for support.

Perhaps the most enduring theoretical approach to conceptualizing household structure in later life assumes a rational evaluation of living arrangement options in light of preferences, resources, and the availability of alternative opportunities (Burr & Mutchler, 1992; Wolf & Soldo, 1988). Rational choice theory assumes that older people engage in an ongoing evaluation of their living circumstances with respect to their preferred goals. Alternative living arrangement opportunities are assessed in light of the resources that affect one's ability to maintain or alter one's residential setting. In practice, this evaluation likely occurs primarily at key life course transition points. Events most likely to prompt a reevaluation of household structure include a change in family circumstances such as the death of a spouse, or a change in personal resources such as the onset of disability.

Greatly complicating decisions about household structure is the fact that any given household is the result not only of the choices made by a single individual but also potentially of multiple individuals' opportunities, preferences, and constraints. Those who are married or partnered evaluate and respond not to a single set of conditions but to both partners' sets of constraints and preferences. Household decisions may reflect intergenerational decision making as well. An older couple may be capable of living as a pair and satisfied doing so, but their adult daughter may need to live with them because she is unable to make ends meet in an independent household. An older widow may prefer to live alone, but her children may feel strongly that she lacks the physical capability to do so and pressure her to live with them. Acknowledging the linked decision making that occurs throughout the family system and that shapes household composition is a challenging but critical part of understanding living arrangement patterns in later life.

**Preferences** The choices that people make about where to live and whom to live with are typically described as partially a function of preferences or "tastes" for various living arrangements (i.e., what living arrangements would provide the greatest satisfaction?). Social scientists acknowledge a general preference for independence in living arrangements. All else being equal, older people in the United States prefer to live alone or exclusively with a spouse or partner, once their children are grown. Living with adult children or other relatives, or moving to a nursing home, is considered less preferable (Shanas, 1979; Wister & Burch, 1987). Given the growing cultural diversity of the older population, this assumed preference for living alone or with a spouse only has been called into question. Indeed, research has demonstrated considerable variability in living arrangement preferences and in perceptions of obligation to share living quarters across generations (Burr & Mutchler, 1999; Lee, Peek, & Coward, 1998). Attributes such as race, ethnicity, immigration history, and level of acculturation appear to shape these preferences and predispositions (Angel, Angel, & Himes, 1992; Burr & Mutchler, 1993b). Moreover, research in Asian and Latin American countries suggests that the cultural underpinnings of preferences for intergenerational coresidence may be breaking down. For instance, increasing numbers of seniors in Japan and China express a preference for living independently (Logan, Bian, and Bian, 1998; Takagi, Silverstein, and Crimmins, 2007).

**Availability of Alternatives** Household composition choices also reflect the availability of others with whom to live (i.e., are there family members or others with whom a shared residence could be established?). Life course trajectories and events are critical in shaping these choices. Older individuals who do not live alone most typically live with their spouses, with their adult children, or with both. As such, demographic events occurring throughout the life course, such as marriage and union formation, union dissolution, and childbearing, largely determine the availability of others with whom one could live. Individuals who never married or who divorced and did not remarry do not have a spouse with whom to live in old age, and are far more likely to live with other relatives or alone. Individuals who have several children are more likely to have at least one with whom they could live compatibly.

Availability of alternatives is also a function of processes of geographic dispersion within the family system. Adult children move away from the communities in which they grew up, leaving their aging parents behind. Many retirees relocate to the Sun Belt or other "amenity" destinations, leaving the communities in which extended family members and support networks are established. Geographic mobility results in aging adults and their extended family members often being geographically separated. When older individuals who are geographically distant from family care networks become frail, widowed, or in need of more assistance, they may move to be closer to (or live with) support networks such as adult children (Litwak & Longino, 1987). Together, the life course processes associated with marriage, marital dissolution, having children, dying, and geographic mobility that occur in the lives of older individuals and in the lives of their close family members combine to define the living arrangement options available to an individual at any given time.

**Resources** Household composition decisions are based also on the financial and other resources available to the older individual. Sufficient economic resources are necessary to live independently; these resources are strongly shaped by life course trajectories earlier in life. The accumulation of assets, such as an owned home and a private pension, is shaped by decisions made earlier in life about educational attainment, employment, and consumption. Individuals who obtain higher levels of education and who develop a stable and well-compensated work career are more likely to reach old age with resources that facilitate realizing their living arrangement preferences. In contrast, those with unstable or poorly compensated lifetime work careers may have even fewer resources in later life. Those with low levels of economic security may be unable to maintain an independent household and may have no choice other than to live with extended family members or others.

Health and disability levels also represent resources that factor into living arrangement decisions. Nominal needs for assistance associated with health declines may be readily met through services provided in an older individual's home by family members living nearby, or by paid or volunteer service organizations. Should the needs of the elderly individual be so extensive that he or she cannot be left alone or if needs for assistance occur routinely throughout the day and night, a reconfiguration of the household may be required. The highest level of disease and disability burden is likely to precipitate a move to a nursing home, especially if family members are unable or unwilling to facilitate support within the community.

**Environment** Features of the environmental context may also shape household and family structure in later life. A home that adequately met the needs of a couple for many years may no longer be suitable when they are unable to manage stairs, for example. Evolving challenges in the environment may be countered by making changes to the physical environment, such as renovations that allow a person to live on a single level. Environmental challenges may be met instead through moving to a more suitable environment, where suitability is judged both by the physical features of the living situation and by the social support available. The process of adjusting one's living circumstances to one's current physical capacity, or optimizing "person–environment fit" (Lawton, 1982), can increase independence and allow the aging individual to avoid the exacerbation of disabilities. Indeed, the biopsychosocial model of disability, one example of which is the International Classification of Functioning, Disability, and Health (ICF) put forth by the World Health Organization (WHO, 2002), points out that health conditions and functioning need not result in limits on participation or activity if the environment is adequately supportive. Paradoxically, making social support available within the household environment is one vehicle through which participation and independence may be facilitated.

An additional line of research suggests that features of the community may enter into decisions about household composition. A shortage of housing, high housing costs, and other features of the housing environment may limit the range of housing choices available to older adults as well as to their families. If housing costs—including not only rent or mortgage but also taxes, utilities, and other related costs—are excessively high in a community, then older adults may view opportunities to live with extended family members more favorably. Indeed, younger relatives in the same high-cost community may have few alternatives to living with older relatives. One study established empirically that older individuals and couples who live in high-cost housing markets are more likely to live with other adults; the same study suggests that older single persons who live in communities with lower median rental costs for small apartments are more likely to avoid institutionalization (Mutchler and Burr, 2003). Thus environmental and cost-of-living factors that are beyond the control of families may also shape household structure in later life.

**Mutual Exchange** The formation of extended family households, especially coresidence between aging parents and their adult children, is an important alternative to living alone or solely with a spouse. The extent to which grown children can serve as resources for frail older parents, including contemplating sharing living quarters, depends not only on the needs and resources of the parents but also on the characteristics and life stage of the adult children. Some literature points specifically to the ambiguity in establishing who is being helped in intergenerational households (Choi, 2003; Speare and Avery, 1993), with most empirical literature suggesting that adult children are often the recipients of support in these households rather than the providers of care, except when the parent is very old or suffers from severe functional limitation.

Yet the exchanges occurring within the household involve many different currencies, including not only financial support but also instrumental assistance and other forms of care. For example, an older man may be able to afford living alone, yet he might not be able to keep his home in good repair unless his son lives with him. An older widow may be financially supported by her son and his wife, with whom she lives. Yet her days may be spent caring for the home and for her grandchildren, allowing her son and his wife to work long hours. The reciprocity embedded in such exchanges occurring within the intergenerational household makes it difficult to determine why the household was formed, who is benefiting the most, and how enduring the arrangement will be.

The well-being of older adults is affected in both tangible and symbolic ways by the composition of the families and households within which they are embedded. Coresident family members such as a spouse, adult children, or other relatives can be important sources of social support, instrumental help, and economic assistance. As well, the help and support that older people provide to the people with whom they live—for instance, providing child care within a three-generation household or caring for a disabled loved one—can bring satisfaction and purpose to their lives. Yet the values of independence and privacy are strong in many segments of American society, and these values tend to support the goal of smaller, more individualistic households. Ultimately, the implications of family and household structure for well-being reflect the balance of these disparate practical and symbolic elements that together shape the formation and maintenance of different kinds of households.

## TRENDS AND PATTERNS IN HOUSEHOLD AND FAMILY STRUCTURE

Perhaps the most notable trend in household and family structure in later life is the rising prevalence of living alone. Throughout the last half of the 19th century, and several decades into the 20th, fewer than 10% of all individuals aged 65 and over lived alone (see Figure 1a). By 1950, 10% of older men and 17% of older women were living in one-person households; rates rose decade by decade until 1990, when 16% of older men and more than 40% of older women were living alone. (These calculations are based on individuals living in households and exclude those living in group quarters such as nursing homes, prisons, and the like.) Historians and others debate the relative significance of demographic factors, preferences, and economic resources in shaping this increase, although it is clear that all three sets of factors contributed to this trend. The concurrent timing of the upturn in rates of living alone in the mid-20th century, and the expansion of the Social Security system, supports the contention of some that the rising ability to "purchase privacy" accounts for part of the upswing (Burch and Matthews, 1987; Kobrin, 1976). Demographic changes in marriage and childbearing, along with the well-established gap in expectation of life between men and women, are also significant (Kramarow, 1995). Indeed, among older men and women who are not currently married (most of whom are widows or widowers), the propensity to live alone is quite similar albeit at higher levels throughout the time period considered, rising to approximately 65% by 1990 (see Figure 1b).

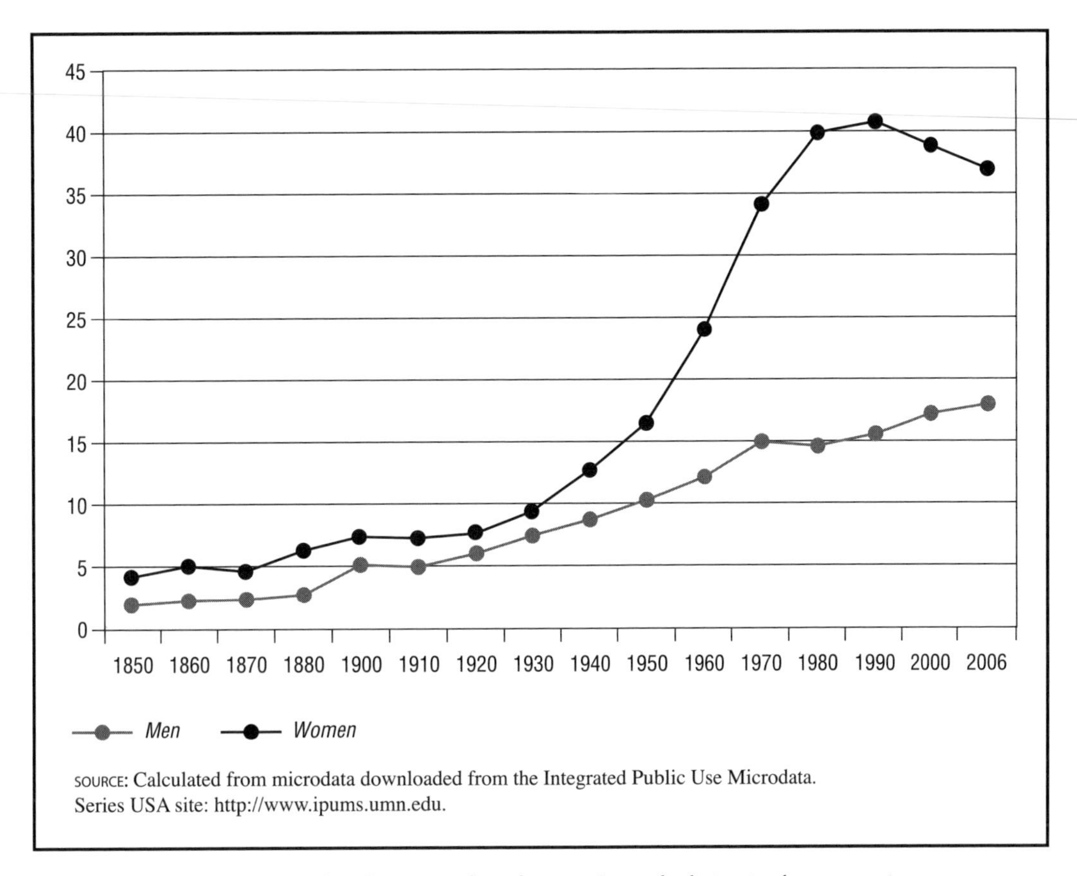


***Figure 1a.*** *Percentage living alone by year and gender, age 65+ only, living in the community.* CENGAGE LEARNING, GALE.

The sizable gender gap between rates of living alone between men and women shown in Figure 1a, a gap that is especially pronounced during the latter decades of the 20th century, is almost entirely the result of the far higher likelihood of older women to have outlived their spouses.

Some investigations by historians have suggested that intergenerational living—that is, three or more generations coresiding under the same roof—was considered desirable in the preindustrial United States, even though it was not commonly observed because demographic conditions made it unlikely that three or more generations in the same family were alive at the same time (Ruggles, 1987). Although demographic conditions in the early 21st century support a situation where three, four, and even five generations are alive at the same time in many families (Matthews and Sun, 2006), intergenerational coresidence occurs at relatively low levels in the United States. The empirical finding that most seniors do live alone or exclusively with a spouse suggests that independent living in later life is indeed viewed favorably by many seniors.

Figures presented in Table 1 show the living arrangements experienced by the population of older individuals in the United States in 2000, as well as within demographic segments of the older population. These tabulations are based on microdata from the U.S. Census of Population and Housing and reflect both composition of the household and whether or not the older individual is the household head. Household headship is assigned to the individual in whose name the home is rented or owned. In these tabulations, both the person listed as the householder and his or her spouse are considered to be "heads of household."

For the entire population aged 65 and over, 70% live in so-called independent households—the older person alone or with his or her spouse only. (Note that these percentages include a small number of seniors—less than one-half of 1%—who also live with their own child under the age of 18.) Another 16% is head of a household that includes other people, most typically the older person's adult child(ren) and/or grandchild(ren). Fewer than 10% are living in the household of someone else (that is, not head of household), and just 6% live in group quarters such as nursing homes, prisons, or mental institutions. Older persons not living alone or exclusively with a spouse will most typically be living with an adult child either in their own home or in the home of the child. For the sample as a whole, fewer than 2% of the seniors live in a household that

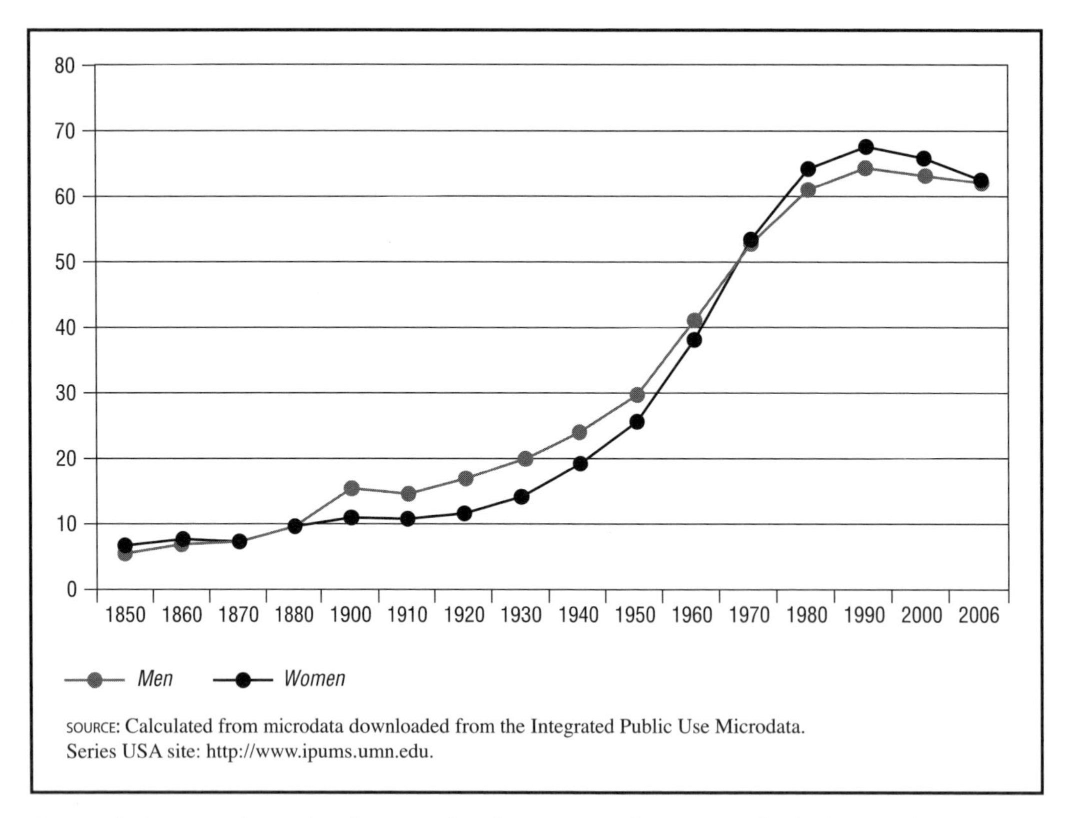


***Figure 1b.*** *Percentage living alone by year and gender, age 65+ only, not married only, living in the community.* CENGAGE LEARNING, GALE.

includes one or more siblings, and fewer than 3% live in a household including another relative, such as a cousin, a niece, or a parent (data not shown).

The pattern of household structure presented here suggests that for the older population as a whole, household headship and independent living are typical. Preferences for independent living, supported by relatively good health and adequate economic resources, commonly result in older persons living on their own in an independent household. "Pseudo-coresidence," or having children live geographically close by but not actually in the same housing unit, can facilitate independent living arrangements even when needs for assistance are high (Zimmer, 2003), as can the use of high-quality and affordable formal in-home services such as homemaker care and visiting nurse care. However, comparisons of household structure patterns across gender, age, and race and ethnic groups suggest that these experiences are not universally shared.

**Gender Differences in Household Structure** As shown in Table 1, older women are considerably more likely to live alone than are older men (36% versus 17%), whereas older men are far more likely to live with a spouse only (57% versus 32%). These patterns largely reflect longer survivorship on the part of women—that is, the greater probability for men that a spouse is available with whom to live—but support the conclusion that both men and women typically live in independent residential situations in later life. Men and women are similarly distributed across most other living arrangements, although women are considerably more likely to live in someone else's household or to live in group quarters. This higher propensity is partly reflective of greater needs for assistance on the part of older women. Older single women also typically have far fewer economic resources than do their male counterparts; indeed, widowhood can trigger a substantial drop in income even for those women who had been part of an economically secure marital unit (Holden, Burkhauser, and Feaster, 1988).

**Age Differences in Household Structure** Table 1 also shows that even among the oldest seniors, residential independence is typical. While 73% of individuals aged 65 to 79 live alone or with a spouse only, even among those aged 80 and over, more than half—64%—live independently. Individuals who are 80 and over are somewhat more likely than their younger counterparts to live in a child's household, and are less likely to head a multigenerational household. Although the oldest individuals are considerably more likely to live in group quarters than are those under age 80, even among these oldest seniors fewer than one out of six lives in a group quarters residence such as a nursing home.

| Living arrangements | Total | Gender: Men | Gender: Women | Age Group: Age 65–79 | Age Group: Age 80+ | Race and Ethnicity[1] Not Hispanic: White alone | Not Hispanic: Black alone | Not Hispanic: Asian alone | Hispanic: All races |
|---|---|---|---|---|---|---|---|---|---|
| Living alone[2] | 28% | 17% | 36% | 25% | 36% | 29% | 30% | 13% | 19% |
| Living with spouse only[2] | 42% | 57% | 32% | 48% | 28% | 46% | 20% | 27% | 26% |
| **Head of Household:** | | | | | | | | | |
| Living with adult children, or grandchildren | 13% | 13% | 13% | 14% | 9% | 10% | 26% | 19% | 24% |
| Living with others | 3% | 3% | 2% | 3% | 2% | 3% | 5% | 3% | 4% |
| **Not head of household:** | | | | | | | | | |
| Living with adult children, or grandchildren | 5% | 3% | 7% | 4% | 8% | 4% | 8% | 31% | 18% |
| Living with others | 3% | 3% | 3% | 3% | 3% | 2% | 5% | 5% | 6% |
| Group quarters | 6% | 4% | 7% | 3% | 14% | 6% | 6% | 2% | 3% |

[1]In the 2000 Census, individuals may report more than one race although the vast majority (98%) of the population aged 65 and over reports a single race. Race and Hispanic ethnicity are reported separately in the Census; a person reporting Hispanic ethnicity may also report any race.
[2]A small share of these households (less than one-half of one percent) include children under age 18.

SOURCE: Created by the author from the Public Use Microdata Sample (PUMS) from the 2000 U.S. Census of Population and Housing.

***Table 1.*** *Living arrangements of U.S. population aged 65 and over, by gender, age group, and race/ethnicity, 2000.* CENGAGE LEARNING, GALE.

**Race and Ethnic Differences in Household Structure** In addition to reflecting differences in resources, including financial, social, and health-based resources, comparisons by race and ethnicity reflect preferences for living arrangements that may be culturally or normatively defined. Members of some groups, such as African Americans, enter old age having experienced socially structured inequality that shape the ways in which family resources are conceptualized and drawn upon. Members of other groups, such as Asian Americans and Latinos, frequently have also experienced discrimination and reduced opportunities throughout their life course. In addition, these groups are heavily composed of first- and second-generation immigrants. Immigrants may use their family networks in distinctive ways throughout the life course (Van Hook and Glick, 2007) to facilitate adaptation to a new culture and environment. Moreover, some older immigrants migrate to the United States for the express purpose of helping and participating in the lives of their adult children and grandchildren, goals that foster intergenerational living arrangements.

Statistics reported in Table 1 support the conclusion that family and household structure take different forms in later life for members of different racial and ethnic groups. For example, living alone is experienced by 29% of non-Hispanic White seniors and 30% of non-Hispanic Black seniors, but only 13% of Asians and 19% of Latinos. Living with a spouse only is most common among Whites, both because they are more likely to have a surviving spouse (as compared to Blacks, for instance) and because they are less likely to live in multigenerational family households. Heading a multigenerational household is most common among African Americans (26%) and Latinos (24%), but least common among Whites (10%). Living in someone else's household is most common among Asians (36%). Living in group quarters is not common for any of the groups but is especially unlikely for Asians and Latinos.

Although not shown separately here, one aspect of family and household composition that is important for many seniors is providing care for a grandchild who lives with them. A considerable amount of scholarly literature has addressed the phenomenon of "skipped-generation" households—that is, households that include grandparents and grandchildren, but not the grandchild's parent(s). These types of households most frequently occur when a child's parents are unavailable or unable to care for them because of institutionalization, imprisonment, substance abuse, or death (Burton and Bengtson, 1985). As many as 2 million grandparents care for grandchildren in skipped-generation households (Simmons and Dye, 2003), and many more provide substantial levels of support and care to their grandchildren in three-generation settings. Grandparents most likely to care for a coresident grandchild are under age 65, female, and a member of a racial or ethnic minority group (especially African Americans).

### LIFE COURSE TRANSITIONS AND HOUSEHOLD COMPOSITION

The aging process frequently involves changes in resources, family networks, and other circumstances that may promote a transition in household structure. A decline in economic resources, or the onset of frailty and emergence of new needs for assistance, may trigger a household adjustment. Some homes can be structurally modified to better align with age-related onset of disability—installing ramps so outside stairs can be avoided, for instance, or remodeling a home so all the living space is on a single floor. Homes that cannot be modified structurally, or disabilities that cannot be accommodated through structural accommodation, need not force a residential move if appropriate personal assistance is secured, in some cases. The modification of household structure—by including a familial caregiver in one's own household, for instance—is one way by which living environments may be modified to accommodate changing abilities in later life.

Adjustments in household structure may also occur based on transitions of others in the network—spouses, children, and grandchildren in particular. One of the most common life course transitions having implications for household structure is the loss of a spouse through death. The older individual whose husband or wife dies often experiences an abrupt transition into living alone. If the surviving widow or widower has the economic and health resources to live alone successfully, this living arrangement may persist for the rest of his or her life. Many older individuals, however, are not prepared to live alone upon the loss of a spouse. Some individuals experience substantial financial strain when a spouse dies and may no longer be able to afford to live alone. Disabled widow(er)s may have been reliant on the deceased spouse for assistance with activities of daily living or instrumental activities of daily living, and may need to identify a substitute source of help. If the new financial, emotional, and assistance-related challenges cannot be met within the household as it is configured following the spouse's death, residential adjustment may need to occur.

Many life course transitions having implications for household structure in later life occur not in the life of the older person, but rather in the lives of close members of his or her family network. Established support networks may be fragmented as close others die, move away, or become frail themselves. Most notably, changes in the resources or life circumstances of adult children are relevant in shaping transitions in household composition of older individuals. Observers note that many adult children continue to live at home with their parents for a prolonged period of time, reflecting both the high cost of establishing an independent household as a young adult and delayed patterns of marriage and family formation (Furstenberg, Kennedy, McLoyd, Rumbaut & Settersten, 2004). As a result, some children may still be living at home as adults move into later life. Others may return home following the breakup of a marriage, when experiencing financial difficulties, or as other challenges to independence occur. The "empty nest" commonly associated with middle age, therefore, extends for some individuals well into later life and may have a recurring quality as adult children come and go. These movements of children and grandchildren in and out of the older household may be experienced as a destabilizing influence; for some families, however, such occurrences give older individuals an important productive role, can provide some financial assistance as resources are shared, and can provide opportunities for reciprocal intergenerational exchange of support.

## IMPACTS ON WELL-BEING

Household structure may shape economic well-being in later life either positively or negatively. Through the pooling of resources and the economies of scale facilitated by a shared residence, older persons may experience a more economically secure lifestyle by living with others than they could achieve on their own. Economic benefits may not necessarily occur, however. As noted previously, many intergenerational households are formed because of economic needs for assistance on the part of the younger generation. Older parents who have the resources to support themselves adequately while living alone may experience economic challenges when sharing a home with other family members, if those household additions do not contribute substantially to the household economy. One example in which this situation may be especially challenging is when grandparents take on responsibility for a grandchild in a skipped-generation household. A grandparent who was getting by economically on his or her own may be unable to cover the many financial costs associated with caring for a dependent child.

Emotional well-being may be affected by household structure as well. Some transitions—for example, transitioning to a one-person household or relinquishing one's own home to move in with a grown child—may be experienced as stressful and require a period of adjustment. Loss of a spouse is widely acknowledged to be a stressful event, often requiring significant role adjustment and potentially leading to short- or long-term depression (Carr et al., 2000); the associated household transition corresponding to the death of a spouse may be a contributing factor in this response.

Household composition may also be related to health outcomes in some cases. For example, researchers determined in a prospective study that older women who live alone are less likely to experience functional decline (Sarwari, Fredman, Langenberg, and Magaziner, 1998). The authors speculate that drawing on the social and emotional resources needed to live alone successfully may promote longevity. Other research has suggested that women who live alone may have greater longevity than those who live with someone other than a spouse

(Davis, Moritz, Newhaus, Barclay, & Gee, 1997). Definitive conclusions regarding health implications of household structure are elusive, given the reciprocal causal pathways linking health outcomes and living arrangement decisions.

## FAMILY AND HOUSEHOLD STRUCTURE IN COMING DECADES

Family and household structures among older adults are likely to be shaped in the future by processes similar to those that have been significant in the past. Demographic influences relating to marriage, childbearing, and other close family relationships will continue to determine the availability of family members who may be sources of support and coresidence opportunities for older individuals, and who, in turn, may require assistance and support from the older individual. Financial and health-related resources will continue to shape evaluations of when it is no longer possible to live independently. Preferences will continue to drive the way that older individuals and their families evaluate options for household structure that will be most appropriate at each stage of life. Because the composition of the older population continues to change, however, the resources, family relationships, and preferences of younger cohorts are different from those characterizing the elderly population of the early 21st century. As one elderly cohort is replaced by another, past patterns of aging are frequently inaccurate predictors of behaviors that may be typical in the future. Changed outlines of family and household structure are likely to result from this process of cohort succession.

Compared to the cohorts of those 65-plus, the middle-aged cohorts of the early 21st century will enter later life having experienced later marriage, more marital disruption, fewer children, and greater acceptance of nonmarital sexual relationships, including cohabitation. While fewer may be living with a spouse as a result of these marital patterns, more may share a household with a cohabiting partner if past living arrangement patterns are carried into later life. More of the older population in coming years will have remained childless, and most will have had smaller families than did their parents. As a result, more may live alone, and fewer will share a household with a child. At the beginning of the 21st century, other relatives, such as siblings, shared households only rarely. However, because many members of the baby boom cohort have more siblings than children, the possibility that conventional forms of household composition may adapt to accommodate changing demographic realities cannot be ruled out.

The resources of the cohorts who will be entering later life in the first few decades of the 21st century are also likely to be distinctive. Estimates suggest that baby boomers, on average, are healthier and better prepared financially for retirement than their parents were (Greenblatt, 2007). Better health and lower levels of disability may result in fewer needs for assistance on the part of incoming cohorts of seniors; if so, residential independence will be more likely for many. Moreover, if they reach later life with better financial security, they may be better able than the older cohorts of the early 21st century to realize their household structure goals. Some evidence suggests, however, that baby boomers are less likely to own a home at midlife than were same-age people a generation earlier. Inasmuch as an owned home is the most significant asset held by most older people, this may reflect a gap in economic security among seniors in the future that could have implications for household structure.

Emerging options for receiving assistance and securing independence may reshape household composition in coming years. It is likely that in the future a wider range of in-home services will be available; if these services are provided at acceptable cost and in a convenient way, then even elders with substantial needs for assistance may be able to live independently. Housing options such as assisted-living and continuing-care communities are likely to be increasingly available. For members of the new cohorts of seniors who prefer independent living arrangements and can afford these options, and especially for those with few familial resources on which to draw, these options are likely to be heavily used and will result in more seniors living in "quasi-independent" households.

An additional factor that will contribute to the reshaping of household and family structure among older people in the future is the growing racial and ethnic diversity of the population. The baby boom includes far more Asians and Latinos than earlier cohorts, and almost one in six boomers is an immigrant, mostly from Latin America or Asia. These diverse populations bring unique life course experiences shaping family composition, the accumulation of resources, and the health and disability trajectories that determine needs for assistance. As well, most of these rapidly growing groups are considered to hold "familistic" values that support intergenerational caregiving and coresidence. Household composition among older Americans in coming years could be modified to include more intergenerational families as a result of these growing ethnic populations. However, to the extent that patterns of higher intergenerational coresidence are primarily a reflection of recent immigration to the United States (Van Hook & Glick, 2007) or of socioeconomic status (Burr & Mutchler, 1993a), household structure differences among race and ethnic groups may not persist assuming high levels of assimilation and acculturation.

**SEE ALSO** Volume 3: *Caregiving; Grandparenthood; Intergenerational Transfers; Parent-Child*

*Relationships, Later Life; Sibling Relationships, Later Life; Singlehood; Social Integration/Isolation, Later Life; Social Support, Later Life; Widowhood.*

## BIBLIOGRAPHY


Angel, R. J., Angel, J. L., & Himes, C. L. (1992). Minority group status, health transitions, and community living arrangements among the elderly. *Research on Aging, 14,* 496–521.

Antonucci, T. C. (1990). Social supports and social relationships. In R. H. Binstock & L. K. George (Eds.), *Handbook of aging and the social sciences* (3rd ed., pp. 205–226). San Diego: Academic Press.

Burch, T. K., & Matthews, B. J. (1987). Household formation in developed societies. *Population and Development Review, 13,* 495–511.

Burr, J. A., & Mutchler, J. E. (1992). The living arrangements of unmarried elderly Hispanic females. *Demography, 29,* 93–112.

Burr, J. A., & Mutchler, J. E. (1993a). Ethnic living arrangements: Cultural convergence or cultural manifestation? *Social Forces, 72,* 169–180.

Burr, J. A., & Mutchler, J. E. (1993b). Nativity, acculturation, and economic status: Explanations of Asian American living arrangements in later life. *The Journals of Gerontology, Series B: Psychological Sciences and Social Sciences, 48,* S55–S63.

Burr, J. A., & Mutchler, J. E. (1999). Race and ethnic variation in norms of filial responsibility among older persons. *Journal of Marriage and the Family, 61,* 674–687.

Burton, L. M., and Bengtson, V. L. (1985). Black grandmothers: Issues of timing and continuity of roles. In V. L. Bengtson & J. F. Robertson (Eds.), *Grandparenthood* (pp. 61–77). Beverly Hills, CA: Sage.

Carr, D., House, J. S., Kessler, R. C., Nesse, R. M., Sonnega, J., & Wortman, C. (2000). Marital quality and psychological adjustment to widowhood among older adults: A longitudinal analysis. *The Journals of Gerontology, Series B: Psychological Sciences and Social Sciences, 55,* S197–S207.

Choi, N. G. (2003). Coresidence between unmarried aging parents and their adult children: Who moved in with whom and why? *Research on Aging, 25,* 384–404.

Davis, M. A., Moritz, D. J., Newhaus, J. M., Barclay, J. D., & Gee, L. (1997). Living arrangements, changes in living arrangements, and survival among community dwelling older adults. *American Journal of Public Health, 87,* 371–377.

De Vos, S. (2003). Revisiting the classification of household composition among elderly people. *Journal of Cross-Cultural Gerontology, 18,* 229–245.

Furstenberg, F. F., Jr., Kennedy, S., McLoyd, V. C., Rumbaut, R. G., & Settersten, R. A., Jr. (2004). Growing up is harder to do. *Contexts, 3,* 33-41.

Greenblatt, A. (2007, October 19). Aging baby boomers. *CQ Researcher, 17,* 865–888.

Himes, C. L., Hogan, D. P., & Eggebeen, D. J. (1996). Living arrangements of minority elders. *The Journals of Gerontology, Series B: Psychological Sciences and Social Sciences, 51,* S42–S48.

Holden, K. C., Burkhauser, R. V., & Feaster, D. J. (1988). The timing of falls into poverty after retirement and widowhood. *Demography, 25,* 405–414.

Kobrin, F. E. (1976). The fall of household size and the rise of the primary individual in the United States. *Demography, 13,* 127–138.

Kramarow, E. A. (1995). The elderly who live alone in the United States: Historical perspectives on household change. *Demography, 32,* 335–352.

Lawton, M. P. (1982). Competence, environmental press, and the adaptation of older people. In M. P. Lawton, P. G. Windley, & T. O. Byerts (Eds.), *Aging and the environment: Theoretical approaches* (pp. 33–59). New York: Springer.

Lee, G. R., Peek, C. W., & Coward, R. T. (1998). Race differences in filial responsibility expectations among older parents. *Journal of Marriage and the Family, 60,* 404–412.

Litwak, E., & Longino, C. F., Jr. (1987). Migration patterns among the elderly: A developmental perspective. *The Gerontologist, 27,* 266–272.

Logan, J. R., Bian, F., & Bian, Y. (1998). Tradition and change in the urban Chinese family: The case of living arrangements. *Social Forces, 76,* 851–882.

Matthews, S. H., & Sun, R. (2006). Incidence of four-generation family lineages: Is timing of fertility or mortality a better explanation? *The Journals of Gerontology, Series B: Psychological Sciences and Social Sciences, 61,* S99–S106.

Mutchler, J. E., & Burr, J. A. (2003). Living arrangements among older persons: A multilevel analysis of housing market effects. *Research on Aging, 25,* 531–558.

Ruggles, S. (1987). *Prolonged connections: The rise of the extended family in nineteenth-century England and America.* Madison: University of Wisconsin Press.

Ruggles, S., Sobek, M., Alexander, T., Fitch, C. A., Goeken, R., Hall, P. K., et al. (2004). Integrated public use microdata series: Version 3.0. (Machine-readable database.) Minneapolis: Minnesota Population Center.

Sarwari, A. R., Fredman, L., Langenberg, P., & Magaziner, J. (1998). Prospective study on the relation between living arrangement and change in functional health status of elderly women. *American Journal of Epidemiology, 147,* 370–378.

Shanas, E. (1979). The family as a social support system in old age. *The Gerontologist, 19,* 169–174.

Simmons, T., & Dye, J. L. (2003, October). *Grandparents living with grandchildren: 2000* (Census 2000 Brief No. C2KBR-31). U.S. Bureau of the Census. Retrieved May 29, 2008, from http://www.census.gov/prod/2003pubs/c2kbr-31.pdf

Speare, A., Jr., & Avery, R. (1993). Who helps whom in older parent–child families? *Journal of Gerontology, 48,* S64–S73.

Takagi, E., Silverstein, M., & Crimmins, E. (2007). Intergenerational coresidence of older adults in Japan: Conditions for cultural plasticity. *The Journals of Gerontology, Series B: Psychological Sciences and Social Sciences, 62,* S330-S339.

Van Hook, J., & Glick, J. E. (2007). Immigration and living arrangements: Moving beyond economic need versus acculturation. *Demography, 44,* 225–249.

Waite, L. J., & Hughes, M. E. (1999). At risk on the cusp of old age: Living arrangements and functional status among black, white, and Hispanic adults. *The Journals of Gerontology, Series B: Psychological Sciences and Social Sciences, 54,* S136–S144.

Wilmoth, J. M. (1998). Living arrangement transitions among America's older adults. *The Gerontologist, 38,* 434–444.

Wister, A. V., & Burch, T. K. (1987). Values, perceptions, and choice in living arrangements of the elderly. In E. F. Borgatta & R. J. V. Montgomery (Eds.), *Critical issues in aging policy: Linking research and values* (pp. 180–198). Beverly Hills, CA: Sage.

Wolf, D. A., & Soldo, B. J. (1988). Household composition choices of older unmarried women. *Demography, 25,* 387–403.

World Health Organization. (2002). *Towards a common language for functioning, disability, and health: ICF.* Retrieved May 28, 2008, from http://www.designfor21st.org/documents/who_icf_2002.pdf

Zimmer, Z. (2003). A further discussion on revisiting the classification of household composition among elderly people. *Journal of Cross-Cultural Gerontology, 18,* 247–250.

***Jan E. Mutchler***

# FONER, ANNE

## *1921–*

***Anne Foner.*** PHOTO BY PEGGY FONER. COURTESY OF ANNE FONER.

Anne Foner illustrates in her own life a key principle she and her colleagues have emphasized in the sociological analysis of aging and society: that the process of aging from birth to death is not immutable but changes as society itself undergoes transformation. She was part of the first wave of adult married women in the United States who returned to school and the workforce when they were in their 30s and 40s, helping to establish a new life course pattern for women in the United States.

Foner received her B.A. in 1941 from Queens College, now part of the City University of New York, as a member of the first graduating class. She did not go on to graduate study until 1960, having spent the intervening years in domestic, volunteer, and part-time work activities. She received a Ph.D. in sociology from New York University in 1969 and went on to teach in the sociology department at Rutgers University. She officially retired in 1991 but continued professional activity well into her 80s.

It was at New York University that she first met Matilda White Riley (b. 1911), with whom she later collaborated on what was Foner's first major published work: a multivolume series on aging and society. The first volume, *Aging and Society I: An Inventory of Research Findings*, was more than a catalog of research on aging. It selected from a voluminous literature and condensed and organized social science findings on people in their middle and later years. It began to suggest broad generalizations about human aging. At the same time, it pointed to limitations in the available studies and called attention to commonly accepted beliefs about aging that did not hold up to careful scrutiny. The third volume, *Aging and Society III: A Sociology of Age Stratification*, coauthored with Riley and Marilyn Johnson, explored the implications of research on aging for understanding age as built into social institutions and affecting individual attitudes and behavior.

In subsequent publications she explored age as an element in social structures and social change and highlighted that it—like sex and race—is a basis of social differentiation and inequality. Like other forms of social stratification, she noted that age-based inequalities in power and privilege are found in all societies, but age systems of inequality are unique. Because aging is inevitable, as people grow up and grow older they confront different opportunities or constraints over the life course—and this can affect how they react to disadvantages or advantages experienced at any given time.

Age-based inequalities, Foner observed, are also the basis of age conflicts. The young may perceive themselves as relatively disadvantaged and may challenge the middle-aged and older adults who seek to protect their privileges. Age conflicts can also stem from differences in worldviews and values arising from the social, political, and economic context of the period in which successive cohorts live out their lives. Generally, age conflicts are played out in institutional spheres such as the family, the workplace, and religious associations, but occasionally they spill out across the whole society—typically over moral issues that do not lend themselves to compromise. Societal-wide age conflicts can lead to change in age systems in the society, a major theme in Foner's work.

According to Foner, change in age systems can affect different elements of these systems. For example, there may be changes in the number of socially recognized age divisions such as the discovery in earlier times of adolescence as a distinct life stage, changes in the relative sizes of different age strata such as the increase in the number of older people and decrease in the proportion of children and adolescents in recent times, or changes in age norms governing attitudes and behavior deemed appropriate for people of given ages. These changes often come about as societies and individuals deal with societal events such as wars and depressions and technological and political transformations.

Sometimes the push for change comes about from coordinated actions of many individuals in organized social movements. At other times the push for change comes about from the uncoordinated actions of many people of a given age reacting to new circumstances in the society. A case in point is the move by many individual married adult women into the paid workforce in the 20th century. In changing their own lives, they also changed societal norms of appropriate behavior for adult women.

Beyond these macro-level issues, Foner focused on individual-level processes, including retirement, intergenerational relationships in the family, transitions over the life course, and age-related political attitudes and behavior. In studying aging from birth to death and recognizing age as a key element in social structure and social change, Foner has helped broaden the understanding of age as a social phenomenon and strengthen its connection to the entire sociological tradition.

**SEE ALSO** Volume 3: *Riley, Matilda White; Theories of Aging.*

**BIBLIOGRAPHY**

Foner, A. (1974). Age stratification and age conflict in political life. *American Sociological Review, 39*, 187–196.

Foner, A. (1978). Age stratification and the changing family. In J. Demos & S. S. Boocock (Eds.), *Turning points: Historical and sociological essays on the family. American Journal of Sociology, 84*(Suppl.), 340–386.

Riley, M. W., & Foner, A. (1968). *Aging and society I: An inventory of research findings.* New York: Russell Sage Foundation.

Riley, M. W., Johnson, M., & Foner, A. (1972). *Aging and society III: A sociology of age stratification.* New York: Russell Sage Foundation.

*Nancy Foner*

# FRAILTY AND ROBUSTNESS

Generally speaking, scientists have used the term *frailty* to describe a state of health in which a person is more susceptible to negative health outcomes, such as serious illness or death, than a person termed *robust.* Different scientific disciplines offer competing yet complementary perspectives on frailty, its causes, and its consequences. However, a consequence recognized by all is that such differences across people imply that everyone can expect their own, unique experience of health across their lifetime and particularly in late life. Some people may "age well" and maintain the ability to perform their day-to-day tasks efficiently, leading active and fulfilling lives through advanced ages. Others may be less fortunate, perhaps losing the ability to perform some activities that they would otherwise like or need to do, and less able to endure the daily challenges that those living independently encounter on a regular basis. Examples of such challenges include the physical task of walking up and down stairs or to the corner store, recovery from an illness or fall, or distressing events such as the death of a spouse. Failure to successfully meet these and other related challenges may serve as important markers for elevated risks of subsequent health declines in late life, including serious disease or death.

Robust older adults are more likely than others to successfully meet these challenges and avoid long-term, negative impacts on their health; frail elders are less fortunate and more likely to suffer greater frequency and severity of illness, adverse events, and, potentially, a shorter life span. Several of the studies reviewed here, particularly those in the medical sciences, consider this susceptibility as a relative inability to recover from common stressors, examples of which might include illness, surgery, a fall, negative psychosocial experiences, or traumatic events. A person who is not frail is thought to be relatively robust to the health risks that could accompany such exposures.

Although such notions of frailty and robustness (in related contexts sometimes called *resilience*) could be characterized in other age groups, the discussion in this entry focuses on the concepts of frailty and robustness in late life. However, even among older adults only, the prevalence of frailty might differ widely, depending on the perceptions of elders, their families, and their health care providers. As a result, researchers and health care providers have worked to specify exactly what these terms mean, what they imply for the clinical care of elders, and the clinical and public health opportunities for development of interventions to enhance health in late life. In addition, the concept of frailty has implications for the study of population health: If the most frail die youngest, then one must be careful when interpreting data characterizing the older population because it would naturally reflect the less frail survivors (Vaupel & Yashin, 1985).

The concepts of frailty and robustness can be illustrated using the following two fictitious case histories. Mr. X is a 75-year-old man who volunteers each week teaching children to read, walks his dog with his wife every day, and controls his high blood pressure with exercise, a low-salt diet, and medication. He interacts regularly with a wide circle of friends and neighbors and is considering joining a bridge club at his church. A month ago, Mr. X had surgery to remove a cataract, recovered well, and is now completely back to his prior level of function. In contrast, Mr. Y is a 75-year-old man who used to walk outside regularly, but he now feels uncertain on the sidewalks and largely restricts his movement to inside his house. He says that he rarely has the energy to socialize with friends and, although he still enjoys tending to his garden, he is worried that he might fall and so keeps only a window-box garden. Mr. Y recently had a small stroke following cataract surgery, which has affected his balance and coordination, and both he and Mrs. Y are concerned about his safety and whether he should continue to live with his wife in their home. Mr. X would be regarded as nonfrail or robust, whereas Mr. Y would be regarded as frail.

Researchers from a variety of scientific disciplines have sought to define frailty and understand the reasons that people vary in their ability to avoid the long-term health risks associated with negative physical or emotional experiences (e.g., the minor surgery in the preceding case histories) and recover to their original level of health. The fact that older adults with similar health vary in their ability to withstand such exposures and either maintain function or falter has led researchers and health care providers to seek an explanation for such differences, and this entry reviews several important studies. Some of this work examines large numbers of older adults to try to improve researchers' ability to predict mortality rates across populations or time, primarily through tailoring statistical methods to account for unseen differences in people, such as frailty, that affects their risk of death. Other studies highlighted here focus on the individual and seek to unravel, at the biological level, the mechanisms that define how resilient a person may be to the numerous negative physical and social incidents that accumulate throughout late life.

Among social scientists, demographers have developed a notion of frailty in their quest to understand differences in mortality across populations or population subgroups. For example, James Vaupel, Kenneth Manton, and Eric Stallard (1979) wanted to improve the way in which demographers calculate mortality rates for a population. Building on prior work, they modified typical calculations for mortality to account for potential differences in the risk of death across people in a population. In particular, they assumed that being frail meant that a person's risk of death was relatively higher than another member of the population who is not frail. Defining frailty in this way is consistent with the core notion outlined previously (i.e., that frailty comprises elevated risk of subsequent poor health but is distinctive in that it is generally not focused on understanding the biological sources and detailed individual mechanisms that produce elevated health risks for individuals). However, some subsequent work has moved in this direction; for example, work by Anatoli Yashin and Ivan Iachine (1997) developed a method to use data on twins to study the relative effect of genes and environment on longevity, and a review that includes twin studies (Christensen, Johnson, & Vaupel, 2006) suggested that life span may, to some degree, be affected by genetic factors.

Many researchers in demography and other social science disciplines have expanded on the preceding work and related ideas. Researchers have also adapted the earlier notion of frailty to study important life-course events that are unrelated to health—these include, for example, childbirth, marriage, or employment. This work uses particular kinds of statistical models that estimate the risk of death or each of these other important life-course events and applies the term *unmeasured* (or unobserved) *heterogeneity* to describe the unspecified individual differences in the probability of such outcomes (Wooldridge 2002, p. 703), which is consistent with the theme underlying earlier use of the term *frailty* in demographic literature.

In the medical sciences, research on frailty is led by gerontologists and geriatricians and can be seen as complementing work in the social sciences by focusing on the identification of specific biological mechanisms and a clinical, diagnosable syndrome that could lead to a range of health outcomes, including death and other clinically significant end points. Several conceptualizations of the geriatric syndrome of frailty have been developed but, although the specifics of each vary somewhat, Howard Bergman et al. (2007) found, "general agreement that the core feature of frailty is increased vulnerability to stressors due to impairments in multiple, inter-related systems" (pp. 731–732). Stressors might include, for example, an episode of illness or distressing events such as the death of a spouse. However, because of the differences in which frailty is theorized to operate, a variety of methods have been proposed to measure frailty. In the following we review several distinct theoretical conceptualizations for the geriatric syndrome of frailty that extend from this core conceptualization of "vulnerability to stressors" and impaired function of multiple biological systems and the empirical measurement approaches that have been suggested to accompany each. Each measurement approach has been associated with a variety of negative health outcomes associated with aging.

Linda Fried et al. (2001) theorized that frailty is a clinically observable syndrome that follows a specific, cyclical pattern. Specifically, they suggested that processes of aging and existing disease can induce loss of muscle mass, followed by declines in strength and endurance, then reduced activity and metabolic function, lower energy use, and, finally, nutritional deficiencies. Closing the cycle, nutritional deficiencies are hypothesized to induce further muscle loss and so on (see p. M147 and Figure 1). Researchers have operationalized this conceptualization in studies by defining as frail a study participant who has at least three of five measured characteristics, including weak grip strength, slow walking speed, exhaustion, low energy expenditure, and weight loss (Bandeen-Roche et al., 2006).

Other researchers have adopted this approach but measured a larger variety of characteristics in defining frail (Puts, Lips, & Deeg, 2005). A contrasting view is provided by Kenneth Rockwood and Arnold Mitnitski (2007), who defined the geriatric syndrome of frailty more broadly as being manifest in the total number of deficits (e.g., diseases, clinical diagnostics, disability measures, and so on) that a person has. That is, they suggested that "The more things individuals have wrong with them, the higher the likelihood that they will be frail" (p. 722). This approach is operationalized by calculating a continuous frailty index equal to the proportion of deficits present. A recent comparison of these two conceptualizations of geriatric frailty and their measurement (Rockwood, Andrew, & Mitnitski, 2007) found that the measures are related (using a variety of statistical tests). However, their discussion points out that the different perspective (i.e., specific cyclical pattern vs. global assessment of deficits) and empirical operationalizations (i.e., a discrete count variable from 1 to 5 vs. a continuous index between zero and 1) mean that each approach has strengths and weaknesses for the study of biological mechanisms and clinical translation of frailty.

Frailty is a concept that is potentially important to a variety of events in later life. First, as suggested by the literature reviewed previously, it is a risk factor for a range of significant health outcomes in late life, which in turn play an important role in decisions that govern numerous events in the later life course. For example, frailty is associated with disability, which could affect decisions about work, the decision of a spouse to provide informal support, the decision by an elder to coreside with children or other family and receive informal support from them, the ability of elders to "age in place" or move to new surroundings, and the degree of social engagement that can be maintained. These are major changes that affect older adults, members of their family, and their social networks. In addition, because they can be associated with health, these changes also affect every taxpayer, because public programs such as Medicare and Medicaid spend many taxpayer dollars on health care for older adults. Conversely, the life-course perspective can also bring numerous insights and stimulate advances in the study of frailty (Kuh, 2007).

This entry closes by revisiting Mr. X and Mr. Y and reconsidering their experiences of health change, both in light of the preceding discussion of frailty and robustness and to illustrate the wide range of factors that determine health in late life. Mr. X was identified as nonfrail because he has maintained the capacity to actively engage with his environment; by volunteering, walking, and effectively managing his health conditions, he demonstrates the ability to respond successfully to a multitude of physical and cognitive challenges. He seeks out additional interaction and challenges in the form of his social activities. Finally, in the face of an acute stressor (his surgery), he regained his prior level of function with no lasting adverse effects. Conversely, Mr. Y exemplifies a frail older adult. He has reduced his level of activity because of his perceived inability to navigate safely outside and his lack of energy. In addition, the surgery experience was followed by a stroke, which (although not necessarily causally related) left him with a markedly reduced level of physical function. At present, frailty research offers the physician and family of each man an integrated perspective on their respective experiences and proposes a rationale for why each man achieved, or suffered, his respective outcome. In the future, as research on frailty progresses, perhaps one day a frailty diagnosis may offer physicians, their patients, and their families an opportunity for treatment. Ultimately, the objective of research on frailty and robustness is to design interventions to increase robustness and prevent frailty.

**SEE ALSO** Volume 3: *Aging; Allostatic Load; Centenarians; Disability and Functional Limitation, Later Life; Genetic Influences, Later Life; Mortality; Oldest Old.*

**BIBLIOGRAPHY**


Bandeen-Roche, K., Xue, Q.L., Ferrucci, L., Walston, J., Guralnik, J. M., Chaves, P., et al. (2006). Phenotype of frailty: Characterization in the women's health and aging studies. *Journals of Gerontology: Series A, Biological Sciences & Medical Sciences, 61*(3), 262–266.

Bergman, H., Ferrucci, L., Guralnik, J., Hogan, D. B., Hummel, S., Karunananthan, S., et al. (2007). Frailty: An emerging research and clinical paradigm—Issues and controversies. *Journals of Gerontology: Series A, Biological Sciences & Medical Sciences, 62*(7), 731–737.

Christensen, K., Johnson, T. E., & Vaupel, J. W. (2006). The quest for genetic determinants of human longevity: Challenges and insights. *Nature Reviews Genetics, 7*(6), 436–448.

Fried, L. P., Tangen, C. M., Walston, J., Newman, A. B., Hirsch, C., Gottdiener, J., et al. (2001). Frailty in older adults: Evidence for a phenotype. *Journals of Gerontology: Series A, Biological Sciences & Medical Sciences, 56*(3), M146–M156.

Kuh, D. (2007). A life course approach to healthy aging, frailty, and capability. *Journals of Gerontology: Series A, Biological Sciences & Medical Sciences, 62*(7), 717–721.

Luthar, S. S. (2006). Resilience in development: A synthesis of research across five decades. In D. Cicchetti & D. J. Cohen (Eds.), *Developmental psychopathology* (2nd ed., pp. 739–795). Hoboken, NJ: Wiley.

McEwen, B. S. (2003). Interacting mediators of allostasis and allostatic load: Towards an understanding of resilience in aging. *Metabolism, 52*(Suppl. 10), 10–16.

Puts, M. T., Lips, P., & Deeg, D. J. (2005). Static and dynamic measures of frailty predicted decline in performance-based and self-reported physical functioning. *Journal of Clinical Epidemiology, 58*(11), 1188–1198.

Rockwood, K., Andrew, M., & Mitnitski, A. (2007). A comparison of two approaches to measuring frailty in elderly people. *Journals of Gerontology: Series A, Biological Sciences & Medical Sciences, 62*(7), 738–743.

Rockwood, K., & Mitnitski, A. (2007). Frailty in relation to the accumulation of deficits. *Journals of Gerontology: Series A, Biological Sciences & Medical Sciences, 62*(7), 722–727.

Vaupel, J. W., Manton, K. G., & Stallard, E. (1979). The impact of heterogeneity in individual frailty on the dynamics of mortality. *Demography, 16*(3), 439–454.

Vaupel, J. W., & Yashin, A. I. (1985). Heterogeneity's ruses: Some surprising effects of selection on population dynamics. *American Statistician, 39*(3), 176–185.

Wooldridge, J. M. (2002). *Econometric analysis of cross-section and panel data.* Cambridge, MA: MIT Press.

Yashin, A. I., & Iachine, I. A. (1997). How frailty models can be used for evaluating longevity limits: Taking advantage of an interdisciplinary approach. *Demography, 34*(1), 31–48.;

***Christopher L. Seplaki***
***Sarah L. Szanton***

# FRIENDSHIP, LATER LIFE

Friendships contribute to health and well-being throughout the life course, including later adulthood. Older adults with close friendships have been found to be healthier, happier, and more socially active than those without close friendships (Rawlins, 2004).

## AGE SIMILARITIES AND DIFFERENCES IN FRIENDSHIP

Friendships in later life are similar to friendships in earlier life stages in some ways. For example, later life friendships continue to provide someone to spend time with, talk to, help with practical tasks, and provide emotional support and companionship. Throughout life, then, friends are people with whom individual share mutual trust and respect, interests and values, and affection and support (Blieszner & Roberto, 2004).

Later life friendships also differ in some ways from earlier friendships. Friendships in childhood, limited by children's cognitive abilities, tend to be rather self-serving, focusing primarily on companionship and enjoyment (Blieszner & Roberto, 2004). Maturing cognitive processes in adolescence increase the importance of mutuality and reciprocity in relationships, and friends come to be seen not only as companions, but as intimate confidants (Berndt, 1996). In young adulthood, friendship networks expand, as new lives and social ties are forged away from home. In later adulthood, in contrast, new friendships are less likely to be formed, although some older adults do attempt to form new ties and many are successful, especially following the death of a spouse (Lamme, Dykstra, & Broese van Groenou, 1996).

In general, social networks tend to shrink rather than expand in later life. Yet this generally does not increase older adults' susceptibility to loneliness because the number of close friends changes little over time; declines in social networks, instead, result from reduced contact with peripheral social ties (Carstensen, Fung, & Charles, 2003). Thus, with increasing age, the number of friends in people's social networks tends to decline, but the remaining friendships tend to be deeper and more fulfilling.

## QUALITATIVE ASPECTS OF FRIENDSHIPS IN LATER LIFE

Qualitative aspects of friendships often influence whether a friendship will withstand the test of time. As people age, friendships based primarily on shared interests may diminish as a result of declining health or transportation difficulties. In contrast, close friendships based on a long history of shared experiences and intimate exchanges are more likely to endure. These long-term friendships provide older adults with a sense of continuity in their lives and, as a result, are highly valued. In fact, older adults' close friendships are less likely to end as a result of increasing distance or decreasing contact, whereas these factors often lead to the dissolution of friendships in younger age groups (Nussbaum, 1994).

Evidence that the quality, rather than the quantity, of social ties is particularly important also can be found in studies that have examined the contributions of contact with friends versus family members toward older adults' well-being. For many older adults, life satisfaction appears to be more strongly related to contacts with friends than with family (Lawton, Winter, Kleban, & Ruckdeschel, 1999). Friendships are voluntary in nature, making interactions with friends enjoyable (Rawlins, 2004). Family relationships, in contrast, are more obligatory in nature, and interactions with family members may be enjoyable at times but routinized or perfunctory at other times. In fact, a study of older adults' daily activities and well-being found that their interactions with friends frequently involved stimulating leisure activities, whereas their interactions with family members frequently involved maintenance tasks (e.g., housework) or passive forms of leisure (e.g., watching television; Larson, Mannell, & Zuzanek, 1986). Not surprisingly, interactions with friends are more strongly related to well-being (Pruchno & Rosenbaum, 2003).

However, family members are most often called on when older adults fall ill to provide sustained aid and care that might strain a friendship (Rawlins, 2004). Friends and family members, therefore, can be regarded as making

***Old Friends.*** *For five decades, this group of eight women has gathered once a month to play cards, enjoy good food, and savor lasting friendships. In January 2006, they celebrated their golden anniversary in Salt Lake City at the same place where they played their first hand of canasta in November 1955.* AP IMAGES.

complementary contributions to older adults' health and well-being by serving as sources of companionship and care (Rook & Ituarte, 1999).

## DEMOGRAPHIC CHARACTERISTICS AND INDIVIDUAL DIFFERENCES THAT INFLUENCE FRIENDSHIPS IN LATER LIFE

Demographic and individual differences influence later life friendships. As is true throughout life, women's friendships are characterized by more intimate self-disclosure, whereas men's friendships typically involve shared activities (Beals & Rook, 2006). As a result, women tend to have closer same-sex friendships than men, and this is particularly true for married people. Most married women have close confidants beyond their spouses, but men typically do not (Phillipson, 1997). Social class also continues to play a role in later life friendships, with middle-class people having more friends than working class older adults (Phillipson, 1997), most likely due to their greater financial resources. Personality factors also affect friendship formation and maintenance in later life. Not surprisingly, extroverts and those who are more open to experience have been found to have larger social networks than introverts and those less open to experience, even among the oldest old (80 years and older; Lang, Staudinger, & Carstensen, 1998).

Other factors (e.g., poor health and mobility, financial problems, residential relocation, transportation difficulties) can impede the formation or maintenance of later life friendships. Although these problems can contribute to or exacerbate relationship tensions (August, Rook, & Newsom, 2007), many older adults report great satisfaction with their social relationships despite these obstacles (Carstensen et al., 2003).

## THEORETICAL PERSPECTIVES ON AGE AND FRIENDSHIP INVOLVEMENT

A strikingly robust finding in social gerontology is an age-related reduction in social network involvement. According to Disengagement Theory (Cumming & Henry, 1961), this decline is a natural aspect of aging that allows older adults to turn inward and reflect on their lives as they prepare for the approaching end of life. According to Activity Theory (Maddox, 1963), in contrast, this decline reflects societal rejection of the elderly, driven by ageist attitudes. The key to successful aging according to this theory is to maintain social activity, replacing lost social roles (e.g., worker) with new ones (e.g., volunteer) if necessary. Neither of these theories, however, fully captures the complex relationship between social involvement and well-being in later life. Whereas some older adults strive for extensive social involvement, many are content with a reduced level of social activity.

Socioemotional Selectivity Theory (Carstensen et al., 2003) contends that the age-related decline in social network involvement is due to people's growing awareness as they age that time left to live is limited, creating a preference to spend one's time with the most meaningful, emotionally rewarding interaction partners. Thus, the reduction in network size reflects the shedding of superficial relationships while the closest and most important relationships remain intact.

Another theoretical perspective on friendships, Social Exchange Theory (Thibaut & Kelley, 1959), posits that healthy friendships are those that have an equitable "give and take," and this remains true in later life. Reciprocity, being able to give back an amount of support equivalent to what was received, may be even more important to relationship satisfaction in friendships than in family relationships (Rook, 1987). However, declines that accompany aging, such as diminishing health or resources, may keep older people from seeking support from friends if they feel unable to reciprocate (Rawlins, 2004).

## CURRENT TRENDS AND FUTURE DIRECTIONS

Losses are increasingly common as one ages, and friendship loss is no exception. In one study of adults over age 65, 25% reported the death of a friend in the preceding year (Aldwin, 1990). Another study found that for those older than age 85, the numbers increase to 59% for men and 42% for women (Johnson & Troll, 1992). But despite the high rates of loss, friendships in later life likely will increase in importance in the future because demographic trends suggest that more older adults will be single, childless, and/or living far from relatives. Friendships are a particularly important source of support and companionship for single people and are especially important when family members are not available (Cantor, 1979; Lang et al., 1998). In one study, neighbors and friends of frail elders assisted with instrumental support tasks such as providing transportation and helping with daily tasks (Barker, 2002). Highly personal forms of care for incapacitated elders, such as bathing or feeding, are, however, typically performed by family members or formal caregivers. More research is needed to determine whether friends can comfortably and effectively perform such support tasks over time (Rook, Sorkin, & Zettel, 2002).

More research examining the diverse forms and functions of friendship in later life is also needed. For example, future research should investigate the patterns of friendships throughout life for sexual minorities (i.e., gay, lesbian, bisexual, and transgendered people; Galupo, 2007) as well as for various ethnic minority groups. Researchers also should investigate the role that intergenerational friendships can play in the social networks of older adults. Although same-age friends are most typical throughout the lifespan, having some friends who are younger may be beneficial for older adults given the increased probability of illness or death among friends who are closer in age. Moreover, as greater numbers of older adults become comfortable accessing the Internet, alternative modes of communication (e.g., e-mail, online chat rooms) may enhance later life friendships when relocation or limited mobility hinder in-person interactions. Finally, some intervention studies have shown promise in terms of helping lonely older adults form friendships (e.g., Stevens, Martina, & Westerhof, 2006); researchers should continue to pursue interventions that have the potential to enhance friendships in later life.

SEE ALSO Volume 3: *Social Integration/Isolation, Later Life; Social Support, Later Life; Theories of Aging.*

### BIBLIOGRAPHY

Aldwin, C. M. (1990). The Elders Life Stress Inventory: Egocentric and nonegocentric stress. In M. A. P. Stephens, J. H. Crowther, S. E. Hobfoll, & D. L. Tennenbaum (Eds.), *Stress and coping in later-life families* (pp. 49–69). Washington, DC: Hemisphere.

August, K. J., Rook, K. S., & Newsom, J. T. (2007). The joint effects of life stress and negative social exchanges on emotional distress. *Journal of Gerontology: Social Sciences, 62,* S304–S314.

Barker, J. C. (2002). Neighbors, friends, and other nonkin caregivers of community-living dependent elders. *Journals of Gerontology: Social Sciences, 57B,* S158–S167.

Beals, K., & Rook, K. S. (2006). Gender differences in negative social exchanges: Frequency, reactions, and impact. In V. H. Bedford & B. F. Turner (Eds.), *Men in relationships: A new look from a life course perspective* (pp. 197–217). New York: Springer.

Berndt, T. J. (1996). Friendships in adolescence. In N. Vanzetti & S. Duck (Eds.), *A lifetime of relationships* (pp. 181–212). Pacific Grove, CA: Brooks/Cole.

Blieszner, R., & Roberto, K. A. (2004). Friendships across the life span: Reciprocity in individual and relationship development. In F. R. Lang & K. L. Fingerman (Eds.), *Growing together: Personal relationships across the lifespan* (pp. 159–182). New York: Cambridge University Press.

Cantor, M. H. (1979). Neighbors and friends. *Research on Aging, 1,* 434–463.

Carstensen, L. L., Fung, H. H., & Charles, S. T. (2003). Socioemotional selectivity theory and the regulation of emotion in the second half of life. *Motivation and Emotion, 27,* 103–123.

Cumming, E., & Henry, W. E. (1961). *Growing old: The process of disengagement.* New York: Basic Books.

Galupo, M. P. (2007). Friendship patterns of sexual minority individuals in adulthood. *Journal of Social and Personal Relationships, 24,* 139–151.

Johnson, C. L., & Troll, L. (1992). Family functioning in late late life. *Journals of Gerontology, 47B,* S66–S72.

Lamme, S., Dykstra, P. A., & Broese van Groenou, M. I. (1996). Rebuilding the network: New relationships in widowhood. *Personal Relationships, 3,* 337–349.

Lang, F. R., Staudinger, U. M., & Carstensen, L. L. (1998). Perspectives on socioemotional selectivity in late life: How personality and social context do (and do not) make a difference. *Journals of Gerontology, 53B,* P21–P30.

Larson, R., Mannell, R., & Zuzanek, J. (1986). Daily well-being of older adults with friends and family. *Psychology and Aging, 1,* 117–126.

Lawton, M. P., Winter, L., Kleban, M. H., & Ruckdeschel, K. (1999). Affect and quality of life: Objective and subjective. *Journal of Aging and Health, 11,* 169–198.

Maddox, G. L. (1963). Activity and morale: A longitudinal study of selected elderly subjects. *Social Forces, 42,* 195–204.

Nussbaum, J. F. (1994). Friendship in older adulthood. In M. L. Hummert, J. M. Wiemann, & J. F. Nussbaum (Eds.), *Interpersonal communication in older adulthood: Interdisciplinary theory and research* (pp. 209–225). Thousand Oaks, CA: Sage.

Phillipson, C. (1997). Social relationships in later life: A review of the research literature. *International Journal of Geriatric Psychiatry, 12,* 505–512.

Pruchno, R., & Rosenbaum, J. (2003). Social relationships in adulthood and old age. In R. M. Lerner, M. A. Easterbrooks, & J. Mistry (Eds.), *Handbook of psychology: Developmental psychology* (Vol. 6; pp. 487–509). Hoboken, NJ: John Wiley & Sons.

Rawlins, W. K. (2004). Friendships in later life. In J. F. Nussbaum & J. Coupland (Eds.), *Handbook of communication and aging research* (2nd ed., pp. 273–299). Mahwah, NJ: Lawrence Erlbaum Associates.

Rook, K. S. (1987). Reciprocity of social exchange and social satisfaction among older women. *Journal of Personality and Social Psychology, 52,* 145–154.

Rook, K. S., & Ituarte, P. H. G. (1999). Social control, social support, and companionship in older adults' family relationships and friendships. *Personal Relationships, 6,* 199–211.

Rook, K. S., Sorkin, D. H., & Zettel, L. A. (2002). The vexing problem of loneliness: Current trends and future projections. *Aging Today.*

Stevens, N. L., Martina, C. M. S., & Westerhof, G. J. (2006). Meeting the need to belong: Predicting effects of a friendship enrichment program for older women. *Gerontologist, 46,* 495–502.

Thibaut, J. W., & Kelley, H. H. (1959). *The social psychology of groups.* New York: Wiley.


***Laura Zettel-Watson***
***Karen S. Rook***

## FUNCTIONAL LIMITATIONS

SEE Volume 3: *Disability and Functional Limitation, Later Life.*

# G

## GAMBLING, LATER LIFE

SEE Volume 2: *Gambling.*

## GAYS AND LESBIANS, LATER LIFE

The study of lesbian, gay, bisexual, and transgender (LGBT) older persons has much to contribute to the understanding of aging in minority communities and under stigmatized conditions. As such, it has much to offer an analysis of aging more generally (de Vries and Blando, 2004), fostering a more holistic and inclusive view of the diverse experiences of older persons and the life course.

### PARAMETERS OF THE POPULATION

In some contexts and situations, the term *LGBT* has been expanded to include: Q, for *queer*, and another *Q* for *questioning*; *I* for *intersex*; another *T* for *two-spirit*. As de Vries (2007) has pointed out, these additions are motivated by a variety of social forces including age and cohort, an increased attention to process, advances in theory and the body of knowledge, and an explicit recognition of the role of culture, as respectively revealed below. For instance, *queer* is a term more commonly endorsed by younger rather than older gay men and lesbians, perhaps in the service of empowerment and neutralizing and/or claiming a pejorative label (Adelman, Gurevitch, de Vries & Blando, 2006). *Questioning* reflects a more fluid appreciation of sexual experiences. *Intersex* derives from the reframing and deeper understanding of those born with genitalia that are neither exclusively male nor female. *Two-spirit* is a term rooted in Native American and Canadian first nations cultures characterizing the presence of both a masculine and feminine spirit within the same body.

Among older adults, the majority of research has focused on gay men and, to a somewhat lesser extent, lesbians. Much is missed by this relatively restricted focus. Miller, Andre, Ebin, and Bessonova (2007) remind readers that bisexuals are not identified by the gender of their partner(s); that is, a bisexual woman whose partner is a woman remains a bisexual rather than lesbian; a bisexual woman whose partner is a man remains a bisexual rather than a heterosexual. Such invisibility dramatically adds to the challenges of the bisexual experience. Intersex persons of the later years have also been neglected in research and analyses; similarly, transgendered persons are rightly critical of the largely superficial and often dismissing ways in which their experiences have been incorporated. As is true to varying degrees for those who identify as lesbian, gay, bisexual, or intersex, a great diversity is meant to be contained within the single *T* category. For example, transgender persons include heterosexual, homosexual, and bisexual persons. They include persons who present as male and/or female in varying situations. They include persons who may be postoperative, preoperative (e.g., transitioning), or nonoperative male-to-female (MTF) or female-to-male (FTM) (Cook-Daniels, 2006).

Within the above constraints and considerations, estimates of the prevalence of LGBT persons in general, and older LGBT persons in particular, vary widely: The legacy of stigma (and hence the reticence to identify as LGBT) and the malleability of sexuality and identity render the validity of such estimates questionable. Cahill, South, and Spade (2000) suggest that the current LGBT population in the United States over the age of 65 may be as large as 3 million people—perhaps expanding to as many as 4 million by the year 2030. These estimates are likely under-representative of this population—a statement of increasing significance with the aging of subsequent cohorts who are known for their questioning of authority and pushing of boundaries.

## STUDYING THE LGBT POPULATION

Perspectives on sexuality and the elderly have been framed by myths declaring older persons are sexually unattractive, neither desirous nor capable of sexual expression. In contrast, the very notion of an LGBT gerontology raises the issue of sexuality directly (de Vries and Blando, 2004). The literature on LGBT aging and older persons has developed in both size and complexity since the early 1980s. Early publications were largely anecdotal and/or clinical, descriptive accounts often depicting older homosexual men and women as socially isolated, depressed, sexually frustrated, unhappy, among a host of other such characteristics (Berger, 1996). As the field grew, the publications became increasingly empirical in nature, although typically still based on small samples of openly disclosing women and men recruited from public and urban centers who were willing to participate in research. Still, the extent to which there can be a representative sample of men and women manifesting characteristics (or representing a variety of terms and constructs) that are stigmatized and in flux remains problematic.

The literature on gay and lesbian older adults frequently comments on the marked cohort effects in communities of LGBT persons and how their lives have been shaped by historical period. The LGBT cohort now in later life are individuals whose expressions of love were "diagnosed" as a psychiatric disorder in the *Diagnostic and Statistical Manual* (the psychiatric diagnosis "bible") until it was changed in 1973. Even in the early 21st century, their committed relationships are the subject of intense debate with threats of constitutional exclusion in the United States. These are individuals who, through the course of their lives, have been labeled as anti-family and immoral by religious groups, and as a security risk or morale threat by military leaders (Kochman, 1997). These are women and men who endured and have seen AIDS decimate their social networks and destroy their communities.

A common and significant reference point defining this cohort is the Stonewall Rebellion or Riot. On the evening of June 27, 1969, a contingent from the New York City Police Department (NYPD) raided the Stonewall Inn, a gay dance bar in Greenwich Village, New York City. These raids were part of a routine pattern of harassment endured by the occupants of this and most other gay and lesbian bars. On this evening, however, the police raid escalated into several nights of street fights and clashes between outraged gay men and a NYPD that was not accustomed to homosexuals fighting back. The events of these evenings were widely reported in and sensationalized by the media; it became known as the Stonewall Rebellion and what many identify as the turning point in the struggle for gay rights in the United States.

## THEMES AND PROMINENT ISSUES IN THE STUDY OF LGBT AGING

The developing research into the lives of older LGBT persons suggests a population both challenged and bolstered by its demography and experiences. de Vries (2006) reported that LGBT older adults are significantly less likely than heterosexual women and men of comparable age to be in partnered relationships and to have children, two of the groups most frequently called upon in the provision of care for an elder in need. For example, a large community survey, including more than 700 participants at least 50 years of age, found that about three-quarters of gay men and about one-half of the lesbians reported their relationship status as single and only one-quarter of gay men and one-half of lesbians had children (Adelman et al., 2006), the majority of whom were born into the previous heterosexual marriages of these individuals. A national survey of LGBT baby boomers found that many reported concerns about where and how their future care might be addressed (MetLife Survey, 2007). At the same time, the literature reveals significant discussions of "chosen families," the strong bonds forged by the inner circle of friends and those on whom an individual might call in a time of need, often in response to alienation from biological kin (Weston, 1991).

Interestingly, income levels appear similar across LGBT and heterosexual aging populations, despite persistent myths of relative LGBT affluence (Badget, 1998). LGBT adults tend to be more highly educated (also supported by census-level data, see Black, Gates, Sanders, and Taylor, 2000), providing a point of contrast to the frequently noted association between income and education. Relatedly, several authors have proposed that LGBT older adults have fashioned a sense of hardiness/competence out of a lifetime of surviving as a sexual minority in an often-hostile heterosexual environment—a strategy of engaging their environment that may bode well for success in the challenges of later life. For example, Friend

***Gay Pride.*** *A man is helped by a transsexual as he marches in the streets of Paris carrying a placard reading "Gay pensioners don't want to retire" during the gay and lesbian parade themed "March of proud gays, lesbians, and transsexuals."* PIERRE ANDRIEU/AFP/GETTY IMAGES.

(1991) has offered a theory of successful aging as applied to older lesbians and gay men, primarily based on such "crisis competence" (Kimmel, 1979) and confronting rigid gender roles and ageist assumptions. Friend suggests that being freed (or excluded) from the relative bounds of traditional gender role definitions have afforded gay men and lesbians the opportunity to engage in behaviors throughout their lives that heterosexuals rarely confront, perhaps until the death of a spouse. A popular example of this may be found in Harvey Fierstein's *Torch Song Trilogy* (1983) in which Arnold, the main character, a gay man in his early middle years, says that he can cook a meal, sew a shirt, hammer a nail—whatever it takes to get through—he can do it himself as has been required of him throughout his life.

There is some suggestion that later life may bring with it some unique physical and mental health issues for this population. Although not unique to LGBT communities, several authors have commented that ageism is particularly strong within gay male communities (e.g., Bergling, 2004). Palmore (1990) proposes that persons subjected to prejudice and discrimination tend to adopt the dominant group's negative image and to behave in ways that conform to that negative image with associated potentially deleterious consequences on mental health and well-being. Herdt and Kertzner (2006) reported evidence of higher levels of depression and psychological distress among midlife and older lesbians and gay men, which they attribute to the accumulation of a lifetime of stigma. Adelman and colleagues (2006), in their large community-based empirical study, found higher rates of chronic disease and disability, not the least of which was HIV/AIDS, among older gay men. Rather than a difference in the constellation of disorders, Barker (2004) notes that older lesbian and bisexual women may suffer an exacerbation of prevalence, earlier onset, and manifestation of common disorders. Health issues for transgender persons are similarly made more complicated by the interaction of the aging body with the introduction of hormones for those who have transitioned from one biological gender to another.

## FUTURE DIRECTIONS

In the early 21st century, the first cohort of openly lesbian, gay, bisexual and transgender persons is approaching the later years, creating their own way with little historical reference to serve as a guide. Dozens of efforts are afoot by LGBT communities to provide and care for the aging pioneers of a population. There are parallels in these efforts to the dramatic and inspiring ways in which the LGBT communities (comprising many of these same, now older adults) rose to the challenge of caring for those dying of AIDS in the early years of the pandemic—a time when families, medical facilities, and governments shamefully retreated from their responsibilities.

As de Vries (2007) has noted, it is the interaction of these historical, demographic, and bio-psycho-social factors that make more complex the issues faced by older LGBT persons and the delivery of services that meet their needs. The discriminatory experiences LGBT adults have experienced in North American health care settings (e.g., Brotman, Ryan, and Cormier, 2003) have led to an unfortunate and understandable reluctance to seek out health care services and to evaluate the delivery of such services negatively. When gay and lesbian support and services are available, still rare and certainly an urban phenomenon, they tend to be more frequently used in comparison with the use of generic, heteronormative senior services (see Quam and Whtiford, 1992) and are evaluated more positively. Moreover, the norms and presumptions of heterosexuality and the "family-centrism" that pervade societal institutions often serve to exclude (or at least not invite) the LGBT elder. For example, non-registered domestic partners have been denied entry to the hospital room in which their loved one was dying. Sadly, older LGBT persons who have struggled to come out and live openly in a frequently hostile environment "often find themselves having to [go] back into hiding when they begin to require health care services" (Brotman, et al, 2003, p. 193). The families that LGBT persons create, either in lieu of or in addition to their biological families, are often not recognized and honored by those outside of these intimate circles (de Vries and Hoctel, 2007).

In some ways, the study of LGBT aging and concerns about the services needed and delivered do not differ from that of other groups bounded by culture or relationship status or some other social construct. Studying the particular context within which members of such groups age, their experiences and the source and type of care they receive and need is a necessary prerequisite to the development and offering of services appropriately tailored and to a full and complete appreciation of the life course.

**SEE ALSO** Volume 3: *Sexual Activity, Later Life; Social Support, Later Life.*

**BIBLIOGRAPHY**

Adelman, M., Gurevitch, J., de Vries, B., & Blando, J. (2006). Openhouse: community building and research in the LGBT aging population. In D. Kimmel, T. Rose, & S. David (Eds). *Lesbian, gay, bisexual, and transgender aging: Research and clinical perspectives* (pp. 247–264). New York: Columbia University Press.

Badget, M. V. L. (1998). Income inflation: The myth of affluence among gay, lesbian, and bisexual Americans. Washington, DC: The Policy Institute of the National Gay and Lesbian Task Force and the Institute for Gay and Lesbian Strategic Studies. Retrieved January 10, 2008, from http://thetaskforce.org

Barker, J. C. (2004). Lesbian aging: An agenda for social research. In G. Herdt & B. de Vries (Eds.), *Gay and lesbian aging: Research and future directions* (pp. 29–72). New York: Springer.

Berger, R. M. (1996). *Gay and gray: The older homosexual man.* (2nd ed.). New York: Harrington Park Press.

Bergling, T. (2004). *Reeling in the years: gay men's perspectives on age and ageism.* Binghamton, NY: Harrington Park Press.

Black, D., Gates, G., Sanders, S., & Taylor, L. (2000). Demographics of the gay and lesbian population in the United States: Evidence from available systematic data sources. *Demography, 37,* 139–154.

Brotman, S., Ryan, B., & Cormier, R. (2003). The health and social service needs of gay and lesbian elders and their families in Canada. *The Gerontologist, 43,* 192–202.

Cahill, S., South, K., & Spade, J. (2000). *Outing age: public policy issues affecting gay, lesbian, bisexual, and transgender elders.* Washington, DC: Policy Institute, National Gay and Lesbian Task Force.

Cook-Daniels, L. (2006). Trans aging. In D. Kimmel, T. Rose, & S. David (Eds)., *Lesbian, gay, bisexual, and transgender aging: research and clinical perspectives.* New York: Columbia University Press.

de Vries, B. (2006). Home at the end of the rainbow: Supportive housing for LGBT elders. *Generations, 29*(4), 65–70.

de Vries, B. (2007). LGBT couples in later life: A study in diversity. *Generations, 31*(3), 18–23.

de Vries, B., & Blando, J. A. (2004). The study of gay and lesbian lives: Lessons for social gerontology. In G. Herdt & B. de Vries (Eds.), *Gay and lesbian aging: research and future directions* (pp. 3–28). New York: Springer.

de Vries, B., & Hoctel, P. (2007). The family friends of older gay men and lesbians. In N. Teunis & G. Herdt (Eds.), *Sexual inequalities and social justice* (pp. 213–232). Berkeley: University of California Press.

Friend, R. A. (1991). Older lesbian and gay people: A theory of successful aging. *Journal of Homosexuality, 20,* 99–118.

Herdt, G., & Kertzner, R. (2006). I do, but I can't: The impact of marriage denial on the mental health and sexual citizenship of lesbians and gay men in the United States. *Sexuality Research and Social Policy, 3*(1), 33–49.

Kimmel, D. C. (1979). Life history interviews of aging gay men. *International Journal of Aging and Human Development, 10* (3), 239–248.

Kochman, A. (1997). Gay and lesbian elderly: Historical overview and implications for social work practice. In J. K. Quam (Ed.), *Social services for senior gay men and lesbians* (pp. 1–25). New York: Haworth Press.

MetLife Mature Market Institute. (2006). *Out and aging: The MetLife study of lesbian and gay baby boomers.* New York: MetLife Mature Market Institute.

Miller, M., Andre, A., Ebin, J., & Bessonova, L. (2007). *Bisexual health: an introduction and model practices for HIV/STI prevention programming.* Washington, DC: National Gay and Lesbian Task Force Policy Institute.

Palmore, E. B. (1990). *Ageism: negative and positive.* New York: Springer.

Quam, J. K., & Whitford, G. S. (1992). Adaptation and age-related expectations of older gay and lesbian adults. *The Gerontologist, 32,* 367–374.

Weston, K. (1991). *Families we choose: lesbians, gays, kinship.* New York: Columbia University Press.

**Brian de Vries**

# GENERATION

SEE *Cohort.*

# GENETIC INFLUENCES, LATER LIFE

Genetic influences are the influences that can be attributed to heredity (family likeness). Heredity is the passing of characteristics (traits) from parents to offspring. Genetic influences in later life are attributed to traits related to aging such as life span and longevity, age at menopause, age at onset of specific diseases in late life (Alzheimer's disease, heart disease, and so on), physical health and cognitive functioning in later life, rate of aging (estimated through tests for biological age), rate-of-change traits, and biomarkers of aging (Finch, 2007).

Genetic influences are also related to effects of the fundamental chemical units of heredity called genes. A gene is a segment of deoxyribonucleic acid (DNA) carrying coded hereditary information. The number of gerontogenes (genes involved in the aging process) remains to be established, but there are no doubts of their existence. For example, in humans one of the forms of a gene coding apolipoprotein E (APOE2) is associated with exceptional longevity (more prevalent among centenarians) and decreased susceptibility to Alzheimer's disease (Finch, 2007; Martin, Bergman, & Barzilai, 2007).

Genetic influences operate through the mechanism of gene action—the way in which genes produce their effect on an organism by influencing biochemical processes during development and aging. Many of the genes within a given cell are inactive much or even all the time (repressed). Different genes can be switched on or off depending on cell specialization (differentiation)—a phenomenon called differential gene expression. Gene expression may change over time within a given cell during development and aging. Changes in differential gene expression are vitally important for cell differentiation during early child development, but they may persist further in later life and become the driving force of the aging process.

Although genes determine the features an organism may develop (genotype), the features that actually develop (phenotype) depend upon the complex interaction between genes and their environment, called gene–environment interaction. Gene–environment interactions are important because genes produce their effects in an indirect way (through proteins), and, therefore, the ultimate outcome of gene action may be different in different circumstances (Ryff & Singer, 2005). Although genes do not change over the life course (creating the impression of causal links), many traits in later life demonstrate very high environmental plasticity; that is, they can be modified in response to an environmental change (Ryff & Singer, 2005). Older adults on average experience poorer health compared to younger adults, so genetic contribution to health, functional status, and cognition are among the most thoroughly studied traits in later life.

## STUDY METHODS AND DESIGNS

Most studies of genetic influences use quantitative genetics (or ACE) models to separate the sources of phenotypic or observed variability into an *additive* genetic component (A), a *common* or shared environment component (C), and a nonshared *environment* element (E). Shared environmental influences are shared nongenetic factors that are transmitted from parents to offspring or are shared by the members of the same family (such as lifestyle or diet). Nonshared environmental influences are nongenetic factors that are different among family members. The genetic contribution to phenotypic variability of trait is measured using heritability estimates. Heritability estimates represent the proportion of phenotypic variation of trait that can be explained by genetic effects. A heritability value of 1.0 (or 100%) means that the trait is fully genetically determined, whereas a value of 0 means that the trait is fully environmentally determined.

Quantitative genetics uses a number of designs in the study of genetic influences, including family design, twin design, and the adoption method. Family design compares the incidence of disease (or other trait) among biological and nonbiological relatives of an affected individual (called proband). The famous statistician Karl Pearson (1857–1936) and Alexander Graham Bell (1847–1922), the inventor of the telephone, were among the first researchers to try to estimate the contribution of genetic factors into the human life span at the beginning of the 20th century (see review in Gavrilov, Gavrilova, Olshansky, & Carnes, 2002). The first comprehensive studies of familial resemblance and longevity go back to the 1930s when the American biostatistician Raymond Pearl published his seminal book, *The Ancestry of the Long-Lived*, which showed that close relatives of nonagenarians (persons in their 90s) live longer than relatives of shorter lived persons (Pearl & Pearl, 1934). This initial finding was later replicated by numerous studies of persons with exceptional longevity, including early 21st century studies of centenarians (Martin et al., 2007).

The twin design is based on the comparison of identical (monozygotic) twins and fraternal (dizygotic) twins. Monozygotic twins are assumed to be genetically identical to each other because they developed from the same fertilized egg. Dizygotic twins are formed from two different fertilized eggs and have only half of their genes in common. If a trait is genetically influenced, then monozygotic twins should show a closer resemblance to each other in regard to that trait compared to dizygotic twins. Franz J. Kallmann was the first researcher to apply twin design to the study of late-life traits and to conduct a survey of old twin pairs (Kallmann & Sander, 1948).

The adoption method is a quasi-experimental design based on cases in which children are adopted away from their biological parents early in life. This gives researchers the opportunity to separate the effects of nature and nurture. The Swedish Adoption/Twin Study of Aging is probably the largest repository of data on adopted twins (Pedersen & Svedberg, 2000).

In addition to the methods of quantitative genetics, molecular genetic methods are used to identify specific genes responsible for genetic influence. In molecular genetic studies of human aging traits, the gene association studies remain the most common research approach (De Benedictis et al., 2001). In these studies the effect of candidate genes on longevity is analyzed by comparing gene frequencies between affected individuals (cases) and unaffected control individuals. The comparison of candidate gene frequencies among centenarians and younger controls is a typical example of such studies. Another molecular genetics approach—the genome-wide linkage scan of genes—is a relatively new direction of research. Linkage analysis is a mapping of genetic loci using observations of related individuals (pairs of affected and nonaffected siblings, for example). This direction of research has a potential for obtaining interesting results, although the success of genome-wide scans of complex human diseases requires large sample sizes and considerable effort and expense.

In addition to common phenotypic traits (such as the presence or absence of disease), the genetic epidemiology of aging incorporates age in the specification of traits under study. The traits that are specific for later life are survival traits and rate-of-change traits (Hadley et al., 2000). A survival trait is defined in terms of the specific age interval over which an individual is at risk for a specific outcome. For example, early-onset and late-onset variants of Alzheimer's disease are associated with different genes and modes of action. Rate-of-change traits are defined as changes in physiological, cognitive, or behavioral traits over a period of time. The study of genetic influences on rate-of-change traits is a rapidly developing area of research in the early 21st century (Pedersen & Svedberg, 2000).

## MAJOR RESEARCH FINDINGS

Longevity is one of the most widely studied broad survival traits. It was shown that siblings and parents of persons with exceptional longevity have significantly lower mortality compared to population-based controls and that the offspring of long-lived parents live longer than the offspring of short-lived parents (Gavrilov, Gavrilova, Olshansky, & Carnes, 2002; Martin et al., 2007). Genetic influences on longevity found in family studies were confirmed in twin and adoption studies (see Gavrilov et al., 2002). Although a strong familial clustering of longevity is now a well-established fact, heritability estimates for life span using standard methods of quantitative genetics are moderate—20% to 30% (Cournil & Kirkwood, 2001).

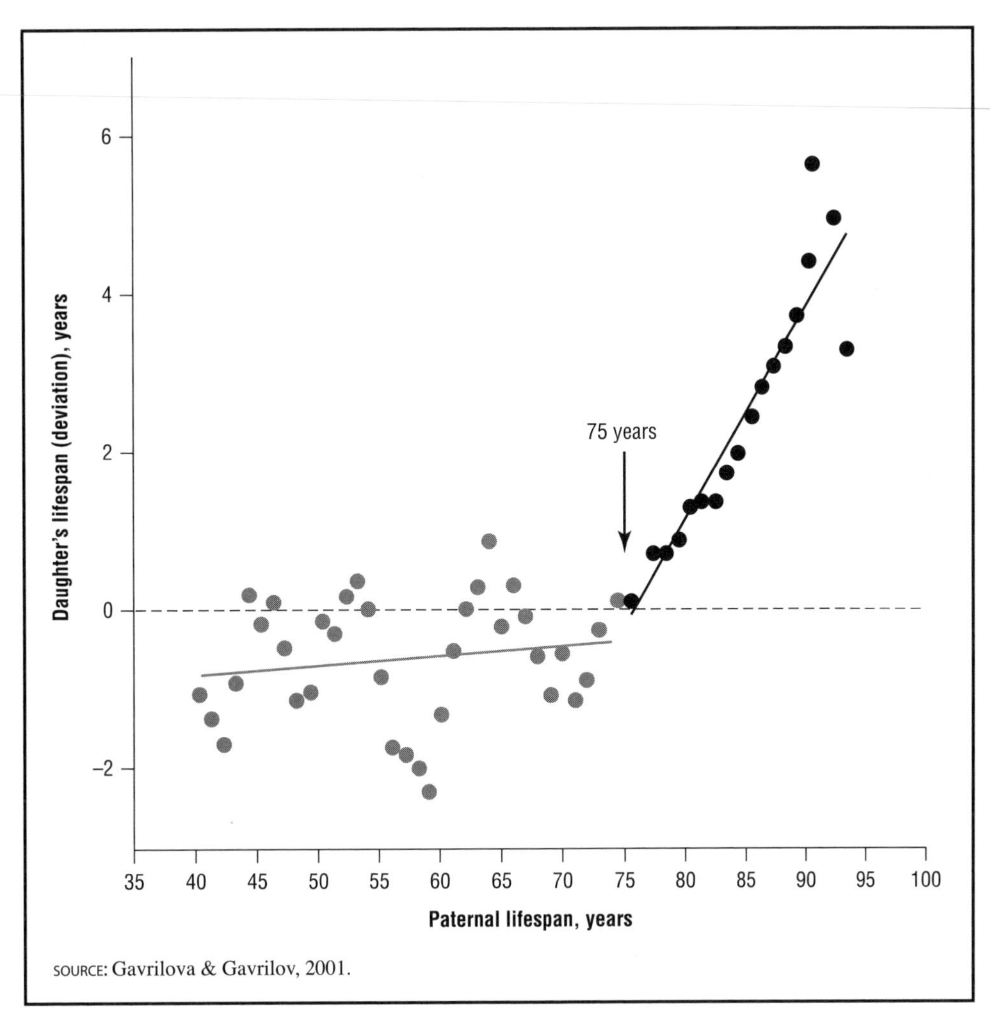


***Figure 1.*** *Daughter's life span (deviation from the cohort mean) as a function of paternal life span. Based on the data for 5,779 daughters from European aristocratic families born between 1800 and 1880 who survived to age 30. Data are smoothed by a 5–year moving average.* CENGAGE LEARNING, GALE.

Heritability estimation by standard methods of quantitative genetics is based on the assumption of linear dependence between offspring and parental traits. A study of more than 10,000 adult men and women from the European aristocracy, however, demonstrated that familial resemblance in life span between parents and children is essentially nonlinear (see Figure 1): very small when parents live shorter lives (30 to 70 years) and very strong in the case of longer lived parents (80+ years), suggesting an unusual nonlinear pattern of life-span inheritance (Gavrilov et al., 2002). These findings may explain the existing longevity paradox: Although the heritability estimates for life span were reported to be rather low (Cournil & Kirkwood, 2001), it is well known that longevity runs in families (Martin et al., 2007). A 2006 study of Danish and Finnish twin cohorts confirmed that genetic influences on human life span are minimal before age 60 but increase thereafter (Hjelmborg et al., 2006).

A review of gene–longevity association studies revealed that different studies often produced inconsistent and even contradictory results (De Benedictis et al., 2001). Most studies of gene–longevity association are based on case-control studies of centenarians, in which the proportion of a certain genotype among long-lived individuals is compared to the same proportion in a presumably shorter lived control group (usually persons of middle age). If the proportion of a particular genotype is higher among long-lived individuals compared to the control group, then it is assumed that this genotype may be associated with longevity. The association of a genotype with longevity in case-control studies is usually measured using odds ratio, which is a measure comparing whether the probability of longevity is the same between two groups. An odds ratio higher than unity means that carriers of a particular genotype have a higher chance of living to 100 compared to non-carriers; alternatively, an odds ratio less than unity means that carriers of a particular genotype have a smaller chance of living to 100 compared to non-carriers.

The APOE gene is the only one that demonstrated consistency in different case-control gene–longevity studies (Finch, 2007). Apolipoprotein E (APOE) is a protein involved in cholesterol transport that binds to LDL receptors and is crucial to blood cholesterol levels (Finch, 2007). The APOE4 gene variant (allele) was found to be associated with heart disease, Alzheimer's disease, and longevity. APOE3 is the most prevalent allele in human populations, whereas APOE4 may vary and is higher than 15% in northern Europe and among aboriginal populations of New Guinea and Australia (Finch, 2007).

A combined analysis of eight APOE findings showed a net odds ratio for extreme longevity of 0.51 for the E3/E4 genotype compared to the common E3/E3 genotype, implying that the E3/E4 genotype reduces by roughly 50% the chances of survival to extreme ages compared to E3/E3 (Melzer, Hurst, & Frayling, 2007). The prevalence of APOE4 decreases with age because of differential survival—the mortality of E4 carriers is 10% to 14% higher and the mortality of E2 carriers 4% to 12% lower compared to E3/E3 and E4/E2 genotypes. It was estimated that individuals with the E4/E4 genotype may have a life expectancy at age 65 that is 5 years shorter than that of individuals with the E2/E2 and E2/E3 genotypes (Ewbank, 2004). Linkage studies of longevity genes are less common compared to association studies. One genome-wide linkage study of U.S. centenarians found a suggestive locus at chromosome 4, although this finding was not replicated in other populations (Melzer et al., 2007).

Parental age is another genetically linked factor affecting longevity. Children conceived by fathers at older ages have more inborn mutations (Vogel & Motulsky, 1997) and may be at higher risk of Alzheimer's disease and prostate cancer in later life. Daughters conceived by fathers age 45 and older live shorter lives (on average), whereas sons seems to be unaffected, suggesting the possible role of mutations on the paternal X chromosome (inherited by daughters only) in the aging process (Gavrilov et al., 2002).

Most chronic diseases in later life are complex multifactorial disorders. Multifactorial disorders are influenced by multiple genes, often coupled with the effects of environmental factors. Many diseases common to old age, such as late-onset Alzheimer's disease, heart disease, and diabetes, are considered to fall into this category. Most genes associated with multifactorial disorders have low penetrance, meaning that genotype carriers' likelihood of developing the disease is low. Thus, the individuals with disease-related genes do not necessarily succumb to the disease (Ryff & Singer, 2005). With a favorable lifestyle and environment, there is an opportunity for an individual with genetic risk factors to delay and even avoid the disease. For example, in the 1960s and 1970s the population of North Karelia in Finland had very high levels of heart disease and a significant proportion of people carrying mutations predisposing them to familial hypercholesterolemia (high blood cholesterol). However, an intensive community-based intervention program directed at lifestyle improvement significantly percent reduced (by 60% to 70%) heart disease and cancer rates over the span of 25 years (Ryff & Singer, 2005). Thus, the genetic risks of diseases in later life can be substantially reduced by proper behavioral, social, and economic measures.

Alzheimer's disease is the most common cause of severe memory loss at older ages. For late-life forms of dementia, the APOE4 allele was found to be strongly associated with both late-onset Alzheimer's disease and accelerated cognitive decline after age 65 (Finch, 2007). The highest cognitive decline was observed in APOE4 carriers with diabetes, carotid atherosclerosis, and peripheral vascular disease. APOE4 carriers with mild cognitive impairment were two to five times more likely to develop Alzheimer's disease compared to carriers of the most common APOE3 genotype. Another APOE allele, the APOE2, was found to be protective against Alzheimer's disease (Finch, 2007).

Many biomarkers of physiological or functional status including handgrip strength, walk speed, systolic blood pressure, pulmonary function, fasting glucose level, and bone degeneration demonstrate a high heritability at older ages (Melzer et al., 2007). Integral estimates of biological age have also been shown to have a strong genetic component, with heritability estimates ranging from 27% to 57%. Age at natural menopause was found to be highly heritable: Data from the two generations of the Framingham Heart Study showed that the crude and multivariable-adjusted heritability estimates for age at natural menopause were 0.49 and 0.52 (Murabito, Yang, Fox, Wilson, & Cupples, 2005). Sex hormone levels play an important role in health and survival at older ages. Studies of male twins ages 59 to 70 found that plasma testosterone levels have substantial genetic variation, whereas estrogen concentrations were largely influenced by environmental factors.

Cognitive functioning also shows a significant genetic component. Most studies of cognitive abilities in later life were conducted using studies of older twins, which showed that the overall cognitive functioning in older age is highly heritable with estimates of heritability equal to 76% in Danish twins 70 and older and 62% in Swedish twins 80 and older (Melzer et al., 2007).

Researchers have also started to collect information on genetic influences at different ages as well as on rate-of-change traits (Pedersen & Svedberg, 2000). Studies show that phenotypic variability has a tendency to increase with age for the majority of traits because of nonshared environmental effects. Genetic contribution to variability in cognitive abilities shows stability until ages 65 to 70 and declines thereafter. A similar pattern was found for self-rated health. Rate-of-change traits usually demonstrate a lower heritability compared to the absolute levels of studied traits. This was found to be the case for such traits as cognitive performance, body mass index, and lipid and lipoprotein levels. Thus, the rate-of-change traits apparently are not significantly affected by genetic factors.

Gene–environment interactions represent one of the most important and promising areas for the studies of the life course. Gene–environment interactions refer to differential genetic sensitivity to specific environmental factors. Genetic factors often act as effect modifiers (or moderators) when effects of socioeconomic or behavioral factors are analyzed. For example, there is no increase in risk for Alzheimer's disease among persons with head injury if they do not carry the APOE4 gene. For carriers of APOE4, however, head injury results in a tenfold increase in the risk of Alzheimer's disease. Similarly, APOE4 was found to be a risk factor for ischemic heart disease, but this applied mainly to smokers (Ryff & Singer, 2005).

It should be noted that heritability estimates for late-life traits may vary significantly across populations and that populations living in less favorable environments generally demonstrate smaller effects of genetic factors on variability of late-life traits. For example, the heritability of forced respiratory volume in Russian twins was found to be much smaller compared to Swedish twins most likely because of differences in environmental influences between Russian and Swedish samples (Whitfield, Brandon, & Wiggins, 2002).

## RESEARCH CHALLENGES AND FUTURE DIRECTIONS

Studies of genetic influences in later life face many methodological challenges. The main problem is that many individuals do not survive to late ages, and this survival is affected by both environmental and genetic factors. Twin studies often suffer from the limitations of cross-sectional design when it is impossible to distinguish selection effects (genetically determined differential survival) from true aging changes (Pedersen & Svedberg, 2000). Studies on exceptional longevity often suffer from the lack of data on living relatives, including parents (Hadley et al., 2000). Inconsistency in the findings of many gene–longevity association studies may be due to the lack of proper control groups in these case-control studies, because cases (centenarians) and controls (young adults) belong to different birth cohorts with different past histories. Thus, a comparison of centenarians and young adults is susceptible to artifacts resulting from differences in genetic makeup between different age cohorts unrelated to differential survival. The collection of longitudinal data (data from the same individuals over time) for twins and adoptees will alleviate the problems posed by cross-sectional designs and help to discriminate between selection processes and true aging changes. The collection of biomarkers (including genetic markers) that is underway in many population surveys and longitudinal studies in the early 21st century will fill the gap in knowledge about the association between specific genetic markers and later life traits. The most promising areas of research—gene–environment interactions in later life and early life genetic influences on late-life traits—are at the beginning of their development and will shape future life-course research on genetic influences in later life (Pedersen & Svedberg, 2000; Ryff & Singer, 2005).

## POLICY ISSUES

The rapid development of molecular genetics and the prospect of individual genome scans raise serious ethical concerns about the proper use of individual genetic information. Should individuals be informed about genetic risks for chronic diseases in later life if this information may result in unnecessary stress? Older persons having genes predisposing them to the risk of certain diseases (such as the APO4 gene) may be unfairly treated by insurance companies. These problems require both the protecting sensitive genetic information and educating the public that having genes predisposing a person to late-onset diseases is not a destiny and that individuals with unfavorable genotypes may never develop the specific disease (Ryff & Singer, 2005). At the same time, knowledge about genetic markers predisposing to late-life diseases may lead to the development of intervention measures specific to individual genetic makeups. Such a personalized approach may eventually become a fixture in medical care.

**SEE ALSO** Volume 3: *Aging; Dementias; Frailty and Robustness; Life Expectancy.*

## BIBLIOGRAPHY

Cournil, A., & Kirkwood, T. B. L. (2001). If you would live long, choose your parents well. *Trends in Genetics, 17*, 233–235.

De Benedictis, G., Tan, Q., Jeune, B., Christensen, K., Ukraintseva, S. V., Bonafè, M., et al. (2001). Recent advances in human gene–longevity association studies. *Mechanisms of Ageing and Development, 122*, 909–920.

Ewbank, D. (2004). From Alzheimer's disease to a demography of chronic disease: The development of demographic synthesis for fitting multistate models. In L. J. Waite (Ed.), *Aging, health, and public policy: Demographic and economic perspectives* (supplement to *Population and Development Review, 30*, pp. 63–85). New York: Population Council.

Finch, C. E. (2007). *The biology of human longevity: Inflammation, nutrition, and aging in the evolution of lifespans.* Amsterdam: Academic Press.

Gavrilov, L. A., Gavrilova, N. S., Olshansky, S. J., & Carnes, B. A. (2002). Genealogical data and the biodemography of human longevity. *Social Biology, 49*, 160–173.

Gavrilova, N. S., & Gavrilov, L. A. (2001). When does human longevity start? Demarcation of the boundaries for human longevity. *Journal of Anti-Aging Medicine, 4*, 115–124.

Hadley, E. C., Rossi, W. K., Albert, S., Bailey-Wilson, J., Baron, J., Cawthon, R., et al. (2000). Genetic epidemiologic studies on age-specified traits. *American Journal of Epidemiology, 152*, 1003–1008.

Hjelmborg, J. v. B., Iachine, I., Skytthe, A., Vaupel, J. W., Mcgue, M., Koskenvuo, M., et al. (2006). Genetic influence on human lifespan and longevity. *Human Genetics, 119*, 312–321.

Kallmann, F. J., & Sander, G. (1948). Twin studies on aging and longevity. *Journal of Heredity, 39*, 349–357.

Martin, G. M., Bergman, A., & Barzilai, N. (2007). Genetic determinants of human health span and life span: Progress and new opportunities. *PLoS Genetics, 3*, 1121–1130.

Melzer, D., Hurst, A. J., & Frayling, T. (2007). Genetic variation and human aging: Progress and prospects. *The Journals of Gerontology, Series A: Biological Sciences and Medical Sciences, 62*, 301–307.

Murabito, J. M., Yang, Q., Fox, C., Wilson, P. W. F., & Cupples, L. A. (2005). Heritability of age at natural menopause in the Framingham Heart Study. *The Journal of Clinical Endocrinology and Metabolism, 90*, 3427–3430.

Pearl, R., & Pearl, R. D. (1934). *The ancestry of the long-lived.* Baltimore: Johns Hopkins Press.

Pedersen, N. L., & Svedberg, P. (2000). Behavioral genetics, health, and aging. *Journal of Adult Development, 7*, 65–71.

Ryff, C. D., & Singer, B. H. (2005). Social environments and the genetics of aging: Advancing knowledge of protective health mechanisms. *The Journals of Gerontology, Series B: Psychological Sciences and Social Sciences, 60*(1), 12–23.

Vogel, F., & Motulsky, A. G. (1997). *Human genetics: Problems and approaches.* (3rd ed.). Berlin: Springer.

Whitfield, K. E., Brandon, D. T., & Wiggins, S. A. (2002). Sociocultural influences in genetic designs of aging: Unexplored perspectives. *Experimental Aging Research, 28*, 391–405.

***Natalia S. Gavrilova***
***Leonid A. Gavrilov***

# GLOBAL AGING

Global aging broadly refers to the process by which the populations of the world's nations are growing increasingly older; indicators of population aging include the proportion of a nation's population that is age 65 or older, as well as trend data showing that the average and median ages of a nation's population have increased over time. Population aging processes throughout the world will have critically important social and economic consequences, including a potential shortage of working-age individuals, heightened demand for costly health care services, adequate housing accommodations and pensions for older adults, and a growing number of older adults relying on their children and grandchildren for social and economic support.

The rapid increase in population aging across the globe signals one of the most important demographic changes in recent history. In the latter half of the 20th century, the world's developed nations completed the demographic transition (Phillipson, 1998). The demographic transition refers to a societal-level shift from high mortality rates and high fertility rates (thus, short life spans and large families) to low mortality rates and low fertility rates (thus longer life expectancies, and smaller families). Countries that proceed through this transition ultimately have relatively high proportions of older persons and low proportions of younger persons (Powell, 2005). This transformation has taken many years to unfold, and is influenced by multiple factors. For example, in Europe and North America, the process of population aging is driven by factors including basic public health measures that steadily reduced the risk of contagious disease and modern medicine that has prolonged lives. In developing nations, by contrast, the demographic transition is still underway. These countries vary widely in how far along they are in the demographic transition; although most developing nations have much younger populations than developed nations, their numbers of older adults are increasing rapidly.

Researchers use a variety of methodological tools to document trends in population aging, and to predict the societal consequences of these demographic changes. Data on population aging processes come from multiple sources. Vital statistics registries, maintained by local governments, track all births and deaths as well as changes in an individual's legal status such as marriage, divorce, and migration (registration of one's place of residence) (Phillipson, 1998). In developed countries with good registration systems (such as the United States and much of Europe), registry statistics are the best data source for enumerating the number of births and deaths in populations (Bengtson and Lowenstein, 2004).

Researchers also use data obtained from population censuses. Censuses are usually conducted by national governments and attempt to enumerate every person in a country (Gavrilov & Gavrilova, 1991). Censuses also gather basic social and demographic information about a nation's population. However, in contrast to vital statistics data that are typically collected continuously and summarized on an annual basis, censuses occur at longer intervals, typically every 10 years. For example, the decennial U. S. Census takes place only once every ten years (Phillipson, 1998). However, the Census Bureau also collects information annually through the American Community Survey. In nations where the vital registration system is incomplete, censuses may be used as an alternative source of information about fertility and mortality. For example, the Chinese census gathers information on births and deaths that occurred in the 18 months immediately preceding the start of the data collection period (Cook & Powell, 2007).

Drawing on these two types of data sources, researchers use a diverse range of measures to study global aging patterns. Demographers typically rely on statistics such as national birth rates (the number of live births for every 100,000 persons in a population), life expectancy projections (average expected length of life at birth), and dependency ratios (the proportion of the population who is of non-working age relative to those who are of working age) to compare and contrast the aging processes of diverse societies.

One important indicator of population aging is the percentage of persons age 65 and older in a population. In the United States, persons ages 65 and older accounted for 13% of the national population in 2000, yet this figure is expected to increase to 20% by 2030 (Estes, 2001). While the proportions of older people in a population are typically highest in developed countries, very steep growth of elderly populations is projected in developing nations (Cook & Powell, 2007). For example, between 2006 and 2030, the number of older people in less developed countries is projected to increase by 140%, compared to an increase of 51% in more developed countries (Krug, 2002).

Population aging not only reflects the proportion of a population that is age 65 and older; demographers also are interested in heterogeneity within the older population. Demographers often count and contrast the "old" (65+) with the "oldest old" (85 and older). The oldest old population is growing at an even more rapid pace than the overall older adult population. Around the world, the 85 and older population is projected to increase 151% between 2005 and 2030, compared to a 104% increase for the overall population age 65 and over, and a 21% increase for the population under age 65 (Bengtson & Lowenstein, 2004). This rapid growth partly reflects the fact that very small numbers of persons were ages 85 and older in prior decades; thus the small number is growing at a proportionally large pace.

The most striking increase will occur in Japan: By 2030 nearly 24% of all older (age 65 and older) Japanese are expected to be at least 85 years old (Kim & Lee, 2007). As will be discussed below, the rise in the oldest old population has important consequences for family relations. For example, the number of four-generation families (that is, families with living children, parents, grandparents and great-grandparents) may become more common as the oldest generation enjoys increasingly long life.

When the proportion of older persons in a population increases, the proportion of younger persons necessarily decreases. This ratio of older persons to younger persons is an important indicator calculated by demographers, as it is often viewed as a potential indication of a society's economic vitality. Demographers often calculate *dependency ratios*, which refer to the number of "dependents" (that is, persons under age 15 and over age 64), relative to those of working age (15 to 64). Interestingly, absolute dependency ratios have changed little over time, but the composition of the dependent population has shifted drastically.

Throughout most of human history, dependent populations had large numbers of young persons (due to high birth rates) and small numbers of older persons, yet in the early 21st century older persons account for a large and growing share of the dependent population. This shift has sweeping implications for policy and culture. For example, a society with a large youthful population would need to invest its national resources in education or job training programs to prepare the young people for the work force. A society with a large older population, by contrast, would need to invest its resources in health care and public pension programs.

## THE SIZE AND GROWTH OF THE WORLD'S OLDER POPULATION

In nearly every nation there is concern about population aging and its consequences for individuals, families, economies, and the state. On one hand, global aging is a triumph of modern times—a desirable consequence of improved public health, sanitation, and social and economic development. On the other hand, long life spans and population that is old often create fiscal strains for societies and families. Although a large proportion of older adults are physically, emotionally, and financially well off, many live with physical disability, cognitive impairment, and financial strain. This disparity creates challenges for governments and families worldwide. These challenges are expected to be most acute for the governments of developing nations because they are experiencing the most rapid growth in the older population.

Population aging can be put into perspective by reviewing a number of statistics that reveal the magnitude of changes that have occurred over the past century. The

United Nations (UN) estimates that the global population of those over 60 years will double, from 542 million in 1995 to around 1.2 billion people by the year 2025 (Krug, 2002, p. 125). Between 2003 and 2004 alone, the world's older adult population grew by 10.3 million persons. Projections suggest that the annual net gain will continue to exceed 10 million over the next decade.

In 1990 only 26 nations worldwide had 2 million or more older persons. By 2000, 31 countries had reached the 2 million older person mark (Cook & Powell, 2007). By 2030 more than 60 countries will have at least 2 million people age 65 or older, according to UN projections. The world is likely to have one billion older people by 2030 (Krug, 2002).

Not only is the total size of the older adult population growing worldwide, but so is the proportion. By 2045, for the first time in history, the global population of persons ages 60 years and over will likely surpass the number of children under age 15 (Powell, 2005). In every region of the world, the rate of population increase for the 65-and-over age group is higher than for the under-14 age group and the 15–64 age group (Bengston & Lowenstein, 2004). As noted earlier, this transformation of the world's dependent population reflects reduced fertility and increased life expectancy. Total fertility rates are expected to decline from 2.82 children per woman worldwide in 1995–2000 to 2.15 children in 2045–2050. Life expectancy worldwide is expected to increase by 11 years, from 65 in 1995–2000 to 76 in 2045–2050—although increases will be more moderate in nations suffering from high rates of HIV/AIDS mortality (Phillipson, 1998).

When absolute numbers are considered, the majority of the world's older adult population lives in developing countries. Even in the world's poorest countries—many of which are plagued by epidemics, AIDS, natural disasters, starvation, and warfare—life expectancy is increasing and the number of older people is growing. By 2015 an estimated two-thirds of the world's elderly population (or roughly 597 million older people) will reside in developing countries (Bengtson & Lowenstein, 2004). In 2005, 1 in 12 people in developing countries were over 60. By 2015, 1 in 10 persons in developing countries will be over 60, and by 2050, 1 in 5 people in developing countries will be over 60.

Throughout most of the globe, older persons are more likely than younger persons to be female. In 2006 there were 82 men for every 100 women over age 60 worldwide (Powell, 2005). In developing countries, the gap is less wide: There are 85 men for every 100 women over 60. However, as age increases, the sex ratio grows even more imbalanced. For persons over age 80, there are only 73 men for every 100 women (Bengston & Lowenstein, 2004). This pattern reflects the fact that men die younger than women, and has important implications for the daily lives of older adults and their families.

## THE CAUSES AND CONSEQUENCES OF GLOBAL AGING

Scholars are not only interested in documenting the pace and level of population aging. They are also concerned with documenting the causes and consequences of such important patterns. As noted earlier, population aging is caused by the relative increase in the older population relative to the younger population. The rise in the number of older persons largely reflects the fact that life expectancy is increasing. Increases in life expectancy are a consequence of changes in how individuals die in the early 21st century. Infant mortality rates have dropped considerably over the past three centuries, and infectious diseases that kill infants, children, and persons of working age have largely been eradicated (or can be treated). Thus, more people are surviving through the difficult early-life years and are living through later life. In later life, the leading causes of disease are conditions that are chronic, meaning older persons can live with diseases such as heart disease or cancer for relatively long time periods. However, these years of survivorship are often marked by physical discomfort, difficult treatment regimens, and expensive health care costs.

These processes have important implications for families, as well as individuals. As people live longer and have fewer children, family structures are transformed, leaving older people with fewer options for care. This erosion of family support has increased demand for federally funded social insurance systems. As social insurance expenditures escalate, countries are carefully evaluating the sustainability of these systems.

Population aging also will have dramatic effects on social entitlement programs, labor supply, trade, and savings around the globe, and may require new fiscal approaches to accommodate a changing world. For example, shrinking ratios of workers to pensioners and people spending a larger portion of their lives in retirement increasingly challenge existing health and pension systems (Bengtson & Lowenstein, 2004; Krug, 2002; Estes, 2001). The expansion of social programs targeted toward the elderly may have the unintended consequence of increasing stigma and perpetuating negative stereotypes of older adults. Younger working adults may perceive that they are funding public programs for the large and growing number of older adults, and may grow to resent their elders (Estes, Biggs, & Phillipson, 2003).

Although many of the challenges of aging are addressed at the national level (as will be elaborated below), population aging can no longer be viewed as a national problem but as one that affects transnational agencies and communities. Local approaches to addressing the challenges of global aging had some meaning in a world where states were in control of their own destinies, and when *citizenship* and *national boundaries* were clear-cut and readily defined concepts. However, through processes of globalization, nations are increasingly interdependent and the aging of one society may have important implications (and require policy shifts) from other nations. For example, an aged population in one nation (such as Germany) may create the need for the importing of labor from other distant countries, such as Turkey. This is just one example of how globalization shapes nations' individual responses to population aging. To illustrate the diverse ways that global aging is unfolding in three non-U.S. contexts, this entry next briefly highlight key trends across the world: Europe, Asia, and Africa.

**Europe** The population structure of western European countries has changed dramatically since the turn of the 20th century. In 1901 just over 6% of the population was age 65+; this figure increased to 18% by 2001 (Powell, 2005). During the same time period, the population of persons under age 16 fell from 35% to 20%. As a result of these changes, dependency rates shifted—with important consequences for the European labor force. For example, in 1950 there were 12 people aged 15 to 64 to support each one of retirement age. It will be only 4-to-1 by 2050 (Powell, 2005). Some economists fear this will lead to bankrupt pensions, lower living standards, and a labor shortage. Nations including France, Germany, Greece, Italy, Russia, and the Ukraine have already seen an absolute decline in the size of their workforces throughout the 20th century. In the United Kingdom, for example, the percentage of people of working age is projected to drop from 64% in 1994 to 58% in 2031 (Powell, 2005).

These population trends have important implications for the European political climate. For example, Germany has the largest total population in Europe and the third oldest population in the world. As such, the German government faces challenging questions about funding public pensions and health care. Aging issues have started to figure prominently in political discussions prior to 2009 elections, as political parties vie for the elderly vote. The Angela Merkel administration (beginning 2007) has been criticized for increasing pensions while opponents talk about a "war of generations" requiring young people to pay for taxation for elder care.

Germany is not alone in its concerns. As the number of workers per pensioner decreases throughout Europe, there will be pressure on pension provision. This is evident in 2008, in such areas as pensions and long-term care, the retreat of the state made evident in the erosion of State Earnings Related Pay, forcing people to devise their own strategies for economic survival in old age (Phillipson, 1998). In the British context that also impinges on global societies in general: Private pensions are slowly being introduced in order to prevent the burden of an aging population. These are ways in which the state continues to rely on apocalyptic projections, the "demographic time bomb," about aging populations in order to justify cuts in public expenditure (Powell, 2005). Despite these worries, there is also widespread understanding of the unique contributions older persons make to society; older people take much of the responsibility for our social and civic life and for the care of children, the sick and the very old in the community.

**Asia** Asia has the largest population of any continent in the world. As such, they provide a fascinating case for studying population aging. China, in particular, has been identified as having four unique characteristics of population aging (Du & Tu, 2000): unprecedented speed; the rapid growth of the aging population before the completion of modernization; fluctuations in the nation's dependency ratio; and a powerful influence of government population policy. Unlike most other nations in the world, the growth of China's elderly population is partly a consequence of the nation's very restrictive population policy. The nation's "one child" policy punished families who gave birth to more than one child, thus contributing to the relatively small youthful population and relatively large older population. Taken together, these factors mean serious concerns for Chinese policy makers.

Kim and Lee (2007) have argued that the rapidly growing elderly population in China and most of Asia has serious economic implications. However, the magnitude of these implications depends on the (in)ability of individual economies to resolve the demographic burden through changes such as increased pension reform, immigration policy, and extension of retirement age. Like European and North American countries, Asia will ultimately have to tackle issues related to pension reform and the provision of long-term health care services (Cook & Powell, 2007).

Japan has already begun to tackle such issues. In 2007, 17% of the Japanese population was over age 65, and this proportion will near 30% by 2022. From 2005 to 2012, Japan's workforce is projected to shrink by around 1% each year—a pace that will accelerate after that. Economists fear that, besides straining Japan's underfunded pension system (Cook & Powell, 2007), the decline of workers and young families will make it harder for Japan to generate new wealth.

The future challenge of providing for the older adult population is especially urgent in the world's two biggest nations—India and China (Kim & Lee, 2007). Only 11% of Indians have pensions, and they tend to be civil servants and the affluent. With a young population and relatively large families, many of the older adult population still count on their children for support. Relying on family support will be even more difficult in China as the population continues to age. By 2030 in China, there will be only two working-age people to support every retiree. Yet only 20% of workers have government- or company-funded pensions or medical coverage (Cook & Powell, 2007). At the same time, older adults will have fewer children upon whom to rely for economic and practical support, a consequence of the one-child policy described above.

**Africa** Economic security, health and disability, and living conditions in later life are policy concerns throughout the world, but the nature of the problem differs considerably from continent to continent and between and within countries—especially within Africa. In Africa older people make up a relatively small fraction of the total population, and traditionally their main source of support has been the household and family, supplemented in many cases by other informal mechanisms, such as kinship networks and mutual aid societies. In 2005 Nigeria was among the 30 countries in the world with the largest populations age 60 and over. Nigeria had the largest older population in sub-Saharan Africa, with more than 6 million people age 60 and over; South Africa had just over 3.4 million. Congo and South Africa are projected to have nearly 5 million older people in 2030. Burkina Faso, Cameroon, Cote d'Ivoire, Madagascar, Mozambique, Niger, Senegal, and Uganda are all projected to have their older populations grow to over one million people by 2030 (International HIV/AIDS Alliance & HelpAge International, 2004).

Very little careful empirical research has been undertaken on long-term trends on the welfare of older people in Africa, yet there are several reasons to believe that traditional caring and social support mechanisms are under intense strain (OECD, 2007). African economies, among the poorest in the world, are still heavily dependent on subsistence agriculture, and average income per capita is lower than it was at the end of the 1960s. Consequently, the region contains a growing share of the world's poor. In addition, reductions in fertility and child mortality have meant that, despite the huge impact of the HIV/AIDS epidemic across much of the region, both the absolute size and the proportion of the population age 60 and over have grown and will continue to grow over the next 30 years (Estes, Biggs, & Phillipson, 2003).

In Africa older people have traditionally been viewed in a positive light, as repositories of information and wisdom. And while African families are generally still intact, social and economic changes taking place can weaken traditional social values and networks that provide care and support in later life. Africa has long carried a high burden of disease, including from malaria and tuberculosis; currently it is home to more than 60% of all people living with HIV—some 25.8 million in 2005. The vast majority of those affected are still in their prime wage-earning years, at an age when, normally, they would be expected to be the main wage earners and principal sources of financial and material support for older people and children in their families. Many older people have had to deal with the loss of their own support while absorbing the additional responsibilities of caring for their orphaned grandchildren. Increasingly, then, it appears that African societies are being asked to cope with population aging with neither a comprehensive formal social security system nor a well-functioning traditional care system in place (International HIV/AIDS Alliance & HelpAge International, 2004).

The key issue that must be addressed by public policy and public health researchers in future decades is that a majority of the world's population of older people (61%, or 355 million) live in poorer African countries. This proportion will increase to nearly 70% by 2025. For many countries, however, population aging has been accompanied by reductions in per capita income and declining living standards. Epstein (2001) notes that between 1950 and the late 1970s, life expectancy increased by at least 10% in every developing country in the world, or on average by about 15 years. However, at the beginning of the 21st century, life expectancy remains below 50 in more than ten developing countries, and since 1970 has actually fallen, or has barely risen, in a number of African countries (Phillipson, 1998).

## THE FUTURE OF GLOBAL AGING

Global aging represents a triumph of medical, social, and economic advances, yet it also presents tremendous challenges for many regions of the world. Population aging strains social insurance and pension systems, and challenges existing models of social support traditionally provided by kin (Bengston & Lowenstein, 2004). It affects economic growth, trade, migration, disease patterns and prevalence, and fundamental assumptions about growing older. Global aging will have dramatic effects on local, regional, and global economies. Phillipson (1998) has argued that the personal consequences of aging are shaped by the rise of globalization; globalization exerts unequal and highly stratified effects on the lives of older people (Phillipson, 1998; Estes, 2001).

In the developed world, the high costs of public programs targeting older persons make such programs a frequent target for budget cuts. In less developed countries, older people (particularly women) are strongly affected by the privatization of health care, and the burden of debt repayments to the World Bank and the International Monetary Fund (IMF) (Estes, 2001). Globalization also has an indirect effect on the lives of older persons, as high levels of cross-national migration disrupt the lives of older adults, especially when their children move across the globe. Older adults also are particularly susceptible to the consequences of global political change and warfare; older persons account for an estimated one-third the world's refugees—a figure estimated at more than 53 million older people worldwide in 2000 (Estes, 2001).

Changes in the age structures of societies also have consequences for the size and characteristics of a nation's labor force (Phillipson, 1998). Nations with older populations often do not have an adequate number of workers and thus may loosen their immigration policies, as a way to increase the size of their youthful populations and thus their supply of workers. Changes in immigration policy, in turn, may alter the very nature of a nation's work force. The foreign-born workforce is growing in most Organization for Economic Cooperation and Development (OECD) countries (OECD, 2007). For example, in the United States, large and growing numbers of medical workers are migrants. Currently, 22% of physicians and 12% of nurses in the United States are foreign-born, with the majority coming from African countries, the Caribbean, and Southeast Asia (OECD, 2007).

Many countries in Asia have developed alternative strategies for addressing the worker shortage that is an inevitable result of population aging. For example, in South Korea and Japan, which have historically strong cultural aversions to immigration, employers such as small factories, construction companies, and health clinics are relying on "temporary" workers from the Philippines, Bangladesh, and Vietnam (OECD, 2007). The implications of global aging also extend to more youthful workers. For example, in China, state industries are struggling over how to lay off unneeded middle-age workers when there is no social safety net to support them (Cook & Powell, 2007).

What really has pushed aging to the top of the global policy agenda, though, is the recognition of increasing fiscal gaps in the United States, Europe, Japan, and elsewhere—and these financial threats could worsen as large proportions of the population reach retirement age. While the Social Security system in the United States is projected to remain solvent until at least 2042, the forecast is more pessimistic for social security programs in Europe. In the United States most citizens have private savings plans to help supplement the often meager payments provided by social security. In much of Europe, however, as many as 90% of all workers rely almost entirely on public pensions to support them in old age (Walker & Naegele, 2000). For example, Austria guarantees 93% of one's earnings after retirement, and Spain offers 94.7%. As noted earlier, declining numbers of youthful workers in industrialized nations means a declining number of persons are paying into the system that ultimately supports retirees (Krug, 2002).

These two key consequences of global aging—the potential labor shortage, and high costs of pensions to growing numbers of older adults—have forced policy makers in several nations to question practices such as mandatory retirement and policies regarding retirement timing (Powell, 2005). Similarly, policy makers are debating at the age at which individuals should be fully entitled to social welfare benefits such as health insurance provision (e.g., Medicare in the United States). Nation states with extensive social programs targeted to the older population—principally health care and income support programs—find the costs of these programs escalating as the number of eligible recipients grows and the duration of eligibility lengthens due to increases in lifespan (Bengtson & Lowenstein, 2003).

Governments may be limited in how much they can reshape social insurance programs by raising the age of eligibility, increasing contribution rates, and reducing benefit levels. Consequently, shortfalls may need to be financed using general revenues. Projections of government expenditures in the United States and other OECD countries show increases in the share of gross domestic product devoted to social entitlements for older populations. In some cases, this share more than doubles as a result of population aging (OECD, 2007).

The financial costs associated with providing for the massive older population are also borne by individuals and families. Family members often must pay for long-term care or medical care of their aged relatives, in those cases where the elderly person does not have sufficient personal resources to cover such expenses. Population aging also has indirect effects on the economic well-being of individuals in a society. For example, the largest component of household wealth in many countries is housing value. Home values could drop sharply if large numbers of older homeowners try to sell houses to smaller numbers of younger buyers.

Global aging affects not only the value of homes, but the living arrangements maintained over the life course. For example, older people's living arrangements reflect their need for family, community, or institutional support. Living arrangements also indicate sociocultural preferences—for example, some choose to live in nuclear households whereas others prefer extended families (Estes, Biggs, & Phillipson, 2003). The number, and often the percentage, of older people living alone are rising in most countries. In some European countries, more than 40% of women age 65 and older live alone (Walker & Naegele, 2000). Even in societies with strong traditions of older parents living with children, such as in Japan, traditional living arrangements are becoming less common. In the past, living alone in older age often was equated with social isolation or family abandonment (Phillipson, 1998). However, research in many cultural settings illustrates that older people, even those living alone, prefer to be in their own homes and local communities (Gilleard & Higgs, 2001). This preference is reinforced by greater longevity, expanded social benefits, increased home ownership, elder-friendly housing, and an emphasis in many nations on community care (Estes, Biggs, & Phillipson, 2003). As people live longer and have fewer children, family structures are also transformed (Bengtson & Lowenstein, 2004). This has important implications in terms of providing care to older people. Most older people in the early 21st century have children, and many have grandchildren and siblings. However, in countries with very low birth rates, future generations will have few if any siblings. As a result of this global trend toward having fewer children, people will have less familial care and support as they age (Bengtson & Lowenstein, 2004).

Although doomsayers believe that an aging population is necessarily plagued with physical and economic problems, Longino (1994) offers a more optimistic perspective. He argues that technological developments, such as better preventive medicine and the development of assistive devices, as well as individual- and family-level adaptation (such as the development of elderly-friendly housing arrangements) mean that the future of aging nations may be quite positive.

The aging of the global population is without parallel in human history (Bengston & Lowenstein, 2004). If the level and pace of population aging persist in the coming decades, by 2050 the number of older people globally will exceed the number of young for the first time in history. As a result, nations throughout the world are confronted with profound challenges pertaining to illness and health care, older adults' access to housing and economic resources, including pension provision. The implications of global aging affect not just older adults, but individuals at all stages of the life course, families, household, governments, and even cross-national relations.

**SEE ALSO** Volume 3: *Demographic Transition Theories; Epidemiologic Transition; Life Expectancy; Mortality; Population Aging.*

**BIBLIOGRAPHY**

Bengtson, V. L., & Lowenstein, A. (Eds.). (2004) *Global aging and challenges to families.* New York: De Gruyter.

Cook, I. G., & Powell, J. L. (2007). *New perspectives on China and aging.* New York: Nova Science.

Du, P., & Tu, P. (2000). Population ageing and old age security. In X. Peng and Z. Guo (Eds.), *The changing population of China*, Oxford, U.K.: Blackwell, pp. 77–90.

Epstein, H. (2001). Time of indifference. *New York Review of Books,* April 12, pp. 33–38.

Estes, C. L. (2001). *Social policy and aging.* Thousand Oaks, CA: Sage.

Estes, C., Biggs, S., & Phillipson, C. (2003). *Social theory, social policy, and ageing.* Buckinghamshire, U.K.: Open University Press.

Federal Reserve Bank of Kansas City. (2004). *Global demographic change: Economic impacts and policy challenges.* Symposium proceedings, August 26–28, 2004. Accessed July 8, 2008, from http://www.kc.frb.org

Gavrilov, L. A., & Gavrilova, N. S. (1991). *The biology of life span: A quantitative approach.* New York: Harwood Academic.

Giddens, A. (1993) *Sociology.* Cambridge, U.K.: Polity Press.

Gilleard, C., & Higgs, P. (2001). *Cultures of ageing.* London: Prentice Hall.

Gruber, J., & Wise, D. A. (Eds.). (1999). *Social security and retirement around the world.* Chicago: University of Chicago Press.

Gruber. J., & Wise, D. A. (Eds.) (2004). *Social security programs and retirement around the world: Micro estimation.* Chicago: University of Chicago Press.

HelpAge International. (2000). *The mark of a noble society.* London: Author.

Hermalin, A. I. (Ed.). (2002). *The well-being of the elderly in Asia: A four-country comparative study.* Ann Arbor: University of Michigan Press.

Holtzman, R. A. (1997). *A World Bank perspective on pension reform.* Paper prepared for the joint ILO-OECD Workshop on the Development and Reform of Pension Schemes, Paris, December.

International HIV/AIDS Alliance and HelpAge International. (2004). *Building blocks: Africa-wide briefing notes: Supporting older careers.* Accessed July 8, 2008, from http://www.helpage.org

International Monetary Fund. (2006) The economics of demographics. *Finance and development 43*, no. 3. Accessed July 8, 2008, from http://www.imf.org

Kim, S., & Lee, J-W. (2007). Demographic changes, saving and current account in East Asia. *Asian Economic Papers, 6*, no. 2.

Kinsella, K., & Velkoff, V. A. (2001). *An aging world: 2001.* Washington, DC: National Institute on Aging and U.S. Census Bureau.

Krug, E. G. (2002). *World report on violence and health.* Geneva: World Health Organisation.

Longino, C. F. (1994). Pressure from our aging population will broaden our understanding of medicine. *Academic Medicine, 72*(10), 841–847.

Lopez, A. D., Mathers, C. D., Ezzati, M., Jamison, D. T., & Murray, C. J. L. (Eds.). (2006). *Global burden of disease and risk factors.* Washington, DC: The World Bank Group.

Manton, K. G., & Gu, X. (2001). Changes in the prevalence of chronic disability in the United States black and nonblack population above age 65 from 1982 to 1999. *Proceedings of the National Academy of Sciences 98*: 6354–6359.

May, T., & Powell, J. L. (2008). *Situating social theory 2.* Philadelphia, PA: Open University Press.

Organisation for Economic Cooperation and Development (OECD) Directorate for Employment, Labour and Social Affairs. (2007). *Disability trends among elderly people: Re-assessing the evidence in 12 OECD countries.* (Interim Report.) Paris: OECD.

Phillipson, C. (1998). *Reconstructing old age.* London: Sage.

Powell, J. L. (2005). *Social theory and aging.* Lanham, MD: Rowman and Littlefield.

United Nations Department of Economic and Social Affairs, Population Division. (2002). *World Population Ageing 1950–2050.* New York: United Nations.

Walker, A., & Naegele, G. (2000). *The politics of old age in Europe.* Philadelphia, PA: Open University Press.

***Jason L. Powell***

# GRANDPARENTHOOD

Grandparenthood constitutes a life-course transition (becoming a grandparent) as well as a life-course stage (being a grandparent). For individuals with multiple grandchildren, one could even speak of "grandparenthoods" because relationships with each individual grandchild differ by the grandchild's lineage (i.e., whether the grandchild is a child of one's daughter or son), birth order, gender, or geographical distance to the grandparent. The experience of grandparenthood also varies over time, both historically and within grandparents' and grandchildren's life course, and across divergent cultural subgroups. From a different perspective, grandparenthood can also be viewed as a social position and a social role akin to parts (positions) in a drama that are played by different actors (role incumbents).

## GRANDPARENTHOOD AS SOCIAL POSITION

Social structures provide a blueprint for what grandparenthood is and how it should be enacted. Societies in North America and Western Europe with their bilateral kinship systems acknowledge grandparents on both the mother's and father's sides, but other societies with patrilineal or matrilineal systems may assign the position of grandparent only to the father's or mother's parents. In addition, individuals other than blood relatives may be viewed as grandparents. Although grandparenthood through adoption is practiced in many societies, grandparenthood through remarriage (stepgrandparents) or grandparenthood through artificial fertility methods are mostly phenomena of modern societies. Because these modern types of grandparenthood lack institutionalization (e.g., there are no separate terms for stepgrandparents acquired through the grandparents' own remarriage or for those acquired through remarriage of the grandparents' children), they can foster ambiguity in individuals' self-perceptions as grandparents (Ikels, 1998).

Social norms prescribe grandparents' rights and obligations. Once again, there is considerable cross-cultural and historical variation. Some traditional societies (e.g., traditional China and to some extent modern rural China), endorsed coresidence of young couples with the husband's parents (Ikels, 1998). In contrast, coresidence with grandparents, although on the rise, remains quite rare in the contemporary United States. Generally, the rights and obligations of grandparenthood are ill defined in modern European and North American societies. Laws pertaining specifically to grandparents' rights and duties are also rare. There is some requirement of economic support in cases of teenage parents, and grandparent visitation rights permit grandparent–grandchild contacts even against parents' wishes, although only under select circumstances (Hill, 2001). One of the more widely accepted norms is that of parental independence and noninterference on the part of grandparents in the parental domain. Consequently, grandparents rarely view themselves as disciplinarians of their grandchildren, and they resent having to take on this function under certain circumstances, for example, when grandparents raise their grandchildren (Landry-Meyer & Newman, 2004). However, even in this regard some variation exists. African-American grandparents seem more inclined to become directly involved in parenting functions and to assume authority roles vis-à-vis their grandchildren than their White counterparts (Vandell, McCartney, Owen, Booth, & Clarke-Stewart, 2003).

Despite this vagueness of social norms, grandparents assume important functions in modern societies. Their involvement in child care and in raising grandchildren reduces the need for formal child care and foster care, and their help in times of family crises assists families and grandchildren in coping with disruptive life events such as divorce. Grandparents also play a significant economic role as consumers of products for children, through their financial support to grandchildren and their parents, and through child care for employed mothers.

Unlike in some preindustrial societies where grandparenthood constituted a basis for social status in the community (Ikels, 1998), social status in the United States and Western Europe is typically linked to individuals' educational and economic achievements. The social significance of grandparenthood is acknowledged through special events such as Grandparents' Day, but one may wonder to what extent these events derive from true esteem for grandparents rather than from marketing initiatives by selected industries (where would greeting card companies be without family events?).

Like parts in a play, social positions need to be filled by actors. To what extent and by whom the position of grandparent is filled depends on fertility and mortality patterns in two successive generations. Increased longevity and relatively low ages at child birth during the middle of the 20th century contributed to a dramatic rise in the supply of living grandparents to grandchildren. In 2000 more than 40% of 10-year-old children had four living grandparents compared with only 6% of children of that age in 1900. The duration of having living grandparents rose as well. In 1900 only about 20% of children age 30 had living grandparents, compared with a projected 80 percent in 2020 (Hagestad & Uhlenberg, 2007). Further increases in longevity will support this trend into the future. However, delays in childbearing during recent decades will undermine it. Because childbearing patterns vary considerably by racial and ethnic group, the experience of grandparenthood is likely to become more diversified. Late grandparenthood is likely to prevail among non-Hispanic Whites and Asians and Pacific Islanders, whereas African Americans and especially Hispanics are likely to continue to become grandparents in middle age.

Thus, by the middle of the 21st century more grandchildren, and especially grandchildren from selected racial and ethnic groups, will again experience grandparents' deaths at earlier ages, have older grandparents during their childhood, and be less likely to have living grandparents well into their adulthood. From the grandparents' perspective, however, the supply of grandchildren has declined over the 20th century from an average of more than 12 in 1900 to between 5 and 6 by the late 1900s (Uhlenberg & Kirby, 1998), and this trend is expected to continue in the 21st century. The number of older individuals remaining without grandchildren (due to childlessness in either the grandparent or parent generation) has varied over the last century. Rates of childlessness were relatively high at the beginning of the 20th century and peaked during the Great Depression, then declined during the baby boom era (ca. 1947–1964) and have increased since the late 20th century. Thus, a noteworthy proportion of individuals especially of White and Asian descent will remain without grandchildren (Szinovacz, 2007).

It has been argued that longer duration of grandparenthood and reduced number of grandchildren will further the intensity and quality of grandparent–grandchild relationships (Hagestad & Uhlenberg, 2007). However, this view may be overly optimistic. Other demographic trends, such as the delay in childbearing age, the continued high divorce rate, and declining fertility, can undermine the quality of intergenerational relationships. Adolescent and older grandchildren may be increasingly exposed to frail and demented grandparents. They may also lose contacts with grandparents especially on their father's side after parents' divorce, and as fewer adult children are available to care for their frail parents, grandchildren may become more involved in grandparents' care. These experiences, too, will vary widely across diverse population groups, leading to considerable heterogeneity in the experience of grandparenthood (Szinovacz, 2007).

## GRANDPARENTHOOD TRANSITIONS

In contrast to most other life-course events, the transition to grandparenthood is a countertransition, that is, a transition contingent on others' behaviors. In rare cases—such as when parents are estranged from their children or when fathers are not even aware that they are fathers—grandparents may even remain ignorant about their transition to grandparenthood. Individuals initiate the transition themselves only when they remarry a partner who already has grandchildren or acquire grandchildren through adoption. Thus, some individuals' aspirations to become grandparents may be thwarted by their children's decisions to delay parenthood or to remain childless, whereas others may enter grandparenthood at a time when they have little desire to become a grandparent. Because most studies have focused on current grandparents rather than on the transition to grandparenthood, very little is known about how this transition transforms grandparents' lives, their marriages, or their relationships with the grandchildren's parents. What little is known suggests that grandparenthood is usually welcomed by the grandparents and tends to strengthen grandmother-mother bonds (Fischer, 1988). However, grandparenthood that comes too early can lead to strain in grandparents' lives and accelerate self-perceptions as aged (Kaufman & Elder, 2003).

The grandparent role is dynamic; it changes over time and varies across relationships with specific grandchildren. Although one's status as grandparent is established with the birth or adoption of the first grandchild, additional grandparenthood transitions occur as children have more children or additional children become parents. Current research provides little insight into the meanings of the first and subsequent grandparent transitions. However, as more grandchildren are born, grandparents need to divide their attention among these grandchildren. Some evidence suggests that frequent visits with the grandchildren from a single child are more common than frequent visits with all grandchildren from multiple sets of children. Conversely, having grandchildren from several children increases the chances of frequent contacts with the grandchildren from at least one child (Uhlenberg & Hammill, 1998). To further understanding of these and other dynamics of the grandparent role, it will be important to explore the interlinkages in the lives of all grandparents and all grandchildren.

## THE GRANDPARENT ROLE

Grandparenthood links the lives of three generations—grandparents, parents, and grandchildren. Consequently, the enactment of the grandparent role depends not only on the grandparents themselves but also on the attitudes and behaviors of parents and grandchildren (Szinovacz, 1998). Considerable evidence indicates that parents mediate grandparent–grandchild relationships, at least until grandchildren reach adulthood. Conflicts between parents or divorce in the middle generation as well as strained relationships between a parent and his or her children-in-law can undermine grandparent–grandchild relationships (Fingerman, 2004). Similarly, divorce on the part of the grandparents themselves has been linked to reduced closeness to grandchildren, possibly because it undermines grandparent–parent relationships (King, 2003).

Although parental mediation is important, it is certainly not the only factor impinging on the frequency or quality of grandparent–grandchild relationships. Other important factors that influence these interactions include geographical distance, urban versus rural background, age and number of grandchildren, and family structure and history. Relationships tend to be closer if grandparents live closer to the grandchildren, if the grandchildren are younger, or if grandparents knew their own grandparents (Chan & Elder, 2000). Grandmothers and grandfathers also approach the role somewhat differently. Some studies suggest that grandmothers maintain closer relationships to their grandchildren, but others demonstrate considerable involvement by grandfathers as well (Mann, 2007). Research further shows that both events in grandparents' and in grandchildren's lives exert some influence on grandparent–grandchild relationships. For example, grandchildren's transition to college seems to further closer ties between grandparents and grandchildren from the perspective of both grandparents and grandchildren (Crosnoe & Elder, 2002).

Numerous studies attest to the variety of grandparenting activities and styles. These studies reveal different types of grandparenting, depending on which dimensions (e.g., frequency and type of activities with grandchildren, role meaning and salience, instrumental assistance, quality of relationships with grandchildren, or influence) were used to create such typologies. Grandparents can be companions, babysitters, providers of emotional support, story tellers, family historians, socialization agents, disciplinarians, or transmitters of values and culture. The latter activity seems particularly important among Native Americans as it serves to maintain tribal traditions.

Variation also exists in how much grandparents become involved in their role. For instance, one study (Mueller, Wilhelm, & Elder, 2002) distinguished among five types of grandparents—influential (those ranging high on contact, activities, intimacy, helping, instrumental assistance, and authority), supportive (grandparents who demonstrate a relatively high level of all functions except for particularly low authority), passive (those with relatively low involvement in any functions), authority oriented (those with relatively low involvement in all functions except for high authority), and detached (those with very low involvement across all functions). Close to 40 percent of grandparents exhibited either the influential or supportive patterns, whereas slightly over 25 percent were detached. This suggests that most grandparents attribute high salience to this role and derive gratification from close contacts with their grandchildren. Thus, claims by some authors that grandparents have opted out of the involved grandparent role (Kornhaber, 1996) remain mainly unsubstantiated.

Another indicator that grandparents continue to play an important role especially in family crises (thus the reference to grandparents as family watchdogs) is the increased prevalence of grandparents raising grandchildren. According to the 2000 U.S. Census, more than 2.4 million grandparents had responsibility for raising grandchildren in their households. Assumption of this responsibility prevails among grandmothers and minorities, especially African Americans, Native Americans and Pacific Islanders, Hispanics, and those of other races. And least common among Whites and Asians (Simmons & Dye, 2003). Grandparents raise grandchildren mostly when the parents are either dead or unable or unwilling to carry out parental responsibilities because of various reasons including illness, drug abuse, or incarceration. Debate continues about how raising grandchildren affects grandparents' lives. Research suggests that grandparents who assume this role score lower on mental health measures (e.g., depression) than other grandparents, but other effects such as the impact on grandparents' physical well-being or economic situation remain unclear. Even though grandparents raising grandchildren typically score lower on physical health and higher on poverty than others of their age, this finding largely reflects the greater vulnerability among grandparent populations who become surrogate parents and not effects of the transition to surrogate grandparenthood (Hughes, Waite, LaPierre, & Luo, 2007; Minkler & Fuller-Thomson, 2005).

## THE FUTURE OF GRANDPARENT RESEARCH

Research has demonstrated that grandparenthood continues to be a significant although not necessarily prestigious role in modern societies and within families. Grandparents are engaged in many activities with their grandchildren and derive satisfaction from their involvement with grandchildren. It is known that such involvement varies across cultures and population subgroups as well as over the life cycle. Nevertheless, most studies remain static by focusing on grandparents at a specific point in time. Longitudinal studies (in which data are collected about individual lives at multiple points over time) are needed to explore how the grandparent role changes over time and in response to specific transitions in the lives of both grandparents and grandchildren. For example, how does the enactment of the role change in response to grandparents' retirement, their own illness, or the illness of a grandparent's spouse? How does it change in response to grandchildren's development, their entry into school, or their dating and marriage?

There is also a lack of information about intrafamilial variations in grandparenthood, that is, how grandparents relate to different grandchildren. Furthermore, little is known about the intricacies of grandparents' relationships with each other. Do close relationships between maternal and paternal grandparents foster relationships with the grandchildren? Will paternal and maternal grandparents compete with each other, especially as the supply of grandchildren declines? More information is needed about differences and similarities in grandfathers' and grandmothers' relationships with their grandchildren. Most important for understanding such differences will be an approach that takes the perspective of the grandparent couple; that is, do married grandparents split grandparenting tasks or do they engage jointly in activities with their grandchildren, and how do married grandparents' activities with grandchildren differ from those of single grandparents?

To answer these questions, it will be essential to rely on a life-course perspective that emphasizes heterogeneity in grandparenting across cultures and over the life span and attends to the interlinked lives of grandparents, parents, and grandchildren. From a policy and programmatic perspective, it will be essential to shift from a focus on intergenerational conflict to a stronger emphasis on enabling grandparents to take on heavy responsibilities for grandchild care without detrimental consequences to the grandparents' or the grandchildren's well-being. All evidence points to the fact that grandparents are not abandoning their grandchildren or other family obligation to pursue leisure interests. However, it is often particularly vulnerable groups of grandparents who face overly demanding care responsibilities, and these grandparents need both social and material supports. The retrenchment of social welfare for the elderly is likely to undermine especially vulnerable grandparents' ability to attend to increasing care responsibilities.

**SEE ALSO** Volume 1: *Grandchildren;* Volume 2: *Social Roles;* Volume 3: *Caregiving; Family and Household Structure, Later Life; Intergenerational Transfers; Parent-Child Relationships, Later Life.*

**BIBLIOGRAPHY**

Chan, C. G., & Elder, G. H. (2000). Matrilineal advantage in grandchild–grandparent relations. *The Gerontologist, 40*, 179–190.

Crosnoe, R., & Elder, G. H. (2002). Life course transitions, the generational stake, and grandparent–grandchild relationships. *Journal of Marriage and the Family, 64*, 1089–1096.

Fingerman, K. L. (2004). The role of offspring and in-laws in grandparents' ties to their grandchildren. *Journal of Family Issues, 25*, 1026–1049.

Fischer, L. R. (1988). The influence of kin on the transition to parenthood. *Marriage and Family Review, 12*, 201–219.

Hagestad, G. O., & Uhlenberg, P. (2007). The impact of demographic changes on relations between age groups and generations: A comparative perspective. In K. W. Schaie, & P. Uhlenberg (Eds.), *Social structures. Demographic changes and the well-being of older persons* (pp. 239–261). New York: Springer.

Hill, T. J. (2001). What's a grandparent to do? The legal status of grandparents in the extended family. *Journal of Family Issues, 22*, 594–618.

Hughes, M. E., Waite, L. J., LaPierre, T. A., & Luo, Y. (2007). All in the family: The impact of caring for grandchildren on grandparents' health. *The Journals of Gerontology: Social Sciences, 62B*, S108–S119.

Ikels, C. (1998). Grandparenthood in cross-cultural perspective. In M. E. Szinovacz (Ed.), *Handbook on grandparenthood* (pp. 40–52). Westport, CT: Greenwood Press.

Kaufman, G., & Elder, G. H. (2003). Grandparenting and age identity. *Journal of Aging Studies, 17*, 269–282.

King, V. (2003). The legacy of a grandparent's divorce: Consequences for ties between grandparents and grandchildren. *Journal of Marriage and the Family, 65*, 1044–1069.

Kornhaber, A. (1996). *Contemporary grandparenting*. Thousand Oaks, CA: Sage.

Landry-Meyer, L., & Newman, B. M. (2004). An exploration of the grandparent caregiver role. *Journal of Family Issues, 25*, 1005–1025.

Mann, R. (2007). Out of the shadows? Grandfatherhood, age and masculinities. *Journal of Aging Studies, 21*, 281–291.

Minkler, M., & Fuller-Thomson, E. (2005). African American grandparents raising grandchildren: A national study using the Census 2000 American Community Survey. *The Journals of Gerontology: Social Sciences, 60B*, S82–S92.

Mueller, M. M., Wilhelm, B., & Elder, G. H. (2002). Variations in grandparenting. *Research on Aging, 24*, 360–388.

Simmons, T., & Dye, J. L. (2003). *Grandparents living with grandchildren: 2000*. Washington, DC: U.S. Bureau of the Census.

Szinovacz, M. E. (1998). Research on grandparenting: Needed refinements in concepts, theories, and methods. In M. E. Szinovacz (Ed.), *Handbook on grandparenthood* (pp. 257–288). Westport, CT: Greenwood.

Szinovacz, M. E. (2007). The future of intergenerational relationships—variability and vulnerabilities (commentary). In K. W. Schaie, & P. Uhlenberg (Eds.), *Social structures. Demographic changes and the well-being of older persons* (pp. 262–282). New York: Springer.

Uhlenberg, P., & Hammill, B. (1998). Frequency of grandparent contact with grandchild sets: Six factors that make a difference. *The Gerontologist, 38*, 276–285.

Uhlenberg, P., & Kirby, J. B. (1998). Grandparenthood over time: Historical and demographic trends. In M. E. Szinovacz (Ed.), *Handbook on grandparenthood* (pp. 23–39). Westport, CT: Greenwood.

Vandell, D. L., McCartney, K., Owen, M. T., Booth, C., & Clarke-Stewart, A. (2003). Variations in child care by grandparents during the first three years. *Journal of Marriage and the Family, 65*, 375–381.

**Maximiliane E. Szinovacz**

# H

## HEALTH BEHAVIORS, LATER LIFE

Understanding the social and behavioral determinants and outcomes of health-related behaviors, such as diet, exercise, and smoking, in later life is crucial to enhancing the lives of a large and increasing older adult population in the United States and around the world. In particular, understanding the causes and effects of specific modifiable health behaviors may increase health-promoting choices in the population, reduce morbidity and early mortality, decrease medical costs, and improve health services and policies aimed at older adults. An overview of patterns and trends in body weight, exercise, smoking, and substance abuse in later life are described here. More information about these health behaviors is presented in the entry on Health Behaviors in Adulthood.

### BODY WEIGHT

Extremes in body weight and body mass index (BMI)—that is, being either underweight or obese—are risk factors for poor health outcomes in later life. BMI is a measure of body fat that is derived from measurement of height and weight. Both high and low BMIs are associated with increased rates of functional impairment and disability; increased prevalence of diseases such as diabetes, hypertension (i.e., high blood pressure), and arthritis; and increases in the amount of care required in later life.

The general life course trend in body weight is that individuals tend to gain weight through middle adulthood into early old age and then plateau or decline in weight at very advanced ages (Jenkins, Fultz, Wray, & Fonda, 2003). This suggests that middle age is a time of life in which weight management is particularly important to overall health and especially to health concerns associated with excess weight. In contrast, older age is often marked by weight loss, sometimes related to disease. Also, being obese for longer lengths of time throughout the life course may have particularly adverse effects on health (Schafer & Ferraro, 2007).

Body weight and diet, like many other health behaviors, are affected by major life events. Widowhood is one example of a life event that may affect health behaviors. For a variety of reasons, such as decreased social contacts and loss-related depressive symptoms, widowed older adults are likely to consume a diet that provides insufficient calories and nutritional diversity (Quandt et al., 2000). Retirement also has an impact on eating behavior. Retirement contributes to older adults eating out less often, likely freeing up time and allowing them to spend more time cooking. However, retirement also may contribute to a more sedentary lifestyle that may counteract any beneficial health effects that eating more meals at home might bring (Chung, Popkin, Domino, & Sterns, 2007).

Being able to function independently is an important component of an older adult's well-being. As such, high BMI is a health risk factor that can have a profoundly negative influence on functional independence. There are several physiological pathways for the influence of obesity on poorer physical functioning in older age. First, excessive body weight typically contributes to inflammation of joint tissue, making ambulating (i.e., movement) painful and difficult (Walford, Harris, & Weindruch, 1987). Second, excessive body weight also increases the amount of mechanical stress placed on body joints, elevating one's risk of osteoarthritis (Clark & Mungai, 1997) and decreasing functioning. Third, excess weight is associated with a sedentary lifestyle, which contributes to both decreased muscle strength and cardiovascular fitness and may eventually result in difficulties with physical functions such as walking several blocks or climbing flights of stairs (Himes, 2000). Fourth, side effects and symptoms associated with a broad range of diseases that are more common among obese persons may make movements difficult.

Being underweight in later life may contribute to or signal adverse health outcomes due to its association with the complex syndrome of frailty—a condition characterized by wasting and a decrease in the body's reserves (Fried, Ferrucci, Darer, Williamson, & Anderson, 2004). One estimate suggests that 2.9% of community-dwelling adults age 70 and older are underweight in the United States (Jenkins, 2004). Low BMI has been suggested as one indicator of the frailty syndrome (Fried et al., 2001). Frailty in older adults corresponds to increased risk for disease, disability, and institutionalization. Being underweight may be a proxy for frailty and thus is associated with an increased prevalence of a range of adverse health outcomes in later life. In sum, obesity is a risk factor for various diseases, whereas being underweight may be a consequence of disease.

Although both extremes in body weight contribute to certain adverse health outcomes, obesity in older age may not necessarily contribute to early mortality. Whereas obesity in middle age is associated with higher disease and mortality rates, especially among some non-White populations, obesity among older adults may indicate a physical robustness, particularly in comparison with being underweight. Rather, older obese persons represent a select population. Obesity contributes to early morality at midlife, and those obese persons who survive to later life are particularly robust. This physical robustness may be in part due to other positive behavioral, environmental, or genetic factors that may contribute to a resistance to the heath problems associated with obesity.

## EXERCISE

Lack of exercise has deleterious effects on health, with a particularly negative impact on physical functioning. Older individuals who do not participate in regular vigorous physical activity are more likely to experience the onset of functional impairment (Jenkins, 2004) due to decreased muscle tone and cardiovascular fitness. Over the past several decades, health professionals and policy makers alike have realized and begun to increase awareness of the benefits of exercise in later life. This is particularly important for future generations of older adults, who are more likely to have worked in sedentary white-collar or technical jobs, compared to prior cohorts who worked in physically active jobs, often in agricultural or manufacturing sectors.

Exercise programs targeted toward older adults have been used as effective interventions to improve health outcomes. In particular, such exercise programs are suggested as effective interventions for frailty (Fried et al., 2004). Exercise may also improve balance among older adults and thereby decrease the likelihood of dangerous falls.

Four broad domains of exercise are recommended for older adults: physical activities that improve endurance, balance, strength, and flexibility (National Institute on Aging, 2007). Improvements in each of these domains are thought to translate to improvements in health. More specifically, participating in activities that improve aerobic capacity aids in the prevention of disease and helps improve mood. Participating in exercises that build musculature may help older adults to function independently longer.

## SMOKING

The effects of smoking on health have been studied extensively, and a substantial and growing body of literature speaks to smoking's detrimental effects on a range of health outcomes. Smoking has been shown to be associated with various life-threatening health conditions such as heart disease (Lahiri & Song, 2000), increases in mortality (Smith, Taylor, Sloan, Johnson, & Desvousges, 2001), and functional difficulties (Ostbye, Taylor, Krause, & Scoyoc, 2002). The health problems associated with smoking are more likely to affect older smokers compared to younger smokers, in part because they have been smoking longer (American Lung Association, 2007). Older smokers, compared to their younger counterparts, also are less inclined to think smoking has or will have a negative impact on their health (Rimer et al., 1990). This attitude likely contributes to the added challenge of creating effective smoking cessation programs for this population.

An additional difficulty is that the current generation of older adults has the highest smoking rate of any other generation in the United States in the early 21st century. (American Lung Association, 2007). Many developed their smoking behaviors during the 1940s and 1950s, when smoking was more socially acceptable and common. This social context shaped how they viewed their behavior and likely influenced their desire to quit. Successful smoking cessation programs should consider the social environment in which these older adults developed their behaviors to better equip them to stop smoking.

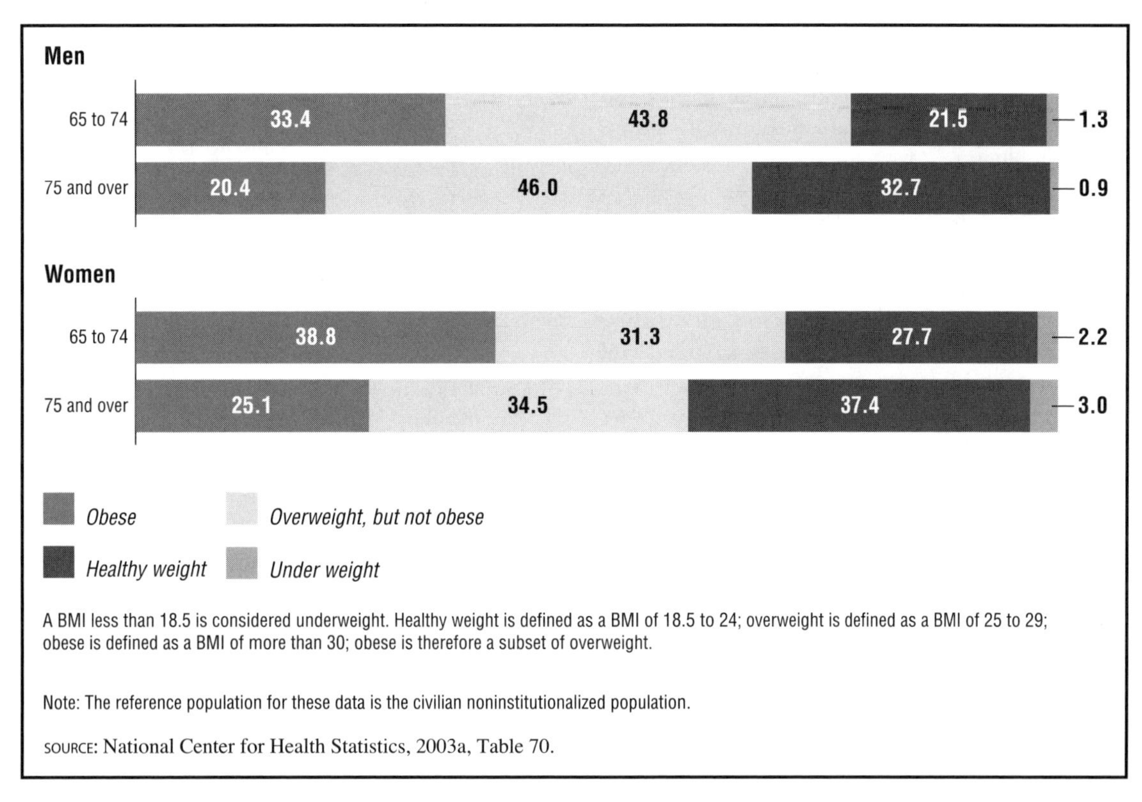


***Figure 1.*** *Percent distribution of people aged 65 and over who were underweight, healthy weight, overweight, and obese by age and sex: 1995–2000.* CENGAGE LEARNING, GALE.

## ALCOHOL AND DRUG USE

The effect of alcohol use on mortality has long intrigued social scientists, health professionals, and policy makers alike. Unlike smoking behavior, however, alcohol use has received much less attention in regard to its effects on disease and morbidity (excluding cardiovascular disease, where fairly substantial attention is given; Perreira & Sloan, 2002). This is unfortunate because the misuse of alcohol, particularly among older adults, may have deleterious effects on various aspects of health and functioning, even while moderate amounts of alcohol consumption may have beneficial effects on certain aspects of cognitive and cardiovascular health. In sum, moderate drinking is associated with better health, whereas abstinence and excessive drinking has negative effects on health and mortality.

The use and especially the misuse of alcohol have different implications for older adults than for their younger counterparts. Interactions of prescription drugs and alcohol are one concern. The body's ability to eliminate drugs from the system becomes less efficient with older age. That, combined with a higher rate of prescription drug usage among older adults, makes alcohol consumption, even in moderation, potentially more problematic among older than among younger populations.

Alcohol and drug usage varies among older adults both in frequency and correlates. Alcohol use, even problematic alcohol use, is much more common than illicit drug use among the elderly population. In 2000 nearly nine times as many older adults reported having a drinking problem (i.e., heavy and binge drinking) than using an illicit drug in the prior month (Substance Abuse and Mental Health Services Administration, 2001). White older adults were more likely to report using alcohol and illicit drugs in the prior month, compared to Hispanic older adults. Both alcohol use and problem drinking were higher among older adult males than older adult females. The most common types of drugs misused by older adults in 2000 were marijuana and prescription drugs (in particular psychotherapeutics; Substance Abuse and Mental Health Services Administration, 2001).

## CONCLUSION

The study of health behaviors in later life is a rapidly expanding and exciting area of research. New data collection efforts are allowing researchers to better understand problems that impact the health of older adults. One example of such data collection efforts are large-scale national surveys that follow older adults as they age, such as the Health and Retirement Study. New technology now enables researchers to easily collect and analyze biomarkers (such as cholesterol, blood sugar levels, and DNA) on large numbers of individuals. Future directions in research should take advantage of such readily available high-quality data to better understand aging patterns and cohort changes in regard to the health behaviors of older adults.

International comparisons among older adults in regard to various health behaviors show some interesting variability. For example, when comparing England and the United States, older adults are similar in regard to smoking behavior, older adults in England tend to drink more heavily, and there is a higher proportion of obesity in the United States (Banks, Marmot, Oldfield, & Smith, 2006). This suggests the need for even further international collaborations, where researchers can approach solutions to problem behaviors differently and learn from one another.

In sum, the cumulative effect of engaging in risky health behaviors may result in poorer health outcomes throughout adulthood and older age. However, it is important to note that changing behaviors and engaging in positive health behaviors such as exercising, smoking cessation, and healthy weight maintenance can still have some positive effects on health even if the behavior change is initiated later in life.

**SEE ALSO** Volume 2: *Obesity, Adulthood;* Volume 3: *Arthritis; Cancer, Adulthood and Later Life; Cardiovascular Disease; Diabetes, Adulthood and Later Life; Frailty and Robustness.*

**BIBLIOGRAPHY**

American Lung Association. (2007). *Smoking among older adults fact sheet.* Retrieved June 26, 2008, from http://www.lungusa.org

Banks, J., Marmot, M., Oldfield, Z., & Smith, J. P. (2006). Disease disadvantage in the United States and England. *Journal of the American Medical Association, 295*(17), 2037–2045.

Clark, D. O., & Mungai, S. M. (1997). Distribution and association of chronic disease and mobility difficulty across four body mass index categories of African-American women. *American Journal of Epidemiology, 145,* 865–875.

Chung, S., Popkin, B. M., Domino, M. E., & Sterns, S. C. (2007). Effect of retirement on eating out and weight change: An analysis of gender differences. *Obesity, 15,* 1053–1060.

Fried, L. P., Tangen, C. M., Walston, J., Newman, A. B., Hirsch, C., Gottdiener, J., et al. (2001). Frailty in older adults: Evidence for a phenotype. *Journals of Gerontology Series A: Biological Sciences and Medical Sciences, 56,* M146–M156.

Fried, L. P., Ferrucci, L., Darer, J., Williamson, J. D., & Anderson, G. (2004). Untangling the concepts of disability, frailty, and comorbidity: Implications for improved targeting and care. *Journals of Gerontology Series A: Biological Sciences and Medical Sciences, 59,* 255–263.

Himes, C. L. (2000). Obesity, disease, and functional limitation in later life. *Demography, 37,* 73–82.

Jenkins, K. R. (2004). Body-weight change and physical functioning among young old adults. *Journal of Aging and Health, 16,* 248–266.

Jenkins, K. R., Fultz, N. A., Wray, L. A., & Fonda, S. J. (2003). Patterns of body weight in middle-aged and older Americans, by gender and race, 1994-2000. *Social and Preventative Medicine, 48,* 257–268.

Lahiri, K., & Song, J. G. (2000). The effect of smoking on health using a sequential self-selection model. *Health Economics, 9,* 491–511.

National Institute on Aging. (2007). *Exercise and physical activity: Getting fit for life.* Retrieved April 29, 2008, from http://www.nia.nih.gov

Ostbye, T., Taylor, D. H., Krause, K. M., & Scoyoc, L. V. (2002). The role of smoking and other modifiable lifestyle risk factors in maintaining and restoring lower body mobility in middle-aged and older Americans: Results from the HRS and AHEAD. *Journal of the American Geriatrics Society, 50,* 691–699.

Perreira, K. M., & Sloan, F. A. (2002). Excess alcohol consumption and health outcomes: A 6-year follow-up of men over age 50 from the Health and Retirement Study. *Addiction, 97,* 301–310.

Quandt, S. A., McDonald, J., Arcury, T. A., Bell, R. A., & Vitolins, M. Z. (2000). Nutritional self-management of elderly widows in rural communities. *The Gerontologist, 40*(1), 86–96.

Rimer, B. K., Orleans, C. T., Keintz, M. K., Cristinzio, S., & Fleisher, L. (1990). The older smoker: Status, challenges and opportunities for intervention. *Chest, 97,* 547–553.

Schafer, M. H., & Ferraro, K. F. (2007). Obesity and hospitalization over the adult life course: Does duration of exposure increase use? *Journal of Health and Social Behavior, 48*(4), 434–449.

Shlipak, M. G., Stehman-Breen, C., Fried, L. F., Song, X., Siscovick, D., Fried, L. P., et al. (2004). The presence of frailty in elderly persons with chronic renal insufficiency. *American Journal of Kidney Diseases, 43,* 861–867.

Smith, V. K., Taylor, D. H. Jr., Sloan, F. A., Johnson, F. R., & Desvousges, W. H. (2001). Do smokers respond to health shocks? *The Review of Economics and Statistics, 83,* 675–687.

Substance Abuse and Mental Health Services Administration. (2001). *The NHSDA report: Substance use among older adults.* Retrieved April 29, 2008, from http://www.oas.samhsa.gov/2k1/

Walford, R. L., Harris, S. B., & Weindruch, R. (1987). Dietary restriction and aging: Historical phases, mechanisms and current directions. *Journal of Nutrition, 117,* 1650–1654.

Walston, J., & Fried, L. P. (1999). Frailty and the older man. *Medical Clinics of North America, 83,* 1173–1194.

***Kristi Rahrig Jenkins***

# HEALTH CARE USE, LATER LIFE

Thanks to the rapid decline in the death rate over the last 150 years, the final stage of the life course now usually begins at age 65. More people reach that milepost than ever before, making old age a common experience shared

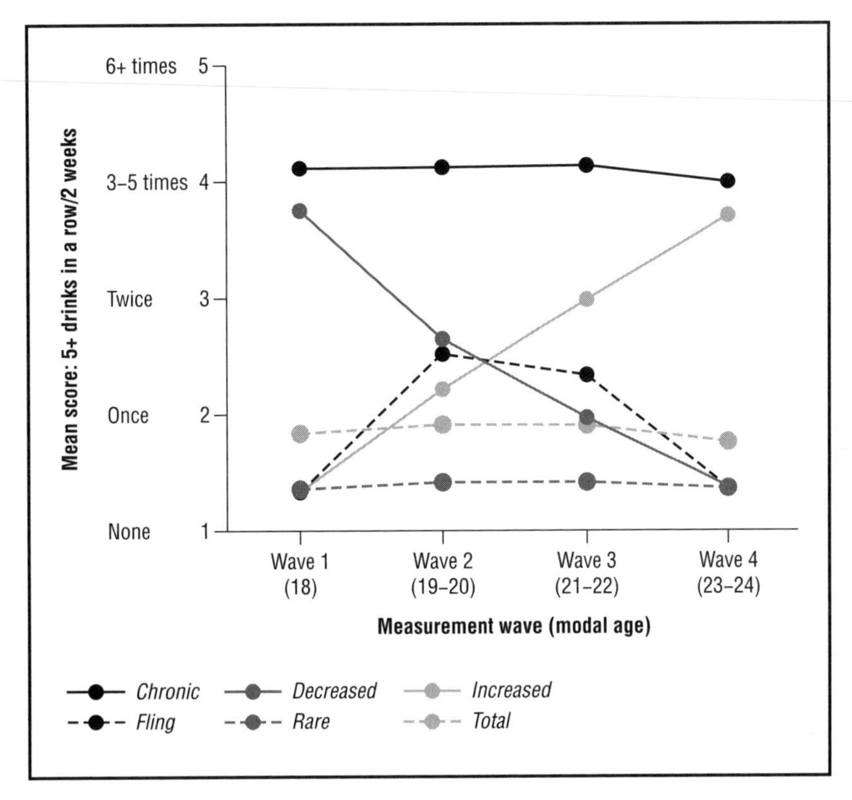


*Figure 1. Health care spending for persons aged 65 and older, by types of service. 2004.* CENGAGE LEARNING, GALE.

by many. The typical view of this stage of the life course is that health and abilities decline, leading to much greater use of health care. Although statistics support this view as a generalization, individuals' experiences vary enormously, with many people remaining robust and able as long as they live, and others suffering from a legacy of poor health and declining faculties accumulated well before old age.

Since the enactment in 1965 of Medicare, the U.S. federally funded program of health insurance for the elderly, health care use by those in later life in the United States has not only been underwritten but also shaped by the program. Because of this federal responsibility, data on health care use by the elderly are more complete and comprehensive than for any other age group. Primary sources of data are the administrative records of the program itself; those of the Medicaid program, which pays for much of nursing home care; nationally representative surveys of the U.S. population, including the elderly, conducted by the National Center for Health Statistics; and surveys of Medicare enrollees conducted by the Centers for Medicare and Medicaid.

Almost the entire elderly population is enrolled in Medicare. In 2005, the U.S. Census Bureau estimated the population 65 and older at about 37 million. Medicare reported that nearly 36 million of them (96.9%) were enrolled in the program. (Since 1972, Medicare has also covered disabled people under 65 and almost 7 million were enrolled in 2005.)

## OVERVIEW OF HEALTH CARE USE IN LATER LIFE

The elderly consume medical services in amounts disproportionate to their numbers in the population. In 2004, people aged 65 and over comprised 12.4% of the U.S. population, but consumed 34% of the nation's personal health care spending, almost $15,000 for each elderly person (Hartman, Catlin, Lassman, Cylus, & Heffler, 2007). Medicare paid half the cost. Private health insurance, Medicaid, and payments by the elderly and their families each accounted for 14 to 16%.

Figure 1 shows the major categories of service covered by these expenditures: inpatient hospital care; outpatient care in physicians' offices and clinics; outpatient prescription drugs; care in nursing homes; and other services. The figure and all expenditures reported in this section are based on National Health Expenditure data, a system of accounts maintained by the Centers for Medicare and Medicaid Services that provides a comprehensive look at the nation's annual health care spending over the past 50 years, with detail by type of service, payer, and age group (Hartman, Catlin, Lassman, Cylus, & Heffler, 2007).

### HOSPITAL CARE

From 1965 to 1983 the rate of hospitalization among the elderly rose steadily, from 249 hospital stays per 1,000 elderly people to 413 per 1,000. With the introduction in 1983 of prospective payment for hospitals, a system of payment rates set in advance and based on diagnosis, which replaced the earlier system of reimbursing costs, hospital stays declined to a low of 334 per 1,000 elderly in 1990. Partly because of the continued aging of the population, use has risen since then, to 360 stays per 1,000 elderly in 2005. The average length of stay has declined steadily for elderly people, from 10.7 days in 1980 to 5.5 days in 2005. Days of hospital care, a combination of the number and length of stays, were 4,098 per 1,000 elderly in 1980, but only 1,988 by 2005. Despite these declines, expenditures for hospital care have risen faster than inflation. In 1987, hospital care for the elderly cost $67 billion, or $2,248 per person; by 2004, the amount was $194 billion, or $5,403 per person (Hartman, et al., 2007.)

### PHYSICIAN AND CLINICAL SERVICES

In 2005, 94% of the noninstitutionalized elderly visited physicians' offices, hospital outpatient departments, and hospital emergency departments (National Center for Health Statistics, 2007). The overwhelming majority of these visits were made to physicians' offices, with about 10% to hospital outpatient and emergency departments (Cherry, Woodwell, & Rechtsteiner, 2007). Spending for these services, the second largest category of health expenditure, grew from $32 billion, or $1,075 per person, in 1987 to $109 billion, or $3,024 per person, in 2004.

### PRESCRIPTION DRUGS

With the advent of medications to prevent and control chronic disease, such as agents to lower blood pressure and cholesterol, the use of prescription drugs has become nearly universal among the elderly. Spending for prescription drugs was $56 billion in 2004, 10.5% of personal health care spending for the elderly, and up from 5.9% in 1987. In 2006, Medicare introduced a prescription drug benefit to help pay the rising costs.

### NURSING HOMES

About 1.4 million people were in nursing homes in 2005, most of them aged 65 and over. Additional elderly people are in psychiatric or chronic disease hospitals, Veterans Administration hospitals, and other long-term care facilities. In general, elderly residents of these institutions suffer from multiple chronic conditions and functional impairments. In 2004 nursing home costs for the elderly amounted to $91 billion.

***Pill use.*** *With the advances in health care, the elderly must often take many pills on a daily basis.* © BRUNO EHRS/CORBIS.

### OTHER HEALTH SERVICES

The aged population uses many additional health services: other professional services (e.g., private-duty nurses, chiropractors, podiatrists, optometrists, therapists), home health, dental, other personal health care, and durable and other medical equipment. The cost of these services and supplies amounted to $82 billion in 2004.

### LONG-TERM CARE

In addition to medical care, many elderly people who have lost some capacity for self-care require a range of social, personal, and supportive services. *Long-term care* is defined as physical care over a prolonged period for people incapable of sustaining themselves without this care. It involves a spectrum of services responding to different needs across a range of chronic illness and disability. These services cross the boundaries between income maintenance and health, social services, and housing programs.

In 2004, 17 million elderly people needed assistance with activities of daily living (ADLs), and instrumental activities of daily living (IADLs), two classifications often used in research (National Center for Health Statistics 2007). ADLs are the basic tasks of everyday life such as eating, bathing, and dressing. IADLs encompass a range of activities that are more complex, such as handling personal finances, shopping, traveling, using the telephone, and taking medications. About 80% of the elderly who need long-term care live at home or in community-based settings such as assisted living facilities (Eckenwiler, 2007). Many are cared for by family and friends, who may themselves be elderly. Research projects in the United States have focused on developing alternative ways to provide long-term care services, such as adult day care, home health, meals-on-wheels, and respite care. Most of these services are aimed at maintaining the independence of the aged or disabled person at home to avoid institutional placement, often viewed as a measure of last resort.

## USE OF SERVICES BY AGE AND GENDER WITHIN THE ELDERLY

The elderly use more health care than younger people, and, within the elderly group itself, the same pattern continues: The oldest old use more health care than younger elderly. Differences by age, gender, and other demographic and socioeconomic characteristics are documented not only by the Medicare program, but also by the surveys of the National Center for Health Statistics. These surveys are the source of the summary tables published each year in the *Statistical Abstract of the United States* (e.g., U.S. Census Bureau, 2008) and in *Health, United States* (see National Center for Health Statistics, 2007), two good starting points for learning about health care use in later life and for identifying the surveys that support in-depth research. (Data not otherwise attributed in this section come from various *Statistical Abstracts.*)

The National Hospital Discharge Survey, which has sampled hospital records annually since 1965, is the nation's benchmark for data on hospital care. Drawing on this survey, Figure 2 shows trends in hospital days per 1000 persons, by age within the 65 and older group (Kozak, DeFrances, & Hall, 2006; Gillum, Graves, & Wood, 1998). The long-term trend described earlier holds true at each age: Hospital use rose until the introduction of prospective payment in 1983, and has declined since then. Throughout the period, however, the youngest elderly used less hospital care than the oldest. In 2004 people aged between 65 and 74 years averaged just over 1,400 hospital days per 1,000, compared with almost 2,500 for those aged between 75 and 84 years, and 3,400 for those 85 and older. As noted earlier, hospital days combine the number of hospital stays during a year and the length of those stays to summarize the time spent in the hospital by the average person in the age group.

Three surveys provide data on the use of physician and clinic care: the National Health Interview Survey, annual since 1957, which collects data from a representative sample of the U.S. population; and the more recent National Ambulatory Medical Care Survey (NAMCS) and National Hospital Ambulatory Medical Care Survey (NHAMCS), which survey physicians' offices, and hospital outpatient and emergency departments, respectively. These surveys show that persons aged between 65 and 74 years old made 725 visits per 100 persons to physicians' offices, hospital outpatient departments, and emergency rooms in 2005, or more than seven visits per person. Persons 75 years old and older made 865 visits per 100 persons. The most common reasons for office visits by the elderly were elevated blood pressure (7.7% of visits), cancer (6.3%), arthritis and related conditions (4.8%), and diabetes (4.5%; Cherry et al., 2007). Suggesting the importance of earlier life stages for health care use in later life, the first four reasons for the elderly were also the most common reasons among people aged between 50 and 64 years of age. Although data from the NAMCS and the National Health Interview Survey are not fully comparable, together they suggest that the elderly's use of outpatient physicians' care has been rising over time.

The National Health and Nutrition Examination Survey (NHANES) and the Medical Expenditure Panel Survey (MEPS, conducted by the Agency for Healthcare Quality and Research, 2002), both based on nationally representative samples, are two more surveys that provide information about the health care use of the elderly. The NHANES focuses primarily on health, not health care use, but asks about prescription drug use. Between 1988 and 1994, 73.6% of people 65 and older reported using at least one prescription drug in the last month; by 1999 to 2002, that figure had risen to 84.7%. Women were more likely than men to report prescription drug use: 88.1% versus 80.1% in the period from 1999 to 2002.

The periodic National Nursing Home Surveys collect information about residents of nursing homes, most of whom are elderly. Most residents, 74% in 2004, are women (National Center for Health Statistics 2007), in large part because women live longer than men, and so outlive their spouses and potential caretakers. Stable during the 1970s and 1980s, rates of nursing home use have declined since then: in 1985 there were 46 residents per

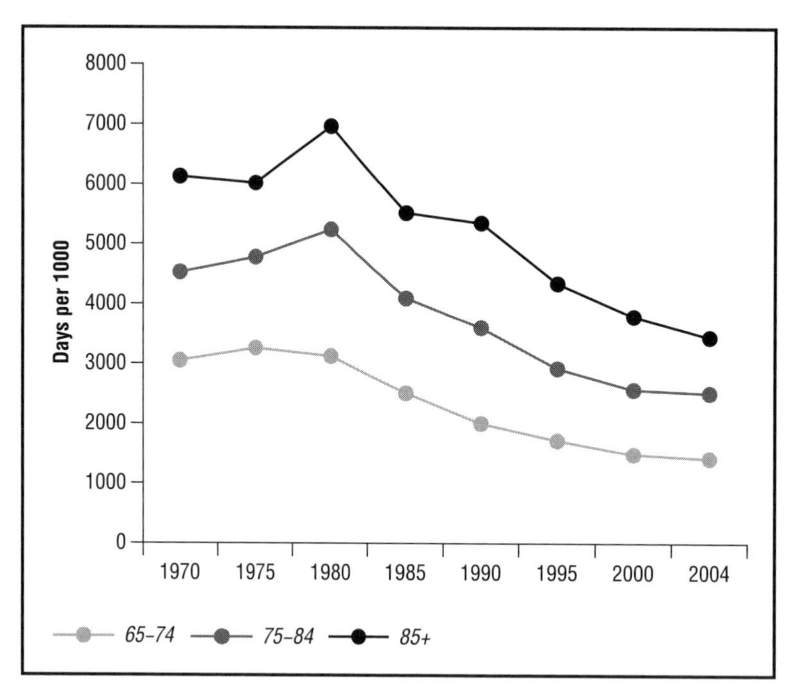


***Figure 2.*** *Annual hospital days per 1,000 persons, by age.* CENGAGE LEARNING, GALE.

1,000 elderly; by 2004, 36 per 1,000. The decline has been particularly marked among those 75 and older, whose rates of nursing home use dropped by a third, from 58 to 36 per 1,000 people for those aged between 75 and 84, and from 220 to 139 per 1,000 people for those 85 and older. The decline is due to a combination of factors, including reduced levels of disability among the elderly (see later discussion in this entry) and the growing range of alternatives to nursing homes discussed earlier in this entry.

### EFFECT OF LIFE COURSE ON HEALTH CARE USE IN LATER LIFE

Use of health care services in later life is determined in large part by the culmination of circumstances and experiences earlier in the life course: genetic endowment and health at birth; socioeconomic advantage or disadvantage, including access to medical care; and the cultural context that shapes personal health habits and the levels and types of health resources available.

A fundamental aspect of good health, and determinant of the need for care, is the ability to function well physically and mentally. Data from the National Health Interview Survey show that, over the period from 1982 to 2002, disability measured by ADLs declined among persons 70 and older, and disability measured by IADLs declined even more (Schoen, Martin, Andreski, & Freedman, 2005). The improvement was not evenly distributed: Differences by race persisted throughout the period, with non-Whites experiencing more disability and differences by education and income widened. ADL limitations actually increased among older adults with an elementary school education, and those in the lowest income group, at the same time that they declined among those with more education and income.

The influence of the earlier life course on health care use in old age is starkly apparent in a comparison of Medicare beneficiaries who were uninsured before age 65 with those who had had private insurance (McWilliams, Meara, Zaslavsky, & Ayanian, 2007b). The comparison is based on the Health and Retirement Study, a longitudinal study supported by the National Institute on Aging that began documenting the lives of its participants in the early 1990s. Before age 65, uninsured adults with cardiovascular disease or diabetes had fewer doctors' visits and hospitalizations than insured adults with the same conditions. After age 65, when enrollment in Medicare gave them better access to care, they had substantially more visits and hospitalizations than previously insured persons. The greater use of services led to better health, although it did not compensate fully for the earlier lack of care (McWilliams, Meara, Zaslavsky, & Ayanian, 2007a).

Health care use and expenditures are commonly highest in the last year of life. Numerous studies have documented that more than 25% of total health care expenditure for the elderly is devoted to caring for the 5% who die each year (Rice & Fineman, 2004). Because attempts to prolong life are typically less aggressive for the oldest old, however, end-of-life health care spending declines at older ages, mainly due to less use of inpatient hospital care, and is lower for those aged between 75 and 84 years old than those 65 to 74, and lower again for those 85 and older (Levinsky, Yu, Ash, Moskowitz, Gazelle, Saynina, & Emmanuel, 2001).

## RACIAL DISPARITIES IN HEALTH CARE USE

The impact of race on health care use has been a particularly active area for research in the last two decades. The *Report of the Secretary's Task Force on Black and Minority Health*, published by the Department of Health and Human Services in 1985, presented authoritative documentation that Blacks received fewer health care services, of lower quality, than Whites. In the intervening years, hundreds of studies have documented these disparities in more detail. The Institute of Medicine summarized the findings in *Unequal Treatment: Confronting Racial and Ethnic Disparities in Health Care* (Smedley, Stith, & Nelson, 2003). Defining disparities as differences in care unrelated to clinical needs, preferences, or availability of care, the report found that:

> A large body of published research reveals that racial and ethnic minorities experience a lower quality of health services, and are less likely to receive even routine medical procedures than are white Americans.... Significantly, these differences are associated with greater mortality among African-American patients.

Because of the higher use of health care by the elderly, and the greater availability of good data, important studies have focused on racial disparities in later life. In 2005, *The New England Journal of Medicine* published three articles, based on data for millions of Medicare enrollees, showing that, despite the attention drawn to the problem, racial disparities in the use of major surgical procedures and in procedures for the management of heart attack had not improved over the decade of the 1990s (Jha, Fisher, Li, Orav, & Epstein, 2005; Vaccarino, Rathore, Wenger, Frederick, Abramson, Barron, et al., 2005). By contrast, differences in preventive care provided through managed care plans did decline (Trivedi, Zaslavsky, Schneider, & Ayanian, 2005).

Since 2003, the Agency for Healthcare Quality and Research has published the annual *National Healthcare Disparities Report* (Agency for Healthcare Quality and Research, 2005). The report compiles current information about differences in the use of services, and their quality, by racial/ethnic group, education, and income, and for special populations such as children, women, the elderly, residents of rural areas, and those with special health care needs. Not all disparities are to the disadvantage of the group: for example, women receive more preventive services than men. Summary tables at the end of each chapter detail racial/socioeconomic differences in receipt and quality of services.

## SOCIOLOGICAL THEORY AND FUTURE RESEARCH

Sociological theory recognizes that the link between illness and use of health care—the *help-seeking process*—is not a straightforward matter of biological need, but is shaped by an individual's symptoms, personality, cultural background, and experiences with the health care system (Cockerham, 2001; Mechanic, 1982). Symptoms that send one person to the doctor are ignored by another, people with the same symptoms and the same willingness to seek help can have quite different experiences in the health care system, and use of health services can serve purposes other than the maintenance of health, for example, providing people with reassurance or reason to put aside other obligations. Experience throughout the life course influences health and health care use in later life. Not only health but health habits are set starting in childhood, and shape health in adulthood. Researchers have found that the characteristics of an individual's prenatal and infant experience are associated with development of chronic diseases many years later. As Kuh and Ben-Shlomo put it (1997): "...throughout the life course exposures or insults gradually accumulate through episodes of illness, adverse environmental conditions and behaviours increasing the risk of chronic disease and mortality."

The most widely used sociological model of health care use organizes these contributing factors into three groups (Andersen, Kravits, & Anderson, 1975). *Predisposing factors* encompass demographic characteristics, such as age and gender, and personal disposition to seek care, which is influenced by upbringing and cultural background. *Enabling factors* refer to income, health insurance, the availability of health facilities and the attitude toward the patient of those who work in them, as well as other factors that make it easy, or difficult, to get care. *Need* originates with a physical or mental condition, but includes the way an individual has learned to interpret and respond to symptoms.

The statistics presented in this entry testify to the centrality of good data to research on health care use in later life. The theory just outlined suggests that, because help-seeking behavior is learned over the life course, and can change with an individual's experiences and circumstances, the most effective way to study it may be to study populations over a period of time, those who do and do not seek care, to identify the important and malleable factors that contribute to decisions to seek care. As essential as good national statistics are, often the only way to learn more about differences in health care use, and the reasons for them, is to study the process as it unfolds in individuals' lives (Mechanic, 1982). Important areas for further research include the processes that lead to successful aging (Rowe & Kahn, 1998), the time and energy devoted to those processes by the elderly and by their friends and family (Russell, Ibuka, & Abraham, 2007), and the conditions conducive to ending the life course with what is recognized, personally and culturally, as a good death (Carr & Khodyakov, 2007). Research in these areas would contribute to making life after 65 not only an increasingly common experience, but also an increasingly satisfying one.

**SEE ALSO** Volume 2: *Policy, Health;* Volume 3: *Cancer, Adulthood and Later Life; Cardiovascular Disease; Chronic Illness, Adulthood and Later Life; Diabetes, Adulthood and Later Life; End of Life Decision-Making; Health Differentials/Disparities, Later Life; Hospice and Palliative Care; Long-term Care; Policy, Later Life Well-Being.*

### BIBLIOGRAPHY

Agency for Healthcare Research and Quality. (2002). *2005 National healthcare disparities report.* Rockville, MD.

Andersen, R., Kravits, J., & Anderson, O. W. (Eds.) (1975). *Equity in health services: Empirical analyses in social policy.* Cambridge, MA: Ballinger Publishing.

Anderson, G., & Horvath, J. (2004). The growing burden of chronic diseases in America. *Public Health Reports, 119,* 263–270.

Carr, D. S., & Khodyakov, D (2007). Health care proxies in later life: Whom do we choose and why? *Journal of Health and Social Behavior 48*(2), 180–194.

Cherry, D. K., Woodwell, D. A., & Rechtsteiner, E. A. (2007). *National Ambulatory Medical Care Survey: 2005 Summary.* (Advance data from vital and health statistics; No. 387.) Hyattsville, MD: National Center for Health Statistics.

Cockerham, W. C. (2001). Medical sociology and sociological theory. In W. C. Cockerham (Ed.) *The Blackwell companion to medical sociology.* Malden, MA: Blackwell.

Eckenwiler, L. (2007). *Caring about long-term care: An ethical framework for caregiving.* Center for American Progress. Retrieved April 9, 2008, from http://www.americanprogress.org/issues/2007/07/caregiving_report.html

Gillum, B. S., Graves, E. J., & Wood, E. (1998). *National Hospital Discharge Survey: Annual summary, 1995.* Hyattsville, MD: National Center for Health Statistics.

Hartman, M., Catlin, A., Lassman, D., Cylus, J., & Heffler, S. (2007, November). U.S. spending, by age, selected years through 2004. *Health Affairs Web Exclusive,* W1–W12. Retrieved April 9, 2008, from http://www.cms.hhs.gov/NationalHealthExpendData/

Jha, A. K., Fisher, E. S., Li, Z., Orav, E. J., & Epstein, A.M. (2005). Racial trends in the use of major procedures among the elderly. *The New England Journal of Medicine, 353,* 683–691.

Kozak, L. J., DeFrances, C. J., & Hall, M. J. (2006). *National hospital discharge survey: 2004 Annual summary with detailed diagnosis and procedure data.* (Advance data from vital and health statistics; No. 162.) Hyattsville, MD: National Center for Health Statistics.

Kuh, D., & Ben-Shlomo, Y. (Eds.) 1997. *A life course approach to chronic disease epidemiology* (pp. 3–14). New York: Oxford University Press.

Levinsky, N. G., Yu, W., Ash, A., Moskowitz, M., Gazelle, G., Saynina, O., & Emanuel, E. J. (2001). Influence of age on medicare expenditures and medical care in the last year of life. *Journal of the American Medical Association, 286,* 1349–1355.

McWilliams, J. M., Meara, E., Zaslavsky, A. M., & Ayanian, J. Z. (2007a). Health of previously uninsured adults after acquiring Medicare coverage. *Journal of the American Medical Association, 298,* 2886–2894.

McWilliams, J. M., Meara, E., Zaslavsky, A. M., & Ayanian, J. Z. (2007b). Use of health services by previously uninsured Medicare beneficiaries. *New England Journal of Medicine, 357,* 143–153.

Mechanic, D. (1982). The epidemiology of illness behavior and its relationship to physical and psychological distress. In D. Mechanic (Ed.), *Symptoms, Illness Behavior, and Help-Seeking* (pp. 1-24). New York: PRODIST.

National Center for Health Statistics. (2007). *Health, United States, 2007 with chart book on trends in health of Americans.* Hyattsville, MD: Author. Retrieved April 9, 2008, from http://www.cdc.gov/nchs/data/hus/hus07.pdf

Rice, D. P., & Fineman, N. (2004). Economic implications of increased longevity in the United States. *Annual Review of Public Health, 25,* 457–473.

Rowe, J. W., & Kahn, R. L. (1998). *Successful aging.* New York: Pantheon Books.

Russell, L. B., Ibuka, Y., & Abraham, K. B. 2007. Health-related activities in the American time use survey. *Medical Care, 45,* 680–685.

Schoen, R. F., Martin L. G., Andreski, P. M., & Freedman, V. A. (2005). Persistent and growing socioeconomic disparities in disability among the elderly: 1982-2002. *American Journal of Public Health, 95,* 2065–2070.

Smedley, B. D., Stith, A. Y., & Nelson, A. R. (Eds.) 2003. *Unequal treatment: Confronting racial and ethnic disparities in health care.* Washington, DC: National Academies Press.

Trivedi, A. N., Zaslavsky, A. M., Schneider, E. D., & Ayanian, J. Z. (2005). Trends in the quality of care and racial disparities in Medicare managed care. *The New England Journal of Medicine, 353,* 692–700.

U.S. Census Bureau. (2008). *Statistical abstract of the United States* (127th ed.) Washington, DC: U.S. Government Printing Office.

U.S. Department of Health and Human Services. (1985, August). *Black and Minority Health: Report of the Secretary's Task Force,* Vol. 1, *Executive Summary.* Retrieved April 9, 2008, from http://eric.ed.gov

Vaccarino, V., Rathore, S. S., Wenger, N. K., Frederick, P. D., Abramson, J. L., Barron, H. V., et al., for the National Registry of Myocardial Infarction Investigators. (2005). Sex and racial differences in the management of acute myocardial infarction, 1994 through 2002. *The New England Journal of Medicine, 353,* 671–682.

***Louise B. Russell***
***Dorothy P. Rice***

# HEALTH DIFFERENTIALS/ DISPARITIES, LATER LIFE

This entry provides a general overview of health disparities occurring in later life, among persons 65 years of age and older. By definition, health disparities are differences in health status among subgroups of the population. They typically refer to the higher rates of disease and mortality experienced by racial and ethnic minorities, and the economically disadvantaged. The World Health Organization (WHO) views health disparities as unjust when they represent conditions that are preventable and avoidable, and which result from inequities in social and economic resources. This entry focuses primarily on health disparities among older African Americans and describes the factors contributing to the health conditions they disproportionately face. The entry reviews data on the major health disparities and the explanations used to understand health disparities, and discusses strategies and interventions used to reduce these health differentials.

## HEALTH DISPARITIES AMONG OLDER MINORITIES

While the overall population of persons 65 and older is growing, the expanding numbers of older minorities comprise a significant segment. According to 2006 U.S. Census data, persons 65 and older numbered 37.3 million with older African Americans comprising 8.3% of this population in the United States, older Hispanics comprising 6.4%, and older Asian Pacific Islanders comprising 3.1%. Less than 1% of older adults were Native Alaskan or American Indian in 2006 (Administration on Aging, 2007a). By the year 2050, it is projected that the older African-American population will increase to 12% of those 65 and older, while older Hispanics will account for 18% and Asians 8% of the elderly population (Federal Interagency Forum, 2008). Contributing to this increase in the older minority population are the higher minority birth rates coupled with improved survival, immigration, the aging population of minority baby boomers, and a substantial increase in the numbers of the oldest old (e.g., those who are 85 years of age and older).

Life expectancy has increased for older racial and ethnic minorities throughout the 20th century. Nonetheless, older Whites can expect to live longer than other racial and ethnic groups. Life expectancy at birth is 68.2 years for African-American men and 74.9 years for African-American women (Arias, 2002). In contrast, older Whites have greater life expectancy at birth: 74.8 years for males and 80.0 years for females. The lower life expectancy at birth is due to the higher rates of infant mortality among African Americans as well as elevated mortality risks during the teen and young adult years, especially for Black men. However, for African Americans surviving to age 65, the gap in life expectancy narrows. At age 65, African-American men and women can expect to live another 15.2 and 18.6 years, respectively (Administration on Aging, 2007a). At age 85 and beyond, the racial gap in life expectancy disappears; older African Americans at this point may have a similar or better life expectancy than older Whites. This mortality crossover at the oldest ages is well-documented (Arias, 2002). Some researchers contend that the racial crossover in mortality results from inaccuracies in data, such as a tendency of older Blacks to overstate their age on surveys (Preston et al., 1996). Conversely, others posit that it reflects the *survival of the fittest* doctrine—that those individuals who withstand early life adversities, such as socioeconomic disadvantage and the threats of illness and crime victimization, yet who still survive until age 65, may be particularly robust and thus survive until very late life (Johnson, 2000).

Race and class disparities are not only apparent in life expectancy data; similar disparities are documented for many chronic health conditions. For example, the proportion of persons diagnosed with hypertension among older African Americans was 68.4% in 2002 and 2003 compared to 45.0% for Hispanics and 49.7% for Whites. Arthritis also had the highest prevalence among older African Americans (53.4%), followed by Whites (48.4%) and Hispanics (42.6%). Diabetes was highest among African Americans (24.5%) and Hispanics (21.9%) and lowest for Whites (14.9%). Similarly, stroke prevalence was highest for African Americans (9.6%) and lower for Whites (8.6%) and Hispanics (8.0%). Cancer and heart disease each have higher prevalence among older Whites, but the mortality risk for these conditions is greater for older racial and ethnic minorities. Specifically with regard to leading causes of death, rates for older African Americans and Hispanics exceed those of Whites for heart disease (32.0%, 32.4%, 31.8%, respectively), cancer (22.7%, 21.0%, 21.5%, respectively), stroke (8.3%, 7.4%, 7.9%, respectively), and diabetes (5.0%, 6.3%, 2.4%, respectively) (Centers for Disease Control, 2007). The rates of HIV and AIDS among persons 50 years and older were also higher among racial and ethnic minorities than Whites. In addition, many older racial and ethnic minorities have more chronic health conditions compared to Whites.

Other health indicators provide additional evidence of health disparities faced by older minorities, and underscore the ways that health disparities affect the daily lives of older adults. Physically unhealthy days is an indicator of the number of days in the past month where poor physical health kept an individual from doing usual activities, performing basic self-care tasks, working, or participating in recreational activities. According to the Behavioral Risk Factor Survey, the number of physically unhealthy days in the past month averaged 6.8 for older African Americans and 6.6 for Hispanics, compared to 5.5 for Whites (Centers for Disease Control, 2007). In addition, older African Americans are more likely than Whites to have disabilities, and the proportion reporting such disabilities increase with increasing age and with decreasing socioeconomic status. Data also indicate that 11.1% of African Americans needed help from others with personal care in comparison to 5.3% for Whites and 8.1% for Hispanics (National Center for Health Statistics, 2007a).

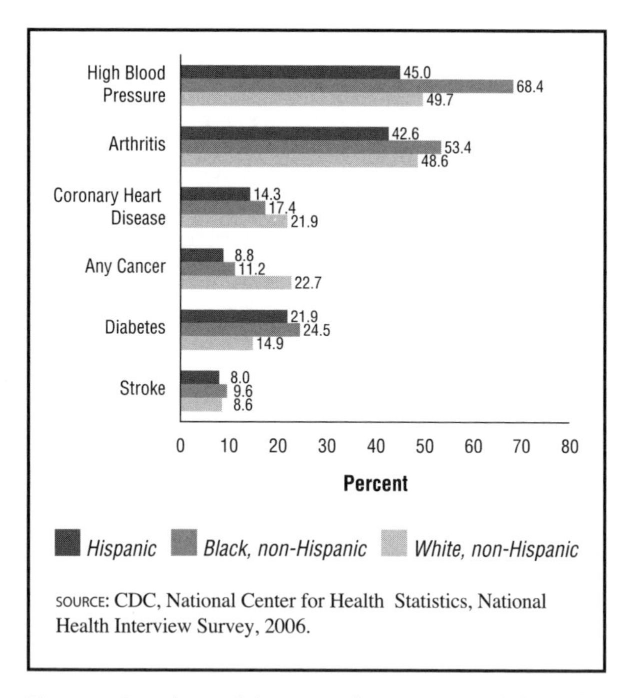


***Figure 1.*** *Prevalence of chronic conditions among adults aged 65 years or older varied by race/ethnicity in 2002–2003.* CENGAGE LEARNING, GALE.

## EXPLAINING HEALTH DISPARITIES CAUSES AND CONTRIBUTING FACTORS

While biological and genetic factors may influence predisposition to disease and mortality, definitive scientific knowledge is lacking on how social and physical environment interface with biology to produce health disparities. Contemporary approaches for understanding health disparities tend to focus on the broader historical, socioeconomic, and cultural factors. John Capitman and associates (2005) contend that these factors both determine the complex and interrelated meanings of social location (race or ethnicity, gender, social class, region, and community) and shape the resources and environments that influence health. For older minorities, health disparities stem from their social location as a minority group, which in turn influences the socioeconomic resources available to them, the social and physical environments in which they live, the health behaviors in which they engage, and their access to quality health care for prevention and treatment of illness and disease. A life course perspective underscores the importance of understanding how circumstances occurring earlier in life have a cumulative impact on health status later in life. Specifically, the major factors contributing to health disparities are cumulative lifetime and current availability of social and economic resources needed for maintaining good health in American society; exposure to toxic physical and social environments; tobacco and alcohol use, eating habits, and amount of physical activity; and access to quality medical care.

## SOCIAL AND ECONOMIC RESOURCES

Numerous studies have documented the important relationship between socioeconomic status and health, with lower socioeconomic status contributing to poorer health outcomes. Socioeconomic status is typically measured by income and wealth, education, and occupation, and is associated with the availability of resources to meet one's daily needs and desires. Lower socioeconomic status increases vulnerability to health risks such as exposure to poor housing and toxic environments, inability to pay for health costs, and lack of knowledge of health resources and health-promoting behaviors. For older racial and ethnic minorities, historical and current patterns of racial and ethnic discrimination have resulted in reduced availability of social and economic resources later in life (Capitman et al., 2005).

As a measure of socioeconomic status, educational attainment among older minorities has increased significantly over the past 4 decades in response to federal and state legislation, as well as local policies and programs that have expanded educational opportunities. Nonetheless, the level of educational attainment levels of older minorities lag behind that of older Whites. Data from 2007 show that 58% of older African Americans and 42% of older Hispanics had finished high school compared to 81% of older Whites (Federal Interagency Forum, 2008). Moreover, 10% of older African Americans and 9% of older Hispanics in 2007 had earned a bachelor's degree or higher, compared to 21% of older Whites (Federal Interagency Forum, 2008). Labor force participation rates do not vary significantly by race and ethnicity among those 65 and older; in 2003 17.0% of African-American men, 18.7 % of White men, and 17.4% of Hispanic men in this age group were in the labor force. Similarly among women 65 and older, rates of labor force participation in 2003 were 10.3% for African Americans, 10.8% for Whites, and 9.4% for Hispanics (He et al., 2005). These data, however, do not reveal racial or ethnic differences in the type or quality of jobs that adults held during their working lives. The data also fail to capture the numbers of older persons who continue to work in household, child care, and other low-wage service jobs that racial and ethnic minorities are apt to hold.

Among all older persons heading households in 2006, Whites had a median income of $41,091, compared to $30,775 for African Americans, $43,035 for Asians, and $29,385 for Hispanics (Administration on Aging, 2007a). Older African Americans (23%) and Hispanics (19%) were more likely than older Whites (8%) to live in poverty, with poverty circumstances varying by gender (Federal Interagency Forum, 2008). In particular, older African-American women were more likely to live in poverty than African-American men, with poverty being more severe for those living alone. Significant racial gaps exist in household net worth encompassing not only income, but also real estate, stocks, bonds, and other assets exclusive of debt. The median household net worth in 2005 for older Whites ($226,900) was more than 6 times that of older African Americans ($37,800). The largest share of income for African Americans 65 and older tends to come from Social Security benefits, which provides income to 82.6% of African Americans in this age group (Wu, 2007).

## PHYSICAL AND SOCIAL ENVIRONMENTS

Where one lives and with whom one lives are additional factors associated with health disparities. Research shows that life expectancy varies by community of residence and the degree of racial concentration. Christopher Murray and colleagues (2006) found that in communities where African Americans comprise the majority population, life expectancy was lower than in communities where the population was largely White. Additional research has examined the association between neighborhoods and health status. Specifically, residing in neighborhoods with few social and economic resources along with exposure to poor housing, crime, and violence contributes to the self-reported health differentials between older African Americans and Whites. Residing in a more affluent neighborhood contributes positively to self-rated health, even after adjusting for one's personal economic resources (Cagney et al., 2005).

Household living arrangements vary by gender and have ramifications for health status in terms of availability of economic resources and social support. Reflecting the gender gap in longevity, 52% of older African-American men in 2006 were most likely to live with their spouse, 18% with other relatives, 4% with nonrelatives, while 26% were most likely to live alone. In comparison, among African-American women, only 23% lived with their spouse, 34% with other relatives, 2% with nonrelatives, while 42% lived alone (Administration on Aging, 2007b). These gender differences in living arrangements result from women's greater likelihood of becoming widowed. They also reflect older men's higher mortality risk and their greater likelihood of remarrying once they are widowed. A multicultural survey of older persons indicated that older African Americans are more likely than other older subgroups to live in multigenerational households and to say that they will care for their grandchildren or aging parents (American Association of Retired Persons, 2001). While living in multigenerational households may bring the advantages of shared resources and social support, such arrangements across the life course may also diminish one's health status through the stress associated with limited financial resources and family caregiving.

Poorer health status among older African Americans, as compared to older Whites, may also be linked to differences in marital status. Among persons 65 and older, African Americans are the least likely to be married because of the lower numbers of marriageable men resulting from high rates of mortality, incarceration, and lower incomes. Marriage provides a protective effect on health, because spouses (particularly wives) monitor each other's health behaviors, such as diet and medication compliance. As such, married people have lower mortality rates than unmarried people at all ages, and the survival advantage of marriage is larger for men. Among persons ages 65 to 74, the death rate per 100,000 for never-married people was 4,029.6, compared with 2,351.4 for ever-married people. Further, among people who had ever married, death rates of currently married people were lower than the rates for the divorced or widowed (He et al., 2005).

## MODIFIABLE HEALTH RISK BEHAVIORS

Health behaviors contribute significantly to poor health outcomes, and a lifetime of poor health behaviors increases risk for disease and a shorter life expectancy. A particular health threat to African-American women is obesity, which increases one's risk for a range of diseases including type 2 diabetes, hypertension, heart disease and stroke, and some cancers. Among White women 20 years and older, 58.7% were overweight, which includes those who were obese, in comparison to 79.1% of African-American women and 71.4% of Mexican-American women. Among men however, African Americans are the least overweight (66.3%), followed by White men (71.6%) and Mexican-American men (71.8%) (National Center for Health Statistics, 2007b). Maintaining a healthy body weight is related to physical activity and balanced nutrition. Data show that a lower proportion of African Americans (21.2%) and Hispanics (20.0%) engage in regular leisure time activity, relative to Whites (31.6%) (National Center for Health Statistics, 2007b). Additional data indicate that older African Americans (25%) and older Hispanics (26%) are also less likely than their White (31%) counterparts to eat the recommended five or more servings of fruits and vegetables daily (Centers for Disease Control, 2007). Healthy eating and physical fitness practices may reflect cultural and personal preferences as well as reduced access to high-quality, affordable foods and safe spaces for recreation and physical activity in many minority neighborhoods.

## DIFFERENTIAL ACCESS AND QUALITY OF HEALTH CARE

The disparities in health status found among older racial and ethnic minorities reflect, in part, differential access and quality of health care throughout their life span. These health care disparities are troubling given that older persons are eligible for health care coverage through the government-sponsored Medicare program. In 2006, the majority (94%) of persons 65 and older were covered by Medicare (Agency for Health Care Research and Quality, 2008). Despite Medicare coverage, access and utilization of health care systems are also shaped by geographical proximity to health care facilities and having access to transportation. Further, in many instances, Medicare-covered health services require co-pays for care and prescription medication. Research shows that elderly racial and ethnic minorities are more likely to delay receiving health care assistance because of these direct and indirect costs, even though they were covered by Medicare (Agency for Health Care Research and Quality, 2008).

Health disparities in later life also stem from the poorer quality of care received by racial and ethnic minorities, as documented in the 2003 landmark report, *Unequal Treatment*, for the Institute of Medicine by Brian Smedley and colleagues. Additional research by Jose Escarce and Thomas McGuire (2004) found that White Medicare beneficiaries were twice as likely as African Americans to receive coronary artery bypass surgery and were about twice as likely to receive nonsurgical revascularization. In another study, Dorothy Dunlop and colleagues (2008) documented lower rates of arthritis-related hip and knee surgeries among older African Americans, while Douglas Keith and colleagues (2008) found that older minorities and those with low education had less access to kidney transplantation Other studies have noted differential quality of health care associated with hospitals and the racial characteristics of their patients. Hospitals with high volumes of elderly African-American patients provided poorer quality care for patients with acute myocardial infarction and pneumonia and had a higher rate of mortality after heart attacks than did hospitals with predominantly older White patients (Jha et al., 2007).

The underlying reasons for the differences in health care quality for older minorities in America are not completely understood, although racial discrimination by health care providers is cited as one possible explanation. In other instances, health care providers in hospitals serving predominantly minority populations are less likely to be board certified and may lack the resources, equipment, and technology necessary for provision of quality care.

Utilization of available health care by older racial and ethnic minorities is also apt to be influenced by cultural factors as well as past experiences of discrimination in the health care system. Older African Americans, in particular, are apt to be familiar with the historical patterns of racial segregation and discrimination that affected all sectors of society, including health care, and in many instances continue to do so. Nancy Keating and associates (2004) note that African Americans are less likely to report confidence and trust in their specialty physician than Whites. In examining health services utilization among older African Americans, Ronica Rooks and Diane Brown (2008) found that older African Americans were less likely than their White counterparts to express trust in hospitals or in heath care professionals, and were less likely to believe that African Americans receive the same quality of care as Whites.

## CLOSING THE HEALTH STATUS GAP

The four major categories of factors contributing to health disparities described above also give rise to opportunities for reducing and ultimately eliminating health disparities experienced by older racial and ethnic minorities. Efforts target modifiable health behaviors such as improving nutrition, increasing physical activity, and reducing cigarette smoking. Other efforts focus on improving health literacy among older persons, motivating them to take part in regular screenings and health-promotion activities, assisting them with disease management, and encouraging their participation in clinical research. Barriers to accessing quality health care are addressed through programs that offer transportation, reduce the costs of prescription drugs, coordinate patient navigation, provide cultural competence in health care settings, and increase racial and ethnic diversity in the health professions workforce. Additional programs aim to reduce the impact of poor housing and toxic neighborhood environments on health in later life. However, while many of these efforts have been successful in their specific settings, widespread adoption and sustainability are lacking. Efforts are needed to reach racial and ethnic minorities with the necessary resources early in life to develop and maintain good health, so that health disparities do not evolve later in life. Most important, a national agenda is needed to address the broader social and economic issues that are largely responsible for health disparities occurring across the life span.

**SEE ALSO** Volume 3: *Genetic Influences, Later Life; Health Care Use, Later Life; Life Expectancy; Neighborhood Context, Later Life; Poverty, Later Life.*

**BIBLIOGRAPHY**


Administration on Aging. (2007a). *A profile of older Americans: 2007.* Washington, DC: U.S. Department of Health and Human Services. Retrieved June 12, 2008, from http://www.aoa.gov/prof/Statistics/profile/2007/2007profile.pdf

Administration on Aging. (2007b). *A statistical profile of Black older Americans aged 65 plus.* Washington, DC: U.S. Department of Health and Human Services. Retrieved June 12, 2008, from http://www.aoa.dhhs.gov/press/prodsmats/fact/pdf/Facts-on-Black-Elderly2008.doc

Agency for Health Care Research and Quality. (2008). *2007 National health care and disparities reports.* Rockville, MD: U.S. Department of Health and Human Services. Retrieved June 12, 2008, from http://www.ahrq.gov/qual/qrdr07.htm

American Association of Retired Persons. (2001). *In the middle: A report on multicultural boomers coping with family and aging issues.* Washington, DC: Belden, Russonello, & Stewart. Retrieved June 12, 2008, from http://assets.aarp.org/rgcenter/il/in_the_middle.pdf

Arias, E. (2002). United States life tables, 2000. *National Vital Statistics Report, 51*(3). Retrieved June 12, 2008, from http://www.cdc.gov/nchs/data/nvsr/nvsr51/nvsr51_03.pdf

Cagney, K.A., Browning, C.R., & Wen, M. (2005). Racial disparities in self-rated health at older ages: What difference does the neighborhood make? *Journals of Gerontology, Series B: Psychological Sciences and Social Sciences, 60*(4), 181–190.

Capitman, J.A., Bhalotra, S., & Ruwe, M. (2005). *Cancer and elders of color: Opportunities for reducing health disparities.* Burlington, VT: Ashgate.

Centers for Disease Control and the Merck Company Foundation. (2007). *The state of aging and health in America, 2007.* Whitehouse Station, NJ. Retrieved June 12, 2008, from http://www.cdc.gov/aging/pdf/saha_2007.pdf

Dunlop, D.D., Manheim, L.M., Song, J., Sohn, M.W., Feinglass, J.M., Chang, H.J., et al. (2008). Age and racial/ethnic disparities in arthritis-related hip and knee surgeries. *Medical Care, 46*(2), 200–208.

Escarce, J.J., & McGuire, T.G. (2004). Changes in racial differences in use of medical procedures and diagnostic tests among elderly persons: 1986–1997. *American Journal of Public Health, 94*(10), 1795–1799.

Federal Interagency Forum on Aging-Related Statistics. (2008). *Older Americans 2008: Key indicators of well-being.* Washington, DC: U.S. Government Printing Office.

He, W., Sengupta, M., Velkoff, V.A., & DeBarros, K.A. (2005). *65 plus in the United States: 2005.* Washington, DC: U.S. Government Printing Office.

Jha, A.K., Orav, E.J., Li, Z., & Epstein, A.M. (2007). Concentration and quality of hospitals that care for elderly Black patients. *Archives of Internal Medicine, 167*(11), 1177–1182.

Johnson, N.E. (2000). The racial crossover in comorbidity, disability, and mortality. *Demography, 37*(3), 267–283.

Keating, N.L., Gandhi, T.K., Orav, E.J., Bates, D.W., & Ayanian, J.Z. (2004). Patient characteristics and experiences associated with trust in specialist physicians. *Archives of Internal Medicine, 164*(9), 1015–1020.

Keith, D., Ashby, V.B., Port, F.K., & Leichtman, A.B. (2008). Insurance type and minority status associated with large disparities in prelisting dialysis among candidates for kidney transplantation. *Clinical Journal of the American Society of Nephrology, 3*(2), 463–470.

Murray, C.J., Kulkarni, S.C., Michaud, C., Tomijima, N., Bulzacchelli, M.T., Iandiorio, T.J., et al. (2006). Eight Americas: Investigating mortality disparities across races, counties, and race-counties in the United States. *Public Library of Science Medicine, 3*(9), 260.

National Center for Health Statistics. (2007a). *Early release of selected estimates based on data from the 2006 National Health Interview Survey.* Retrieved June 12, 2008, from http://www.cdc.gov/nchs/about/major/nhis/released200706.htm

National Center for Health Statistics. (2007b). *Health, United States, 2007: With chartbook on trends in the health of Americans.* Hyattsville, MD. Retrieved June 12, 2008, from http://ncbi.nlm.nih.gov/books/bv.fcgi?rid=healthus07.TOC

Preston, S.H., Elo, I.T., Rosenwaike, I., & Hill, M. (1996). African-American mortality at older ages: Results of a matching study. *Demography, 33*(2), 193–209.

Rooks, R., & Brown, D.R. (2008). *Perceived discrimination and mistrust among middle-aged and older African Americans and Whites in the U.S. health care system: The Cancer Attitudes and Awareness Study.* Manuscript under review.

Smedley, B.D., Stith, A.Y., & Nelson, A.R. (Eds.). (2003). *Unequal treatment: Confronting racial and ethnic disparities in health care.* Washington, DC: National Academies Press.

Wu, K.B. (2007). *African Americans age 65 and older: Their sources of retirement income in 2005.* Washington, DC: American Association of Retired Persons Public Policy Institute. Retrieved June 12, 2008, from http://assets.aarp.org/ rgcenter/econ/fs137_aaincome.pdf


*Diane R. Brown*

# HEALTH LITERACY

Health literacy is critical for understanding the challenges facing older adults' ability to navigate the health care system and is increasingly important as health care systems place greater responsibility on patients to manage their own health care. Health literacy measures help identify patients at risk for inadequate health care and guide development of interventions to improve their outcomes. Thus they are essential for understanding and addressing disparities in health care resource utilization and outcomes associated with age and other demographic variables.

Health literacy has been conceptualized in several ways. A common definition focuses on individuals' abilities: "the capacity to obtain, process, and understand basic health information and services needed to make appropriate health decisions" (U.S. Department of Health and Human Services, 2000). These abilities include skills required to read text, interpret complex documents such as insurance forms, and understand and manipulate numbers (often referred to as *numeracy*). Health knowledge relevant to understanding health information is sometimes included in the definition of health literacy (Baker, 2006). Health literacy is also closely linked with education, in part because core literacy skills are systematically imparted during schooling. However, there is general agreement that health literacy is not reducible to educational attainment, especially for older adults because of their many years of literacy-related experiences after formal schooling (Baker et al., 2007). Health literacy is also related to more general cognitive abilities such as working memory, in part because language comprehension processes (e.g., word recognition, drawing inferences) depend heavily on these abilities. The finding that performance on standard health literacy measures is predicted by performance on general cognitive measures (Levinthal et al., in press) provides evidence for this assertion.

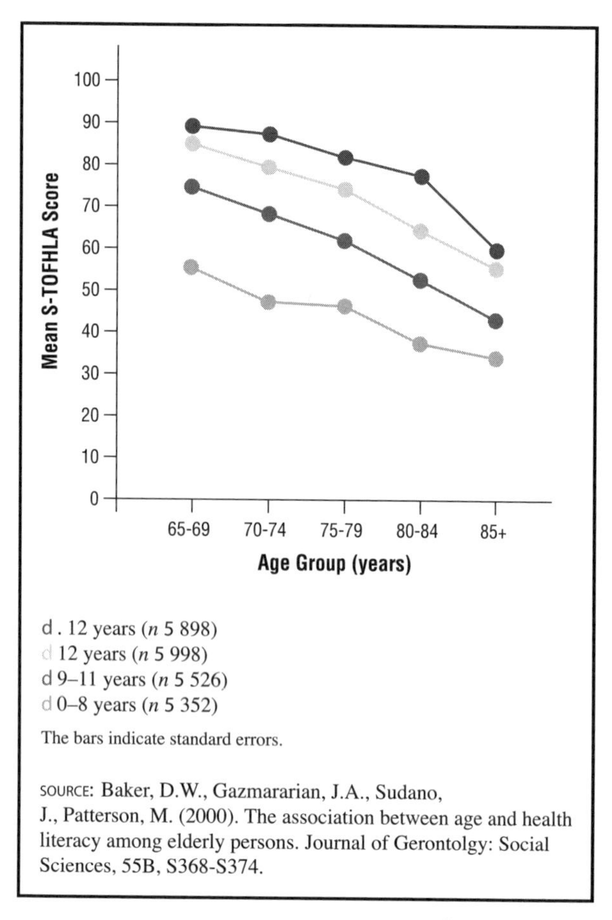


SOURCE: Baker, D.W., Gazmararian, J.A., Sudano, J., Patterson, M. (2000). The association between age and health literacy among elderly persons. Journal of Gerontolgy: Social Sciences, 55B, S368-S374.

***Figure 1.*** *Mean scores on the Short Test of Functional Health Literacy in Adults for five age groups, stratified according to years of school completed.* CENGAGE LEARNING, GALE.

Health literacy has also been defined functionally, as the relationship between an individual's abilities on the one hand and the demands placed on these abilities by specific health care contexts on the other (Nielsen-Bohlman, Panzer, & Kindig, 2004). According to this view, even highly skilled readers may experience low health literacy when confronted with complex or unfamiliar health tasks. Functional approaches often take a broader view of the resources that individuals bring to health care tasks, including community-level factors such as social networks (Nielsen-Bohlman et al., 2004).

Although health literacy is conceptualized in different ways, measures of health literacy focus on individual-level abilities, perhaps because these relatively stable abilities are easier to measure than dynamic functional relationships between abilities and context (Baker, 2006). Perhaps most common is the Rapid Estimate of Adult Literacy in Medicine (REALM), which measures the ability to pronounce medically related words varying in complexity (Davis et al., 1993). Performance on this test is assumed to be a proxy for a larger set of comprehension and reasoning processes that define health literacy. The Test of Functional Health Literacy in Adults (TOFHLA; Baker, Williams, Parker, Gazmararian, & Nurss, 1999) is more directly related to health literacy abilities because it measures comprehension of actual health documents (by means of a cloze procedure, which involves filling in missing words in the texts). Other approaches take a more comprehensive approach to measuring literacy skills. The Health Activities Literacy Scale, based on the National Adult Literacy Survey, sampled a wide range of texts that serve a variety of purposes (health promotion, prevention, treatment) and ordered them in terms of processing difficulty to be broadly representative of health literacy demands (Rudd, 2007). Other measures are designed for practical rather than research purposes, such as identifying patients with inadequate literacy in clinical contexts. The Newest Vital Sign is a brief assessment of how well patients understand a nutrition label that focuses on numeracy skills. It functions well as a screening instrument but is less likely to predict health outcomes compared to the Short Test of Functional Health Literacy in Adults (STOFHLA; see Baker, 2006).

Estimates based on these measures suggest that about half of the U.S. population has less than adequate health-related literacy (difficulty finding, understanding, or reasoning about basic health information). The proportion of adults with less than adequate health literacy increases with age and is higher for African American and Hispanic middle-age and older adults compared to non-Hispanic White or Asian adults (Paasche-Orlow et al., 2005). These differences may partly reflect differences in health status (e.g., African American adults are more likely than White Americans to have some chronic conditions), as well as differences in the amount or quality of educational attainment. Age-related differences in health literacy also reflect age-related differences in general cognitive abilities, which may impair comprehension processes (Levnithal et al., in press). Finally, elderly immigrants may face special challenges related to health literacy because of limited English proficiency and perhaps limited education in their native language.

Differences in health literacy are associated with health-related knowledge, self-care behaviors, and health outcomes, especially among older adults. Older adults with lower health literacy know less about their illness and treatments (Gazmararian, Williams, Peel, & Baker, 2003), which may partly reflect poor comprehension of health information conveyed by documents such as medication instructions (Davis et al., 2006) and health care providers (Schillinger et al., 2003). They also tend to be less successful at taking medication (Gazmararian et al., 2006), and, perhaps not surprisingly, they tend to have worse health outcomes such as increased hospitalization (for review, see DeWalt et al., 2004) and even mortality (Baker, 2007).

There is great interest in improving health behaviors and outcomes among older adults with low health literacy. This goal requires understanding why older adults have trouble navigating the health care system. Perhaps the most common approach has been to simplify health information provided to patients with low health literacy in order to address the well-documented gap between the difficulty of health documents (e.g., medication instructions, consent forms) and patients' average reading skills (McCray, 2005). Difficulty is usually measured by readability formulae that summarize word and sentence length, and sometimes word frequency, so this strategy usually involves using short, common words. However, improving document readability has had only limited success in improving comprehension among low-literacy adults, perhaps because this strategy does not address dimensions of text such as information organization and familiarity that are known to influence comprehension (McCray, 2005).

Pictorials and other visual-graphic media are also used to support comprehension (usually augmenting text) because they reduce the need for reading processes such as recognizing words. If more explicit than text, pictures also reduce the need to draw inferences to understand the text. However, the evidence for pictorial benefits among older adults with low health literacy is mixed (Houts, Doak, Doak, & Loscalzo, 2006).

The studies on improving health documents suggests the need for research that is guided by theories that integrate health literacy with theories of language comprehension and cognitive aging to identify what comprehension processes are impaired among older adults with low health literacy and how interventions can support these processes.

Communication between health care providers and their patients with low health literacy has also been addressed to improve provider/patient concordance (agreement) about self-care goals and plans for accomplishing these goals. "Teachback" strategies, such as asking patients to demonstrate their understanding so that providers can check comprehension, have been proposed as an important method of improving patient comprehension. Routine use of these strategies has been recommended as a "universal precaution" because they may improve comprehension regardless of patients' literacy level, coupled with the fact that it is difficult to identify patients with low health literacy during clinical encounters (Paasche-Orlow, Schillinger, Greene, & Wagner, 2006). However, effects of these strategies on patient comprehension and outcomes have not been systematically investigated.

Multimedia approaches to improving both written and spoken communication to patients have been included as part of multifaceted patient education interventions to improve health behaviors and outcomes among diverse patients (Murray et al., 2007). These approaches have had some success in improving health outcomes for patients with lower health literacy skills, perhaps because multifaceted interventions address multiple dimensions of health literacy.

Information technology such as electronic medical records and web-based health services also has the potential to address multiple health literacy-related barriers to health care. Health information is increasingly available on public web sites and on portals provided by specific health care practices. Unfortunately, Internet-based information may be just as difficult to understand as printed sources of information because average readability often exceeds recommended grade levels (McCray, 2005). Information technology can also facilitate patients' access to tailored information, as well as support patient/provider communication by addressing barriers such as limited patient contact time. However, the impact of these systems on diverse patients is underinvestigated. In addition, because technology has been less accessible to patients from low socioeconomic backgrounds who are at risk for poor health literacy, it may increase disparities in health care associated with health literacy (McCray, 2005).

Finally, patients' literacy-related skills may be improved by adapting principles from adult literacy education, rather than designing environments to reduce demands on these skills (Nielson-Bohlman et al., 2004). Literacy training may provide more general benefits compared with design-based interventions to the extent that they improve literacy skills that patients can use across a variety of contexts. However, training programs are intensive and target relatively small groups of patients, whereas redesigned health information and services can be made available to many patients.

To summarize, health literacy has been conceptualized both as a set of individual abilities necessary to understand and use health-related information and more functionally as the relationship between patients' abilities and the demands on these abilities imposed by specific health contexts. The most common measures of health literacy focus on individual abilities, essentially measuring reading ability. Studies employing these measures have documented inadequate health literacy as a pervasive problem that is linked to a variety of important patient health behaviors and outcomes. There is a need for health literacy theories that are both more precise (specifying comprehension processes and how these depend on patient cognition and health knowledge) and more comprehensive (integrating community- as well as individual-level analyses of patient resources). Such theories will help specify pathways by which health literacy is linked to health behaviors and outcomes and guide more integrated approaches to improving health literacy among older adults. Particularly promising are community-based interventions that leverage health information technology to improve access to information and services.

SEE ALSO Volume 3: *Cognitive Function and Decline; Health Care Use, Later Life.*

### BIBLIOGRAPHY


Baker D. W. (2006). The meaning and the measure of health literacy. *Journal of General Internal Medicine, 21,* 878–883.

Baker, D. W., Williams, M. V., Parker, R. M., Gazmararian, J. A., & Nurss, J. (1999). Development of a brief test to measure functional health literacy. *Patient Education and Counseling, 38,* 33–42.

Baker, D.W., Wolf, M.S., Feinglass, J., Thompson, J.A., Gazmararian, J., & Huang, J. (2007). Health literacy and mortality among elder persons. *Archive of Internal Medicine, 167,* 1503–1509.

Davis, T. C., Long, S. W., Jackson, R. H., Mayeaux, E. J., George, R. B., Murphy, P.W., et al. (1993). Rapid estimate of adult literacy in medicine: A shortened screening instrument. *Family Medicine, 25,* 391–95.

Davis, T. C., Wolf, M. S., Bass, P. F., Middlebrooks, M., Kennen, E., Baker, D. W., et al. (2006). Low literacy impairs comprehension of prescription drug warning labels. *Journal of General Internal Medicine, 21,* 847–851.

DeWalt, D. A., Berkman, N. D., Sheridan, S., Lohr, K. N., & Pignone, M. P. (2004). Literacy and health outcomes: A systematic review of the literature. *Journal of General Internal Medicine, 19,* 1228–1239.

Gazmararian, J. A., Kripalani, S., Miller, M. J., Echt, K. V., Ren, J., & Rask, K. (2006). Factors associated with medication refill adherence in cardiovascular-related diseases: A focus on health literacy. *Journal of General Internal Medicine, 21,* 1215–1221.

Gazmararian, J. A., Williams, M. V., Peel, J., & Baker, D. W. (2003). Health literacy and knowledge of chronic illness. *Patient Education and Counseling, 51,* 267–275.

Houts, P. S., Doak, C. C., Doak, L. G., & Loscalzo, M. J. (2006). The role of pictures in improving health communication: A review of research on attention, comprehension, recall, and adherence. *Patient Education and Counseling, 61,* 173–190.

Levinthal, B. R., Morrow, D. G., Tu, W., Wu, J., Young, J., Weiner, M., et al. (in press). Cognition and health literacy in patients with hypertension. *Journal of General Internal Medicine.*

McCray, A. T. (2005). Promoting health literacy. *Journal of the American Medical Informatics Association, 12,* 152–163.

Murray, M. D., Young, J., Hoke, S., Tu, W., Weiner, M., Morrow, D. G., et al. (2007). Pharmacist intervention to improve medication adherence in heart failure: A randomized trial. *Annals of Internal Medicine, 146,* 714–725.

Nielsen-Bohlman, L., Panzer, A. M., & Kindig, D. A. (Eds.). (2004). *Health literacy: A prescription to end confusion.* Washington, DC: National Academies Press.

Paasche-Orlow, M. K., Parker, R. M., Gazmararian, J. A., Nielsen-Bohlman, L. T., & Rudd, R. R. (2005). The prevalence of limited health literacy. *Journal of General Internal Medicine, 20,* 1–10.

Paasche-Orlow, M. K., Schillinger, D., Greene, S. M., & Wagner, E. H. (2006). How health care systems can begin to address the challenge of limited literacy. *Journal of General Internal Medicine, 21,* 884–887.

Rudd, R. E. (2007). Health literacy skills of U.S. adults. *American Journal of Health Behavior, 31,* S8–S18.

Schillinger, D., Piette, J., Grumbach, K., Wang, F., Wilson, C., Daher, C., et al. (2003). Closing the loop: Physician communication with diabetic patients who have low health literacy. *Archives of Internal Medicine, 163,* 83–90.

U.S. Department of Health and Human Services. (2000). *Healthy people 2010: Understanding and improving health and objectives for improving health.* (2nd ed., 2 vols). Washington, DC: U.S. Government Printing Office.


***Daniel G. Morrow***

## HEARING LOSS

SEE Volume 3: *Sensory Impairments.*

# HOMELESS, LATER LIFE

SEE Volume 2: *Homeless, Adults.*

# HOSPICE AND PALLIATIVE CARE

Hospice and palliative care improves the quality of life of patients and their families who are affected by life-threatening illness by preventing and relieving suffering through pain and symptom relief, as well as by providing emotional, practical, and spiritual support.

## A BRIEF HISTORY OF THE MODERN HOSPICE AND PALLIATIVE CARE MOVEMENT

The modern hospice and palliative care movement can be traced back to Dame Cicely Saunders (1918–2005), who founded St. Christopher's Hospice in London in 1967. She was a nurse, who later trained as a social worker and eventually became a physician. Saunders began working with terminally ill patients in the 1940s and decided to make it her life's work to develop a better model of care for these individuals. In 1963 Saunders was invited to speak at Yale University, where she introduced the idea of holistic hospice care to a group of students and faculty. This new approach to end-of-life care focused on pain and symptom control for terminally ill patients. Using photographs, Saunders demonstrated the dramatic differences that she and her team were seeing in patients who were receiving hospice care. Following the presentation, Florence Wald (b. 1917), the dean of the Yale School of Nursing, invited Saunders to become a visiting faculty member at Yale—an invitation Saunders gladly accepted. Then, in 1968, Wald took a sabbatical to work at St. Christopher's Hospice and to gain firsthand experience with Saunders's new and innovative model of care.

In 1974 the Connecticut Hospice, the first hospice in the United States, was founded, followed shortly thereafter by an inpatient facility at Yale Medical Center. By the late 1970s hospice programs were being tested across the country in order to determine exactly what a hospice should be and what type of care it should provide. The first legislation establishing the Medicare hospice benefit, which allowed Medicare patients to choose hospice care in lieu of curative treatments if they had a prognosis of less than 6 months to live, was passed by the U.S. Congress in 1982 and made permanent in 1986. In the early 21st century, most states provide hospice care as part of their Medicaid programs, which was the catalyst for the significant growth in the number of hospices around the country. It was also during this time that hospices transitioned from grassroots, volunteer-based organizations into the more traditional health care model that is used today. In 2008 there were more than 4,500 hospices nationwide, including some that are part of larger health care systems and others that are independent, as well as both for-profit and nonprofit hospices. In addition, hospices service a variety of illnesses, are found in both large and small communities, and continue to strive to provide the best possible end-of-life care for terminally ill patients and their families.

## HOSPICE CARE AND PALLIATIVE CARE: WHAT THEY ARE AND WHY THEY ARE IMPORTANT

The National Hospice and Palliative Care Organization (NHPCO), which was originally the National Hospice Organization, was founded in 1978. The NHPCO is the largest nonprofit membership organization in the United States, representing both hospice and palliative care professionals and programs. This organization is dedicated to improving end-of-life care and increasing access to hospice care for all individuals, with the ultimate goal of dramatically improving quality of life for both the dying patient and his or her family caregivers. Because hospice care is truly a set of principles, rather than a simple construct, it can be rather difficult to define; however, author Stephen Connor (1998) offered this definition based on the work done by the NHPCO:

> [Hospice care is] a coordinated program providing palliative care to terminally ill patients and supportive services to patients, their families, and significant others 24 hours a day, seven days a week. Comprehensive/case managed services based on physical, social, spiritual, and emotional needs are provided during the last stages of illness, during the dying process, and during bereavement by a medically directed interdisciplinary team consisting of patients/families, health care professionals and volunteers. Professional management and continuity of care is maintained across multiple settings including homes, hospitals, long term care, and residential settings. (p. 184)

*Palliative care,* as defined by the NHPCO, is as follows:

> [Palliative care is] treatment that enhances comfort and improves the quality of an individual's life during the last phase of life.... no specific therapy is excluded from consideration.... the test of palliative care lies in the agreement between the individual, physician(s), primary caregiver, and the hospice team that the expected outcome is relief from distressing symptoms, the easing of pain, and/or the enhancing of quality of life.

Notice that the term *palliative care* is included in the definition of hospice care. This is because hospice care is considered one type of palliative care—one with the specific focus of providing comfort and a better quality of life for individuals near the end of their lives for whom cure is no longer an option. In a sense, these two terms are interchangeable for patients at the end of their lives; however, palliative care can be instituted at an earlier phase of the illness. In general, to qualify for hospice care, a patient must be certified as having a prognosis of less than 6 months to live; however, patients can choose to begin palliative treatments prior to becoming eligible for hospice care. Once a patient has been enrolled in hospice care, Medicare covers the cost of all services provided by the hospice including, but not limited to, nursing visits, medications, and medical equipment. Hospices are reimbursed by Medicare at a set rate per day—$135.11 for routine home care in 2008—and the average length of stay nationally is approximately 59 days (NHPCO, 2007). However, it is important to note that the median length of stay for patients enrolled in hospice is approximately 21 days and that this measure is considered a more accurate picture of the average hospice experience for patients and their families (NHPCO, 2007). Some regional differences have been seen in median length of stay in hospice, with Louisiana, Mississippi, Alabama, South Carolina, North Carolina, and New Mexico reporting on average a 30- to 45-day length of stay (Last Acts, 2002). Both hospice care and palliative care share a common philosophy that includes the following principles (Last Acts, 2002):

1. Respect for the choices of the dying person.
2. Attention to all aspects of the dying person's life, including spiritual, emotional, physical, psychological, and social needs.
3. Providing support for the family members of the patient.
4. Provision of health care by an interdisciplinary team in all care settings.
5. Striving to provide the best possible care at the end of life.

One reason for the increase in attention to the topics of hospice and palliative care is because of the reality that most deaths in the United States do not actually occur in the way that most people report they would like them to. Approximately 50% of all Americans die in hospitals, with their deaths often preceded by stays in intensive care units and numerous physician visits, whereas another 20 to 25% of Americans die in nursing homes, a proportion that is currently on the rise (Last Acts, 2002). This leaves approximately 25% of Americans who die at home, despite that more than 70% say that their home, where they can be surrounded by friends and family, is their preferred location of death (Last Acts, 2002). Additionally, research has shown that hospice care may prolong the lives of terminally ill patients. In the sample for one study (Connor, Pyenson, Fitch, Spence, & Iwasaki, 2007), hospice patients survived, on average, 29 days longer than nonhospice patients. Out of the six disease categories that were studied, four showed significant increases in survival time (the two groups that did not differ were breast and prostate cancer patients): (a) for congestive heart failure patients, survival time increased by 81 days; (b) for lung cancer patients, 39 days; (c) for pancreatic cancer patients, 21 days; and (d) for colon cancer patients, 33 days.

## THE ROLE OF FAMILIES IN HOSPICE AND PALLIATIVE CARE

Although it is beyond the scope of this entry to examine in detail the role of family caregivers for patients who are receiving hospice and palliative care services, it does merit some attention, especially because they play a critical role in the decision regarding whether to utilize these services. In one study (Chen, Haley, Robinson, & Schonwetter, 2003), patients with advanced cancer were surveyed on decision making in regard to hospice care. Whereas half of these patients reported that they were first introduced to hospice as a treatment option by a health care provider (e.g., physicians, nurses, and social workers), a surprising 20% indicated that it was a family member who initiated the discussion. This study also found that when it comes to making the final decision to obtain hospice care, family members were reported to make this decision in more than 40% of cases. Not surprisingly, Chen and colleagues found that the characteristic that most influenced who aided the patient in making the final decision about whether to enter hospice was their marital status: Patients who were married were more likely to have their families make the decision, whereas patients who were widowed, divorced, separated, or single tended to make the final decision for themselves.

It is important to mention the impact that providing care at the end of life can have on family members. Ezekiel Emanuel and colleagues (Emanuel et al., 1999; Emanuel, Fairclough, Slutsman, & Emanuel, 2000) conducted national studies that documented the high levels of assistance provided by family caregivers of terminally ill patients and the burdens experienced by those families in the context of terminal illnesses. They showed that burden and depression are higher in family caregivers of patients with substantial care needs regardless of the specific terminal illness, as compared to family caregivers of patients with lower levels of care needs. Consistent with this finding, another study (Haley, LaMonde, Han, Narramore, & Schonwetter, 2001) found that hospice caregivers for terminally ill patients with either lung cancer or dementia showed high rates of depression, lower life satisfaction, and poorer self-rated health than noncaregiving controls, with few differences in caregiver well-being across disease type. Haley and colleagues also found that many families report experiencing benefits from caregiving, such as a sense of satisfaction and feelings of closeness to their relatives.

One of the main tenets of hospice care is the continued support for the family caregivers provide after the death of the patient. The NHPCO (2007) reported that, on average, bereavement services are utilized by approximately two family members per hospice death. Additionally, in the year following the death of the patient, an average of seven contacts, including follow-up phone calls, visits, and mailings, are received by these family members. Roughly 94% of all hospices offer bereavement services to everyone in the community, regardless of whether their loved one used hospice services; community members who never had family enrolled into a hospice program accounted for approximately 17% of the individuals that utilize bereavement programs (NHPCO, 2007).

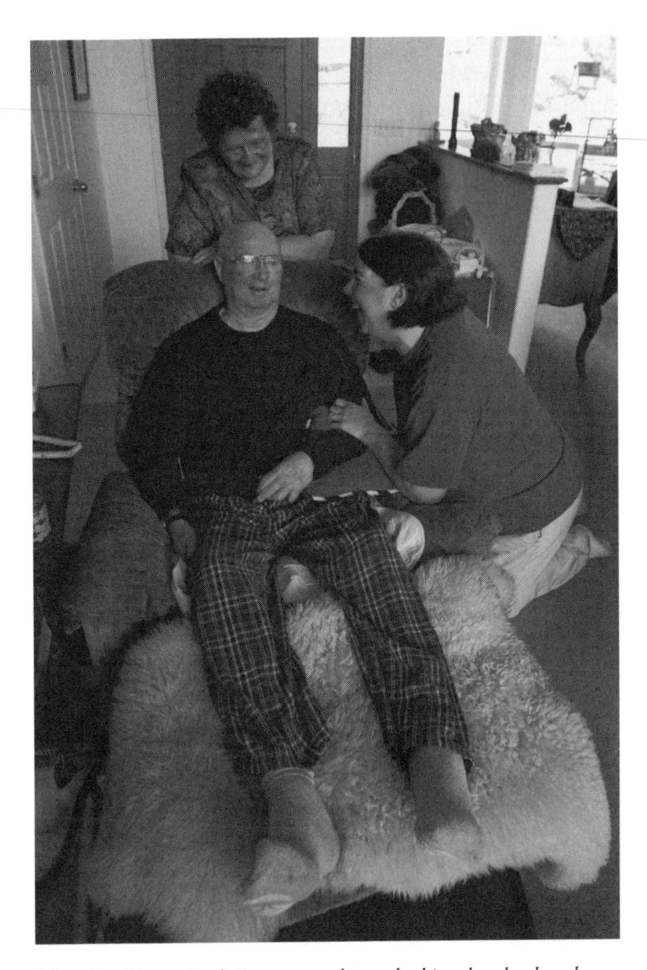

***Hospice Care.*** *Ruth Sauer stands overlooking her husband, Merle, as longtime caregiver Brigitte Webb shares a laugh with him in the Sauer's home. When he came home from the hospital after several bouts of pneumonia for what doctors said would be the last time, hospice care came home with them.* **AP IMAGES.**

## TRENDS IN HOSPICE AND PALLIATIVE CARE

There are some promising trends in the utilization of hospice and palliative care services, including, but not limited to, increased enrollment, location of death, patient diversity, program growth, and cost-effectiveness. The NHPCO (2007) reported that, in 2006, approximately 1.3 million patients received hospice services, which is a significant increase (162%) from approximately 495,000 in 1997. Furthermore, approximately 36% of all individuals who died in the United States in 2006 were enrolled in a hospice program (NHPCO, 2007).

As previously noted, there is a gap between where Americans would like to die and where most deaths actually occur, at home versus at a hospital. In the general population, approximately 50% of deaths occur in a hospital setting (Last Acts, 2002); however, this number is significantly reduced to only about 9% for individuals enrolled in a hospice care program (NHPCO, 2007). Additionally, 74.1% of hospice patients died in a setting that they identified as *home* (47.1% in a private residence, 22.5% in a nursing home, and 4.6% in a residential facility; NHPCO, 2007), as compared to approximately 50% of the general population (Last Acts, 2002). The remaining 17% of hospice patient deaths occurred in inpatient hospice facilities, which are typically a combination of acute and residential care and can be located either in stand-alone facilities or within a dedicated hospital space (NHPCO, 2007).

During the early days of the hospice movement in the United States, cancer patients accounted for the vast majority of hospice admissions, but in 2008 they made up only 44.1% of the hospice population (NHPCO, 2007). With the increase in deaths due to chronic illnesses in this country, the face of hospice care is beginning to change. In 2006 the primary diagnosis of all noncancer patients (55.9% of the total hospice population) under hospice care were heart disease (12.2%); debility unspecified or "failure to thrive" (11.8%); dementia, including Alzheimer's disease (10.0%); lung disease (7.7%); stroke or coma (3.4%); kidney disease (2.9%); motor neuron diseases (2.0%); liver disease (1.8%); HIV or AIDS (0.5%); and other diagnoses (3.7%; NHPCO, 2007). The inclusion of so many chronic illnesses into the hospice model of care has cleared the way for clinicians and researchers to examine the unique challenges each illness presents and how palliative care treatment options can be introduced and implemented in an aging population.

In 2007 almost 80% of hospice patients were over the age of 65 and approximately 33% were age 85 or older; both numbers are expected to increase as the baby boom generation continues to age (NHPCO, 2007). One study (Connor, Elwert, Spence, & Christakis, 2007), using the data from all Medicare beneficiaries age 65 and older who died in 2002, provided some important information on current hospice utilization trends. This study found that women were more likely to enroll in hospice care than their male counterparts (30% compared to 27%), that individuals who identified themselves as White used hospice services more frequently than individuals who identified themselves as Black (29% compared to 22%), and that, overall, 28.6% of older Americans use hospice services in their last year of life.

Although the utilization of hospice services by minority populations is still relatively low, research has demonstrated a slight increase (19.1% of the hospice population in 2006 compared to 17.8% in 2005) in these numbers, particularly in individuals who identify themselves as African American or multiracial (NHPCO, 2007). Many people believe that the underutilization of hospice services by minorities, particularly African Americans, is due to the distrust of the medical system; however, there is evidence to suggest that the issue is far more complicated. Research has suggested that cultural attitudes and preferences for aggressive treatment at the end of life as well as a lack of education at all levels within minority communities about hospice services are both barriers to the utilization of hospice care.

Ever since the first hospice opened in the United States, there has been tremendous growth in the number of hospice programs nationwide. In 2006 there were approximately 4,500 hospice and palliative care programs in existence nationwide. This is an increase of about 50% between 1997 and 2006, with the majority of this growth seen in small, independent hospices (NHPCO, 2007). The increase in the number of hospice and palliative care organizations, coupled with findings that the use of hospice services simultaneously saves money for Medicare (an average of $2,309 per hospice patient) and provides quality care to terminally ill patients and their families, indicates that this relatively young health care model should remain the gold standard in end-of-life care as the American population continues to age.

## THE FUTURE OF HOSPICE AND PALLIATIVE CARE

Although the number of minorities enrolled in hospice and palliative care programs is increasing slightly, this group should still be considered an underserved population that merits further examination. Additional research is needed in the areas of preferences for, and barriers to, the use of hospice and palliative care services for minorities and other medically underserved populations. This area of research should also consider the needs of the frail older population and residents of nursing homes, particularly those who do not have family caregivers involved in their care.

It is essential that the societal perception of hospice and palliative care programs remain an accurate reflection of the model of care that is being provided to patients and their families. The most straightforward way to do this is through increased community education, directed at individuals of all ages as well as health care workers, about the availability of and services provided by local hospice and palliative care organizations. Along these same lines, it is imperative that the health care system is prepared to deal with the aging baby boom generation that has begun to reach retirement. A national survey of more than 1,500 bereaved family members found that those whose loved ones died under hospice care reported higher life satisfaction, fewer concerns with care, and fewer unmet needs than those whose loved ones died in a hospital or nursing home setting (Teno et al., 2004). Although it may seem that the take-home message from this research is that nursing homes and hospitals are incapable of providing quality end-of-life care, that is not the case. Rather, the lesson is that improvements need to be made in the education of health care providers on proper end-of-life care in all health care settings; hospitals, hospices, and nursing homes need to work in tandem to provide a continuum of care for all individuals with terminal illnesses, as well as their families, as they move through the health care system.

**SEE ALSO** Volume 3: *Caregiving; Death and Dying; End of Life Decision-Making; Health Care Use, Later Life; Long-term Care; Widowhood.*

### BIBLIOGRAPHY

Chen, H., Haley, W. E., Robinson, B. E., & Schonwetter, R. S. (2003). Decisions for hospice care in patients with advanced cancer. *Journal of the American Geriatric Society, 51*(6), 789–797.

Connor, S. R. (1998). *Hospice: Practice, pitfalls, and promise.* Washington, DC: Taylor & Francis.

Connor, S. R., Elwert, F., Spence, C., & Christakis, N. A. (2007). Geographic variation in hospice use in the United States in 2002. *Journal of Pain and Symptom Management, 34*(3), 277–285.

Connor, S. R., Pyenson, B., Fitch, K., Spence, C., & Iwasaki, K. (2007). Comparing hospice and nonhospice patient survival among patients who die within a 3-year window. *Journal of Pain and Symptom Management, 33*(3), 238–246.

Emanuel, E. J., Fairclough, D. L., Slutsman, J., Alpert, H., Baldwin, D., & Emanuel, L. L. (1999). Assistance from family members, friends, paid caregivers, and volunteers in the care of terminally ill patients. *New England Journal of Medicine, 341*(13), 956–963.

Emanuel, E. J., Fairclough, D. L., Slutsman, J., & Emanuel, L. L. (2000). Understanding economic and other burdens of terminal illness: The experience of patients and their caregivers. *Annals of Internal Medicine, 132*(6), 451–459.

Haley, W. E., LaMonde, L. A., Han, B., Narramore, S., & Schonwetter, R. S. (2001). Family caregiving in hospice: Effects on psychological and health functioning among spousal caregivers of hospice patients with lung cancer or dementia. *The Hospice Journal, 15*(4), 1–18.

Kapo, J., Morrison, L. J., & Liao, S. (2007). Palliative care for the older adult. *Journal of Palliative Medicine, 10*(1), 185–209.

Last Acts National Program. (2002, November). *Means to a better end: A report on dying in America today.* Washington, DC: Author. Retrieved May 25, 2008, from http://www.rwjf.org/files/

National Hospice and Palliative Care Organization. (n.d.). *About NHPCO.* Retrieved May 25, 2008, from http://www.nhpco.org/i4a/

National Hospice and Palliative Care Organization. (2007, November). *NHPCO facts and figures: Hospice care in America.* Retrieved May 25, 2008, from http://www.nhpco.org/files/

Taylor, D. H., Jr., Ostermann, J., Van Houtven, C. H., Tulsky, J. A., & Steinhauser, K. (2007). What length of hospice use maximizes reduction in medical expenditures near death in the U.S. Medicare program? *Social Sciences & Medicine, 65*(7), 1466–1478.

Teno, J. M., Clarridge, B. R., Casey, V., Welch, L. C., Wetle, T., Shield, R., et al. (2004). Family perspectives on end-of-life care at the last place of care. *Journal of the American Medical Association, 291*(1), 88–93.

***Allison M. Burton***
***Rachel Marks***

## HUMAN CAPITAL

SEE Volume 1: *Human Capital.*

# I

## INHERITANCE

An inheritance or bequest is the transfer of accumulated and unconsumed wealth after the death of one generation to the next generation. Wealth is defined as the value of property or assets owned. It is often measured as net worth or the sum of all property and financial assets, less any liabilities on those assets. Wealth, then, for successive generations is a function of one's own savings from income (or life-cycle savings) and inheritances received from the prior generation. Economists are concerned that inheritances may lead to increased wealth inequality because very few families hold the majority of the nation's wealth. Also, individuals who receive inheritances may be less motivated to work and save and thus, aggregate productivity declines, which has an effect on the overall economy.

The life-cycle hypothesis suggests that, ideally, there should be either no inheritances, or only accidental inheritances, which have a negligible effect on productivity and wealth inequality. In terms of wealth accumulation, the life cycle hypothesis suggests that families accumulate assets throughout their working years, and then later consume these assets in their retirement years. The extensive use of inheritances, however, suggests that families are motivated to leave an inheritance, which gives rise to the study of bequest motives, who receives inheritances, and how inheritances affect the economy as a whole.

### HISTORICAL TRENDS IN INHERITING WEALTH

Prior to the Industrial Revolution, the wealth distribution (including land) was highly skewed, with very few families owning the vast majority of wealth, and the majority of families owning very little wealth. In England economic growth was very slow, and thus inheritance played a major role in wealth accumulation and in the creation of societal wealth inequality. A slow growth rate meant that there were relatively few other opportunities to accumulate one's own fortune. Inheritances were dynastic, meaning that the purpose was to keep the family's wealth intact across generations. The main mechanism of inheritance then was called *primogeniture*, meaning that the eldest son inherited the bulk of the estate. Often the estate was entailed, which essentially cast the heir as more of a tenant than an owner of the property as legally he had to transmit the principal value of the estate to his eldest son. In this way, the dynastic family's wealth and power were maintained and even increased generation after generation. This system increased wealth inequality as the eldest son's siblings inherited very little.

In America, however, primogeniture never really took hold. Land was plentiful and the agricultural economy was fast-growing, which allowed individuals to create their own fortunes rather than depend upon an inheritance. The Industrial Revolution also played a role by causing the economy to expand rapidly, which allowed greater means for individuals to accumulate their own wealth, thereby decreasing wealth inequality somewhat. Thus inheritances as a means of wealth accumulation became less important in all countries that experienced the industrial revolution. Within several generations, the primogeniture forms of inheritance were replaced with *multigeniture* inheritance (e.g., equal share inheritance by all the sons), and in 1948 the Married

Women's Property Act allowed married daughters to receive an equal share of inheritance that was protected from their husbands. This bequest system still dominates into the early 21st century.

Jeffrey Rosenfeld (1979) claims that surviving spouses (wives) have gone from being a minor to a major beneficiary in the span of less than 100 years. By 1950 spouses became the primary beneficiary and often the executor of their husbands' wills. Rosenfeld attributes this change in bequest customs to "gains in longevity and patterns of mobility which made married people less dependent upon the descent group [previous generation(s) of family] and more reliant upon one another" (1979, p. 65). Men and women became egalitarian partners in marriage and, thus, each other's primary beneficiary. This practice has become normative, and children do not contest the will when the spouse receives the inheritance.

## THE AMOUNT OF WEALTH ACCUMULATION DUE TO INHERITANCES

Of major importance to researchers and policy makers is decomposing wealth accumulation into inherited wealth and noninherited wealth, as each has very different economic policy implications for programs such as public transfer programs, social insurance, and government taxes. Using the life-cycle model, Laurence Kotlikoff and Lawrence Summers (1981) found that life-cycle wealth accumulation makes up 20% of total wealth accumulation, whereas transfers and bequests make up 80%. Franco Modigliani (1988) measured transfers directly by asking for the amount of transfers received. He estimated that life cycle wealth from savings makes up 80% of total wealth accumulation whereas transfers and bequests make up 20%. The range of findings, from 20 to 80% of wealth coming from transfers, is too broad to use successfully in developing economic policy.

William Gale and John Scholz (1994) argue that the majority of transfers are inter vivos (while still alive) rather than bequests and that earlier models did not take this into account. They estimated that 43% of total transfers are inter vivos transfers, and that bequests constitute 31% of total wealth. Donald Cox and Frederic Raines (1985) reestimated using a slightly different formula and found that inter vivos transfers accounted for 58% of total transfers. They found that inter vivos transfers are three times as large as inheritances. Again, there is no consensus on the assumptions and elements of the models and therefore no consensus on the composition of wealth. There is disagreement over what should be included as inter vivos transfers—cash gifts, college tuition, the down payment on a home, the purchase or gift of a car, and so on.

## BEQUEST MOTIVES

Intergenerational transfers that occur because parents care about the welfare of their children are called altruistic bequests, and can be added to a life-cycle model such that parents spend some portion of their savings on bequests to their children. B. Douglas Bernheim (1991) found evidence that private savings are strongly influenced by the bequest desire. Altruistic bequests are hypothesized to equalize opportunities among offspring such that children who have less will receive a larger inheritance. The exchange model hypothesizes that parents provide bequests in exchange for care while they are still alive. This would also suggest an unequal bequest pattern unless all children provide an equal amount of help to the parents. The strategic bequest model argues that parents use threat of disinheritance to control children's behavior.

Research has found weak support for intentional bequest transfers. Cox (2003) finds that bequests are made equally to both sons and daughters regardless of their financial situation, which does not support altruistic bequest theory. This implication is shared by the literature that emphasizes bequests are entirely accidental. It may be that individuals over-save because length of life is uncertain and they do not want to spend their last days in poverty. Alternatively, it may be that parents want to treat all children equally despite differences in their economic situation. John Laitner (2001) finds that models fit best when one assumes that altruistic bequests are quite rare.

There is little consensus on bequest motives. One reason for the lack of consensus is that data on inheritances are very rare. Surveys of retrospective bequests received will not adequately include the amount of earnings the bequest has provided. The primary method has been to determine the amount bequeathed in a single year and then to "blow up" this amount based on assumptions regarding ages at which bequests are made and received in an econometric life-cycle model. The models make very restrictive assumptions, and there is no consensus on what goes into the models—and as these models are sensitive to the assumptions made, results vary.

Current research has continued using life-cycle models, except that many of the restrictive assumptions have been loosened. For example, Laitner (2001) developed a model that allows for mixtures of inter vivos transfers and bequests. Ignacio Ocampo and Kazuhiro Yuki (2006) allow for intragenerational heterogeneity in terms of age, ability, earnings shocks, and inherited bequest. Chengze Fan (2001) introduces a Markovian game framework. These studies do little to resolve the lack of consensus because theoretical work is lacking. Inheritance scholars need first to agree on a theory of inheritances and bequest motives before determining the best way to model bequests and bequest motives.

## IMPACT OF INHERITANCES ON THE ECONOMY OR WEALTH INEQUALITY

If the life-cycle hypothesis held true and individuals' wealth only came from earnings and individuals consumed all their savings prior to dying, then the only wealth inequality would be due to age. Sixty-year-olds would have accumulated more wealth than 30-year-olds, and not have decumulated as much wealth as 80-year-olds. However, wealth is more unequally distributed than income. Edward Wolff (1996) estimated that the top 5% of wealth-holders accounted for 56% of wealth in the United States in 1995. According to Melvin Oliver and Thomas Shapiro (1995), less than 5% of the population reported inheriting extensive amounts of money in the early 1960s, but there was a strong correlation between reporting extensive bequests and having a high income. In 1970 four out of every five of the richest Americans were born to wealth, suggesting that wealth inequality is driven by inheritances.

In fact there is some evidence that inheritances do increase wealth inequality. The life-cycle model assumes no inheritances. Some families choose to leave inheritances, however, and thus save beyond their own lifetime needs. Laitner (2001) finds that dynastic bequest motivated households, or households that desire to keep wealth in the family, continue to build wealth until death. Thus, compared to households that follow the life-cycle model, the average inheritance is larger, which will increase wealth inequality. Burkhard Heer (2001) found that accidental bequests, which occur when the bequestor dies earlier than expected, caused a small increase in wealth inequality.

## INHERITANCE TAXES

Estate taxes are designed to redistribute wealth and increase equality. Because inheritances are not earned through merit, but by accident of birth, it is considered a good candidate for redistributive taxes. Heer (2001) finds that, indeed, the estate tax does reduce wealth inequality. U.S. policy appears to be inconsistent, reflecting Americans' ambivalence, in taxing inheritances. The cutoff level at which a deceased individual had to pay estate taxes increased from $170,000 in 1980 to $600,000 in 1987. This means that estate taxes were increasingly targeting only the very wealthy. If the estate tax cutoff had been lower, a greater proportion of the population would have paid estate taxes, leading to smaller inheritances for more families and thus decreasing wealth inequality. The tax cut enacted in June 2001 reduces the estate tax gradually, repeals it in 2010, and then reinstates it in its pre-2001 form at the beginning of 2011.

## FUTURE DIRECTIONS

An important future research direction is to examine racial inequality in inheritance. Research has shown that when net worth is used as an indicator of well-being, racial inequality is even more severe than other indicators suggest. Oliver and Shapiro (1995) found that 25% of White families compared to 60% of Black families had zero or negative assets in 1992. Racial differences in wealth may be due to racial differences in inheritance. African Americans born prior to the late 1960s were subject to residential, educational, and occupational segregation. This effectively precluded Blacks from accumulating wealth. Robert Avery and Michael Rendall (2002) investigated inheritances between a cohort of Black and White Americans. They found that life-cycle wealth accumulation is much more equal than inheritances. They forecasted that one-third of Whites compared to less than 1 in 20 African Americans would receive an inheritance of at least $25,000 (1989 dollars).

Changes in the institution of the family also may change bequest behavior. As of 2008, economic models treat the family as a single unit that makes bequest decisions with complete consensus. Cox (2003) asks how gender in the family might influence bequest decisions. Now that there are so many broken families, multiple families, stepfamilies, and half brothers and sisters in families, how might this family complexity affect bequest decisions? Among the elderly who live in retirement homes, there is a trend toward leaving bequests to their friends (Rosenfeld, 1979). As the population ages and more and more elderly live in retirement communities or assisted living communities rather than with their families, this might become even more normative.

Lastly, Keith Blackburn and Giam Cipriani (2005) examine the impact that the upcoming demographic transition (aging of the population) will have on wealth accumulation. Their model demonstrates that the demographic transition is linked to the flow of intergenerational wealth as development progresses. The upcoming demographic transition will place a burden on workers and it is possible that taxing inheritances, rather than earnings, may reduce some of that burden (Heer, 2001). Future directions suggest that the life-cycle model needs to incorporate inheritances so as to develop the best aging policies at the individual, family, and population levels.

**SEE ALSO** Volume 3: *Intergenerational Transfers; Pensions; Wealth.*

**BIBLIOGRAPHY**

Avery, R. B., & Rendall, M. S. (2002). Lifetime inheritances of three generations of Whites and Blacks. *American Journal of Sociology, 107*(5), 1300–1346.

Bernheim, B. D. (1991). How strong are bequest motives? Evidence based on estimates of the demand for life insurance and annuities. *Journal of Political Economy, 99*(5), 899–927.

Blackburn, K., & Cipriani, G. P. (2005). Intergenerational transfers and demographic transition. *Journal of Developmental Economics, 78*(1), 191–214.

Cox, D. (2003). Private transfers within the family: Mothers, fathers, sons, and daughters. In A. H. Munnell & A. Sundén (Eds.), *Death and dollars: The role of gifts and bequests in America* (pp. 168–196). Washington, DC: Brookings Institution Press.

Cox, D., & Raines, F. (1985). Interfamily transfers and income redistribution. In M. David & T. Smeeding (Eds.), *Horizontal equity, uncertainty, and economic well-being.* Chicago: University of Chicago Press.

Fan, C. S. (2001). A model of intergenerational transfers. *Economic Theory, 17*(2), 399–418.

Gale, W. G., & Scholz, J. K. (1994). Intergenerational transfers and the accumulation of wealth. *Journal of Economic Perspectives, 8*(4), 145–160.

Heer, B. (2001). Wealth distribution and optimal inheritance taxation in life cycle economies with intergenerational transfers. *Scandinavian Journal of Economics, 103*(3), 445–465.

Kotlikoff, L. J., & Summers, L. H. (1981). The role of intergenerational transfers in aggregate capital accumulation. *Journal of Political Economy, 89*(4), 706–732.

Laitner, J. (2001). Secular changes in wealth inequality and inheritance. *The Economic Journal, 111*(474), 691–721.

Modigliani, F. (1988). The role of intergenerational transfers and life cycle saving in the accumulation of wealth. *Journal of Economic Perspectives, 2*(2), 15–40.

Ocampo, I. P., & Kazuhiro, Y. (2006). Savings, intergenerational transfers, and the distribution of wealth. *Macroeconomic Dynamics, 10*(3), 371–414.

Oliver, M. L., & Shapiro, T. M. (1995). *Black wealth/white wealth: A new perspective on racial inequality.* New York: Routledge.

Rosenfeld, J. P. (1979). *The legacy of aging: Inheritance and disinheritance in social perspective.* Norwood, NJ: Ablex.

Wolff, E. N. (1996). International comparisons of wealth inequality. *Review of Income and Wealth, 42*(4), 433–451.

*Erin Ruel*

# INTERGENERATIONAL RELATIONSHIPS

SEE *Caregiving; Family and Household Structure, Later Life; Grandparenthood; Inheritance; Intergenerational Transfers; Parent-Child Relationships, Later Life.*

# INTERGENERATIONAL TRANSFERS

Intergenerational transfers are usually defined as help—in the form of money, gifts in-kind, or time—between relatives. Examples include a parent's expenditure for a child's college tuition or an adult child's time spent running errands for an older parent. Most of the research literature in this area focuses on transfers between relatives living in separate households, partly because the household is usually considered the primary spending unit in economic analyses. This interhousehold focus also reflects the data sources available to researchers; more information is available on transfers *between* households than *within* them.

But one can imagine many intergenerational transfers that take place within households as well. The most obvious example is the gift of shared housing—parents who let their grown children live at home for free (or who take their own parents into their home) are making an intergenerational transfer. Further, there is no logical age constraint on what constitutes an intergenerational transfer; the time and money that a mother devotes to her infant might just as well be counted. However, conventions in the research literature are such that attention usually is limited to children who are old enough to live on their own.

A key definitional issue is that intergenerational transfers are usually restricted to assistance that is private (indeed, a synonym is *private transfers*) as distinct from governmental transfers, such as Social Security or publicly provided education, which also shuffle resources from one generation to another. This convention is not universal, however. For instance, Ronald Lee (1994) uses the term *intergenerational transfer* to encompass any source of transfer, be it private or public. In what follows, the term is used to refer to private transfers only.

Another defining characteristic of intergenerational transfers is whether a transfer occurs before or after a person is deceased. Intergenerational transfers take the form of either inter vivos transfers (i.e., transfers between two living people) or bequests. Because the latter is covered in a separate entry, this entry focuses mainly upon inter vivos transfers. Listed below are the primary reasons why intergenerational transfers are important:

- They account for substantial money and time expended by households.
- They affect the distribution of economic well-being in a population.
- They can interact with public transfers, possibly diluting their effectiveness.

- They can help young people overcome difficulties borrowing money.
- They can affect incentives to save.
- Their patterns can sometimes reveal the underlying motives for them (e.g., pure altruism versus two-way exchange).

**The prevalence and size of intergenerational transfers** Intergenerational transfers constitute a substantial sum of money no matter how they are defined, but obviously the exact figure depends upon the exact measure at hand. William Gale and John Scholtz (1994) provide a variety of estimates of private transfers in the United States. One estimate, which counts monetary support flowing between households, plus college payments and bequests, amounted to a little more than $200 billion in 1986. To put that number in perspective, it was roughly equal to aggregate consumer spending on cars and trucks that year. Gale and Scholtz report that up to 30% of U.S. households were involved in private transfers, either as givers, recipients, or both.

The figures cited above deal just with private transfers to children who are out of the house, but exclude the costs of raising dependent children. For a child born in 1999, the U.S. Department of Agriculture estimates that a middle-income family can expect to pay about $160,000 on food, shelter, and other necessities over 17 years of dependency (Lino, 2000).

Though financial transfers receive most of the attention in the literature, time-intensive help also has been shown to be an important form of intergenerational transfer. For instance, Kathleen McGarry and Robert Schoeni (1995) find that up to one-third of people in their 50s who have a living parent provide time-related assistance to them. Among those who provide time, the commitment is substantial—averaging more than 400 hours annually.

Intergenerational transfers are particularly important in developing countries, which usually lack the publicly provided social safety nets that high-income welfare states provide. For instance, the predominant form of social security in low-income countries is old-age support from children. Donald Cox and Marcel Fafchamps (2008) canvass several studies of developing countries and find that, for the modal country, about 40% of households either give or receive private transfers. Among recipient households, private transfers hover around one-quarter to one-third of total income.

Intergenerational transfers are associated with saving and capital formation, because one possible motivation for saving would be to leave an estate for one's children (Kotlikoff & Summers, 1981). There are, of course, alternative reasons for saving—the accumulation of wealth for financing one's retirement being the most prominent. Exactly how much wealth accumulation is fueled by the desire to make intergenerational transfers is a matter of some contention: Estimates have ranged from 20% to 80%. Gale & Scholtz (1994) argue that the true proportion is likely to lie within these two extremes.

**Patterns of intergenerational transfers** Private transfers have been found to flow from rich to poor in every country ever studied. In this sense they act like publicly provided social safety nets by helping to equalize the distribution of economic well-being.

Further, private and public transfers can interact—a point first made by Gary Becker (1974) and Robert Barro (1974). To see how, imagine that your indigent grandmother can no longer take care of herself and that you are considering taking her into your home and providing care for her yourself. But then, you find that she qualifies for Medicaid-funded nursing home care that is of comparable quality, so you choose that route instead. Opting for the publicly provided care is an example of the so-called *crowding out* of private transfers by public transfers.

The logic of crowding out implies provocatively unexpected outcomes. In the above example, Medicaid does not improve your grandmother's well-being because it merely supplants the private transfers she would have received otherwise. Instead, *you* are the true beneficiary of the program because your burden of caring is eased.

Most empirical studies suggest that the prospect of complete crowding out is remote, but that partial crowding out occurs. For instance, in the studies of developing countries surveyed by Cox and Fafchamps (2008), the modal response to a $1 increase in public transfers was a 25-cent fall in private transfers. In the United States, estimated crowding out is even weaker. Some studies even indicate that private transfers could rise in response to an increase in the income of the dependent family member (Cox, 1987).

**Motivations for private transfers** One obvious, and compelling, motivation for private transfers is familial altruism—the donor gives because he or she cares about the recipient's well-being. But another possible motive is exchange, that is, private transfers are given in compensation for some service that another family member provides. Elderly parents, for instance, might promise bequests in exchange for care and attention they receive from their adult children (Bernheim, Shleifer, & Summers, 1985). Inter vivos transfers might also be part of a two-way exchange of money for services (Cox, 1987). Exchange theory could explain occasional findings of a positive association between recipient income and transfers received if, for instance, children with higher wages required larger private transfers in order to compensate them for the services they provide to their parents.

Some researchers have advanced a more nuanced approach of mixed motives—a blend of altruism and self-interest (Lucas & Stark, 1985). Cox, Bruce Hansen, and Emmanuel Jimenez (2004) find support for this idea—altruistic motives appear to prevail when recipients are in exceptionally dire straits; otherwise, patterns are more consistent with nonaltruistic motives such as exchange.

**The effects of age, gender, and relatedness** The aforementioned findings are concerned with income-related patterns of intergenerational transfers, but intergenerational transfers are affected by other variables, too; they follow distinct age trajectories (which often differ from one country to the next), for instance, and they are often targeted to female-headed households (Cox & Fafchamps, 2008). Further, there is evidence of nepotism in private transfers; closer relatives are favored, and, in the eyes of survey respondents, transfers to nonrelatives are more likely to be viewed as loans rather than gifts (Cox, 2004).

Some of these effects appear to have straightforward explanations. When looking at age patterns in the United States, for instance, private transfers are disproportionately allocated toward younger households. Such a pattern would make sense if younger people, who have not yet established the requisite track record to enable them to borrow from financial institutions, rely on familial transfers to help them overcome these borrowing constraints (Cox, 1990). Another life course-related influence is the function of private transfers as old-age support, particularly in developing countries with little in the way of formal pensions. An example is Vietnam, where much of private transfers tend to flow from young to old (Cox, 2004), a pattern that contrasts with that of developed countries such as the United States.

Those interested in life course patterns of intergenerational transfers should consult the work of Lee (1994) and Laurence Kotlikoff (1992). These authors take a comprehensive approach to resource flows among the generations, taking into account not only private transfers, but public transfers (such as Social Security) and private saving as well.

Further, any discussion of intergenerational transfers over the life course would be incomplete without recognition of the extensive—and essential—contributions of sociologists, demographers, and social psychologists. A key concept from sociology is that of norms: practices, traditions, and values enforced by societal or familial sanctions or rewards (or perhaps feelings of guilt) that affect one's behavior. Return, for instance, to the above example of contemplating whether to care for one's indigent grandmother. Key questions in the caregiving decision might be, "What is expected of me?" or "What is the most socially acceptable thing to do?" There is extensive evidence of strong gender norms in caregiving; women are more involved in caring for elderly parents than men, for instance. Life course factors enter into such decisions as well, as in, for instance, when adult children become sandwiched between the demands of caring for their elderly parents *and* children of their own. In addition to these forces, the exigencies of demography impinge upon caregiving; parents of the baby boom cohort have more children upon which to rely on in old age than their lower-fertility counterparts from earlier and later cohorts, for instance. (A particularly useful survey of social and demographic factors in caregiving is Colleen Johnson's *Perspectives on American Kinship in the later 1990s* [2000].)

**Evolutionary Biology as an Approach to Age, Gender, and Relatedness** Much of economic theory to date has taken a generic parent-child approach to intergenerational transfers, rather than considering, say, mothers versus fathers or sons versus daughters. But emerging evidence confirms that biological attributes such as motherhood and fatherhood indeed matter, even controlling for standard economic variables such as income or wealth. For instance, nearly all economic studies of the allocation of resources within households indicate that putting more money in the hands of mothers rather than fathers has the repercussion of benefiting of children.

The generic approach—for instance, positing a household inhabited by what amounts to spouses one and two rather than fathers and mothers—misses the biology, but still makes sense within a strictly economic framework because economics is about the effects of incomes and prices, not about motherhood or fatherhood per se. In contrast, however, evolutionary biology is about the nature of, say, motherhood, and some economists have availed themselves of insights from that discipline in order to complement and build upon strictly economic models of the family. (See, for example, surveys by Theodore Bergstrom in "Economics in a Family Way.")

To understand how a biological perspective can be potentially useful, consider a study of the expansion of public pensions to poor Black households in postapartheid South Africa. Esther Duflo (2003) estimated the effects of the income boost to the elderly on the health of young children (one-quarter of South African Black children under age 5 live with their grandparents). Duflo found that the presence of only one kind of grandparent—the maternal grandmother—affected child health. Strictly economic considerations turned out to be insufficient in explaining this trend, but biological considerations can. If relatedness matters, then it may be noteworthy that, of all four grandparents, only the maternal grandmother can be 100% certain that the grandchild is a genetic relative.

Further, it turns out that several studies have uncovered a key role for maternal grandmothers. For example, Rebecca Sear and colleagues (2002) found that the mortality risk of young Gambian children depended more on the availability of maternal grandmothers than any other grandparent (and more than even fathers)—despite the fact that the villages investigated were patrilocal (suggesting a more prominent role for paternal grandparents).

This evolutionary approach to intergenerational transfers is quite simple, yet it generates an array of predictions concerning age, gender, and relatedness in familial transfers. It is one possible path to furthering knowledge about intergenerational transfers. The key idea emanates from a twist on the Darwinian dictum of "survive and reproduce," proposed by William Hamilton (1964), whereby survival and reproduction are envisioned to occur at the level of the gene, as opposed to the organism. A mother's altruism toward her child, therefore, is thought to be impelled by her behaving as if she seeks to perpetuate her genes.

Melding this simple idea to the facts of reproductive biology generates a wide variety of predictions and explanations. For example, a postmenopausal grandmother would be expected to be more altruistic toward her still-fertile granddaughter than vice versa, since the grandmother, no longer capable of bearing children, can only further the interests of her genes by providing assistance to relatives.

These kinds of hypotheses are controversial and are the subject of ongoing research. There is much more to family behavior than these types of evolutionary forces; economic incentives, societal pressures and norms, legal systems, religion, and culture are all likely to figure prominently into intergenerational transfer behavior. It is also possible that these kinds of cultural forces complement biological factors. For instance, the introduction of cash crops in northern Tanzania raised the value of land, and fathers began to bequeath their holdings to sons rather than to more distant relatives (such as nephews) as they did before land prices rose (Gulliver, 1961). The practice was immediately codified into law. Thus, the region's current inheritance practices may be rooted in biology and culture.

It is also important to point out that individual choice can supercede evolutionary pressure. For example, a father may feel driven, partly for biological reasons, to provide for his son's education, yet may still deliberately withdraw financial support if he does not think his son is working hard enough. Evolutionary explanations do not carry any presumption that a behavior is laudable. For instance, parental transfers to stepchildren have been found to be smaller than transfers to genetic children (Case, Lin, & McLanahan, 2000) and abuse of stepchildren has been found to be more severe than that of genetic children (Daly & Wilson, 1988).

The evolutionary perspective is but one example of the inherent interdisciplinary nature of intergenerational transfers. The subject has captured the attention of myriad disciplines: economics, evolutionary biology, sociology, anthropology, psychology, demography, and more. Accordingly, anyone interested in researching this subject would be well-advised to integrate findings from various disciplines into their approach in order to expand upon what the existing literature has to offer.

**SEE ALSO** Volume 3: *Caregiving; Family and Household Structure, Later Life; Grandparenthood; Inheritance; Parent-Child Relationships, Later Life; Social Security; Social Support; Wealth.*

### BIBLIOGRAPHY


Barro, R.J. (1974). Are government bonds net wealth? *Journal of Political Economy, 82*(6), 1095–1117.

Becker, G.S. (1974). A theory of social interactions. *Journal of Political Economy, 82*(6), 1063–1093.

Bergstrom, T.C. (1996). Economics in a family way. *Journal of Economic Literature, 34*(4), 1903–1934.

Bernheim, B.D., Shleifer, A., & Summers, L.H. (1985). The strategic bequest motive. *Journal of Political Economy, 93*(6), 1045–1076.

Bowles, S., & Posel, D. (2005). Genetic relatedness predicts South African migrant workers' remittances to their families. *Nature, 434*(7031), 380–383.

Case, A., Lin, I.-F., & McLanahan, S. (2000). How hungry is the selfish gene? *Economic Journal, 110*(466), 781–804.

Cox, D. (1987). Motives for private income transfers. *Journal of Political Economy, 95*(3), 508–546.

Cox, D. (1990). Intergenerational transfers and liquidity constraints. *Quarterly Journal of Economics, 105*(1), 187–217.

Cox, D. (2004). Private interhousehold transfers in Vietnam. In P. Glewwe & D. Dollar (Eds.), *Economic growth and household welfare: Policy lessons for Vietnam* (pp. 559–596). Washington, DC: The World Bank.

Cox, D. (2007). Biological basics and economics of the family. *Journal of Economic Perspectives, 21*(2), 91–108.

Cox, D., & Fafchamps, M. (2008). Extended family and kinship networks: Economic insights and evolutionary directions. In T.P. Schultz & J. Strauss (Eds.), *The handbook of development economics* (Vol. 4) (pp. 3711–3784). Amsterdam: Elsevier Press.

Cox, D., Hansen, B.E., & Jimenez, E. (2004). How responsive are private transfers to income? Evidence from a laissez-faire economy. *Journal of Public Economics, 88*(9-10), 2193–2219.

Daly, M., & Wilson, M. (1988). *Homicide.* New York: Aldine de Gruyter.

Duflo, E. (2003). Grandmothers and granddaughters: Old-age pension and intrahousehold allocation in South Africa. *World Bank Economic Review, 17*(1), 1–25.

Gale, W.G., & Scholtz, J.K. (1994). Intergenerational transfers and the accumulation of wealth. *The Journal of Economic Perspectives, 8*(4), 145–160.

Gulliver, P.H. (1961). Land shortage, social change, and social conflict in East Africa. *The Journal of Conflict Resolution, 5*(1), 16–26.

Hamilton, W.D. (1964). The genetical evolution of social behavior (I and II). *Journal of Theoretical Biology, 7*(1), 1–52.

Johnson, C.L. (2000). Perspectives on American kinship in the later 1990s. *Journal of Marriage and the Family, 62*(3), 623–639.

Kotlikoff, L.J. (1992). *Generational accounting: Knowing who pays, and when, for what we spend.* New York: The Free Press.

Kotlikoff, L.J., & Summers, L.H. (1981). The role of intergenerational transfers in aggregate capital accumulation. *Journal of Political Economy, 89*(4), 706–732.

Lee, R. (1994). Population age structure, intergenerational transfer, and wealth: A new approach, with applications to the United States. *Journal of Human Resources, 29*(4), 1027–1063.

Lino, M. (2000). *Expenditures on children by families, 1999 annual report.* Washington, DC: U.S. Department of Agriculture, Center for Nutrition Policy and Promotion. Retrieved July 3, 2008, from http://www.cnpp.usda.gov/publications/Crc/crc1999.pdf

Lucas, R.E.B., & Stark, O. (1985). Motivations to remit: Evidence from Botswana. *Journal of Political Economy, 93*(5), 901–918.

McGarry, K., & Schoeni, R.F. (1995). Transfer behavior in the Health and Retirement Study: Measurement and the redistribution of resources within the family. *Journal of Human Resources, 30*(Suppl.), 184–226.

Sear, R., Steele, F., McGregor, I., & Mace, R. (2002). The effects of kin on child mortality in rural Gambia. *Demography, 39*(1), 43–63.

**Donald Cox**

# L

## LEISURE AND TRAVEL, LATER LIFE

The study of leisure in later life has a long history. In 1961 Robert Havighurst found that participation in leisure activities contributes to life satisfaction as people age. In the 1970s and 1980s a considerable body of knowledge was accumulated by scholars in North America and around the world (Howe, 1988). Much of that work was grounded in three gerontological theories: disengagement theory (Cumming & Henry, 1961), activity theory (Havighurst, 1961), and continuity theory (Atchley, 1988). In many respects the transition to retirement and later life and the accompanying role losses were a natural fit for scholars interested in leisure, because retirement often brings free time to enjoy hobbies, travel, and a leisure-oriented life style.

### ACTIVITY THEORY

Taking a lead from the popularity of activity theory in gerontology, much early research on leisure and later life was based on the premise that higher levels of participation in a range of activities contribute to greater life satisfaction in later life (Havighurst, 1961; Kelly, Steinkamp, & Kelly, 1987; Riddick, 1985). That premise was consistent with conceptualizations of leisure as a form of activity; researchers found that higher levels of participation in leisure activities were linked with higher levels of life satisfaction, which frequently was measured by using the Life Satisfaction Index (Neugarten, Havighurst, & Tobin, 1961).

Statistical models were developed, and when health and income were controlled, leisure participation was found to account for higher levels of life satisfaction than did other life-style factors. However, researchers came to recognize that leisure includes more than activities, and so they raised questions about the relevance of activity theory in studying leisure in later life. Similarly, in mainstream gerontology, researchers found that not all activities contributed equally to later life satisfaction. Larry Peppers (1976) found that participation in pursuits characterized as "active social" yielded higher levels of life satisfaction than did participation in pursuits characterized as "sedentary isolated." Other researchers (Lemon, Bengston, & Peterson, 1981) questioned the inconsistent findings among studies that used activity theory to predict life satisfaction and concluded that it did not explain the complexity of everyday life.

Thus, even though there is a consensus about the value of leisure participation in later life, current theorizing recognizes that not all leisure is universally and equally beneficial. Scholars generally find that different types of activity provide different benefits (Kelly, 1987), social interaction is often a key characteristic of the most satisfying forms of leisure (Nimrod, 2007), and the meaning of the activity to the individual is of the utmost importance (Gibson, Ashton-Shaeffer, Green, & Autry, 2003–2004).

### DISENGAGEMENT THEORY

Although the original articulation of disengagement theory stated that role loss and withdrawal from the community are negative and inevitable experiences for older adults, leisure researchers recognize that disengagement may be positive in that it provides opportunities for individuals to engage in generativity and integration (Kleiber & Ray, 1993). In contrast to the pervasive view that leisure simply involves socializing and activity, Douglas Kleiber (2001) argued that leisure characterized by relaxation may give individuals an opportunity to reflect on their lives. Kleiber, building on the developmental psychologist Erik Erikson's stage theory, suggested that that type of leisure may allow midlife individuals to identify ways in which they can leave a legacy for future generations (generativity) and allow persons in the later years to put their lives into context (ego-integrity).

The work of Kleiber (2001) and others dovetails with the core components of Paul and Margret Baltes' (1990) theory of selective optimization with compensation. Both disengagement and selective optimization with compensation theories suggest that withdrawing from some activities and relationships is strategic because it lets individuals focus on the people and activities that are most meaningful to them as well as providing time for leisure contexts that facilitate the developmental tasks of later life.

### CONTINUITY THEORY

The theme of continuity is important in the study of late-life leisure. John R. Kelly (1982) suggested that individuals build a leisure repertoire in childhood and that as people move through the life course, the choice of leisure activities remains relatively constant. This hypothesis is consistent with the tenets of continuity theory (Atchley, 1988), which states that consistency in identity is maintained by expanding one's earlier social roles and adopting new roles. Kelly's work also underscores the importance of leisure throughout the life course: Building a full and diverse leisure repertoire in childhood has implications for a person's activities and well-being in later life (Yoesting & Burkhead, 1973). However, adults do change and develop new leisure interests as they age. Many individuals regard retirement as an opportunity to engage in many new pursuits, including international travel (Gibson, 2002). However, a core set of interests seems to persist throughout life (Mobily, Lemke, & Gisin, 1991).

### LEISURE AND LIFE TRANSITIONS

Leisure also is related to important life transitions, such as the transition to retirement. Gerontological research originally focused primarily on men's retirement, reflecting gendered patterns of employment over the life course (Szinovacz, 1992). However, with more women in the paid work force for much of their lives—especially among recent cohorts—this research focus is changing (Erdner & Guy, 1990). However, Toni Calasanti (1993, 1996) questioned whether women ever retire from their household responsibilities. Nonetheless, mainstream thinking still views retirement as freedom to do all the things individuals have always wanted to do, including travel and all their favorite activities. However, Barrie Hawkins (1990–1991) warned that most people never prepare adequately for a leisure-oriented life after retirement; this is where the crisis may occur among people who have been socialized into work roles and are uncertain how to make the transition to a life without work.

Another transition that may affect or be affected by a person's leisure pursuits is spousal bereavement. Ian Patterson and Gaylene Carpenter (1994) found that once the initial stages of bereavement pass, leisure plays an important role in the lives of widows and widowers by giving them ways to reconnect with others. The extent to which caregiving strains inhibit leisure is also an important topic of inquiry (Bedini & Phoenix, 1999). At a time when caregivers could benefit from the buffering effects of leisure on stress (Dupuis & Pedlar, 1995), they often are isolated from their friends and favorite leisure pursuits. Nancy Gladwell and Leandra Bedini (2004) examined the ways caregiving responsibilities affect leisure travel and found that caregivers often forgo vacations. Frequently, they would like to take the care recipient on vacation with them, but the logistics are often difficult.

### THE ROLE OF TRAVEL

Travel in later life is another common research focus, although many researchers are concerned with the business of travel and the senior traveler as a viable market segment (Javalgi, Thomas, & Rao, 1992). Although some of these studies have provided social scientists with insights into the variety of types of travel, choice of destinations, and motivations (Shoemaker 1989, 2000), they have not shown how travel contributes to later life satisfaction. Many individuals are avid travelers in later life and regard it as a meaningful experience (Gibson, 2002).

As part of the search for meaningful travel, the concept of educational travel has become popular among midlife and later-life individuals. In a study of participants in Elderhostel (a large not-for-profit educational travel organization for older adults), David Thomas and Frank Butts (1998) found that intellectual stimulation and social interaction are the most satisfying aspects of educational excursions. Older individuals also frequently travel to see friends and family and report participation in multigenerational activities such as grandtravel, in which grandparents take their grandchildren on trips (Lago & Poffley, 1993). It is of interest to scholars whether baby boomers have distinct travel and leisure patterns. An American Association of Retired Persons report suggests that boomers are much more interested in adventure travel than their predecessors were (Davies, 2005).

## SOCIAL ROLES, HEALTH, AND CIVIC ENGAGEMENT

Researchers are expanding their definitions of leisure and exploring the ways in which social roles and health shape the experience of leisure in later life. There is a focus on investigating the meaning of different leisure experiences and how they contribute to well-being in later life, such as the experiences of grandmotherhood (Wearing, 1996) and grandfatherhood (Scratton & Holland, 2006). Physical activity has become a popular focus in response to concern about inactivity over the life span (Sasidharan, Payne, Orsega-Smith, & Godbey, 2006) and the fact that recent cohorts of older adults are more likely than their predecessors to participate in competitive and recreational sports. Studies of competitive athletic events held expressly for older adults (e.g., National Seniors Game Competition) reveal that participation brings both physical and emotional benefits to participants, including the benefit of being part of a social community (Lyons & Dionigi, 2007).

***American Hiking Society Trip.*** *Two retirees dig holes to install bridge railings on the Virginia Creeper Trail within the Mt. Rogers National Recreation Area in southwestern Virginia, July 2004, during a volunteer vacation trip organized by the American Hiking Society.* AP IMAGES.

Another line of research into social involvement in community in later life involves volunteering, civic engagement, and building social capital through leisure (Maynard & Kleiber, 2005). Loss of social capital has become a concern (Putnam, 2000), and many scholars see older adults as people who are playing an active role in maintaining a sense of community and filling volunteer roles in local organizations. Scholars in many Asian countries are focusing on the experiences of older adults in relation to leisure and tourism (Lee, 2005), reflecting the rapidly growing older populations in those nations. In many ways this research is building on work from the 1980s that established that it is not just the activity but the meaning of activity that is the most important constituent of leisure in later life and that at the foundation of much of this meaning is the social context. These developments have taken researchers back to Kelly's (1987) contention that leisure is both social and existential.

**SEE ALSO** Volume 3: *Retirement; Theories of Aging; Time Use, Later Life.*

### BIBLIOGRAPHY


Atchley, R. C. (1988). *Social forces and aging: An introduction to social gerontology*. Belmont, CA: Wadsworth.

Baltes, P. B., & Baltes, M. M. (1990). Psychological perspectives on successful aging: The model of selective optimization with compensation. In P. Baltes & M. Baltes (Eds.), *Successful aging: Perspectives from the behavioral sciences*. New York: Cambridge University Press.

Bedini, L. A., & Phoenix, T. L. (1999). Addressing leisure barriers for caregivers of older adults: A model leisure wellness program. *Therapeutic Recreation Journal* (Third Quarter), 222–240.

Calasanti, T. M. (1993). Bringing in diversity: Toward an inclusive theory of retirement. *Journal of Aging Studies, 7*(2), 133–150.

Calasanti, T. M. (1996). Gender and life satisfaction in retirement: An assessment of the male model. *Journal of Gerontology, 51*(1), S18–S29.

Cumming, E., & Henry, W. E. (1961). *Growing old: The process of disengagement*. New York: Basic Books.

Davies, C. (2005). *2005 travel & adventure report: A snapshot of boomers' travel & adventure experiences*. American Association of Retired Persons. Retrieved May 20, 2008, from http://www.aarp.org/research/

Dupuis, S. L., & Pedlar, A. (1995). Family leisure programs in institutional care settings: Buffering the stress of caregivers. *Therapeutic Recreation Journal, 29*(3), 184–205.

Erdner, R. A., & Guy, R. F. (1990). Career identification and women's attitudes toward retirement. *International Journal of Aging and Human Development, 30*(2), 129–139.

Gibson, H. (2002). Busy travelers: Leisure-travel patterns and meanings in later life. *World Leisure, 44(2)*, 11–20.

Gibson, H., Ashton-Shaeffer, C., Green, J., & Autry, C., (2003–2004). Leisure in the lives of retirement-aged women: Conversations about leisure and life. *Leisure/Loisir. 28*(3/4), 203–230.

Gladwell, N. J., & Bedini, L. A. (2004). In search of lost leisure: The impact of caregiving on leisure travel. *Tourism Management, 25*(6), 685–693.

Havighurst, R. (1961). The nature and values of meaningful free-time activity. In R. Kleemeier (Ed.), *Aging and leisure*. New York: Oxford University Press.

Hawkins, B. (1990–1991). Challenges for leisure services in a graying America. *Leisure Information Quarterly, 17*(3), 1–5.

Howe, C. Z. (1988). Selected social gerontology theories and older adult leisure involvement: A review of literature. *Journal of Applied Gerontology, 6*(4), 448–463.

Javalgi, R. G., Thomas, E. G., & Rao, S. (1992). Consumer behavior in the U.S. pleasure travel marketplace: An analysis of senior and nonsenior travelers. *Journal of Travel Research, 31*(2), 14–19.

Kelly, J. R. (1982). *Leisure*. Englewood Cliffs, NJ: Prentice-Hall.

Kelly, J. R. (1987). *Freedom to be: A new sociology of leisure*. New York: Macmillan.

Kelly, J. R., Steinkamp, M. W., & Kelly, J. R. (1987). Later-life satisfaction: Does leisure contribute? *Leisure Sciences, 19*, 189–200.

Kleiber, D. (2001). Developmental intervention and leisure education: A life span perspective. *World Leisure, 43*(1), 4–10.

Kleiber, D., & Ray, O. (1993). Leisure and generativity. In J. R. Kelly, (Ed), *Activity and aging: Staying involved in later life* (pp. 106–118). Thousand Oaks, CA: Sage.

Lago, D., & Poffley, J. (1993). The aging population and the hospitality industry in 2010: Important trends and probable services. *Journal of Hospitality & Tourism Research, 17*(1), 29–47.

Lee, M. K. 2005). Pre- and post-retirement leisure in South Korea and the implications for life satisfaction. *World Leisure Journal, 47*(4), 23–31.

Lemon, B., Bengston, V., & Peterson, J. (1981). An exploration of the activity theory of aging: Activity types and life satisfaction among in-movers to a retirement community. In C. Kart & B. Manard (Compilers), *Aging in America: Readings in social gerontology* (pp. 15–38). Sherman Oaks, CA: Alfred.

Lyons, K., & Dionigi, R. (2007). Transcending emotional community: A qualitative examination of older adults and masters' sports participation. *Leisure Sciences, 29*(4), 375–389.

Maynard, S., & Kleiber, D. (2005). Using leisure services to build social capital in later life: Classical traditions, contemporary realities, and emerging possibilities. *Journal of Leisure Research, 37*, 475–493.

Mobily, K. V., Lemke, J. H., & Gisin, G. J. (1991). The idea of leisure repertoire. *Journal of Applied Gerontology, 10*(2), 208–223.

Neugarten, B. L., Havighurst, R. J., & Tobin, S. S. (1961). The measurement of life satisfaction. *Journal of Gerontology, 16*, 134–143.

Nimrod, G. (2007). Retirees' leisure: Activities, benefits, and their contribution to life satisfaction. *Leisure Studies, 26*(1), 65–80.

Patterson, I., & Carpenter, G. (1994). Participation in leisure activities after the death of a spouse. *Leisure Sciences, 16*, 105–117.

Peppers, L. G. (1976). Patterns of leisure and adjustment to retirement. *The Gerontologist, 16*(5), 441–446.

Putnam, R. D. (2000). *Bowling alone: The collapse and revival of American community*. New York: Simon & Schuster.

Riddick, C. C. (1985). Life satisfaction determinants of older males and females. *Leisure Sciences, 7*(1), 47–63.

Sasidharan, V., Payne, L., Orsega-Smith, E., & Godbey, G. (2006). Older adults' physical activity participation and perceptions of well-being: Examining the role of social support for leisure. *Managing Leisure, 11*(3), 164–185.

Scratton, S., & Holland, S. (2006). Grandfatherhood and leisure. *Leisure Studies, 25*, 233–250.

Shoemaker, S. (1989). Segmentation of the senior pleasure market. *Journal of Travel Research, 27*, 14–21.

Shoemaker, S. (2000). Segmenting the mature market: 10 years later. *Journal of Travel Research, 39*, 11–26.

Szinovacz, M. (1992). Leisure in retirement: Gender differences in limitations and opportunities. *World Leisure and Recreation, 34*(1), 14–17.

Thomas, D. W., & Butts, F. B. (1998). Assessing leisure motivators and satisfaction of international Elderhostel participants. *Journal of Travel and Tourism Marketing, 7*(1), 31–38.

Wearing, B. (1996). Grandmotherhood as leisure. *World Leisure and Recreation, 38*(4), 15–19.

Yoesting, D. R., & Burkhead, D. I. (1973). Significance of childhood recreation experience on adult leisure behavior. *Journal of Leisure Research, 5*, 25–36.

*Heather J. Gibson*

## LIFE EXPECTANCY

Life expectancy is a demographic indicator that summarizes the level of mortality of a population or cohort. It is calculated on the basis of a set of age-specific mortality rates (deaths per population number by age), which describe how the risk of mortality varies with age in a given population or cohort, and indicates the number of years that an individual can expect to live given this set of age-specific mortality rates. Life expectancy can be calculated at any age (e.g., the life expectancy at age 65, which indicates the number of additional years that an individual age 65 can expect to live), but it is most often calculated at birth. In this case, it is interpreted as the number of years that a newborn can expect to live under a given set of age-specific mortality rates. It can also be interpreted as the average life span or mean age at death produced by a given set of age-specific mortality rates.

Life expectancy is a useful mortality indicator because it summarizes complex, age-varying risks of mortality in one single indicator that is easy to interpret (average number of years a person can expect to live). It thus allows convenient comparisons of mortality levels across nations, population subgroups, time periods, and birth cohorts. However, this summary conceals information about the age pattern of mortality. When interpreting life expectancies, one needs to keep in mind that not everyone dies at the same age and that two populations with identical levels of life expectancy may experience quite different age patterns of mortality.

Life expectancies can be calculated for actual birth cohorts of individuals. In this case, cohort life expectancy summarizes a mortality experience that spans about a century, from the year when these individuals are born until 100 or more years later when the last members of the birth cohort die. Cohort life expectancies are rarely calculated, however, because they require mortality data for a period spanning 100 years or more, which are rarely available. Moreover, cohort life expectancies can be calculated only for cohorts that are now extinct and thus summarize past mortality risks rather than current risks. For more timely information, demographers calculate period life expectancies, which summarize mortality rates experienced over a short period of time, typically a calendar year. The period life expectancy at birth corresponds to the number of years that a newborn can expect to live under the age-specific mortality rates of that period. It is calculated by simulating a hypothetical cohort of individuals that would experience at each age the mortality risks of a given period. Under such a scenario, individuals born today will be exposed, when they reach older ages, to the mortality risks experienced by today's older individuals. Period life expectancies conveniently summarize the age-specific mortality risks of a period, but when mortality is rapidly changing, they provide little information about the average life span or mean age at death of actual cohorts of individuals. Because mortality tends to decline over historical time, the life expectancy for a given year typically underestimates the life expectancy for the cohort born that year.

## HISTORICAL TRENDS IN LIFE EXPECTANCY

Little is known about levels of life expectancy before the 18th century, but evidence from skeletal remains, burial inscriptions, parish registers, and records for unusual subgroups, such as monks or the aristocracy, provides some information about historical trends. Estimates of life expectancy at birth for the prehistoric period and antiquity are in the range of 20 to 30 years (Acsádi & Nemeskéri, 1970). These low levels of life expectancy are due in part to extremely high levels of child mortality, which have a large impact on life expectancy. It is estimated that for the prehistoric and early historic period, the percentage of newborns that died before age 5 was in the range of 44 to 60% (Hill, 1995). For the medieval period, a study of monks in England in the 15th century suggests a life expectancy at birth of about 22 years (Hatcher, Piper, & Stone, 2006), although the extent to which this estimate can be applied to the broader population is not clear. Estimates for England as a whole, generated from English parish registers, show that in the 16th century, life expectancy at birth was fluctuating in the range of 30 to 40 years (Wrigley & Schofield, 1981).

The first accurate estimates of life expectancy at the national level, based on exhaustive counts of population and deaths, come from Sweden. Figure 1 shows trends in life expectancy at birth, for males and females, since the earliest available year (1751). Levels of life expectancy at birth in Sweden in the second half of the 18th century were no better than levels found in England two centuries earlier. Improvements in life expectancy started during the 19th century, especially after 1850. Between 1850 and 2000, life expectancy at birth increased steadily from about 45 years to about 80 years. This rapid increase in life expectancy was initially due to reductions in infant and child mortality. Since 1950, however, reductions in old-age mortality have played a more important role. In light of the historical record, improvements in life expectancy in a country such as Sweden appear dramatic and relatively recent. Data for less developed countries show that, in many cases, the improvements in life expectancy have been even more rapid. Figure 1 shows estimates of life expectancy for India in the 20th century. Starting from levels in the early 20s around 1900, similar to estimates for the prehistoric period, India tripled its life expectancy, reaching levels in the early 60s by the end of 20th century.

A number of factors have been proposed to explain these dramatic increases in life expectancy. Factors can be organized in four categories: (a) improvements in standards of living (including improvements in nutrition and housing conditions), (b) advances in medical technology (including drugs, vaccines, and surgeries), (c) public health measures (such as the establishment of sewage systems and improvements in the supply and quality of drinking water), and (d) improvements in personal health behaviors (including personal and household hygiene). Explanations for improvements in life expectancy vary depending on time and place. Medical technology does not appear to initially have played a large role in more developed countries because, with a few exceptions, effective vaccines, drugs, and surgeries were not available on a wide scale until well into the 20th century, when life expectancy had already increased by a significant amount. These initial improvements are attributed to a combination of improvements in standards of living, which led to better nutrition, and to public health measures, which then led to better sanitation and water quality. The relative contribution of these two factors, however, is still debated.

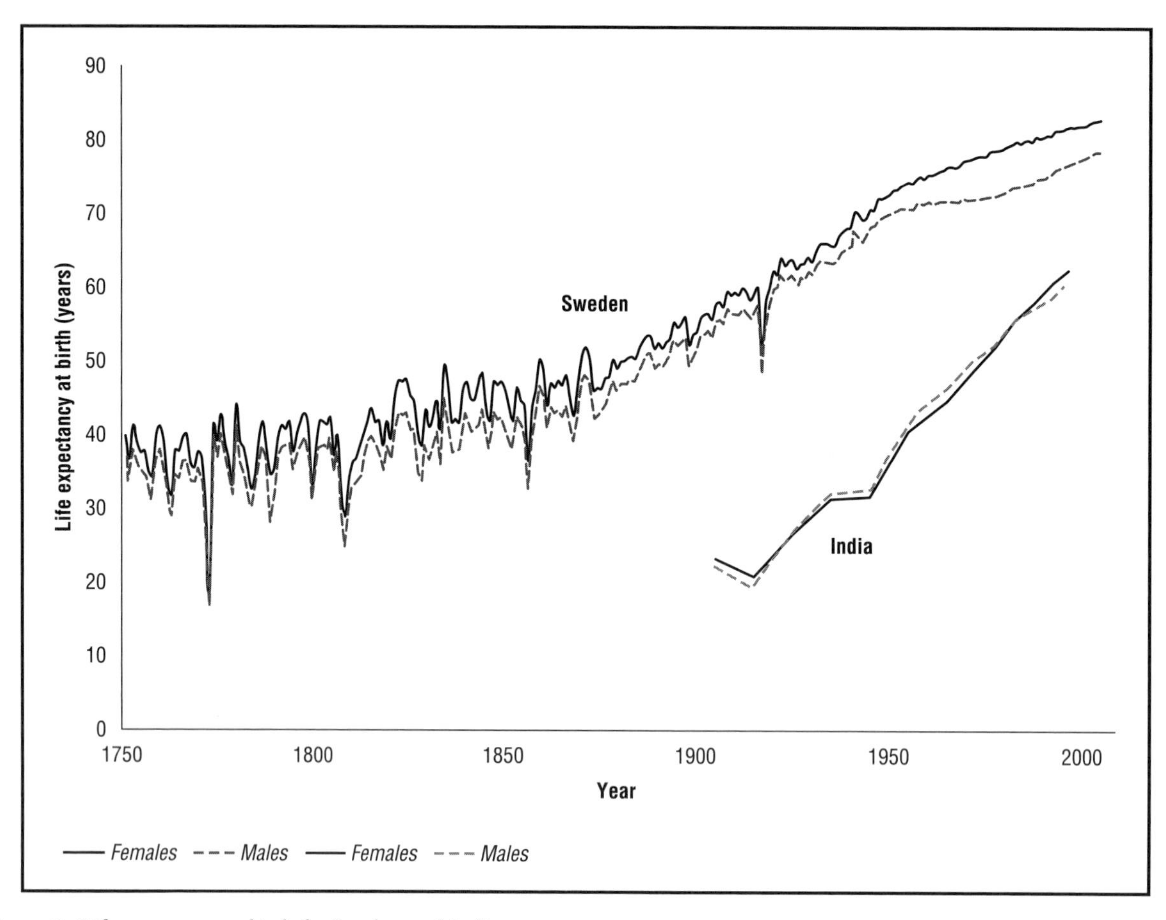


***Figure 1.*** *Life expectancy at birth for Sweden and India.* CENGAGE LEARNING, GALE.

Around the turn of the 20th century, greater acceptance of germ theory led to important changes in personal health practices, which, together with the introduction of drug-based therapies in the 1930s and 1940s, explain the continued increase in life expectancy. (The germ theory doctrine simply holds that infectious diseases are caused by microorganisms.) Increases in life expectancy in more developed countries after 1970 are mostly due to better prevention, management, and treatment of cardiovascular diseases. In contrast with the experience of more developed countries, less developed countries were often able to achieve spectacular increases in life expectancy with few improvements in standards of living. These fast increases are explained primarily by public health campaigns, such as large-scale immunization campaigns, antimalarial programs, and other government programs.

In spite of impressive progress globally during the 20th century, there are still wide discrepancies in life expectancy across nations. For the period between 2005 and 2010, the estimated life expectancy at birth for the world as a whole is 67 years, but values for individual countries range from 40 to 42 in Swaziland and Mozambique to 82 and 83 in Iceland and Japan. Also, global progress does not imply that life expectancy will necessarily increase with time. A number of countries in sub-Saharan Africa have experienced sharp declines in life expectancy during the late 20th century as a consequence of the AIDS epidemics. Also, in Russia and other eastern European countries, a reversal in life expectancy occurred starting in the mid-1960s. Among Russian males, life expectancy at birth in 2006 was 60.35 years, which is lower than its highest point of 64.89 years in 1964. This reversal appears to be primarily due to alcohol consumption and its consequences.

## FUTURE PROSPECTS

Life expectancy is projected to continue increasing in the coming decades. Figure 2 shows estimates of life expectancy at birth by region for the period between 2005 and 2010, along with projected values for the period between 2045 and 2050. Every region of the world is expected to experience some increase, although the amount of increase varies by region. The smallest projected increases are for more developed regions. This does not necessarily imply that these regions will experience a slowdown in mortality decline. Mortality declines produce smaller increases at higher levels of life expectancy than similar

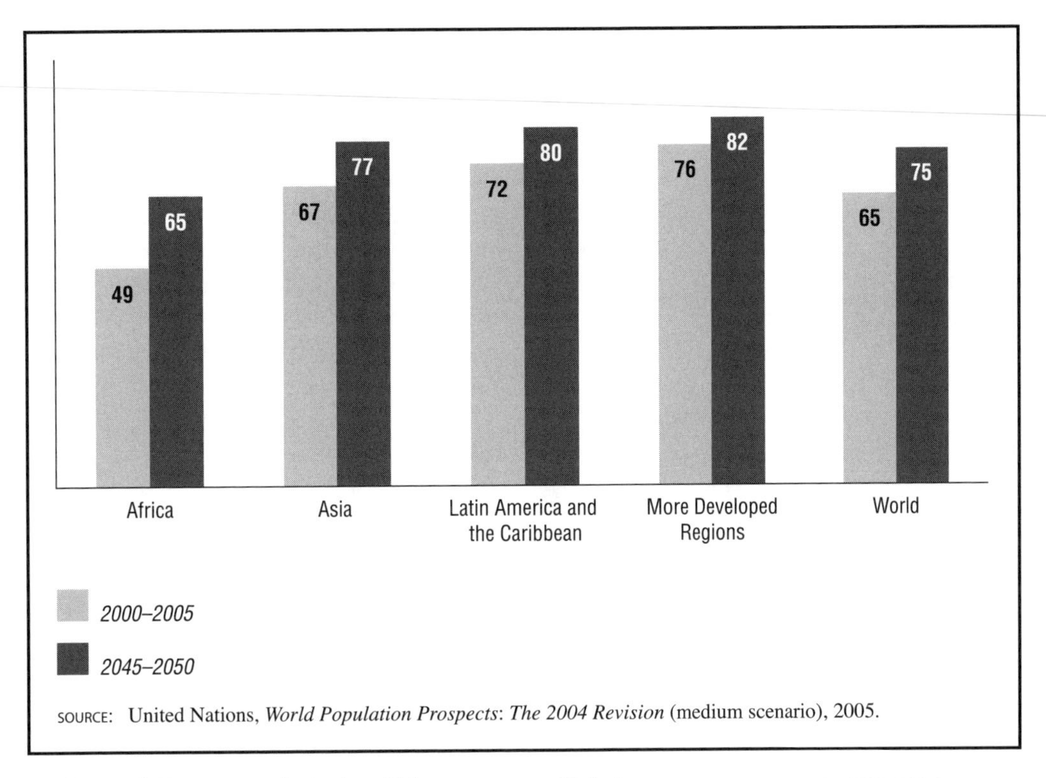


***Figure 2.*** *Trends in Life Expenctancy, by Region. Life expectancy at birth, in years.* CENGAGE LEARNING, GALE.

mortality declines at lower levels of life expectancy. Starting from the lowest level of life expectancy, Africa is expected to experience the largest increase in the coming decades. Note that these life expectancy forecasts are based on extrapolation of past trends. Unforeseen events, such as epidemics or technological breakthroughs, could produce different values than those presented in Figure 2.

## GENDER DIFFERENCES IN LIFE EXPECTANCY

Females typically experience higher levels of life expectancy than males. According to the World Health Organization, in 2006, life expectancy at birth was higher among females in every country of the world (Barford, Dorling, Smith, & Shaw, 2006). Nonetheless, the magnitude, and sometimes the direction, of gender differences in life expectancy have varied greatly over time and place.

Figure 1 presents data on male versus female life expectancy in Sweden and India. In Sweden during the 19th century and the first half of the 20th century, female life expectancy exceeded male life expectancy by only about 2 to 3 years. In the second half of the 20th century, however, the female advantage increased to reach 6.2 years in 1978, followed by a decrease in more recent years. In India, females experienced slightly higher levels of life expectancy around 1900, but progressively lost their advantage thereafter. This advantage was recovered in the 1990s, although girls still experienced higher mortality at infant or child ages in 2005 and 2006. In 2006, the largest gender differential in life expectancy was observed in Russia, with a male disadvantage of 13 years.

Gender differences in life expectancy are explained by a complex combination of biological and behavioral factors. Hormonal and genetic factors appear to contribute to males' lower life expectancy, by making them more vulnerable to infectious and cardiovascular diseases. Males' lower life expectancy is also explained by gender differences in behaviors and lifestyles, such as drinking, smoking, driving, occupation, and overall attitudes toward health. Smoking, in particular, explains to a large degree the increase in the male–female gap for life expectancy during the 1950s and 1960s in many developed countries. In some countries where life expectancy was lower among females, such as India during the second half of the 20th century, the female disadvantage seems to be related to the preference given to sons with respect to food allocation and medical care. Female disadvantages in life expectancy were also relatively common in European countries during the late 19th century and seem to be also related to women's lower status, as well as maternal mortality.

Future trends in gender differences in life expectancy are highly uncertain, but it is generally believed that the

## BIOLOGICAL LIMITS TO HUMAN LIFE

It is useful to make the distinction between maximum theoretical life span (the highest possible age at death that an individual could experience) and maximum theoretical average life span (the highest possible life expectancy at birth that a population could attain).

Researchers have not reached consensus on the existence of, or numerical values for, upper limits to maximum life span or maximum average life span. Although it has been claimed that a life expectancy at birth higher than 85 years is highly unlikely (Olshansky, Carnes, & Cassel, 1990), data show that Japanese females have already exceeded that limit, with a value of 85.81 years in 2006 (Statistics Bureau of Ministry of Internal Affairs and Communication, 2007). Also, the life expectancy at birth for both sexes in Japan, which was 82 years in 2005, is projected to exceed the 85-year threshold by 2025 and reach 87 years by 2050 (United Nations, 2007). Although these projections are merely extrapolations of past mortality trends, the absence of a slowdown in mortality decline in recent years suggests that, although future gains in life expectancy may be smaller than in the past, life expectancy does not appear to be approaching a limit.

Theory is of little help for determining a value for the maximum theoretical life span, but data on recorded ages at death provide useful information. The highest-ever recorded and verified age at death is for Jeanne Calment, a French woman who died in 1997 at the age of 122 years (Robine & Allard, 1999). Although this constitutes the all-time worldwide record, trends in the highest age at death recorded each year in individual countries show an extension of maximum life span since the 1970s. For example, data for Sweden show that the maximum recorded age at death increased during the period from 1861 to 1999, from about 101 years to about 110 years, with an acceleration after 1970 (Wilmoth, Deegan, Lundström, & Horiuchi, 2000). This has been interpreted as evidence that there is no sign of humankind approaching a finite limit to maximum life span.

**BIBLIOGRAPHY**

Olshansky, S. J., Carnes, B. A., & Cassel, C. (1990). In search of Methuselah: Estimating the upper limits to human longevity. *Science, 250*, 634–640.

Robine, J.-M., & Allard, M. (1999). Jeanne Calment: Validation of the duration of her life. In B. Jeune & J. W. Vaupel (Eds.), *Validation of exceptional longevity* (pp. 145–161). Odense, Denmark: Odense University Press.

Statistics Bureau of Ministry of Internal Affairs and Communication. (2007). *Statistical handbook of Japan 2007*. Retrieved June 5, 2008, from http://www.stat.go.jp/English

United Nations. (2007). *World population prospects: The 2006 revision*. New York: Author.

Wilmoth, J. R., Deegan, L. J., Lundström, H., & Horiuchi, S. (2000). Increase of maximum life-span in Sweden, 1861–1999. *Science, 289*, 2366–2368.

female advantage in life expectancy will continue to decrease in developed countries, due to the fact that male and female behaviors (smoking, in particular) have become more similar. In many developing countries, however, it is predicted that the female advantage will increase in a fashion similar to what was observed in developed countries during the mid-20th century, because males have been differentially adopting many of the behaviors producing excess mortality.

### SOCIOECONOMIC DIFFERENTIALS IN LIFE EXPECTANCY

Levels of life expectancy at the national level can mask important within-country differences by socioeconomic status (SES), race and ethnicity, marital status, area of residence, and other variables. The study of mortality disparities and their causes is important, because it allows the identification of disadvantaged subgroups and the formulation of policies aimed at reducing these disparities.

Whether SES is measured using education, occupation, income, or a combination of these variables, there is ample evidence that groups with lower SES experience lower levels of life expectancy than groups with higher SES. In the United States in 2000, for example, the difference in life expectancy at age 25 between individuals with only a high school education or less and individuals with any college was 7 years (Meara, Richards, & Cutler, 2008).

A multitude of factors potentially contributes to the observed socioeconomic differentials. The factors that are most often cited include housing conditions, occupational hazards, health behaviors (e.g., smoking, alcohol use, diet, and exercise), access to and utilization of health care, and psychosocial stress. It is also possible that the relationship between SES and life expectancy is spurious and that other variables, such as poor health or social background, may cause both lower SES and lower life expectancy. There is no agreement about the validity of these various explanations.

In the decades leading up to the 21st century, there is evidence that socioeconomic differentials in life expectancy have increased in some developed countries, including the United States and Great Britain. In these countries, the life expectancy among higher socioeconomic groups has increased faster than among lower socioeconomic groups. This pattern is attributed in part to faster adoption of healthy lifestyles (better diet and more exercise) and better access to medical innovations in the area of prevention and treatment of cardiovascular diseases among individuals with higher SES. Differential trends in smoking by social class may also have contributed to the widening gap. Not all developed countries, however, have experienced a widening gap in life expectancy. In Canada, for example, the gap between people in low- and high-income areas declined between 1971 and 1996 (Wilkins, Berthelot, & Ng, 2002). Among French males, the gap between the life expectancy of managers and that of manual workers remained constant between 1980 and 1991 (Cambois, Robine, & Hayward, 2001).

In multiethnic or multiracial countries, levels of life expectancy typically differ by race and ethnicity. Perhaps the best-known example of such differentials is the Black–White differential in the United States. In 2003 the White advantage in life expectancy was 6.3 years for males and 4.5 years for females (Harper, Lynch, Burris, & Smith, 2007). Other countries where race and ethnic differentials have been documented include Brazil, South Africa, and the United Kingdom. Race and ethnic differences in life expectancy appear to be due in part to the fact that race and ethnic groups differ with respect to SES. Other factors that may play a role besides socioeconomic factors include cultural factors (which may shape health behaviors in distinct ways and may also shape norms and beliefs about social relationships), neighborhood effects, psychosocial stress associated with minority status and discrimination, and genetic factors. When studying the life expectancy of race and ethnic groups that are foreign-born, it is important to also consider the *healthy migrant* effect (i.e., healthier individuals may be more likely to migrate than their less healthy counterparts). The healthy migrant effect makes it difficult to interpret differences in life expectancy between foreign-born and native-born groups.

Another well-known differential in life expectancy is the differential by marital status. Studies have repeatedly shown that, in various countries and time periods, life expectancy is higher among married individuals than among unmarried individuals. There are two hypotheses for explaining this differential. The first hypothesis stresses the role of selection into marriage. According to this hypothesis, individuals who are in poor health may be less likely to marry, which could explain the lower life expectancy of the unmarried. Other individual characteristics, such as education, may both affect the likelihood of marrying and the risk of death and explain the observed differentials. The second hypothesis stresses the beneficial or protective effect of marriage on survival. Marriage may influence health behaviors (e.g., smoking, diet, and alcohol use) in positive ways, reduce psychosocial stress, and provide a more supportive social environment, which together may reduce mortality risks. Scholars agree that both selection and protection are operating factors, but the respective contribution of these two mechanisms has not been well established.

Another source of within-country variation in life expectancy is one's area of residence. The amount of variation depends on the choice of geographical unit for calculating these differences. In France, for example, the life expectancy disparity between the highest and lowest life expectancy at the *région* level (21 units) in 1994 was 4.5 years for males and 2.6 years for females. At the *département* level (94 units), the disparity was 6.2 years for males and 3.4 years for females (Valkonen, 2001; a *département* is on average four times the size of a U.S. county, and a *région* typically contains four *departments*). In the United States in 1999, the life expectancy disparity at the county level was 18.2 years for males and 12.7 years for females (Ezzati, Friedman, Kulkarni, & Murray, 2008). Regional differences in life expectancy are explained to a large extent by differences in the socioeconomic and ethnic and racial makeup of the population of these subnational areas. The healthy migrant effect, arising from both internal and international migration, is also likely to play a role. The possible causal effects of area, such as environmental factors (e.g., climate, air pollution, and water quality) and quality of health services, are difficult to quantify.

Although life expectancy is the product of a complex set of factors that are difficult to identify and evaluate, it remains a simple, and perhaps the least ambiguous, measure of human welfare.

**SEE ALSO** Volume 3: *Active Life Expectancy; Age Structure; Death and Dying; Demographic Transition Theories; Epidemiologic Transition; Mortality; Population Aging.*

## BIBLIOGRAPHY

Acsádi, G., & Nemeskéri, J. (1970). *History of human life span and mortality.* Trans. K. Balás. Budapest: Akadémiai Kiadó.

Barford, A., Dorling, D., Smith, G. D., & Shaw, M. (2006). Life expectancy: Women now on top everywhere. *British Medical Journal, 332*(7545), 808.

Cambois, E., Robine, J.-M., & Hayward, M. D. (2001). Social inequalities in disability-free life expectancy in the French male population, 1980–1991. *Demography, 38*(4), 513–524.

Ezzati, M., Friedman, A. B., Kulkarni, S. C., & Murray, C. J. L. (2008). The reversal of fortunes: Trends in county mortality and cross-county mortality disparities in the United States. *Public Library of Science Medicine, 5*(4), 557–568.

Guillot, M. (2002). The dynamics of the population sex ratio in India, 1971–96. *Population Studies, 56*(1), 51–63.

Harper, S., Lynch, J., Burris, S., & Smith, G. D. (2007). Trends in the Black–White life expectancy gap in the United States, 1983–2003. *Journal of the American Medical Association, 297*(11), 1224–1232.

Hatcher, J., Piper, A. J., & Stone, D. (2006). Monastic mortality: Durham priory, 1395–1529. *The Economic History Review, 59*(4), 667–687.

Hill, K. (1995). The decline of childhood mortality. In J. L. Simon (Ed.), *The state of humanity* (pp. 37–50). Cambridge, MA: Blackwell.

Meara, E. R., Richards, S., & Cutler, D. M. (2008). The gap gets bigger: Changes in mortality and life expectancy, by education, 1981–2000. *Health Affairs, 27*(2), 350–360.

Olshansky, S. J., Carnes, B. A., & Cassel, C. (1990). In search of Methuselah: Estimating the upper limits to human longevity. *Science, 250*(4981), 634–640.

Robine, J. M., & Allard, M. (1999). Jeanne Calment: Validation of the duration of her life. In B. Jeune & J. W. Vaupel (Eds.), *Validation of exceptional longevity.* Odense, Denmark: Odense University Press.

Statistics Bureau of Ministry of Internal Affairs and Communication. (2007). *Statistical handbook of Japan 2007.* Retrieved June 5, 2008, from http://www.stat.go.jp/English

United Nations. (2007). *World population prospects: The 2006 revision.* New York: Author.

Valkonen, T. (2001). Trends in differential mortality in European countries. In J. Vallin, F. Meslé, & T. Valkonen (Eds.), *Trends in mortality and differential mortality* (pp. 185–328). Starsbourg: Council of Europe.

Wilkins, R., Berthelot, J.-M., & Ng, E. (2002). Trends in mortality by neighborhood income in urban Canada from 1971 to 1996. *Health Reports, 13*(Suppl.), 45–72.

Wilmoth, J. R. (1998). The future of human longevity: A demographer's perspective. *Science, 280*(5362), 395–397.

Wrigley, E. A., & Schofield, R. S. (1981). *The population history of England, 1541–1871: A reconstruction.* Cambridge, MA: Harvard University Press.

***Michel Guillot***

# LIFE REVIEW

SEE Volume 3: *Wisdom.*

# LIFE SPAN

SEE Volume 3: *Centenarians; Death and Dying; Life Expectancy; Mortality; Oldest Old.*

# LIFELONG LEARNING

Ancient and contemporary societies all over the world have understood the importance of learning continuously throughout life. The concept of lifelong learning, broadly defined as the process by which people consciously acquire formal or informal education throughout their lives for personal or career development, is not new. The imperative for societies to promote and organize continuous learning, however, is a recent development. Since the 1970s a steady flow of official documents, policy statements, and program initiatives have been implemented to support learning activities across the life course. Educators, employers, policy makers, and the public have recognized that knowledge obtained and skills learned by late adolescence or young adulthood are not enough to successfully adapt to rapidly changing cultural, social, political, and economic environments. Although lifelong learning has become a key principle of 21st century national and international educational policies, defining and equitably implementing this nebulous and multifaceted concept is a significant challenge.

## CONCEPT OF LIFELONG LEARNING

There is no universal definition of lifelong learning. It is an all-encompassing, generic term that overlaps with closely related concepts, such as continuing and adult education (Aspin & Chapman, 2000). Adult education typically refers to learning in structured programs, among people older than traditionally aged undergraduate college or university students. The age at which a learner becomes an adult varies greatly across sociohistoric and cultural systems, which have diverse political and economic priorities. Continuing education also serves adult learners, but does not normally include basic instruction programs, such as English as a second language (ESL) classes or preparation for high school equivalency exams. Continuing education students enroll in various postsecondary programs, such as university credit courses, workforce training, and formal personal enrichment classes offered on campuses and online. Lifelong learning encompasses continuing as well as adult education, and has burgeoned into a global concept that includes all forms of teaching and learning that equip individuals to encounter a broad range of working and living experiences (Jarvis, 2001).

Although diverse forms of learning from cradle to grave have taken place throughout history, up to the

1960s, education was predominantly equated with the schooling of young people (Mendel-Añonuevo, Ohasko, & Mauch, 2001). A few marginal institutions served adults' educational needs, but the main purpose of education was to socialize young people and prepare young adults (mainly males) for full-time employment. The 1972 United Nations Educational, Scientific, and Cultural Organization (UNESCO) report "Learning to Be" was one of the first attempts to institutionalize the idea of lifelong education, the conceptual precursor to lifelong learning. Also known as the Faure Report, this comprehensive vision advocated the right and necessity for all individuals to learn for their social, cultural, political, and economic development and recommended integrating adult education into a redesigned system, not simply tacking it onto the end of school education (Faure, 1972).

In 1973 the Organization for Economic Co-operation and Development (OECD) advocated a similar concept of recurrent education. Known as the Clarifying Report, this document proposed replacing the front-end model of education that concentrates organized learning on childhood and adolescence with an educational system that redistributes learning opportunities over the entire life course. The Clarifying Report advocated alternating education with other activities, such as work, leisure, and retirement, over the life course. Although reports from the UNESCO and the OECD articulated slightly different tactics and strategies for promoting lifelong education, they shared the belief that initial training and education should be followed by learning opportunities accessible to all citizens regardless of age, sex, race, ethnicity, or social class.

In 1996 the UNESCO's Delors Report advocated a semantic and substantive shift from lifelong education to lifelong learning. In the early 1970s lifelong education was conceived as a strategy for improving collective life as well as personal skills. Emphasizing the role of social institutions and structures, the goal of lifelong education was to develop more humane communities and individuals in the midst of social change (Bagnall, 2000). In contrast, the predominant interpretation of lifelong learning in the 1990s and 2000s has a stronger focus on individual skill acquisition in the face of a rapidly changing workplace (Jarvis, 2007). The economically motivated conception of lifelong learning has drawn sharp criticism since the late 1990s because of its emphasis on "learning to earn" and neglect of broader social contributions.

## LIFE COURSE THEORIES FOR LIFELONG LEARNING

Theories of lifelong education and learning are fragmented across several academic disciplines, including behavioral psychology, educational philosophy, and cognitive neuroscience. Indeed, it is questionable whether a comprehensive theory of lifelong learning is even possible given the vast number of factors that shape the process and context of lifelong learning (Jarvis, 2006).

The life course perspective, which is a framework for studying people over time in historical context, offers one integrative approach to examining lifelong learning. By focusing on the developmental pathways people establish through constraints and incentives, the life course perspective highlights how events experienced early in life influence later life transitions and outcomes (Elder, 1994). Age stratification theory and the theory of cumulative advantage and disadvantage, both reflecting key insights of a life course perspective, offer insight into lifelong learning.

Matilda White Riley's (1911–2004) age stratification theory (1996) begins with the assumption that age, like gender and race, is a basis for grouping people into social categories and channeling them through different role expectations and opportunity structures. Such age-grading assigns education to the young, work and family responsibilities to the middle-aged, and leisure in retirement to the old, with each age-segregated life segment occurring within a distinct set of social institutions. The current approach to education, for example, involves an intensive concentration in the first 25 years of life, but lacks systematic attempts to update skills and knowledge throughout adulthood. In the United States there is a tendency to focus expectations and resources on early education, viewing education like a measles immunization: once given, it lasts a lifetime (Harootyan & Feldman, 1990). As the life course becomes more fluid, however, alternating periods of employment, formal education, and leisure across the life course will become a greater possibility.

The theory of cumulative advantage and disadvantage is also a useful lens through which to examine lifelong learning. This theory proposes that individuals who have early opportunities for success often build on that success to perpetuate and increase their advantages into later life (Merton, 1973). Just as the accumulation of advantage provides stratified access to material and psychological rewards, negative life events can have an enduring and multiplying impact over the life course (O'Rand, 1996). The theory of cumulative advantage and disadvantage may be used as a tool to understand how lifelong learning can be a mechanism for individual empowerment and for social exclusion (Hamil-Luker, 2005).

## TRENDS IN LIFELONG LEARNING

As evinced by the increasing numbers of adult learners and programs offered, lifelong learning has experienced burgeoning growth since the 1970s. Between 1971 and

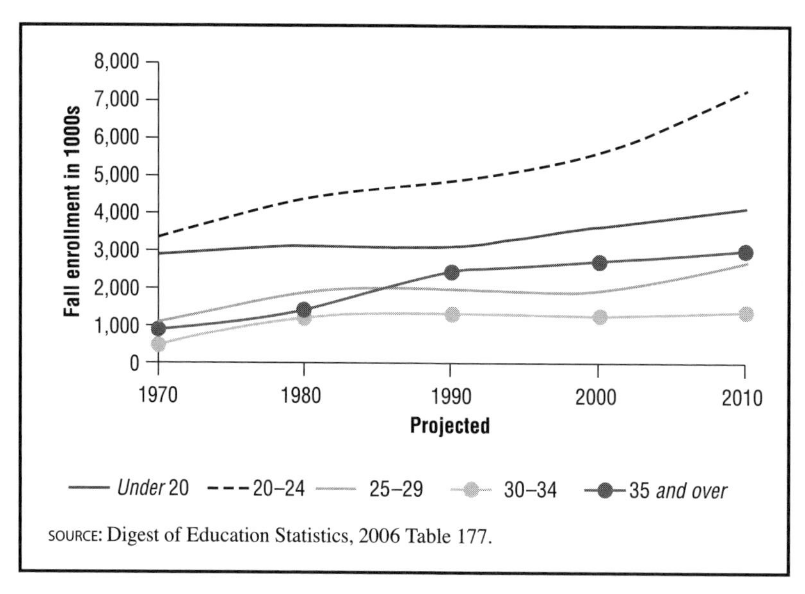

SOURCE: Digest of Education Statistics, 2006 Table 177.

***Figure 1.*** *Total fall enrollment in degree-granting institutions by age, 1970–2010.* CENGAGE LEARNING, GALE.

1991, full- and part-time enrollment of students aged 35 and older at colleges and universities rose by 248% (National University Continuing Education Association, 1995). Enrollment trends for degree-granting institutions are presented in Figure 1. As shown here, since the mid-1970s universities have admitted substantial numbers of students over the age of 24. Although traditional aged students will continue to enroll in degree-granting institutions in the largest numbers into 2010, the greatest percent increase will be among those aged 35 and over (Snyder, Dillow, & Hoffman, 2007). From 2004 to 2014, the U.S. Department of Education projects a rise of 11% in enrollments of persons under 25, but an increase of 15% in the number aged 25 and over (Snyder, Dillow, & Hoffman, 2007).

In addition to the increasing numbers of adults pursuing university coursework, 88 million adults in 2000 and 2001 enrolled in basic skills classes, work training programs, or personal development courses (Kim, Hagedorn, Williamson, & Chapman, 2004). Excluding full-time programs, 44% of adults in the United States participated in formal adult educational activities in 2004 and 2005 (O'Donnell, 2006). Middle-aged workers are also increasingly likely to reenter vocational training (Elman & O'Rand, 1998). As a further indicator of the growing importance of lifelong learning, federal funding for adult education increased from approximately $201 million in 1991 to $585 million in the fiscal year of 2005 (U.S. Department of Health and Education, 2005).

Numerous economic, technological, and demographic developments have contributed to the proliferation of lifelong learning policies and participation (Sticht, 1998). The most powerful influence is the recognition among governments that an educated workforce can contribute to sustained economic growth, productivity gains, and national competitiveness in a global, knowledge-based marketplace. In its *Strategic Plan: 1998–2002*, for example, the U.S. Department of Education includes the goal of ensuring "access to post-secondary education and lifelong learning" so "adults can strengthen their skills and improve their earning power over their lifetime" (1997, p. 41).

New technological developments and rapidly dropping prices for personal computers, Internet access, and other technological tools have facilitated lifelong learning in homes, workplaces, and schools. Growing numbers of individuals engage in distance learning, where teachers and students are separated over space and time but have interactive communication. Raising the standard for what it means to be literate in the United States in the early 21st century, basic skills include new information and communication technologies.

The aging of the population in most developed nations has contributed to a growth in learning activities among older adults (Hamil-Luker & Uhlenberg, 2002). An overall increase in education levels, improved nutrition, and medical care have contributed to more disability-free years of life. This, in turn, has resulted in greater leisure time and interest in educational activities among older adults. Furthermore, neuroscience research has helped combat the myth of inevitable intellectual decline with age, showing that the brain has a lifelong capacity to reshape itself in response to experience (Bruer, 1999). Mental agility and

| Characteristic | Any Adult Education | Work-Related | Personal Interest | ESL | Basic Skills | Part-time College | Part-time Vocational | Apprenticeship |
|---|---|---|---|---|---|---|---|---|
| **Age** | | | | | | | | |
| 16–24 | 53 | 21 | 27 | 2 | 6 | 9 | 2 | 3 |
| 25–34 | 52 | 32 | 22 | 2 | 2 | 7 | 2 | 3 |
| 35–44 | 49 | 34 | 22 | 1 | 1 | 4 | 1 | 1 |
| 45–54 | 48 | 37 | 20 | – | – | 3 | 1 | 1 |
| 55–64 | 40 | 27 | 21 | – | – | 1 | 1 | – |
| 65+ | 23 | 5 | 19 | – | – | – | – | – |
| **Sex** | | | | | | | | |
| Male | 41 | 24 | 18 | 1 | 1 | 4 | 1 | 2 |
| Female | 47 | 29 | 24 | 1 | 1 | 4 | 1 | 1 |
| **Years of schooling** | | | | | | | | |
| No high school degree | 22 | 4 | 11 | 2 | 7 | – | 1 | 1 |
| High school degree | 33 | 17 | 16 | 1 | 1 | 2 | 1 | 2 |
| Some college/voc/associate | 51 | 31 | 25 | 1 | – | 6 | 2 | 1 |
| Bachelor's degree | 60 | 44 | 29 | – | – | 6 | 1 | – |
| Graduate/prof education | 66 | 51 | 30 | – | – | 7 | 1 | – |
| **Household income** | | | | | | | | |
| $20,000 or less | 28 | 11 | 16 | 1 | 2 | 2 | 1 | 2 |
| $20,001–$35,000 | 36 | 18 | 17 | 2 | 2 | 4 | 1 | 1 |
| $35,001–$50,000 | 42 | 23 | 22 | 1 | 1 | 2 | 1 | 1 |
| $50,001–$75,000 | 48 | 33 | 21 | – | – | 5 | 1 | 1 |
| $75,001 + | 58 | 39 | 27 | – | 1 | 5 | 2 | 1 |
| **Occupation** | | | | | | | | |
| Professional/managerial | 70 | 56 | 29 | – | – | 8 | 1 | 1 |
| Sales/service/clerical | 48 | 31 | 22 | 1 | 2 | 5 | 2 | 1 |
| Trade and labor | 34 | 19 | 13 | 2 | 2 | 2 | 2 | 3 |

Note: Estimate rounds to 0 or 0 cases in sample.

***Table 1.*** *Percentage of adults who participated in adult education by type of activity and demographic characteristics; National Household Education Survey 2004–2005.* CENGAGE LEARNING, GALE.

learning ability do not uniformly decline with advancing age, offering new learning opportunities for those in the *third age.*

Although there has been tremendous growth in lifelong learning, only a small fraction of those who could reap benefits are participating. The 2003 National Assessment of Adult Literacy, for example, found that 14% of Americans aged 16 or older in the United States have below basic literacy. More than half of the 120 million U.S. workers aged 25 to 64 do not possess a postsecondary degree (Neurohr, 2007). Cross-national survey data on literacy and numeracy suggest that the skills of U.S. adults do not compare favorably with their peers from other countries (Lemke & Gonzalez, 2006). Although increasing lifelong learning opportunity is frequently heralded as a way to solve these deficiencies, the proliferation of adult education and training programs may in fact contribute to increased social and economic exclusion. Groups who are already privileged disproportionately take advantage of educational and training opportunities. As shown in Table 1, those with the highest levels of education, income, and occupational prestige are the most likely to participate in lifelong learning. Furthermore, different groups are channeled into different types of academic and career-training programs. Adults aged 55 to 64, for example, are less likely to receive work-related training than those aged 25 to 54, but they are equally likely to enroll in personal interest courses. As employer demand for highly skilled workers grows and as the already well-educated pursue further training, those without favorably valued skills may fall further and further down socioeconomic and political ladders.

## FUTURE DIRECTIONS FOR LIFELONG LEARNING

From the highest levels of government to the lowest levels of impoverishment, there is widespread endorsement of the view that lifelong learning can resolve many of the economic, cultural, social, and political problems in the 21st century. Implementing lifelong learning, however, is hampered by lack of shared understanding of the term, difficulty in measuring it, diversity of learning opportunities, and lack of empirical research on outcomes. Most education research still focuses on basic education for children and young adults, with comparatively little effort on studying adult education. A multitude of publications focus on motivations and cognitive development of individual learners, but neglect structural barriers, public policies, and the larger social and historic context in which learning occurs or fails to occur. Furthermore, the majority of statements about lifelong learning are formulated in positive terms, ignoring problems of access and issues of equity.

Discussions and debates over lifelong learning must be accompanied by evidence of how it works and the contributions it makes to societies. While there is some research on the economic benefits of lifelong learning for individuals, there is limited research on the institutional and national returns to investments in lifelong learning as well as the non-economic benefits that accrue to individuals. Furthermore, future research should assess the process by which lifelong learning is used as a mechanism of social exclusion. By examining program offerings and patterns of behavior among learners, researchers can identify segments of the population to be served and combat the tendency for lifelong education to contribute to inequality in the realms of employment, earnings, citizenship, health, consumption, and individual well-being (Field, 2006).

Although policy statements and experimental initiatives on lifelong learning have flourished, a redesigned education system in which people of all ages update their knowledge and skills over time has not been achieved. Translating endorsement of a concept into policy application is difficult (Istance, Schuetze, & Schuller, 2002). Indeed, the widespread provision of lifelong learning will entail a revolution in education systems.

**SEE ALSO** Volume 2: *Educational Attainment;* Volume 3: *Wisdom.*

### BIBLIOGRAPHY

Aspin, D. N., & Chapman, J. D. (2000). Lifelong learning: Concepts and conceptions. *International Journal of Lifelong Education, 19,* 2–19.

Bagnall, R. (2000). Lifelong learning and the limitations of economic determinism. *International Journal of Lifelong Education, 19,* 20–35.

Bruer, J. T. (1999). The myth of the first three years: A new understanding of early brain development and lifelong learning. New York: The Free Press.

Center for Educational Research and Information. (1973). *Recurrent education: A strategy for lifelong learning.* Paris: Organization for Economic Co-operation and Development.

Delors, J., et al. (1996). *Learning, the treasure within: Report to UNESCO of the international commission on education for the 21st century.* Paris: United Nations Educational, Scientific, and Cultural Organization.

Elder, G. H., Jr. (1994). Time, human agency, and social change: Perspectives on the life course. *Social Psychology Quarterly, 57,* 4–15.

Elman, C., & O'Rand, A. M. (1998). Midlife work pathways and educational entry. *Research on Aging, 20,* 475–505.

Faure, E. (1972). *Learning to be: The world of education today and tomorrow.* Paris: United Nations Educational, Scientific, and Cultural Organization (UNESCO).

Field, J. (2006). *Lifelong learning and the new educational order.* Sterling, VA: Trentham Books.

Hamil-Luker, J., & Uhlenberg, P. (2002). Later life education in the 1990s: Increasing involvement and continuing disparity. *Journal of Gerontology: Psychological and Social Sciences, 57,* S324–S331.

Hamil-Luker, J. (2005). Women's wages: Cohort differences in returns to education and training over time. *Social Science Quarterly, 86,* 1261–1278.

Harootyan, R. A., & Feldman, N. S. (1990). Lifelong education, lifelong needs: Future roles in an aging society. *Educational Gerontology, 16,* 347–358.

Istance, D., Schuetze, H. G., & Schuller, T. (2002). *International perspectives on lifelong learning: From recurrent education to the knowledge society.* Philadelphia: Open University Press.

Jarvis, P. (2001). *The age of learning: Education and the knowledge society.* Sterling, VA: Kogan Page.

Jarvis, P. (2006). *Towards a comprehensive theory of human learning.* New York: Routledge.

Jarvis, P. (2007). *Globalization, lifelong learning, and the learning society: Sociological perspectives.* New York: Routledge.

Kim, K., Hagedorn, M., Williamson, J., & Chapman, C. (2004). *National Household Education Surveys program of 2001: Participation in adult education and lifelong learning, 2000–01.* Washington, DC: National Center for Education Statistics, U.S. Department of Education, and the Institute of Education Sciences.

Lemke, M., & Gonzales, P. (2006). *U.S. student and adult performance on international assessments of educational achievement.* Washington, DC: National Center for Education Statistics, U.S. Department of Education, and the Institute of Education Sciences.

Mendel-Añonuevo, C., Ohsako, T., & Mauch, W. (2001). *Revisiting lifelong learning for the 21st century.* Hamburg, Germany: United Nations Educational, Scientific, and Cultural Organization (UNESCO) Institute for Education.

Merton, R. K. (1973). The Matthew Effect in science. In N.W. Storer (Ed.), *The Sociology of science.* Chicago: University of Chicago Press.

National University Continuing Education Association (NUCEA). (1995). New and older college student profile. *NUCEA News, 11*(6), 3.

Neurohr, J. (2007). *Lifelong learning: New strategies for the education of working adults.* Washington, DC: U.S. Federal News Service.

O'Donnell, K. (2006). *National Household Education Surveys program of 2005: Adult education participation in 2004–05.* Washington, DC: National Center for Education Statistics, U.S. Department of Education, and the Institute of Education Sciences.

O'Rand, A. (1996). The precious and the precocious: Understanding cumulative disadvantage and cumulative advantage over the life course. *The Gerontologist, 36,* 230–238.

Pugsley, R. S. (1999). Lifelong-learning policies in the United States: Converging perspectives. In A. Tuijnman & T. Schuller (Eds.), *Lifelong learning policy and research: Proceedings of an international symposium* (pp. 129–141). London: Portland Press.

Riley, M. W. (1996). Age stratification: Age, aging, and the aged. In the *Encyclopedia of gerontology* (pp. 81–92). San Diego, CA: Academic Press.

Riley, M. W. (1998). *The hidden age revolution: Emergent integration of all ages.* Syracuse, NY: Center for Policy Research.

Riley, M. W., & Riley, J. W. (2000). Age integration: Conceptual and historical background. *The Gerontologist, 40*(3), 266–270.

Snyder, T. D., Dillow, S. A., & Hoffman, C. M. (2007). *Digest of education statistics, 2006.* Washington, DC: U.S. Government Printing Office.

Sticht, T. G. (1998). *Beyond 2000: Future directions for adult education.* Washington, DC: U.S. Department of Education.

U.S. Department of Education (2004). *Fiscal year 2005 budget summary.* Washington, DC: Author.

U.S. Department of Education. (1997). *Strategic plan: 1998–2002.* Washington, DC: U.S. Government Printing Office.

***Jenifer Hamil-Luker***

# LONELINESS, LATER LIFE

Loneliness has been defined as a sense of dissatisfaction with the number or quality of one's social relationships. Although loneliness may include an objective lack of social relationships, it has been more broadly conceptualized as a subjective discrepancy between desired and actual relationships (De Jong-Gierveld, 1987; Perlman & Peplau, 1981).

Two main dimensions of loneliness are social isolation and emotional isolation. Social isolation refers to a perceived lack of social ties and dissatisfaction with the number or frequency of one's social interactions, resulting in persons feeling left out, marginalized, or bored. Emotional isolation, by contrast, refers to the content and quality of relationships, representing a sense of disconnection, lack of intimacy, or loss of significant relationships. Emotional loneliness is experienced as a more profound and distressing feeling of "utter aloneness" (Weiss 1973, p. 21) and as an intense, emotionally painful experience that diminishes psychological well-being. A less studied component of loneliness has been described by Lars Andersson (1986) as existential estrangement, referring to a sense of aloneness arising out of awareness of one's own finiteness and mortality.

## OVERVIEW OF RESEARCH ON LONELINESS

Research on loneliness has been traced as far back as the late 1700s. In the 1950s, David Riesman's (1953) influential book, *The Lonely Crowd,* and the English translation of Émile Durkheim's (1951) classic, *Suicide,* established social isolation as a significant individual experience and as a characteristic of modern societies. Within the study of aging, early studies were influenced by disengagement theory, which described old age as a time of loss and gradual but inevitable detachment from social roles and relationships. Modernization theory and structural-functionalist perspectives on families reinforced the image of older adults as cast off from society and isolated from their kin and communities. In response, a number of researchers sought to document the ongoing social connection of older adults, redefining loneliness as a problematic individual experience that diminishes psychological well-being and is neither universal nor inevitable in old age. This research was focused on identifying the *deficits* associated with loneliness, including social losses, life transitions, and structural circumstances, as exemplified by Helena Lopata's (1925–2003) landmark research on loneliness among older widows.

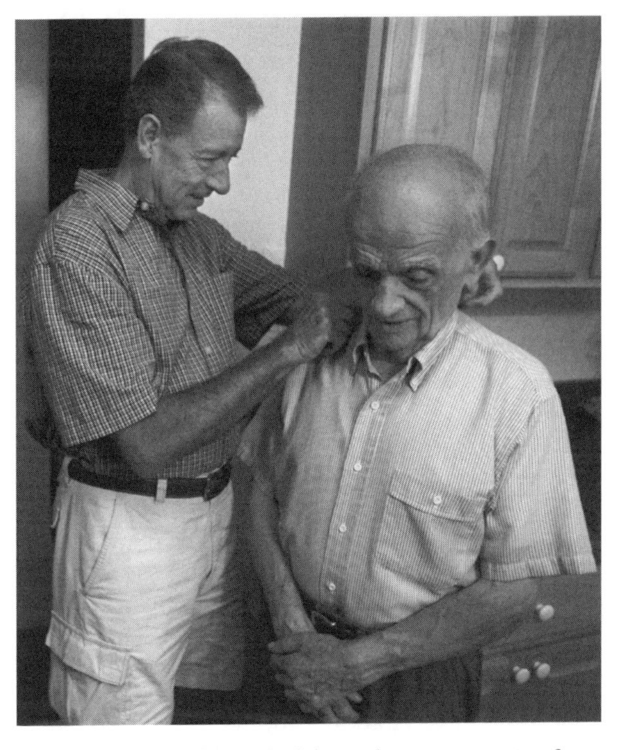

***Lonely Nation.*** *Bob Moody, left, a volunteer companion for Rocky Lepore, fixes Lepore's collar before they go for a walk in Chicago. Moody is a member of "Little Brothers-Friends of the Elderly," a group that provides companionship for isolated elderly people in several American cities.* AP IMAGES.

Researchers also examined the role of physical and social environments in shaping loneliness, including living arrangements and senior housing, relations and contact with kin, and social networks and activities. These studies documented the extent and correlates of loneliness among older adults, but found few consistent links between objective circumstances and subjective reports of loneliness. These observations led to new and more precise definitions and measures of loneliness, which emphasized its subjective nature and its distinctness from other kinds of psychological distress and from objective indicators of social isolation.

## CONTEMPORARY RESEARCH CONTRIBUTIONS

Since the late 1980s, theorizing about loneliness has expanded to better conceptualize the complexity of loneliness, while research has continued to attend to the objective and subjective factors linked with loneliness. Ami Rokach's and Heather Brock's (1997) phenomenological approach has revealed the multifaceted experiences of loneliness through a five-factor *experiential conceptualization of loneliness* that includes emotional distress, social inadequacy and alienation, interpersonal isolation, and self-alienation, as well as the potentially positive growth related to loneliness. This model has been used to describe loneliness in different age groups and populations, though it has been tested only with nonprobability samples that may not describe the general population. By focusing on qualitative aspects of loneliness, Rokach's work has shed light on the benefits of recognizing and dealing with loneliness and the dangers of repressing or denying it. Particularly intriguing is its recognition of the potential of loneliness for positive outcomes such as motivating change and growth (Rokach et al., 2007).

Pearl Dykstra and Jenny De Jong-Gierveld (1994) in the Netherlands have also examined the complexity of loneliness, focusing on the underlying cognitive dimensions of loneliness and applications to large-scale studies of older adults. Their work has explored the important role of individual preferences, expectations, and perceptions in defining evaluations of loneliness. Differences among older adults are partly shaped by individual preferences regarding social networks and the importance of having an intimate partner relationship; loneliness reflects the cognitive discrepancy between actual and preferred relationships. Objective circumstances (such as health problems, disability, cognitive or sensory declines, or depression) may predispose older persons to loneliness, or they may represent barriers to actions that could reduce or ameliorate loneliness (Dykstra, 1995).

## MEASURING LONELINESS

Existing methods for measuring loneliness reflect these different conceptualizations of loneliness and the complexity of the concept itself. The most basic measures have asked respondents, "How often do you feel lonely?" (in a specified time period) or "Rate yourself on the following scale of loneliness." Single, direct questions are believed to tap into self-awareness of feeling lonely, especially with regard to emotional isolation. In large surveys, a single question provides an inexpensive measure of loneliness that is highly correlated with standard scales. The reliance on self-reporting, however, may underrepresent the true prevalence of loneliness. As loneliness is seen as an undesirable and stigmatized condition, individuals may be reluctant to disclose their feelings in response to a direct question.

Two commonly used scales for measuring the severity and intensity of loneliness, without explicitly referring to loneliness, are the University of California, Los Angeles, (UCLA) scale and the De Jong-Gierveld loneliness scale. The UCLA scale consists of 20 statements that provide a unidimensional assessment of social relations. Shorter versions have also been used successfully in research, including a three-item scale designed specifically for use in large telephone surveys with older adults. De Jong-Gierveld's (1987) 11-item loneliness scale, and a more recently developed six-item version, incorporate both positively and negatively worded items and measure overall loneliness as well as the components of social and emotional loneliness.

## PREVALENCE AND CORRELATES OF LONELINESS

A primary research concern has been to estimate the prevalence of loneliness in the general population (and within specific vulnerable subgroups) and to identify the factors associated with greater risks of loneliness. Estimates of loneliness in older populations vary, but roughly 5–15% of adults over age 65 report feeling severely or often lonely and as many as 40–50% of adults aged 80 and older report moderate or serious loneliness (Weeks, 1994). The relation between age and loneliness has been described as U-shaped, with the highest levels found among the oldest old but relatively low levels among most older adults (Pinquart & Sorenson, 2001). After accounting for structural circumstances, older adults seem to report less loneliness than those at younger ages and less than one might expect based on their objective circumstances, possibly due to more selective social networks and an increased acceptance of loneliness as a part of their life (Schnittker, 2007).

Marital status, intimate partner relations, and other family relations are central predictors of loneliness. Close ties serve as a source of social support and as a buffer against stresses. Loneliness is more prevalent among widowed persons (particularly in the initial period of bereavement), and there is some evidence of greater loneliness among older adults who are divorced or have never married, particularly men. Gender differences in loneliness are inconsistent and highly related to marital status. Childlessness, however, is not consistently linked with loneliness after accounting for other factors (Koropeckyj-Cox, 1998). In general, the quality and closeness of social contacts are more important than quantity, and contacts with friends and neighbors are more influential than contact with kin, particularly among unmarried elders.

Living alone is related to loneliness, in part because of its connection with being unmarried. Higher levels of loneliness are found among elders living in nursing homes, and loneliness itself increases the risk of nursing home admission. Various studies have linked loneliness with poor physical health, including high blood pressure (Hawkley et al., 2006), Alzheimer's disease (Wilson et al., 2007), and suppressed immune function (Kennedy, Keicolt-Glaser, & Glaser, 1988), as well as with assessments of having worse health than expected (Victor et al., 2005) and a higher body mass index (Lauder et al., 2006). It is also correlated with depression (Cacioppo et al., 2006), other forms of psychological distress, and suicide (Kennedy & Tanenbaum, 2000).

## FUTURE RESEARCH DIRECTIONS

As populations continue to grow older, understanding loneliness as a component of psychological well-being and quality of life in old age will remain important. Changes in relationships and families are likely to present additional challenges, with smaller families and an increased prevalence of divorce, cohabitation, and childlessness among currently aging cohorts. These variations, combined with an increased emphasis on seeking personal self-fulfillment within intimate and family relationships, may increase the risks of loneliness in the future, particularly as nonfamilial community ties have weakened. Continued interest in loneliness will also be motivated by concern about enhancing physical and mental health and reducing the potentially preventable, negative consequences of loneliness.

The increased availability of large-scale studies of aging, including longitudinal data (where individuals are observed at more than one point in time), presents several avenues for future research. First, the influence of the life course perspective in research on loneliness is remarkably limited. Loneliness is usually studied through cross-sectional comparisons of current feelings, with relatively little attention to past experiences. A few studies have examined age, marital status, and childlessness in a larger life course context—by separating, for example, marital history from current status or permanent childlessness from having no surviving children. Some have used longitudinal data to examine changes over time. Future research will need to further explore how loneliness itself is experienced over the life course and how earlier or sustained episodes of loneliness or hardship (as well as coping and recovery) shape the preferences, evaluations, and strategies for dealing with day-to-day challenges. The life course perspective provides a conceptual framework for better integrating qualitative, experiential insights and new theoretical ideas about ambivalence in relationships into one's understanding of loneliness.

Second, further cross-national research may help to illuminate both the similarities and differences in cross-cultural experiences of loneliness. As De Jong-Gierveld and Betty Havens (2004) have recently noted, assessments of loneliness depend "on the prevailing (social) standards as to what constitutes an optimal network of relationships" and on the context in a particular society of "integrating or mediating structures" available to persons throughout the life course and in old age (p. 110). The prevalence, meanings, and implications of loneliness across societies are significant areas to explore for future research, particularly with regard to developing countries that are experiencing rapid aging and economic and social change. Cross-national, comparative research may provide an opportunity to reexamine and sharpen conceptualizations of loneliness as a "culture bound" phenomenon (Perlman 2004, p. 186).

**SEE ALSO** Volume 3: *Mental Health, Later Life; Singlehood; Social Integration/Isolation, Later Life; Social Support, Later Life; Suicide, Later Life.*

## BIBLIOGRAPHY

Andersson, L. (1986). A model of estrangement—Including a theoretical understanding of loneliness. *Psychological Reports, 58*, 683–695.

Cacioppo, J. T., Hughes, M. E., Waite, L. J., Hawkley, L. C., & Thisted, R. A. (2006). Loneliness as a specific risk factor for depressive symptoms: Cross-sectional and longitudinal analyses. *Psychology and Aging, 21*(1), 140–151.

De Jong-Gierveld, J. (1987). Developing and testing a model of loneliness. *Journal of Personality and Social Psychology, 53*(1), 119–128.

De Jong-Gierveld, J., & Havens, B. (2004). Cross-national comparisons of social isolation and loneliness: Introduction and overview. *Canadian Journal on Aging, 23*(2), 109–113.

Durkheim, E. (1951). *Suicide: A study in sociology.* (J. A. Spaulding & G. Simpson, Trans.). Glencoe, IL: Free Press.

Dykstra, P. A. (1995). Loneliness among the never married and formerly married: The importance of supportive friendships and desire for independence. *Journals of Gerontology: Social Sciences, 50B*, S321–S329.

Dykstra, P. A., & De Jong-Gierveld, J. (1994). The theory of mental incongruity, with a specific application to loneliness among widowed men and women. In R. Erber & R. Gilmour (Eds.), *Theoretical frameworks for personal relationships* (pp. 235–259). Hillsdale, NJ: Lawrence Erlbaum.

Hawkley, L. C., Masi, C. M., Berry, J. D., & Cacioppo, J. T. (2006). Loneliness is a unique predictor of age-related differences in systolic blood pressure. *Psychology and Aging, 21*(1), 152–164.

Kennedy, G. J., & Tanenbaum, S. (2000). Suicide and aging: International perspectives. *Psychiatric Quarterly, 71*(4), 345–362.

Kennedy, S., Keicolt-Glaser, J., & Glaser, R. (1988). Immunological consequences of acute and chronic stressors: Mediating role of interpersonal relationships. *British Journal of Medical Psychology, 61*(1), 77–85.

Koropeckyj-Cox, T. (1998). Loneliness and depression in middle and old age: Are the childless more vulnerable? *Journal of Gerontology Series B: Social Sciences, 53,* S302–S312.

Lauder, W., Mummery, K., Jones, M., & Caperchione, C. (2006). A comparison of health behaviours in lonely and non-lonely populations. *Psychology, Health, & Medicine, 11*(2), 232–245.

Perlman, D. (2004). European and Canadian studies of loneliness among seniors. *Canadian Journal on Aging, 23*(2), 181–188.

Perlman, D., & Peplau, L. A. (1981). Towards a social psychology of loneliness. In S. W. Duck & R. Gilmour (Eds.), *Personal Relationships 3: Personal Relationships in Disorder* (pp. 31–56). London: Academic Press.

Pinquart, M., & Sorenson, S. (2001). Influences on loneliness in older adults: A meta-analysis. *Basic and Applied Social Psychology, 23*(4), 245–266.

Riesman, D. (1953). *The lonely crowd: A study of the changing American character.* Garden City, NY: Doubleday.

Rokach, A, & Brock, H. (1997). Loneliness: A multidimensional experience. *Psychology: A Journal of Human Behavior, 34*(1), 1–9.

Rokach, A., Matalon, R., Rokach, B., & Safarov, A. (2007). The effects of gender and marital status on loneliness of the aged. *Social Behavior and Personality, 35,* 243–254.

Victor, C. R., Scambler, S. J., Bowling, A., & Bond, J. (2005). The prevalence of, and risk factors for, loneliness in later life: A survey of older people in Great Britain. *Ageing & Society, 25*(3), 357–375.

Weeks, D. J. (1994). A review of loneliness concepts, with particular reference to old age. *International Journal of Geriatric Psychiatry, 9*(5), 345–355.

Weiss, R. S. (1973). *Loneliness: The experience of emotional and social isolation.* Cambridge, MA: MIT Press.

Wilson, R. S., Krueger, K. R., Arnold, S. E., Schneider, J. A., Kelly, J. F., Barnes, L. L., et al. (2007). Loneliness and risk of Alzheimer disease. *Archives of General Psychiatry, 64*(2), 234–240.

*Tanya Koropeckyj-Cox*

## LONGEVITY

**SEE** Volume 3: *Centenarians; Death and Dying; Life Expectancy; Mortality; Oldest Old.*

## LONG-TERM CARE

Long-term care (LTC) encompasses the wide variety of services and support involved in the sustained delivery of health and social care to individuals with functional deficits due to disability or old age, according to Rosalie Kane and Robert Kane (1987). Although children and younger adults with disabilities or chronic health conditions may require LTC, it is much more common and most often associated with frailty in the later part of the life course. As individuals age, functional limitations increase and, for some, interfere with their ability to manage self-care needs without assistance. Individuals' LTC needs vary from a few deficits that demand regular but episodic assistance to those requiring total personal care. For example, many elderly individuals have occasional but persistent needs for help with instrumental activities of daily living, such as doing household chores, preparing meals, and running errands. When such needs are met, individuals retain independence and their capacity to age-in-place at home. At the other end of the spectrum, very frail elders may require assistance with most or all of the activities of daily living such as bathing, dressing, eating, toileting, and transferring in and out of chairs or beds. Some elders retain the physical capacity to perform those tasks for themselves but have cognitive deficits (such as Alzheimer's or other dementias) that require reminders and constant supervision to preserve their safety.

Different dimensions of LTC can be distinguished by (a) the population that needs assistance; (b) the source of provision (informal or formal); (c) the type, complexity, and intensity of services that individuals receive; and (d) the diverse settings in which LTC is provided. Due to population growth, the numbers of nonelderly individuals needing LTC will grow in coming decades whereas, among the elderly, the age group at highest risk for needing LTC (85+) is projected to more than triple from 6 million (in 2005) to 21 million people by 2050 (Feder, Komisar, & Friedland, 2007). Frail elders receive most of the home-based LTC they need from their families, with paid formal care filling the remaining gaps. When informal LTC occurs in the private sphere of the household, Tony Calasanti and Katherine Slevin (2001) point out, it has a taken-for-granted aspect that escapes much public attention. It is usually only when LTC is formalized because it requires private or public financing, involves public policy or regulation, or entails a move from home to a specialized residential care site that the costs and arrangements of LTC capture public attention. Consequently, the study of LTC populations, providers, policy, and services can inform debates around a range of issues, from gender patterns in providing and receiving care to later life financial stability to the merits and challenges of publicly funded social programs.

### TRENDS IN LTC

Individuals' LTC needs can be provided informally by family and friends or formally through purchase from public or private sources or may be supplied by voluntary organizations. Family provision has always dominated LTC for frail elders. Even at the turn of the millennium, with a greater array of formal LTC services and providers than ever before, Ari Houser (2007b) indicated that most LTC is organized and rendered informally by family and friends who are not paid for their services. In fact, families provide an estimated 85% of all LTC (Kitchener & Harrington, 2004). Although informal LTC is unpaid, it has tremendous value. In 2006 the total economic value of informal LTC in the United States was estimated at $350 billion (Houser, 2007b).

Functional declines that often accompany aging mean that, as individuals get older, their likelihood of needing LTC increases (see Figure 1). Gender differences also shape the character of LTC, because women live longer and have higher rates of disability than men. As a result, elderly women require more LTC than men (79% of women compared to 58% of men) and for about a year and a half longer than their male counterparts (Houser, 2007b). A familiar pattern is married women who care for ailing spouses until they die and then require LTC themselves, a pattern typical in most developed countries. For older women, living alone increases the risk of social isolation, poverty (Ginn, Street, & Arber, 2001), and receiving LTC in a formal setting, such as a nursing home (NH; Freedman, 1996).

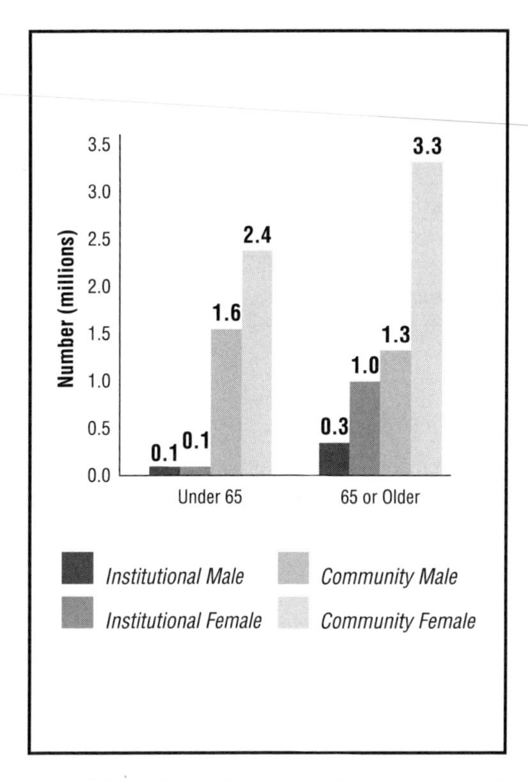


***Figure 1.*** *U.S. adults needing help with everyday activities, by age, gender, and setting.* CENGAGE LEARNING, GALE.

Beyond differences in men's and women's LTC needs, LTC provision is also highly gendered. Strong cultural norms dictate that women—wives, daughters, daughter-in-laws, and sisters—care for parents or disabled relatives. As Francesca Cancian and Stacey Oliker (2000) explain, the idea that women should be almost exclusively responsible for providing LTC has roots in the 19th century ideology of "separate spheres" in which the home was the domain of women and men worked solely outside the home and reflects the assumption that women are "naturally" more nurturing and better suited to the task. Yet men provide informal LTC too (mainly for their spouses), albeit at much lower rates than women (Arber & Ginn, 1995; Calasanti & King, 2007). Compared to the kinds of intimate, often hands-on LTC women are mainly responsible for, men's LTC provision has long been presumed to be more instrumental, encompassing tasks such as financial support or help with house maintenance. However, recent scholarship challenges the notion that men necessarily perform LTC that differs greatly from what women do (Carroll & Campbell, 2008; Russell, 2007), although the amount of hours spent on such activities does differ.

Political forces also perpetuate gender inequality in LTC provision, particularly in the United States. Several European countries have policies supporting informal LTC. For example, German social insurance provides universal home care benefits, including cash allowances for LTC (even for services provided by family members) and also provides the safety net of formal LTC. However, resistance to big government coupled with powerful private business interests curtailed such efforts in the United States. Thus, the public LTC programs developed in the United States favor modest benefits, include formal provision, and provide little acknowledgement or support for informal LTC (Cancian & Oliker, 2000). The gendered nature of informal LTC has long-term effects of its own, because when women spend time out of paid work to provide LTC, the lack of public policy support means their socially necessary work is uncompensated. Women may lose wages by accepting part-time or more flexible, lower-paying jobs or by leaving the workforce altogether, putting their own financial security in old age at risk (Ginn, Street, & Arber, 2001).

## FORMAL LTC

When informal LTC is unavailable or needs for LTC assistance outstrip informal caregivers' capacity to meet them, formal services often bridge areas of LTC need. Widespread availability of formal services that help frail elders remain in their own homes is a fairly recent LTC innovation. Typical home-based LTC includes home health care, personal care and housekeeping services, transportation assistance, meals-on-wheels, adult day centers,

| | 1973–74 | 1977 | 1985 | 1995 | 1997 | 1999 | 2004 |
|---|---|---|---|---|---|---|---|
| Homes | 15,700 | 18,900 | 19,100 | 16,700 | 17,000 | 18,000 | 16,100 |
| Beds | 1,177,300 | 1,402,400 | 1,624,200 | 1,770,900 | 1,820,800 | 1,879,600 | 1,730,000 |
| Current residents | 1,075,800 | 1,303,100 | 1,491,400 | 1,548,600 | 1,608,700 | 1,628,300 | 1,492,200 |
| Occupancy rate | 91.4% | 92.9% | 91.8% | 87.4% | 88.4% | 86.6% | 86.3% |

SOURCE: CDC/NCHS, National Nursing Home Survey, various years.

***Table 1.*** *Trends in NH facilities, beds, residents and occupancy rates, 1973–2004.* CENGAGE LEARNING, GALE.

Alzheimer's respite care, and other local services available for purchase. However, not all LTC services are routinely available in every community or to every individual (Mor et al., 2007). Rural communities, in particular, often lack the formal home-based LTC services that are available in more urban areas. Lack of alternative services (Coburn, Bolda, & Keith, 2003) and patterns of traditional LTC admissions make NHs particularly critical sites of LTC in rural communities (Phillips, Holan, Sherman, Leyk Williams, & Hawes, 2004). Even where home-based services are available, many individuals cannot afford all services they need. Voluntary and nonprofit providers and Medicaid funding to purchase home- and community-based services can fill some gaps, providing essential LTC home-based services for frail elders at risk of NH placement. When LTC can no longer be managed at home, moves to specialized residential LTC sites often ensue. These can include institutional care provided in NHs (also called skilled nursing facilities) or increasingly popular and somewhat less institutional residential care settings such as assisted living, continuing care retirement communities, board and care homes, residential care facilities, and adult foster homes.

## NURSING HOMES

Until recently the most typical residential site for formal LTC in later life was the NH. Yet ending up in a NH when frailty occurs is not inevitable. Eighty-eight percent of U.S. NH residents were 65 or older in 2004, yet only 2% of the 65 to 84 population lives in NHs. Individuals who are long-stay residents in such homes are often extremely frail, and residents have become more frail over time. Preferred alternatives such as home-based services and assisted living have become more widely available, helping all but the most frail elders who can afford it to avoid institutionalization in NHs. In recent years, elderly Blacks have had higher rates of NH utilization than Whites, reversing historical trends; assisted living, in contrast, is dominated by White residents (Institute of Medicine, 2008). Almost four in five NH residents in 2004 needed assistance with four or five activities of daily living. Nearly half of residents had dementia, and more than half were confined to a bed or wheelchair (Houser, 2007a). Two-thirds of NH residents 65 to 84 and 82% of residents 85 and older were women. At the time of admission more than half of residents were widowed; only 20% were married or living with a partner (Houser, 2007a), reflecting the inevitable after-effects of patterns of spousal LTC provided at home. Because many elders with high LTC needs cannot afford to purchase LTC on their own, Medicaid eligibility entitles low-income individuals to NH levels of care. In the United States, retired women receive just over half the income that men counterparts receive; widowed women's incomes are even lower, according to Debra Street and Janet Wilmoth (2001), making the risk of admission to NHs especially high for low-income widows.

Formal LTC is in a state of transformation, as new residential LTC sites such as assisted living compete with NHs for clients, as more supportive home care services become available, and as reimbursement policies change. The NH industry has been reconfigured (see Table 1) to respond to changes in Medicare and Medicaid reimbursement policies (Street, Quadagno, Parham, & McDonald, 2003) and growing consumer preferences for LTC alternatives that permit individuals to remain in their own homes or other community settings, retaining their independence for as long as possible. The number of NHs peaked in the mid-1980s, but licensed NH beds increased until the late 1990s. Since then both the number of facilities and beds nationwide have declined, NH occupancy rates have stabilized, and NHs have been transformed from dominantly custodial residential LTC sites to increasingly skilled medical environments. Though entering a NH in the 1970s typically represented the last home for individuals before they died, Frederic Decker (2007) noted that by 2004 temporary admission to a NH to receive skilled nursing services and recuperate for a time-limited stay after an acute illness was nearly as common as a long-stay residential NH admission.

The number of NH residents in 1985 was nearly the same as two decades later, at the same time as the national over 85 population—the age group at highest risk for needing LTC—grew by more than 80% (Houser, 2007a). Medicaid reforms have reallocated resources previously used to reimburse predominantly NH-based LTC, substituting home- and community-based services such as homemaking services, respite care, and services that provide appropriate but less expensive care in less restrictive environments. Medicare NH reimbursement policies have also contributed to more short-stay NH admissions, reducing the length of expensive hospital stays after an acute hospitalization (Street, Quadagno, Burge, & McDonald, 2003). However, trends of declining NH residency also coincide with people's desire to age in place in their own homes or to receive LTC services in more homelike, less institutional environments (Street, Burge, Quadagno, & Barrett, 2007).

High levels of formal LTC are expensive, no matter where the care is delivered, but that is especially true in NHs. In 2007 the average cost of a private room in a U.S. NH was $213 per day, or $77,747 annually; the average cost of a semiprivate room was $189 per day, or $68,985 annually (Metlife Mature Market Institute, 2007). The high cost of NH care has driven two trends. First, many individuals seek lower-cost alternatives, patching together needed services provided in their homes or making a move at about half the annual cost of semiprivate care in a NH (MMMI, 2007). Second, individuals who enter NHs as private-pay residents—even individuals of average means—can quickly consume a lifetime of savings and become impoverished. In 2007 poor frail elders or impoverished NH residents became entitled to Medicaid LTC when they met NH level of care needs and their assets were less than $2000 for individuals or $3000 for couples and their income ranged from Supplementary Security Income level $623 for a single individual per month up to 300% of the individual Supplementary Security Income level ($1,869 monthly, depending on income limits set by each state (Kaiser Commission on Medicaid and the Uninsured, Kaiser Family Foundation [KFF], 2007). When that happens, any income the individual receives (such as pensions or Social Security) is first applied toward the cost of NH care (except for a nominal personal allowance), and Medicaid pays the balance.

## KEY ISSUES IN LTC PROVISION

In 2005, public insurance—either Medicare or Medicaid—paid for the majority of formal LTC provided in NHs. Sixty-three percent of the total cost of all NH care was from public sources whereas only 26% was paid out of pocket, with the remainder purchased through private insurance or other sources (KFF, 2007). Medicaid pays the greatest share of LTC costs, purchasing 44% of all NH care (KFF, 2007) and 55% of home health care (Feder et al., 2007). Medicaid Home- and Community-Based Services (HCBS) waivers allow (but do not require) state Medicaid programs to pay for home-based services that delay or prevent the need for NH admission for physical therapy, assistance with maintaining the home, day care, meals, respite care, and other similar services. Since 1990 Medicaid expenditures shifted from 13% for HCBS and 87% for NH to 41% for HCBS and 59% for NH in 2006 (KFF, 2007). The Older American's Act (OAA; passed in 1965 and reauthorized several times since) also provides funds to states for community-based services designed to support independent living, such as adult day care and meals-on-wheels. Because OAA-financed operations offer home-based services to individuals without the stringent Medicaid eligibility criteria, they are important LTC resources for individuals with modest incomes. However, due to limited funding, OAA services and Medicaid HCBS services often involve long waiting lists.

The greater availability of formal, home-based LTC services, whether purchased privately or provided under Medicaid or OAA programs, has not supplanted informal LTC. Rather, availability of home-based services has been accompanied by an increase in informal care. A comparison of U.S. national data from 1984 to 1999 found that families were providing proportionately more care in 1999 than previously, whereas proportionate use of formal care had declined. Increasingly, family members were caring for relatives who were older and had greater disability (Spillman & Black, 2005), likely because the ability to purchase at least some home-based LTC services enables families to persist in offering high levels of often complex care.

To put the U.S. experience in perspective, a study of 12 developed countries (Australia, Austria, Canada, Germany, Ireland, Japan, Luxembourg, Netherlands, Norway, Sweden, the United Kingdom, and the United States) found that, even in countries with more extensive provisions for publicly funded services, much LTC is provided informally by unpaid relatives and friends. Most developed countries have moved toward providing publicly funded LTC in the home, thereby allowing people to age-in-place (Organisation for Economic Co-operation and Development, 2005). Both of these transnational patterns—high levels of informal care and moving publicly supported, formal LTC out of institutional settings to the home or community—are consistent with recent U.S. LTC experiences.

The impending old age of the baby-boom generation will likely mean a growing disabled population needing LTC over the coming decades, but that need will not necessarily be accompanied by more resources. Despite efforts to promote the purchase of private long-term care insurance, less than 8% of individuals 50 and older are covered, with coverage limited mainly to the most affluent. Many individuals cannot afford to purchase private LTC insurance or prioritize other kinds of spending. Some cannot purchase LTC insurance due to underwriting practices that minimize insurers' risks by eliminating individuals with particular health problems from eligibility. Others do not purchase private LTC insurance because they are uncertain how to value a relatively expensive product in terms of very uncertain future needs. Regardless of the reason, private LTC insurance is not yet widespread nor does it that seem likely under current policy and market conditions (Feder et al., 2007). More older individuals and limited capacity to pay will surely put additional fiscal and service strains on the LTC system, which is already underfunded and unable to meet all of the LTC needs for frail elders (Kasper, Lyons, & O'Malley, 2007; Mor et al., 2007). Funding concerns, quality assurance, and creating and maintaining a high-quality LTC workforce are three critical issues for LTC in the United States and around the world.

Although other developed countries face similar challenges to their capacity to fund and provide enough high-quality LTC, given aging populations and economic uncertainty, Mary Jo Gibson and Donald Redfoot (2007) indicate that in the United States the fiscal pressures seem even more immediate. Debates about LTC are cast in somewhat different terms depending on the country in question. For example, in Germany the debate is over how to improve services and maintain the financial viability of the LTC insurance program, whereas in the United States much of the debate centers on scaling back publicly funded services (Gibson & Redfoot, 2007).

The quality of LTC care has long concerned researchers, policy makers, and families of frail elders alike. In the mid 1980s a scathing Institute of Medicine report (1986) was the catalyst to NH quality standards legislation and reform incorporated in the 1987 Omnibus Budget Reconciliation Act. Twenty years later NH quality standards were still problematic, and oversight of the quality of care in other LTC sites almost entirely lacking (Institute of Medicine, 2001). Although the United States has a nationwide NH quality standard, the logistics of multilevel regulation (federal/state) can be difficult to manage and uneven in application. U.S. researchers have devoted considerable effort to understanding the conditions that create or undermine high-quality LTC in NH and other LTC settings, finding that workforce issues, such as adequate staffing and staff training are central to high-quality care (Institute of Food and Agricultural Sciences, 2007; Kasper et al., 2007). However, the political will and resource streams required to improve the LTC workforce had not yet materialized in the early 2000s. Overwhelmingly, direct LTC workers are women, mostly single, many with less than a high school education, and disportionately Black, Hispanic, and non-U.S.-born (Institute of Medicine, 2008). An Institute of Medicine Report (2008) noted that the ability to recruit and retain direct care workers (certified nursing assistants, personal and home care aides, geriatric aides, orderlies) is "dire" for these essential positions that command low wages and few benefits despite the high emotional and physical demands of such jobs.

## LTC IN THE FUTURE

In countries with aging populations, meeting the challenges of creating an appropriately trained workforce to provide adequate levels of high-quality LTC in the settings in which individuals prefer to receive it and then paying for it is a source of ongoing debate. As baby boomers approach old age, there is growing interest in finding acceptable, affordable LTC strategies. Baby boomers are likely to have different expectations about where and how LTC should be delivered that may be an engine for innovation. At the same time, achieving adequacy and flexibility in both formal and informal LTC provision will be challenging. Women's high levels of labor force participation will limit their availability as informal LTC providers, and there is little on either the policy or economic horizon that suggests a windfall in public LTC funding.

One proposal for affordable, high-quality LTC would be publicly funded payments to active retired persons who provide LTC care in noninstitutional settings (Organisation for Economic Co-operation and Development, 2005). A trend toward longer retirement in most developed countries and larger groups of disability-free people over the age of 50 who are not in paid work create a pool of potential LTC providers. Using public policy to encourage this group to provide LTC for frail elders may allow their working children to continue employment, thereby contributing to the economy and simultaneously reducing the need for more expensive institutional services.

Another way LTC needs may be addressed in the future is through technological advances. For example, some segments of the population that currently lack access to LTC services (whether traditionally underserved or geographically/financially disadvantaged) could benefit from information and communications technologies such as in-home monitoring, telemedicine, and reminder services. Already, wearable, user-activated, medical alert pendants are in widespread use. Mobility aids such as well-designed walkers and powered wheelchairs improve frail elders' capacity to move around and enact self-care (Alwan & Nobel, 2007). New technologies, such as stair-climbing wheelchairs and environmental fall detection, may transform LTC in the future. Although the contours of the LTC provision landscape will continue to evolve, the need for LTC will also increase throughout the world in response to population aging. As long as there are old people, there will be a need for LTC (however it is arranged) to address issues of frailty and the need for assistance in later life and for people and institutions willing to provide it.

**SEE ALSO** Volume 2: *Policy, Health;* Volume 3: *Assisted Living Facilities; Assistive Technologies; Disability and Functional Limitation, Later Life; Frailty and Robustness; Health Care Use, Later Life; Policy, Later Life Well-Being; Retirement Communities.*

**BIBLIOGRAPHY**

Alwan, M., & Nobel, J. (2007). *State of technology in aging services.* Washington, DC: Center for Aging Services Technologies.

Arber, S., & Ginn, J. (1995). Gender differences in informal caring. *Health and Social Care in the Community, 3*(1), 19–31.

Calasanti, T., & King, N. (2007). Taking "women's work" like a man: Husbands' experiences of care work. *The Gerontologist, 47*(4), 516–527.

Calasanti, T., & Slevin, K. (2001). *Gender, social inequalities, and aging.* Walnut Creek, CA: Alta Mira Press.

Cancian, F. M., & Oliker, S.J. (2000). *Caring and gender.* Thousand Oaks, CA: Pine Forge Press.

Carroll, M., & Campbell, L. (2008). Who now reads Parsons and Bales? Casting a critical eye on the gendered styles of caregiving literature. *Journal of Aging Studies, 22*(1), 24–31.

Centers for Disease Control and Prevention, National Center for Health Statistics. National Nursing Home Survey. (n.d.). *Nursing Home Trends.* Retrieved May 25, 2008, from http://www.cdc.gov/nchs/

Coburn, A. F., Bolda, E. J., & Keith, R.G. (2003). Variations in nursing home discharge rates for urban and rural nursing facility residents with hip fracture. *Journal of Rural Health, 19*(2), 148–155.

Decker, F. H. (2005). *Nursing Homes, 1977–1999: What has changed, what has not?* Hyattsville, MD: National Center for Health Statistics.

Feder, J., Komisar, H. L., & Friedland, R. B. (2007). *Long-term care financing: Options for the future.* Washington, DC: Georgetown University Long-Term Care Financing Project.

Freedman, V. A. (1996). Family structure and the risk of nursing home admission. *Journals of Gerontology Series B: Psychological Sciences and Social Sciences, 51*(2), S61–S69.

Gibson, M. J., & Redfoot, D. L. (2007). Comparing long-term care in Germany and the United States: What can we learn from each other? Washington, DC: American Association of Retired Persons.

Ginn, J., Street, D., & Arber, S. (Eds.). (2001). *Women, work and pensions: International issues and prospects.* Buckingham, England: Open University Press.

Houser, A. (2007a). *Long-term care.* Washington, DC: American Association of Retired Persons Public Policy Institute.

Houser, A. (2007b). *Women and long term care.* Washington, DC: American Association of Retired Persons Public Policy Institute.

Institute for the Future of Aging Services. (2007). *The long-term care workforce: Can the crisis be fixed? Problems, causes and options.* Washington, DC: Institute of Food and Agricultural Sciences.

Institute of Medicine. (1986). *Improving the quality of care in nursing homes.* Washington, DC: National Academy Press.

Institute of Medicine. (2001). *Improving the quality of long term care.* Washington, DC: National Academy Press.

Institute of Medicine. (2008). *Retooling for an aging America: Building the health care workforce.* Washington, DC: National Academy Press.

Kaiser Commission on Medicaid and the Uninsured, Kaiser Family Foundation. (2007). *Medicaid and long term care services and supports: Fact sheet.* Washington, DC: Henry J. Kaiser Family Foundation.

Kane, R. A., & Kane, R.L. (1987). *Long term care: Principles, programs, and policies.* New York: Springer.

Kasper, J., Lyons, B., & O'Malley, M. (2007). *Long term care services and supports: The future role and challenges for Medicaid.* Kaiser Commission on Medicaid and the Uninsured. Washington, DC: Henry J. Kaiser Family Foundation.

Kitchener, M., & Harrington, C. (2004). The U.S. long-term care field: A dialectic analysis of institution dynamics. *Journal of Health and Social Behavior, 45,* 87–101.

Mor, V., Zinn, J., Gozalo, P., Feng, Z., Intrator, O., & Grabowski, D. C. (2007). Prospects for transferring nursing home residents to the community. *Health Affairs, 26*(6) 1762–1771.

Metlife Mature Market Institute. (2007). *The Metlife market survey of nursing home and assisted living costs.* Westport, CT: Author.

Organisation for Economic Co-operation and Development. (2005). *Ensuring quality long-term care for older people.* Paris: Author.

Pandya, S. (2005). *Nursing homes: Fact sheet.* Washington, DC: American Association of Retired Persons Public Policy Institute.

Phillips, C. D., Holan, S., Sherman, M., Leyk Williams, M., & Hawes, C. (2004). Rurality and nursing home quality: Results from a national sample of nursing home admissions. *American Journal of Public Health, 94*(10), 1717–1722.

Russell, R. (2007). Men doing women's work: Elderly men caregivers and the gendered construction of care work. *The Journal of Men's Studies, 15*(1), 1–18.

Spillman, B. C., & Black, K. J. (2005). *Staying the course: Trends in family caregiving.* Washington, DC: American Association of Retired Persons.

Street, D., Burge, S., Quadagno, J., & Barrett, A. (2007). The salience of social relationships for resident well-being in assisted living, *The Journal of Gerontology: Series B, Psychological Sciences and Social Sciences, 62,* S129–S134.

Street, D., Quadagno, J., Parham, P., & McDonald, S. (2003). Reinventing long-term care: The effect of Medicare and Medicaid on Florida nursing homes, 1989–1997. *The Gerontologist, 43,* 118–131.

Street, D., & Wilmoth, J. (2001). Social insecurity: Women and pensions in the U.S. In J. Ginn, D. Street, & S. Arber (Eds.), *Women, work and pensions: International issues and prospects.* Buckingham, U.K.: Open University Press.

***Debra Street***
***Sarah Desai***

## LOPATA, HELENA
### *1925–2003*

Helena Znaniecka Lopata was born in Poznań, Poland, and came to the United States with her family in 1939, when the Nazis occupied her country. Her father was the famed sociologist Florian Znaniecki (1882–1958), who coauthored the classic study, *The Polish Peasant in Europe and America* (1918–1920). Lopata received her Ph.D. in 1954 from the University of Chicago, and was a professor of sociology and director of the Center for the Comparative Study of Social Roles at Loyola University. Her tenure at Loyola University lasted from 1969 until 1997 when she retired. Over her lifetime, she published 20 books and scores of journal articles. In addition to her work on social roles and the life course, discussed below, she wrote on time, grief, loneliness, women's work, and the cosmopolitan community of scholars, of which she considered herself a member.

***Helena Lopata.*** COURTESY OF JUDITH WITTNER, PROFESSOR DEPARTMENT OF SOCIOLOGY LOYOLA UNIVERSITY.

In order to understand Lopata's approach to the life course, one must understand her theory of social roles, which builds upon the concept of social circles developed by her father, Florian Znaniecki. Znaniecki saw social circles as networks of social cooperation and collective action. Rights, privileges, duties, and obligations between the members of the social circle and the person at its center—the wife, mother, or widow, to name the roles that interested Lopata—allowed that central person to negotiate with members of the circle to define and execute her role. This perspective on roles replaced a static and individualist concept with one that was both collective and fluid. In Lopata's role theory, the entire social circle through its reciprocal relationships with the named role incumbent produces and enacts the role. For example, the mother role includes both "the person defined as the mother *and* the circle with rights and duties" (personal communication, July 2002).

Lopata envisioned the life course as a "shifting agglomeration of roles that marks a person's passage through life" (Wittner 2003, p. 174). In her life course analysis, that shifting agglomeration—biography—intersects with historical changes, so that even as women moved among their roles as wives, workers, mothers, empty nesters, and widows, the wider contexts within which they acted were also changing. Lopata's shorthand term for historical change was *modernization*, the term her father and his contemporaries favored. This term refers to the movement from a simpler time to a time of increasingly complex institutions such as the economy and the system of education, which offered women release from immersion in family life. Lopata focused on the potential and actual advantages of modernizing society to women and muted any concern with power and conflict. Her empirical studies documented how women were moving from lives defined almost totally by family relations to more complex involvements in multiple institutional contexts. To Lopata, these more complex involvements saved women from potentially damaging dependency on husbands and families, mitigated the losses incurred at different life stages (the departure of children, the death of a husband), and enriched their lives and self-concepts.

Lopata's method of life course analysis was based on her theory of social roles. She focused on the intersections of biography and history at the turning points in women's lives. She explored the ways that traditional social supports for women were declining and also the ways that women were constructing new networks of support and new self-concepts at these critical junctures. This method is apparent in two major bodies of empirical work on the life course that Lopata produced over her lifetime.

Lopata's first empirical work was her study of housewives in suburban Chicago, which she initiated in 1956. *Occupation: Housewife*, published in 1971, was pathbreaking in its choice of subject matter, the lives of American housewives. Lopata's unerring instinct for timely sociological questions led her to this topic long before other sociologists understood how changes in women's lives were central to the emerging transformations of U.S. society. In *Occupation: Housewife*, Lopata explored how young wives and mothers in the new suburbs of postwar America left behind social circles of support that women had enjoyed in close-knit urban neighborhoods. Isolated from families and friends, they became emotionally and economically dependent on their husbands. Lopata found that some women remained trapped in these "flattened" life spaces inside families, whereas others negotiated more flexible marital roles and moved on to professional careers and wider institutional connections, remaking their lives as traditional social supports slipped away. In *City Women* (1984) and *Circles and Settings* (1994), Lopata furthered her notion of the life course as a sequence of stages through which women moved historically as well as individually, from traditional extended family systems, through a transitional period marked by the disorganization of long-established roles, to the emerging modern stage of greater equality in families and wider access to the male-dominated public sphere.

Lopata's research on widows forms a second body of empirical work to which she applied her theoretical framework. As in her studies of housewives, Lopata focused on the historically changing experience and meanings of widowhood. Where once American widows had been embedded in and dependent for support on extended kin networks, particularly those of in-laws, in contemporary society their duties and rights as widows within their social circle were narrowed, making the widow role temporary. Her research revealed that after briefly mourning with and assisting the new widow, circle members left the widow to rebuild her identity as an unmarried woman without their help. Nevertheless, Lopata interpreted this contemporary practice as essentially progressive, arguing that, like the suburban housewives she studied earlier, contemporary widows were increasingly likely to lead multidimensional lives, returning to school, entering the labor force, and constructing new roles and circles of support that allowed them to make successful and satisfying transitions to their postmarital lives.

In her empirical and theoretical work on women's lives, Lopata explored how women inhabited and transformed their social roles during the last half of the 20th century. The story she tells is about slow progress toward a society of autonomous but interdependent women linked together with men in multidimensional social circles beyond families, circles that they themselves had helped to construct. By focusing on women's responses to a shifting social order, Lopata showed the positive side to the vast changes they confronted. By fashioning alternative life courses in response to change, women were, she believed, leading the way toward creating a more egalitarian and democratic public sphere.

**SEE ALSO** Volume 2: *Roles; Znaniecki, Florian;* Volume 3: *Widowhood.*

## BIBLIOGRAPHY

Lopata, H. (1971). *Occupation: Housewife*. New York: Oxford University Press.

Lopata, H. (1973). *Widowhood in an American city*. Cambridge, MA: Schenkman.

Lopata, H. (1976). *Polish Americans: Status competition in an ethnic community*. Engelwood, NJ: Prentice-Hall.

Lopata, H. (1979). *Women as widows: Support systems*. New York: Elsevier.

Lopata, H. (1984). *City women: Work, jobs, occupations, careers.* New York: Praeger.

Lopata, H. (1991). Which child? The consequences of social development on the support systems of widows. In B. Hess & E. Markson (Eds.), *Growing old in America*. New Brunswick, NJ: Transaction.

Lopata, H. (1993). The interweave of public and private: Women's challenge to American society. *Journal of Marriage and the Family, 55*, 220–235.

Lopata, H. (1994). *Circles and settings: Role changes of American women*. Albany: State University of New York Press.

Lopata, H. (1996). *Current widowhood: Myths and realities.* Thousand Oaks, CA: Sage.

Wittner, J. (2003). Occupation sociologist: Theory, research, and life experience in the work of Helena Lopata. *Symbolic Interaction, 26*(1), 173–185.

***Diana Guelespe***
***Judith Wittner***

# M-N

## MARRIAGE IN LATER LIFE

Marital status is an important influence on the physical and mental health and economic well-being of older adults. Extensive research has documented the positive effects of marriage on health (e.g., Lillard & Panis, 1996; Ross, Mirowsky, & Goldsteen, 1990; Smith & Zick, 1994; Umberson, 1992; Waite, 1995). Individuals who are married tend to have lower mortality rates (Goldman, 1993; Ross et al., 1990), better physical health (Waldron, Hughes, & Brooks, 1996), and better psychological well-being, compared to their unmarried counterparts (Barrett, 2000). The protective effect of marriage on both physical and mental health has particular importance for older individuals. The number of older married adults is increasing along with life expectancy, and marriage potentially influences health behaviors, the likelihood of having a spousal caregiver, and financial resources, all of which have been shown to affect physical and mental health in older adults (Ross et al., 1990; Tower & Kasl, 1996). The following discussion of marital status in later life focuses on (a) a demographic portrait of married versus unmarried adults aged 65 and older in the United States, (b) the connection between marriage and health, (c) the impact of widowhood on health among older adults, and, finally, (d) marital satisfaction in later life.

### MARITAL STATUS

According to the U.S. Census Bureau (2004a), older married persons constitute almost 16% of all married people in the United States. Approximately 13% of the U.S. population is over 65, and older individuals are slightly underrepresented among the married population. More than half of adults over age 65 in the United States were currently married in 2003, and nearly one-third were widowed (U.S. Census Bureau, 2004a), the vast majority of whom were women (80%). This translates into dramatically reduced income for these women, as 90% of those widowed had personal earnings of less than $5,000 per year. In terms of ethnicity, older non-Hispanic Blacks were more likely to be widowed than non-Hispanic Whites, Asians, or Hispanics (U.S. Census Bureau, 2004a), reflecting Blacks' elevated mortality risks relative to other ethnic groups in the United States.

Divorce is far less common in the older population than in younger age groups, likely reflecting cohort rather than age trends because divorce was relatively rare when current cohorts of older adults were young married persons. Approximately 8% of older adults are currently divorced (U.S. Census Bureau, 2004a). The majority of older divorced persons are female, reflecting women's greater survival and the fact that men are more likely to remarry—thus "exiting" the pool of divorced persons. As with those who were widowed, most had personal earnings of less than $5,000 per year. Finally, older non-Hispanic Blacks were more likely than non-Hispanic Whites, Asians, and Hispanics to be divorced (U.S. Census Bureau, 2004a).

Marital status has direct effects on the living arrangements of persons over age 65. Women's greater likelihood to both become and remain widowed translates into a large number of female-headed households among older adults. Women over the age of 65 are almost four times more likely than men to head a household without a spouse (U.S. Census Bureau, 2005). The living arrangements of married older persons also differ by ethnicity. Non-Hispanic Black, Hispanic, and Asian older married persons are more likely than their non-Hispanic White counterparts to live with other family household members (U.S. Census Bureau, 2004b). The differences in household composition are likely to be due to differences in cultural ideals, health status, and the economic resources required to maintain an independent household (Peek, Coward, & Peek, 2000).

## MARRIAGE AND HEALTH

A substantial body of research reveals that being married is strongly linked to positive health outcomes (Ross & Mirowsky, 1989; Umberson, 1987). Two general explanations are offered for the connection between marriage to health: selection and protection. The first process, social selection, refers to the tendency of healthy individuals to marry or to have better marital prospects. Thus, having better health, which leads to a longer life, also makes marriage more likely. Being married, however, may cause people to have better health. This process is referred to as protection. The protection argument suggests that there are beneficial influences of marriage on social, psychological, and physical resources that are connected with physical health, mental health, and mortality (Christakis & Allison, 2006; Schone & Weinick, 1998; Stimpson, Kuo, Ray, Raji, & Peek, 2007). If protection mechanisms are at play, the statistical association between marital status and health reflects the fact that health shapes marital status, rather than vice versa.

In general, although there is some evidence of selection (Lillard & Panis, 1996; Waldron et al., 1996), there is more substantial support for marriage being protective of health (Smith & Zick, 1994; Waite, 1995). There are three dominant mechanisms through which marriage is hypothesized to affect health: (a) risky/healthy behaviors, (b) social support, and (c) economic resources. First, marriage is associated with reducing risky or dangerous behaviors, such as smoking, drinking, and not wearing seat belts (Schone & Weinick, 1998; Umberson, 1987). In addition, some evidence shows that marriage is associated with individuals' performing health-enhancing behaviors, such as regular visits to the doctor, exercise, and eating well (Schone & Weinick). Second, marriage may provide social support. Being married, at least in a healthy and supportive marriage, is associated with feeling loved, esteemed, and cherished (Ross & Mirowsky, 1989). In addition, individuals who are married are more likely to report that they have a confidant (Ross et al., 1990). Furthermore, support from one's spouse also influences recovery from illness and facilitates coping behaviors (Ducharme, 1994; Schröder, Schwarzer, & Endler, 1997). The emotional benefits of marriage depend, however, on the quality of the marital relationship, with healthy marriages providing the richest rewards (Gove, Hughes, & Style, 1983; Umberson, Williams, Powers, Liu, & Needham, 2006). Third, marriage is associated with increases in financial resources. Married individuals have higher household incomes, on average, than single individuals (Smith & Zick, 1994; Waite, 1995). The pooling of resources and economies of scale, where two can live almost as cheaply as one, potentially influences health, because economic well-being is strongly related to health (D. R. Williams, 1990).

How these protective effects translate into health outcomes is most apparent with the example of mortality. The effects of marriage on mortality are well established in the United States as well as other countries (Brockmann & Klein, 2004; Lillard & Panis, 1996). Married adults have lower mortality than never married, widowed, or divorced individuals. In the early 1990s researchers reported that mortality rates were 250% higher for unmarried men than married men and 50% higher for unmarried women than married women (Ross et al., 1990). These findings additionally corroborated the widely believed assertion that marriage is more protective for men than for women. For example, the transition into marriage is thought to be beneficial for both men and women, but men experience immediate reductions in mortality whereas women do not. Furthermore, the transition out of marriage increases mortality rates for men, but for women the effects seems to be more gradual (Brockmann & Klein, 2004).

Since the late 1990s, however, researchers have challenged the broad claim that married adults have better health. Rather, the focus of studies on marriage and health has shifted to examining the effects of marital history on health, particularly marital transitions and marital quality. First, one group of researchers suggests that the link between marriage and health can be viewed from two different perspectives: resource and crisis. The resource model argues that marriage brings greater support, both financial and emotional, and better health behaviors. The main emphasis of the crisis model is that differences in health due to marital status reflect stress and strain revolving around the event of marital dissolution. Thus, the crisis model suggests that individuals who transition from married to divorced or widowed may experience a brief decline in health, but after a specified period the unmarried individuals' health statuses will be similar to those who remained in a married state. Kristi Williams and Debra Umberson (2004) showed with nationally representative data in the United States that the health of the continually divorced and never married is similar to that of the married. These researchers also found that transitions appear to more negatively affect men's health than women's. They argue that these findings support the crisis model—that marital status differences in health reflect stresses of divorce and widowhood rather than resources provided by marriage. These

***You May Kiss the Bride.*** *Lee Becker, 91, and Velma Becker, 84, now Mr. and Mrs. Lee Becker, kiss at the end of their wedding.* AP IMAGES.

findings are generally upheld in data from other countries as well (Brockmann & Klein, 2004).

Second, research on the influence of marital quality on the relationship between marriage and health yields further challenge to the idea that marriage is beneficial to health under any condition. Research on marital quality focuses more on mental health than on physical health. K. Williams (2003) argued that, in addition to the deeply ingrained idea that marriage is more beneficial to men, the notion that marital quality affects women more than men has rarely been challenged in research. She showed with nationally representative data from the United States that the effects of marital status, marital transitions, and marital quality had very similar effects on psychological well-being for men and women. One key and expected finding with regard to both genders is that exiting marriage is related to increased depression only among adults who have high marital quality. For those with poor marital quality, exiting marriage is associated with a decline in depression. In summary, the long-held tenet that marriage is protective of health, although generally upheld, does have certain conditions under which it is "truer" than under others.

## WIDOWHOOD AND HEALTH

Of particular interest to researchers is the relationship of spousal loss to health. Research has suggested that widowhood is associated with poor health outcomes, especially depression (Mendes de Leon, Kasl, & Jacobs, 1994; Turvey, Carney, Arndt, Wallace, & Herzog, 1999). With increased longevity comes the issue of increased time spent potentially without a spouse. In addition, a continued high divorce rate coupled with the aging of the baby boom generation may also lead to increased divorce rates among older adults. It is important to separately explore the health effects of these life transitions in order to better understand their significance.

More than 10.5 million adults over the age of 65 are widowed. Multiple health issues can accompany the transition to widowhood. The loss of a spouse, in addition to being emotionally devastating, can mean the loss of one's primary caregiver, social support, and financial resources (Martikainen & Valkonen, 1996; Smith & Zick, 1994). Widowhood may be followed by increased health service use and accompanying health conditions such as depression, limitations in activities of daily living, and fair or poor self-rated health (Bennett, 2006; Lillard & Panis, 1996). Further evidence suggests that widowhood has significant short-term negative effects on health, but not as much evidence has been found for long-term effects, and these effects tend to be stronger for men than women (K. Williams & Umberson, 2004).

For example, evidence from the Changing Lives of Older Couples Study, a prospective study of spousal bereavement, suggests that widowhood was a significant predictor of depressive symptoms in both men and women age 65 and older. The effect of widowhood on mental health was dependent, however, on marital quality (Carr et al., 2000). For individuals who reported a higher level of dependence on their spouse, anxiety levels increased over the two waves of data, whereas for those who reported less dependence on their spouse, anxiety levels decreased. The results of this study also indicated that adjustment to widowhood was most difficult for those who responded that the quality of their marital relationship was high. Respondents who reported more conflict in their relationships had less difficulty making the adjustment to widowhood.

## MARITAL SATISFACTION

Although the evidence regarding the relationship between health and marriage applies to all life course stages, marital satisfaction within the marriage varies depending on life stage. Early years of marital relationships are associated with high satisfaction; marital satisfaction appears to decline in the middle years; and in later years, marital satisfaction rises again (Charles & Carstensen, 2002; Levenson, Carstensen, & Gottman, 1993; Orbuch, House, Mero, & Webster, 1996). There are two general explanations for the decline of satisfaction after the early years of marriage that focus on incompatibility and conflict and the presence of children. The median length of first marriages that end in divorce is 8.2 years for men and 7.9 years for women (Kreider, 2005). That is, roughly half of marriages that end in divorce half do so during the first 8 years. Moreover, conflict in general and controversy over children-related issues are typically higher in younger marriages than in older ones (Levenson et al., 1993). Older marriages, in general, are characterized by reduced conflict in conjunction with an increase in potential for pleasure, especially with respect to children. Researchers concluded that for middle-age couples, parenthood is a greater source of probable conflict than it is among older couples, for whom having children is a potentially greater source of pleasure, reflecting the fact that grown children typically place fewer demands on their parents than do young or adolescent children.

In addition, the early years of marriage often include high levels of both positive and negative experiences (Charles & Carstensen, 2002), whereas in the middle years, spouses describe fewer positive aspects but still high levels of conflict. Finally, in the later years, reports of conflict decline, whereas reports of positive aspects of marriage increase. Researchers emphasize that conflict over children is the driving force behind low satisfaction with marriage in the middle years but that other factors besides children leaving home influence satisfaction in the later years, such as conflict resolution, friendship, and selection.

First, increased length of marriage is associated with the development of better conflict resolution skills. One example of this using an observational system for coding emotional behavior is that older couples used expressions of affection along with expressions of discontent and disagreement during arguing, whereas younger couples used more negative expression (Carstensen, Gottman, & Levenson, 1995). Second, length of marriage is related to the tendency to cite "friendship" as an important characteristic of marriage (Charles & Carstensen, 2002). One study that examined perceptions of successful marriages reported that both men and women cited the same three criteria for what they perceived as the reason for the success of their marriage: commitment, liking their spouse, and having their best friend for a spouse (Lauer, Lauer, & Kerr, 1990). Finally, there is the argument that selection is an important part of the relationship between satisfaction and marriage in late life. For example, marriages that have a high degree of conflict often end in divorce. Orbuch et al. (1996) argued, however, that levels of satisfaction tend to rise after the period when most marriages end in divorce (satisfaction tends to rise after about 20 years according to some studies), whereas the median length of marriages that end in divorce is 8 years (Kreider, 2005).

Finally, there is very little research exploring the effects of race and ethnicity on marital satisfaction (Broman, 1993). Using nationally representative data, Broman found that Blacks were less likely to be satisfied with their marriages and less likely to feel that their marriages were harmonious. He argued that race variations in three factors may be responsible for this finding: spousal support, amount of household work, and financial satisfaction. He found that Blacks experienced lower spousal support and financial satisfaction. These effects, however, did not entirely account for the effect of race on marriage. In addition, the relationship between race and marital satisfaction was found for women only. Thus, Black women were less satisfied with their marriages than White women.

In conclusion, the picture of marriage in later life appears to be a relatively positive one. Although caregiving and widowhood are aspects of life that most older adults ultimately deal with, late-life marriage is a generally positive experience. Future research needs to examine older marriages among ethnic and racial minorities; this need is becoming increasingly important as minority groups, especially older Hispanics, are increasing both in number and proportion of the older population in the United States. Another important research direction is the use of longitudinal data to examine the connection between marriage and health over the life course. Studies are beginning to focus on short-term transitions into and out of marital states, and future analyses should continue to take advantage of longitudinal data to examine long-term effects of transitions. As the "institution" of marriage continues to change and the U.S. population (especially baby boomers) begin reaching older ages, the availability of caregivers, or the caregiver pool, may diminish. This will have far-reaching effects on the system of informal and formal long-term care in the United States.

**SEE ALSO** Volume 2: *Cohabitation; Marriage; Remarriage;* Volume 3: *Caregiving; Sexual Activity, Later Life; Social Integration/Isolation, Later Life; Social Support, Later Life.*

## BIBLIOGRAPHY


Barrett, A. E. (2000). Marital trajectories and mental health. *Journal of Health and Social Behavior, 41,* 451–464.

Bennett, K. M. (2006). Does marital status and marital status change predict physical health in older adults? *Psychological Medicine, 36,* 1313–1320.

Brockmann, H., & Klein, T. (2004). Love and death in Germany: The marital biography and its effect on mortality. *Journal of Marriage and the Family, 66,* 567–581.

Broman, C. L. (1993). Race differences in marital well-being. *Journal of Marriage and the Family, 55,* 724–732.

Carr, D., House, J. S., Kessler, R. C., Nesse, R. M., Sonnega, J., & Wortman, C. (2000). Marital quality and psychological adjustment to widowhood among older adults: A longitudinal analysis. *The Journals of Gerontology, Series B: Psychological Sciences and Social Sciences, 55,* S197–S207.

Carstensen, L. L., Gottman, J. M., & Levenson, R. W. (1995). Emotional behavior in long-term marriage. *Psychology and Aging, 10,* 140–149.

Charles, S. T., & Carstensen, L. L. (2002). Marriage in old age. In M. Yalom & L. L. Carstensen (Eds.), *Inside the American couple: New thinking/new challenges* (pp. 236–254). Berkeley: University of California Press.

Christakis, N. A., & Allison, P. D. (2006). Mortality after the hospitalization of a spouse. *The New England Journal of Medicine, 354,* 719–730.

Ducharme, F. (1994). Conjugal support, coping behaviors, and psychological well-being of the elderly spouse. *Research on Aging, 16,* 167–190.

Goldman, N. (1993). Marriage selection and mortality patterns: Inferences and fallacies. *Demography, 30,* 189–208.

Gove, W. R., Hughes, M., & Style, C. B. (1983). Does marriage have positive effects on the psychological wellbeing of the individual? *Journal of Health and Social Behavior, 24,* 122–131.

Hobbs, F. B., with Damon, B. L. (1996). *65+ in the United States.* Current Population Report No. P23-190. Washington, DC: U.S. Census Bureau. Retrieved June 5, 2008, from www.census.gov/prod/

Kreider, R. M. (2005). *Number, timing, and duration of marriages and divorces: 2001.* Current Population Report No. P70-97. Washington, DC: U.S. Census Bureau. Retrieved June 5, 2008, from www.census.gov/prod/

Lauer, R. H., Lauer, J. C., & Kerr, S. T. (1990). The long-term marriage: Perceptions of stability and satisfaction. *The International Journal of Aging and Human Development, 31,* 189–195.

Levenson, R. W., Carstensen, L. L., & Gottman, J. M. (1993). Long-term marriage: Age, gender, and satisfaction. *Psychology and Aging, 8,* 301–313.

Lillard, L. A., & Panis, C. W. A. (1996). Marital status and mortality: The role of health. *Demography, 33,* 313–327.

Martikainen, P., & Valkonen, T. (1996). Mortality after the death of a spouse: Rates and causes of death in a large Finnish cohort. *American Journal of Public Health, 86,* 1087–1093.

Mendes de Leon, C. D., Kasl, S. V., & Jacobs, S. (1994). A prospective study of widowhood and changes in symptoms of depression in a community sample of the elderly. *Psychological Medicine, 24,* 613–624.

Orbuch, T. L., House, J. S., Mero, R. P., & Webster, P. S. (1996). Marital quality over the life course. *Social Psychology Quarterly, 59,* 162–171.

Peek, M. K., Coward, R. T., & Peek, C. W. (2000). Race, aging, and care: Can differences in family and household structure account for race variations in informal care? *Research on Aging, 22,* 117–142.

Ross, C. E., & Mirowsky, J. (1989). Explaining the social patterns of depression: Control and problem solving—or support and talking? *Journal of Health and Social Behavior, 30,* 206–219.

Ross, C. E., Mirowsky, J., & Goldsteen, K. (1990). The impact of the family on health: The decade in review. *Journal of Marriage and the Family, 52,* 1059–1078.

Schone, B. S., & Weinick, R. M. (1998). Health-related behaviors and the benefits of marriage for elderly persons. *The Gerontologist, 38,* 618–627.

Schröder, K. E. E., Schwarzer, R., & Endler, N. S. (1997). Predicting cardiac patients' quality of life from the characteristics of their spouses. *Journal of Health Psychology, 2,* 231–244.

Smith, K. R., & Zick, C. D. (1994). Linked lives, dependent demise? Survival analysis of husbands and wives. *Demography, 31,* 81–93.

Stimpson, J. P., Kuo, Y.-F., Ray, L. A., Raji, M. A., & Peek, M. K. (2007). Risk of mortality related to widowhood in older Mexican Americans. *Annals of Epidemiology, 17,* 313–319.

Tower, R. B., & Kasl, S. V. (1996). Depressive symptoms across older spouses: Longitudinal influences. *Psychology and Aging, 11,* 683–697.

Turvey, C. L., Carney, C., Arndt, S., Wallace, R. B., & Herzog, R. (1999). Conjugal loss and syndromal depression in a sample of elders aged 70 years or older. *The American Journal of Psychiatry, 156,* 1596–1601.

Umberson, D. (1987). Family status and health behaviors: Social control as a dimension of social integration. *Journal of Health and Social Behavior, 28,* 306–319.

Umberson, D. (1992). Gender, marital status, and the social control of health behavior. *Social Science and Medicine, 34,* 907–917.

Umberson, D., Williams, K., Powers, D. A., Liu, H., & Needham, B. (2006). You make me sick: Marital quality and health over the life course. *Journal of Health and Social Behavior, 47,* 1–16.

U.S. Census Bureau. (2004a). Table A1. Marital status of people 15 years and over, by age, sex, personal earnings, race, and Hispanic origin: 2003. In *Current Population Survey, 2003 annual social and economic supplement.* Retrieved March 20, 2005, from www.census.gov/population

U.S. Bureau of the Census. (2004b). Table F1. Family households, by type, age of own children, age of family members, and age, race, and Hispanic origin of householder: 2003. In *Current Population Survey, 2003 annual social and economic supplement*. Retrieved March 20, 2005, from www.census.gov/population/

U.S. Bureau of the Census. (2005). Table 62. Families by type, race, and Hispanic origin: 2003. In *Statistical abstract of the United States: 2004–2005*. Retrieved March 20, 2005, from www.census.gov/prod

Waite, L. J. (1995). Does marriage matter? *Demography, 32*, 483–507.

Waldron, I., Hughes, M. E., & Brooks, T. L. (1996). Marriage protection and marriage selection: Prospective evidence for reciprocal effects of marital status and health. *Social Science and Medicine, 43*, 113–123.

Williams, D. R. (1990). Socioeconomic differentials in health: A review and redirection. *Social Psychology Quarterly, 53*, 81–99.

Williams, K. (2003). Has the future of marriage arrived? A contemporary examination of gender, marriage, and psychological well-being. *Journal of Health and Social Behavior, 44*, 470–487.

Williams, K., & Umberson, D. (2004). Marital status, marital transitions, and health: A gendered life course perspective. *Journal of Health and Social Behavior, 45*, 81–98.

***M. Kristen Peek***

# MAYER, KARL ULRICH

***1945–***

Karl Ulrich Mayer, a German sociologist, has accomplished seminal work in linking life course research to analyses of institutions and social change. Mayer was born in Eybach, Germany. He received academic training in sociology and related subjects at the University of Tübingen; Gonzaga University (BA, 1966); Fordham University (MA, 1967); the University of Konstanz (Dr. rer. soc., 1973), and the University of Mannheim (Ph.D., with a thesis on habilitation, 1977). He held positions at the universities of Frankfurt and Mannheim, the National Survey Research Center (ZUMA), Nuffield College, Oxford, and various visiting professorships (e.g., at the European University Institute in Florence). Between 1983 and 2005, he was a director at the Max Planck Institute for Human Development in Berlin, heading the Center for Sociology and the Study of the Life Course. Since 2003 he has been a professor of sociology and, in addition, the director of the Center for Research on Inequalities and the Life Course (CIQLE) at Yale University—a responsibility he undertook in 2005.

***Karl–Ulrich Mayer.*** PHOTO COURTESY OF KARL ULRICH MAYER.

From early on in his career, Mayer was interested in questions of social stratification and mobility. His interest in life course research developed out of his early empirical studies, including an analysis of the retrospective part of the 1971 German micro census, when he noticed the very different life chances of various birth cohorts. A pioneer of quantitative life course research in Germany, Mayer is probably best known for being the principal investigator of the German Life History Study (GLHS). This study, most of the time based at the Max Planck Institute for Human Development, lasted for more than 20 years and provides detailed retrospective information about the lives of 11,400 men and women born between 1919 and 1971. The data cover nearly the entire 20th century, and enable researchers to explore the long-term effects of events on later life at least for the older cohorts. The GLHS is probably the most comprehensive single data source on social conditions before, during, and after the division of Germany. The data can show how experiences in the German Democratic Republic and during the transformation after 1989 affected individual life courses; this topic has become a prominent part of Mayer's work.

The GLHS is based upon a conceptual framework Mayer has used throughout his research. It conceptualizes the life course as a succession of activities and events occurring in various domains of life from birth to death. The individual life course is seen as a multilevel process embedded in families and groups, featuring continuities between events earlier and later in the life course as well as feedback effects of individual behavior on the macro level of society. A core element of this concept is the regulation of the life course by social institutions, most notably institutions of the welfare state. As a guideline for rigorous empirical research, Mayer views the life course not as an entity shaped by a grand normative structure but looks rather at sequences of specific life transitions that may be influenced by a variety of institutions.

Focusing on the later stages of the life course, Mayer was also co-principal investigator of the Berlin Aging Study (BASE), a multidisciplinary in-depth study of older adults aged 70 to more than 100 years who lived in former West Berlin. In the main study (1990–1993), a sample of more than 500 individuals was closely examined with regard to their mental and physical health, psychological functioning, and socioeconomic situation. The study has been continued as a longitudinal study.

Beyond the sociology of aging and the life course, Mayer's research has contributed profoundly to contemporary knowledge in the areas of social stratification, mobility, and the sociology of elites; social demography (though he has always opposed simple ideas of an unmediated impact of demographic changes on social life); occupational structures and labor market processes; and methods of survey research. He has been one of the rather few sociologists linking sophisticated individual-level research with macro-level social theory, and he has shown a constant interest in international comparisons. To date he has coauthored and edited about 30 books and has published more than 200 articles. From 1996 to 2004 he was coeditor of the *Kölner Zeitschrift für Soziologie und Sozialpsychologie.*

Following his theoretical interest in institutions, he has been concerned with questions of practical reforms of (higher) education and training, and he has been particularly successful in developing research infrastructure. He started the German General Social Survey, has built up close linkages between social science and official statistics, and has helped to found a number of prominent research institutions. He was also a member of the German Science Council. Mayer has been a member of a number of academies of science and has received academic awards such as the Distinguished Scholar Award from the American Sociological Association Section on Aging and the Life Course.

**SEE ALSO** Volume 2: *Individuation/Standardization Debate.*

**BIBLIOGRAPHY**

Baltes, P. B., & Mayer, K. U. (Eds.). (1999). *The Berlin Aging Study: Aging from 70 to 100.* New York: Cambridge University Press.

Diewald, M., Goedicke, A., & Mayer, K. U. (Eds.). (2006). *After the fall of the wall: Life courses in the transformation of East Germany.* Stanford, CA: Stanford University Press.

Hillmert, S., & Mayer, K. U. (Eds.). (2004). *Geboren 1964 und 1971: Neuere Untersuchungen zu Ausbildungs- und Berufschancen in Westdeutschland* [Born in 1964 and 1971: Investigations on chances of education and occupation in West Germany]. Wiesbaden, Germany: Verlag für Sozialwissenschaften.

Mayer, K. U. (Sec. Ed.) (2001). Biographies. In N. J. Smelser & P. B. Baltes (Eds), *International encyclopedia of the social and behavioral sciences.* Oxford, U.K.: Elsevier Science.

Mayer, K. U., & Müller, W. (1986). The state and the structure of the life course. In A. B. Sørensen, F. E. Weinert, & L. R. Sherrod (Eds.), *Human development and the life course: Multidisciplinary perspectives* (pp. 217–245). Hillsdale, NJ: Erlbaum.

Mayer, K. U., *Lebensverläufe und sozialer Wandel* [Life courses and social change]. (1990). Opladen, Germany: Westdeutscher Verlag.

***Steffen Hillmert***

# MEDIA AND TECHNOLOGY USE, LATER LIFE

Computer-based technological developments in the latter part of the 20th century fundamentally altered the fabric of social and economic life and will likely continue to do so. The prime market segments for such technological innovations tend to be persons in the young and young adult stages of the life course. It is important to ask, therefore, how older persons have been affected by these technological developments, to examine how elders might participate in and benefit from new technologies, and to understand factors associated with technology adoption and use by the older population. Owing to the wide range of technological applications, the focus in this entry is on computer- and home-based information and communication technology, omitting areas such as assistive technology (considered elsewhere in this volume), technology in the workplace, and technological applications for vehicular transportation.

## MODES OF TECHNOLOGY USE

Developments in communication and information technology are having far-reaching implications for social interaction, social networks, and social support. E-mail, text and instant messaging, Voice over Internet Protocol (VoIP), two-way video communications, news groups, chat rooms, social networking sites (e.g., Facebook), and dating websites (e.g., Match.com) enable persons to initiate, maintain, or extend social relationships, unimpeded by constraints of geographical distance. The

***Teaching Internet to the Elders.*** *A junior at Standley Lake High School teaches a retiree to use the Internet during a class at the school in Westminster, CO. An innovative program spearheaded by EarthLink, an Internet service provider, brought the students and AARP members together.* AP IMAGES.

Internet is of particular relevance to older adults who wish to be in contact with dispersed networks of family and friends and for those who may be isolated because of mobility limitations. Research consistently shows that the primary way online elders use the Internet is for e-mail, including intergenerational communication with children and grandchildren (Fallows, 2004; Fox, 2004).

Internet-based communication also has special relevance to caregivers of older persons and others seeking social support. Online support groups enable caregivers to overcome barriers imposed by time and distance. Unlike face-to-face support groups, the asynchronous character of the communication does not require other network members to be immediately and concurrently available. Numerous online support groups exist, and research on the effects of participating in them suggests that such access is generally beneficial for caregiver well-being (Smyth & Kwon, 2004).

The Internet is especially well suited to information gathering, a process facilitated by the availability of powerful search engines. The value of this aspect of technology to the elderly is demonstrated by findings showing that information gathering is another major way they make use of the Internet. Prominent among the specific types of information sought is information about health, which is understandable given the higher prevalence of health problems at the latter stages of the life course (Fox, 2004, 2006).

By virtue of their flexibility, new technologies also have the potential to contribute to the intellectual enrichment of older persons. Distance learning courses offered via two-way interactive television and online courses open up educational opportunities for elders who may be unable to enroll in traditional courses. In the early 21st century, however, older adults were somewhat less likely than the general population to be enrolled in any form of adult education and lifelong learning courses, and only a very small proportion of persons 65 and older is enrolled in any type of online distance learning course (Cutler, 2006).

Existing and emerging technologies also have the capacity to collect information about the status of older persons on a real-time basis via monitoring and surveillance. Telehealth and telemedicine technology can monitor a person's condition and provide data to flag significant changes and initiate appropriate responses. Health status data collected in the home can be transmitted both to health care providers and to family or other informal caregivers, regardless of their physical proximity to the older person (Whitten, 2006). Similarly, efforts underway to develop "smart" houses are attempting to harness the power of technology to monitor conditions in the home environment, movement through the house, health status, needs for self-care, and wandering

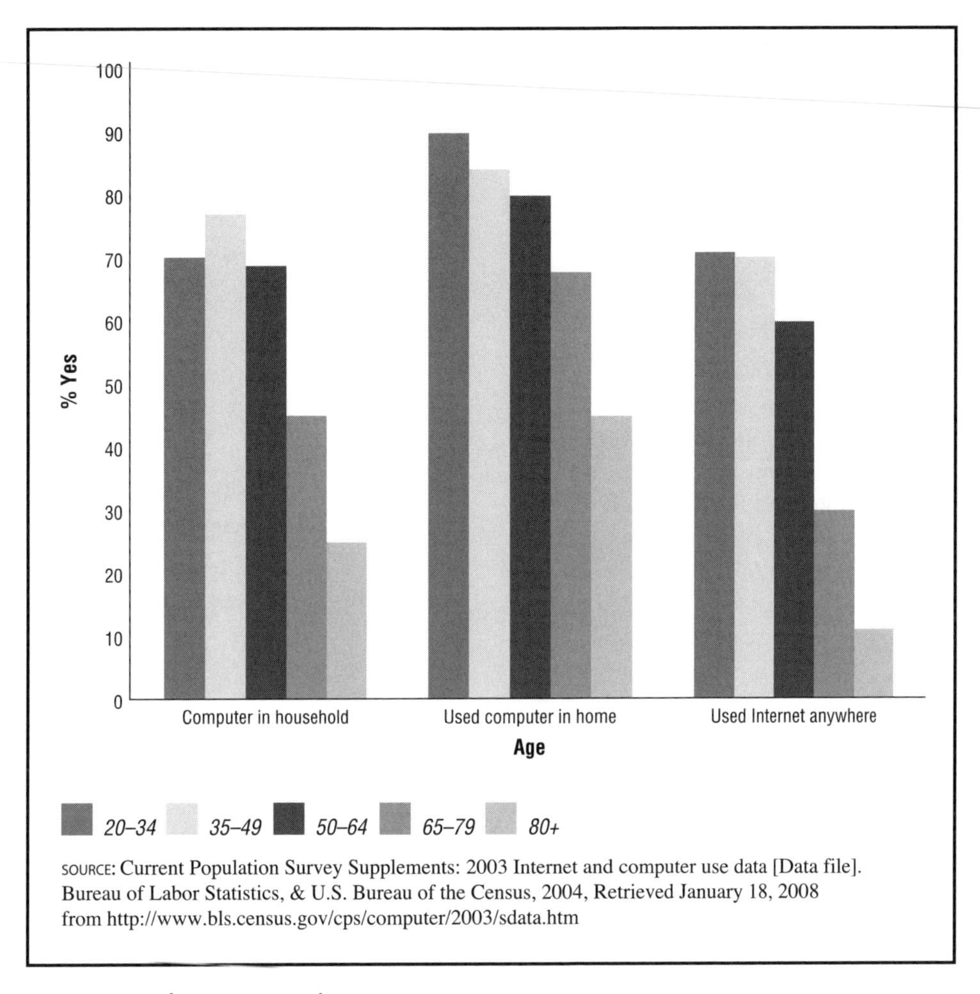


***Figure 1.*** *Computer access and Internet usage by age, 2003.* CENGAGE LEARNING, GALE.

from the home (Horgas & Abowd, 2004). These applications are particularly important because efforts to slow the rate of growth of health care costs have resulted in a shift in the locus of care from hospitals to home-based and other community-based settings.

Finally, forms of e-commerce range from the direct electronic deposit of checks to paying bills and conducting other financial transactions electronically to ordering goods and services over the Internet. Direct-deposit services benefit elders who may find it difficult to get to a bank because of functional or transportation limitations or who are concerned about the security of mailed checks or about their personal safety when going to a bank. Being able to shop for and purchase goods and services online has several advantages: It provides access for those with impaired mobility, shopping is not temporally limited, and there are no geographical constraints on the businesses that can be accessed. Because older people take longer to process information (Mayhorn, Rogers, & Fisk, 2004), online purchases may also present less time pressure than would the same transaction conducted in person or over the phone. As convenient as online commerce is, smaller percentages of older persons than of younger and middle-age persons currently make use of e-commerce, although such usage by elders is increasing (Fox, 2004).

## FACTORS IN THE USE OF TECHNOLOGY BY OLDER PERSONS

Older persons have traditionally tended to be late adopters of new technology (Horrigan, 2007; Rogers, 2003). For example, despite trends over time toward increasing computer and Internet use by older persons (U.S. Census Bureau, 2007, Table 1128), age differences persist. The data in Figure 1 show that older adults are less likely to live in households that have a computer, are less likely to have used the computer if there is one, and are far less likely to have made use of the Internet at any location (Bureau of Labor Statistics & U.S. Census Bureau,

2004). Attempts to determine if these access and usage differences can be accounted for by compositional factors associated with age (e.g., socioeconomic, demographic, and health differences) show that the age differences persist even after taking relevant variables into account (Cutler, Hendricks, & Guyer, 2003). Although computer and Internet use are prime examples of the negative relationship between age and technology use, similar age differences are evident for other modalities such as automatic teller machine (ATM) and cell phone use.

Research aimed at understanding the lower use of technology among older persons has considered several broad sets of factors (Cutler, 2006). Behavioral scientists have focused their efforts on problems with product design and instructions and with barriers erected by age-related decrements in cognitive, sensory, and motor functioning (Schieber, 2003). The role of social-psychological factors has been less systematically studied and is less well understood, but scattered evidence indicates that variables such as levels of interest, comfort, and control are associated with age differences in technology use. Expectations of others likely contribute to age differences, as ageist attitudes about the capabilities of older persons may foster reticence to try new technologies (Cutler, 2005). Finally, among older persons, socioeconomic and demographic variables have been shown to play a key and consistent role in explaining variation in access to and use of computers and the Internet: Availability and use tend to be lower among women and persons who are widowed, among persons with lower incomes and education levels, and among those who have one or more disabilities (Bureau of Labor Statistics & U.S. Census Bureau, 2004).

## THE FUTURE

Will age differences in technology use diminish in the future, or will they persist? Research has demonstrated that one of the most important factors in how attitudes shape technology use is experience. In school and in workplace settings, as well as at home, both the young and the middle aged will have had much greater exposure to computer-based information technology than current cohorts of older persons. The proliferation of cell phones and related communications technology and familiarity with automated systems such as ATMs among the young and middle-aged means that these and similar skills will be brought with them to their later years. Then, too, adopting and using new technology is related to socioeconomic factors. That future cohorts of older persons will have higher levels of educational attainment and perhaps greater levels of economic security also suggests that age differences in technology usage may diminish somewhat in coming years.

On the other hand, age-related changes in cognitive, sensory, and motor functioning need to be considered. The changing levels of performance that accompany normal aging may work against adoption and use of tomorrow's new, enhanced, and perhaps miniaturized but more complicated technologies, just as these changes have worked against use by older persons of early 21st-century technologies. Technological gadgetry and wizardry can also be expensive, beyond the financial reach of many elders, and perhaps less salient in their hierarchy of needs. For example, the potential benefits of smart houses are impressive, but more fundamental for some elders are basic housing issues of availability, affordability, and adequacy (Cutler & Hendricks, 2001). For older persons living on limited, fixed incomes, the fruits of technological change may prove to be inaccessible, thereby perpetuating the age-based "technological divide."

**SEE ALSO** Volume 3: *Assistive Technologies; Lifelong Learning; Social Integration/Isolation, Later Life; Time Use, Later Life.*

**BIBLIOGRAPHY**

Bureau of Labor Statistics & U.S. Census Bureau. (2004). *Current population survey supplements: 2003 Internet and computer use data.* Retrieved January 18, 2008, from http://www.census.gov

Cutler, S. (2005). Ageism and technology. *Generations, 29*(3), 67–72.

Cutler, S. (2006). Technological change and aging. In R. Binstock & L. George (Eds.), *Handbook of aging and the social sciences* (6th ed., pp. 257–276). San Diego, CA: Academic Press.

Cutler, S., & Hendricks, J. (2001). Emerging social trends. In R. Binstock & L. George (Eds.), *Handbook of aging and social sciences* (5th ed., pp. 462–480). San Diego, CA: Academic Press.

Cutler, S., Hendricks, J., & Guyer, A. (2003). Age differences in home computer availability and use. *Journal of Gerontology: Social Sciences, 58*, S271–S280.

Fallows, D. (2004) *The Internet and daily life.* Retrieved May 14, 2008, from http://pewinternet.org

Fox, S. (2004). *Older Americans and the Internet.* Retrieved May 14, 2008, from http://www.pewinternet.org

Fox, S. (2006). *Online health search 2006.* Retrieved May 21, 2008, from http://pewinternet.org

Horgas, A., & Abowd, G. (2004). The impact of technology on living environments for older adults. In R. Pew & S. Van Hemel (Eds.), *Technology for adaptive aging* (pp. 230–252). Washington, DC: National Academies Press.

Horrigan, J. (2007). *A typology of information and communication technology users.* Retrieved May 21, 2008, from http://www.pewinternet.org

Mayhorn, C. B., Rogers, W. A., & Fisk, A. D. (2004). Designing technology based on cognitive aging principles. In D. C. Burdick & S. Kwon (Eds.), *Gerotechnology: Research and practice in technology and aging* (pp. 42–53). New York: Springer.

Rogers, E. (2003). *Diffusion of innovations* (5th ed.). New York: Free Press.

Schieber, F. (2003). Human factors and aging: Identifying and compensating for age-related deficits in sensory and cognitive function. In N. Charness & K. W. Schaie (Eds.), *Impact of technology on successful aging* (pp. 113–133). New York: Springer.

Smyth, K., & Kwon, S. (2004). Computer-mediated communication and its use in support groups for family caregivers. In D. C. Burdick & S. Kwon (Eds.), *Gerotechnology: Research and practice in technology and aging* (pp. 97–116). New York: Springer.

U.S. Census Bureau. 2007. *Statistical abstract of the United States: 2008, information and communications.* Washington, DC: Author. Retrieved May 21, 2008, from http://www.census.gov

Whitten, P. (2006). Telemedicine: Communication technologies that revolutionize healthcare services. *Generations, 30*(2), 20–24.

***Stephen J. Cutler***

# MEDICARE/MEDICAID

SEE Volume 2: *Policy, Health;* Volume 3: *Long-term Care.*

# MENTAL HEALTH, LATER LIFE

Consideration of mental health in a life course perspective is useful, as it helps place diverse forms of psychopathology into an important context. Most mental health problems tend to be initially diagnosed early in life, during adolescence or in young adulthood. It should be noted that the risk of first diagnosis of a mental illness declines with age. One exception, which follows a late onset and escalating trajectory, applies to the dementias, including Alzheimer's disease. A second psychological problem that escalates in late life among White males is suicidal thoughts and, ultimately, suicide itself.

Stressful life events may be expected to contribute to mental health problems. Older adults experience major normative stressors such as serious illness and social losses, including retirement and the death of loved ones. Nevertheless, they show great resilience in the face of these stressors and to threats of impending death.

The disciplinary orientations of researchers and clinicians play an important role in approaches taken to mental health and illness in late life. In terms of diagnosis and treatment of mental illness, psychiatric orientations emphasize the biological origins of these illnesses. Indeed, treatment of many, if not most, mental illnesses involves pharmaceutical intervention. There have been major advances in cognitive neuroscience that have helped elucidate the role of brain structure and function in psychopathology.

Psychologists tend to focus on the important interactions between environmental forces and biological susceptibility, in the development and manifestations of mental health problems. These are referred to as the diathesis stress theories of mental disorders. Developmental and social psychologists, as well as sociologists, have also focused on the stress process, whereby stress exposure may pose risks for mental illness, while coping resources and social supports may ameliorate the adverse effects of stressors on mental health. Indeed, research reveals that stressful life events can exacerbate existing psychological disorders, such as anxiety, depression, and *positive symptoms* of schizophrenia (e.g., auditory, visual, or olfactory hallucinations) (Holmes, 2006). Furthermore, social resources and supports can help diminish the number and intensity of symptoms in already existing psychiatric disorders.

Considering mental health within the life course perspective is useful because it helps to distinguish special challenges faced by older people living with chronic mental illness from those facing mental health problems for the first time in late life. These distinctions are often overlooked in the literature dealing with general mental health or on mental health at a particular life stage. Most instances of serious psychiatric disorders among older people reflect the aging of individuals with long-term psychiatric illness. In fact, some mental disorders of young adulthood tend to improve with age, such as positive symptom schizophrenia, anxiety disorders, and obsessive-compulsive disorders (Holmes, 2006). This may be due to changes, with aging, in the level of neurotransmitters and other brain processes. For example, an excess level of the neurotransmitter dopamine, responsible for positive symptoms of schizophrenia, declines with aging. Yet, one cannot rule out cohort differences in rates of diagnosis of various psychiatric disorders, because research is often reported based on cross-sectional studies. It should also be recognized that diagnostic criteria for mental disorders have evolved over time.

Abnormal psychology and psychiatry provide a vast array of diagnostic entities that apply to issues of mental health and aging. It is beyond the scope of this entry to review all of the disorders included in the fourth edition of the *Diagnostic and Statistical Manual of Mental Disorders*, also known as the DSM-IV, the official diagnostic manual of the American Psychiatric Association. Instead, this entry will focus on a selected number of disorders that include the more prevalent psychiatric disorders of late life, and will also provide a few illustrations of less frequent but notable disorders or clinical problems.

Accordingly, this review will include diagnostic criteria, etiology, course of illness, treatment, and management of selected mental health problems. The mental health problems and issues selected for inclusion in this entry are (a) common emotional problems in aging; (b) adjustment disorders; (c) mood disorders (depression, suicide, and mania); (d) dementias; (e) anxiety disorders; (f) post-traumatic stress disorder (PTSD); (g) mental health and resilience in late life; (h) treating mental illness through psychotherapy and pharmacotherapy; and (i) systems of caring for the mentally ill older population. This entry will also discuss the status of delivery of mental health services to the elderly. (The term *elderly* simply refers to individuals who are age 65 or older.) Current gerontological terminology designates persons ages 65 through 74 as the *young old* and those age 85 and older as the *oldest old*, while the 10-year age group between 75 and 84 constitutes an intermediate group between the young old and oldest old. In addition, those 100 years old and beyond are referred to as *centenarians*. These demarcations may change in the future as people live longer and healthier lives.

## COMMON EMOTIONAL PROBLEMS

Emotional problems associated with old age are generally related to experiences of stressful life events that are common during this stage in the life course. Such emotional problems include anger, sadness, helplessness, and loneliness, and may reflect the shared human experience of dealing with personal and social losses. These emotional states cause distress and discomfort, and may represent clear mental health problems of late life. To the extent that most of these emotional reactions generally resolve themselves over time, they are not considered as formal psychiatric diagnostic categories. However, when such negative emotions do persist and interfere with the older individual's functioning, they are designated as "adjustment reactions" in the DSM-IV.

In this section of the entry, there will be a brief review of some of the normative stressors of aging that are generally associated with the experience and manifestation of these emotional problems. These stressors include the death of a close family member or loved one, caregiving, and coping with life-threatening physical illness. In addition, traumatic stressors will be considered, including man-made and natural disasters, in a later section of the entry discussing PTSD.

**Death of Close Family Members** The loss of loved ones, including spouses, siblings, and even adult children, is part of the life experience of many elderly people. Widowhood may include a unique form of bereavement that affects the lifestyle, social position, and social support of older people (Lopata, 1996). Bereavement has been characterized in the mental health literature as including several stages, particularly when the death of a loved one is anticipated. In the latter instance, older adults are likely to exhibit *anticipatory grief reactions*. *Grief reaction*, which occurs shortly after the loss of a loved one, involves sadness and expression of negative emotions, including depressive ideation, loss of interest in enjoying life, restlessness, and sleep and appetite disturbances. In the aftermath of the individual's anniversary of death, grief reactions may also be manifested and are referred to as *anniversary reactions* (Butler et al., 1998).

Reactions to bereavement are often culturally shared expressions. Most religions have developed rituals, where the community can express social support for the person who is bereaved and show acceptance of their grief reactions. Such rituals often acknowledge that a period of time must elapse before the bereaved individual can return to normal social roles. In addition, members of the community also express their empathy and sharing of emotions. The inability to express one's grief could result in adverse psychological consequences. In addition to generating emotions of sadness, bereavement is also likely to lead to intense feelings of loneliness. This linkage between loss of one's social network, particularly in widowhood, and feelings of loneliness, has been confirmed both in U.S.-based and international studies. Similar findings have been reported based on the Finnish elderly (Jylhä, 2004) and among the Swedish aged population (Berg, Mellström, Persson, & Svanborg, 1981), indicating that the loss of a spouse is a significant contributor to loneliness.

**Caregiving** Another important example of stressful life situations that are likely to lead to emotional problems in late life is caregiving. Much of the extensive caregiving literature has focused on elderly spouses providing care to someone with Alzheimer's disease or other debilitating conditions (Zarit & Zarit, 2007). Such elderly caregivers are simultaneously coping with the loss of companionship and social support from the person for whom they are caring, and the intense physical and psychological demands of caregiving. Just as sadness and loneliness are prevalent emotions among the bereaved, elderly caregivers often experience anger and helplessness as they confront role strain and the inevitable decline that they are witnessing in their loved one. Many elderly caregivers must simultaneously confront their own frailty and personal losses, even as they are attempting to cope with the illness of a close family member. Effective strategies, such as marshaling support and instrumental coping to meet challenges head-on, have been found to diminish the adverse mental health consequences of caregiving stress. There are notable cultural influences on stressors associated with caregiving and the emotional responses to the caregiving experience. Norms of obligation differ internationally, and available social supports to the elderly caregiver are also shaped by cultural context. For example, Japanese caregivers had traditionally been expected to care for their elders at home; but with growing industrialization, they now face difficult choices that include institutionalizing elders, with resultant feelings of guilt, sadness, and even anger (Young, McCormick, & Vitaliano, 2002).

**Facing Life-Threatening Illness** In addition to well-recognized problems posed by caregiving to the elderly, being a recipient of care presents its own challenges. Older adults suffering from life-threatening or disabling illness confront personal losses and stigma. This is in addition to engaging in adaptive tasks of ensuring that they receive responsive and adequate care from formal, as well as informal, caregivers. The disability cascade represents a sequence of events leading from chronic illness (e.g., severe arthritis), to physical impairment (e.g., pain), to functional limitations and disability (e.g., mobility problems) that alter the lives of many older adults. As the elderly confront these illness-related losses, and are no longer able to independently perform activities of daily living, they frequently experience emotions of sadness, helplessness, loss of control and self-efficacy, and diminished self-esteem. The need to give up valued social roles and activities also elicit negative emotions, both when it is due to physical illness and when it is based on environmental or societal displacement of the elderly, as may occur through involuntary retirement.

## ADJUSTMENT DISORDERS

Adjustment disorders of late life refer to time-limited, but often severe, maladaptive reactions to stressful life events. Adverse psychological responses may include depression, anxiety, fearfulness, physically or verbally acting out, or destructive behaviors. To the extent that the stressful life situation (e.g., acute physical illness, problems with family members) may resolve itself, symptoms that are reactions to the stressor are also more likely to dissipate. However, for some older adults, reactions continue, and symptoms initially diagnosed as adjustment reactions may be reclassified as a chronic mental disorder. Where the stressful event has permanent consequences, such as amputation for a diabetic patient, or the death of one's spouse, individuals exhibiting initial adjustment disorders are likely to gradually develop new coping skills, which eventually result in improved psychological functioning.

Older adults requiring institutional placement, particularly in nursing homes, often exhibit psychological distress or behavioral symptoms that are diagnosed as an adjustment disorder, or perhaps more accurately, as an adjustment reaction. Among elderly patients in hospitals, who are referred for psychiatric diagnosis and treatment, approximately 20% are diagnosed with adjustment disorders. It is notable that patients exhibiting cognitive impairment seldom receive this diagnosis, based on their assumed chronic and irreversible brain pathology. Such patients are generally not expected to overcome stress-induced psychological problems. Adjustment disorders are ultimately confirmed by their transitory nature. Longitudinal research in 2008 profiling community-dwelling older persons offers evidence that recent stressors, occurring during the past year, are most likely to trigger depressive symptoms. It is notable, however, that an accumulation of negative life events over a 4-year period also contributed to depressive symptoms.

Research on stressful life events, such as widowhood, suggests that strong initial grief reactions, anxiety, and depressive symptoms generally dissipate within a 1-year period, with most older adults returning to their prior levels of psychological well-being (Wilcox et al., 2003). Criteria for diagnosis of adjustment disorders, according to the DSM-IV, include an identifiable stressor antecedent to the symptoms, a determination that a patient's response exceeds the *usual* responses to such stressors, and significant impairments in the patient's ability to function. Additional specific criteria that are listed in the DSM-IV manual require that the stress-related disturbance does not meet the criteria of schizophrenia or mania, personality disorder (such as schizoid, avoidant, or dependent personality disorders), or symptoms of bereavement, and that once the stressor has terminated, the symptoms subside within 6 months.

Among older adults, medical illness and hospitalization are among the most common stressors related to a diagnosis of adjustment disorders. It is notable that patients who develop adjustment disorders frequently have prior symptomatology or a history of mental health problems (Lantz, 2006).

Psychotherapy is considered the treatment of choice for adjustment disorders. However, few older patients are actually referred for psychotherapy (Butler et al., 1998). Furthermore, those who are referred often choose not to go for treatment. Studies show that brief goal-directed therapy as well as cognitive behavioral therapy (CBT) are effective in easing adjustment disorders (Lantz, 2006). However, these data are based primarily on older adults suffering from depressive symptoms. Few of the older adults in these studies had isolated diagnoses of adjustment disorders.

Adjustment disorders are typically expected to resolve within a 6-month period, with some improvement anticipated after 3 months. Those with poor resolution are likely to have experienced multiple or extreme stressors while also having limited social supports. In terms of extreme adverse reactions, suicide attempts have been reported (Smyer & Qualls, 1999). At the same time, there is growing evidence of resilience in late life. Studies of older persons dealing with highly stressful events, such as a cancer diagnosis (Bergeman & Wallace, 1999) and long-term cancer survivorship (Deimling, Kahana, Bowman, & Schaefer, 2002), reveal that many can retain their earlier levels of psychological well-being.

## MOOD DISORDERS: DEPRESSION, SUICIDE, AND MANIA

Depression in old age bears many similarities to depression diagnosed early in life, but it also has several distinctive characteristics and thus may present challenges for accurate diagnosis. Depression is recognized as the most frequent psychiatric diagnosis in old age. Nevertheless, in a life course perspective, it is notable that depression is also the most frequent diagnosis of mental health problems in younger age groups. In fact, depression rates are lower in old age than at other points during the adult life course. Thus, prevalence rates for depression are highest in midlife, with women portraying significantly higher rates of depression than do their male counterparts (Lewinsohn, Hops, Roberts, Seeley, & Andrews, 1993). At older ages, depression rates are lower and gender differences also become less marked, although women continue, at all life stages, to report greater depressive symptomatology than men, as shown in cross-sectional studies.

Typically, late-life depression is initially diagnosed in a primary care setting. Recognizing symptoms of depression and referral of patients for more specialized care presents special challenges. Symptoms of depression are often difficult to distinguish from symptoms of cognitive impairment, on the one hand, and from symptoms of physical illness, such as fatigue, on the other. Among the elderly, both somatic symptoms of depression (disturbances in eating, sleeping, and libido) and problems in memory and cognition are frequently observed, and may be reflecting underlying physical illness, reactions to stressful life events, or early-stage dementia.

Depression is a complex disorder with diagnostic classifications dependent on the number of symptoms, their duration, and severity. Severe cases of clinical depression may also include suicidal ideation and psychotic features such as hallucinations or delusions. According to the DSM-IV, a diagnosis of major depressive disorder requires the presence of depressed mood, or inability to derive pleasure in life, lasting for a minimum of 2 weeks. Furthermore, four additional symptoms of depression from among a specific list of nine categories must also be present. The DSM-IV also attempts to rule out symptoms that may be due to the direct physiological effects of substance abuse, of medication, or of a general medical condition. It also differentiates between major depression and symptoms of bereavement, after the loss of a loved one. Additional criteria for arriving at a diagnosis of depression are listed in the DSM-IV.

There are numerous categorizations in the DSM-IV that are relevant to depressive disorders in later life. Mild symptom clusters are referred to as elevations in depressive symptomatology. Such elevations are regularly observed in research on socially disadvantaged groups and are often the result of stressful life events. They are often measured based on responses to the Center for Epidemiological Studies depression scale (CES-D), a scale that is commonly used in sample surveys to assess depressive symptoms among community-dwelling adults (Radloff, 1977). The DSM-IV clinical classification for mild forms of depression is called *dysthymia*, which affects 2% of elderly adults.

Clinically significant depression is generally diagnosed as *major depressive disorder*. This may be manifested in a single episode or in recurrent episodes of clinical depression. Additionally, manic-depressive or bipolar disorder may be diagnosed when there are alternating episodes of mania and depression. A milder version of bipolar disorder is referred to as *cyclothymia*, when individuals cycle between sadness and lethargy, on the one hand, and spells of energy and euphoria on the other. However, the magnitude of alternating depression and mania are more muted in cyclothymia. Depression may also coexist with other psychiatric disorders. These include anxiety disorders, obsessive-compulsive disorder, PTSD, schizophrenia, and hypochondria (Holmes, 2006). There are additional descriptions in the DSM-IV of specific reactions among the elderly. These were described earlier as anticipatory grief, grief reactions, and anniversary reactions (associated with the death of a loved one). Diagnosis of depression in these cases is often a matter of severity of symptoms. When symptoms resolve in a relatively short period, the mental health problem may be designated as an adjustment reaction.

Depression is the most frequently identified and most extensively studied mental health problem among older adults. About 2% of older adults have suffered from a major depressive disorder (Beekman et al., 1995). However, clinically significant symptoms of depression, which do not reach the criterion for a diagnosis of major depressive disorder, occur much more frequently. About 15% of community-dwelling elderly persons and 40% of elderly persons living in long-term care facilities manifest such problems (Gatz, 2000). Furthermore, suicide, which is considered one of the ultimate adverse outcomes of depression, also tends to increase with age, particularly among

White males (McIntosh, Santos, Hubbard, & Overholser, 1994).

Risk factors for depression are multidimensional. Focusing on biological etiology, neurotransmitter deficiency (insufficient serotonin and norepinephrine) has been viewed as a key cause of depressive problems. Genetic predispositions clearly play a role in both brain structure and function. Additional evidence for risk factors is based on the strong association of late-life depressive episodes with prior history of depression, major or minor. Cerebrovascular disease has also been associated with late-life depressive episodes. Individuals who have had strokes in the left prefrontal area of the brain are more likely to develop depressive symptoms than are people who had other forms of brain disease (Alexopoulos et al., 1997). Additionally, environmental factors, such as loss of a loved one or burdensome caregiving responsibilities, which represent stressful late-life situations, have also been linked to depressive symptomatology (Bodnar & Kiecolt-Glaser, 1994). Studies have also shown that individuals of lower socioeconomic status are more likely to develop depression (Fiske & Jones, 2005). This association suggests that stress exposure associated with limited economic resources could contribute to the development of depression.

## DEMENTIA

Dementias represent highly prevalent mental health problems in late life. They involve gradual and progressive decline in memory and cognition to the point where individuals are unable to cope with their environment (Youngjohn & Crook, 1996). The dementias include a variety of neurodegenerative diseases such as Alzheimer's disease, vascular dementia, Pick's disease, later stages of Parkinson's disease, Huntington's disease, and others. Alzheimer's disease is the most prevalent of these conditions. Depressive symptoms have been consistently found to contribute to cognitive impairment, which needs to be distinguished from dementia, because the former (depression) is reversible (Jorm, 2000). Conversely, older persons can react to cognitive decline with feelings of depression.

## ANXIETY DISORDERS

Anxiety has been found, in epidemiological studies, to decline with age (Kessler et al., 1994). Nevertheless, varying levels of anxiety present major mental health problems for large numbers of elderly persons. Given that older adults endure normative stressors of chronic illness, disability, and social losses, it is understandable that emotions reflecting worry, agitation, arousal, or fear would frequently accompany stressful life situations. Anxiety experienced in late life is often associated with other negative emotions, including loneliness and depression. Furthermore, anxious elderly persons are likely to report poorer health and more activity limitations (de Beurs et al., 1999). It is important to note that, in addition to psychological manifestations, there are strong physiological components to anxiety. Arousal and anxiety can be brought about by a biochemical imbalance in the brain (i.e., insufficient GABA), even in the absence of stressful life events (Holmes, 2006).

Experiences and expressions of anxiety on a temporary basis, in response to stressful life situations, are common. However, the experience of anxiety in the absence of environmental triggers, or the continuing experience of anxiety after the triggers are no longer present, are classified as anxiety disorders by the DSM-IV. There has been considerable controversy in establishing whether such anxiety disorders increase or decrease in old age (Lauderdale, Kelly, & Sheikh, 2006). There are indications from research showing that rates of anxiety disorders do not, in fact, increase with age (Manela, Katona, & Livingston, 1996). These findings may reflect the development of resilience in the elderly, based on a lifetime of learning to cope with numerous stressful life situations. It should be noted that epidemiological studies differ widely in their estimates of anxiety disorders in late life, particularly based on the criteria used for establishing prevalence rates (e.g., 1 month, 6 months, or 12 months). Longitudinal studies of the same individuals over time are few, as compared to cross-sectional studies. This leaves an open question as to whether anxiety changes within the same individuals over time, or whether cohort effects are being observed.

Classification of anxiety disorders in the clinical literature and the DSM-IV encompasses a broad spectrum of mental health problems. These problems include (a) generalized anxiety disorder (GAD); (b) phobic disorders; (c) panic disorders; (d) acute stress disorders; (e) obsessive-compulsive disorders; and (f) PTSD.

GAD is characterized by hyperarousal within the individual (e.g., elevated heartbeat, respiration, and other symptoms) and involves excessive worry and anxiety that persists most of the time, for at least a 6-month period. Symptoms include restlessness, irritability, difficulty concentrating, and sleep difficulties. Typically there is no clear trigger for the anxiety. Worries may center on problems that might occur in the future. Studies indicate that symptoms of this disorder most commonly occur in young adulthood (Holmes, 2006). It is notable that GAD in older adults is characterized by a chronic course, with most of those treated for this problem having manifested symptoms earlier in their lives (Blazer, George, & Hughes, 1991).

Phobias refer to irrational fears of specific objects or social situations that interfere with an individual's ability to function effectively in their environment. Such irrational fears are relatively common in the general population, with estimates of up to 10% of the population experiencing some type of phobia at any one time. Phobias of spiders, elevators, air travel, and of social situations are particularly common, with women reporting more frequent instances of phobias than their male counterparts (Hollander & Simeon, 2004). Phobias interfere with daily functioning, because those suffering from them tend to avoid situations where they might encounter the object of their fears. Consequently, they never adjust to the feared object. Prevalence of phobias is slightly less frequent among older adults than among younger age groups. Nevertheless, on an absolute basis, phobias are relatively common problems in late life as well as in earlier points in the life course. Types of phobias reported by older adults do not differ significantly from those reported by younger age groups. However, on some occasions, what appears to be a phobia in a young adult, such as getting onto a bus, constitutes a justifiable concern for an older person who has difficulty in ambulation or climbing steps.

### POST-TRAUMATIC STRESS DISORDER (PTSD)

Unlike GADs, where there is often an unknown origin for the symptoms, PTSD represents a form of anxiety disorder where there is a clear and identifiable origin (Dohrenwend, 1998). Symptoms in this case are found in the aftermath of major natural or man-made disasters, such as earthquakes and wars, or extreme personal trauma, such as a rape or other forms of abuse. Subsequent to experiencing personal or social catastrophes, distress represents a normal response to abnormal situations. Symptoms of PTSD often linger on, even in the long-term aftermath of the original trauma, when threats are no longer present. In considering PTSD in a life course perspective, two major categories become relevant. One set of problems is encountered among those older adults who are exposed to traumatic situations such as wars or natural disasters in late life. A second category is noted, where persons suffered traumatic stress exposure earlier in life. These latter individuals may exhibit long-term, renewed, or new psychological symptoms as they encounter old age.

There are three symptom clusters necessary for the diagnosis of PTSD in the aftermath of a traumatic event. These include intrusiveness, avoidance, and hyperarousal. These symptoms have to persist for at least 1 month's duration. PTSD is further categorized as acute (less than a 3 month duration), chronic (3 months or longer), or delayed onset (where trauma-related symptoms appear at least 6 months after the traumatic event). Intrusiveness is exemplified by nightmares, and daytime intrusive thoughts that are reminiscent of the trauma. Avoidance or numbing refer to a tendency to avoid facing anything related to the traumatic event and feeling numb when forced to face it. Hyperarousal is manifested in excessive vigilance to events and objects that could possibly or remotely pose a threat.

The majority of research dealing with late-life trauma exposure has focused on natural disasters, including floods, earthquakes, hurricanes, tornadoes, and volcanic eruptions. Many of these studies have been conducted outside of the United States (Liu et al., 2006; Armenian et al., 2000). These studies typically involve only short-term follow-ups and suggest remarkable resilience on the part of elderly trauma victims, particularly where social supports are available. Thus, older survivors of the 1988 Armenian earthquake reported less intrusiveness, but more symptoms of hyperarousal, relative to younger survivors (Goenjian et al., 1994). Notably, the overall severity of PTSD in this sample did not differ by age, illustrating the resilience of older adults.

Examples of PTSD in late life, based on having experienced trauma earlier in life, typically derive from community surveys of older persons who had lived through wartime trauma. Such studies have focused on elderly survivors of the Holocaust (Kahana, Harel, & Kahana, 2005) and on elderly war veterans, including survivors of Pearl Harbor (Wilson, Harel, & Kahana, 1988). The Pearl Harbor study showed a decline in PTSD symptoms over time, since the trauma. Other studies were done on soldiers who had experienced wartime captivity (Dikel, Engdahl, & Eberly, 2005). Among those individuals, substantial numbers continue to manifest PTSD, even in the long-term aftermath of the original trauma. Others have shown healing after their initial experience of PTSD, but symptoms may have reemerged when they encountered negative life events of old age that served as reminders of the earlier trauma or of personal vulnerability (Kuch & Cox, 1992). Thus, one can discern several life course trajectories that this disorder may take, in the aftermath of the traumatic event. The extent of trauma exposure appears to be related to the likelihood of exhibiting symptoms of PTSD later in life (Yehuda, Southwick, Giller, Ma, & Mason, 1992). This finding has been observed both in studies of Holocaust survivors and with war veterans.

Focus on traumatic events that happened to older adults in the United States relates primarily to victims of crime. Among elderly individuals seeking treatment after criminal victimization, about one-third reported symptoms of PTSD (Gray & Acierno, 2002). It is important to note, however, that clinical populations who present for treatment are more likely to consist of individuals experiencing significant symptoms than are nonclinical samples of community-dwelling crime victims.

In considering life course trajectories of PTSD, one can discuss four typologies: (a) the *resilient* survivor, who feels strong and powerful after coping with and surviving the traumatic experience; (b) the *untainted* survivor, where the individual simply goes on with life and tries to leave the past behind; (c) the *conditionally vulnerable* survivor who adapts well, but after facing new threats, reacts with a flare-up of PTSD symptoms; and (d) the *vulnerable* survivor, who has an almost lifelong history of PTSD subsequent to the original trauma (Kahana, Harel, & Kahana, 2005). The existence of these subgroups may help researchers understand why clinicians often report long-lasting effects or exacerbation of PTSD symptoms with aging, whereas community-based studies tent to show either no increase or an actual decline in PTSD symptoms over the life course (Wilson, Harel, & Kahana, 1988).

## MENTAL HEALTH AND RESILIENCE IN LATE LIFE

In considering the mental health of the elderly, the resilience and adaptability of this group deserves attention. Older adults are likely to experience diverse normative stressors, presented by chronic illness and disability. In addition, with increasing life expectancy, there is also an increasing incidence of social losses. These may reflect deaths of friends and family of the same generation and even loss of adult children. Relocation of longtime friends and neighbors constitutes yet another set of losses. Although the number of reported life events declines with aging, the magnitude of events likely to be experienced by older adults presents threats to the self and to one's identity (Thoits, 1991). In addition, stressors of late life may be superimposed on trauma, which older adults might have experienced earlier in their lives. Thus, many of the oldest old the early 21st century may have lived though the Great Depression (1929–1939), World War II (1939–1945), and the immigrant experience.

Considering the accumulation of stressors in late life and threats of impending mortality, older adults generally exhibit good mental health. Studies of community-based samples of older adults reveal relatively low rates of mental health problems (Smyer & Qualls, 1999). These comparisons are likely to reflect cohort differences in coping with stressful life situations. The research of the authors of this entry has explored late-life adaptation of those elderly who had experienced major trauma early in life. In a study comparing psychological well-being of survivors of the Nazi Holocaust with other immigrants to the United States, the authors found that 40 years after experiencing trauma, survivors portrayed signs of both stress and resilience (Kahana, Harel, & Kahana, 2005). Survivors exhibited somewhat more sleep disturbances and somewhat lower morale than did their less traumatized counterparts (i.e., the other immigrants). However, they also showed a high level of social functioning, community involvement, marital stability, and they raised highly achieving children. These findings fit well with the focus of the psychological literature on resilience in late life (Glantz & Johnson, 1999). In a recent set of studies completed in 2008, the authors of this entry have considered the mental health of elderly survivors of three prevalent cancers (prostate, breast, and colorectal). This research revealed that whereas worries about one's future persist, many survivors consider cancer to be a life-changing experience. Rates of depression are not highly elevated in this group, and there is also evidence of posttraumatic growth and transformation associated with the experience of cancer survivorship.

The authors' research has also focused on considering the impact of increasing frailty, and of stressful life events, among community-dwelling older adults who participated in our long-term panel study. Respondents in the study exhibited good mental health, and high levels of social engagement and health promotion (Kahana, Lawrence, Kahana, Kercher, Wisniewski, Stoller et al., 2002). Proactive adaptations include exercise, planning ahead, and helping others. These adaptations were found to enhance psychological well-being, notwithstanding the normative stressors of aging. The findings of this research, comparing urban White with urban African-American elderly, did not reveal significant differences in the mental health of these groups (Kahana et al., 1999).

## TREATING MENTAL ILLNESS AND PSYCHOLOGICAL DISORDERS IN LATE LIFE

In considering approaches to treating diverse mental health problems in late life, psychotherapy and pharmacotherapy are two major approaches documented in the scientific literature. Environmental interventions will also be noted in the concluding section of this entry, as the broader societal approaches to caring for the mentally ill are discussed.

**Psychotherapy** Older persons can benefit from diverse forms of psychotherapy, as is the case with younger persons. Therapies typically employed with older persons include CBT, interpersonal therapies, and group therapy. A careful review of advances in psychotherapy with older adults has been provided by Patricia Arean (2003). These therapies are also utilized with younger people. In addition, *reminiscence and life review* therapy has been utilized with older adults (Butler et al., 1998). The basic therapeutic process is similar for both younger and older people, assuming there are no major cognitive impairments among the older patients. However, the life issues discussed will be different for the old versus the young, with older people more apt to discuss illness, physical disability, death and dying, and bereavement. Nevertheless, even here, similarities are shared with the old and the young, such as interpersonal relationships, family issues, assertiveness issues, and competent coping techniques.

A potential problem facing psychotherapists is their lack of experience in dealing with elderly patients. Younger therapists may not be attuned to later-in-life issues that confront older people. Many clinical training programs do not focus sufficiently on the elderly; as a result, seeing an older patient in therapy is often a new experience for many young therapists. Offering mental health professionals courses in gerontology, clinical geropsychology, and internship experiences working with the elderly can help remedy this situation. A number of graduate programs are now providing such training.

Early views regarding psychotherapy with the elderly were pessimistic. Sigmund Freud (1856–1939) felt that individuals over the age of 50 were unsuitable for his form of therapy (i.e., psychoanalysis). However, as the field moved forward from psychodynamic orientations to newer forms of behavioral therapies, there has been an upsurge of interest in the applications of these newer therapies to the elderly. In the clinical psychology literature, success has been reported in applying behavioral therapies to older persons suffering from depressive disorders (Gallagher & Thompson, 1982). The effectiveness of behavioral techniques in treating agitation has also been documented (Newton & Lazarus, 1992). In dealing with adjustment disorders, brief psychotherapy has been successfully implemented (Horowitz & Kaltreider, 1980).

**Pharmacotherapy** When recurrent symptoms of psychological distress cannot be alleviated by psychotherapy, older patients can benefit from the use of psychotropic drugs. Such drugs are commonly prescribed for older persons suffering from agitation, depression, mania, other psychotic disorders, dementia, anxiety, and sleep disorders. In general the same class of drugs is prescribed for older patients as for younger ones, depending on the psychiatric disorder (e.g., benzodiazepines, such as Valium, for both younger and older patients suffering from anxiety). However, most of the research on the effects of drugs has been conducted on younger adults who do not suffer from various medical conditions associated with aging and who are, therefore, not on medications for these conditions. Consequently, there is insufficient information on side effects or on dosage regulation for older adults. Many clinical trials testing new drugs exclude elderly individuals. Because comorbid illnesses are prevalent among older adults, a careful review of the patient's medical history and medications is necessary before prescribing psychotropic drugs, thereby preventing possible drug interaction effects.

Clinicians should also note that older persons have greater sensitivities to psychotropic drugs and should generally be given lower dosages than for younger patients, to avoid possible toxicities. More specifically, the medications need to be more accurately calibrated in older adults to insure optimal effectiveness. Concerns have been expressed about compliance in the use of medication among older adults (Avorn, 1988). Efforts to correct this problem include the use of pill boxes that alert the patient regarding which pills have to be taken and when. Having noted caution applying to medication use by older adults, it is important to also acknowledge documented benefits of mixed therapies that use both psychotherapy and drug therapy in treating mental health problems among the aged (Pampallona et al., 2004).

Having provided a general review of psychotherapy and pharmacotherapy with older adults, this entry now turns to discussing the treatment of prevalent mental health problems in late life, recognizing that treatment often involves a combination of psychotherapeutic and pharmacological modalities. Treatment of depression, GADs, and dementia are discussed below.

**Depression** Treatment of depression involves both psychotherapeutic interventions and pharmacotherapy. Regarding mild and moderate depression, psychotherapy appears to be the treatment of choice. Research supports the effectiveness of cognitive behavioral therapy (CBT), group therapy, and other brief therapeutic efforts (Laidlaw, Thompson, & Gallagher-Thompson, 2004). Additionally, social interventions aimed at reducing stress and enhancing social supports for elders facing serious illness, caregiving responsibilities for an ill spouse, or bereavement, can reduce the risk for developing depression. Religious and spiritual support have also been found to reduce depressive symptoms in the face of stressors (Boswell, Kahana, & Dilworth-Anderson, 2006). In more severe cases of depression, the use of drug therapy has become standard (Salzman, 1998). When depression is accompanied by suicidal thoughts, electroconvulsive therapy (ECT) is utilized, to bring about a quick remission. ECT is safe and has been effectively used with elderly patients suffering from depression. Reversible side effects of this treatment include temporary memory loss. Transcranial magnetic stimulation (TMS) has also been added as a promising intervention for depression in late life (Holmes, 2006).

Preventive efforts to reduce the incidence of future depressive episodes have focused on monitoring patients with prior histories of depression, and engaging them in various stress reduction efforts. Early recognition of adverse reactions to serious medical illness episodes can be useful in forestalling more severe consequences of illness. Primary care physicians can play an important role in the recognition and early treatment of depressive symptoms among older adults, because they are the first professionals to treat older adults. It has been suggested that offering mental health services in primary care settings can enhance access of elderly members and minorities to mental health care (Ayalon, Areán, Linkins, Lynch, & Estes, 2007).

**Generalized Anxiety Disorders** Both similar and different issues for those dealing with depression arise in the treatment and management of GADs. Treatment of these conditions typically involves collaborative care by physicians and psychologists, including pharmaceutical and psychotherapeutic interventions. Among psychotherapeutic interventions, CBT is most frequently used. It is recommended that modifications for use with older adults also be implemented. These modifications may account for age-associated memory changes (Babcock, Laguna, Laguna, & Urusky, 2000). Based on concerns about side effects of medications, psychopharmacological interventions have not been recommended as the initial therapy of choice. With regard to treatment of phobias, CBT has been found to be effective. Desensitization therapy is particularly effective, and involves gradual exposure to the feared object (Barlow & Brown, 1996).

**Dementia** Regarding treatment of the dementias, there is a lack of consensus about techniques that can be successfully utilized. One technique that has been used since the 1960s is *reality orientation therapy*, which helps the patient become better attuned to what is happening in their environment, to learn about the daily news, and to improve cognitive skills that have declined. An alternative approach, which became popular in the 1970s, is *validation fantasy therapy*, which gives comfort to older dementia patients by empathizing with them and validating their feelings. Currently, more precise memory and cognitive retraining programs are being conducted with both dementia patients (Malone & Camp, 2007) and with community-dwelling older adults, who would like to improve their memory and cognition (Small, LaRue, Komo, & Kaplan, 1997). Self-help books on this topic are currently popular in bookstores. There have also been extensive efforts to treat symptoms of dementia with environmental interventions (Regnier & Pynoos, 1992). Group psychotherapy has also been used successfully for some time with older patients who have mild dementia.

## CARING FOR MENTALLY ILL OLDER ADULTS

Even as resilience and mental health are recognized in late life, one cannot lose sight of the severe problems faced by those who do suffer from mental illness. With the rapid growth of the elderly population in the United States and worldwide, the sheer number of older adults needing mental health services will grow.

Since the 1960s to 1970s, there has been a major movement to deinstitutionalize severely mentally ill individuals (Brown, 1985). Consequently, most older individuals suffering from a mental illness are now living in the community. Unfortunately, the promise of the community mental health movement has not been fulfilled. Only about half of those old persons with severe psychiatric disorders are receiving any mental health services (George, 1992). Some older adults with mental illness, and those suffering from dementia or Alzheimer's disease, are generally being cared for in nursing homes. The quality of care in nursing homes has been widely criticized, and few facilities enable residents to utilize expert mental health services (Smyer, Shea, & Streit, 1994).

The Nursing Home Reform Act of 1987 reflects an effort by Congress to improve the quality of care in nursing homes through regulatory reform. Part of the implementation of this plan relates to screening older patients prior to admission, with the goal of offering admission primarily to patients with dementia, and screening out those who do not have dementia, but who suffer from other forms of mental illness. An important goal of the Nursing Home Reform Act also relates to reducing or eliminating inappropriate treatments, including chemical and physical restraints in nursing homes. This concern has been warranted, as studies demonstrate that some individuals living in nursing homes have received antipsychotic medication even though they did not have a diagnosis of mental illness (Spore, Smyer, & Cohen, 1991). By contrast, substantial portions of other patients who did have a diagnosis of mental illness did not receive medications.

The undertreatment of mental disorders in late life partly reflects the fragmentation of services, along with some reluctance by mentally ill older adults and their caregivers to utilize available services. This underutilization of mental health services may be due to perceived stigma associated with mental illness, particularly among today's older cohorts.

For older adults who are suffering from late-onset mental health problems and are not long-term psychiatrically ill persons, primary care physicians serve most often as mental health service providers. This raises problems about adequate differential diagnosis and referral for psychotherapy. Questions have also been raised about the level of expertise of primary care physicians in prescribing psychotropic medications. Currently, few studies document the mental health service use trajectories of older adults suffering from different forms of mental illness.

In developing an agenda for improved mental health services for older adults, there are several promising avenues toward progress. However, implementation of both proven and innovative services has been slow. Community-based mental health outreach services that identify isolated older adults with mental illness have shown promise but are not widely used. Environmental interventions for cognitively impaired older adults are more extensively used, but still reach only a relatively small segment of elders who can benefit from it.

Part of the challenge toward improving mental health care in later life relates to enhanced training of mental health professionals. Well-trained professionals from different disciplines are needed to serve a growing population of diverse older adults with a wide variety of mental health problems. Research advances can also lead to improvements in the lives of older mentally ill persons. Such research can offer evidence-based guidelines for the best practices in the treatment for those with mental illness.

SEE ALSO Volume 2: *Trauma;* Volume 3: *Caregiving; Chronic Illness, Adulthood and Later Life; Cognitive Functioning and Decline; Dementias; Loneliness, Later Life; Quality of Life; Stress in Later Life; Suicide, Later Life; Widowhood.*

## BIBLIOGRAPHY

Alexopoulos, G. S., Meyers, B. S., Young, R. C., Campbell, S., Silbersweig, D., & Charlson, M. (1997). "Vascular depression" hypothesis. *Archives of General Psychiatry, 54*(10), 915–922.

American Psychiatric Association. (2000). *Diagnostic and statistical manual of mental disorders: DSM-IV-TR.* (4th ed.). Washington, DC: Author.

Areán, P. A. (2003). Advances in psychotherapy for mental illness in late life. *American Journal of Geriatric Psychiatry, 11*(1), 4–6.

Armenian, H. K., Morikawa, M., Melkonian, A. K., Hovanesian, A. P., Haroutunian, N., Saigh, P. et al. (2000). Loss as a determinant of PTSD in a cohort of adult survivors of the 1988 earthquake in Armenia: Implications for policy. *Acta Psychiatrica Scandinavica, 102*(1), 58–64.

Avorn, J. (1988). Medications and the elderly. In J. Rowe & R. Besdine (Eds.), *Geriatric medicine.* (2nd ed.). Boston: Little, Brown.

Ayalon, L., Arean, P. A., Linkins, K., Lynch, M., & Estes, C. L. (2007). Integration of mental health services into primary care overcomes ethnic disparities in access to mental health services between black and white elderly. *American Journal of Geriatric Psychiatry, 15*(10), 906–912.

Babcock, R. L., Laguna, L. B., Laguna, K. D., & Urusky, D. A. (2000). Age differences in the experience of worry. *Journal of Mental Health and Aging, 6,* 227–235.

Barlow, D. H., & Brown, T. A. (1996). Psychological treatments for panic disorder and panic disorder with agoraphobia. In M. Mavissakalian & R. F. Prien (Eds.), *Long-term treatments for anxiety disorders* (pp. 221–240). Washington, DC: American Psychiatric Press.

Beekman, A. T. F., Deeg, D. J. H., van Tilburg, T., Smit, J. H., Hooijer, C., & van Tilburg, W. (1995). Major and minor depression in later life: A study of prevalence and risk factors. *Journal of Affective Disorders, 36*(1-2), 65–75.

Berg, S., Mellström, D., Persson, G., & Svanborg, A. (1981). Loneliness in the Swedish aged. *Journal of Gerontology, 36*(3), 342–349.

Bergeman, C. S., & Wallace, K. A. (1999). Resiliency in later life. In T. L. Whitman, T.V. Merluzzi, & R. D. White (Eds.), *Life span perspectives on health and illness* (pp. 207–226). Mahwah, NJ: Erlbaum.

Blazer, D., George, L. K., & Hughes, D. (1991). The epidemiology of anxiety disorders: An age comparison. In C. Salzman & B.D. Lebowitz (Eds.), *Anxiety in the elderly: Treatment and research* (pp. 17–30). New York: Springer.

Bodnar, J. C., & Kiecolt-Glaser, J. K. (1994). Caregiver depression after bereavement: Chronic stress isn't over when it's over. *Psychology and Aging, 9*(3), 372–380.

Boswell, G., Kahana, E., & Dilworth-Anderson, P. (2006). Spirituality and healthy lifestyle behaviors: Stress counterbalancing effects on the well-being of older adults. *Journal of Religion and Health, 45*(4), 587–602.

Brown, P. (1985). *The transfer of care: Psychiatric deinstitutionalization and its aftermath.* Boston: Routledge & Kegan Paul.

Butler, R. N., Lewis, M. I., & Sunderland, T. (1998). *Aging and mental health: Positive psychosocial and biomedical approaches.* (5th ed.). Boston: Allyn & Bacon.

De Beurs, E., Beekman, A. T. F., van Balkom, A. J. L., Deeg, D. J. H., van Dyck, R., & van Tilburg, W. (1999). Consequences of anxiety in older persons: Its effect on disability, well-being, and use of health services. *Psychological Medicine, 29*(3), 583–593.

Deimling, G. T., Kahana, B., Bowman, K. F., & Schaefer, M. L. (2002). Cancer survivorship and psychological distress in later life. *Psycho-Oncology, 11*(6), 479–494.

Dikel, T. N., Engdahl, B., & Eberly, R. (2005). PTSD in former prisoners of war: Prewar, wartime, and postwar factors. *Journal of Traumatic Stress, 18*(1), 69–77.

Dohrenwend, B. P. (1998). *Adversity, stress, and psychopathology.* New York: Oxford University Press.

Fiske, A., & Jones, R. S. (2005). Depression. In M. L. Johnson (Ed.), *The Cambridge handbook of age and ageing* (pp. 245–251). New York: Cambridge University Press.

Gallagher, D. E., & Thompson, L. W. (1982). Treatment of major depressive disorder in older adult patients with brief psychotherapies. *Psychotherapy Theory, Research, and Practice, 19*(4), 482–490.

Gatz, M. (2000). Variations on depression in later life. In S. H. Qualls & N. Abeles (Eds.), *Psychology and the aging revolution: How we adapt to longer life* (pp. 239–258). Washington, DC: American Psychological Association.

George, L. K. (1992). Community and home care for mentally ill older adults. In J. E. Birren, R. B. Sloane, & G. D. Cohen (Eds.), *Handbook of mental health and aging* (2nd ed., pp. 794–815). San Diego, CA: Academic Press.

Glantz, M. D., & Johnson, J. L. (Eds.). (1999). *Resilience and development: Positive life adaptations.* New York: Kluwer Academic/Plenum.

Goenjian, A. K., Najarian, L. M., Pynoos, R. S., Steinberg, A. M., Manoukian, G., Tavosian, A. et al. (1994). Post-traumatic stress disorder in elderly and younger adults after the 1988 earthquake in Armenia. *American Journal of Psychiatry, 151*(6), 895–901.

Gray, M. J., & Acierno, R. (2002). Symptoms presentations of older adult crime victims: Description of a clinical sample. *Journal of Anxiety Disorders, 16*(3), 299–309.

Hollander, E., & Simeon, D. (2004). Anxiety disorders. In R. E. Hales & S. C. Yudofsky (Eds.), *Essentials of clinical psychiatry* (2nd ed., pp. 339–422). Washington, DC: American Psychiatric Publishing.

Holmes, D. (2006). *Abnormal psychology.* Mason, OH: Thomson.

Horowitz, M. J., & Kaltreider, N. B. (1980). Brief psychotherapy of stress response syndromes. In T. Karasu & L. Bellak (Eds.), *Specialized techniques in individual psychotherapy* (pp. 162–183). New York: Brunner/Mazel.

Jorm, A. F. (2000). Is depression a risk factor for dementia or cognitive decline? A review. *Gerontology, 46*(4), 219–227.

Jylhä, M. (2004). Old age and loneliness: Cross-sectional and longitudinal analyses in Tampere Longitudinal Study on Aging. *Canadian Journal on Aging, 23*(2), 157–168.

Kahana, B., Harel, Z., & Kahana, E. (2005). *Survivors of the Holocaust: Aging and adaptation.* New York: Kluwer/Springer.

Kahana, E., Kahana, B., Kercher, K., King, C., Lovegreen, L., & Chirayath, H. (1999). Evaluating a model of successful aging for urban African-American and white elderly. In M. Wykle & A. B. Ford (Eds.), *Serving minority elders in the 21st century* (pp. 287–322). New York: Springer.

Kahana, E., Lawrence, R., Kahana, B., Kercher, K., Wisniewski, A., Stoller, E. et al. (2002). Long-term impact of preventive proactivity on quality of life of the old-old. *Psychosomatic Medicine, 64*(3), 382–394.

Kessler, R. C., McGonagle, K. A., Nelson, C. B., Hughes, M., & Eshleman, S. (1994). Lifetime and 12-month prevalence of DSM-III-R psychiatric disorders in the United States: Results from the National Comorbidity Survey. *Archives of General Psychiatry, 51*(1), 8–19.

Kuch, K., & Cox, B. J. (1992). Symptoms of PTSD in 124 survivors of the Holocaust. *American Journal of Psychiatry, 149*(3), 337–340.

Laidlaw, K., Thompson, L.W., & Gallagher-Thompson, D. (2004). Comprehensive conceptualization of cognitive behavior therapy for late-life depression. *Behavioral and Cognitive Psychotherapy, 32*(4), 389–399.

Lantz, M. (2006). Adjustment disorders in late life. In M. E. Agronin & G. J. Maletta (Eds.), *Principles and practice of geriatric psychiatry* (pp. 421–428). Philadelphia: Lippincott, Williams, & Wilkins.

Lauderdale, S. A., Kelly, K., & Sheikh, J. I. (2006). Anxiety disorders in the elderly. In M. E. Agronin & G. J. Maletta (Eds.), *Principles and practice of geriatric psychiatry* (pp. 429–448). Philadelphia: Lippincott, Williams, & Wilkins.

Lewinsohn, P. M., Hops, H., Roberts, R. E., Seeley, J. R., & Andrews, J. A. (1993). Adolescent psychopathology: I. Prevalence and incidence of depression and other DSM-III-R disorders in high school students. *Journal of Abnormal Psychology, 102*(1), 133–144.

Liu, A., Tan, H., Zhou, J., Li, S., Yang, T., Wang, J. et al. (2006). An epidemiological study of post-traumatic stress disorder in flood victims in Hunan China. *Canadian Journal of Psychiatry, 51*(6), 350–354.

Lopata, H. Z. (1996). *Current widowhood: Myths and realities.* Thousand Oaks, CA: Sage.

Malone, M. L., & Camp, C. (2007). Montessori-based dementia programming: Providing tools for engagement. *Dementia, 6*(1), 150–157.

Manela, M., Katona, C., & Livingston, G. (1996). How common are the anxiety disorders in old age? *International Journal of Geriatric Psychiatry, 11*, 65–70.

McIntosh, J. L., Santos, J. F., Hubbard, R. W., & Overholser, J. C. (1994). *Elder suicide: Research, theory, and treatment.* Washington, DC: American Psychological Association.

Newton, N. A., & Lazarus, L. W. (1992). Behavioral and psychotherapeutic interventions. In J. E. Birren, R. B. Sloane, & G. D. Cohen (Eds.), *Handbook of mental health and aging* (2nd ed., pp. 699–721). San Diego, CA: Academic Press.

Pampallona, S., Bollini, P., Tibaldi, G., Kupelnick, B., & Munizza, C. (2004). Combined pharmacotherapy and psychological treatment for depression: A systematic review. *Archives of General Psychiatry, 61*(7), 714–719.

Radloff, L. S. (1977). The CES-D scale: A self-report depression scale for research in the general population. *Applied Psychological Measurement, 1*(3), 385–401.

Regnier, V., & Pynoos, J. (1992). Environmental interventions for cognitively impaired older persons. In J. E. Birren, R. B. Sloane, & G. D. Cohen (Eds.), *Handbook of mental health and aging* (2nd ed., pp. 764–789). San Diego, CA: Academic Press.

Salzman, C. (1998). Treating depression in the elderly. In N. Brunello, S. L. Langer, & G. Racagni (Eds.), *Mental disorders in the elderly: New therapeutic approaches* (Vol. 13, pp. 25–30). New York: Karger.

Small, G. W., LaRue, A., Komo, S., & Kaplan, A. (1997). Mnemonics usage and cognitive decline in age-associated memory impairment. *International Psychogeriatrics, 9*(1), 47–56.

Smyer, M. A., & Qualls, S. H. (1999). *Aging and mental health.* Malden, MA: Blackwell.

Smyer, M. A., Shea, D. G., & Streit, A. (1994). The provision and use of mental health services in nursing homes: Results from the National Medical Expenditure Survey. *American Journal of Public Health, 84*(2), 284–287.

Spore, D. L., Smyer, M.A., & Cohen, M.D. (1991). Assessing nursing assistants' knowledge of behavioral approaches to mental health problems. *The Gerontologist, 31*(3), 309–317.

Thoits, P.A. (1991). On merging identity theory and stress research. *Social Psychology Quarterly, 54*(2), 101–112.

Wilcox, S., Aragaki, A., Mouton, C. P., Evenson, K. R., Wassertheil-Smoller, S., & Loevinger, B.L. (2003). The effects of widowhood on physical and mental health, health behaviors, and health outcomes: The women's health initiative. *Health Psychology, 22*(5), 513–522.

Wilson, J., Harel, Z., & Kahana, B. (1988). *Human adaptation to extreme stress: From the Holocaust to Vietnam.* New York: Plenum Press.

Yehuda, R., Southwick, S., Giller, E. L., Ma, X., & Mason, J. W. (1992). Urinary catecholamine excretion and severity of

PTSD symptoms in Vietnam combat veterans. *Journal of Nervous and Mental Disease, 180*(5), 321–325.

Young, H. M., McCormick, W., & Vitaliano, P. (2002). Evolving values in community-based long-term care services for Japanese Americans. *Advances in Nursing Science, 25*(2), 40–56.

Youngjohn, J. R., & Crook, T. H. (1996). Dementia. In L. L. Carstensen, B. A. Edelstein, & L. Dornbrand (Eds.), *The practical handbook of clinical gerontology* (pp. 239–254). Thousand Oaks, CA: Sage.

Zarit, S. H., & Zarit, J. M. (2007). *Mental disorders in older adults: Fundamentals of assessment and treatment.* (2nd ed.). New York: Guilford Press.

***Boaz Kahana***
***Eva Kahana***

## MOEN, PHYLLIS
### *1942–*

Phyllis Moen is an internationally recognized life-course scholar of work, family, aging, and gender. Born in Hazelhurst, Georgia, her path to the academy was unconventional and informed her later interests in the role of timing and the interplay between work and family as key factors shaping the life course. Married at age 18 and the mother of two young children by age 20, she completed correspondence and night courses to earn her bachelor's degree while living on a small farm in Crookston, Minnesota. She was widowed unexpectedly at age 35 and had to raise her children as a single parent. She completed her Ph.D. in 1978 at the University of Minnesota (with mentors Reuben Hill, Bob Leik, and Jeylan Mortimer). She spent the next 25 years as a faculty member in two departments (Human Development and Sociology) at Cornell University, where she was honored in 1992 with an endowed chair as the Ferris Family Professor of Life Course Studies. Cornell colleagues and esteemed scholars of the life course and human development, such as Glen Elder, Jr., Urie Bronfenbrenner, and Robin M. Williams, Jr., substantially influenced her life-course scholarship. Moen left Cornell in 2003 to join the sociology department of the University of Minnesota, where she currently holds a McKnight Presidential Chair.

Dr. Moen's research agenda considers the links between existing and often outdated institutions (especially work, family, gender, and retirement), social transformations (economic, demographic, social and technological, as well as policy shifts), and the life biographies, health, and well-being of individuals and families. Her life-course framework promotes understanding of the organizational arrangements and pathways perpetuating gender and age disparities in life quality, particularly health, well-being, and satisfaction. Investigating patterns of continuity and change in roles and relationships has been one of the linchpins of Moen's research. Indeed, she has spearheaded several important longitudinal studies, including the Women's Roles and Well-Being Study, the Cornell Retirement and Well-Being Study, and the Ecology of Careers Panel Study.

Moen's scholarship demonstrates how gender and age, as master statuses, are embedded in social structures and conventional thinking, shaping the life choices and life chances of men and women as they enter, persist in, exit, and sometimes reenter and re-exit roles and relationships over time. Her book, *The Career Mystique: Cracks in the American Dream* (2005; with Patricia Roehling), summarizes and builds on this work and was named the "Best Professional and Scholarly Publication in Sociology in 2005" by the Association of American Publishers.

One of Moen's most significant scholarly contributions is her illumination of the importance of *linked lives*, or the ways the life domains such as work and family are intertwined. Her many studies of the various linkages between husbands and wives, where the couple rather than the individual serves as the unit of analysis, have contributed to our understanding of the work, family, and retirement experiences of dual-earner couples. *It's about Time: Couples and Careers* (2003) chronicles the adaptive strategies of couples trying to manage two jobs and their family life in a world based on the (one job per family) career mystique.

Phyllis Moen has published more than 70 articles in many prominent scholarly journals: *The American Sociological Review, American Journal of Sociology, The Gerontologist, Social Problems, Journal of Marriage and the Family, Social Forces, Sociological Quarterly,* and *Journal of Health and Social Behavior.* She is the author, coauthor, or editor of eight books, including *Examining Lives in Context: Perspectives on the Ecology of Human Development* (1995), *A Nation Divided* (1999), and *Social Integration in the Second Half of Life* (2001). Her research has been funded by government agencies, including the National Institute for Child Health and Human Development, National Institute on Aging, and National Science Foundation, and private foundations (Alfred P. Sloan Foundation, Atlantic Philanthropic).

Moen's influence on life-course sociology is also evidenced through her professional leadership. She served a term as director of the sociology program at the National Science Foundation in the late 1980s, was elected president of the Eastern Sociological Association (2003–2004), and has chaired both the Family (1994–1995) and Aging and Life Course Sections (2006) of the American Sociological Association. She has played a pivotal role in establishing a number of important research institutions, including the Bronfenbrenner Life Course Center at Cornell University

(1992). Within that center she helped establish (with Karl Pillemer) the Cornell Gerontology Research Institute. With support from the Alfred P. Sloan Foundation, Moen created the interdisciplinary Cornell Careers Institute. Dr. Moen co-founded (with Erin L. Kelly) the Flexible Work and Well-Being Center at the University of Minnesota in 2005 to study ways to offer employees greater control over the time and timing of their work.

SEE ALSO Volume 2: *Careers.*

BIBLIOGRAPHY

Moen, P. (Ed). (2003). *It's about time: Couples and careers.* Ithaca, NY: Cornell University Press.

Moen, P., Dempster-McClain, D., & Walker, H. A. (1999). *A nation divided: Diversity, inequality, and community in American society.* Ithaca, NY: Cornell University Press.

Moen, P., Elder,.G. H. Jr., Lüscher, K. (Eds.). (1995). *Examining lives in context: Perspectives on the ecology of human development.* Washington, DC: American Psychological Association.

Pillemer K., Moen, P., Wethington, E., & Glasgow, N. (Eds.). (2000). *Social integration in the second half of life.* Baltimore, MD: Johns Hopkins University Press.

*Noelle Chesley*

## MORBIDITY

SEE Volume 3: *Arthritis; Cancer, Adulthood and Later Life; Cardiovascular Disease; Chronic Illness, Adulthood and Later Life; Diabetes, Adulthood and Later Life; Disability and Functional Limitation, Later Life; Life Expectancy; Mortality; Self-Rated Health.*

## MORTALITY

The study of mortality reveals patterns about the number of deaths in a population. Mortality, along with fertility, is one of the major stages in the life course that all individuals experience; all are born and will die. Opposed to a more sociological study of death and dying that generally focuses on societal values, norms, and attitudes regarding death, mortality research is typically studied from a population or demographic perspective. As such, it is primarily concerned with key demographic questions: How is mortality measured? How does mortality change over time? Who is dying and why are they dying? What are people dying from?

Decreases in mortality in the 20th century have been one of the most notable world achievements. Advances in social conditions, nutrition, public health, and medicine have led to fewer deaths in infancy and early childhood and have led to mortality occurring at increasingly older ages. On average, individuals living in the early 21st century can expect to live approximately 30 years longer than comparable individuals living a century ago. While decreases in mortality is a positive trend, it brings with it new challenges and concerns. Reductions in mortality across the world are partially responsible for increases in aging populations and substantial growth in the overall world population.

The study of mortality is important because it provides insights into both historical and current population dynamics. It allows researchers to better understand the economic, social, and political conditions that influence population growth in a society. An understanding of mortality allows us to assess population health and to understand the changes in living conditions throughout time and between different societies. Importantly, a focus on mortality provides information on social and environmental problems associated with population growth.

### MEASUREMENT

The accurate and reliable measurement of death is paramount to the study of mortality. Mortality is often measured through mortality rates, which are simply expressed as the number of deaths per 1,000 persons in a given year for a given population. Mortality rates also can be used to examine deaths by specific causes or for specific age, gender, or race/ethnic groups to provide a more complete understanding of the structure of a population. For instance, a researcher may want to know how many deaths occurred in the United States among 65- to 75-year-olds in order to understand both population growth and aging trends. Often, mortality rates are used to construct life-expectancy tables, which provide among other information, the expected probable age of death for each specific age category. For example, the use of a life-expectancy table can inform researchers that in 2005, a 65-year-old male in the United States was expected to live an average of 17.2 more years (NCHS, 2007).

The measurement of mortality is not always simple, because deaths can be caused by diseases, degenerative processes, the physical environment, the social environment, or a combination of factors. The death certificate is a particularly useful, official legal document that records causes of death. Death certificates also include information such as age, sex, race/ethnicity, and additional demographic characteristics. They are an invaluable resource for researchers seeking to understand health trends and aiming to develop health intervention strategies.

The causes of death that are listed on death certificates have been standardized through the World Health Organization (WHO) into the International Classification of Diseases (ICD), a periodically updated system that is used to ensure consistency across countries in the collection of (health) and mortality data. But there are often inaccuracies in death certificates and there are temporal changes in the classification of causes of death. Errors may also result from misdiagnoses, inadvertent omission of diseases, difficulties when several diseases are involved, or biases in reporting the underlying causes due to the physician's knowledge and experience in determining causes of death. For example, Alzheimer's Disease has only recently been identified as a major cause of death that is becoming more regularly reported on death certificates and remains subject to underreporting contingent on the severity of the disease and co-occurrence with other diseases.

In addition to causes of death, researchers are also interested in the "actual" causes of death. Whereas causes of death are limited to pathological conditions such as specific diseases, homicides, or accidents, "actual" causes of death are based on potentially modifiable factors that lead to the death (McGinnis & Foege, 1993). For instance, while a cause of death may be lung cancer, the actual cause of death may be due to excessive tobacco smoking. Actual causes of death are also prone to mismeasurement. It is difficult to ascertain actual causes of death with certainty because most diseases and injuries are linked to numerous causes and conditions.

## HOW DOES MORTALITY CHANGE OVER HISTORICAL TIME?

Mortality is often studied through a historical perspective to understand how death causes and correlates have changed over time. The epidemiologic transition is a framework that is used to understand the relationships between mortality rates and major causes of death throughout history. The general hypothesis suggests that as nations modernize, they tend to follow similar trajectories characterized by improvements in social, economic, and health conditions. Following these changes, mortality rates decline and life expectancy increases. Better social conditions with advances in sanitation and public health reduce infectious diseases and disproportionally benefit infants, children, and women of childbearing ages. Advances in infant, childhood, and maternal mortality mean that people live to older ages. In general, the epidemiologic transition suggests that as societies modernize, infectious diseases such as influenza, pneumonia, and smallpox are replaced with degenerative, stress-related, and manmade diseases such as heart disease and cancers that affect older aged populations.

## WHO IS DYING AND WHY?

Death rates vary by social demographic characteristics such as age, gender, race/ethnicity, social institutions, and socioeconomic status. A focus on sociodemographic categories highlights the relevance of social conditions and structural positions on mortality, identifies the impact of social processes, and informs public policy decisions about how societal changes can influence health and mortality trends in the future.

**Age** Mortality rates differ by age and generally show a J-shaped curve of deaths with age. First, there are higher rates of mortality for infants because of the increased vulnerability found during childbirth and in the first year of life. Death during the first year of life is an important variable of consideration and is often measured as the infant mortality rate, or deaths among infants under age one per 1,000 live births. As of 2007 the United States had an infant mortality rate of 6.5 per 1,000 live births, compared to high rates in middle Africa with a rate of 141 in Angola and low rates including 2.6 in Singapore and 2.8 in Japan (Population Reference Bureau, 2007). This is followed by a sharp decrease in mortality risk with very few deaths occurring during childhood and early adolescence, with the lowest levels of mortality occurring around age 10. Next, there is an increase in death between the ages of 15 and 24 because of the increased number of deaths associated with accidents, homicide, and suicide among this age group, particularly among males. Finally, this is followed by increasing rates of mortality into older age categories, with large increases occurring after age 85. Whereas in the past people were likely to die at any age, current age trends reduce the highest risks of mortality to a narrow age range concentrated at older ages; these trends will have large impacts on overall population structures and lead to larger elderly populations.

**Gender** Gender differences in mortality vary by country, but in general, women tend to live longer than men. This is particularly true in developed countries where advances in maternal mortality have virtually eliminated medically preventable deaths during childbirth. Indeed, in 2000, developed countries had a maternal mortality rate of 20 deaths per 100,000 live births, compared to a rate of 400 for developing countries (WHO, 2004). In the United States females have experienced substantial longevity advantages over the past century. Between 1920 and 1950, females experienced increased advantages in mortality rates over men with increasing gains in most causes of death. The gap continued to increase between 1950 and 1970, primarily due to higher rates of diabetes-related mortality for males. 1970 to 1979 showed a steadily increasing (albeit slower) difference in the sex gap, with peak differences of 7.8 years occurring in 1975 and 1979 (Arias, 2007). This has been followed by a steady erosion of mortality advantages for women explained by social and behavioral changes, including lower infant mortality rates that benefit males because of their higher infant mortality rates, increases in female smoking, and the accumulation of social and environmental stress associated with more women in the workforce (Verbrugge, 1980).

The gender gap in mortality is often explained through both social/environmental and biological explanations. Biological approaches suggest that women are protected through reproductive physiology, hormones, and genetic advantages that reduce risks of major degenerative causes of death. For example, male sex hormones may predispose men toward aggressiveness that leads to more fatal accidents and violent deaths (Waldron, 1985). Social approaches emphasize that mortality differentials are associated with behavioral differences linked to gender socialization, self-protective behaviors, and/or differences in exposure or vulnerability to stressors (Nathanson, 1984). Socialization processes include the processes through which individuals develop an awareness of social norms and values. Socialized gender differences are linked to access to food and health care, social networks, occupational hazards, and participation in health-related behaviors. For instance, men are less likely to use preventative care than women. Men are also more likely to engage in harmful behaviors including alcohol abuse, drunk driving, violent behaviors, and cigarette smoking—the single most important cause of higher mortality for males.

**Race/Ethnicity** Socially and economically disadvantaged race/ethnic groups have higher mortality rates in most societies. For example, African Americans in the United States have higher risks of death for nearly every major cause of death, live approximately 7 years less than European Americans, and experience even wider mortality gaps with Asian Americans, who are socioeconomically advantaged. This relationship is often explained through the confluence of structural socioeconomic disadvantage and individual lifestyle behaviors. But race/ethnic differences are also linked to other negative factors, including racism, increased physiological stress responses to adverse conditions, compromised access to health care, dangerous or deprived physical environments, deleterious health behaviors, and small social support networks (Hummer, 1995).

Interestingly, the U.S. Latino foreign-born population has been shown to have more favorable mortality than U.S.-born residents. While Latino immigrants typically have similar socioeconomic standing to non-Hispanic Blacks, they do not suffer the accompanying health disadvantages and have mortality rates similar or better than non-Hispanic Whites. This is an "epidemiologic paradox" that continues to confound many researchers, but is likely to be due to a combination of data issues and nativity factors including health behaviors, support systems, health status upon migration, and illness-related return migration (Palloni & Arias, 2004).

**Social Institutions** Social institutions such as marriage and religion have a large impact on mortality. Generally, married individuals have lower mortality than those who are not married. Marriage is linked with numerous positive support factors including emotional and financial benefits. Married individuals benefit from higher incomes, higher social prestige, and stable employment (Rogers, 1995; Smith & Waitzman, 1994). Marriage is linked to care-giving relationships, social integration, and social networks. Also, marriage is linked with better eating habits, medical compliance, and overall healthier behaviors (Ross, Mirowsky, & Goldsteen, 1990). For instance, married individuals are less likely to smoke cigarettes, to abuse alcohol, and to use illicit drugs (Umberson, 1992). Unmarried men have high levels of mortality from social pathologies including accidents, suicide, homicide, and other risk-taking behaviors (Rogers, 1995).

Increased religious participation is associated with mortality advantages. Compared to those that attend religious services at least once a week, those that do not attend religious services have nearly twice the risk of death (Hummer, Rogers, Nam, & Ellison, 1999). Religious activity is associated with health behaviors and lifestyles, with religious individuals less likely to smoke cigarettes, drink alcohol, and to engage in risky behaviors. Religion is also linked to increased levels of social integration, psychological resources, coping resources, positive emotions, physiological effects, and potential financial support (Hummer et al., 1999; McCullough, Hoyt, Larson, Koenig, & Thoresen, 2000).

**Socioeconomic Status** Higher status individuals have lower mortality rates and live longer in nearly every society. Socioeconomic status is measured by a variety of indicators including income, education, and occupation. Each of these measures indicates that high levels of socioeconomic status lead to lower levels of mortality. Increases in education are linked with lower levels of mortality in a graded fashion, with each education category at a lower risk than each preceding education category (Adler, Boyce, Chesney, Cohen et al., 1994). Education provides individuals with information to determine avoidable risks and income provides a means to purchase better health. High levels of education are linked with higher levels of health knowledge that promote healthy behaviors. Also, educational attainment indicates access to knowledge and skills that are associated with successful employment, higher earnings, accurate knowledge about health, and a greater sense of control.

Compared to the unemployed (those without jobs but who are actively seeking employment), employed individuals are healthier. Although the rewards of employment are health-enhancing, there is a health selection effect with those in poor health (and ultimately, at an elevated risk of mortality) more likely to be unemployed or not actively seeking employment. Income is a link between education and mortality that can directly affect mortality through the purchase of health care, adequate housing, and a nutritious diet (Elo & Preston, 1996). Income may also be indirectly linked to mortality through healthy behaviors or the stressors associated with poverty or financial distress. In addition to income, the employed have access to social networks, health insurance, and workplace amenities (i.e., gyms or health promotion services) that promote both physical and mental health. Specific occupations also affect mortality, with higher levels of occupational status and prestige linked to lower levels of mortality. For example, the commercial fishing and construction industries are perennially ranked as some of the most dangerous jobs in the United States due to a high propensity of on-the-job accidents. In addition to workplace hazards, the link between occupational status and mortality is also likely to be due to the physical demands of a job, workplace stress that may affect other negative health behaviors, and exposure to hazardous materials or toxins.

Low socioeconomic status may also have higher levels of mortality because of structural access to resources that can have lasting effects throughout the life course. For instance, low education and parental income during childhood may place a child at risk due to poorer schools, unhealthy foods, and unsafe play areas that may subsequently influence negative health behaviors. Cumulative disadvantage theories suggest that early risk factors can influence both short-term and long-term health outcomes. Although it is possible to overcome initial hardships, it is more likely that an accumulation of disadvantages is likely to hinder an individual's chances of good health. Additionally, poor living conditions are often associated with less access to parks, health care facilities, or healthy foods, and with higher levels of social and psychological stressors and crime that are both indirectly and directly linked to mortality outcomes.

## WHAT ARE PEOPLE DYING FROM?

Death rates are often calculated as either occurring from a general category of all causes or they are broken down into deaths due to specific causes. A focus on cause-specific mortality allows researchers to better understand health at a population level. As indicated by the epidemiologic transition, modernization leads to a shift in the causes of death to more "manmade" types of disease. For example, the most frequent causes of death in the United States include: diseases of the heart, malignant neoplasms (cancer), cerebrovascular diseases (stroke), chronic lower respiratory diseases, accidents, and diabetes mellitus. Research on actual causes of disease has suggested that nearly half of all deaths could be attributed to modifiable and preventable behaviors (Mokdad, Marks, Stroup, & Gerberding, 2004).

The leading "actual" causes of death in the United States include, in ranked order from high to low: tobacco use, poor diet/physical inactivity, alcohol consumption, microbial and toxic agents, motor vehicles, firearms, sexual behavior, and illicit drug use (McGinnis & Foege, 1993; Mokdad et al., 2004). Tobacco is considered the foremost actual cause of death and it is linked to cancers, cardiovascular diseases, and chronic lung diseases, with approximately 18% of all deaths in the United States attributable to smoking in 2000 (Mokdad et al., 2004). Increasing frequency of cigarette smoking is associated with higher risks of mortality and current and former smokers are at higher risks than never smokers (Rogers, Hummer, & Nam, 2000). Diet and inactivity are associated with obesity, heart disease, cancer, and diabetes. Both low and high levels of body weight have higher risks of death, but for different causal reasons. Individuals who are underweight have higher levels of mortality primarily due to other diseases or malnutrition that cause them to be underweight. And individuals who are obese have higher levels of mortality than those who are considered normal or slightly overweight because of links to cardiovascular disease, cancer, and diabetes.

## FUTURE OF MORTALITY RESEARCH

One of the main goals of mortality research is to understand mortality differentials and to reduce health disparities. Researchers are dedicated to understanding the reasons for race/ethnic, gender, and socioeconomic differences in mortality. One way to address these disparities is to develop and use more reliable and accurate measurements of important variables. For instance, researchers will continue to examine the role of important factors such as knowledge, money, power prestige, and social networks as "fundamental causes of disease" that shape exposures to risk and mortality (Link & Phelan, 1995). Measurement of socioeconomic status will benefit from more specific operationalizations. For example, measures of wealth and income portfolios are often better measures than simple measures of occupational income, and specific occupational tasks and decision-making tasks will further explain the relevance of occupations. Further measurements that will also bolster current mortality research include detailed information on the physical and built environment and advanced measurements of social networks and social relationships. Current mortality research has also begun to include more biological markers, to understand the complex interplay between social and biological characteristics. Accordingly, future research will continue to include biological data that accurately measures stress hormones, genetic information, anthropometry, metabolism, cardiovascular markers, nutrition, chromosomes, neurotransmitters, and inflammatory markers.

Finally, the future of mortality research will benefit from an explicit life course perspective. This is essential to fully understand disease pathways and the causes of mortality outcomes. A life course perspective will provide insights into the importance of changes in socioeconomic status, health, social networks, physical environment, stressors, and environmental exposure on mortality. Researchers will be better able to understand the relationship between early life conditions and later life mortality. It is highly likely that economic and living conditions during childhood will have lasting impacts on later life decisions and opportunities. New advances in data collection will allow researchers to examine individuals throughout their lives to determine how health-related behaviors, social environment, and economic conditions influence patterns of mortality.

**SEE ALSO** Volume 3: *Age Structure; Death and Dying; Demographic Transition Theories; Epidemiologic Transition; Health Differentials/Disparities, Later life; Life Expectancy; Population Aging; Suicide, Later Life.*

**BIBLIOGRAPHY**

Adler, N. E., Boyce, W. T., Chesney, M. A., Cohen, S., Folman, S., Kahn, R. L. et al. (1994). Socioeconomic status and health: The challenge of the gradient. *American Psychologist, 49*(1), 15–24.

Arias, E. (2007). United States life tables, 2004. *National Vital Statistics Reports, 56*(9), 1–39.

Elo, I. T., & Preston, S. H. (1996). Educational differentials in mortality: United States, 1979–85. *Social Science & Medicine, 42*(1), 47–57.

Hummer, R. A. (1995). Black-white differences in health and mortality: A review and conceptual model. *The Sociological Quarterly, 37*(1), 105–125.

Hummer, R. A., Rogers, R. G., Nam, C. B., & Ellison, C. G. (1999). Religious involvement and U.S. adult mortality. *Demography, 36*(2), 273–285.

Link, B. G., & Phelan, J. (1995). Social conditions as fundamental causes of disease. *Journal of Health and Social Behavior, 35*(extra issue), 80–94.

McCullough, M. E., Hoyt, W. T., Larson, D. B., Koenig, H. G., & Thoresen, C. (2000). Religious involvement and mortality: A meta-analytic review. *Health Psychology, 19*(3), 211–222.

McGinnis, J. M., & Foege, W. H. (1993). Actual causes of death in the United States. *JAMA, 270*(18), 2207–2212.

Mokdad, A. H., Marks, J. S., Stroup, D. F., & Gerberding, J. L. (2004). Actual causes of death in the United States, 2000. *JAMA, 291*(10), 1238–1245.

Nathanson, C. A. (1984). Sex differences in mortality. *Annual Review of Sociology, 10*, 191–213.

National Center of Health Statistics (NCHS) (2007). *Health, United States, 2007. With chartbook and trends in the health of Americans.* Hyattsville, MD: U.S. Government Printing Office.

Palloni, A., & Arias, E. (2004). Paradox lost: Explaining the Hispanic adult mortality advantage. *Demography, 41*(3), 385–415.

Population Reference Bureau. (2007). *2007 World population data sheet.* Washington, DC: Population Reference Bureau.

Rogers, R. G. (1995). Marriage, sex, and mortality. *Journal of Marriage and the Family, 57*(2), 515–526.

Rogers, R. G., Hummer, R. A., & Nam, C. B. (2000). *Living and dying in the USA: Behavioral, health, and social differentials of adult mortality.* San Diego: Academic Press.

Ross, C. E., Mirowsky, J., & Goldsteen, K. (1990). The Impact of the Family on Health: The Decade in Review. *Journal of Marriage and the Family, 52*(4), 1059–1078.

Smith, K. R., & Waitzman, N. J. (1994). Double jeopardy: Interaction effects of marital and poverty status on the risk of mortality. *Demography, 31*(3), 487–507.

Umberson, D. (1992). Gender, marital status and the social control of health behavior. *Social Science & Medicine, 34*(8), 907–917.

Verbrugge, L. M. (1980). Recent trends in sex mortality differentials in the United States. *Women Health, 5*(3), 17–37.

Waldron, I. (1985). What do we know about causes of sex differences in mortality? A review of the literature. *Population Bulletin UN, 18*, 59–76.

*Jarron M. Saint Onge*

# NEIGHBORHOOD CONTEXT, LATER LIFE

Older adults are more vulnerable to changing social and economic conditions in their neighborhoods than younger people (Glass & Balfour, 2003). This vulnerability may translate into poorer health, increased disability, less frequent use of health care services, and poorer prognosis for recovery from a chronic disease. There are several reasons why this might be true. First, the cognitive and physical declines associated with normal aging and chronic disease mean that older people will be less able to cope with transportation issues, declining physical infrastructure, and the loss of commercial and social services that can accompany neighborhood change. As residential and economic change modifies an older person's surroundings, he or she may have a more difficult time finding services and overcoming new physical barriers. Physical challenges and cognitive decline may make even a familiar and stable neighborhood more difficult to negotiate.

Second, older adults may be more vulnerable to local conditions because the social space of older people is smaller and tends to be more geographically constrained. As people age, social ties and social networks contract as children leave home, work is left behind, and friends and family die or move away. Neighbors, local volunteer opportunities, and social groups often become the foundation of an older person's social network and social support system. Thus, the social resources of the residential community will have a much larger impact on an older person. Finally, older people who stay in their homes after retirement have been exposed to the local environment for much longer periods of time than younger residents. The cumulative impact of environmental assaults or other neighborhood conditions may appear only later in life after continuous exposure to the risks posed by local environments.

This entry examines the neighborhood and community conditions researchers believe may have an impact on the health of older people. It also examines the types of measures social scientists use to capture these community conditions and how neighborhood and community conditions may affect health. Many theories suggest that there are mechanisms that link where one lives to one's health. This entry focuses on those theories that have special relevance to the lives of older adults, and will conclude with a review of evidence on a variety of health outcomes including mortality, disability, the onset of chronic disease, and perceived health. This final section also assesses whether scientific research actually supports the notion that older people are more vulnerable to the economic and social conditions in their neighborhoods.

## CHARACTERISTICS OF THE RESIDENTIAL COMMUNITY

Communities and neighborhoods have different levels of material and social resources that may affect the daily lives of individuals. Material resources include the built environment, or the nature and quality of transportation, buildings, and physical infrastructure such as lighting, sidewalks, and streets. Other aspects of the built environment include parks and recreation areas, open-air playgrounds and pedestrian walkways, community spaces such as town squares, band shells, or other shared physical resources. Well-lit streets and sidewalks, for instance, are of great benefit to an older person with mobility issues.

Another set of material resources that have an impact on the well-being of individuals is the availability of commercial, government, and institutional goods and services. Easily accessible and well-stocked grocery stores are an example of the type of retail establishments that can benefit individuals. The quality of local services such as public transportation and health care matter a great deal, particularly to people who have lost the ability to drive or who must see their health care provider often. Government services also may vary substantially. Police and fire protection are not consistent across all neighborhoods and communities. Local tax revenues and the volume of crime influence the quality of policing. The distribution of commercial goods and services is also quite uneven across communities. Particularly for persons in rural areas, who are more likely to be over 65, and those in poor neighborhoods, simple access to high-quality food within reach of one's home may be a problem.

Social resources are more difficult to describe but no less important to the well-being of individuals. Places of worship, local social groups such as Kiwanis and the Knights of Columbus, social and emotional support groups, bridge leagues, and recreational groups are all examples of the social resources communities have that allow people to remain engaged and socially active. Similarly social services such as elder care, home health care, meals-on-wheels, home visitation, and other related geriatric services often have their origin in a community organization such as the local church. Many communities do not have the resources or people necessary to support these types of voluntary organizations. For people who have lost a spouse or lack other family and friends, these informal social networks can be critical not only in keeping them connected to the larger world, but in providing basic social services such as meals, transportation, and companionship for little or no charge.

People also have very different perceptions of the quality, warmth, and safety of their neighborhoods and communities that may or may not be tied to a measurable reality. Older people often perceive residential change, rapid economic growth, or increasing ethnic diversity as threatening to their way of life or community. Perceptions, then, can determine how willing individuals are to venture out of their homes or take part in community-wide activities.

## MEASURING RESIDENTIAL CHARACTERISTICS

Social scientists find a variety of ways to measure the characteristics of neighborhoods and communities that can then be linked to individual measures of health and well-being. The most popular method is to use the economic characteristics of neighborhoods, such as poverty, household structure, ethnic composition, median income, the proportion of owner-occupied households, and residential instability, to act as approximations of the available material and social resources. Poor neighborhoods with few owner-occupied housing units are thought to lack material and social resources also.

These types of data are widely available at the neighborhood level (defined either as a census tract or census block group) in the United States, either from the decennial Census or the American Community Survey. Data from other surveys that ask about health and well-being can be linked to data from the Census if one knows the address of the respondent to the original survey. Data analysts can then link together the characteristics of places people live to their individual characteristics and health outcomes. Neighborhood-level economic and demographic data, as measured by the Census, are limited because there is an implicit assumption that poverty and residential instability are always related to poorer material and social resources. Nevertheless, they are the most efficient way to describe communities because the data are widely available and periodically updated for all neighborhoods in the United States. These indicators also can be easily linked to other types of data because residential addresses can be matched directly to Census data.

Data about material and social resources in a neighborhood may also be gathered directly from commercial establishments, government services such as law enforcement, and social entities such as churches. For instance, local law enforcement agencies often provide information about crime incidence by neighborhood or street address. Other administrative data also may be useful, such as birth, death, and marriage records. Retail service information can be acquired through commercial data services such as Claritas, which sell information about store locations and local demographics. Other data can be gathered on a smaller scale for social institutions such as churches by buying specialized mailing lists or directory services. When used in combination with Census data, these types of information provide an integrated profile of the material and social environments that surround older adults.

The third way researchers gather information about the local environment is through a method called systematic social observation (SSO). SSO is a standardized approach for directly observing the physical, social, and economic characteristics of neighborhoods, one block at a time. Researchers create videotape and observer logs to characterize city blocks. Observers count and code such things as the number of boarded up or burnt out buildings, incidences of graffiti, and illegal activities such as drug selling and prostitution. This method is very effective at capturing the built environment in a more thorough way because observers both count and rate the quality of buildings and streets. It is also an effective way of capturing street-level interactions that are not often captured in other types of data collection (Raudenbush & Sampson, 1999).

Finally, respondents can be asked about their perceptions of various aspects of the neighborhood. Neighborhood surveys often ask respondents questions about their perceptions of the social organization, social cohesion, and disorder in their residential neighborhoods. Social cohesion is used to describe the strength of psychological and social relationships between members of a community. The organization of social relationships, such as how community groups such as the local Boy Scout council or School Board draw different members of the community together, will affect social cohesion. Social disorder is a term used to describe both the feeling of neighborhood disintegration and its behavioral and physical manifestations such as public drinking, street violence and boarded up or burnt out buildings. Typical questions about these concepts may ask about the ability of neighbors to control unwanted behaviors such as drug use and fighting. The purpose of these questionnaires is to assess perceptions rather than objective realities. A neighborhood may appear safe from observation but its inhabitants may perceive changes and threats that are not visible from other sources of data collection. Neighborhood surveys also are a good way to assess whether individuals feel close to their neighbors socially and whether they feel integrated into their communities (Raudenbush & Sampson, 1999).

## POTENTIAL LINKS BETWEEN NEIGHBORHOODS AND INDIVIDUAL HEALTH

The remaining question to address is how geographic environments and changes in those environments affect individual health. Much of what researchers know about the links between geographic context and health are the result of studying poverty and health disparities. Spatial differences in poverty in the United States have been of particular concern. Residential segregation by income and race has always been a feature of the American landscape. The result is that the physical and environmental quality of neighborhoods varies substantially within a single city and across the country. Within that context, researchers usually agree on four primary mechanisms, although there is some disagreement about which is most important. First and foremost, the local environment may affect all forms of health and health care-seeking behavior. For example, poorly-lit streets without sidewalks and inadequate recreational facilities will limit the amount of walking or exercising people are willing and able to do. Also, the availability of high-quality, nutritious food can modify dietary intake.

Some researchers have argued that local social norms fostered by concentrated poverty and disadvantage as well as an individual's social networks may encourage cigarette smoking, drinking, and illegal drug use. This type of influence has been documented for young people but is usually not found among older persons. Similarly if local health care facilities are sparse or not easily accessible, individuals may find it difficult to find and use appropriate health care. This can either exacerbate existing health conditions or forestall the diagnosis of emerging conditions. In any case, the environment imposes constraints on or provides opportunities for individuals to engage in behavior that contribute to better health.

Rich social engagement and strong social networks have been demonstrated to facilitate healthy aging. Older persons who remain active in community life and who have family and friends who visit and help with basic activities of daily life live longer and are less likely to be disabled. Social engagement enhances brain function and is likely to lead to a more active lifestyle. In studies of the elderly from mid-life to older ages, researchers have found that those persons who remain socially active and continue to have contact with friends and neighbors show fewer signs of dementia and are less likely to lose both hearing and vision. In communities and neighborhoods with rich social resources, often called *social capital,* social engagement is easier.

Poor, transient communities or those undergoing rapid economic change often lack these deep social networks. Thus, the second way in which communities can affect health is because they may fail to provide inhabitants with the opportunities to remain engaged. The density and quality of social resources in a local community will also affect trust among neighbors as they have more opportunities to interact and remain friends. Several researchers have proposed a different but related pathway from the community social environment to individual health. Christopher Browning and Kathleen Cagney (2002), among others, suggest that collective efficacy—or the ability of the community to affect community-level outcomes such as social disorder (including public drinking) or the preservation of public places—is positively related to both the maintenance of social capital and the quality of community relationships. Neighbors who feel they can work together to solve community problems, such as crime and unwanted commercial activity, will feel more engaged and better supported by each other. Collective action also fosters trust among neighborhoods and further enhances residents' feelings of security and social connectedness.

The biological and emotional stress associated with living in dangerous or disordered environments can lead to poor health directly by modifying the production of stress hormones, which are thought to lead to a higher incidence of heart disease, impair brain activity, and impair immunity to infectious disease. Chronic stress often leads to perpetual elevation of these stress hormones, which is implicated in the onset of diabetes and the functioning of the central nervous system. People can be stressed in two ways by poor and disordered environments. First, the presence of physical and social disorder may make people feel as if they are constantly in danger of attack. Street crime and crumbling infrastructure will heighten this feeling of vulnerability because people believe they cannot control what happens to them in their own homes or on the street. Social disorder may also lead to a greater number of stressful life events for individuals. People in poor neighborhoods are more likely to be the victim of a crime, lose a loved one to violence or drug abuse, and suffer a house fire or eviction (Boardman, 2004). Perceived and actual vulnerability combine to affect mental health directly and physical health through the endocrine and neurological systems.

The last pathway from the local environment to health leads directly through the physical environment itself. Residents of poorer neighborhoods and communities are less likely to be able to control land use. Industrial land use, mixed zoning, and more deliberate waste dumping often make poor communities environmentally hazardous. The health consequences of air, soil, and water contamination are well-known. Neighborhoods with little political or economic power often cannot forestall these dangerous forms of pollution. Political power in the community is central to preventing unwanted land use yet is often undermined by limited economic resources and the lack of community activism. Individuals in these communities often do not have the wherewithal to move away to more desirable neighborhoods. Older adults are likely to have the longest exposure to environmental hazards and have fewer resources enabling them to move.

## RESEARCH ON THE HEALTH OF THE ELDERLY

Despite the clear connections between the local environment and the health of older adults, the actual evidence is often less clear. For some health indicators, researchers find a strong and consistent link between place of residence and the health outcome, whereas for other outcomes the effect is less straightforward. The effects of different aspects of the residential environment on the health of older adults very much depends on how health is defined. In addition, it is difficult to make broad generalizations from existing research because the measures used to characterize the residential environment are inconsistent.

Very few researchers have found any effect of the local environment, measured either by material and social resources or by perceptions, on mortality rates among older adults. Most of the residential effects on mortality are observed before age 65 (Waitzman & Smith, 1998). The only exception to this is among older persons who have Mexican ancestry or who were born in Mexico (Eschbach et al., 2004). The lack of mortality effects among the elderly in general may be true because many of the fatal assaults on health that occur in socioeconomically disadvantaged neighborhoods, such as violence or unhealthy behaviors, happen in early adulthood. It is less clear why these effects can be found among different ethnic groups.

Similarly, there is mixed evidence as to whether local economic and social circumstances are associated with disability and physical function in later life. Many authors have found that once something is known about individuals and the families they live in, the social and economic environment does not seem to matter (Feldman & Steptoe, 2004; Robert, 1998). Other authors suggest that physical disability in older adults is, in fact, higher in communities where the built environment is poor (Balfour & Kaplan, 2002). In this case the difference may have to do with how one thinks about the residential environment. In studies that include measures of the built environment, the authors directly measure those aspects of the residential environment that can be challenging to a person who is disabled or partially disabled.

In studies of hospitalization and survival following a heart attack, the neighborhood social and economic environment seems to matter when both younger and older people are included in the study (Borrell et al., 2004). This suggests that both subsequent mortality and the rehospitalization of persons who have had a heart attack or other cardiovascular-related events such as a stroke are higher for those living in disadvantaged neighborhoods. In a study restricted to persons over age 70, however, no differences were found in the occurrence of diseases such as strokes, congestive heart failure, or heart attack among people who live in different types of neighborhoods (Wight et al., 2008).

Finally, there is one health indicator on which all researchers agree. The majority of studies have found that all types of environmental and neighborhood stressors are linked to poorer perceived health among older adults. When asked about their health, older persons who live in challenging environments, whether measured by perception or reality, are more likely to say that they are in poor or fair health (Cagney, Browning, & Wen, 2005; Robert & House, 2000). This suggests that the local conditions have the greatest effect on the mental health of older adults. The social and physical isolation associated with living in a disadvantaged neighborhood will have a direct impact on how they feel about themselves and their well-being. The physical consequences may then flow from this feeling of vulnerability and deprivation.

**SEE ALSO** Volume 3: *Aging in Place; Health Differentials/Disparities, Later Life.*

**BIBLIOGRAPHY**

Balfour, J. L., & Kaplan, G. (2002). Neighborhood environment and loss of physical function in older adults: Evidence from the Alameda County Study. *American Journal of Epidemiology, 155*(6), 507–515.

Boardman, J. (2004). Stress and physical health: The role of neighborhoods as mediating and moderating mechanisms. *Social Science and Medicine, 58*(12), 2473–2483.

Borrell, L. N., Roux, A. V. D., Rose, K., Catellier, D., & Clark, B. (2004). Neighborhood characteristics and mortality in the Atherosclerosis Risk in Communities Study. *International Journal of Epidemiology, 33*(2), 398–407.

Browning, C. R., & Cagney, K. A. (2002). Neighborhood structural disadvantage, collective efficacy, and self-rated physical health in an urban setting. *Journal of Health and Social Behavior, 43*(4), 383–399.

Cagney, K., Browning, C., & Wen, M. (2005). Racial disparities in self-rated health at older ages: What difference does the neighborhood make? *Journals of Gerontology, Series B: Psychological Sciences and Social Sciences, 60*(4), 181–190.

Eschbach, K., Ostir, G. V., Patel, K. V., Markides, K. S., & Goodwin, J. S. (2004). Neighborhood context and mortality among older Mexican Americans: Is there a barrio advantage? *American Journal of Public Health, 94*(10), 1807–1812.

Feldman, P. J., & Steptoe, A. (2004). How neighborhoods and physical functioning are related: The roles of neighborhood socioeconomic status, perceived neighborhood strain, and individual health risk factors. *Annals of Behavioral Medicine, 27*(2), 91–99.

Glass, T., & Balfour, J. (2003). Neighborhood, aging, and functional limitations. In I. Kawachi & L. F. Berkman (Eds.), *Neighborhoods and health* (pp. 3003–3334). New York: Oxford University Press.

Haan, M., Kaplan, G. A., & Camacho, T. (1987). Poverty and health: Prospective evidence from the Alameda County Study. *American Journal of Epidemiology, 125*(6), 989–998.

LeClere, F. B., Rogers, R., & Peters, K. (1997). Ethnicity and mortality in the United States: Individual and community correlates. *Social Forces, 76*(1), 169–198.

Patel, K., Eschbach, K., Rudkin, L., Peek, M. K., & Markides, K. (2003). Neighborhood context and self-rated health in older Mexican Americans. *Annals of Epidemiology, 13*(9), 620–628.

Raudenbush, S. W., & Sampson, R. (1999). Ecometrics: Toward a science of assessing ecological settings, with application to the systematic social observation of neighborhoods. *Sociological Methodology, 29*, 1–41.

Robert, S. (1998). Community-level socioeconomic status effects on adult health. *Journal of Health and Social Behavior, 39*(1), 18–37.

Robert, S., & House, J. (2000). Socioeconomic inequalities in health: Integrating individual-, community-, and societal-level theory and research. In G. L. Albrecht, R. Fitzpatrick, & S. C. Scrimshaw (Eds.), *The handbook of social studies in health and medicine* (pp. 115–135). Thousand Oaks, CA: Sage.

Ross, C. E., & Mirowsky, J. (2001). Neighborhood disadvantage, disorder, and health. *Journal of Health and Social Behavior, 42*(3), 258–276.

Sampson, R. J., & Raudenbush, S. (1999). Systematic social observation of public spaces: A new look at disorder in urban neighborhoods. *American Journal of Sociology, 105*(3), 603–651.

Waitzman, N. J., & Smith, K. R. (1998). Phantom of the area: Poverty-area residence and mortality in the United States. *American Journal of Public Health, 88*(6), 973–976.

Wen, M., Browning, C. R., & Cagney, K. A. (2003). Poverty, affluence, and income inequality: Neighborhood economic structure and its implications for health. *Social Science and Medicine, 57*(5), 843–860.

Wen, M., & Christakis, N. (2005). Neighborhood effects of posthospitalization mortality: A population-based cohort study of the elderly in Chicago. *Health Services Research, 40*(4), 1108–1127.

Wight, R. G., Cummings, J., Miller-Martinez, D., Karlamangla, A., Seeman, T. E., & Aneshensel, C. S. (2008). A multilevel analysis of urban neighborhood socioeconomic disadvantage and health in late life. *Social Science and Medicine, 66*(4), 862–872.

***Felicia LeClere***

***Bernice Neugarten.*** © MATTHEW GILSON. REPRODUCED BY PERMISSION.

# NEUGARTEN, BERNICE
## *1916–2001*

Bernice L. Neugarten was a monumental figure in the field of adult development and aging. In a career spanning more than 50 years, Neugarten wrote or edited over 160 published manuscripts, including the books *Middle Age and Aging* and *Age or Need?* Neugarten's ideas forever changed understandings of human development as she turned attention to middle and later life during a time when most scientific inquiry focused on children. Nearly three dozen papers that embody her most important contributions are collected in *The Meanings of Age: Selected Papers of Bernice L. Neugarten.*

Born in a small Nebraska town, Neugarten was educated at the University of Chicago, where she ultimately earned a doctoral degree in Human Development. After taking time to raise children and pursue other writing and research, she returned to the University of Chicago as a faculty member in the Committee on Human Development and eventually served as its chair. In 1980 Neugarten founded the doctoral program in Human Development and Social Policy at Northwestern University in Chicago.

Neugarten had a knack for finding catchy phrases to express provocative ideas. One example is the distinction between the "young-old" and "old-old"—between those who are relatively healthy, affluent, and active and those who are not, regardless of their chronological age. This notion challenged common images of aging and old age as negative and pathological. It was also meant to reflect the great individual differences that exist among older people, differences produced by the unique experiences and interests that come with long lives.

Although age is a convenient way to classify ourselves and others, Neugarten argued that age often poorly predicts psychological, biological, and social statuses. She also speculated that an aging society, which is produced by longer life expectancy and better health, brings the potential of an "age-irrelevant society" and a more "fluid life cycle," in which age becomes less meaningful in determining experiences in work, education, family, and leisure. Neugarten also warned that an aging society brings the potential for politics of "age divisiveness," because younger groups may turn against unprecedented numbers of elders.

Neugarten's 1965 paper "Age Norms, Age Constraints, and Adult Socialization," published with Joan Moore and John Lowe, is one of the most frequently cited social science articles of the 20th century. Using data from the landmark Kansas City Study of Adult Life, on which Neugarten was a key investigator, this paper introduced the concepts of "social clocks" and "age timetables." It investigated individuals' awareness of being "early," "on-time," or "late" with respect to major life transitions and individuals' judgments about the appropriateness of a variety of recreation, appearance, and consumption behaviors at different ages. Neugarten emphasized that these age norms and expectations act as "prods and breaks" on behavior, in some cases prompting it and in other cases preventing it.

Neugarten often said that she was struck by the amount of psychological change rather than stability in adult life. Adulthood cannot be understood simply by projecting forward those concerns important in childhood and adolescence. She begged scholars to consider the many new psychological issues that emerge throughout adulthood. For example, Neugarten noted the "changing time perspective" at midlife, when people begin to think in terms of time-left-to-live rather than time-since-birth; and the "personalization of death," during which men begin to "rehearse" for illness and women for widowhood.

Throughout her career, Neugarten emphasized the active roles that people play in shaping their lives; yet she also acknowledged that people's actions are significantly shaped by the social settings and historical time in which they live. People cannot be understood in isolation from their environments, and the study of lives requires collaboration between psychology and sociology.

In later work Neugarten advocated that age-based public policies be replaced, or at least better balanced, by need. She was also intrigued by the ethical issues associated with longer lives, including how medical care for very old people might be handled in more effective and humane ways, as well as how the presence of large numbers of elders presents both challenges and opportunities for families and societies.

Toward the end of her life, Neugarten made the controversial statement that gerontology would eventually disappear as a field. Aging is a lifelong process that begins at birth, not at an arbitrary point in later life. From a policy standpoint, age-related entitlements were being questioned, and from the standpoint of providers, recognition of the difficulty of designing and delivering services based solely on age was growing. For Neugarten, the common practice of "chopping up" the life cycle into distinct periods worked against the need to understand the complexity and beauty of the whole.

SEE ALSO Volume 3: *Aging; Oldest Old.*

**BIBLIOGRAPHY**

Neugarten, B. L. (Ed.). (1968). *Middle age and aging: A reader in social psychology.* Chicago: University of Chicago Press.

Neugarten, B. L. (Ed.). (1982). *Age or need? Public policies and older people.* Beverly Hills, CA: Sage Publications.

Neugarten, B. L., Moore, J., & Lowe, J. (1965). Age norms, age constraints, and adult socialization. *American Journal of Sociology, 70,* 710–717.

Neugarten, D. A. (Ed.). (1996). *The meanings of age: Selected papers of Bernice L. Neugarten.* Chicago: University of Chicago Press.

*Richard A. Settersten, Jr.*

## NURSING HOMES

SEE Volume 2: *Policy, Health;* Volume 3: *Assisted Living Facilities; Long-term Care; Retirement Communities.*

# O

## OBESITY, LATER LIFE

SEE Volume 2: *Obesity, Adulthood.*

## OLD AGE

SEE Volume 3: *Aging; Oldest Old.*

## OLDER AMERICANS ACT

SEE Volume 3: *Policy, Late-Life Well Being.*

## OLDER DRIVERS

Modern society now faces the challenge of meeting the transportation needs of a rapidly expanding population of older adults. For nearly all of history, older adults have accounted for a very small percentage of the total population. Now the oldest old, or persons 85 and older, are the fasting growing segment of the population. For example, in 1998 the 65 to 74 age group was 8 times larger than in 1900, the 75 to 84 age group was 16 times larger, and the 85 and over age group was 33 times larger (Hu, Jones, Reuscher, Schmoyer, & Fruett, 2000). This large population of older persons has been responsible for creating new business, housing, social service, and medical trends. Changing demographics have had, and will continue to have, enormous implications for transportation. Given that family sizes have declined over the past century, ever-increasing numbers of older adults will need to meet their own mobility needs for as long as possible.

In addition to the dramatic increase in the older population, two major changes in transportation demographics have occurred for older drivers: (a) Older drivers are driving more miles than ever before; the current cohort of older drivers is driving more than past cohorts (i.e., so the number of miles driven on average by a 75-year-old in the early 21st century is greater than the number of miles driven by the same in prior years) and (b) there has been an increase in the proportion of women drivers. As of 2008, almost half of all licensed drivers are women. Although men still account for the majority of miles driven, the increasing number of women in the workforce, along with the increase of women's economic independence and the increase in their vehicle ownership, represent major demographic changes, and these changes have implications for aging and transportation. For example, many older women can take over the driving role, thus extending the mobility and independence of both older adults.

### SIGNIFICANCE OF DRIVING FOR THE OLDER ADULT

Mobility is a critical component of independence and quality of life. Both older and younger persons depend on the automobile for most of their travel. In 1990 between 75% and 95% of all trips made by older persons were made by private automobile. Rates were higher for the young old (in this case, those between the ages of 60

***Senior Transportation.*** *Ninety-one-year-old Elsie Emslie sits behind the steering wheel of her car. Emslie has 75 years of experience behind the wheel of a car and takes an annual driving assessment offered through the Tampa Bay area's Getting in Gear program for older adults.* AP IMAGES.

and 64) and gradually decreased with advancing age. However, even for the very old (85 and older), more than three fourths of their trips were made by private automobile. Because the cost of providing alternative transportation has been so high, particularly in the United States, it is important for older persons to retain their driving privileges for as long as they can safely do so.

Historically research on older drivers has gone through several phases. In the 1970s, research questions focused on whether older drivers presented a safety risk to other road users by being on the road. Subsequently, researchers focused on identifying age-related risk factors for crash involvement. Although there was a predominant perception that older drivers represented a safety risk, from a population perspective there is no significant increase in crash risk until drivers reach the ages of 75 to 80 (Evans, 1988). Even though most older drivers are not at increased crash risk, there continues to be a focus on understanding the age-related changes that elevate risk on an individual level. Research has tried to balance safety concerns within the broader context of transportation and meeting the mobility needs of older adults. Topics of research include understanding how mobility changes with age and what factors influence these changes, identifying methods for detecting functional changes and correcting them when possible, and discovering how the transportation system may be altered to better serve older adults.

## CHANGES IN MOBILITY WITH AGE

As people grow older, they may experience declines in various modes of functioning. Specifically, sensory and cognitive abilities may be affected, which may impair mobility in general and driving in particular (Guralnik, Fried, & Salive, 1996). Mobility encompasses a range of abilities, from being able to move one's body, to the extent of one's life space (ranging from very constrained, such as living only within one's home, to unconstrained, such as traveling to other countries), to the avoidance of negative events such as falls and automobile crashes.

Many older drivers reduce their driving over time to avoid potentially challenging or bothersome driving situations or contexts in which they do not feel safe, such as driving at night, in the rain, or during rush hour (Ball, Owsley, Myers, & Goode, 1998). Such restrictions in driving habits, sometimes culminating in the decision to stop driving altogether (most often the decision to stop driving is a personal choice; however, the concern of others may weigh in this decision) can pose a threat to independence and may lead to isolation, depression, and reduced access to health care (Fonda, Wallace, & Herzog, 2001) and other resources that positively impact qualify of life, such as employment and social activities (Marottoli, Cooney, Wagner, Doucette, & Tinetti, 2000). Significant decreases in mobility can occur over periods as short as 3 years (Wood et al., 2005), and declining sensory and cognitive performance appear to be important predictors of driving cessation and mobility decline (Edwards et al., 2008). Reduced mobility and any resulting social isolation can seriously undermine the quality of life for older persons and accelerate declines in personal health. With increasing concerns about rising health care costs, assuring accessible transportation for older persons could prove a beneficial investment.

## IDENTIFYING RISK FACTORS FOR DRIVING COMPETENCE

Older adults rely heavily on automobiles to maintain their mobility, and a driver's license is an important symbol of independence. However, older drivers (particularly those ages 75+) are involved in more traffic convictions, crashes, and fatalities per mile driven than most other age groups (Evans, 1988). Furthermore, due to increasing frailty, older adults are more likely to be killed or injured in a collision of equivalent severity than more robust younger persons (Hu et al., 2000). When injured, older adults have lengthier hospital stays and higher mortality rates (Sartorelli et al., 1999). Thus the older traffic injury victim represents a costly problem in terms of both acute and continued health care costs.

Because most individual older drivers are as safe on the road as middle-age drivers, it is important to understand the factors responsible for increased crash risk for some older persons. Many potential risk factors have been evaluated, including age itself, visual function, cognitive function, physical function, medical conditions, and medications. For example, the relationship between visual function and driving safety has become much clearer over the past 20 years. In general, normal age-related changes in visual function do not result in increased crash risk. Visual acuity, although necessary for reading distant road signs, is only weakly related to crash risk. Severe visual field loss in both eyes, although not common, elevates crash risk, as does contrast sensitivity loss (a measure of how faded or washed out an image can be before it becomes indistinguishable from its background) from cataracts, even if present in only one eye (Owsley, Stalvey, Wells, Sloane, & McGwin, 2001). Glaucoma and cataracts, when accompanied by visual function impairment, also have been associated with increased crash risk. Physical functioning can also impact driving behavior. For example, Richard Marottoli (1994) found that older persons with multiple lower limb abnormalities or who perform poorly on a rapid walk test had more self-reported crashes and citations.

Although adequate visual and physical functioning clearly are needed for safe driving, recent research suggests that cognitive factors play a significantly larger role in crash risk than visual sensory variables. With respect to visual information processing, an increasing body of work, including several large field studies with differing driving environments, has shown that impairments on a specific measure of the speed of processing, the Useful Field of View test is consistently a strong predictor of driving ability (Clay et al., 2005). This test measures the presentation of time needed to correctly identify and locate important visual information in the visual field. Thus someone who can process visual information quickly can respond to potential hazards across a larger visual area than an individual who processes information more slowly. Other cognitive measures, including tests of executive function, memory, and reasoning, have also been related to increased crash risk. Furthermore, although medical diagnoses themselves are not always good predictors of driving competence, some diagnoses or the medications used to treat them are helpful as triggers for a more comprehensive evaluation of the cognitive abilities they may impair.

## INTERVENTIONS TO MAINTAIN DRIVING COMPETENCE

Cataracts is the leading cause of visual impairment in older adults. Fortunately, cataract surgery has become common, and older adults who undergo cataract surgery are 50% less likely to be involved in a motor vehicle crash than those who need (but do not elect to have) the surgery (Owsley, Sloane, McGwin, & Ball, 2002). As a general rule, a reasonable strategy to help maintain driving competence is to aggressively treat all chronic medical conditions to promote public health and slow functional decline in an aging population.

Approaches to prevent cognitive decline, including exercise, nutrition, and cognitive training or brain fitness programs, have also received considerable study during the past decade. Research on cognitive training has shown that enduring improvements are indeed possible (Willis et al., 2006) and that improved driving abilities can result from such programs (Roenker, Cissell, Ball, Wadley, & Edwards, 2003).

Research suggests that the complex public health issue of older driver remediation necessitates a comprehensive approach. Such an approach might include retesting of drivers referred for assessment because of poor driving history, concern of family members, or physician request; expansion of voluntary programs that include driver assessment, education, training, referral for appropriate intervention, and counseling regarding driving cessation and alternative transportation; and insurance discounts as incentives for participation in such programs. Such programs are becoming more widespread.

## FUTURE DIRECTIONS

Research and its translation are now underway on many fronts: safer roadways, safer automobiles, better alternative transportation services, better driver regulation procedures, greater access to proven driver rehabilitation programs, and the development of creative new partnerships for providing safe mobility to older people. Accessible transportation for older adults in the future will rely on actions taken by federal agencies, Congress, and states, counties, and cities. Older persons, caregivers, social agencies, insurance companies, airlines, bus operators, and local businesses need to anticipate and adapt to the changing demographics and resulting needs for transportation, and particularly for the preferred mode of transportation, driving.

Public policy aimed at promoting referral-based driver assessment, fostering the development of effective interventions, and supporting the creation and expansion of voluntary driver improvement programs would go a long way toward improving the safe mobility of older adults. The American Association for Retired Persons has a educational senior driver program, attendance of which results in an insurance discount. Posit Science Corporation has a cognitive training program called Insight that is based on the speed of processing training. This company is working with insurance partners to make the program available to their insured older drivers. Although the need for action in these areas is driven by the aging population, the results ultimately will improve safety and mobility for all age groups.

**SEE ALSO** Volume 3: *Aging; Cognitive Functioning and Decline; Disability and Functional Limitation, Later Life; Media and Technology Use, Later Life; Sensory Impairments.*

**BIBLIOGRAPHY**

Ball, K., Owsley, C., Myers, R., & Goode, K. T. (1998). Cognitive abilities and cognitive function in a diverse population: Pilot findings from the active study. *Gerontologist, 54.*

Clay, O. J., Wadley, V. G., Edwards, J., Roth, D. L., Roenker, D., & Ball, K. K. (2005). Cumulative meta-analysis of the relationship between useful field of view and driving performance in older adults: Current and future implications. *Optometry & Vision Science, 82*(8), 724–731.

Edwards, J. D., Ross, L. A., Ackerman, M., Small, B. J., Ball, K. K., Dodson, J. E., et al. (2008). Longitudinal predictors of driving cessation among older adults from the ACTIVE clinical trial. *Journals of Gerontology, Series B: Psychological Sciences and Social Sciences, 63*(1), 6–12.

Evans, L. (1988). Older driver involvement in fatal and severe traffic crashes. *Journal of Gerontology, 43,* S186–S193.

Fonda, S. J., Wallace, R. B., & Herzog, A. R. (2001). Changes in driving patterns and worsening depressive symptoms among older adults. *Journals of Gerontology, Series B: Psychological Sciences and Social Sciences, 56*(6), S343–S351.

Guralnik, J. M., Fried, L. P., & Salive, M. E. (1996). Disability as a public health outcome in the aging population. *Annual Review of Public Health, 17,* 25–46.

Hu, P. S., Jones, D. W., Reuscher, T., Schmoyer, R. S., Jr., & Fruett, L. F. (2000). Projecting fatalities in crashes involving older drivers, 2000–2025. *ORNL Reports,* 6963.

Marottoli, R. A., Cooney, L. M., Wagner, D. R., Doucette, J. & Tinetti, M. E. (1994). Predictors of automobile crashes and moving violations among elderly drivers. *Annals of Internal Medicine, 121*(11), 842–846.

Marottoli, R. A., Mendes de Leon, C. F., Glass, T. A., Williams, C. S., Cooney, L. M., & Berkman, L. F. (2000). Consequences of driving cessation: Decreased out-of-home activity levels. *Journals of Gerontology, Series B: Psychological Sciences and Social Sciences, 55,* S334–S340.

Owsley, C., Sloane, M., McGwin, G., Jr., & Ball, K. (2002). Timed instrumental activities of daily living tasks: Relationship to cognitive function and everyday performance assessments in older adults. *Gerontology, 48*(4), 254–265.

Owsley, C., Stalvey, B., Wells, J., Sloane, M., & McGwin, G., Jr. (2001). Visual risk factors for crash involvement in older drivers with cataract. *Archives of Ophthalmology, 119*(6), 881–887.

Roenker, D. L., Cissell, G. M., Ball, K. K., Wadley, V. G., & Edwards, J. D. (2003). Speed-of-processing and driving simulator training result in improved driving performance. *Human Factors, 45*(2), 218–233.

Sartorelli, K. H., Rogers, F. B., Osler, T. M., Shackford, S. R., Cohen, M., & Vane, D. W. (1999). Financial aspects of providing trauma care at the extremes of life. *Journal of Trauma, 46*(3), 483–487.

Willis, S. L., Tennstedt, S. L., Marsiske, M., Ball, K., Elias, J., Mann Koepke, K., et al. (2006). Long-term effects of cognitive training on everyday functional outcomes in older adults: The ACTIVE Study. *Journal of the American Medical Association, 296*(23), 2852–2854.

Wood, K. M., Edwards, J. D., Clay, O. C., Wadley, V. G., Roenker, D. L., & Ball, K. K. (2005). Sensory and cognitive predictors of functional ability in older adults. *Gerontology, 51,* 131–141.

***Karlene Ball***

# OLDEST OLD

Of increasing interest to researchers are elders considered to be very old. Their position as the fastest growing segment of the older population and status of having exceeded their life expectancy have fostered interest in understanding who they are and how they differ from those in young-old age groups. Yet to date, most research has been at the descriptive level concerning people in the United States, Germany, and Sweden. Theoretical developments in psychology and sociology have broadened the understanding of these elders, underscoring their unique position in the age structure.

## WHO ARE THE OLDEST OLD?

Although age 65 is the socially constructed and recognized milestone determining old age since 1935, the average life span has increased 20 years since then in developed countries

(United Nations Division for Social Policy and Development, 2003). In reaction to this increasing lifespan, some scholars have pointed out the need for finer gradations of *old,* defined as the young-old and oldest old (Neugarten, 1974; Laslett, 1991). Two common means exist for defining the oldest old for the purpose of empirical research. The first approach defines the oldest old category as the time point at which 50% of a birth cohort has died. In developed countries, this would be age 80. Another demographic approach to defining the oldest old is more differentiated and begins where half of those in a birth cohort who have reached age 50 or age 60 have died. The average age for the oldest old group would then be 85 in developed countries (Baltes & Smith, 2002). With various definitions of oldest old, a need has been recognized for a consistent definition to promote research on this specific age group.

**Historical Development of the Oldest Old Age Group in the United States** In 1900, men and women who were 65 years old could expect to live an additional 12 years, with 13% reaching the age of 85. By the year 2000, 42% of those reaching age 65 could expect to live to age 85 (Costa, 2003). One explanation for this increase in life expectancy is a reduction in risk factors and adversities such as infectious disease, poor nutrition, low socioeconomic status, and occupational accidents that can lead to early death or impaired functioning. Findings from a study that explored these early factors suggest that up to one-fifth of the increase between 1900 and 1999 in the probability of someone aged 65 living to age 85 may be due to improvements in early life conditions. The remaining increase can be attributed in part to improvement in medical care, decline in pollution, rise in refrigeration and reduced use of salt as a food preservative (Costa, 2003). Costa suggests that reduction in mortality for future cohorts will be tied to further innovation in medical care as there are fewer early life insults with the exception of pollution.

## SIGNIFICANCE OF THE OLDEST OLD

An increase in life expectancy and decline in fertility have contributed to an aging society in developed countries. With the aging of the baby boomers, American society has grown old rapidly, resulting in a dramatic increase in the demographic projections for the oldest old. Whereas the age group 85 and older increased by 274% between 1960 and 1994, those over 65 years old increased 100% and the entire U.S. population increased only 45% in that same period. By 2020, there will be 7 million people aged 85 years and older in the United States (U.S. Census Bureau, 2003). Figures 1 and 2 display the population distribution by age over a 200-year period (1880–2080). It is clear that the coming decades will bring many more people into the very old age groups and fewer into the younger age periods.

This increase in numbers of the very old comes with an attendant increase in the need for services. Significant increases in the prevalence and incidence of senile dementia among the oldest old as well as the greater level of physical dependence due to increased limitations in activities of daily living have imposed a great burden on both informal caregivers and the public health care system. This burden will only increase as the number of very old people increases.

## IMPORTANT THEORETICAL PERSPECTIVES ON THE OLDEST OLD

Although multiple losses through the death of friends and family as well as physical and social decline may be considered almost normative transitions among the very old, this view is not universal. Other perspectives emphasize positive characteristics of growing old such as wisdom, generosity, and self-acceptance. A lifespan developmental view is a perspective that emphasizes development throughout life, even into very old age. This perspective views all stages as being important and as incorporating a balance of gains as well as losses.

This positive perspective has also prompted theorists to view aging in terms of success. Originally developed in the 1980s, successful aging was portrayed as a complex process involving personal, social, and environmental factors. In the 1990s, researchers proposed two levels of successful aging, one for the young-old and one for the oldest old.

Other gerontological theories also have contributed to the understanding of successful aging. *Socioemotional theory* (Carstensen, 1993) views the reduction in social networks and social contacts in later life in a positive light. As elders come closer to the end of their lives, they choose to spend time with fewer people. They prefer to interact with those they feel close to and with whom they have an emotional bond. The selection, optimization, and compensation (SOC) model (Baltes, 1997) provides an explanation for how older people use selective compensatory efforts to deal with deficits, as they begin to experience cognitive decline. Goals are selected and pursued within the context of existing ability. With increasing levels of frailty in this age group, Baltes and Smith (2002) suggest that successful aging in the oldest old group might be measured by the individual's ability to offset inevitable loss through selection, optimization, and compensation strategies.

Successful aging is also intertwined with resilience. With some evidence indicating that age-related decline can be minimized or reversed (Staudinger, Marsiske, & Baltes, 1995), resilience is an important component of aging.

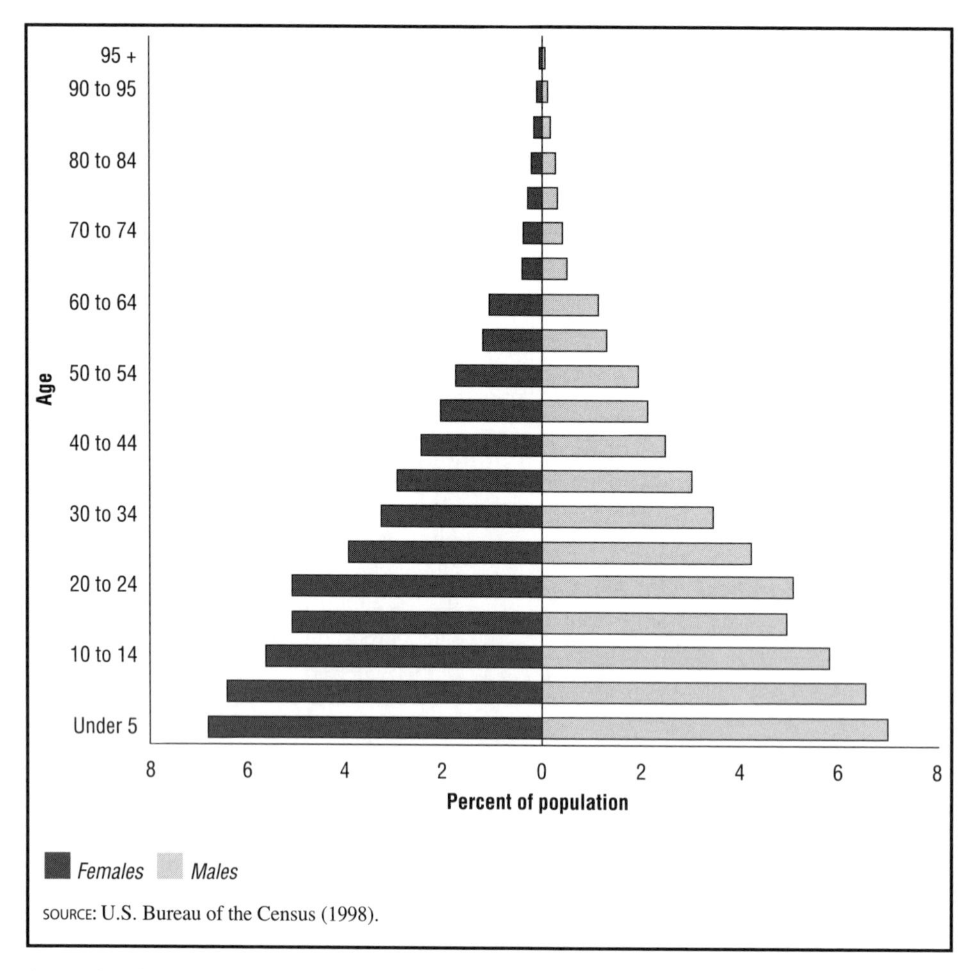


***Figure 1.*** *Population distribution by age and sex in the United States, 1880.* CENGAGE LEARNING, GALE.

Resilience is a construct that combines multiple domains: social, emotional, spiritual, cognitive, and physical. Many elders have a positive sense of well-being and demonstrate adaptability and resilience at any stage of life (Dyer & McGuinness, 1996; Staudinger, Marsiske, & Baltes, 1995).

## DEMOGRAPHIC DESCRIPTION

**Race and Ethnicity** Among the oldest old, the greatest percentage in 2002 were non-Hispanic Whites (86.4%), compared with Blacks (7%), those of Hispanic origin (4%), and Asians (1.8%), thus reflecting much less diversity than that of U.S. population as a whole. By 2010, the oldest old age group will be composed of 84.3% non-Hispanic Whites, 7.8% Blacks, 5.3% of Hispanic origin, and 2% Asians (U.S. Census Bureau, 2003). Compared with the race and ethnic distribution of the overall U.S. population, Whites are overrepresented and Blacks underrepresented among the oldest old, reflecting higher mortality rates among Blacks than in Whites.

**Marital Status** The pattern of marital status is changing with advancing age with declining numbers of married elders in the very old group. Although 63% of young-old aged between 65 and 74 are married and living with a spouse and 20% are widowed, 27% of the oldest old are married and living with a spouse and 53% are widowed. Among both groups, about 4% never married. Young-old are almost three times as likely as the oldest old to be divorced (9% and 3%, respectively; Kreider & Simmons, 2003). In addition to age, gender imbalance in life expectancy also influences marital status among the oldest old. Although 9% of women and 45% of men among the oldest old are married and living with their spouse in 2000, 72% and 35% are widowed, respectively. Oldest old men are five times as likely as their female counterparts to be married (Kreider & Simmons, 2003). This gender gap reflects both men's greater likelihood of dying and their greater likelihood of remarrying after widowhood, relative to their female counterparts.

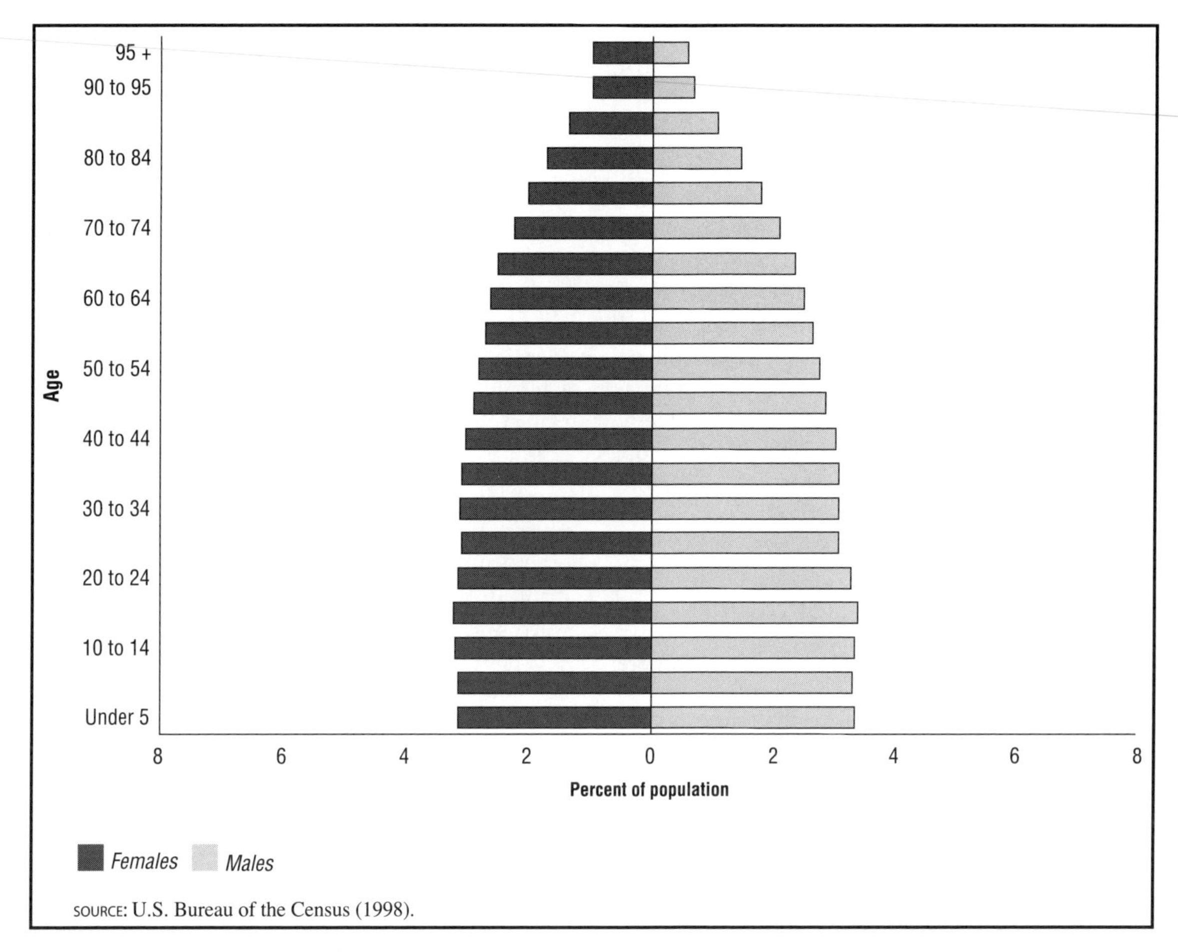


*Figure 2. Estimated population distribution by age and sex in the United States, 2080.* CENGAGE LEARNING, GALE.

**Living Arrangements** No national figures are available for people 85 years and older who live in the community. For those 75 years old and older in 2002, 40% of elders lived alone while 45% lived with a spouse and 15% lived with other people (U.S. Census Bureau, 2003). Even though similar proportions of elders aged 75 and older lived alone, for White and Black elders (40% and 39%, respectively) racial variations are present in living arrangements. Some 46% of White people who are 75 years old and older live with a spouse compared with 30% of elderly Black people. More Black elders age 75 and older live with other people (31%) compared with White elders (14%; U.S. Census Bureau, 2003). For Hispanic elders aged 75 and over, 25% live alone, 45% live with spouses, and 30% live with other people (U.S. Census Bureau, 2003).

Although most of the oldest old continue to live in the community, people in this age group constitute the largest proportion of residents of long-term care facilities. In 1999, 47% of such residents were among the oldest old, compared with 32% for elders aged between 75 and 84 years old and 12% for those aged between 65 and 74 years old (Bernstein, Hing, Moss, Allen, Siller, & Tiggle, 2003). Overall, though, the proportion of all elders living in long-term care facilities is declining. About 18% of the oldest old lived in such facilities in 2000, down from 25% in 1990 (Hetzel & Smith, 2001)

**Socioeconomic Status** The oldest old are more likely than young-old to be poor. The poverty rate was 15.3% for elders aged between 75 and 84 years old and 19.8% for the oldest old in 1995 (U.S. Bureau of the Census, 1996). In addition, economic status varies widely by gender and race. The poverty rates range from 19.7% for oldest old women living in metropolitan areas to 31.6% of those living outside metropolitan areas. Oldest old men living inside metropolitan areas reported lower poverty (12.1%) than those living outside metropolitan areas (20.8%; U.S. Bureau of Census, 1996).

Living arrangement is also related to poverty among the oldest old. Both men and women living alone are more likely to be poor than those living in families. Among Black oldest old living alone, 67.8% of women and 53.2% of men are living in poverty (U.S. Bureau of the Census, 1996).

Educational attainment, one of the crucial determinants for socioeconomic status, is lower among the oldest old than young-old. In 2002, 61% of oldest old men and 57% of oldest old women had at least a high school education whereas 73% of men and 74% of women aged between 65 and 74 years old completed high school (Smith, 2003). Even though no significant gender difference exists in the proportion of high school graduates, elderly men received more college education than elderly women. (Smith, 2003). These patterns reflect cohort differentials, whereby more recent cohorts achieved more schooling than their predecessors.

## SOCIAL AND PSYCHOLOGICAL DIMENSIONS OF THE OLDEST OLD

**Physical Health** Chronological age may have a more significant influence on health for those older than age 85 than for younger age groups (Friedrich, 2001). Although younger age groups vary widely, the oldest old show more consistent decreases in physical health and cognitive abilities. A study suggests that a decrease in health and well-being may slow down after reaching age 95 (Kulminski, Ukraintseva, Akushevich, Arbeev, Land, & Yashin, 2007). Drawing on longitudinal findings from the Berlin Aging Study where behavioral and social changes were reported on this age group, Baltes and Smith (2002) noted that the oldest old display a "level of bio-cultural incompleteness, vulnerability and unpredictability. The people in this age group are at the limits of their functional capacity, a state that makes them very different than all other age groups" (p. 2).

**Social Networks** The young-old list significantly more people in their social networks than do the very old (Smith & Baltes, 1999) because the very old are less socially embedded than younger adults are. In examining social contacts among young-old and very old people, Field and Minkler (1988) found that involvement within the family and friendship patterns does not change over time for the young-old or very old. Another longitudinal study (Dunkle & Haug, 2001) found similar results. Although many women are without spousal support because they have been widowed, they have confidants, family, and friends who are available to provide support.

## PSYCHIATRIC ILLNESS

Elders who are in the oldest old age group are at higher risk for mental disorders due to multiple functional disabilities, medical illness, and increasing vulnerabilities to various stressors with age, resulting from declining health and dwindling social relationships. The oldest old dwelling in the community report higher levels of depressive symptoms than their young-old counterparts (Blazer, 2000; Blazer, Burchett, Service, & George, 1991; Stallones, Marx, & Garrity, 1990). Even so, no clear age-related trend was present in the prevalence of depression in old age as found in a German sample in which the age of the subjects ranged from 70 to 100 (Helmchen, Baltes, Geiselmann, Kanowski, Linden, Reischies, Wagner, Wernicke, & Wilms, 1999). Conflicting evidence from a longitudinal study among the oldest old (Dunkle & Haug, 2001) suggests increasing depressive symptoms over a 9-year period from ages 85 to 94.

Worry, a common issue for older people, is a significant factor influencing mental health. Consistent with other studies including predominantly young-old participants (Skarborn & Nicki, 1996), for the oldest old, worry was strongly associated with depressive symptoms and poor mental health (Dunkle & Haug, 2001; Roberts, Dunkle, & Haug, 1994).

## PSYCHOLOGICAL AND COGNITIVE FUNCTIONING

With advanced old age, more old people show decline or dysfunction in several aspects of psychological functioning. The BASE (Berlin Aging Study) data show that advancing age negatively affects intellectual performance, which subsequently affects subjective well-being. The effect of age is not so great in other psychological arenas such as self, personality, and social relationships. In general, older adults are less responsive to social expectations and can behave more in accordance with their feelings.

Memory, a major component of cognitive functioning, remains relatively intact until the late stages of cognitive decline, which is more prevalent among the very old, especially those with limited formal education. These very old elderly with poor cognitive function experience an accelerated decline in cognitive function and increased susceptibility to senile dementia. In particular, Alzheimer's disease affects predominantly the oldest old and increases even in advanced ages, frequently leading to institutionalization. It is also related to social class membership. Members of the lower classes are more frequently diagnosed with senile dementia than those of higher classes even when education is controlled (Helmchen et al., 1999). In 2000, 1.8 million people aged 85 and older had Alzheimer's disease, comprising 40% of 4.5 million people with Alzheimer's disease. This number of the oldest old with Alzheimer's disease is expected to increase to 8 million by 2050 (Hebert, Scherr, Bienias, Bennett, & Evans, 2003).

## FUTURE DIRECTIONS

Important considerations for future research include clarification of the definition of the oldest old group, and the need for further research using nationally as well as internationally representative samples with attention to racial/ethnic subgroups, as well as differentiation between those aged between 85 and 99 and those of centenarians. To date, most research has been of a descriptive nature, attempting to demarcate those older than 85 years of age from those younger. Further research is needed to connect behavioral observations and the social context of the oldest old to understand the mechanisms that support quality of life for these elders.

**SEE ALSO** Volume 3: *Age Structure; Aging; Baltes, Margret and Paul; Centenarians; Frailty and Robustness; Global Aging; Neugarten, Bernice; Wisdom.*

### BIBLIOGRAPHY


Baltes, P. (1997). On the incomplete architecture of human ontogeny: Selection, optimization, and compensation as foundation of developmental theory. *American Psychologist, 52,* 366–380.

Baltes, P., & Smith, J. (2002). New frontiers in the future of ageing: From successful ageing of the young-old to the dilemmas of the fourth age. Plenary lecture for the Valencia Forum Valencia, Spain, April 1-4, 2002. Retrieved May 27, 2008 from http://www.mpib-berlin.mpg.de/en/forschung/lip/Baltes-Xmith.pdf

Bernstein, A. B., Hing, E., Moss, A. J., Allen, K. F., Siller, A. B., & Tiggle, R. B. (2003). *Health care in America: Trends in utilization.* Hyattsville, MD: National Center for Health Statistics.

Blazer, D. G. (2000). Psychiatry and the Oldest Old. *The American Journal of Psychiatry, 157,* 1915–1924.

Blazer, D., Burchett, B., Service, C., & George, L. (1991). The association of age and depression among the elderly: An epidemiologic study. *Journals of Gerontology: Med Science, 46,* M210–M215.

Carstensen, L. L. (1993). Motivation for social contact across the life-span: A theory of socioemotional selectivity. In J. Jacobs (Ed.), *Nebraska Symposium on Motivation* (Vol. 40, pp. 209–254). Lincoln: University of Nebraska Press.

Costa, D. (2003) *Becoming oldest-old: Evidence from historical U.S. Data.* Chestnut Hill, MA: Center for Retirement Research at Boston College.

Dunkle, R. B., & Haug, M. R. (2001). *The oldest old in everyday life: Self perception, coping with change, and stress.* New York: Springer Publishing Company.

Dyer, J. G., & McGuiness, T. M. (1996). Resilience: Analysis of the concept. *Archives of Psychiatric Nursing, 10,* 276–282.

Field, D., & Minkler, M. (1988). Continuity and change in social support between young-old and old-old or very old age. *Journal of Gerontology: Psychological Sciences, 43,* 100–106.

Friedrich, D. (2001). *Successful aging: Integrating contemporary idea, research findings and intervention strategies.* Springfield, IL: Charles C Thomas.

Hebert, L. E., Scherr, P. A., Bienias, J. L., Bennett, D. A., & Evans, D. A. (2003). Alzheimer disease in the U.S. population. *Archives of Neurology, 60,* 1119–1122.

Helmchen, H., Baltes, M., Geiselmann, B., Kanowski, S., Linden, M., Reischies, F. M., et al. (1999). Psychiatric illnesses in old age. In P. Baltes, & K. Mayer (Eds.), *The Berlin Aging Study: Aging from 70-100.* Cambridge, U.K.: Cambridge University Press, 167–196.

Hetzel, L., & Smith, A. (2001). *The 65 years and over population: 2000, Census 2000 Brief.* Washington, DC: U.S. Census Bureau.

Kreider, R., & Simmons, T. (2003). *Marital status: 2000. Census 2000 brief.* C2KBR-30. U.S. Census Bureau.

Kulminski, A., Ukraintseva, S., Akushevich, I., Arbeev, K., Land, K., & Yashin, A. (2007). Accelerated accumulation of health deficits as a characteristic of aging. *Experimental Gerontology, 42,* 963–970.

Laslett, P. (1991). *A fresh map of life: The emergence of the Third Age.* Cambridge, MA: Harvard University Press.

Neugarten, B. L. (1974). Age groups in American society and the rise of the young-old. *Annals of the American Academy of Politics and Social Sciences, 9,* 187–198.

Roberts, B., Dunkle, R., & Haug, M. (1994). Physical, psychological, and social resources as moderators of the relationship of stress to mental health of the very old. *Journal of Gerontology: Social Sciences, 49,* S35–S43.

Skarborn, M., & Nicki, R. (1996). Worry among Canadian seniors. *International Journal of Aging & Human Development, 43,* 169–178.

Smith, D. (2003). *The older population in the United States: March 2002.* P20–546. U.S. Census Bureau.

Smith, J., & Baltes, P. (1999). Trends and profiles of psychological functioning in very old age. In P. Baltes & K. Mayer (Eds.), *The Berlin Aging Study: Aging from 70–100* (pp. 197–226). Cambridge, U.K.: Cambridge University Press.

Stallones, L., Marx, M. B., & Garrity, T. F. (1990). Prevalence and correlates of depressive symptoms among older U.S. adults. *American Journal of Preventive Medicine, 6,* 295–303.

Staudinger, U. M., Marsiske, M., & Baltes, P. B. (1995). Resilience and reserve capacity in late adulthood: Potentials and limits of development across the life span. In D. Cicchetti & D. J. Cohen (Eds). *Developmental psychopathology: Vol. 2. Risk, disorder and adaptation* (pp. 801–847). New York: Wiley.

United Nations Division for Social Policy and Development. (2003). *The aging of the world's population.* New York: United Nations.

U.S. Bureau of the Census. (1996). *Current population reports, special studies, P23-190, 65+ in the United States.* Washington, DC: U.S. Government Printing Office.

U.S. Census Bureau. (2003). *Statistical Abstract of the United States: 2003* (123rd ed.). Washington, DC: U.S. Government Printing Office.


*Ruth E. Dunkle*

# P-Q

## PAIN, ACUTE AND CHRONIC

Pain is defined as "an unpleasant sensory and emotional experience associated with actual or potential tissue damage" (Price 1988, p. 6) and is "whatever the patient says it is, existing whenever the patient says it does" (McCaffery & Beebe 1989, p. 7). These definitions highlight pain as a multidimensional and subjective phenomenon.

Several different types of pain exist. The most basic distinction is whether pain is acute or persistent (sometimes referred to as chronic). *Acute pain* results from injury, surgery, or disease-related tissue damage (Panda & Desbiens, 2001), is typically brief, subsides with healing, and is usually associated with autonomic activity (e.g., tachycardia, which is an accelerated heartbeat, and sweat). Conversely, *persistent pain* is typically prolonged (lasting more than 3–6 months), may or may not be associated with a diagnosable disease process, and autonomic activity is usually absent (American Geriatrics Society, 2002; Harkins, 2002; Panda & Desbiens, 2001). Persistent pain can lead to functional loss, reduced quality of life, mood disruptions, and behavior changes, especially when untreated (Gordon, Pellino, Miaskowski, McNeill, Paice, Laferriere, & Bookbinder, 2002). Persistent and acute pain often coexist among older adults due to high rates of comorbidity.

### PREVALENCE

Physical pain is a significant problem for many older adults, affecting an estimated 50% of community-dwelling older adults and 85% of long-term care facilities (American Geriatrics Society, 2002; Herr, 2002; Sha, Callahan, Counsel, Westmoreland, Stump, & Kroenke, 2005). The high prevalence rate is related to the high rate of chronic health disorders among older adults, particularly painful musculoskeletal conditions such as arthritis (Helme & Gibson, 1999). A high prevalence of more acute conditions, such as cardiovascular disease, infection, and other painful diseases and syndromes, also exists in this age group (Feldt, Warne, & Ryden, 1998). Cancer, in particular, is associated with significant pain for a third of patients with active disease and two-thirds with advanced disease (Reiner & Lacasse, 2006). Huffman and Kunik (2000) found that of 86% of rural community-dwelling older adults reporting pain during the previous year, 59% reported multiple pain complaints. Thus, pain among older adults is common and is often complicated by co-occurring presence of different types, locations, and causes of pain.

### HOW AND WHY SOCIAL SCIENTISTS STUDY PAIN

Social scientists study pain for several reasons. Pain has major implications for older adults' health, functioning, and quality of life (American Geriatrics Society, 2002) and is associated with depression, withdrawal, sleep disturbances, impaired mobility, decreased activity engagement, and increased health care use (Gordon et al., 2002; Herr, 2002). Other geriatric conditions commonly exacerbated by pain include falls, weakness, malnutrition, difficulty walking, and slowed rehabilitation (American Geriatrics Society, 2002; Gordon et al., 2002). Hence pain has implications for physical, functional, and mental health among older adults, concepts that social scientists frequently investigate. In 2001 the Joint Commission on

Accreditation of Health Care Organizations (JCAHO) recognized pain assessment as the fifth vital sign and required health care professionals to evaluate and document pain assessment systematically. This policy change is relevant for medical sociologists who track trends in health and who may observe its impact in prevalence or consequences of pain across the life course.

## STUDY OF PAIN OVER THE LAST SEVERAL DECADES: MAIN PAIN MEASUREMENT TOOLS

As fundamental human experiences, pain and relief of pain have been a focus of daily life and medical care for centuries. Medical study of pain began in the 1800s with the advent of anesthesia, but interdisciplinary study was not initiated until the 1970s with the formation of the International Association for the Study of Pain and the American Pain Society. Pain studies in older adults began in the 1990s, followed by a growing body of research on physical and mental health consequences of pain in elders and measurement issues.

Patients' self-reports of pain are considered the gold standard, because no biological test exists. Although pain is multidimensional, few assessment tools evaluate all of these dimensions. The McGill Pain Questionnaire is one commonly used, comprehensive tool that measures pain affect and evaluation (through 78 word descriptors), pain location (using a body map), and pain intensity (based on a single question rating subjective pain on a six-point scale).

Pain intensity is the most commonly assessed dimension, measured with tools such as the visual analogue scale (VAS), the verbal descriptor scale (VDS), and the Faces Pain Scale (FPS) (Herr, 2002). The VAS, widely used in hospital settings, asks patients to rate pain intensity on a scale from zero to ten but requires ability to discriminate subtle differences in pain intensity, which may be difficult for some older adults to complete. Alternatively, the VDS asks patients to select a word that best describes present pain (e.g., no pain to worst pain imaginable), has been found a reliable and valid measure of pain intensity, and is reportedly easiest to complete and most preferred by older adults (Herr, 2002; Taylor, Harris, Epps, & Herr, 2005). The FPS, initially developed to assess pain intensity in children, has been used to measure pain intensity, particularly among cognitively impaired older adults. It consists of seven cartoon faces depicting least pain to most pain possible (Bieri, Reeve, Champion, Addicoat, & Ziegler, 1990). Among adults, the FPS is considered more appropriate than other pictorial scales because the cartoon faces are not age, gender, or race specific.

## ADVANCES MADE IN PAIN ASSESSMENT IN INDIVIDUALS WITH DEMENTIA

Recognition is growing about the problem of pain in elderly adults, particularly, in the difficulties associated with assessing and managing pain in elders with dementia. Patients with dementia cannot adequately report pain due to deficits in cognitive and verbal skills (i.e., confusion and impaired memory, judgment, attention, and language), which worsen as the disease progresses. No evidence exists, however, that this population physiologically experiences less pain than do other older adults (American Geriatrics Society, 2002). Instead, cognitively impaired elders may fail to interpret sensations as painful, are less able to recall pain, and may not be able to verbalize it to care providers (American Geriatrics Society, 2002). Thus, they are at risk for inadequately assessed and managed pain.

Because ability to self-report is diminished in persons with dementia, observational assessment of pain behaviors is necessary. Several measures have been developed to assess pain in persons with dementia. In 2006 Herr, Bjoro, and Decker completed a comprehensive state-of-the-science review of 14 existing measures and summarized their strengths and limitations. In general, pain behaviors include guarded movement, bracing, rubbing the affected area, grimacing, vocalizations, and restlessness.

Promising behavioral observation measures include the Pain Assessment in Advanced Dementia (PAINAD) (Warden, Hurley, & Volicer, 2003) and the Non-Communicative Patient's Pain Assessment Instrument (NOPPAIN) (Snow, Weber, O'Malley, Beck, Bruera, Ashton et al., 2004). Both are short, easy-to-use clinical tools for rating presence and intensity of pain among people with dementia. The PAINAD measures five pain indicators: breathing, negative vocalizations, facial expressions, body language, and consolability. The NOPPAIN measures pain noises, pain words, pain faces, bracing, rubbing, and restlessness. Preliminary studies suggest that both tools are reliable and valid measures (Taylor, Harris, Epps, & Herr, 2005; Warden et al., 2003). More recent data supported validity of the NOPPAIN against established microanalytic pain behavior analysis (Horgas, Nichols, Schapson, & Vieites, 2007).

When assessing pain in patients with advanced dementia, it is important to recognize that it is not possible to definitively determine an individual's pain through behavior alone (Horgas, et al., 2007). Instead, behavioral indicators should be used to trigger a comprehensive pain assessment protocol (Miller, Talerico, Rader, Swafford, Hiatt, Miller et al., 2005). The American Society for Pain Management Nursing's Task Force on pain assessment in nonverbal patients (including patients with dementia) recommends a comprehensive, hierarchical approach, including the following: (a) self-report, (b) look for potential causes of pain, (c) observe patient's behavior, (d) obtain surrogate reports of pain or changes in patient's behaviors/activities, and (e) give pain medications and determine whether pain indicators are reduced or eliminated (Herr, Coyne, Key, Manworren, McCaffery, Merkel et al., 2006). The recent interdisciplinary expert consensus panel also supports the need for comprehensive pain assessment, including self-report, behavioral, and proxy measures in persons with dementia (Hadjistavropoulos, Herr, Turk, Fine, Dworkin, Helme et al., 2007).

## FUTURE DIRECTIONS

Pain researchers have made giant strides over the past few decades, recognizing prevalence and developing multiple strategies for measuring pain in older adults. Further work is needed, however, to determine the most useful tools for this population and evaluate their sensitivity to change over time or in response to treatment. Specifically for patients with dementia, more work is needed to develop and test strategies to alleviate pain because pharmaceutical studies typically exclude people with dementia from drug trials, preventing these vulnerable elders benefit of research outcomes (Ancill, 1995).

Moreover, little is known about pain assessment and treatment in subsections of the elderly population. For instance, how do race and sex differences in pain play out in late life? Does type of dementia influence pain expression? Does what we know about pain assessment in persons with dementia extend to other populations with intellectual and developmental disabilities or adults who remain noncommunicative for other reasons (e.g., communication difficulties as a result of a stroke)?

Pain, a common problem for older adults, has an important impact on the life course. Although much has been learned, more research and interdisciplinary collaboration are warranted to improve measurement and management of pain and to minimize deleterious outcomes associated with this phenomenon.

SEE ALSO Volume 3: *Arthritis; Chronic Illness, Adulthood and Later Life; Dementias; Disability and Functional Limitation, Later Life; Hospice and Palliative Care; Mental Health, Later Life.*

### BIBLIOGRAPHY

American Geriatrics Society Panel on Persistent Pain in Older Persons (2002). The management of persistent pain in older persons. *Journal of the American Geriatrics Society, 50,* S205–S224.

Ancill, R. (1995). Psychopharmacological studies in demented elderly: Methodological and ethical concerns. *Human Psychopharmacology, 5,* 53–61.

Bieri, D., Reeve R. A., Champion, G. D., Addicoat L., & Ziegler, J. B. (1990). The Faces Pain Scale for the self-assessment of the severity of pain experienced by children: Development, initial validation, and preliminary investigation for ratio scale properties. *Pain, 41,* 139–150.

Feldt, K. S., Warne, M. A., & Ryden, M. B. (1998). Examining pain in aggressive cognitively impaired older adults. *Journal of Gerontological Nursing, 24,* 14–22.

Gordon, D. B., Pellino, T. A., Miaskowski, C., McNeill, J. A., Paice, J. A., Laferriere, D. et al. (2002). A 10-year review of quality improvement monitoring in pain management: Recommendations for standardized outcome measures. *Pain Management Nursing, 3,* 116–230.

Hadjistavropoulos, T., Herr, K., Turk, D., Fine, P., Dworkin, R. H., Helme, R. (2007). An interdisciplinary expert consensus statement on assessment of pain in older persons. *Clinical Journal of Pain, 23*(Suppl. 1), 1–43.

Harkins, S. W. (2002). What is unique about the older adult's pain experience? In D. K. Weiner, K. Herr, & T. E. Rudy (Eds.), *Persistent pain in older adults: An interdisciplinary guide for treatment* (pp. 4-17). New York: Springer.

Helme, R. D., & Gibson, S. J. (1999). Pain in older people. In I. K. Crombie, P. R. Croft, S. J. Linton et al., (Eds.), *Epidemiology of pain* (pp. 103–112). Seattle: IASP Press.

Herr, K. (2002). Chronic pain: Challenges and assessment strategies. *Journal of Gerontological Nursing, 28,* 20–27.

Herr, K., Bjoro, K., & Decker, S. (2006). Tools for assessment of pain in nonverbal older adults with dementia: A state-of-the-science review. *Journal of Pain and Symptom Management, 31,* 170–192.

Herr, K., Coyne, P. J., Key, T., Manworren, R., McCaffery, M., Merkel, S. et al. (2006). Pain assessment in the nonverbal patient: Position statement with clinical practice recommendations. *Pain Management Nursing, 7,* 44–52.

Horgas, A. L., Nichols, A. L., Schapson, C. A., & Vieites, K. (2007). Assessing pain in persons with dementia: Relationships between the NOPPAIN, self-report, and behavioral observations. *Pain Management Nursing, 8,* 77–85.

Huffman, J. C., & Kunik, M. E. (2000). Assessment and understanding of pain in patients with dementia. *The Gerontologist, 40*(5), 574-581.

McCaffery, M., & Beebe, A. (1989). *Pain: Clinical manual for nursing practice.* Philadelphia: Mosby.

Miller, L. L., Talerico, K. A., Rader, J., Swafford, K., Hiatt, S. O., Miller, S. M. et al. (2005). Development of an intervention to reduce pain in older adults with dementia. *Alzheimer's Care Quarterly, 6,* 154–167.

Panda, M., & Desbiens, N. A. (2001). Pain in elderly patients: How to achieve control. *Consultant, 41,* 1597–1604.

Price, D. D. (1988). *Psychological and neural mechanisms of pain.* New York: Raven Press.

Reiner, A., & Lacasse, C. (2006). Symptom correlates in the gero-oncology population. *Seminars in Oncology Nursing, 22,* 20–30.

Sha, M. C., Callahan, C. M., Counsel, S. R., Westmoreland, G. R., Stump, T. E., & Kroenke, K., (2005). Physical symptoms as a predictor of health care use and mortality among older adults. *The American Journal of Medicine, 118*(3), 301–306.

Snow, A. L., Weber, J. B., O'Malley, K. J., Cody, M., Beck, C., Bruera, E. et al. (2004). NOPPAIN: A Nursing assistant-administered pain assessment instrument for use in dementia. *Dementia and Geriatric Cognitive Disorders, 17,* 240–246.

Taylor, L. J., Harris, J., Epps, C. D., & Herr, K. (2005). Psychometric evaluation of selected pain intensity scales for use with cognitively impaired and cognitively intact older adults. *Rehabilitation Nursing, 30,* 55–61.

Warden, V., Hurley, A. C., & Volicer, L. (2003). Development and psychometric evaluation of the Pain Assessment in Advanced Dementia (PAINAD) scale. *Journal of the American Medical Directors Association, 4,* 9–15.

***Ann L. Horgas***
***Amanda F. Elliott***

# PARENT-CHILD RELATIONSHIPS, LATER LIFE

Relationships with adult children are among the most significant sources of emotional support and assistance for older persons, particularly for the widowed. The components of the relationship include the extent of contact and emotional support, exchange and assistance, and sometimes coresidence. Researchers have most commonly studied these bonds in terms of the positive association between parents and children but more recently are recognizing the potential for the simultaneous existence of conflict and ambivalence.

## SHARED AFFECTION AND CONTACT

Shared affection and contact are the cornerstones of intergenerational relationships. Most older persons have at least one child living nearby. Among those who do not live with their child, approximately three-quarters live within a 35-minute drive of at least one, and half have two children within this geographic range (Lin & Rogerson, 1995). Nearly 80% report weekly contact with at least one of their children. However, not all children live close by, and distant living is also common for elderly parents and adult children. Among those elders born prior to World War I, one quarter have no living child closer than 100 to 200 miles, and half have at least one child living more than 200 miles away (Climo, 1992). "Distant" children, those who are not geographically proximate, may not see their parents frequently, but the quality of the parent–child relationship is just as high as for those who live near one another (Rossi & Rossi, 1990). In other words, distance does not erode the relationship. The typical distant child visits twice per year. Whereas only 10% visit less than once per year, one-third visit three times per year or more. Average visits last for four days but range from one day to six weeks (Climo, 1992).

Scholars have identified three types of parent–child relationships: tight-knit, sociable, and detached. The most common types are the tight-knit and sociable. Tight-knit relationships are characterized by high levels of affection, opportunity to see one another, and exchange of resources. Sociable relationships also have high affection and opportunity to see one another but do not include an exchange of resources. However, tight-knit relationships are more common with mothers than fathers (31% of relationships with mothers versus 20% of relationships with fathers are tight-knit whereas 28% of relationships with mothers and 23% of relationships with fathers are sociable). In addition, relationships with fathers are more likely to be detached than relationships with mothers (27% versus 7%). These ties are characterized by low affection, few opportunities to see one another, and low exchange of resources. With increasing age, children and parents are more likely to have relationships that are sociable rather than tight-knit, reflecting a decrease in exchange of resources from parents to children (Connidis, 2001).

Intergenerational relationships tend to be heavily gendered. Women of both generations are more likely than men to maintain intergenerational relationships across adulthood (Fingerman, 2003). Overall children tend to feel closer to their mothers than to their fathers, and daughters report closer ties to both parents than do sons (Rossi & Rossi, 1990). In addition, women consistently express stronger filial norms than men from young adulthood to old age (Gans & Silverstein, 2006). However, gender differences in parental perceptions of relationships with sons and daughters are eliminated once a within-family analysis is used in current generations of parents whose first-born children are in middle school (Proulx & Helms, 2008). That is, few gender differences emerge in parents' perceptions of continuities and changes in their relationships with first-born children within individual families.

## EXCHANGE AND ASSISTANCE

Parents and adult children give and receive different resources. The flow of *financial* aid and services (such as babysitting) tends to be unidirectional, from parents to children. In contrast, parents seek companionship, appreciation, affection, and care giving from their children. Once adult children are married, the wife's parents tend to provide and receive more assistance than the husband's parents (Goetting, 1990; Lee, Spitze, & Logan, 2003; Shuey & Hardy, 2003). This is the result of parent–child relationships being embedded in a larger system of gender relationships, as discussed earlier (Proulx & Helms, 2008; Shuey & Hardy, 2003). Parental aid to married

***Woman Feeds Her Father.*** *Children often become caregivers to their elderly parents.* ED KASHI/CORBIS.

children is most concentrated in the early years of marriage and decreases over time as adult children become more self-sufficient. Services to adult children tend to be highest when grandchildren are preschool age and in need of babysitting (Goetting, 1990).

Reciprocity tends to be at the root of filial responsibility. Adult children provide care for their elderly parents in exchange for all of the assistance and care that their parents gave to them while growing up (Connidis, 2001). Research from the early 2000s suggests, however, that filial norms tend to weaken after mid-life (Gans & Silverstein, 2006). They may peak at mid-life as a manifestation of filial maturity and then decrease as a result of parent care anxiety and an altruistic desire to spare younger generations from the burden of parent care. Whereas filial norms have weakened over historical time, they also have been strengthened recently in later-born generations: The baby boom generation that reached mid-life in the 1990s was more familistic than the period that they aged into, despite the opposite historical trend of weakening norms across time (Gans & Silverstein, 2006). This may be the beginning of continued high levels of familism in the subsequent generations..

CORESIDENCE

Shared living arrangements are a third component of parent and adult child relationships. Approximately 16% of parents 60 years of age and older live with an adult child. However, these rates increase significantly beyond the age of 75 for women and age 80 for men and are highest for mothers over 90 years of age (Schmertmann, Boyd, Serow, & White, 2000). Older parents are more likely to move in with a child, usually a daughter, following a decline in health, income losses, or the loss of a former caregiver or spouse. Parents may also move in with children due to a desire for companionship (Wilmoth, 2000).

Contrary to popular expectations, coresidence is more a function of adult children living with parents than vice-versa. An adult child's need for support is a key motivator for living with parents. The growing trend for adult children to return to their parent's home has been termed the *refilling of the empty nest.* Returning home is considered appropriate for a divorced daughter, both with and without children, and for the period between finishing college and starting a full-time job or following unemployment (Mitchell, 2000). Children who return home are expected to save their money and eventually seek independence. Coresident children also tend to provide more assistance to parents than those living on their own (White & Rogers, 1997). However, living together tends to increase strain between parents and adult children, particularly for younger children who are unemployed (White & Rogers, 1997).

## WHY ARE THEY IMPORTANT TO STUDY?

Relationships with one's parents and children are among the most important relationships that adults experience. Among a variety of types of relationships, adults rated their relationships with their parents and children as having the highest levels of obligation (Rossi & Rossi, 1990). They are a central source of satisfaction across the life course and, along with marriage, form the bedrock of the family. This is evidenced by the fact that adults most often spend holidays and major celebrations with their parents (or parents-in-law) and children (Merrill, 2007). As stated earlier, parents and adult children are also an important source of exchange and assistance to one another. Parents are the most likely sources of financial assistance and help with babysitting to adult children and their families while they are gaining independence. Likewise, as parents grow older, it is their adult children who are most likely to provide companionship and assistance to them as they become more limited in the tasks that they can perform.

Relationships between mothers and adult daughters are the most widely studied of the intergenerational relationships (Fingerman, 2003). This is a reflection of women's continued kin-keeping roles in the family and the relative importance of family in women's lives. These relationships are believed to be closer than any other family bonds. Studies focus on communication between mothers and daughters and even on mother-in-law and daughter-in-law relationships (Merrill, 2007).

## TRENDS AND PATTERNS

The exchange of resources between parents and their adult children differ somewhat by race and class. Whereas parents from the middle class are more likely to provide financial help to their adult children, working-class families are more likely to provide hands-on services to one another such as babysitting for grandchildren and caring for elderly family members. Coresidence, whether with parents or parents-in-law, is also more common in the working class due to reduced incomes (Goetting, 1990). Black and White children are more likely to help their parents financially relative to Hispanic children even when holding income constant (Wong, Capoferro, & Soldo, 1999). In addition, Asian Americans and African Americans endorse norms of intergenerational assistance to older kin more than do European Americans and Latinos (Coleman, Ganong, & Rothrauff, 2006).

Support and affective ties also change over the life course. Support to adult children is at its peak when grandchildren are preschool age and adult children need greater assistance. Parents assume and expect that their adult children will become increasingly independent as they grow older. Affection between parents and children is at its lowest when children are adolescents and then peaks when children are in their 20s. It drops off slightly again before leveling off when children are in their 30s (Rossi & Rossi, 1990). For both parents and adult children, one's satisfaction in the relationship is strongly associated with the belief that the other person is independent.

There has been an historical trend toward an increase in the number of years that parents and adult children spend with one another, due to an increase in life expectancy. Longer life expectancy also has resulted in an increase in the number of generations living at any one time. However, there has not been the expected increase to four or five generations living simultaneously, due to older ages at marriage and at first birth among recent cohorts of adults (Connidis, 2001).

## THEORIES OF INTERGENERATIONAL RELATIONSHIPS

The main theory driving research on parent and adult child relationships is referred to as the *intergenerational solidarity perspective*. This theory, which focuses on the solidarity or strength of intergenerational bonds, states that solidarity has six separate components:

1. associational solidarity (the type and frequency of interaction and activities);
2. structural solidarity (opportunities for and barriers to interaction);
3. functional solidarity (the exchange of assistance and support);
4. affectual solidarity (intimacy and distance);
5. consensual solidarity (the agreement between generations on opinions and values);
6. normative solidarity (the extent to which family members share expectations of family life).

Since its inception, however, scholars have criticized the model for its emphasis on family cohesion without recognition of conflict between parents and adult children. As a result, the model has been modified to become the *family solidarity-conflict model*. This version of the model recognizes that conflict is a normal aspect of family relations and that it influences both how family members perceive one another and their willingness to help one another (Bengtson, Giarrusso, Mabry, & Silverstein, 2002). Solidarity and conflict are not seen as separate ends of a single continuum, however. Family relationships can exhibit both high solidarity and high conflict simultaneously, or low solidarity and low conflict.

The most recent concept used in studying parent–child relationships in later life is referred to as *ambivalence* (Bengtson, Giarrusso, Mabry, & Silverstein, 2002; Connidis & McMullin, 2002). It refers to the contradictions in relationships such as the presence of both conflict and solidarity or positive and negative sentiments. Connidis and McMullin argued that life-course scholars need to examine conflict as a separate dimension of relationships beyond incorporating it into normative assumptions of solidarity. For example, they argued that there is conflict embedded in the social structure, such as the organization of family and work based on gender, which affects relationships.

## THE FUTURE

Parent–child relationships in later life are different from earlier stages in the life course. They are affected by a long joint history and a shared experience of life-course stages. Parents and children share a history of fulfilling support and exchange of resources to one another, although norms of filial obligation decrease after adults reach mid-life. Filial anxiety about care-giving may increase in the future if older parents and spouses need assistance simultaneously.

Family relationships, including those between parents and children, are growing more complex in recent generations, given the high levels of divorce and remarriage. Now family members have not only their own biological parents and children to turn to in their kin network but also a growing web of stepparents and stepchildren as well as both current and former in-laws. Research on parent and adult children relationships is moving in the direction of examining the nature of such bonds and differences in support and exchange as a result (Lee, Spitze, & Logan, 2003). For example, although a good deal is known about relationships between young children and their stepparents, there is far less information about those relationships in later life or about relationships with newly married older parents and their partners.

In the future, research will look more toward the overlapping life trajectories of parents and their adult children. As parents and adult children live longer, they share more life-course experiences such as grandparenthood. Adult children will also have more years with healthy elders than ever before, which may result in interesting new findings in parent–child relationships.

**SEE ALSO** Volume 3: *Caregiving; Family and Household Structure, Later Life; Grandparenthood; Intergenerational Transfers.*

## BIBLIOGRAPHY


Bengtson, V. L., Giarrusso, R., Mabry, J. B., & Silverstein, M. (2002). Solidarity, conflict and ambivalence: Complementary or competing perspectives on intergenerational relationships? *Journal of Marriage and the Family, 64*, 568–576.

Climo, J. (1992). *Distant parents.* New Brunswick, NJ: Rutgers University Press.

Coleman, M., Ganong, L. H., & Rothrauff, T. C. (2006). Racial and ethnic similarities and differences in beliefs about intergenerational assistance to older adults after divorce and remarriage. *Family Relations, 55,* 576–587.

Connidis, I. A. (2001). *Family ties and aging.* Thousand Oaks, CA: Sage.

Connidis, I. A., & McMullin, J. A. (2002). Sociological ambivalence and family ties: A critical perspective. *Journal of Marriage and the Family, 64*, 558–567.

Fingerman, K. L. (2003). *Mothers and their adult daughters.* Amherst, NY: Prometheus Books.

Gans, D., & Silverstein, M. (2006). Norms of filial responsibility for aging parents across time and generations. *Journal of Marriage and the Family, 68*(4), 961–976.

Goetting, A. (1990). Patterns of support among in-laws in the United States. *Journal of Family Issues, 11*(1), 67–90.

Lee, E., Spitze, G., & Logan, J. R. (2003). Social support to parents-in-law: The interplay of gender and kin hierarchies. *Journal of Marriage and the Family, 65*, 396–403.

Lin, G., & Rogerson, P. (1995). Elderly parents and the geographic availability of their adult children. *Research on Aging, 17*(3), 303–331.

Merrill, D. M. (2007). *Mothers-in-law and daughters-in-law: Understanding the relationship and what makes them friends or foe.* Westport, CT: Praeger.

Mitchell, B. A. (2000). The refilled "nest": Debunking the myth of families in crisis. In E. M. Gee & G. M. Guttman (eds.), *The overselling of population aging: Apocalyptic demography, intergenerational challenges, and social policy* (pp. 80–99). Don Mills, Ontario: Oxford University Press.

Norgard, T. M., & Rodgers, W. L. (1997). Patterns of in-home care among elderly Black and White Americans. *Journal of Gerontology: Social Sciences, 52B*, S93–S101.

Proulx, C. M., & Helms, H. M. (2008). Mothers' and fathers' perceptions of change and continuity in their relationships with young adult sons and daughters. *Journal of Family Issues, 29*(2), 234–261.

Rossi, A. S., & Rossi, P. H. (1990). *Of human bonding Parent–child relations across the life course.* New York: Aldine de Gruyter.

Schmertmann, C. P., Boyd, M., Serow, W., & White, D. (2000). Elder-child coresidence in the United States: Evidence from the 1990 census. *Research on Aging, 22*(1), 23–42.

Shuey, K., & Hardy, M. A. (2003). Assistance to aging parents and parents-in-law: Does lineage affect family allocation decisions? *Journal of Marriage and the Family 65*(2), 418–431.

White, L. K., & Rogers, S. L. (1997). Strong support but uneasy relationships: Coresidence and adult children's relationships with their parents. *Journal of Marriage and the Family, 59*(1), 62–76.

Wilmoth, J. M. (2000). Unbalanced social exchanges and living arrangement transitions among older adults. *The Gerontologist, 40*(1), 64–74.

Wong, R., Capoferro, C., & Soldo, B. J. (1999). Financial assistance from middle-aged couples to parents and children: Racial-ethnic differences. *Journal of Gerontology: Social Sciences, 54B*(3), S145–S153.

**_Deborah M. Merrill_**

# PENSIONS

Pension plans are fringe benefits offered by some employers to provide workers with cash payments on retirement. In 2006 about 24% of Americans age 65 and older received pension benefits from past private-sector employers, and about 11% received benefits from past public-sector employers (Purcell, 2007a). Median annual benefits in 2006 were about $7,200 among older adults receiving private pensions and $14,400 for those receiving pensions from government employers (Purcell, 2007a).

Two basic types of employer-sponsored pension plans are now prevalent. Defined benefit (DB) plans, formerly the most common type, promise specific monthly retirement benefits that usually continue until one's death. Defined contribution (DC) plans, which are now more common, function essentially as individual tax-deferred retirement savings accounts to which both employers and employees usually contribute. Cash balance plans are hybrids that combine features of DB and DC plans. Each plan type affects individual retirement incomes and employer costs differently and raises distinct research and policy issues.

## HOW BENEFITS ACCUMULATE

DB plans base payments on formulas that usually depend on earnings and the number of years an individual worked for his or her employer. A typical formula in the private sector sets annual benefits equal to 1% of average annual salary for each year of service. For example, someone who worked 25 years for an employer would earn 25% of his or her salary during retirement. Most public-sector plan formulas are more generous, with typical multipliers of around 1.5%. Sometimes the earnings base includes all years that the participant worked for the employer, but more commonly it includes only the most recent years, such as the past five. A few plans set benefit payments equal to some fixed annual amount per year of service, regardless of earnings.

DC plans do not promise specific retirement benefits. Instead, employers that provide 401(k)-type plans—the most common type of DC plan—contribute to a retirement account in the participant's name; the amount of the contribution is typically a specific percentage of salary. Other DC plans include deferred profit-sharing plans and employee stock ownership plans. Only private for-profit firms may offer 401(k) plans, named after the section of the tax code that governs them. Equivalent plans are known as 403(b) plans in the nonprofit sector and 457(b) plans in the public sector. Employees may also contribute to their retirement accounts and defer taxes on their contributions until they withdraw funds from their accounts. Employer contributions sometimes depend on how much the participant contributes. For example, some employers match worker contributions up to a specific amount, providing few benefits to employees who contribute little to their retirement plans. Account balances grow over time with contributions and investment returns.

Hybrid pension plans combine features of DB and DC plans. In cash balance plans, the most common type of hybrid plan, employers set aside a given percentage of salary for each employee and credit interest on these contributions. Interest credit rates are generally tied to some benchmark, such as the U.S. treasury bill rate. Benefits are expressed as an account balance, as in DC plans, but these balances are only bookkeeping devices. Plans pay benefits from funds invested in a pension trust on behalf of all participants.

In all plan types, participants must usually remain with the employer a specific number of years before their benefits *vest*, meaning that ownership transfers from the employer to the employee. Federal law limits the vesting period. According to the Employee Retirement Income Security Act (ERISA) of 1974, benefits in most private-sector DB and hybrid plans must fully vest within 5 years if vesting occurs all at once or 7 years if it occurs gradually over time. In private-sector DC plans, employer contributions must fully vest within 3 years, or 6 years if vesting occurs gradually. Employee contributions, however, vest immediately and never revert back to the employer. Federal law does not limit vesting periods in state and local government plans; 5- or 10-year vesting is common in the public sector.

## BENEFIT RECEIPT

DB plan benefits are generally paid in monthly installments to retirees who have reached the plan's eligibility age and continue until the retiree's death. Surviving spouses also receive benefits unless both partners waive survivor protection in exchange for higher payouts while the plan participant is alive. Federal law generally requires DB plans to offer these payment schemes, known as lifetime annuities, although some DB plan sponsors permit retirees to receive benefits as lump-sum payments. Few private-sector plans adjust benefits paid during retirement for inflation, so that the pension's purchasing power plunges over time for many retirees. If the price level increases 3% every year, for example, the real value of the pension benefit received at age 80 for a retiree who began collecting at age 60 would amount to only 55% of the original benefit's value. However, cost-of-living escalators that increase annual pension payments at the same rate as the growth in the consumer price index are common in the public sector. Most DB plans also pay reduced benefits to participants who retire before the plan's normal retirement age and have reached the early retirement age set by the plan. (Some employers offer disability benefits to employees who are forced by health problems to stop working before reaching retirement age, but these plans are less common than retirement plans.)

Cash balance plans must also offer a lifetime annuity with an expected value equal to the participant's account balance. Most participants, however, choose to receive their benefits as lump-sum distributions (Schieber, 2003).

DC plan beneficiaries receive the funds that have accumulated in their accounts, generally as lump-sum distributions—either a one-time payment or a series of payments over a set period. Few DC plan sponsors offer annuities. Beneficiaries can use their account balances to purchase an annuity from an insurance company, but few people do so, partly because the terms offered by insurance companies are not very favorable.

DC plan participants can collect whenever they separate from the employer. Distributions received before age 59 and one-half years, however, are subject to a 10-percent penalty, unless they are rolled over into an Individual Retirement Account (IRA) or lifetime annuity. Many plans allow departing employees to keep their balances in the plan and withdraw at a later date. People must begin withdrawing from their 401(k) plans after they reach age 70 and one-half years, unless they are still working.

Benefits from DB, cash balance, and DC plans are generally subject to ordinary income tax when they are received. Participants may, however, deduct any after-tax contributions they made to the plan.

## COVERAGE RATES

In 2007, 51% of private-sector workers—about 57 million people—participated in employer-sponsored retirement plans (Bureau of Labor Statistics [BLS], 2007b). (This total excludes the self-employed, workers in private households, and government workers.)

In the public sector, pension coverage is nearly universal (Munnell & Soto, 2007a). Private-sector coverage rates are higher among unionized workers and full-time workers and lower among low-wage workers, Blacks, and Hispanics, who are more likely to work in less-skilled occupations than other social groups. In 2006, for example, 55% of non-Hispanic Whites participated in employer-sponsored pension plans, compared with only about 44% of Blacks and 28% of Hispanics (Purcell, 2007b). Coverage rates are similar for men and women.

## CHANGES IN COVERAGE

Although overall pension coverage rates among private-sector workers remained fairly steady over the last quarter of the 20th century, a dramatic shift from DB to DC plans took place. Between 1980 and 2007, the share of private-sector workers participating in DB plans fell from 39 to 20%, whereas the share participating in only DC plans increased from 8% to 31%. Assets in private DC plans nearly doubled between 1997 and 2007, growing from $2.3 trillion to $4.4 trillion, whereas private DB plan assets increased only modestly, rising from $1.8 trillion to $2.4 trillion (Investment Company Institute, 2007). Private-sector DB plan coverage remains high, however, among unionized workers (67%) and workers in firms with 100 or more employees (32%; BLS, 2007b). The decline in the heavily unionized manufacturing sector, increases in the administrative costs of complying with the complex federal regulations that govern DB plans, and accounting rule changes that now require employers to report pension liabilities on their balance sheets have contributed to the erosion in DB plan coverage (Gustman & Steinmeier, 1992; Munnell & Soto, 2007b; Munnell & Sunden, 2004).

Conversions to cash balance plans, which are classified as DB plans for legal and regulatory purposes, have compounded the decline in traditional DB plans. Cash balance plans, which did not exist before 1985, provided coverage for 23% of all private-sector workers in DB plans in 2005 (BLS, 2007a).

DB plans continue to dominate in the public sector, which employs about one sixth of the workforce. In 2004, 86% of state and local government employees and nearly all federal government employees participated in defined benefit plans (Munnell & Soto, 2007a). The federal government and some state and local governments also offer supplemental DC plans. As of 2007, recent efforts by some jurisdictions, including the state of California, to move to DC plans have not been very successful, primarily because of the opposition of powerful public unions.

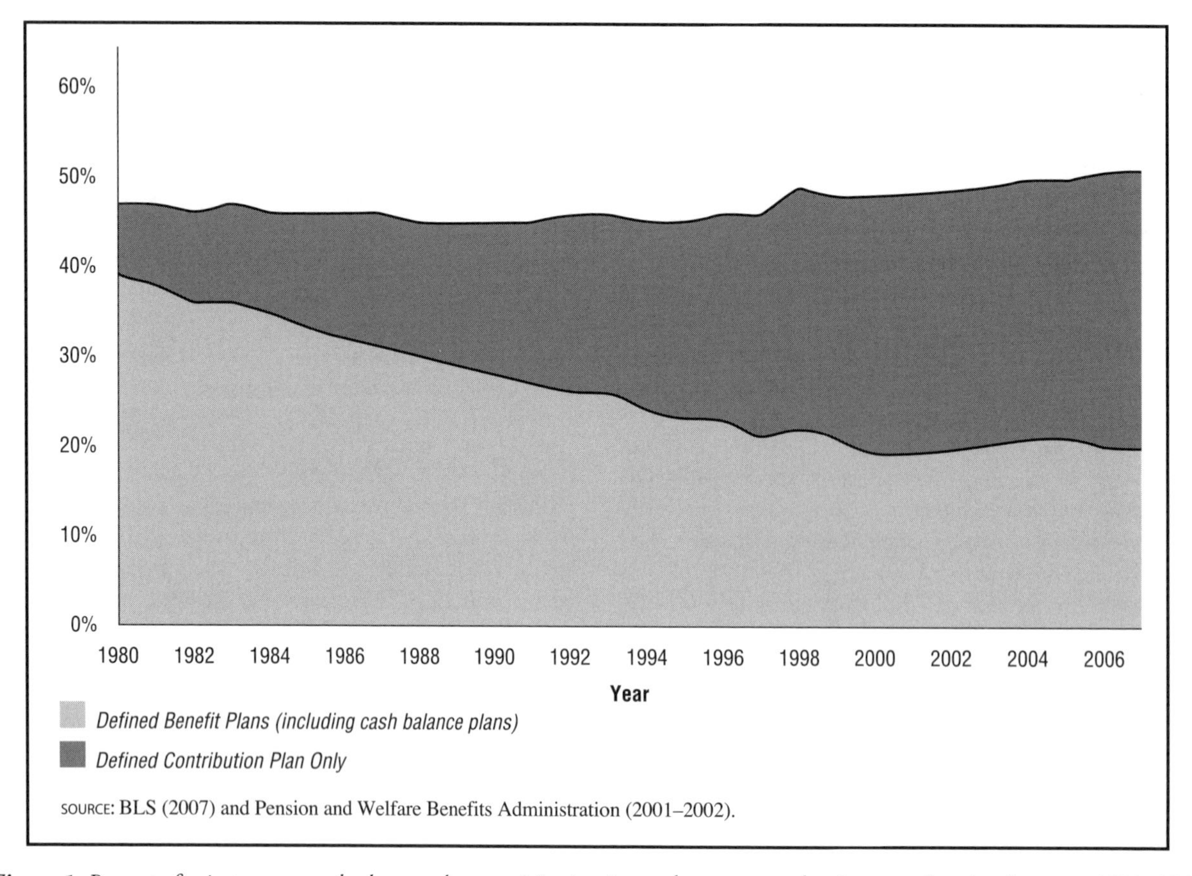


SOURCE: BLS (2007) and Pension and Welfare Benefits Administration (2001–2002).

***Figure 1.*** *Percent of private wage and salary workers participating in employer-sponsored retirement plan, by plan type, 1980–2007.* CENGAGE LEARNING, GALE.

## KEY RESEARCH ISSUES

An important research question is the impact of pensions on retirement decisions. Most traditional DB plans, which became popular in the 1960s and 1970s when many employers wished to hire younger, lower-paid workers, encourage early retirement, and penalize workers who remain on the job after they become eligible to receive pension benefits. DB benefit formulas typically pay more for more years of service, but workers forego a year of retirement benefits for every year that they remain on the job past the plan's retirement age. The increase in annual benefits from an additional work year does not fully offset the loss from the reduction in the number of pension payments, thus lowering lifetime benefits. These retirement incentives are becoming counterproductive as the workforce ages and firms strive to retain older workers.

DC and cash balance plans do not discourage work at older ages because they express benefits as account balances that can continue to grow throughout the worker's career. In fact, workers in DC plans generally retire about 2 years later than those in DB plans (Friedberg & Webb, 2005).

Another key question is how the decline in traditional DB plans affects retirement security. There are advantages and disadvantages to both DB and DC plans, and the net effect of the shift to DC plans is not yet clear. By providing a guaranteed benefit that lasts from retirement to death, DB plans offer retirement income security for workers who remain with a single employer for most of their careers.

However, workers who often change employers and those with spotty work histories do not earn many benefits in DB plans. DB plan benefits accumulate rapidly in the years immediately before retirement age. Additional work years increase benefits by adding an additional percentage of pay and by raising the value of previously accumulated benefits by both real wage growth and inflation. Consider, for example, a worker with 30 years of tenure with her employer who earns $80,000 per year and participates in a DB plan that provides a pension equal to 1% of final salary for each year of service. If she works 1 more year at the same salary, her annual pension will increase by $800 (i.e., 1% of $80,000). If her salary increases by 5% the next year, then her annual pension will grow by $800, plus an additional $1,240 (5% of $80,000, multiplied by 0.31). Consequently, workers in DB plans generally lose substantial benefits if they are laid off or if the firm goes out of business late in their career. The federal government insures DB benefits that have already been earned (see sidebar on the Pension Benefit Guaranty Corporation), but participants forego the rapid run-up in pension benefits that they would have received if they remained employed until the plan's retirement age.

Workers in DC plans, by contrast, do not necessarily lose benefits if they change jobs because their account balances can continue earning investment returns after they separate from their employer. DC plans, then, are well suited to the early 21st century's increasingly mobile workforce.

DC plan participants face other kinds of risks, especially the uncertainty surrounding investment returns. Workers with bad investment luck or who make unwise choices may end up with little retirement income. Another drawback is that workers generally must sign up with their employer to participate in DC plans, and then they must agree to have funds withheld from their paycheck. Only 77% of eligible private-sector workers at firms that offer DC plans participated in 2007 (BLS, 2007b), and only 6% contributed the maximum amount allowed by law in 2003 (Kawachi, Smith, & Toder, 2006).

To accumulate substantial retirement savings, DC plan participants must also resist the temptation to cash in their account balances when they change jobs. For example, only 45% of people age 21 to 57 in 2003 who received a lump-sum distribution from an employer plan rolled any part of it into another retirement account (Verma & Lichtenstein, 2006).

DC plan retirees also run the risk of spending their balances too quickly, leaving them with inadequate income at very old ages, or spending too slowly and not making the most of their retirement savings (Butrica & Mermin, 2007). DB plan beneficiaries do not generally face these risks, because most receive lifetime annuities that provide regular monthly payments from retirement until death. Relatively few employers allow DC plan participants to convert their balances into lifetime annuities, and annuities purchased from insurance companies are expensive because only those people who live the longest tend to purchase them.

Although the growing popularity of cash balance plans among employers has been controversial, these plans may provide more retirement security than either DC plans or traditional DB plans (Johnson & Uccello, 2004). Unlike traditional DB plans, benefits in cash balance plans accumulate gradually over the course of the career, enabling workers who change jobs frequently to accumulate substantial retirement benefits. They also contain many of the advantages of traditional DB coverage, including automatic enrollment, federal government insurance of benefits, and mandatory annuity options for benefit payout. Additionally, benefits in cash balance plans are subject to less investment risk than DC balances.

## PENSION BENEFIT GUARANTY CORPORATION (PBGC)

The federal government's Pension Benefit Guaranty Corporation (PBGC) insures private-sector defined benefit (DB) plans, including hybrid plans, assuming responsibility for pension payments up to a certain amount if the employer declares bankruptcy. It does not insure defined contribution plans. In 2007, PBGC guaranteed annual DB plan benefits up to $49,500 per participant to those who began collecting at age 65, but less to those who collected earlier. In return, plan sponsors must pay PBGC monthly premiums and adhere to specific funding requirements by setting aside money each year to cover expected future benefits.

Because of certain exceptions to the funding rules, however, many private-sector plans are underfunded, with insufficient reserves to cover expected payouts. In 2006 the shortfall among underfunded single-employer plans totaled $350 billion, about 28% of total liabilities (PBGC, 2006). Increased underfunding by private-sector plans raises PBGC's expected liabilities, weakening the agency's financial position. In 2007, PBGC's assets fell $14.1 billion short of expected liabilities, an improvement over 2006. Nonetheless, employer bankruptcies could force the PBGC to assume responsibility for many unfunded pension liabilities, threatening the agency's solvency and raising the possibility of a taxpayer bailout. The 2006 Pension Protection Act (PPA) tightened funding requirements and increased the insurance premiums paid by plan sponsors to fund PBGC, improving the agency's financial outlook. Added regulation could lead more employers to terminate their DB plans and further undermine traditional pension coverage, however.

**BIBLIOGRAPHY**

Pension Benefit Guaranty Corporation. *Annual report.* Retrieved April 11, 2008, from http://www.pbgc.gov

## KEY POLICY ISSUES

Attention has focused on boosting retirement savings for the nearly two fifths of private-sector workers employed at firms that do not offer a retirement plan (BLS, 2007b). One approach has been the Saver's Credit, enacted by the U.S. Congress in 2001, which provides federal government matches of up to 50% of the first $2,000 in retirement savings by low-income adults. The government contribution, however, comes as a nonrefundable tax credit and thus does not benefit savers who do not earn enough to pay taxes.

Some proposals would expand the Saver's Credit by providing a refundable tax credit to low-income savers. Other proposals would require employers to allow workers to make payroll-deduction deposits to IRAs or 401(k) plans, perhaps with a government match. These proposals would not force employers to contribute.

Other efforts have focused on boosting DC plan participation and contributions among workers offered coverage by their employers. The 2006 Pension Protection Act (PPA) made it easier for employers to automatically enroll workers in DC plans, which can substantially increase participation rates (Choi, Laibson, Madrian, & Metrick, 2004; Gale, Iwry, & Orszag, 2006). Only about one third of employers automatically enrolled participants in 2007, although about half of remaining employers said they were at least somewhat likely to do so in the coming year (Hewitt Associates, 2007).

PPA also made recent increases in 401(k)-plan contribution limits permanent. In 2008 individuals may contribute up to $15,500 per year to their 401(k) plans, and participants age 50 and older may contribute an additional $5,000. Some argue that these limits should be raised even higher, but higher contribution limits do not appear to boost savings much (Kawachi et al., 2006). About 70% of the tax benefits from new DC-plan contributions in 2004 went to taxpayers in the top 20% of the income distribution, and more than half went to the top 10% (Burman, Gale, Hall, & Orszag, 2004).

Because few DC plans allow participants to collect their benefits as lifetime annuities, the decline in DB plan coverage may substantially reduce the future number of retirees with guaranteed payment streams outside of Social Security. One solution might be to promote deferred annuities that do not begin making payments until age 80 or 85 but then continue until one's death, insuring people against the risk of running out of money if they live to a very old age.

Improved financial literacy—people's ability to make appropriate decisions in managing their personal finances—is an important goal. As responsibility for retirement planning falls increasingly on families and individuals, the ability to make informed financial decisions is becoming more urgent. People need to decide how much to save in DC plans, how to invest their contributions, and how to convert their account balances into payment streams that will support them in retirement. Yet, only 43% of surveyed workers in 2007 said they have tried calculating how much money they will need for retirement, and many appear to underestimate retirement needs (Employee Benefit Research Institute, 2007). Financial literacy, generally measured by knowledge of financial terms and concepts, is particularly low among Blacks, Hispanics, and people with limited education. Better access to professional investment advice at work could improve retirement planning.

Other related policy initiatives have centered on efforts to improve phased retirement options. Many workers say they would prefer to switch to part-time work with their current employer as they grow older, rather than moving directly from full-time work to complete retirement (American Association of Retired Persons, 2003). However, few workers can afford to cut back their hours without collecting retirement benefits. Federal law limits employers' ability to make DB plan payments to active workers. PPA eased these restrictions, but most employers are still unable to pay DB plan benefits to workers on the payroll younger than age 62.

**SEE ALSO** Volume 3: *Policy, Later Life Well-Being; Retirement; Social Security; Wealth.*

**BIBLIOGRAPHY**


American Association of Retired Persons. (2003). *Staying ahead of the curve 2003: The AARP working in retirement study.* Washington, DC: Author.

Bureau of Labor Statistics. (2007a). *National Compensation Survey: Employee benefits in private industry in the United States, 2005.* Washington, DC: U.S. Department of Labor. Retrieved March 19, 2008, from http://www.bls.gov/ncs/

Bureau of Labor Statistics. (2007b). *National Compensation Survey: Employee benefits in private industry in the United States, March 2007.* Washington, DC: U.S. Department of Labor. Retrieved March 19, 2008, from http://www.bls.gov/ncs/

Burman, L. E., Gale, W. G., Hall, M., & Orszag, P. R. (2004). *Distributional effects of defined contribution plans and individual retirement accounts.* Washington, DC: Urban-Brookings Tax Policy Center.

Butrica, B. A., & Mermin, G. B. T. (2007). Do annuities help older Americans manage their spending? *Older Americans Economic Security Brief, 14.* Washington, DC: Urban Institute.

Choi, J., Laibson D., Madrian, B. C., & Metrick, A. (2004). For better or for worse: Default effects and 401(k) savings behavior. In D. A. Wise (Ed.), *Perspectives on the economics of aging* (pp. 81–121). Chicago: University of Chicago Press.

Employee Benefit Research Institute. (2007). *The retirement system in transition: The 2007 Retirement Confidence Survey* (Issue Brief No. 304). Washington, DC: Author. Retrieved February 24, 2008, from http://www.ebri.org/pdf

Friedberg, L., & Webb, A. (2005). Retirement and the evolution of pension structure. *Journal of Human Resources, 40*(2), 281–308.

Gale, W. G., Iwry, J. M., & Orszag, P. R. (2006). The automatic 401(k): A simple way to strengthen retirement security. In P. R. Orszag, J. M. Iwry, & W. G. Gale (Eds.), *Aging gracefully: Ideas to improve retirement security in America* (pp. 19–32). New York: Century Foundation Press.

Gustman, A. L., & Steinmeier, T. L. (1992). The stampede toward defined contribution pension plans: Fact or fiction? *Industrial Relations, 31*(2), 361–369.

Hewitt Associates. (2007). *Trends and experience in 401(k) plans.* Lincolnshire, IL: Author.

Investment Company Institute. (2007). *The U.S. retirement market, second quarter 2007.* Retrieved February 24, 2008, from http://www.ici.org/stats

Johnson, R. W., & Uccello, C. E. (2004). Cash balance plans: What do they mean for retirement security? *National Tax Journal, 62*(2, Part 1), 315–328.

Kawachi, J., Smith K. E., & Toder, E. J. (2006). *Making maximum use of tax-deferred retirement accounts.* Washington, DC: The Urban Institute. Retrieved February 24, 2008, from http://www.urban.org

Munnell, A. H., & Soto, M. (2007a). State and local pensions are different from private plans. *State and Local Pension Plans, 1.* Retrieved February 24, 2008, from http://crr.bc.edu

Munnell, A. H., & Soto, M. (2007b). *Why are companies freezing their pensions?* Retrieved March 19, 2008, from http://crr.bc.edu

Munnell, A. H., & Sunden, A. (2004). *Coming up short: The challenge of 401(k) plans.* Washington, DC: Brookings Institution Press.

Purcell, P. (2007a). *Income and poverty among older Americans in 2006.* Washington, DC: Congressional Research Service.

Purcell, P. (2007b). *Pension sponsorship and participation: Summary of recent trends.* Washington, DC: Congressional Research Service.

Schieber, S. (2003). *The shift to hybrid pensions by U.S. employers: An empirical analysis of actual plan conversions.* Pension Research Council Working Paper No. 2003-23. Retrieved February 24, 2008, from http://rider.wharton.upenn.edu/

Verma, S., & Lichtenstein, J. (2006). *Pension lump-sum distributions: Do boomers take them or save them?* Retrieved February 24, 2008, from http://assets.aarp.org/rgcenter/

***Richard W. Johnson***

# POLICY, LATER LIFE WELL-BEING

The well-being of older adults is a consequence of lifetime experiences and may be shaped by such policies as public pensions and health insurance programs. Such policies contribute to the health and economic security of older people by instilling confidence that the resources one needs to maintain optimal levels of health and independence are available and secure. These policies include a range of public programs that depend on revenue (taxation) to (re)distribute income and provide services through public expenditures, with such programs generally comprising the largest social programs of national *welfare states,* both in the United States and throughout other developed countries as well.

Income security requires having sufficient income to meet individual needs and some discretionary purchases from a combination of public and private sources. National public pension systems, such as Social Security in the United States, provide direct universal benefits to pensioners in the form of regular guaranteed income (Social Security Administration, 2007). Income support to alleviate poverty is also a feature of many public pensions systems, usually provided through means-tested programs such as Supplemental Security Income (SSI) in the United States. Unlike universal entitlement to benefits under social insurance, eligibility for poverty-based programs usually requires individuals to meet a means-test by proving they have no resources to support themselves—virtually no assets of their own and insufficient income to meet subsistence needs—often a highly bureaucratic and demeaning process.

In most countries, tax policies provide an important source of fiscal welfare by offering preferential tax treatment for certain behaviors governments want to encourage, such as saving for children's higher education or retirement, buying health or long-term care insurance, or purchasing a home. For example, this includes lowering taxes on personal income (known as tax expenditures or tax subsidies) for working-age individuals who save for retirement in particular types of tax-sheltered accounts (e.g., IRAs, 401(k) plans) or who participate in private-sector pension plans (U.S. Congress, 1999). Governments also insure and regulate private pension plans to ensure that private-sector employers can meet current and future pension obligations. Because the institution of retirement depends on having sufficient income to sustain consumption in old age, policies that determine the generosity and stability of both public and private pensions are critical components to late-life well-being for all but the wealthiest older individuals.

As people grow older, the onset of age-related and chronic conditions increases their need for routine access to affordable medical care, making national health insurance an important factor in health security. In most developed countries, health insurance is universal. In the United States, however, eligibility for public health insurance is based on age. Medicare was designed to provide insurance coverage for medical care delivered to individuals 65 and older (Moon, 2006). Very frail older individuals may also require long-term care to sustain their well-being at the highest possible levels. Consequently, most countries have publicly funded long-term care policies, although such programs are usually more fragmented and less comprehensive than public health insurance and pension programs. In the United States, only poor individuals are entitled to publicly funded long-term care. Medicaid, a means-tested insurance program, expends nearly half of its public funding to pay for long-term care for poor elders. Because care is so expensive—more than $75,000 annually in 2008—even many middle income individuals who pay their own way when they enter a nursing home consume a lifetime of savings fairly quickly to pay for their care. Individuals admitted to nursing homes who must sell their homes and use up their entire savings are described as "spending down" to poverty; impoverishment must occur before they qualify for means-tested assistance for nursing home care under Medicaid.

Each country's welfare state represents its unique combination of policies designed to improve its citizens' social welfare; policies that address late-life well-being are no different in that regard. Among the many differences within countries and across nation-specific policies are: (a) the basis for claiming the benefit (age or need); (b) the basis of eligibility (through contributions or payroll taxes as a worker, through general taxation as a citizen, or as the dependent spouse, partner, or child of a beneficiary); (c) whether the program is *universal* and delivers valuable benefits for all income groups (e.g., Social Security, Medicare) or *selective*, targeted to provide benefits only for individuals with low income (e.g., Medicaid, SSI); and (d) the scope and generosity of benefits delivered. The public/private mix of benefits—that is, the proportion of benefits paid through public programs or through private-sector arrangements—are other policy choices that shape the character of welfare states and, by extension, late-life well-being (Béland & Gran, in press).

Rules governing the three main types of welfare state programs—social insurance, social assistance, and fiscal welfare—determine who pays for benefits and who gets benefits, and the generosity of benefits individuals receive. Age is often used with other criteria to establish eligibility for public benefits. Social Security, for example, at its inception required beneficiaries to be at least 65 years old to be automatically eligible for benefits that were linked to prior earnings and length of work history. To ensure that older workers did indeed retire, however, a strict earnings test for anyone under the age of 70 meant that if beneficiaries earned more than the allowable amount ($9,600 maximum for individuals taking early benefits from age 62–64, and $15,500 for individuals from ages 65–69 in 1999), Social Security benefits

| | Benefit type | Funding Source | Beneficiaries |
|---|---|---|---|
| **Social Assistance** | | | |
| Medicaid | Means-tested health insurance | General revenue, state taxes | Aged, blind, and disabled poor |
| Supplemental Security Income (SSI) | Means-tested cash income | General revenue | Aged, blind, and disabled poor |
| **Social Insurance** | | | |
| Medicare | Universal health insurance for the elderly | Payroll taxes | Social Security recipients and spouses aged 65 and older |
| Social Security | Universal cash pensions | Payroll taxes | Income for workers 62 and older and their dependents |
| **Fiscal Welfare** | | | |
| Tax expenditures for occupational pensions | Tax break for employees | General revenue | Workers in firms offering pensions |
| Tax expenditures for retirement savings | Tax break for income-earners | General revenue | Individuals who contribute to retirement savings accounts |
| Tax expenditures for mortgage interest | Tax break for homeowners | General revenue | Individuals who purchase homes |

SOURCE: Adapted from Quadagno (2008).

***Table 1.*** *Selected welfare state policies that impact late-life well being.* CENGAGE LEARNING, GALE.

would be forfeited. In 2000 the retirement test was eliminated for workers between the ages of 65 and 69, but remains in effect for individuals younger than normal retirement age (66 for individuals born from 1943 to 1954 and rising to 67 for individuals born in 1960 or later) with earnings from employment, and age remains a commonly used standard for Social Security entitlement and for other public benefits such as Medicare. For some means-tested benefits such as long-term care under Medicaid and income under SSI, a combination of age and means testing (targeting only low-income and low-asset individuals) determine eligibility.

## THE OLD-AGE WELFARE STATE

Social assistance policies such as SSI and Medicaid are critically important for the older poor individuals who receive them. For the vast majority of older individuals, however, late-life well-being depends on social insurance benefits such as Social Security and Medicare and the private income streams related to fiscal welfare that subsidize private-sector pensions and retirement savings (Quadagno, 2008). Policies (or their absence) are most fundamentally about who shoulders responsibility for late-life well-being: the state, the family, or the individual? (Uhlenberg, 1992). Throughout human history, most older individuals worked their entire lifetimes or depended on families for support in old age. Policies designed explicitly to enhance older adults' well-being are relatively recent, following the new risks and needs for older individuals that accompanied the shift from rural agriculture and household production to industrialized employment and urbanization. Mutual aid societies and some benevolent employers assisted displaced older workers when paid employment became impossible, from around the last two decades of the 19th century and for the first several decades of the 20th, but such piecemeal assistance could not keep pace with the need given the increased longevity and work/retirement patterns that developed in the 20th century (Uhlenberg, 1992). Wealthy industrialized countries made commitments to meet that need by creating public pensions systems, launching "the old-age welfare state" (Myles, 1989).

While the "old-age" welfare state refers mainly to national pension systems, maturing welfare states developed a range of public policies that contributed to late-life well-being as governments assumed collective responsibility for enhancing social welfare. Although national public pension programs were implemented at different times, ranging from the 1890s for Germany and New Zealand, to the 1930s for the "laggard" United States, by the early 1970s all developed countries had mature public pension systems and comprehensive welfare states, albeit with varying eligibility rules and generosity of benefits (Quadagno & Street, 2005). Welfare states' policies protected individuals and their families from the risks of lost income due to unemployment, disability, divorce, poor health, retirement, and the death of a parent or spouse. Such policies provide income and social services; they also structure social relations. Rules and policies determine eligibility for benefits, shaping the levels and forms of redistribution across social classes and within and across generations (Esping-Andersen, 1990). Welfare state policies that improve the social welfare and skill sets of younger individuals and their families set the stage for future well-being in old age (Street, 2007), even when they are not explicitly designed to do so.

## DEVELOPMENT OF THE OLD-AGE WELFARE STATE IN THE UNITED STATES

In the midst of the Great Depression, when more than half of older Americans were impoverished, President Franklin Roosevelt's New Deal ushered in the U.S. welfare state. Its cornerstone was the Social Security Act of 1935, the first national welfare program. It created two programs explicitly designed to address the income needs of older individuals: Social Security and Old Age Assistance. Old Age Assistance provided income for the aged poor, while Social Security, a contributory social insurance program, provided pensions for retired workers age 65 and older. From its outset, Social Security has been adapted to address changing risks and needs and was soon expanded to include benefits for widows and spouses of retired workers in 1937. By the 1950s Disability Insurance benefits were added, and in the 1970s changes to Social Security permitted retirement with reduced benefits at age 62.

Another major U.S. welfare state expansion during President Lyndon B. Johnson's War on Poverty directly affected older individuals when Medicare and Medicaid were created in 1965. Medicare, the federal health insurance program for older Americans, originally provided health insurance for physician visits and hospital stays. Lack of coverage for prescription drugs, and the costs of deductibles and co-pays, left potentially large out-of-pocket expenses for beneficiaries. Medicaid, a joint federal/state insurance program for the poor, uses age and need as criteria for entitlement. Its coverage of nursing home care is particularly important for older beneficiaries and has turned the program into the dominant payer of long-term care in the United States (Kaiser Family Foundation [KFF], 2007b). A more recent health-related policy expansion that affected late-life well-being was the 2003 passage of Medicare "Part D," which extended prescription drug coverage to older Americans (KFF, 2007a).

Medicare has always had deductibles, co-pays, and, more importantly, gaps in essential coverage that have had to be paid out of pocket, and Social Security was never intended as the sole source for retirement income. Retirement income security usually depends on additional income from private-sector pensions and/or individual retirement savings. Health security often requires benefits from other sources (either Medicaid or commercial Medigap insurance) to fill gaps in Medicare coverage for expensive health care. Tax expenditures play an important role in encouraging private, individual provision to enhance health and income security. For example, mortgage-interest tax subsidies help individuals become homeowners. The largest single asset for most individuals, a home, provides a source of wealth that can be used to augment retirement income, either by selling it or by taking out a reverse mortgage. For older individuals who are "house rich" and income poor, reverse mortgages provide the option of taking the equity value out of homes in the form of lump sum or monthly payments that depend on borrowing based on the value of the home and the age of the homeowner, while permitting the individual to remain in their home for their lifetimes. Other national fiscal welfare policies that influence security in later life include tax breaks for such private employment benefits as group health insurance and for income placed into private-sector pensions/retirement savings plans.

## CURRENT POLICY CONCERNS

Early public policies served as the foundations for the modern welfare states that addressed life course needs and risks of 20th century industrial economies. Current trends in demographic, political, economic, and social circumstances around the world are the basis for new debates on policies to meet 21st century needs for late-life well-being. Population aging, projections of program costs, and the size of public direct expenditure programs such as Social Security and Medicare have contributed to a sense of urgency about policy reform. High proportions of women in the paid labor market, changing family forms, patterns in men's employment that depart from traditional trajectories (less lifetime employment, shorter job tenures, low or stagnant wages), the impending retirement of the large baby boom cohort, and concerns about the housing and equity markets are all factors that contribute to uncertainty in the capacity of policy to meet new and evolving needs of the U.S. population. These concerns are further fueled by critics of public provision who prefer more private, market-based approaches. Recent trends in a political era dominated by neoliberals who advocate limited government and market solutions for social welfare have leaned toward reforming policies to move away from collective provision and toward more individual responsibility for late-life well-being (Ginn, Street, & Arber, 2001; Hacker, 2006; O'Rand, 2003).

While individual responsibility may be appealing on the surface, a deeper look reveals that many older adults, particularly women who are widowed or single and racial/ethnic minorities, have incomes below the poverty line. Such low incomes are often a function of disadvantages experienced over the life course, including structural race and gender disadvantages associated with lifelong employment opportunities (such as employment sector, wage level, and tenure) (Shuey & O'Rand, 2006). While Social Security addresses some of the problems associated with low lifetime incomes and periods out of paid work, gaps in publicly subsidized private pension coverage create categories of disadvantaged pensioners. Many public pension systems, developed when it was taken for granted that most women would receive pensions as dependents of employed breadwinning men, still fail to adequately address either women's increased employment or their disproportionate responsibility for unpaid care work (Harrington Meyer & Herd, 2007). Because it is normative for women to take time out of paid work to care for children and frail elders, they typically have lower lifetime earnings than men, and are disadvantaged in terms of later life income unless public policies take their socially necessary but unpaid care work into account. Realistically, adapting and reforming public pensions systems to compensate for the realities of women's typical life experiences will probably be necessary, because it would be unrealistic for private employers to take on that responsibility (Ginn, Street, & Arber, 2001).

Moreover, employers since the early 1990s have moved to replace traditional defined-benefit private pensions (which feature pooled risk-sharing and guaranteed benefits) with defined-contribution plans (which feature individual risk and uncertain benefits). Both potential sources of retirement income receive tax subsidies, yet a majority of workers lack private pension coverage altogether (Herd & Kingson, 2005). Although defined-contribution plans offer portability and ownership for a mobile workforce, they come with high risks. This is a particular concern when equity markets and housing markets are unsettled because it exposes individuals to potentially low retirement income in the wake of poor investment choices, inadequate levels of participation and savings (whether due to choice or a lack of surplus funds available for saving), or simple bad luck in equities markets, even if investment decisions are sound.

Advocates of preserving public programs such as Social Security and Medicare observe that they are an essential floor of protection to minimize poverty, preserve the quality and security of older individuals' lives, have low costs of program administration, share risks (by pooling all workers' contributions to provide somewhat higher rates of return for workers with lower lifetime incomes, and by insuring benefits for survivors and dependents, or for individuals who become disabled), and can adapt to meet future needs (Harrington Meyer, 2005; Herd & Kingson, 2005). Critics of large public expenditure programs raise the specter of impending bankruptcy in the face of population aging and highlight the potential for greater returns (and possibly higher retirement income) if individuals could channel their current Social Security payroll taxes to private investment instead.

While there are benefits and risks with both positions, one thing that is indisputable is that in the long run some adjustments will need to be made to the programs. Advocates of privatization, however, have been unable to dismantle public social insurance programs (Quadagno & Street, 2006). Proposals to reform social insurance programs such as Social Security to cope with population aging range from the incremental to the radical. Some reformers favor small adjustments to payroll tax rates, slowed benefit increases, or gradually raising the age of eligibility for benefits. Others prefer substantial privatization restricting public responsibility for late-life well-being to means-tested health and pension programs for low income individuals. While Medicare and Social Security will likely survive into the foreseeable future, health and income security in later life will undoubtedly depend on policy adjustments that meet 21st century realities.

## OTHER POLICIES AFFECTING LATE-LIFE WELL-BEING

Health and income security are profoundly influenced by the ways other modern welfare state policies interact with earlier life course experiences, shaping an individual's potential educational attainment, occupational status, employment history, and family status. Consequently, social welfare policies that address *needs* and *risks* for younger individuals are critically important to establish a foundation that can sustain well-being later in life, independent of the contributions of age-based programs such as Social Security and Medicare. Social policies that meet earlier *needs* such as high-quality education to prepare for employment opportunities that create surplus funds available for savings, or to create safe and affordable housing and communities, shape earlier life course experiences in ways that create opportunities for individuals to live the kinds of lives that increase their chances for a comfortable old age. So do social policies designed to mitigate some of the *risks* of working-age adults and their families. Unemployment insurance helps downsized workers (laid off from jobs in globalizing economies where unemployment risks are growing) to bridge the income gap until they find their next jobs, disability insurance sustains individuals who become unable to work, and health insurance provides immediate access to medical care for effective interventions when a person becomes sick or injured (Street, 2007). Earlier life course interventions have indirect effects on later life well-being, amplifying the effects of such policies as public pensions and health insurance.

Large government expenditure programs that are national in scope are obviously implicated in the quality of later life. Less obvious but important contributions are made by myriad policies implemented on a more modest scale. A few examples include:

- Local policies relating to the funding and comprehensiveness of public transportation, important when elders no longer drive;
- Policies influencing workplace issues, such as age discrimination, because many individuals reaching retirement age in uncertain economic times want the option to continue working; and
- Issues of home ownership affordability for seniors on fixed incomes, with concerns driven by escalating local property taxes.

## LATE-LIFE WELL-BEING IN THE FUTURE

Researchers recognize that the connections between the quality of later life and policies designed to enhance that quality are intertwined across levels of government and in a state of flux. Tensions between individual responsibility and collective provision are evident in most national debates about the interactions of age, need, and policy. Women's changing roles, population aging, burgeoning national debt, slowed growth of the domestic economy, uncertainty in equity and housing markets, and international insecurity create a very complex policymaking environment. Given unprecedented population aging, policy debate has too often centered myopically only on public policies that can be tweaked, stretched, or transformed to provide for soon-to-be-retiring baby boomers. Beyond public resistance to tax increases to fund public policies, complicated taxing and spending arrangements focus most policy attention on direct public expenditure programs, while obscuring the expense and inefficiencies created by using tax expenditures. Uncertain national economic conditions and the sheer size and complexity of policies that enhance the well-being of older adults create challenges for transforming and updating policies.

Despite ongoing debates about their merits, flaws, and affordability in the future, universal programs such as Social Security and Medicare are effective enough to create widespread, intergenerational, public support (Hudson, 2005; Street & Cossman, 2006; Williamson,

McNamara, & Howling, 2003). There is no doubt that public health and pension programs are expensive, but their payoff has been substantial. The public policies of modern welfare states have contributed to increased longevity, more stable retirement income, better access to health care and improved quality of life for older individuals throughout the developed world—precisely the payoffs to expect from large public investments in social welfare. While policies critical to late-life well-being will undoubtedly undergo policy changes in the future (as they have in the past), it seems unlikely they will be dismantled in the face of the obvious need for income and health security in old age. If retirement is to remain an institutionalized stage of the life course, policies that provide pension income and health insurance will remain essential.

**SEE ALSO** Volume 2: *Policy Health;* Volume 3: *Pensions; Poverty, Later Life; Health Care Use, Later Life; Long Term Care; Social Security.*

**BIBLIOGRAPHY**

Béland, D., & Gran, B. (Eds.). (2008). *Public and private social policy: Health and pension policies in a new era.* Houndmills, U. K.: Palgrave Macmillan.

Esping-Andersen, G. (1990). *The three worlds of welfare capitalism.* Princeton, NJ: Princeton University Press.

Ginn, J., Street, D., & Arber, S. (Eds.). (2001). *Women, work, and pensions: International issues and prospects.* Buckingham, U.K.: Open University Press.

Hacker, J. S. (2006). *The great risk shift: The assault on American jobs, families, health care, and retirement and how you can fight back.* Oxford, U.K.: Oxford University Press.

Harrington Meyer, M. (2005). Decreasing welfare, increasing old age inequality: Whose responsibility is it? In R. B. Hudson (Ed.), *The new politics of old age policy* (pp. 65–89). Baltimore, MD: Johns Hopkins University Press.

Harrington Meyer, M., & Herd, P. (2007). *Market friendly or family friendly? The state and gender inequality in old age.* New York; Russell Sage Foundation.

Herd, P., & Kingson, E. R. (2005). Reframing Social Security: Cures worse than the disease. In R. B. Hudson (Ed.), *The new politics of old age policy* (pp. 183–204). Baltimore, MD: Johns Hopkins University Press.

Hudson, R. B. (Ed.). (2005). *The new politics of old age policy.* Baltimore, MD: Johns Hopkins University Press.

Kaiser Family Foundation. (2007a, February). *Medicare at a glance.* Retrieved June 5, 2008, from http://www.kff.org/medicare/upload/1066-10.pdf

Kaiser Family Foundation. (2007b, October). *Medicaid enrollment and spending trends.* Retrieved June 5, 2008, from http://www.kff.org/medicaid/upload/7523_02.pdf

Moon, M. (2006). *Medicare: A policy primer.* Washington, DC: Urban Institute Press.

Myles, J. (1989). *Old age in the welfare state: The political economy of public pensions* (Rev. ed.). Lawrence: University of Kansas Press.

O'Rand, A. (2003). The future of the life course: Late modernity and life course risks. In J. T. Mortimer & M. J. Shanahan (Eds.), *Handbook of the life course* (pp. 693–701). New York: Kluwer Academic/Plenum.

Quadagno, J. (2008). *Aging and the life course* (4th ed.). Boston: McGraw-Hill.

Quadagno, J. & Street, D. (2005) Antistatism in American welfare state development. *Journal of Policy History, 17,* 52–71.

Quadagno, J., & Street, D. (2006). Recent trends in U.S. social welfare policy: Minor retrenchment or major transformation? *Research on Aging, 28,* 303–316.

Shuey, K. M., & O'Rand, A. M. (2006). Changing demographics and new pension risks. *Research on Aging, 28,* 317–340.

Social Security Administration. (2007, October). *Social Security: A brief history.* Retrieved June 5, 2008, from http://www.socialsecurity.gov/history/pdf/2007historybooklet.pdf

Street, D. (2007). Too much, too little, just right? Policy disconnects in an aging society. *Public Policy and Aging Report, 17*(3), 7–10.

Street, D., & Cossman, J. S. (2006). Greatest generation or greedy geezers? Social spending preferences and the elderly. *Social Problems, 53,* 75–96.

Uhlenberg, P. (1992). Population aging and social policy. *Annual Review of Sociology, 18,* 449–474.

U.S. Congress. Joint Economic Committee. (1999, August). *Tax expenditures: A review and analysis.* Retrieved June 5, 2008, from http://www.house.gov/jec/fiscal/tax/expend.htm

Williamson, J. B., McNamara, T. K., & Howling, S. A. (2003). Generational equity, generational interdependence, and the framing of the debate over Social Security reform. *Journal of Sociology and Social Welfare, 30*(3), 3–14.

***Debra Street***
***K. Thomas D'Amuro***

# POLITICAL BEHAVIOR AND ORIENTATIONS, LATER LIFE

Students of politics have long recognized that the effectiveness and stability of democratic systems of government rest upon the broad-based political activity of their citizens. Such activity is not only necessary for the election of officeholders who will serve as representatives of the people, but is also necessary to maintain a common sense of legitimacy among those over whom the government exercises authority. The study of political behavior and orientations is the study of democratic activity on the part of individual citizens, and the beliefs they hold that help to shape their activity. The political behavior of an individual consists of his or her efforts to participate in the electoral system, influence officeholders and policy makers, organize and join with those who share their political interests, protest or support government policy, express political opinions, persuade fellow citizens to believe or behave in a certain way, or take other actions relative to politics or the political system.

Political behavior is motivated and guided by the individual's political orientations, a set of attitudes and beliefs regarding political ideology, policy preferences, partisanship, and identifications with other politically relevant ideas, symbols, and groups. Political behavior and orientations in individuals have most frequently been studied through the use of large-scale surveys that ask respondents to report their level of participation in political activities and their opinions about political subject matter.

## AGING AND POLITICS

In the more than 6 decades that such surveys have been conducted, it has become evident that people of different ages participate in the political system at different rates. For example, research has consistently shown that the most basic and often studied measure of mass political behavior, the rate at which citizens exercise their right to vote, appears to arc upward throughout most of the life course. Propensity to vote starts out relatively low as young people enter the electorate, increases rapidly in young adulthood, continues to increase at a decelerating pace throughout middle age, peaks and levels off at around the age of retirement, and then slowly begins to decline only as individuals enter advanced old age (Rosenstone & Hansen, 1993). U.S. Census data on voter turnout in national elections from 1998 to 2004 show the same relationship between age and voter turnout, with the highest rates of participation consistently occurring in the 65 to 74 age group (U.S. Census Bureau, 2008).

The relationship between aging and political orientations is much less clear. As one might expect, orientations that have a motivating or enabling influence on an individual's propensity to participate, such as interest in political affairs, knowledge about politics, and strength of partisan (one political party) affiliation, do seem to increase in intensity with age (Delli Carpini & Keeter, 1996). However, the concept of political orientations also includes the ideological and partisan direction of beliefs and affiliations, and those do not seem to vary systematically by age. Despite conventional wisdom to the contrary, people do not become significantly less liberal and more conservative in their ideology as they age (Alwin & Krosnick, 1991).

As John Campbell and John Strate (1981) report, "The political orientations of older people are not peculiar. Knowing that someone is old will not help very much in predicting how conservative he or she is, in most important respects" (pp. 590–591). Identification with one or another political party, in particular, seems to be a remarkably stable trait; the partisan attachments formed early in one's political life tend to persist well into adulthood (Jennings & Markus, 1984). There is little evidence, and little reason to expect, that the ideology, partisanship, or policy attitudes of a diverse cohort of people would converge as they age together.

Although most research suggests that growing older is associated with increasing levels of many types of political activity over most of the life course, the question of how and why—and even if—this is the case is a matter of some dispute. A few studies, most notably that by Warren Miller and J. Merril Shanks (1996), challenge the notion that aging affects political behavior at all during the middle years of life. They propose, instead, a lengthy plateau in the rising life course arc of voting turnout; aside from dramatic positive growth in voting in the first few elections in which a young adult is eligible and a significant decline in turnout in advanced old age, they posit that the shape of the age-voting relationship is essentially flat across most of the life course. Questions and controversies such as these remain because of competing theories about the mechanics of political socialization and the nature of the survey data upon which the aging and politics research is based.

## THEORETICAL FOUNDATIONS

Scholars have proposed four different theoretical models of the effects of age on political behavior and orientations (Sears, 1983). The *life cycle model* posits periodic changes in political orientations and behavior because of transitions through different age-related social roles and statuses, as well as gradual changes characterized by political maturation, socialization, and habituation. As individuals age, they are shaped by their education, their social interactions and experiences, and their use of the news media to learn about politics and keep abreast of political issues, events, and personalities. The process of aging may result in a growing ability to understand abstract political concepts, an accumulation of experience and knowledge about politics that makes participation easier and more meaningful for the individual, and the development and reinforcement of habits of political activity.

Transitions through the stages of the life course help to structure the social roles that individuals play and thus the stake they hold in society and the resources they bring to the political system. The changing structure of incentives, opportunities, and resources that accompanies changing status helps to mold political beliefs and actions as citizens age. With the onset of advanced old age, biological changes can lead to gradual declines in hearing, eyesight, balance, mobility, and cognitive functioning, making it more difficult to follow politics in the news media and interfere with the ability to participate in political activity. While the life cycle model does not seem to apply to the partisan and ideological patterns of orientations in the population, it is arguably the best description of the relationship between aging and political behavior, which would explain why most political scientists who have considered the issue have found gradually increasing levels of political activity through the entire adult life span.

Life cycle model opponents rely implicitly on another model, the *impressionable years model*, to provide the foundation for their counterargument. The impressionable years model emphasizes the importance of an individual's formative political experience in late adolescence and early adulthood; it hypothesizes that orientations toward politics and the propensity for political activity are characteristics that are developed relatively early in adult life and resist change in later stages of the life course. An individual undergoes formal and informal political socialization in early adulthood, generally considered to be between the ages of 17 and 25 (Schuman & Scott, 1989), leading to a great deal of change in political behavior and orientations during that portion of the life course. Once the individual reaches political maturity, however, the effects of those socialization experiences crystallize and set the stage for later behavior and orientations toward politics. According to the impressionable years model, the differences in socialization experiences between birth cohorts are what result in differences in political generations, and those generational or cohort differences must be responsible for the appearance of aging effects in cross-sectional studies.

The two remaining models leave much less room for any relationship between age and politics. The *lifelong openness model* asserts that changes in attitudes and behavior are equally likely at any point in the life course, and that such changes bear no relation to the age of the individual but rather arise irregularly over the course of one's life from periodic exposure to historical events or the idiosyncratic interaction with one's political and social environment. The *persistence model* implies a much different effect; political orientations are developed and crystallized not during early adulthood but, rather, during childhood and are set in place by the time an individual reaches adulthood. In that case, survey data collected on those age 18 and older would show no relationship between advancement through the life course and change in political behavior and orientations, even in early adulthood.

## METHODOLOGICAL CHALLENGES

To further complicate the theoretical tension between the life cycle and impressionable years models, the study of aging and politics is impeded in practice by the statistical confounding of aging, period, and cohort effects in survey data. Period effects occur when the historical ebbs and flows of political events shift the overall behavior and orientations of entire citizenries. Cohort effects, as represented by the impressionable years model, occur when these events are experienced by young people in their politically formative years and create patterns of behavior and orientations among the members of that particular generation that remain throughout their lives. Age, period, and cohort are statistically confounded because, for example, in survey data collected during a single period, the effects of age and cohort perfectly mask one another. An individual's chronological age at a given point in time is both a marker for his or her position in the life course as well as his or her membership in a particular generation (Glenn, 1976). What appears to be a statistical relationship between age and behavior in a snapshot survey might actually be, as impressionable years model proponents have argued, attributable to the different formative experiences of successive generations rather than to the process of growing older and traversing the life course. Perhaps it is not that older people vote more, it is that the more recent generations have been socialized to vote less. Likewise, it may not be that people become more conservative as they age, but that earlier generations entered adulthood having been socialized in a more conservative era.

The utility of chronological age as a marker of position in the life course is threatened not only by cohort effects, but by the nature of the marker itself. The age number is merely a rough surrogate for the myriad psychological, social, and biological processes that individuals experience as they grow older. The measure of a person's age in years is a rough indicator of these processes because aging not only occurs gradually as individuals develop and mature and accumulate experience, but it has a periodic nature as well, in which gradual development is punctuated by important life course transitions. Plus, the rate at which different individuals develop varies considerably, as does the timing of those critical milestones along the life course (e.g., graduation, marriage, homeownership, parenthood, promotion, empty nesting, retirement, widowhood, and advanced old age). Nevertheless, short of being able to account for individual differences in development and life course transition timing, chronological age is usually the best measure available.

## LIFE SPAN CIVIC DEVELOPMENT

The most compelling research to attempt to address the theoretical and methodological challenges described above was conducted by Strate and his colleagues (1989) and strongly supports the life cycle model of aging with regards to political participation. They used

## AMERICAN ASSOCIATION OF RETIRED PERSONS (AARP)

AARP (formerly The American Association of Retired Persons) was founded in 1958 but traces its roots to the National Retired Teachers Association (NRTA), founded by Ethel Percy Andrus (1884–1967) in 1947 to provide life insurance to its members. As of 2008 AARP is the largest voluntary organization in the United States with nearly 40 million members aged 50 and over. It is commonly considered an aging interest group, but it is also a member benefit group as was its NRTA predecessor, providing discounts on goods and services and marketing products such as automobile and health insurance to its members. AARP does engage in political advocacy on behalf of its members, but its size and the diversity of its membership makes it difficult for the organization to take stands on contentious issues. Since its disastrous involvement in the 1988 debate over the Medicare Catastrophic Coverage Act, in which it assumed a pro-Act position that was later repudiated by many of its own members, it has tended to act cautiously and avoid taking strong controversial positions that might alienate some of its members.

**BIBLIOGRAPHY**

Pratt, H.J. (1993). *Gray agendas: Interest groups and public pensions in Canada, Britain, and the United States*. Ann Arbor: University of Michigan Press.

a large cross-sectional time series of survey data from the 1952 through 1984 American National Election Studies in an attempt to disentangle the effects of age, historical period, and cohort on voting. They found that, even after controlling for period and cohort effects across 32 years worth of data, age has strong direct and indirect positive curvilinear effects on behavior. The indirect effects of age consist of age-related increases in other factors that positively influence political behavior, such as income, strength of partisanship, church attendance, attachment to one's community, a sense of government responsiveness, and civic competence, which they define as "knowledge and habits of knowledge acquisition relevant to politics" (Strate et al. 1989, p. 450).

In other words, older people tend to vote at higher levels in the later stages of life not because of when they matured politically, but because the process of aging results in a growing availability of resources to expend in political activity, an expanding stake in the political order, deepening attachments to social and political issues and groups, an enhanced sense of the efficacy of one's political actions, a heightened interest in politics, greater diligence in monitoring politics in the print media, and an increasing knowledge and understanding of politics, all of which motivate and enable higher levels of political activity. Strate and his colleagues found that the effects of aging on voting, when properly accounted for, match, and perhaps even exceed the universally accepted strong effects of education on voting. In some ways aging is a substitute for formal education; while college-educated young adults participate at much greater rates than their less-educated counterparts, there are decreasing differences in rates of participation between those who were and were not college-educated across the middle of the life course, and the difference disappears entirely in the late stages of life.

### HOW POLICIES MAKE CITIZENS

Subsequent research has helped to further illuminate the life cycle model by considering the ways in which age structures individual interactions with political institutions. For example, Steven Rosenstone and John Hansen (1993) found that as individuals grow older, they become increasingly likely to be contacted by a political party during election campaigns. This type of mobilization is an important source of motivation to participate that arises from the political context rather than the individual, yet it is positively influenced by the individual's age. Of course, parties employ optimization strategies to guide their efforts in turning out the vote, and they recognize that contacts with older citizens are more likely to be effective toward that end.

Andrea Campbell (2002) found that senior citizen political involvement in the United States is strongly augmented by their status as recipients of Social Security benefits. Social Security not only provides resources to older individuals that can be expended in the pursuit of political activity, but it signifies the strong stake in government policy that they hold, which motivates them to act in politically relevant ways to protect that stake. The pull of Social Security in the later stages of life is so strong that it helps to overcome disadvantages faced by those with lower incomes. Similar to the effects of education, those with higher incomes generally participate at levels higher than do those with lower incomes. This disparity is dramatically reduced among Social Security beneficiaries; because they rely to a greater extent on those benefits, lower-income seniors are more urgently mobilized to participate at higher rates then their socioeconomic status would suggest. Not surprisingly,

Campbell also found an uncommon indicator that the position in the life course of those in later life, and thus their status as beneficiaries, has a directional effect on their orientation toward Social Security policy. Older Americans almost unanimously support the maintenance of Social Security benefits, as one would expect.

## THE ELECTORAL BLUFF

What effect does political activity by older adults have on democracy? Obviously, heightened participation by those in later life helps lend legitimacy and stability to democratic systems, as all conventional political participation does. But aside from support for age-based program such as Social Security, there is no reason to believe that the increased activity by older adults can be marshaled in a particular ideological or partisan direction. As Robert Binstock (2000) points out, people in later life are "heterogeneous in socioeconomic and political characteristics... [and] unlikely to cast their ballots in a monolithic or even cohesive fashion." The exception, he notes, would be if political parties or candidates endorsed "sharply different policies on aging.... In such circumstances the votes of older persons might tend to cohere" (p. 30). Barring these unlikely circumstances, the ability of age-based interest groups to swing elections and influence officeholders may be illusory. Even the political power of such a huge organization as the American Association of Retired Persons (AARP) is more likely to be based upon the perceived threat of cohesive activity by its members, a phenomenon Binstock calls "the electoral bluff" (2000, p. 24), than on any actual ability to marshal the orientations and behavior of its members in one direction or another.

Political behavior, then, appears to be quite susceptible to life course effects, as are political orientations that encourage and facilitate participation, but the partisan and ideological directions of those orientations are not, with the exception of support for policies whose benefits accrue based on the age of the recipient. In short, individuals in democratic systems such as the United States become more likely to fit the mold of the ideal citizen—motivated, informed, and active—as they age. They enter retirement with a lifetime's accumulation of resources, habits, and motivations to participate, and also with a renewed resource (more free time) and a fresh incentive (protection of their Social Security benefits). Only very late in the life course, when the physical rigors of old age begin to make their effects felt, when difficulty seeing, hearing, and walking makes participation more difficult, do individuals begin to decrease their levels of activity.

**SEE ALSO** Volume 2: *Policy, Health;* Volume 3: *Policy, Later Life Well-Being; Social Security; Time Use, Later Life; Volunteering, Later Life.*

**BIBLIOGRAPHY**

Alwin, D. F., & Krosnick, J. A. (1991). Aging, cohorts, and the stability of sociopolitical orientations over the life span. *American Journal of Sociology, 97*(1), 169–195.

Binstock, R. H. (2000). Older people and voting participation: Past and future. *The Gerontologist, 40*(1), 18–31.

Campbell, A. (1971). Politics through the life cycle. *The Gerontologist, 11*(2), 112–117.

Campbell, A., Converse, P. E., Miller, W. E., & Stokes, D. E. (1960). *The American voter.* New York: Wiley.

Campbell, A. L. (2002). Self-interest, Social Security, and the distinctive participation patterns of senior citizens. *American Political Science Review, 96*(3), 565–574.

Campbell, A. L. (2003). *How policies make citizens: Senior political activism and the American welfare state.* Princeton, NJ: Princeton University Press.

Campbell, J. C., & Strate, J. M. (1981). Are old people conservative? *The Gerontologist, 21*(6), 580–591.

Day, C. L. (1994). The older American voter. In R. J. Manheimer (Ed.), *Older Americans almanac: A reference work on seniors in the United States* (pp. 147–165). Detroit, MI: Gale Research.

Delli Carpini, M. X., & Keeter, S. (1996). *What Americans know about politics and why it matters.* New Haven, CT: Yale University Press.

Glenn, N. D. (1976). Cohort analysts' futile quest: Statistical attempts to separate age, period, and cohort effects. *American Sociological Review, 41*(5), 900–904.

Glenn, N. D., & Grimes, M. (1968). Aging, voting, and political interest. *American Sociological Review, 33*(4), 563–575.

Jennings, M. K., & Markus, G. B. (1984). Partisan orientations over the long haul: Results from the three-wave political socialization panel study. *American Political Science Review, 78*(4), 1000–1018.

Jennings, M. K., & Niemi, R. G. (1981). *Generations and politics: A panel study of young adults and their parents.* Princeton, NJ: Princeton University Press.

Miller, W. E., & Shanks, J. M. (1996). *The new American voter.* Cambridge, MA: Harvard University Press.

Rosenstone, S. J., & Hansen, J. M. (1993). *Mobilization, participation, and democracy in America.* New York: Macmillan.

Schuman, H., & Scott, J. (1989). Generations and collective memories. *American Sociological Review, 54*(3), 359–381.

Sears, D. O. (1983). The persistence of early political predispositions: The roles of attitude object and life stage. In L. Wheeler & P. Shaver (Eds.), *Review of personality and social psychology* (Vol. 4, pp. 79–116). Beverly Hills, CA: Sage.

Strate, J. M., Parrish, C. J., Elder, C. D., & Ford, C. C. (1989). Life span civic development and voting participation. *American Political Science Review, 83*(2), 443–464.

U.S. Census Bureau. (2008). *Voting and registration data.* Retrieved June 16, 2008, from http://www.census.gov/population/www/socdemo/voting.html

Verba, S., & Nie, N. H. (1972). *Participation in America: Political democracy and social equality.* New York: Harper & Row.

Wolfinger, R. E., & Rosenstone, S. J. (1980). *Who votes?* New Haven, CT: Yale University Press.

*Thomas B. Jankowski*

# POPULATION AGING

An individual's age is determined by the time elapsed since she or he was born. A population has an age, too, and the world's population is getting older. A population's age is determined by the age distribution of its individual members. In aging populations, the older segment of the population (usually those aged 65 or older) represents a relatively large proportion of the total population. The populations of all developed and many developing countries are aging. This unprecedented demographic trend is a consequence of relatively recent declines in mortality and fertility and has profound and long-term consequences for social issues such as health, economic productivity, and health care. This entry will describe young and old populations, explain the demographic processes that cause populations to age, and discuss the demographic and social consequences of population aging.

## WHAT OLD AND YOUNG POPULATIONS LOOK LIKE

A population's age is actually a facet of its age-gender structure. The age-gender structure of a population refers to the age distribution of men and women in the population. This can be represented graphically using a population pyramid (sometimes called an age-gender pyramid). A population pyramid depicts either the number or percentage of people in a population at each age. Examples of population pyramids are shown in Figure 1. The bars on the right-hand side of each pyramid represent the age distribution of women and the bars on the left-hand side represent the age distribution of men.

A young population has a greater proportion of the population concentrated at the younger ages. This gives the population pyramid its wide base and triangular shape. The pyramid on the left in Figure 1 is typical of the population of less developed countries and provides a good example of a young population. In contrast, an old population has a greater proportion of the population concentrated at older ages. The pyramid on the right in Figure 1 represents the population of more developed countries and is a good example of an old population. Population pyramids for old populations tend to look more rectangular than the triangular shape of a young population. One way to describe the aging of a population is to refer to the rectangularity of its population pyramid over time. Regardless of their shape, the graphical depictions shown in Figure 1 are called *pyramids*.

The age distribution of a population can be summarized statistically using the median age. Median age refers to the midpoint of an age distribution where 50% of the population is older and 50% are younger than that value. In an old population, the relatively large numbers of people in the older age groups tends to increase the median age. In a young population, the concentration of people in younger age groups produces a lower median age. The median age of the world population is 28 (United Nations, 2007). The country with the highest median age is Japan (43 years), whereas the country with the lowest median age is Uganda (15 years). The United States has a median age of 36.

A third way to characterize the age of a population is to examine the proportion of the population in the older age groups. In the more developed countries, age 65 is usually considered the threshold for advanced age because this is the age at which adults generally become eligible for full Social Security benefits. In less developed countries, age 60, or sometimes an even younger age, is used as the beginning of old age. Because of recent growth in the older population, especially in more developed countries, the older population is commonly stratified into three age groups. Persons aged 65 to 74 are generally fairly independent and healthy. Consequently, they are commonly referred to as the *young old*. Persons aged 85 and older—the *oldest old* group—tend to experience numerous health problems resulting in considerable frailty and dependence. The 10-year age group between 75 and 84 constitutes an intermediate group between the young old and the oldest old. A population with a relatively large proportion of its members in the oldest segments of the population may be classified as an old population. Conversely, young populations have a relatively small proportion of their members in these old-aged categories. The country with the highest proportion of its population aged 60 and over is Japan (27.9%), whereas the United Arab Emirates has the lowest percentage of its population aged 60 and over (1.7%) (United Nations, 2007). With respect to the size of the proportion of persons 60 and over, the United States is ranked 43rd among the nations of the world with 17.2% of the population aged 60 and over.

## HOW POPULATIONS AGE

An aging population is one in which the older population grows at a faster rate than the total population. Consequently, the proportion of the population at older ages increases over time, prompting a secular increase in the median age. Population aging in more developed

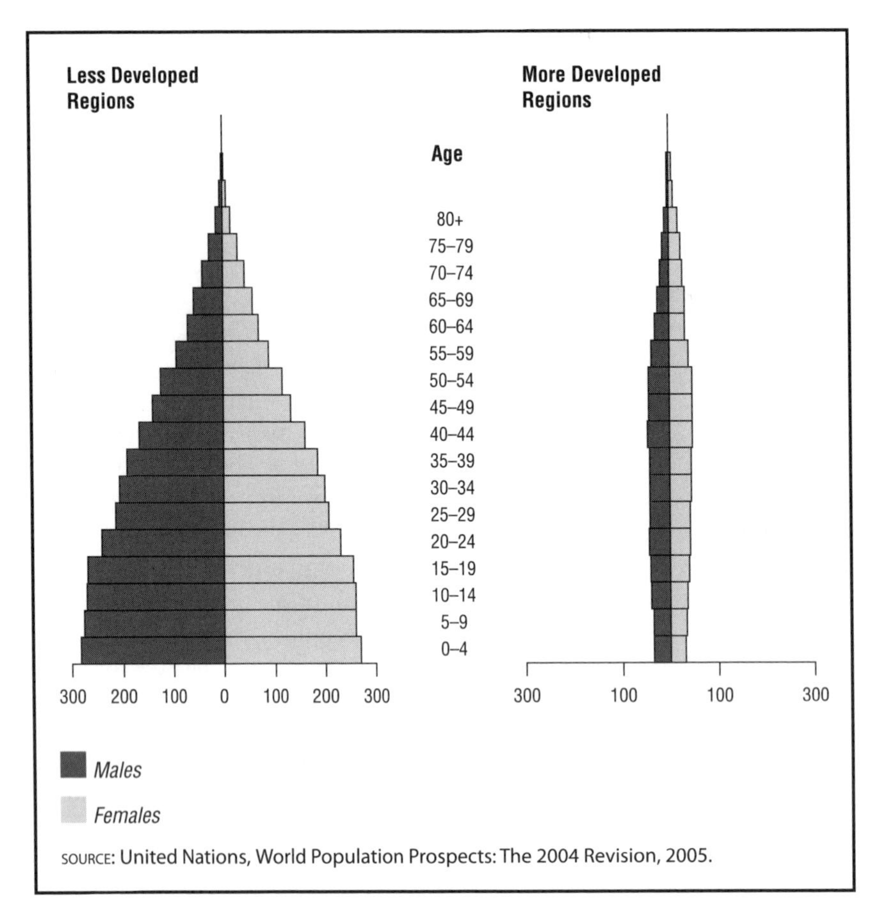


***Figure 1.*** *Age Distribution of the World's Population. Population structures by age and sex in the millions, 2005.* CENGAGE LEARNING, GALE.

countries occurred as a result of the historical shift from high fertility and mortality to low fertility and mortality. This demographic transition occurred in three stages (Gill, Glazer, & Thernstrom, 1992). The first stage is characterized by high mortality and fertility and prevailed for most of human history. During the second stage, both fertility and mortality declined. Declines in mortality generally preceded declines in fertility generating dramatic population growth. During the third stage, both mortality and fertility reached low, stable levels.

The transition from high fertility and mortality to low fertility and mortality produces a systematic shift in the age-gender structure resulting in population aging. In populations with high fertility rates, each successive birth cohort tends to be larger than the one preceding it, creating a high proportion of young people in a population. As fertility declines, subsequent birth cohorts are similar in size, reducing the proportion of the population concentrated at young ages. When mortality is high, birth cohorts suffer considerable attrition with few cohort members surviving until old age. Consequently, older adults constitute a relatively small proportion of the population, making the median age of the population relatively young. Initial declines in mortality generally occurred at the youngest ages resulting in improved survival for infants and young children and ironically producing a younger population. However, subsequent declines in mortality benefit middle-aged and older adults, resulting in disproportionately high growth rates for these age groups and an increase in the median age. The dramatic increases in life expectancy that occurred during the 20th century in developed countries, and in most less developed countries, mean that people routinely survive to older ages, increasing the numbers of older adults in a given population.

The population of the United States provides a good illustration of an aging population. During the 100-year period between 1900 and 2000, the United States, along with other industrialized countries, made the transition from a young population to an old population. The median age of the U.S. population rose from 22.9 years in 1900 to 35.3 years in 2000. Over that 100-year period, the number of adults aged 65 and older grew from 3.1 million to 35.0 million. In any growing population, the number of older adults (and indeed any age group) will increase. A truer indicator of population aging is the growth of the older population relative to that of the total population. Between 1900 and 1950, the population of the United States approximately doubled (76 million to 151 million), while the older population quadrupled (3 million to 12 million). Between 1950 and 2000, the total U.S. population grew from 151 million to 281 million, while the older population grew from 12 million to 35 million. Consequently, the proportion of the population aged 65 and older increased from 4.1% in 1900 to 12.4% in 2000. The relative size of the oldest age group (those 85 and older) increased even more dramatically, from only 0.2% of the population in 1900 to 1.5% of the population in 2000 (roughly a sevenfold increase!).

While the demographic transition during the 20th century provides a good description of historical demographic changes in more developed countries, the extent to which this model applies to less developed countries has been the source of considerable debate (Weeks, 2005). In the majority of less developed countries, both mortality and fertility have declined, but have not reached the low sustained levels observed in more developed countries. There are two consequences of this pattern in less developed countries. First, the populations of many less developed societies have begun to age, especially countries in South America and Asia. (Many countries in Africa sustain high fertility rates resulting in very young populations.) The second consequence of the intermediate levels of mortality and fertility decline in less developed countries is that population growth in these societies remains rapid.

Although population aging at the national level is driven primarily by fertility and mortality patterns, migration can exert a significant influence on local populations. One migration pattern that can result in local population aging is the in-migration of older adults. Florida maintains the highest proportion of older adults of any state in the United States (17.6% aged 65 and over) due to a large and sustained influx of older migrants. Local populations also can age as a result of the out-migration of younger people. For example, the populations of some Midwestern states, such as North and South Dakota, have aged considerably since the 1980s as younger people have moved to other states seeking economic opportunities.

## SEX RATIO

Upon examining the population pyramids shown in Figure 1, one might notice that they are not symmetrical, especially at the top (the older ages). This lack of symmetry occurs because there are rarely the same number of men and women in a population. The sex ratio, defined as the number of males per 100 females, is a helpful way to describe the gender composition of a population. This statistic can be calculated by dividing the number of men by the number of women and multiplying this total by 100.The current sex ratio for the total U.S. population is 97.2 indicating that women outnumber men. The sex ratio varies considerably by age. Because male births outnumber female births, the sex ratio at young ages tends to favor males. For example, the sex ratio for those under 5 years of age is 104.8. Because women experience lower age-specific mortality, the sex ratio decreases for older age groups and favors women. The sex ratio for young adults (20 to 39) is 103.9 but drops to 97.0 for those in middle age (40 to 59). Older adults (65 and older) have a sex ratio of 72.9; whereas among the oldest segment of the population (85 and older), the sex ratio drops below 50 at 47.6.

**BIBLIOGRAPHY**

U.S. Census Bureau. *Annual estimates of the population by sex and 5-year age groups for the United States: April 1, 2000 to July 1, 2007.* Retrieved June 12, 2008, from http://www.census.gov/popest

## CONSEQUENCES OF POPULATION AGING

Population aging has two important demographic consequences. First, population aging has a profound influence on the gender composition of populations. Women have lower rates of mortality in almost all current societies (Waldron, 2005). In more developed countries (those with the oldest populations), the gender differences in mortality are particularly pronounced. For example, women in the United States have an average life expectancy at birth of 80.4 years compared to 75.2 years for men (Kung et al., 2008). One important consequence of women's greater longevity is that women outnumber men in most populations. In the United States women outnumber men by 4.3 million (U.S. Census Bureau, 2008); worldwide, there are 70 million more women than men (United Nations, 2007). The sex ratio—the number of men per 100 women—declines dramatically with advancing age. In fact, among those 85 and older, women outnumber men by approximately two to one.

A second demographic consequence of population aging is the effect this shift has on the relative numbers of old and young people in a society. The dependency ratio (sometimes called the support ratio) is a helpful way to summarize the extent of the population most likely to need social support and is defined as the ratio of the combined child population (0 to 14 years) and older population (65 years and over) to the rest of the population (15 to 64 years). The dependency ratio can be decomposed into the youth dependency ratio (the ratio of the 0- to 14-year-old population to the 15- to 64-year-old population) and the old-age dependency ratio (the ratio of the 65 and older population to the 15- to 64-year-old population). In younger populations, the youth dependency ratio is a far larger component of the dependency ratio compared to the old-age dependency ratio. For example, in the population of Africa, older adults comprise less than 10% of potential dependents (United Nations, 2007). In older populations, such as those in European countries and the United States, the youth dependency ratio and the old-age dependency ratio are approximately equal, indicating that older adults account for roughly half of potential dependents (United Nations, 2007). The composition of the dependent population has important implications for the type and extent of both formal and informal (filial) support systems needed in a given society.

## CURRENT AND FUTURE RESEARCH ON POPULATION AGING

Population aging also has profound social consequences that are currently the foci of considerable research activity. Perhaps the most urgent set of questions being investigated by social researchers concerns the impact of a rapidly growing number of older adults on population health and systems of health care. The decline in mortality that has occurred in most parts of the world precipitated a shift in the primary causes of death from acute infectious and parasitic diseases (such as influenza and malaria that can strike any age group) to degenerative and chronic conditions (such as heart disease and cancer, which occur mostly at older ages) (Omran, 1971). Heart disease is now the leading cause of death in more developed nations (Syme, 2000); and in the United States, heart disease and cancer account for approximately half of all deaths (Kung et al., 2008). The shift from acute to chronic disease raises a number of questions about the future of population health and presents a new set of challenges to health care systems in countries with aging populations.

A key question has emerged as a consequence of increasing longevity: How will additional years added to life expectancy affect population health? The risk of chronic illness rises precipitously with age. In the United States the vast majority of older adults report at least one chronic condition and about half report multiple chronic conditions (He et al., 2005). One potential consequence of declining mortality at older ages is an increase in the prevalence of chronic comorbidity triggering an epidemic of impairment and disability in aging populations. A second alternative is that declines in mortality at older ages are accompanied by declining severity of chronic illness and an attenuation of their disabling consequences (Robine & Michel, 2004).

As evidence of the second alternative, Kenneth Manton and his colleagues (1997) reported significant declines in the prevalence of disability throughout the 1980s and early 1990s. These findings have been echoed by other studies that have reported lower rates of disability (Freedman et al., 2002) and better self-assessments of health (Martin et al., 2007). While many members of the older population appear to be benefiting from improvements in the treatment of chronic illness and its sequelae, these positive trends are not enjoyed to the same extent among racial and ethnic minority groups and among poorer segments of the population, creating considerable health disparities in later life (Crimmins & Saito, 2001).

Recent mortality decline has provoked a debate about the possibility of an upper limit to human life expectancy (Olshansky, Carnes, & Cassel, 1990). Assuming that point has not yet been reached and that future increases in longevity are likely, trends in chronic disease and disability in the older population will undoubtedly be scrutinized carefully to determine whether there is an inflection point at which increased longevity leads to a greater prevalence of morbidity. As the populations of less developed countries continue to age, there will be considerable interest in the impact of chronic disease and disability on the health status of older populations in these countries.

A second set of social issues inspired by population aging focuses on the increasing need for social support generated by a growing older population. One of the key services needed by older adults is health care. Because chronic conditions often persist over a substantial period of one's life, chronically ill persons require extensive medical care. According to the Centers for Disease Control and Prevention (2008), treatment of chronic disease accounts for the majority of health care expenditures in the United States. This finding, coupled with sharply rising health care expenditures in recent years, raises concerns about the cost of meeting the health care needs of an aging population. The financial ramifications of population aging have been a point of contention, however, as several studies have found weak or no effects of population aging on health care expenditures (Getzen, 1992; Werblow, Felder, & Zweifel, 2007). The capacity of the U.S. heath care system to meet the medical needs of the aging baby boom cohort will certainly be at the forefront of social scientists' and health care providers' research agendas in the coming decades.

SEE ALSO Volume 3: *Age Structure; Aging; Demographic Transition Theories; Epidemiologic Transition; Global Aging; Life Expectancy.*

**BIBLIOGRAPHY**


Bodenheimer, T. (2005). High and rising health care costs. Part 1: Seeking an explanation. *Annals of Internal Medicine, 142*(10), 847–854.

Centers for Disease Control and Prevention. (2008). *Chronic disease overview.* Retrieved June 18, 2008, from http://www.cdc.gov/nccdphp/overview.htm

Crimmins, E., & Saito, Y. (2001). Trends in healthy life expectancy in the United States, 1970–1990: Gender, racial, and educational differences. *Social Science and Medicine, 52*(11), 1629–1641.

Freedman, V. A., Martin, L. G., & Schoeni, R. F. (2002). Recent trends in disability and functioning among older adults in the United States: A systematic review. *Journal of the American Medical Association, 288*(24): 3137–3146.

Freedman, V. A., Schoeni, R. F., Martin, L. G., & Cornman, J. (2007). Chronic conditions and the decline in late-life disability. *Demography, 44*(3), 459–477.

Getzen, T. E. (1992). Population aging and the growth of health expenditures. *Journal of Gerontology: Social Sciences, 47*(3), 98–104.

Gill, R. T., Glazer, N., & Thernstrom, S. A. (1992). *Our changing population.* Englewood Cliffs, NJ: Prentice-Hall.

He, W., Sengupta, M., Velkoff, V.A., & DeBarros, K. A. (2005). *65 plus in the United States: 2005.* Washington, DC: U.S. Government Printing Office.

Kung, H.-C., Hoyert, D. L., Xu, J., & Murphy, S. L. (2008). Deaths: Final data for 2005. *National Vital Statistics Reports, 56*(10). Hyattsville, MD. Retrieved June 18, 2008, from http://www.cdc.gov/nchs/data/nvsr/nvsr56/nvsr56_10.pdf

Lee, R. (2003). The demographic transition: Three centuries of fundamental change. *Journal of Economic Perspectives, 17*(4), 167–190.

Manton, K., Corder, L., & Stallard, E. (1997). Chronic disability trends in elderly United States populations: 1982–1994. *Proceedings of the National Academy of Science, 94,* 2593–2598.

Martin, L. G., Schoeni, R. F., Freedman, V. A., & Andreski, P. (2007). Feeling better? Trends in general health status. *Journals of Gerontology, Series B: Psychological Sciences and Social Sciences, 62,* 11–21.

Olshansky, S. J., Carnes, B., & Cassel, C. K. (1990). In search of Methuselah: Estimating the upper limits to human longevity. *Science, 250*(4981), 634–640.

Omran, A. (1971). The epidemiological transition: A theory of the epidemiology of population change. *Milbank Memorial Fund Quarterly, 49*(4), 509–538.

Robine, J.-M., & Michel, J. P. (2004). Looking forward to a general theory on population aging. *Journals of Gerontology, Series A: Biological Sciences and Medical Sciences, 59*(6), 590–597.

Schoeni R. F., Martin, L. G., Andreski, P., & Freedman, V. A. (2005). Persistent and growing disparities in disability among the elderly: 1982–2002. *American Journal of Public Health, 95*(11), 2065–2070.

Syme, S. L. (2000). Forward. In L. F. Berkman & I. Kawachi (Eds.), *Social epidemiology* (pp. ix–xii). New York: Oxford University Press.

United Nations (2007). *World population ageing 2007.* Retrieved June 18, 2008, from http://www.un.org/esa/population/publications/WPA2007/wpp2007.htm

U.S. Census Bureau. (2008). *Annual estimates of the population by sex and 5-year age groups for the United States: April 1, 2000 to July 1, 2007.* Retrieved June 18, 2008, from http://www.census.gov/popest/national/asrh/NC-EST2007-sa.html

Waldron, I. (2005). Gender differences in mortality: Causes and variation in different societies. In P. Conrad (Ed.), *The sociology of health and illness: Critical perspectives* (7th ed., pp. 38–54). New York: Worth.

Weeks, J. R. (2005). *Population: An introduction to concepts and issues* (9th ed.). Belmont, CA: Thomson Wadsworth Learning.

Werblow A., Felder, S., & Zweifel, P. (2007). Population ageing and health care expenditure: A school of "red herrings"? *Health Economics, 16*(10), 1109–1126.


***Chuck W. Peek***

# POVERTY, LATER LIFE

Although public programs such as Social Security have successfully reduced the poverty rate among older adults in the United States, economic hardship is a familiar experience for many older Americans. The risk of experiencing poverty in any given year is relatively low for American adults, though the accumulation of that risk across the life course is considerably higher (Rank & Hirschl, 1999b). As a result, a sizeable proportion of the older adult population has experienced poverty at some point during adulthood, experiences that may affect one's economic security in the long term.

Because so many people live for many years after they have retired, the issue of post-retirement economic support is of great importance for seniors, their families, and society at large. The longer the time spent in retirement, in the absence of receiving a wage, the more likely that economic resources will be depleted at some point. Sufficient personal retirement planning can offset this risk, as can social policies that recognize the importance of ensuring a base level of economic support. Fundamental to the discussion of economic well-being is the determination of what it means to be poor and the determination of an appropriate poverty threshold for persons and their families.

Though controversial both in definition and in measurement, poverty is commonly used as an indicator of economic deprivation (Citro & Michael, 1995). Because the poverty measure based on income is a relatively easy way to gauge economic status and is uniformly applied across the United States, it is the most frequently cited measure of economic well-being. In addition to a discussion of the definition and measurement of poverty, this entry includes an examination of elderly poverty rate trends over time in the United States and of specific subpopulations particularly at risk within the older population.

## DEFINITION AND MEASURE

Poverty measures are based on comparing the level of income considered adequate for the living expenses of an individual or family to the amount of their pretax income; income includes earnings, pensions, and all other forms of cash receipts. Two slightly different poverty measures exist in the United States: the *poverty threshold* and the *poverty guidelines* (Department of Health and Human Services, 2008). The poverty threshold is created by the Census Bureau for statistical purposes and takes into account both family size and the age of the householder. The simpler poverty guideline is used for administrative purposes, such as determining eligibility for government programs.

Both poverty measures assume that certain economies of scale come with larger households and calculate poverty based on the number of persons in each family. The poverty threshold additionally considers whether the householder of a one- or two-person family is an older adult. For householders over age 65, the poverty threshold is 8–10% lower compared to families headed by younger persons, based on the fact that the food plan costs used in the development of the poverty methodology in the 1960s were found to be lower for aged adults (Fisher, 1997). In 2006 the poverty threshold for a senior living alone was $9,669; the equivalent value for a two-person family in which the householder was over age 65 was $12,201 (U.S. Census Bureau, 2007b).

Although using the same consistent measure across time is useful both in trend analysis of poverty and in providing a consistent benchmark for public policy, this measurement has fallen under some heavy criticism. The criticisms that are particularly salient for older adults are based on the calculations used to determine both income as well as cost of living needs (Citro & Michael, 1995). Some critics stress the need to consider in-kind benefits in the calculations; for example, programs such as Medicare or low-income housing may play a significant role in easing a senior's financial burden and could be considered a type of income. Including the value of these types of benefits in the calculation of income would result in a lower poverty rate. Other critics argue that the thresholds used to define poverty status are too low, especially for seniors, many of whom face significant medical costs and are especially vulnerable to fluctuations in other expenses, such as housing costs. Basing the calculation of poverty on costs that disproportionately affect seniors, such as health care costs, might have the result of increasing the estimation of economic hardship for the older population.

## THEORETICAL CONSIDERATION

The life-course perspective is relevant to understanding poverty in later life in part because a good predictor of late-life poverty is whether (and for how long) a person experienced poverty in earlier years (Rank & Hirschl, 2001). Moreover, many of the factors that contribute to poverty (e.g., employment history) are the result of lifelong processes. Indeed, the experience of poverty is not a single static event but rather a dynamic process reflecting a series of evolving factors contributing to late-life poverty.

Across the lifespan, many people experiencing poverty do so for relatively short spells of time and move in and out of poverty. For some, the experience of poverty can be chronic, whereas others manage to exit poverty (Rank & Hirschl, 2001). Though persons ages 65 and older have fewer episodes of poverty compared to younger persons, seniors have a higher chance of being chronically poor compared to younger adults (Iceland, 2003). In other words, if an older person is poor, he or she has a lower chance of exiting poverty than does his or her younger counterpart.

Factors that directly affect poverty in late life are determined across the adult lifespan, such as the accumulation of human and social capital. Human capital refers to the accumulation of acquired workplace skills, which can affect that individual's ability to participate in the economy and increase returns from the labor market (Becker, 1964). Human capital theory can be used to explain the pattern of individual earnings across the life course, whereby earnings are lowest for younger persons and then rise rapidly with age as new capital is acquired (McKernan & Ratcliffe, 2002). The pace of this rise begins to slow toward retirement age as the increase of human capital slows, resulting in a decrease in earnings near retirement ages (McKernan & Ratcliffe, 2002). This pattern is reflected in poverty spells, in which older adults have higher chronic poverty rates and lower exit rates from poverty (Iceland, 2003; McKernan & Ratcliffe, 2002).

In addition to human capital, other sources of wealth can accumulate over the life course and may be drawn on by elders faced with economic hardships. One such source is social capital, which refers to an individual's access to social resources created through relationships within social networks (Coleman, 1988). Resources that may be especially useful for seniors include information exchange (e.g., information about available public assistance) as well as intergenerational assistance (e.g., in-kind assistance for parents provided by children), among other resources. Social capital may offset shortfalls in other types of capital and buffer some of the effects of economic hardship.

## HISTORICAL AND DEMOGRAPHIC TRENDS

An examination of poverty rates in the United States over time suggests that overall poverty rates have declined since data collection began in 1959 (Iceland, 2003). Figure 1 examines this trend by age groups and shows a decline of poverty rates among older adults from more than one-third (35%) of elders in 1959 to 9.4% in 2006 (U.S. Census Bureau, 2007a). In large part this drastic decline in poverty rates for elders can be attributed to the success of the Social Security and Medicare programs (Rank & Hirschl, 1999a).

Though poverty-trend data suggest that most older adults are not poor, there is evidence that many elders live just above the poverty line, near the edge of poverty. In 2003 an additional 6.7% of elders lived in families with incomes between 100% and 125% of the poverty line (He, Sengupta, Velkoff, & DeBarros, 2005). Often living on fixed incomes, elders considered to be near poor may have no additional resources to offset economic risks such as higher property taxes or increasing health care expenses. This suggests that in addition to the current number of older adults living in poverty, many more elders are economically vulnerable.

Cross-sectional data collected at one point in time fail to capture the dynamic paths in and out of poverty that happen across the life course, and recently researchers have begun to analyze the paths of poverty with longitudinal datasets. For example, Rank and Hirschl (1999b) examined the lifetime risk of poverty and found that by the age of 30, about 27% of persons in the United States will have experienced poverty at some point. They contrasted this to persons over age 65, where more than one-half of older adults will have experienced a spell of poverty. More dramatically, about two-thirds of persons ages 85 and older had experienced poverty in their adult lifetimes.

## POCKETS OF POVERTY

In addition, there are significant differences within older adults as a group where pockets of poverty highlight a disproportionate risk of poverty for certain subgroups,

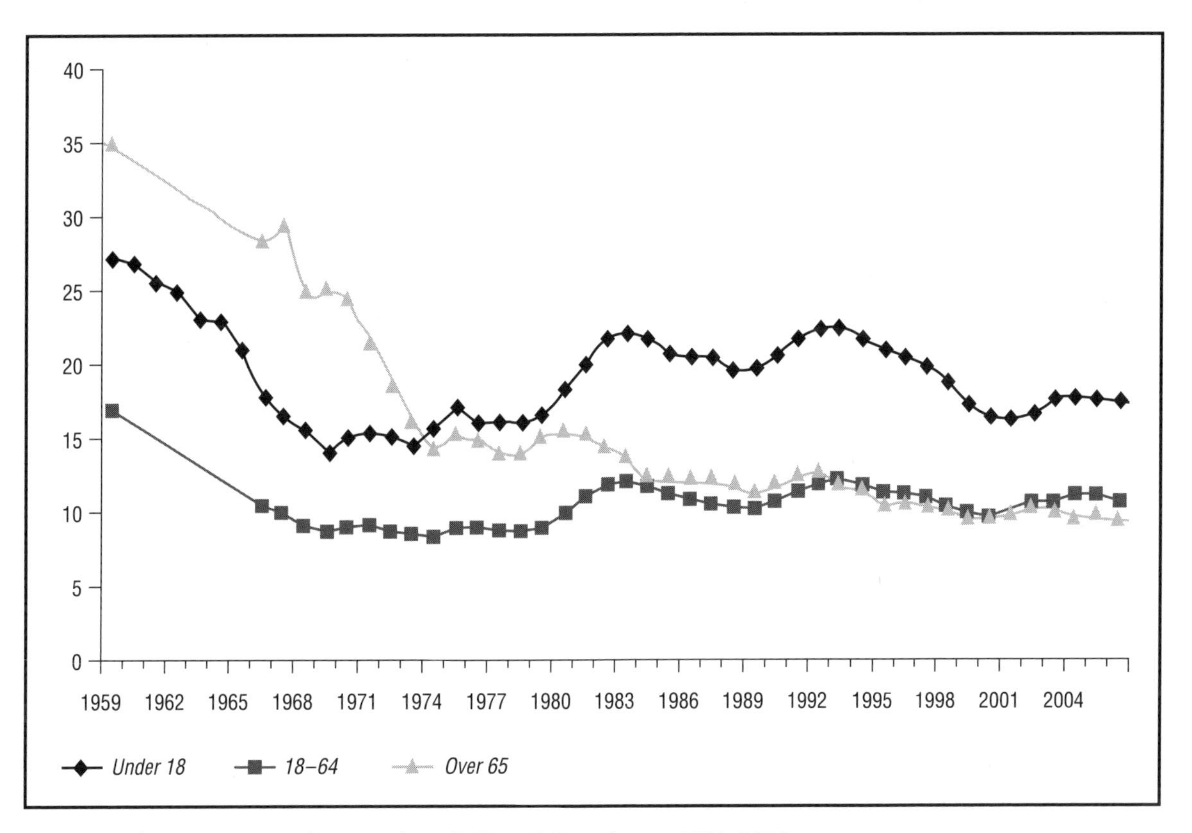


***Figure 1.*** *Trends in poverty rates (in percent) in the United States by age, 1959–2006.* CENGAGE LEARNING, GALE.

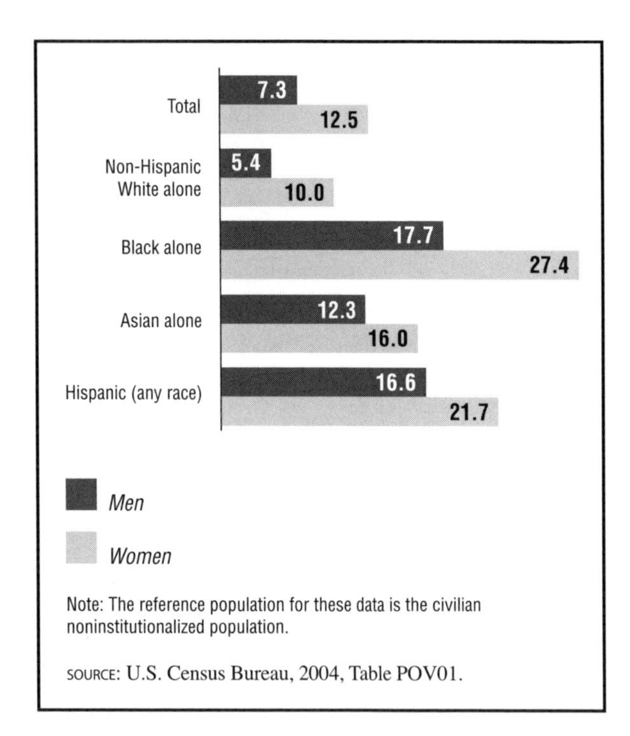


***Figure 2.*** *Percent of people aged 65 and over in poverty by sex, race, and origin, 2003.* CENGAGE LEARNING, GALE.

such as women and minorities. Although the evidence clearly shows that these groups are particularly vulnerable to spells of poverty, it is important to note that there is heterogeneity within these groups.

Marital status is significant for both older men and women; older unmarried adults have higher individual poverty rates compared to older married persons. A particularly striking subsample of this group is older women, whose poverty is intricately linked to marital patterns. For many reasons, including childrearing and other caretaking responsibilities, women often take lengthy periods of time off from the labor force, resulting in limited access to post-retirement income security plans for older women. Married women's eligibility for spouses' income tempers their lack of benefits based on their own work history. However, it has been shown that widowhood often precipitates a drop in economic well-being among women, even if women were not poor before the husband's death (Sevak, Weir, & Willis, 2003–2004).

In addition, the number of persons who will have experienced poverty by later life differs starkly by race: Hispanics and African-American elders have higher poverty rates compared to non-Hispanic. The percentage of older Black persons falling below the poverty line in 2006 was nearly one-quarter (23%) compared to only 7% of non-Hispanic Whites. Hispanic elders have a similarly high poverty rate; 19% of this population falls below the poverty threshold. Though comparatively older Asians are not as likely to be poor, still 12% of Asian elders fall below the poverty line. In addition, the cumulative lifetime risk of poverty is striking if examined by race. By the time Blacks reach the age of 75, more than 90% of them will have experienced at least 1 year in poverty, compared to 52% for Whites (Rank & Hirschl, 1999b).

It is important to note that poverty rates are calculated for the family; therefore, the composition of the household and each member's individual resources shape these differential experiences. The risk of poverty may be offset to some extent by adjusting household composition. For example, a widow with few economic resources of her own would be poor if she lives alone; if she moves in with her economically secure daughter, she would not be classified as poor. By contrast, an older couple who has income above the poverty line on their own may fall below the poverty cutoff when a grandchild moves in with them, due to the associated increase in expenses.

## CONCLUSION

Despite significant and marked improvements in poverty rates of older adults across time, the risk of poverty remains a real possibility for many older adults in the United States (Rank & Hirschl, 1999b). Although arguments can be made against the current measurement of poverty used by researchers today, the high risk of late-life poverty must be central in any discussion of later-life issues. The cumulative risk of poverty across the life course has implications for the well-being of adults in later life, by shaping adults' lifelong accumulation of wealth, pension resources, and Social Security credits.

Several unanswered questions on this topic should be addressed by future research. First, what are the long-term implications of hardship that occurs in childhood or young adulthood? For example, it may be that older adults who experienced poverty as children have a higher risk of chronic disease in later life. Second, what can we expect with respect to poverty levels among baby boomers when they reach later life? Boomers have had patterns of pension coverage, earnings histories, and asset accumulation that differ from those of their parents, which may place them at higher (or lower) risk of poverty when they retire. Additionally, how well does the current poverty measurement reflect economic hardship among older adults? Research on measurement improvements and understanding how low incomes are associated with subjective experiences of hardship is needed.

**SEE ALSO** Volume 3: *Pensions; Policy, Later Life Well-Being; Social Security; Wealth.*

**BIBLIOGRAPHY**

Becker, G. S. (1964). *Human capital.* (2nd ed.). New York: Columbia University Press.

Citro, C. F., & Michael, R. T. (Eds.). (1995). *Measuring poverty: A new approach.* Washington, DC: National Academy Press.

Coleman, J. S. (1988). Social capital in the creation of human capital. *American Journal of Sociology, 94,* S95–S120.

Department of Health and Human Services. (2008). *The 2008 HHS poverty guidelines.* Retrieved May 21, 2008, from http://aspe.hhs.gov

Fisher, G. M. (2007). *The development of the Orshansky poverty thresholds and their subsequent history as the official U.S. poverty measure.* Poverty Measurement Working Paper Series, U.S. Census Bureau. Retrieved April 24, 2008, from http://www.census.gov/hhes

He, W., Sengupta, M., Velkoff, V. A., & DeBarros, K. A. (2005). 65+ in the United States: 2005 (*Current Population Reports* P23–209). Washington, DC: U.S. Department of Census.

Iceland, J. (2003). Dynamics of economic well-being: Poverty 1996–1999 (*Current Population Reports* P70–91). Washington, DC: U.S. Census Bureau.

McKernan, S., & Ratcliffe, C. (2002). *Transition events in the dynamics of poverty.* Washington, DC: Urban Institute.

Rank, M. R., & Hirschl, T. A. (1999a). Estimating the proportion of Americans ever experiencing poverty during their elderly years. *The Journals of Gerontology, 54B*(4), S184–194.

Rank, M. R., & Hirschl, T. A. (1999b). The likelihood of poverty across the American adult life span. *Social Work, 44*(3), 201–216.

Rank, M., & Hirschl, T. (2001). The occurrence of poverty across the life cycle: Evidence from the PSID. *Journal of Policy Analysis and Management, 20*(4), 737–755.

Sevak, P., Weir, D. R,. & Willis, R. J. (2003–2004). The economic consequences of a husband's death: Evidence from the HRS and AHEAD. *Social Security Bulletin, 65*(3), 31–44.

U.S. Census Bureau. (2007a). Historical poverty tables. *Current Population Survey, Annual Social and Economic Supplements.* Retrieved February 22, 2008, from http://www.census.gov

U.S. Census Bureau. (2007b). *Poverty thresholds 2006.* Retrieved April 22, 2008, from http://www.census.gov

***Kerstin Gerst***
***Jan E. Mutchler***

# QUALITY OF LIFE

Quality of life is a complex concept because it represents a social construct of a uniquely European and North American origin. Although definitions of what constitutes life quality may vary widely when compared across cultures, health systems, philosophies, religions, and jobs; social scientists approach the task of measuring *the quality of life* from a perspective that evolved over centuries of change in the European world view and that reflects people's perception of their place in the world community. At a minimum, an acceptable quality of life requires that an individual have food, water, clothing, and shelter beyond that required to simply survive and that he or she be healthy enough to engage in the daily activities to maintain this level of existence for an extended period. Beyond this minimal level, all measures of life quality are subjective and can only be evaluated and understood within the social context in which they occur. While all societies have a vested interest in maintaining a healthy population, the idea that it is possible to actively intercede and positively influence the quality of life at the individual, national, and even global level is a self-directed, modern, Western approach to problem resolution. To understand this concept it is necessary to see it as part of an evolving social conscience on the part of modern Western society.

## HISTORICAL EVOLUTION OF THE CONCEPT OF QUALITY OF LIFE

Scholars' understanding of the quality of life for populations in prehistoric eras remains speculative as it must be inferred from fossil records. Throughout recorded history, however, conceptualizations of quality of life typically reflect social thinking on what represents the "ideal" life attainable at that time. Historically, literal biblical interpretations dominated Western thought and behaviors for most aspects of life well into the 18th century, and Judeo-Christian principles continued to strongly influence behaviors into the early 21st century. Under this biblical tradition people's quality of life is exemplified by the life of Adam and Eve in the Garden of Eden. After the fall of humankind, this level of happiness, health, and plenty became unattainable, and an individual was forced to improve his quality of life through the sweat of his brow.

This view of quality of life gained depth and complexity as Europe, particularly England and France, formalized political science in the 17th century. This period was marked by philosophical debates that began over the roles, rights, and obligations of society, of rulers, and of citizens and how nation states collectively served the needs of their community. Thomas Hobbes and his classic publication *Leviathan* (1651) may be the best known of these early writers. He introduces the argument that to survive humans need to abide by a "social contract" that ties them explicitly to a sovereign ruler and requires them to surrender their natural rights in exchange for the peaceful existence that only life under a sovereign-led state can offer. Without this submission to a central authority, humankind could only exist in its natural state, where the quality of life was "solitary, poor, nasty, brutish, and short." In Hobbes' argument for the "Divine Rights of Kings," quality of life was completely

***Garden of Eden.*** *This 16th century painting illustrates how quality of life had once been exemplified by the life of Adam and Eve in the Garden of Eden.* © FRANCIS G. MAYER/CORBIS.

dependent upon the people's acceptance of an organized government controlled by a sovereign.

While Hobbes's work drew a number of criticisms, it was not until the early 18th century and the emergence of the Enlightenment that Hobbes's basic thesis on the absolute power of monarchy was significantly revised. *The Social Contract* written by Jean-Jacques Rousseau and published in 1762 formed a complete contrast to Hobbes's writings. Rousseau saw society emerging not as an escape from brutality and chaos but from a shared interest among people to cooperate as populations grew larger. This cooperation led them to work together to improve the quality of life for all. Rather than seeing the natural state as brutish, Rousseau argued that humankind in this state was free; neither good nor bad, and through cooperation people devised social contracts that improved the quality of life for the group. Rousseau's concept of the social contract represented an important conceptual shift, allowing people to directly influence their quality of life, something largely impossible under either a literal biblical interpretation or the Hobbesian perspective. Prevailing philosophies of the Enlightenment argued that quality of life would improve as manmade inequalities were overcome.

The following century, however, was defined by an industrial rather than a cultural revolution. The 19th century saw great gains in commerce, personal wealth, trade, expansionism, and the emergence of the European empires. However, such economic developments also were accompanied by increasing levels of social and economic inequality, which, in turn, created clear divides in the quality of life across society. Extreme differences in poverty, status, and social class resulted in social unrest, riots, and deportation laws; thus, society sought to explain how these inequalities could exist and sought new measures of quality of life. The 18th century also was marked by the belief that science represented the future; the scientific method was seen as the obvious way to explore quality of life. This represented a major philosophical shift, moving quality of life out of the realm of philosophy and into one of scientific inquiry, largely uninterested in debating social contracts, but instead seeking ways to physically measure why some groups excelled at the expense of others.

The publication of Darwin's *Origin of the Species* in 1859 provided a "scientific" explanation for inequality within a particular social community. Darwin's biological model of evolution and adaptive change became a framework that explained inequality, poverty, industrialization, and colonial exploitation as a simple extension of the natural order. The idea of Social Darwinism was first introduced by Oscar Schmidt in 1875, less than five years after the publication of Darwin's work. It explained in the starkest of terms why some groups advance and other do not: "The free will of the morally elevated man is no common property of all mankind" (Schmidt 1875, p. 300). The implication of such writings was that civilized persons are civilized because they are naturally predisposed to be so and savages are savages because they are born as such. Consequently, a high quality of life was the direct result of biological superiority, and the poor were destined to live in poverty "as a consequence of their own retardation" (Schmidt 1875, p. 298).

This idea that some groups succeed because they are inherently superior was quickly embraced as an explanation for inequality in industrialized society. These interpretations drew heavily on early work by Hebert Spencer, particularly *Social Statics* (1851). Spencer is perhaps best known for introducing the term "survival of the fittest," in his *Principles of Biology* (1864), and this phrase came to justify harsh business and social decisions as being "*just a part of the natural order.*" Although Spencer's ideas are among the most misunderstood and misused concepts in the social sciences, they made a lasting impact on the way Western society perceives inequality. Spencer saw people as intrinsically good and capable of perfection, but he also emphasized individual responsibility regardless of social barriers and institutional inequalities. His writings suggested that it was possible to "scientifically" justify gross inequalities in the quality of life between members of the same society. In essence the privileged members of society achieve a high quality of life because they evolve to the point where they deserve it (Spencer, 1883). Consequently, not only are the privileged not faulted for their high quality of life, they are also not held responsible for helping poorer members of society overcome inequality. Because quality of life is directly dependent upon people's personal progress and achievements, their quality of life improves only through their own hard work and self improvement.

This fundamental perspective of individual responsibility continues to influence Western perspectives of how quality of life is evaluated at both the individual and societal level. The underlying assumption of much research is that every person has the capacity to achieve a high quality of life, but inequality is unavoidable as some people naturally excel, whereas others lag behind due to personal weakness. While the quality of life a person enjoys, good or bad, is a direct consequence of his or her individual achievements, members of society can help others improve their quality of life, but only if those others prove worthy of such help. In other words, rather than giving people fish to improve their quality of life, teach them how to fish. With this knowledge, they should then be able to take care of themselves. If they cannot, then this inability must be due to personal flaws or weaknesses; consequently, their current quality of life may represent the best they are capable of attaining.

## MEASURING QUALITY OF LIFE

Scholars' ability to systematically define and operationalize *quality of life* through the use of a standardized measure is difficult because of variations inherent between people and societies. Despite these challenges, there is a genuine need to try to capture quality of life in a systematic manner. Definitions vary from ones as broad as that used by the World Health Organization where quality of life is "the individual's perception of their position in life in the context of the culture and value systems in which they live and in relation to their goals" to narrowly focused instruments such as the Wong-Baker Faces scale that measure life quality (in this case, physical pain) at a precise moment in time (Wong & Whaley, 1986). These measures were designed to provide a comparative basis by which researchers can evaluate and ultimately strive to eliminate inequalities in individuals' well-being. Without some mechanism to measure quality of life, it becomes virtually impossible to develop policy, allocate resources, or make informed decisions regardless of the ultimate success of these efforts. Typically, quality of life measures can be divided into two broad categories: (a) individual measures that normally take the form of overall quality of life as well as medical or health measures of life quality; and (b) societal-level measures of the quality of life in a country, region, or area.

## MEASURING QUALITY OF LIFE FROM A MEDICAL PERSPECTIVE

The measures and scales used by the Western medical system represent one of the most common approaches to studying quality of life. Because good health is fundamental to life quality and because both disease and the treatment of sickness can disrupt the feeling of well being, quality of life in a medical context refers to "the patient's ability to enjoy normal life activities" (Hecht & Shiel, 2003). Other formal definitions offer similar summaries. The National Cancer Institute (NCI) at the National Institutes of Health (NIH) has developed descriptions such as "the overall enjoyment of life," whereas *Stedman's Medical Dictionary* offers a more detailed assessment stating that quality of life involves "a patient's general well-being, including mental status, stress level, sexual function, and self-perceived health status."

Despite widespread agreement that health influences quality of life, its formal measurement is relatively new. One of the earliest attempts to collect information and classify quality of life was done in New York City in 1937 (New York Heart Association, 1939), when researchers attempted to define the health of elderly persons receiving public assistance. Formal measurements were based upon researchers' observations of the older persons' level of disability. A more complex index of elderly health was introduced in 1947 by F. D. Zeman, incorporating both the observed level of elderly disability and occupational background (i.e. skilled, unskilled). At about the same time, other scales were developed, such as Karnofsky's 100-point scale that evaluated quality of life among cancer patients. The scale assessed the patients' ability to engage in daily activities, their need for caregiving, and their need for medical treatment (Karnofsky & Burchenal, 1948). By the late 1950s medical scales that measured the quality of life had become far more complex. The PULSE scale (Moskowitz & McCann, 1957) represented an early attempt to incorporate emotional and cognitive states as part of overall health and quality of life measures, while the 1958 Index of Activities of Daily Living (Benjamin Rose Hospital, 1958, 1959) became the foundation for future measures of functional ability. This scale included the Instrumental Activities of Daily Living (IADL) scale introduced by Michael P. Lawton and Elaine M. Brody in 1969, one of the most commonly used measures of quality of life in both the medical and social sciences. Currently, literally hundreds of scales are available for measuring life satisfaction, particularly with respect to managing conditions such as HIV/AIDS, breast cancer, depression, and virtually any serious health condition. Jordan Matthew Prutkin (2002) provides a thorough and instructive review of the history of quality of life measures and represents an excellent source for more information.

## INDIVIDUAL MEASURES OF OVERALL QUALITY OF LIFE OR LIFE HAPPINESS

Psychological conditions, such as happiness or emotional satisfaction, are also frequently captured by quality of life assessments. Many social and health surveys ask a basic series of questions such as "How happy would you say you are?"; "How satisfied are you with the way your life has turned out?"; "How happy are you with the quality of your marriage?"; and so on. These kinds of satisfaction questions typically have respondents rate their feelings on a scale often ranging from "very dissatisfied" to "very satisfied." Because they use a standard metric, these measures offer a straightforward tool to compare levels of life quality both within and across samples. This is a powerful tool for evaluating overall life quality at the individual level. However, such measures reflect subjective appraisals. As such, one's response to a question may be biased by current stressors or by one's mood on the day of interview. Survey participants who have recently experienced emotional traumas such as disease, death, or divorce may evaluate their satisfaction based upon these immediate events, rather than stepping back and evaluating life quality across their entire life course.

Perhaps one of the most ambitious efforts to measure an individual's quality of life is the World Health Organization Quality of Life (WHOQOL) project, begun in 1991. WHO sought to create an instrument that would measure comparative quality of life across nations and across cultures. The project represents an effort to introduce cultural competence into the measurement of quality of life by allowing variations in cultures and value systems to be integrated into the assessment of personal goals, living standards, and concerns. Currently the WHO has developed a 26-item instrument—WHOQOL-BREF, a tool that touches on the domains of physical health, psychological health, social relationships, and environment. The WHOQOL-BREF is relatively easy to use, and it offers researchers an opportunity to compare local data with data obtained globally.

## MACRO OR SOCIETAL MEASURES OF QUALITY OF LIFE

Measuring the quality of life for a nation or a society has a long history, as such indicators were traditionally tied to the economic strength or potential of a nation. From works such as the classic *Wealth of Nations* by Adam Smith to ongoing economic surveillance systems, such as those used by the World Bank or the Social Weather-station series, quality of life is measured through broad summary measures such as gross domestic product (GDP), life expectancy, literacy rates, and employment statistics. For example, the *Tables of Economic and Social Indicators* have been used by the World Bank (2008) since 1950 to rank developed and developing nations based upon their economic stability. Similarly, the United Nations (2008) *Demographic Yearbook* has collected information on population size and composition, births, deaths, marriage, and divorce on an annual basis since 1948. These kinds of resources allow comparative measures on quality of life to be developed across nations. Longevity, fertility, infant mortality, and GDP all represent direct indicators of quality of life. However,

## SUCCESSFUL AGING

Successful aging consists of three interrelated elements: an active lifestyle, a relatively low risk of disease, and high levels of physical and cognitive functioning. Early societies recognized the value of successful aging, ascribing special status to long-lived people. For example, in the Hebrew Bible, extreme old age was a characteristic of key patriarchs, revealing the esteem conferred on such people. In the modern world, with worldwide increases in longevity, many old people now suffer from chronic disease and disability. As a result, long life can be viewed negatively—as an outcome of medical interventions (e.g., pacemakers, bypass surgery)—or positively—as a trait of those old people who successfully negotiate the aging process through exercise, good diet, and the benefit of genetic advantages. Life course scholars interested in successful aging now seek to identify mechanisms that will lead to improved health and greater longevity for older adults. Most scholars agree that healthy lifestyle changes represent immediate returns to old people in terms of successful aging and benefit all people regardless of their genetic makeup and current health status.

**BIBLIOGRAPHY**


Benet, S. (1974). *Abkhasians: The long living people of the Caucasus.* New York: Holt Rinehart & Winston.

Hayflick, L. (1965). The limited in vitro lifetime of human diploid cell strains. *Experimental Cell Research 37*, 614–636.

New England Centenarian Project. Retrieved January 5, 2008, from http://www.bumc.bu.edu/Dept/Home.aspx?DepartmentID=361

Okinawa Centenarian Study. Retrieved January 5, 2008, from http://www.okicent.org

Olshansky, S. J., & Carnes, B. A. (2001). The quest for immortality: Science at the frontiers of aging. New York: Norton.

Rowe, J. W., & Kahn, R. L. (1998). *Successful aging.* New York: Pantheon Books.


these snapshot measures reflect European and North American notions of what "quality" is, and these measures, in turn, shape both how scholars and laypersons assess the quality of life worldwide. They also guide where policy makers focus resources to make changes. Some Asian societies often have different perspectives on the concept of *life quality*, hold different attitudes toward birth and death, and propose different ideas about the direction their societies should take in their efforts to achieve the highest quality of life possible. Measures such as those developed by the World Bank and the United Nations are useful but they, like the concept of quality of life itself, are constantly being refined as scholars learn more, obtain better sources of information, and broaden their definitions to include non-Western perspectives of what defines a life of quality.

### CONCLUSION

Conceptualizations of quality of life reflect individuals' beliefs about how they stand in relation to other members of society. The approach to conceptualizing quality of life is guided by hundreds of years of philosophical debate, as well as more recent changes in how one defines *well-being* in a period of development and innovation. There is no one definitive definition of *quality of life*; however, what most definitions share is an effort to evaluate life quality in terms of equity and in terms of how an individual lives relative to other members of his or her recognized community.

**SEE ALSO** Volume 3: *Social Integration/Isolation, Later Life; Social Support, Later Life.*

### BIBLIOGRAPHY


Benjamin Rose Hospital (Staff). (1958). Multidisciplinary study of illness in aged persons I. *Journal of Chronic Diseases, 7*(4), 332–345.

Benjamin Rose Hospital (Staff). (1959). Multidisciplinary study of illness in aged persons II. *Journal of Chronic Diseases, 9*(1), 55–62.

Hobbes, T. (1946). *Leviathan, or The matter, forme, and power of a common wealth ecclesiasticall and civil*, ed. Michael Oakeshott. Oxford: Basil Blackworth. (Original work published 1651).

Inter-University Consortium for Political and Social Research. (2008). *World tables of economic and social indicators series.* Retrieved June 13, 2008, from http://www.icpsr.umich.edu/cocoon/ICPSR/SERIES/00076.xml

Karnofsky, D. A., & Burchenal, J. H. (1948). The clinical evaluation of chemotherapeutic agents in cancer. In C. M. Macleod (Ed), *Evaluation of chemotherapeutic agents* (pp. 191–205). New York: Columbia University Press.

Lawton, M. P., & Brody, E. M. (1969). Assessment of older people: Self-maintaining and instrumental activities of daily living. *Gerontologist, 9*, 179–186.

Moskowitz, E., & McCann, C. B. (1957). Classification of disability in the chronically ill and aging. *Journal of Chronic Diseases, 5*(3), 42–46.

New York Heart Association Criteria Committee. (1939). *Nomenclature and criteria for diagnosis of diseases of the heart.* New York: Author.

Rousseau, J-J. (1984). *A discourse on inequality*, (M. Cranston, Trans.). Harmondsworth, U.K.: Penguin Books. (Original work published 1754)

Rousseau, J-J. (1988). *The social contract.* Amherst, NY: Prometheus Books. (Original work published 1762)

Schmidt, E. O. (1875). *The doctrine of descent and Darwinism.* London: H. S. King. Retrieved June 27, 2008, from http://www.books.google.com/books?id=TntIAAAAMAAJ

Spencer, H. 1874. *The study of sociology.* New York: D. Appleton. Retrieved June 27, 2008, from http://www.books.google.com/books?id=C-ItAAAAIAAJ

Spencer, H. (1904). *The principles of biology.* New York: D. Appleton. (Original work published 1864)

Spencer, H. (1910). *Social statics.* London: Watts. (Original work published 1851)

United Nations Statistics Division. (2008). *Demographic yearbook.* Retrieved June 13, 2008, from http://unstats.un.org/unsd/demographic/products/dyb/dyb2.htm

van der Post, L. (1961). *The heart of the hunter.* London: Hogarth Press.

Wong, D., & Whaley, L. (1986). *Clinical handbook of pediatric nursing.* (2nd ed.). St. Louis: C. V. Mosby, p. 373. Retrieved June 13, 2008, from http://painconsortium.nih.gov/pain_scales/index.html

Zeman, F. D. (1947). The functional capacity of the aged: Its estimation and practical importance. *Journal of the Mount Sinai Hospital, 14*, 721–728.

***James W. McNally***

# R

## RELIGION AND SPIRITUALITY, LATER LIFE

Religion has been an important topic in the social and behavioral sciences since their inceptions. From the beginning, sociologists and psychologists have focused on very different aspects of religion. Émile Durkheim (1858–1917) set the stage for sociological views of religion, defining it as "a unified system of beliefs and practices which unite into one single moral community, called a Church, by all who adhere to them" (1912/1951, p. 44). Durkheim believed that religion serves important functions for both societies and individuals: stabilizing and integrating societies and providing a moral compass for believers. William James (1842–1910), the father of psychological inquiry in religion, had a very different focus. His primary premises are that religious feelings are psychological facts that benefit individuals by transforming their personalities, their understanding of the meaning of life, and their values. He contended that religious or spiritual feelings are experienced most frequently during times of solitude, contemplation, and personal ritual. Unlike Durkheim, James had no respect for organized religion. In his words, "When a religion has become orthodox, then the time of spiritual value is over" (1902/1997, p. 72). These very different views of religion are the cornerstone of modern conceptions of religion and spirituality. It remains true that sociologists are the primary investigators of religion and psychologists more often focus on spirituality.

Before proceeding, a caveat is in order. The vast majority of research on social and psychological facets of religion and spirituality is based on samples from North America and Western Europe, especially the United States. Thus, knowledge about the life course dynamics of religion and spirituality is limited to specific countries and specific religious traditions.

### DEFINITIONS AND MEASUREMENT

Scholars disagree about how to define religion and spirituality and, especially, about the extent to which they are distinct versus overlapping. Increasingly, however, scholars rely on the definitions offered by Hill and Pargament (2003), who view religion and spirituality as having in common the "search for the sacred, a process through which people seek to discover, hold on to, and, when necessary, transform whatever they hold sacred in their lives" (p. 65). The difference between religion and spirituality is that the former rests on the beliefs and practices of a community of believers—a community that shares religious beliefs, practices, and identity. In contrast, spirituality is more often defined as a search for the sacred that can, but need not, rest on religious traditions.

Individuals cannot be neatly sorted into those who are religious and those who are spiritual, however. Research that includes measures of both religious participation and spiritual practices outside of organized religion consistently reports strong positive relationships between the two. That is, the vast majority of people who participate in organized religion also engage in personal spiritual practices. Nonetheless, a sizable minority of the population does not participate in organized religion but report that they believe in God or a higher power and engage in personal spiritual practices (Zinnbauer et al., 1997).

Religious involvement takes multiple forms. A panel of experts identified 11 dimensions of religious participation relevant to health (Idler et al., 2003): religious affiliation (e.g., denomination), religious history and socialization, public religious practices (e.g., attending services), private religious practices (e.g., prayer/meditation, reading sacred texts), religious social support, religious coping, beliefs and values, religious commitment, forgiveness, daily spiritual experiences, and self-ratings of religiousness. Although these dimensions are especially relevant for research on the relationship between religion and health, according to Idler et al. they also comprise a relatively comprehensive view of religious participation in general. Based on data on all 11 dimensions from a nationally representative sample of American adults, the correlations across dimensions of religious involvement are positive but relatively weak (Idler et al., 2003). This pattern indicates that the dimensions are distinct, probably have different antecedents and consequences, and may exhibit different dynamics over the life course.

Because the scientific study of spirituality is quite recent, fewer measures are available and it is unclear whether there are distinct dimensions. Nonetheless, some dimensions of religious involvement listed above can be spiritual practices that occur outside of organized religion. Private "religious" practices (e.g., prayer, meditation), daily spiritual practices, and forgiveness, for example, can be practiced outside of any religious tradition.

## RELIGIOUS INVOLVEMENT: AGE AND LIFE COURSE PATTERNS

The United States is, without question, the most religious nation in the Western world. A 2004 survey of a representative sample of American adults found that 66% reported that "I have no doubt that God exists," 74% prayed several times a week or more, and 49% attended religious services once a month or more (Association of Religious Data Archives, 2008). In this and other surveys from the early 21st century, older adults reported even higher percentages. In a 2001 Gallup poll, for example, 60% of Americans ages 50 to 64, 67% of those ages 65 to 74, and 75% of those ages 75 and older reported that religion is very important to them (Gallup, 2002). In that same poll, 44% of people ages 50 to 64, 50% of those ages 65 to 74, and 60% of those ages 75 and older reported that they had attended religious services in the past week. In contrast to the United States, levels of religious participation are much lower in Europe and other Westernized societies (Crockett & Voas, 2006).

Because these surveys are based on cross-sectional data, it is not clear whether these age differences are due to an increase in religious participation across the life course or whether older cohorts have been more involved in religion than younger cohorts throughout their lives. Two types of studies have investigated whether the positive association between age and religious participation represents age or cohort effects. There are theoretical reasons to expect both patterns. The "life cycle" hypothesis suggests that as adults enter late life they increasingly turn to religion to find meaning in the lives they have lived and prepare for death (e.g., Erikson, 1982), suggesting an aging effect. In contrast, the "secularization hypothesis" argues that since World War II, religious participation has declined across cohorts as a result of increasing levels of education and the prestige of science (Presser & Chaves, 2007).

In the first type of study, investigators assemble repeated cross-sectional surveys collected over decades and longer and use these data to determine whether age groups exhibit the same levels of religious participation regardless of when they were born—or if different birth cohorts report different levels of religious involvement, regardless of age. These studies focus exclusively on rates of attending religious services, and the results are mixed. In the United States, disagreement continues about whether rates of religious service attendance have declined substantially since World War II (e.g., Presser & Chavez, 2007) or declined only slightly (e.g., Putman, 2000). One study found no decline in attendance between 1990 and 2006 (Presser & Chaves, 2007). These studies provide minimal support for the secularization hypothesis and no support for the life cycle hypothesis. In contrast, church attendance in Europe has declined dramatically since World War II (Crockett & Voas, 2006), providing strong support for secularization there.

Second, a few studies used longitudinal or retrospective data to trace intraindividual patterns of religious involvement across the life course. Ingersoll-Dayton, Krause, and Morgan (2002) used retrospective interview data to identify distinct patterns of religious involvement in multiple dimensions. Four trajectories were identified for each: stable, increasing, decreasing, and curvilinear (i.e., U-shaped) patterns. Stable and curvilinear patterns were most common. The curvilinear patterns were generally tied to specific events, with increases often triggered by the birth of children and adverse life experiences and decreases most often resulting in disillusionment with clergy or church members. Using longitudinal data from adolescence until age 32, Stolzenberg, Blair-Loy, and Waite (1995) examined patterns of religious services attendance over time. They reported substantial change in attendance over the course of adolescence and early adulthood, with both increases and decreases very common. These changes in attendance are linked in complex ways with changes in marital status and the birth and ages of children. Some of these role transitions also operate differently for men and women; for example,

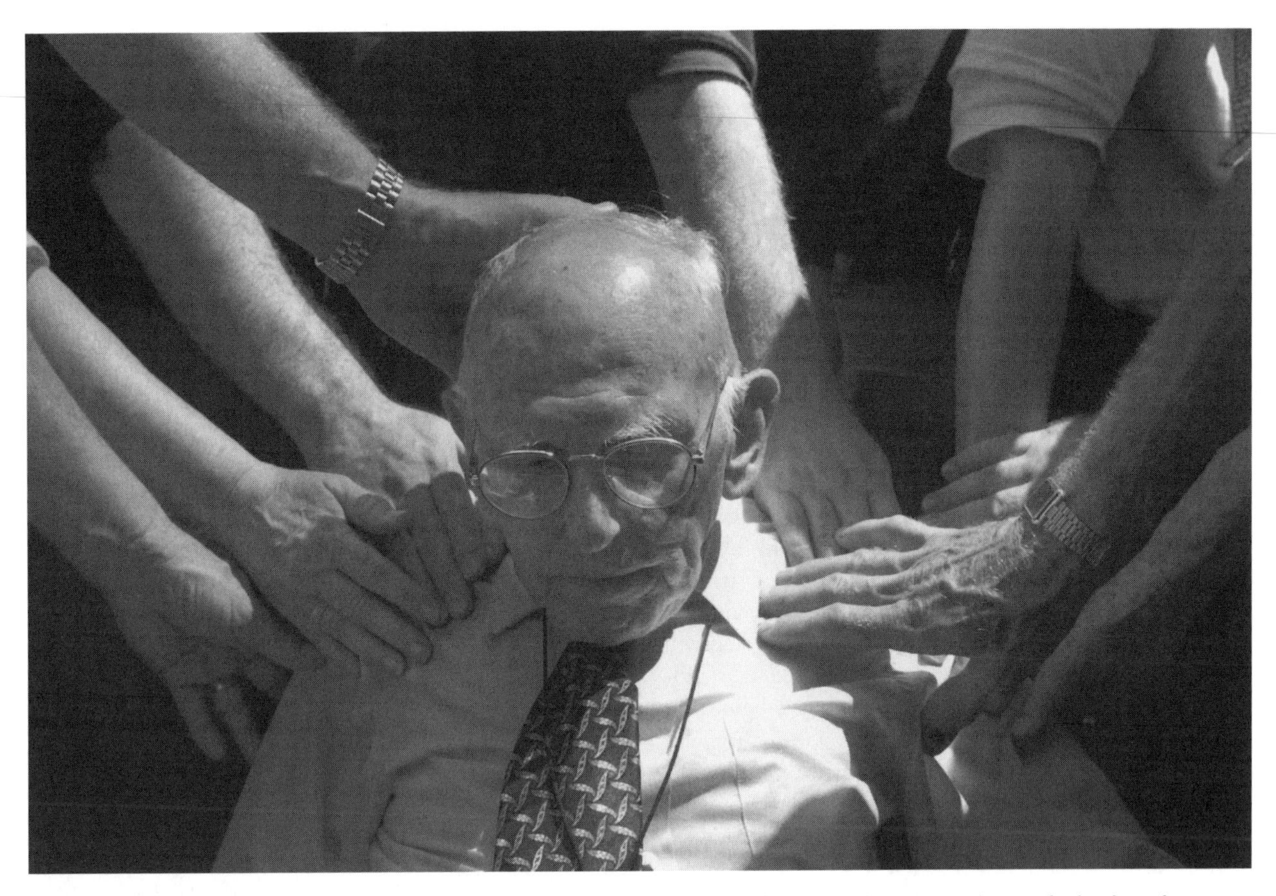

***Belated Call.*** *Ed Schreiber, 96, prays during the traditional laying on of hands at his ordination in the Cumberland Presbyterian denomination on June 21, 2000, in Adairville, KY. Schreiber, of Nashville, TN, began his seminary studies at age 92.* AP IMAGES.

divorce tends to be followed by increased church attendance for women and decreased attendance for men. Finally, Paul Wink (2003) examined a composite index of religiosity in a longitudinal study of two cohorts, born 10 years apart, from childhood through early old age. Seven measurements were taken over approximately 50 years. In both cohorts, religious involvement was overwhelmingly stable over the life course.

Age patterns of religious involvement take different forms, depending on the research design. There are substantial differences across cross-sectional, repeated cross-sectional, and longitudinal studies. Although longitudinal data are preferable, the few studies available suggest that length of observation and the time interval between measurements affect research results. With regard to the latter point, in the longitudinal study that examined the dynamics of religious involvement between adolescence and young adulthood, frequent changes in levels of church attendance were observed. In the longitudinal study spanning 50 years, however, overwhelming stability was observed. In this study, however, measurements were often a decade or more apart; thus, substantial unobserved change could occur between measurements. Perhaps the most interesting aspect of both groups of studies, however, is what was *not* found. There is little evidence that the higher rates of religious participation reported by older adults are a result of cohort differences. At the same time, studies of intraindividual change fail to observe meaningful increases in religious involvement in late adulthood.

In addition to age differences, gender and race/ethnicity also are strongly related to religious participation. Women report higher levels of religious involvement than men at all ages (Idler et al., 2003). In the United States, African Americans report the highest levels of religious involvement of any racial/ethnic group, especially in comparison to Whites (Idler et al., 2003). Again, these racial/ethnic differences are found throughout adulthood.

One form of religious participation, attending religious services, would seem to be more dependent on health than other more private and personal forms. Detailed reports of levels of religious attendance during late life indicate that attendance is lower among the oldest-old (i.e., age 80 or 85 and older) than among adults ages 65 to 79 (Gallup, 2002). An important longitudinal study of the effects of disability on religious participation, however, found that religious attendance dropped temporarily after the onset of disability but typically rebounded to predisability levels (Idler & Kasl, 1997).

## SPIRITUALITY: AGE AND LIFE COURSE PATTERNS

Although many studies of spirituality, especially among older adults, have appeared since the late 1990s, almost none of them are based on longitudinal data covering sufficient years to provide insights about cohort differences, age changes, and life course patterns of spirituality. The notable exception to this is a series of studies by Wink (2006), Wink and Dillon (2002), and Wink and Scott (2005). Data for these studies are from the Berkeley Growth Studies, which began in the 1920s and followed two cohorts from childhood through late life. Data collection spanned approximately 50 years, with seven times of measurement. Not surprisingly, the Berkeley Growth Studies do not include what are now viewed as standardized methods of assessing spirituality and religion. To examine long-term patterns of religion, spirituality, and other phenomena, trained raters examined the full range of data collected at each time of measurement and generated ratings, using the same metric at each test date. Thus, the aforementioned research was based on ratings of degree of religiousness and degree of spirituality. Because these are composite ratings, it is not possible to examine specific dimensions of religious or spiritual experience.

With regard to spiritual development, these investigators found that, by early adulthood, individuals vary substantially in the extent to which spiritual issues are important to them (Wink & Scott, 2005). Whatever this "baseline" level of spirituality, it tends to remain quite stable until the late 50s or early 60s, after which a demonstrable increase in concern about and exploration of spiritual issues occurs (Wink & Dillon, 2002). Although there is a general pattern of increasing spirituality during later life, some individuals exhibit greater increases than others—and a few show no increase at all. The major predictors of increases in spirituality in later life are (a) a history of sustained religious involvement, (b) openness to new experience—a personality characteristic measured in early adulthood, and (c) an accumulation of multiple negative life events or stressors across the adult life course (Wink & Dillon, 2002). The strong relationship between sustained religious involvement during adulthood and increased spirituality in later life highlights the fact that religion and spirituality can never be viewed as either/or commitments. For most American adults, religion and spirituality are overlapping commitments. Women are rated as having higher levels of spirituality at all ages (Wink & Dillon, 2002), although an increase in spirituality in late life is true for both men and women.

An important part of Wink and colleagues' research agenda has been to compare the effects of religiosity and spirituality on well-being. Overall, religiosity is associated with more elements of well-being than spirituality. Specifically, religiosity is associated with closer, more satisfactory interpersonal relationships, greater community involvement, higher levels of life satisfaction, and less death anxiety. Spirituality is not related to these outcomes (Wink, 2006). Similarly, high levels of religiosity lessen the effects of physical illness on depression (Wink, 2006). Spirituality does not exhibit this buffering effect. In contrast, however, higher levels of spirituality are associated with a greater sense of personal growth, and religiosity is not.

The Berkeley Growth Studies have made unique and important contributions to knowledge about life course patterns of both religiosity and spirituality. Nonetheless, these studies also have serious limitations. For example, the participants in these studies were all White, and socioeconomic variability was limited. Also important is the fact that the measurement strategies forced upon investigators by the age and design of the studies would be judged unacceptable by current standards. Clearly, there is much left to learn about age changes, cohort differences, and life course patterns of spirituality.

**SEE ALSO** Volume 2: *Durkheim, Émile;* Volume 3: *Social Integration/Isolation, Later Life.*

### BIBLIOGRAPHY

Association of Religious Data Archives. (2008) *U.S. Surveys.* Retrieved May 21, 2008, 2008, from http://www.thearda.com/Quickstats

Crockett, A., & Voas, D. (2006). Generations of decline: Religious change in 20th-century Britain. *Journal for the Scientific Study of Religion, 45,* 567–584.

Durkheim, É. (1951). *The elementary forms of religious life.* New York: Oxford University Press. (Original work published 1912)

Erikson, E. H. (1982). *The life cycle completed.* New York: Norton.

Gallup, G. H., Jr. (2002, June 4). *The religiosity cycle: Religion and social trends.* Retrieved May 21, 2008, from http://www.gallup.com/poll/

Hill, P. C., & Pargament, K. I. (2003). Advances in the conceptualization and measurement of religion and spirituality: Implications for physical and mental health research. *American Psychologist, 58,* 64–74.

Idler, E. L., & Kasl, S. V. (1997). Religion among disabled and nondisabled persons II: Attendance at religious services as a predictor of the course of disability. *The Journals of Gerontology, Series B: Psychological Sciences and Social Sciences, 52,* S306–S316.

Idler, E. L., Musick, M. A., Ellison, C. G., George, L. K., Krause, N., Ory, M. G., et al. (2003). Measuring multiple dimensions of religion and spirituality for health research: Conceptual background and findings from the 1998 General Social Survey. *Research on Aging, 25*, 327–365.

Ingersoll-Dayton, B., Krause, N., & Morgan, D. (2002). Religious trajectories and transitions over the life course. *International Journal of Aging and Human Development, 55*, 51–70.

James, W. (1997). *The varieties of religious experience.* New York: Touchstone. (Original work published 1902)

Presser, S., & Chaves, M. (2007). Is religious service attendance declining? *Journal for the Scientific Study of Religion, 46*, 417–423.

Putman, R. D. (2000). *Bowling alone: The collapse and revival of American community.* New York: Simon and Schuster.

Stolzenberg, R. M., Blair-Loy, M., & Waite, L. J. (1995). Religious participation in early adulthood: Age and family life cycle effects on church membership. *American Sociological Review, 60*, 84–103.

Wink, P. (2006). Who is afraid of death? Religiousness, spirituality, and death anxiety in late adulthood. *Journal of Religion, Spirituality, and Aging, 18*, 93–110.

Wink, P., & Dillon, M. (2002). Spiritual development across the adult life course: Findings from a longitudinal study. *Journal of Adult Development, 9*, 79–94.

Wink, P., & Scott, J. (2005). Does religiousness buffer against the fear of death and dying in late adulthood? Findings from a longitudinal study. *The Journals of Gerontology, Series B: Psychological Sciences and Social Sciences, 60*, P207–P214.

Zinnbauer, B. J., Pargament, K. I., Cole, B., Rye, M. S., Butter, E. M., Belavich, T. G., et al. (1997). Religion and spirituality: Unfuzzying the fuzzy. *Journal for the Scientific Study of Religion, 36*, 549–564.

***Linda K. George***

# REMINISCENCE

SEE Volume 3: *Wisdom.*

# RESIDENTIAL MOBILITY, LATER LIFE

Residential mobility, defined as a change of address, occurs during the life course of almost every person in the Western world, and is experienced in the United States by a majority of people after 60 years of age. Most changes of address, however, are over short distances; these are local "housing adjustments." Most of these short moves have relatively little impact on the movers' activities, time use, social roles, or social networks. They are, in other words, mundane, and while they contribute to socioeconomic and environmental changes, such as housing price trends, most have only minor consequences for older people's lives (Longino & Warnes, 2005). The exception to this generalization is moves into local long-term-care settings.

Two other categories of mobility have more radical consequences for older people's lives. First, long-distance moves across important political boundaries substantially alter people's daily activities, social contacts, and life prospects. This type of move is called "internal migration." It is internal to national boundaries and crosses state or county lines, the defining characteristic of migration. In the context of later life it is sometimes referred to as "retirement migration" (Haas, Bradley, Longino, Stoller, & Serow, 2006). Following this type of move, there is often a need to find new doctors, churches, volunteer activities, and friends. It has an important impact on the lives of the movers. Second, "international migration" from one national culture to another is an additional and even more radical type of move.

## MIGRATION SELECTIVITY

"Who Moved among the Elderly" was the title of the first comprehensive census analysis of the population characteristics of older mover types (Biggar, 1980). J. C. Biggar's article made a very strong statement, showing that there were distinctive profiles among the various elderly mobility categories (nonmovers, local movers, intrastate migrants, and interstate migrants). Residentially mobile local movers, in contrast to nonmovers, had lower average incomes, and a higher proportion of local movers were living dependently with others. By contrast, interstate migrants were younger on average, more often married, more likely to live in their own homes, and had higher average incomes and education than persons in the other mobility categories.

L.E. Hazelrigg and M. A. Hardy (1995) extend Biggar's work by comparing the income characteristics of older migrants with nonmigrant age peers at their destinations. They found that the migrants were economically better off. They attributed this to the tendency of migrants to move to locations with a somewhat lower cost of living than at their origin. Cost of living and income are higher in large cities and their suburban counties where many migrants originate. Also, some important selectivity factors are at work. Moving is costly, and this tends to screen out those who cannot afford to make a distant move. Further, lifestyle-driven amenity migrants tend to move soon after retirement, before there is any decay in their retirement income relative to more recent retirees. As a caution, W. J. Serow (2001) adds that where destinations have a strong attraction to tourists, cost of living tends to be higher and so do incomes. W. H. Walters (2002) provides a reminder

***Snowbirds.*** *Carol Waugh (L), Bob Passaro, and JoAnn Warnke ride in the back of a truck after a round of golf at the 18-hole desert golf course at Slab City. A former military base in the California desert, Slab City was known as Camp Dunlap during World War II, 80 miles southeast of Palm Springs. Thousands of "Snowbirds," retired people seeking warm weather in the winter, descend upon Slab City from November to April every year.* KATIE CALLAN/CORBIS.

that it is fairly common for studies to include personal attributes of migrants and seek to infer mobility motivation from them.

## PATTERNS OF MIGRATION IN THE UNITED STATES

One way of describing migration destinations is to rank the states or counties that received the largest proportions of later life migrants. Between 1960 and 2000 the U.S. census asked where one lived exactly 5 years before the census: in the same house, in another county in the same state, in another state, or abroad. Using this 5-year item, the numbers and proportions of interstate and intrastate migrants can be compared over time. Interstate migration has held very steady for migrants age 60 and older at 4.0% to 4.6% (Longino, 2006). Short-distance migration within states has declined since 1960 for persons of all ages. Census microdata, a small sample of long-form census records, has been handy for making such comparisons. Since 2000, this program has been replaced by the American Community Survey, an annual survey of 1% of the U.S. population, which asks where one lived 1 year (not 5 years) before. Thus, the observed patterns will shift as future migration studies will assume this new metric.

One of the major features of interstate late-life migration is that the migrants coming from many states are concentrated in only a few destinations, a result of highly focused flows into certain states. In 2000 more than half of older migrants (54%) arrived in just 10 states, having lived in other states 5 years before. In descending order, these states were Florida, Arizona, California, Texas, North Carolina, Georgia, Nevada, Pennsylvania, New Jersey, and Virginia (Longino, 2006).

Using the 2000 census microdata files, the top 100 counties or county groups have been ranked in terms of net interstate migration. Although these substate destinations tend to be within the leading destination states, there is greater variety than is commonly assumed. Ocean County, New Jersey, for example, has consistently received enough retirees from New York and Pennsylvania to keep it among the top 100 interstate destinations for several decades (Longino, 2006). The 100 counties in

2000 sending the largest numbers of interstate migrants to other states were nearly all metropolitan and suburban counties, and more than half (58) were outside the Sun Belt.

## CONCEPTUAL MODELS OF LATER LIFE MIGRATION

Attempts to understand the dynamics of general migration began in the late 19th century with a seminal paper presented at the Royal Statistical Society of London by E. G. Ravenstein (1885) and elaborated some 70 years later by Everett S. Lee (1966). This decision model emphasized the attractions of the destination and the repulsions of the origin—pushes and pulls. R. F. Wiseman (1980) applied this framework to later life migration, and it has been very useful for examining the triggering mechanisms, needed resources, and feedback loops involved in residential adjustment. He identified two categories of older migrants. "Amenity" migrants are younger and have richer economic and social capital resources. "Assistance" migrants are the opposite, and often with more severe health problems. W. H. Haas and W. J. Serow (1993) expanded further, focusing on amenity migrants. C. F. Longino et al. (2008), in a national, prospective study, found that family and community ties at the origin hold back migration, and having vacation homes and regular vacation sites tend to encourage it.

P. H. Rossi (1955) may have been the first to carefully analyze age and mobility, showing that younger people move for many reasons related to their need to establish educational, work, and family statuses. It was just a matter of time until Rossi's approach was extended to later life mobility that is related to retirement and health.

E. Litwak and C. F. Longino (1987) were the first to present a developmental context for understanding the patterns of older interstate migration that are now commonly reported in demographic studies. They argued that retirement and health put older people under pressures to make three basic types of moves. The first type involves persons who are recently retired; these are often amenity-driven moves. A second type includes persons who are usually somewhat older than amenity migrants and who are experiencing moderate forms of disability (Miller, Longino, Anderson, James, & Worley, 1999), a situation often compounded by widowhood. Movement toward family members is one result (Silverstein & Angelelli, 1998). These migrants are said to be making assistance-motivated moves. A third type is an institutional move when health problems overwhelm the capability of the family to care for older relatives in the community. These are nursing home moves. The concept of life course stage applies here to populations and not necessarily to individual persons. Because migration is a youthful phenomenon, even in later life, there are more amenity-motivated than assistance-seeking migrants, but an individual may experience any combination of the three moves, or none at all.

A final conceptual framework that began to emerge during the 1990s is what has been referred to as the place identity model (Cutchin, 2001). Some migrants never put down roots but remain emotionally tied to their former communities. Some of them have problems changing from being a vacationer to being a permanent resident after they arrive. Indeed, some put on an "ageless self" identity when joining the ranks of the active retirees in their new communities, maintaining the energy levels of productive middle-aged persons (McHugh, 2000).

The overwhelming finding of assessment studies, in which older migrants are interviewed about their experience, is that retired migrants make positive assessments of their own moves, the main exception being that women express some dissatisfaction with their reduced contacts with friends, children, and metropolitan facilities (Warnes, King, Williams, & Patterson, 1999). Most moves are undertaken after careful and extended thought and planning.

## PROSPECTS

Most commentators suggest that later life migration will grow in the foreseeable future, as a consequence of increased affluence and home ownership, further advances in telecommunications and transport, increased longevity, and the progressive transition from family-oriented to individualistic lifestyles. The baby boomers, that large segment of the U.S. population born between 1946 and 1964, will also swell the older population as they retire. This growth in the total number of migrations in the retirement-aged population may imply an increased number of migrants to many of the early 21st century's most popular destinations.

However, there may also be many previously unnoticed destinations that by the year 2030 will swell with retirees. Property costs may escalate in well-established locations in response to growing demand (Serow, 2001), as entrepreneurs quickly develop alternative opportunities. A substantial dispersal of some of the preferred destinations appears likely, and indeed is evident in Florida's decline from receiving a 26% to a 19% share of older interstate migrants nationally between 1980 and 2000 (Longino, 2006).

An alternative scenario is also possible. Another popular prediction is that the sharp division between the working and retirement ages will progressively dissolve. Some say that part-time, temporary, or full-time employment is necessary for the highest standard of living in later life. If income generation comes increasingly to be linked to positive retirement, then it may be important for the older person to remain in the region in which they have good employment-related connections (Longino & Warnes, 2005).

SEE ALSO Volume 3: *Aging in Place; Assisted Living Facilities; Long-term Care; Neighborhood Context, Later Life; Retirement Communities.*

BIBLIOGRAPHY

Biggar, J. C. (1980). Who moved among the elderly, 1965–1970: A comparison of types of older movers. *Research on Aging, 2,* 73–91.

Cutchin, M. P. (2001). Deweyan integration: Moving beyond place attachment in elderly migration theory. *International Journal of Aging and Human Development, 52,* 29–44.

Haas, W. H., III, Bradley, D. E., Longino, C. F., Jr., Stoller, E. P., & Serow, W. J. (2006). In retirement migration, who counts? A methodological question with economic policy implications. *The Gerontologist, 46,* 815–820.

Hazelrigg, L. E., & Hardy, M. A. (1995). Older adult migration to the Sunbelt: Assessing income and related characteristics of recent migrants. *Research on Aging, 17,* 209–234.

Lee, E. S. (1966). A theory of migration. *Demography, 3,* 47–57.

Litwak, E., & Longino, C. F., Jr. (1987). Migration patterns among the elderly: A developmental perspective. *The Gerontologist, 27,* 266–272.

Longino, C. F., Jr. (2006). *Retirement migration in America* (2nd ed). Houston, TX: Vacation Publications.

Longino, C. F., Jr., Bradley, D. E., Stoller, E. P., & Haas, W. H. III (2008). Predictors of non-local moves among older adults: A prospective study. *Journal of Gerontology: Social Sciences* 63(B), S7-S14.

Longino, C. F., Jr., & Warnes, A. M. (2005). Migration and older people. In M. L. Johnson (Ed.), *The Cambridge handbook of age and ageing* (pp. 538–545). Cambridge, U.K.: Cambridge University Press.

McHugh, K. E. (2000). The "ageless self"? Emplacement of identities in Sun Belt retirement communities. *Journal of Aging Studies, 14,* 103–115.

Miller, M. E., Longino, C. F., Jr., Anderson, R. T., James, M. K., & Worley, A. S. (1999). Functional status, assistance, and the risk of a community-based move. *The Gerontologist, 39,* 187–200.

Ravenstein, E. G. (1885). The laws of migration. *Journal of the Statistical Society of London, 48,* 167–235.

Rossi, P. H. (1955). *Why families move: A study in the social psychology of urban residential mobility.* Glencoe, IL: Free Press.

Serow, W. J. (2001). Retirement migration counties in the southeastern United States: Geographic, demographic, and economic correlates. *The Gerontologist, 41,* 220–227.

Silverstein, M., & Angelelli, J. J. (1998). Older parents' expectations of moving closer to their children. *The Journals of Gerontology, Series B: Psychological Sciences and Social Sciences, 53,* S153–S163.

Walters, W. H. (2002). Place characteristics and later-life migration. *Research on Aging, 24,* 243–277.

Warnes, A. M. (1992). Migration and the life course. In T. Champion & T. Fielding (Eds.), *Migration processes and patterns: Vol. 1. Research progress and prospects* (pp. 175–187). London: Belhaven Press.

Warnes, A. M., King, R., Williams, A. M., & Patterson, G. (1999). The well-being of British expatriate retirees in southern Europe. *Ageing and Society, 19,* 717–740.

Wiseman, R. F. (1980). Why older people move: Theoretical issues. *Research on Aging, 2,* 141–154.

*Charles F. Longino, Jr.*

# RETIREMENT

Retirement is defined broadly as the departure event in an individual's life course from a phase of the occupational life cycle (Atchley, 1993, 1996). Rather than a mere withdrawal from paid work, retirement in contemporary social contexts is a complex process inextricably linked with social structures and individual life adjustments. Typically, retirement involves reliance on pension instead of salary as the primary means of financial support and adapting to new options in later life such as leisure pursuits, voluntary activities, and second careers (Szinovacz, 2003). Furthermore, many contemporary workers do not make a clear-cut break from full-time jobs one day to complete retirement the next. Pathways to retirement in the early 21st century are diverse and individualized processes that connect working lives to lives in complete retirement (Quadagno & Hardy, 1996).

## MEASUREMENT AND THE IMPORTANCE OF STUDYING RETIREMENT

Mainly because of the diversity in the pathways taken into retirement, there is no single generally agreed-on way to measure a person's retirement status. Nonetheless, researchers often rely on either one or both of two major criteria to measure retirement status: (a) a person's self-definition of current work status and (b) objective indicators concerning a person's retirement status. The objective indicators consist mainly of receipt of pension income as one's main source of income, total cessation of formal employment, departure from a career job of adulthood that had lasted 10 years or longer, and a significant reduction in hours or days worked for wages (Gendell & Siegel, 1992).

When measuring a person's retirement status, retirement researchers have faced three major challenges: women's retirement status, discouraged workers, and the increased complexity of contemporary workers' pathways to complete retirement. First, because of employment interruptions of greater frequency and longer duration, women's work histories tend to be more irregular than those of men. This general tendency makes women's transition from employment to retirement less clear and thus more difficult to measure than that of men (Szinovacz, 2003). Second, there is difficulty in measuring the retirement status of older discouraged workers. A discouraged worker refers to an unemployed person who is eligible to participate in the labor force but has given up seeking employment primarily because of the unavailability of employment options that she or he considers suitable (Schulz, 2001).

Although discouraged workers are not counted among those currently in the labor force, they are also not counted in unemployment rates because of the somewhat voluntary nature of their nonworking status. Thus, controversy exists as to how many older people who consider themselves retirees actually fall into the discouraged worker category (Bjørnstad, 2006). Third, the increasing complexity of the transition from full-time employment to complete retirement makes it difficult to measure a person's retirement status. In the early 21st century, only about half of older workers move from full-time employment to complete withdrawal from the labor force in a single step. The other half pass through a period of partial retirement on the way to complete retirement, or reverse the retirement process by reentering the labor force. As many as one-third of retirees become reemployed, often within 1 to 2 years of their first retirement (Hardy, 2006).

As most industrial countries, including the United States, have faced the challenges of population and workforce aging, retirement has become an increasingly important issue. In the United States the upcoming retirement of the baby boomers, the generation born between 1946 and 1964, has led to two major concerns. The first concern is the potential loss of a significant number of skilled and experienced workers who are vital to the maintenance of economic productivity (Hardy, 2006; Rix, 2004). Because of the impending retirement of such a large cohort, U.S. labor force growth is expected to decrease from 1.1% per year in the 1990s to 0.36% per year during the period between 2010 and 2020 (Organisation for Economic Co-operation and Development [OECD], 2005). The second concern is the anticipated fiscal burden on the rest of the society. The retirement of the baby boomers is expected to increase public expenditures associated with Medicare, Medicaid, and Social Security. In response to these concerns, much effort has been made to examine these issues with a focus on current and projected future trends in employment rates especially among those ages 55 and older. Therefore, it is important to study the influence of current policies on the patterns of retirement for the baby boomers as well as how new employment practices and public policies may improve the boomers' working lives and the quality of their life in retirement (Munnell & Sass, 2007).

## HISTORY OF RETIREMENT AS A SOCIAL INSTITUTION

Retirement as a social institution developed and became widespread during the 20th century, particularly among the industrialized countries (Atchley, 1996; Williamson & Pampel, 1993). In the industrialized countries of the early 21st century, most workers leave the labor force between the ages of 55 and 65 (Social Security Administration, 2006–2008). For instance, between 1990 and 1995, the median age for men's retirement was 60.4 in Germany, 62.3 in Sweden, 64.7 in Japan, and 62.1 in the United States. Women's median retirement age for the same period was 59.1 in Germany, 62.4 in Sweden, 62.3 in Japan, and 62.6 in the United States (Gendell & Siegel, 1992).

Retirement began to be institutionalized only after the Industrial Revolution of the 19th century (Costa, 1998). Two main factors led to the institutionalization of retirement during the 20th century. The first was a mutual agreement between employers and workers fixing the age for withdrawing from employment. Employers needed to replace high-salaried older workers with lower-salaried younger ones in order to speed up production and get more out of workers. Workers' unions agreed to fixing the age for mandatory retirement in exchange for greater job security until reaching that age. Although ages for mandatory retirement rules varied by sectors and economy and occupations, they were set mostly between 55 and 60 (Atchley, 1993). The second factor was the need to find a way to support the increasing number of older workers, many of whom were finding it very difficult to obtain work. In the 1880s Otto von Bismarck, the Prussian chancellor of Germany, introduced the world's first public pension system. It called for a massive intergenerational income redistribution scheme designed to help meet the income needs of workers ages 65 and over. Soon many other European nations were introducing similar schemes (Shulz & Myles, 1990).

In the United States the institutionalization of retirement picked up steam during the 1920s with the introduction of old-age pension schemes in many states and with the expansion of corporate pension schemes; much more important, however, was the introduction of a federal old-age pension scheme embodied in the Social Security Act of 1935. The introduction of this national public pension program made leaving the labor force much more attractive to older workers starting in the

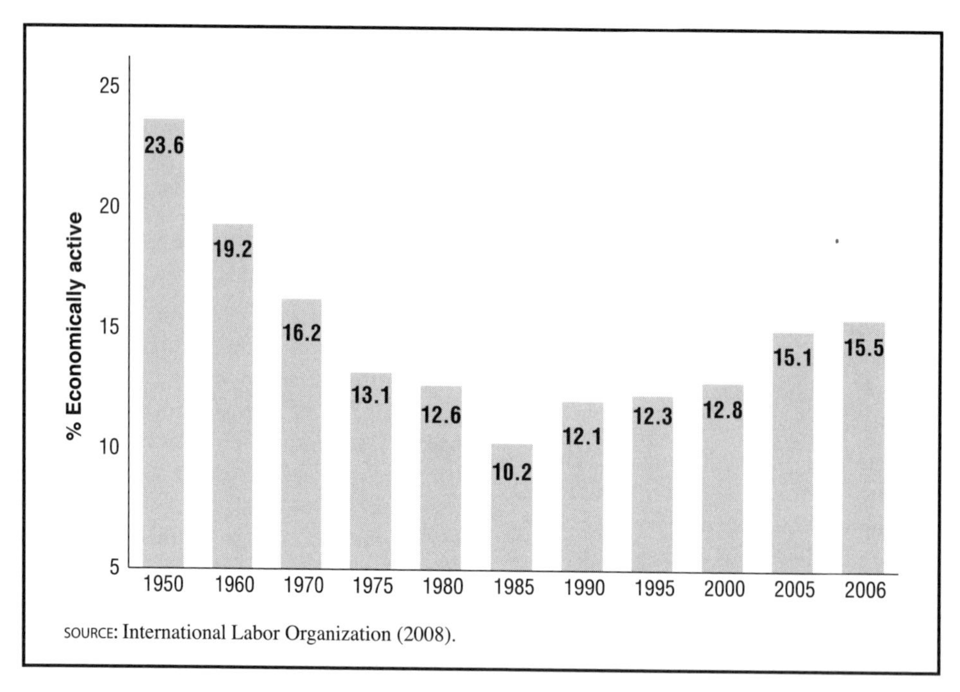


***Figure 1.*** *Civilian labor force participation rates in the U.S. for people age 65 and for the years 1950 through 2006.* CENGAGE LEARNING, GALE.

1940s. The pension program at first provided only small benefits. Later, increases in benefit levels meant that Social Security replaced a larger part of a worker's pre-retirement income. The availability of retirement options gradually restructured the time workers spent in the labor force before leaving to spend time in various leisure activities and other efforts directed at self-fulfillment in later life (Atchley, 1993). In 1890, 68% of men over age 65 were in the labor force, but that figure dropped to 54% by 1930. In 1950, after Social Security had been in place for several years, the portion of men over age 65 in the labor force dropped further to 46% and continued to decline to below 17% by 1989. The average retirement age of men dropped from 74 in 1910 to 67 in 1950. It continued to drop through the mid-1980s, when the average age stood at 62 (National Academy on an Aging Society, 2000).

In the United States, there was a trend toward an increasing prevalence of "early retirement" through the mid-1980s (Clark & Quinn, 2002). Early retirement refers to withdrawal from the labor force before age 65, the age of eligibility for retirement with the full benefit of Social Security. One factor driving the trend of early retirement was a change in Social Security policy in 1961 allowing workers to start receiving their pensions at age 62, albeit with about a 25% reduction of the benefit they would be entitled to receive if they waited until age 65 (Gall, Evans, & Howard, 1997). Also, to save on the high salaries of older workers, many companies were offering early retirement packages, including bonuses, to workers between the ages of 55 and 60. About 9 out of 10 U.S. pension plans, particularly for white-collar workers, provide financial incentives for early retirement (Clark & Quinn, 2002).

In 1950, as Figure 1 shows, 23.6% of workers (men and women combined) ages 65 and older remained in the labor force. By 1960, the figure was down to 19.2%. It steadily decreased until the mid-1980s. In 1985 the labor force participation of men and women ages 65 and older reached a low of 10.2% (International Labour Organization, 2008). That year, almost 25% of those 51 to 59 years of age did not work. During the 1980s, about 75% of all new Social Security beneficiaries each year retired before their 65th birthday, and most began collecting retirement benefits at age 62.5 (Quinn & Burkhauser, 1994; Toossi, 2002). Figure 1 also shows, however, that since the early 1990s the long-range trend toward earlier and earlier retirement has reversed. By 2000, the labor force participation rate for people, both men and women, ages 65 and older (12.8%) became higher than that of 1980 (12.6%). The participation rate rose further to 15.5% by 2006 (International Labour Organization, 2008).

At least for now, the early retirement trend among older Americans certainly appears to be over (Hardy, 2006; Quinn, 1997a). The end of this trend is largely attributable to three factors. The first is the strong macroeconomic performance of the U.S. economy through the 1990s (OECD, 2005). Second, 1983 amendments to the Social Security Act started to delay the age of eligibility for full benefits and increased the financial penalty for receiving early benefits at age 62 (Munnell & Sass, 2007). The final factor is employment practices and public policy initiatives that have increased older workers' options regarding pathways to full retirement (Butrica, Schaner, & Zedlewski, 2006).

## COMMON PATTERNS OF RETIREMENT

Throughout much of the 20th century, Americans viewed retirement as an event that occurred once in a lifetime and involved an immediate and complete withdrawal from full-time employment (Rix, 2004). Retirement in the 21st century, in contrast, has come to be characterized by a variety of pathways to complete retirement. Retirement research has developed four conceptual categories of retirement behavior based on the observed patterns and trends in the United States: (a) partial retirement, (b) bridge employment, (c) unretirement, and (d) joint retirement. These conceptual categories are not a mutually exclusive set of retirement behaviors; rather they are common occurrences that retirement researchers have noted.

Partial retirement, also known as phased retirement, is a generic term broadly referring to the process of gradually phasing into complete retirement though reduced work hours and job responsibilities, which may even involve changing one's workplace and occupation (Clark & Quinn, 2002). From 1960 to 2002 the proportion of older men who worked part-time rose from 30% to 43.6%, whereas that of women rose from 44% to 58.2% (Rix, 2004). About 40% of men and 35% of women ages 55 to 64 who received income from a pension in 2005 were still employed as of March 2006 (Hardy, 2006). Watson Wyatt Worldwide (2004) found that 57% of those workers currently in partial retirement entered into the arrangement voluntarily in order to have more leisure time. Brown (2005) reported that about 76% of workers ages 50 to 65 plan to continue working after age 65 primarily because of financial reasons. Such a gradual pathway to complete retirement enables older workers to adjust better to life in retirement and simultaneously allows employers to make gradual changes instead of coping with the abrupt departure of a well-integrated employee (Rix, 2004).

Bridge employment, a growing labor force participation pattern among older workers in the early 21st century, refers to work between their career jobs and complete retirement, which is either part-time or lasts fewer than 10 years, or both (Quinn, 1997b). Although used as a form of partial retirement, bridge employment is considered a distinct category of retirement because it involves an exit and reentry to the labor force, rather than a mere gradual reduction of hours or days worked (Clark & Quinn, 2002). As of 2004, about 73% of men and 46% of women ages 51 to 61 had a full-time career job.

By 2005, among those who had already retired from full-time career jobs, about 60% of workers, men and women combined, reentered the labor market and worked at a bridge job. More than half of these bridge jobs were part-time (Cahill, Giandrea, & Quinn, 2006).

The term *unretirement* refers to workers who reenter the labor force because of unwarranted optimism about their financial security, which had led them to retire too early, or because of unexpected financial shocks in retirement (Hardy, 2006). Unretirement is most common among retirees in their early to mid-50s, typically occurs within the first 2 years of first retirement, and lasts an average of 4 years. About 24% of those in this age group who originally retired from their career jobs unexpectedly reenter the labor force (Maestas, 2004). Unretirement usually involves jobs similar to bridge employment. They generally require fewer work hours, pay lower wages than a career job, and are more likely to involve a shift from being an employee to being self-employed (Hayward, Hardy, & Liu, 1994).

Joint retirement is a pattern of retirement that involves a simultaneous sequence of work and final withdrawal from the workforce by a working couple. Research has suggested that availability of employer-provided retiree health insurance is an important factor in the retirement decision, particularly for older workers. The likelihood of joint retirement—timing retirement together—more than doubles when wives have employer-provided retiree health insurance (Kapur & Rogowski, 2007).

## PLANNING AND TIMING OF RETIREMENT

Retirement involves more than a decision to withdraw from the labor force; it also involves a decision as to when and how to retire. Quinn and Burkhauser (1994) reported that 65% of men and 55% of women were able to retire near their desired retirement ages. Only about 10% of men and women were able to or had to retire before their desired retirement ages. About 25% of men and 32% of women needed to remain in the labor force longer than they had planned to. Retirement researchers have identified four major factors that largely determine the timing of a person's retirement: (a) availability of adequate retirement income, (b) health status and accessibility to health insurance, (c) job satisfaction, and (d) employment and retirement policies.

First, an adequate income, through a combination of Social Security, a private pension, and interest income, directly affects the feasibility of retirement. Financial status also impacts worker health and job satisfaction. When given a choice, assuming financial security and adequate health insurance, most people elect to retire as soon as they can (Flippen & Tienda, 2000).

Second, a person's health status, including physical and mental functional limitations and accessibility to health insurance, is an important factor in the retirement decision, especially among those for whom retirement is least attractive (Moon, 2002). Poor health, when combined with an adequate retirement income, usually results in early retirement. In contrast, the combination of poor health and an inadequate income often does not lead to early retirement particularly among low-income workers (Mutchler, Burr, Massagli, & Pienta, 1999).

About 55% of retirees between the ages of 51 and 59 report that a health condition or impairment substantially limits the amount or type of work they can do. In addition, retirees are three times more likely to be in fair to poor health than their employed counterparts (National Academy on an Aging Society, 2000).

The third factor affecting retirement timing is workers' satisfaction with their jobs, which is often determined by the workers' attachment to the job, organizational commitment, and the nature of a job (Taylor & Doverspike, 2003). Some workers retire to escape undesirable working conditions such as boring, repetitive, and stressful jobs and work environments. Workers who have a positive attitude toward retirement and leisure but are dissatisfied with their jobs are likely to retire early. Employees with a high school education or less tend to show lower job satisfaction and thus retire earlier than well-educated employees (Quinn & Burkhauser, 1994).

Fourth, public policies and employment practices affect the timing of retirement. For example, the 1986 amendment to the federal Age Discrimination in Employment Act, which abolished mandatory retirement, has protected workers both in the private and public sectors from forced retirement based on their age. This policy allows workers to choose to stay at work longer if they elect to do so. Prior to 1986, mandatory retirement rules in most workplaces influenced retirement age for many workers (Rix, 2004). Federal policy increasing the age of eligibility for full Social Security benefits from age 65 to 67 by the year 2027 is creating an added incentive to delay the timing of retirement (Neumark, 2003).

## GENDER AND RACIAL INEQUALITIES IN RETIREMENT

When comparing men and women, financial security provided mainly through Social Security benefits creates the single largest gender difference in decision and timing of retirement (Flippen & Tienda, 2000; Ruhm, 1996). On average, retired women's pension benefits make up only about 60% of that of retired men (Belgrave & Bradsher, 1994). Women's likelihood of lower-paying employment tends to keep them from being entitled to adequate retirement pensions (Moen, 1996; O'Grady-LeShane, 1996). Thus, women's marital status influences their financial security in retirement and the decision and timing of the retirement. Furthermore, because of their assumption of family care obligations, women are more likely to have a discontinuous work history, which results in their lower financial security (Pienta, Burr, & Mutchler, 1994). Married women are more likely than single women to be able to retire early because their financial security in retirement tends to rely on their husbands' pension eligibility. Single women are likely to remain in the labor force longer than married women because the pension benefits they are entitled to are often inadequate as a result of their having had relatively low-paying jobs. This general tendency, however, may partly decline in the future because women of the early 21st century are less likely to have interrupted work histories than those in the past. Nevertheless, the gender gap in pay and access to employer pension coverage still persist (Szinovacz, 2003).

Racial minorities—African Americans and Hispanics in particular—have shown different retirement patterns than White men. African Americans tend to work in less secure jobs that often offer low pay, few benefits, and a high risk of disability (Taylor & Doverspike, 2003). Compared with White men, African American men have fewer options in the decision and timing of retirement mainly because of their higher disability rates and poorer health (Hogan & Perrucci, 1998). Also, when compared with the general population, a smaller proportion of African American workers report that their employers pay into a pension plan on their behalf (Employee Benefit Research Institute, 2003; Gallo, Bradley, Siegel, & Kasl, 2000). Both their public and private pension benefits tend to be lower. African Americans and Hispanics are much more likely than White males to experience involuntary labor market exit because of poor health and are likely to retire without sufficient financial security (Flippen & Tienda, 2000; Gibson, 1987). One study found that they are much less likely than retired White men to receive any form of retirement benefits and much more likely to receive disability benefits and public assistance (Hayward, Friedman, & Chen, 1996).

When compared with White women, African American women are more likely to have worked steadily most of their adult lives, but they retire later than their White counterparts, largely for economic reasons (Szinovacz, 2003). Greater probability of widowhood and lower wages result in more than half of African American women ages 62 to 64 being in the labor force, compared with one-third of White women in that age span. Furthermore, retirement induced by labor market problems is much more common among African American women than among White women (Belgrave & Bradsher, 1994).

## SATISFACTION WITH RETIREMENT

Traditionally, a widely held belief in American society, particularly among men, was that full-time participation in the labor force was important to a sense that one was leading a full and meaningful life. This belief contributed to the view that retirement was likely to represent a personal crisis and have a number of adverse personal consequences (Atchley, 1993). Retirement, however, is not usually a negative event; retirement research from the late 1990s has identified the positive effects of retirement on life satisfaction and health, especially during the first year postretirement (Reitzes, Mutran, & Fernandez, 1998). Indeed, the majority of older adults in the 2002 Health and Retirement Study expressed high levels of satisfaction with retirement (61.5%), although others said they were only somewhat satisfied (32.9%), and some reported dissatisfaction (5.6%; Butrica et al., 2006).

Generally, there are four factors that strongly influence satisfaction with life in retirement: (a) financial security, (b) health, (c) preparation and planning for retirement, and (d) active engagement (Reitzes et al., 1998; Szinovacz, 2003). Not surprisingly, retirees with higher incomes, or at least adequate finances, report that they are more satisfied with their lives and develop a more positive identity as retirees than do those with lower incomes (Szinovacz, 2003).

Given the observed positive relations between health status and earned income, programs that improve health status during the working years may, in turn, increase earned income in retirement. Those who believe that they know more about their financial planning, including Social Security and health care coverage such as Medicare, are more likely to have prepared for retirement (Taylor & Doverspike, 2003). Conversely, those without definite retirement plans tend to find themselves bored or depressed (Ekerdt, Kosloski, & DeViney, 2000). Participating in productive activities at older ages is associated with better physical and mental health and lower mortality (Lum & Lightfoot, 2005). One study reported that 58% of volunteers said that an important reason for helping others was to render their own lives more satisfying. Activities other than work that provide autonomy, some sense of control, and the chance to learn new things are all related to retirement satisfaction (Szinovacz, 2003). Conversely, activities that involve less problem solving, are less complex, and are less fulfilling have all been associated with distress and depression in retirement (Ross & Drentea, 1998).

## PHASES OF RETIREMENT PROCESSES

Atchley (1993, 1996) has proposed a widely cited conceptual model illustrating the phases of the retirement process in six distinctive stages: (a) preretirement, (b) honeymoon, (c) disenchantment, (d) reorientation, (e) stability, and (f) the terminal phase. In the preretirement phase, becoming aware of retirement approaching, workers begin saving money, envision postretirement activities such as hobbies, and prepare for general changes to their social lives. The honeymoon phase comes immediately after the actual event of retirement. Retired people typically enjoy their free time during this phase by doing activities such as extended travel. This phase of retirement life requires disposable income, which is a problem for some older people. In the disenchantment phase, the retired person may begin to feel depressed about life and the lack of interesting things to do.

After the traveling, cleaning, and doing the things most desired, some retirees get tired and bored. Often retirees next go through a fourth phase referred to as reorientation in which they develop a more realistic attitude about how to deal with retirement. Retirees reevaluate their choice of activities and make decisions about what is most important. This phase involves using their life experiences to develop a realistic view of alternatives given their resources. Reorientation also involves exploring new avenues of involvement in an effort to create a set of realistic choices that establish a structure and a routine for living in retirement with at least a modicum of satisfaction. During the fifth phase, referred to as stability, the retired person establishes a new set of daily life routines and enjoys them. Typically, volunteer work, visiting, or some other routine is developed that keeps the retiree happy and feeling important.

The sixth and terminal phase of life in retirement is marked primarily by illness or disability that prevents the retiree from actively caring for himself or herself. Also, with increasing frequency the fifth stage sometimes ends because of reemployment. Because workers are retiring earlier than they used to, many are young and healthy enough to return to the labor force, thus terminating retirement, at least temporarily.

## THEORETICAL FRAMEWORKS OF RETIREMENT

Retirement research has made extensive use of the following four distinctive theoretical frameworks to account for postretirement well-being in society: (a) disengagement theory, (b) activity theory, (c) continuity theory, and (d) the life course perspective. Disengagement theory focuses primarily on the smooth functioning of a society rather than on individual adjustment or attitudes. This theory suggests that as individuals age it is both necessary and positive for them to disengage from society. Early approaches focused on the loss of the work role occasioned by retirement and suggested that this loss would undermine individuals' identities and lead to their social withdrawal (Cumming & Henry, 1961).

Activity theory (which dates from the 1950s) argues that it is not retirement per se but involvement in fulfilling or alienating activities that influences well-being. This theory indicates that retirement leads to a loss of sense of control, mainly because of a reduction in problem-solving activities. Retirees, however, do not report more distress than full-time workers (Ross & Drentea, 1998). Continuity theory emphasizes the importance of maintaining focal identities over life transitions such as retirement. Thus, pronounced lifestyle changes following retirement, as well as experiences of simultaneous life events that lead to disruption in salient identities, are likely to reduce well-being. Atchley (1993, 1996) argued that there is considerable continuity in identity and self-concept over the retirement transition and that this continuity contributes to retirement adaptation. That retirement does not necessarily constitute an identity crisis is upheld by accumulating evidence showing that, on average, retirees are satisfied with their lives (Elder & Johnson, 2003).

A more recent and nuanced view of retirement adaptation derives from the life course perspective and its integration with selected assumptions from other theories. The life course perspective draws attention to four concepts that seem crucial to understanding postretirement well-being: (a) contextual embeddedness of life transitions, (b) interdependence of life spheres, (c) timing of life transitions, and (d) trajectories and pathways (Dannerfer & Uhlenberg, 1999; Setterstein, 2003).

Contextual embeddedness of life transitions refers to the experiences under which the transition occurs, including selected attributes, current and past statuses and roles, as well as societal context. It is also assumed that life spheres are interdependent, so that experiences in one sphere (e.g., employment) influence and are influenced by experiences in other spheres (e.g., family). Furthermore, the experience of life transitions is contingent on their timing in terms of cultural prescriptions, personal expectations, and occurrences in other life spheres. The notion of trajectories and pathways points to the historical context of life experiences (historical time), their development over time (trajectories), and the interrelationships among diverse life transitions (pathways).

## FUTURE RESEARCH DIRECTIONS

The 21st century has found many Americans, particularly baby boomers, ill prepared for retirement (Moody, 2006). Because of changes in the age of eligibility for Social Security benefits, workers born after 1960 will not eligible for the full benefit until age 67. Of workers 55 and older, however, about 44% believe that they will be eligible for full Social Security benefits 1 to 4 years before they actually will be. One-half of workers 55 and older have less than $50,000 saved for retirement (Employee Benefit Research Institute, 2006).

In response to the aging of the population and the workforce, policy makers in the United States, along with those of most other industrialized nations, have been seeking ways to reduce the anticipated fiscal burden of the growing number of retirees on the public resources, younger populations, and the national economies. Part of the public effort is, as in the cases of the United Kingdom and Sweden, to privatize exiting public old-age pension programs by introducing individual accounts (OECD, 2005). Another way to deal with the growing number of older people is to look for ways to postpone retirement for older workers. In years ahead, facilitating efforts by employers to retain older workers longer than they currently do is expected to be the subject of much research (DeLong, 2004). The older workers of the early 21st century are healthier, better educated, and more highly skilled than those in any previous times (Rix, 2004). They should be able to work longer, but will they?

The ever-changing diverse pathways into retirement is another promising research topic. It would also be of use to address and untangle the patterns and trends in retirement being driven by changes in the national and global economy (Hardy, 2006).

Another direction for future retirement research is the effort to come to a clearer understanding of the biological, psychological, and social aspects of aging, which are likely to influence the retirement behaviors of current and future older workers. Much research has been done to identify a variety of age-related changes in physical functioning, but further research is needed on specifically how these age-related biological changes connect to job requirements in different types of occupations (Szinovacz, 2003).

Retirement research has paid considerable attention to the role of public and private pensions in retirement behaviors and satisfaction, but little research has been done on workplace flexibility. This line of research is expected to lead to a greater variety of partial retirement options and more supportive work environments for current and future older workers (Shepard, Clifton, & Kruse, 1996).

Researchers also need to put more effort into figuring out what types of employment training and education and workplace designs will increase the number of workers who elect to work well beyond their mid-60s. Finally, there is a need for research on how and why selected policies influence (or fail to influence) workers' retirement decisions. Social scientists know very little about the diversity of work patterns in later life or about how aging affects work performance in various work settings (Van Dalen & Henkens, 2002). Some jobs provide opportunities for personal growth and creative expression; other jobs subject workers to physical strain, emotional stress, and hazardous conditions. Careful study of workplace interventions is needed to facilitate efforts to make work less stressful for older workers, to increase work satisfaction, to reconfigure jobs, and to understand how technology is changing the workplace.

SEE ALSO Volume 2: *Careers; Policy, Employment; Employment, Adulthood; Job Change;* Volume 3: *Pensions; Social Security; Theories of Aging.*

### BIBLIOGRAPHY


Atchley, R. C. (1993). Critical perspectives on retirement. In T. R. Cole, W. A. Achenbaum, P. L. Jakobi, & R. Kastenbaum (Eds.), *Voices and visions of aging: Toward a critical gerontology* (pp. 3–19). New York: Springer.

Atchley, R. C. (1996). Retirement. In J. E. Birren (Ed.), *Encyclopedia of gerontology* (Vol. 2, pp. 437–449). San Diego, CA: Academic Press.

Belgrave, L. L., & Bradsher, J. E. (1994). Health as a factor in institutionalization: Disparities between African Americans and Whites. *Research on Aging, 16*, 115–141.

Bjørnstad, R. (2006). Learned helplessness, discouraged workers, and multiple unemployment equilibria. *The Journal of Socio-Economics, 35*, 458–475.

Brown, S. K. (2005, March). *Attitudes of individuals 50 and older toward phased retirement* (AARP Research Report). Retrieved May 21, 2008, from http://assets.aarp.org/rgcenter

Butrica, B. A., Schaner, S. G., & Zedlewski, S. R. (2006, May). *Enjoying the golden work years* (Perspectives on Productive Aging No. 6). Washington, DC: Urban Institute. Retrieved May 21, 2008, from http://www.urban.org

Cahill, K. E., Giandrea, M. D., & Quinn, J. F. (2006). Retirement patterns from career employment. *The Gerontologist, 46*, 514–523.

Clark, R. L., & Quinn, J. F. (2002). Patterns of work and retirement for a new century. *Generations, 26*(2), 17–24.

Costa, D. L. (1998). *The evolution of retirement: An American economic history, 1880–1990*. Chicago: University of Chicago Press.

Cumming, E., & Henry, W. E. (1961). *Growing old: The process of disengagement*. New York: Basic Books.

Dannerfer, D., & Uhlenberg, R. (1999). Paths of the life course: A typology. In V. L. Bengtson & K. Warner Schaie (Eds.), *Handbook of theories of aging*. New York: Springer.

DeLong, D. W. (2004). *Lost knowledge: Confronting the threat of an aging workforce*. Oxford, U.K.: Oxford University Press.

Ekerdt, D. J., Kosloski, K., & DeViney, S. (2000). The normative anticipation of retirement by older workers. *Research on Aging, 22*, 3–22.

Elder, G. H., Jr., & Johnson, M. K. (2003). The life course and aging: Challenges, lessons, and new directions. In R. A. Settersten Jr. (Ed.), *Invitation to the life course: Toward new understandings of later life* (pp. 49–81). Amityville, NY: Baywood.

Employee Benefit Research Institute. (2003). *The 2003 Minority Retirement Confidence Survey: Summary of findings*. Retrieved April 7, 2008, from http://www.ebri.org/pdf/

Employee Benefit Research Institute. (2006). *Will more of us be working forever?: The 2006 Retirement Confidence Survey.* Retrieved May 8, 2008, from http://www.ebri.org/pdf

Flippen, C., & Tienda, M. (2000). Pathways to retirement: Patterns of labor force participation and labor market exit among the pre-retirement population by race, Hispanic origin, and sex. *The Journals of Gerontology, Series B: Psychological Sciences and Social Sciences, 55*, S14–S27.

Gall, T. L., Evans, D. R., & Howard, J. (1997). The retirement adjustment process: Changes in the well-being of male retirees across time. *The Journals of Gerontology, Series B: Psychological Sciences and Social Sciences, 52*, P110–P117.

Gallo, W. T., Bradley, E. H., Siegel, M., & Kasl, S. V. (2000). Health effects of involuntary job loss among older workers: Findings from the Health and Retirement Survey. *The Journals of Gerontology, Series B: Psychological Sciences and Social Sciences, 55*, S131–S140.

Gendell, M., & Siegel, J. S. (1992). Trends in retirement age by sex, 1950–2005. *Monthly Labor Review, 115*(7), 22–29.

Gibson, R. C. (1987). Reconceptualizing retirement for black Americans. *The Gerontologist, 27*, 691–698.

Hardy, M. A. (2006). Older workers. In R. H. Binstock & L. K. George (Eds.), *Handbook of aging and the social sciences* (6th ed., pp. 201–216). Boston: Academic Press.

Hayward, M. D., Friedman, S., & Chen, H. (1996). Race inequities in men's retirement. *The Journals of Gerontology, Series B: Psychological Sciences and Social Sciences, 51*, S1–S10.

Hayward, M. D., Hardy, M. A., & Liu, M.-C. (1994). Work after retirement: The experience of older men in the U.S. *Social Science Research, 23*, 82–107.

Hogan, R., & Perrucci, C. C. (1998). Producing and reproducing class and status differences: Racial and gender gaps in U.S. employment and retirement income. *Social Problems, 45*, 528–549.

International Labour Organization. (2008). *LABORSTA Internet: Total economically active population*. Retrieved January 22, 2008, from http://laborsta.ilo.org/

Kapur, K., & Rogowski, J. (2007). The role of health insurance in joint retirement among married couples. *Industrial & Labor Relations Review, 60*, 397–407.

Lum, T. Y., & Lightfoot, E. (2005). The effects of volunteering on the physical and mental health of older people. *Research on Aging, 27*, 31–55.

Maestas, N. (2004, July). *Back to work: Expectations and realizations of work after retirement* (University of Michigan Retirement Research Center Working Paper No. 2004-085). Retrieved April 7, 2008, from http://www.mrrc.isr.umich.edu/publications

Mayer, K. U. (2001). *The sociology of the life course and life span psychology: Diverging or converging pathways.* Ann Arbor, MI: Society for the Study of Human Development.

Moen, P., Sweet, S., & Swisher, R. (2005). Embedded career clocks: The case of retirement planning. In R. Macmillan (Ed.), *The structure of the life course: Standardized? individualized? differentiated?* (pp. 237–265). Oxford, England: Elsevier.

Moen, P. (1996). A life course perspective on retirement, gender, and well-being. *Journal of Occupational Health Psychology, 1,* 131–144.

Moody, H. R. (2006). *Aging: Concepts and controversies.* (5th ed.). Thousand Oaks, CA: Pine Forge Press.

Moon, M., with P. Herd. (2002). *A place at the table: Women's needs and Medicare reform.* New York: Century Foundation Press.

Munnell, A. H., & Sass, S. A. (2007, June). *The labor supply of older Americans* (Center for Retirement Research at Boston College Working Paper No. 2007-12). Retrieved May 21, 2008, from http://crr.bc.edu/images

Mutchler, J. E., Burr, J. A., Massagli, M. P., & Pienta, A. (1999) Work transitions and health in later life. *Journal of Gerontology: Social Sciences, 54B,* S252–2261.

National Academy on an Aging Society. (2000, June). *Who are young retirees and older workers?* (Data Profile: Young Retirees and Older Workers Series No. 1). Retrieved May 21, 2008, from http://ihcrp.georgetown.edu/agingsociety

Neumark, D. (2003). Age discrimination legislation in the United States. *Contemporary Economic Policy, 21,* 297–317.

O'Grady-LeShane, R. (1996). Older women workers. In W. H. Crown (Ed.), *Handbook on employment and the elderly* (pp. 103–109). Westport, CT: Greenwood Press.

Organisation for Economic Co-operation and Development. (2005). *Ageing and employment policies: United States.* Paris: Author.

Pienta, A. M., Burr, J. A., & Mutchler, J. E. (1994). Women's labor force participation in later life: The effect of early work and family experiences. *The Journals of Gerontology, Series B: Psychological Sciences and Social Sciences, 49,* S231–S239.

Quadagno, J., & Hardy, M. (1996). Work and retirement. In R. H. Binstock & L. K. George (Eds.), *Handbook of aging and the social sciences* (4th ed., pp. 325–345). San Diego, CA: Academic Press.

Quinn, J. F. (1997a). Retirement trends and patterns in the 1990s: The end of an era? *Public Policy and Aging Report, 8*(3), 10–14.

Quinn, J. F. (1997b). The role of bridge jobs in the retirement patterns of older Americans in the 1990s. In D. L. Salisbury (Ed.), *Retirement prospects in a defined contribution world* (pp. 25–39). Washington, DC: Employee Benefit Research Institute.

Quinn, J. F., & Burkhauser, R. V. (1994). Retirement and labor force behavior of the elderly. In L. G. Martin & S. H. Preston (Eds.), *Demography of aging* (pp. 50–101). Washington, DC: National Academy Press.

Reitzes, D. C., Mutran, E. J., & Fernandez, M. E. (1998). The decision to retire: A career perspective. *Social Science Quarterly, 79,* 607–619.

Rix, S. E. (2004, February). *Aging and work: A view from the United States* (AARP Public Policy Institute Paper No. 2004-02). Retrieved May 21, 2008, from http://assets.aarp.org/rgcenter

Ross, C. E., & Drentea, P. (1998). Consequences of retirement activities for distress and the sense of personal control. *Journal of Health and Social Behavior, 39,* 317–334.

Ruhm, C. J. (1996). Gender differences in employment behavior during late middle life. *The Journals of Gerontology, Series B: Psychological Sciences and Social Sciences, 51,* S11–S17.

Schulz, J. H. (2001). *The economics of aging.* (7th ed.). Westport, CT: Auburn House.

Schultz, J., & Myles, J. (1990). Old-age pensions: A comparative perspective. In R. Binstock & L. George (Eds.), *Handbook of aging and the social sciences* (pp. 398–414). New York: Academic Press.

Settersten, R. A. (1998). Time, age, and the transition to retirement: New evidence on life-course flexibility? *The International Journal of Aging and Human Development, 47,* 177–203.

Settersten, R. A., Jr. (2003). Rethinking social policy: Lessons of a life course perspective. In R. A. Seetersten, Jr. (ed.) *Invitation to the life course: Toward new understanding of later life* (pp. 191–222). New York: Baywood Publishing.

Shepard, E. M., Clifton, T. J., & Kruse, D. (1996). Flexible work hours and productivity: Some evidence from the pharmaceutical industry. *Industrial Relations, 35*(1), 123–139.

Social Security Administration. (2006–2008). *Social security programs throughout the world, 2006–2007.* Retrieved May 21, 2008, from http://www.socialsecurity.gov/policy

Szinovacz, M. E. (2003). Contexts and pathways: Retirement as institution, process, and experience. In G. A. Adams & T. A. Beehr (Eds.), *Retirement: Reasons, processes, and results* (pp. 6–52). New York: Springer.

Taylor, M. A., & Doverspike, D. (2003). Retirement planning and preparation. In G. A. Adams & T. A. Beehr (Eds.), *Retirement: Reasons, processes, and results* (pp. 53–82). New York: Springer.

Toossi, M. (2002). A century of change: The U.S. labor force, 1950–2050. *Monthly Labor Review, 125*(5), 15–28.

Van Dalen, H. P., & Henkens, K. (2002). Early-retirement reform: Can it and will it work? *Ageing and Society, 22,* 209–231.

Watson Wyatt Worldwide. (2004). *Phased retirement: Aligning employer programs with worker preferences—2004 survey report.* Washington, DC: Author.

Williamson, J. B., & Pampel, F. C. (1993). *Old-age security in comparative perspective.* New York: Oxford University Press.

***Masa Higo***
***John B. Williamson***

# RETIREMENT COMMUNITIES

The U.S. Census Bureau projects that the U.S. older adult population aged 65 years and older will more than double from 34.9 million in the year 2000 to 71.4 million in the year 2040. Partially because of this, retirement communities and other elder-friendly housing is expected to grow in numbers also. While only about 5% of the U.S. older adult population currently lives in planned retirement communities, the industry is growing steadily. Broadly defined, retirement communities are housing facilities for older adults that offer at least minimal services for the residents. Often these communities have minimum age requirements for admittance.

While older adults are typically classified as one group, their individual needs and physical abilities vary greatly. Even within a single individual, needs change from decade to decade as an individual ages. Young retirees may be fit and active compared to the oldest adults who may labor with life's daily tasks. These changing needs can be a struggle within traditional living contexts. Different types of retirement communities are available to serve older adults' changing physical and emotional needs. Some types of retirement communities seek to ease the physical and life changes accompanying the aging process by providing services and programs, such as transportation and health services. Others provide recreational activities for retirees. Some retirement communities go a step further and cater their services or programs to specific subgroups. For example, retirement community options for gay, lesbian, bisexual, and transgender (GLBT) older persons are becoming increasingly available for the approximately 4 million of them who will be reaching retirement age by the year 2030. GLBT retirement communities provide services and support to individuals who might otherwise avoid seeking needed care in a traditional venue for fear of prejudicial treatment.

The United States has a great variety of retirement communities. There are currently six planned retirement community types. These include retirement new towns, retirement villages, retirement subdivisions, congregate housing, continuing care retirement communities (CCRCs), and university-linked retirement communities. The six planned retirement community types can be categorized broadly as either service-oriented or recreation-oriented communities. An additional broad retirement community category exists: unplanned retirement communities, commonly called naturally occurring retirement communities (NORCs). Because a substantial number of older adults reside in NORCs, they warrant mentioning despite being unplanned communities that generally do not provide supportive services for their older adult residents.

NORCs are fully age-integrated housing facilities with at least half of their residents aged 60 or older. The term *naturally occurring retirement community* was coined in 1985 by Michael Hunt, a researcher and professor at the University of Wisconsin-Madison. Because NORCs are not designed as retirement communities, the facilities may lack accessible design elements, such as grab bars and no-step entries, and supportive services. Often these communities evolve by hosting long-term residents aging-in-place in addition to others who moved there upon retirement because of market forces. In the early 1990s, it was established that over one quarter (27%) of the U.S. elderly resided in NORCs. This number is expected to continue to grow.

Service-oriented communities include congregate housing, CCRCs, and university-linked retirement communities. These differ from recreation-oriented communities in their offerings, in their target markets, and market areas. Target markets are demographic groups that facilities attempt to attract. Generally, service-oriented communities appeal to those over age 75. This market is predominantly women and those who need or recognize the need for functional assistance in the future. The geographic region from which residents are drawn is much smaller than for recreation-oriented communities. For service-oriented communities, new residents often come from within 15 miles of their previous homes. The exception to this rule is in the southeastern United States where residents may come from much further away.

Recreation-oriented communities consist of retirement new towns, retirement villages, and retirement subdivisions. These have target markets of older adults who are often younger than 75 years of age. These preretirees or young retirees are typically more active individuals who desire recreational activities and low- or no-maintenance living. This market usually consists of more couples, whereas unmarried persons (typically widows) make up the majority of residents in the service-oriented communities. Recreation-oriented communities attract residents from large regional and even national market areas.

**Retirement new towns** These towns originated in 1960 with the New Year's Day grand opening of Sun City, Arizona. This large-scale development opened the doors quite literally on the *active retirement* concept. Modern retirees were encouraged to reject stereotypical sedentary activities such as sitting on a park bench, and instead were offered numerous activities and an idyllic lifestyle.

Retirement new towns are most often found in Sunbelt and western states. While the lifestyle offered is focused on active leisure, these retirement communities supply both active and passive recreational activities. Active recreational options include sports such as golf, swimming, and tennis. Passive recreational choices might include crafts, games, and educational programs. Also, new towns have the most integrated and comprehensive retail, financial, and medical services.

New towns are privately developed. Largest in size among retirement communities, new town populations

***Senior Generation Gap.*** *Characterized Residents dine in the formal dining room at San Francisco Towers retirement community in San Francisco, CA. As residences designed for a generation that came of age during the Great Depression make way for one that entered adulthood amid postwar prosperity, more and more retirement communities are experiencing culture clashes. Often, squabbles arise when administrators propose raising monthly fees to pay for the spa cuisine, wellness classes and computer–ready apartments demanded by comparatively spry 70-year-olds.* AP IMAGES.

range from 5,000 to 46,000 residents, as found in Arizona's Sun City, which is the world's largest retirement development. Other examples of retirement new towns include Sun City Center near Tampa, Florida, and Leisure World in Laguna Hills, California.

**Retirement villages** Such villages are smaller, with fewer services than new towns. These privately developed retirement communities typically have from 1,000 to 5,000 residents. More moderately-sized, these communities cannot support large-scale retail and service facilities. While some incorporate these services to some extent, the level they are included varies. Often, services are conveniently located nearby in the host community.

Both passive and active recreational opportunities are widely available to residents. These might include shuffleboard, performances, and classes. Retirement village residents are predominately retired couples in their late 60s. While more common in Sunbelt states, they can be found in northern climates also. Some examples of retirement villages are Leisure Village West in Ocean County, New Jersey, and Leisure Village in Camarillo, California.

**Retirement subdivisions** These subdivisions attract residents with the lifestyle available in the host community or the area's appealing climate. Commonly, these developments are located in urban Sunbelt areas. This housing type relies on the surrounding community for services and amenities. Because retirement subdivisions offer fewer services and amenities themselves, they are often less expensive than new towns or retirement villages.

Generally small or medium-sized, retirement subdivisions are planned by for-profit developers. The types of housing in these subdivisions can vary from conventional single-family homes to mobile homes. Often, residents in these developments are healthy, married couples in their early 70s. Some examples of retirement subdivisions are Orange Gardens in Kissimmee, Florida, and Riviera Mobile Home Park in Scottsdale, Arizona.

**Congregate housing** Definitions vary for this type of housing. Frequently, congregate housing consists of independent living apartments with some supportive services provided. Because these facilities' residents tend to be older elderly individuals, independent living can be prolonged with the help of supportive services, such as meal, shopping, and housekeeping services. Congregate housing residents tend to be widowed women aged 75 and older. While a variety of supportive services are available, personal care services are usually not; this is the main difference distinguishing congregate housing from assisted living facilities, which offer extensive help with daily living tasks. Though passive recreational activities may be available, congregate housing does not usually offer active recreational activities.

Traditionally, congregate housing has been developed by government, religious, or fraternal agencies. More recently, private for-profit organizations entered the congregate housing market. These for-profit developments are higher priced than nonprofit developments. The least expensive variety is government subsidized developments. Congregate housing examples include the Hyatt Hotel's subsidiary Classic Residence, which can be found in Maryland, Texas, New Jersey, and California.

**Continuing care retirement communities** CCRCs are senior living facilities minimally offering three care levels: active (or independent) living, assisted living, and nursing home care. In addition to these three levels of care, commonly called the continuum of care, CCRCs offer a wide selection of social and recreational activities and health care services. Often these social and recreational activities include shows, classes, and outings. While these facilities offer abundant passive recreational activities, active recreational activities are nonexistent or limited, perhaps including only low-intensity exercise classes. Also, CCRCs offer many other on-site amenities such as coffee shops, grocery stores, and beauty shops.

The health care aspect is what distinguishes CCRCs from other retirement community options. In addition to housing specifically geared for assisted living or nursing care, residential care options are becoming increasingly available. This program allows staff to provide health and personal care services to independent living residents in their apartments. Such services enable frail residents the option to age-in-place rather than moving into assisted living. CCRC residents are commonly older, in their mid-80s.

Among CCRCs, there are two versions: life-care communities and life-care look-alikes. Life-care communities guarantee residents nursing care should the need arise. Life-care look-alikes only guarantee a priority spot on nursing bed waiting lists. Traditionally, CCRCs were developed by nonprofit groups, but recently for-profit agencies such as Marriott Corporation have entered the market. Nonprofit options tend to be less expensive than for-profit options. Examples of CCRCs include Maple Knoll Village in Springdale, Ohio, and Oakwood Village Retirement Communities in Madison, Wisconsin.

**University-linked retirement communities** Such communities are a relatively new concept. As of 2008, more than 60 college campuses throughout the United States offer this retirement community option. Some university-linked retirement communities are loosely tied to their universities, whereas others have stronger, mutually enriching associations. The more integrated retirement communities offer residents university services such as the opportunity to attend classes, or the opportunity to utilize university health services and, when available, the university-linked hospital facility. The university is enhanced through older adult residents mentoring, volunteering, guest lecturing, and other forms of direct involvement. Students benefit from the employment, internship, volunteer, and research opportunities these retirement communities provide. Rather than focusing on entertainment, university-linked retirement communities provide opportunities for personal growth. Arguably, this can be seen as a more meaningful way to spend retirement time.

University-linked retirement communities come in three types depending on the level of integration with the university affiliate. In the first type, the affiliated university is not involved in the development or operation of the retirement community. The university's role is to provide social and academic programs for the residents. In the second type, the university provides support, usually providing land or financing, to the retirement community in addition to programming. In the third type, the university is fully linked with the retirement community. The university owns, supervises, and runs the retirement community. Also, the university provides the social and academic programs and activities. Campus-affiliated retirement communities include the University of Michigan in Ann Arbor and the University of Florida in Gainesville.

Retirement communities are anticipated to grow in number in the future. These communities are a constantly evolving residential and lifestyle option for older adults. As a group, the baby boomer generation entering later life has greater wealth and higher education than preceding cohorts of older adults. Research shows educated older adults are more likely to enroll in educational programs upon retirement. As a result, university-linked retirement communities, despite their newness, are anticipated to be an increasingly attractive option for retirees. Also, more specialized retirement communities, such as those for GLBT persons, are anticipated to grow in number.

Like the rest of the world, the United States is expecting tremendous growth in its older adult population. Even though older adults often are classified into a single category, there is much variation within that category. Equally, much variety is needed in living arrangements to appeal to this large and dynamic group. This implies both opportunities for growth in all service-oriented and recreation-oriented retirement community types.

**SEE ALSO** Volume 3: *Assisted Living Facilities; Neighborhood Context, Later Life; Residential Mobility, Later Life.*

**BIBLIOGRAPHY**

Campbell, N., & Memken, J. (2007). Accessible housing availability for the growing U.S. elderly population. *Housing and Society, 34*(1), 101–115.

Harrison, A., & Tsao, T.-C. (2006). Enlarging the academic community: Creating retirement communities linked to academic institutions. *Planning for Higher Education, 34*(2), 20–30.

Howard, D., Sloane, P., Zimmerman, S., Eckert, J.K., et al. (2002). Distribution of African Americans in residential care/ assisted living and nursing homes: More evidence of racial disparity? *American Journal of Public Health, 92*(8), 1272–1278.

Hunt, M. (n.d.). *A typology of retirement communities: Emerging themes*. Unpublished manuscript, University of Wisconsin—Madison.

Isn't this gay, dear?: Retirement communities (gay retirement homes). (2002). *The Economist, 365*(8300), 54.

Larson-Keagy, E., & McHugh, K. (2005). These white walls: The dialectic of retirement communities. *Journal of Aging Studies, 19*(2), 241–256.

Lowy, L. (1987). Major issues of age-integrated versus age-segregated approaches to serving the elderly. *Journal of Gerontological Social Work, 10*(3-4), 37–46.

MacLarne, C., Landsberg, G., & Schwartz, H. (2007). History, accomplishments, issues, and prospects of supportive service programs in naturally occurring retirement communities in New York state: Lessons learned. *Journal of Gerontological Social Work, 49*(1-2), 127–144.

Masotti, P., Fick, R., Johnson-Masotti, A., & Macleod, S. (2006). Healthy naturally occurring retirement communities: A low-cost approach to facilitating healthy aging. *American Journal of Public Health, 96*(7), 1164–1170.

Pastalan, L., & Schwarz, B. (Eds.). (1994). University-linked retirement communities: Student visions of elder care. Binghamton, NY: Haworth Press.

Poulin, J. (1984). Age segregation and the interpersonal involvement and morale of the aged. *The Gerontologist, 24*(3), 266–269.

Streib, G. (2002). An introduction to retirement communities. *Research on Aging, 24*(1), 3–9.

***Nichole M. Campbell***

# RILEY, MATILDA WHITE
## *1911–2004*

Matilda White was born in Boston on April 19, but spent most of her childhood and adolescence in Maine. While attending high school she met a fellow student, Jack Riley, who became her childhood sweetheart and lifelong partner. Riley received a bachelor's degree from Radcliffe College in 1931 and married Jack Riley that summer. They later had two children. Riley received a doctorate of science from Bowdoin College in 1972. Matilda and Jack Riley's professional collaboration began in the 1930s and continued throughout their marriage. Jack Riley died in 2002, months before their 71st wedding anniversary. Matilda White Riley died in Maine on November 14.

Matilda White Riley was one of the most influential figures in the establishment of the sociology of aging and the life course. In her long career she comprehensively reviewed and synthesized the state of the science, made seminal scholarly contributions, and designed and directed the primary source of funding for aging research in the social and behavioral sciences.

Riley's career was punctuated by a number of firsts. In 1939 Riley and her father established the Market Research Company of America, pioneering the use of sophisticated sampling and survey techniques to understand and predict consumer behavior. From 1949 to 1960 Riley served as the first executive director of the American Sociological Association. In 1979 she became the first associate director for social and behavioral research at the newly established National Institute on Aging (NIA) at the National Institutes of Health (NIH). For the next 20 years Riley directed the social and behavioral grants programs at NIA and worked with the other NIH institutes to incorporate social and behavioral research. From 1973 to 1981 she also served on the faculty at Bowdoin College in Maine; she was the first woman to achieve the rank of full professor there.

Riley's scholarly legacy is based largely on three enduring theories of age, the life course, and social structure. During the early 1970s Riley directed a state-of-the-science review and synthesis of social factors and aging. After reviewing what was known, Riley developed age stratification theory (Riley, Johnson, & Foner, 1972). She argued that age is a basis of stratification, functionally equivalent to other forms of stratification, such as socioeconomic status, race and ethnicity, and gender. The defining characteristics of stratification systems are that the strata can be arranged hierarchically in terms of their social value and that rewards and responsibilities are allocated differentially across strata. Riley argued that old age is the least valued age stratum and that older adults are allocated fewer rewards (e.g., financial support, public esteem, valued social roles) than are those in other age strata. Although historical conditions change and old age may no longer be at the bottom of the age stratification hierarchy, the enduring truth of age stratification theory lies in the recognition that age is more than a personal characteristic; it is a fundamental element of social structure.

Riley's second important contribution was the concept of structural lag, which refers to the ongoing mismatch between the characteristics and needs of societal members and the structural arrangements of a society (Riley, Kahn, & Foner, 1994). Riley posited that social, cultural, and historical changes occur—and, most important, alter people's lives—more quickly than social structure can be modified to meet the needs generated by those changes. For example, structural arrangements for day care for children lagged decades behind the massive entry of mothers into the labor force. Because personal well-being is highly dependent on structural supports, structural lag makes the life course more difficult than it would be otherwise.

Although both age stratification theory and structural lag implicitly apply to people of all ages, Riley's third important contribution focuses explicitly on the life course. She noted that most people assume that they will have a life course in which major tasks are sequenced by age or life stage. Thus, people assume that the proper "order" of life is to complete one's education, work and raise a family, and then retire for a period of sustained leisure. Riley argued that this age-segregated life course creates unnecessary strains for individuals and harms society by precluding social contributions by people in certain age groups, especially older adults. Riley advocated an alternative, age-integrated life course in which education, productive activity, and leisure are pursued in tandem throughout the life coursc (Riley & Riley, 2000). Transformation of the life course to achieve age integration cannot occur unless the structural arrangements of society are changed drastically; this would include everything from changes in age-based laws and programs to the shift to a labor force dominated by part-time workers.

Matilda White Riley's life served as an illustration of a personal and professional journey at odds with social conditions. Her scholarly legacy has led to a greater understanding of the intersection of social structure and personal biography.

**SEE ALSO** Volume 3: *Foner, Anne; Theories of Aging.*

**BIBLIOGRAPHY**

Riley, M. W., Johnson, M. E., & Foner, A. (1972). *A sociology of age stratification* (Vol. 4). New York: Russell Sage Foundation.

Riley, M. W., Kahn, R. L., & Foner, A. C. (Eds.). (1994). *Age and structural lag: Society's failure to provide meaningful opportunities in work, family, and leisure.* New York: Wiley.

Riley, M. W., & Riley, J. W. (2000). Age integration: Conceptual and historical background. *The Gerontologist, 40,* 266–270.

*Linda K. George*

# ROSSI, ALICE S.

***1922–***

Alice Schaerr Rossi, the sociologist and educator, was one of the early analysts of the role of women in modern American society, and an esteemed researcher of life course issues. An activist as well as a scholar, in 1966 she became one of the founders of the National Organization for Women, and an organizer of Sociologists for Women in Society, becoming its first president. She was elected president of the American Sociological Association in 1982 (and was its third woman president). Rossi's political and feminist roles were formative in the development of her scholarly attention to sex and gender in all domains of life, with shifts in theoretical paradigms informing each next generation of research over a 40-year period.

Born in 1922 in New York City, Rossi received a BA at Brooklyn College of the City University of New York in 1947. She earned a PhD in sociology in 1957 at Columbia University on the basis of her dissertation "Generational Differences in the Soviet Union." In this work, she compared Russians reared before the revolution and those after the revolution, in terms of their life course history and its consequences.

Rossi attributes some of her initial interest on certain life course perspectives to her association with Bernice Neugarten (b. 1916), whom Rossi met when she was a research associate in the Committee on Human Development at the University of Chicago (1964–1967). Neugarten's work on aging inspired Rossi to develop a research agenda exploring different stages of parenting. Rossi's work, reported in "Transition to Parenthood" in the *Journal of Marriage and the Family* (1968), had considerable influence in the field of family sociology. It viewed family roles in terms of stages including the "honeymoon" stage (marriage to first birth), early parenting, late parenting, and post-parenting, with insights about changes in different life stages. This was reprinted in 14 anthologies and was widely cited by others scholars, thus becoming a *citation classic* in 1986. Her book *Gender and the Life Course* (1985) also made her a major figure in life course analysis.

Her interests in the intersections of social and biological factors were developed through participation in a MacArthur Foundation supported research network on midlife development, spanning the years between 1989 and 1999. In the period following the research she and other network members produced hundreds of journal articles, and a final summary volume in 2003. She edited a book, *Sexuality across the Life Course* (1994), with commissioned articles on topics across the life course and a 70 page introductory chapter on a biosocial

***Alice Rossi.*** *NOW founder Alice Rossi speaks at a podium.* NATIONAL ORGANIZATION FOR WOMEN, INC.

perspective on the life course (blending biological and physiological variables with psychological, sociological, or historical variables). She did a major review of research and theory on the menopausal transition and analyzed menstrual and menopausal symptoms that respondents had reported in a national survey the MacArthur network launched in 1995. This became an important chapter in the study's summary volume, *How Healthy Are We? A National Study of Well-being at Midlife* (2003). Another study Alice Rossi did, with her husband and colleague Peter Rossi (1921–2006), gave major attention to changes due to aging and changes associated with birth cohort differences and was reported in *Of Human Bonding: Parent-Child Relations across the Life Course* (1990).

A cluster of Alice Rossi's scholarly work informed and was informed by her political activities. Her service on former U.S. president Jimmy Carter's (b. 1924) Commission on International Women's Year in 1977 led to a panel study of how participation in the Houston Conference had an impact on women delegates' political aspirations, which she reported in *Feminists in Politics* (1982). Her political concerns for abortion law reform in the 1950s through the 1970s led to her designing questions for national surveys about conditions of public approval for legalizing abortion. These survey questions were used in numerous public opinion polls over a 30-year period. Her earlier publications include the path-breaking analyses of social restrictions on women's access to male-dominated occupations. Among these writings were *Women in Science: Why So Few?* (1965), *Barriers to the Career Choice of Engineering, Medicine, or Science among American Women* (1965), and *Equality between the Sexes: An Immodest Proposal* (1964), a study of the social barriers women face. She also edited a widely used anthology titled *The Feminist Papers* (1973), a collection of feminist articles through history.

As of 2008 Rossi is a professor emerita at the University of Massachusetts where she was Harriet Martineau Professor of Sociology from 1974 to 1991. Prior to that she was professor and chair of the Department of Sociology and Anthropology at Goucher College (1969–1971), a research associate at the Department of Social Relations at Johns Hopkins University (1967–1969), and a research associate (or associate professor) at the University of Chicago (1964–1967). She also held other research posts at Harvard University, the National Opinion Research Center, and Cornell University.

She is the recipient of numerous awards and honorary degrees, and was elected a fellow of the American Academy of Arts and Sciences in 1986. She also served as president of the Eastern Sociological Society in 1973. Alice and Peter Rossi, who died in 2006, were married in 1951. They had two daughters and a son.

SEE ALSO Volume 2: *Menopause; Parent-Child Relationships, Adulthood;* Volume 3: *Sexuality, Later Life.*


**BIBLIOGRAPHY**

Rossi, A. S. (1964). Equality between the sexes: An immodest proposal. *Daedalus*, 607–652.

Rossi, A. S. (1965). Barriers to the career choice of engineering, medicine, and science among American women. In J.A. Mattfield and C. G. Van Aken (Eds.), *Women and the Scientific Professions*. Cambridge: Massachusetts Institute of Technology Press.

Rossi, A. S. (1965). Women in science: Why so few?. *Science*, 1196–1202.

Rossi, A. S. (1968). Transition to parenthood. *Journal of Marriage and the Family, 30*, 26–39.

Rossi, A. S. (1973). *Feminist papers: From Adams to de Beauvoir.* New York: Columbia University Press.

Rossi, A. S. (1980). *Generational differences in the Soviet Union.* New York: Arno Press.

Rossi, A. S. (1982). *Feminists in politics: A panel analysis of the first National Women's Conference.* New York: Academic Press.

Rossi, A. S. (1985). *Gender and the life course.* New York: Aldine.

Rossi, A. S. (1994). *Sexuality across the life course.* Chicago: University of Chicago Press.

Rossi, A. S. (2003). Social responsibility in family and community. In O. G. Brim, C. D. Ryff, & R. C. Kessler (Eds.), *How healthy are we? A national study of well-being at midlife* (pp. 550–585). Chicago: University of Chicago Press.

Rossi, A. S. (1990). Rossi, A., & Rossi, P. H. *Of human bonding: Parent-child relations across the life course.* Hawthorne, NY: Aldine de Gruyter.


*Cynthia Fuchs Epstein*

# RYDER, NORMAN B.

## *1923–*

Norman Burston Ryder is a Canadian-born demographer and sociologist who spent most of his career in the United States. His work is so firmly grounded in a life-course perspective that his methods and modes of thought have influenced analysis of all parts of the age spectrum. His work is notable for its use of birth cohorts in the analysis of social change, for its insistence on the processional nature of decision making, and for its focus on the population aggregate as a determinant and consequence of behavior throughout the life course.

***Norman Ryder.*** OFFICE OF POPULATION RESEARCH, PRINCETON UNIVERSITY.

Ryder was born in Hamilton, Ontario. He received his bachelor of arts degree from McMaster University in 1944 and a master of arts degree in economics from the University of Toronto in 1946. Studying on a Milbank Memorial Fund Fellowship at Princeton University, he received another master's degree in economics in 1949 and a doctorate in sociology in 1951. His dissertation, *The Cohort Approach: Essays in the Measurement of Temporal Variations in Demographic Research*, was published in 1980 by Arno Press as part of a series of important dissertations in the social sciences. After graduation, Ryder returned to Canada to work for the Dominion Bureau of Statistics in Ottawa and to hold a faculty position at the University of Toronto. A few years later he returned to the United States. After a brief stay at the Scripps Foundation for Research in Population Problems in Oxford, Ohio, working on the design for the first Growth of American Families survey, he moved in 1956 to the University of Wisconsin. In 1971 he returned to Princeton University and the Office of Population Research, where he remained until his retirement in 1989. Ryder was president of the Population Association of America in 1972–73 (Petersen & Petersen, 1985; van der Tak, 1991).

Ryder is perhaps most widely known for his use of cohorts in the analysis of social change (Ryder, 1965). A cohort is a group of people experiencing a given event in the same period. For example, a birth cohort is the group of people born in the same year, and a marriage cohort is the group of people marrying in the same year. Ryder was not the first demographer to use cohorts in demographic analysis (Whelpton, 1949). He generalized the idea, however, using it to analyze mortality as well as fertility in his dissertation (Ryder, 1980). In that same work he also investigated marriage cohorts as well as birth cohorts and conducted the analysis by parity status of the woman, *parity* being the medical term for the number of babies a woman has birthed.

In a widely cited paper, "The Cohort as a Concept in the Study of Social Change" (1965), Ryder connected the notion of cohorts with the less technical but more widely used concept of a generation and discussed the demographic use of cohorts in the context of a generation as defined by sociologist Karl Mannheim (1952) and historian José Ortega y Gasset (1933). Thus, an established life course of transitions at customary ages may be disrupted by period events such as wars, depressions, or inventions. Such a disruption, occurring to birth cohorts at various ages, may cause the birth cohort to modify their subsequent life course in differing ways. Ryder's observations on cohorts set off a continuing project that tries to statistically separate the effects of age, period, and cohorts on a dependent variable (Mason & Fienberg, 1985; Yang, Fu, & Land, 2004).

The greater part of Ryder's career was spent on the analysis of fertility decisions. In this work he was always alert to the Markovian nature of life—that is, what has happened before, whether intentional or not, conditions the decisions one makes subsequently. Ryder's first published paper, one in which he invents parity progression ratios—that is, birth probabilities conditional on parity—makes exactly that point (Stolnitz & Ryder, 1949). The bulk of Ryder's work on fertility analyzes decision making using surveys, especially the several National Fertility Surveys (Ryder & Westoff, 1971; Westoff & Ryder, 1977a). Attention to careful measurement of both dependent and independent variables has always been a hallmark of Ryder's work. The measurement of contraceptive use, whether a given birth was wanted, and the intention to have a subsequent birth were all important themes in his research (Ryder 1973, 1976; Westoff & Ryder, 1977b).

Finally, Ryder has always been alert to issues of aggregation in demographic studies. His classic paper "Notes on the Concept of a Population" (1964a) takes very seriously the reality of the population as more than a simple aggregation of its elements. In this paper, individuals are nested in birth cohorts and cohorts are nested in populations. In a subsequent paper (1964b), he details how rates at one level translate into rates at another. His sense of the interdependence of these levels extends to the policy arena. His "Two Cheers for ZPG" (1972) argues that insisting on zero population growth now and henceforth would lead to fertility booms and busts that would continue for a very long time.

Ryder's career has been that of a gifted technical demographer and a wide-ranging sociologist with a clear eye on what is important.

**SEE ALSO** Volume 2: *Mannheim, Karl;* Volume 3: *Age, Period, Cohort Effects; Cohort.*

**BIBLIOGRAPHY**

Mannheim, K. (1952). The problem of generations. In P. Kecskemeti (Ed.), *Essays on the sociology of knowledge* (pp. 276–322). New York: Oxford University Press.

Mason, W. M., & Fienberg, S. E. (Eds.). (1985). *Cohort analysis in social research: Beyond the identification problem.* New York: Springer-Verlag.

Ortega y Gasset, J. (1933). *The modern theme* (J. Cleugh, Trans.). New York: Norton.

Petersen, W., & Petersen, R. (1985). Ryder, Norman B. In *Dictionary of demography: Biographies* (pp. 884–885). Westport, CT: Greenwood Press.

Ryder, N. B. (1964a). Notes on the concept of a population. *The American Journal of Sociology, 69*, 447–463.

Ryder, N. B. (1964b). The process of demographic translation. *Demography, 1*, 74–82.

Ryder, N. B. (1965). The cohort as a concept in the study of social change. *American Sociological Review, 30*, 843–861.

Ryder, N. B. (1972). Two cheers for ZPG. *Daedalus, 2*(4), 45–62.

Ryder, N. B. (1973). A critique of the National Fertility Study. *Demography, 10*, 495–506.

Ryder, N. B. (1976). The specification of fertility planning status. *Family Planning Perspectives, 8*, 283–290.

Ryder, N. B. (1980). *The cohort approach: Essays in the measurement of temporal variations in demographic research.* New York: Arno Press.

Ryder, N. B., & Westoff, C. F. (1971). *Reproduction in the United States, 1965.* Princeton, NJ: Princeton University Press.

Stolnitz, G. J., & Ryder, N. G. (1949). Recent discussion of the net reproduction rate. *Population Index, 15*, 114–128.

van der Tak, J. (1991). Interview with Norman B. Ryder. In *Demographic destinies: Interviews with presidents and secretary-treasurers of the Population Association of America* (PAA Oral History Project, Vol. 1, pp. 325–342). Washington, DC: Population Association of America.

Westoff, C. F., & Ryder, N. B. (1977a). *The contraceptive revolution.* Princeton, NJ: Princeton University Press.

Westoff, C. F., & Ryder, N. B. (1977b). The predictive validity of reproductive intentions. *Demography, 14*, 431–453.

Whelpton, P. K. (1949). Cohort analysis of fertility. *American Sociological Review, 14*, 735–749.

Yang, Y., Fu, W. J., & Land, K. C. (2004). A methodological comparison of age-period-cohort models: The intrinsic estimator and conventional generalized linear models. *Sociological Methodology, 34*, 75–110.

***Hal Winsborough***

# S

## SECOND DEMOGRAPHIC TRANSITION

SEE Volume 3: *Demographic Transition Theories.*

## SELF

The term *self* has been applied in many ways by philosophers, sociologists, and psychologists. Sociologists tend to use the term *identity* whereas psychologists use the term *self,* but this disciplinary distinction is blurred (Howard, 2000). Theorists in both disciplines focus on different aspects of the self in their research and theories. In one study, for example, two psychologists (Leary and Tangney, 2003) explored whether the term *self* was used in a consistent fashion in entries in a computerized database of published psychological studies (PsycInfo). The researchers found more than 66 different applications, including many hyphenated terms used to denote diverse facets and processes related to the self (e.g., self-esteem, self-monitoring). Following this review, Leary and Tangney concluded that the term *self* is best used as an organizing construct to integrate theory and research on the personal characteristics and descriptions, subjective experiences and beliefs, personal life stories, and typical behaviors (projects, goals, interests, life routines) of an individual.

Sociologists traditionally consider the social and relational roots of the self and identity over the life course (Howard, 2000; Rosenberg, 1981). According to sociological perspectives, the self is shaped by interactions with cultural, historical, and social systems of influence (e.g., family, school, occupation, religion). As individuals progress through the life course, they are assigned to and actively adopt different roles within these systems. Such roles might include daughter, student, worker, mother, parent, friend, voter, caregiver, or senior citizen. Each of these roles carries social expectations regarding appropriate behavior and beliefs for role holders. Individuals adopt these *social expectations* as their own beliefs and aspirations, and compare themselves with others in similar social roles and groups (i.e., *reference groups*). In turn, members of the social groups give feedback to the individual about their status. Sociologists view transitions in work and family roles, physical appearance, social age categories, and participation in society as sources of change in the self.

By contrast, psychologists consider the dynamic intersection between the inborn or personal characteristics of individuals and their social contexts. They focus on underlying cognitive, emotional, and motivational processes associated with adapting to personal aging and changing roles and life circumstances. According to psychological theory, individuals actively select their social contexts and significant others (such as peers, siblings, or spouse) and evaluate their interactions with these significant others (*reflected appraisal*). In addition, individuals remember their earlier life experiences and construct their own autobiography. In addition to *social comparison* (that is, comparing one's self with others, as a way to evaluate one's own abilities and attributes), individuals also make *temporal comparisons* with their personal past experience and their personal hopes and fears about the future (*possible selves*). These different but complementary approaches contribute to a variety of research on the self during adulthood.

This entry primarily focuses on research on the self in midlife and old age. It focuses on two central areas of investigation, the *self-concept* and *possible selves*, and reviews findings about the content, structure, and functions of these constructs and whether these facets change over time. Before moving to these two topics, we briefly review the multiple components and dimensions of the self, to provide background to subsequent material.

## THE MULTIPLE DIMENSIONS OF THE SELF

Scholars have long conceptualized the self as a system that involves many components and levels. The psychologist William James (1890) is credited as being the first to distinguish between the *self-as-knower* (the "I," or subject) and the *self-as-known* (the "me," an object of reflection). The self-as-knower encompasses all of the processes involved in monitoring and being aware of our momentary relationship with the environment and our location in space. This aspect of the self also underlies our experiences of emotion, pain, hunger, and bodily sensations and the impression that we can somehow control or direct our feelings and thoughts.

In contrast, the self-as-known refers specifically to people's knowledge and general beliefs about themselves. Individuals describe, interpret, evaluate, and construct their self as an "object." The self-as-known may be kept private or disclosed to others. It is protected from threat, enhanced, and adjusts to changes in social context, personal relationships, and personal needs. The self-as-known thus includes one's sense of identity and perceived social roles, personal knowledge of one's own life, and autobiographical memories, as well as personal theories, beliefs, goals, and life narratives.

Although the distinction made by James almost a century ago was widely adopted by theorists, until recently most research focused on the known rather than the knowing self. However, contemporary cognitive and social neuroscientists interested in investigating aspects of consciousness, self-monitoring, empathy and the ability to synchronize with the actions of others are revitalizing research on the self-as-knower (e.g., Harmon-Jones and Winkielman, 2007).

In contemporary research on the known self, the terms *self-concept* and *identity* are frequently used synonymously to refer to sub-components of the self. Early theories of adulthood and aging sometimes used the terms *self* and *personality* interchangeably. There is a growing consensus, however, that *personality* can be considered a separate component of the self (e.g., Hooker and McAdams, 2003). Adult personality is often described in terms of a profile of five core dispositions or traits (extraversion, neuroticism, conscientiousness, agreeableness, openness to new experience; e.g., Pervin and John, 1999). Self-related knowledge, beliefs, and processes are distinguished from personality traits; the potential amount of self-relevant information stored in memory is large and varied. Furthermore, whereas individual differences in the core personality traits appear to have a substantial biogenetic basis and to be relatively persistent across the lifespan, differences in self-related knowledge, beliefs, and processes are based more on cultural, historical, and social influences and thus are more susceptible to change during the course of an individual's life.

## SELF-CONCEPT

According to James, the *self-concept* is integral to the definition of self-as-known. Researchers have used the term in both a narrow and a broad way, however (Demo, 1992). Narrow definitions focus on the thematic content of self-descriptions and identification with social groups and social roles. Broad definitions also include self-evaluations (e.g., self-esteem), general beliefs about personal competence and ability to achieve goals and perform social roles (self-efficacy, agency), and the memories and stories of one's own life.

Theories about the nature of the self-concept and how it might change in adulthood and old age originate in the fields of sociology and psychology. Theorists who adopt a broad definition make proposals about changes in content, organization, and function. Sociological frameworks typically address issues related to the social construction of identity and the influence of social roles (e.g., Howard, 2000; Stryker, 2007). Sociologists, in particular, consider differences associated with structural or sociodemographic characteristics such as gender, race, socioeconomic, and age. In comparison, psychologists have focused primarily on self-related processes. They ask whether these processes change during adulthood and examine the consequences of individual differences in self-concept for health, well-being, and longevity.

For example, some psychologists believe that older adults are motivated to maximize positive emotions and minimize negative experiences and that this is observed in their specific selection of social partners (Carstensen, 1993). Older adults prefer to reduce their social networks in order to spend more time with people with whom they feel close. Young adults, in contrast, are motivated to obtain information about the world and to expand their social contacts in order to do this regardless of potential emotional costs. Sociologists, on the other hand, might interpret the reduction in size of the social network as a response to changed roles within society and social expectations, such as retirement or widowhood.

## THEMATIC CONTENT IN MIDLIFE AND OLD AGE

Self-descriptions given in response to questions such as "Tell me something about yourself; Who are you?" contain the important characteristics of self-related knowledge that an individual considers uniquely distinguish him- or herself from others (Markus and Nurius, 1986). Self-descriptions may communicate to a listener an overall picture of an individual's identity, behavior, goals, values, interests, and personal characteristics (Epstein, 1990; McAdams, 2006).

In old age, themes or specific descriptions that were relatively unimportant in young and middle adulthood gain in salience or importance to the individual (Breytspraak, 1984). Erik Erikson (1959), for example, proposed that midlife and old age is characterized by the developmental tasks of generativity (versus self-absorption) and integrity (versus despair). He suggested that these tasks are manifested in reflections about the past, one's legacy, contributions to others, and thoughts about death. Others have added three themes to this description: (a) loss of professional status, (b) coping with physical decline, and (c) the process of dying. Some theorists suggest that the reorganization of personal life narratives and self-descriptions is the major task of midlife. Others argue that post-retirement and the period of young old age is another period of change due to a decrease in professional and family roles and obligations. After age 70, there is increased room for new self-definitions in such domains as hobbies and personal interests. In advanced old age if individuals face increasing physical declines that put constraints on pursuing hobbies and interests, self-descriptions are often characterized by a life review and reflections about having lived a long life. Thus, the self-descriptions of very old persons may rely on experiences, achievements, and events that happened in the past rather than in the present or the future.

The family represents another important theme in older persons' self-descriptions. Laura Carstensen's socioemotional selectivity theory (Carstensen, 1993) suggests that people are increasingly selective with regard to their social partners when approaching the end of life. Whereas social partners become less important for gaining information as one ages, emotion regulation becomes an increasingly important motive for social contact. Family members and relatives, usually long-standing members of one's social convoy (Antonucci, 1990), might have heightened emotional importance in old age as the number of same-aged friends decrease due to their health-related problems, reduced mobility, or because they have died. Family stories about relationships and changes in relationships are central to the self.

Empirical research is equivocal as to whether self-descriptions change with age. Few if any studies have examined the same individuals longitudinally from early in adulthood into old age. Most research asks if people in different age groups differ, but this cross-sectional design confounds age with cohort effects. That is, it is not possible for researchers to discern whether the changes observed reflect age differences (e.g., maturation processes) or one's membership in a specific birth cohort (e.g., baby boomer versus member of "greatest generation"). The content of the self-concept (i.e., attitudes, beliefs) of an older person reflects influential social forces when they were younger, together with new themes that that emerge with age. It is not possible to disentangle these two aspects in cross-sectional studies. Lifespan researchers generally reserve the term *change* to reports of longitudinal evidence and otherwise refer to *age-related differences* for cross-sectional studies.

McCrae and Costa (1988) found age-related differences in the self-definition of persons between 32 and 84 years of age: With increasing age, themes such as age, health, life events, life situations, hobbies/interests, and attitudes were mentioned more frequently, whereas family roles, social relationships, neuroticism, personality traits, and daily living routines were mentioned less frequently. George and Okun (1985), however, found no significant age-related differences in their cross-sectional comparison of the content of the self-definitions of three age groups (45–54, 55–64, and over 65 years). Likewise, Filipp and Klauer (1986) reported no age differences in a cross-sectional comparison of five male cohorts (born between 1905 and 1945). A longitudinal analysis of the changes in self-definitions over 26 months, however, showed that the themes, social roles, political or religious attitudes, body image, and social style were increasingly reported to be self-defining, while emotionality and autonomy were mentioned less frequently.

Charles and Pasupathi (2003) examined variability in the self-descriptions of adults aged 18 to 94 over the course of a week and asked whether this situational variability was associated with daily mood. Older women showed less day-to-day variability than younger women, especially when they reported being together with the same people. There were no age-related differences between young and older men, and overall, men varied less from day-to-day. Greater variability in self-descriptions was related to more frequent and more intense experience of negative affect. This is one of the few studies of the ways that day-to-day context shapes self-descriptions. The findings point to the value of this methodology as a way to examine the construction of life stories and the self-concept, particularly during periods of the life course associated with transitions in roles and change in family, work, and health contexts.

Freund and Smith (1999) examined the spontaneous self-descriptions of old and very old persons in the context of the Berlin Aging Study (BASE), a heterogeneous sample of old (70–84 years) and very old (85–103 years) adults in Berlin, Germany. Participants included a broad spectrum of themes in their descriptions, but health, personal characteristics and activities, and aspects of life review dominated. The majority of the sample considered current hobbies and interests, social participation, and daily living routines as self-defining domains. There were more similarities than differences between the old (70–84 years) and the very old (85–103 years) in the content of the self-descriptions. As is to be expected, very old participants generally did not mention outdoor activities that require good health and physical mobility, but instead discussed their health. Participants over 85 years also mentioned themes about family/relatives and interpersonal style less frequently than the younger age group (70–84 years).

Although family was one of the most salient themes, the very old persons (85–100+ yrs) referred to it less frequently. One possible explanation of this finding is that extremely close social partners, such as a husband or wife, might be highly integrated into one's self in very old age. This integration of close family members into one's self might take place to such a degree that they are perceived as part of oneself rather than "external" social partners who deserve a special mention. Widowed, divorced, and single older adults, however, did mention other social partners not belonging to their family (i.e., friends, acquaintances) more frequently than married persons. Not being married in old age might make relationships with other social partners more important.

These descriptive analyses of the content of the self-descriptions offer insights into the age-specific topics and challenges that face midlife and older adults. The analyses of life narratives collected using more open-ended methods provide additional insight into themes, including outcomes of life review, explanations for personal transitions, perceived "second chances" in life, and stories of personal redemption (e.g., Birren and Schroots, 2006; McAdams, 2006). Comparison of life narratives over time also offers a window on the process of constructing and reorganizing the self-concept. Birren and Schroots (2006), for example, suggest that the process of life review late in life is particularly important for the integration of self-knowledge. Life review may be a means by which individuals are able to face the inevitable aspects of physical dependency in very old age with pride and dignity.

## AGE IDENTITY AND PERCEPTIONS OF AGING

One theme of particular interest to lifespan developmental psychologists and life course sociologists is the individual's perception and evaluation of their own aging process. Sociological theory views physical appearance as a cue to social categorization (e.g., gender, race, age). Although there is much research on gender and racial identity, until recently there has been relatively little about the effects of physical aging on age identity and change in self-concept. Some research, however, considers stereotypes about physical attractiveness and physical appearance in old age and individuals' perceptions about the personal meaning of "getting older."

*Subjective age* is a multidimensional construct that indicates how old a person feels and into which age group a person categorizes him or herself (e.g., Settersten and Mayer, 1997). After early adulthood, most people say that they feel younger than their chronological age and the gap between subjective age and actual age generally increases as one ages. On average, for example, 90-year-olds in relatively good health report feeling between 12 and 20 years younger (Baltes and Smith, 2003). Age identity has several distinctive features. Unlike many other social categories (e.g., race, gender), all middle-aged and older adults were previously members of the categories child, adolescent, and young adult. As people get older, their knowledge and expectations about the characteristics of members in the category of seniors or older adults may or may not be renewed. Whereas some aspects of age identity may be positively valued (e.g., acquiring seniority in a profession or becoming a grandparent) others may be less valued depending on societal context. Perceived physical age (i.e., the age one looks in a mirror) is one aspect that requires considerable self-related adaptation in social and cultural contexts that value young bodies. In contemporary western society, older women more frequently describe inconsistencies between their subjective age and the image of their body reflected in a mirror than do older men.

Asking people how satisfied they are with their own aging captures an evaluative component of age identity. A large survey on the perceptions of aging in Americans over the age of 65 found that 87% were satisfied with life in general, yet considerably fewer people (64%) reported that getting older was better than they had expected, and 46% indicated that they felt old and tired. Feeling younger and being satisfied with one's own aging are expressions of *positive self-perceptions of aging*. They reflect age identity and the operation of self-related processes that enhance well-being. Psychologists suggest that positive self-perceptions of aging might sustain levels of social activity and engagement, enhance self-esteem and well-being, and boost bio-physiological functioning. Levy (2003) found that older individuals who are able to adapt to and accept changes in their appearance and physical capacity in a positive way evidenced higher well-being, better health, and longer life spans.

## EVALUATION AND STRUCTURE OF THE SELF

Two aspects of the self are considered essential for positive well-being and for maintaining a sense of overall personal continuity and cohesion. The first is the extent to which individuals consider their own attributes and life stories to be good or bad (positive or negative), and the second is the level of multifacetedness or differentiation of the self-concept.

Obviously, whether or not individuals believe that they have positive qualities is very important for their general sense of self-worth and emotional well-being (Epstein, 1990; Swann, Rentfrow, and Guinn, 2003). The majority of individuals in all age and cohort groups report a global sense of positive self-esteem (cf., Bengtson, Reedy, and Gordon, 1985; Crocker, 2004). Indeed, feeling worthless as a person over an extended time is a sign of pathological change, especially depressive illness.

*Multifacetedness* refers to the number of self-defining themes in an individual's self-concept and the richness and depth of information in these themes. Several researchers argue that having a multifaceted self-concept means that an individual has multiple alternatives available to them to compensate for potential loss (e.g., Leary and Tangney, 2003). For example, if a person indicates that helping others is an important feature of their self-concept but mentions only one example ("I often volunteer at my club"), this self-defining theme might be vulnerable if going to the club becomes impossible due to declining physical health. If, however, the theme "helping others," apart from active volunteer work, contains additional aspects such as helping the neighbor, giving advice, organizing the volunteer efforts of others from home, or helping family members, then the theme can be maintained in the self-concept. Similar to proposals about multifacetedness, some scholars suggest that the self becomes more integrated and that this integration involves increases in cognitive and emotional complexity (Diehl, Hastings, and Stanton, 2001).

Using cross-sectional data from the Berlin Aging Study, Freund and Smith (1999) found that multifaceted self-descriptions guarded against late-life depression, but did not bolster positive emotional well-being if the older person was physically frail. One interpretation of this finding is that multifacetedness might also be associated with the compartmentalization of the self-concept (e.g., Showers and Zeigler-Hill, 2003; see also Diehl, et al., 2001). For example, with increasing age, those themes and aspects that were previously highly salient to the self, but for some reason became obsolete, are not deleted entirely but rather separated from current themes. Over time, this process of compartmentalizing personal themes and aspects of self-knowledge could have both positive and negative effects on well-being. If the personal value placed on the category of past themes outweighs the perceived importance of present themes, then despite a general sense of life satisfaction, very old individuals will nevertheless experience a sense of personal loss. They are no longer the person that they were. The challenge of maintaining a positive view of life in very old age is daunting (Baltes and Smith, 2003).

## PROCESSES THAT SUPPORT, ENHANCE, AND PROTECT THE SELF

Many processes associated with enhancing, supporting, and protecting the self are proposed in the sociological and psychological literature. These processes include:

1. maintaining self esteem by carefully selecting activities and social partners that verify one's sense of mastery and competence;
2. avoiding contexts that threaten self-esteem;
3. comparing interests and performance with social peers;
4. regulating mood and emotional experiences to maximize positive and minimize negative feelings;
5. engaging in satisfying personal projects;
6. and working on personal goals that are compatible with one's self-concept (Leary and Tangney, 2003).

Research suggests that although all of these processes are present throughout adulthood, there are often subtle changes associated with increasing age (e.g., Brandtstädter and Lerner, 1999). The projects, goals, and hobbies that individuals pursue are reorganized and new priorities are established throughout the life course. The diagnosis of a chronic illness, for example, often contributes to new priorities and new goals. Such goals might range from giving up smoking, exercising more, or reducing work stress to focus on family life. In addition, people adjust the standards that they strive to achieve to accommodate changes in their physical capacity. Levels of aspiration thus tend to decrease with age. Instead of striving to run a marathon in three and a half hours, for example, the goal is to be capable of jogging a few miles three times per week and to avoid injury.

Strategies of comparison (social and temporal) used to evaluate oneself may also change with age in order to protect the self. Rather than compare one's self with people who are better off (i.e., upward comparison), older adults instead prefer to make downward comparisons with those who are not doing as well as themselves. This strategy can serve to bolster a sense of well-being in many contexts. For example, even though a person might be in the hospital, there may be fellow patients who are not seen as recovering as quickly as oneself. Some older adults who complain that they see themselves as being slower at doing math or reading than they remember from their earlier years, nevertheless gain comfort by comparing their own ability to some of their peers with mild dementia.

The strategies used to cope with difficulties also tend to become more emotion-focused than problem-focused with age. Individuals find ways to cope that prioritize emotional well-being over finding a concrete solution to the problem. This is similar to the proposals of Carstensen's socioemotional selectivity model (1993; Carstensen, Isaacowitz, and Charles, 1999). Cross-sectional studies show that older adults focus on emotionally meaningful goals (such as contact with others close to them), whereas young adults are more likely to pursue goals that expand their horizons or generate new social contacts. Carstensen and colleagues suggest that these changes in preferences are linked to perceived time left in life. Because future time is inevitably limited in old age, young and older adults are motivated to select different goals.

## POSSIBLE SELVES

Possible selves are highly personalized, hoped-for and feared images of the self that function as incentives for action (Markus and Herzog, 1991). As temporal extensions of the self-concept, they guide decisions about what goals to work on, where to invest time and effort, what to avoid or resist, and what to abandon. Possible selves also reflect an individual's motivation to try to control the direction of her or his future life: motivations such as self-improvement, self-maintenance, and efforts to minimize loss and maximize well-being (Baltes and Carstensen, 1991; Cross and Markus, 1991; Hooker, 1999; Markus and Herzog, 1991; Ryff, 1991). People change and recalibrate their possible selves in response to changes in life circumstances, specific life events (e.g., widowhood, diagnosis of illness), and social expectations.

Although most research on possible selves, as conceptualized by Markus and colleagues, has been undertaken with college students and adolescents, this aspect of the self-concept in old age has received some attention because it offers an important window on the adaptive capacity and motivational system of older individuals (Dunkel and Kerpelman, 2006; Hooker and McAdams, 2003). Theories about the aging self suggest differences in the *number*, *content*, and *dynamics* of possible selves between the middle-aged, young old, and oldest old (e. g., Markus and Herzog, 1991). Lifespan psychologists suggest that, for the majority of the oldest old, declining health and losses in life quality are inevitable and that this places strong constraints on achieving new goals (Baltes and Smith, 2003). Life course sociologists point to the social expectations associated with transitions and life events in midlife and old age. These transitions heighten awareness of personal constraints (e.g., health, financial) and the closeness of one's own death. This influences the types of personal goals and projects selected and the temporal extension of these goals (e.g., Carstensen, Isaacowitz, and Charles, 1999). The awareness of a limit to the personal time left to live is reflected in the overall temporal focus of the self-concept and this is reflected in an individual's possible selves.

**The Content of Possible Selves in Old Age** Whereas concerns about the social, interpersonal, and occupational self are prominent domains in the future scenarios of young and middle-aged adults, in later life the domain of health becomes more salient (Hooker, 1992; 1999). Cross and Markus (1991), however, reported that while the fears of 60-year-olds were about health and lifestyle constraints (e.g., becoming physically dependent), their hoped-for selves were about personal characteristics. Similarly, in interviews with men and women aged over 85 years, Troll and Skaff (1997) found that perceived changes in personality characteristics (and especially positive changes) were mentioned more often than changes in physical health, everyday competence, and lifestyle. Other researchers suggest that strivings for satisfying interpersonal relationships are important in old age (e.g., Antonucci, 1990; Carstensen, et al., 1999).

Smith and Freund (2002) examined data from the Berlin Aging Study and found that the possible selves of adults aged 70 to 103 years were highly personalized and varied. Contrary to suggestions that late adulthood is a period of disengagement from making future plans in favor of life review, participants in BASE generated varied future scenarios that covered a range of domains. Possible selves associated with personal characteristics, health, and social relationships predominated. The majority of participants had at least one matched possible self (i.e., a hope-for and a feared scenario for the same theme).

Hopes and fears about health and personal characteristics were mentioned more than ones about family and social relationships. Furthermore, participants ages 80 years and older reported fewer hopes related to their social relationships, compared to the 70–79 year olds. In current self-descriptions, Freund and Smith (1999) found that BASE participants frequently mentioned their activities and interests. In the possible selves scenarios of the same participants, however, this domain was less prominent and was rarely mentioned as a feared self. Given the realistic constraints associated with declines in health, activities and interests may be things that people are prepared to abandon (or to leave out of their future-self images) because they can gain esteem from memories of past acts and present achievements. Although concerns about cognitive functioning (memory, dementia) are often thought to occupy the minds of older adults, this domain was mentioned rarely in the future-self images of BASE participants.

Research on subgroups of older adults with specific illnesses, such as Alzheimer's disease (Cotrell and Hooker, 2005) and Parkinson's disease (Frazier, Cotrell, and Hooker, 2003), suggests that health-related changes in objective life circumstances play a significant role in the content and functioning of possible selves. While the central late-life task of dealing with declining health represented a focal domain in the possible selves of the majority of participants in these studies, a wide range of other domains also are evident, especially those associated with identity (personal characteristics) and attachment (social relationships, positive contacts with family and friends). Hoped-for selves were not just expressions about avoiding undesirable outcomes or maintaining the current status: Expressions of desires to experience something new or experience something again predominated. As in younger age groups, the possible selves of many individuals also showed a degree of motivation for change.

**The Dynamics of Possible Selves** Possible selves are a dynamic part of the self concept in very old age. Several theorists (e.g., Hooker, 1999; Markus and Herzog, 1991) propose that possible selves are acquired, maintained, transformed, and given up over time. In longitudinal studies, researchers find evidence of both stability and change in the profile of domains included in possible of selves over time. Whereas individuals' concerns about long-term projects associated with family well-being or health maintenance may be stable over time, their specific hopes and fears about short-term issues may change considerably. Changes in health status and life circumstances play a role in giving up possible selves linked to activities and interests and those older adults who lose social partners may reduce their hopes and fears about social relationships. Over time, older individuals may also be less motivated to strive for maintenance and instead focus managing their losses.

A further aspect relates to the extent to which the structure of possible selves in old age changes over time. Is there, for instance, a trend toward more integrated or compartmentalized possible selves? A trend toward a highly integrated (dedifferentiated) structure might involve the addition or maintenance of matched hopes and fears over time or a restriction of matched possible selves to highly salient late-life domains like health. A trend toward compartmentalization (differentiation), in contrast, might involve the addition or maintenance of more fears than hopes or the increased domination of possible selves by fears.

Smith and Freund (2002) examined the dynamics of the possible selves of participants in the Berlin Aging Study over four years. They found that some images were stable while others were added and deleted over time. The large majority of BASE participants showed some aspects of change in their future possible selves. New hopes and fears were added; other aspects were lost over time. They also observed changes in the extent to which hopes and fears within a domain were matched, and a progression toward adding matches in the domain of health.

Theory suggests that hoped-for possible selves organize and energize the adoption of behaviors (Cross and Markus, 1991; Hooker, 1992; Hooker and Kaus, 1992; Whaley, 2003). This reflects another aspect of the dynamics of possible selves. For example, individuals who want to be good grandparents might have a possible self in the domain of social relations that motivates them to think about different ways of participating in the lives of their grandchildren. This simulation may facilitate a decision to engage in relevant activities (e.g., babysitting) and fuel long hours of continued patience with energetic grandchildren. In contrast, researchers propose that feared possible selves disorganize behavior and cause inaction because they provide the individual with a vivid undesired image without necessarily specifying means and strategies of how to avoid it (Hooker, 1992).

Hoppmann, Gerstorf, Smith, and Klumb (2007) examined whether possible selves in three salient life domains (health, cognition, and social relationships) are associated with the performance of daily activities in those domains. Using time-sampling information from 83 participants of the Berlin Aging Study, they demonstrated that domain-specific possible selves translate into daily behavior and are related with concurrent affective experiences and subsequent mortality hazards in old and very old age. Hopes in the domains of health and social relations were positively associated with the performance of health-related and social activities. Although participants with health-related hopes reported lower overall levels of positive affect, in general the performance of possible self-related activities in daily life was associated with elevations in concurrent positive affect. Older adults who report hopes appear to have elaborate images of what to do in the service of their desired future selves and this helps them to actually perform domain-specific activities (Cross and Markus, 1991; Hooker, 1992; Whaley, 2003). In contrast, older adults who report feared possible selves may feel trapped by vivid images of undesired situations and lack the means and strategies to avoid them. In addition, older adults may perceive low control over feared outcomes particularly in the domains of health and cognition (Hooker, 1992). This might apply less to the domain of social relations. Alternatively, older adults may successfully avoid situations that are related to their feared selves.

Hoppmann and colleagues found no association between hopes and daily activities in the cognitive domain. One reason for this finding might be that by the time individuals reach old age, they can draw on life-long experiences to help them decide how to stay in good health (e.g. physical activity, medical check-ups) and maintain satisfying relationships (e.g. calling friends, solving social conflicts), but have little experience with cognitive decline. For most persons, cognitive decline accumulates slowly over many decades and usually does not constrain everyday functioning unless pathological change also occurs. For this reason, possible selves about cognitive functioning in general may be less effectively implemented. Alternatively, many older adults may perceive little control over cognitive decline.

**The Function of Possible Selves** Psychologists typically consider the motivational and evaluative functions of possible selves in old age. For example, they ask whether possible selves a) indicate desires for self improvement (gain), self maintenance, or efforts to minimize or prevent losses; b) indicate the individual's preferences about what to approach and avoid in the future; and c) contribute to a positive sense of well-being (Cross and Markus, 1991; Markus and Herzog, 1991). Discrepancy-reducing theories of mood, for example, propose that engaging in activities that are instrumental in either minimizing the distance between an actual and a desired situation or maximizing the perceived distance from a feared scenario contributes to experiences of positive affect.

Some researchers suggest that whereas middle-aged adults focus on achieving hoped-for selves (e.g., acquiring material possessions), older adults are more concerned with ensuring predictability (i.e., maintenance) and preventing or avoiding feared selves such as illness and dependency. Markus and Ruvolo (1989) proposed that when a domain gains in personal salience, an individual develops countervailing hopes and fears in that domain. Hopes are linked to strategies outlining what to do to attain domain-specific goals and the matched fears offset or balance these hopes with images of what could happen if the desired states were not realized. Matched hopes and fears in a domain indicate a high level of motivational control in that domain and the availability of means and strategies for working on future goals (Markus and Ruvolo, 1989). Knowing in which domains older adults have hopes and fears and in which domains matched possible selves are constructed can therefore tell us much about the operation of the system.

Which characteristics (content and structure) of possible selves are linked to well-being in late life? Cross and Markus (1991) found that at all ages persons who reported low life satisfaction generated more hopes about personal characteristics (i.e., indicating a desire to change present self characteristics), compared with those high in life satisfaction who generated more hopes in the occupational, family, and health domains. Smith and Freund (2002) found that hopes were less related to well-being than were feared self images. Developing and maintaining balanced possible selves, particularly in old age, might also serve as a resource for well-being.

Older adults who prioritize health in their current and future self-descriptions may be vulnerable to losses in well-being. The maintenance of matched hopes and fears about health, for example, might reflect chronic worry and rumination rather than a motivational force. This interpretation is analogous to a report by Niedenthal, Setterlund, and Wherry (1992). They suggested that a large number of highly interrelated possible selves (matched hopes and fears can be viewed as a special case of interrelated possible selves) may have detrimental emotional consequences when individuals are confronted with negative events. Similarly, Showers and colleagues (2003) found that the compartmentalization of positive and negative self images (and especially an increased focus on positive images) in the context of stressful life changes minimized the impact of negative life events on well-being.

?A3B2 tlsb=0.01w?>A working self concept that includes future guides for bolstering self-esteem and a sense of past and present mastery is an important aspect of the self in later life. While individuals may gain esteem from past feats in some domains (e.g., skills, family), other aspects of the self require continuous input (I'm still a nice person and accepted by others). For most older adults, health becomes self-defining. Those individuals who suffer from debilitating illnesses or lack well-functioning support networks to assist them to cope with poor health are at risk. The dynamic interplay of possible self content in relation to new challenges associated with changes in life circumstances and the relationship between current self-descriptions and future scenarios remains to be investigated. Such studies will further a current understanding of the role of future-oriented motivational systems in the maintenance of identity and well-being in very old age.

**SEE ALSO** Volume 1: *Identity Development; Social Development;* Volume 2: *Agency; Personality;* Volume 3: *Age Identity.*

**BIBLIOGRAPHY**

Antonucci, T. C. (1990). Social supports and social relationships. In R. H. Binstock & L. K. George (Eds.), *Handbook of aging and the social sciences* (3rd ed., pp. 205–226). San Diego, CA: Academic Press.

Baltes, M. M., & Carstensen, L. L. (1991). Possible selves across the life span: Commentary. *Human Development, 34,* 256–260.

Baltes, P. B., & Smith, J. (2003). New frontiers in the future of aging: From successful aging of the young old to the dilemmas of the fourth age. *Gerontology, 49,* 123–135.

Bengtson, V. L., Reedy, M. N., & Gordon, C. (1985). Aging and self-conceptions: Personality processes and social contexts. In J. E. Birren & K. W. Schaie (Eds.), *Handbook of the psychology of aging* (pp. 544–593). New York: Van Nostrand Reinhold.

Birren, J. E., & Schroots, J. J. F. (2006). Autobiographical memory and the narrative self over the life span. In J. E. Birren and K. Warner Schaie (Eds.) *Handbook of the psychology of aging* (6th ed. pp. 477–499). Burlingham, MA: Elsevier Academic Press

Brandtstädter, J., & Lerner, R. M. (1999). *Action & self-development: Theory and research through the life span.* Thousand Oaks, CA: Sage Publications, Inc.

Breytspraak, L. M. (1984). *The development of self in later life.* Boston: Little, Brown & Co.

Carstensen, L. L. (1993). Motivation for social contact across the life span: A theory of socioemotional selectivity. In J. Jacobs (Ed.). *Nebraska symposium on motivation: 1992: Developmental perspectives on motivation, 40,* 209–254. Lincoln: University of Nebraska Press.

Carstensen, L. L., Isaacowitz, D. M., & Charles, S. T. (1999). Taking time seriously: A theory of socioemotional selectivity. *American Psychologist, 54,* 165–181.

Charles, S. T., & Pasupathi, M. (2003). Age-related patterns of variability in self-descriptions: Implications for everyday affective experience. *Psychology and Aging, 18*(3), 524–536.

Cotrell, V., & Hooker, K. (2005). Possible selves of individuals with Alzheimer's Disease. *Psychology and Aging, 20*(2), 285–294.

Crocker, J., & Park, L. E. (2004). The costly pursuit of self-esteem. *Psychological Bulletin, 130,* 392–414.

Cross, S., & Markus, H. (1991). Possible selves across the life span. *Human Development, 34*(4), 230–255.

Demo, D. H. (1992). The self-concept over time: Research issues and directions. *Annual Review of Sociology, 18,* 303–326.

Diehl, M., Hastings, C. T., & Stanton, J. M. (2001). Self-concept differentiation across the adult life span. *Psychology and Aging, 16*(4), 643–654.

Dunkel, C., & Kerpelman, J. (2006). *Possible selves: Theory, research and applications.* Hauppauge, NY: Nova Science Publishers.

Epstein, S. (1990). Cognitive-experiential self-theory. In A. Pervin (Ed.), *Handbook of personality: theory and research* (pp. 165–192). New York: Guilford Press.

Erikson, E. H. (1959). Identity and the life cycle. New York: International Universities.

Filipp, S. H., & Klauer, T. (1986). Conceptions of self over the life span: Reflections on the dialectics of change. In M. M. Baltes & P. B. Baltes (Eds.), *The psychology of control and aging* (pp. 167–205). Hillsdale, NJ: Erlbaum.

Frazier, L. D., Cotrell, V., & Hooker, K. (2003). Possible selves and illness: A comparison of individuals with Parkinson's disease, early-stage Alzheimer's disease, and healthy older adults. *International Journal of Behavioral Development, 27*(1), 1–11.

Freund, A. M., & Smith, J. (1999). Content and function of the self-definition in old and very old age. *Journals of Gerontology: Psychological Sciences, 54,* 55–67.

George, L. K., & Okun, M. A. (1985). Self-concept content. In E. W. Busse, J. L. Maddox, J. B. Nowlin, & J. C. Siegler (Eds.), *Normal aging III: Reports from the Duke Longitudinal Studies 1975–1984* (pp. 267–282). Durham, NC: Duke University Press.

Harmon-Jones, E., & Winkielman, P. (Eds.). (2007). *Social neuroscience: Integrating biological and psychological explanations of social behavior.* New York: Guilford Press.

Hooker, K. (1992). Possible selves and perceived health in older adults and college students. *Journals of Gerontology, 47*(2), 85–95.

Hooker, K., (1999). Possible selves in adulthood: Incorporating teleonomic relevance into studies of self. In T. M. Hess & F. Blanchard-Fields (Eds.). *Social cognition and aging* (pp. 97–122). San Diego, CA: Academic Press.

Hooker, K., & Kaus, C. R. (1992). Possible selves and health behaviors in later life. *Journal of Aging and Health, 4,* 390–411.

Hooker, K., & McAdams, D. P. (2003). Personality reconsidered: A new agenda for aging research. *Journals of Gerontology Series B: Psychological Sciences and Social Sciences, 58 B,* 296–304.

Hoppmann, C. A., Gerstorf, D., Smith, J., & Klumb, P. L. (2007). Linking possible selves and behavior: Do domain-specific hopes and fears translate into daily activities in very old age? *Journals of Gerontology: Series B: Psychological Sciences and Social Sciences, 62*(2), 104–111.

Howard, J. A. (2000). Social psychology of identities. *Annual Review of Sociology, 26,* 367–393.

James, W. (1890). *Principles of psychology* (Vol. 1). New York: Holt.

Leary, M. R., & Tangney, J. P. (Eds.). (2003). *Handbook of self and identity.* New York: The Guilford Press.

Levy, B. R. (2003). Mind matters: Cognitive and physical effects of aging self-stereotypes. *Journals of Gerontology: Series B: Psychological Sciences and Social Sciences, 58(4),* 203–211.

Markus, H. R., & Herzog, A. R. (1991). The role of the self-concept in aging. *Annual review of gerontology and geriatrics, 11,* 110–143.

Markus, H., & Nurius, P. (1986). Possible selves. *American Psychologist, 41,* 954–969.

Markus, H., & Ruvolo, A. (1989). Possible selves: Personalized representations of goals. In L. A. Pervin (Ed.), *Goal concepts in personality and social psychology* (pp. 211-241). Hillsdale, NJ: Erlbaum.

McAdams, D. P. (2006). The redemptive self: Generativity and the stories Americans live by. *Research in Human Development, 3*(2–3), 81–100.

McCrae, R. R., & Costa, P. T., Jr. (1988). Age, personality and the spontaneous self-concept. *Journal of Gerontology: Social Sciences, 43,* 177–185.

Niedenthal, P. M., Setterlund, M. B., & Wherry, M. B. (1992). Possible self-complexity and affective reactions to goal-relevant evaluation. *Journal of Personality and Social Psychology, 63*, 5–16.

Pervin, L. A., & John, O. J. (Eds.). (1999). *Handbook of personality.* (2nd ed.). New York: Guilford Press.

Rosenberg, M. (1981). The self-concept: Social product and social force. In M. Rosenberg and R. H. Turner (Eds.). *Social psychology: Sociological perspectives* (pp. 593–624). New York: Basic Books.

Ryff, C. D. (1991). Possible selves in adulthood and old age: A tale of shifting horizons. *Psychology and Aging, 6*(2), 286–295.

Settersten, R. A., Jr., & Mayer, K. U. (1997). The measurement of age, age structuring, and the life course. *Annual Review of Sociology, 23*, 233–261.

Showers, C. J., Zeigler-Hill, V. Organization of self knowledge: Features, functions, and flexibility. In M. R. Leary & J. P. Tangney (Eds.). (2003). *Handbook of self and identity* (pp. 47–67). New York: Guilford Press.

Smith, J., & Freund, A. M. (2002). The dynamics of possible selves in old age. *Journals of Gerontology: Series B: Psychological Sciences and Social Sciences, 57*(6), 492–500.

Stryker, S. (2007). Identity theory and personality theory: Mutual relevance. *Journal of Personality, 75*(6), 1083–1102.

Swann, W. B. Jr., Rentfrow, P. J., & Guinn, J. S. Self verification: The search for coherence. In M. R. Leary & J. P. Tangney (Eds.). (2003). *Handbook of self and identity.* (pp. 367–383). New York: Guilford Press.

Troll, L. E., & Skaff, M. M. (1997). Perceived continuity of self in very old age. *Psychology and Aging, 12*(1), 162–169.

Whaley, D. E. (2003). Future-oriented self-perceptions and exercise behavior in middle-aged women. *Journal of Aging and Physical Activity, 11*(1), 1–17.

***Jacqui Smith***

# SELF-RATED HEALTH

Survey respondents are often asked for a self-rating of their global or overall health by answering the single question, "How would you rate your health?" The usual response categories are: excellent, very good, good, fair, or poor. This simple question has been the focus of a large and still rapidly growing body of U.S. and international research on adult and old-age populations. Responses have been used to track the health of populations over time; to compare health levels of countries, regions, and population subgroups; to predict the later health, disability, and even mortality of individuals in populations; and to compare perceptions of health among cohorts with different life course experiences. They have thus had continuing relevance to the study of health by all of the three life course parameters of age, period, and cohort.

## CONCEPT AND MEASUREMENT

Epidemiological surveys whose purpose is to measure the health status of populations often begin with this subjective rating of overall health prior to asking a series of more specific and objective questions about the individual's medical history and current health status, including functional limitations, health service use, symptoms, and medications. In many other types of surveys, such as those concerned with employment, the economy, or political opinion, self-ratings of health may be included as the single measure of health status. It has become a familiar question that respondents find easy to answer. The wording of these survey items may vary quite a bit (Bjorner, Fayers, & Idler, 2005); one common variant includes a specific age comparison ("Compared to other people your age, how would you rate your health?"). Older persons generally rate their health better on average when directed to compare themselves to other elderly persons than they do when making simple global ratings; one study finds that among middle-aged and elderly Danes, cross-sectional and longitudinal global self-ratings of health decline with age, but that age-comparative self-ratings do so much less or not at all (Andersen, Christensen, & Frederiksen, 2007). Because the age-comparative question conceals potentially important differences by age, some researchers argue that the simple global question is to be preferred (Vuorisalmi, Lintonen, & Jylhä, 2006).

## RESEARCH FINDINGS

Self-ratings of health are frequently used to track changes in population health over time or to make international comparisons. For decades, the National Center for Health Statistics has included the self-rated health question in its surveys, such as the National Health Interview Survey (NHIS). Similarly, the World Health Organization's Study on Global Ageing and Adult Health uses self-ratings of health as a comparative indicator of population health.

Such ratings, not surprisingly, show a strong relationship to age. Figure 1 shows that the percent of NHIS respondents reporting fair or poor health is higher for each older age group, ranging in 2005 from under 5% for 18- to 24-year-olds to 35% for those 85 and over; self-ratings of health mirror the increasing prevalence of chronic disease and functional limitations with age. Figure 1 also shows a trend of decline in the proportion reporting fair or poor health among the population aged 45 to 84, with relative stability for those younger and older. There was an especially sharp improvement in self-reported health in the young elderly group, aged 65 to 74, in the period from 1982 to 1990, when the proportion went from more than one-third to just one-quarter

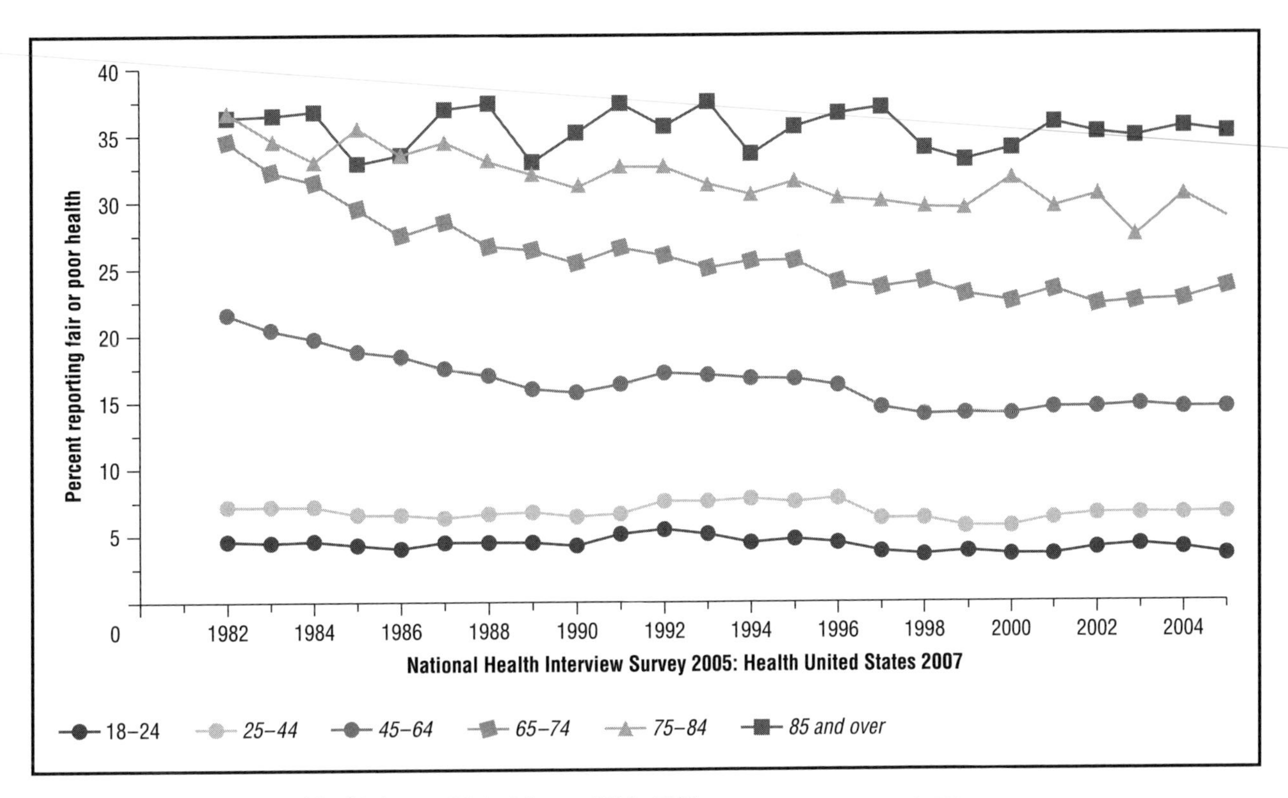


***Figure 1.*** *Respondent-assessed health by age: United States, 1982–2005.* CENGAGE LEARNING, GALE.

reporting less than good health. Self-ratings of health thus also mirror improvements in functional ability in the elderly during this period (Manton, Corder, & Stallard, 1997).

The objective health correlates of self-rated health are key to understanding what these subjective ratings are actually measuring. The Duke Longitudinal Studies of Normal Aging, begun in the 1950s, compared elderly respondents' global self-ratings to physicians' global ratings for the same individuals. While there was a significant amount of agreement between study participants and their physicians, indicating that participants and physicians were taking at least some of the same factors into account, analyses also found that that older individuals more often rated their health as better than the physicians did, a tendency that became more pronounced as people got older, and also that self-ratings were good predictors of future health (Maddox & Douglass, 1973).

In cross-sectional studies (or one-time, snapshot studies), self-rated health is associated with medical diagnoses, physical function, physical symptoms such as chest pain and breathlessness, musculoskeletal pain, and biomarkers such as albumin, total to HDL cholesterol ratio, hemoglobin, and creatinine (Bjorner et al., 2005; Jylhä, Volpato, & Guralnik, 2006). Self-ratings of health also are associated with psychosocial characteristics such as marital status (Joutsenniemi et al., 2006), social support (Cheng & Chan, 2006), poor socioeconomic status in childhood and adulthood (Hyde, Jakub, Melchior, Van Oort, & Weyers, 2006), and depression (Ruo et al., 2006). Self-ratings of health thus appear to reference a very wide range of experiential phenomena, from physiological states "under the skin," to emotional distress, the supportiveness of microlevel social relationships, and even the lifelong advantage or disadvantage of macrolevel social position.

In each of these associations, self-ratings of health reflect the expected direction of association; that is, illness or social disadvantage is associated with poorer ratings of health. The association of self-rated health with age, however, is more complicated. While cross-sectionally, as in Figure 1, poorer ratings of health are typical for older age, comparisons of self-ratings of health and actual physical health status among older and younger respondents reveal that older persons tend to rate their health relatively more positively, in comparison with younger persons at any given level of health status. This difference could arise because as people get older, they adjust to chronic illness over time and recalibrate what "health" means. Or it could be attributable to cohort differences deriving from the hardship or health disadvantage that many of the elderly persons of the early 21st century experienced in early life. Or it could be attributable to the selective survival of those with better self-ratings of health—those with the poorest health having already died prior to old age, leaving the relatively healthy among the survivors. There is empirical support for all three explanations (Idler, 1993).

Such research tends to dispel the stereotype of hypochondriasis (that is, excessive preoccupation or worry about having a serious illness) among elderly persons; the older persons of the early 21st century are more likely to underemphasize health complaints than to overemphasize them. To the extent that there are cohort differences, however, these patterns may not hold for the future. A comparison of preboomers' and post–World War II baby boomers' self-ratings of health found, after adjusting for objective health status, that baby boomers reported poorer self-rated health and more rapid decline per year in self-rated health (Chen, Cohen, & Kasen, 2007), suggesting heightened expectations for health and functioning of the postwar cohorts, and that health optimism in old age may be less prevalent in the future.

Self-ratings of health are valuable simply as cross-sectional indicators of health status in populations, but their usefulness increased beginning in 1982 with a Canadian study that showed self-rated health to be a strong predictor of mortality over seven years in a large representative sample of elderly persons. Males and females who rated their health as poor were nearly three times as likely to die as those who rated their health as excellent, even when sociodemographic factors, Manitoba Health Services data on diagnoses, physician visits, and hospitalizations, and respondent self-reports of conditions were included in the analysis. Respondents who rated their health as fair and even good also had significantly higher risks of mortality compared with those who rated their health as excellent, even after adjustment for age, gender, and health status.

Since this initial publication there have been more than 100 such studies appearing in international public health, epidemiology, and social science journals in health, nearly all of which have had similar findings (Idler & Benyamini, 1997). A meta-analysis (that is, a report that systematically synthesizes the findings of prior studies) found significantly higher relative risks of mortality for those who reported good (1.23), fair (1.44), and poor (1.92) health, compared with those who reported excellent health (DeSalvo, Bloser, Reynolds, He, & Muntner, 2006). In other words, persons with poor health were 1.92 times as likely to die during the study period, compared to those with excellent self-rated health. The continuing production of such studies is attributable to the frequency with which the self-rated health item is included in health surveys with longitudinal follow-up of mortality; these are by their nature secondary analyses of existing data with long follow-up periods. Many but not all of these studies have employed samples of older persons. Thus self-ratings of health have proven themselves to be both a useful indicator of the current health status of populations and valid predictors of mortality over follow-up periods as long as 12 or more years.

Population-based longitudinal studies have increasingly turned their attention to assessing how well self-ratings of health predict a range of health outcomes that logically precede mortality; researchers have studied a variety of other health end points including onset of coronary heart disease, withdrawal from the labor force, and functional disability (Bjorner et al., 2005), as well as the consequences of such end points for health services utilization and expenditures (DeSalvo, Fan, McDonell, & Fihn, 2005). At the same time, self-ratings of health are starting to be employed in smaller clinical research situations, such as emergency departments (Wong, Wong, & Caplan, 2007), for the purpose of predicting mortality, morbidity, and recovery and assessing quality of life outcomes in specific patient groups. A related area is the assessment of the quality of life of family caregivers who are coping with the needs of their cognitively or physically impaired elderly family members. An increasing body of research shows the health impact of caregiving and the need for assessments in which self-ratings of health of the caregivers themselves play a central role. It is likely that there will continue to be new applications and analyses of the concept of self-rated health as a single item, or embedded in multidimensional quality of life measurements, in representative population samples of elderly persons, in patient samples, and in caregiver samples.

## FUTURE RESEARCH

A number of innovative new approaches show promise for increasing understanding of the meaning and predictiveness of self-ratings of health. The turn to more clinically based research is advantageous because the objective health status of patient groups may be easier to determine and accurately adjust for, and because the implications for quality of life and the use and cost of health services are tangible. Population-based research, however, will continue to have the advantages of large sample sizes, long-term follow-up, and comparability with other studies. Several studies from the early 21st century show the importance of the concept of trajectories of self-rated health. P. Diehr and D. L. Patrick (2003) have proposed including death as a sixth (and worst) category when the outcome is self-rated health; an end point including the categories of excellent, very good, good, fair, poor, and death would then account fully for all members of the sample and not produce misleading results because of attrition. G. A. Kaplan, P. T. Baltrus, and T. E. Raghunathan (2007) use a 30-year follow-up of an earlier study to construct self-rated health trajectories as sensitive indicators of health over the life course.

At the other extreme of follow-up periods, another study used a daily diary approach to understand the close relationship among symptoms, positive and negative affect, and self-ratings of health (Winter, Lawton, Langston, Ruckdeschel, and Sando, 2007). Given the development of new statistical techniques for the analysis of longitudinal data, and the availability of self-ratings of health in multiple waves of data, it is probable that future research in self-rated health will lean heavily on the concept of trajectories, both short term and long term.

Another individual-focused approach uses an experimental design for understanding the psychology of self-ratings. P.G. Williams, M. S. Wasserman, and A. J. Lotto (2003) used computer-based Stroop tasks to investigate the cognitive processing of self-ratings of health. Stroop tasks require participants to identify the color that is being used when a word printed in that color appears on a computer screen; the participant's ability to identify the color is impeded to a greater or lesser extent by the "distraction" that the meaning of the word presents, which delays attention to the color of the letters. The study showed that participants who rated their health as poor or fair took longer to identify the color of illness-related words compared with non-illness words and compared with participants with good health, showing that health-relevant information is processed differently by those who rate their health differently.

Finally, two other studies combine the advantages of the large, representative population-based study with the specificity of the patient samples. The Centers for Disease Control and Prevention (CDC) has used the Behavioral Risk Factor Surveillance System to track the self-rated health of diabetics in the United States; they find that fair or poor self-rated health is three times more likely among diabetics than among non-diabetics in the U.S. population, and that the prevalence of fair/poor health increased from 1996 to 2005 (CDC, 2006). A second paper tracking disease subgroups within populations used data from the Epidemiologic Follow-up Study to the National Health and Nutrition Examination Survey to identify diagnostic groups on the basis of both self-reported history and symptoms, and the standardized physician's examination and laboratory tests given to respondents (Idler, Leventhal, McLaughlin, and Leventhal, 2004). This study found that self-ratings of health were strong predictors of mortality in the circulatory disease diagnostic group, but did not predict mortality at all in a group with no diagnoses, even when age matched and health status was controlled; moreover, within the circulatory disease group there was a stronger effect for self-ratings among those who had experienced symptoms or had a history of the disease, in comparison with those who were diagnosed only on the day of the exam. These approaches suggest that more homogeneous, disease-based subgroups within large population samples may hold considerable promise for closer examination of risk factors and trajectories, particularly when the disease is chronic, potentially disabling, and requires daily management to avoid exacerbations and the costly use of emergency health care. As a group, these new directions in research, some at the individual level with a focus on the cognitive basis for self-ratings, and others at the population level describing the arc of these ratings over time, promise to keep interest in this simple variable high.

## CONCLUSION

Self-rated health is a widely used indicator of health status in cross-sectional population and clinical studies, as well as a significant predictor of mortality and other health outcomes in longitudinal studies. It is strongly associated with more objective measures of health status, such as functional limitations; diagnoses, especially of chronic conditions; and the use of health services, but it appears to incorporate additional information beyond these indicators, such as emotional distress, socioeconomic status, and social support. Self-ratings of health may represent a higher order of integration of all information available to the respondent, as well as their trajectory and perceived prognosis. Or it may represent a fundamental sense of health identity that underlies and colors new health events, influences the reporting of symptoms, and motivates health behaviors that result in measurable health outcomes. Given its brevity and its utility, it is likely to continue to stay in wide use in surveys and assessment instruments, which will in turn lead to further research.

**SEE ALSO** Volume 2: *Disability, Adulthood;* Volume 3: *Age, Period, Cohort Effects; Health Differentials/ Disparities, Later Life; Mental Health, Later Life.*

## BIBLIOGRAPHY

Andersen, F. K., Christensen, K., & Frederiksen, H. (2007). Self-rated health and age: A cross-sectional and longitudinal study of 11,000 Danes aged 45–102. *Scandinavian Journal of Public Health, 35*, 164–171.

Bjorner, J., Fayers, P., & Idler, E. (2005). Self-rated health. In P. Fayers & R. Hays (Eds.), *Assessing quality of life in clinical trials: Methods and practice* (2nd ed., pp. 309–323). Oxford: Oxford University Press.

Centers for Disease Control and Prevention. (2006, November 17). Self-rated fair or poor health among adults with diabetes—United States, 1996–2005. *Morbidity and Mortality Weekly Report, 55*, 1224–1227.

Chen, H., Cohen, P., & Kasen, S. (2007). Cohort differences in self-rated health: Evidence from a three-decade, community-based, longitudinal study of women. *American Journal of Epidemiology, 166*, 439–446.

Cheng, S.-T., & Chan, A. C. M. (2006). Social support and self-rated health revisited: Is there a gender difference in later life? *Social Science & Medicine, 63*, 118–122.

DeSalvo, K. B., Bloser, N., Reynolds, K., He, J., & Muntner, P. (2006). Mortality prediction with a single general self-rated health question: A meta-analysis. *Journal of General Internal Medicine, 21*, 267–275.

DeSalvo, K. B., Fan, V. S., McDonell, M. B., & Fihn, S. D. (2005). Predicting mortality and healthcare utilization with a single question. *Health Services Research, 40*, 1234–1246.

Diehr, P., & Patrick, D. L. (2003). Trajectories of health for older adults over time: Accounting fully for death. *Annals of Internal Medicine, 139*, 416–420.

Hyde, M., Jakub, H., Melchior, M., Van Oort, F., & Weyers, S. (2006). Comparison of the effects of low childhood socioeconomic position and low adulthood socioeconomic position on self rated health in four European studies. *Journal of Epidemiology and Community Health, 60*, 882–886.

Idler, E. L. (1993). Age differences in self-assessments of health: Age changes, cohort differences, or survivorship? *Journals of Gerontology, Series B: Psychological Sciences and Social Sciences, 48*, S289–S300.

Idler, E. L., & Benyamini, Y. (1997). Self-rated health and mortality: A review of twenty-seven community studies. *Journal of Health and Social Behavior, 38*, 21–37.

Idler, E. L., Leventhal, H., McLaughlin, J., & Leventhal, E. (2004). In sickness but not in health: Self-ratings, identity, and mortality. *Journal of Health and Social Behavior, 45*, 336–356.

Joutsenniemi, K. E., Martelin, T. P., Koskinen, S. V., Martikainen, P. T., Härkänen, T. T., Luoto, R. M., et al. (2006). Official marital status, cohabiting, and self-rated health: Time trends in Finland, 1978–2001. *European Journal of Public Health, 16*, 476–483.

Jylhä, M., Volpato, S., & Guralnik, J. M. (2006). Self-rated health showed a graded association with frequently used biomarkers in a large population sample. *Journal of Clinical Epidemiology, 59*, 465–471.

Kaplan, G. A., Baltrus, P. T., & Raghunathan, T. E. (2007). The shape of health to come: Prospective study of the determinants of 30-year health trajectories in the Alameda County Study. *International Journal of Epidemiology, 36*, 542–548.

Maddox, G. L., & Douglass, E. B. (1973). Self-assessment of health: A longitudinal study of elderly subjects. *Journal of Health and Social Behavior, 14*, 87–93.

Manton, K. G., Corder, L., & Stallard, E. (1997). Chronic disability trends in elderly United States populations: 1982–1994. *Proceedings of the National Academy of Sciences of the United States of America, 94*, 2593–2598.

National Center for Health Statistics. *National Health Interview Survey*. Retrieved April 24, 2008, from http://www.cdc.gov/nchs/nhis.htm

Ruo, B., Bertenthal, D., Sen, S., Bittner, V., Ireland, C. C., & Hlatky, M. A. (2006). Self-rated health among women with coronary disease: Depression is as important as recent cardiovascular events. *American Heart Journal, 152*, 921.e1–921.e7.

Vuorisalmi, M., Lintonen, T., & Jylhä, M. (2006). Comparative vs. global self-rated health: Associations with age and functional ability. *Aging—Clinical and Experimental Research, 18*, 211–217.

Williams, P. G., Wasserman, M. S., & Lotto, A. J. (2003). Individual differences in self-assessed health: An information-processing investigation of health and illness cognition. *Health Psychology, 22*, 3–11.

Winter, L., Lawton, M. P., Langston, C. A., Ruckdeschel, K., & Sando, R. (2007). Symptoms, affects, and self-rated health: Evidence for a subjective trajectory of health. *Journal of Aging and Health, 19*, 453–469.

Wong, D. D., Wong, R. P. C., & Caplan, G. A. (2007). Self-rated health in the unwell elderly presenting to the emergency department. *Emergency Medicine Australasia, 19*, 196–202.

World Health Organization. *Study on Global Ageing and Adult Health*. Retrieved April 24, 2008, from http://www.who.int/healthinfo/systems/sage/en/index.html

***Ellen L. Idler***

## SENESCENCE

SEE Volume 3: *Aging.*

## SENSORY IMPAIRMENTS

Sensory impairments, specifically vision and hearing impairments, are among the most common chronic conditions in later life. Vision impairment affects between 9% and 18% and hearing loss affects between 24% and 33% of older adults. Older adults may also experience a concurrent loss of vision and hearing referred to as *dual sensory impairment*. Research has shown that between 5% and 21% of the older adult population has dual sensory impairment (Brennan, Horowitz, & Su, 2005). Sensory impairments are the major cause of activity limitations and disability in older adults. For instance, several studies have demonstrated that vision loss significantly predicts functional disability in older adults even after controlling for age, gender, and co-occurring health conditions (Horowitz, 1994). As the older adult population will be increasing over the next 30 years, so will the number of individuals who experience sensory impairments and consequent disability in later adulthood.

## CAUSES OF SENSORY IMPAIRMENTS

Vision impairment or chronic vision loss among older adults occurs due to age-related eye diseases such as macular degeneration, cataracts, glaucoma, and diabetic retinopathy and can occur on a continuum ranging from minimal vision loss to complete blindness. Moderate and significant vision loss is termed *low vision* and is defined as a significant reduction of visual function that cannot be corrected to the normal range by ordinary eyeglasses, contact lenses, medical treatment, or surgery (Faye, 2000). A person with low vision may have severely reduced visual acuity or contrast sensitivity or a significantly obstructed field of vision.

Age-related hearing loss among older adults is called *presbycusis* and refers to the loss of auditory sensitivity with aging (Glass, 2000). The loss associated with presbycusis is usually greater for high-pitched sounds, but age-related hearing loss is also defined by general difficulty in understanding conversations especially when background noise is present. Causes of presbycusis are changes in the inner and middle ear or complex changes along the nerve pathways leading to the brain. As in the case of vision impairment, hearing loss generally occurs on a continuum ranging from mild hearing loss to profound hearing loss equaling deafness.

## THE ASSESSMENT OF SENSORY IMPAIRMENTS

For the purpose of the assessment of vision and hearing impairments, both clinical assessment methods and self-report measures are available. The clinical assessment of low vision, conducted by either an optometrist or ophthalmologist specializing in low vision, entails the assessment of visual acuity, contrast, and visual field through the use of vision charts and history taking. The clinical assessment of hearing loss entails an evaluation by an audiologist, who presents sounds in a sound-proof room and records the reaction to the sounds on a chart called an audiogram, which is a graphical representation of how well a certain person can perceive different sound frequencies. Based on the audiogram, the audiologist can determine the level of hearing loss.

In addition to these clinical measures, questionnaires that assess vision or hearing loss of varying degrees from the perspective of the patient have been developed. These self-report instruments determine the patients' functional status in the area of vision or hearing based on the amount of difficulty they experience in performing vision-related activities of daily living or the amount of difficulty they have processing auditory information. In the area of vision, the most widely used instruments include such validated measures as the Functional Vision Screening Questionnaire (Horowitz, 1996), The National Eye Institute Visual Functioning Questionnaire (Mangione et al., 2001), and the Veterans Affairs Low-Vision Visual Functioning Questionnaire (Stelmack et al., 2004). The following instruments are cited in the literature for the purpose of assessing hearing loss in older adults: the Hearing Handicap Inventory for the Elderly (Weinstein & Ventry, 1983), the Hearing Measurement Scale (Noble & Atherley, 1970), and the Communication Profile for the Hearing Impaired (Garstecki & Erler, 1999).

Clinical assessments and self-report instruments are used not only in the evaluation of older adults for the purpose of screening and providing appropriate interventions but also to assess sensory functioning for research purposes. However, in the case of both vision and hearing impairment, some population-based surveys such as the National Health Interview Survey conducted by the National Center for Health Statistics assess participants' vision and hearing loss through the use of single-item measures that are designed to assess vision and hearing impairment based on a specific definition of vision and hearing loss. For example, vision loss is defined as self-reported blindness in one or both eyes or other trouble seeing even when using glasses (Adams & Marano, 1995).

## RISK FACTORS FOR SENSORY IMPAIRMENTS

Research has identified several risk factors that are associated with the development of age-related eye diseases causing vision loss and the development of hearing loss. The first category of such factors can be described as environmental and behavioral risk factors. Hearing loss, for instance, can be caused by exposure to loud noise over long periods of time, smoking, a history of middle ear infections, and exposure to certain chemicals. In the case of vision loss, smoking and unprotected exposure to sunlight represent a risk factor in the etiology of both cataracts and macular degeneration. Moreover, individuals with diabetes are at risk not only for diabetic retinopathy (an eye disease that affects half of all individuals diagnosed with diabetes) but also for developing cataracts and glaucoma.

There are also several demographic factors that are associated with an increased occurrence or prevalence of vision and hearing loss. Hence, these factors are responsible for several demographic disparities in sensory impairments. As pointed out previously, the likelihood of experiencing a vision and/or hearing impairment significantly increases with age. Research consistently finds that increased age functions as a predictor of both vision and hearing impairments (e.g., Horowitz, Brennan, & Reinhardt, 2005). In fact, among older adults about 17% of adults age 65 to 74 years and 26% of adults age 75 and older report some form of vision impairment, and persons 65 years and older are eight times more likely to have a hearing impairment than persons ages 18 to 34. The prevalence of hearing impairment has also been found to differ according to gender, with a higher number of older men experiencing hearing loss than older women. The poorer hearing in men can generally be attributed to greater levels of exposure to occupational and recreational noise compared to older women.

Studies of gender difference in the prevalence rates of vision loss have been less consistent; some studies have found a higher prevalence of vision impairment among women (Rodriguez et al., 2002) whereas others have not (e.g., Muñoz et al., 2000). A recent re-analyses of several population-based studies conducted by the Eye Disease Prevalence Research Group (2004), however, revealed that gender differences in prevalence rates varied according to ethnic groups. The prevalence rates for non-Hispanic White women were higher when compared to non-Hispanic White men. Yet this gender difference did not emerge in Hispanics and non-Hispanic Blacks. In contrast, hearing loss has been found to be most common in White men, followed by White women, Black men, and Black women (Helzner et al., 2005).

Other research has shown that overall African Americans are more likely to be visually impaired and more likely to have diabetic retinopathy and glaucoma when compared to Whites, who are more likely to have vision loss resulting from macular degeneration (E. G. West et al., 1997). There is also research that supports the high prevalence rates of vision impairment among Hispanic populations (Muñoz et al., 2002). In addition, overall Whites are more than twice as likely as Blacks and non-Hispanics are more than twice as likely as Hispanics to be hard of hearing (Holt, Hotto, & Cole, 1994). Moreover, there is evidence that lower education and income are associated with both higher rates of vision impairment and a higher prevalence of hearing loss. Finally, there is some evidence that hearing impairment is greater at all ages among individuals living in rural areas.

***Hearing Dog.*** *Sheri Abt walks Murphy near her home in Brainerd, MN. Abt, who suffers from a profound hearing loss, received Murphy two weeks before from Dogs for the Deaf, an international hearing dog training and placement organization based in Oregon.* AP IMAGES.

## LONG-TERM EFFECTS OF SENSORY IMPAIRMENTS

Research in the area of sensory impairments has also investigated the long-term effects of both vision and hearing impairment for older adults. Evidence shows that over time both vision and hearing impairment increasingly affect an older adult's functional ability and interaction with the physical and social environment. These sensory impairments individually or combined can lead to social isolation (e.g., Wahl & Oswald, 2000), cognitive decline, which is due to a reduced ability to participate in stimulating events (Peters, Potter, & Scholer, 1988), and decreased mobility as well as higher risk of falls and hip fracture (Campbell, Crews, Moriatry, Zack, & Blackman, 1999).

Moreover, consistent relationships have been documented between age-related sensory impairments and decreased emotional well-being, such as an increase in affective disorders, reduced feelings of self-worth and lower morale, and increased depression. There is strong evidence from a number of studies that approximately one-third of older adults who are visually impaired experience clinically significant depressive symptoms (e.g., Horowitz, Reinhardt, & Kennedy, 2005) compared to between 8% and 16% of their nonvisually impaired counterparts (Blazer, 2003).

## THE FUTURE OF THE STUDY OF SENSORY IMPAIRMENTS

The experience of a vision and hearing impairment may not inevitably lead to the long-term consequences discussed previously, because services for the hearing impaired and vision rehabilitation services can prevent or alleviate many of the effects associated with these impairments. These services provide equipment and training to reduce the functional limitations associated with sensory impairments. Based on an assessment of the remaining visual function, services for people with vision loss may include the prescription of appropriate optical (e.g., magnifiers) and adaptive aids (e.g., special lighting). Services for people with hearing loss may entail the fitting of an appropriate hearing aid. People with vision loss can also receive instructions in skills of daily living and mobility skills. In addition, services for older adults may also include counseling with a mental health professional in an individual or group setting to help effectively cope with the emotional consequences of sensory impairments.

Some research evidence supports the effectiveness of such interventions for improved functional status and emotional well-being (e.g., Brody et al, 1999; Watson, Dc l'Aune, Stelmack, Long, & Maino, 1997). However, more research in the area of evaluations of the effectiveness of services for older adults with sensory impairments is needed, especially research employing controlled evaluation designs. Moreover, past research has demonstrated a lack of awareness of available services among older adults (see, e.g., The Lighthouse, 1995). However, very little is known about why this lack of awareness exists. Hence, future research needs to investigate not only the factors that may lead to a lack of awareness of available services but also the specific barriers that older adults of various socioeconomic backgrounds face when trying to access these important services. Also, more studies in the area of sensory impairments need to focus on the combined impact of concurrent sensory impairments (i.e., dual sensory impairments) and other comorbidities on the quality of life of older adults.

Finally, in the near future the research community working with and studying older adults with sensory impairments needs to be prepared to investigate the characteristics and needs of the cohort of aging baby boomers. The older adult cohort of baby boomers may be less likely to accept disability and dependency associated with disability as a normal part of aging than the present cohort of older adults. In the future, a change in perceptions by society may occur that in the present generally has internalized negative stereotypes about the helplessness of individuals with sensory impairments.

**SEE ALSO** Volume 3: *Assistive Technologies; Disability and Functional Limitation, Later Life.*

### BIBLIOGRAPHY

Adams, P. F., & Marano, M. A. (1995). *Current estimates from the National Health Interview Survey, 1994.* Washington, DC: National Center for Health Statistics.

Blazer, D. G. (2003). Depression in late life: Review and commentary. *Journals of Gerontology: Medical Sciences, 58,* M249–M265.

Brennan, M., Horowitz, A., & Su, Y.-p. (2005). Dual sensory loss and its impact on everyday competence. *The Gerontologist, 45,* 337–346.

Brody, B. L., Williams, R. A., Thomas, R. G., Kaplan, R. M., Chu, R. M., & Brown, S. I. (1999). Age-related macular degeneration: A randomized clinical trial of a self-management intervention. *Annals of Behavioral Medicine, 21,* 322–329.

Campbell, V. A., Crews, J. E., Moriarty, D. G., Zack, M. M., & Blackman, D. K. (1999). Surveillance for sensory impairment, activity limitation, and health-related quality of life among older adults—United States, 1993–1997. *MMWR: CDC Surveillance Summaries, 48,* 131–156.

Eye Disease Prevalence Research Group. (2004). Causes and prevalence of visual impairment among adults in the United States, *Archives of Ophthalmology, 122,* 477–485.

Faye, E. (2000). Functional consequences of vision impairment: Vision function related to eye pathology. In B. Silverstone, M. A. Lang, B. P. Rosenthal, & E. F. Faye (Eds.), *The Lighthouse handbooks on vision impairment and vision rehabilitation* (pp. 791–798). New York: Oxford University Press.

Garstecki, D. C., & Erler, S. F. (1999). Older adult performance on the Communication Profile for the Hearing Impaired. *Journal of Speech, Language, and Hearing Research, 42,* 785–796.

Glass, L. E., (2000). Dual vision and hearing impairment in adults. In B. Silverstone, M. A. Lang, B. P. Rosenthal, & E. F. Faye (Eds.). *The Lighthouse handbooks on vision impairment and vision rehabilitation* (pp. 469–486). New York: Oxford University Press.

Helzner, E. P., Cauley, J. A., Pratt, S. R., Wisniewski, S. R., Zmuda, J. M., Talbot, E. O., et al. (2005). Race and sex differences in age-related hearing loss: The Health, Aging and Body Composition Study. *Journal of the American Geriatrics Society, 53,* 2119–2127.

Holt, J., Hotto, S., & Cole, K. (1994). Demographic aspects of hearing impairment: Questions and answers. Retrieved May 21, 2008, from http://www.gallaudet.edu

Horowitz, A. (1994). Vision impairment and functional disability among nursing home residents. *The Gerontologist, 34,* 316–323.

Horowitz, A. (1996). *Validation of the functional vision screening questionnaire for older people.* Poster presented at Vision 96, the International Conference on Vision, Madrid, Spain.

Horowitz, A. (2004). Prevalence and consequences of age-related vision impairment. *Topics in Geriatric Rehabilitation, 20,* 185–195.

Horowitz, A., Brennan, M., & Reinhardt, J. P. (2005). Prevalence and risk factors for self-reported visual impairment among middle-aged and older adults. *Research on Aging, 27,* 307–325.

Horowitz, A., & Reinhardt, J. P. (2000). Mental health issues in visual impairment: Research in depression, disability, and rehabilitation. In B. Silverstone, M. A. Lang, B. P. Rosenthal, & E. F. Faye (Eds.), *The Lighthouse handbooks on vision impairment and vision rehabilitation* (pp. 1089–1110). New York: Oxford University Press.

Horowitz, A., Reinhardt, J. P., Kennedy, G. (2005). Major and subthreshold depression among older adults seeking vision rehabilitation services. *American Journal of Geriatric Psychiatry, 13,* 180–187.

The Lighthouse Inc. (1995). *The Lighthouse National Survey on Vision Loss: Experiences, attitudes and knowledge of middle-aged and older Americans.* New York: Author.

Mangione, C. M., Lee, P. P., Gutiérrez, P. R., Spritzer, K., Berry, S., & Hays, R. D. (2001). Development of the 25-item National Eye Institute Visual Function Questionnaire. *Archives of Ophthalmology, 119,* 1050–1058.

Muñoz, B., West, S. K., Rodriguez, J., Sanchez, R., Broman, A. T., Snyder, R., & Klein, R. (2002) Blindness, visual impairment and the problem of uncorrected refractive error in the Mexican-American population: Proyecto VER. *Investigative Ophthalmology and Vision Science, 43,* 608–614.

Muñoz, B., West, S. K., Rubin, G. S., Schein, O. D., Quigley, H. A., et al. (2000). Causes of blindness and visual impairment in a population of older adults: The Salisbury Eye Evaluation. *Archives of Ophthalmology, 118,* 819–825.

Noble, W., & Atherley, G. (1970). The hearing measurement scale: A questionnaire assessment of auditory disability. *Journal of Audiological Research, 10,* 229–250.

Peters, C. A., Potter, J. F., & Scholer, S. G. (1988). Hearing impairment as a predictor of cognitive decline in dementia. *Journal of the American Geriatrics Society, 36,* 981–986.

Rahmani, B., Tielsch, J. M., Katz, J., Gottsch, J., Quigley, H., Javitt, J., & Sommer A. (1996). The cause-specific prevalence of visual impairment in an urban population: The Baltimore Eye Survey. *Ophthalmology, 103,* 1721–1726.

Rodriguez, J., Sanchez, R., Muñoz, B., West, S. K., Broman, A. T., Snyder, R. W., et al. (2002). Causes of blindness and visual impairment in a population-based sample of U.S. Hispanics. *Ophthalmology, 109,* 737–743.

Stelmack, J. A., Szlyk, J. P., Stelmack, T. R., Demers-Turco, P., Williams, R. T., Moran, D., et al. (2004). Psychometric properties of the Veterans Affairs Low-Vision Visual Functioning Questionnaire. *Investigative Ophthalmology and Visual Science, 45,* 3919–3928.

Wahl, H. W., & Oswald, F. (2000). The person-environment perspective of vision impairment. In B. Silverstone, M. A. Lang, B. P. Rosenthal, & E. F. Faye (Eds.), *The Lighthouse handbooks on vision impairment and vision rehabilitation* (pp. 1069–1088). New York: Oxford University Press.

Watson, G. R., De l'Aune, W. R., Stelmack, J., Long, S., & Maino, J. (1997). Veterans' use of low vision devices for reading. *Optometry and Visual Science, 74,* 260–265.

Weinstein, B. E., & Ventry, I. M. (1983). Audiometric correlates of the Hearing Handicap Inventory for the Elderly. *Journal of Speech and Hearing Disorders, 48,* 379–384.

West, S. K., Muñoz, B., Rubin, G. S., Schein, O. D., Bandeen-Roche, K., Zeger, S., et al. (1997). Function and visual impairment in a population-based study of older adults, the SEE project. *Investigative Ophthalmology and Visual Science, 38,* 72–82.

***Verena R. Cimarolli***

# SEXUAL ACTIVITY, LATER LIFE

Research on sexual activity and sexual health in late life is in its infancy, but strong linkages are already emerging between the sexuality of older adults and other domains of life. For instance, mental and physical health are strongly associated with older adults' sexual activities and problems (Laumann, Das, & Waite, 2008; Lindau et al., 2007), as are socioeconomic status, marital status, the quality of intimate relationships (Laumann et al., 2008), and social connectedness (Cornwell & Laumann, 2008). These linkages point to the central role of sexuality, as both a cause and an indicator of overall wellness in later life and of healthy aging.

## THEORIZING SEXUALITY IN LATE LIFE

While sexuality among the elderly has not yet been adequately theorized, several conceptual frameworks for adult sexuality are helpful. Laumann, Gagnon, Michael, and Michaels (1994) develop an integrated model that emphasizes three sets of factors: (a) an individual's social network—both the sexual relationship itself and the broader web of "stakeholder" ties, such as those with friends and family, in which the relationship is embedded; (b) social norms or "scripts," which structure sexual patterns—such as culturally specific notions that sexual interest declines naturally with age (Waite, Laumann, Das, & Schumm, in press), or that masturbation lowers a man's virility (Das, Parish, & Laumann, 2007); and (c) individual choice, borrowed from economic choice theory, in which people draw on available resources and information to maximize "utility."

A second framework, guiding the Kinsey Institute's empirical studies, is the dual control model of sexual response (Bancroft & Janssen, 2000; Bancroft, Loftus, & Long, 2003). The model conceives of human sexual response as an adaptive mechanism, strongly responsive to a person's current life situation, and comprised of cognition, central brain mechanisms including sexual arousal, and physiological processes such as erectile dysfunction in men and lubrication problems in women.

A third framework is the interactive biopsychosocial model of health (Lindau, Laumann, Levinson, & Waite, 2003). This model extends the conceptual framework proposed by Laumann et al. (1994) by integrating social influences with biological and psychological "capital" or endowments, with variation in each domain affecting the others. Sexual health is conceptualized as "jointly produced" by the interaction of an individual's capital endowments with those of his or her significant others.

## DATA ON SEXUALITY

Knowledge about sexuality in later life has been limited by a lack of nationally representative data sources. Most research to date focuses on clinical or community samples, such as the Massachusetts Male Aging Study, which do not represent the larger population of older adults. Clinical samples typically are comprised of persons already seeking medical and psychological care, whereas community samples are often limited to small geographic regions. Available cross-sectional studies include the 29-country Global Study of Sexual Attitudes and Behaviors, which obtained information on the prevalence and correlates of sexual problems among women and men aged 40 to 80 (Laumann et al., 2005; Nicolosi et al., 2004). The study used random sampling methods but suffered from low response rates. On average, roughly 19% of persons contacted ultimately completed the survey. The 1996 Swedish sex survey (Fugl-Meyer & Fugl-Meyer, 1999) and the 1992 and 1999 Finnish sex studies (Haavio-Mannila, Kontula, & Kuusi, 2001) included a range of sexual, social, and health-related questions. These surveys are nationally representative of all adult individuals in those nations, but included only small subsamples of older adults.

More recently, the 2005–2006 National Social Life, Health, and Aging Project (NSHAP) collected data on sexuality, health, social factors, and biological measures, among women and men aged 57 to 85 living in the United States (Lindau et al., 2007), and had a high response rate (75.5%). Many of the research findings discussed later in this entry are based on the NSHAP study.

## MEASURES

A key challenge facing researchers studying sexuality at any age is the relative lack of consensus on the specific behaviors and problems to examine. The 1992 National Health and Social Life Survey (NHSLS) defined sex as: "any mutually voluntary activity with another person that involves genital contact and sexual excitement or arousal ... even if intercourse or orgasm did not occur" (Laumann et al. 1994, p.67). This broad definition avoids equating sex solely with penile intercourse (which would exclude, for instance, sex between two women) and orgasm (because some sexual events may not culminate in orgasm for either partner). The NHSLS asked respondents about a wide range of sexual behaviors, including frequency of any sex and of vaginal sex, masturbation, and subjective responses to sex. Respondents were also asked about frequency of sexual thoughts, the subjective appeal of various sexual practices, and general attitudes about sexuality. Many of these items were replicated in the NSHAP, including the frequency of sex with a marital, cohabiting, or other partner; frequency of vaginal intercourse; condom use; and oral sex; as well as hugging, kissing, or other forms of intimate contact (Waite et al., in press).

There are divergent opinions on how to obtain information on sexual problems. One commonly used list of problems is based on the diagnostic categories identified in the American Psychiatric Association's *Diagnostic and Statistical Manual of Mental Disorders* (fourth edition, text revision, 2000 [*DSM–IV–TR*]). This list includes: (a) disorders of desire, such as low interest in sex and objections to having the genitals touched; (b) disorders of sexual arousal, including female sexual arousal problems (vaginal dryness, lubrication difficulties) and male erectile problems; (c) orgasmic disorders, such as inability to reach climax among both sexes and premature ejaculation among men; and (d) pain during sex. The World Health Organization's *International Statistical Classification of Diseases and Related Health Problems* (10th revision, 2nd edition, 2004 [*ICD–10*]) adds to this list lack of pleasure in sex (sexual anhedonia) and excessive sexual drive, that is, nymphomania or satyriasis.

Another controversial issue in measuring sexual problems is the length of time for which symptoms must be present for one to consider it a "dysfunction." In the study of Bancroft et al. (2003), only women sexually active in the preceding month were asked about their frequency of sexual activities and problems, because, the study authors argued, women would not be able to accurately recall experiences prior to that time. Rosen and Laumann (2003) counter, however, that focusing on such short time frames may not effectively differentiate between occasional versus chronic sexual problems. Both the NHSLS and NSHAP resolve this issue by asking about problems lasting "several months or more" over the past year.

A final measurement-related controversy involves the importance of the respondent's subjective distress as a component of a sexual dysfunction. Based on their interpretation of the *ICD–10* and *DSM–IV–TR* definitions of dysfunction, and the recommendations of the first International Consensus Development Conference on Female Sexual Dysfunction (Boston, 1998), Basson et al. (2000, 2004) strongly recommend inclusion of a personal distress criterion in the definition. Bancroft et al. (2003), however, demonstrate that sexual difficulties are often correlated more with distress about the intimate relationship than about one's own sexual response. Such sexual difficulties, they argue, may thus represent adaptive psychosomatic responses to difficult situations. That is, these reactions may be sexual "problems" rather than medical "dysfunctions." Thus, measures not taking distress into account may result in overestimates of the prevalence of dysfunction. Finally, Rosen and Laumann (2003) note that, in contrast with sexual problems per se, measures of distress have yet to undergo rigorous psychometric tests. Based on these debates, the International Consultation on Erectile Dysfunction (Lue et al., 2004) recommended, for each dysfunction, a per se definition based on the presence (and degree) of a sexual problem, and a second definition including personal distress, to assess the impact of the dysfunction on the individual and his or her relationships.

## BASIC TRENDS

Basic trends in the sexual practices and health of older adults can be obtained from a comparison of reports of sexuality among 1992 NHSLS respondents aged 55 to 60 and 2005–2006 NSHAP respondents aged 57 to 64 and 75 to 85 (Laumann et al., 1994; Waite et al., in press). The oldest NHSLS respondents and the youngest NSHAP respondents are similar in age. First, the percentage who have a stable sexual partner is similar among the oldest NHSLS respondents (55 to 60) and the youngest NSHAP group (57 to 64)—ranging from 65% to 75% for women and 84% to 95% among men (reanalysis of NHSLS raw data; Waite et al., in press). Among the oldest NSHAP respondents (75 to 85), this decreases sharply to 40% among women, but more moderately to 78% among men—a gender difference probably attributable to women's greater chances of being widowed rather than married, a consequence of their greater longevity and the age difference between spouses. In contrast, for sex in the preceding year, while the proportion sexually active is similar (84%) for the oldest NHSLS and youngest NSHAP men, it drops sharply to 38% in the oldest NSHAP men. The same decline is apparent among women, from 59% to 62% among the younger groups to 17% in the oldest.

At all ages, sex usually takes the form of vaginal sex, exceeded in frequency, in the NSHAP sample, only by foreplay. Masturbation declines with age—among men from a high of between 48% and 63% (oldest NHSLS and youngest NSHAP group) to a low of only 28% (oldest NSHAP group), and among women from 22% and 32% to 16%. Among those reporting sex in the preceding year, NSHAP prevalences of oral sex are also lower than for vaginal sex, but decline with age only moderately among women (from 53% to 36%). Among NSHAP men, in contrast, oral sex prevalence starts out relatively higher (62%), but then declines sharply (to 28% among the oldest men). This suggests that neither masturbation nor oral sex serves as a replacement for intercourse among the elderly, because those in the oldest groups report the least partnered sex, the lowest level of masturbation, and—among those having any sex—the least oral sex. Note, however, that these changes in prevalence across age cohorts might be affected by changes in cohort preferences for these sexual practices, in addition to aging processes. For example, there is decided shift in the popularity of oral sex in the NHSLS when comparing the oldest age cohort (those born in the 1930s) with those born later (see Laumann et al., 1994, pp. 101–107). Such a shift might be attributable to society-wide changes in sexual mores regarding specific sexual practices.

Among those who reported any sexual activity in the previous year, at any age, women also tended to report more sexual problems than men. The only problems less common among women than men are climaxing too early and performance anxiety. Intriguingly, among NSHAP respondents who do have sex, there appears to be little increase in sexual problems with age—with the notable exceptions of erectile problems and inability to climax among men. These results suggest maintenance of sexual capacity with age rather than inevitable decline, at least among those who remain sexually active.

## FUTURE DIRECTIONS

Two important avenues to advancing knowledge of sexuality in later life have emerged in the early 21st century. First, efforts are underway to collect longitudinal data—or data that tracks individuals over multiple points in time. Most importantly, preliminary work has begun on a second wave of the NSHAP—the only study to link late-life sexuality with health, social factors, and other life dimensions. A second direction is the increasing incorporation of biomeasures in population-based surveys. Conceptual models such as the interactive biopsychosocial model (Lindau et al., 2003), described above, propose complex interactions between social and physiological correlates of sexuality. The NSHAP obtained levels of the three important sex hormones—testosterone, progesterone, and estradiol—along with a range of other physiological indicators, which should prove useful in exploring the ways that physiological, social, emotional, and physical factors work together to affect sexuality at older ages, and *changes* in sexual functioning toward the end of life.

## CONCLUSION

Social science research has uncovered strong linkages between older individuals' sexual practices and problems and health, quality of life, and satisfaction with intimate relationships. Given these linkages, proper treatment of sexual problems is likely to enhance overall well-being. The enormous popularity of drugs to treat erectile dysfunction provides clear evidence of this. And sexual problems may suggest underlying physiological or disease processes that would benefit from medical intervention. Information on the social distribution and correlates of sexual problems at this age is critical both for targeting service delivery to populations at greater risk and in medical treatment (Laumann et al., 2008). More generally, these findings point to the central position of late-life sexuality as a nexus where social life and connectedness, culturally influenced attitudes and practices, and biological processes associated with aging and physical functioning come together (Waite et al., in press). As such, understanding sexual patterns, their context, and their meanings for older individuals is central to promoting healthy aging in later ages.

**SEE ALSO** Volume 3: *Marriage, Later Life; Singlehood; Sleep Patterns and Behavior; Social Support, Later Life.*

### BIBLIOGRAPHY


Addis, I. B., Van Den Eeden, S. K., Wassel-Fyr, C. L., Vittinghoff, E., Brown, J. S., & Thom, D. H., for the Reproductive Risk Factors for Incontinence Study at Kaiser (RRISK) Study Group. (2006). Sexual activity and function in middle-aged and older women. *Obstetrics and Gynecology, 107*, 755–764.

American Psychiatric Association. (2000). *Diagnostic and statistical manual of mental disorders.* (4th ed., text revision). Washington, DC: Author.

Bancroft, J. (1999). Central inhibition of sexual response in the male: A theoretical perspective. *Neuroscience and Biobehavioral Reviews, 23*, 763–784.

Bancroft, J. (2002). Biological factors in human sexuality. *The Journal of Sex Research, 39*, 15–21.

Bancroft, J., & Janssen, E. (2000). The dual control model of male sexual response: A theoretical approach to centrally mediated erectile dysfunction. *Neuroscience and Biobehavioral Reviews, 24*, 571–579.

Bancroft, J., Loftus, J., & Long, J. S. (2003). Distress about sex: A national survey of women in heterosexual relationships. *Archives of Sexual Behavior, 32*, 193–208.

Basson, R., Althof, S., Davis, S., Fugl-Meyer, K., Goldstein, I., Leiblum, S., et al. (2004). Summary of the recommendations on sexual dysfunctions in women. *The Journal of Sexual Medicine, 1*, 24–34.

Basson, R., Berman, J., Burnett, A., Derogatis, L., Ferguson, D., Fourcroy, J., et al. (2000). Report of the International Consensus Development Conference on Female Sexual Dysfunction: Definitions and classifications. *The Journal of Urology, 163*, 888–893.

Cawood, E. H. H., & Bancroft, J. (1996). Steroid hormones, the menopause, sexuality, and well-being of women. *Psychological Medicine, 26*, 925–936.

Cornwell, B., & Laumann, E. O. (2008, January). *Sexual networks and sexual dysfunction: The relevance of non-intimate social ties.* Paper presented at the International Sunbelt Social Network Conference, St. Pete Beach, FL.

Ellingson, S., Laumann, E. O., Paik, A., & Mahay, J. (2004). The theory of sex markets. In E. O. Laumann, S. Ellingson, J. Mahay, A. Paik, & Y. Youm (Eds.), *The sexual organization of the city* (pp. 3–39). Chicago: University of Chicago Press.

Fugl-Meyer, A. R., & Fugl-Meyer, K. S. (1999). Sexual disabilities, problems, and satisfaction in 18–74 year old Swedes. *Scandinavian Journal of Sexology, 2*, 79–105.

Graham, C. A., Ramos, R., Bancroft, J., Maglaya, C., & Farley, T. M. M. (1995). The effects of steroidal contraceptives on the well-being and sexuality of women: A double-blind, placebo-controlled, two-centre study of combined and progestogen-only methods. *Contraception, 52*, 363–369.

Haavio-Mannila, E., Kontula, O., & Kuusi, E. (2001). *Trends in sexual life: Measured by national sex surveys in Finland in 1971, 1992, and 1999 and a comparison to a sex survey in St. Petersburg in 1996* (The Population Research Institute Working Paper E 10/2001). Helsinki: Family Federation of Finland.

Laumann, E. O., Das, A., & Waite, L. J. (2008, August). *Sexual dysfunction among older adults: Prevalence and risk factors from a nationally representative probability sample of men and women 57 to 85 years of age.* Paper presented at the annual meeting of the American Sociological Association, Boston.

Laumann, E. O., Gagnon, J. H., Michael, R. T., & Michaels, S. (1994). *The social organization of sexuality: Sexual practices in the United States.* Chicago: University of Chicago Press.

Laumann, E. O., Nicolosi, A., Glasser, D. B., Paik, A., Gingell, C., Moreira, E. D., et al. (2005). Sexual problems among women and men aged 40–80 y: Prevalence and correlates identified in the Global Study of Sexual Attitudes and Behaviors. *International Journal of Impotence Research, 17*, 39–57.

Lindau, S. T., Laumann, E. O., Levinson, W., & Waite, L. J. (2003). Synthesis of scientific disciplines in pursuit of health: The interactive biopsychosocial model. *Perspectives in Biology and Medicine, 46*, S74–S86.

Lindau, S. T., Schumm, L. P., Laumann, E. O., Levinson, W., O'Muircheartaigh, C. A., & Waite, L. J. (2007, August 23). A study of sexuality and health among older adults in the United States. *The New England Journal of Medicine, 357*, 762–774.

Lue, T. F., Basson, R., Rosen, R., Giuliano, F., Khoury, S., & Montorsi, F. (2004). *Sexual medicine: Sexual dysfunction in men and women.* Paris: Health Publications.

Nicolosi, A., Laumann, E. O., Glasser, D. B., Moreira, E. D., Paik, A., & Gingell, C. (2004). Sexual behavior and sexual dysfunctions after age 40: The Global Study of Sexual Attitudes and Behaviors. *Urology, 64*, 991–997.

Rosen, R. C., & Laumann, E. O. (2003). The prevalence of sexual problems in women: How valid are comparisons across studies? *Archives of Sexual Behavior, 32*, 209–211.

Sanders, S. A., Graham, C. A., Bass, J. L., & Bancroft, J. (2001). A prospective study of the effects of oral contraceptives on sexuality and well-being and their relationship to discontinuation. *Contraception, 64*, 51–58.

Waite, L. J., Laumann, E. O., Das, A., & Schumm, L. P. (in press). Sexuality: Measures of partnerships, practices, attitudes, and problems in the National Social Life, Health, and Aging Project. *The Journals of Gerontology, Series B: Psychological Sciences and Social Sciences.*

World Health Organization. (2004). *International statistical classification of diseases and related health problems.* (10th revision, 2nd ed., Vols. 1–3). Geneva: Author.

***Linda J. Waite***
***Aniruddha Das***
***Edward O. Laumann***

# SHANAS, ETHEL

***1914–2005***

Ethel Shanas was born on September 6 in Chicago, Illinois, where she grew up and received her education (A.B., 1935; M.A., 1937; Ph.D., 1947) from the University of Chicago. After receiving her doctorate from the Department of Sociology, she remained at the University of Chicago on the Committee on Human Development as a research associate and instructor (1947–1952). She was a senior research analyst for the city of Chicago (1952–1953) and lecturer in social sciences at the University of Illinois at Chicago (1954–1956). From 1956 to 1961 she served as the senior study director at the National Opinion Research Center and research associate/associate professor in the Department of Sociology at the University of Chicago. She joined the University of Illinois at Chicago as a full professor of sociology starting in 1965 and as a full professor at the School of Public Health of the university's Medical Center starting in 1973. Shanas retired from academia in 1982. She lived with her husband, Lester "Steve" Perlman, in Evanston, Illinois, until her death on January 20, 2005.

Shanas taught graduate and undergraduate courses in sociology of aging and medical sociology. Using social surveys, she investigated health status and incapacity, family help patterns, living arrangements, generational relationships, financial status, and work/retirement patterns of persons 65 years of age and older living in the community. She used findings from her two national surveys to compare subgroups of older persons—across countries (in 1962, older persons in the United States, Britain, and Denmark), across time periods (data from 1962 and 1975, older persons in the United States), and across racial groups (in 1975, White and Black older persons in the United States).

Many researchers in the mid-20th century concentrated their efforts on the younger life stages, and, as a result, little was known about older people, and myths about them abounded. Additionally, federal programs began to provide older persons with benefits and services once provided by their families, and the myth of family abandonment reared its ugly head. From the 1950s through the 1970s, Shanas used survey findings to debunk many of these myths. She showed that old age is not synonymous with poor health, abandonment by family, being isolated and lonely, living in poverty, or being institutionalized.

Shanas found that the majority of persons 65 and older are relatively healthy and socially integrated through their families, friends, and work life. She also found that the family provides most of the care to its older members when they become sick and incapacitated and that institutionalization is undertaken only as a last resort.

Findings from her 1962 and 1975 surveys demonstrated that older persons are not a homogeneous group but make up two distinct life stages, the old and the very old, each with its own distinguishing characteristics. The younger group has enough income from work or retirement programs to be taken seriously in the consumer market. The majority lives independently with a spouse and sees at least one adult child often. The very old group includes more women, more widowed, and more frail and incapacitated persons, because women outlive men and sickness and incapacity are associated with advanced age.

Shanas served as a consultant to the United Nations and numerous federal agencies and a delegate to the White House Conferences on Aging. In her capacity as consultant she helped establish the Long-Term Care Minimum Data Set. Her service to professional organizations was extensive, including stints as president of the Illinois Sociological Society, the Midwest Sociological Society, and The Gerontological Society of America (GSA); vice president of the International Sociological Association's Research Committee on Aging; and secretary of the International Association of Gerontology.

Her collaborative efforts across cultures and disciplines are evident in the book *Old People in Three Industrial Societies* (Shanas et al., 1968) and in the two editions of the *Handbook of Aging and the Social Sciences* (Binstock & Shanas, 1976, 1985), which included perspectives from a broad array of social sciences. She developed an index of incapacity, which she used in her research, and during her tenure as president of GSA, President Richard M. Nixon signed the Research on Aging Act establishing a National Institute on Aging. This had been a goal of hers and of GSA. Additional contributions include her service on the editorial boards of professional journals and the other publications she edited and wrote. Her students benefited immensely from her organizational, writing, and editing skills, the grant-supported positions and professional travel she provided them, the high expectations she set for them, and her support and encouragement as they strived to meet those expectations.

Elected a fellow of the American Sociological Association and GSA, Shanas was the Keston Memorial Lecturer at the University of Southern California (1975) and received GSA's Kleemeier Award (1977; see Shanas, 1979), the National Council on Family Relations' Burgess Award (1978), and GSA's Brookdale Award (1981). In 1979 she was elected to membership in the National Academy of Sciences' Institute of Medicine.

Shanas successfully combined a meaningful career and family life during a period when women had few supports for career development and advancement. She provides an excellent role model for persevering and overcoming barriers in attaining one's goals and making major contributions to a chosen field of study.

**SEE ALSO** Volume 3: *Oldest Old; Policy, Later Life Well-Being.*

**BIBLIOGRAPHY**

Binstock, R. H., & Shanas, E. (Eds.). (1976, 1985). *Handbook of aging and the social sciences.* (1st and 2nd eds.). New York: Van Nostrand Reinhold.

Shanas E. (1962). *The health of older people: A social survey.* Cambridge, MA: Harvard University Press.

Shanas, E. (1978). Research grants studies: National survey of the Black aged (Grant No. 57823). *Social Security Bulletin, 41*(7), 33–35.

Shanas, E. (1979). Social myth as hypothesis: The case of the family relations of old people (Robert W. Kleemeier award lecture). *The Gerontologist, 19,* 3–9.

Shanas, E. (1982). *National survey of the aged* (DHHS Publication No. OHDS 83-20425). Washington, DC: U.S. Department of Health and Human Services, Office of Human Development Services, Administration on Aging.

Shanas, E., Townsend, P., Wedderburn, D., Friis, H., Milhøj, P., & Stehouwer, J. (1968). *Old people in three industrial societies.* New York: Atherton Press.

*Gloria D. Heinemann*

# SIBLING RELATIONSHIPS, LATER LIFE

Sibling relationships have been of great interest since earliest recorded history. For most people, it is the longest lasting of all their relationships, beginning when one sibling is first aware of the other and ending only at one sibling's death. As such, it is a unique kind of relationship.

Although they may extend over the entire life span, sibling relationships have been studied most extensively in their earlier phases, that is, in infancy, childhood, adolescence, and young adulthood. Once individuals leave their parents' home to marry and establish their own households, family studies have tended to focus on spousal relationships and parent–child relationships. However, in the decades around the turn of the 21st century, more attention has been paid to sibling relationships in middle age and old age, possibly because people and their siblings are living longer and with increasing recognition of the importance of such relationships.

## IMPORTANCE OF SIBLING RELATIONSHIPS IN OLD AGE

One might ask whether enough elderly people have living siblings to make it worthwhile to look at their sibling relationships. Clearly, as people grow older, some of their siblings do die—a small yet significant proportion of older adults have no living brothers or sisters. However, Victoria Bedford and Paula Avioli (2006) reported that in a sample of older adults, more than 80% of elders in the 65 to 84 age range still have one or more living siblings, as do 78% of those over age 85. Similarly, Victor Cicirelli (2002) found that 73% of a sample of adults over age 70 had living siblings, with about half of their original siblings still alive.

It is important to study sibling relationships in old age for several reasons. First, most siblings have some degree of genetic heritage in common as well as a shared family history that extends over a long time period. In old age, people tend to become concerned about reviewing earlier events and relationships in their lives and putting them into a mature perspective. Siblings who have shared a common past can be invaluable sources of information in clarifying memories of earlier events and people in the kin network. Second, siblings are often important sources of social support in old age, improving morale, giving advice when needed, and helping with some tangible services. Third, siblings can serve as role models for how to negotiate the last portion of the life span, dealing with such issues as retirement, health problems, and the dying process. Fourth, increases in longevity (or life span) mean that more people will have living siblings in old age than ever before. Finally, the large baby boom generation approaching old age at the beginning of the 21st century also tends to have larger sibships than the previous generation. At the same time, they have less stable marriages and fewer children, making the relationships with siblings potentially more important in old age.

## AREAS OF SIBLING RESEARCH

Researchers have gathered information about sibling relationships in old age using a wide variety of methods, including large-scale surveys, individual in-depth interviews, checklists, observations, and responses to psychological tests. Early research in the 1970s focused on how many siblings, living and dead, older adults had, how far away they lived, how often they were in contact, and whether they felt close, rivalrous, or indifferent. On average, older adults were in contact with their sibling at least monthly; relatively few were out of touch. Most reported positive feelings toward their siblings, either feeling close or very close. A large-scale study of sibling relationships over the entire adult age span (White & Riedmann, 1992a, 1992b) found that feelings of closeness between siblings were relatively stable across adulthood and old age, although amount of contact tended to decline. (Feelings toward half- and step-siblings were somewhat less close.)

However, some studies have found that sibling relationships grew stronger in the retirement years once children left home and became established. In general, rivalry and conflict between siblings tends to be low in old age, although some think that it remains beneath the surface and can recur under the right conditions. Finally, having a good relationship with a sibling in old age has been associated with better physical health, higher self-esteem, better morale, less loneliness, and less anxiety and depression (Cicirelli, 1995). However, it has not been determined whether a good sibling relationship is a contributing cause or a result of the latter conditions.

Many studies have tried to relate the older individual's sibling structure (i.e., the number of siblings, their birth order, gender, and the age spacing between them) to such things as intelligence, achievement in life, personality traits, and the nature of the sibling relationship itself (e.g., Conley, 2004). Most researchers tend to agree that relationships between pairs of sisters are the closest, with brother–brother relationships least close and sister-brother relationships in between.

Because the relationships between siblings vary greatly, some researchers have tried to classify them into types. For example, Deborah Gold (1989) identified five types of sibling relationships: the intimate (who are unusually close and devoted to each other), the congenial (who are close and friendly and see each other often), the loyal (who base their relationships on shared family values and see each other at family events), the apathetic (who have little interest and see each other infrequently), and the hostile (who have strong negative feelings of resentment and anger). Most sibling relationships are of the first three types.

A number of studies have investigated the extent to which siblings provide help and care for one another in old age. The great majority of elders say that they are ready to help their sibling if needed, although somewhat fewer say that they themselves would rely on a sibling for help. In actual fact, relatively few older adults act as primary caregivers for a sibling, and when they do it is usually because the sibling does not have a spouse or adult children who are available (Cicirelli, Coward, & Dwyer, 1992). However, more elders give siblings help that is of a secondary and occasional nature, such as help with transportation or housework. In any case, older adults seem to feel a sense of security just knowing that a sibling could be called on for help if a need should arise.

Relationships between siblings are not always constant but seem to grow closer or less close depending on ongoing events in their lives (such as divorce, death of a spouse, or a move). In general, relationships among surviving siblings appear to become closer following the death of other siblings or parents. Sibling relationships also may involve a certain degree of ambivalence, where harmonious feelings can coexist with conflict (Connidis & McMullin, 2002; Fingerman, Hay, & Birditt, 2004).

## SOME THEORETICAL APPROACHES

A number of different theories have been proposed to try to explain why sibling relationships persist over time in spite of geographic separation and the existence of other close relationships. One theoretical perspective views the sibling relationship as part of a family network of relationships (the family systems approach in psychology) or in the context of a larger kin network (the social constructionist framework in sociology). In the family systems approach (Minuchin, 1974), the relationship that an individual has with one sibling is influenced by the relationship that individual has with other siblings and by the relationship of other siblings with one another. (Earlier in the life span, the sibling subsystem, the parent–child subsystem, and the parent subsystem all interact with and influence one another; in later life, only the sibling subsystem remains but earlier influences of other portions of the system may still be evident.) In the social constructionist approach (Walker, Allen, & Connidis, 2005), sibling relationships are worked out within the broader context of the norms and practices of the larger kin network and social group. Thus sibling relationships may be closer or less close, depending on gender, social class, ethnicity, and so on, as these are interpreted within a particular kin network.

Attachment theory (Cicirelli, 1995) as applied to siblings suggests that the original attachment of the child to the mother, whether secure or insecure, serves as a prototype for the relationship with siblings. Secure

| Age | One or more living sister | One or more living brother | Any living sibling |
|---|---|---|---|
| 40–49 (n=232) | 70.7 | 73.3 | 99.6 (n=235) |
| 55–64 (n=171) | 67.8 | 69.0 | 91.2 (n=182) |
| 65–74 (n=95) | 77.9 | 65.3 | 80.3 (n=117) |
| 75–84 (n=136) | 58.3 | 64.0 | 83.8 (n=99) |
| 85+ (n=51) | 52.9 | 37.3 | 78.9 (n=38) |

SOURCE: The 1986 Data of the General Social Survey Cumulative File.

***Table 1.*** *Percent of respondents with siblings in later life.* CENGAGE LEARNING, GALE.

attachments explain sibling closeness and helping behavior, whereas insecure anxious attachments may account for ambivalent sibling relationships, and disturbed insecure attachments may account for hostile or abusive relationships. The attachment bond is thought to continue throughout life and is responsible for siblings' need for occasional contact and resulting positive feelings.

Exchange theory has also been used to explain sibling relationships in adulthood. That is, siblings strive to maintain a balance in the relationship between what each gives to the relationship and what each receives in return. The relationship suffers when the imbalance becomes too great.

## RESEARCH

Some recent studies have explored the factors associated with closer sibling relationships in old age. Genetic similarity was found to be important, with identical twins living closer, having more contact, exchanging more support, and feeling emotionally closer than fraternal twins, who in turn had a closer relationship than non-twin siblings (Neyer, 2002). Birth order was also found to be important, with firstborns having more sibling contact than later-borns (Pollet & Nettle, 2007). Major life events were also found to be associated with closer sibling relationships. Elders who experienced the death of a parent in childhood felt closer to their siblings in old age than those who grew up in intact families (Mack, 2004), and loss of a spouse in later adulthood was related to increased sibling contact and sibling support (Guiaux, von Tilburg, & van Groenou, 2007).

Another area of sibling research is concerned with the effects of a sibling's death on the views of older adults about death in general (Cicirelli, 2002). Those who had more deceased siblings tended to have less fear of the dying process itself, perhaps through seeing how their deceased siblings handled their decline and death, but a greater fear of the destruction of the body after death. However, those who saw death as involving an afterlife tended to have closer relationships to their living siblings. In general, elders felt closer to their remaining living siblings following sibling death; those who had a poor relationship with deceased siblings were more likely to experience depressive symptoms in old age.

## AREAS FOR FUTURE RESEARCH

As noted earlier, sibling relationships in old age have not been extensively studied, and there are a number of areas of study where further work is needed. First, just who is considered to be a sibling needs to be more carefully defined in future studies. Most past research has looked at full biological siblings and assumed that they were reared in intact families. However, with the increasing prevalence of alternative family types, relationships with half-siblings, step-siblings, adoptive siblings, and fictive or social siblings need to be examined more carefully. Factors that may influence the nature of the interpersonal relationship between siblings include the degree of genetic similarity (ranging from all genes in common in the case of identical twins, to none in the case of adoptive or step-siblings), whether they are legally regarded as siblings, whether they were reared together or apart (including the amount of time they lived together in childhood). Research is needed on how these factors influence the sibling relationship in later life, as well as the factors that contribute to closer relationships.

Another area where further research is needed involves looking more closely at the nuances of sibling relationship in old age in order to determine what things contribute to maintaining a close sibling relationship in the last portion of life. If there is ambivalence in the sibling relationship, what kinds of things are sources of problems, and how can they be dealt with to improve the sibling relationship?

More information is needed about how the relationship between a sibling pair functions within the entire sibling group and in the context of the larger family network. For example, little is known about how spouses (or partners) influence the sibling relationship in old age, whether dislike of a spouse may interfere with sibling contact or influence feelings, and so on.

Finally, studies of changes in sibling relationships over time as the baby boom generation moves into old age would be of great interest. Researchers need to determine the effect of smaller numbers of children and more failed marriages compared to the previous generation on sibling relationships.

SEE ALSO Volume 2: *Family and Household Structure, Adulthood;* Volume 3: *Caregiving; Social Support, Later Life.*


**BIBLIOGRAPHY**

Bedford, V. H., & Avioli, P. S. (2006). "Shooting the bull": Cohort comparisons of fraternal intimacy in midlife and old age. In V. H. Bedford & B. F. Turner (Eds.), *Men in relationships: A new look from a life course perspective* (pp. 81–101). New York: Springer.

Cicirelli, V. G. (1995). *Sibling relationships across the life span.* New York: Plenum.

Cicirelli, V. G. (2002). *Older adults' views on death.* New York: Springer.

Cicirelli, V. G., Coward, R. T., & Dwyer, J. W. (1992). Siblings as caregivers for impaired elders. *Research on Aging, 14,* 331–350.

Conley, D. (2004). *The pecking order: Which siblings succeed and why.* New York: Pantheon Books.

Connidis, I. A., & McMullin, J. A. (2002). Sociological ambivalence and family ties: A critical perspective. *Journal of Marriage and Family, 64,* 558–567.

Fingerman, K. L., Hay, E. L., & Birditt, K. S. (2004). The best of ties, the worst of ties: Close, problematic, and ambivalent social relationships. *Journal of Marriage and Family, 66,* 792–808.

Gold, D. T. (1989). Sibling relationships in old age: A typology. *International Journal of Aging and Human Development, 28,* 37–51.

Guiaux, M., van Tilburg, T., & van Groenou, M. B. (2007). Changes in contact and support exchange in personal networks after widowhood. *Personal Relationships, 14,* 457–473.

Mack, K. Y. (2004). The effects of early parental death on sibling relationships in later life. *Omega, 49,* 131–148.

Minuchin, S. (1974). *Families and family therapy.* Cambridge, MA: Harvard University Press.

Neyer, F. J. (2002). Twin relationships in old age: a developmental perspective. *Journal of Social and Personal Relationships, 19,* 155–177.

Pollet, T. V., & Nettle, D. (2007). Birth order and face-to-face contact with a sibling: Firstborns have more contact than laterborns. *Personality and Individual Differences, 43,* 1796–1806.

Walker, A. J., Allen, K. R., & Connidis, I. A. (2005). Theorizing and studying sibling ties in adulthood. In V. L.Bengtson et al. (Eds.), *Sourcebook of family theory and research,* (pp. 167–181). Thousand Oaks, CA: Sage.

White, L. K., & Riedmann, A. (1992a). Ties among adult siblings. *Social Forces, 71,* 85–102.

White, L. K., & Riedmann, A. (1992b). When the Brady Bunch grows up: Step/half and full sibling relationships in adulthood. *Journal of Marriage and the Family, 54,* 197–208.


*Victor Cicirelli*

# SINGLEHOOD

In research on the life course and aging, singlehood usually is defined in terms of a person's legal marital status; it is considered the status of never having been legally or officially (heterosexually) married. In popular discourse and in some research studies, however, the term *single* often is used as a synonym for *unmarried* (Connidis, 2001) or may be applied more broadly to someone without a current partner (not married, cohabiting, or otherwise romantically or intimately involved) or someone looking for a partner (Koropeckyj-Cox, 2005).

These inconsistencies in the way singlehood is defined reflect changes in attitudes and social norms that have transformed the meanings and significance of marriage in European and American societies and in many other countries around the world. In the last three decades of the 20th century and the first decade of the 21st, life paths have become more varied and complex and a greater variety of relationships have become available to formally single adults, including nonmarital cohabitation, living-apart-together relationships, same-sex enduring partnerships (and in some countries and states legally recognized same-sex marriages), and other sexually intimate relationships (Cooney & Dunne, 2001). This diversity challenges earlier assumptions and generalizations about singlehood with regard to living arrangements, past life history, sexuality, and relationships and raises important questions about these and other dimensions that may be more informative than formal marital status for understanding well-being in midlife and old age.

## HISTORICAL PREVALENCE AND SIGNIFICANCE OF SINGLEHOOD

Historical patterns related to the timing and likelihood of marriage have shaped the life courses of past and current cohorts of older adults. Singlehood and relatively late marriages were common historically in northern and western Europe, particularly in the middle to late 19th century and the early 20th century (Hajnal, 1982) and also were characteristic of the United States, Canada, and Australia in that period. Getting married was regarded as an important rite of passage into adulthood and into socially sanctioned sexual activity and childbearing, and economic stability and maturity were regarded as prerequisites. Late ages at marriage meant that singlehood was normative in young adulthood. Median ages at first marriage in 1900 were about 26 years for men and 22 years for women (U.S. Census Bureau, 2006), and about 40% of men and 31% of women over age 15 never married (U.S. Census Bureau, 2004).

Lifelong singlehood and celibacy has a long history in religious vocations and the priesthood, and the single status was associated with valued social roles in the extended family and community, particularly for women (Watkins, 1984). During the Victorian era and the industrial revolution, economic circumstances (and immigration in the United States) reinforced a pattern of delayed marriage. Adolescents and young adults contributed to the family economy, and stem family living arrangements were common in which a never-married adult child remained in the parental home, contributing income and helping to care for aged parents (Guinnane, 1991; Hareven, 1982). The economic hardships and uncertainties of the Great Depression continued this pattern of late marriage and economic interdependence into the 1930s.

After World War II, economic prosperity and government programs for returning veterans stimulated a shift toward earlier marriage and higher fertility rates, and marriage was transformed from an economic and social institution into a more private, intimate, and procreative relationship (Cherlin, 2004; Coontz, 2005). Social attitudes and popular images promoted normative expectations of heterosexual marriage, parenthood, and domesticity, and single and childless adults, along with gay men and lesbians, were regarded with pity or disapproval (Coontz, 2005; May, 1988, 1995). In 1950 the median age at marriage in the United States had declined to about 23 years for men and 20 for women (U. S. Census Bureau, 2006). For adults over age 65, this fluctuation has meant that the prevalence of singlehood has varied from 8.5 and 7% of women and men, respectively, in 1960, reflecting the lower marriage rates of the Depression era, to just over 4% of women and men in 2000, reflecting the aging of those who were young adults during the postwar baby boom (He, Sengupta, Velkoff, & DeBarros, 2005).

Since the 1960s ages at marriage and the proportions remaining single have been increasing, and the lives of never-married adults have come to reflect a wider variety of possible life paths that may include nonmarital cohabitation, nonmarital childbearing, and same-sex relationships (Cooney & Dunne, 2001). As a result of these social changes, the meanings and implications of singlehood over the life course have varied across cohorts of older men and women.

## OVERVIEW OF RESEARCH ON SINGLEHOOD

The postwar context provided the milieu in which many of the foundational social scientific theories of family and aging were developed, including structural functionalism in the sociology of the family, attachment theory in psychology, and disengagement theory and activity theory in the study of aging. Each of these theories emphasized the centrality and symbolic significance of relationships, particularly in childhood and marriage. In sociological research, the structural-functionalist perspective in particular conceptualized heterosexual marriage as universal and all but mandatory; those who remained single and/or childless were regarded as deviant or incomplete (Cherlin, 2008). Erik Erikson's (1963) early formulations of the stages of adult development also emphasized marriage and childbearing as central to achieving the normative tasks of intimacy, generativity, and integrity, although his later work acknowledged the potential for generative activities that did not require procreation (Erikson, 1982).

Gerontological research has defined family structure as a primary indicator of resources for social and instrumental support in old age. Those without kin have been seen as potentially isolated and vulnerable, stimulating interest in using survey data to assess and compare the relative well-being of never-married, unmarried, and/or childless older adults (Keith, 1986; Lawton, Moss, & Kleban, 1984; Ward, 1979). Single adults have been compared with their married peers on a variety of measures of relative well-being, sometimes combining all the unmarried and sometimes distinguishing between the never married and the formerly married (widowed or divorced). In general, single older adults have been described as more socially isolated, more lonely and depressed, and more likely to live in a nursing home in old age, although research findings on gender differences and on subjective measures of well-being have been mixed.

Several studies in the 1970s and 1980s used more qualitative approaches to examine the lives of single older adults on their own terms and in a variety of circumstances. Those studies documented the diversity of experiences of single older adults and examined individuals and families within their larger social and historical contexts (Allen & Pickett, 1987). One of the most influential was Peter Stein's (1976) typology of singlehood, which provided a multidimensional view of variations among single adults that took into account whether the single status was chosen or involuntary and whether it was perceived as temporary or stable.

These dimensions of choice and time horizon have helped explain the variability in the psychological well-being, behaviors, and perspectives of single adults (Connidis, 2001; Dykstra, 1995). Robert Rubinstein (1986), an anthropologist, looked specifically at the experiences of older men living alone, including a substantial number who were single, and the factors related to greater vulnerability or more positive well-being. The sociologist Katherine Allen (1989; see also Allen & Pickett, 1987) documented the diverse life paths of older never-married women born in the early 1900s, particularly their family relationships, caregiving roles, and social ties. Other researchers provided in-depth portraits of generally invisible subpopulations that were composed disproportionately of never-married older adults, including marginalized older men living in single-room occupancy hotels (Cohen & Sokolovsky, 1989) and older lesbians (Kehoe, 1989). Those studies expanded research on aging and singlehood by providing a glimpse of the growing and previously hidden diversity among older adults.

In the last decade of the 20th century and the first decade of the 21st, research on singlehood, aging, and the life course continued to broaden, reflecting contemporary trends and the aging of new cohorts; their varied experiences of singlehood show the influence of the dramatic social changes that occurred in their lifetimes (Connidis, 2001).

## KEY THEMES IN CONTEMPORARY RESEARCH

A persistent thread in research on marital status in later life is the legacy of structural functionalism that has defined unmarried older adults as a disadvantaged group because of their lack of a spouse and their official marital status (Waite, 1995; Waite & Gallagher, 2000). This research has used large surveys to examine how marital status, particularly singlehood, is related to various measures of objective circumstances and subjective well-being. These studies span a number of countries, including the United States, Canada, the Netherlands, the United Kingdom, and Germany, with comparable findings. A prominent theme in this research is the fundamental importance of gender in shaping the experiences of singlehood and the impact of marriage selection (the processes by which individuals are selected into marriage on the basis of their valued social characteristics) and larger structural circumstances on the relative well-being of single adults.

In general, highly educated women constitute an important subset among the never married (Barrett, 1999); remaining single gave those women greater independence to pursue higher education, more continuous work careers, and greater career advancement compared with their ever-married peers. Despite their educational and work histories, however, single women's earnings and retirement incomes have been lower than those of men (Koropeckyj-Cox & Call, 2007). Single men, in contrast, are somewhat less educated and have lower incomes compared with those who have married, likely reflecting a preference for marrying more advantaged men. Median household and per capita wealth are lower among all unmarried older adults, including the never married, compared with their married peers (Lupton & Smith, 1994, cited in Waite, 1995). These economic disadvantages reflect lower relative earnings among single adults (particularly women) as well as the cumulative effects of having to cover food, housing, and other expenses on a single income (i.e., lacking the economies of scale enjoyed by larger households). Higher mortality and poorer health are linked with being unmarried, reflecting the selection of healthier individuals into marriage and the potential benefits of the marital relationship for physical and mental health, particularly for men (Waite, 1995). The disadvantages for never-married adults appear greatest in countries where singlehood is rarer and more marginalized (Kisker & Goldman, 1987). Never-married older adults are somewhat less likely to live alone than are those who are divorced or widowed, often living with siblings or other relatives (Choi, 1996; Stull & Scarisbruck-Hauser, 1989). However, being single and childless in old age generally is linked with a greater reliance on formal paid services or living in a nursing home (Freedman, 1996).

Research on the social support networks and contacts of single older adults is mixed. Some studies have described never-married adults as more isolated (Gubrium, 1975), less socially connected, and less likely to have a confidant than their ever-married peers (Barrett, 1999; Marks, 1996). However, single women have more contact with relatives and larger social networks than do single men (Barrett, 1999). Single adults have been described as representing the extremes of social interaction, from those who are highly integrated and active (particularly single women) to those who are more isolated and vulnerable (Seccombe & Ishii-Kuntz, 1994). Over the life course, many single adults cultivate and maintain contact with friends who later may provide emotional and some kinds of instrumental support (Dykstra, 1990; Rubinstein, 1987; Rubinstein, Alexander, Goodman, & Luborsky, 1991; Seccombe & Ishii-Kuntz, 1994). Jenny DeJong Gierveld (2003) and other European scholars (e.g., Borell & Karlsson, 2003) have also noted the emergence of living-apart-together relationships, which provide companionship and social support for single adults while maintaining independence. For older single women, living-apart-together arrangements also offer the benefits of a relationship while avoiding some of the traditionally gendered expectations of marriage, including additional housework or looking after a partner.

There are also consistent gender differences in various measures of relative subjective well-being among single older adults. Unmarried men are generally more lonely and depressed than married men are, whereas never-married women are similar to those who are married and report less loneliness and depression than do their formerly married peers (Koropeckyj-Cox, 1998). Single men are significantly lonelier than single women (Dykstra, 1995; Zhang & Hayward, 2001). This gender difference can be explained by women's greater contact with kin and friends (Pinquart, 2003). Pearl Dykstra

(1995) noted that a lack of friendships is a stronger predictor of loneliness than is being single. Those who prefer singlehood and express a low desire for a partner show the most positive well-being, reflecting the importance of perceptions of singlehood as a chosen versus an involuntary status (Dykstra, 1995).

A growing body of qualitative research has explored the meanings of singlehood, with a focus on never-married White women, a group that appears to be relatively advantaged with regard to education, careers, and subjective well-being. These studies often incorporate feminist approaches and criticize comparative methods for reinforcing marriage-centered heteronormative assumptions and "a bias for the norm" (McDill, Hall, & Turell, 2006, p. 41; see also Allen, 1989; Davies, 2003). Their findings highlight the significance of independence and choice and report generally high levels of satisfaction and social integration (Baumbusch, 2004; McDill et al., 2006) as well as the complex identity work (Reynolds & Taylor, 2005; Reynolds, Wetherell, & Taylor, 2007), ambivalence about singlehood (Lewis & Moon, 1997), and varied life transitions in the lives of single women (Davies, 1995). Other studies have explored the lives of lesbians, many of whom are technically classified as never married and may not be in a current relationship; their life courses, identities, relationships, and experiences of aging reveal both similarities to and divergences from those of single heterosexual women (Jones & Nystrom, 2002; Rosenfeld, 1999).

## FUTURE RESEARCH DIRECTIONS

The transformations of marriage and greater variety of relationships and life paths have called into question the usefulness of singlehood as an analytic and conceptual category, particularly as it was defined in earlier studies. Definitions that are based on official legal marital status are no longer necessarily informative as they may mask very different histories and current relationships. However, the continuing symbolic significance of marriage as a status marker (Cherlin, 2004) with legal recognition and benefits argues for varied approaches to understanding families, relationships, well-being, and the life course that take into account the different dimensions of marital, residential, and relationship statuses. Also, research on the life course should attend to both similarities and differences among groups, such as never-married and late-marrying adults, cohabiting and living-apart-together couples, and never-married mothers and those who have cohabited, married, or divorced. Future research will have to attend to how these dimensions shape health, psychological well-being, social functioning and connectedness, and resources differentially over the life course.

Although both survey-based research and qualitative research on singlehood have been expanding, this is still a relatively neglected area, particularly with regard to the experiences of racial-ethnic and sexual minorities (Allen & Walker, 2006; Barrett, 1999). Further, there are few in-depth studies of never-married men despite their numerical growth and the more negative implications of singlehood for men (Cooney & Dunne, 2001). Future research should explore these important axes of diversity and the way they intersect with one another and with gender and age relations. The growing body of work in the qualitative traditions, including constructionist, feminist, phenomenological, and narrative approaches, has contributed many insights into the life course, aging, gender, and social relationships, but those observations often are limited by narrow samples. Future research would benefit from integrating these conceptual frameworks into large-scale representative and comparative survey projects.

**SEE ALSO** Volume 2: *Family and Household Structure, Adulthood;* Volume 3: *Cohort; Loneliness, Later Life; Sexual Activity, Later Life; Social Integration/Isolation, Later Life.*

**BIBLIOGRAPHY**


Allen, K. R. (1989). *Single women/family ties: Life histories of older women.* Newbury Park, CA: Sage.

Allen, K. R., & Pickett, R. S. (1987). Forgotten streams in the family life course: Utilization of qualitative retrospective interviews in the analysis of lifelong single women's family careers. *Journal of Marriage and the Family, 49*(3), 517–526.

Allen, K. R., & Walker, A. J. (2006). Aging and gender in families: A very grand opening. In T. M. Calasanti & K. F. Slevin (Eds.), *Age matters: Re-aligning feminist thinking* (pp. 155–174). New York: Routledge.

Barrett, A. E. (1999). Social support and life satisfaction among the never married: Examining the effects of age. *Research on Aging, 21,* 46–72.

Baumbusch, J. L. (2004). Unclaimed treasures: Older women's reflections on lifelong singlehood. *Journal of Women and Aging, 16*(1/2), 105–121.

Borell, K., & Karlsson, S. G. (2003). Reconceptualizing intimacy and ageing: Living apart together. In S. Arber, K. Davidson, & J. Ginn (Eds.), *Gender and ageing: Changing roles and relationships* (pp. 47–62). Maidenhead, England: Open University Press.

Cherlin, A. J. (2004). The deinstitutionalization of marriage. *Journal of Marriage and the Family, 66,* 848–861.

Cherlin, A. J. (2008). *Public and private families: An introduction.* (5th ed.). New York: McGraw-Hill.

Choi, N. K. (1996). The never married and divorced elderly: Comparison of economic and health status, social support, and living arrangement. *Journal of Gerontological Social Work, 26,* 3–25.

Cohen, C. I., & Sokolovsky, J. (1989). *Old men of the Bowery: Strategies for survival among the homeless.* New York: Guilford Press.

Connidis, I. A. (2001). *Family ties & aging*. Thousand Oaks, CA: Sage.

Cooney, T. M., & Dunne, K. (2001). Intimate relationships in later life: Current realities, future prospects. *Journal of Family Issues, 22*, 838–858.

Coontz, S. (2005). *Marriage, a history: From obedience to intimacy or how love conquered marriage*. New York: Viking.

Davies, L. (1995). A closer look at gender and distress among the never married. *Women and Health, 23*, 13–30.

Davies, L. (2003). Singlehood: Transitions within a gendered world. *Canadian Journal on Aging, 22*(4), 343–352.

DeJong Gierveld, J. (2003). Social networks and social well-being of older men and women living alone. In S. Arber, K. Davidson, & J. Ginn (Eds.), *Gender and ageing: Changing roles and relationships* (pp. 95–110). Maidenhead, England: Open University Press.

Dykstra, P. A. (1990). *Next of (non)kin: The importance of primary relationships for older adults' well-being*. Amsterdam: Swets & Zeitlinger.

Dykstra, P. A. (1995). Loneliness among the never and formerly married: The importance of supportive friendships and a desire for independence. *Journal of Gerontology: Psychological Sciences and Social Sciences, 50*(5), S321–S329.

Erikson, E. H. (1963). *Childhood and society* (2nd ed.). New York: Norton.

Erikson, E. H. (1982). *The life cycle completed*. New York: Norton.

Freedman, V. A. (1996). Family structure and the risk of nursing home admission. *Journal of Gerontology: Psychological Sciences and Social Sciences, 51*(2), S61–S69.

Gubrium, J. F. (1975). *Living and dying at Murray Manor*. New York: St. Martin's Press.

Guinnane, T. W. (1991). Rethinking the Western European marriage pattern: The decision to marry in Ireland at the turn of the century. *Journal of Family History, 16*(1), 47–64.

Hajnal, J. (1982). Two kinds of preindustrial household formation systems. *Population and Development Review, 8*(3), 449–494.

Hareven, T. (1982). *Family time and industrial time: The relationship between the family and work in a New England industrial community*. New York: Cambridge University Press.

He, W., Sengupta, M., Velkoff, V. A., & DeBarros, K. A. (2005). *Sixty five plus in the United States: 2005*. U.S. Census Bureau, Current Population Report P23–209. Washington, DC: U.S. Government Printing Office.

Jones, T. C., & Nystrom, N. M. (2002). Looking back … looking forward: Addressing the lives of lesbians 55 and older. *Journal of Women and Aging, 14*(3–4), 59–76.

Kehoe, M. (Compiler). (1988). *Lesbians over 60 speak for themselves*. New York: Haworth Press.

Keith, P. M. (1986). Isolation of the unmarried in later life. *Family Relations, 35*(3), 389–395.

Kisker, E. E., & Goldman, N. (1987). Perils of single life and benefits of marriage. *Social Biology, 34*(3–4), 135–152.

Koropeckyj-Cox, T. (1998). Loneliness and depression in middle and old age: Are the childless more vulnerable? *Journal of Gerontology: Psychological Sciences and Social Sciences, 53*, S303–S312.

Koropeckyj-Cox, T. (2005). Singles, society, and science: Sociological perspectives. *Psychological Inquiry, 16*, 91–97.

Koropeckyj-Cox, T., & Call, V. R. A. (2007). Characteristics of older childless persons and parents: Cross-national comparisons. *Journal of Family Issues, 28*, 1362–1414.

Lawton, M. P., Moss, M., & Kleban, M. H. (1984). Marital status, living arrangements, and the well-being of older people. *Research on Aging, 6*(3), 323–345.

Lewis, K. G., & Moon, S. (1997). Always single and single again women: A qualitative study. *Journal of Marital and Family Therapy, 23*, 115–131.

Lupton, J., & Smith, J. P. (1994). *Marriage, assets, and savings*. Working Paper 99-12. Santa Monica, CA: RAND Corporation. Retrieved on June 24, 2008, from www.rand.org/pubs

Marks, N. F. (1996). Flying solo at midlife: Gender, marital status, and psychological well-being. *Journal of Marriage and the Family, 58*(4), 917–932.

May, E. T. (1988). *Homeward bound: American families in the cold war era*. New York: Basic Books.

May, E. T. (1995). *Barren in the promised land: Childless Americans and the pursuit of happiness*. New York: Basic Books.

McDill, T., Hall, S. K., & Turell, S. C. (2006). Aging and creating families: Never-married heterosexual women over forty. *Journal of Women and Aging, 18*(3), 37–50.

Pinquart, M. (2003). Loneliness in married, widowed, divorced, and never-married older adults. *Journal of Social and Personal Relationships, 20*(1), 31–53.

Reynolds, J., & Taylor, S. (2005). Narrating singleness: Life stories and deficit identities. *Narrative Inquiry, 15*(2), 197–215.

Reynolds, J., Wetherell, M., & Taylor, S. (2007). Choice and chance: Negotiating agency in narratives of singleness. *Sociological Review, 55*(2), 331–351.

Rosenfeld, D. (1999). Identity work among lesbian and gay elderly. *Journal of Aging Studies, 13*, 121–144.

Rubinstein, R. L. (1986). *Singular paths: Old men living alone*. New York: Columbia University Press.

Rubinstein, R. L. (1987). Never-married elderly as a social type: Re-evaluating some images. *The Gerontologist, 27*(1), 108–113.

Rubinstein, R. L., Alexander, B. B., Goodman, M., & Luborsky, M. (1991). Key relationships of never married, childless older women: A cultural analysis. *Journal of Gerontology: Psychological Sciences and Social Sciences, 46*(5), S270–S277.

Seccombe, K., & Ishii-Kuntz, M. (1994). Gender and social relationships among the never-married. *Sex Roles, 30*, 585–603.

Stein, P. J. (1976). *Single life: Unmarried adults in social context*. Englewood Cliffs, NJ: Prentice-Hall.

Stull, D. E., & Scarisbruck-Hauser, A. (1989). Never-married elderly: A reassessment with implications for long-term care policy. *Research on Aging, 11*(1), 124–139.

U.S. Census Bureau. (2004). No. HS-11. Marital status of the population by sex: 1900 to 2000. In *Statistical abstract of the United States: 2003*. Retrieved May 24, 2008, from http://www.census.gov/statab

U.S. Census Bureau. (2006). Table MS-2: Estimated median age at first marriage, by sex: 1890 to the present. In *Current population survey, 2004*. Retrieved May 24, 2008, from www.census.gov/population

Waite, L. J. (1995). Does marriage matter? *Demography, 32*(4), 483–507.

Waite, L. J., & Gallagher, M. (2000). *The case for marriage: Why married people are happier, healthier, and better off financially.* New York: Doubleday.

Ward, R. A. (1979). The never-married in later life. *Journal of Gerontology, 34,* 861–869.

Watkins, S. C. (1984). Spinsters. *Journal of Family History, 9*(4), 210–225.

Zhang, Z., & Hayward, M. D. (2001). Childlessness and the psychological well-being of older parents. *Journal of Gerontology: Psychological Sciences and Social Sciences, 56B,* S311–S320.

***Tanya Koropeckyj-Cox***

# SLEEP PATTERNS AND BEHAVIOR

Sleep, a behavior common to all people, has been described as "a reversible behavioral state of perceptual disengagement from and unresponsiveness to the environment" (Carskadon & Dement 2005, p. 13). Sleep behavior usually includes being in a resting state, being quiet, and having one's eyes closed. It was once considered a passive state during which the body and brain were inactive. This view changed during the mid-20th century when technological advances in humans' ability to record brain waves and other bodily functions, known as polysomnography, led to the discovery that sleep is an active process during which the brain is anything but passive.

## NREM AND REM SLEEP

Polysomnography, which involves applying electrodes to a person's head and body to record brain wave activity, eye movement, and neck muscle tension, allows researchers and clinicians to distinguish sleep from wake. Measurement of eye movement is used to divide sleep into two states: non-rapid eye movement (NREM) and rapid eye movement (REM) sleep.

During NREM, people experience little or no eye movement, muscle tone, and physiological arousal. Unlike with REM sleep, dreaming is rare. NREM sleep is composed of four stages defined by distinct brain wave activity patterns. Stage one is characterized by low-voltage brain wave activity between 4 and 6 cycles per second (Morgan, 2000). During stage one, people are drowsy and may deny that they were sleeping if awakened. Stage two is defined by the appearance of sleep spindles (0.5 to 1.5-second bursts of 12 to 14 cycles per second brain wave activity) and K-complexes (large, slow peaks of activity followed by smaller valleys lasting at least 0.5 second) (Morgan, 2000). Stages three and four are typically grouped together and referred to as slow wave sleep. Brain wave activity is the slowest at 1 to 4 cycles per second and, unlike REM or other NREM stages, is very uniform (Morgan, 2000). In stage three, 20 to 50% of brain wave activity is slow wave, whereas in stage four, more than 50% is slow wave activity (Carskadon & Rechtschaffen, 2005).

During REM sleep, people experience rapid eye movement, loss of muscle tone, brain wave activity similar to stage one NREM sleep, and high levels of physiological arousal (i.e., increased pulse rate, blood pressure, and respiration rate). REM sleep is the state when most people dream.

People enter sleep through NREM and proceed to cycle through all four stages of NREM before an REM episode will occur. A full sleep cycle including both NREM and REM typically lasts 90 to 120 minutes (Carskadon & Dement, 2005). People typically experience four to five sleep cycles per night, and approximately 80% of the total sleep period is NREM. The length of NREM and REM sleep change over the course of the night. Specifically, as people cycle through NREM and REM, REM and stage two NREM episodes increase, whereas stages three and four NREM decrease (Carskadon & Dement, 2005).

## MEASURING SLEEP

Polysomnography is considered the gold standard method for measuring sleep because it allows clinicians and researchers to study the sleep stages and their transitions—known as sleep architecture (Carskadon & Rechtschaffen, 2005). Actigraphy, which consists of a wristwatch-like device, is also used to measure sleep objectively. Actigraphy does not record brain wave activity, but instead measures limb movements. The premise underlying actigraphy is that people's movement is limited during sleep; therefore, movement is a proxy measure of sleep (i.e., a high level of movement signals that the person is awake, whereas little or no movement indicates that they are asleep). Although actigraphy is not as informative as polysomnography, it can be used to capture people's sleep patterns in their home environments for a few days to a few weeks or even longer. Mobile versions of polysomnography are available for home use. However, home-based polysomnography is typically used to collect information for only a night or two, because it is expensive and cumbersome (requiring the attachment of electrodes each evening).

Sleep diaries are the most commonly used subjective measure of sleep and provide important information on people's perceptions of their sleep. Different versions are available, but no version has been shown to be superior.

Sleep diaries ask people to provide estimates of their sleep from the night before and generally include information on people's bedtimes and when they wake up, how long they took to fall asleep, how many times they awoke during the night and for how long, and the total amount of time they spent sleeping. Sleep diaries are generally collected for 1 to 2 weeks. Although they do not indicate sleep stages or movement during the night, sleep diaries are widely used because they are the cheapest and most efficient way to measure sleep.

## SLEEP IN LATER LIFE

Sleep and sleep architecture are not static but change as people age. As babies people have shorter NREM-REM cycles (about 50 minutes), begin sleep with REM rather than NREM, and sleep for most of a given 24-hour period. Distinct NREM stages do not appear until several months post-birth. During adolescence people experience 40% less slow wave sleep than they did as children (Carskadon & Dement, 2005). During later life these sleep architecture changes continue: First, people report poorer sleep quality across their life spans, especially during midlife to later life; second, the total amount of sleep decreases from an average of 7 hours to 6 hours per night (Nau, McCrae, & Lichstein, 2005); third, the daily amount of sleep is more variable; fourth, older adults report more arousals during the middle of the night with eight awakenings per night on average (Morgan, 2000); and fifth, these increased arousals are associated with older adults spending more time in stages one and two and less time in stages three and four (i.e., slow wave sleep). Although these changes occur in both men and women, men have significantly worse sleep architecture deterioration. Despite this, some research indicates that women are more likely to complain about their sleep and seek help for poor sleep (Morgan, 2000). Finally, older adults have more frequent shifts in sleep stages than do younger adults.

## INSOMNIA

A major focus of sleep research is insomnia occurring in later life. Insomnia involves a complaint of difficulty initiating sleep, maintaining sleep, or non-restorative sleep that lasts at least 1 month and causes difficulty with daytime functioning (American Psychiatric Association, 2000). Non-restorative sleep involves the complaint of poor quality sleep even though the person has had adequate circumstances and opportunity for sleep. Insomnia complaints are more common and more severe in older adults. Whereas insomnia in younger adults is typically transient, insomnia in later life is often chronic and related to several factors, including changes in sleep architecture and health.

At all ages, however, insomnia is a risk factor for depression, anxiety, and substance abuse. Insomnia can be a warning sign to a clinician for other psychological disorders. The reverse is also true: People with other psychological disorders often develop insomnia. People with depression, anxiety, and substance abuse issues frequently report difficulty initiating sleep, maintaining sleep, or non-restorative sleep; however, the factors that initially precipitate the insomnia are different. For people with depression, their low mood may exacerbate their sleep difficulties. People with anxiety experience excessive worry, which can cause them to have difficulty falling asleep and staying asleep. Also people who abuse either legal or illegal substances may experience different side effects from the drugs, which may induce symptoms of insomnia.

Although insomnia may initially be a risk factor and symptom of these and other psychological disorders, the insomnia, many times, becomes a separate disorder. This means that an individual may continue to suffer from insomnia even though the initial psychological disorder has been effectively treated. The insomnia develops a life of its own because the individual begins to develop cognitions and behaviors that contribute to poor sleep. For example, the individual may begin to associate the bedroom with poor sleep because he or she has had difficulty falling asleep in the past. If this association is strong, the individual may have difficulty falling asleep because he or she associates the bedroom with being awake. In addition, the individual may begin to nap during the day or increase caffeine intake to cope with the insomnia. These behaviors may initially help the individual; however, in the long term, they maintain the insomnia. Cognitive behavioral treatment for insomnia targets these types of cognitions and behaviors.

Insomnia is also a warning sign of other sleep disorders, including apnea. Sleep apnea is characterized by partial pauses or complete cessation in breathing during the night. People with sleep apnea experience these partial or complete pauses five or more times per hour throughout the night. The poor breathing during the night is typically unknown to the person. The person will report, however, symptoms of insomnia, such as non-restorative sleep and difficulty with daytime functioning. Clinicians who suspect apnea or another sleep disorder, which may have the initial appearance of insomnia, will refer a patient for a sleep study. A sleep study involves an overnight visit to a sleep laboratory during which the patient's sleep is measured with polysomnography.

## INSOMNIA TREATMENT

Insomnia is treated in multiple ways for older adults. Sleep medications are the most common treatment. Although medications are beneficial for short-term difficulties, older individuals experience insomnia for 7 to 12 years on average (McCrae et al., 2003). Sleep medications may not be the best option for these individuals because they do not treat the behaviors contributing to the maintenance of chronic insomnia (i.e., negative thinking about sleep). With chronic medication use, older individuals are susceptible to developing a new condition, hypnotic dependent insomnia, characterized by dependency on the sleep medication and a worsening of insomnia (called rebound insomnia) and increased anxiety during withdrawal.

Cognitive behavioral treatment successfully treats insomnia without dependency concerns. Specifically, it has been shown to decrease total wake time during the night. In addition to relaxation, most treatment packages utilize sleep education, sleep hygiene, stimulus control, and sleep restriction: Sleep education reviews age-related changes in sleep and realistic expectations; sleep hygiene involves reviewing behaviors that may contribute to poor sleep (e.g., caffeine use); stimulus control focuses on associating the bedroom environment with sleep; and sleep restriction involves limiting time in bed. People with insomnia spend large amounts of time awake in bed in the hopes of catching up on sleep. By restricting time in bed, people reduce the time spent awake in bed worrying about not sleeping. Finally, relaxation is used to decrease arousal, which increases the likelihood of sleep.

Older adults also experience other sleep disorders at a higher rate including sleep-related breathing disorders, periodic leg movements (repetitive leg movements during sleep), and restless leg syndrome (irresistible urges to move one's legs, especially when resting). Reason for the increased prevalence is uncertain. Medical devices (to help breathing) and medications are typically recommended to decrease symptoms. Insomnia is highly comorbid with these disorders because they promote nocturnal awakenings. Unfortunately, after these disorders are treated, the insomnia often persists because of the learned awakening behavior.

## FUTURE DIRECTIONS

Sleep research continues to be a priority. People sleep for one-third of their lives; however, researchers still do not know everything that happens during sleep or how people's bodies differ during sleep and while awake. Research indicates that respiration, heart rate, and multiple other physiological behaviors change during sleep. However, scientific understanding of the exact mechanisms underlying these changes remains incomplete.

**SEE ALSO** Volume 3: *Mental Health, Later Life; Sexual Activity, Later Life.*

## BIBLIOGRAPHY


American Psychiatric Association. (2000). *Diagnostic and statistical manual of mental disorders.* (4th ed.). Washington, DC: Author.

Ancoli-Israel, S. (2005). Actigraphy. In M. Kryger, T. Roth, & W. Dement (Eds.), *Principles and practice of sleep medicine* (pp. 1459–1467). Philadelphia: Elsevier; Saunders.

Bliwise, D. (2005). Normal aging. In M. Kryger, T. Roth, & W. Dement (Eds.), *Principles and practice of sleep medicine* (pp. 24–38). Philadelphia: Elsevier; Saunders.

Carskadon, M., & Dement, W. (2005). Normal human sleep: An overview. In M. Kryger, T. Roth, & W. Dement (Eds.), *Principles and practice of sleep medicine* (pp. 13–23). Philadelphia: Elsevier; Saunders.

Carskadon, M., & Rechtschaffen, A. (2005). Monitoring and staging human sleep. In M. Kryger, T. Roth, & W. Dement (Eds.), *Principles and practice of sleep medicine* (pp. 1359–1377). Philadelphia: Elsevier; Saunders.

Edinger, J. D., Hoelscher, T. J., Marsh, G. R., Lipper, S., & Ionescu-Pioggia, M. (1992). A cognitive-behavioral therapy for sleep-maintenance insomnia in older adults. *Psychology and Aging, 7*(2), 282–289.

Javaheri, S. (2005). Sleep and cardiovascular disease: Present and future. In M. Kryger, T. Roth, & W. Dement (Eds.), *Principles and practice of sleep medicine* (pp. 1459–1467). Philadelphia: Elsevier; Saunders.

McCrae, C. S., Rowe, M. A., Tierney, C. G., Dautovich, N. D., DeFinis, A. L., & McNamara, J. P. H. (2005). Sleep complaints, subjective and objective sleep patterns, health, psychological adjustment, and daytime functioning in community-dwelling older adults. *Journal of Gerontology: Psychological Sciences, 60*(4), 182–189.

McCrae, C. S., Wilson, N. M., Lichstein, K. L., Durrence, H. H., Taylor, D. J., Bush, A. J., et al. (2003). "Young old" and "old old" poor sleepers with and without insomnia complaints. *Journal of Psychosomatic Research, 54*(1), 11–19.

Morgan, K. (2000). Sleep and aging. In K. Lichstein & C. Morin (Eds.), *Treatment of late-life insomnia* (pp. 3–26). Thousand Oaks, CA: Sage

Morin, C. M., Colecchi, C., Stone, J., Sood, R., & Brink, D. (1999). Behavioral and pharmacological therapies for late-life insomnia. *Journal of the American Medical Association, 281*(11), 991–999.

Morin, C. M., Kowatch, R. A., Barry, T., & Walton, E. (1993). Cognitive-behavior therapy for late-life insomnia. *Journal of Consulting and Clinical Psychology, 61*(1), 137–146.

Nau, S., Cook, K., McCrae, C., & Lichstein, K. (2005). Treatment of insomnia in older adults. *Clinical Psychology Review, 25*(5), 645–672.

Ohayon, M. M. (2002). Epidemiology of insomnia: What we know and what we still need to learn. *Sleep Medicine Reviews, 6*(2), 97–111.

Vitiello, M., Moe, K., & Prinz, P. (2002). Sleep complaints cosegregate with illness in older adults: Clinical research informed by and informing epidemiological studies of sleep. *Journal of Psychosomatic Research, 53*(1), 555–559.


***Christina McCrae***
***Pamela Dubyak***

# SOCIAL INTEGRATION/ ISOLATION, LATER LIFE

Dating back to the work of late 19th-century sociologist Emile Durkheim, social scientists have studied people's social embeddedness. The quality and number of one's personal relationships, active involvement in voluntary organizations, and social integration in general are the result of the individual's choices and actions, yet also are shaped by societal circumstances and contexts. Sociologists have studied whether social changes such as changes in family form and the so-called breaking up of the nuclear family (Popenoe, 1993) have led to declining levels of civic engagement and social integration (Putnam, 1995).

## DEFINING SOCIAL ISOLATION

Social isolation refers to the absence of close personal relationships with other people. Isolated people do not have others with whom they maintain regular contact, and many maintain only a very small number of relationships that entail only superficial contact. Social isolation refers to the objective characteristic of a situation, or the actual number of persons in one's life, rather than subjective characteristics, such as one's perception that their social ties are insufficient. An important question facing life course sociologists, and especially social gerontologists, is: To what extent is an individual truly "alone"? One can envision a continuum ranging from complete social isolation at one end to being fully integrated in social relationships and social contexts at the other. The latter end may encompass social contexts such as the household, the family, local organizations such as the church or voluntary organizations, or a virtual context in which people maintain geographically distant contact by means of modern communication techniques, including e-mail or communication using social networking web sites.

Although people who live alone may appear to be at risk of social isolation, many maintain a satisfying network of meaningful social relationships outside their household. Conversely, people in a strained or frosty marriage may feel social isolation, especially if they have few friends or a limited social network outside of the marriage. A social network consists of the set of people with whom one has a direct personal relationship. It might include close family members (e.g., spouse, children), distant relatives (e.g., cousins, in-laws), and a variety of nonkin relationships (e.g., neighbors, friends, colleagues, fellow club members).

## THEORETICAL APPROACHES

Old age is a stage in the life course that may be viewed as marked by social isolation. Part of the reason why older people are vulnerable to social isolation is that there are few social expectations about the roles for older adults to fulfill. This perspective, called *disengagement theory*, posits that older people will withdraw themselves from society—as they retire from work outside the house and as friends and family members die—thus resulting in deterioration of their social networks (Cumming, Dean, Newell, & McCaffrey, 1960). Although disengagement theory has garnered little empirical support in recent years, it has provided the foundation for the development of socioemotional selectivity theory (Carstensen, 1992). This theory proposes that as they face the end of life, older people specifically disengage from their more and casual distant relationships and instead place greater emphasis on their closest personal ties. Older people are believed to find their emotional engagement with core network members to be particularly rewarding in maintaining their social identity and sharing joys and sorrows. Although the size of older adults' social networks may decline, levels of satisfaction are as high as ever, because older adults' needs change and they prefer the company and support of a smaller, although close-knit, group of significant others.

Older people vary widely in their needs and resources, however (Baltes & Carstensen, 1996). The life-course approach offers a framework for understanding heterogeneity in late life. Life transitions and the trajectories in which they are embedded are a central concern of life-course studies. Many transitions follow socially structured sequences, and many life transitions are intertwined. For example, older adults may move to a residential care facility after death of the spouse who had previously been providing care. The extent to which an older adult is socially isolated or integrated also is shaped by social contexts. In other words, individuals are not simply *excluded*, but there are specific population groups who are most susceptible to the experiences of marginalization and, in turn, social isolation. For example, people whose spouses have died may be excluded from activities with married couples. Specific life events in old age that diminish social integration include widowhood or widowerhood, death or incapacitation of network members, and lack of important resources—such as good health or an ability to travel—both of which help older adults to maintain their relationships (Antonucci & Akiyama, 1987; Morgan, 1988).

## METHODS FOR STUDYING SOCIAL INTEGRATION

Social scientists use a variety of methods for mapping social networks. Mapping personal networks can provide data showing to what extent people are socially isolated versus integrated (Broese van Groenou & van Tilburg,

2007). Some of these methods focus on the exchange of emotional, instrumental, and material support within relationships, whereas others focus on emotional nature of one's interpersonal ties. A third approach is to document the number and type of formal role relationships one has (e.g., spouse, sibling, worker). Researchers typically select a method that reflects their specific research interests. A key component of all three methods is that a single respondent is asked to provide information about the people in his or her social network; that is, the other network members do not provide assessments of the relationship. As a first step, respondents are usually asked to identify by name those persons (if any) whom they believe make up their network. This procedure results in an assessment of individual's network size, which can vary from no one to a large number of people.

Measures of isolation and integration may reflect both objective and subjective aspects of one's social networks. The number of people in one's network is considered an objective characteristic. By contrast, the feeling that one is loved and supported is considered a subjective measure. Key concepts may be measured in either objective or subjective terms. For example, social isolation may reflect on objective factors, such as having no close relationships, and loneliness may reflect subjective characteristics, such as feeling one has unsatisfying relationships. The two do not necessarily overlap; socially isolated people are not necessarily lonely, and lonely people are not necessarily socially isolated in an objective sense. Where a person ends up on the subjective continuum—ranging from not at all lonely to severely lonely—may also depend on his or her subjective standards and expectations and not only on the actual number of persons in one's network (Perlman & Peplau, 1981). Some people with few social contacts might feel lonely; others might feel sufficiently embedded. An example of the latter situation is that of a person who cherishes his or her privacy and actively seeks to avoid undesired social contacts.

***Isolation.*** *Seniors can feel isolated after losing a spouse.* DOUG CROUCH/PHOTOGRAPHER'S CHOICE RR/GETTY IMAGES.

## HOW MANY PEOPLE ARE SOCIALLY ISOLATED?

Estimates of the proportion of the general population that is socially isolated depend upon the definition of a social "tie." For example, one study (Höllinger & Haller, 1990) revealed that between 5% and 23% of the respondents in Germany and Austria stated that they had "no friends." These differences may reflect sociocultural differences in how people define the term *friendship*. In some contexts, friendship might refer to a relationship with a person whom one likes very much and with whom one shares a wide range of activities. In other cases, however, friendship refers to merely being casual acquaintances and sharing only a specific interest or activity.

McPherson, Smith-Lovin, and Brashears (2006) reported that about half the U.S. population say that they do not have anyone with whom they can discuss important matters. The authors of that study concluded that many people in the United States may have weak or nonexistent ties to members of their communities and neighborhoods. However, they also acknowledged that they had limited information on each person's social networks and thus might have overestimated the number of social isolates (or people who did not have a close confidant with whom to share their thoughts). The present author adds the further critique that having "no confidant" is not necessarily the same thing as being socially isolated. For example, one study of older adults living in London revealed that 13% did not have a confidant; however, all had at least one personal network member (Bowling, Grundy, & Farquhar, 1995). In many studies that adopted other methods for assessing social integration, much larger network sizes were observed. Typical network sizes ranged from about 5 to 10 people; in some studies, higher averages were observed. This indicates that most people are surrounded by a set of people to whom they can turn for help, advice, or emotional support. Consequently, in these studies, only a small number of socially isolated people is observed. Another study of 3,000 Dutch older adults (van Tilburg, 1998) found that only 6 respondents could not identify any network members; the average network size was around 14 people.

Life-course scholars agree that the number of one's social contacts gradually decreases with advancing age. This decrease is partly due to functional or social loss: spousal bereavement, physical and cognitive impairments, or the death of other members of the network. Among older people living at the beginning of the 21st century these events often occur only at an advanced age; age 75 is sometimes taken as a marker for the average age at which a downward development of social integration begins. Given that many older adults start this phase of life with a large personal network, few will end their life socially isolated. Furthermore, losses may be accompanied by gains. For example, retirement enables people to pursue new activities and relationships, as they fill their nonwork hours with friendships and hobbies. Further, increases in life span enable many grandparents to develop emotionally close relationships with their grandchildren when they mature. Increased demands for personal care among older adults may strengthen ties between care givers and care recipients.

## CONSEQUENCES OF SOCIAL ISOLATION

The negative consequences of being socially isolated have been documented extensively. People with few contacts may have difficulty in finding a job: Labor market marginality leads to poverty and social isolation, which in turn reinforce the risk of long-term unemployment (Gallie, Paugam, & Jacobs, 2003). Vast evidence suggests that social isolation can threaten one's psychological health, indicated by an elevated risk of depression, loneliness, and suicide among people with few or weak social ties. Furthermore, isolated people lack the health advantages of being connected to other people. Networks contribute to a healthy lifestyle, provide access to information for disease prevention, reduce psychological stress, and enhance beneficiary physiologic responses (Berkman, Glass, Brisette, & Seeman, 2000). Finally, people who lack social ties are more likely to die prematurely, compared with findings in people with more extensive contacts (Berkman & Syme, 1979). It is not the mere presence of relationships that matter but also the frequency with which one maintains contact, how geographically proximate one's network members are, and how emotionally close and fulfilling these relationships are.

## FUTURE DIRECTIONS

Personal relationships are shaped by sociohistorical context. As such, future studies focusing on aging baby boomers may reveal patterns very different from the ones detected among current cohorts of older adults. Two macrosocial changes may have particularly powerful ramifications: changing family structures and the weakening of the geographical foundation of networks.

Decreasing family size and changing family structure (i.e., increasing rates of divorce and remarriage) have typically been interpreted as a sign of decreasing importance of the family. Despite pessimistic assessments of how such changes may affect the social lives of older adults, most research reveals that levels of intergenerational contact and support have not declined concomitantly (Bengston, 2001). However, in the second half of the 20th century the number of childless people has increased. As such, older adults may have fewer—but not necessarily poorer quality—social ties in the future. Furthermore, family structures are becoming increasingly complex, and traditional definitions of "family" need to be revised. Relatively high rates of remarriage following divorce (and to a lesser extent, widowhood) have created a growth in the number of stepfamilies. In stepfamilies, family members' roles, norms, and obligations are less clearly defined than in first-marriage families. The loosening of the role-based character of primary kinship is exemplary for other types of personal relationships. Social bonds may be more flexible and fluid. However, not all social observers are optimistic that these social changes will be beneficial to older adults; Allan (2001) has countered that these changes may lead to a fragmented and less predictable social life that in turn may increase the risk of isolation.

A second and related development is the weakening of the geographic basis of relationships. With increasing geographic mobility and widespread reliance on the Internet, networks have transformed from local communities to virtual communities (Wellman, 1999). Among future older generations, social networks may ultimately comprise a mixture of traditional networks, consisting of local kin, friends, and members of social organizations, as well as global networks of long-distance relationships based on shared interests. Although some people profit from technological developments that expand the traditional boundaries of social networks, others will have greater difficulty accessing, initiating, and maintaining such long-distance relationships.

These new family and network structures have predominantly been created in the second half of the 20th century among people who will become the next generation of older people. It is unknown to what extent these developments will lead to an increasing number of socially isolated people. Are the risks of social isolation anchored in the life course? For example, is vulnerability accumulated across various domains of life, such as when people have a small family, live in a deprived neighborhood, and have a history of divorce or nonemployment? Are deficits in personal networks treatable in old age? These questions will direct the future research agenda.

**SEE ALSO** Volume 2: *Durkheim, Émile; Social Support, Adulthood;* Volume 3: *Childlessness; Loneliness, Later Life; Marriage, Later Life; Singlehood; Widowhood.*

**BIBLIOGRAPHY**

Allan, G. (2001). Personal relationships in late modernity. *Personal Relationships, 8,* 325–339.

Antonucci, T. C., & Akiyama, H. (1987). Social networks in adult life and a preliminary examination of the convoy model. *Journal of Gerontology, 42,* 519–527.

Baltes, M. M., & Carstensen, L. L. (1996). The process of successful aging. *Aging & Society, 16,* 397–422.

Bengtson, V. L. (2001). Beyond the nuclear family: The increasing importance of multigenerational bonds. *Journal of Marriage and the Family, 63,* 1–16.

Berkman, L. F., Glass, T., Brisette, I., & Seeman, T. E. (2000). From social integration to health: Durkheim in the new millennium. *Social Science and Medicine, 51,* 843–857.

Berkman, L. F., & Syme, S. L. (1979). Social networks, host resistance and mortality: A nine-year follow-up study of Alameda County residents. *American Journal of Epidemiology, 109,* 186–204.

Bowling, A., Grundy, E., & Farquhar, M. (1995). Changes in network composition among the very old living in inner London. *Journal of Cross-Cultural Gerontology, 10,* 331–347.

Broese van Groenou, M. I., & van Tilburg, T. G. (2007). Network analysis. In J. E. Birren (Ed.), *Encyclopedia of gerontology* (2nd ed., Vol. 2, pp. 242–250). San Diego, CA: Elsevier.

Carstensen, L. L. (1992). Social and emotional patterns in adulthood: Support for socioemotional selectivity theory. *Psychology and Aging, 7,* 331–338.

Cumming, E., Dean, L. R., Newell, D. S., & McCaffrey, I. (1960). Disengagement: A tentative theory of aging. *Sociometry, 23,* 23–35.

Gallie, D., Paugam, S., & Jacobs, S. (2003). Unemployment, poverty and social isolation: Is there a vicious circle of social exclusion? *European Societies, 5,* 1–32.

Höllinger, F., & Haller, M. (1990). Kinship and social networks in modern societies: A cross-cultural comparison among seven nations. *European Sociological Review, 6,* 103–124.

McPherson, M., Smith-Lovin, L., & Brashears, M. E. (2006). Social isolation in America: Changes in core discussion networks over two decades. *American Sociological Review, 71,* 353–375.

Morgan, D. L. (1988). Age differences in social network participation. *Journal of Gerontology, 43,* S129–S137.

Perlman, D., & Peplau, L. A. (1981). Towards a social psychology of loneliness. In R. Gilmour & S. W. Duck (Eds.), *Personal relationships in disorder* (pp. 31–56). London: Academic.

Putnam, R. D. (1995). Bowling alone: America's declining social capital. *Journal of Democracy, 6,* 65–78.

Popenoe, D. (1993). American family decline, 1960–1990: A review and appraisal. *Journal of Marriage and the Family, 55,* 527–542.

van Tilburg, T. G. (1998). Losing and gaining in old age: Changes in personal network size and social support in a four-year longitudinal study. *Journal of Gerontology, 53B,* S313–S323.

Wellman, B. (1999). *Networks in the global village: Life in contemporary communities.* Boulder, CO: Westview.

*Theo van Tilburg*

# SOCIAL SECURITY

Social Security provides critical protections throughout the lives of virtually all persons in the United States. Enacted in 1935, Social Security—the Old Age, Survivors and Disability Insurance (OASDI) program—does more to secure family incomes and reduce poverty than any other policy or program, public or private. In addition to ensuring a measure of dignity and self-sufficiency in retirement and old age, Social Security protects against other life-altering events—including the death or disability of a worker, spouse, or parent.

As a social insurance program, Social Security is predicated on the idea that society is inherently interdependent—parents nurturing children, younger generations caring for their predecessors, and the healthy providing for the infirm. Indeed, as this entry emphasizes, Social Security is best understood as a program that protects citizens and cohorts across the entire life course.

After defining several terms, the progression of this legislation since its inception in 1935 is reviewed. The benefits and costs of Social Security are then discussed, including its economic impact for elderly, disabled, surviving, and child beneficiaries. Next, this entry describes the program's financing problem and discusses the use of declarations of *crisis* to advance an ideological position that supports privatizing the program. This entry observes that relative to other industrial nations, the United States is better positioned to expend resources on its public retirement pension programs. Finally, this entry concludes by noting that there are many reasonable options for addressing the projected financing problem and by highlighting the need for interventions to further strengthen protections across the course of life, an area likely to be of special interest to life course researchers.

## SOCIAL INSURANCE AND SOCIAL SECURITY DEFINED

Individuals and families in all societies are subject to economic risks such as unemployment, illness, disability, retirement, divorce, and more. In all societies, risks are addressed through some mix of private (family, savings, private insurance, charity, employment-based health care, and pensions) and public (welfare, social insurance, and government mandates) mechanisms. Social insurance is one very important approach to protecting against identifiable risks that could overwhelm the finances of individuals and families. Whereas welfare programs give immediate relief to extreme financial problems, social insurance programs in the United States—including Medicare, Social Security, unemployment insurance, and worker's compensation—seek to *prevent* financial distress. Built on the principle of universal coverage, social insurance provides a social means of pooling risks. Using insurance principles, the costs and risks of coverage are spread across a broad population. (In the case of Social Security, the risk is spread across all working Americans.) In exchange for modest work-related contributions over many years, social insurance provides a floor of protection against predictable risk (Ball, 2000).

Unlike private insurance plans, social insurance plans do not "cream off" the best risks and try to keep the most expensive risks out of their insurance pools. To the contrary, because social insurance programs seek to provide widespread basic protection, they embrace all citizens and try to assure a basic level of security. Hence, whereas profit-driven private health insurance often seeks to exclude persons with serious illnesses, a social insurance system seeks their inclusion. Because social insurance systems do not exclude bad risks, it is essential that the participation be mandatory to maintain a financially viable system. Also, the participation of the entire workforce prevents those who might opt out from eventually having to be rescued by taxpayers through welfare programs (Ball, 2000). Benefits eligibility is earned through a worker's payroll tax contributions. Hence, benefits are considered an earned right, another factor supporting the dignity of beneficiaries and the political stability of social insurance programs.

In other national contexts, Social Security often refers to a system of social insurance, public assistance (welfare), and related social interventions. In the United States, Social Security commonly refers to OASDI, the program that provides cash benefits to retired, disabled, and surviving and other family members and is sometimes used to describe Medicare programs. Except when otherwise indicated, in this entry the term is used to refer solely to OASDI. Social Security also represents an ideal, a value to be achieved by a civilized society seeking to provide widespread basic protection against what Franklin D. Roosevelt (1882–1945) called "the vicissitudes of life." Indeed, the OASDI program, as the next section highlights, is rooted in such a vision.

## HISTORY

Faced with unprecedented economic dislocation, President Roosevelt and the New Deal reformers of the 1930s saw the need and opportunity to prepare an economic security bill that would address unemployment and old-age insecurity. With Roosevelt's popularity boosted by the early successes of the New Deal, in 1934 he established the Committee on Economic Security. Chaired by Secretary of Labor Frances Perkins (1882–1965), the Committee on Economic Security report served as the basis for the Social Security Act of 1935, which established two social insurance programs, three income-tested welfare programs, and several public health and social service programs. In a January 17, 1935, message to Congress, Roosevelt commended the Committee on Economic Security proposals to Congress as a plan that "is at once a measure of prevention and a method of alleviation":

> We can never insure one hundred percent of the population against one hundred percent of the hazards and vicissitudes of life, but we have tried to frame a law that will give some measure of protection to the average citizen and his family.... This law, too, represents a cornerstone in a structure which is being built but is by no means complete. (American Rhetoric, 1935)

That final sentence, of course, is critical—the Social Security Act represents a structure to be built on and, by inference, to further extend protections against many of the unprotected risks citizens encounter over their lives. Following enactment, a favorable political consensus prevailed allowing the incremental expansion of Social Security and related programs from 1939 through the mid-1970s.

**Incremental Expansion** Benefits were extended in 1939 for the wives of retired workers and for the surviving wives and children of deceased workers. These survivor benefits were made available to men in 1950. The 1950 amendments to the Social Security Act established social insurance as the nation's dominant means of protecting older Americans against loss of income in retirement. Coverage was extended to regularly employed domestic and farm workers and benefits increased, assuring that Social Security benefits would generally be more available and of greater value than benefits provided through the federal-state welfare program for the aged funded under the original Social Security Act.

In 1956 disability insurance protections for permanently and severely disabled workers ages 50 to 64 were added, eventually extending to all workers under age 65 in 1960. The 1956 amendments also gave women the right to accept permanently reduced retired workers benefits between ages 62 and 64, an option extended to men in 1961. The high rate of poverty—an estimated 39% in 1959—and those near poverty among the old combined with a growing economy to provide political rationale for substantial benefit increases from 1965 through 1972. In 1972 an automatic annual cost-of-living allowance was incorporated into the law, a provision that ensures that benefits, once received, maintain their purchasing power from year to year. Although critically important for helping to stabilize the incomes of the old, disabled, and surviving family members, this provision made the financing of the program more sensitive to economic change (Berkowitz, 1991).

**Financing Problems Emerge** Conservatively financed and carefully monitored, Social Security and Medicare are the only federal programs whose anticipated revenues and expenditures are projected out to 75 years in the future. These projections provide an early warning system so that policy makers can make needed adjustments in a timely manner. The financial stability of Social Security rests on the authority and taxing power of government. This power is reinforced by the self-interest of political leaders, protecting the promised benefits, and assuring the program's continuity and financial integrity (Kingson, in press). Moreover, an implied covenant, arising from a deeply embedded sense of mutual responsibility in civilization, reinforces and underlies "the fundamental obligations of the government and citizens of one time and the government and citizens of another to maintain a contributory social insurance system" (Brown, 1977, pp. 31–32).

From time to time, financing problems emerge requiring legislation, with the last major ones occurring in the mid-1970s and early 1980s. Another financing problem is on the horizon, due to a number of factors, including the aging of the baby boomers, the erosion of the payroll tax base due to growing income inequality, increases in life expectancy at age 65, and the long-term declines in birth rates since the 1960s. Fortunately, the Social Security financing problem is less problematic than the previous one.

## UNDERSTANDING BENEFITS AND COSTS OF SOCIAL SECURITY

A cross-sectional (i.e., *time-freeze*) perspective may present a different picture of the benefits and costs of Social Security than a perspective that views the transfers Social Security structures over time (i.e., a longitudinal perspective). For example, at one point in time Social Security can be understood primarily as a program that taxes the young to pay for retired older Americans. However, viewed over time, there is a reciprocity of giving and receiving, such that workers at one time make payroll tax contributions to support current beneficiaries with the promise and expectation that the same will be done for them and their family members when they achieve eligibility. Similarly, those receiving benefits are either disabled or retired, or else they are spouses or young dependents of retired, disabled, and deceased workers—each of whom have made contributions into the program and helped to build the economy during their active work lives (Kingson, Hirshorn, & Cornman, 1986.).

Social Security affects virtually all Americans, as taxpayers and as beneficiaries, covering 165 million workers and their families and providing benefits each month to 50 million beneficiaries in January 2008—including 31.7 million retired workers, 2.4 million spouses of retired workers, 4.4 million aged widow(er)s, 7.1 million disabled workers, 152,000 spouses of disabled workers, 153,000 spouses of deceased workers caring for dependent children, and—what most people are surprised to learn—4.1 million children. In 2008, 3.3 million of these children were mostly under age 18 and the dependents of disabled, deceased, and retired workers. However, there are another 800,000 severely disabled adult children, also dependent on disabled, deceased, and retired workers, whose developmental and other severe disabilities began before age 22. Contrary to what many people believe, working persons do not pay into a personal saving account that determines the benefits that they and their families receive. Rather, the Social Security Administration maintains a record for each worker of earnings subject to the payroll tax. This earnings history is used to determine eligibility and benefit amounts.

## THE BENEFITS

Monthly Social Security benefits are not huge, nor are they insignificant. In January 2008, the maximum monthly benefit for persons first retiring at age 65 was $2,030. Average monthly benefits in January 2008 were as follows:

- Retired worker alone: $1,066
- Aged couple with both receiving benefits: $1,761
- Widowed mother and two children: $2,221
- Aged widow(er) alone: $1,040
- All disabled workers: $1,004
- Disabled worker, spouse, and one or more children: $1,761
- Children of deceased workers: $936

Social Security benefits are based on a progressive benefit formula, structured to assure that people who work consistently at low and modest wage levels receive a substantially larger rate of return on their payroll tax payments (roughly twice the size) than those with substantially higher earnings. Benefits to low-wage earners replace about 54% of their average lifetime earnings, adjusted to capture changes in standards of living over the life of workers. This amount decreases to 40% for individuals earning average wages and 28% for workers whose earnings are nearer to the program's maximum taxable income (National Academy of Social Insurance, 2008). In providing larger returns to lower-income workers, the benefit structure recognizes that these workers may have limited access to private savings accounts and employer-based pension plans.

There is of course much more to know about Social Security benefits than this overview provides, much of it quite complex, as seen below:

- Covered workers may accept reduced retirement benefits when they turn 62 or monthly benefits that are about 5 to 7% larger for each year their receipt of benefits is postponed, up until age 70.
- Full retirement age—66 for workers born from 1943 to 1954—is scheduled to gradually increase to age 67 for workers born in 1960 or later.
- Severely disabled workers are eligible to receive monthly benefits if their condition meets the disability eligibility criteria.
- Special rules apply to the timing of benefit receipt for widows and spouses of retired workers.
- Under special circumstances, grandchildren and severely disabled widow(er)s between the ages of 50 and 59 can be eligible for benefits.

Although the above are the most obvious and direct benefits of Social Security, the program's indirect benefits should not be overlooked. In underwriting the economic security of the old, the program frees up middle-aged adult children to devote more resources to their young children. A joining institution, it is based on and gives expression to important values widely shared in America—the idea that people have responsibilities to honor their parents and protect their families, their neighbors, and themselves. As former Senator Bill Bradley (b. 1943) once observed, Social Security is arguably the best expression of community in America.

**Economic Impact across the Life Course** Few recognize that Social Security is the foundation of most families' retirement, disability, and life insurance protection and that it provides protections across the entire course of life (Herd & Kingson, 2005). Ask most Americans to envision a recipient of Social Security and the prevailing image would most likely be of an elderly person in their twilight years, enjoying retirement supported by the Act's cash benefits. Although it is true that Social Security has transformed old age in America, it is important to not discount the impact of Social Security on the 30% of recipients (and their family members) who are not retired workers. Some examples are given below:

- Social Security does more than any other federal program, with the exception of the Earned Income Tax Credit, to reduce poverty among children, lifting 1.3 million out of poverty (Lavery & Reno, 2008).
- A 30-year-old worker earning around $30,000 holds Social Security life insurance protection for her or his spouse and two young children with a present value of $443,000 and disability protections insurance protection equivalent to $414,000.
- Soldiers fighting in Iraq and Afghanistan and virtually all working adults are covered by Social Security. If they are disabled, they receive benefits, as do their dependents and their families if they die.
- Without Social Security benefits, 55% of the 7.1 million severely disabled workers and their 153,000 spouses would live in poverty.
- Social Security is the foundation of the nation's retirement income system. It is the only pension protection available to 6 out of 10 private-sector workers (Ball, 2000).
- Without Social Security, the poverty rate among the old would increase to nearly 50%.

Because its benefits are based on a progressive benefit formula, Social Security is particularly important for low- and moderate-income households with persons ages 65 and over (see Table 1) and also for older women and minority populations:

- For the bottom 60% of the elderly income distribution—those 16.2 million households with incomes under $25,587 in 2004—Social Security provides over 70% of all household income.
- Social Security provides 90% of household income to approximately 54% and 62% of African American and Hispanic unmarried seniors, respectively (National Academy of Social Insurance, 2008).

The security of beneficiaries is protected by annual cost-of-living protection, which assures that benefits, once received, maintain their purchasing power into advanced old age. Indeed, the program's adequacy features—the

| All members over age 65 | | QUINTILES | | | | |
|---|---|---|---|---|---|---|
| | All Aged Units | Units Under $10,399 (Q1) | $10,399–$16,363 (Q2) | $16,363–$25,587 (Q3) | $25,587–$44,129 (Q4) | $44,129 and over (Q5) |
| Number of units (in millions) | 27.0 | 5.3 | 5.5 | 5.4 | 5.4 | 5.4 |
| Percent of Total Income From: ** | | | | | | |
| Social Security(OASDI) | 38.6 | 82.6 | 83.4 | 66.6 | 47.5 | 18.9 |
| Railroad retirement | 0.5 | 0.3 | 0.4 | 0.6 | 1.0 | 0.3 |
| Government employee pension | 9.0 | 0.8 | 2.1 | 5.5 | 10.4 | 9.9 |
| Private pension/annuity | 10.2 | 0.7 | 2.2 | 6.0 | 10.1 | 10.9 |
| Income from assets | 12.6 | 2.3 | 3.8 | 6.0 | 8.4 | 17.8 |
| Earnings | 26.3 | 1.2 | 2.8 | 7.1 | 15.7 | 40.1 |
| Public assistance (welfare) | 0.6 | 8.4 | 1.6 | 0.9 | 0.2 | 0.1 |
| Other | 2.4 | 2.0 | 1.5 | 2.7 | 2.6 | 1.9 |

* All members of households are 65 or over. Aged units are married couple living together—at least one of whom is 65—and nonmarried persons 65 or older.
** Details may not sum to totals due to rounding error.

SOURCE: Social Security Administration (2006).

***Table 1.*** *Importance of various sources of income to elderly households (aged units), 2004**. CENGAGE LEARNING, GALE.

desire to provide widespread protection and do a bit more for those who have worked many years but at low wages—have driven its success.

This is not to suggest that the economic security of the old cannot be improved. Despite the successes Social Security has had in maintaining living standards and alleviating poverty among elderly populations, specific groups are still vulnerable– specifically women who are very old, those who are unmarried or divorced, and elderly African American and Hispanic populations. For example, although only about 10% of those 65 and older live below the federal poverty level (U.S. Census Bureau, 2006), closer examination reveals the following:

- Median household income declines as women age, dropping from $16,474 for those ages 65 to 69 to $13,172 for women 75 and older—a 20% drop between these age groups and, alarmingly, 63% and 55% lower than men in the same age ranges (He, Sengupta, Velkoff, & DeBarros, 2005).
- Nineteen and a half percent of Hispanics (men and women) and 23.7% of African Americans, 65 and older fell below the poverty line in 2006, compared to 8.8% of Caucasians (He et al., 2005).
- Forty and four-fifths percent of Hispanic and 40.3% of African American women 65 and older who are living alone fall below the poverty line, compared to 16.9% of non-Hispanic White women over 65 and living alone (He et al., 2005).

There are myriad reasons for the elevated percent of poverty among elderly women, including the persistent gender gaps in wages, societal expectations that women will leave work to perform caregiving duties (for both children and aging parents), and lower rates of private pensions and savings compared to men (National Organization for Women Foundation [NOW], 2007). Many women rely on the spouse or survivors benefits to augment their Social Security—specific benefits provided to spouses after 10 years of marriage—helping to reduce the percentage of poverty among married women to 3% compared to 15% of unmarried women (NOW, 2007). Due to higher divorce rates, resulting in shorter marriages and a lower number of women marrying, it is estimated that the percentage of poverty among unmarried women will grow over time (NOW, 2007). Although Social Security has done much to underwrite the economic security of individuals and families across the course of life, policy makers and life course researchers should not lose sight of groups that remain at risk.

## THE COSTS OF SOCIAL SECURITY

Current benefits are funded primarily from the taxes paid by current workers, with the promise that current workers will themselves receive benefits when they become eligible. Employed persons contribute 6.2% of their gross earnings (with an equal employer match) up to a maximum taxable ceiling ($102,000 in 2008) into two trust funds—the Old Age and Survivors Insurance and Disability Insurance, or what is more conveniently referred to as the combined OASDI trust fund. Self-employed persons make contributions equivalent to those made by regularly employed persons and their employers. The maximum taxable ceiling is adjusted yearly for changes in average wages. The goal is for Social Security to receive a constant share of national earnings. Additional revenues come from treating a portion of Social Security benefits as taxable income and from the interest earned from investing the growing OASDI trust fund assets in government bonds.

In calendar year 2007, the combined OASDI trust fund received about $780 billion from all sources—$652 billion from payroll tax revenues, $17 billion from treating Social Security benefits as taxable income, and $101 billion in interest payments for treasury bonds and other federal securities held by Social Security trust funds. In turn, $591 billion were expended—$582 billion on benefit payments, $3.9 billion on the portion of the railroad retirement program that is essentially part of Social Security, and $5.5 billion on administrative expenses. Social Security is one of the most efficient federal programs with less than 1% (0.9%) of trust fund revenues spent on administration (Board of Trustees, 2007).

**The Politics of Social Security Financing** Unlike the mid-1970s and early 1980s, Social Security does not face an immediate risk of taking in less revenue than it needs to expend within the next few years, nor is it likely to within the next 20 to 25 years, even if Congress takes no action (Altman, 2005). However, a significant long-term problem is projected by Social Security's actuaries and its Board of Trustees.

The most commonly accepted estimates suggest that OASDI has sufficient funds to meet all obligations until 2041. Outlays are projected to exceed tax revenues (payroll tax receipts and taxes on benefits) in 2017. However, income from all sources, including interest on trust fund investment, is projected to exceed expenditures through 2027. After that, timely payment of benefits will require drawing down the OASDI assets, depleting them after 2041. Of course, the size of the actual problem could grow or shrink, depending on economic and demographic changes (Board of Trustees, 2007).

Even if Congress failed to act before 2041, Social Security's dedicated stream of income after 2041 would be sufficient to pay about 78 cents of every dollar promised over the remaining 75-year estimating period. In other words, trust fund depletion—although it would be a disaster for the politicians—would not mean that Social Security would cease to pay any benefits.

Theoretically, the financing problem could be addressed immediately by raising the Social Security payroll tax on employers and employees from 6.2% to 7.2% or by immediately reducing all future benefits by about 14%. No one seriously advocates either approach, but it does provide a very rough indication of the size of the financing problem. Moreover, relative to other industrial nations, population aging is not placing the United States under excessive pressure and Americans are not heavily taxed even though their per capita income is among the highest, $34,681 in 2000 U.S. dollars, as compared to the equivalent of $25,056 in France, $24,215 in Germany, and $28,030 in the United Kingdom (Organisation for Economic Cooperation and Development [OECD], 2007).

Comparative data published by the OECD (2007) indicate that in the early 21st century there are approximately 21 persons ages 65 and over in the United States per 100 persons of working age, compared to 26 in Germany, 28 in France, 29 in Italy, 28 in Japan, 27 in the United Kingdom, and 30 in Sweden. By 2030, when the youngest of the U.S. baby boomers will reach age 65, this elderly dependency ratio will grow to 37 per 100 in the United States, 39 per 100 in France, 49 per 100 in Germany, 48 per 100 in Japan, and 39 per 100 in the United Kingdom. Other nations carry much higher tax burdens than the United States. For example, federal expenditures, as a percent of gross domestic product, are generally much lower than other OECD nations—16.2% in 2003, compared to 28.7% in France, 27.6% in Germany, 24.2% in Italy, 31.3% in Sweden, and 20.1% in the United Kingdom (OECD, 2007). In short, compared to their major trading partners, the United States is better positioned to make adjustments in its public pension system (i.e., Social Security).

Even so, the existence of a long-term financing problem has served as a vehicle for those who disagree with the social insurance approach to argue for dramatic change. Persistent claims that Social Security is unfair and unsustainable (Peterson, 1996), a previously soaring stock market, and anxiety about the future of the program has undermined faith in the program, especially among young adults (Altman, 2005).

George W. Bush (b. 1946) seized on these concerns in the 2000 U.S. presidential election and throughout his two terms, proposing that a portion of payroll taxes be diverted to individual accounts, with some hoping that this might be the first step to a fully privatized system. He favored a more "market approach as a 'solution' to Social Security's financing troubles. Individual accounts would not only cure Social Security's bankruptcy blues, they would allow Americans more choice, increase savings, and bigger returns on their retirement investments—all while making the program more equitable for women and minorities" (Herd & Kingson, 2005, p. 188). Those advocating partial privatization did not emphasize how the diversion of payroll taxes into private accounts would actually make the projected shortfall much worse and require huge reductions in benefit guarantees, especially for the young (Diamond & Orszag, 2005).

As it became clear that the traditional Social Security program and its benefits were threatened, strong opposition built up. Ultimately, public education, a stagnant stock market, and concerns about how privatization proposals would grow the federal debt all combined with the declining favorability ratings of the president to, once again, shift the politics of Social Security. By 2007 proposals to partially privatize Social Security were no longer politically viable. Nonetheless, as previously discussed, a real financing problem exists. To address public concern and to provide lead time for the public to adjust to whatever changes need to be made, this financing problem will need to be addressed before too many years pass.

## CONCLUSIONS

In a speech given on June 30, 1961, John F. Kennedy (1917–1963) stated the following about some realities of Social Security: "A Nation's strength lies in the well-being of its people. The social security program plays an important part in providing for families, children, and older persons in time of stress, but it cannot remain static. Changes in our population, in our working habits, and in our standard of living require constant revision" (Social Security Administration, n.d.).

In the early 21st century, Social Security policy discussion reflected deep divisions in the philosophy of the extent to which the individual versus the national community should bear the risk of preparing for their retirement, disability, or survivorship—with the Bush administration seeking to move the program toward a more individualistic, privatized model and the traditional supporters of the social insurance approach successfully fending off this effort.

At some point in the next 20 years, preferably sooner rather than later, attention will turn toward addressing the projected financial shortfall in Social Security. Simultaneously, serious attention also needs to be directed at how to strengthen benefits for today's and tomorrow's young and old, especially those remaining at significant economic risk. Along with many others—some liberal, some conservative, and some moderates (Altman, 2005; Ball, 2006; Diamond & Orszag, 2005; Schulz & Binstock, 2006; Steuerle & Bakija, 1994)—the authors conclude with two broad assertions:

- The financing problem may be addressed in several different ways without radically altering the program's basic commitments and structure. For example, Social Security trust fund investments could be diversified, allowing for a small portion of the trust fund assets to be invested by an independent board in a broad selection of private equities and larger returns from trust fund investments. The ceiling on wages subject to the payroll tax—now only 84% of all earnings—could be restored to cover 90% of earnings, as was the case in 1983 following the last major financing reform. Small increases in payroll taxation (e.g., by 0.25% on employee and employer in 2040) could be scheduled 30 or more years in the future. Retirement ages can be further adjusted or the benefit formula trimmed to reduce benefits for the most well-off. Plainly, there will be no pain-free solutions. What is important to recognize is that there are many ways to put together a financing reform that does not undermine the social insurance approach.
- Consideration should also be given to selective expansions of protection by, for example, reducing the minimum length of marriage from 10 to 7 years to assist divorced spouses to qualify for spousal and survivor benefits (NOW, 2007); adjusting the special minimum benefit formula to improve the adequacy of benefits for low-wage workers who have been in the labor force many years (Reno, 2007); implementing a one-time benefit increase at age 85 to protect the very old, a group still at significant economic risk (Reno, 2007); and restoring student benefits for surviving children, ages 18 to 21 (Reno, 2007).

This entry has emphasized that Social Security is best understood as "a work in progress" whose purpose is to provide widespread basic economic protection against risks to which all Americans are subject in the course of their lives. Life course research and scholarship has much to contribute to the understanding of the benefits, costs, public perceptions, and even politics of Social Security and the implications of change for tomorrow's elders, workers, and children.

**SEE ALSO** Volume 3: *Intergenerational Transfers; Pensions; Policy, Later Life Well-Being; Retirement.*

## BIBLIOGRAPHY


Altman, N. J. (2005). *The battle for social security: From FDR's vision to Bush's gamble*. Hoboken, NJ: Wiley.

American Rhetoric Online Speech Bank. (1935). *Franklin Delano Roosevelt: Speech upon signing the Social Security Act*. Retrieved May 19, 2008, from http://www.americanrhetoric.com/speeches/

Ball, R. M. (2000). *Insuring the essentials: Bob Ball on Social Security*. New York: Century Foundation Press.

Ball, R. M. (2006). Meeting Social Security's long-range shortfall: A golden opportunity for the new Congress. Retrieved May 19, 2008, from www.robertball.org

Berkowitz, E. D. (1991). *America's welfare state: From Roosevelt to Reagan*. Baltimore, MD: Johns Hopkins University Press.

Berkowitz, E. D. (1997). The historical development of Social Security in the United States. In E. R. Kingson & J. H. Schulz (Eds.), *Social Security in the 21st century*. New York: Oxford University Press.

Board of Trustees, Federal Old Age and Survivors Insurance and Disability Insurance Trust Funds. (2007). *2007 annual report of the trustees of the Federal Old Age and Survivors Insurance and Federal Disability Insurance Trust Funds.* Washington, DC: U.S. Government Printing Office. Retrieved May 19, 2008, from http://www.socialsecurity.gov/OACT/

Brown, J. D. (1977). *Essays on Social Security.* Princeton, NJ: Princeton University Press.

Diamond, P. A., & Orszag, P. R. (2005). *Saving Social Security: A balanced approach.* Washington, DC: Brookings Institution Press.

Harrington Meyer, M., & Herd, P. (2008). Is poverty a disappearing problem for older women? *The Huffington Post.* Retrieved May 19, 2008, from http://www.huffingtonpost.com/

He, W., Sengupta, M., Velkoff, V. A., & DeBarros, K. A. (2005). *65+ in the United States: 2005.* Retrieved May 19, 2008, from http://www.census.gov/prod/

Herd, P., & Kingson, E. R. (2005). Selling Social Security reform: A story of framing and reform. In R. B. Hudson (Ed.), *Future of age based public policy.* Baltimore: Johns Hopkins University Press.

Kingson, E. R. (2001). Social Security: Past, present, and future. In M. E. Crahan, L. R. Jacobs, W. A. Joseph, G. Nzongola-Ntalaja, & J. A. Paul (Eds.), *The Oxford companion to the politics of the world.* New York: Oxford University Press.

Kingson, E. R. (in press). Social Security. In *Encyclopedia of social work.* Silver Spring, MD: National Association of Social Workers.

Kingson, E. R., & Berkowitz, E. D. (1993). *Social Security and Medicare: A policy primer.* Westport, CT: Auburn House.

Kingson, E. R., Hirshorn, B. A., & Cornman, J. C. (1986). *Ties that bind: The interdependence of generations.* Cabin John, MD: Seven Locks Press.

Kingson, E. R., & Schulz, J. H. (1997). (Eds.). *Social Security in the 21st century.* New York: Oxford University Press.

Lavery, J., & Reno, V. P. (2008). Children's stake in Social Security. *Social Security Brief, 27.* Retrieved May 19, 2008, from http://www.nasi.org/usr_doc/

National Academy of Social Insurance. (2008). *Social Security: An essential asset and insurance protection for all.* Retrieved May 19, 2008, from http://www.nasi.org/usr_doc/

National Organization for Women Foundation. (2007). *NOW foundation testimony at Congressional briefing on Social Security and women.* Retrieved May 19, 2008, from http://www.nowfoundation.org/issues/

Organisation for Economic Co-operation and Development. (2007). *Selection of OECD social indicators: How does your country compare?* Retrieved May 19, 2008, from http://www.oecd.org/dataoecd/

Peterson, P. G. (1996). *Will America grow up before it grows old? How the coming Social Security crisis threatens you, your family, and your country.* New York: Random House.

Reno, V. P. (2007). Building on Social Security's success. *Economic Policy Institute Briefing Paper, 208.* Retrieved May 19, 2008, from http://www.sharedprosperity.org/bp208/

Reno, V. P., & Lavery, J. (2005). Options to balance Social Security funds over the next 75 years. *Social Security Brief, 18.* Retrieved May 19, 2008, from http://www.nasi.org/usr_doc/

Schulz, J. H., & Binstock, R. H. (2006). *Aging nation: The economics and politics of growing older in America.* Westport, CT: Praeger.

Sherman, A. (2005). Social Security lifts 1 million children above the poverty line. Retrieved May 19, 2008, from http://www.cbpp.org/

Social Security Administration. (2006). *Income of the population 55 or older, 2004.* Retrieved from http://www.ssa.gov/policy/

Social Security Administration. (n.d.). Social Security history: Presidential quotes, John Fitzgerald Kennedy. Retrieved May 19, 2008, from http://www.ssa.gov/history/

Steuerle, C. E., & Bakija, J. M. (1994). *Retooling social security for the 21st century: Right and wrong approaches to reform.* Washington, DC: Urban Institute Press.

U.S. Census Bureau. (2006). *Age and sex of all people, family members, and unrelated individuals iterated by income-to-poverty ratio and race: 2005 below 100 percent of poverty—Black alone.* Retrieved May 19, 2008, from http://pubdb3.census.gov/macro/

White, J. (2001). *False alarm: Why the greatest threat to Social Security and Medicare is the campaign to save them.* Baltimore, MD: Johns Hopkins University Press.

***Eric R. Kingson***
***Jenni Bartholomew***

# SOCIAL SELECTION-CAUSATION DEBATE

The life-course perspective focuses on temporal components of individual biography, investigating how lives unfold over many years. As a consequence, life-course scholars are often interested in how differences arise between social groups, particularly in the later years (Dannefer, 1987; O'Rand & Henretta, 1999). Studies of inequality in later life, however, are often challenged by a methodological and theoretical conundrum: Are differences between groups caused by some intervening event/factor, or do individuals end up in particular social groups because of their preexisting characteristics? This is the essence of the social causation–social selection debate and is central to social scientists' understanding of the temporal dynamics of the life course and the origins of later-life inequality.

## DEFINING SOCIAL CAUSATION AND SOCIAL SELECTION

The temporal orientation of the life-course perspective means that later life must be studied in relation to other periods of the life span, tracing connections across individuals' lives (Settersten, 2006). To study these temporal relations, life-course scholars conceptualize individuals' biographies in terms of transitions and trajectories. *Transitions* represent relatively discrete changes in roles or statuses, for example, starting a new job or getting married; *trajectories* denote sequences of transitions—or long-term patterns of stability and change—in these roles or statuses, such as a work career or marital history. Thus, scholars interested in understanding the origins of inequality have often looked to transitions as differentiating membership between social groups and how these groups differ on some outcome trajectory (e.g., income, health, education, marital stability). There is considerable debate, however, as to whether experiencing a transition and belonging to one social group versus another represents a cause or effect of disparate life experiences.

In the most simplistic sense, individuals who experience a given transition become members of a group, whereas those who do not experience that transition are not members of the group. Thus, if members of these groups differ from one another on some outcome, one might conclude that the transition that defined the groups caused the difference. This is known as *social causation*. Differences between two social groups, however, do not necessarily reflect the effect of group membership, because individuals do not randomly experience transitions or randomly become members of one group versus another. Therefore, some of the identified "consequences" of a given transition and associated group membership may merely represent a continuation of a trajectory that predated the transition and may have in fact contributed to the experience of that transition itself. That is, differences among individuals may put them at different risks of experiencing a transition, of becoming a member of one social group versus another. Thus, individuals may self-select or drift into certain groups. This is known as *social selection*. A prominent example from the research literature helps to illustrate these concepts.

## AN EXAMPLE OF SOCIAL CAUSATION AND SOCIAL SELECTION: MARRIAGE AND HEALTH

A large body of research documents that married individuals have better health in later life than individuals who are not married. Married persons rate their health more favorably, have better objective physical and mental health, and have lower mortality risks than divorced, widowed, or never-married persons (Waite, 1995; Waite & Gallagher, 2000). It may be that something about being married *causes* better health. It also is possible, however, that people in better health are more likely to get and stay married; that is, they are *selected* for marriage and would have had good health whether they were married or not.

Studies that support the social causation perspective theorize that marriage is a social institution that promotes and maintains good health through a number of different mechanisms (Waite, 1995). Marriage provides access to the emotional and social support of a spouse and increases social ties to others. Married people, in some respects, lead more orderly, regimented lives than the unmarried, getting more regular sleep, balanced meals, and physician visits, which promotes their health and well-being (Umberson, 1987). Moreover, marriage curbs negative health behaviors, as the level of alcohol and drug use declines among individuals once they marry. Married persons also have higher incomes and accumulate more wealth than their unmarried peers, which permits the purchase of more and better quality health care, a benefit that is especially important for women and racial/ethnic minorities (Waite & Gallagher, 2000). Thus, because married individuals have access to social support and wealth, and because they engage in behaviors that are health promoting, health differences between the married and nonmarried are *caused* by the former group being married. An important caveat to this discussion is that marriage may be beneficial for health only when the relationship is of high quality (Hawkins & Booth, 2005).

As noted previously, however, healthier individuals may be more likely to experience the transition into marriage in the first place, and differences between the married and nonmarried may represent social selection. Studies supporting this perspective find that personal characteristics increase both the likelihood individuals will marry and that they will have good health. Socioeconomic status is an often-identified selection agent, because more educated persons—who have better health behaviors and greater earnings that permit purchase of high-quality health care—are more likely to get and remain married. Thus, people with characteristics associated with better health are more likely to be *positively selected* into marriage. Similarly, individuals with characteristics associated with poor health are less likely to get and remain married. For example, less educated people are less likely to marry and, if they do marry, are more likely to divorce, in part because financial problems are a leading cause of marital discord. Likewise, individuals with alcohol and drug problems and those prone to conflict or with psychiatric problems are also less likely to get married and, if they do marry, more likely to divorce (Waite, 1995). Less educated individuals and those with fewer socioeconomic resources are also more likely to become widowed because their spouses are more likely to die at younger ages. Individuals with these and other characteristics that undermine health are said to be *negatively selected* for marriage.

Reconciling which side of the social causation–selection debate is supported by the weight of the empirical evidence is complicated by differences in the samples and measurement and analytic techniques across studies. Nevertheless, there appears to be more support for the social causation hypothesis; that is, being married causes good health. Accounting for differences in socioeconomic status generally does not eliminate the greater health and lower mortality of the married, as would be expected if social selection was operating. Although such prior studies are suggestive, it is difficult to assess directly whether people in good health are selected for marriage, because most existing longitudinal data sets do not have measures of health prior to marriage. One exception is a study that used historical data on male undergraduates at Amherst College to test whether men with beneficial health profiles were more likely to marry and how their mortality experiences differed from those who did not marry (Murray, 2000). Men with favorable health profiles at admission to college were more likely to get married, consistent with the selection hypothesis. Even after controlling for health in early adulthood, however, married men had lower risks of mortality than unmarried men—a finding supporting the social causation hypothesis. Thus, although one cannot deny that some social selection is operating (at least for men), being married causes individuals to accrue additional advantages that promote the maintenance of good health and well-being.

## SOCIAL CAUSATION AND SOCIAL SELECTION AS LIFE-COURSE PROCESSES

Although social causation and social selection are often presented as competing hypotheses for the origins of inequality between groups in later life, both hold validity as explanations of later-life inequality. Thus, in some respects, the social selection–social causation debate is frequently a false debate; both social causation and selection processes can be operating—albeit at different points in the life course. Social selection processes often occur early in the life course, when individuals nonrandomly experience transitions that anchor their position in adulthood, whereas social causation processes are predominant in mid- and later life. The temporality of these processes is evident from the example of marriage and health, but prior research has documented a number of other instances, including the relationships between adolescent pregnancy and low socioeconomic status (Hoffman, Foster, & Furstenberg, 1993), premarital cohabitation and the risk of divorce (Lillard, Brien, & Waite, 1995), and religious participation and family relations, health, and delinquency in adolescence (Regnerus & Smith, 2005).

Indeed, the temporal orientation of the life-course perspective is attractive precisely because it permits theoretically different mechanisms to be operating at different points in individuals' lives. For example, concerning the relationship between adolescent pregnancy and low socioeconomic status, prior studies have found that girls from impoverished backgrounds are more likely to become pregnant and give birth as adolescents (*selection*), whereas in midlife these adolescent mothers have slightly lower socioeconomic standing compared to women from similar backgrounds that did not experience an adolescent birth (*causation*; Hoffman et al., 1993).

Although discussion of social causation and selection often concerns differences between two discrete groups, this discussion can be extended to consider how trajectories dynamically interact with one another across the life course. That is, the development of one trajectory may influence the simultaneous development of another. For example, a consistent finding across studies is that individuals in disadvantaged economic circumstances—those with low levels of educational attainment, low incomes, less wealth, and unstable work histories—have worse health outcomes than those in better circumstances (Mulatu & Schooler, 2002; Smith, 1999). The social causation hypothesis is that socioeconomic status influences the development of health over time, because persons with fewer resources are less able to avoid threats to health (e.g., infection, poor working conditions) and have less access to health care services to deal with these threats.

The social selection hypothesis, by contrast, is that persons in poor health are less likely to complete their education and less able to be regularly employed, which limits their ability to earn and accumulate financial resources. Poor health also increases medical expenses and thereby depletes savings. Again, whereas individuals in poor health are selected into lower socioeconomic strata, primarily in early life, prior studies overwhelmingly demonstrate that socioeconomic trajectories also influence health trajectories, especially in mid- and later life (Mulatu & Schooler, 2002).

## RESEARCH CHALLENGES

Although a good deal of progress has been made in examining social causation and selection hypotheses on a variety of topics, several research challenges remain in examining these issues in later life. Perhaps foremost among these challenges is the general absence of longitudinal data spanning the lives of individuals from early childhood into old age across a number of birth cohorts. The absence of such longitudinal data is problematic because many years often precede the measurement of the presumed causal agent, and many years intercede the observation of hypothesized outcomes. Although the discussion of social causation and selection is often a theoretical one, longitudinal data are necessary to disentangle how hypothesized causation and selection processes generate later-life inequalities. Many longitudinal studies, such as the Health and Retirement Study (HRS), are age-bounded, sampling individuals in mid- and later life when selection processes have already left their imprint on individuals' life experiences. Even the most sophisticated statistical techniques cannot compensate for the absence of information earlier in the life course, and studies that pool data across cohorts to simulate trajectories confront additional methodological problems.

The temporal orientation of the life-course perspective highlights the need to move beyond age-specific studies toward more integrated data collection efforts that permit the prospective measurement of individuals' choices and decisions across the life span (Elder, Johnson, & Crosnoe, 2003; Settersten, 2006). Accordingly, as panel studies of younger individuals, such as the National Longitudinal Study of Adolescent Health (Add Health), mature, they will provide additional leverage to understanding how life-course processes generate inequalities among older individuals.

Although such long-view data sets are ideal, the time and financial resources required to collect and store such data for studies of later life are immense, and ongoing data collection efforts, such as Add Health, remain many years from being able to study later-life outcomes directly. As a result, age-specific studies focused on older adults such as the HRS are likely to remain a substantial source of research in the coming decades (Settersten, 2006). It is important to recognize that another type of social selection further challenges social scientists' ability to understand the mechanisms that generate later-life inequalities: *selective mortality* (George, 2005). Simply put, many of the most socially and economically disadvantaged persons in the population do not live long enough to be eligible for inclusion in studies that begin observation in mid- and later life (George,2005).

Thus, analyses of life-course processes are *conditional* on survival to older ages, representing a limited range of experiences, and potentially fail to detect social selection, as well as sequential inequality and divergent causal processes (see, for example, Willson, Shuey, & Elder, 2007). Studies that aim to document the origin of differences between social groups may be limited in their ability to do so because the greater risk of mortality for one group may serve to make the two groups appear more similar over time. Rather than being a solely methodological issue, selective mortality has theoretical implications: Selective mortality introduces an additional life-course process and associated substantive questions that must be examined (George, 2005) because it undermines researchers' ability to test empirically life-course theories and hypotheses concerning social causation and selection.

**SEE ALSO** Volume 2: *Health Differentials/Disparities, Adulthood; Social Class;* Volume 3: *Marriage, Later Life; Mortality; Self-Rated Health.*

**BIBLIOGRAPHY**

Dannefer, D. (1987). Aging as intracohort differentiation: Accentuation, the Matthew effect, and the life course. *Sociological Forum, 2,* 211–236.

Elder, G. H., Jr., Johnson, M. K., & Crosnoe, R. (2003). The emergence and development of life course theory. In J. T. Mortimer & M. J. Shanahan (Eds.), *Handbook of the life course* (pp. 3–19). New York: Kluwer Academic/Plenum Publishers.

George, L. K. (2005). Socioeconomic status and health across the life course: Progress and prospects. *The Journals of Gerontology, Series B: Psychological Sciences and Social Sciences, 60,* S135–S139.

Hawkins, D. N., & Booth, A. (2005). Unhappily ever after: Effects of long-term, low-quality marriages on well-being. *Social Forces, 84*(1), 451–471.

Hoffman, S. D., Foster, E. M., & Furstenberg, F. F., Jr. (1993). Reevaluating the costs of teenage childbearing. *Demography, 30,* 1–13.

Lillard, L. A., Brien, M. J., & Waite, L. J. (1995). Premarital cohabitation and subsequent marital dissolution: A matter of self-selection? *Demography, 32,* 437–457.

Mulatu, M. S., & Schooler, C. (2002). Causal connections between socio-economic status and health: Reciprocal effects and mediating mechanisms. *Journal of Health and Social Behavior, 43,* 22–41.

Murray, J. E. (2000). Marital protection and marital selection: Evidence from a historical-prospective sample of American men. *Demography, 37,* 511–521.

O'Rand, A. M., & Henretta, J. C. (1999). *Age and inequality: Diverse pathways through later life.* Boulder, CO: Westview Press.

Regnerus, M. D., & Smith, C. (2005). Selection effects in studies of religious influence. *Review of Religious Research, 47*(1), 23–50.

Settersten, R. A., Jr. (2006). Aging and the life course. In R. H. Binstock & L. K. George (Eds.), *Handbook of aging and the social sciences* (6th ed., pp. 3–19). Boston: Academic Press.

Smith, J. P. (1999). Healthy bodies and thick wallets: The dual relation between health and economic status. *The Journal of Economic Perspectives, 13*(2), 145–166.

Umberson, D. (1987). Family status and health behaviors: Social control as a dimension of social integration. *Journal of Health and Social Behavior, 28,* 306–319.

Waite, L. J. (1995). Does marriage matter? *Demography, 32,* 483–507.

Waite, L. J., & Gallagher, M. (2000). *The case for marriage: Why married people are happier, healthier, and better off financially.* New York: Doubleday.

Willson, A. E., Shuey, K. M., & Elder, G. H., Jr. (2007). Cumulative advantage processes as mechanisms of inequality in life course health. *American Journal of Sociology, 112,* 1886–1924.

*David F. Warner*

# SOCIAL SUPPORT, LATER LIFE

Social relationships are extremely important for survival and well-being across the life span. Émile Durkheim (1897/1951) made this important observation in his sociological study of suicide, which revealed that social isolation or the lack of social integration was associated with increased suicide risk. Many theorists believe that social relationships are important for survival and health because of the support they provide. Social support is a broad construct that includes different types and qualities of support. In general, social support includes the help and sense of belonging people receive from their social ties (e.g., spouse, children, and coworkers), and it is an important contextual factor that influences health. Social support is particularly central for successful aging as people become more invested in their social networks and rely on them for help. There are several important themes or debates in this area that will be highlighted in this entry: (a) How does one determine when a social relationship or interaction is supportive? (b) Do individuals perceive social relationships and interactions differently, and what accounts for those differences? (c) How and why are social relationships important for health? This entry will first provide a definition and measurement of social support followed by a summary of research on the predictors and implications of social support for health. Finally, new and future areas of research will be outlined.

## DEFINITION AND MEASUREMENT OF SOCIAL SUPPORT

First, in order to understand whether a relationship or interaction is supportive, it is important to know how social relationships and support are defined. The convoy model of social relations, developed by the psychologists Robert L. Kahn and Toni C. Antonucci in 1980, provides a useful framework for understanding social relationships and support across the life span. According to this model, individuals are accompanied by "convoys" of close social partners who provide support as well as irritations across the life span. The term *convoy* is also referred to as a "social network." The convoy or social network usually includes one's spouse, other immediate family (parents, children, siblings), and best friends.

These social convoys are distinguished by structural as well as functional qualities. Structural aspects of the convoy refer to factors such as number of relationships, whereas functional aspects include perceived support and the positive as well as negative qualities of relationships. Personal (e.g., age, gender, race) and situational (e.g., role expectations, resources, demands) factors influence structural and functional aspects of the convoy, which, in turn, affect the individual's health and well-being. Researchers have consistently found that functional aspects of support are more important than structural aspects in affecting well-being. In addition, negative aspects of relationships are more highly associated with well-being than are the positive aspects, perhaps because they occur less often and are consequently more salient.

Thus, whereas social networks refer to the structural aspects of social relationships, social support refers to the content and quality of social relationships. Support is defined as an interaction that involves aid, affect, or affirmation. Aid is defined as informational and instrumental support. Informational support, for example, involves the practical advice and information individuals receive from others. Instrumental support refers to activities such as helping with finances and activities of daily living such as getting groceries and driving. Affect involves emotional support, which includes the love, care, and affection a person receives from others as well as their willingness to listen when the person has troubles. Affirmation refers to a sense of belonging and being accepted by others.

Because support can be interpreted in so many ways, researchers introduced the concept of relationship quality, which is the evaluation of relationships as positive and/or negative. Positive aspects of relationships include feeling loved, cared for, and understood, for example. In contrast, negative aspects of relationships include demands, criticism, unsolicited advice, and the like. In addition, supportive behaviors can at times be interpreted negatively. For example, certain types of support may be interpreted as overprotective or unwanted, and may increase feelings of dependency.

A relatively new area in the social support research that is gaining momentum is the field of ambivalence. While social support literature traditionally examined positive relations to the exclusion of negative or examined positive and negative qualities separately, this area of work recognizes that the same relationship can have both positive and negative qualities. Ambivalence refers to having both positive and negative sentiments about the same relationship. For example, spouses may view one another as extremely supportive but also highly irritating. Researchers have found that ambivalent feelings are normative in close social ties, especially among spouses and in the parent–child relationship.

Another aspect of close social ties gaining increased attention includes social control. Researchers define social control as the indirect and direct ways that close social ties control an individual's health behaviors. For example, relationships may encourage healthful behaviors such as exercise or discourage unhealthful behaviors such as smoking. Indirect social control occurs because relationships involve responsibilities and role obligations that may discourage self-destructive behaviors. Direct social control involves explicit persuasion or sanctions. Social control is considered different from support because although it may lead to improvements in health, it may not be considered supportive. Social control is particularly important to examine in older adulthood because older adults often experience chronic health problems that demand changes in health behaviors.

The measurement of support is particularly complicated because support includes not only several types of interactions but also subjective perception. For example, a gesture that is interpreted by one individual as supportive may be interpreted by another as intrusive. The interpretation of support depends on who is receiving the support, the type of support provided, the context in which the support is given, and who is providing the support. Support can be measured as support actually received or perceived to be available. For example, people may report whether someone drives them to the doctor or they may be asked whether their social ties would help if they needed a ride to the doctor. In addition, support can be measured with surveys and observational methods. Example survey assessments of actual support received inquire about the support received during a stressful experience. Observational studies of support received have coded supportive behaviors during a stressful laboratory experience. In addition to these measures of support actually received, support can also be measured as the perceived availability of support or perceptions of the quality of support. For example, individuals may report the extent to which they experience positive qualities including feeling loved, cared for, and listened to, as well as negative qualities such as feeling criticized and burdened with demands. These types of assessments can also be combined to form a measure of ambivalence.

## TYPES OF SUPPORT RELATIONSHIPS

Older people rely on their relationships with friends and family for social support, but they expect different types of support from different close social partners. For example, individuals often expect both instrumental and emotional support from spouse and family but expect primarily emotional support from friends. Two of the dominant models of support preferences in the literature include Cantor's hierarchical compensatory model (1979) and Weiss's functional specificity model (1974). According to the hierarchical compensatory model, people prefer to receive all types of support from spouses, followed by children and friends. In contrast, the functional specificity model suggests that different relationships serve specific functions irrespective of the type of relationship. Thus one relationship cannot fulfill all functions, and it is important to have diversity in social networks (friends and family). For example, a married woman living with a spouse may feel lonely in the absence of a best friend. Research suggests that daily well-being may be more highly associated with friend relationships than with family relations among the elderly, possibly because of the voluntary nature of friendship compared to the obligatory nature of family support. Topics of conversation among friends may also be more engaging and challenging than those with family.

## VARIATIONS IN SUPPORT BY PERSONAL CHARACTERISTICS

People have different perceptions of support and receive different types of support depending on several personal characteristics including age, gender, race, and socioeconomic status. Older people report more positive and less negative relationships with others than do younger adults. Research suggests that these outcomes may be based on improved emotion regulation and the elimination of problematic relationships. Emotion regulation involves attempts to control either the experience or the expression of emotion. A new line of work in this field suggests that people may also treat older adults more positively because older adults engage in fewer irritating behaviors or because there is less time remaining in the relationship. Indeed, in the laboratory, researchers have found that individuals are less confrontational when interacting with older adults.

Numerous gender-based social support differences have also been found. Women have a larger number of close social network members than do men that are both more positive and more negative than men's. Women tend to feel more burdened than men by the problems of others, perhaps because people are more likely to rely on women for support. Women tend to experience greater daily distress and interpersonal problems than do men. Men also tend to rely on spouses for support, whereas women rely on spouses along with friends and family for support.

Social support also varies by race and socioeconomic status. Researchers have found that African Americans have smaller networks that are composed of more family members than do Whites. These differences in the composition of networks may lead to variations in the support provided and/or received. Research shows that African Americans report less satisfaction in their marital relations and are expected to provide more support to network members. People with lower socioeconomic status (e.g., lower education or income) may experience more stressors that lead to strains in their social ties.

## SOCIAL AND PSYCHOLOGICAL PREDICTORS OF SUPPORT

Research shows that whether a person provides support depends on a variety of psychological and situational factors. Research regarding links between personality and support reveals that individuals who score high on neuroticism scales tend to perceive greater negativity in their relationships. Another important determinant of support provided is the support history of the relationship, which is referred to as the "support bank." People are more likely to provide support if they received it previously, doing so as a means of maintaining reciprocity. Long-term relationships do not demand immediate reciprocity, whereas short-term and/or new relationships require more immediate reciprocity. Individuals usually perceive that they give more than they receive. Friend relationships that are perceived to be inequitable or are nonreciprocal are especially troublesome.

## IMPLICATIONS OF SUPPORT FOR HEALTH

After Durkheim, Engel (1977), a physician, recognized through interacting with patients that it was not only biology that contributed to their health problems but their social context as well. In response, he developed the biopsychosocial model of health, which incorporated the social context as an important determinant of health and disease. During this same period, two influential papers by Cassel (1976) and Cobb (1976) suggested ways that social support may influence health. According to Cassel, support has a direct effect by protecting individuals from disease, whereas Cobb suggested that social support influences health indirectly by reducing the negative effects of stress. Similarly, Cohen and Wills (1985) suggested that social support buffers the influence of stressors on well-being. These papers gave rise to two theoretical perspectives that guide the literature on social support and health: the main effect and buffering theories.

According to the main effect theory, there is a direct association between relationship quality and health, irrespective of one's stress level. Social support may influence health directly by improving health behaviors and increasing self-efficacy, for example. Indeed, research has shown that social support leads to overall better well-being and increased feelings of control.

In contrast, stress buffering theories state that social relations are particularly influential under stressful life circumstances by either preventing stress or reducing negative reactions to it. Researchers have found support for this model in the context of several types of life stressors, including lower levels of education, stressful life events, and chronic illness. For example, the literature indicates that stress has a less detrimental impact on health when people have socially supportive relationships. A variation of the stress buffering theory is referred to as the matching hypothesis, which suggests that support is most helpful if the support type matches with the particular stressor. For example, giving emotional support to someone in financial distress may not be as helpful as loaning him or her money. Next, the links between social support and specific health-related outcomes of physical health, mental health, and cognitive ability are discussed.

**Physical Health** Research shows strong links between social support and physical health. More supportive relations lead to reductions in the biological stress response (e.g., blood pressure, heart rate), whereas negative interactions lead to increases in the biological stress response. In particular, lower positive relations and greater negative relations are associated with increased heart rate, blood pressure, stress hormones (cortisol), functional limitations, and health problems, including lower self-rated health. Theorists suggest that the chronic stress response (e.g., increased cortisol levels) leads to wear and tear on the body and eventually to chronic health problems and death.

Social support is also associated with mortality. Researchers have found that the implications depend on the type of support, whether support is provided or received, and the type of relationship. For example, controlling for initial health status, receiving greater instrumental support is often associated with increased mortality. Researchers suggest that this may be due to the reinforcement of the sick role and the encouragement of dependency. Along these same lines, providing support may be better for health than receiving support. Controlling for health status, married people who provided support had lower mortality rates than those who received support. In addition, feelings of companionship in marriage and supportive relations at work were associated with lower mortality rates among women. At the same time, other researchers have found no association between relationship quality in specific relations (e.g., parent–child, neighbors, friends) and mortality.

Researchers who have examined the buffering effects of social support in the context of illness have found mixed results. Higher quality spousal relationships (high positive, low negative) are associated with increased survival rates among people with congestive heart failure. Some research suggests, however, that support may lead to increased mortality rates among people who have illnesses. It is also important to recognize that social relationships can encourage negative health behaviors such as eating fatty foods, smoking, and drinking. Indeed, researchers have found that obesity is contagious in social networks and that it tends to spread among network members over time, perhaps because of health behaviors or alterations in normative weight expectations. Social networks that encourage unhealthful behaviors may be particularly problematic for older adults because they have been members of their social networks for longer. Thus, they may be even more vulnerable to chronic health conditions not only because of their age but also because of cumulative negative health effects of their network members.

**Mental Health** Social support has important implications for psychological well-being. In general, positive aspects of relationships are associated with greater well-being, whereas negative aspects are associated with lower well-being. The quality of the spousal relationship is more highly associated with well-being than the quality of other family and friend relations from young adulthood to old age. Whereas spouses and family are important for overall well-being, friends often voluntarily provide companionship, increasing feelings of daily well-being.

**Cognitive Ability** Social support may reduce declines in cognitive ability associated with mild cognitive impairment and dementia. Social support may influence cognition by improving positive affect and creating greater complexity. Close social relations may also encourage positive health behaviors and compliance with medical treatment, thus delaying the onset or progress of mild cognitive impairment. Negative aspects of relationships most likely have important implications for cognitive impairment. Research indicates that chronic stress is associated with cognitive impairment. Researchers have also suggested that early family adversity may contribute to cognitive impairment in old age.

**Dual Effects** Research suggests that social control may have the dual effect of increasing distress while simultaneously improving health behaviors and functioning. For example, social control is associated with greater depression but more frequent physical exercise among Japanese elderly. Overall, it is important to note that social relationships, support, and control may have bidirectional and dual effects.

**Implications of Health for Social Support** A person's mental and physical health may influence the social support he or she receives. Not surprisingly, people who are more depressed report increases in negative social relations over time, perceive their interactions more negatively, and elicit more conflict. At the same time, depressed individuals may burden their close relationships with high demands for support. Similarly, people who are physically ill often experience a decrease in support, become less socially active, and cause discomfort among their social partners. Indeed, researchers found that spousal support declined over time among women with breast cancer.

## FUTURE OF THE FIELD

Research innovations in social support research draw on important methodological advances. Researchers are increasingly collecting daily diary accounts of support, which involve either daily phone calls or written surveys, to examine support interactions experienced every day for a period ranging from several days to a month. These allow for interesting examinations of within-person associations regarding the predictors of support (e.g., mood) and the consequences of support for well-being.

Another increasingly popular method is to include multiple reports of support (e.g., both spouses, multiple family members). Studies of multiple family member and dyadic data allow researchers to examine the support given and received from multiple perspectives. Research shows that although people are in the same relationship, they can have very different views of the relationship. For example, parents often report greater investment and closeness to their children than do their children. Likewise, parents report greater irritation with their children than do their children with them. Research on the spousal relationship indicates that support of which the spouse is unaware (invisible support) may be more beneficial for health. Thus, dual report data allows for the examination of reciprocity as well as support received and perceived.

Researchers are also increasingly recognizing the importance of including biological stress markers in their studies of social support. Several of the ongoing national data sets include measures of social support as well as biological indicators of health such as blood pressure, heart rate, and physical assessment of body mass index.

Finally, an exciting area involves the combination of several social support measures into profiles to understand the combinations of supportive or unsupportive others that exist in a single person's social network. For example, a person may have an extremely supportive best friend relationship along with negative spouse and child relationships. These profiles allow for a more comprehensive picture of social networks. Researchers have also begun to use the profile technique to understand how the combination of structural and support aspects of relationships work together to create different social network patterns. For instance, a person may have few network members who are extremely supportive or extremely dense social networks that tend to be negative. Diverse relationship profiles (e.g., married with children and friends) usually are associated with the greatest well-being. Relationships are heterogeneous, and these new methods allow researchers to capture the dynamic nature of social networks.

In sum, social support is a multifaceted construct with great complexity in the types of interactions it refers to, the perceptions of those interactions, and the influence it has on health. Social support varies widely by the characteristics of the person, the relationship, and the particular social context. Social support also has important implications for physical and psychological health. Thus, social support is also particularly important to consider in applied settings for older adults. Including supportive others in efforts to improve health behaviors and health status is essential. It is also important, however, for practitioners to know that relationships vary widely in their supportive qualities. Thus, before considering including relationships in prevention and interventions, researchers should ask older adults which relationships they consider as most supportive. Overall, social support is an ever-growing and dynamic construct that is used widely in many disciplines and is extremely important to include in any study of health and the social context.

SEE ALSO Volume 2: *Durkheim, Émile;* Volume 3: *Family and Household Structure, Later Life; Friendship, Later Life; Loneliness, Later Life; Marriage, Later Life; Sibling Relationships, Later Life; Social Integration/Isolation, Later Life.*

**BIBLIOGRAPHY**


Antonucci, T. C. (2001). Social relations: An examination of social networks, social support, and sense of control. In J. E. Birren & K. W. Schaie (Eds.), *Handbook of the psychology of aging* (5th ed., pp. 427–453). San Diego, CA: Academic Press.

Birditt, K. S., & Antonucci, T. C. (2007). Relationship quality profiles and well-being among married adults. *Journal of Family Psychology, 21*, 595–604.

Birditt, K. S., Fingerman, K. L., & Almeida, D. M. (2005). Age differences in exposure and reactions to interpersonal tensions: A daily diary study. *Psychology and Aging, 20*, 330–340.

Blazer, D. G. (1982). Social support and mortality in an elderly community population. *American Journal of Epidemiology, 115*, 684–694.

Bolger, N., Zuckerman, A., & Kessler, R. C. (2000). Invisible support and adjustment to stress. *Journal of Personality and Social Psychology, 79*, 953–961.

Brown, S. L., Nesse, R. M., Vinokur, A. D., & Smith, D. M. (2003). Providing social support may be more beneficial than receiving it: Results from a prospective study of mortality. *Psychological Science, 14*, 320–327.

Cantor, M. H. (1979). Neighbors and friends: An overlooked resource in the informal support system. *Research on Aging, 1*, 434–463.

Carstensen, L. L., Isaacowitz, D. M., & Charles, S. T. (1999). Taking time seriously: A theory of socioemotional selectivity. *American Psychologist, 54*, 165–181.

Cassel, J. (1976). The contribution of the social environment to host resistance. *American Journal of Epidemiology, 104*, 107–123.

Cobb, S. (1976). Social support as a moderator of life stress. *Psychosomatic Medicine, 38*, 300–314.

Cohen, S., Underwood, L. G., & Gottlieb, B. H. (Eds.). (2000). *Social support measurement and intervention: A guide for health and social scientists.* Oxford, U.K.: Oxford University Press.

Cohen, S., & Wills, T. A. (1985). Stress, social support, and the buffering hypothesis. *Psychological Bulletin, 98*, 310–357.

Connidis, I. A., & McMullin, J. A. (2002). Ambivalence, family ties, and doing sociology. *Journal of Marriage and Family, 64*, 594–601.

Coyne, J. C., Rohrbaugh, M. J., Shoham, V., Sonnega, J. S., Nicklas, J. M., & Cranford, J. A. (2001). Prognostic importance of marital quality for survival of congestive heart failure. *The American Journal of Cardiology, 88*, 526–529.

Cutrona, C. E. (1996). *Social support in couples: Marriage as a resource in times of stress.* Thousand Oaks, CA: Sage Publications.

Durkheim, É. (1951). *Suicide: A study in sociology* (J. A. Spaulding & G. Simpson, Trans.). Glencoe, IL: Free Press. (Originally work published 1897.)

Engel, G. L. (1977, April 8). The need for a new medical model: A challenge for biomedicine. *Science, 196*, 129–136.

Kahn, R. L., & Antonucci, T. C. (1980). Convoys over the life course: Attachment, roles, and social support. In B. P. Baltes & O. G. Brim (Eds.), *Life-span development and behavior* (Vol. 3, pp. 253–286). New York: Academic Press.

Robles, T. F., & Kiecolt-Glaser, J. K. (2003). The physiology of marriage: Pathways to health. *Physiology and Behavior, 79*, 409–416.

Rook, K. S., & Ituarte, P. H. G. (1999). Social control, social support, and companionship in older adults' family relationships and friendships. *Personal Relationships, 6*, 199–211.

Simons, R. L. (1983–1984). Specificity and substitution in the social networks of the elderly. *International Journal of Aging and Human Development, 18*, 121–139.

Uchino, B. N. (2004). *Social support and physical health: Understanding the health consequences of relationships.* New Haven, CT: Yale University Press.

Walen, H. R., & Lachman, M. E. (2000). Social support and strain from partner, family, and friends: Costs and benefits for men and women in adulthood. *Journal of Social and Personal Relationships, 17*, 5–30.

Weiss, R. S. (1974). *Loneliness: The experience of emotional and social isolation.* Cambridge, MA: MIT Press.


***Kira S. Birditt***

## SPOUSAL CAREGIVING

SEE Volume 3: *Caregiving; Family and Household Structure, Later Life.*

## STRESS IN LATER LIFE

This entry focuses on patterns of late life exposure to stressors and the effects of such stressors on older adults. Stressors may be specific, discrete life events or enduring life situations that tax the adaptive capacities of the individual. These events or situations generally refer to negative or unwelcome environmental demands or stimuli. Selye's (1956) classic conceptualization of stress refers to a state of physiological arousal that follows when environmental demands exceed the individual's response capacities. Stress and its consequences in the context of the widely studied stress paradigm are considered (Pearlin, Menaghan, Lieberman, & Mullan, 1981). Internal resources (such as coping styles) and external resources (such as social support) as well as proactive behaviors may ameliorate the adverse psychological effects of stress exposure (Kahana & Kahana, 2003a). Attention to the life course paradigm can enhance an understanding of ways that older adults respond to and cope with stressful life situations in late life. Findings from empirical studies are discussed, focusing on both conceptual and methodological challenges and advances characterizing the field of stress research. Longitudinal studies have been conducted by Eva Kahana, Boaz Kahana, and colleagues on stress, coping, and health in late life (Kahana & Kahana, 2003b).

Prior work called attention to both vulnerability and resilience of older adults who endured extreme trauma, such as the Holocaust, earlier in their life course (Kahana, Harel & Kahana, 2005) and examined responses of older adults to challenges of life threatening illness (Deimling, Kahana, Bowman & Schaefer, 2002; Kahana, Deimling, Sterns & Kahana, in press). In examining life course perspectives on stress, the focus is on stress exposure and the consequences of such exposure, including diminished psychological well-being, social functioning, physical health, and quality of life. Subsequently, buffers (or protective factors) of the stress model are considered, including coping resources, coping strategies, and proactive behavioral adaptations. To illustrate the discussion both U.S.-based and international research are cited.

## MULTIDISCIPLINARY APPROACH TO STRESS RESEARCH

Stress exposure and its impact on elderly individuals can best be understood using a multidisciplinary lens. Sociologists have contributed to stress research by recognizing the role of broad social forces and arrangements in shaping stress exposure. Social and political arrangements that differ across societies and nations also shape potential stressors, such as retirement.

An understanding of stress research in late life also benefits from social psychological orientations that consider the role of "meaning making" in determining how the self responds to stressful life circumstances (McLeod & Lively, 2007). Social psychologists often use the symbolic interactionist perspective as a framework for studying the interaction between individual selves and the social environment and interpret stress effects as a function of these interactions. These interactions have been referred to as "symbolic interactionism" (Blumer, 1969). A guiding assumption in this framework is that individuals can and do play active roles in anticipating and responding to stressful life situations (Thoits, 2006). Active responses may include cognitive maneuvers such as reinterpreting the stressful situation and behavioral adaptations such as marshaling social support (Kahana & Kahana, 2003b). This focus on planfulness and agency that individuals exercise, in spite of situational constraints, is a key tenet of the life course perspective.

Interdisciplinary explorations of the stress process would be incomplete without acknowledging biological influences (Selye, 1956). Stress affects nearly every organ within the human body. The biological system operates to maintain survival during stressful situations, but also opens avenues for disease and disabilities. Stress affects physiological processes and has been implicated in lowering serotonin levels, thereby increasing the likelihood of psychological depression. Stress also reduces the body's immune system, making the individual more susceptible to viruses, infections, and also to chronic diseases (Kiecolt-Glaser & Glaser, 1991). Such biological stress outcomes, in turn, affect individual behaviors that have additional consequences for health.

## STRESS EXPOSURE IN LATE LIFE

Older adults experience acute (one time) stressful life events and chronic (ongoing) stressors that are unique to their life stage (Kahana & Kahana, 2003b). Minor but prevalent stressors of daily living, referred to as "hassles" in the stress literature, will not be extensively discussed here as they are generally not problematic in the lives of older adults. The incidence and prevalence of acute stressors is not greater in old age than during young adulthood or midlife (Pearlin, Mullan, Semple & Skaff, 1990). However, stressors that affect identity or social networks are more common in old age as compared to earlier life course stages. Exposure to chronic illness, attendant physical impairment, and functional limitations increase for most elderly persons, resulting in a highly stressful downward spiral referred to as the disability cascade (Verbrugge & Jette, 1994). The disability cascade may result in adverse psychological consequences, such as an increase in depressive symptoms. Elderly individuals who encounter health-related stressors may also identify themselves as disabled (Kelley-Moore, Schumacher, Kahana & Kahana, 2006).

In addition to illness-related stressors, social losses are also normal stressors of later life (Kahana & Kahana, 1996, 2003b). With older age there is an increased likelihood of becoming widowed and of experiencing the death of age peers among both family and friends. These losses create broken attachments, and society may devalue older adults, who have a diminished social network (Pearlin & Mullan, 1992). Stress exposure also poses problems because, unmitigated, it is likely to have adverse effects on quality of life outcomes (George, 2005). Nevertheless, subjective well being and life satisfaction have been found to be stable over the life course and do not decline in old age (Fujita & Diener, 2005). In the early literature on stress and coping (Holmes & Rahe, 1967), both positive (e.g., vacations, birthdays) and negative (e.g., divorce, death) life events were considered potential stressors, based on the life changes they each entail. However, there is far more evidence about adverse consequences of negative rather than positive events and, furthermore, older adults tend to be exposed to more negative than positive life events. For example, marriage, the birth of a child, and a new job are normative positive life events for young adults, but are much less likely to occur in old age. Older people are more likely to be confronted by "exit" events, representing losses, than younger people, who are more likely to experience "entrance" events that may be viewed as challenges.

In considering stressors of late life in the context of increasing life expectancy and an aging society, it is important to recognize that the traditionally defined period of old age in the United States, starting with eligibility for Social Security (at age 65 in 2008), encompasses almost 20 years for those attaining average life expectancy and possibly 30 or more years for long-lived elderly. Stressors experienced by the young-old (65–74), the old-old (75–84) and the oldest-old (85+) may differ, based on work, family life cycles, and exposure to illness and disability.

## RECENT AND CUMULATIVE LIFE EVENTS

Research on stress exposure in late life, following traditions of general stress research, has been based on diverse definitions, which may yield different portrayals of the degree and type of stress experienced by elderly persons. The classic approach to empirical stress research relied on a count of negative recent life events weighted by the amount of life change attributed to each event by judges or by the respondent (e.g., Holmes & Rahe, 1967). In more recent research, a list of events is typically presented to respondents and the number of life events. In 1976 Kiyak, Liang, and Kahana designed the Geriatric Scale of Life Events to ensure that events were age appropriate. If stress exposure is measured as the number of events one experiences, old age does not necessarily yield a larger number of recent life events than do earlier periods in the life course (Wheaton, 1990). In fact, research on the epidemiology of stress reveals that the percentage of persons with one or more life events during the past year is inversely related to age in the general population; that is, older people experience fewer life events than younger persons (Goldberg & Comstock, 1980). This may be readily linked to the placement of older adults in the life course where subsequent to retirement, they fill fewer social roles related to work, and even to family, after adult children leave the home.

When conceptualizing stress exposure in terms of discrete life events, it is important to recognize that stressful life events have cumulative effects and extend across the life course. According to this view of life stress, older adults, by definition, will have accumulated more events than persons of younger ages. The study of cumulative life stress represents an important, but relatively underutilized, approach to understanding stress in late life. In this tradition significant life crises are measured across the life course and may be combined with chronic stressors and recent life events. Indeed, chronic stressors and cumulative life events have been found to have a major impact on quality of late life (Turner, Wheaton, & Lloyd, 1995).

Stress exposure, as measured by recent life events, has been associated with negative physical health and mental health consequences (Dohrenwend, 1998). Stress exposure poses special challenges to the old-old because of their greater vulnerability and more limited coping resources or social supports. While adverse psychosocial effects of stress have been extensively studied, there is an absence of longitudinal data on the changing patterns of stress exposure posed by negative life events over time. Prior research (Turner, Wheaton, & Lloyd, 1995) has demonstrated that cumulative stressors are better predictors of adverse outcomes than are single stressors. The cumulative approach to the study of life events benefits from its comprehensiveness. However, this approach has also been critiqued for not allowing sufficient consideration of contextual influences and coping efforts in dealing with specific life events (George, 2005). The following discussion addresses the impact of exposure to chronic stressors and singular normative life events in late life.

## CHRONIC STRESSORS

Stress researchers now recognize that chronic or enduring stressors exert a significant effect on well being and thus comprise an important aspect of stress exposure. In fact, chronic stressors are stronger predictors of adverse health outcomes than acute stressors (McGonagle & Kessler, 1990). Many of these chronic stressors, such as poverty, are more clearly anchored in the social position of the individual than they are related to age (Wheaton, 1994). Structural influences shape individuals' social positions and, over time, can lead to cumulative disadvantage (Dannefer, 2003). Chronic stressors can also include "non-events" or the absence or unavailability of desired events, such as an unfulfilled desire to become a grandparent. In the case of the elderly, social losses, including widowhood or death of elderly friends and relatives, may result in social isolation, which constitutes a stressful experience, based on absence of desired and gratifying social contacts.

Older adults experience less exposure to some forms of chronic stress than do younger persons. Older adults are less likely to report interpersonal tension (a form of chronic stress) and are less likely to argue with family members (Birditt, Fingerman, & Almedia, 2005). This may indicate both better social skills and better emotion regulation in later life. Alternatively this finding could reflect reduced involvement in social roles in late life. Furthermore, it has been suggested that, when elders do encounter chronic stressors, their appraisal process—or how they perceive and interpret a particular event—produces heightened reactivity, resulting in a greater negative reaction (Mroczek & Almeida, 2004).

Some major stressors deserve special attention because they bring about extensive and often enduring changes in the life of older adults. These stressors have been investigated as unique events rather than simply as components of cumulative stress exposure. Four such stressors include retirement, caregiving, widowhood, and trauma due to natural or manmade disasters.

**Retirement** One of the emblematic age-related changes that is a normal stressor of later life is the relinquishing of work roles. Retirement has been studied extensively by gerontological researchers and presents an excellent case to illustrate variation in response to potential late life stressors. If work roles are valued and retirement is involuntary and even unanticipated, it poses a major disruption in lifestyle, valued activities, and relationships of an older person. Based on legal protections against age discrimination in employment, involuntary or forced retirement is no longer the norm in the United States (Marshall & Taylor, 2005). However, in many other countries, including Japan and Western European counties such as the Netherlands, involuntary retirement remains the norm, which may reflect ageism and pose stressful life situations for the elderly.

For older persons who have been engaged in routine, physically demanding, or even demeaning work roles, and who do not value their work roles, retirement may be a welcome and positively anticipated transition (Wheaton, 1990). Retirement for these elderly, who typically are of lower socioeconomic status, represents freedom from chronic stressors of a demanding and unrewarding work life, and they are pleased to adopt new leisure-oriented social roles. In a longitudinal study of urban elders and retirees to the Sunbelt states of the southern United States, retirement was rarely mentioned as a major stressor experienced in the past (Kahana et al., 1999).

When individuals experience early, involuntary retirement that does not fit into their expected life course trajectory, they may appraise it as a chronic stressor. If retirement fits into the individual's chosen life trajectory, high levels of retirement satisfaction are reported, even if life after retirement does not match anticipated experiences (Fitzpatrick, Vinick & Bushfield, 2005).

In a longitudinal study of retiring civil servants in London, Mein and colleagues (2003) found that retirement did not have any adverse effects on physical or mental health. Rather, those who continued to work after age 60 experienced deteriorated mental health. Analysis of European data from the SHARE (Survey of Health, Ageing, and Retirement in Europe) project shows that many workers seek retirement to escape from unfavorable jobs (Siegrist et al., 2007).

**Caregiving** Normative stressors of advanced old age include caregiving to an ill spouse, sibling, or adult child. An extensive literature documents the burdens of caregiving particularly for caregivers of those suffering from dementia and Alzheimer's disease (Kiecolt-Glaser, Dura, Speicher, Trask, & Glaser, 1991). Characteristics of the patient (e.g., disruptive behavior), the context of caregiving (at home or in a long-term care facility), and resources of the caregiver (e.g., social supports) influence both the appraisals of caregiving and the consequences of caregiving stress (Pearlin et al., 1990). In addition to stressors posed by caregiving, older adults must also deal with competing role demands on the one hand and with psychological strains such as low self-esteem on the other. Gerontological research has focused extensively on the special burdens of elderly spouses who are coping with their own frailty, even as they provide care to their spouse.

Effective coping strategies can diminish the stressful effects of caregiving, such as physical health problems and poor mental health. Gerontological literature has also noted stresses experienced by grandparents who are raising grandchildren. Frequently, such grandparents are racial or ethnic minorities who face additional stressors posed by economic or neighborhood-related hardships (Nicholson Grinstead et al., 2003).

Cultural factors also influence both caregiver stress and the process of coping with stress. For example, Latino caregivers encounter greater stress exposure due to the earlier onset of disabilities among Latino elders (Aranda & Knight, 1997). Research comparing caregivers in the United States with those in other countries, such as Japan, has revealed both commonalities and differences in stressors of caregiving and coping responses to such stressors (Wallhagen & Yamamoto-Mitani, 2006). Comparative research suggests that American caregivers need more anticipatory socialization (or preparation for their new role as caregiver), whereas Japanese caregivers encounter greater difficulty in accepting services provided by others. Obligations for caregiving in the home are generally strong in Japan, and are traditionally the responsibility of the wife of the eldest son. With the growing aged population of Japan, traditional patterns of caregiving are shifting, and institutions are increasingly being utilized for services to frail elders. These social changes pose special stressors by creating ambiguity in role expectations.

**Widowhood** Widowhood is a normative stressor of late life, particularly for women. About one half of women ages 65 and older are widows, but only about 15% of men of similar ages are widowers. Widowhood has wide ranging reverberations for stress exposure in late life. Bereavement and loss of a life partner are generally viewed as extremely stressful experiences. Studies have consistently demonstrated adverse effects of widowhood on mental health and psychological well-being (Wilcox et al., 2003). However, after the initial period of adverse reaction, most bereaved spouses return to their baseline levels of psychological well being.

In addition, widowhood often results in further social losses, as friends and family may distance themselves from the widowed individual. For women, widowhood also entails exposure to financial stressors, as survivors' benefits are typically only a fraction (about one-half) of the husband's pension (Smith & Zick, 1996). In terms of coping with widowhood, widows often employ role substitution, where they engage in higher levels of informal social participation than their non-widowed counterparts (Utz, Carr, Nesse, & Wortman, 2002). For some men and women, the experience of widowhood also depends on their ability to marshal assistance from adult children.

Van Den Brink et al. (2004), in their longitudinal analysis on the effects of widowhood on elderly men in three European countries (Finland, the Netherlands, and Italy), found that men who were widowed within the past five years experienced more difficulties in independent activities of daily living (ADL) than those widowed for longer periods of time. The Swedish Panel Study of Living Conditions of the Oldest Old found that engagement in leisure activities served as a buffer that diminished the psychological and physiological impacts of widowhood (Silverstein & Parker, 2002).

**Traumatic Stress** The study of exposure to overwhelming traumatic events such as natural disasters, war, and interpersonal violence has developed into a specialized field of scientific inquiry. Such traumatic events represent extreme forms of stress exposure for all ages and result in physical morbidity illness, post-traumatic stress disorder (PTSD), and other mental health problems (Van der Kolk, McFarlane, & Weisaeth, 2007).

Researchers differentiate between the impact of traumatic stress occurring in old age and the long-term consequences of enduring traumatic experiences earlier in life. Natural disasters have a pronounced, immediate effect on physical health and psychological well being of aged survivors.

Many international research studies center on traumatic stress, focusing on the impact of manmade as well as natural disasters on the elderly. Chung et al. (2004) studied the results of experiencing an aircraft crash or train accident. The impact of these traumatic events on elderly groups did not vary from that of the younger population. Their findings are similar to earlier studies of natural disasters such as floods, earthquakes, and volcanoes. In a comparative study of post-traumatic stress as a result of the 1988 earthquake in Armenia, the proximity of the individual to the epicenter of the quake was a stronger predictor of stress level than the victim's age (Goenjian et al., 1994).

Turning to the study of human disasters, wartime combat often diminishes well-being in later life. Young adults who were prisoners of war may experience post-traumatic symptoms throughout the remainder of their life course (Chung et al., 2004). Studies conducted by Israeli researchers show that stress from earlier trauma in young adulthood, such as the Holocaust, may recur if the individual encounters war-related stressors in later life (Solomon & Prager, 1992). Research comparing elderly survivors of the Holocaust with immigrants to the United States and to Israel revealed different typologies of trauma survivorship, ranging from the "resilient" to the "vulnerable" survivor (Kahana, Harel, & Kahana, 2005). Those survivors who report being socially integrated are most likely to exhibit resilience. Whereas international literature focused extensively on war and natural disasters, researchers in the United States have documented adverse effects of individual stress exposure, in situations where older adults are victims of abuse or crime (McCabe & Gregory, 1998).

## COPING WITH STRESS IN LATER LIFE

Understanding how the adverse affects of stress exposure on quality of life may be ameliorated is an important part of the study of the stress process. External and internal coping resources that facilitate effective coping are reviewed in this section, followed by a discussion of general coping strategies and specific proactive behaviors.

**Coping Resources** Social supports and economic resources are among the most widely studied external resources available to older adults (Kahana & Kahana, 2003b; Thoits, 1995). Self-efficacy (or effectiveness), mastery, and optimism are valuable internal psychological resources for coping. Each of these resources will be discussed below.

***Social Supports.*** The effectiveness of coping strategies used by individuals in stressful life situations is strongly influenced by the social and environmental resources they possess. Social supports can encourage and reassure individuals as they confront stressful life situations. Social support includes the availability and receipt of instrumental, emotional, and/or informational support. Research indicates that perceived support, or one's belief in the availability of support, serves as a stronger stress buffer than does the actual receipt of support (Wethington & Kessler, 1986). For older adults, receiving instrumental support can be threatening, because it underscores their neediness and vulnerability, potentially resulting in lower self esteem.

Having a confidante or a close human relationship has been found to be a consistent buffer of stress (Cohen & Wills, 1985). In old age, bereavement, and particularly widowhood, may be a major stressor as well as a major loss of significant social support (Lopata, 1995). One of the important ambiguities in the stress and coping literature is that the same phenomena may be alternatively viewed as stressors or as buffers in the stress paradigm (Kahana, 1992). The mechanisms whereby social support serves as a coping resource are not yet well understood. Potential pathways include social supports that enhance effective coping, mastery, and self esteem or encourage engagement in healthy lifestyle behaviors (Thoits, 1995). In very old age, increasing levels of stress exposure and a decline in personal coping resources may be counterbalanced by availability of social resources and supports (Martin, Grunendahl, & Martin, 2001).

***Self-efficacy or Mastery.*** *Self-efficacy* represents an important internal coping resource, as it relates to individuals' appraisals of their own effectiveness in dealing with stressors through productive coping behaviors (Bandura, 1986). Limited social resources have been associated with reduced self efficacy, but these associations diminish in late life (Gecas, 1989). Self efficacy, which some also refer to as *mastery* (Bandura, 1986), represents an important, situation-specific coping resource, as it results in positive outcome expectations and can thus facilitate instrumental, problem-focused coping in late life. This is particularly important because older adults experience many uncontrollable events; yet, to cope effectively with stressful situations, they must maintain a belief that they can cope well with problems at hand. Mastery, or self efficacy, can mediate both earlier and later life economic hardships that affect elders' later physical and mental health (Pudrovska et al., 2005).

***Optimism.*** Optimism also serves as an important coping resource in late life. This characteristic shares, in common with self efficacy, an underlying propensity for positive outcome expectations. Persons with optimistic life orientations experience better outcomes after confronting stressful illness situations, ranging from breast cancer to coronary bypass surgery (Scheier & Carver, 1985). These findings have also been confirmed in international research such as the Zutphen Elderly Study (Giltay et al., 2006). In a longitudinal follow up of 887 men in the Netherlands, this study found optimism to be relatively stable over time and a significant predictor of reduced mortality from cardiovascular illness. The value of optimistic dispositions has been studied primarily in the context of stressful life situations. Optimism is a better predictor of subsequent physical and mental health among older individuals facing stressors, such as caregiving demands, than it is among their less stressed counterparts (Robinson-Whelen et al., 1997). Personality characteristics such as extroversion and openness to experiences are also coping resources and can result in positive reappraisals of life experiences and stressors, leading to more effective coping efforts (Costa, 1996). While there is an implied link between coping resources and coping strategies, the mechanism by which these coping resources ameliorate adverse effects of stress are not well understood.

**Coping Strategies** Direct coping efforts in stressful life situations have been categorized along multiple dimensions. To capture the complexity of coping responses, Skodol (1998) identifies six coping categories that crosscut much of the literature: (a) planful problem solving, (b) support seeking, (c) focusing on the positive, (d) distraction or distancing, (e) wishful thinking or escape, and (f) acceptance. The most widely accepted categories of coping strategies are active (or problem-focused) coping efforts and emotion-focused efforts (Lazarus & Folkman, 1984). Active coping efforts are most useful when individuals face stressors that are controllable, such as difficulties with coworkers. In contrast, emotion-focused efforts, and cognitive reappraisals, may be most effective when confronting stressors that cannot be readily controlled, such as the death of a spouse (Lent, 2007).

Research on age differences in the use of coping strategies is limited. Some studies suggest that older adults are more likely to use emotion-focused "palliative" coping than are their younger counterparts (Folkman, Lazarus, Pimley, & Novacek, 1987). In regard to gender differences, men exhibited more problem-focused than emotion-focused coping (Folkman & Lazarus, 1980). The type of problem being addressed was a key determinant of coping strategies selected, with stressful work situations eliciting more problem-focused coping and health challenges eliciting more emotion-focused coping. Work by Folkman and Lazarus (1980) also underscored the important role played by appraisals in shaping coping efforts. Appraisal or evaluation of stressors, based on perception of the degree of threat they pose, serves as a key determinant of types of coping strategies invoked to respond to the stressor (Folkman & Lazarus, 1980).

Traditional ideas of coping based on the work of Folkman and Lazarus focus on appraisals of the problem, followed by consideration of (a) problem-focused or task-oriented coping, (b) emotion-focused coping aimed at managing emotional distress, and (c) avoidance coping, wherein individuals employ various strategies to escape or focus away from the problem situation. These traditional categorizations offer a shared lens for classifying coping, but they also suffer from some conceptual ambiguities. For example, they do not fully separate appraisal from coping, they do not distinguish the goals of coping from the methods of coping, and they do not address the propensity of individuals to engage in multiple coping efforts, either concurrently or sequentially. Because many studies have applied Folkman and Lazarus's 1980 formulations, a review of their findings as well as alternative conceptualizations of coping in late life follow.

Studies of coping with chronic illness in late life have been reviewed by Poon, Basford, Dowzer, and Booth (2003). Problem-focused strategies have been generally judged as more effective than emotion-focused or avoidant coping strategies, even when dealing with chronic illness. However, some studies offer evidence of benefits of emotion-focused or avoidance-oriented coping, particularly when dealing with uncontrollable events such as life-threatening illness.

The most widely used assessment tool for categorizing coping responses has been the "Ways of Coping Checklist" developed by Folkman and Lazarus (1985). This instrument includes 66 items, referring to thoughts or actions that an individual uses to deal with a self-selected problem situation that occurred in the past month. Based on factor analyses, problem-focused and emotion-focused coping subscales have been identified.

**Proactive Adaptations and Resilience** Approaches to conceptualization and assessment of coping strategies have yielded inconsistent results in predicting quality of life outcomes in response to stress exposure (George, 2005). Such results may be due to the over-inclusiveness of using problem-focused versus emotion-focused categorizations. Knowing that a person did something instrumental about a problem may be insufficient without specifying what adaptations or behaviors were used. Accordingly, in dealing with an illness diagnosis, a patient may seek health information, engage in health promotion, seek a second opinion, marshal social support from family, or focus on family or work roles to compensate for future inability to fulfill such roles. Classifying these different modes of behavior only as problem-focused coping does not allow for sufficient discrimination between alternative behavioral strategies. It also fails to link the literature on coping with stress to the extensive parallel literature on health promotion, prevention, and self care (Ory & Defriese, 1998).

To address this limitation, the model of Preventive and Corrective Proactivity (PCP) was proposed to explore the broad array of behavioral adaptations older adults use in dealing with normative stressors of aging (Kahana & Kahana, 1996, 2003a; Kahana, Kahana & Kercher, 2003). Most of the literature on coping with stress has been based on assessments of self-reported propensity toward active or passive coping, emotional or cognitive coping, or approach versus avoidance coping (Aldwin, 2000).

The PCP model (Figure 1) considers specific proactive behavioral responses to stressful life situations faced in late life, including chronic illness, social losses, and person-environment incongruence (Component A) (Kahana & Kahana, 1996, 2003a). Preventive behaviors such as health promotion, planning ahead, and helping others (Component C1), contribute to the development of external social resources (Component C). such adaptations may delay the onset of some stressors, such as ill health or disability. Furthermore, corrective adaptations, such as marshaling support, role substitution, and environmental modifications (Component C2), may counteract adverse effects of stressors on quality of life outcomes (Component E). Proactive behavioral adaptations thus add to the benefits that older adults derive from internal resources such as hopefulness and self esteem (Component B). Longitudinal studies of successful aging provide support for the proposed model. They demonstrate the benefits of exercising, planning, and marshaling support in ameliorating the impact of stressors on quality of life outcomes (Kahana et al., 2002; Kahana, Kahana, & Kelley-Moore, 2005).

The positive psychology movement (Seligman, Steen, Park & Peterson, 2005) called attention to the importance of resilience and adaptive capacities of persons, even in the face of great adversity. This movement focuses on the need and capacity for restoring emotional well-being rather than simply diminishing symptoms of distress. Empirical research shows that posttraumatic growth, transformation, and transcendence often emerge after experiencing

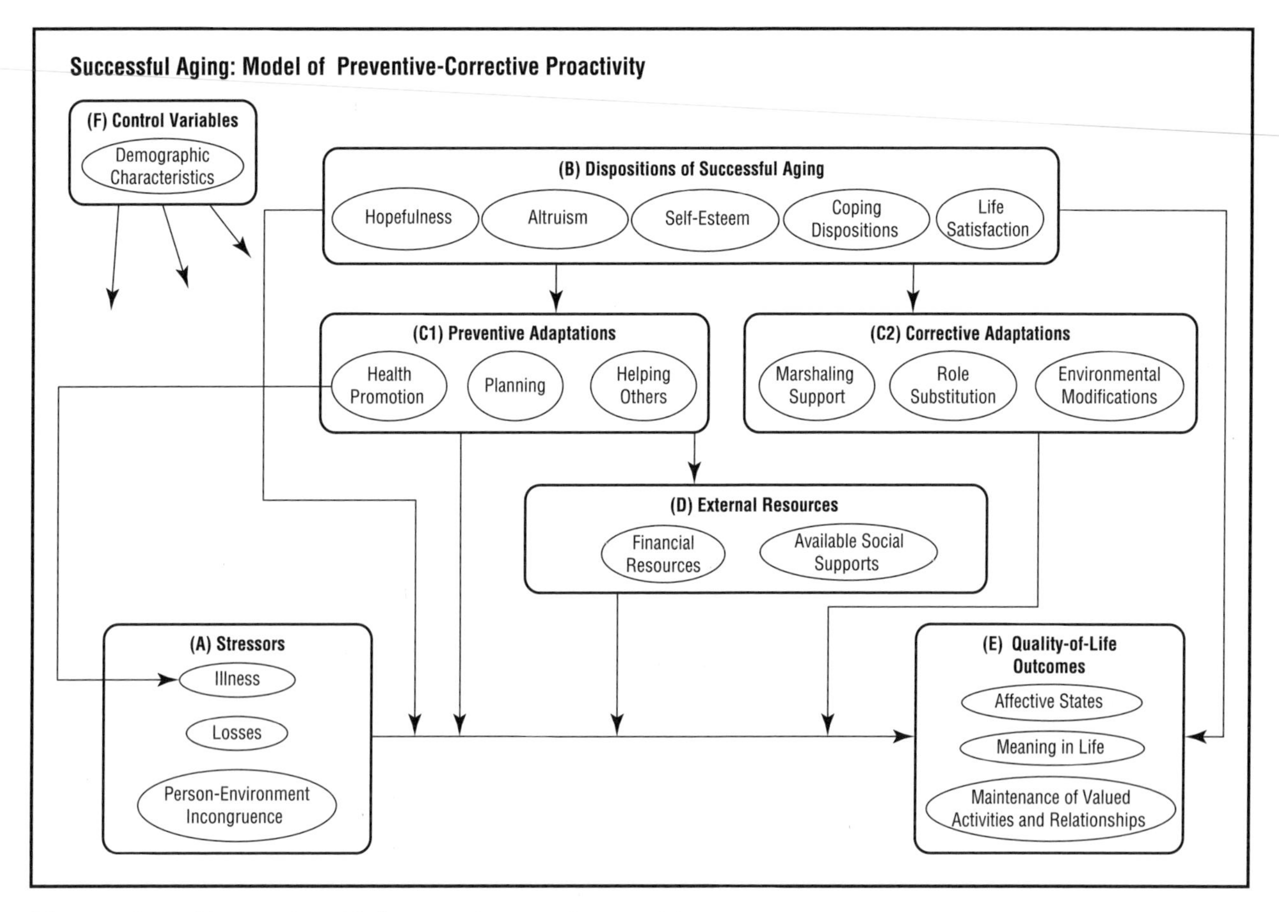


***Figure 1.*** *Successful aging. A model of preventative–corrective proactivity.* CENGAGE LEARNING, GALE.

stressors, such as life threatening illness (Calhoun & Tedeschi, 2006). In evaluating potential strengths of older people and their resilience in dealing with stress exposure, *wisdom* is a unique coping resource that may contribute to life satisfaction in late life, even for older adults encountering major stressors (Ardelt, 1997).

## MECHANISMS LINKING STRESS EXPOSURE AND PSYCHOSOCIAL OUTCOMES

In considering late life responses to stress, certain potential mechanisms may be responsible for adverse psychological and social outcomes. One possible explanation of negative quality of life is older adults' increased exposure to certain stressors. They are more likely to experience both chronic illness and social losses than their younger counterparts. Kahana and Kahana (2003b) refer to these prevalent stressors of late life as normative stressors of aging. In addition to more normative stressors, older adults may be at risk for negative outcomes, based on diminished resources or greater vulnerability.

Researchers have debated whether greater stress exposure leads to greater vulnerability and plays a major role in explaining adverse outcomes in late life. Some researchers argue for the importance of comprehensive and sophisticated measures of stress exposure that transcend the traditional focus on stressful life events (Turner, Wheaton, & Lloyd, 1995). It has also been argued that greater vulnerability of the aged to stressful life events is influenced by the greater severity and lack of controllability of events that they experience. Serious illness, caregiving, and widowhood exemplify such stressors.

An important challenge in understanding the extensive research on consequences of stress in later life relates to placing physical health alternatively as a stressor or as an outcome of stress exposure. Because physical health problems are normative late life stressors, they are often studied as sources of stress exposure, with mental health outcomes as a result of stress (Poon et al., 2003). However, stressful life events, and particularly traumatic stressors, also are likely to have an impact on physical health (Thoits, 1995).

## SOCIAL AND DEMOGRAPHIC INFLUENCES ON COPING WITH STRESS AND STRESS OUTCOMES IN LATE LIFE

Risk factors for stress exposure are not shared equally among all elderly. Women, elderly minorities, the unmarried, and individuals of lower socioeconomic status (SES) experience higher rates of stress exposure that accumulate throughout the life course, leading to more intense inequality in late life (Thoits, 1995). Poon et al. (2003) analyzed the role of demographic influences on coping with chronic disease and found that three overarching sociodemographic factors affect coping and management of health conditions: education, gender, and personality.

Low educational levels are associated with higher rates of stress exposure and poorer coping strategies. Higher levels of education may facilitate instrumental problem-focused coping among older adults facing health problems (DeKlerk et al., 1997). Individuals possessing higher education are more likely to utilize positive coping strategies that include health management, medication compliance, and mastery of assistive techniques when dealing with stressful health situations. Education was negatively related to resigned helplessness in coping (Krogh et al., 1992). Those with lesser education tend to misunderstand treatment strategies and have more restrictive communication with health care professionals, thus exacerbating their health problems and leading to further health inequalities (Poon et al., 2003).

Individuals of low SES often live in poor neighborhoods that increase exposure to environmental stressors. Living within a central city neighborhood is a strong predictor of psychological distress, related to the perceived neighborhood disorder. Low income neighborhoods are plagued with high crime levels, drugs, vandalism, and high noise levels, which residents are powerless to change. The environmental stressors of low-income neighborhoods lead to increased susceptibility to chronic health problems such as asthma, arthritis, and high blood pressure. Those experiencing more disadvantages will have resulting risk factors that accumulate throughout the life course (Ferraro & Kelley-Moore, 2003), leading to inequalities in stress exposure.

Important interactions among SES, gender, and minority status can increase stress exposure in late life. Women are more likely than men to be poor, with racial stratification among women making the situation more problematic for minorities. Overall, women live longer, poorer, more disabled lives than do men (Harrington Meyer & Herd, 2007). Racial and ethnic minorities are further disadvantaged because they experience worse health and more chronic health conditions than the White population (Hayward, Friedman, & Chen, 1996). Additionally, minorities are at increased risk for entering into poverty; they are more likely to have higher rates of unemployment, lower income levels, fewer assets, and poorer health. Women and minorities often lack the capital to mitigate the risk of poverty. The stress and effects of disadvantage persist into retirement (Hayward, Friedman & Chen, 1996).

The retirement years leave many women living in increased levels of poverty. Throughout the life course, women generally carry the burden of unpaid care work, which has tremendous implications for old age security. Social Security rewards marriage and steady employment (Harrington Meyer & Herd, 2007). The number of women, specifically African American women, who reach retirement age and are ineligible for spousal Social Security benefits is increasing. Additionally, with private pensions moving toward defined contribution plans, women will lose access to spousal protections and must rely on their own pensions and Social Security (Harrington Meyer & Herd, 2007).

British researchers found that demographic characteristics and exposure to adverse life events interact to shape adverse results of stress over the life course (Grundy & Holt, 2000). Thus, for example, women may be more sensitive to network-related events (or stressful events befalling their significant others), whereas men may be more adversely affected by financial stressors (Conger, Elder, Simons, & Ge, 1993). In terms of coping strategies, some research shows that women employ less effective coping methods (Poon et al., 2003).

Gender differences have been consistently reported in depressive symptoms, which reflect major psychological consequences of stress exposure (Turner & Avison, 1989). Women consistently report higher levels of depressive symptoms than do their male counterparts. Research suggests that these gender differences reflect greater vulnerability of women rather than their higher levels of stress exposure (McLeod & Kessler, 1990). Alternatively it has been argued that women's stress exposure may be underestimated, as they are particularly sensitive to negative events endured by significant others (Thoits, 1995). Research with both male and female elderly cancer patients underscores the importance of events endured by the family, particularly spouses and adult children, relative to personal stress exposure when living with cancer (Kahana et al., in press).

Disadvantaged social groups respond differently to stressful life situations (Thoits, 1995). Personality may shape the coping strategies employed by individuals; general outlook on life, hardiness, locus of control, and neuroticism affect coping styles in both a positive and negative manner. Individuals possessing higher levels of self-esteem and mastery generally experience more positive effects from coping. Avoidance and passive coping are associated with greater dysfunction and depressive symptoms. Individuals who are optimistic are more likely to employ effective coping strategies and, as a result, adjust to illness more easily than pessimists (Poon et al., 2003).

## UNDERSTANDING STRESS IN A LIFE COURSE PERSPECTIVE

The stressfulness of specific events generally depends on appraisals of the person experiencing it (Lazarus & Folkman, 1984). Such appraisals can best be understood by placing stressors in the context of the life course (Settersten, 1999). Sociologists thus emphasize socially recognized and shared life transitions (e.g., retirement) that are intertwined with age-related role changes (e.g., empty nest) throughout life. Understood in this context, the stressfulness of specific normative and non-normative events is likely to increase when the event takes place off-time rather than on time; that is, events that occur at the normal or expected point in the life course are less stressful than those that occur sooner or later than anticipated. Accordingly, major normative life transitions during late life include retirement and widowhood. The impact of both of these events is likely to be exacerbated if they occur at earlier points in the life course (Lopata, 1995). There may be fewer role models for adapting to the multiple social and psychological changes brought about by such stressful life events during middle age and for young-old individuals.

Another important life course concept that shapes appraisal of stress is related to cohorts, or members of the same group. Earlier cohorts of older adults who had lived through the Great Depression or World War II may respond to financial threats or challenges more strongly than would their counterparts who did not have similar traumatic experiences related to financial deprivation (Elder, 1974). Similarly, computer-based transactions may create stress for older cohorts, who must cope with unfamiliar tasks, whereas the computer is a welcome resource to more recent cohorts who are experienced in using computers and the Internet.

Sociologists have acknowledged the importance of using life course perspectives in understanding how people cope with stress (Settersten, 1999). Late life adaptation also represents a central concept in the study of developmental psychology. Accordingly, human development has been defined in terms of the changing adaptive capacities of individuals throughout the life span (Baltes, 1987). However, data regarding life course differences in coping with stress are typically based on cross-sectional studies, comparing young adults and older persons. Age differences in coping have been interpreted as reflecting life-stage-related developmental changes in coping skills and recognition that differential stress exposure throughout life may elicit different coping resources (Lazarus & Folkman, 1984).

## CHALLENGES AND OPPORTUNITIES FOR STRESS RESEARCH IN THE FUTURE

The stress paradigm has served as a flexible and robust conceptual framework that has generated an extensive and useful body of empirical research. As its fundamental tenet, this paradigm proposes that adverse life events or life situations threaten quality of life of individuals. However, adverse stress effects may be ameliorated by social and personal resources and proactive behaviors (Kahana & Kahana, 2003). Elements of the stress paradigm have been well articulated in conceptual frameworks presented by Pearlin et al. (1981), with later refinements offered by numerous scholars, including Thoits (1995), George (2005), Lazarus and Folkman (1984), Kahana and Kahana (1996), and Wheaton (1994). Refinements of the stress process model have expanded conceptualization and measurement of stress exposure. They also helped identify a broader array of relevant personal and social resources and proactive behaviors that can help ameliorate adverse effects of stress exposure. Developments in understanding possible positive outcomes in the aftermath of stressful life experiences has also moved the field forward. Empirical research utilizing the stress paradigm is becoming increasingly sophisticated. Longitudinal studies with better measures of coping and adaptations are likely to help clarify mechanisms that link stress exposure and buffers to quality of life in old age.

This review highlights the important roles played by exposure to adverse life events and life situations in placing individuals at risk for physical, psychological, and social problems. These adverse effects can be reduced by availability of social and psychological resources and proactive behavioral adaptations (Kahana & Kahana, 2003a). The nature of stressors confronted, changes throughout the life course, and resources are also influenced by life course transitions. Social policy can have an important impact, both on the distribution of social resources and the level of stress exposure experienced by individuals. In addition, practical interventions can serve useful functions in strengthening individual coping skills to insure that stressors may be confronted in ways that maintain good quality of life.

**SEE ALSO** Volume 2: *Social Support, Adulthood; Trauma;* Volume 3: *Aging; Allostatic Load; Caregiving; Mental Health, Later Life; Oldest Old; Retirement; Self; Social Integration/Isolation, Later Life; Widowhood; Wisdom.*

**BIBLIOGRAPHY**


Aldwin, C. M. (2000). *Stress, coping, and development: An integrative perspective.* New York: Guilford Press.

Aranda, M. P., & Knight, B. G. (1997). The influence of ethnicity and culture on the caregiver stress and coping process: A sociocultural review and analysis. *The Gerontologist, 37*(3), 342–354.

Ardelt, M. (1997). Wisdom and life satisfaction in old age. *Journals of Gerontology, 52B*, 15–27.

Baltes, P. B. (1987). *Theoretical propositions of life span development-psychology on the dynamics between growth and decline.* Washington, DC: American Psychological Association.

Bandura, A. 1986. *Social foundations of thought and action: A social cognitive theory.* Englewood Cliffs, NJ: Prentice Hall.

Birditt, K. S., Fingerman, K. L., & Almeida, D. M. (2005). Age differences in exposure and reactions to interpersonal tensions: A daily diary study. *Psychology and Aging, 20*(2), 330–340.

Blumer, H. (1969). *Symbolic interactionism: Perspective and method.* Englewood Cliffs, NJ: Prentice-Hall.

Calhoun, L. G., & Tedeschi, P. C. (2006). *Handbook of posttraumatic growth: Research and practice.* New York: Routeledge.

Chung, M. C., Werrett, J., Easthope, Y., & Farmer, S. (2004). Coping with post-traumatic stress: Young, middle-aged, and elderly comparisons. *International Journal of Geriatric Psychiatry, 19*(4), 333–343.

Cohen, S., & Wills, T. A. 1985. Stress, social support, and the buffering hypothesis. Psy*chological Bulletin, 98*(2), 310–357.

Conger, R. D., Elder, G. H., Simons, R. L., & Ge, X. (1993). Husband and wife differences in response to undesirable life events. *Journal of Health and Social Behavior, 34*, 71–88.

Costa, P. T., Somerfield, M. R., & McCrae, R. R. (1996). Personality and coping: A reconceptualization. In M. Aeidner & N. S. Endler (Eds.), *Handbook of coping: Theory, research, applications* (pp. 44–61). New York: Wiley.

Dannefer, D. (2003). Cumulative advantage/disadvantage and the life course: Cross-fertilizing age and social science theory. *The Journals of Gerontology Series B: Psychological Sciences and Social Sciences, 58*, S327–S337.

Deimling, G., Kahana, B., Bowman, K., & Schaefer, M. (2002). Cancer survivorship and psychological distress in later life. *Psycho-Oncology, 11*, 479–494.

DeKlerk, M. M. Y., Huijsman, R., & McDonnell, J. (1997). The use of technical aids by elderly persons in the Netherlands: An application of the Andersen and Newman model. *Gerontologist, 37*(3), 365–373.

Dohrenwend, B. (1998). *Adversity, stress, and psychopathology.* London: Oxford University Press.

Elder, G. H. (1974). *Children of the Great Depression: Social change in life experience.* Chicago: University of Chicago Press.

Ferraro, K. F., & Kelley-Moore, J. A. (2003). Cumulative disadvantage and health: Long-term consequences of obesity? *American Sociological Review, 68*(5), 707–729.

Fitzpatrick, T. R., Vinick, B. H., & Bushfield, S. (2005). Anticipated and experienced changes in activities after husbands retire. *Journal of Gerontological Social Work, 46*(2), 69–84.

Folkman, S., & Lazarus, R. S. (1980). An analysis of coping in a middle-aged community sample. *Journal of Health and Social Behavior, 21*(3), 219–239.

Folkman, S., & Lazarus, R. S. (1985). If it changes it must be a process: A study of emotion and coping during three stages of a college examination. *Journal of Personality and Social Psychology, 48*, 150–170.

Folkman, S., Lazarus, R. S., Pimley, S., & Novacek, J. (1987). Age differences in stress and coping processes. *Psychology and Aging, 2*(2), 171–184.

Fujita, F., & Diener, E. (2005). Life satisfaction set point: Stability and change. *Journal of Personality and Social Psychology, 88*(1), 158–164.

Gecas, V. (1989). The social psychology of self-efficacy. *Annual Review of Sociology, 15*, 291–316.

George, L. K. (2005). Stress and coping. In M. L. Johnson (Ed.), *The Cambridge handbook of age and aging* (pp. 292–300). New York: Cambridge University Press.

Giltay, E. J., Zitman, F. G., & Kromhout, D. (2006). Dispositional optimism and the risk of depressive symptoms during 15 years of follow-up: The Zutphen Elderly study. *Journal of Affective Disorders, 91*(1), 45–52.

Goenjian, A. K., Najarian, L. M., Pynoos, R. S., Steinberg, A. M., Manoukian, G., Tavosian, A. et al. (1994). Posttraumatic stress disorder in elderly and younger adults after the 1988 earthquake in Armenia. *American Journal of Psychiatry, 151*(6), 895–901.

Goldberg, E. L., & Comstock, G. W. (1980). Epidemiology of life events: Frequency in general populations. *American Journal of Epidemiology, 111*(6), 736–752.

Grundy, E., & Holt, G. (2000). Adult life experiences and health in early old age in Great Britain. *Social Science & Medicine, 51*(7), 1061–1074.

Harrington Meyer, M., & Herd, P. (2007). *Market friendly or family friendly? The state and gender inequality in old age.* New York: Russell Sage.

Hayward, M. D., Friedman, S., & Chen, H. (1996). Race inequities in men's retirement. *Journals of Gerontology Series B: Psychological Sciences and Social Sciences, 51*(1), S1–S10.

Holmes, T., & Rahe, R. (1967). The social readjustment scale. *Journal of Psychosomatic Research, 11*, 213–218.

Kahana, B., Deimling, G., Sterns, S., & Kahana, E. (in press). Physical impairment and psychological transformation among elderly cancer survivors. *Proceedings of European Congress of Physical and Rehabilitation Medicine, Bruges, Belgium, June 3–6, 2008.*

Kahana, B., Harel, Z., & Kahana, E. (2005). *Survivors of the Holocaust: Aging and adaptation.* New York: Kluwer/Springer Press.

Kahana, E. (1992). Stress research, and aging: Complexities, ambiguities, paradoxes, and promise. In M. Wykle, E. Kahana, & J. Kowal (Eds.), *Stress and health among the elderly* (pp. 239–256). New York: Springer Publishing.

Kahana, E., & Kahana, B. (1996). Conceptual and empirical advances in understanding aging well through proactive adaptation. In V. Bengston (Ed.), *Adulthood and aging: Research on continuities and discontinuities* (pp. 18–40). New York: Springer Publishing.

Kahana, E., & Kahana, B. (2003a). Patient proactivity enhancing doctor-patient-family communication in cancer prevention and care among the aged. *Patient Education & Counseling, 50*, 67–73.

Kahana, E., & Kahana, B. (2003b). Contextualizing successful aging: New directions in an age-old search. In R. Settersten (Ed.), *Invitation to the life course: A new look at old age* (pp. 225–255). Amityville, NY: Baywood Publishing.

Kahana, E., Kahana, B., Adams, S., Hammel, R., & York, J. (2008, March). *Redefining the self and signaling to others: A semiotic analysis of narratives among aged cancer survivors.* Presented at the 5th Annual Meeting of the American Psycho-Oncology Society, Los Angeles, CA.

Kahana, E., Kahana, B., & Kelley-Moore, J. (2005, August). Coping with disability in late life: A longitudinal study of proactive adaptations. Presented at the American Sociological Association Annual Meeting, Philadelphia.

Kahana, E., Kahana, B., Kelley-Moore, J., Adams, S., Hammel, R., & Kulle, D. et al. (In press). Toward advocacy in cancer care among the old-old: Cautionary personal actions and bold advice to others. *Journal of American Geriatric Society.*

Kahana, E., Kahana, B., & Kercher, K. (2003). Emerging lifestyles and proactive options for successful aging. *Ageing International, 28*(2), 155–180.

Kahana, E., Kahana, B., Kercher, K., King, C., Lovegreen, L., & Chirayath, H. (1999). Evaluating a model of successful aging for urban African American and white elderly. In M. Wykle (Ed.), *Serving minority elders in the 21st century* (pp. 287–322). New York: Springer Publishing.

Kahana, E., Lawrence, R., Kahana, B., Kercher, K., Wisniewski, A., & Stoller,. (2002). Long-term impact of preventive proactivity on quality of life of the old-old. *Psychosomatic Medicine, 64*(3), 382–394.

Kelley-Moore, J., Schumacher, J., Kahana, E., & Kahana, B. (2006). When do older adults become disabled? Acquiring a disability identity in the process of health decline. *Journal of Health & Social Behavior, 47*, 126–141.

Kiecolt-Glaser, J. K., Dura, J. R., Speicher, C. E., Trask, O. J., & Glaser, R. (1991). Spousal caregivers of dementia victims: Longitudinal changes in immunity and health. *Psychosomatic Medicine, 53*(4), 345–362.

Kiecolt-Glaser, J. K., & Glaser, R. (1991). Stress and immune function in humans. In A. R. Felten & N. Cohen (Eds.), *Psychoneuroimmunology II* (pp. 849–867). San Diego, CA: Academic Press.

Kiyak, A., Liang, J., & Kahana, E. (1976). *A methodological inquiry into the Schedule of Recent Life Events.* Paper presented at the meetings of the American Psychological Association, Washington, DC.

Krause, N. (2006). Social relationships in late life. In R. H. Binstock & L. K. George (Eds.), *Handbook of aging and the social sciences* (6th ed., pp. 181–200). New York: Academic Press.

Krogh, V., Trevisan, M., Jossa, F., Bland, S., Jalowiec, A., & Celentano, E. et al. (1992). Coping and blood pressure. *Journal of Human Hypertension, 6*(1), 65–70.

Lazarus, R. S. (2006). Emotions and interpersonal relationships: Toward a person-centered conceptualization of emotions and coping. *Journal of Personality, 74*(1), 9–46.

Lazarus, R. S., & Folkman, S. (1984). *Stress, appraisal, and coping.* New York: Springer Publishing.

Lent, R. W. (2007). Restoring emotional well-being. In M. Feuerstein (Ed.), *Handbook of cancer survivorship* (pp. 231–247). New York: Springer Publishing.

Lopata, H. Z. (1995). *Current widowhood: Myths and realities.* Thousand Oaks, CA: Sage Publications.

Marshall, V. W., & Taylor, P. (2005). Restructuring the life course. In M. L. Johnson (Ed.), *The Cambridge handbook of age and aging* (pp. 572–582). New York: Cambridge University Press.

Martin, M., Grunendahl, M., & Martin, P. (2001). Age differences in stress, social resources, and well-being in middle and older age. *The Journals of Gerontology Series B: Psychological Sciences and Social Sciences, 56*, P214–P222.

McCabe, K. A. & Gregory, S. S. (1998). Elderly victimization: An examination beyond the FBI's index crimes. *Research on Aging, 20*, 363–372.

McGonagle, K. A., & Kessler, R. C. (1990). Chronic stress, acute stress, and depressive symptoms. *American Journal of Community Psychology, 18*(5), 681–706.

McLeod, J. D., & Kessler, R. C. (1990). Socioeconomic differences in vulnerability to undesirable life events. *Journal of Health and Social Behavior, 31*, 162–172.

McLeod, J. D., & Lively, K. J. (2007). Social psychology and stress research. In W. Avison, J. McLeod, & B. Pescosolido (Eds.), *Mental health: Social mirror* (pp. 275–303). New York: Springer Publishing.

Mein, G., Martikainen, P., Hemingway, H., Stansfeld, S., & Marmot, M. (2003). Is retirement good or bad for mental and physical health functioning? Whitehall II longitudinal study of civil servants. *Journal of Epidemiology and Community, 57*(1), 46–49.

Mroczek, D. K., & Almeida, D. M. (2004). The effect of daily stress, personality, and age on daily negative affect. *Journal of Personality, 72*(2), 355–378.

Nicholson Grinstead, L., Leder, S., Jensen, S., & Bond, L. (2003). Review of research on the health of caregiving grandparents. *Journal of Advanced Nursing, 44*(3), 318–326.

Ory, M. G., & Defriese, G. H. (Eds.). (1998). *Self-care in later life: Research, program, and policy issues.* New York: Springer Publishing.

Pearlin, L. I., Menaghan, E. G., Lieberman, M. A., & Mullan, J. T. (1981). The stress process. *Journal of Health and Social Behavior, 22*(4), 337–356.

Pearlin, L., & Mullan, J. (1992). Loss and stress in aging. In M. Wykle, E. Kahana, & J. Kowal (Eds.), *Stress and health among the elderly* (pp. 117–132). New York: Springer Publishing.

Pearlin, L. I., Mullan, J. T., Semple, S. J., & Skaff, M. M. (1990). Caregiving and the stress process: An overview of concepts and their measures. *The Gerontologist, 30*(5), 583–594.

Poon, L. W., Basford, L., Dowzer, C., & Booth, A. (2003). Coping with comorbidity. In L. W. Poon, S. H. Gueldner, & B. M. Sprouse (Eds.), *Successful aging and adaptation with chronic diseases* (pp. 116–150). New York: Springer Publishing.

Pudrovska, T., Schieman, S., Pearlin, L. I., & Nguyen, K. (2005). The sense of mastery as a mediator and moderator in the association between economic hardship and health in late life. *Journal of Aging and Health*, 33(5), 634–660.

Robinson-Whelen, S., Cheongtag, K., MacCallum, R. C., & Kiecolt-Glaser, J. (1997). Distinguishing optimism from pessimism in older adults: Is it more important to be optimistic or not to be pessimistic? *Journal of Personality and Social Psychology, 73*(6), 1345–1353.

Scheier, M. F. & Carver, C. S. (1985). Optimism, coping, and health-assessment and implications of generalized outcome expectancies. *Health Psychology, 4*(3), 219–247.

Seligman, M. E. P., Steen, T. A., Park, N., & Peterson, C. (2005). Positive psychology progress: Empirical validation of interventions. *American Psychologist, 60*(5), 410–421.

Selye, H. (1956). *The stress of life.* McGraw-Hill, New York.

Serido, J., Almeida, D. M., & Wethington, E. (2004). Chronic stressors and daily hassles: Unique and interactive relationships with psychological distress. *Journal of Health and Social Behavior, 45*(1), 17–33.

Settersten, R. A. (1999). *Lives in time and place: The problems and promises of developmental science.* New York: Baywood Publishing.

Siegrist, J., Wahrendorf, M., von dem Knesebeck, O., Jürges, H., & Börsch-Supan, A. (2007). Quality of work, well-being, and intended early retirement of older employees—Baseline results from the SHARE study. *The European Journal of Public Health, 17*(1), 62–68.

Silverstein, M., & Parker, M. G. (2002). Leisure activities and quality of life among the oldest old in Sweden. *Research on Aging, 24*(5), 528–547.

Skodol, A. E. (1998). Personality and coping as stress-attenuating or stress-amplifying factors. In B. P. Dohrenwend (Ed.), *Adversity, stress, and psychopathology* (pp. 377–389). New York: Oxford University Press.

Smith, K. R., & Zick, C. D. (1996). Risk of mortality following widowhood: Age and sex differences by mode of death. *Social Biology, 4*, 59–71.

Solomon, Z., & Prager, E. (1992). Elderly Israeli Holocaust survivors during the Persian Gulf War: A study of psychological distress. *American Journal of Psychiatry, 149*, 1707–1710.

Thoits, P. A. (1995). Stress, coping, and social support processes: Where are we? What next? *Journal of Health and Social Behavior, 35*(Extra Issue), 53–79.

Thoits, P. A. (2006). Personal agency in the stress process. *Journal of Health and Social Behavior, 47*, 309–323.

Turner, R. J., & Avison, W. R. (1989). Gender and depression: Assessing exposure and vulnerability to life events in a chronically strained population. *The Journal of Nervous and Mental Disease, 177*(8), 443–455.

Turner, R. J., Wheaton, B., & Lloyd, D. A. (1995). The epidemiology of social stress. *American Sociological Review, 60*, 104–124.

Utz, R. L., Carr, D., Nesse, R., & Wortman, C. B. (2002). The effect of widowhood on older adults' social participation. *The Gerontologist, 42*, 522–533.

Van Den Brink, C. L., Tijbuis, M., Van Den Bos, G. A. M., Giampaoli, S., Kivinen, P., & Nissinen, A. (2004). Effects of widowhood on disability onset in elderly men from three European countries. *Journal of American Geriatrics Society, 52*, 353–358.

Van der Kolk, B. A., McFarlane, A., & Weisaeth, L. (2007). *Traumatic stress: The effects of overwhelming experience on mind, body, and society.* New York: Guilford Press.

Verbrugge, L. M., & Jette, A. M. (1994). The disablement process. *Social Science & Medicine, 38*, 1–14.

Wallhagen, M. I., & Yamamoto-Mitani, N. (2006). The meaning of family caregiving in Japan and the United States: A qualitative comparative study. *Journal of Transcultural Nursing, 17*(1), 65–73.

Wethington, E., & Kessler, R. C. (1986). Perceived support, received support, and adjustment to stressful life events. *Journal of Health & Social Behavior, 27*(1), 78–89.

Wheaton, B. (1990). Life transitions, role histories, and mental health. *American Sociological Review, 55*(2), 209–223.

Wheaton, B. (1994). Sampling the stress universe. In W. R. Avison & I. H. Gotlib (Eds.), *Stress and mental health: Contemporary issues and prospects for the future* (pp. 77–114). New York: Plenum.

Wilcox, S., Aragaki, A., Mouton, C. P., Evenson, K. R., Wassertheil-Smoller, S., & Loevinger, B. L. (2003). The effects of widowhood on physical and mental health, health behaviors, and health outcomes: The women's health initiative. *Health Psychology, 22*(5), 513–522.

***Eva Kahana***
***Boaz Kahana***
***Rachel Hammel***

# STRUCTURAL LAG

**SEE** Volume 3: *Riley, Matilda White.*

# SUICIDE, LATER LIFE

Suicide is the willful taking of one's own life. Theories of elderly suicide include two broad categories: individual-based psychiatric and social perspectives. The first links suicide in the elderly to an enduring personal trait, such as a fundamental incapacity to adapt or cope, or recurrent depression (Nisbet, 2000). The second emphasizes social risk and protective factors outside of the individual psyche as linked to suicide risk. These include physical illness and supportive social networks. These perspectives are viewed as complementary. For example, an elderly person who has had a lifelong depression problem might ultimately commit suicide only after a severe external life crisis such as the death of a spouse.

## PSYCHIATRIC PERSPECTIVE

Affective psychiatric illness, especially severe depression, is the leading predictor of elderly suicide and is independent of some important secondary predictors, including social factors and physical health (Conwell, Duberstein, & Caine, 2002). The best research studies in this area are those that rigorously compare the psychological and social worlds of suicides (*cases*) with those of nonsuicidal persons (*controls*). A meta-analysis (or integrative summary analysis) of 19 case-control studies dealing with psychiatric risk factors for elderly suicide determined that the strongest predictor of suicide was depressive illness, including manic depression. Eight studies found "very large" associations, and five detected moderate or small associations. Severe physical illness, pain, and visual impairment produced significant, although weaker, risk ratios (measures of the relative importance of risk factors) in 13 studies (Grek, 2007). Unfortunately, psychiatric-oriented studies on elderly suicide tend not to include a broad or varied range of social risk and protective factors, making it difficult to weigh the relative contributions of psychiatric versus social factors.

## INDIVIDUAL-LEVEL RISK AND PROTECTIVE FACTORS

There are many social reasons to expect that elderly people would have a high rate of suicide, relative to younger persons. First, sociological research dating back to the findings of Émile Durkheim (1858–1917) reveals that social support is a key buffer against suicide risk. Similar to arguments made in modern disengagement theory, the Durkheimian model of elderly suicide views social integration, measured in relation to bonds to people and institutions such as marriage, work, and the family, as declining with age (Stack, 2000). With retirement comes the loss of social relationships with coworkers and the purpose associated with the routines of employment. Friends and spouses die, thus contributing to loneliness and weakened social support networks. Many people lose ties to their familiar home environment as they move into small quarters in nursing homes. Incomes tend to decrease with retirement, resulting in financial strain. Health costs can rise, making it difficult to pay for necessary medical care and prescription medicine. Age-related health stressors include memory loss, blindness, and battles with long-term terminal illnesses such as cancer, strokes, and paralysis. These health problems can further limit one's social participation and interactions. Although these stress factors affect most elderly people, there is wide variation in suicide rates among subgroups of the elderly. For example, elderly women are more apt to lose a spouse than elderly men, but elderly women have a lower suicide rate (Stack, 2000). Table 1 provides data on the suicide rates (per 100,000) for gender-, race-, and age-specific groups between 1950 and 2004.

**Gender** Older men's suicide rates are typically 5 or more times that of elderly women. The male to female ratio narrowed between 1950 and 1970 from 5.6 to 4.8, but since 1970 it has widened. In fact, elderly men commit suicide at a rate nearly 8 times that of elderly women. The gender gap in elderly suicide remains a puzzle. Many risk factors for elderly women are the same (e.g.,

| Group | 1950 | 1960 | 1970 | 1980 | 1990 | 2000 | 2004 |
|---|---|---|---|---|---|---|---|
| White Males | | | | | | | |
| 65+ | 55.8 | 46.7 | 41.1 | 37.2 | 44.2 | 33.3 | 31.2 |
| 65–74 | 53.2 | 42.0 | 38.7 | 32.5 | 34.2 | 24.3 | 24.2 |
| 75–84 | 61.9 | 55.7 | 45.5 | 45.5 | 60.2 | 41.1 | 37.1 |
| 85+ | 61.9 | 61.3 | 45.8 | 52.8 | 70.3 | 61.6 | 48.4 |
| Black Males | | | | | | | |
| 65+ | 9.0 | 9.9 | 8.7 | 11.4 | 14.9 | 11.5 | 11.3 |
| 65–74 | 10.0 | 11.3 | 8.7 | 11.1 | 14.7 | 11.1 | 9.8 |
| 75–84 | * | * | * | 10.5 | 14.4 | 12.1 | 15.0 |
| 85+ | * | * | * | * | * | * | * |
| White Females | | | | | | | |
| 65+ | 9.9 | 8.8 | 8.5 | 6.4 | 6.8 | 4.3 | 4.0 |
| Black Females | | | | | | | |
| 65+ | * | * | 2.6 | * | 1.9 | 1.3 | * |
| Ratio WM/BM | | | | | | | |
| 65+ | 6.2 | 4.7 | 4.7 | 3.3 | 3.0 | 2.9 | 2.8 |
| Ratio WF/BF | | | | | | | |
| 65+ | * | * | 3.3 | * | 3.6 | 3.3 | * |
| Ratio WM/WF | | | | | | | |
| 65+ | 5.6 | 5.3 | 4.8 | 5.8 | 6.5 | 7.7 | 7.8 |

Note: * = counts are inadequate to calculate reliable rates (CDC, 2006).

***Table 1.*** *Suicide rates per 100,000. By gender, race and age group, elderly population, USA, 1950–2004.* CENGAGE LEARNING, GALE.

depression level) or greater (e.g., poverty, living alone, widowhood, physical illness, and disabilities) than those for elderly men (Canetto, 1995; Stack, 2000). However, elderly women benefit from a series of protective factors: They are more likely than their male peers to seek appropriate levels of psychological help, to use less lethal methods of suicide, to have stronger social networks, to have better and more flexible coping abilities, and to be institutionalized in nursing homes where committing suicide is more difficult. For example, in 2004 42.9% of elderly women and 78.7% of elderly men ages 65 to 74 used guns in their suicide. National data from the General Social Surveys showed that 49% of elderly men approve of suicide in the case of terminal illness, compared to only 33% of elderly women. The greater cultural support among elderly men also contributes to their higher suicide rate.

**Race** Elderly White males have a much higher suicide rate than elderly Black males. However, the gap has narrowed from a ratio of 6.2 in 1950 to 2.8 in 2004, wherein White rates declined while Black rates rose. Further, elderly White females have a suicide rate at least triple that of elderly Black females. The reasons are largely unknown. It should be noted that caution needs to be exercised in interpreting official data on elderly suicide by race. The cause of death is ascertained by county medical examiners and coroners. It has been argued that suicides are often misclassified as unintentional poisonings, and this is apparently especially true of elderly Blacks. For example, the ratio of unintentional poisonings to official suicides is 5 times greater for Black males over 65 than for their White counterparts. With adjustments for these and other probable misclassifications of suicides, the racial gap in suicide narrows (Rockett, Samora, & Coben, 2006).

**Social Support** Indicators of supportive social networks and religious ties were investigated in some research, but their associations with suicide (as protective factors) were small compared to psychiatric morbidity (Grek, 2007). An analysis of the National Mortality Followback Surveys, which sought to identify the characteristics associated with 354 elderly suicides from a sample of 5,870 elderly deaths, determined that after controlling for a variety of factors (including gender, race, and depression), social networks variables affected suicide risk. For example, participation in religious activities lowered risk by 18%, whereas living alone increased risk 2.01 times. Change of residence in the last year of life can disrupt social support networks. Elderly persons who moved recently were 1.8 times more apt to die of suicide than their counterparts. Being male increased risk 2.6 times, whereas being White increased risk 6.7 times. All these relationships are independent of socioeconomic confounders or control variables.

**Marital Integration** Divorced men and women in all age brackets of the elderly generally have a suicide rate of at least double that of their married counterparts. For example, divorced men between 75 and 79 have a suicide rate of 103 per 100,000, 3.2 times that of their married age-matched peers. Divorced elderly women ages 75 to 79 have a suicide rate of 10.7 per 100,000, 2.4 times that of married women of the same age. The ratios are nearly as large for the widowed versus the elderly married. However, whereas marriage protects the elderly from suicide, it protects the middle-aged age groups more so. Elderly spouses are more apt than middle-aged spouses to be ill or disabled and, as such, provide less social support.

**Opportunity Factors: Guns and Nursing Homes** Opportunities for committing suicide vary according to the availability of lethal means and the presence of motivated rescuers who will intervene to stop suicide attempts. From the National Mortality Followback Surveys, elderly persons who had a firearm available in their home were 4.6 times more likely to die from suicide than elderly persons who did not have a gun available. Elderly persons who resided in nursing homes were 59% less apt to die by suicide than elderly persons who resided elsewhere. The elderly in nursing homes are under greater surveillance than their counterparts, just as married people are relative to singles.

## OTHER RISK AND PROTECTIVE FACTORS

Suicide rates vary by region. State-level studies of elderly suicide are important for various reasons, including the notion that various social welfare policies affecting the financial status of the elderly are set at the state level. For example, states in which incomes for the elderly are higher and in which religion is stronger tend to have lower suicide rates. States in which guns are more available tend to have higher elderly suicide rates. For example, the two states with the lowest elderly rates are Rhode Island (7.25 per 100,000) and Massachusetts (6.48 per 100,000). Both have high church attendance rates and high proportions of Catholics. States with the highest elderly suicide rates are Nevada (32.12 per 100,000), Idaho (26.15 per 100,000), and Montana (25.87 per 100,000), states with relatively easy access to guns and low religiosity rates.

**Imitation** The elderly are as vulnerable as youth to copycat effects (i.e., imitation) due to highly publicized suicide stories in the mass media. The impact of a suicide story in the news on the elderly rate almost doubles if the story involves an elderly person. One can speculate that elderly persons identify with the victim in the story.

**Cohort Effects** Cohort analysis traces the suicide rates of persons born in a certain time period (e.g., the baby boomers) as they age over the life course. Large birth cohorts are viewed as being at a disadvantage relative to small cohorts. The former experience more competition in social and economic life, producing more so-called failures. The large baby boom cohort has been marked by relatively high suicide rates. It is anticipated that when this cohort retires, the elderly suicide rates will increase accordingly (Conwell et al., 2002). In contrast, the recent fall in elderly suicide rates is related to the advantageous characteristics of members of the Great Depression (1929–1939) birth cohort, a relatively small birth cohort.

## NEW DIRECTIONS IN RESEARCH

Directions for future research in this area include those involving prevention, assisted suicide, and suicide ideation.

**Prevention** Approximately 40% of elderly persons who committed suicide reportedly saw a physician during the last month of life, a figure much greater than that for nonelderly suicides. The potential for suicide prevention, then, through physician screening for depression, is higher for the elderly than the nonelderly populations (Harwood & Jacoby, 2002). The most common method of elderly suicide is by use of firearms.

**Assisted Suicide** Elderly suicide rates may increase as assisted suicide becomes more widely available. In physician-assisted suicide, a physician provides the means of suicide, which are then employed by the patient. Physician-assisted suicide first became legal in Oregon in the late 1990s. Physicians provide a prescription for a lethal drug, which the patient then obtains and uses for the suicide. However, there is no evidence that rates of physician-assisted suicide are increasing in the Netherlands, the first nation that legalized physician-assisted suicide (Harwood & Jacoby, 2002).

**Suicide Ideation** Suicide ideation refers to talking about the idea of taking one's own life. The predictors of suicide ideation among the elderly are similar to the predictors of completed suicide. Depression is the main predictor of such suicidal thinking. Other antecedents include physical disability, pain, and visual and hearing impairment. Social isolation indicators, such as divorce and widowhood, also foster suicide ideation. In turn, suicide ideation is the best single predictor of suicide among the elderly. However, this association may reflect a spurious statistical relationship. Depression predicts both ideation and completed suicide. It is very common to think about suicide before completing it.

Toll-free state and national suicide hotlines are available to the general public at any time. The effectiveness of these and other policy interventions on preventing elderly suicide is difficult to ascertain and is largely unknown. A web page with helpful information on prevention is provided by the American Association of Suicidology (2008).

**SEE ALSO** Volume 3: *Chronic Illness, Adulthood and Later Life; Death and Dying; Mental Health, Later Life; Mortality; Social Integration/Isolation, Later Life.*

**BIBLIOGRAPHY**

American Association of Suicidology. (2008). *Dedicated to the understanding and prevention of suicide.* Retrieved May 17, 2008, from www.suicidology.org

Canetto, S. S., & Lester, D. (Eds.). (1995). Elderly women and suicidal behavior. In *Women and suicidal behavior* (pp. 215–233). New York: Springer.

Centers for Disease Control. (2006). *Health, United States, 2006: With chartbook on trends in the health of Americans.* Washington, DC: Author. Retrieved May 14, 2008, from http://www.cdc.gov/nchs/

Conwell, Y., Duberstein, P. R., & Caine, E. (2002). Risk factors for suicide in later life. *Biological Psychiatry, 52*(3), 193–204.

Grek, A. (2007). Clinical management of suicidality in the elderly: An opportunity for involvement in the lives of older patients. *Canadian Journal of Psychiatry, 52,* 47S–57S.

Harwood, D., & Jacoby, R. (2002). Suicidal behavior among the elderly. In K. Hawton & K. van Heeringen (Eds.), *The international handbook of suicide and attempted suicide* (2nd ed., pp. 276–291). New York: Wiley.

*National Suicide Prevention Lifeline 1-800-273-TALK.* Retrieved May 17, 2008, from http://www.suicidepreventionlifeline.org

Nisbet, P. (2000). Age and the life span. In R. Maris, A. Berman, & M. Silverman (Eds.), *Comprehensive textbook of suicidology* (pp.127–144). New York: Guilford Press.

Rockett, I. R. H., Samora, J. B., & Coben, J. H. (2006). The Black–White suicide paradox: Possible effects of misclassification. *Social Science and Medicine, 63*(8), 2165–2175.

Stack, S. (2000). Suicide: A 15-year review of the sociological literature. Part II: Modernization and social integration. *Suicide and Life-Threatening Behavior, 30*(2), 163–176.

***Steven Stack***

# T

## TECHHNOLOGY USE, LATER LIFE

SEE Volume 3: *Media and Technology Use, Later Life.*

## THEORIES OF AGING

Social gerontology is a multidisciplinary field grounded in the sociology of aging and life course but informed by psychology, demography, epidemiology, anthropology, economics, history, and the humanities, among other disciplines. A central aim of social gerontology since its inception has been to understand and improve the lives of older adults. Thus social gerontologists are interested in the impact of socioeconomic, political, and cultural forces and conditions on the processes of aging and in the statuses and well-being of older people. Social gerontology explores the ways in which the older population and the diversity of the aging experience affect and are affected effected by social structures. Research in social gerontology addresses many domains of social life and behavior, including family relationships, health and disability, and older adults' social participation. Social gerontologists are also interested in social inequality across the life course, the unequal treatment of older people, and the deleterious effects of ageism. The recognition of diversity and inequality has been crucial to the development of the field and are incorporated in theory and practice.

This entry reviews current theoretical developments in social gerontology and the sociology of aging. Presented here are the field's major theories or theoretical perspectives, each theory's intellectual origins, what the theory tries to explain, the theory's key concepts, and how the theory has been used in recent research. Before discussing specific theories, however, it is useful to provide some background on what is meant by theory in social gerontology, the history of theorizing in this field, and issues of epistemology (approaches to knowledge) as they relate to the underlying assumptions of different theoretical perspectives. The challenges of theory building are also discussed, including the reluctance of researchers to integrate data with theory and synthesize theoretical insights with existing knowledge, or to pay attention to theory at all.

### WHAT THEORY IS

Theory refers to the construction of explicit explanations that account for empirical findings. Theories of aging help to systematize what is known, explain the *how* and *why* behind the *what* of data, and change the existing order to solve problems, such as age-related disabilities or lack of income security. The systematic progression of knowledge (i.e., explanation) over time is the standard by which any field of scholarly or scientific research is judged. If empirical results are not presented within the context of more general explanations or theory, the process of building, revising, and interpreting how and why phenomena occur is limited. It is through the ability to explain specific empirical findings with more general theories that knowledge develops.

In building theory, researchers rely on previous explanations of behavior that have been organized and ordered in some way. Whenever researchers begin a project, they are operating under some implicit theory about how a set of phenomena may be related, and these expectations or hunches are derived from previous explanations. Yet too often research agendas proceed without any stated theory about how things work. Especially in the area of public policy applications or program interventions in gerontology, it is crucial to specify the theoretical assumptions of a research investigation or program intervention before investing large sums of money in it. If the theory is inadequate, it is unlikely the research intervention program or public policy will achieve its objectives. If the research findings are not backed by tested theoretical assumptions, then it is difficult to judge whether an intervention policy is grounded in supportable assumptions about why things happen.

## WHAT GERONTOLOGISTS NEED TO EXPLAIN

Social gerontologists focus on three sets of issues as they attempt to analyze and understand the phenomena of aging (Bengtson, Rice, & Johnson, 1999). The first set concerns the aged: the population of those who can be categorized as elderly in terms of their actual or expected life span. Most gerontological research in decades leading up to the 21st century has focused on the functional problems of aged populations, seen in human terms as medical disability or barriers to independent living. A second set of issues focuses on aging as a developmental process. Here the principal interest is in the situations and problems that accumulate during the life span and cannot be understood separate from developmental experiences and processes across a lifetime. A third set of issues involves the study of age as a dimension of structure and behavior within species. Social gerontologists are interested in how social organizations are created and changed in response to age-related patterns of birth, socialization, role transitions, and retirement or death. The phenomena to be explained relate to how institutions such as labor markets, retirement and pension systems, health care organizations, and political institutions take into account or deal with age. Although these three emphases are quite different in focus and inquiry, they are nonetheless interrelated in social gerontological research and practice. Theoretical engagement helps to distinguish among these basic categories of interest.

## CHALLENGES IN THEORY DEVELOPMENT

The field of social gerontology has accumulated many findings and has developed several important traditions of theory. Yet analysis of published findings in aging research suggests many researchers and practitioners are relatively unconcerned about theories of aging (Bengtson, Burgess, & Parrott, 1997). In social gerontology of the early 21st century, there are several problems that impede theory building and the development of a corpus of cumulative knowledge. First is the problem of tacit assumptions. Social gerontologists approach their research or study with certain assumptions and tacit theoretical orientations, even if not made explicit. In their eagerness to exploit new data sources and analytic techniques and generate findings for the solution of the problems associated with aging, researchers often neglect to clearly spell out their theoretical assumptions. One of the purposes that theories on aging should achieve is to lay out these tacit assumptions and orientations in an explicit and systematic way.

A second problem is reducing theory to empirical generalizations. Skepticism about the importance of theory as well as the proliferation of single-aspect research, which tends to lack theoretical grounding, has led some gerontology researchers to substitute empirical generalization for theory. Propositional statements based on empirical generalizations are about specific events in particular empirical settings rather than about more general processes that occur across a range of contexts. Often empirical generalizations are little more than summaries of research findings that require a theory to explain them. There is a need to raise these empirical generalizations to the level of explanation.

A third problem concerns disciplinary boundaries. Social gerontology has evolved into a broad academic enterprise. In addition to sociology, the fields of social psychology and psychology, demography, anthropology, political science, epidemiology, history, and the humanities are represented among social gerontology researchers. The field of social gerontology itself is in need of integration, because so many more factors are now recognized to be involved in human aging (Birren, 1999). For the mountains of data to yield significant new insights, an integrating framework is essential. However, this cannot be done without theories and concepts that are broader and more general in scope. This lack of integration in theories of aging is also an artifact of disciplinary specialization. The various disciplines study a growing diversity of outcomes; hence there is little overlap in theoretical explanations. This poses a further challenge for integrating theory and findings across the sciences when distinct areas of inquiry pursue knowledge under different epistemological assumptions.

A fourth issue, although not necessarily a problem, is to recognize that theory development is also a social enterprise. It has long been observed that science is a social endeavor that cannot be separated from social and professional considerations (Kuhn, 1962). Science reflects the concerns, careers, and competitiveness of collective groups of practitioners. Moreover, like the aging process itself, theoretical development processes—and the explanations that ensue—are embedded in institutional and historical contexts. W. Andrew Achenbaum (1995) observed how the development of gerontological theories paralleled the historical construction of gerontology around new scientific methods and medical practices. Not surprisingly, the biomedicalization of aging remains a guiding research paradigm. One must be mindful of the connections between scientific inquiry and the social milieu at particular points in time that influence how a subject matter is conceived. Since the mid-1908s, interpretive and critical social gerontologists have called attention to these connections (Hendricks & Achenbaum, 1999), cautioning researchers to be more reflective on their own values or biases as they interpret findings, develop explanations, and make policy recommendations.

## THE STRUCTURE OF THEORIES IN SOCIAL GERONTOLOGY

Theories in social gerontology differ in several respects: (a) their underlying assumptions (particularly about human nature—specifically, whether human behavior is essentially determined, and thus predictable, or whether individuals are essentially creative and agentic, that is, producers of the social world); (b) their subject matter (reflecting specific disciplinary interests, or whether the focus is on macro-level institutions or on micro-level interactions); (c) their epistemological approach (positivistic, interpretive, or critical); (d) their methodological approach (deductive or inductive); and (e) their ultimate objectives (whether they aim largely to describe things, explain or even predict them, or change the way things are).

The classical definition of a scientific theory is essentially a deductive one, starting with definitions of general concepts and putting forward a number of logically ordered propositions about the relationships among concepts. Concepts are the building blocks of theory. Concepts are linked to empirical phenomena through operational definitions, from which hypotheses are derived and then tested against empirical observations. A general theory allows researchers to logically deduce a number of fairly specific statements, or explanations, about the nature and behavior of a large class of phenomena. Because such theories are useful in predicting and hence manipulating people's environments, they are considered essential for the design of programs aimed at ameliorating problems associated with aging, especially by government funding agencies. Some researchers have generated explanations of aging phenomena using inductive or grounded theoretical approaches (Strauss & Corbin, 1990) and qualitative methods, starting with the data and leading into the final stages of analysis to the emergence of key concepts and how they relate to one another. Research using quantitative methods can also proceed inductively, starting with data and developing theory.

Mainstream gerontological research is scientific in its approach to knowledge. However, interpretive and critical perspectives and qualitative and narrative methods have become more common. In modern social gerontology there is debate over positivistic approaches where knowledge is gained from the scientific method, or whether social theories can be scientific at all. Many social gerontologists believe there are nonscientific ways to look at, interpret, and develop knowledge about aging. Researchers using interpretive approaches, as opposed to positivistic approaches, focus on describing and understanding how social interactions proceed and on the subjective meanings of age and aging phenomena. From this perspective, a theory is useful to the extent that it provides a deeper understanding of particular social events and settings (Gubrium & Holstein, 1999). The assumption is that individuals are active agents and can change the nature of their social environments. Thus there cannot be general theories of aging reflecting fixed or natural laws of human social organization (Turner, 2003).

The critical theory perspective questions positivism and the search for scientific natural laws as a principal source of knowledge. Within this perspective, the understanding of meanings and the analysis of power and domination and the constraints imposed by social structures or forces are termed *critical knowledge*. Critical knowledge is equally as important as objective knowledge in understanding phenomena (Bengtson et al., 1997).

## DEBATES OVER EPISTEMOLOGY

To understand the controversies in social gerontology surrounding forms of knowledge and the use of theory, one must concern themselves with epistemology: *how one knows what they think they know*. Is there a reality out there? Are social phenomena real facts? Or is reality itself socially constructed through the collaborative definitional and meaning-sharing activities of people who observe it (Marshall, 1999)? Critical theorists note that values cannot be separated from facts and that all research is value-laden. Such concerns are metatheoretical, and they have been the subject of a great deal of debate in recent years among scholars in social gerontology. Metatheories—technically, theories of theories—are concerned with more fundamental epistemological and metaphysical questions addressing such things as the nature of human activity about which humans must develop theory; the basic nature of human beings or the fundamental nature of society; or the appropriate way to develop theory and what kind of theory is possible, such as scientific theories, interpretative frameworks, general concepts that sensitize and orient, or critical approaches (Turner, 2003).

Because they are incommensurate, perhaps one effective way to deal with these issues in social gerontology is to regard each perspective as providing different lenses to address the different problems at hand, thereby enriching one's understanding of the multiple facets of aging. It should be remembered, however, that although scientific, interpretive, and critical approaches to knowledge are different in their objectives and methods, all of these theoretical approaches do involve a set of concepts, which are the building blocks of any theory. Increasingly, scholars in social gerontology are weighing the prospect of finding a common currency of ideas and concepts that would allow a synthesis to emerge.

## EARLY THEORIZING IN SOCIAL GERONTOLOGY

In gerontology's short history, considerable intellectual effort has been invested in theory development. Early researchers on aging, such as Granville Stanley Hall (1844–1924), Edmund Cowdry (1888–1975), Ralph Linton (1893–1953), Talcott Parsons (1902–1979), and Robert Havighurst (1900–1991), integrated empirical findings into theoretical insights and established the foundations of gerontology. As social gerontology developed in the post–World War II (1939–1945) period, it drew theoretical insights from the prevailing theoretical paradigm of the time, structural functionalism and symbolic interactionism, and later Marxism and rational choice.

**Disengagement Theory** Drawn from structural functionalism, disengagement theory was the first explicitly scientific theory of aging (Cumming & Henry, 1961). This theory attempted to explain age-related decreases in social interaction, psychological involvement, and the supposedly inevitable process of aging individuals withdrawing from society. The theory postulated that aging individuals and social structures would mutually disengage as individuals approached death, an adaptation seen as beneficial for the individual and society. This general theory of aging was elegant, multidisciplinary, parsimonious, and intuitively provocative (Achenbaum & Bengtson, 1994). However, its ambitious propositions were roundly criticized (Hochschild, 1975), particularly its unfalsifiability claims. The theory had attempted to explain both macro- and micro-level changes with one grand theory, but when tested against the cited data, its validity and generalizability claims could not be supported. Whereas many older people do appear to disengage or withdraw from their social connections and activities, many do not. One outcome of the profound criticism of disengagement theory was to curtail further attempts to develop a general theory of aging. Nevertheless, disengagement theory had a significant effect in social gerontology by prompting development of alternative theories of aging, particularly activity theory.

**Activity Theory** An implicit theory in gerontology for decades, activity theory was formalized by Bruce Lemon, Vern Bengtson, and James Peterson (1972) in response to the challenge posed by disengagement theory. Based on symbolic interactionism, activity theory postulates that older people who are more active will be more satisfied with their lives. Activity theory places strong emphasis on ongoing social interaction in the development of self-concept. It argues that one's self-concept is related to one's roles and that with old age comes a loss of roles (e.g., retirement and widowhood). In order to maintain a positive sense of self, older persons must substitute new roles for those lost in old age. Well-being in late life results from increased activity in newly acquired roles. Activity theory provides a conceptual justification for a central assumption underlying many programs and interventions for the elderly—that social activity in and of itself is beneficial and results in greater life satisfaction. Activity theory has received considerable empirical support but is vulnerable to several criticisms. First, the theory assumes that all older persons need and desire high levels of social activity. Some older people may prefer to be couch potatoes. Second, the theory overlooks variations in the meaning of particular activities in the lives of older people. The ideas of activity theory can be readily discerned in the more recent *successful aging* paradigm put forth by John Rowe and Robert Kahn in 1998. Not unlike activity theory, successful aging has been criticized for its excessive individualism and its discounting of social diversity and inequalities (Schmeeckle & Bengtson, 1999).

**Modernization Theory** As formulated by Donald Cowgill (1974), modernization theory attempts to explain variations in age status both historically and across societies. Its historical roots are in structural functionalism. Focusing on the macrostructural conditions of older adults in different sociocultural settings, the theory postulates that the status of the aged is inversely related to the level of societal industrialization. Whereas the elderly held high status in preindustrial societies as a result of their control of scarce resources and their knowledge of tradition, they have lower status in present industrialized societies. Four elements of industrialization are implicated in the reduced status of older people: economic technology, urbanization, mass education, and health technology. Modernization theory is elegant and parsimonious in capturing the general socioeconomic processes as they relate to the status of the aged; yet like most general theories, it cannot be documented empirically except at the most superficial levels. For example, historical research examining the loss of authority of elders, timing and sequencing of proportion of the aged, and the appearance of retirement are at variance with tenets of modernization theory. Although no longer used as a general explanation of the status of the aged, it has been applied in more narrowly defined settings, such as in Isabella Aboderin's (2004) qualitative study of the intergenerational relations and the status of elders under conditions of poverty in urban Ghana in the late 1990s.

**Social Competence and Breakdown Theory** Social competence and breakdown theory attempts to explore both normal and problematic aspects of aging. Based on symbolic interactionism, Joseph Kuypers and Vern Bengtson (1973) sought to explain the negative consequences that can accompany crises that often occur with advancing age. They conceptualized how a negative spiral of feedback can occur: (1) an elderly individual, whose self-concept may already be vulnerable because of role loss or negative stereotypes concerning aging, experiences a health-related crisis; (2) experiencing a health-related crisis leads to labeling of the older person as dependent by the social environment—health professionals or family; (3) atrophy of previous competency skills occurs; and (4) the individual adopts the self-concept of being sick, inadequate, or incompetent. This leads to further vulnerability, leading to another negative cycle and further negative consequences for social and psychological competence. The process can be reversed and competence promoted by providing improved environmental supports while facilitating expression of personal strength. Although useful for sensitizing practitioners in dealing with the problems of aging, the social competence and breakdown model has yet to be tested in empirical studies.

## CONTEMPORARY THEORIES IN SOCIAL GERONTOLOGY

Additional theories emerged in a second period of theorizing in social gerontology and the sociology of aging, including the political economy of aging perspective (Estes, Gerard, Jones, & Swan, 1984), which draws from Marxist thinking and conflict theory in sociology and exchange theory (Dowd, 1975), a rational choice perspective. Since the late 1980s, these theories, as well as earlier theories (activity and modernization theories), have been refined and reformulated, and new theoretical perspectives have emerged. Prominent among the latter are the life course perspective, cumulative advantage and disadvantage theory, and socioemotional selectivity theory. In reviewing theory development in social gerontology, Jon Hendricks (1992) suggested more recent theoretical work reflects an effort to synthesize the distinct micro- or macro-level approaches of earlier theorizing. Also, there has been a shift among a subgroup of social gerontologist toward socially constructed and ideological considerations in theoretical conceptualizing. The growing presence in the field of social constructivism, critical perspectives, feminist theories of aging, political economy of aging perspectives, and postmodernist perspectives reflects this trend.

**The Age Stratification (Age and Society) Theory** This perspective represents one of the oldest traditions of macro-level theorizing in social gerontology. Matilda Riley, Anne Foner, and Joan Waring (1988) traced this perspective's intellectual roots to structural functionalism, particularly the works of sociologists Pitirim Sorokin (1889–1968), Karl Mannheim (1893–1947), and, later, Parsons. This theory seeks to explain (a) cohort flow, or the movement of different age cohorts across time in order to identify similarities and differences between them; (b) the interdependence of age cohorts and social structures; and (c) the asynchrony between structural and individual change over time. Its major concepts are age cohorts, age roles, age-graded social structures, age segregation or integration, and structural lag. Structural lag occurs when social structures cannot keep pace with the changes in population dynamics and individual lives.

Since the late 1980s, Riley and colleagues have refined this perspective, now referred to as the *age and society paradigm*. A current example of structural lag is the discordance between the increasing needs of elderly parents for caregiving support, concurrent reductions in state resources to provide long-term care services, and the resultant increased demands placed on families to provide parent care even as adult children are less able to do so because of employment demands. Using this theoretical perspective, Riley and Karyn Loscocco (1994) argued that a more age-integrated society brought about by policy changes can compensate for structural lag. Restructuring the social institutions of work, education, and the family through such things as extended time off for education or family, for example, can bring social structures in balance with individuals' lives.

**Life Course Theory** This perspective is perhaps the most widely cited theoretical framework in social gerontology in the early 21st century. Its proponents argue that to understand the present circumstances of older adults, one must take into account the major social and psychological forces that have operated throughout the course of their lives (George, 1996). Although there is debate as to whether the life course is a theory or an orienting perspective, it represents a convergence of thinking in sociology and psychology about processes at both macro- and micro-social levels of analysis and for both populations and individuals over time. This multidisciplinary perspective draws content and methods from sociology, psychology, anthropology, and history. Researchers using this perspective are attempting to explain (a) the dynamic nature, context, and process of aging; (b) age-related transitions and life trajectories; (c) how aging is related to and shaped by social contexts, cultural meanings, and social structural location; and (d) how time, period, and cohort shape the aging process for individuals as well as for social groups (Bengston & Allen, 1993; Elder & Johnson, 2003). Although studies so far have not incorporated all four of these life course perspective dimensions in their empirical analyses, new methodological advances suggest such a multilevel, cross-time model in the future.

Glen Elder and Monica Johnson (2003) identified five basic principles that guide life course research. The first is that *development and aging are lifelong processes*; relationships, events, and processes of earlier life stages have consequences for later life relationships, processes, and outcomes. The second principle concerns the *interdependence of lives over time*, especially in the family, where individuals are linked across generations by bonds of kinship and processes of intergenerational transmission. For example, economic declines can have reverberating effects on the interconnected life paths of family members. The third principle concerns *agency* in human development and the idea that individuals make choices within the constraints of social structures and historical conditions. The fourth principle concerns the impact of *history and place* on aging. Researchers now recognize the necessity of nesting individual lives and family processes in social and historical contexts. A fifth principle emphasizes *historical time*, the importance of transitions and their timing relative to structural and historical contexts. There can be "a best fit" in the timing of individual development and family life stage and their temporal convergence with structural and historically created opportunities.

**Cumulative Advantage and Disadvantage Theory** Cumulative advantage and disadvantage theory applies a life course approach to the analysis of stratification among the aged. The theory seeks to explain how inequality in old age is produced. The theory derives from Robert Merton's (1988) original observation of the *Matthew effect* on scientific careers. As applied to the status of older people, the metaphor implies that those already advantaged (across a range of domains, such as health or wealth) will accumulate more benefits, whereas those who are disadvantaged early will accumulate more loss. In the 1970s and 1980s, two themes emerged in social gerontology that the cumulative advantage and disadvantage perspective was uniquely positioned to examine: the heterogeneity or diversity of older persons and the poverty and inequality among the aged. A central concept is intracohort heterogeneity. Structural or institutional arrangements operate to stratify cohorts as they allocate differential opportunities for the accumulation of value and reward. Inequality is seen as the product of institutional arrangement as well as aggregated individual actions over time. People who begin in a position of social advantage generally are better positioned to acquire additional resources than those who begin life at the bottom of the stratification system (Quadagno & Reid, 1999). It is important to explain the within-cohort differences over time along significant life course trajectories in terms of health, family, work, income, and wealth.

There are, however, flaws in this theory according to some researchers. In expanding the scope of cumulative advantage and disadvantage theory, Kenneth Ferraro, Tetyana Shippee, and Markus Schafer (in press) argue that accumulating advantage is not necessarily oppositional to accumulating disadvantage. Cumulative advantage and disadvantage theory ignores power relationships that determine how resources are allocated. A political economy of aging perspective would counter the idea of attributing inequality to structural arrangements and constraints and argue instead that inequality is the product of economic and political forces and power arrangements. Finally, the perspective as currently conceptualized makes no allowance for agency.

**Social Exchange Theory** This micro-level theory has been useful in many studies in social gerontology and the sociology of aging, particularly those focused on intergenerational social support and transfers. Developed and extended by James Dowd's "Aging as Exchange" in 1975, the social exchange theory of aging draws from sociological formulations by George Homans (1910–1989) and Peter Blau (1918–2002) and work in economics that assumes a rational choice model of decision-making behavior. The positivist tradition underlies this perspective; the interpretation of exchange events is not considered. Applied to aging, this perspective attempts to account for exchange behavior between individuals of different ages as a result of the shift in roles, skills, and resources that accompany advancing age. It explicitly incorporates the concept of power differentials. A central assumption here is that the various actors (such as parent and child or elder and youth) each bring resources to the interaction or exchange and that resources need not be material and will most likely be unequal. A second assumption is that the actors will only continue to engage in the exchanges for as long as the benefits are greater than the costs and while there are no better alternatives.

This theoretical approach also assumes that exchanges are governed by norms of reciprocity—that is, when a person gives something, he or she trusts that something of equal value will be reciprocated. A major contribution of the theory is its ability to explain exchanges of contact and social support as well as how these exchanges are influenced by emotional, social, or financial report. However, simplistic formulations of social exchange theory may ignore the fact that many interactions are not driven solely by rationality but rather by irrational motivations such as altruism or affection. Also, the theory is premised on the assumption of an imbalance in the relative power of the parties to the exchange. Finally, in contrast to social constructionist theories, the quality and the meaning of the exchange are ignored.

**Continuity Theory** Continuity theory (Atchley, 1989) proposes that despite some disruptions of established roles and behavior patterns across the life span, individuals are inclined to maintain as much as possible the same habits, personalities, and lifestyles they developed in earlier years. Individuals are also predisposed to continue many activities and major tasks into older age. Further, individuals in later life make adaptations that allow them to gain a sense of continuity between the past and the present. The theory posits that it is this sense of continuity across the life span that contributes to well-being in later life. Continuity theory's implicit reference to trajectories and their constitutive roles, identities, values, and behaviors across life stages finds parallels in aspects of the life course perspective. Assumptions contained in a person's perceptions of the meaning of time—their own constructions or culture-bounded views—may call into question the usefulness of continuity theory. Gary Kenyon, Jan-Eric Ruth, and Wilhelm Mader (1999) questioned whether continuity theory is about aging per se or whether it reflects a cohort, cultural, or period effect based on an unexamined belief in a linear view of time.

**Life Span Development Theory** Life span development theory is one of the most widely cited explanatory frameworks in the psychology of aging as well as social gerontology. The framework conceptualizes ontogenetic development as biologically and socially constituted and as manifesting both developmental universals (homogeneity) and interindividual variability (e.g., differences in genetics and in social class). This perspective also proposes that the second half of life is characterized by significant individual differentiation, multidirectionality, and intraindividual plasticity or adaptability. Using the life span development perspective, Paul Baltes and Jacqui Smith (1999) identified three principles regulating the dynamics between biology and culture across the ontogenetic life span: First, evolutionary selection benefits decrease with age; second, the need for culture increases with age; and third, the efficacy of culture decreases with age. Their focus is on how these dynamics contribute to the optimal expression of human development and the production of outcomes of adaptive fitness. Drawing from evolutionary theory and ontogenetic theories of learning, Baltes and Smith also postulated that a condition of loss, limitation, or deficit could play a catalytic role for positive change.

**Selective Optimization with Compensation Theory** Life span development theory has produced one overall theory to explain how individuals manage adaptive (successful) development in later life. The theory identifies three fundamental mechanisms or strategies: selection, optimization, and compensation (Baltes & Carstensen, 1999). This is a model of psychological and behavioral adaptation in which the central focus is on managing the dynamics between gains and losses as one ages. Selection refers to the increasing restriction of an individual's life to fewer domains of functioning because of age-related loss in the range of adaptive potential. Optimization reflects the idea that people engage in behaviors that augment or enrich their general reserves and maximize their chosen life courses. Like selection, compensation results from restriction of the range of adaptive potential and becomes operative when specific behavioral capacities are lost or are reduced below a standard required for adequate functioning. This lifelong process of selective optimization with compensation enables people to age successfully.

**Socioemotional Selectivity Theory** In this theory, Laura Carstensen (1992) combined insights from developmental psychology—particularly the selective optimization with compensation model—with social exchange theory to explain why the social exchange and interaction networks of older persons are reduced over time (a phenomenon that disengagement theory tried to explain). Through mechanisms of socioemotional selectivity, individuals reduce interactions with some people as they age while increasing emotional closeness with significant others, such as an adult child or a sibling. Carstensen's theory provides a concise developmental-behavioral explanation for selective interaction in old age. This theory explains the change in social contact by the self-interested need for emotional closeness with significant others, which leads to increasingly selective interactions with others in advancing age. Such chosen interactions reflect the levels of reward these exchanges of emotional support achieve for older persons.

**Social Constructionist Theories** Social constructionist theories are among the more frequently cited perspectives in social gerontology. Social constructionist theories draw from a long tradition of micro-level analysis in the social sciences: symbolic interactionism (Mead, 1934), phenomenology (Berger & Luckmann, 1966), and ethnomethodology (Garfinkel, 1967). Using hermeneutic or interpretive methods, social constructionism focuses on individual agency and social behavior within larger structures of society and particularly on the subjective meanings of age and the aging experience. Key concepts of social constructionist theories of aging include social meaning, social realities, social relations, attitudes toward aging and the aged, and life events.

Researchers working in this tradition emphasize their interest in understanding, if not explaining, individual processes of aging as influenced by social definitions and social structures. Examples include Jaber Gubrium's 1993 study of the subjective meanings of quality of care and quality of life for residents of nursing homes and how each resident constructs meanings from her or his own experiences. These meanings emerge from analyses of life narratives but cannot be measured by predefined measurement scales, such as those used by most survey researchers. Sharon Kaufmann (1994) examined how frailty is socially produced through the interaction of older individuals, their caregivers, and their health professionals. One critique of social constructionist theories is that their micro-level focus obscures macro-level effects such as cohort, historical, and age stratification influences. As well, this perspective ignores structure and may minimize the role of power.

**Feminist Theories of Aging** Feminist theories of aging, or feminist gerontology, give priority to gender as an organizing principle for social life across the life span that significantly alters the experience of aging, often in inequitable ways (Calasanti, 1999). This theoretical perspective also challenges what counts as knowledge and how it functions in the lives of older women and men. Current theories and models of aging are regarded as insufficient because they fail to address gender relations, the experience of women in the context of aging and caregiving demands, or issues of race, ethnicity, or class. At the macro-level of analyses, feminist theories of aging combine with political economy and critical perspectives to examine differential access to the key material, health, and caring resources that substantially alters the experience of aging for women and men. For example, feminist researchers seek to explain the higher rates of poverty among older women compared to men and propose changes in the ideologies and institutions that perpetuate it. From a feminist perspective, family caregiving can be understood as an experience of obligation, structured by the gender-based division of domestic labor and the devaluing of unpaid work (Stroller, 1993). At the micro-level, feminist perspectives hold that gender should be examined in the context of social meanings, reflecting the influence of the social constructivist approach.

**Political Economy of Aging Theory** This perspective, which draws originally from Marxism (Marx, 1967), conflict theory (Simmel, 1966), and critical theory (Habermas, 1971), attempts to explain how the interaction of economic and political forces determines how social resources are allocated and how variations in the treatment and status of older adults can be understood by examining public policies, economic trends, and social structural factors (Estes, 2001). A political economy perspective applied to aging maintains that socioeconomic and political constraints shape the experience of aging, resulting in the loss of power, autonomy, and influence of older persons. Life experiences are seen as being patterned not only by age but also by class, gender, and race and ethnicity. These structural factors, often institutionalized or reinforced by economic and public policies, constrain opportunities, choices, and experiences of later life. Another focus of the political economy of aging perspective is how ageism is constructed and reproduced through social practices and policies and how it negatively affects the well-being of older people (Bytheway, 1995).

**Critical Theories of Aging** Critical perspectives are reflected in several theoretical trends in contemporary social gerontology, including the political economy of aging, feminist theories, theories of diversity, and humanistic gerontology. Coming primarily out of the Frankfurt School of Critical Theory (Habermas, 1971), and poststructuralism (Foucault, 1977), these perspectives share a common focus on criticizing the process of power as well as traditional positivistic approaches to knowledge. Critical gerontology has developed two distinct patterns, one that focuses on humanistic dimensions of aging and the other on structural components. Harry Moody (1993) postulated four goals of the humanistic strand of critical theory: (a) to theorize subjective and interpretive dimensions of aging, (b) to focus on praxis (involvement in practical change) instead of technical advancement, (c) to link academics and practitioners through praxis, and (d) to produce emancipatory knowledge.

A second strand emphasizes that critical gerontology should create positive models of aging focusing on the strengths and diversity of age, in addition to critiquing positivist knowledge (Bengtson et al., 1997). To reach the goals of critical gerontology, researchers focus on the key concepts of power, social action, and social meanings in examining the social aspects of age and aging. Social constructionism, feminist theories, and critical perspectives have gained prominence in social gerontological theorizing, mirroring theoretical developments in sociology and the humanities. Not uncommonly, social gerontologists combine insights from all three perspectives to guide their research and interpret findings. At the same time, these theoretical perspectives pose a challenge to the scientific assumptions that have traditionally guided gerontological research.

**Postmodernist Theories** Postmodernist perspectives in aging, sometimes referred to as a postpositivist or post-Enlightenment perspective, follow the work of Michel Foucault (1926–1984), Jean-François Lyotard (1924–1998), and Richard Rorty (1931–2007). There are various strands of postmodernism (economic, feminist, cultural, and deconstructionist), but almost all challenge the Enlightenment's emphasis on individual freedom, rationality, progress, and the power of science to better the human condition. They see science and knowledge as inexorably linked to social control and power. Most postmodernists reject the canons of science; the assumption that reason can provide an objective, reliable, and universal foundation for knowledge; and the idea that reality has a unitary nature that can be definitively observed and understood. This position of extreme relativity toward truth causes postmodernists to challenge the relevance or even the possibility of theory. Postmodernism has been strongly attacked for its antitheoretical stance and for having provided a great deal of criticism of existing theory but offering little that can actually replace it. What postmodernism has contributed is to make social theorists aware of the limits of using a modern metaphor to understand contemporary circumstances and the limits of methodological approaches developed under the modernist metaphor (Pescosolido & Rubin, 2000).

## CONCLUSION

The goal in this entry was, first, to examine the state of theory and knowledge building in social gerontology and assess its prospects for future development and, second, to present an overview of the major theories in the field. Although theory development remains crucial from the perspective of science, many in social gerontology seem to question the importance, or even the validity, of theory. Others may see theorizing as an impediment to getting on with practical matters of solving the problems widely experienced by older people and their families.

In the quest to understand the diverse phenomena of aging, social gerontologists focus on three sets of issues: aging, the aged themselves, and age as a dimension of structure and social organization. Societal aging poses new problems for gerontologists. Developing knowledge that informs policies that can effectively deal with the challenges posed by growing numbers of elders will be crucial in the coming decades. There are good reasons for theory development in the field of social gerontology.

Yet theory development has lagged. This entry then identified specific problems that impede the development of theory and cumulative knowledge building. First, researchers need to make explicit their assumptions and theoretical orientations when presenting their results and interpretations. Second, there has been a proliferation of single aspect research findings—too frequently generated by overly narrow research inquiries—that lack theoretical grounding and explanation. There is a need to raise these empirical generalizations to an explanatory level and integrate explanations and understandings with previous knowledge and explanations. Third, there is the need to cross disciplinary boundaries and develop multidisciplinary and interdisciplinary causal explanations of broader theoretical scope. Fourth, researchers need to be more sensitive to the social dimensions of scholarly research and values that imbue paradigmatic frameworks, affecting the kinds of questions asked, the analytic approaches and methods chosen, and the interpretations put forth. This entry then provided an overview of the major theories in social gerontology.

In the 1990s and 2000s the scientific approach to knowledge in social gerontology has been criticized by those who espouse social constructionist or critical approaches. They argue that general explanatory laws cannot account for people's day-to-day experience and meanings and such laws are rendered impossible because of individual choice making. More fundamentally, critical and postmodernist theorists reject the Enlightenment ideals of reason and progress; they critique science as a source of subordination. Within social gerontology, debates over epistemology and the limitations of science and positivism continue.

Yet it may be possible to accommodate these seemingly incommensurate epistemological positions. Perhaps explanation and understanding in the complex field of social gerontology should draw from a range of theories and theoretical perspectives, depending on the problem at hand. This diversity of theoretical perspectives can offer complementary insights. However, in order for this to happen, it is important that researchers pay more attention to the accumulated knowledge of the field and to be explicit in their theoretical perspectives and insights. After all, there is nothing so practical as a good theory.

**SEE ALSO** Volume 3: *Bengtson, Vern; Baltes, Margret and Paul; Demographic Transition Theories; Epidemiologic Transition; Elder, Glen H., Jr.; Riley, Matilda White;*

Volume 2: *Marx, Karl; Social Structure; Sociological Theories.*

## BIBLIOGRAPHY


Aboderin, I. (2004). Decline in material family support for older people in urban Ghana, Africa: Understanding processes and causes of change. *Journals of Gerontology, Series B: Psychological Sciences and Social Sciences, 59*, 128–137.

Achenbaum, W. A. (1995). *Crossing frontiers: Gerontology emerges as a science.* New York: Cambridge University Press.

Achenbaum, W. A., & Bengtson, V. L. (1994). Re-engaging the disengagement theory of aging: On the history and assessment of theory development in gerontology. *The Gerontologist, 34*, 756–763.

Atchley, R. C. (1989). A continuity theory of normal aging. *The Gerontologist, 29*(2), 183–190.

Baltes, M. M., & Carstensen, L. L. (1999). Social-psychological theories and their applications to aging: From individual to collective. In V. L. Bengtson & K. W. Schaie (Eds.), *Handbook of theories of aging* (pp. 209–226). New York: Springer.

Baltes, P. B., & Smith, J. (1999). Multilevel and systemic analyses of old age: Theoretical and empirical evidence for a fourth age. In V. L. Bengtson & K. W. Schaie (Eds.), *Handbook of theories of aging* (pp. 153–173). New York: Springer.

Bengtson, V. L., & Allen, K. R. (1993). The life course perspective applied to families over time. In P. G. Boss, W. J. Doherty, R. LaRossa, W. R. Schumm, & S. K. Steinmetz (Eds.), *Sourcebook of family theories and methods: A contextual approach.* New York: Plenum Press.

Bengtson, V. L., Burgess, E. O., & Parrott, T. M. (1997). Theory, explanation, and a third generation of theoretical development in social gerontology. *Journals of Gerontology, Series B: Psychological Sciences and Social Sciences, 52*(2), 72–88.

Bengtson, V. L., Rice, C. J., & Johnson, M. L. (1999). Are theories of aging important? Models and explanations in gerontology at the turn of the century. In V. L. Bengtson & K. W. Schaie (Eds.), *Handbook of theories of aging* (pp. 3–20). New York: Springer.

Berger, P. L., & Luckmann, T. (1966). *The social construction of reality: A treatise in the sociology of knowledge.* Garden City, NY: Doubleday.

Birren, J. E. (1999). Theories of aging: A personal perspective. In V. L. Bengtson & K. W. Schaie (Eds.), *Handbook of theories of aging* (pp. 459–471). New York: Springer.

Blau, P. M. (1964). *Exchange and power in social life.* New York: Wiley.

Bytheway, B. (1995). *Ageism.* Buckingham, U.K.: Open University Press.

Calasanti, T. M. (1999). Feminism and gerontology: Not just for women. *Hallym International Journal of Aging, 1*(1), 44–55.

Carstensen, L. (1992). Social and emotional patterns in adulthood: Support for socioemotional selectivity theory. *Psychology and Aging, 7*(3), 331–338.

Cowdry, E. V. (Ed.). (1939). *Problems of aging.* Baltimore, MD: Williams and Wilkins.

Cowgill, D. O. (1974). Aging and modernization. A revision of the theory. In J. F. Gubrium (Ed.), *Late life: Communities and environmental policy* (pp. 126–146). Springfield, IL: Thomas.

Cumming, E., & Henry, W. (1961). *Growing old: The process of disengagement.* New York: Basic Books.

Dowd, J. J. (1975). Aging as exchange: A preface to theory. *Journal of Gerontology, 30*(5), 584–594.

Elder, G. H., Jr., & Johnson, M. K. (2003). The life course and aging: Challenges, lessons, and new directions. In R. A. Settersten, Jr. (Ed.), *Invitation to the life course: Toward new understandings of later life* (pp. 49–81). Amityville, NY: Baywood.

Estes, C. L. (Ed.). (2001). Political economy of aging: A theoretical framework. In *Social policy and aging: A critical perspective.* Thousand Oaks, CA: Sage.

Estes, C. L., Gerard, L. E., Jones, J. S., & Swan, J. H. (1984). *Political economy, health, and aging.* Boston: Little, Brown.

Ferraro, K. F., Shippee, T. P., & Schafer. M. H. (in press). Cumulative inequality theory for research on aging and the life course. In V. L. Bengtson, M. Silverstein, N. M. Putney, & D. Gans (Eds.), *Handbook of theories of aging.* (3rd ed.). New York: Springer.

Foucault, M. (1977). *Discipline and punish: The birth of a prison,* Trans. A. Sheridan. New York: Pantheon.

Garfinkel, H. (1967). *Studies in ethnomethodology.* Englewood, NJ: Prentice-Hall.

George, L. K. (1996). Missing links: The case for a social psychology of the life course. *The Gerontologist, 36*, 248–255.

Gubrium, J. F. (1993). *Speaking of life: Horizons of meaning for nursing home residents.* Hawthorne, NY: Aldine de Gruyter.

Gubrium, J. F., & Holstein, J. A. (1999). Constructionist perspectives on aging. In V. L. Bengtson & K. W. Schaie (Eds.), *Handbook of theories of aging* (pp. 287–305). New York: Springer.

Habermas, J. (1971). *Knowledge and human interests,* Trans. J. J. Shapiro. Boston: Beacon Press.

Hall, G. S. (1922). *Senescence: The last half of life.* New York: Appleton.

Havighurst, R. J., & Albrecht, R. (1953). *Older people.* New York: Longmans, Green.

Hendricks, J. (1992). Generations and the generation of theory in social gerontology. *International Journal of Aging and Human Development, 35*(1), 31–47.

Hendricks, J., & Achenbaum, A. (1999). Historical development of theories of aging. In V. L. Bengtson & K. W. Schaie (Eds.), *Handbook of theories of aging* (pp. 21–39). New York: Springer.

Hochschild, A. R. (1975). Disengagement theory: A critique and a proposal. *American Sociological Review, 40*(5), 553–569.

Homans, G. C. (1961). *Social behavior: Its elementary forms.* New York: Harcourt, Brace, & World.

Kaufmann, S. R. (1994). The social construction of frailty: An anthropological perspective. *Journal of Aging Studies, 8*, 45–58.

Kenyon, G. M., Ruth, J.-E., & Mader, W. (1999). Elements of a narrative gerontology. In V. L. Bengtson & K. W. Schaie (Eds.), *Handbook of theories of aging* (pp. 40–58). New York: Springer.

Kuhn, T. (1962). *The structure of scientific revolutions.* Chicago: University of Chicago Press.

Kuypers, J. A., & Bengtson, V. L. (1973). Social breakdown and competence: A model of normal aging. *Human Development, 16*(3), 181–201.

Lemon, B. W., Bengtson, V. L., & Peterson, J. A. (1972). An exploration of the activity theory of aging: Activity types and life satisfaction among in-movers to a retirement community. *Journal of Gerontology, 27,* 511–523.

Linton, R. (1942). Age and sex categories. *American Sociological Review, 7*(5), 589–603.

Lyotard, J. F. (1984). *The postmodern condition: A report on knowledge,* Trans. G. Bennington & B. Massumi. Minneapolis: University of Minnesota Press.

Mannheim, K. (1952). The problem of generations. In P. Kecskemeti (Ed.), *Karl Mannheim: Essays in sociology of knowledge.* London: Routledge and Kegan Paul. (Original work published 1928)

Marshall, V. W. (1999). Analyzing social theories of aging. In V. L. Bengtson & K. W. Schaie (Eds.), *Handbook of theories of aging* (pp. 434–455). New York: Springer.

Marx, K. (1967). *Capital: A critique of political economy.* New York: International Publishers. (Original work published 1867)

Mead, G. H. (1934). *Mind, self, and society.* Chicago: University of Chicago Press.

Merton, R. K. (1988). The Matthew effect in science, II: Cumulative advantage and the symbolism of intellectual property. *Isis, 79*(4), 606–623.

Moody, H. R. (1993). Overview: What is critical gerontology and why is it important? In T. R. Cole, W. A. Achenbaum, P. L. Jakobi, & R. Kastenbaum (Eds.), *Voices and visions of aging: Toward a critical gerontology.* New York: Springer.

Parsons, T. (1942). Age and sex in the social structure of the United States. *American Sociological Review, 7*(5), 604–616.

Pescosolido, B. A., & Rubin, B. A. (2000). The web of group affiliations revisited: Social life, postmodernism, and sociology. *American Sociological Review, 65*(1), 52–76.

Quadagno, J., & Reid, J. (1999). The political economy perspective in aging. In V. L. Bengtson & K. W. Schaie (Eds.), *Handbook of theories of aging* (pp. 344–358). New York: Springer.

Riley, M. W., Foner, A., & Waring, J. (1988). Sociology of age. In N. J. Smelser (Ed.), *Handbook of sociology.* Newbury Park, CA: Sage.

Riley, M. W., & Loscocco, K. A. (1994). The changing structure of work opportunities: Toward an age-integrated society. In R. P. Abeles, H. C. Gift, & M. G. Ory (Eds.), *Aging and quality of life.* New York: Springer.

Rorty, R. (1994). Method, social science, and social hope. In S. Seidman (Ed.), *The postmodern turn: New perspectives on social theory.* Cambridge, U.K.: Cambridge University Press.

Rowe, J. W., & Kahn, R. L. (1998). *Successful aging.* New York: Pantheon.

Schmeeckle, M., & Bengtson, V. L. (1999). Successful aging. Conclusions from a longitudinal study: Cross-sectional perspectives. *Contemporary Gerontology, 5*(3), 87–90.

Simmel, G. (1966). *Conflict and the web of group affiliations,* Trans. K. H. Wolff. Glencoe, IL: Free Press. (Original work published 1908)

Sorokin, P. A. (1947). *Society, culture, and personality.* New York: Harper.

Strauss, A., & Corbin, J. (1990). *Basics of qualitative research: Grounded theory procedures and techniques.* Newbury Park, CA: Sage.

Stroller, E. P. (1993). Gender and the organization of lay health care: A socialist-feminist perspective. *Journal of Aging Studies, 7,* 151–170.

Turner, J. H. (2003). *The structure of sociological theory.* Belmont, CA: Wadsworth Thomson Learning.



***Norella M. Putney***
***Vern L. Bengtson***


# TIME USE, LATER LIFE

Time is an essential resource for older adults in modern life, particularly because they have so much of it. This especially applies to those older adults who can rely on pensions and retirement income, rather than working for pay. Indeed, most older adults lead lives that meet the classical definition of *leisure* by Greek philosophers, namely freedom from the necessity of work. Thus, older adults should expect to have maximal freedom in choosing how they spend their time, within the constraints posed by physical or financial limitations. Time is an important resource to examine because its management and the choices of activities people choose to occupy it with expresses their values and motivations across the life course. As illustrated here, one can also see how demographic and other factors seem to shape people's lives, such as becoming retired, providing elder care, or going to college.

## MEASURING PEOPLE'S TIME USE: TIME ESTIMATES VERSUS TIME DIARIES

There are two main types of data sources from which to infer patterns and trends in how time is spent: time estimates and time diaries. Most researchers have come to rely mainly on the more elaborate and comprehensive technique of the time diary, because with diaries, they can assess *all* daily activities—not merely individual work or free-time activities. Having equivalent measures for younger adults of working age further allows researchers to document how people's daily life changes as they retire or grow older.

**Bureau of Labor Statistics (BLS) Work Estimates** The BLS has the oldest time series of relevant data on employment status and work hours; some statistics date back 100 years or more. These data have advantages over more commonly used time diaries because they broaden one's understanding by (a) extending back to earlier points in

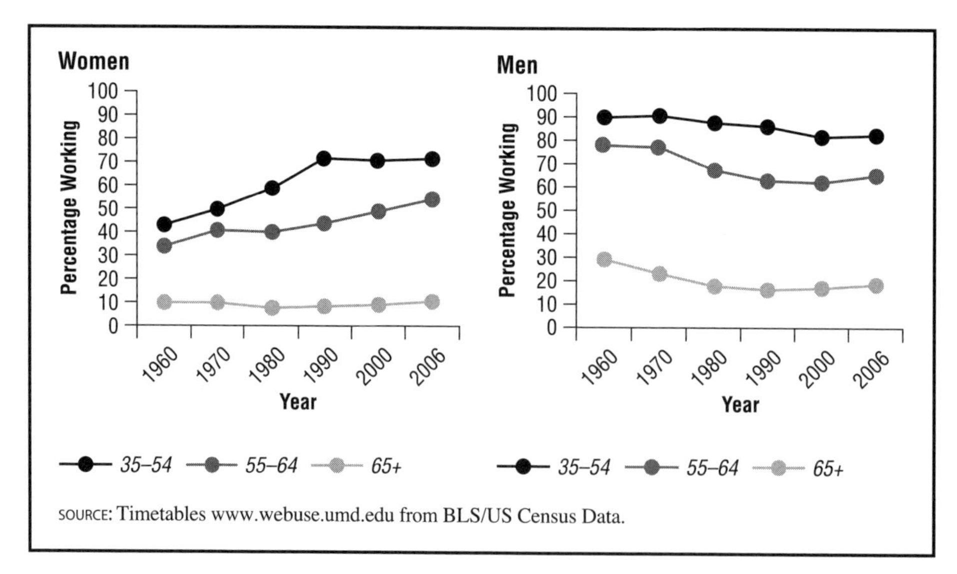


***Figure 1.*** *Changes in proportions working at a paid job by age: 1960–2006.* CENGAGE LEARNING, GALE.

history, (b) having larger sample sizes, and (c) covering specialized or more detailed activities. Figure 1 shows decennial trends in employment status since 1960, which documents the steady increases in the percentage of younger women employed in a given year (from 42.5% in 1960 to 71.5% in 2006 for those ages 35 to 54, and from 34% in 1960 to 54.5% in 2006 for those ages 55 to 64). In contrast, one sees steady declines for men (from 91% in 1960 to 84% in 2006 for those ages 35 to 54, and from 79% in 1960 to 66% in 2006 for those ages 55 to 64).

The contrasts for those past the nominal retirement age of 65 can be seen to be quite different, however. For older men, there is the decrease from a 29% employment rate in 1960 to 19% in 2006, but for older women, there is no change—the 10% in 1960 remained steady in 2006. Thus, current cohorts of older women are not taking part in the gendered work revolution evidenced among younger women, with their rate of being employed only half that of older men. Moreover, even those older women who do work put in less than half the work time (3 weekly hours) of senior employed men (8 hours).

**General Social Survey (GSS) Free-Time Activities** The GSS has been asking questions about older and younger people's participation in eight free time activities since 1972. These GSS data allow researchers to examine time-use trends since 1972 within age groups and patterns of change as one ages. Thus, it is possible to examine how older adults in the early 21st century are different than past generations of older adults and how they differ from younger age groups.

In the area of socializing, the GSS data show slight increases among older adults in visits with friends and with relatives but decreasing visits with neighbors and at bars—trends that mirror historical trends for adults under age 65. At the same time, the GSS participation rates in all four of these forms of socializing activity do decline as adults get older. By far, the greatest declines with age are found for sexual activity—from 36 occasions per year for those 55 to 64, to 18 occasions per year for those between 65 and 74, to 6 occasions per year for those 75 and older. Overall occasions of sex among older adults, however, have not declined since 1989.

GSS data on religious services attendance also show stark life course differences. Younger adults' participation has declined over the past 35 years, whereas attendance at religious services among older adults has remained fairly steady during this time period. However, religious attendance does also decline with advanced age, especially as older adults reach their mid-80s. Similarly, reading newspapers has not declined for older adults in their 60s and 70s, but it has declined dramatically for younger adults and declined only somewhat for persons in their 80s. In contrast, estimated TV viewing among older adults has increased slightly since the 1970s, and viewing is one activity that does increase with age into one's 80s.

## TIME DIARY STUDIES

In time-diary accounts, respondents are asked not to estimate or to make complex, vague, and changing calculations but to simply recall all of their activities sequentially for a specific period, usually the previous day. This mode of data collection generally takes 10 to 15 minutes to complete over the telephone. This not only reduces the respondents' recall period and reporting burden but also ensures that the resulting account respects the zero-sum property of time; that is, activities must total to exactly 24 hours a day. For example, if time spent on paid work decreases, then it must be *zeroed out* by increases in time spent on other activities.

Considerable evidence supports the basic reliability and validity of such diary data. Various diary accounts are consistent with each other and with other ways of collecting time data (such as observational or "beeper" studies, in which respondents are paged electronically throughout the day, which have yet to be done with representative samples of older people). Indeed, the diary can be seen as a type of social microscope, offering unique insights into the minutiae of daily life, much as the biological microscope allowed scientists to examine aspects of life not earlier observable.

Moreover, in the process of collecting such data, researchers have been able to obtain detailed information about who participated in activities, what other activities were taking place at the same time (multitasking), where and when activities took place, and any number of other aspects of an activity (including how much people enjoy the activity). Time diaries provide the dynamic feature of watching everyday life unfold across the 24 hours of a typical day.

This is not to say that the diary is without flaws. Respondents can still distort, embellish, or even lie about what they do. Many, when asked to recall, simply cannot remember and may substitute a habitual activity (i.e., what they "usually" do) for what actually took place. The method also demands much time and effort from both interviewer and respondent, although survey respondents usually enjoy the process of spontaneously recalling their daily activities over the telephone once underway.

One of the controversies surrounding time-diary data collections is whether certain types of individuals (e.g., busy people) fail to respond to the diary. Robinson (1985) found that busier people (e.g., people who worked more or slept less or watched less TV) in an initial survey were actually *more* likely to participate in a follow-up diary survey. Gershuny (2000) similarly concluded that nonresponse was not associated with an individual's activity patterns.

**Scientific Support for the Time Diary Method** Time estimates from surveys may overestimate time spent in a variety of activities. For example, Verbrugge and Gruber-Baldine (1993) reported average estimated weekly activity totals of 187 hours (versus the 168 hours actually available in a week), and their list of activities did not include time for church-going, shopping, and adult education. In one national survey (Hawes, Talarzyk, & Blackwell, 1975), estimated weekly activities averaged more than 230 hours. Godbey and Chase (1983) found almost half of all respondents overestimated the actual number of times they used a fitness center by more than 100%, when compared to the center log-in records.

Past research has shown that time diary estimates of paid work hours are typically lower than survey estimates derived from the Current Population Survey (Robinson & Bostrom, 1994). Robinson and Gershuny found consistent overreporting of paid work hours by employed people not only in the United States but also in 10 other Western countries. Robinson and Godbey (1999) showed even more serious overestimation of time spent doing housework and doing volunteer activity and underestimation of time sleeping and free time. This is consistent with the hypothesis of social desirability bias so prominent in public opinion and attitude studies; this hypothesis holds that people will overstate their time spent on prestigious or socially valued activities and understate their time spent on activities associated with fun, relaxation, or laziness.

Older adults were not included in the first national diary study in 1965, but they were included in the subsequent national diary studies conducted in 1975, 1985, and between 1992 and 1995 (Robinson and Godbey, 1999). These later diary studies had modest sample sizes overall and small samples of older adults, in particular. In the annual American Time Use Survey (ATUS), which began in 2003 and is the most recent of the BLS diary surveys, more than 9,000 older adults have been interviewed. (The ATUS data from 2003 through 2005 are shown in Table 1.)

**Diary Patterns and Trends** Table 1 shows the ATUS activity times of men and women age 65 and older in comparison to two younger age groups, those age 55 through 64 and 35 through 54. Those in the age range between 55 and 64 may be seen as a transitional age group; they may be undergoing "anticipatory socialization" into the world of retirement. This middle-age group thus acts as a bridge between those aged 35 to 54 and those age 65 and older—the usual age of retirement.

Figure 1 first reveals the dramatic decline in older adults' time spent in paid work and commuting by 6 to 10 hours per week for those ages 55 to 64. This drops another 15 to 20 hours per week on average after age 64. These declines are mainly offset by increases in housework (4 hours more per week), sleep (4 hours more per week), TV watching (8 hours more per week), reading (5 hours more per week), hobbies (1 hour more per week), and relaxation (about 3 hours more per week). Activities that show smaller age-related increases are eating and

| Time Uses/ Activities (Age) | Women 35–54 | 55–64 | 65– | Age Diff. +/– | Men 35–54 | 55–64 | 65– | Age Diff. +/– |
|---|---|---|---|---|---|---|---|---|
| **A. CONTRACTED TIME** | | | | | | | | |
| 1. Paid Work | 25.4 | 19.8 | 3.3 | **–21** | 38.1 | 28.1 | 6.5 | **–32** |
| 2. Commute | 2.0 | 1.4 | 0.2 | **–2** | 3.1 | 2.4 | 0.5 | **–3** |
| 2x. Education | 0.9 | 0.4 | 0.3 | **–1** | 0.5 | 0.2 | 0.1 | **0** |
| **B. COMMITTED TIME** | | | | **–24** | | | | **–35** |
| 3. Housework | 17.8 | 19.0 | 23.0 | **+5** | 10.2 | 12.5 | 13.8 | **+4** |
| 4. Child care | 6.7 | 2.6 | 1.3 | **–5** | 3.5 | 1.2 | 0.8 | **–3** |
| 5. Shopping | 7.2 | 7.6 | 6.7 | **–1** | 4.7 | 5.0 | 6.3 | **+2** |
| **C. PERSONAL CARE** | | | | **–1** | | | | **+3** |
| 6. Sleeping | 58.5 | 58.3 | 62.3 | **+4** | 57.2 | 57.7 | 62.0 | **+5** |
| 7. Eating | 7.2 | 8.2 | 9.2 | **+2** | 8.0 | 9.3 | 10.2 | **+2** |
| 8. Grooming | 8.6 | 9.8 | 9.6 | **+1** | 6.6 | 7.3 | 8.2 | **+2** |
| **D. FREE TIME** | | | | **+7** | | | | **+9** |
| 9. Religion | 0.9 | 1.3 | 1.5 | **+1** | 0.7 | 0.8 | 1.1 | **0** |
| 10. Organizations | 1.8 | 1.7 | 2.1 | **0** | 1.3 | 1.3 | 1.9 | **+1** |
| 11. Social Events | 0.9 | 0.9 | 0.8 | **0** | 0.9 | 0.9 | 0.7 | **0** |
| 12. Visiting | 4.7 | 5.4 | 5.1 | **0** | 3.8 | 3.7 | 4.2 | **0** |
| 13. Fitness Activity | 1.3 | 1.1 | 1.1 | **0** | 2.0 | 2.3 | 2.2 | **0** |
| 14. Hobbies | 0.7 | 1.4 | 2.0 | **+1** | 0.8 | 1.1 | 2.0 | **+1** |
| 15. TV | 14.4 | 17.6 | 25.1 | **+11** | 18.7 | 22.2 | 29.3 | **+11** |
| 16. Radio/records | 0.2 | 0.2 | 0.5 | **0** | 0.5 | 0.4 | 0.7 | **0** |
| 17. Reading | 2.2 | 4.3 | 7.1 | **+5** | 1.7 | 3.0 | 6.7 | **+5** |
| 18. Home Comm. | 2.1 | 2.4 | 2.6 | **0** | 1.7 | 1.9 | 2.1 | **0** |
| 19. IT | 0.7 | 0.8 | 0.8 | **0** | 1.1 | 1.2 | 1.0 | **0** |
| 20. Rest/relax | 1.7 | 2.3 | 4.3 | **+3** | 2.0 | 2.9 | 5.5 | **+4** |
| 21. Free travel | 1.9 | 2.1 | 1.9 | **0** | 1.9 | 2.1 | 2.2 | **+3** |
| **E. TOTAL FREE** | **34.1** | **41.5** | **54.2** | **+20** | **36.6** | **43.5** | **59.6** | **+23** |
| 22. Total travel | 8.7 | 7.6 | 5.5 | **–3** | 7.7 | 7.8 | 6.4 | **–1** |

SOURCE : Timetables www.webuse.umd.edu based on BLS/US Census Data.

***Table 1.*** *Time/activity differences by age (in hours per week from 2003–2005).* CENGAGE LEARNING, GALE.

grooming. In addition to the work decline, there is the expected decline in the amount of time spent providing childcare. Thus, the main changes in free time are concentrated on TV, reading, and relaxing and hence do not generally extend to other free-time activities. No declines are found in organizational activity, fitness (sports) activities, or attending movies and other social events; however, total travel outside the home does decline, probably a function of the decreased need to commute to work.

Of particular interest to researchers is the increase in time spent doing housework for both older men and women. With fewer family members and smaller homes to care for, why would more time be devoted to housework in these empty-nest years? Even though married men's hours of housework and shopping increase from 10 to over 13 hours per week as they age, older married women continue to do almost two-thirds of the total housework.

Also of interest is the rather dramatic increase in TV viewing past retirement. Of the 20 or more hours of increased free time for those age 65 and older, about half of it is spent on TV. However, in percentage of free time, the increase in TV's share of free time only rises from 42% to 46% among women age 65 and older, whereas for men it declines slightly from 51% to 49%—thus closing the gender gap in TV viewing time.

Finally, it is important to note that many of the age differences in activity noted in Table 1 reflect differences not in age per se but in hours spent at work. When the increases in housework, sleep, TV, and reading are adjusted for this employment status, the age differences are almost a nonfactor. In other words, older adults who continue to work show activity patterns quite similar to workers under age 65.

**Differences by Background Factors** Among older adults, average paid work hours decline from 8 hours for those ages 65 to 72, to 3 hours for those between 73 and 79, to less than an hour for those 80 and older. Housework hours also decline but only slightly, from 18 hours to 15 hours for those 80 and older. Sleeping hours increase by about 5 hours, but only for those 85 and older, and TV, relaxing, and reading hours also increase—each by about 4 hours per week. Both free time and overall travel decline almost 4 hours past age 84.

Table 1 shows many of the same gender patterns as revealed among younger adults, as noted earlier in the finding for women's domination of housework (and childcare). In contrast, older men continue to do two-thirds of the paid work. In terms of personal care, sleep hours of men and women remain virtually identical, whereas men spend more time eating and women more time grooming. Older men have about 5 more hours of free time than older women, almost all of which they devote to TV viewing, with more time spent exercising and relaxing as well. Even with less free time, older women manage to find slightly more free time for religion, organizational activity, socializing, and reading. Similar to observed racial differences among younger adults, older Blacks spend more time grooming, attending church, watching TV, and relaxing than older Whites, who in turn spend more time doing housework, eating, and reading than older Blacks.

In terms of role factors, the differences are less pronounced than for preretirement groups. Employed seniors spend 10 fewer hours per week watching TV, 3 hours less reading, and about an hour less time on hobbies and in home communication, compared to their nonworking peers. Married seniors work about 3 more hours, but they spend about 3 hours less time asleep or watching TV than those not married; there are no differences on housework or on other free time activities.

In terms of status factors, higher education and income are associated with spending twice as much time working compared to those with lower levels of education and income. There are no differences in time spent in housework, childcare, or shopping. College-educated and older adults in the highest income category spend 5 fewer hours per week sleeping than those with lower education and income, which is offset by 2 to 3 more hours eating meals but no notable difference in grooming time. As with adults under age 65, the most sizable free-time activity differences were found for media use, with the college-educated and highest income earners watching about 5 fewer hours of TV each week (again offset by 4 to 5 more hours reading and about an hour more of computer use). Higher educated and income groups also spend more of their free time traveling, including travel that is tied more to organizational meetings. They also spend less time relaxing.

**Historical Trends** Little time-diary data are available about historical trends in time use among older adults. Nonetheless, some fairly clear patterns emerge, and these generally parallel the trends shown in Table 1—patterns also noted in analyses conducted on these earlier diary studies of older adults (Robinson, 1997). Since between 1975 and 1985, changes among older adults have been concentrated in a few activities. Older adults sleep more then in the past (older women sleep 2 more hours and older men sleep 5 more hours per week). Older adults are also watching more television than in the past (3 to 5 more hours on average per week). These increases are offset by smaller decreases in a number of personal care and free-time activities such as eating, grooming, visiting, fitness activity, hobbies, and home communication. These results largely mirror those trends found among working-age persons. There is one important exception: No decline in housework time was documented among older adults.

## POLICY ISSUES AND TIME FOR OLDER ADULTS

As is true for people under age 65, time-diary coverage of all daily activity in a society might be thought to have far-reaching policy implications. However, it is difficult to develop policy interventions to adjust for time use and the potential health consequences thereof. For example, the National Sleep Foundation has raised general alarms about sleep deprivation as a national crisis. However, time-diary studies show no decrease in sleep since the late 1960s. National recommendations are holding steady at the recommended and legendary "8 hours a day" figure for older adults, as well as younger adults.

Readers and leisure advocates may be alarmed at the fact so much of older adults' free time is devoted to TV viewing, making them an ideal target for "Turn Off Your TV Week," which prompts people to leave their TVs off for one designated week each year and find more concentration, challenge, and gratification in other activities. Ironically, diary research suggests that although people rate TV in general as relatively low on the "fun meter" the programs they watched on the diary day rated far higher in enjoyment, actually above the levels for other free-time activities. Moreover, although viewing hours do rise dramatically for older adults, this rise does not equal the heavily increased proportion of free time that occurred when viewing hours for younger adults rose between 1965 and 1975.

Many policy ideas and findings about increasing the quality of daily lives of older people were brought out in the pioneering studies of Baldes and Baldes (1990), and future generations of social gerontologists and policy makers can draw insights from their efforts to weigh policy options to help optimize time use and daily life activities during the so-called golden years.

**SEE ALSO** Volume 3: *Leisure and Travel, Later Life; Volunteering, Later Life.*

**BIBLIOGRAPHY**

Baltes, P., & Baltes, M. (1990). *Successful aging: Perspectives from the behavioral sciences.* New York: Cambridge University Press.

Godbey, G., & Chase, D. R. (1983). The accuracy of self-reported participation rates: A research note. *Leisure Studies, 2,* 231–235.

Gershuny, J. (2000). *Changing times: Work and leisure in postindustrial society.* Oxford, U. K.: Oxford University Press.

Hawes, D., Talarzyk, W., & Blackwell, R. (1975). Consumer satisfactions from leisure time pursuits. In M. Schlinger (Ed.), *Advances in consumer research.* Chicago: Association for Consumer Research.

Juster, F. T., & Stafford, F. P. (1985). *Time, goods, and well-being.* Ann Arbor: Survey Research Center, Institute for Social Research, University of Michigan.

Robinson, J. P. (1985). The validity and reliability of diaries versus alternative time use measures. In F. T. Juster & F. Stafford (Eds.), *Time, goods, and well-being* (pp. 33–62). Ann Arbor: Survey Research Center, Institute for Social Research, University of Michigan.

Robinson, J. P. (1997). Freeing up the golden years. *American Demographics, 19*(10), 20–24.

Robinson, J. P., & Bostrom, A. (1994). The overestimated workweek? What time diary measures suggest. *Monthly Labor Review, 117*(8), 11–23.

Robinson, J. P., & Gershuny, J. I. (1994). Measuring hours of paid work: Time diary versus estimate questions. In *Bulletin of Labor Statistics* (pp. xi–xvii). Geneva, Switzerland: International Labor Office.

Robinson, J. P., & Godbey, G. (1999). *Time for life: The surprising ways Americans use their time.* (2nd ed.). University Park: Pennsylvania State University Press.

Verbrugge, L., & Gruber-Baldine, D. (1993). *Baltimore study of activity patterns.* Ann Arbor: Institute of Gerontology, University of Michigan.

***John Robinson***
***Steven Martin***
***Andrew Caparaso***

## VISION PROBLEMS

SEE Volume 3: *Sensory Impairments.*

## VOLUNTEERING, LATER LIFE

Volunteering is a form of helping activity that occurs throughout the life course. Volunteering is considered by many observers to be an important activity for the support and vibrancy of local communities, for the well-being of individuals, and for maintaining the foundations of democracy in part because trust and norms of reciprocity are central to this form of government (Wilson & Musick, 1999). More than 150 years ago, Alexis de Tocqueville (1835–1840) was among the first to observe that the United States was replete with countless examples of selfless helping activity occurring within communities even while its people and its ethos heavily promoted individualism and self-sufficiency. This paradox remains a characteristic of American society today.

### DEFINING AND STUDYING VOLUNTEERING

Wilson (2000) defines volunteering as "any activity in which time is given freely to benefit another person, group, or organization" (p. 215). One advocacy group, the Independent Sector (2001), estimates that in the year 2000 the economic value of all types of formal and informal volunteering among persons in the United States was nearly $240 billion. Johnson and Schaner (2005) estimate that in 2002 persons age 55 and over contributed $162 billion, or $2,698 per person, worth of helping in the form of volunteering and unpaid help given to others. Older women provided about $3,000 worth of volunteering, on average, annually and older men provided about $2,400. They also estimate that the value of formal volunteering alone for this age group was $44 billion. Combining both formal and informal types of volunteering, these authors show that about three out of every four older persons provided some form of unpaid help. These data provide an economic benchmark for the valuable contributions that older persons make to American society.

The remainder of this entry focuses primarily on formal volunteering, typically structured through affiliation with a group or organization. Informal volunteering, or informal helping, as it is sometimes called, is help given to others in a person's social network without receiving pay. This type of helping tends to be unstructured and is geared toward relatives, friends, and neighbors.

### HISTORICAL AND DEMOGRAPHIC TRENDS

The number of people volunteering in the United States has fluctuated over time, causing some observers to express concern that Americans may be losing their civic consciousness. Nevertheless, volunteering among all age groups is relatively high in the United States. For example, between 1989 and 2005 volunteering among adults increased by 32%; most of this growth occurred among three age groups: older teenagers (16 to 19 years old), middle-aged adults (45 to 64 years old), and older adults (65 years old and older) (Corporation for National and Community Service, 2006). These increases may be attributable to a renewed sense of community brought on by national tragedy (the 9/11 terrorists attacks) or to media coverage of national disasters, such as hurricanes and massive wildfires. As well, increased recruitment efforts among nonprofit organizations may explain some of the increase. Some characteristics unique to the current generation of older persons may also explain the increase, including rising average levels of education and income and generational differences in commitment to communities related to the historical context in which a person grew up (Corporation for National and Community Service, 2006).

Among the three age groups that are most likely to volunteer, older persons are somewhat less likely to volunteer than persons in the other two groups. In 2005 the proportions of volunteers for each age group were as follows: 23.5% for persons 65 years old and over, 30% for persons 45 to 64 years old, and 28.4% for persons 16 to 19 years old. Research confirms a curvilinear relationship between age and volunteering, whereby the likelihood of volunteering increases through young adulthood until reaching a high point in middle age where it then levels off with a slight downturn in later life due in part to reduced health resources among the elderly (Corporation for National and Community Service, 2006). Individuals in the age 65 and older group are nevertheless more likely than those in the other age groups to volunteer more than 100 hours annually.

In 2002, nearly 20 million persons over age 55 volunteered, and the average number of hours committed annually to volunteering among this age group was 169 (Zedlewski & Schaner, 2006). This same study, using nationally representative survey data of the U.S. population, demonstrated that more than 33% of those persons aged 65 to 75 who were not working were volunteers, and that for the same age group nearly 46% of persons who were working also volunteered. Persons who work, even those in the later stages of the life course, are more likely to volunteer than persons who do not work.

Among all age groups, Whites are the most likely to volunteer, followed by African Americans and Hispanics. In addition, married persons are more likely to volunteer than nonmarried persons, and part-time workers are more likely to volunteer than full-time workers or those who are unemployed. Finally, adults living with children, especially older children, contribute more volunteer activity than those living in households without children (Wilson, 2000).

People of all ages, including the elderly, volunteer for a range of organizations and groups, including religious organizations (45% of older volunteers did so for a religious group). Other organizations include civic and political groups, educational and cultural organizations, and other community organizations. Hospitals and other health care organizations are common sources of volunteer activity, but fewer than 11% of older persons volunteered in 2005 for these types of organizations (Corporation for National and Community Service, 2006).

## CENTRAL THEMES IN THE STUDY OF VOLUNTEERING

Studies on volunteering have centered around three themes: explanations of volunteering, the relationship between aging and volunteer activity, and the health benefits of volunteering. Explaining why people volunteer, irrespective of their age, is important both to scholars and to organizations that rely on volunteers in order to conduct their business (Wilson, 2000). Since the late 1980s social psychologists have spent considerable effort evaluating the motives that underlie volunteering activity. Some argue that volunteering is a learned activity in which the value of volunteering is taught to children by their parents and in schools; thus an intergenerational link commits people to a career in volunteering that often spans the life course. Research that employs values as a predictor of volunteer behavior has seen only limited success, in part because of the wide range of volunteer activities in which people engage and the varieties of meaning they attach to those activities.

Bradley (1999–2000) argues there are at least three categories of motivation for volunteering among older persons. The first is that volunteering provides a sense of purpose to one's life and allows older persons to give back to the community; this allows older people to make a difference while providing meaningful activity. The second category is personal growth; many older persons desire to pursue individual goals and interests such as increasing knowledge about a political issue or social problem and volunteering is one mechanism for achieving these goals. The third category is continued productivity. Volunteering for a formal organization provides structure in one's day (there is a reason to get up in the morning), and the volunteer accrues social rewards related to helping others (social status).

Some sociologists, economists, and gerontologists argue that volunteering is similar to any other form of work, except that it is unpaid. As with paid work, to be a volunteer requires skills that come from education and work experience. People with higher levels of education have more skills, and they are more likely to learn about or be aware of problems that need attention, and they are also more likely to be asked to volunteer. Having a job provides persons with a social network where civic skills may be learned and applied, yielding more volunteering

(Wilson, 2000). It has been hypothesized that when older persons retire from work, they might replace at least some of their paid work hours with unpaid volunteering hours (Chambre, 1984). Relatively little research evidence supports this idea. Instead, the evidence seems to show that persons who were volunteers before retirement are more likely to volunteer after retirement; in other words, there is continuity across the life course when it comes to volunteering rather than a substitution of one form of work for another (Mutchler, Burr, & Caro, 2003).

Another important factor in explaining volunteering behavior concerns the contribution of a person's social network and social relationships. The odds of volunteering increase for those persons who know a lot of other people; who are members of social, political, and professional organizations; and, as noted above, who have prior volunteering experience (Wilson 2000, p. 223). For the elderly, belonging to a religious organization is the most important conduit to the volunteer role because many volunteer opportunities occur within the context of the religious organization itself. Also, religious organizations provide a social network for learning about volunteering opportunities.

The relationship between aging and activity has a long history of investigation in the social sciences. When social scientists think about volunteering, they often consider it as falling under the umbrella of successful aging, which was given a renewed emphasis and attention by Rowe and Kahn (1998). One of the three important tenets of the successful aging paradigm is that older persons should remain active and engaged in their communities. Volunteering is certainly one mechanism for remaining active and engaged.

Two prominent theories of the relationship between activity of all kinds and aging yield diametrically different predictions. Activity theory suggests that as people age they will remain active within the limits of their health and functional status. Disengagement theory suggests that as people age they will remove themselves from many of the roles they once held and will eventually recede entirely from meaningful social pursuits. A relatively new theory called socioemotional selectivity offers a more nuanced way of framing the issue (Carstensen, 1992). This theory suggests that as people age they do reduce some of their social roles and the activities associated with these roles, but they choose among options available to them, deciding which activities to commit to and which to leave behind. Their choices are seen as being driven at least in part by those roles and activities that have the most meaning to them.

Hendricks and Cutler (2004) set out to investigate this possibility as it relates to volunteer activity and aging. From socioemotional selectivity theory, they hypothesize that as people move into the later stages of the life course they will reduce the number of volunteer activities in which they engage, and they will reduce the total number of hours of volunteering. They also hypothesize, however, that older persons will focus more intently on a few volunteer activities and commit significant amounts of time to just these few. Their results, based on national data generated by the U.S. Bureau of the Census, show just this. This research is intriguing but the analysis used cross-sectional data (data collected at a single point in time). To have greater confidence in these results, researchers will need to test these hypotheses with panel data; these are data that follow a group of individuals over relatively long periods of time.

In regard to the relationship between volunteering and health in later life, a growing body of research shows that there is a significant benefit to health and longevity for persons who volunteer, and this benefit appears to accrue most substantially to older persons (Corporation for National and Community Service, 2007a). Thus, volunteering in later life has positive effects not only for community and society but also for the volunteer. Of course, if volunteering improves the health status of older persons, as research shows, then this returns another benefit to society through reduced health care costs and the postponement of disability and dependency.

## PRODUCTIVE AGING

Social scientists have long been interested in studying social, leisure, and productive activities across the life course. Productive aging is defined as engaging in activity that produces socially valued goods and services, whether paid or not. Thus, working in the labor market for pay later in life would be one form of productive aging. Other forms include formal volunteering, providing care to persons with acute or chronic illness, child care (especially grandparenting), and informal helping (Bass & Caro, 2001). Some observers suggest that managing one's health through self-care and obtaining education later in life also are forms of productive aging. Productive aging itself falls under the rubric of successful aging (Rowe & Kahn, 1998). One of the three tenets of the successful aging paradigm is that older persons remain active and engaged in their communities. Engaging in productive activities is one way for older persons to maintain or increase their well-being.

***Pet Meals on Wheels.*** *Meals on Wheels volunteer Harriet Waring delivers pet food to a senior person's home in Fort Worth, TX. Meals on Wheels had recently started a nationwide program to provide seniors not only with meals but with pet food, because people were so needy they were feeding their meals to their dogs and cats.* AP IMAGES.

A significant amount of research shows that older persons who volunteer report higher levels of life satisfaction and happiness than persons who do not volunteer (e.g., Wheeler, Gorey, & Greenblatt, 1998). The effect is likely related to the sense of purpose that older persons find in their volunteer roles and their ability to act on their desire to give something back to members of their community, as discussed above. The number of depressive symptoms (e.g., feeling sad, inability to sleep or eat) is lower among persons who volunteer than among nonvolunteers (Wilson & Musick, 1999).

Based on data that observes persons at multiple points in time, research shows that volunteers experience higher levels of self-reported health and physical health (e.g., Lum & Lightfoot, 2005. Volunteers demonstrate higher levels of functional status (less disability) than nonvolunteers of a similar age. Evidence also shows that persons who volunteer have more social roles (e.g., worker, parent) and that more social roles leads to better health outcomes. Volunteering even appears to reduce the negative consequences of having undergone serious medical procedures and reduces chronic pain (Corporation for National and Community Service, 2007a).

A number of studies show that the risk of death is reduced for those who volunteer but that the positive effect may operate only for those older persons who volunteer a moderate amount compared to those who do not volunteer as well as those who devote a large amount of time to volunteering (e.g., Musick & Wilson, 1999). Thus a new hypothesis was developed called the threshold hypothesis suggesting that benefits do not accrue to individuals after a certain level of activity is achieved.

There are several reasons why volunteering has a positive effect on health and general well-being, especially among the elderly. First, being a volunteer provides a social network whereby information about healthy behavior and health care services may be enhanced. Also, these networks may provide a form of social support that researchers believe helps to reduce the negative association between stress and health. Second, volunteering provides the volunteer with enhancements to their self-esteem and self-efficacy. These psychological attributes also help persons cope with stress. Third, older people may benefit more from volunteering than younger people because their volunteering is seen as discretionary, that is, older persons are able, when their personal resources allow, to choose volunteering activities that have intrinsic value for them (e.g., volunteering for a church or synagogue or for a cultural organization). By contrast, young and middle-aged adults often volunteer for activities that may seem obligatory to them, such as volunteering for a professional organization related to their work or for an organization that relates to their roles as parents, such as a school or sports team (Van Willigen, 2000).

## THE FUTURE OF VOLUNTEERING RESEARCH AND UNANSWERED QUESTIONS

By 2008 more than 70 million persons made up the baby boom generation (persons born between 1946 and 1964). In the year 2011 the leading edge of the baby boom generation will reach the normative age of retirement (age 65). What will this mean for the nation's need for motivated and skilled volunteers? Baby boomers are, on average, healthier and have more income and education than earlier generations of middle-aged persons, and many also have what may be called activist roots. Will this translate into more volunteer activity? Will boomers volunteer for the same types of activities as their parents, and will they volunteer with a greater or lesser commitment? Nonprofit organizations that rely on volunteers would like to have answers to these questions and scholars would like to know if their theories and research findings based on studies of previous generations of older volunteers will be relevant to this new generation of volunteers (Corporation for National and Community Service, 2007b). Fortunately, evidence shows that baby boomers volunteer more than members of other generations at the same point in the life course. Given that research shows that volunteers tend to age as volunteers, this is likely to translate into substantial volunteer effort in old age for the baby boomers.

More research is needed about the potential for older persons to volunteer, both in the current generation of older persons and for generations to follow. Is it possible that an untapped army of volunteers is out there waiting to be asked to help? Some evidence suggests this is the case, but many older people who might like to volunteer are constrained either by their health and functional status limitations or because they lack skills and experiences that many nonprofit organizations need. What would it take to get more elderly involved? Will such programs as Foster Grandparents and Senior Corps continue to be effective avenues for volunteer activity?

Little research exists comparing the volunteer activity, benefits of volunteering, and motivations for volunteering among different race and ethnic groups. Given the growth of Hispanic and Asian groups in the United States, heavily influenced by the process of rapid immigration, understanding the volunteering potential and experiences of persons from these groups has enormous importance for the well-being of the elderly and for society.

**SEE ALSO** Volume 3: *Religion and Spirituality, Later Life; Social Integration/Isolation, Later Life; Time Use, Later Life.*

### BIBLIOGRAPHY

Bass, S. A., & Caro, F. G. (2001). Productive aging: A conceptual framework. In N. Morrow-Howell, J. Hinterlong, & M. Sherraden (Eds.), *Productive aging: Concepts and challenges* (pp. 37–78). Baltimore: Johns Hopkins University Press.

Bradley, D. B. (1999–2000). A reason to rise each morning: The meaning of volunteering in the lives of older adults. *Generations, 23*(4), 45–50.

Carstensen, L. L. (1992). Social and emotional patterns in adulthood: Support for socioemotional selectivity theory. *Psychology and Aging, 7,* 331–338.

Chambre, S. M. (1984). Is volunteering a substitute for role loss in old age? An empirical test of activity theory. *The Gerontologist, 24,* 292–298.

Corporation for National and Community Service, Office of Research and Policy Development. (2006). *Volunteer growth in America: A review of trends since 1974.* Washington, DC: Author. Retrieved March 13, 2008, from http://www.nationalservice.gov/pdf/06_1203_volunteer_growth.pdf

Corporation for National and Community Service, Office of Research and Policy Development. (2007a). *The health benefits of volunteering: A review of recent research.* Washington, DC: Author. Retrieved March 13, 2008, from http://www.nationalservice.gov/pdf/07_0506_hbr.pdf

Corporation for National and Community Service, Office of Research and Policy Development. (2007b). *Keeping baby boomers volunteering: A research brief on volunteer retention and turnover.* Washington, DC: Author. Retrieved March 13, 2008, from http://www.nationalservice.gov/pdf/07_0307_ boomer_report.pdf

Hendricks, J., & Cutler, S. J. (2004). Volunteerism and socioemotional selectivity in later life. *The Journals of Gerontology, Series B: Psychological Sciences and Social Sciences, 59,* S251–S257.

Independent Sector. (2001). *Giving and volunteering in the United States: Key findings.* Retrieved April 14, 2008 from http://www.independentsector.org/PDFs/GV01keyfind.pdf

Johnson, R. W., & Schaner, S. G. (2005, September). *Value of unpaid activities by older Americans tops $160 billion per year* (Perspectives on Productive Aging No. 4). Washington, DC: Urban Institute. Retrieved March 19, 2008, from http://www.urban.org/UploadedPDF/311227_older_americans.pdf

Lum, T. Y., & Lightfoot, E. (2005). The effects of volunteering on the physical and mental health of older people. *Research on Aging, 27,* 31–55.

Musick, M. A., Herzog, A. R., & House, J. S. (1999). Volunteering and mortality among older adults: Findings from a national sample. *The Journals of Gerontology, Series B: Psychological Sciences and Social Sciences, 54,* S173–S180.

Mutchler, J. E., Burr, J. A., & Caro, F. G. (2003). From paid worker to volunteer: Leaving the paid workforce and volunteering in later life. *Social Forces, 81,* 1267–1293.

Rowe, J. W., & Kahn, R. L. (1998). *Successful aging.* New York: Pantheon.

Tocqueville, A. de. (2004). *Democracy in America* (A. Goldhammer, Trans.). New York: Library of America. (Original work published 1835–1840.)

Van Willigen, M. (2000). Differential benefits of volunteering across the life course. *The Journals of Gerontology, Series B: Psychological Sciences and Social Sciences 55,* S308–S318.

Wheeler, J. A., Gorey, K. M., & Greenblatt, B. (1998). The beneficial effects of volunteering for older volunteers and the people they serve: A meta-analysis. *International Journal of Aging and Human Development, 47,* 69–79.

Wilson, J. (2000). Volunteering. *Annual Review of Sociology, 26,* 215–240.

Wilson, J., & Musick, M. (1999). The effects of volunteering on the volunteer. *Law and Contemporary Problems, 62,* 141–168.

Zedlewski, S. R., & Schaner, S. G. (2006, May). *Older adults engaged as volunteers* (Perspectives on Productive Aging No. 5). Washington, DC: Urban Institute. Retrieved March 13, 2008, from http://www.urban.org/UploadedPDF/311325_older_volunteers.pdf

***Jeffrey A. Burr***

# WEALTH

Wealth is the value of property owned by a household at any time. It is usually measured as *net worth,* or total assets less total debts. Total assets include the family home, vacation homes, other real estate, vehicles, and other assets. This also includes financial assets such as savings accounts, checking accounts, stocks, bonds, mutual funds, and retirement accounts. Liabilities include mortgages, car loans, credit card debt, school loans, informal debt such as loan repayment to a friend or family member, and any other outstanding liabilities. Net financial assets, or *financial wealth,* is an alternative measure of wealth. Financial wealth is wealth that can be liquidated relatively easily for immediate use. Wealth is distinct from *income,* a flow of funds into the household from wages, salaries, government transfer payments (e.g., social security income), or investments. Studies of inequality and the distribution of financial well-being often focus on income and how income changes over time. However, wealth may be an even more important indicator of well-being because it provides both direct financial benefits and other advantages. Indeed, wealth is among the most fundamental indicators of well-being because it is relatively enduring and related in some way to most other measures of achievement (Keister 2000, 2005). It can improve educational attainment and occupational opportunities and can enhance political influence. It serves as a financial buffer against the loss of a primary breadwinner's income and provides needed resources in extreme circumstances such as a medical emergency or a natural disaster. Wealth can also be passed to future generations to extend these advantages indefinitely.

Wealth has been difficult to study until relatively recently because data on assets and debts have been limited. Wealth data are challenging to collect because most wealth is owned by a relatively small group of families who are not always willing to share information about their assets according to Seymour Spilerman (2000). As a result, Melvin L. Oliver & Thomas M. Shapiro (2006) point out, income data served as a proxy for wealth until wealth data became more widely available over the past three decades. Although surveys have made improvements in the collection of wealth information, some problems remain. It is still difficult to sample the wealthiest families and include respondents from hard-to-locate populations such as unemployed Black males (Oliver & Shapiro 2006). Some of the currently used sources of U.S. wealth data include the Panel Study of Income Dynamics (PSID), the Survey of Consumer Finances (SCF), and the Survey of Income and Program Participation (SIPP) (Keister & Moller 2000). The Luxembourg Wealth Study (LWS), launched in late 2007, contains standardized wealth data from ten countries and includes the 2001 SCF and PSID for the U.S.

## TRENDS IN WEALTH INEQUALITY

Although the benefits of wealth are significant, they are not enjoyed uniformly in the United States because asset ownership is highly concentrated (Keister 2000, 2005; Wolff 1998). Between 1995 and 2004 mean net worth increased 72% to $448,000, while the median increased only 31% to $93,000. In 2004 the top 1% of households owned 33% of net worth, and the top 10% owned 70% of net worth. The number of billionaires listed in the Forbes 400 has increased from about 95 in 1993 to 300 in 2000, and these families grew increasingly wealthy (Keister 2005). At the same time, 16% of households had zero or negative net worth, that is, their debts exceed their assets (Keister 2005; Bucks et al. 2006). The United States is also among the most unequal countries in terms of wealth ownership. While wealth inequality was consistently more severe in Europe for many decades, by the early 1990s the United States had surpassed all industrial societies in the extent of family wealth inequality. Estimates from the Survey of Financial Characteristics of Consumers (SFCC) and the SCF for 1964–2001 suggest a very small number of households in the United States have historically controlled the vast majority of household wealth (Keister 2005).

One promising finding suggests that the proportion of families owning some form of wealth increased to 97.9% and has risen continuously since 1995 with the exception of a slight halt in 2001 (Bucks et al. 2006). Asset ownership increased most for those at the lowest quintile of the wealth distribution, families with household heads under 35 or over 65 years old, for nonWhite or Hispanic families, families with a non-working head, renters, and families in the bottom quartile of the wealth distribution; asset ownership levels were already at nearly 100% for all other demographic groups. However, despite a rise in the ownership of any asset for these groups, most saw a decline in median value of all assets (Bucks et al. 2006).

Wealth mobility, or movement from one segment of the wealth distribution to another, is relatively rare. Researchers study both inter-generational (comparing parents and their children) and intra-generational mobility (observing changes in a person's wealth from early-life to later-life). The evidence suggests that significant wealth mobility has been rare since the early history of the United States. Modern patterns also provide evidence that wealth mobility is limited (see Keister 2005 for details on wealth mobility patterns). While it is relatively unlikely that any individual is going to make a large and significant change in wealth position, there is evidence that considerable wealth mobility does occur in the United States. In other words there are large numbers of people who make very large changes in their wealth status over time (Keister 2005). An important caveat is that much of the mobility that does occur does not constitute movement across great spans of the distribution.

## DETERMINANTS OF SAVING AND ACCUMULATION

While basic facts about the distribution of wealth have become taken for granted, an understanding of the processes that account for wealth inequality is still limited. Until recently, efforts to explain wealth inequality typically focused on the role of aggregate influences such as market fluctuations and demographic trends. Evidence suggests that because the wealthy are more likely to own stocks, wealth inequality worsens when the stock market booms. Similarly when real estate values increase, those who own houses and other land improve their position. Because those who are already well-off are more likely to own appreciable land, wealth inequality tends to worsen. With rising land values, however, the middle class has historically benefited more than they do with stock booms because homeownership has been more common among middle class families. Changes in portfolio behavior, that is, in the combination of assets families own, thus have important implications for wealth ownership and inequality. In fact, because stock ownership has become more common among middle class families, stock market booms in the late 1990s had less of an effect on wealth inequality than they would have if middle class stock ownership had remained at previous levels.

Researchers have begun to identify the specific individual and family characteristics that contribute to saving and accumulation, which are factors that affect position in the wealth distribution. Family background contributes to wealth accumulation and mobility in a number of ways. Intergenerational transfers, or inheritance, increase both wealth accumulation and mobility. There is evidence that intergenerational transfers account for anywhere from 20% to 80% of the net worth of current families, although it is likely that most inherited wealth occurs through intervivos (money transferred while parents are living) rather than bequests (which occur after parental death). Divorce or separation directly affects the amount of assets flowing into the family, and indirectly affects children's school performance, educational attainment, and other wealth-related processes (Keister 2005).

Sibship size (i.e., total number of siblings) can also affect adult wealth and chances for upward wealth mobility (Keister 2003). When there are funds to be transferred across generations, children with many siblings generally inherit less compared with children in smaller-sized families. Parents' financial and nonfinancial resources (e.g., time) are also more limited in large families, which negatively affects children's educational quality and attainment. Educational attainment is an important predictor of wealth ownership, as education provides access to stable, high-paying sources of employment and income, which can then provide the monetary basis for investment and future wealth.

Religious upbringing also influences wealth directly though savings or investment behavior as well as indirectly through fertility behaviors or well-being (Keister 2007, 2008). Religion may also provide social contacts that improve opportunities to accumulate wealth via information or investment assistance (Keister 2007). In recent decades, for example, Catholics have been highly upwardly mobile. In contrast, Conservative Protestants have been overrepresented in the bottom of the wealth distribution because they tend to have large families, relatively low education, and low levels of female labor force participation. Moreover, Conservative Protestants tend to share the belief that money belongs to God, and people are tasked with using money to do God's work. Therefore personal wealth accumulation tends to be a low priority for Conservative Protestants.

An individual's environmental and family context also matters for wealth accumulation. Both past and current research has supported the implications of kin networks for individual spending behaviors, savings potential, and, subsequently, the amount of wealth acquired (Stack 1974). Increased incidence of poor kin causes constraints for wealth accumulation, N. S. Chiteji & Darrick Hamilton (2002) explain, as helping out family takes precedence over saving, and assets that would otherwise go toward increasing the wealth of the primary family unit are given away. Birth cohort, economic trends, and geography can also influence wealth and wealth accumulation through access to resources and employment (Keister 2005). Baby boomers, for example, were more likely to postpone marriage and childbearing than their parents, which explains in part why the boomers have more wealth than their parents at the same age (Keister & Deeb-Sossa 2001).

The type of employment an individual has can affect wealth, as managerial and professional occupations often pay more than skilled- or unskilled-labor positions (McGrath and Keister 2008). Certain occupations may also influence wealth through increased investment resources or opportunity, such as through retirement plans. Education, occupation, or upbringing also can influence how financially literate a person is and, consequently, can facilitate higher rates of wealth accumulation from high-return investments.

Race also has a notable effect on individuals' wealth acquisition. Analysis of wealth distribution in the United States reveals a sizeable disparity between the net worth of Black and Hispanic households as compared to that of White households. Evidence of the Black-White wealth gap in particular has been supported using multiple data sets and numerous indicators over nearly a 20-year period. Analysis of the 1992 and 1994 PSID revealed Black families had less net worth than White families at every income category; even within the $15,000-and-under per year income category, median net worth was $10,000 for Whites and zero for Blacks (Conley 1999, 2001). Analyses of wealth data also suggest that Black-White wealth differences are persistent across age groups, including among the elderly (Ozawa & Tseng 2000). Although nonWhite and Hispanic families have experienced recent growth in both mean and median total wealth, African-American families experienced only an increase in the mean value of net worth, indicating wealth increased mainly for those already at the top of the distribution (Bucks et al. 2006).

The relationship between race and wealth is particularly complicated because race is confounded with other patterns. Disparities in portfolio behavior, housing ownership, and asset composition between Blacks and Whites play important roles (Conley 2001). The vast majority of Black wealth (72.2%) is held in consumable assets while only 25% is in income-producing assets; comparatively, a full 50% of Whites' wealth is in income-producing assets (Oliver & Shapiro 1989). Whites are also four times more likely to own higher-return-producing assets in the form of stock or IRA accounts (Oliver & Shapiro 1989). Blacks' lesser preferences for and access to higher-return investments contributes to this trend (Keister 2000). Home equity represents the largest share of wealth for both Blacks and Whites—62% and 42%, respectively—but median home equity is 1.7 times higher for Whites (Oliver & Shapiro 1989). Homes owned by Blacks experience slower rates of appreciation due to the increased likelihood the home is located in a more urban, less desirable neighborhood (Conley 2001, Flippen 2004). Despite the difference in home quality, Blacks also tend to pay higher mortgages (Conley 2001).

Differential rates and incidences of inheritance have also been cited as important determinants of the Black-White wealth gap; 24% of White households receive bequest inheritances of mean value $115,000 while only 11% of Black households receive inheritances of mean value $32,000 (Wolff 1998, Avery & Rendall 2002). Researchers speculate historically lower rates of marriage for Blacks also result in lower rates of asset transfers (Oliver & Shapiro 1989). A comparison of several wealth-predicting models reveals that socioeconomic differences, parental wealth/inheritance differences, and asset differences all progressively account for some of the disparity between Black and White wealth, although part of the gap continues to be unexplained (Conley 2001).

Research comparing the wealth of immigrants and native-born groups assessed why race has a primary effect on wealth while nativity seems to be secondarily determinative as well as why the lack of intergenerational inheritance tends to effect Blacks' future wealth accumulation but not that of immigrants. Although Native Americans fare better wealth-wise than immigrants, the disparity between these two groups is much smaller than observed wealth differences by race, education, or age (Hao 2007). Comparing the distribution of wealth by nativity status reveals a very similar pattern, although immigrants fare slightly worse in the middle part of the distribution (Hao 2007). A comparison of Black, White, Asian, and Hispanic wealth distributions reveals two distinct patterns: Asians and Whites follow a similar distribution, whereas Blacks and Hispanics follow a different one, which results in universally lower net-worth values. As a single group, Blacks experience the greatest disadvantage in the wealth distribution, particularly above the 70th percentile (Hao 2007).

## FUTURE DIRECTIONS

Researchers must identify levels of wealth inequality and explore changes in inequality for various groups. Current data on wealth ownership are much more reliable than data ever were in the past. Yet there are important improvements that could be made to data collection and interpretation that would dramatically improve the understanding of wealth inequality and its implications. For instance, better samples, particularly samples that include large and more representative groups of high-wealth households, would allow researchers to better represent the full distribution of wealth. Current wealth samples do not accurately represent the top of the distribution because only a small number of families from that part of the distribution are likely to be included. This poses an issue for accurate data, because the top of the distribution is precisely where the bulk of wealth is held. Naturally, this is an extremely challenging proposition, as the wealthy are more likely than others to be reluctant to participate in a survey. Moreover, very wealthy people may be unaware of the size of their fortunes, particularly if a third party manages their wealth.

However, the Survey of Consumer Finances (SCF) has made an effort to include an over-sample of high-income households in its survey to address this problem. Other surveys might consider imitating this procedure. Moreover, all survey researchers, including those responsible for the collection of the SCF, might consider over-sampling high-*wealth* households rather than high-*income* households given that the correlation between income and wealth is high but very far from perfect.

Future research might also usefully expand on the study of the determinants of saving and accumulation. There are numerous unanswered questions regarding why people save money and why, when they do save, some people experience higher returns than similar others. A related area in which future research could make an important contribution is on how cultural orientation affects wealth ownership. Evidence shows that unique values regarding work and money combined with amenable demographic behaviors (e.g., educational attainment, stable marriage, and high female labor force participation) allowed Roman Catholics to be upwardly mobile in the wealth distribution in recent decades. However, little is known about the practices that lead some religious groups to accumulate relatively high-value wealth portfolios. For example, Mormons tend to be religiously conservative, but there is little evidence that they are asset-poor. Contrasting Mormons with other Conservative Protestants (CP) might provide useful insight into the behaviors and values that affect saving behavior and wealth ownership.

It would also be useful to explore whether some religious groups have closer social networks that compensate for lack of accumulation. Similarly, the growth of suburban megachurches has created a growing group of people who call themselves Conservative Protestants, but who have higher SES than the typical American CP. As these churches continue to grow, they will provide a useful contrast to the group of CP denominations currently being studied (Keister 2007, 2008). Similarly, people born in Jewish families tend to have relatively high net worth, but the processes that account for this are not well understood. Moreover, differences in wealth accumulation among Reform, Conservative, and Orthodox Jews could inform understanding of the relationship between religious values and wealth ownership and help differentiate religious influences from ethnic processes. Researchers also know very little about the effects of other religious beliefs—including Asian religions, Islam, and Eastern Orthodox religions—on wealth.

Finally, prior research has overlooked two other very important questions. First, little exploration of international comparisons of wealth ownership has been done. Data difficulties have made it problematic to compare empirical evidence across national boundaries and, as a result, researchers have very little evidence of transnational trends. The newly-available LWS data (see first section above) may help launch data analysis in this direction. Second, the policy implications of wealth inequality and changing patterns of inequality have attracted relatively little attention. Future research should identify the degree to which wealth inequality is responsive to policy changes and which policy changes affect inequality. Another future challenge for wealth research and policy is to determine how lower-income households or families facing large amounts of debt can successfully begin and maintain the wealth-acquisition process.

**SEE ALSO** Volume 2: *Consumption, Adulthood and Later Life; Debt; Saving;* Volume 3: *Inheritance; Intergenerational Transfers; Pensions.*

**BIBLIOGRAPHY**

Avery, R. B., & Rendall, M. S. (2002). Lifetime inheritances of three generations of Whites and Blacks. *The American Journal of Sociology, 107*(5), 1300–1346.

Bucks, B. K., Kinnickell, A. B., & Moore, K. B. (2006). Recent changes in U.S. family finances: Evidence from the 2001 and 2004 Survey of Consumer Finances. *Federal Reserve Bulletin, 92,* A1–A38.

Chiteji, N. S., & Hamilton, D. (2002). Family connections and the Black-White wealth gap among middle-class families. *The Review of Black Political Economy,* Summer Issue, 9–28.

Conley, D. (1999). *Being Black, living in the red: Race, wealth, and social policy in America.* Berkeley: University of California Press.

Conley, D. (2001). Decomposing the Black-White wealth gap: The role of parental resources, inheritance, and investment dynamics. *Sociological Inquiry, 71*(1), 39–66

Flippen, C. (2004). Unequal returns to housing investments? A study of real housing appreciation among Black, White, and Hispanic households. *Social Forces, 82*(4), 1523–1551.

Hao, L. (2007). *Color lines, country lines: Race, immigration, and wealth stratification in America.* New York: Russell Sage Foundation.

Keister, L. A. (2000). *Wealth in America: Trends in wealth inequality.* Cambridge, U.K.: Cambridge University Press.

Keister, L. A. (2003). Sharing the wealth: The effect of siblings on adults' wealth ownership. *Demography, 40*(5), 21–542.

Keister, L. A. (2005). *Getting rich: America's new rich and how they got that way.* New York: Cambridge University Press

Keister, L. A. (2007). Upward wealth mobility: Exploring the Roman Catholic advantage. *Social Forces, 85*(3), 1195–1226.

Keister, L. A. (2008, March 5). Conservative Protestants and wealth: How religion perpetuates asset poverty. *American Journal of Sociology, 113*(5), 1237–1271.

Keister, L. A., & Deeb-Sossa, N. (2001). Are baby boomers richer than their parents? Intergenerational patterns of wealth ownership in the U.S. *Journal of Marriage and the Family, 62*, 569–579.

Keister, L. A., & Moller, S. (2000). Wealth inequality in the United States. *Annual Review of Sociology, 26*, 63–81.

McGrath, D., & Keister, L. A. (2008). Nonstandard work and asset ownership. *Work and Occupations.*

Oliver, M. L. & Shapiro, T. M. (1989). Race and wealth. *Review of Black Political Economy, 17*(4), 5–25.

Oliver, M. L., & Shapiro, T. M. (2006). *Black wealth/White wealth: A new perspective on racial inequality.* New York: Taylor & Francis Group.

Ozawa, M. N., & Tseng, H-Y. (2000). Differences in net worth between elderly Black people and elderly White people. *Social Work Research, 24*(2), 96–108.

Shapiro, T. M. (2004). *The hidden cost of being African American.* New York: Oxford University Press.

Spilerman, S. (2000). Wealth and stratification processes. *Annual Review of Sociology, 26*, 497–524.

Stack, C. (1974). *All our kin: Strategies for survival in a Black community.* New York: Harper and Row.

Wolff, E. N. (1998) Recent trends in the size distribution of household wealth. *Journal of Economic Perspectives 12*(3), 131–150.

***Lisa A. Keister***
***Lane M. Destro***

# WIDOWHOOD

One of the most common stressful events in later life is widowhood, which has significant social and psychological implications. Widowhood is the marital status that a man or woman gains once his or her spouse has died. A widow is a woman whose spouse has died, and a widower is a man whose spouse has died. It is useful to distinguish between widowhood and bereavement. Bereavement can be seen as the situation or state of having experienced the death of someone significant in one's life—in this case, a spouse. Bereavement is generally thought to be a short-term state that primarily has personal consequences and meanings. Research into bereavement often examines the events following the death for up to 2 years. Widowhood, by contrast, refers to an ongoing and frequently long-term state, which has both social and personal consequences and meanings. Despite the usefulness of this distinction, much of the research on widowed people does not distinguish between bereavement and widowhood. However, for this entry the term *widowhood* is used.

Widowhood is one of the most deeply distressing life events experienced by adults, and it becomes more likely as people age. In European and North American societies it is also more common among women than men. The fact that men usually die at earlier ages than women and women tend to marry men slightly older than themselves partially explains this phenomenon. In the United States in 2005, 18% of men and 52% of women ages 75 to 84 years were widowed, and 32% of men and 75% of women aged 85 and over were widowed (U.S. Census Bureau, 2006). Similar patterns are observed elsewhere as well. For example, according to the Office for National Statistics (ONS; 2005, 2006) in the United Kingdom, 16% of men and 45% of women 65 years old and over were widowed in 2004. In 2003, 27% of men and 63% of women 75 years old and over were widowed.

## HOW WIDOWED PEOPLE DIFFER FROM OTHER MARITAL STATUS GROUPS

In the United States widowed women account for the largest marital status group among women ages 65 years and over (42%) and is the second largest marital status group for men (32%). In comparison, the divorced and separated (approximately 10% for both men and women) and the never married (4% for both men and women) account for much smaller proportions of the older population (U.S. Census Bureau, 2006) and are broadly similar to those found in the United Kingdom (ONS, 2005, 2006). Widowed, divorced, and never-married people share some of the problems that living alone brings (Cramer, 1993), and widowed and divorced people also share the difficulties that marital dissolution brings (Prigerson, Maciejewski, & Rosenheck, 1999). Widowed and married people also share other commonalities, such as having (in general) a loving marital relationship. However, there are aspects of widowhood that make it and its effects unique. Widowed people are the only group whose partners have died and who have had no choice in the marital dissolution. They are also more likely to be older than other groups experiencing marital dissolution.

## EARLY RESEARCH AND THEORY

Although the vast majority of research on widowhood has been conducted since the mid-20th century, two earlier classic studies of bereavement are worthy of mention because they have significantly influenced research in widowhood. Sigmund Freud (1856–1939) described the differences between grief and melancholia in his 1917 seminal paper *Mourning and Melancholia.* He understood that the death of a loved one sometimes caused depression and that there was important psychological work to do to ameliorate the effects of grief, coining the term *grief work.*

Erich Lindemann (1944) studied the effects of bereavement following the Coconut Grove fire, a nightclub fire in Boston, Massachusetts, that killed nearly 500 people. He distinguished between normal and morbid grief, and his work formed the basis of much of the later theorizing in bereavement and, to some extent, in widowhood. Normal grief is that which people typically experience following the death of a loved one. Morbid grief, by contrast, is grief that lasts longer and is more severe because of the complications that are associated with it—it is grief that is seen as pathological. However, the systematic study of widowhood is believed to have started with Peter Marris (1958), when he examined normal grief among widowed women in London, England. He found that there was a lower rate of morbid grief among these women than among those who had experienced other types of traumatic bereavement, yet there were also shared experiences, such as sensing the deceased's presence.

Colin Murray Parkes (1996) conducted the first study that followed bereaved people through their first year of bereavement and synthesized the results, along with results of two other important studies, in *Bereavement: Studies of Grief in Adult Life.* In this Parkes identified the determinants of grief, the features of grief, and recommended strategies for helping the bereaved. Although Parkes described his studies in terms of bereavement, he focused primarily on younger widows and thus had much to say about widowhood, both at younger and older ages.

The first author widely recognized for her research specifically on widowhood was Helena Lopata (b. 1925) beginning in the 1970s. She published *Widowhood in an American City* (1973), a study describing the experiences of older widowed women in Chicago, Illinois, which examined both the emotional and the social consequences of losing a husband. Dale Lund (2001) is another widely recognized researcher, who has focused his attention on the effects of spousal loss among men. In Europe, Margaret Stroebe has influenced thinking about both widowhood and bereavement from the 1980s onward, eventually publishing the *Handbook of Bereavement Research* in 2001. At the end of the 20th century, a team of researchers at the University of Michigan developed the Changing Lives of Older Couples (CLOC) study, a large survey that tracked the experiences of older widows and widowers over a 4-year period following the death of their spouse (Carr, House, Wortman, Nesse, & Kessler, 2001).

## THEORETICAL PERSPECTIVES

Most of the theoretical work on widowhood has focused on bereavement rather than on widowhood itself; therefore, this section discusses those aspects of bereavement theory most relevant to widowhood. Historically a number of researchers have developed theories that explain the ways in which people adapt to bereavement, including spousal loss. Many of these have resembled stage theories, which suggest that people must experience sequential emotional states such as anger, depression, numbness, disorganization, and reorganization in order to adapt successfully to loss. In addition, a number of scholars have emphasized the importance of grief work in the adaptation process. Grief work involves working through the feelings, memories, and thoughts associated both with the death itself and with the spouse. However, Lopata (1996) among others have suggested that these approaches are unhelpful and even potentially harmful because they imply that these stages are necessary conditions to successful adaptation.

## THE DUAL PROCESS MODEL OF BEREAVEMENT

In 1999, Stroebe and Henk Schut developed a conceptual model to explain the ways in which people adapt to bereavement, and indeed this model was developed originally with widowhood in mind. The Dual Process Model (DPM) of coping with bereavement describes two types of coping behaviors or experiences: loss-oriented coping and restoration-oriented coping. In the former, coping comprises grief work, as described earlier. This may involve avoiding making changes to one's life—for example, continuing to set the dinner table for two rather than for one. Grief may also intrude into everyday life; seeing someone who resembles the deceased, for instance, may lead to tears. This type of coping may also involve moving to a new home or disposing of the husband's or wife's possessions.

In contrast, restoration-oriented coping consists of attending to life changes, such as changing the names on one's bank account. It also involves doing new things, such as joining a club and taking on new roles or beginning new relationships. Finally it involves avoiding things that remind one of grief; so, for example, people may stay away from the house or keep busy so they have no time to think about how upset they are feeling. Key to the DPM model is oscillation, which is the process whereby coping switches between loss- and restoration-oriented tasks. In 2006 the DPM was brought together with cognitive stress theory (Lazarus & Folkman, 1984) to develop an integrative risk factor framework (Stroebe, Folkman, Hansson, & Schut, 2006). Cognitive stress theory describes the relationship among stress, coping, and outcome. Central to this theory is appraisal or evaluation of the stressor, in this instance either or both bereavement and widowhood. The aim of the integrative framework is to allow exploration of the ways that individual differences influence adaptation to bereavement and therefore identify those individuals who will deal with bereavement and widowhood normally as well as those who would benefit from some form of intervention.

## CONTINUING BONDS

Another important theoretical perspective is that of continuing bonds with the deceased (Klass, Silverman, & Nickman, 1996). Until work was published on this perspective, the general view was that it was important to sever ties with the deceased as a means of adapting to the new situation. One of the difficulties with the earlier approach was that it did not reflect what most people normally did when dealing with their bereavement and widowhood. Widows normally would keep possessions belonging to their deceased husbands, for example. Both widows and widowers quite normally felt their spouses' presence, in a way that was not associated with pathology or distress. The work of Dennis Klass, Phyllis Silverman, and Steven Nickman (1996) suggested that maintaining a bond with the deceased was common among healthy grieving people. Their book, *Continuing Bonds: New Understandings of Grief*, examined these ideas in detail. In it, for example, Lopata discussed the ways in which older widows idealized their deceased husbands and tended to forget their faults and foibles whereas Miriam and Sidney Moss (1996) discussed the triadic relationship between the widowed person, their new spouse, and their deceased spouse.

Since 2005 other scholars, such as Stroebe and Schut (2005), have begun to discuss whether it is better, in terms of outcome, to relinquish or to continue to hold a bond with the deceased. They suggest that it is not possible to say that one path is more beneficial than another and that it may, instead, depend on the individuals concerned. For some it may be important to maintain bonds, whereas for others it may be necessary to relinquish them. The key may be to distinguish between continuing bonds and grief intensity.

## ANTICIPATION AND SOCIAL CAUSATION

Two other theoretical perspectives are also important to note: anticipatory bereavement and social causation. The theory of anticipatory bereavement suggests that some widowed people experience the effects of bereavement before their spouse has died (Dessonville-Hill, Thompson, & Gallagher, 1988). Among widows who have an ill spouse, this may not be surprising. For example, many spouses die from terminal illnesses such as cancer or from dementia. It is distressing to watch one's spouse die. However, even among those who do not expect their spouses to die, there may be higher levels of depression than those who do not go on to become widowed (Bennett & Morgan, 1992). Thus, it appears that anticipatory bereavement cannot be understood only in terms of caring for a sick spouse. It may also be explained by the fact that, for women in particular, husbands are generally older and are expected to die sooner. The other theoretical perspective is social causation; this perspective suggests that it is the effects of widowed status rather than, or in addition to, the bereavement itself that causes declines in psychological well-being (Wade & Pevalin, 2004). Society does not treat single people, including widowed people, as well or grant them as much status as those who are married. Thus, widowed people are disadvantaged financially, socially, and psychologically.

## THE CONSEQUENCES OF WIDOWHOOD

Traditionally much of widowhood literature has focused on those people for whom experiences of grief and widowhood might be described as pathological. But for the majority of widowed people, especially those who are older, widowhood is a high-probability event and an event that, although distressing, cannot be described as pathological but rather as normative. Among younger people widowhood is less common and not a normative event. In these circumstances, younger people have fewer shared experiences to draw on, and the effects may differ—something that is addressed later in this entry.

However, in general, the evidence suggests that widowed people experience lowered morale and mood following the loss of their spouse. Depressive feelings may be elevated among widowed people for at least 2 years following their loss, and mood may not return to its pre-widowhood levels. However, only a relatively small proportion of widowed people meet the criteria for clinical depression, especially in the long term. Widowed people may miss their spouse and feel sad, but at the same time they carry on with their new lives and find satisfaction. The evidence for physical health is less clear. Some research suggests that there are short-term effects on physical health. For example, sleep and eating habits may be disrupted. Health maintenance behaviors may also be affected; physician consultations, for example, may increase or, conversely, decrease. Changes in these behaviors may be dependent on whether the deceased (often the wife) was the gatekeeper for health-related behaviors. For instance, wives often monitor their husbands' diets and medication

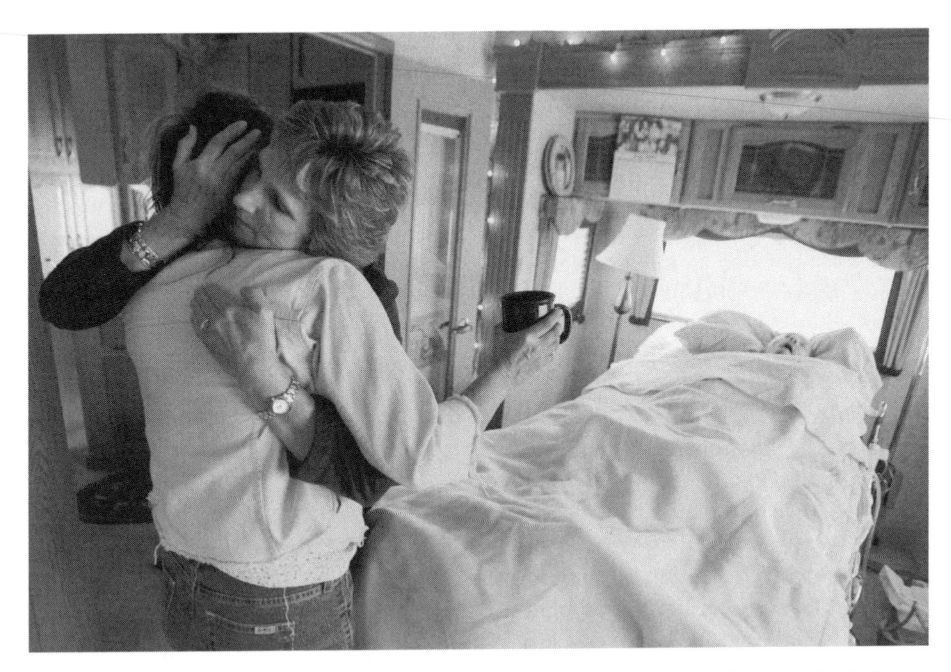

***Cancer Caregiver.*** *Hospice nurse Joni Connelly comforts Nancy Warner as her husband of five days, Dick, lies unconscious in their Post Falls, Idaho, trailer. Marriage was a priority for Dick, who realized his body was beginning to give up its fight against cancer. He was a hospice patient for four and a half months before he died, with Nancy, his wife and caregiver, by his bedside.* AP IMAGES

regimens, and the loss of a spouse may hurt a husband's ability to keep up with these two important health behaviors. There is also evidence, among men in particular, of increased mortality across all causes of death, which includes suicide, but especially in accidental deaths. The popular view of people dying from a broken heart is borne out to some extent by data from death certificates (Parkes, Benjamin, & Fitzgerald, 1969). The evidence suggests that men, rather than women, are more likely to die prematurely following the death of their spouse, and this is across all causes of death (Jones & Goldblatt, 1987).

## SOCIAL CONSEQUENCES

Widowed people also report social consequences of widowhood. Widowed women talk often about changes in friendships. They report losing or being shunned by their married friends and of turning to other widowed women for companionship. The social lives of widowed men also change. Traditionally men's social networks revolved around work. Frequently other social activities, with both family and friends, were arranged by their wives. When their wives die, men must forge new social relationships or face a reduced social circle. The social circle may be increased if the widow(er) remarries. This is more common among men than women. For many women of the pre-World War II (1939–1945) birth cohorts, there is no desire to remarry and resume the traditional gender role of caretaker (Bennett, Hughes, & Smith, 2002).

## GENDER DIFFERENCES

Throughout this discussion there has been evidence of gender differences in the responses to widowhood. Men and women, including the widowed, believe that men fare worse as widowed people than women. They attribute this to men's poorer domestic and social skills and the notion that men, in the European and North American developed nations, bottle up their feelings. Some research suggests that this might be the case, at least with respect to emotional responses. Margaret Stroebe, Robert Hansson, Wolfgang Stroebe, and Henk Schut (2001) found that, on balance, when the most carefully controlled studies were considered, widowed men were more vulnerable following spousal loss, although this difference was small. However, some studies show that the differences may be due not to the experience of emotional stress but rather with the language used in expressing emotional feelings. To preserve masculinity, men may use masculine language such as control and self-sufficiency to express emotional feelings (Bennett, 2007).

## IDENTITY

Identity is one aspect that is challenged by widowhood. For many married people, being married and part of a couple is a central part of their identity. Once a partner has died, society views that person as a widow and as a person alone. Yet the widowed person still sees herself or himself as a wife or a husband and as maintaining a bond with the deceased.

Thus, a widowed person's identity is challenged. At the same time they may see themselves both as a widow(er) and as a wife or husband whose spouse has died. Some changes and reconstructions of identity are required. For men it appears that this is undertaken in ways that allow masculinity to be preserved at a time when it is most under threat. Women, by contrast, maintain their self-identity as wife, while at the same time incorporating an independent and self-sufficient self in the face of social challenges.

## SOCIAL SUPPORT

Social support is known to influence coping in stressful situations in general and, as a consequence, a number of studies have examined the effects of social support on adaptation to widowhood. One of the most carefully controlled studies of social support was conducted with data from the CLOC study. A main effect for social support in simple terms means that the more social support a person has, the better his or her well-being. In addition, if social support has a buffering or mediating effect, then social support will enhance coping with the stressful situation. Stroebe, Zech, Stroebe, and Abakoumkin (2005) found evidence for a main effect for social support but no effects of buffering or social support as a protective factor. They found that social support, though helpful, does not reduce the impact of loss or quicken the pace of adaptation. This may be because bereavement, unlike other types of stressors, is one that (among older adults) is part of the normal aging experience rather than one that is unexpected and abnormal. Social support for widowed people comes from a variety of formal and informal sources. For many, social support is provided informally through family and friends. For some it is provided more formally through welfare and health services or through bereavement counseling. The key to effectively coping with widowhood may be to ensure a good fit between the needs of the widowed person and the support offered. Difficulties may arise when this fit is poor; not only may under-provision be problematic, but over-provision may be inappropriate as well.

The age at which people become widowed may influence the ways in which they respond to widowhood and the ways in which society responds to them. Younger widowed people often face additional challenges. For example, they may have children to care for and, therefore, have to manage their own grief alongside that of their children. There may be greater financial strain as one parent becomes both caregiver to children and breadwinner. Social circumstances also may change; younger widowed people caring for children may feel particularly isolated as they are unable to socialize as often as they wish. Younger widows may be more interested in repartnering than older widows, and yet this may be more difficult if there are children around.

## FACTORS THAT CONTRIBUTE TO OUTCOMES

This discussion has focused on the normal experiences of widowhood. However, there are some factors that contribute to the successful (or unsuccessful) adaptation into widowhood. The circumstance of the death is thought to have some bearing on adaptation. Those people who are widowed as a consequence of violent or traumatic causes may have a poorer outcome, as Lindemann's (1944) early work showed. There is not clear evidence as to whether a sudden or prolonged death is harder to come to terms with (Lopata, 1996). Among older spouses, there may be some recognition that one of them is likely to die and that it is more likely to be the husband. Thus, as has been mentioned earlier, there may be anticipation of the death. The older the spouse, the more likely widowhood becomes. Among younger spouses, by contrast, death is an unlikely event and, thus, may be more difficult to adjust to. For many widowed people, having the opportunity to say goodbye is important but in many cases is simply not possible. Those people who feel responsible, whether with justification or not, for their spouse's death may find adaptation more difficult. Those who had an ambivalent relationship with the deceased may also find adaptation more problematic. Those who keep to themselves, especially in the context of emotional expression, are also less able to cope well.

Some circumstances and personal characteristics appear to be helpful. For example, those who have been caring for a sick spouse may feel some relief mixed with grief. Those who are able to find new meaning and new identities are better able to deal with widowhood. Among men, those who have had previous experience with domestic responsibilities (e.g., looking after children or a sick spouse) appear to be better equipped at adapting to widower status. People who continue to communicate to what they believe is their deceased spouse's presence appear to cope better than those who do not.

Younger widowed men and women may face additional challenges in adapting to widowhood. Many widowed women talk about the changes in friendships that occur as a consequence of widowhood. This is particularly important among younger widows who may face a double burden of isolation. They may have child care responsibilities that tie them to the home and, as with older widowed women, married friends may drift away. American and British society is more accepting and equipped for couples than for those on their own.

## PRACTICE AND INTERVENTION

There have been a number of supports designed for widowed people. Stroebe et al. (2001) make clear the distinction between grief counseling and grief therapy. The former refers to helping a bereaved person through the process of normal grieving; the latter refers to interventions designed to assist in complicated or pathological grief. In the United States, Phyllis Silverman's (1986) Widow-to-Widow program provides mutual help, whereby widowed people help other widowed people adjust to life as a widow. In the United Kingdom there is a national self-help organization, Cruse, that provides support for widowed people. Lund et al. (2004) has taken the DPM model of coping with bereavement and applied it to an intervention.

## FUTURE OF WIDOWHOOD RESEARCH

The future of widowhood research is very exciting. There are increasing opportunities to study widowhood longitudinally, especially with studies such as the CLOC. It is important to distinguish the effects of widowhood from those of bereavement and from preexisting social and psychological states. Much of the research on widowhood has focused on men and women born before World War II. These men and women grew up with experiences of traditional gender roles, with most men going out to work while women raised the family. These patterns are slowly changing. It is unlikely that the experiences of widowed men and women will be exactly the same when new studies take place with widowed people born after the 1950s. Profound changes also are occurring in the patterns of marital relationships. People are cohabiting more, marrying later, and divorcing and remarrying more frequently. These complex marital histories are likely to make studying widowhood more complex.

**SEE ALSO** Volume 2: *Family and Household Structure, Adulthood;* Volume 3: *Caregiving; Death and Dying; Singlehood.*

## BIBLIOGRAPHY


Bennett, K. M. (2007). "No sissy stuff": Towards a theory of masculinity and emotional expression in older widowed men. *Journal of Aging Studies, 21*, 347–356.

Bennett, K. M., Hughes, G. M., & Smith, P. T. (2002). The transition from married to widowed status in women widowed in later life. *Proceedings of the Conference of the British Society of Gerontology 2002, 20.*

Bennett, K. M., & Morgan, K. (1992). Activity and morale in later life: Preliminary analyses from the Nottingham Longitudinal Study of Activity and Ageing. In N. Norgan (Ed.), *Physical activity and health*. Cambridge, U.K.: Cambridge University Press.

Carr, D., House, J. S., Wortman, C., Nesse, R., & Kessler, R. C. (2001). Psychological adjustment to sudden and anticipated spousal loss among older widowed persons. *Journals of Gerontology Series B: Psychological Sciences and Social Sciences, 56*(4), S237–S248.

Cramer, D. (1993). Living alone, marital status, gender, and health. *Journal of Community and Applied Social Psychology, 3*, 1–15.

Dessonville-Hill, C., Thompson, L. W., & Gallagher, D. (1988). The role of anticipatory bereavement in older women's adjustment to widowhood. *The Gerontologist, 28*(6), 792–796.

Freud, S. (1953–1974). Mourning and melancholia. In *The standard edition of the complete psychological works of Sigmund Freud* (Vol. 14), trans. J. Strachey. London: Hogarth. (Original work published in 1917)

Jones, D. R., & Goldblatt, P. O. (1987). Cause of death in widow(er)s and spouses. *Journal of Biosocial Science, 19*(1), 107–121.

Klass, D., Silverman, P. R., & Nickman, S. L. (Eds.). (1996). *Continuing bonds: New understandings of grief.* Washington, DC: Taylor & Francis.

Lazarus, R. S., & Folkman, S. (1984). *Stress, appraisal, and coping*. New York: Springer.

Lindemann, E. (1944). The symptomatology and management of acute grief. *American Journal of Psychiatry, 101*, 141–148.

Lopata, H. Z. (1973). *Widowhood in an American city.* Cambridge, MA: Schenkman.

Lopata, H. Z. (1996). *Current widowhood: Myths and realities.* Thousand Oaks, CA: Sage.

Lund, D.A. (Ed.). (2001). *Men coping with grief.* Amityville, NY: Baywood.

Lund, D. A., Caserta, M., Vries, B. D, & Wright, S. (2004). Restoration after bereavement. *Generations Review, 14*(4), 9–15.

Marris, P. (1958). *Widows and their families*. London: Routledge & Paul.

Moss, M. S., & Moss, S. Z. (1996). Remarriage of widowed persons: A triadic relationship. In D. Klass, P.R. Silverman, & S.L. Nickman (Eds.), *Continuing bonds: New understandings of grief.* Washington, DC: Taylor & Francis.

Office for National Statistics. (2005). *Population trends 121.* London: Author.

Office for National Statistics. (2006). *Population trends 125.* London: Author.

Parkes, C. M. (1996). *Bereavement: Studies of grief in adult life* (3rd ed.). New York: Routledge.

Parkes, C. M., Benjamin, B., & Fitzgerald, R. G. (1969). Broken heart: A statistical study of increased mortality among widowers. *British Medical Journal, 1*, 740–743.

Prigerson, H. G., Maciejewski, P. K., & Rosenheck, R. A. (1999). The effects of marital dissolution and marital quality on health and health service use among women. *Medical Care, 37*(9), 858–873.

Silverman, P. R. (1986). *Widow to widow*. New York: Springer.

Stroebe, M. S., Folkman, S., Hansson, R. O., & Schut, H. (2006). The prediction of bereavement outcome: Development of an integrative risk factor framework. *Social Science and Medicine, 63*(9), 2440–2451.

Stroebe, M. S., Hansson, R. O., Stroebe, W., & Schut, H. (Eds.). (2001). *Handbook of bereavement research: Consequences, coping, and care.* Washington, DC: American Psychological Association.

Stroebe, M. S., & Schut, H. (1999). The Dual Process Model of coping with bereavement: Rationale and description. *Death Studies, 23*(3), 197–224.

Stroebe, M. S., & Schut, H. (2005). To continue or relinquish bonds: A review of the consequences for the bereaved. *Death Studies, 29*(6), 477–494.

Stroebe, W., Zech, E., Stroebe, M. S., & Abakoumkin, G. (2005). Does social support help in bereavement? *Journal of Social and Clinical Psychology, 24*(7), 1030–1050.

U.S. Census Bureau. (2006). *Current population survey, 2006 annual social and economic supplement.* Washington, DC: Author.

Wade, T. J., & Pevalin, D. J. (2004). Marital transitions and mental health. *Journal of Health and Social Behavior, 45*(2), 155–170.

***Kate M. Bennett***

# WISDOM

Wisdom has been hailed as a human virtue across history. Folklore suggests that wisdom increases with age. The scholarly view of wisdom has shifted across time from emphasizing proper conduct in living one's life to focusing on individuals' particular mental capacities and knowledge as well as their socioemotional sensitivity in understanding fundamental life issues. To encompass both moral and social-cognitive aspects of wisdom, Paul B. Baltes and Jacqui Smith (1990) referred to wisdom as an orchestration of mind and virtue. In the past, thorny definitional and measurement issues kept all but the heartiest social science researchers from tackling this complex, value-laden topic. Fortunately, however, the empirical examination of wisdom grew rapidly during the 20th century. The relation of wisdom to aging has been central to its examination in lifespan psychology, life course sociology, and gerontology.

## DEFINITION

In the social sciences, an important distinction is made between implicit and explicit wisdom (Sternberg, 1998). *Implicit wisdom* refers to conceptions of wisdom that individuals with certain personal attributes (e.g., age, gender, culture) carry in their minds. For example, a young woman in Austria may have a different conception (i.e., implicit theory) of what wisdom entails compared with the thoughts of an old man in Japan. Among other issues, research on implicit theories of wisdom addresses whether older and younger individuals conceive of wisdom differently.

*Explicit wisdom* refers to what wisdom *actually is* based on experts' theories (e.g., philosophical writings, theoretical and empirical investigations). Researchers who examine explicit wisdom define and measure individuals' relative levels of wisdom. For example, research addresses whether older individuals have a greater level of wisdom than younger persons. Although definitions of wisdom vary in their specifics, several central aspects appear consistently across the multidimensional definitions of wisdom in the literature. Definitions generally include an integration of positive social-cognitive aspects (e.g., rich knowledge base, reflective attitude), socioemotional qualities (e.g., compassion), and the ability to manifest these capacities in real-world contexts.

One well-accepted definition is that wisdom is expertise in the *fundamental pragmatics of life* (Baltes & Smith, 1990). This involves having rich factual knowledge about human nature and the life course, rich procedural knowledge about ways of dealing with life problems, an understanding of the lifespan contextual nature of issues, a view of different values as relative, and tolerance for uncertainty. This definition does not include age per se; its focus on expertise suggests that age may be a necessary if not sufficient condition for the development of wisdom. Monika Ardelt's definition (2003) of wisdom has also been very influential. She argues that wisdom involves the intersection of three broad components: cognition, reflection, and affect. Ardelt also claims that age alone does not promote wisdom, but her research suggests that wisdom in late life is associated with greater life satisfaction.

Several other authors have contributed key aspects to current definitions of wisdom. For example, R. J. Sternberg's (1998) definition of wisdom from his *Balance Theory* is distinct in including metacognitive style: knowing that one does not know everything. L. Orwoll and M. Perlmutter's (1990) view of wisdom describes it as a mature personality style. Some debate continues in the literature about whether wisdom is best seen as a form of expertise, or behavior, or whether it is an aspect of personality development. J. E. Birren and L. M. Fisher (1990) introduced the notion that regardless of whether wisdom is largely expertise or a matter of personality, it is not simply something one thinks or feels. Wisdom must manifest itself practically in response to life's most challenging issues and problems. These authors also suggest that wisdom should increase with life experience (and therefore age) but note that wisdom is not exclusively found in old age. Baltes and Staudinger (2000) have summarized the relation between age and wisdom by referring to age as one of several *facilitative contexts* for the development of wisdom.

Besides the distinction between implicit and explicit wisdom, scholars have further delineated explicit wisdom. For example, W. L. Randall and G. M. Kenyon (2001) describe *ordinary* and *extraordinary* wisdom. Ordinary wisdom refers to finding meaning in life. This involves accepting and valuing life's experiences including one's own personal life story. Extraordinary wisdom involves cognitive abilities, life experience, relationship skills, striving to live a good life, and spiritual-mystical understanding of the meaning of human existence. A very different delineation has been suggested by Staudinger. She operationalizes the distinction between general and personal wisdom. *General wisdom* is concerned with life in general (e.g., as described in the Berlin Wisdom Paradigm [Baltes & Smith, 1990), whereas *personal wisdom* refers to wisdom as expressed in relation to one's own life. She suggests that one must first gain general wisdom before moving on to the more difficult task of being wise in relation to one's own personal circumstances.

## CONCEPTUAL DEVELOPMENT AND MEASUREMENT OF WISDOM

Early conceptualizations of wisdom in the social sciences often allied wisdom with aging and viewed it as developing through evaluative recall of one's own life experiences. Lifespan theorist Erik H. Erikson (1902–1994) linked age and wisdom in his eighth stage of ego development, integrity versus despair. Erikson theorized that the final stage of adult development involves looking back over one's life and integrating all that has happened, both positive and negative. This is expected to lead to either a sense of integrity and wisdom, or a feeling of despair that life was not worth living. This focus on reminiscence and integration of one's view of life as a path to wisdom is also present in Robert Butler's (1963) notion of the *life review.* Life review may occur at any juncture in life but is expected to occur in late adulthood as one becomes increasingly aware of mortality. Using reminiscence as a tool to make meaning of one's life as an integrated whole is regarded as an aspect of wisdom. Although these ideas were seldom empirically tested, they remain central to theorist's conceptualizations of wisdom.

As researchers became interested in empirically measuring wisdom, an important conceptual development was the identification of implicit and explicit wisdom as distinct constructs. Research on implicit wisdom assesses what people *think or believe* wisdom is, based on their experience of living in society, learning its language and meanings. The focus of implicit wisdom research has been to document the content of different individuals' implicit theories. A review of the implicit theories literature (Bluck & Glück, 2005) shows that implicit wisdom includes five aspects: cognitive ability, insight, reflective attitude, concern for others, and real-world skills. Implicit theory research has used methods such as having individuals rate a list of personal attributes for their similarity to their concept of wisdom, to assess why certain individuals are viewed as wise, analysis of the types of individuals who are nominated by other people as being wise, assessment of various target individuals for level of wisdom using experimental manipulations (e.g., target is male versus female), and content-coding of autobiographical wisdom experiences. This latter methodology draws on the tradition of collecting reminiscences or autobiographical memory narratives from older adults that reflect instances of intergenerational sharing of life knowledge.

Explicit theory approaches to wisdom assess the level of wisdom that individuals display. Experts' definitions of wisdom are operationalized as criteria used for measuring individuals' level of wisdom. The distinction between implicit (i.e., the views of laypersons) and explicit theories (i.e., the views of expert scholars) persists in the literature and does have utility. Note, however, that explicit and implicit forms of wisdom show considerable overlap in terms of what they consider to be the central aspects of wisdom. Explicit wisdom has been measured through the use of scenarios describing fundamental life issues to which individuals provide open-ended responses (i.e., the Berlin Wisdom Paradigm), and scalar self-assessments (self-report scales on which individuals report their own wisdom level). Some researchers have created composite wisdom scores by combining individuals' performance on several existing measures (e.g., *Openness to Experience, Ego Development*) that together are viewed as approximating wisdom whereas others have attempted to measure wisdom directly.

## MAJOR RESEARCH FINDINGS: IMPLICIT AND EXPLICIT WISDOM

Some major research findings from the social science literature on wisdom are briefly summarized here. Findings from the literature on implicit wisdom are reviewed followed by findings on explicit wisdom.

The common person's view of wisdom (i.e., implicit theory) is important in that it provides him or her with a lens for judging other people's personality or actions as wise or unwise, and also for understanding their own personal development. In a review of empirical literature on implicit theories (Bluck & Glück, 2005), five components of wisdom emerged as central. These were (a) high level of cognitive ability, (b) insight into life and life's problems, (c) reflective attitude, (d) concern or compassion for others, and (e) possession of the real-world skills to manifest the aforementioned qualities in everyday life. Highlights from studies of implicit wisdom are presented to provide a more detailed sense of this literature and its methodology.

One traditional method for assessing individuals' views is to have them generate words they feel are related wisdom, or to rate lists of descriptors of wisdom (generated by the participants or the researcher) in terms of their typicality for wisdom. For example, Birren and Fischer (1990), M. Chandler and S. Holliday (1990), and Sternberg and J. Jordan (1998) have all used methods in which participants generate and/or judge what they see as *typical* characteristics of wisdom. Participants are often laypeople but sometimes include particular groups (e.g., professors in different disciplines, individuals from different cultural backgrounds or of different ages) so as to examine group differences.

Another method involves asking participants to nominate people they know and consider wise. Nominations can include both personally or publically known people. For example, researchers found that certain religious figures (e.g., Buddha, Jesus, and Mother Teresa [1908–1997]) and socially and politically influential people (e.g., former South African president Nelson Mandela [b. 1918] and American civil rights leader Martin Luther King, Jr. [1929–1968]) were frequently seen as wise (Paulhus, Wehr, Harms, and Strausser, 2002). Nominees were often older than the nominators, were more often men than women (although this may change in the future), and were seen as providing guidance. This fits with the common view that wise individuals can provide good counsel or advice.

An additional approach to studying implicit theories of wisdom is to ask participants to judge experimentally manipulated targets (e.g., texts, videos) for wisdom. For example, to judge male-versus-female or young-versus-old target individuals. Findings have been somewhat inconsistent, but chronological age of the target is sometimes a predictor of higher wisdom ratings. These studies can be limited if they fail to disentangle the role of possible other, subtle, cues including facial and vocal expressions or quality of advice given.

Finally, Susan Bluck and Judith Glück have collaboratively developed the *Wisdom of Experience* method as a way to study individual's views of wisdom, specifically how individuals view wisdom in their own life. This approach is based on life story and reminiscence theory. It relies on gathering autobiographical memory narratives concerning times when people feel they said, thought, or did something wise. Findings show that wisdom narratives involve certain types of life situations (i.e., important life decisions, negative events, management of enduring difficulties). Content coding of autobiographical memories reveal three forms of wisdom the authors categorize as empathy and support, self-determination and assertion, and knowledge and flexibility. The term *empathy and support* refers to seeing others' perspectives and helping them to resolve difficulties. *Self-determination and assertion* refers to taking control and standing by one's own values and priorities. *Knowledge and flexibility* consists of relying on one's experience, compromising, and being tolerant of uncertainty. Adolescents are most likely to show empathy and support, individuals in early midlife are most likely to describe self-determination and assertion, and older adults are most likely to exhibit knowledge and flexibility when asked to describe an instance of wisdom from their own life.

Across studies of implicit theories of wisdom, having high cognitive ability, insight, reflective attitudes, compassion, and the ability to integrate and to show such behaviors in the real world emerge as consistent aspects of individuals' conceptions of what it is to be wise. Of note, however, is the finding that not all individuals hold the same implicit theory. The central aspects of wisdom tend to vary in their relative emphasis in different groups, such as by age, gender, and culture. For example, studies of implicit theories of wisdom provide insight into the common stereotype that older adults are wiser than younger adults. Although some research (e.g., descriptor studies) finds support for this idea, others do not. In particular, older adults themselves are less likely to believe that wisdom comes with age. More common is the notion that wisdom is based on life experiences. M. Takahashi and W. F. Overton (2005) have described cultural differences in what they term as Eastern and Western cultures' Asian, European, and American views of wisdom, and Glück, J. M. Baron, D. P. McAdams, and Bluck (2005) provided evidence from a large-scale survey that men and women within North American and European culture also have slightly different implicit theories of what wisdom entails and how it develops.

The focus turns now to research on explicit wisdom. Those investigating explicit wisdom face the onerous task of developing defensible ways of measuring it. These researchers must defend that they know what wisdom is and that they know how it can be reliably measured. This has led to considerable productive debate. Some suggest that wisdom should be restricted to the humanities (e.g., philosophy, religion) but perseverance by social scientists has resulted in a small but growing body of empirical research on explicit wisdom particularly in the fields of psychology and sociology.

The *Berlin Wisdom Paradigm* (Baltes & Smith, 1990; Baltes & Staudinger, 2000) provided the first systematic method for research on explicit wisdom. Five theory-based criteria are used for assessing wisdom in individuals' responses to hypothetical scenarios about fundamental life problems. Wisdom is defined as expert knowledge about the meaning and conduct of life and one's score across five criteria provides represents one's level of wisdom. Two criteria are central to all types of expertise: rich factual knowledge and rich procedural knowledge. Three others are metacriteria uniquely necessary to wisdom: lifespan contextualism, value relativism, and tolerance for uncertainty. In a typical study, participants think aloud in response to hypothetical problems, such as, "Imagine that someone gets a call from a good friend who says that he or she cannot go on anymore and wants to commit suicide." Trained coders reliably assess participants' open-ended responses using the five wisdom criteria. Baltes and Staudinger (2000) review findings from several cross-sectional studies using this procedure showing that wisdom appears to be stable, but does not increase, across age groups in adulthood.

Monika Ardelt's (2003) conceptualization of wisdom differs in various ways, notably that she more fully embraces the virtue aspect of wisdom (e.g., compassion). She has developed a reliable and valid three-dimensional wisdom scale (3D-WS) that assesses wisdom as a latent construct that encompasses indicators of cognitive, reflective, and affective personality characteristics. A benefit of the scale is its potential for use in large-scale survey research. Ardelt has also found that older adults are not necessarily wiser than their younger counterparts but that wisdom may be a contributor to successful aging in those who do attain it.

Jeffrey D. Webster (2007) has developed a self-assessed wisdom scale (SAWS) for directly assessing wisdom (i.e., not a latent construct as in Ardelt's work). The multidimensional scale assesses experience, openness, emotion regulation, reminiscence, and humor. Individuals scoring high on the SAWS also scored high on related constructs such as generativity and ego integrity but again, no relationship appears simply between wisdom and age. Thus, wisdom has not been directly related to aging.

Some researchers have examined what factors may lead to wisdom across one's life. Longitudinal analyses conducted by P. Wink and M. Dillon (2003) using a composite measure of wisdom have found that wisdom in late life is related to spirituality-religiosity earlier in adulthood. The link between wisdom and spirituality is also implicit in the approach that Michael R. Levenson, Patricia Jennings, Carolyn Aldwin, and Ray Shiraishi (2005) have taken, viewing self-transcendence as a central aspect of wisdom. These researchers also developed the Adult Self-Transcendence Inventory. In one longitudinal study, the development of wisdom in individuals who had experienced trauma was linked to their ability to cope with and find benefit in their difficult experiences. Thus wisdom may arise from difficult life experiences but only when they are coped with effectively and perceived in a certain manner. Identification of the factors that lead to wisdom across adulthood has begun but much is left to understand about wisdom and its development across the lifespan.

## FUTURE DIRECTIONS

In the past, social scientists avoided the study of wisdom as too complex, philosophical, and not approachable through scientific method. Happily, research on wisdom has come of age as evidenced by the publication of a *Handbook of Wisdom* (Sternberg & Jordan, 2005). Where do we go from here? The distinction between implicit and explicit theories has been useful thus far. In future, however, investigation of wisdom might benefit from a blurring of this conceptual boundary. Research might fruitfully begin to focus on the overlap of implicit and explicit wisdom, for example asking questions such as whether individuals who tend to view wisdom a certain way in their own life or in other people (i.e., implicit theories) tend to show greater levels of explicit wisdom in response to life situations.

Another future direction is one that is guided by the past. The wisdom literature has long focused on the notion that wisdom comes with age. Research on both implicit and explicit theories of wisdom, however, has usually found that age itself is not perceived to, nor does it actually, lead to wisdom. Still, it seems imprudent to close the book on the relation of wisdom to age. Studies should continue to investigate the development of wisdom using new methodologies focused on age as but one of several facilitative contexts (educational opportunities and personal childhood background have also been seen as facilitative contexts) for the development of wisdom. Why do some older adults develop wisdom while others do not? Is wisdom in later life a protective factor in dealing with age-related losses? These questions provide fruitful directions for future research.

Finally, understanding the ecology of wisdom is an area for future expansion. That is, a wise person, as Sternberg and Jordan (2005) suggested, adapts to and shapes his or her environment. People develop different views of wisdom within differing cultural and historical environments. Explicit wisdom is manifest as an interaction between the individual and his or her socially shared environment. Thus, investigating the types of environments that promote or discourage wisdom provides a further avenue for productive research. Bluck and Glück's (2005) wisdom of experience procedure seems particularly useful for conducting research from an ecological standpoint. Limited efforts have been made to teach wisdom but some remain skeptical that wisdom can be easily learned. Further understanding the personal characteristics of wise individuals as well as the contexts that elicit wisdom will be crucial to promote wisdom though policy and practice in the future.

**SEE ALSO** Volume 3: *Baltes, Margret and Paul; Lifelong Learning*

### BIBLIOGRAPHY

Ardelt, M. (2003). Empirical assessment of the three-dimensional wisdom scale. *Research on Aging, 25*, 275–324.

Baltes, P. B., & Smith, J. (1990). Toward a psychology of wisdom and its ontogenesis. In R. Sternberg (Ed.), *Wisdom: Its nature, origins, and development* (pp. 87-120). Cambridge, MA: Cambridge University Press.

Baltes, P. B., & Staudinger, U. (2000). Wisdom: A metaheuristic (pragmatic) to orchestrate mind and virtue toward excellence. *American Psychologist, 55*, 122–136.

Birren, J. E., & Fischer, L. M. (1990). Conceptualizing wisdom: The primacy of affect-cognition relations. In R. J. Sternberg (Ed.), *Wisdom: Its nature, origins, and development* (pp. 317-332). New York: Cambridge University Press.

Bluck, S., & Glück, J. (2004) Making things better and learning a lesson: "Wisdom of experience" narratives across the lifespan. *Journal of Personality, 72,* 543–572.

Bluck, S., & Glück, J. (2005). From the inside out: People's implicit theories of wisdom. In R. Sternberg & J. Jordan (Eds.), *A handbook of wisdom: Psychological perspectives* (pp. 84-109). New York: Cambridge University Press.

Butler, R.N. (1963). The life review: An interpretation of reminiscence in old age. *Journal for the Study of Interpersonal Processes, 26,* 65-76.

Chandler, M., & Holliday, S. (1990). Wisdom in a postapocalyptic age. In R. Sternberg (Ed.), *Wisdom: Its nature, origins, and development* (pp. 121-141). New York: Cambridge University Press.

Glück, J., Bluck, S., Baron, J. M., & McAdams, D. P. (2005). The wisdom of experience: Autobiographical reports across adulthood. *International Journal of Behavioral Development, 29,* 197–208.

Levenson, M. R., Jennings, P. A., Aldwin, C. M., & Shiraishi, R. W. (2005) Self-transcendence: Conceptualization and measurement. *International Journal of Aging and Human Development 60,* 127–143.

Orwoll, L., & Perlmutter, M. (1990). The study of wise persons: Integrating a personality perspective. In R. J. Sternberg (Ed.), *Wisdom: Its nature, origins, and development* (pp. 160-180). New York: Cambridge University Press.

Paulhus, D. L., Wher, P., Harms, P. D., & Strausser, D. I. (2002). Use of exemplar surveys to reveal implicit types of intelligence. *Personality and Social Psychology Bulletin, 28,* 1051–1062.

Randall, W. L., & Kenyon, G. M. (2001). *Ordinary wisdom: Biographical aging and the journey of life.* Westport, CT: Praeger.

Staudinger, U. M., Dorner, J., & Mickler, C. (2005). Wisdom and personality. In R. Sternberg & J. Jordan (Eds.), *A handbook of wisdom: Psychological perspectives* (pp. 191-219). New York: Cambridge University Press.

Sternberg, R. J. (1998). A balance theory of wisdom. *Review of General Psychology, 2,* 347–365.

Takahashi, M., & Overton, W. F. (2005). Cultural foundations of wisdom: An integrated developmental approach. In R. Sternberg & J. Jordan (Eds.), *A handbook of wisdom: Psychological perspectives* (pp. 32-60). New York: Cambridge University Press.

Webster, J. D. (2007). Measuring the character strength of wisdom. I*nternational Journal of Aging and Human Development, 65,* 163–178.

Wink, P., & Dillon, M. (2003). Religiousness, spirituality, and psychosocial functioning in late adulthood: Findings from a longitudinal study. *Psychology and Aging, 18,* 916-924.

***Susan Bluck***
***Jacqueline M. Baron***

# *Appendices*

# *Glossary*

**401(k):** a retirement investment plan that allows an employee to put a percentage of earned wages into a tax-deferred investment account selected by the employer.

**Activities of daily living (ADLs) and instrumental activities of daily living (IADL):** ADLs are activities usually performed for oneself in the course of a normal day including bathing, dressing, grooming, eating, using the telephone, taking medications, and other personal care activities. IADLs are more complex daily tasks (light housework, preparing meals, taking medications, shopping for groceries or clothes, using the telephone, and managing money) that enable an older adult to live independently in the community. Inability to perform these tasks is considered in indication of functional limitation or disability.

**Acute pain:** severe physical discomfort that comes on quickly, is generally treatable, and lasts a relatively short time. It is often a response to a specific injury.

**Additivity:** in multivariate statistical analyses, the property of having only main effects and no interaction effects and thus being represented by an additive model without multiplicative terms.

**Adolescence:** the transitional period of physical and psychological development from the onset of puberty to maturity.

**Adoption and Foster Care Analysis and Reporting System (AFCARS):** a program that collects case-level information on all children in foster care for whom State child welfare agencies have responsibility for placement, care or supervision, and on children who are adopted under the auspices of the State's public child welfare agency.

**Adoption and Safe Families Act (ASFA) of 1997:** signed into law by President Clinton on November 19, 1997, AFSA was enacted by Congress in an attempt to correct problems that were inherent in the foster care system that deterred the adoption of children with special needs.

**Adoption Assistance and Child Welfare Act of 1980:** this act was passed by Congress in 1980. Its purposes were: to correct or alleviate problems in the foster care system; to promote permanency rather than multiple foster placement; and to encourage social workers to work toward reunification of the family and to avoid long-term foster care for the children if possible.

**Advance directive:** these documents assert one's medical treatment preferences and the designation of a surrogate decision-maker in the event that a person should become unable to make medical decisions on their own behalf. Advance directives generally fall into three categories: living will, power of attorney and health care proxy.

**Advanced placement (AP) course:** a college-level academic course offered at high schools across the United States and Canada. Demonstrated mastery in a course may exempt a student from taking a similar introductory-level course in college.

**Adversity:** economic, psychological, environmental or social difficulties that may pose challenges for one's life chances and both physical and psychological well-being.

**Affirmative action:** a policy or a program that seeks to redress past discrimination through active measures to ensure equal opportunity, as in education and employment.

**Age Discrimination in Employment Act of 1967:** prohibited discrimination against workers ages 40 to 65, and made it illegal for employers to fire, demote, or reduce the salary of older workers without showing good cause.

**Age-mate:** a peer who shares one's chronological age or who belongs to a shared birth cohort.

**Aid to Families with Dependent Children (AFDC):** formerly named Aid to Dependent Children (1935-1960), AFDC is a federally funded, and usually state or county administered, welfare assistance program that provides supplemental aid to qualifying households that include one or more minor children.

**Allele:** one member of a pair or series of genes that occupy a specific position on a specific chromosome.

**Alzheimer's disease:** the most common form of dementia, a neurologic disease characterized by loss of mental ability severe enough to interfere with normal activities of daily living, lasting at least 6 months, and not present from birth. AD usually occurs in old age, and is marked by a decline in cognitive functions such as remembering, reasoning, and planning.

**American Association of University Women (AAUW):** founded in 1881, this national organization advances equity for women and girls through advocacy, education, and research. It has a nationwide network of 100,000 members, 1,300 branches, and 500 college and university partners.

**American Community Survey:** to begin in 2010, a survey carried out by the U.S. Census Bureau that replaces the long form of the decennial census. It is an ongoing statistical survey, and thus more current than information obtained by the long form.

**American Educational Research Association (AERA):** founded in 1916, this national organization is concerned with improving the educational process by encouraging scholarly inquiry related to education and evaluation and by promoting the dissemination and practical application of research results. Its more than 26,000 members are educators; administrators; directors of research; persons working with testing or evaluation in federal, state and local agencies; counselors; evaluators; graduate students; and behavioral scientists.

**American Federation of Teachers (AFT):** a labor union founded in 1916 to represent the economic, social, and professional interests of classroom teachers. It is an affiliated international union of the AFL-CIO. The AFT has more than 3,000 local affiliates nationwide, 43 state affiliates, and more than 1.4 million members.

**American Psychological Association (APA):** scientific and professional organization representing psychology in the United States. With 148,000 members, APA is the largest association of psychologists worldwide.

**Americans with Disabilities Act (ADA) of 1990:** signed into law in 1990, this wide-ranging civil rights law prohibits discrimination based on disability. It affords similar protections against discrimination to Americans with disabilities as the Civil Rights Act of 1964. Disability is defined as "a physical or mental impairment that substantially limits a major life activity."

**Antenatal:** occurring before birth; prenatal.

**Anthropometry:** the formal measurement of living human individuals for the purposes of understanding human physical variation.

**Antimiscegenation:** practices, historically enforced by law, that banned interracial marriage and sometimes interracial sex between whites and members of other races.

**Antiretroviral:** an agent or process effective against a retrovirus; e.g., a drug to treat HIV.

**Ascriptive:** a status or characteristics determined at birth.

**Asperger's Disorder:** a pervasive developmental disorder, usually of childhood, characterized by impairments in social interactions and repetitive behavior patterns.

**Asphyxia:** impaired or impeded breathing.

**Assortative mating:** long-term romantic pairings, often with the purpose of reproduction, among two persons with similar ethnic, religious, educational, or socioeconomic backgrounds.

**At-risk:** a demographic term to describe a person who is a likely candidate for a given event; e.g., a woman who is past the age of menarche is "at risk" for giving birth.

**Atrophy:** a wasting or decrease in size of a body organ, tissue, or part owing to disease, injury, or lack of use.

**Autonomy:** the capacity to assert control and exercise free will in a given social context.

**Baby boom generation:** the cohort of men and women born during the post-war era. In the United States, this cohort includes persons born between 1946 and 1964.

**Biography:** an account of the life history of an individual.

**Biomarker:** a distinctive biological or biologically derived indicator of a process, event, or condition; e.g., cholesterol level.

**Birth cohort:** a group of individuals born at the same point in history.

**Birth weight:** the weight of an infant at its birth. It is closely related to gestational age and is closely linked to risk of infant mortality.

**Body mass index (BMI):** a statistical measure of the weight of a person scaled according to height. Also called Quetelet index.

**Built environment:** the man-made surroundings that provide the setting for human activity, ranging from the large-scale civic surroundings to personal places.

**Bureau of Labor Statistics:** the principal fact-finding agency for the U.S. government in the broad field of labor economics and statistics. The BLS is an independent national statistical agency, under the Department of Labor, that collects, processes, analyzes, and disseminates essential statistical data to the American public, the U.S. Congress, other Federal agencies, State and local governments, business, and labor representatives.

**"Burnout":** slang term for a person who regularly smokes marijuana.

**Caseload:** the number of clients or cases handled in a given period, as by a clinic or social services agency.

**Casework:** social work devoted to the needs of individual clients or cases.

**Caseworker:** a professional, usually trained in social work, devoted to serving the needs of individual clients or cases.

**Centenarian:** a person who is 100 years old or older.

**Cerebrovascular:** pertaining to the blood vessels and, especially, the arteries that supply the brain.

**Child and Dependent Care Credit (federal tax credit):** a nonrefundable Federal tax credit available to United States taxpayers. Taxpayers who care for a qualifying individual are eligible. The purpose of the credit is to allow the taxpayer (or their spouse, if married) to be gainfully employed.

**Child Care and Development Fund (CCDF):** federal program that provides block grant funding to support early care and education services for nearly two million children in the United States each month. It assists low-income families, families receiving temporary public assistance, and those transitioning from public assistance in obtaining child care so they can work or attend training/education.

**Child rearing:** the act of raising and socializing one's children.

**Childbearing:** the act of giving birth to an infant.

**Childhood Disintegrative Disorder:** a disintegrative psychosis, also known as Heller's syndrome. A rare condition characterized by late onset (>3 years of age) of developmental delays in language, social function, and motor skills. The cause is unknown.

**Chronic Obstructive Pulmonary Disease (COPD):** a disease of the lungs where the airways become narrowed. This leads to a limitation of the flow of air to and from the lungs causing shortness of breath. The limitation of airflow is not fully reversible and usually gradually gets worse over time.

**Chronic pain:** severe physical discomfort that persists or progresses over a long period of time and is often resistant to medical treatments.

**Cloze procedure:** a method for testing a person's ability to comprehend written text by guessing missing words that have been deleted at regular intervals from the text.

**Cohort:** a group of individuals who experience a significant life event at the same point in time, such as birth, school graduation, or marriage.

**Cohort effect:** variation in the characteristics of an area of study (such as political attitudes, or family formation behavior) over time among individuals who are defined by some shared temporal experience or common life experience, such as year of birth.

**Coming out, to come out:** the voluntary public announcement of one's sexual orientation and gender identity.

**Commodification:** process of turning an act, emotion, or idea (e.g., a work of art) into a product that can be bought, sold, and/or mass-produced.

**Communal:** a group of interacting people living in a common location.

**Community-dwelling (as in "community-dwelling older adults"):** persons who are not residing in a hospital, long-term care facility, or nursing home. Those residing in their own homes in the community.

**Comorbidity:** the presence of one or more disorders (or diseases) in addition to a primary disease or disorder.

**Compulsory education:** schooling which children are required by law to receive and governments to provide.

**Conflict theory:** sociological perspective that emphasizes the role of coercion and power, a person's or group's ability to exercise influence and control over others, in producing social order. It states that a society or organization functions so that each individual participant and its groups struggle to maximize their benefits, which inevitably contributes to social change such as changes in politics and revolutions.

**Congenital anomalies:** a physical condition which is present at the time of birth which varies from the standard presentation. Also known as "birth defect."

**Consumer credit counseling:** a process offering education to consumers about how to avoid incurring debts that cannot be repaid. This process typically focuses on debt counseling and may involve negotiating with creditors to establish a debt management plan (DMP) for a consumer.

**Co-payment; co-pay:** a payment made by an individual who has health insurance, usually at the time a service is received, to offset some of the cost of care.

**Coreside, coresiding:** sharing a home with another individual.

**Coresidence:** the process of living in the same household or home as at least one other individual.

**Cost-of-living:** related to the average cost of the basic necessities of life, such as food, shelter, and clothing.

**Course work:** activities and learning carried out by students at university or middle/high school that contributes towards their overall grade, but which is assessed separately from their final exams.

**Cronyism:** partiality to long-standing friends, especially by appointing them to positions of authority, regardless of their qualifications. A practice that is contrary to the principle of meritocracy.

**Curriculum differentiation:** the practice of tailoring teaching environments and practices to create appropriately different learning experiences for different students.

**Defined benefit plan:** a retirement plan that guarantees a worker a certain payout at retirement, according to a fixed formula which usually depends on one's salary and the number of years' membership in the plan.

**Demagogue:** one who uses a political strategy for obtaining and gaining political power by appealing to the popular prejudices, emotions, fears and expectations of the public.

**Dementia:** the progressive decline in cognitive function due to damage or disease in the brain beyond what might be expected from normal aging.

**Democratization:** the transition to a more democratic political regime. May also refer to a transition to more egalitarian distribution of social and economic resources.

**Demographic and Health Surveys (DHS):** nationally-representative household surveys that provide data for a wide range of monitoring and impact evaluation indicators in the areas of population, health, and nutrition. DHS has been conducted in roughly 75 nations.

**Dependent Care Expense Account (DCEA):** a workplace benefits program that workers to set aside part of their pre-tax salary to pay primarily for childcare expenses of dependent children.

**Developmental task:** biological, social, or cognitive transitions that typically occur at a particular life stage, that are considered a pre-requisite for healthy maturation.

**Dichotomy:** division into two mutually exclusive, opposed, or contradictory groups. In statistical analyses, variables such as "male versus female" are considered a dichotomy.

**Disassociation:** a state of acute mental distress in which certain thoughts, emotions, sensations, and/or memories are compartmentalized, diagnosed mostly in individuals with a history of trauma.

**Discouraged workers:** a person of legal employment age who is not actively seeking employment, usually due to giving up looking, or no success looking.

**Disparity:** a stark difference between two social groups; typically used to describe inequitable health and health care access among poor versus wealthy Americans.

**Domestic partnership:** a legal or personal relationship between two individuals who live together and share a common domestic life but are neither joined by a traditional marriage nor a civil union.

**Drop out:** to stop one's formal education prior to the receipt of a degree.

**Duke Longitudinal Studies of Aging:** survey begun in 1956 that monitored the physical, mental, social and economic status of approximately 800 older adults.

**Duration:** the length of time spent in a particular role or social status.

**Earned Income Tax Credit:** a refundable tax credit. For tax year 2007 in the United States, a filer with one qualifying child could receive a maximum credit of $2,853. For two or more qualifying children, the maximum credit was $4,716. Grandparents, aunts, uncles, and siblings can also claim a child as their qualifying child provided they have shared residence with the child for more than half the tax year.

**Ecological systems theories of human development:** theoretical framework, developed by Urie Bronfenbrenner, specifying four types of nested environmental systems, with bi-directional influences within and between the systems. The four systems are: microsystem (immediate environments), mesosystem (connections between immediate environments), exosystem (external environmental settings), and macrosystem (larger cultural context). A fifth system was later added: Chronosystem (the patterning of environmental events and transitions over the life course).

**Ecology:** the scientific study of the distribution and abundance of life and the interactions between organisms and their environment.

**Elementary and Secondary Education Act of 1965:** a United States federal statute which funds primary and secondary education. The funds are authorized for professional development, instructional materials, resources to support educational programs, and parental involvement promotion. The Act has been reauthorized every five years since its enactment; its current reauthorization is the No Child Left Behind Act of 2001.

**Empirical:** a central concept in the social sciences, holding that all evidence must be dependent on evidence or consequences that are observable by the senses. Empirical data is data that is produced by a survey, experiment, observation, or other formal means of data collection.

**Empty nester:** a person whose children have left the family home, and who thus resides either alone or with one's spouse only.

**Enculturation:** the process whereby an established culture teaches an individual by repetition its accepted norms and values, so that the individual can become an accepted member of the society and find his or her suitable role.

**Endogamous:** the process of marrying or mating within one's own social group.

**English as a second language (ESL):** a formal educational program that teaches the English language to non-native English speakers.

**Entropy:** inevitable and steady deterioration of a system or society.

**Epidemiologic paradox:** the documented pattern whereby Latinos have physical health outcomes as good if not better than Whites in the United States, despite their generally poor socioeconomic resources.

**Epidemiology:** the study of social, demographic, and economic factors affecting the health and illness of populations.

**Epigenetic:** changes in gene expression that are stable between cell divisions, and sometimes between generations, but do not involve changes in the underlying DNA sequence of the organism.

**Equity theory:** framework used to explore satisfaction in terms of perceptions of fair/unfair distributions of resources within interpersonal relationships. Persons who perceive that they are under- or over-awarded are believed to experience more distress than those who feel their inputs and outputs are equal.

**Esoteric:** being understood by or meant for only the select few who have special knowledge or interest.

**Ethnocentric:** tendency to look at the world primarily from the perspective of one's own culture. Often involves the belief that one's own race or ethnic group is the most important and/or that some or all aspects of its culture are superior to those of other groups.

**Ethnography:** a research method where data are collected by observing at first hand the behavior and practices of a social group. Participant observation or interviewing strategies are typically used.

**Etiology:** the study of causation, often used to describe the causal factors contributing to disease onset.

**Eugenics:** a social philosophy proposing the possibility of improving the qualities of the human species or a human population, esp. by such means as discouraging reproduction by persons having genetic defects or presumed to have inheritable undesirable traits (negative eugenics) or encouraging reproduction by persons presumed to have inheritable desirable traits (positive eugenics).

**Exacerbate:** to amplify the effect of; often to make the consequences of an event better or worse.

**Executive function:** a set of cognitive abilities that control and regulate one's abilities and behaviors, including goal-directed behavior, initiating or stopping actions, monitoring and changing behavior as needed, and performing novel tasks and situations.

**Externalizing behaviors:** unhealthy or troubled behaviors, typically performed by young people, that involving directing anger and aggression outward (i.e., toward other individuals). Includes attention problems, aggressive behavior, and rule-breaking actions.

**Extracurricular:** activities performed by students that fall outside the realm of the normal curriculum of school or university education.

**Failure to thrive syndrome:** a medical term denoting poor weight gain and physical growth failure over an extended period of time in infancy. Term may encompass poor physical growth of any cause, and does not imply abnormal intellectual, social, or emotional development.

**Fair Labor Standards Act (FLSA) of 1938:** a federal law that established a national minimum wage, guaranteed time and a half for overtime in certain jobs, and prohibited most employment of minors in "oppressive child labor." Also called the Wages and Hours Bill.

**Family and Medical Leave Act of 1993:** a United States labor law allowing an employee to take unpaid leave due to a serious health condition that makes the employee unable to perform his job or to care for a sick family member or to care for a new son or daughter (including by birth, adoption, or foster care).

**Fecundity:** the biological capacity to reproduce.

**First grade:** the first year of formal schooling following kindergarten. In the United States, first grade typically begins at age 6.

**Flextime:** a variable work schedule which allows an employee to select the hours he or she will work, typically a condensed work week. Those working a condensed week may work 4, 10 hour days, rather than 5, 8 hour days. Those who work a 5 day week may work hours other than the typical "9–5."

**Fluency:** ability to express oneself readily and effortlessly both verbally and in writing. Often used to describe level of proficiency in a language, particularly one other than an individual's native language.

**Foster care:** system by which a certified, stand-in "parent(s)" cares for minor children or young people who have been removed from their birth parents or other custodial adults by state authority.

**Foundation for Child Development:** the oldest private, independent, grantmaking foundation in the nation with a sustained focus on improving the life prospects of children. Dedicated to the principle that all families should have the social and material resources to raise their children to be healthy, educated and productive members of their communities.

**Fragile Families and Child Wellbeing Study:** a survey following a cohort of nearly 5,000 children born in large U.S. cities between 1998 and 2000 (roughly three-quarters of whom were born to unmarried parents).

**Framingham Heart Study:** a cardiovascular study based in Framingham, Massachusetts. The study began in 1948 with 5,209 adult subjects from Framingham, and is now on its third generation of participants. Study findings have informed now-common knowledge concerning heart disease, such as the effects of diet, exercise, and common medications such as aspirin.

**Gender gap:** a disparity between the experiences of men and women; typically used to describe men's earnings advantage, and women's life expectancy advantage.

**Gender-appropriate behavior:** behavior that is consistent with the social norms dictating socially acceptable "male" and "female"-typed behavior.

**Gene-environment interaction:** term used to describe any phenotypic effects that are due to interactions between the environment and genes. Researchers increasingly believe that neither genetics nor environment are solely responsible for producing individual variation, and that virtually all traits show gene-environment interaction.

**Generation:** offspring that are at the same stage of descent from a common ancestor (e.g. mothers and daughters are of different generations). Informally used as a synonym for birth cohort.

**Generation next:** cohort of persons born between 1981 and 1988. Also referred to as Generation Y.

**Generation X:** cohort of persons born between 1966-1980.

**Generativity:** developmental stage, to be attained at midlife, that is believed to be critical for psychological maturation. Coined by Erik Erikson, it refers to the process of nurturing the accomplishments of younger persons, and minimizing attention to personal accomplishments.

**Geriatrics:** branch of internal medicine that focuses on health care of the elderly. It aims to promote health and to prevent and treat diseases and disabilities in older adults.

**Gerontology:** the study of the social, psychological and biological aspects of aging. It is distinguished from geriatrics, which is the branch of medicine that studies the disease of the elderly.

**Globalization:** the development of social and economic relationships stretching worldwide.

**Goals 2000: Educate America Act (1994):** act of the U.S. government that provides resources to states and communities to ensure that all students reach their full potential. States submit applications to develop school improvement plans, and make subgrants to local schools, and awards for preserves and professional development.

**Gun-Free Schools Act:** federal act in the United states stating that any student who brings a weapon to school must be expelled for a period of no less than one year.

**Heterogeneous:** consisting of diverse components or subgroups.

**Heterogeneity:** diversity in a subgroup.

**Homogamous:** a romantic pairing or marriage between two persons sharing social traits such as race, ethnicity, or educational attainment.

**Homophily:** the tendency of individuals to associate and bond with similar others.

**Hospice care:** a philosophy of care that recognizes death as the final stage of life and seeks to enable patients to continue an alert, pain-free life and to manage other symptoms so that their last days may be spent with dignity and quality, surrounded by their loved ones.

**Human capital:** the set of skills which an employee acquires on the job, through training and experience, or through formal education, which increase that employee's value in the marketplace.

**Identity:** an individual's conceptualization of one's self as a discrete, separate entity. The content of one's identity is shaped by one's interactions with significant others, social context, and group memberships.

**Improving America's Schools Act of 1994:** a federal act targeted at reforming education. It included provisions or reforms for: the Title 1 program, providing extra help to disadvantaged students, holding schools accountable for their results at the same level as other students, charter schools, safe and drug-free schools, technology, and increases in funding for bilingual and immigration education.

***In loco parentis*:** latin phrase for "in the place of a parent." Refers to the legal responsibility of a person or organization to take on some of the functions and responsibilities of a parent. For example, colleges and schools may act in the best interests of the students as they see fit, in the absence of parental intervention.

**Incidence rates:** the rate at which new events occur in a population. The numerator is the number of new events occurring in a defined period; the denominator is the population at risk of experiencing the event during this period. Typically used to summarize the onset of disease in a population.

**Individualism:** a moral, political, or social outlook that stresses independence, self-reliance and individual liberty.

**Individuals with Disabilities Education Act (IDEA) of 2004:** a federal law ensuring services to children with disabilities throughout the nation. IDEA governs how states and public agencies provide early intervention, special education and related services to more than 6.5 million eligible infants, toddlers, children and youth with disabilities.

**Industrial Revolution:** the transformation of the U.S. economy in the late 19th century to one reliant on agriculture and home production, to one reliant on manufacturing and mass production of goods.

**Inflation:** the overall general upward price movement of goods and services in an economy, usually as measured by the Consumer Price Index and the Producer Price Index in the United States.

**In-group:** the social group to which one belongs, and which one views as superior to other social groups.

**Innate:** a personal characteristic that is present since birth. Also considered an essential and important trait of an individual.

**Institutional racism:** a form of racism (i.e., discrimination on the grounds of race) which occurs specifically in institutions such as corporations, school systems, financial organizations, and universities.

**Internalizing behaviors:** behavior problems that manifest by turning inward and potentially harming one's self.

**Jim Crow laws:** state and local laws enacted primarily in the Southern United States between 1876 and 1965. They mandated *de jure* segregation in all public facilities, with "separate but equal" accommodations for black Americans and members of other non-white racial groups. In practice, this led to treatment and accommodations that were inferior to those provided for white Americans, systematizing a number of economic, educational and social disadvantages.

**K–12:** referring to the U.S. school grades of kindergarten through grade 12, the final year in the formal secondary school system.

**Life chances:** the opportunities each individual has to improve their quality of life. The concept was introduced by German sociologist Max Weber. It is a probabilistic concept, describing how likely it is, given certain factors, that an individual's life will turn out a certain way.

**Life cycle:** a progression through a series of differing stages of development. A term used by developmental psychologists, whereas sociologists use the related phrase "life course."

**Life span:** the typical length of time that any particular organism can be expected to live.

**Life table:** a numerical table which shows, for a person at each age, what the probability is that they die before their next birthday. These data are used to calculate life expectancy, or the average number of years an individual can expect to live in the future.

**Lifelong:** referring to characteristics or experiences that last over the entire life course.

**Limited English proficient (LEP):** students who perform in the bottom one-half to one-quarter on standardized tests that measure knowledge of the English language. Through the Bilingual Education Act of 1968, these students are often provided with instruction in the public schools that supplements or replaces regular classroom instruction.

**Linked lives concept:** a key principle of the life course paradigm. It holds that human lives both shape and are shaped by one's relationships with other individuals, particularly family members.

**Longitudinal studies:** mode of data collection that involves repeated observations of the same items or individuals over long periods of time–often many decades.

**Long-term-care facility:** a residential facility, typically inhabited by older persons or persons with chronic illness or disability who cannot care for themselves for long periods of time. Provides residents with services to meet their medical and non-medical needs.

**Luxembourg Income Study (LIS):** a cross-national database of micro-economic income data from 30 countries on 4 continents.

**Male climacteric:** also known as andropause or "male menopause." Stage experienced by midlife men, marked by relatively low levels of testosterone, loss of libido and potency, nervousness, depression, impaired memory, the inability to concentrate, fatigue, insomnia, hot flushes, and sweating. Empirical evidence in support of this concept is weak and controversial.

**Mandatory retirement:** based on their age, older persons who hold certain jobs may be required by statute to step down, or retire. The practice is justified by the argument that certain occupations are either too dangerous (military personnel) or require high levels of physical and mental skill (airline pilots). Many view the practice as a form of age discrimination.

**Marriage market:** the pool of eligible candidates that an individual may plausibly consider for marriage. Marriage markets typically are defined by geographic proximity, age, gender, education, and race/ethnicity. Marriage rates are low when one faces a small or inappropriate marriage market.

**Means-testing:** an investigative process which determines whether an individual or family is eligible to receive certain types of government benefits, such as welfare or Medicaid. The "test" can consist of quantifying the party's income, or assets, or a combination of both.

**Mediating variables:** a variable, or measure used in statistical analyses, that partially accounts for the causal relation between the purported independent and dependent variable. For example, the effect of parental poverty on one's own adult health is mediated by, or partially explained by, one's own educational attainment.

**Medicalization:** the process by which health or behavior conditions come to be defined and treated as medical issues. For example, the widespread availability of antidepressants contributes to the medicalization of depression; where it is considered a medical disorder to be treated, rather than a normal response to stressful social circumstances.

**Meta-analysis:** a statistical technique for amalgamating, summarizing, and reviewing previous quantitative research. Researchers amass many published studies on a single topic, such as, the effect of gender on depressive symptoms, and then develop a statistical summary of the results obtained from all studies, and ultimately draw a conclusion about general pattern.

**Middle-aged:** describes persons who have completed young adulthood, but have not yet reached old age. Generally believed to be ages 40 to 60.

**Middle-income:** those individuals or households whose income is generally in the middle of the overall national income distribution.

**Midlife:** life stage including persons who have completed young adulthood, but have not yet reached old age. Generally believed to be ages 40 to 60.

**Moderating variable:** a variable, or measure used in statistical analysis, that affects the direction and/or strength of the relation between an independent or predictor variable and a dependent or criterion variable. For example, the effect of education on earnings may be moderated by gender; each additional year of education may bring higher income for men versus women.

**Modernization:** the process through which a nation or region becomes "modern," and thus guided by science rather than religion; manufacturing and service economies are more common than agricultural; and attitudes and values reflect individualism rather than collectivities.

**Mortality rate:** a measure of the number of deaths (either all causes, or due to a specific cause) in some population, scaled to the size of that population, per unit time. For example, the annual mortality rate in the United States was approximately 826 deaths per 100,000 persons in 2007.

**Narcissism:** a personal trait involving excessive self-regard and self-focus.

**National Assessment of Educational Progress (NAEP):** known as "the Nation's Report Card," it is the only nationally representative and continuing assessment of what students in the U.S. know and can do in various subject areas. Since 1969, assessments have been conducted periodically in reading, mathematics, science, writing, U.S. history, civics, geography, and the arts.

**National Center for Early Development and Learning (NCEDL):** a national early childhood research project supported by the U.S. Department of Education, NCEDL focuses on enhancing the cognitive, social, and emotional development of children from birth through age eight.

**National Center for Education Statistics (NCES):** a division of the U.S. Department of Education and the Institute of Education Sciences, NCES is the primary federal entity for collecting and analyzing data related to education.

**National Center for Health Statistics:** a part of the U.S. Centers for Disease Control and Prevention (CDC), NCHS is the United States' principal health statistics agency. It designs, develops, and maintains a number of systems that produce data related to demographic and health concerns. These include data on registered births and deaths, and national surveys of health.

**National Coalition Against Domestic Violence (NCADV):** a grassroots non-profit membership organization working since 1978 to end violence in the lives of women and children. Provides a national network for state coalitions and local programs serving battered women and their children, public policy at the national level, technical assistance, community awareness campaigns, general information and referrals, and publications on the issue of domestic violence.

**National Council on Measurement in Education (NCME):** a professional organization for individuals involved in assessment, evaluation, testing, and other aspects of educational measurement. Members are involved in the construction and use of standardized tests; new forms of assessment, including performance-based assessment; program design; and program evaluation.

**National Education Association (NEA):** the largest labor union in the United States, representing public school teachers and other support personnel, faculty and staffers at colleges and universities, retired educators, and college students preparing to become teachers.

**National Heart, Lung, and Blood Institute (NHLBI):** a division of the National Institutes of Health (NIH), NHLBI supports research that advances understanding of the diagnosis, progression, treatment, and prevention of diseases of the heart, blood vessels, lung, and blood; blood resources; and sleep disorders.

**National Household Education Survey (NHES):** national survey designed to collect information from households on a variety of educational issues, including early childhood education, school readiness, school safety and discipline, early childhood program participation, parental involvement in education, and children's civic engagement. Conducted by the National Center for Education Statistics (NCES), the NHES obtains data from parents and children.

**National Institute of Mental Health (NIMH):** a division of the National Institutes of Health (NIH), NIMH aims to reduce the burden of mental illness and behavioral disorders through research on mind, brain, and behavior.

**National Institute on Aging (NIA):** a division of the National Institutes of Health (NIH), NIA leads a broad scientific effort to understand the nature of aging and to extend the healthy, active years of life.

**Nativism:** practice or policy of favoring native-born citizens over immigrants.

**Neophyte:** a beginner; novice.

**Nepotism:** the showing of favoritism toward relatives and friends, based upon that relationship, rather than on an objective evaluation of ability, meritocracy or suitability. Often considered a factor contributing to cumulative advantage among already advantaged social groups.

**No Child Left Behind Act of 2001:** a controversial United States federal law that is intended to improve the performance of U.S. primary and secondary schools by increasing the standards of accountability for states, school districts, and schools, as well as providing parents more flexibility in choosing which schools their children will attend. The law requires all states to develop content standards and to measure progress of students through annual testing in English/Language Arts, Mathematics, and Science in grades 3 through 8, and once in high school.

**No-fault divorce:** the dissolution of a marriage requiring neither a showing wrong-doing of either party. It is granted upon a petition by either party to a family court, without requiring the petitioner show that the respondent is at fault, and despite respondent's potential objections to the dissolution.

**Nonmarital:** the state of being unmarried. Often used to describe childbearing that occurs among unmarried persons (e.g., nonmarital childbearing).

**Nonminority:** a member of a majority social group. In the United States, nonminority typically refers to non-Hispanic whites, while minority refers to Blacks, Asians, Hispanics, and Native Americans.

**Norms:** widely accepted, socially constructed expectations for human behavior. Adherence to these expectations is enforced through formal and informal social sanctions (i.e., rewards and punishments). Norms often are specific to specific social groups; that is, specific expectations guide the appropriate behavior for individuals based on their age, gender, social class, etc.

**Numeracy:** an ability to understand and work with numbers and other mathematical concepts. Also called numerical literacy.

**Offending:** violating a rule or law.

**Off-site:** taking place or occurring not on site (e.g., employees of a corporation who work in their own homes are working off-site).

**Off-time:** a behavior or transition that occurs at an age that departs from normative time tables. Usually refers to transitions that occur early, and thus for which one is ill-prepared (e.g., giving birth at age 16 among modern American teens).

**Old-age:** pertaining to later stages of the life course, esp. age 65 and older.

**One-drop rule:** a historical colloquial term in the United States that holds that a person with any trace (i.e., "one drop" of blood) of African ancestry cannot be considered White. Unless the person has an alternative non-White ancestry that he or she can claim, such as Native American, Asian, Arab, Australian aboriginal, the person must be considered Black.

**On-site:** taking place or occurring on site (e.g., employees of a particular firm who work at the corporate offices are working on-site).

**On-the-job:** activities the occur when one is holding a job or working at a work site; e.g., on-the-job training involves the pursuit of job skills in one's current employment setting.

**Ontological:** pertaining to the study of being or existence and its basic categories and relationships.

**Operationalization:** the process of defining an abstract or vague concept so as to make the concept measurable in form of (variables) consisting of specific observations.

For example, "social status" often is measured as number of years of education completed, or current household income.

**Organization for Economic Co-operation and Development (OECD):** formed in 1948, an international organization of thirty countries that accept the principles of representative democracy and free market economy. Initially formed to administer the Marshall Plan, for the reconstruction of Europe after World War II.

**Out-group:** social groups that one is not a part of, and thus are devalued; opposite of in-group.

**Out-of-wedlock:** occurring outside of marriage; e.g., births that occur to unmarried persons.

**Pandemic:** an epidemic of infectious disease that spreads through human populations across a large region, such a continent, or even worldwide; e.g., bubonic plague.

**Paradigm:** the set of practices and guiding philosophies that define a scientific discipline during a particular period of time.

**Parity:** the number of liveborn children a woman has delivered.

**Parochial:** of or relating to a church parish. Often used to describe Catholic or "parochial" school.

**Partograph:** a tool that can be used by midwifery personnel to assess the progress of labor and to identify when intervention is necessary.

**Part-time:** describing work hours that are less than full time; usually fewer than 35 hours per week.

**Pathology:** the study and diagnosis of disease through examination of organs, tissues, bodily fluids and whole bodies. May also refer to departure or deviation from a normal condition; e.g., high levels of crime are considered an indication of neighborhood pathology.

**Perinatal:** pertaining to the period immediately before and after birth. Exact time points vary, yet typically ranges from the 20th to 28th week of gestation and ends 1 to 4 weeks after birth.

**Perpetuate:** cause to continue; e.g., economic strains following divorce can perpetuate symptoms of divorce-related distress.

**Personal Responsibility and Work Opportunity Reconciliation Act of 1996:** also referred to as "welfare reform," this controversial Federal act gives states the power to reform their own programs to move people from welfare to work. A key part of PRWORA is the change of federal Aid to Families with Dependent Children (AFDC) funding from matching funding to the Temporary Assistant to Needy Families (TANF) block grant.

**Pervasive Developmental Disorder:** five developmental disorders characterized by delays in the development of multiple basic functions including socialization and communication. The most commonly known PDD is (1) Autism, with the remaining identified as (2) Rett syndrome, (3) Childhood disintegrative disorder, (4) Asperger syndrome, and (5) Pervasive Developmental Disorder Not Otherwise Specified (or PDD-NOS).

**Pharmacotherapy:** treatment of disease through the use of drugs.

**Phonology:** subfield of linguistics which studies the sound system of a specific language or set of languages.

**Planful competence:** cluster of personal characteristics associated with positive social and emotional development over the life course, according to sociologist John Clausen. Its three components are: self-confidence, dependability, and intellectual investment.

**Policymaker:** a person with power to influence or determine policies and practices at an international, national, regional, or local level.

**Polygyny:** a mating practice in which a male has more than one female sexual partner.

**Population Association of America (PAA):** an organization of professionals working in the population field, including demographers, sociologists, economists and public health professionals.

**Postdivorce:** experiences that occur after one formally dissolves a marriage.

**Postindustrial economy:** a period of growth within an industrialized economy or nation in which the relative importance of manufacturing lessens and that of services, information, and research grows.

**Postneonatal:** refers to time period from the end of the first month of an infant's life to a year after birth.

**Postretirement:** experiences that occur after one formally exits the paid labor force.

**Post-traumatic stress disorder (PTSD):** an anxiety disorder that can develop after exposure to one or more terrifying events in which grave physical harm occurred or was threatened. A severe and ongoing emotional reaction to an extreme psychological trauma.

**Poverty line:** the minimum level of income deemed necessary to achieve an adequate standard of living in a given country. In the United States, the level takes into consideration age, household size, and the cost of expenses such as food.

**Preadolescence:** the period prior to adolescence, typically prior to age 12.

**Predispose:** to make one susceptible to some outcome; for example, obesity predisposes one to diabetes risk.

**Preindustrial:** the historical period before industrialization, specif. before the Industrial Revolution.

**Pre-K:** experiences, particularly schooling, that takes place prior to kindergarten.

**Preschool-age:** the period prior to starting kindergarten, typically prior to age 5.

**Prevalence rate:** the proportion of people in a population who have a disease at a given time: the numerator is the number of existing cases of disease at a specified time and the denominator is the total population.

**Primary stressor:** the root origin of a series of other problematic life circumstances, called secondary stressors; e.g., the primary stressor of job loss may trigger the secondary stressor of financial strains.

**Programme for International Student Assessment (PISA):** begun in 2000, a system of international assessments that focus on 15-year-olds' capabilities in reading literacy, mathematics literacy, and science literacy. PISA is organized by the Organization for Economic Cooperation and Development (OECD).

**Proliferation:** a rapid and often excessive spread or increase, often used to describe stress; e.g., poverty leads to the proliferation of related stressors such as poor nutrition, medical care, and neighborhood quality.

**Prosocial:** circumstances when someone acts to help another person, particularly when they have no goal other than to help a fellow human.

**Proximal, distal influences:** refers to potentially causal influences; proximal are immediate or direct effects, while distal influences are more far removed; e.g., poverty is a distal influence on obesity; poor nutrition is a proximal influence.

**Proxy:** a person authorized to act on another's behalf; e.g., persons who are in a coma may have their health care wishes conveyed by a proxy.

**Psychometric:** the theory and technique of educational and psychological measurement, which includes the measurement of knowledge, abilities, attitudes, and personality traits.

**Psychosocial stressor:** a distressing event or experience which compromises one's psychological or social well-being.

**Public Schools Accountability Act of 1999 (California act):** law enacted in California that authorizes the creation of an educational accountability system for California public schools. Its primary goal is to help schools improve and to measure the academic achievement of all students.

**Qualitative:** research method that focuses on processes, and obtaining the point of view of research subjects. Typically small, focused samples rather than large random sample. Four common methods include: (1) participation in the setting, (2) direct observation, (3) in depth interviews, and (4) analysis of documents and materials.

**Quasi-experimental:** research method that shares characteristics of true experiments, yet lacks the random assignment. Often involves "natural experiments" such as comparing human behavior both pre- and post- an historical event; e.g., comparing depressive symptoms reported in surveys conducted in the first 9 months of 2001, versus those reported after September 11, 2001.

**Recidivism:** the act of a person repeating an undesirable behavior after they have either experienced negative consequences of that behavior, or have been treated or trained to extinguish that behavior. Often used to describe the process of returning to prison after one has been released.

**Reciprocity:** the act or strong strong social expectation that people will respond to each other in similar ways — responding to gifts and kindnesses from others with similar benevolence of their own, and responding to harmful, hurtful acts from others with either indifference or some form of retaliation. Often used when studying caregiving and intergenerational transfers.

**Reflexivity:** process of exploring the ways in which a researcher's involvement with a particular study influences, acts upon and informs such research.

**Religiosity:** a comprehensive term describing the numerous aspects of religious activity, dedication, and belief.

**Repudiation:** act of rejecting or disowning or disclaiming as invalid; e.g., research purporting to show racial differences in innate intelligence has been repudiated on methodological and ethical grounds.

**Resilience:** the positive capacity of people to cope with stress and catastrophe. May describe persons bouncing back to high levels of psychological well-being after experiencing a major stressor and a spell of psychological distress.

**Retirement-age:** referring to persons age 65 and above.

**Rett's Disorder:** a neurodevelopmental disorder that is classified as a pervasive developmental disorder by the DSM-IV. Characteristics include deceleration of the rate of head growth; small hands and feet; repetitive hand movements; cognitive impairment; and problems with socialization.

**Sample survey:** research method used to collect quantitative information about characteristics of a subsample of a population.

**School-age:** referring to children ages 6 to 17, or ages at which young people in the United States traditionally are enrolled in school.

**School-to-work:** describing the transition from full-time education to full-time employment.

**Secondary stressor:** a stressful event or condition that results from a primary, or preceding, stressor; e.g., the primary stressor of divorce may lead to a secondary strain of moving to a new neighborhood.

**Secularization:** the process of transformation by which a society migrates from close identification with religious institutions to a more separated relationship.

**Selective attrition:** the tendency of some people to be more likely to drop out of a study than others. Those who drop out of (or "attrite from") share characteristics that make them distinct from those who remain in the sample. Thus, observed differences between sample means of the wave 1 and wave 2 sample may reflect the fact that the two populations are fundamentally different, due to characteristics of those who attrite versus remain in the study.

**Self-actualization:** developing or achieving one's full potential. Considered the pinnacle of psychologist Abraham Maslow's hierarchy of needs.

**Senescence:** the biological processes of a living organism approaching an advanced age. Often used to describe physical declines among older adults.

**Senile dementia:** the mental deterioration (loss of intellectual ability) that is associated with old age. Two major types of senile dementia are identified: those due to generalized atrophy (Alzheimer type) and those due to vascular problems (mainly strokes).

**Service sector:** the part of industry or business which deals with the marketing and selling of intangible products rather than physical goods.

**Smith-Hughes Act of 1917:** act of the United States Congress that promoted vocational agriculture to train people "who have entered upon or who are preparing to enter upon the work of the farm," and provided federal funds for this purpose.

**Social exclusion:** the alienation or disenfranchisement of certain people within a society, often due to one's social class, educational status, relationships in childhood, and living standards. Exclusion may limit one's opportunities to succeed.

**Social learning:** a theory that explains how people learn social behavior, through observation. If people observe positive, desired outcomes in another's behavior, they are more likely to model, imitate, and adopt the behavior themselves.

**Social norms:** widely-agreed upon expectations for appropriate social behavior. Violation of expectations may be socially sanctions. Expectations are often specific to one's age, gender, or birth cohort.

**Social safety net:** term used to describe a collection of services provided by the state, such as welfare, unemployment benefits, universal healthcare, homeless shelters, the minimum wage and sometimes subsidized services such as public transport, which prevent individuals from falling into poverty beyond a certain level.

**Social Security Act of 1935:** the federal retirement plan enacted by U.S. Congress in 1935. The original purpose (unchanged today) of the Act was to adopt a system that required the current working generation to contribute to the support of older, retired workers. The Act was passed in response to old-age dependency resulting from Depression-generated phenomena.

**Socialization:** the process of learning to become a member of one's society.

**Socioeconomic status (SES):** indication of an individual's or family's economic and social position relative to others, usually based on income, education, occupation, or some combination thereof.

**Soft drug use vs. hard drug use (or soft drugs vs. hard drugs):** categories of non-prescription psychoactive drugs. Hard drug generally refers to drugs illegal for nonmedical use that lead to profound and severe addiction, as opposed to soft drugs that has weaker or no physical withdrawal symptoms.

**Stigma:** the phenomenon whereby an individual with an attribute, which is deeply discredited by his/her society, is rejected as a result of the attribute. Common stigmas in the United States are obesity, mental illness, and substance use.

**Stonewall Rebellion:** series of violent conflicts between lesbian, gay, bisexual, and transgendered individuals and New York City police officers that began during a June 28, 1969 police raid, and lasted several days. Conflicts were centered at the Stonewall Inn and are widely recognized as the catalyst for the modern-day movement towards gay rights.

**Stratification:** the hierarchical arrangement of social groups within a society. Typically used to describe differences on the basis of one's social class, caste, or and strata within a society.

**Stressor:** an agent, condition, or other stimulus that causes stress to an organism.

**Sub-Saharan:** geographical term used to describe the area of the African continent which lies south of the Sahara, or those African countries which are fully or partially located south of the Sahara.

**Subsidize:** to aid or promote with public money, such as housing or job programs that are partially funded with public funds.

**Sudden infant death syndrome (SIDS):** a syndrome marked by the symptoms of sudden and unexplained death of an apparently healthy infant aged one month to one year.

**Sun Belt:** region of the United States generally considered to stretch across the South and Southwest (the geographic southern United States). The Sun Belt has seen substantial population growth in recent decades, partly fueled by a surge in retiring baby boomers who migrate domestically. Includes the states of Alabama, Arizona, California, Florida, Georgia, Louisiana, Mississippi, Nevada, New Mexico, South Carolina, and Texas.

**Supplemental Security Income (SSI):** a monthly stipend provided to aged (legally deemed to be 65 or older), blind, or disabled persons based on need, paid by the United States government.

**Survey of Income and Program Participation (SIPP):** a statistical survey conducted by the United States Census Bureau. The main objective of the SIPP is to provide accurate and comprehensive information about the income of American individuals and households and the participation of these people in income transfer programs. Designed as a continuous series of panels, with a sample size from approximately 14,000 to 37,000 households. Each panel lasts from 2.5 to 4 years. The SIPP sample is a multistage-stratified sample of the U.S. civilian noninstitutionalized population. The respondents are all household members 15 years or older.

**Taxonomy:** the practice and science of classification.

**Temporary Assistance to Needy Families (TANF):** U.S. federal assistance program, commonly known as "welfare." It began on July 1, 1997, and succeeded the Aid to Families with Dependent Children program, providing cash assistance to indigent American families with dependent children. Before 1996, eligibility was determined simply by entitlement. Now, states are given grants to run their own programs. TANF was created by the Personal Responsibility and Work Opportunity Act, which provides a maximum of 60 months of benefits within one's lifetime.

**Total fertility rate (TFR):** the average number of children that would be born to a woman over her lifetime if she were to experience the exact current age-specific fertility rates (ASFRs) through her lifetime, and she were to survive from birth through the end of her reproductive life. It is obtained by summing the single-year age-specific rates at a given time.

**Trajectory:** a path of action. In life course sociology, trajectories are joined by transitions. For example, progressing through school grades is an educational trajectory, while entering the work force and receiving promotions is considered a career trajectory.

**Transitions:** the point of movement from one role or status to another. For example, the school-to work transition involves the movement from the role of student to worker; the transition to parenthood involves movement from the status of childless person to parent.

**Turning points:** the real or perceived movement from one role or status to another. A turning point may be based on observable roles or behaviors, such as the graduating high school, or may be internal and perceived, such as believing that one is an adult, rather than a child.

**Typology:** the systematic classification of types or subgroups; such as a typology of personality groups.

**United Nations Children's Fund (UNICEF):** United Nations Children's Fund or UNICEF is an international organization that provides many types of assistance and help to children and mothers throughout the world. It is funded by governments and private donations.

**United Nations Development Programme:** the United Nations' global development network. Headquartered in New York City, the organization has country offices in 166 countries, where it works with local governments to meet development challenges and develop local capacity. UNDP provides expert advice, training, and grant support to developing countries, with increasing emphasis on assistance to the least developed countries.

**Unretirement:** the process of returning to full-time or part-time work after one has exited the labor force due to retirement.

**Upward mobility:** a change and increase in one's social standing, typically described in terms of education, income, or occupational status. Typically refers to intergenerational mobility, or the movement from one's parent's social class to one's own achieved social class in adulthood.

**Variance:** one measure of statistical dispersion, averaging the squared distance of its possible values from the expected value (mean). Whereas the mean is a way to describe the location of a distribution of a measure, the variance is a way to capture its scale or degree of being spread out.

**Venereal diseases:** an illness that has a significant probability of transmission between humans or animals by means of sexual contact, including vaginal intercourse, oral sex, and anal sex.

**Video deficit:** a psychological phenomenon exhibited among toddlers. Toddlers are less successful at repeating tasks they watch on a video screen compared to the same tasks observed in real life. This video deficit reinforces the importance of human interaction in the development of young children.

**Welfare:** government programs which seek to provide a minimum level of income, service or other support for disadvantaged peoples.

**Well-being:** the physical, emotional, social, and psychological quality of life enjoyed by an individual.

**Workforce:** all persons in a population who is available to work and of working age.

**Working-age:** the population group most likely to be economically productive in a society. It is defined as the population group ages 15 to 64.

**Working-class:** social class grouping that typically includes reference to education, occupation, culture, and income. It is commonly used to refer to a group of people who are employed for wages, especially as manual workers.

**Workplace:** a place, such as an office or factory, where people are employed.

**Workweek:** the legal workweek varies from nation to nation. It is the consecutive set of days, not including the weekend, in which most paid work activities occur. In the United States the workweek lasts 5 days, Monday through Friday.

**World Fertility Surveys (WFS):** survey of human fertility initiated in 1972 and completed in 1984. The WFS provided information for 42 developing countries and 20 developed countries. As part of the survey nearly 350,000 women between the ages of 15 and 49 were interviewed. The WFS objectives were to help developing countries assess fertility levels, to collect data comparable between countries, and to promote national competence in survey methodology. The WFS was followed by the Demographic and Health Surveys.

**World Health Organization (WHO):** a part of the United Nations system, the WHO provides leadership on global health matters by setting the global health research agenda, including norms and standards. The WHO influences the health policy of nations around the world. The WHO also provides technical support to countries and monitoring and assessing health trends.

**World Wide Web; the web:** a system of Internet servers that contain and support HTML (HyperText markup language) documents. HTML documents can be linked to one another, as well as to graphics, audio, and video files. This means you can jump from one document to another simply by clicking on hyperlinks on a Web page. Web browsers (such as Netscape and Firefox) make it easy to access the World Wide Web.

**Young-old and oldest-old:** two subgroups of the older, or age 55+ population. The young-old are the 55-to-75 age group. The oldest-old are age 85 and older. The young-old are distinguished from the middle-aged primarily by retirement, and distinguished from the old-old by continued vigor and active social involvement.

# *Research Methods*

## I. INTRODUCTION AND OVERVIEW

Life course researchers face the formidable challenge of answering the question, Why and how do individuals' lives turn out the way they do? Although most people, at one time or another, want to find out what makes people tick, social scientists are unique in that they use rigorous scientific methods to documents patterns of human thought and behavior. Rather than simply observing one person, or asking an individual about his or her life, life course sociologists are interested in documenting behavior at the *population level*, and also are interested in identifying *subgroup differences*, such as race, ethnic, gender, and birth cohort differences in how human lives unfold. Life course sociologists also are interested in the study of *whole lives*, rather than studying isolated stages, such as adolescence or old age only. They seek to uncover how early life experiences shape one's adulthood and later years; as such, documenting causal relationships is a critical goal. These substantive aims are the guiding force beyond life course researchers' choice of appropriate research methods. *Research methods* refer to the diverse modes of investigation used to gather empirical (or factual) material about social behavior.

This entry briefly summarizes the research goals of life course scholars, discusses how research goals guide the selection of one's research method, describes the main qualitative and quantitative research methods used by life course scholars, summarizes analytic strategies used by quantitative researchers, and offers examples of important life course studies that exemplify the broad range of research methods available. The topic of research methods is an extremely complex and challenging one; scholars can devote years to learning about methods and perfecting their analytic skills, and they often must have strong backgrounds in statistics in order to successfully carry out life course research. This entry focuses on the ideas behind research methods, rather than the precise statistical techniques and software packages used to conduct research. After reading this entry, however, students of the life course should be able to read and understand research articles using a wide range of methods and should be able to select an analytic approach that best fits with their own substantive research goals.

### GOALS OF LIFE COURSE RESEARCH

Social scientists typically have three broad goals: to describe social reality; to identify correlations between two or more behaviors or characteristics; and to test causal hypotheses. *Describing social reality* might involve describing population-level trends, such as documenting the proportion of all 18-year-olds in the United States who have graduated high school, or calculating the average age at which people first marry. Social scientists also describe subgroup differences in social reality, by comparing individuals from different birth cohorts, racial or ethnic groups, or nations. For instance, life course sociologists might examine whether the proportion of people who cohabit prior to marriage is higher in Sweden than in the United States. Researchers might also investigate whether Blacks and Whites differ in their rates of infant mortality or in their overall life span.

Most researchers calculate simple *descriptive statistics* as a way to describe reality: Descriptive statistics include the *mean* (or average) value of some population-level attribute, or a *frequency distribution*, which refers to the proportion of people in a population who fall into each of several mutually exclusive categories, such as the proportion who are single versus married. In order to evaluate whether two subpopulations are different from one another, analysts can use formal statistical tests to ascertain whether subpopulation means or frequency distributions are significantly different from one another. Statistical tests such as *t-tests* can be used to compare means, while *chi-square tests* can be used to assess whether the frequency distribution of a particular attribute differs significantly across subgroups.

A second goal is to detect whether a *correlation*, or a statistical relationship, exists between two or more behaviors and characteristics. Two constructs are correlated if a change in one construct is associated with a systematic change in the second construct. A correlation may be *positive*, where both constructs change in the same direction, or *negative*, where the constructs change in opposite directions. For example, height and weight are usually positively correlated; as height increases, one's body weight also tends to increase. By contrast, absenteeism and school grade point average are negatively or inversely correlated; the more days a child is absent from school, the lower his or her school grades. A data analyst would calculate a *zero-order correlation* to detect the strength and direction of the relationship between two attributes. A correlation of 0 means that two constructs are completely unrelated, whereas a correlation of 1 means that the two constructs are perfectly related. For example, the correlation between height and weight is usually about .70, which is quite high. Importantly, *correlation is not causation*. A zero-order correlation cannot tell us what variable "caused" the other; it simply tells us the strength and positive or negative direction of the relationship. A third goal is to *test causal hypotheses*. A causal hypothesis is a statement that differences in one behavior or event produce a difference or a change in another behavior. When developing causal hypotheses, researchers typically identify an independent variable and a dependent variable. An *independent variable* is a measure that is purported to have an effect on another measure. The measure affected is the *dependent variable*. It is very difficult, however, to establish causation in the social world; there are too many competing hypotheses and characteristics to take into consideration. It is not always clear which construct is the independent variable and which is the dependent variable. Nevertheless, data analysts use a variety of strategies to try to ascertain causation. *Experiments*, described below, are considered the single best way to establish causation. Yet statistical analyses of survey data, especially longitudinal data, where data are collected at multiple points in time, can also be used to evaluate causal hypotheses.

An important guideline when trying to establish causal relations is to think logically and sensibly about human behavior. For instance, some studies have shown that age is negatively correlated with political liberalism—that older persons endorse more conservative political views than their younger counterparts. It is plausible, then, for a young scholar to hypothesize that advanced age may "cause" an individual to cast a vote for a Republican rather than a Democratic political candidate. The reverse is implausible; one's political identity cannot "cause" one's age! In most cases, however, the answer is not so simple. For example, if a researcher finds a positive correlation between body mass index (an indication of one's weight-to-height ratio) and depressive symptoms, can one then necessarily conclude that gaining weight causes a person to become depressed? An equally plausible hypothesis is that unhappy people cope by overeating, or they may lack the energy to maintain an effective exercise regimen.

A further challenge is to figure out whether a purported independent variable *really* predicts the dependent variable, or whether a variety of intervening factors account for the observed statistical association. The most widely used strategy for figuring out whether a correlation between variables is a causal connection is the use of statistical controls, meaning some variables are held "constant" when researchers try to identify and isolate the effect of the purportedly causal variable. For example, some scholars have documented that maternal deprivation is correlated negatively with psychological adjustment in adults. Is it really the case that parent–child separation has direct long-term consequences for the child's well-being? Or is there some other plausible explanation?

Thoughtful researchers would try to generate a list of possible alternative explanations and then would statistically "control" for these measures in their analysis of data. For example, one source of maternal deprivation is a child's hospitalization. Children who are in poor health may be separated from their parents during long hospitalizations; it is plausible that the child's poor health accounts for the observed statistical linkage between maternal deprivation and the child's adult mental health. Likewise, mothers may be separated from their children if they themselves have a mental health problem or if they are imprisoned. Both of these maternal characteristics may expose a child to multiple stressors, which may in turn carry serious long-term consequences. This example reveals the difficulty and complexity of testing causal hypotheses about life course processes and outcomes.

## SELECTING A RESEARCH METHOD

Before a social scientist can describe patterns of human behavior, he or she must first collect and analyze data.

Data collection is a systematic procedure for amassing information about a well-defined population on some well-defined topic. Data collection and analysis methods typically are classified as either "qualitative" or "quantitative." The choice of a research approach should always be motivated by the researchers' substantive goals and questions. Qualitative researchers usually are interested in rich descriptions of social phenomena, but are less concerned with ascertaining causal ordering. For this reason, they obtain rich, in-depth data on small samples, usually by observing them firsthand or by conducting unstructured face-to-face interviews.

Quantitative researchers, by contrast, typically are interested in documenting large-scale patterns, identifying subgroup differences, tracking changes over time, and testing causal hypotheses. For this reason, most quantitative researchers rely on large-scale structured surveys. Experimentation is another method used by quantitative researchers to document causal relationships, although life course sociologists rarely use experiments; rather, this is the preferred method of psychologists. The next sections provide glimpses into each of these research approaches and examples of how each method can be used to investigate questions at the core of life course scholarship.

**Qualitative Research.** Qualitative researchers aim to obtain an in-depth understanding of human behavior, thoughts, and feelings. Simply put, they investigate the *why* and *how* of social behavior, not just *what, where*, and *when*. Such researchers thus need smaller but focused samples rather than large random samples. Qualitative research is well suited to generating rich descriptions of social processes and obtaining individuals' own accounts, interpretations, and explanations for their behavior. However, because qualitative studies often focus on small, highly focused populations—such as homeless persons, cult members, Amish persons, and other statistically rare groups—the study findings are seldom generalizable to larger populations. As a result, qualitative research often has poor *external validity*.

Qualitative researchers typically rely on three methods for studying human lives: participant observation, direct observation, and in-depth interviews. *Participant observation* occurs when the researcher takes part in the activities of the group or community being studied. In doing so, the researcher often wins the trust of his or her research subjects and thus can elicit frank and honest insights from them. However, findings from participant observation studies have been critiqued on the grounds that they are not "objective." Further, such studies can raise ethical issues; social scientists often need to hide their true identity because research subjects may not always be forthright and honest with a scientist, for fear of reproach or in some cases (such as in studies of deviant subcultures) for fear that they could be subject to legal action.

The classic example of participant observation is Laud Humphreys's *Tea Room Trade* study (1970), which investigated the social behavior and relationships of gay men. At the time that Humphreys conducted his study, homosexuality was still a stigmatized identity and few people would come forth to talk openly about their sexuality. Many gay men were married and leading "straight" lives. Humphreys studied gay men by participating in the activities that happened at bathhouses, the public restrooms where gay men would meet for sex. Humphreys took on the role of "lookout" or guard, meaning that he would warn the others if he noticed police, children, or others were coming to use the restroom. Although this study is considered a classic study of gay men's behavior in the mid-20th century, it is also criticized because Humphreys did not confess that he was a researcher. Still, this approach enables life course researchers to study social contexts and behaviors that are stigmatized and "hidden" in modern society.

*Direct observation* is similar to participant observation, except the researcher does not join the activities or group under observation. The investigator also informs the research subjects that they are part of a study. In both participant and direct observation, the social scientists do more than simply observe; they take copious notes or recordings and try to detect patterns in the behavior they witness. One of the best examples of direct observation is the sociologist Annette Lareau's study *Unequal Childhoods* (2003). Lareau investigated parents' child-rearing practices in poor, working-class and middle-class families. She shadowed 12 families for about a month, engaging in "intensive 'naturalistic' observation" of parenting habits and family culture. She watched the parents and children interact after school, during family meals, and just going about their daily activities at home. Lareau found that parenting methods vary by social class more than by race. Middle-class parents, whether Black or White, engaged in a process of "concerted cultivation" designed to draw out their children's talents and skills. Working-class and poor families, by contrast, relied on "the accomplishment of natural growth." These parents believed their kids would turn out just fine, as long as basic comfort, food, and shelter were provided. Lareau's observations allowed her to uncover an important pathway through which social class shapes child outcomes: parental engagement.

*In-depth interview* is the process in which researchers ask probing questions of their subjects and either tape-record, videotape, or transcribe the subjects' words. The questions used are typically "open ended," meaning that research subjects can answer the questions any way they like. Researchers may start their investigation with a preset list of questions, but the interviews often take on a life of their own and have the flow of a natural conversation. Although surveys also ask questions of their respondents, survey questions tend to be "closed ended" and heavily scripted; respondents are asked to select the response option that best represents their views. The same set of survey questions is also used for all study participants, so a survey cannot capture the same idiosyncratic responses that an in-depth interview can.

Because of the open-ended nature of in-depth interviews, this approach often uncovers findings that could not have been detected with closed-ended surveys. Research subjects may hold beliefs or may engage in practices that the researchers had never before thought about and thus would never dream to have asked a question about. This is the case with Kathryn Edin and Maria Kefalas's 2005 study *Promises I Can Keep: Why Poor Women Put Motherhood Before Marriage.* Over a span of 5 years, Edin and Kefalas talked in-depth with 162 low-income single mothers in Philadelphia to learn how they think about marriage and family. In particular, they wanted to know why poor urban women continue to have babies out of wedlock, often knowing that having a child will hurt their own educational and work prospects—as well as impairing the child's chances for economic success.

Edin and Kefalas found that the young women do not get pregnant by accident but enter teen parenting knowingly. The authors observed that

> to most middle class observers ... a poor woman with children but no husband, diploma or job is either a victim of her circumstances or undeniable proof that American society is coming apart at the seams.... But in the social world inhabited by poor women, a baby born into such conditions represents an opportunity to prove one's worth. (p. 6)

While the poor women they studied perceived marriage as a "luxury"—"something they aspired to but feared they might never achieve"—having children is viewed as a necessity and "an absolutely essential part of a young woman's life" (p. 6). Such insights could not have been gleaned from a survey that simply asked women their age at first birth and whether the birth of their child was intended. Edin and Kefalas also characterized a subpopulation that may not have participated in sample surveys, as they often did not have home telephones, and might have distrusted survey researchers who asked curt questions about their life choices. Taken together, qualitative studies are particularly good at investigating the role that personal agency and preferences play in the life course, by obtaining firsthand observations and holding in-depth conversations.

**Quantitative Analysis.** The vast majority of life course researchers use quantitative research techniques, particularly the use of multivariate methods to analyze survey data. A small yet growing number of sociologists also are starting to use experimental designs.

***Experiments.*** Experimentation is a mode of investigation that typically is employed by psychologists. Historically, sociologists have not conducted experiments because most such studies take place in artificial laboratory settings and thus do not capture the important ways that macrosocial and historical context shape social lives. Sociologists, however, have recognized the many unique methodological strengths of experiments, including the ease with which causation can be ascertained.

The experiment is the most highly controlled of all research methodologies and thus has very high *internal validity*. Internal validity means that the study findings cannot plausibly be accounted for by some extraneous influence or by a variable that was not statistically controlled. By design, all potential extraneous influences are held constant in experiments. First, the researcher must first manipulate one or more of the independent variables hypothesized to have a causal impact on the dependent variable. The experimenter creates at least two levels of each independent variable—although more than two levels are possible. Next, the researcher must assign subjects randomly to the two groups or treatments. Random assignment is crucial because it is a way to eliminate extraneous influences.

The sociologist Devah Pager (2003) designed an innovative experiment to examine the long-term consequences of prison on the lives of felons. She conducted a field study, meaning that she used the procedure of random assignment, but she did so in a real-life setting. To evaluate the effect of a criminal record on one's job prospects, she hired actors and sent them on a job search. She sent pairs of young, well-groomed, well-spoken college men with identical resumes to apply for 350 advertised entry-level jobs in Milwaukee, Wisconsin. Two of the pairs were White men, and two were Black men. The only difference between the two men in each pair was that one said that he had served an 18-month prison sentence for cocaine possession. The independent variable Pager manipulated was whether one had a prison sentence; by ensuring that all applicants were identical in terms of their job qualifications, mode of dress, demeanor, age, and gender, she essentially "held constant" the possible factors that could pose a threat to alternative causal influences.

Pager's study found that a criminal mark had a detrimental effect on one's job prospects. More importantly, though, she documented that this effect was much more harmful to Black men than White men. For the Black testers, their callback rate from employers was 5% if they had a criminal record and 14% if they had a clean record. By contrast, for Whites the callback rate was 17% for those with the criminal record and 34% for those with a clean record. Pager's study is a powerful demonstration that a critical life transition—such as becoming a felon—affects the life course differently based on one's race. Despite the importance of Pager's work, however, relatively few topics that are central to life course research are suitable for experimental designs.

***Surveys.*** Surveys make up the foundation of life course research. Surveys are so important that the encyclopedia includes three separate entries describing the different types of surveys conducted and provides summaries of nearly 24 different surveys that provide the data for many highly influential life course studies. This section briefly recaps the basic characteristics of surveys, including their strengths and the variety of forms they take.

A survey is a procedure for collecting information by asking members of some population a set of standard questions and recording their responses. One type of survey, a *census*, is administered to all persons in a nation's population. For example, the U.S. Census is conducted every 10 years, and information about each and every American is recorded. Data from the census are considered the single best data source for describing the characteristics of the U.S. population. For instance, researchers use census data to document that the U.S. population nearly quadrupled between 1900 and 2000, climbing from 76.1 million to 281 million. Census data also reveal that the proportion of the U.S. population that is elderly (over age 65) jumped from 4.1% in 1990 to 12.4% in 2000 (U.S. Bureau of the Census, 2002).

The vast majority of surveys, however, are sample surveys, meaning that a subsample (or a percentage of the pool of eligible survey participants) participates. The highest quality surveys are *random-sample surveys*, meaning that every person in the sampling frame is equally likely to be selected for participation. Participants are drawn from a sampling frame, or the full range of persons who are potential subjects of research. Some surveys, including general-interest surveys conducted by the U.S. government, such as the Current Population Survey, are administered to a subsample of the total U.S. population. Other surveys, however, have a much more tightly defined sample frame. For instance, the Wisconsin Longitudinal Study (WLS) interviewed a randomly selected one-third sample of all persons who were high school seniors in the state of Wisconsin in 1957. While the WLS enables life course scholars to document the experiences of only a single birth cohort, other surveys are designed to characterize the experience of multiple birth cohorts, thus enabling researchers to examine the impact of social change on human lives. For example, the Health and Retirement Study (HRS) began in 1992 as a random-sample survey of preretirement age men and women born between 1931 and 1941, with new younger cohorts brought in at subsequent waves. The HRS data can be used to answer questions such as: Are there cohort differences in the age at which people retire or in the economic well-being of retirees?

Some surveys are conducted in a *face-to-face setting* or over the *telephone*, with hired interviewers asking subjects a standard set of questions. Surveys also can be administered via a *self-administered mail questionnaire*. Here, subjects are mailed a survey instrument to complete and return. Mail surveys have the disadvantage of low response rate (i.e., a low proportion of persons send back their completed survey), yet face-to-face interviews have the downside of high cost and the possibility that subjects may not be truthful in answering the interviewers' questions. Interviewers can help to ensure that high-quality data are collected, however, by explaining the question to interview subjects and prodding them to answer a question that they might want to skip.

Surveys typically consist of a series of *closed-ended questions*, meaning that study participants are forced to select their response from several preset categories. The content of most surveys is far ranging and diverse, often asking about social background, work and family experiences, physical and mental health, social relationships, political participation, and financial characteristics. Nearly each and every response can be quantified in some way; this process of transforming social and psychological concepts into quantifiable, easily observed measures is called *operationalization*. Operationalization enables researchers to conduct statistical analyses of survey data.

For instance, one's educational accomplishments typically are measured as "number of years of school completed," while one's level of mental health can be assessed and given a numerical score using a standard measure such as the Center for Epidemiologic Studies Depression (CES-D) scale (Radloff, 1977). Even seemingly qualitative experiences, such as being married or living in a dangerous neighborhood, can be quantified. Marital status is generally measured as a series of categories, and each category—married, single, or widowed—is assigned a numerical value. Likewise, contextual factors such as living in a dangerous neighborhood can be quantified by assessing the number of crimes that happen on one's city block or the proportion of families receiving federal aid who live in one's census tract. These measures, in turn, can be used by researchers seeking to document correlations and evaluate causal hypotheses, as discussed above.

Surveys are well suited for obtaining self-reported information on attitudes, values, and past behaviors. They also are the most effective method for documenting within-person change over time and historical change, because the same survey questions can be administered at multiple points in time, thus enabling comparisons. Surveys are not particularly good, however, at assessing behavior that happened in the distant past, because subjects may have difficulty in accurately recalling their past experiences. For life course researchers, this is particular problematic. Life course researchers have documented a pattern called *retrospective recall bias*; people will sometime reconstruct their past so that it is consistent with their current mood or feelings. For instance, a person who is now depressed may say that his or her childhood was very unhappy, even if he or she actually felt quite happy during that period.

Survey designs may be cross-sectional or longitudinal. A *cross-sectional survey* is conducted at one point in time; it captures a snapshot of a group of people at one historical moment. Some studies, however, are *repeated cross-sections*, meaning that a snapshot will be taken at multiple points in time, although different persons are interviewed at each time point. This approach allows researchers to document historical changes in values, attitudes, and behaviors. The General Social Survey is one of the nation's most widely used repeated cross-sectional surveys. A new sample of American adults is interviewed every two years. Thus, researchers can examine such questions as: Have attitudes toward abortion changed over the past three decades? Such data, however, do not allow researchers to explore whether and how an individual's own attitudes toward reproductive rights change as they age.

A *longitudinal study* involves reinterviewing the same people at multiple points in time. This enables researchers to examine within-person change and also adopt a whole-life approach to conducting research. Some of the most widely respected and influential studies of the life course draw on longitudinal data. John A. Clausen's *American Lives* study (1993) is based on data from the Berkeley and Oakland Growth Studies. In the late 1920s, a group of children were recruited into a study on child and adolescent development and were subsequently tracked over a 60-year period. The WLS, mentioned earlier, obtained data on a cohort of Wisconsin high school graduates when they were ages 18, 35, 53, and 64. Both of these rich data sources allow researchers to explore the long-term consequences of early choices and experiences.

## STRATEGIES FOR ANALYZING SURVEY DATA

Life course scholars often use sophisticated statistical methods to investigate causal relationships among the characteristics assessed on surveys. A complete understanding of these statistical techniques requires a strong background in algebra and, for some methods, calculus. For this reason, a comprehensive description of data analysis methods is beyond the scope of this entry. This brief "nonmathematical" introduction is intended to help readers identify: (a) how to choose a research method suitable to their research question and data availability; and (b) how to interpret coefficients and empirical results when reading quantitative studies in social science journals and books. Before reading this section, however, readers are advised to first review the encyclopedia entries on Variables and Correlation Versus Causation. Readers also may want to familiarize themselves with a statistical analysis software package such as SPSS, SAS, or Stata; these are among the most widely used (and user-friendly) software packages for conducting the types of analyses described below.

**Ordinary Least Squares Regression.** Ordinal least squares (OLS) regression is the most widely used statistical technique used to evaluate causal hypotheses about the life course. This method allows researchers to predict a *continuous* life course outcome, such as years of schooling, earnings, one's score on a self-esteem or depressive symptoms scale, or the number of functional limitations one has. In general, OLS regression is used to answer questions such as: How well can one predict the value of one variable, such as annual income ($Y$), by knowing the values of another variable, such as level of education ($X$)? The regression equation is written as: $Y = a + b_1X_1 + b_2X_{2\ldots} + e$ where $Y$ is the dependent variable, $X$ is the independent variable, $b$ is the slope or regression coefficient, and $a$ is the intercept (the value of $Y$ when all independent variables equal zero). The $e$ is the error term.

For example, life course researchers interested in income inequality may want to identify characteristics that affect one's yearly income. Here, education ($X_1$) is measured as a continuous variable (e.g., 0 to 24 years of schooling), gender ($X_2$) is a dichotomous (or two-category) variable where female = 1 and male = 0, and income ($Y$) is the continuous outcome variable: INCOME = $10{,}000 + 200X_1 + -1{,}000X_2$. This equation shows that for a man ($X_2 = 0$) with 0 years of education, one's annual income would be $10,000. With each additional year of schooling, his income would go up by $200 (because $b_1 = 200$) when sex is statistically controlled or "held constant." Being female, however, would be associated with a $1,000 decrease in income (because $b_2 = -1{,}000$), when education is held constant.

**Logistic Regression.** Logistic regression, also referred to as logit models, is a special form of regression that is used when a study's outcome measure is *categorical. Binary* logistic regression is used when an outcome measure or dependent variable is a dichotomous or "dummy" variable, scored as 0 or 1. *Multinomial* logistic regression is used when the dependent variable has three or more mutually exclusive categories. For instance, binary models are used to predict whether one is married versus single, whereas multinomial models are used to predict whether one is married, separated, divorced, widowed, or never married.

Binary logistic regression models usually are used for predicting whether or not an event has happened to an individual, such as death, graduation, marriage, or release from prison. This method also is used to document whether one holds a specific social role, such as part-time worker, full-time worker, or unemployed person. It also is used to identify the predictors of some outcome that is generally considered qualitatively good or bad, such as being obese versus normal weight, and having high blood pressure versus normal blood pressure. The predictor variables used in such analyses may be either categorical (e.g., high school graduate or higher = 1; high school dropout = 0), or continuous (e.g., education in years equals 0 through 24). The model is based on transforming data by taking their natural logarithms so as to reduce nonlinearity.

A mortality study can serve as an example of how logistic regression works. In studies of mortality (that is, whether one is dead or alive) in which age of death is not known, logistic regression models are frequently used. In such cases, one might have survey data on study participants at Year 1 (e.g., 1990) and then data from follow-up interviews at Year 10 (e.g., 2000). Perhaps the researcher knows that one of the original respondents from 1990 has died by the time of the 2000 interviews, yet the person's age of death is not known. In such a model, all the people who died between 1990 and 2000 would be coded as 1 (i.e., they experienced the "event" of death); all those who survive are coded as 0 (i.e., they did not experience the "event" of death). The analyst would then use the independent variables measured at Year 1 to assess the odds or likelihood that a respondent has died between 1990 and 2000. The interpretation of the independent variables depends on how they are presented in a given table.

Results for logistic regression are generally presented in one of two ways. One strategy is to present the beta values, or coefficients, before they are exponentiated. The other way shows the exponentiated beta values, or the odds ratio. For example, Table 1 includes data on the effects of different levels of educational attainment on the odds of dying, between interview at Time 1 (1990) and interview at Time 2 (2000). The independent variable of interest is educational attainment. The "reference group" or "omitted category" (that is, persons who provide a benchmark for evaluating relative differences) is persons who have 12 years of education. For the reference group, the relative odds of dying (or being in the "1" category of the dependent variable) always equals 1. The other variables are interpreted "relative to" the reference group. To interpret the parameter estimate for high school dropouts, one calculates exp $^{.1758}$ = 1.19. (This can be calculated on a calculator using the $e^x$ key.) What does this mean? Relative to persons with a high school education only, persons who were high school dropouts were 1.19 times as likely to die between 1990 and 2000. The table generally shows that increased education is associated with reduced odds of death.

A multinomial logistic regression is very similar to binary logistic regression. The main difference is that the dependent variable may include more than two categories. For instance, rather than predicting the odds of death in 2000, a researcher might predict the odds of death due to cancer, death due to heart disease, and death due to other causes. The reference group would be "alive." Coefficients are interpreted the same as in the binary logistic regression example. The one difference is that the output would show as many columns of results as there are nonzero categories of the dependent variable.

**Event History Analysis.** Event history analysis, also referred to as hazard models, survival analysis, or duration analysis, is a strategy ideally suited to addressing life course questions about timing. This approach is used to assess how long an individual exists in a given state before making a transition to another state. It is similar to logistic regression analysis in that it allows researchers to predict movement from one dichotomous state to another, such as the movement from dead to alive, single to married, or prisoner to parolee. Whereas logistic regression predicts *whether* one held a specific role or had made a particular transition, event history can be used to specify *how old* one was when they made such a transition, or *how much time* one spent in a particular role before moving into a new role, such as how long one was married prior to having a first birth. To

| Variable | Parameter estimate(B) | Odds (expB) |
|---|---|---|
| <12 yrs education | .1758 2 | 1.19 |
| 12 education (reference) | ***** | 1.00 |
| 13-15 yrs education | -.0307 | .969 |
| 16+ yrs education | -.0838 | .919 |

***Figure 1.*** CENGAGE LEARNING, GALE.

conduct these analyses, however, researchers must have data on the age at which a person makes a transition into the new state (for people who do make the transition—not all do). The specific equations used in event history analysis vary. A basic model is: $\log h(t) = a + b_1x_1 + b_2x_2$. *Here, b* is the slope or regression coefficient, while *a* is the intercept. The $a$, $b_1$, and $b_2$ are the constants to be estimated, while x is the observed value of some characteristic measured in the survey. In this equation $h(t)$ is the hazard rate. A hazard rate can be generally described as the probability that an event will occur at a particular time to a particular individual, given that the individual is "at risk" at that time. "At risk" means that one is a plausible candidate for the life transition of interest. For example, those women at risk of making the transition to motherhood are women who have not already given birth. Persons at risk of returning to prison are those who have already exited prison; those who are still in jail are not at risk of returning.

When interpreting coefficients from an event history analysis, scholars generally follow the rules that apply to logistic regression models. Table 2 shows results for a proportional hazard model (i.e., one variant of a hazard model). These data are used to examine prison recidivism, or whether a person returns to prison following his or her release. In this study, men were tracked for a year after leaving prison. The event of interest is "first arrest after release." Also of interest is the timing of the arrest (how many months was a man out of prison before his new arrest?). The coefficients indicate not only whether or not a transition was made but also the "speed" of the transition. When reading results for hazard models, one should know the time unit that is the basis of analysis (e.g., number of months before returning to prison, number of years after age 15 that a person marries). See, for example, the data in Table 2. Interpreting the coefficients in this table is much like interpreting unstandardized regression coefficients. The coefficient of -.069 for age at release means that each additional year of life reduces the log of the hazard by .069, controlling for other variables. One can also exponentiate the betas to make the findings more "intuitive." The coefficient for number of prior arrests is .095. Exponentiating this (as in logistic regression) gives the value of 1.10. This means that each additional prior arrest increases the hazard of recidivism by 10%.

Hazard models are preferable to logistic regression models for two reasons. First, hazard models allow researchers to incorporate timing data. Thus, analysts do not simply estimate the predictors of whether one died between 1990 and 2000; rather, they predict one's age at death, or age of transition. Additionally, this approach allows some predictor variables to change over time; that is, it allows use of *time-varying covariates.* When a researcher analyzes a longitudinal data set, they might have indicators of a person's health status, marital status, or employment status for every year. They can then set up their data file so that they have yearly specific indicators of health, for instance. Certainly, this is preferable to assuming that one's health status or marital status at Time 1 will persist for the entire course of the observation period.

| Independent Variable | b | t |
|---|---|---|
| Age at release | -.069 | 2.94** |
| Received financial assistance upon release | -.325 | -1.76 |
| Number of prior arrests | .095 | 3.21** |

*Figure 2.* CENGAGE LEARNING, GALE.

Hazard models can take on many mathematical forms; these forms represent notions about time. One characteristic along which models differ is *functional form,* or one's assumptions about the distribution of events over time. The most basic model is the proportional hazard model. This model does not impose a "functional form," meaning that the analyst does not impose on the data any assumptions about the odds of making a transition over time. There are specific models, such as the Gompertz, in which the researcher does make assumptions about the functional form. For instance, Gompertz models are based on the assumption that the odds of making a transition increase with duration (e.g., advanced age, number of months since exiting prison). Not surprisingly, this form is often used to study adult mortality. The odds of dying increase with advanced age. This form would not work, however, if a researcher was studying transitions from singlehood into marriage. Certainly, the odds of marrying do not increase steadily and monotonically over the life course.

Sometimes researchers want to explore the transition from one state to a variety of possible alternative and mutually exclusive states; such analyses would require the use of *multistate hazard models.* These models are similar to multinomial logistic regression models in that analysts are predicting movement into one of several competing states (e.g., dead due to cancer, dead due to heart disease, dead to other causes, or alive). In sum, hazard models are the best method for examining the factors that influence when individuals make important life transitions such as marriage, first birth, first full-time job, retirement, and ultimately, death.

**Other Advanced Statistical Methods.** Life course researchers may select from a variety of other complex statistical methods, based on their research question. Two additional approaches are elaborated elsewhere in the encyclopedia: Network analysis is described in a separate entry, and twin study designs are discussed in the Genetic Influences entries. This section briefly describes three methods that enable researchers to tackle issues at the core of life course studies: multilevel modeling, structural equation modeling, and latent growth curve analyses. Rather than describing how to interpret coefficients, as was done for the methods discussed above, a conceptual overview is provided along with examples of life course research using these analytic techniques.

*Multilevel modeling* is a statistical approach used by analysts who want to examine the ways that both individual-level and group-level characteristics affect one's life course outcomes. This approach is based on the assumption that individual lives are shaped by social contexts such as their neighborhoods, schools, and families. This method requires that researchers use data that characterize both the individual (e.g., a student in a particular school) and the group (e.g., characteristics of a school that a particular child attends). Thus, multilevel models can identify differences *within* and *between* diverse social contexts. For example, researchers may examine whether living in a neighborhood with a high poverty rate is associated with elevated levels of stress among individuals living there. Researchers recognize, however, that individuals do not randomly assign themselves to neighborhoods; persons who live in poor or crime-ridden neighborhoods may have other traits that are associated with elevated stress levels, and these traits matter above and beyond one's residential locale.

Several early-21st-century studies based on the National Longitudinal Study of Adolescent Health (Add Health) data have used multilevel modeling techniques such as hierarchical linear modeling in order to estimate the effects of both school- and individual-level characteristics on the life course trajectories of adolescents. For example, Igor Ryabov and Jennifer Van Hook (2007) used these data and techniques to examine whether the ethnic and social-class composition of one's high school affected Latino students' academic achievement, and whether these effects vary by the student's generational status. They found that the socioeconomic composition of the school but not the racial composition was an important predictor of Latino adolescents' scores on a standardized aptitude test. They also found that the effects of school composition on the teen's grade point average (GPA) varied by the person's generational status. School socioeconomic status (SES) had a positive effect and school minority composition a negative effect on GPA for foreign-born Latinos only. The authors reasoned that high levels of social capital in immigrant families help buffer children from the disadvantages associated with the schools they attend. In sum, multilevel models allow researchers to explore the ways in which social place and context shape the individual life course.

*Structural equation modeling* (SEM), also referred to as path analysis, is another strategy that enables researchers to explore questions about the multiple direct and indirect influences on the life course. The best way to develop a conceptual understanding of SEM is to think about how these models are similar to, yet expand upon, OLS regression models. SEM is generally used in one of the following three cases. First, a researcher may want to examine two-way causation, or a nonrecursive relationship. For example, rather than doing an OLS regression that predicts the effect of media violence on aggressive behavior, a researcher may also consider the possibility that aggressive behavior leads one to seek out violent media. Second, a researcher may have multiple measures of a construct and may be interested in the effect of the overall construct as well as the degree to which each of its distinct indicators influence the life course. For example, a researcher may believe that a factor called "social background" influences children's school performance, where social background is a construct made up of father's education, mother's education, household income, and number of siblings. Third, a researcher may be interested in both direct and indirect effects of an independent variable on some outcome variable. Many research articles using SEM display indirect and direct effects in a *path diagram*, or a visual image of the set of hypothesized relationships.

SEM techniques enabled the sociologists William H. Sewell and Robert M. Hauser (1975) to identify the ways that parents' social class affects their children's educational and occupational attainment. Using data from the Wisconsin Longitudinal Study, a study that has tracked all Wisconsin high school graduates from the class of 1957 for more than 50 years, the researchers wanted to determine why and how family background affects children's achievements. SEM allowed them to consider a detailed composite measure of parents' social class encompassing education, occupational status, earnings, and farm status. The researchers also found that parents' SES affected a son's educational and occupational outcomes *indirectly*. Boys from higher SES homes received more encouragement from their high school teachers, peers, and parents, and also received better grades. These positive high school experiences, in turn, led to more lofty educational and career aspirations. These high aspirations, in turn, were associated with achieving higher status jobs after completing school. By using elaborating SEM models, the researchers were able to identify the pathways through which social class is transmitted from parents to children.

*Latent growth curve* analyses enable researchers to track within-person change over time. In this modeling strategy, the data analyst must have observations from study participants for at least three points in time. The researcher can then not only document the factors that predict one's value on some variable at the first wave of data collection, but can also pinpoint the factors that are associated with trajectories of improvement and decline over time. This is a complex strategy, but it is becoming increasingly popular as more and more data sets obtain multiple observations of their study participants.

Some excellent examples of the use of growth curve models are studies by the research team of K. A. S. Wickrama, Frederick O. Lorenz, and Rand D. Conger. They studied a sample of 451 farm families in Iowa over a 10-year period, exploring the ways that family and economic factors affect health and well-being. They have found that declines in marital quality are associated with downward trajectories in physical health (Wickrama, Lorenz, Conger, & Elder, 1997); that changes in one's level of workplace control are associated with changes in men's physical and mental health during midlife (Wickrama, Surjadi, Lorenz, & Elder, 2008); and that parents' parenting style affected their teenage children's health trajectories, yet the effects operated indirectly, via the child's perception of parental support (Wickrama, Lorenz, & Conger, 1997). These studies demonstrate the importance of linked lives; generations of parents and children influence one another, while diverse life domains such as work, marriage, and health are intertwined. Latent growth curve models also allow life course researchers to move away from static one-time snapshots of health and well-being and instead document that health declines and improvements are shaped by changes in one's larger social and role networks.

## CONCLUSION

Life course research is guided by four key assumptions: that social lives are shaped by history, that the timing of key life events matters, that individuals are planful and guide their own life courses, and that life domains are interlinked. Researchers have access to a broad range of methods that allow them to describe the human condition, assess interrelationships among individual's characteristics, and evaluate claims about causation. Investigators may choose to conduct in-depth open-ended interviews to understand the ways in which individuals think about their lives and make choices. They may rely on large-scale surveys to document the ways in which social history, race, class, gender, and national origin shape the life course. Despite the diversity of research approaches taken, successful life course researchers typically follow one golden rule: They use the data and methods best suited to addressing their own unique research aims.

### BIBLIOGRAPHY

Allison, P. D. (1984). *Event history analysis: Regression for longitudinal event data.* Beverly Hills, CA: Sage Publications.

Allison, P. D. (1999). *Multiple regression: A primer.* Thousand Oaks, CA: Pine Forge Press.

Clausen, J. A. (1993). *American lives: Looking back at children of the Great Depression.* New York: Free Press.

Edin, K., & Kefalas, M. (2005). *Promises I can keep: Why poor women put motherhood before marriage.* Berkeley: University of California Press.

Hoyle, R. H. (Ed.). (1995). *Structural equation modeling: Concepts, issues, and applications.* Thousand Oaks, CA: Sage Publications.

Humphreys, L. (1970). *Tea room trade: Impersonal sex in public places.* Chicago: Aldine Publishing.

Lareau, A. (2003). *Unequal childhoods: Class, race, and family life.* Berkeley: University of California Press.

Miller, J. E. (2005). *The Chicago guide to writing about multivariate analysis.* Chicago: University of Chicago Press.

Mueller, R. O. (1996). *Basic principles of structural equation modeling: An introduction to LISREL and EQS.* New York: Springer.

Pager, D. (2003). The mark of a criminal record. *American Journal of Sociology, 108,* 937–975.

Radloff, L. S. (1977). The CES-D scale: A self-report depression scale for research in the general population. *Applied Psychological Measurement, 1,* 385–401.

Ryabov, I., & Van Hook, J. (2007). School segregation and academic achievement among Hispanic children. *Social Science Research, 36,* 767–788.

Sewell, W. H., & Hauser, R. M. (1975). *Education, occupation, and earnings: Achievement in the early career.* New York: Academic Press.

U.S. Bureau of the Census. (2002, July). *U.S. Summary: 2000* (Census 2000 Profile No. C2KPROF/00-US). Retrieved August 13, 2008, from http://www.census.gov/prod/2002pubs/c2kprof00-us.pdf

Vogt, W. P. (2005). *Dictionary of statistics and methodology: A nontechnical guide for the social sciences* (3rd ed.). Thousand Oaks, CA: Sage Publications.

Wickrama, K. A. S., Lorenz, F. O., & Conger, R. D. (1997). Parental support and adolescent physical health status: A latent growth-curve analysis. *Journal of Health and Social Behavior, 38,* 149–163.

Wickrama, K. A. S., Lorenz, F. O., Conger, R. D., & Elder, G. H., Jr. (1997). Marital quality and physical illness: A latent growth curve analysis. *Journal of Marriage and the Family, 59,* 143–155.

Wickrama, K. A. S., Surjadi, F. F., Lorenz, F. O., & Elder, G. H., Jr. (2008). The influence of work control trajectories on men's mental and physical health during the middle years: Mediational role of personal control. *The Journals of Gerontology, Series B: Psychological Sciences and Social Sciences, 63,* S135–S145.

Yamaguchi, K. (1991). *Event history analysis.* Newbury Park, CA: Sage Publications.

*Deborah Carr*

## II. CORRELATION VS. CAUSATION

Research projects concerning the life course and human development require particular attention to methodological concerns. One of the most important of these is the distinction between correlation and causation. *Correlation* means that two variables or observations are associated with one another, or that one observation/event occurs or changes when the other does (Babbie, 2001). For example, one might find that frequencies of outdoor weddings decrease at the same time that the number of people visiting the beach decreases. Therefore, frequency of outdoor weddings is correlated with beach attendance. Although these two observations vary together, or correlate, a decrease in outdoor wedding frequency does not cause beach attendance to decrease or vice versa. *Causation* means that one observation results from another, either directly or indirectly (Blalock, 1964). While frequency of outdoor weddings and beach attendance are correlated, their relationship is spurious (or noncausal). It is simply the case that both outdoor weddings and beach attendance decrease during the winter months. The discomfort of cold weather causes not only a decrease in beach attendance but also a decrease in outdoor weddings. A lower frequency of outdoor weddings and lower beach attendance are *correlated*, but both effects are primarily *caused* by cold weather.

The distinction between correlation and causation may seem fairly obvious in the example of outdoor weddings and beach attendance, but causation is often much more difficult to assess. When studying the events and trajectories of human lives, the distinction between correlation and causation is very important. For example, one may notice that an increase in the frequency of socializing with friends and family in a sample of individuals is correlated with better health in that sample (House, Umberson, & Landis, 1988). One's initial conclusion might be that those who have extensive social support networks are healthier. Thus, an active social support network causes, at least in part, better health. What if, however, those who are healthier are more likely to socialize to begin with? Or, perhaps increased social interaction causes better mental health, which, in turn, causes better physical health? Perhaps these causal pathways also vary by age, gender, race, or class.

## CONDITIONS FOR CAUSATION

There are three commonly accepted criteria for establishing causation in the social sciences (Babbie, 2001). First, the causal force must precede the result in time. So, in the above example of the causal relationship between social interaction and health, an individual must have social support prior to an improvement in physical health. Second, the two observations or events must be correlated. For social support to cause improved health, a researcher must observe an association between social support and health, or note that the two vary with one another. The third criterion for causation is that there are no other possible explanations for the correlated relationship (nonspuriousness). A researcher must demonstrate that all alternative explanations are irrelevant. The combination of correlation, temporal order, and nonspuriousness establishes grounds for causation.

## VARIABLES AND PATHWAYS TO CAUSATION

To help clarify the distinction between correlation and causation, it is crucial to have a basic understanding of the various types of "third variables" that are associated with causal pathways (McClendon, 1994). A simple causal pathway may predict that better access to health care (*independent variable*) causes better physical health (*dependent variable*). An individual's residential location may act as an *antecedent* variable, or a variable that precedes and affects the independent variable and thus the overall causal process. For example, an individual living in an urban area would be more likely to have better access to hospitals and better medical care. Therefore, residential location might be associated with an individual's access to medical facilities (via hospitals) and thus subsequently an individual's physical health (see Figure 1, A). In this case, it would be important to control for the effects of residential location when considering an individual's access to health care and physical health.

What if informal social support in the form of social interaction makes individuals feel happier and thus have better health? Happiness, or better mental health, would be an example of an *intervening* or *mediating* variable (see Figure 1, B). More informal social support (independent variable) leads to happiness (mediating variable), which in turn leads to improved physical health (dependent variable). Another "third variable" in the causal process is the *moderating* variable, or a variable that interacts with the independent variable to produce varying outcomes. For example, gender likely moderates the impact of social support on health (see Figure 1, C). Although social support (independent) still continues to have an impact on health (dependent variable), the exact nature of this effect differs for men and women (moderating variable). For example, women tend to socialize more with family and friends and have more diverse social networks than men do (Moore, 1990). Social interaction may have greater health benefits for women than for men. Culture/ethnicity, age, and a variety of other variables also moderate the impact of social support on health.

Third variables that are unrelated to the causal process one is studying yet are correlated with the independent and dependent variable are called *extraneous* variables. To follow from the previous example, one might study the relationship between social support and

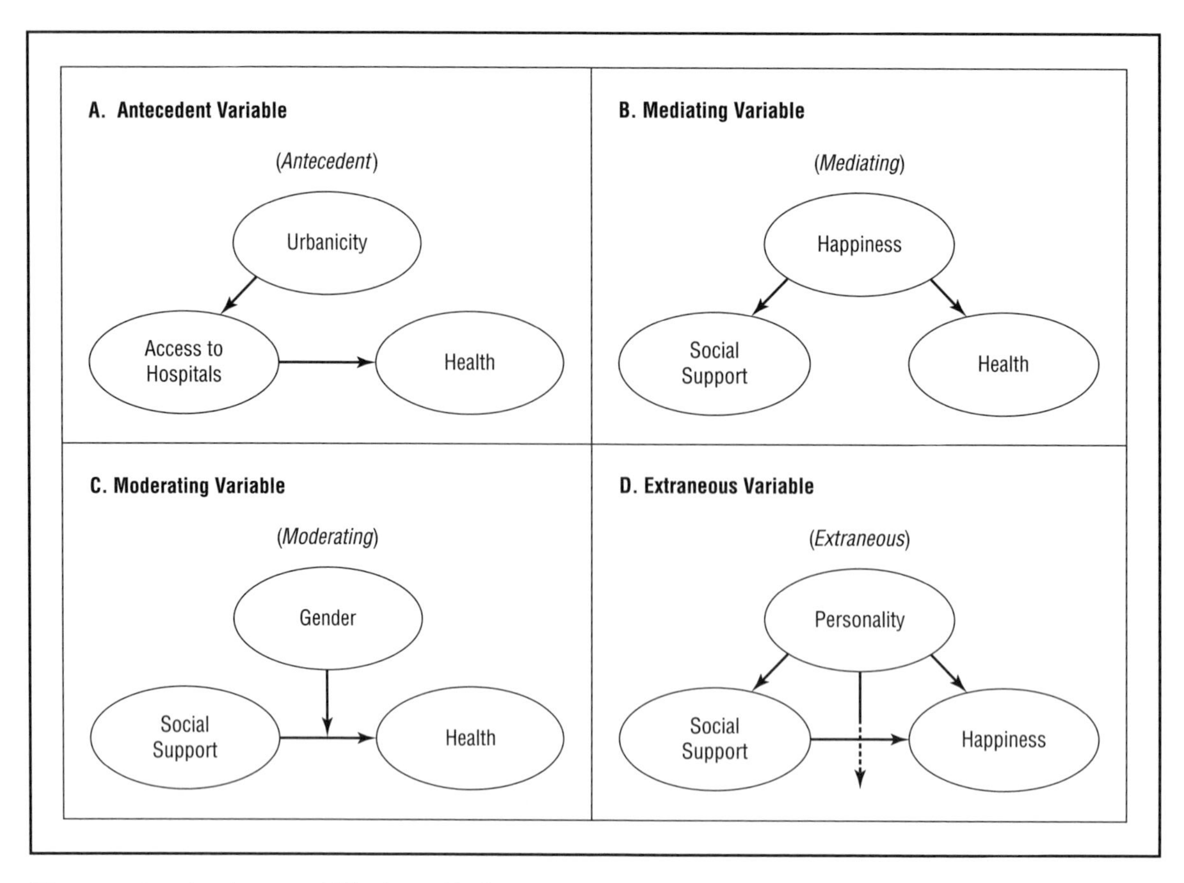


***Figure 1.*** *Causal pathways and "third variables."* CENGAGE LEARNING, GALE.

happiness. Although there may be a relationship between social support and happiness, there could be a third variable that is affecting both the independent and dependent variable in a way that decreases or eliminates the relationship between them. For example, personality may affect how an individual acts and also how that individual feels. A more outgoing personality could cause an individual to engage in more social interactions. An optimistic personality could cause a higher level of happiness. Taking into account an individual's personality may decrease the strength of the original relationship between social support and happiness or even eliminate it altogether. In this case, personality is an extraneous variable (see Figure 1, D). After one takes into account the individual's personality, the correlation between social support and happiness might decrease or disappear entirely. An extraneous variable is the most serious threat to causality and must be taken into account in developing a causal model.

### THEORIES AND HYPOTHESES: CORRELATIONAL VERSUS CAUSAL RELATIONSHIPS

To best anticipate possible causal pathways, researchers use theories and hypotheses. A *theory* is a general framework of propositions or a perspective about a social phenomenon that provides a basis for causal predictions. A *hypothesis* is a specific prediction about a social phenomenon often derived from a larger theoretical orientation/proposition and testable with research and analyses. Not all hypotheses are causal in nature. Because it can be very difficult to establish causality in the social sciences, many hypotheses predict only correlation. Researchers then offer a number of possible causal explanations when they interpret their data. The life course perspective, for example, does not necessarily generate causal hypotheses and thus is often classified by scholars as an orientation or framework, rather than a concrete theory (Heinz & Marshall, 2003). Within a life course framework, however, scholars propose a number of specific theoretical causal pathways to predict both correlation and causation such as childhood development theory, activity theory, theory of reciprocity, and age stratification theory (see Elder, 1998).

Drawing from societal norms regarding women and minorities as caregivers, a researcher might hypothesize a correlation between gender (women), race/ethnicity (minorities), and care for aging parents that contributes to the accumulation of disadvantage over the life course for certain groups (Dannefer, 2003). This hypothesis is a simple correlation prediction drawn from a feminist perspective and knowledge about societal expectations. By using a specific theory, however, a researcher is better able to construct a causal hypothesis. Drawing from the theory of reciprocity (the idea that individuals have an inclination and desire to maintain reciprocal relationships with friends and family in terms of giving and receiving support and assistance throughout their lives), a researcher could hypothesize that an adult child will feel increased obligation and desire to provide care for an elderly parent if he or she received a great amount of support (financial, emotional, etc.) from that parent while growing up (Hareven, 1994). In this case, a researcher would predict not only that childhood and adolescent family experiences will be correlated with adults' decisions to care for aging parents but also that those experiences earlier in the life course have *causal* influence on adult behavior. Researchers should use theory to clarify whether their hypotheses predict correlation or causation and also to interpret their results in terms of causal (or noncausal) pathways.

## CORRELATION AND CAUSATION: METHODOLOGICAL DISTINCTIONS

Once researchers hypothesize causal pathways, they must collect data in specific ways to test their predictions. Social science researchers use three main types of methodology to collect data: ethnography, surveys, and experiments. Each of these three methodological approaches gathers data in a specific manner to help increase knowledge of the causal process. *Ethnography* is a form of social research that focuses on rich, detailed descriptions of social phenomena (Babbie, 2001). Typically, the primary goal of ethnographies is not to provide an empirical test of a causal hypothesis but rather to explore the intricate ways in which a variety of social and situational factors contribute to an individual's experience or concept of that experience. An ethnographer determines causality by first evaluating the credibility or "believability" of an explanation and then eliminating alternative explanations (Babbie, 2001). For example, an ethnographic account may investigate the ways in which older individuals formulate their expectations about aging as well as their identities in later life (Furstenberg, 2002). By understanding the process of idea formation, ethnographers gain insight into the many complex variables that contribute to a particular outcome.

*Surveys* collect less in-depth detail than ethnographies but typically yield a wider variety of information. A broader information base allows survey researchers to investigate a wider array of theorized outcomes. Surveys use telephone, mail, Internet, and/or face-to-face interviews to reach a larger number of people. Two main types of surveys, cross-sectional and longitudinal, provide varying amounts of data for life course research and causality. *Cross-sectional surveys* collect data at only one point in time, so they are not suitable for establishing a clear case for causation. Using cross-sectional survey results to look at causal relationships is like looking at a still photograph of a race car to determine the speed of the car (Babbie, 2001, p. 101). Cross-sectional methods are not able to disentangle the complicated effects of one's age, one's historical period, and/or one's cohort on an outcome variable (Alwin, 2002; Glenn, 1976). Thus, while one can examine information about 12th graders in the year 2008, one cannot compare them to other generations of 12th graders, to other age groups, or to themselves at different ages across the life course using cross-sectional surveys. *Longitudinal surveys*, however, yield data that are better suited for establishing causation because they collect data over many points in time. By examining change over time, researchers are able to determine that one event preceded another temporally and can also rule out spurious relationships (Babbie, 2001). Longitudinal surveys also allow researchers to disentangle the effects of age, period, and cohort in life course research (Glenn, 1976).

*Experiments* provide one of the best methods for determining a causal relationship. Using a controlled or natural environment, an experiment applies a stimulus (or observes individuals in a situation) and then directly observes the outcome. Researchers can place stricter controls on an experiment in order to identify cause and effect more specifically and accurately (Babbie, 2001). While they are excellent for establishing causation, controlled experiments are often less realistic and less likely to be indicative of actual life course experiences. An experiment about the mental stress of newly married couples, for example, cannot take into account every aspect of the couples' history or the myriad of other stressful events that may be going on in their life outside of the breadth of the study. Overall, however, whether in a controlled or natural environment, experiments are a strong method for establishing causation. Experiments and longitudinal surveys are two of the best ways to test causation, while ethnographies and cross-sectional surveys provide important contextual detail.

## CONCLUSION

Studies of the life course and human development involve extensive webs of interconnections among individuals and within the social world. The process of disentangling causal pathways from mere correlations can seem like a daunting task. Using tools of social research, however, such as characteristics of causation, theory and hypotheses, and careful methodology, researchers can begin to investigate the social world through a more specific lens. Although a great deal of social research builds upon correlations between variables, life course and human development research provides a unique stage for investigating intricate causal processes. By focusing explicitly on the differences between correlation and causation, researchers will be better able to specify and interpret their models and thus gain a greater understanding of the human social world.

**BIBLIOGRAPHY**

Alwin, D. F. (2002). Age-period-cohort model. In D. J. Ekerdt (Ed.), *Encyclopedia of aging* (Vol. 1, pp. 43–45). New York: Macmillan Reference USA.

Babbie, E. (2001). *The practice of social research* (9th ed.). Belmont, CA: Wadsworth Thomson Learning.

Blalock, H. M., Jr. (1964). *Causal inferences in nonexperimental research.* Chapel Hill: University of North Carolina Press.

Dannefer, D. (2003). Cumulative advantage/disadvantage and the life course: Cross-fertilizing age and social science theory. *The Journals of Gerontology, Series B: Psychological Sciences and Social Sciences, 58,* S327–S337.

Elder, G. H., Jr. (1998). The life course as developmental theory. *Child Development, 69,* 1–12.

Furstenberg, A.-L. (2002). Trajectories of aging: Imagined pathways in later life. *The International Journal of Aging and Human Development, 55,* 1–24.

Glenn, N. D. (1976). Cohort analysts' futile quest: Statistical attempts to separate age, period, and cohort effects. *American Sociological Review, 41,* 900–904.

Hareven, T. K. (1994). Aging and generational relations: A historical and life course approach. *Annual Review of Sociology, 20,* 437–461.

Heinz, W. R., & Marshall, V. W. (Eds.). (2003). *Social dynamics of the life course: Transitions, institutions, and interrelations.* New York: Aldine de Gruyter.

House, J. S., Umberson, D., & Landis, K. R. (1988). Structures and processes of social support. *Annual Review of Sociology, 14,* 293–318.

McClendon, M. J. (1994). *Multiple regression and causal analysis.* Prospect Heights, IL: Waveland Press.

Moore, G. (1990). Structural determinants of men's and women's personal networks. *American Sociological Review, 55,* 726–735.

Morton, L. W. (2003). Rural health policy. In D. L. Brown & L. E. Swanson (Eds.), *Challenges for rural America in the twenty-first century* (pp. 330–344). University Park: Pennsylvania State University Press.

*Christine A. Mair*
*Feinian Chen*

## III. VARIABLES

The term *variables* broadly refers to measurable characteristics that can vary across time, individuals, groups, and institutions. Babbie (2001) defines a variable as a grouping of attributes or a set of mutually exclusive attributes. In conducting research, we attempt to determine the distribution of attributes across a population. For example, a society is considered *old* if between 8–10% of its population is 65 years or older. The United States consists of 12.6% elderly people in 2000, and thus, is defined as an old society (Gavrilov & Heuveline, 2002). *Operationalization* links variables with concepts and is the process by which researchers define and quantify the variability of a characteristic (or concept) to study social behaviors systematically. This encyclopedia entry briefly outlines the definition of variables, their common usage, and their importance for studying life course processes.

### LEVEL OF MEASUREMENT

*Good* measurement of a variable is characterized by the following: (a) inclusiveness or exhaustiveness, that is, all possible responses or states must be represented by a category; (b) mutual exclusiveness, that is, no response or state should be able to be placed in more than one category; and (c) precision, that is, more, rather than fewer categories should be defined when feasible. For example, for the variable *gender,* all individuals can be categorized into males and females (i.e., inclusiveness). The categories are also mutually exclusive because a person only can be placed into one category. Finally, taken together, the classification of males and females precisely defines gender.

Variables are categorized into four distinct types of measurement that include nominal, categorical, interval, and ratio variables and provide researchers with different levels of information (Stevens, 1946). *Nominal variables* are basic representations of data that denote specific characteristics of observations without quantifying or ranking the amount of difference between the categories. Nominal variables may include gender (male and female), race (White, Black, other), and marital status (single, married, divorced, widowed). *Ordinal variables* are a second class of variables that rank and order observational units. For example, a person's level of life satisfaction can be ranked according to her or his subjective assessments of being very satisfied, satisfied, unsatisfied, or very unsatisfied. Although more information is provided by ordinal variables compared with results using nominal variables, the degree of difference between the ordered levels cannot be determined. Nominal and ordinal variables are both considered to be categorical variables and are essential in studying discrete changes over an individual's life course.

A third type of measurement is termed *interval level.* A variable measured at the interval level provides information on the distance between the rankings of distinct categories. Interval variables are valuable because they allow researchers to quantify changes in the variable at different levels (values) of the variable accurately. For instance, in terms of income, the difference between ten and twenty thousand dollars is considered the same as the difference between $20,000 and $30,000 (i.e., $10,000).

Finally, ratio variables are similar to interval variables except that the former has a meaningful zero point (e.g., weight). Interval and ratio variables are considered continuous variables and capture important changes in the levels of individual growth and human development across age.

## RELATIONSHIPS BETWEEN VARIABLES

In addition to categorizing variables according to the level of measurement, variables also can be distinguishable based on how they relate to one another. In particular, an important goal of conducting research is to establish causal relationships between variables and allow researchers to draw inferences based on data. The key variable to be explained in an empirical study is called the dependent variable—sometimes referred to as an outcome—whereas independent variables are those thought to best explain variations in the dependent variable. In simple terms, independent and dependent variables operationalize what scientists refer to as cause and effect, respectively. As a substantive example, life course researchers have long been interested in understanding how the age of first marriage (independent variable) affects marital stability (dependent variable). Causal order is clear in this case because marital stability does not affect age at first marriage, but such relationships are not always as straightforward in the social science research. However, life course studies have played a critical role in conceptualizing and establishing the casual link between variables that can develop over extended periods of time.

Life course studies have highlighted the importance of mediating (intervening) and moderating variables—those that influence the association between an independent and dependent variables—which provide greater understanding of how and why a social relationship may exist. *Mediating variables* explain how and/or why these relationships occur whereas *moderating variables* affect the strength and/or direction of these relationships. For example, researchers want to learn the relationship between women's employment status and children's intellectual development. Socioeconomic status (SES) can be a mediating factor because SES explains how women's employment can affect children's intellectual development. After controlling for SES, the effect of women's employment on children's intellectual outcome may be reduced. Age can be a moderating factor because the effects of women's employment status on children's intellectual outcomes can be different for younger and older women. For a greater perspective of the life course and human development, the impact and interpretation of individual life experiences change across time, location, and other macrocontexts. Therefore, incorporating mediating and moderating variables helps scholars to understand fully the complex associations between dependent and independent variables.

All types of variables can be collected from both cross-sectional and longitudinal data. Although cross-sectional data are widely available and provide useful measurements of observational units, they are limited to collecting information from subjects at only a single time point and thus researchers cannot ascertain causal direction. In addition, variables from cross-sectional data are less suitable for life course research because they do not capture change in observations from multiple time points. In contrast, life course scholars often rely on longitudinal data to study stability and change among variables related to long-term processes of human development. We will provide examples and demonstrate how different types of variables are used in life course research.

## DYNAMIC VARIABLES IN LIFE COURSE RESEARCH

The theoretical and conceptual progress in life course research has benefited greatly from advancement in how variables are operationalized in research. Variables in a life course perspective can be categorized into the following interrelated groups: (a) as discrete events; (b) as continuous processes; and (c) in a social context. Broadly, life course research recognizes the importance of the timing, sequence, and durations of an individual's life transitions and social roles in the domains of education, family, work, and residence (Elder, 1992). The following section outlines how life course variables are conceptualized and measured to capture the events and experiences of human development.

**Life Course as Discrete Events** Studies of human growth and development demonstrate how the life course is marked by discrete events that shape individuals' social roles, behaviors, and life experiences. As people age, they enter and exit various life stages and roles—called *transitions*— that both define an individual's unique character and represents a shared life cycle that unfolds from childhood to adulthood. Although many life events are common and normative experiences, life transitions can become defining variables in an individual's life course. Transitions such as becoming employed, married, having children, retiring, and becoming widowed are just some examples of categorical variables that have generated enormous amounts of new research and provided a greater understanding of discrete life-changes.

The strength of the life course approach for studying role and status transitions is demonstrated in the literature on becoming a caregiver. Most research concurs that caregiving during adulthood is an important life course transition that involves significant change in family roles, obligations, and time allocation. By using information from longitudinal data, life course scholars show that transitioning into a caregiving role, transitioning out, or remaining a caregiver across survey intervals are distinct variables that may have broad implications for ones' well-being (e.g., Marks, Lambert, & Choi, 2002). For instance, knowing whether an individual recently became a caregiver to his or her spouse or ended this care after the institutionalization or death of a parent offers valuable information on the effects of a discrete role transition beyond the knowledge of an individual's current status.

Likewise, consider the ways marital status is often measured in the literature. Conventional studies typically ascertain marital status by asking survey respondents whether they are currently single, married, divorced, or widowed. In comparison, life course researchers focus on marital status at more than one time point to develop categorical variables that incorporate the continuity and change in status (i.e., transitions) over time. In doing so, scholars can disaggregate multiple trajectories—in this case marital transitions—to identify persons who become married, divorced, widowed, or remarried (Williams & Umberson, 2004). From an empirical standpoint, however, disaggregating trajectories (regardless of the transitions) often require extensive data that are collected from multiple surveys over an extended period, which is usually expensive and time consuming. Life history calendars are also useful for collecting information on life transitions.

**Life Course as Continuous Processes** Measuring life course experiences as discrete events is informative but not fully representative of human development. Therefore, one must also consider variables that measure life course concepts as continuous processes of stability and change. As such, continuous variables are typically used to maximize the level or quantity of change that characterize a person's life beyond his or her past, present, or future status. Just as transitions to parenthood or retirement are critical turning points marked by role adjustments, the timing, duration, and sequence of such events can be crucial in defining the success or failure of an individual's path in life. Accordingly, measuring the accumulation of the age, length, and ordering of role occupancies has proven to be fertile territory for studies implementing life course variables for advancing our understanding of immediate and long-term causal relationships.

To revisit the example of marital status, recent life course research shows that the timing and duration of marital status(es) can have equal or greater explanatory power than simply the transition(s) from one marital status to another. In an innovative study focusing on the culmination of marital experiences, researchers demonstrated that the theoretical concept of a marital trajectory could be bridged with its measurement (Dupre & Meadows, 2007). Using longitudinal data and variables, those authors showed that the age of marriage (timing) and lengths of marriage and divorce (durations) in marital status(es) exert varying degrees of support or harm to one's health. For example, women who marry early or divorce are more likely to experience chronic disease, yet prolonged periods of divorce for women become less consequential to their health. For men, the timing of marriage is much less significant compared with the protective effects of an extended marriage (duration).

Variables quantifying the life course as a continuous process also are reflected in the culmination of an individual's current life status. Again, health is an accurate example of such an accumulation of life events and experiences. Despite the somewhat widespread emphasis on the biological determinants predicting health and longevity, social scientists highlight strong evidence that links the interaction between an individual's genetic makeup and the person's social environment. For example, many studies show that early experiences, including family origin, education, employment, and lifestyle, are significantly associated with health outcomes at old ages. Cumulative disadvantage theory shows that individual differences arising from economic standing, exposure to health risks, and other factors that accumulate from early ages increase over the life course to produce widening inequalities (Dannefer, 2003).

In conclusion, the innovation and use of life course variables in the literature continues to shed new light on how individuals age in a social environment. Both categorical and continuous variables will remain the foundation for constructing individual and contextual measures of complex relationships derived from ever-evolving life course concepts. However, the development of dynamic variables also requires advanced methods to analyze life course processes.

## BIBLIOGRAPHY

Babbie, E. (2001). *The practice of social research* (9th ed.). Belmont, CA: Wadsworth.

Dannefer, D. (2003). Cumulative advantage/disadvantage and the life course: Cross-fertilizing age and social science theory. *Journals of Gerontology, Series B: Psychological Sciences and Social Sciences, 58B,* S327–S337.

Dupre, M. E., & Meadows, S. O. (2007). Disaggregating the effects of marital trajectories on health. *Journal of Family Issues, 28,* 623–652.

Elder, G. H., Jr. (1992). The life course. In E. Borgotta & M. Borgatta (Eds.), *The life course* (pp. 1120–1130). New York: MacMillan.

Gavrilov, L. A., & Heuveline, P. (2002). Aging of population. In P. Demeny & G. McNicoll (Eds.), *The encyclopedia of population* (pp. 32–37). New York: Macmillan Reference USA.

Marks, N. F., Lambert, J. D., & Choi, H. (2002). Transitions to caregiving, gender, and psychological well-being: Prospective evidence from a U.S. national study. *Journal of Marriage and Family, 64,* 657–667.

Stevens, S. S. (1946). On the theory of scales of measurement. *Science, 103,* 677–680.

Williams, K., & Umberson, D. (2004). Marital status, marital transitions, and health: Gendered life course perspective. *Journal of Health and Social Behavior, 45,* 81–98.

*Guangya Liu*
*Feinian Chen*

# *Annotated Bibliography*

*Compiled by Deborah Carr*

This annotated bibliography focuses on scholarly studies that have had a powerful influence on the development of life course theory, or on important empirical studies of life course and human development. This small selection is not exhaustive, yet these books and one documentary film offer scholars a glimpse into the foundations of and recent applications of the life course paradigm.

## VOLUME 1, CHILDHOOD AND ADOLESCENCE

Aries, P. (1962). *Centuries of childhood: A social history of family life.* New York: Vintage Books.

A path breaking study of elite families in France from the 16th to 19th centuries. This study generated the theory of "parental investment." Aries argued that both the financial and emotional costs of childrearing rose during this time period. Greater emotional involvement led to parent's heightened investments in infant survival. As a result, infant mortality rates declined, child survival rates rose, and privileged families were forced to adopt fertility control in order to avoid the production of too many "costly" children. These ideas have important implications for understanding social class differences in parenting style, fertility, and family relations.

Bronfenbrenner, U. (1979). *Ecology of human development: Experiments by design and nature.* Cambridge, MA: Harvard University.

In this classic treatise on human development, Erikson delineated four types of nested systems that shape human lives:*microsystem* (such as the family or classroom); *mesosytem* (two microsystems in interaction, such as work-family conflict); *exosystem* (external environments which indirectly influence development, such as the influence of parent's workplace on child well-being); and *macrosystem* (the larger socio-cultural context). Bronfenbrenner's "bioecological" approach to human development broke down barriers among the social sciences, and built bridges between the disciplines.

Clausen, J. (1993). *American lives: Looking back at the children of the Great Depression.* New York: Free Press.

This study explores the early life factors that set the stage for happy, successful adult lives. Clausen traces the life histories of participants in the Berkeley Longitudinal Studies over a 60-year span,from childhood into old age.Drawing on survey data and in-depth interviews, he argues that adolescents who exhibit "planful competence" go on to experience the most successful work and family lives. Planful competence comprises self-confidence, dependability, and intellectual investment. The study reveals the important ways that both agency and structure shape the adult life course.

Coleman, J. S. (1961). *Adolescent society: The social life of teenagers and its impact on education.* New York: Free Press.

Writing about high schools in the latter half of the 1950s, Coleman showed how the organization of school life reinforces teenage "anti-learning" norms. Ten high schools in northern Illinois were selected from communities which represented a range of sizes and social class backgrounds. This classic study was among the first to show that children and adolescents maintain social worlds that are distinct from their parents'—with their own distinctive norms, values, and practices.

Erickson, E. H. (1950). *Childhood and society.* New York: W. W. Norton.

In this highly influential work, Erikson articulates his theory of psychosocial development and proposes that well-adjusted adults must pass through eight developmental stages from infancy to late adulthood. In each stage the person confronts, and, ideally, masters new challenges. Each stage builds on the successful completion of prior stages. Each challenge that is not successfully resolved is expected to reappear as a problem in the future.Erikson offered an influential theory as to why individuals who had been thwarted in the healthy resolution of early phases (such as establishing healthy levels of trust and autonomy in toddlerhood) had such difficulty with the crises that came in adulthood.

Furstenberg, F. F., Brooks-Gunn, J., & Morgan, S. P. (1987). *Adolescent mothers in later life.* New York: Cambridge University Press.

This landmark study traces the life histories of approximately 300 teenage mothers and their children over a 17-year period. Drawing on interview data and case studies, the authors provide a vivid account of the impact of early childbearing on young mothers and their children. The data reveal that the detrimental effects of early childbearing largely reflect the poor resources the women had prior to giving birth.However, the children of single mothers often revealed very bleak prospects, due largely to the single mothers' material disadvantage in adulthood. The study also highlights the remarkable heterogeneity of both mothers' and children's life course, with many showing unexpected resilience.

MacLeod, J. (1995). *Ain't no makin' it: Aspirations and attainment in a low-income neighborhood* (Expanded Edition). New York: Westview.

In this modern classic, MacLeod chronicles the experiences of two groups of teenage boys in a low-income housing project: the Hallway Hangers, a group of mainly White boys, and the Brothers, a group of mostly Black boys. Through observations and in-depth interviews, MacLeod finds that the Brothers had higher educational and occupational aspirations than did the Hangers. His sociological explanation is that the black teens can attribute obstacles to racism, which inspires them to work harder, while the white teens viewed their futures as bleak and immutable. This study shows how race, class, gender, and sociohistorical context shape one's real and perceived opportunities.

## VOLUME 2, ADULTHOOD

Apted, M. (1997). *The up series.* London: First Run Features.

This film documentary series follows the lives of 12 men and women in the United Kingdom who were first interviewed when they were age 7, in the 1964 film *7 Up*. Apted re-interviews the young people every seven years, and presents their experiences in the follow-up films *14 Up*, *21 Up*, *28 Up*, *35 Up*, *42 Up*, and most recently *49 Up*. The young people came from diverse social class backgrounds, and grew up under a period of rapid social and economic change. The film series is a fascinating glimpse into the ways that race, gender, social class, opportunities, constraints, and personality shape—but do not determine—one's life course. Viewers will be surprised to witness the ups and downs in the young people's lives.

Easterlin, R. (1987). *Birth and fortune: The impact of numbers on personal welfare.* Chicago: University of Chicago.

This controversial demographic study proposes an innovative explanation for the low birth rates during the Depression era, high birth rates during the Baby Boom years of the 1950s, and low birth rates during the Baby Bust years of the 1970s. Easterlin argues that cohort size, or the number of persons born in one's birth year, affect life choices—particularly childbearing—because large cohorts experience difficult competition in their work and schooling experiences. Cohort size also affects one's relative income, or the standard of living that one enjoys in adulthood, relative to the standards they enjoyed in childhood.This study shaped the way that social scientists understand generational differences in adult lives.

Elder, G. H. (1999). *Children of the Great Depression* (25th anniversary). Boulder, CO: Westview Press.

Originally published in 1974, this classic study of the life course presented the first longitudinal study of a Depression cohort. The 25th anniversary edition of the much acclaimed work includes a new chapter which documents how World War II and the Korean War changed the lives of California youth who were born in 1920–1921 and members of a younger birth cohort (1928–1929). The book also reviews the project's contributions to theory and method in the study of lives. The analyses are based on data from the Oakland Growth and Berkeley Guidance Studies of the Institute for Human Development at the University of California.

Hareven, T. (1982). *Family time and industrial time.* Cambridge: Cambridge University Press.

The myth that industrialization broke down traditional family ties is a commonly-held misperception among Americans. Hareven, a social historian, dispels this myth and illustrates how the family survived and became an active force in the modern factory. This book documents how families adapted to changes in work and industry. Hareven reconstructs family and work patterns among immigrants as well as native textile laborers over two generations during a crucial period in the transformation of American industry from the late 19th century. This study reveals how macrosocial changes and individual-level experiences are closely intertwined.

Laub, J. H., & Sampson, R. J. (2006). *Shared beginnings, divergent lives: Delinquent boys to age 70.* Cambridge, MA: Harvard University Press.

This fascinating study reveals that a criminal past does not necessarily mean a criminal future. The authors analyze newly collected data on crime and social development up to age 70 for 500 men who were in reform school during the 1940s. Born in Boston in the late 1920s and early 1930s, these men were the subjects of the classic study *Unraveling Juvenile Delinquency* by Sheldon and Eleanor Glueck (1950). *Shared Beginnings* represents the longest longitudinal study of age, crime, and the life course to date. By blending life-history narratives and survey data, the authors offer new insights into life course trajectories of crime, and identify those factors that either reinforce or derail criminal careers.

McAdam, D. (1988). *Freedom summer.* New York: Oxford University Press.

This study of youth activism in the 1960s exemplifies the core themes of the "sociological imagination." In 1964, more than 1000 volunteers—mostly White, privileged, Northern college students—went to Mississippi to launch voter-registration drives. Within 10 days, three participants were murdered by local segregationists, and dozens more endured beatings and arrests. Drawing on questionnaires and interviews with hundreds of the volunteers, McAdam shows how both social background factors and historical context shaped student activism. Many volunteers continued to participate in the women's, anti-nuclear, environmental and other social movements through adulthood, revealing the far-reaching impact of early adult political socialization.

Mills, C. W. (2000). (orig. 1959). *The sociological imagination.* New York: Oxford University Press.

Considered one of the most influential books in sociology, this book sets forth Mills' thesis that human lives reflect the intersection of "biography" and "history." The "sociological imagination" is a way of observing human behavior that emphasizes the linkages between widespread "social" issues" and more personal "private issues." This seminal work provides the foundation for the life course paradigm, especially the notion that human lives are shaped by sociohistorical context.

Putnam, R. D. (2000). *Bowling alone: The collapse and revival of American community.* New York: Simon and Schuster.

This modern classic describes declines in "social capital" in the United States since 1950, and its implications for every-day-life. Citing data such as declining enrollments in community activities (like bowling leagues), civic organizations, and even voter turnout, Putnam argues that Americans' declining trust in social institutions, the rise of women's employment, and the pervasiveness of the Internet,have led to a fraying of social integration. Although critics have argued that social integration and engagement is as high as ever in the late 20th and early 21st century, Putnam clearly shows the importance of social integration and support for the well-being of Americans.

## VOLUME 3, LATER LIFE

Cowgill, D. O., & Holmes, L. D. (1972). *Aging and modernization.* New York: Appleton-Century-Crofts.

In this highly influential work, the authors argue that modernization leads to declines in status of the elderly. They cite historical evidence showing that in early societies, elderly persons were held in high esteem, yet in modern societies older persons are afforded much lower status. With technological advances, new skills are cherished, and the contributions of the elderly are devalued. This book has generated much research, and its key arguments continue to be debated today, when internet use and computer literacy are parts of daily life.

Cumming, E., & Henry, W. (1961). *Growing old: The process of disengagement.* NY: Basic Books.

This book articulated one of the most widely debated theories of aging: disengagement theory. This thesis, which draws on functionalist perspectives in sociology, holds that "normal" aging involves a gradual and inevitable "disengagement" from one's social roles. Older adults in poor health, the authors argue, should gradually pull away from their work and family roles and relationships; this disengagement will allow them to prepare for their own deaths. This disengagement also is beneficial to society, as it creates work opportunities for younger cohorts, and allows others to prepare for the deaths of loved ones. These ideas are widely refuted, given sweeping evidence that active engagement promotes health among the elderly. However, it provides an interesting perspective for understanding the way views of aging have shifted in recent decades.

Hochschild, A. (1978). *The unexpected community: Portrait of an old age subculture.* Berkeley, CA: University of California Press.

This qualitative study provides a nuanced and in-depth analysis of a retirement community in San Francisco, where the older adults live without loneliness or isolation. Hochschild identifies the distinctive strengths of this community of older adults, and suggests ways that this community provides a model for other older people. This book shows how older adults form their own subcultures and reveals that old age need not be a time of sadness, incapacitation and social isolation.

Lopata, H. Z. (1973). *Widowhood in an American city.* Cambridge, MA: Schenkman.

Considered one of the earliest and most comprehensive studies of late-life widowhood. Lopata conducted surveys and in-depth interviews with widowed women in Chicago, and documented several important findings that guide bereavement research today. She found that severe grief is not universal, nor is it experienced equally by all women—gender, social class, work and family roles, and the nature of one's marriage all conditioned the way women adjusted to the loss of their husbands, often after decades of marriage.

Neugarten, B. L., & Neugarten, D. A. (1996). *Meanings of age: Selected papers.* Chicago: University of Chicago.

Covering more than 40 years of scholarship, this volume brings together Bernice Neugarten's most important contributions in four areas: Age as a Dimension of Social Organization; The Life Course; Personality and Adaptation; and Social Policy Issues. Neugarten pioneered the study of age, the social clock, and social timing and is noted for changing negative stereotypes about aging through her studies of personality, aging, competencies of middle-aged and older people, and generational relations.

Riley, M. W., et al. (1968–1972). *Aging and society.* New York: Russell Sage.

This three volume series is a highly influential work on how chronological age and aging processes both affect and are affected by social and psychological processes. *Volume 1: An Inventory of Research Findings* (1968) provides a review and synopsis of empirical studies of aging and midlife. The vast majority of studies cited were conducted post-1960, revealing the remarkable increase in social gerontology research that flourished in the late 20th century. *Volume 2: Aging and the Practicing Professions* (1969) explored the effects of aging on professional workers. *Volume 3: Age Stratification* (1972), considered the most influential volume, sets forth the central tenets of age stratification theory. This theory proposes that age—like gender and race—is a source of stratification in society. Volume 3 set the stage for the development of the life course paradigm, including the key themes of "linked lives," the importance of transitions and trajectories, the influence of historical context on individual lives.

Rossi, A., & Rossi, P. (1990). *Of human bonding: Parent-child relations across the life course.* NY: Aldine de Gruyter.

The authors analyze data from a study of three generations of family members residing in the greater Boston area. They document important aspects of family relationships, including both the emotional nature of their social ties, but also actual and perceived obligations among family members. An important strength is that they explore the ways that gender shapes family relations, and they show that maternal grandmothers and granddaughters share a particularly close bond. This book clearly illustrates the importance of "linked lives" for one's life course experiences.

# Index

*Boldface page numbers refer to the main entry on the subject. Italic page numbers refer to illustrations, charts, and photos.*

## C

## D

## E

# I

## P

## Q



## R

## S

## T

## U

## V

## Y



## Z